about the author

James Halliday is Australia's most respected wine writer. Over the past thirty-odd years he has worn many hats: lawyer, winemaker and grape grower, wine judge, wine consultant, journalist and author. He has discarded his legal hat, but actively continues in his other roles, incessantly travelling, researching and tasting wines in all the major wine-producing countries. He judges regularly at wine shows in Australia, the UK, the US, South Africa and New Zealand.

James Halliday has written or contributed to more than 50 books on wine since he began writing in 1979 (notable contributions include those to the *Oxford Companion* and the *Larousse Encylopedia of Wine*). His books have been translated into Japanese, French and German, and have been published in the UK and the US as well as Australia.

His most recent works include *Classic Wines of Australia and New Zealand*, *An Introduction to Australian Wine*, *Wine Atlas of Australia and New Zealand* and *Collecting Wine: You and Your Cellar*.

Co-founder of the wine website www.winepros.com.au, Halliday is proving to be as popular on the World Wide Web as he is in other media.

james halliday's

australian

wine

companion

2004 EDITION

HarperCollinsPublishers

HarperCollins*Publishers*

First published as *Australia and New Zealand Wine Companion* in Australia in 1997
This edition published in 2003
by HarperCollins*Publishers* Pty Limited
ABN 36 009 913 517
A member of HarperCollins*Publishers* (Australia) Pty Limited Group
www.harpercollins.com.au

Copyright © James Halliday 2003

HarperCollins*Publishers*
25 Ryde Road, Pymble, Sydney, NSW 2073, Australia
31 View Road, Glenfield, Auckland 10, New Zealand
77–85 Fulham Palace Road, London W6 8JB, United Kingdom
2 Bloor Street East, 20th floor, Toronto, Ontario M4W 1A8, Canada
10 East 53rd Street, New York NY 10022, USA

ISBN 0 7322 7625 X
ISSN 1448-3564

Cover photography by Getty Images
Cover design by Christa Edmonds, HarperCollins Design Studio
Typeset in Bembo 8/9.5 by HarperCollins Design Studio
Printed and bound in Australia by Griffin Press on 60gsm Bulky Paperback White
5 4 3 2 1   03 04 05 06

contents

introduction

the pace of growth in the Australian wine industry continues unabated; it is a pace which means growth pains for all sectors, from grape growers to small wineries to the largest producers. Some temporary relief has come from the size of the 2003 harvest, which is around 14 per cent down on 2002. This is the first time for 7 years that there has been a decrease on the prior year. I say more about this in the 2003 vintage report on page xxxiii.

Exports remain the principal pressure valve. The 2002 calendar year figures suggest that Australia may now be the fifth-largest wine producer in the world, edging past Argentina, and the third-largest exporter by value, edging past Spain. (Direct comparisons are difficult, because the Australian figures become available up to two years earlier than those of our competitors. Full details appear in the 372-page *Statistical Compendium of Global Wine Production and Trade*, published by the Centre for International Economic Studies, University of Adelaide, email cies@adelaide.edu.au.

The domestic pathways from grape to glass are becoming ever more congested. There simply aren't enough quality wholesale distributors, and the chances of a new producer finding a good distributor are slight. Retail shelves are similarly overloaded, a problem severely exacerbated by the ever-growing market share held by the two giants, Coles Myer (Liquorland, Vintage Cellars, Theos, etc) and Woolworths (Safeway, First Estate, etc). The power of these two chains caused the largest Australian company, Southcorp, to buckle at the knees in early 2003, leading to the forced departure of its chief executive, Keith Lambert, several temporary suspensions of its share trading, and the final appalling profit figures which saw its share price tumble to $3 a share from a high of around $8 less than two years previously.

But it's not only the big companies which face growth pains. The vineyard area in Australia has increased from 77 682 hectares in 1996 to 158 594 hectares in 2002. In 1988 the figure was 57 707 hectares, and it was 52 042 hectares 50 years earlier. Thus the growth in 8 years is many times greater than that over the last 65 years.

One might be expected to conclude that massive falls in grape prices, and a prolonged oversupply situation, would place many growers in jeopardy. Even before the impact of the drought on the 2003 harvest became apparent, the Winemakers' Federation of Australia (see p. xxxvi) was forecasting a balance between supply and demand in 2005, and grape shortages – particularly from cooler regions and particularly for white grapes – by 2006.

Nonetheless, the uncertain demand and lower prices for grapes have been a factor in the extraordinary proliferation of new wineries. Incidentally, in this book, wineries and brands are co-extensive: less than 80 per cent of producers actually have a winery; the remainder rely on contract winemaking services.

Indeed, there are some significant 'virtual wineries', owning neither vineyards nor wineries.

That to one side, there are 240 new winery entries in this book; added to the first-time entries in the 2003 *Companion*, it means 428 new entrants in two years. Even more scary for those contemplating their own business is the fact that I have at least some information on another 200 or more wineries, mostly new, hiding their light under a bushel. Which raises a point: if you, the reader, know of a winery which is not in this book, please encourage it to get in touch by email to me at jpaulag@ozemail.com.au.

New wineries mean more wines, and more wines mean more tasting notes. In the 2003 *Companion* there were 2400 tasting notes in a book of 538 pages. This book has 592 pages, and 2705 tasting notes; I in fact wrote up another 400 notes (which were dropped for space reasons), and created a total of just on 5000 for the 12-month period in handwritten form (excluding another 4000 or so written notes from wine shows).

The distribution of points for the 5000 formal notes was as follows:

94 points and above	7 %
90–93 points	17 %
87–89 points	20 %
84–86 points	18 %
80–83 points	18 %
76–79 points	17 %
75 points and below	3 %

Space constraints have thus resulted in an entirely disproportionate representation for wines scoring 84 points or more (62 per cent of the total) and almost no record of the remaining 38 per cent. So if you think my points and rating are ridiculously high, bear in mind that you are seeing only part of the iceberg.

Given that the book cannot grow further in size, that there will almost certainly be another 200-plus new winery entries next year, and that the winery ratings and tasting note ratings only represent part of the total picture, I am working on a format for 2005 which will significantly increase the total information and present it in a more balanced form. A bit like the Australian Wine Show system, it's not yet broken, but it will be unless radical pre-emptive action is taken.

There is no cause to be alarmed; going backwards, the 2002 edition was the last to include New Zealand, and the 2001 edition was the last to include background notes on the making of each wine tasted. So if you have those editions, keep them, and certainly keep this 2004 edition.

—JAMES HALLIDAY

how to use this book

the *Wine Companion* is arranged with wineries in alphabetical order. The entries should be self-explanatory, but here I will briefly take you through the information for each entry.

winery entries

grosset ★ ★ ★ ★ ★

King Street, Auburn, SA 5451 **region** Clare Valley
phone (08) 8849 2175 **fax** (08) 8849 2292 **open** Wed–Sun 10–5 from 1st week of September for approx 6 weeks
winemaker Jeffrey Grosset **production** 8500 cases **est.** 1981
product range ($24.50–50 CD) Watervale Riesling, Polish Hill Riesling, Semillon Sauvignon Blanc, Piccadilly Chardonnay, Gaia (a Cabernet blend), Reserve Pinot Noir.
summary Jeffrey Grosset served part of his apprenticeship at the vast Lindeman Karadoc winery, moving from the largest to one of the smallest when he established Grosset Wines in its old stone winery. He now crafts the wines with the utmost care from grapes grown to the most exacting standards; all need a certain amount of time in bottle to achieve their ultimate potential, not the least the Rieslings and Gaia, among Australia's best examples of their kind. At a Riesling summit held in Hamburg in the latter part of 1998, Grosset was voted Riesling Winemaker of the Year. Exports to the US, Europe and Asia mean a continuous shortage of the wines in all markets.

winery name   Grosset

Although it might seem that stating the winery name is straightforward, this is not necessarily so. To avoid confusion, wherever possible I use the name that appears most prominently on the wine label, and do not refer to any associated trading name.

ratings ★ ★ ★ ★ ★

The winery star system may be interpreted as follows:

★★★★★ Outstanding winery regularly producing exemplary wines.
★★★★☆ Extremely good; virtually on a par with a five-star winery.
  ★★★★ Consistently produces high-quality wines.
  ★★★☆ A solid, reliable producer of good wines.
    ★★★ Typically good, but may have a few lesser wines.
    ★★☆ Adequate.
    NR Normally ascribed where I have not tasted wines from the producer in the past 12 months.

If the ratings seem generous, so be it. The fact is that Australia is blessed with a marvellous climate for growing grapes, a high degree of technological skill, and a remarkable degree of enthusiasm and dedication on the part of its winemakers. Across the price spectrum, Australian wines stand tall in the markets of the world. I see no reason, therefore, to shrink from recognising excellence.

address King Street, Auburn, SA 5451
phone (08) 8849 2175 **fax** (08) 8849 2292

The details are usually those of the winery and cellar door but in a few instances may simply be of the winery; this occurs when the wine is made at another winery under contract and is sold only through retail.

region Clare Valley

The mapping of Australia into Zones and Regions with legally defined boundaries is now well underway. This edition sees radical changes (and additions) to the regional names and boundaries. Wherever possible the official 'Geographic Indication' name has been adopted, and where the registration process is incomplete, I have used the most likely name. Occasionally you will see 'Warehouse' as the region. This means the wine is made from purchased grapes, in someone else's winery. In other words, it does not have a vineyard or winery in the ordinary way.

cellar door sales hours   open Wed–Sun 10–5 from 1st week of September for approx 6 weeks

Although a winery might be listed as not open or only open on weekends, some may in fact be prepared to open by appointment. Many will, some won't; a telephone call will establish whether it is possible or not. Also, virtually every winery that is shown as being open only for weekends is in fact open on public holidays as well. Once again, a telephone call will confirm this.

winemaker Jeffrey Grosset

In the large companies the winemaker is simply the head of a team; there may be many executive winemakers actually responsible for specific wines.

production 8500 cases

This figure (representing the number of cases produced each year) is merely an indication of the size of the operation. Some wineries (principally but not exclusively the large companies) regard this information as confidential; in that event, NFP (not for publication) will appear. If the information was not available, no production entry will appear.

year of establishment   est. 1981

A more or less self-explanatory item, but keep in mind that some makers consider the year in which they purchased the land to be the year of establishment, others the year in which they first planted grapes, others the year they first made wine, others the year they first offered wine for sale, and so on. There may also be minor complications where there has been a change of ownership or a break in production.

price range and product range ($24.50–50 CD) Watervale Riesling, Polish Hill Riesling, Semillon Sauvignon Blanc, Piccadilly Chardonnay, Gaia (a Cabernet blend), Reserve Pinot Noir.

The **price range** covers the least expensive through to the most expensive wines usually made by the winery in question (where the information was available). Hence there may be a significant spread. That spread, however, may not fully cover fluctuations that occur in retail pricing, particularly with the larger companies. Erratic and often savage discounting remains a feature of the wine industry, and prices must therefore be seen as approximate.

For Australia, this spread has been compounded by the introduction on 1 July 2000 of the Goods and Services Tax (GST) of 10 per cent and the special and uniquely discriminatory Wine Equalisation Tax (WET) of 29 per cent imposed on top of one another in a tax-on-tax pyramid.

I have indicated whether the price is cellar door (CD), mailing list (ML) or retail (R). By and large, the choice has been determined by which of the three methods of sale is most important to the winery. The price of Australian wines in other countries is affected by a number of factors, including excise and customs duty, distribution mark-up and currency fluctuations. Contact the winery for details.

product range

Particularly with the larger companies, it is not possible to give a complete list of the wines. The saving grace is that these days most of the wines are simply identified on their label by their varietal composition.

> **summary** Jeffrey Grosset served part of his apprenticeship at the vast Lindeman Karadoc winery, moving from the largest to one of the smallest when he established Grosset Wines in its old stone winery. He now crafts the wines with the utmost care from grapes grown to the most exacting standards; all need a certain amount of time in bottle to achieve their ultimate potential, not the least the Rieslings and Gaia, among Australia's best examples of their kind. At a Riesling summit held in Hamburg in the latter part of 1998, Grosset was voted Riesling Winemaker of the Year. Exports to the US, Europe and Asia mean a continuous shortage of the wines in all markets.

My summary of the winery. Little needs to be said, except that I have tried to vary the subjects I discuss in this part of the winery entry.

🍂 The vine leaf symbol indicates the 240 wineries that are new entries in this year's listing.

tasting notes

> **Grosset Watervale Riesling**
> ♟♟♟♟♟ **2002** Light straw-green; the bouquet is intense, yet not exuberant, with some slate and spice aromas still in the course of the earliest stages of development; the long, clean and vibrant palate has crisp apple and lime flavours accompanied by excellent acidity. As often happens, is showing more in its youth than the Polish Hill, but in the course of time the positions will likely reverse. **rating: 96**
> **best drinking** 2003–2013 **best vintages** '81, '86, '90, '93, '94, '95, '96, '97, '98, '99, 00, '01, '02
> **drink with** Fish terrine • $38

> **wine name** Grosset Watervale Riesling

In most instances, the wine's name will be prefaced by the name of the winery.

> **ratings**

Two ratings are given for each wine; the ratings apply to the vintage reviewed, and may vary from one year to the next.

Points scale	Glass symbol	
98–100	–	Perfection which exists only as an idea.
94–97	♟♟♟♟♟	As close to perfection as the real world will allow.
90–93	♟♟♟♟♟	Excellent wine full of character; of gold medal standard.
85–89	♟♟♟♟	Very good wine; clear varietal definition/style; silver medal standard.
80–84	♟♟♟♟	Good fault-free, flavoursome wine; bronze medal standard.

In the introduction I explain in some detail why the vast majority of wines are scored at four glasses or more. Suffice it here to say I have elected to focus on the wines to buy and enjoy, rather on those to avoid.

♈♈♈♈♈ 2002 Light straw-green; the bouquet is intense, yet not exuberant, with some slate and spice aromas still in the course of the earliest stages of development; the long, clean and vibrant palate has crisp apple and lime flavours accompanied by excellent acidity. As often happens, is showing more in its youth than the Polish Hill, but in the course of time the positions will likely reverse. **rating:** 96

The tasting note opens with the vintage of the wine tasted. With the exception of a very occasional classic wine, this tasting note will have been made within the 12 months prior to publication. Even that is a long time, and during the life of this book the wine will almost certainly change. More than this, remember that tasting is a highly subjective and imperfect art. NV = non-vintage.

best drinking   2003–2013

I will usually give a range of years or a more specific comment (such as 'quick-developing style'), but whatever my best drinking recommendation, always consider it with extreme caution and as an approximate guide at best. When to drink a given wine is an intensely personal decision, which only you can make.

best vintages   '81, '86, '90, '93, '94, '95, '96, '97, '98, '99, '00, '01, '02

Self-explanatory information, but a note of caution: wines do change in the bottle, and it may be that were I to taste all the vintages again, I would demote some and elevate some not mentioned.

drink with   Fish terrine

Again, merely a suggestion – a subliminal guide to the style of wine.

price • $38

This is a guide only.

key to regions

1 Lower Hunter Valley
2 Upper Hunter Valley
3 Hastings River
4 Mudgee
5 Orange
6 Cowra
7 Swan Hill
8 Murray Darling
9 Riverina
10 Perricoota
11 Hilltops
12 Canberra District
12a Gundagai
13 Tumbarumba
14 Shoalhaven
15 Henty
16 Grampians
17 Pyrenees
18 Ballarat
19 Bendigo
19a Heathcote
20 Goulburn Valley
21 Central Victorian High Country
22 Rutherglen and Glenrowan
23 King Valley
24 Alpine Valleys and Beechworth
25 Gippsland
26 Mornington Peninsula
27 Yarra Valley
28 Geelong
29 Sunbury
30 Macedon Ranges
31 Northern Tasmania
32 Southern Tasmania
33 Mount Gambier
34 Coonawarra
35 Wrattonbully
36 Mount Benson
37 Padthaway
38 Langhorne Creek
39 McLaren Vale
39a Kangaroo Island
39b Southern Fleurieu Peninsula
40 Adelaide Hills
41 Eden Valley
42 Adelaide Plains
43 Barossa Valley
44 Riverland
45 Clare Valley
46 Southern Eyre Peninsula
47 Great Southern
48 Pemberton and Manjimup
49 Blackwood Valley
50 Margaret River
51 Geographe
52 Peel
53 Perth Hills
54 Swan District
55 South Burnett
55a Queensland Coastal
56 Granite Belt

wine regions of australia

WESTERN
AUSTRALIA

Perth

Darwin

NORTHERN
TERRITORY

QUEENSLAND

SOUTH
AUSTRALIA

NEW SOUTH
WALES

Brisbane

55

56   55a

Adelaide

45
43
41
42 40   44
46
39
39a   39b   38
37
35
36
34
33   15
8
7
10
19
17
16   18
20
19a 21
30 29
28   27
26

VIC.

9
12a
11
12
5
4   2
1
6
3

A.C.T

22
21a 23   24
25
13
14

Sydney

Melbourne

Launceston

TAS.
31

32

Hobart

0   250   500 km

australia's geographical indications

the process of formally mapping Australia's wine regions continues to ever-so-slowly inch forward. The division into states, zones, regions and subregions follows; those regions or subregions marked with an asterisk are variously in an early or late stage of determination. In two instances I have gone beyond the likely finalisation: it makes no sense to me that the Hunter Valley should be a zone, the region Hunter, and then subregions which are all in the Lower Hunter Valley. I have elected to stick with the traditional division between the Upper Hunter Valley on the one hand and the Lower on the other.

I am also in front of the game with Tasmania, dividing it into Northern and Southern, and, to a lesser degree, have anticipated that the Coastal Hinterland region of Queensland will seek recognition under this or some similar name. Those regions and subregions marked with an asterisk have taken, or are likely to take, steps to secure registration; they may or may not persevere.

state/zone	region	subregion
New South Wales		
Big Rivers	Murray Darling	
	Perricoota	
	Riverina	
	Swan Hill	
Central Ranges	Cowra	
	Mudgee	
	Orange	
Hunter Valley	Hunter	Allandale*
		Belford*
		Broke Fordwich
		Dalwood*
		Pokolbin*
		Rothbury*
Northern Rivers	Hastings River	
Northern Slopes		
South Coast	Shoalhaven Coast	
	Southern Highlands	
Southern New South Wales	Canberra District	
	Gundagai	
	Hilltops	
	Tumbarumba	
Western Plains		

state/zone	region	subregion
South Australia		
Adelaide (Super Zone, above Mount Lofty Ranges, Fleurieu and Barossa)		
Mount Lofty Ranges	Adelaide Hills	Gumeracha* Lenswood Piccadilly Valley
	Adelaide Plains Clare Valley	Auburn* Clare* Hill River* Polish Hill River* Sevenhill* Watervale*
Fleurieu	Currency Creek Kangaroo Island Langhorne Creek McLaren Vale Southern Fleurieu	Clarendon*
Limestone Coast	Coonawarra Mount Benson Penola* Padthaway Wrattonbully*	
The Peninsulas	Southern Eyre Peninsula	
Lower Murray	Riverland	
Far North		
Barossa	Barossa Valley Eden Valley	High Eden Springton*
Victoria		
Central Victoria	Bendigo Central Victorian High Country* Goulburn Valley Heathcote Strathbogie Ranges	Nagambie Lakes
Gippsland		

state/zone	region	subregion
North East Victoria	Alpine Valleys	Kiewa Valley* Ovens Valley*
	Beechworth Glenrowan* King Valley*	Myrrhee* Whitlands*
	Rutherglen	Wahgunyah*
North West Victoria	Murray Darling Swan Hill	
Port Phillip	Geelong Macedon Ranges Mornington Peninsula Sunbury Yarra Valley	
Western Victoria	Grampians Henty Pyrenees	

Western Australia

Eastern Plains, Inland and North of Western Australia

West Australian South East Coastal	Esperance*	
South West Australia	Blackwood Valley Geographe Great Southern	Albany Frankland River Mount Barker Porongurup
	Manjimup* Margaret River Pemberton*	
Central Western Australia		
Greater Perth	Peel Perth Hills Swan District	Swan Valley*

Queensland

| Queensland | Granite Belt
Coastal Hinterland*
South Burnett | |

Tasmania

Tasmania

Australian Capital Territory

Northern Territory

best of the best of Australian wine 2004

this year follows in the tradition of last year by listing the top wines from well over 5000 tasting notes made between April 2002 and March 2003. The overall pattern and content of the Best of the Best follows that of 2003. I can but repeat what I said then, and in previous years: this is a snapshot extracted from tasting notes, with no rewriting of history, nor any attempt to put in wines of equal merit which, for one reason or another, escaped the tasting net. Or were just below the 94-point cut-off.

There are some notable omissions, most frequently because the wine in question did not cross my tasting table this year. There are also some surprising inclusions: I have resisted the temptation to edit the lists in any way.

I continue last year's Special Value Wines, Ten of the Best New Wineries and Ten Dark Horse Wineries – wineries that deserve to be far better known and appreciated.

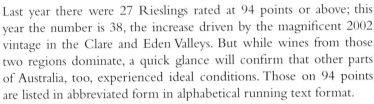

best of the best by variety

riesling

Last year there were 27 Rieslings rated at 94 points or above; this year the number is 38, the increase driven by the magnificent 2002 vintage in the Clare and Eden Valleys. But while wines from those two regions dominate, a quick glance will confirm that other parts of Australia, too, experienced ideal conditions. Those on 94 points are listed in abbreviated form in alphabetical running text format.

2002 Annie's Lane Copper Trail Riesling	96
2002 Cascabel Eden Valley Riesling	96
2002 Ferngrove Vineyards Cossack Riesling	96
2002 Grosset Watervale Riesling	96
2002 Henschke Lenswood Green's Hill Riesling	96
2002 Kilikanoon Morts Block Riesling	96
2002 Petaluma Hanlin Hill Riesling	96
1998 Taylors St Andrews Riesling	96
2002 Carlei Riesling	95
1997 Crawford River Museum Release Riesling	95
2000 Geoff Weaver Lenswood Riesling	95
2002 Grosset Polish Hill Riesling	95
2002 Jim Barry Lodge Hill Riesling	95
2002 O'Leary Walker Polish Hill River Riesling	95
2002 St Hallett Eden Valley Riesling	95
2002 Sevenhill Cellars Riesling	95

2002 Bloodwood, 2001 Capel Vale Whispering Hill, 2002 Cardinham Estate Clare Valley, 2002 Claymore Joshua Tree Clare Valley, 2002 Claymore Joshua Tree Watervale, 2002 East Arm, 2002 Frankland Estate Isolation Ridge, 2001 Karrivale Gibraltar Rock, 2002 Lamont, 2002 Leasingham Bin 7, 2002 Leconfield Old Vines, 2002 Leo Buring Clare Valley, 2002 Leo Buring Leonay, 2002 Mount Horrocks Watervale, 2001 Murdock, 2002 O'Leary Walker Watervale, 1997 Peter Lehmann Eden Valley Reserve, 2002 Tim Adams, 2002 Two Hands The Wolf, 2002 Will Taylor Clare Valley, 2002 Wilson Gallery Series, 2002 Wilson Vineyard DJW.

semillon

Here the pattern is reversed: last year there were 20 wines rating at 94 or above, compared with 11 this year. Once again, the answer lies with the vintage: 2000 and 2001 were better than 2002 in the Hunter Valley, which provided all but three of the wines.

1995 Tyrrell's Reserve HVD Semillon	97
1998 McWilliam's Mount Pleasant Lovedale Semillon	96

1997 Brokenwood ILR Reserve Semillon	95
2002 Keith Tulloch Semillon	95
2001 Rothbury Estate Brokenback Semillon	95
2002 Capercaillie Hunter Valley Semillon	94
2001 Evans & Tate Margaret River Semillon	94
2002 McLeish Estate Semillon	94
2001 Mount Horrocks Semillon	94
2001 Nepenthe Vineyards Semillon	94
1999 Rothbury Ridge Stanleigh Park Vineyard Reserve Semillon	94

sauvignon blanc and blends – and a few others

A substantially larger group than last year, once again reflecting in part the cool vintage conditions prevailing in the majority of the regions responsible for the Sauvignon Blanc or Sauvignon Blanc Semillon blends.

There is also a small but eclectic gathering of six other varietal wines, noteworthy for the fact that two come from Queensland's Granite Belt.

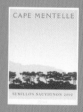

2002 Grosset Semillon Sauvignon Blanc	96
2000 Voyager Estate Tom Price Semillon Sauvignon Blanc	96
2002 Cape Mentelle Semillon Sauvignon Blanc	95
2002 Molly Morgan Semillon Sauvignon Blanc	95
2002 Ralph Fowler Limestone Coast Sauvignon Blanc	95
2002 Bird in Hand Sauvignon Blanc Semillon	94
2002 Briarose Estate Sauvignon Blanc	94
2001 Cape Mentelle Wallcliffe Reserve Sauvignon Blanc Semillon	94
2002 Cullen Sauvignon Blanc Semillon	94
2002 Geoff Weaver Lenswood Sauvignon Blanc	94
2002 Houghton Crofters Semillon Sauvignon Blanc	94
2002 Moondah Brook Semillon Sauvignon Blanc	94
2001 Pfitzner Eric's Vineyard Sauvignon Blanc	94
2002 Pierro Semillon Sauvignon Blanc LTC	94
2002 Stella Bella Sauvignon Blanc	94
2002 The Lane The Gathering Sauvignon Semillon	94
2000 Willow Bridge Estate Winemaker's Reserve Semillon Sauvignon Blanc	94
2002 Xanadu Secession	94
2000 Yarra Yarra Semillon Sauvignon Blanc	94

1993 Ballandean Estate Sylvaner	94
2002 Henschke Joseph Hill Gewurztraminer	94
2002 Hillstowe The Scrub Block Lenswood Pinot Gris	94
2001 Moorilla Estate Gewurztraminer	94

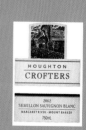

2002 Robert Channon Verdelho 94
2001 Yalumba Eden Valley Viognier 94

chardonnay

Forty-seven wines this year compared with 36 last year. In terms of region of origin, the group is a veritable League of Nations. Those on 94 points are listed in abbreviated form in alphabetical running text format.

2000 Penfolds Yattarna Chardonnay 97
2001 Chalkers Crossing Tumbarumba Chardonnay 96
2001 Howard Park Chardonnay 96
2000 Penfolds Reserve Bin Chardonnay 96
2000 Devil's Lair Chardonnay 95
2001 Grosset Piccadilly Chardonnay 95
2000 Hardys Eileen Hardy Chardonnay 95
2001 Lark Hill Chardonnay 95
2000 Leeuwin Estate Art Series Chardonnay 95
2001 Orlando Jacob's Creek Limited Release Chardonnay 95
2001 Picardy Chardonnay 95
2002 Tuck's Ridge Chardonnay 95

2001 2 Bud Spur, 2001 Ashton Hills, 2001 Bindi, 2001 Bindi Quartz, 2000 Cosham, 1999 Curly Flat, 2002 De Bortoli Yarra Valley, 2001 Domaine Chandon Green Point Reserve, 2001 Dromana Estate, 2001 Gloucester Ridge Premium Reserve, 2001 Hamelin Bay Five Ashes Reserve, 2000 Hay Shed Hill Estate, 2002 Hillcrest, 2001 Lenton Brae, 2001 MadFish, 2001 Mt Lofty Ranges Vineyard, 2001 Narkoojee, 2001 Nepenthe Vineyards, 2001 Orlando Jacob's Creek Premium, 2001 Peacock Hill Vineyard Top Block, 2000 Petaluma Piccadilly Vineyard, 2001 Montrose Stony Creek, 2000 Portree Macedon Ranges, 2002 Rosabrook Estate, 2001 Rosemount Estate Rose Label Orange Vineyard, 2001 Rosemount Estate Roxburgh, 2000 Seppelt Jaluka, 2002 Setanta Emer, 2000 Sharmans, 2001 Shaw & Smith M3 Vineyard, 2001 Stefano Lubiana, 2001 Tower Estate Hunter Valley, 2001 Voyager Estate, 2001 Yalumba Adelaide Hills, 2002 Yeringberg.

sparkling, sweet and rose

Sparkling, rose and sweet white wines. An odd trio, of course, but they all deserve recognition. Three big names are missing from the sparkling list – Pirie, Arras and Yarrabank – purely due to the timing of the release of these wines. Much the same applies to the De Bortoli Noble One.

1995 Jansz Late Disgorged 96
1997 Freycinet Radenti 95
NV Rockford Black Shiraz 95
1999 Domaine Chandon Blanc de Blancs 94

1997 Domaine Chandon Blanc de Noirs	94
1998 Domaine Chandon Brut Rose	94
1999 Domaine Chandon Tasmanian Cuvee	94
1999 Domaine Chandon Vintage Brut	94
NV Hanging Rock Macedon Cuvee	94
1999 Hardys Sir James Vintage	94
NV St Hallett Black	94
1998 Touchwood Coal River Cuvee	94
1999 Yellowglen Vintage Cuvee Victoria	94
1997 Michael Unwin Acrobat Botrytised Riesling	94
2002 Charles Melton Rose of Virginia	94

pinot noir

While this year's total of 38 wines is less than last year's (44), 2001 turned out to be another great vintage for pinot noir in Tasmania, and in parts of southern Australia. With another excellent vintage in the form of 2002 around the corner, Pinotphiles have never had it so good. It must also be pointed out that there are far more producers of pinot noir than there were even a few years ago; that the backbone of mature vines is increasing; and that improved French clones are also having an impact. (Those on 94 points are listed in abbreviated form in alphabetical running text format.)

2000 Pipers Brook Vineyard The Lyre Pinot Noir	97
2001 Bindi Original Vineyard Pinot Noir	96
2001 Curlewis Reserve Pinot Noir	96
2001 Merricks Creek Nick Farr Pinot Noir	96
2001 Moorilla Estate Reserve Pinot Noir	96
2000 Tarrington Vineyards Cuvee Emilie Pinot Noir	96
2001 Bindi Block 5 Pinot Noir	95
2001 Clemens Hill Pinot Noir	95
2001 Coal Valley Vineyard Pinot Noir	95
2001 Elsewhere Vineyard Bay of Eight Pinot Noir	95
2001 Freycinet Pinot Noir	95
2001 Merricks Creek Pinot Noir	95
2001 Seville Estate Reserve Pinot Noir	95
2001 Three Wise Men Reserve Pinot Noir	95

2001 Austin's Barrabool, 2001 Barratt The Reserve, 2000 Chatto, 2001 Cobaw Ridge, 2001 Curlewis, 1998 Curly Flat, 2001 De Bortoli Yarra Valley, 2001 Diamond Valley Estate, 2001 Dromana Estate Reserve, 2001 Elsewhere Vineyard, 2001 Farr Rising Geelong, 2000 Kooyong, 2001 Merricks Creek Close Planted, 2000 Miceli Lucy's Choice, 2001 Milford Vineyard, 2001 Moorilla Estate Black Label, 2001 The Moorooduc, 2001 Paringa Estate, 2001 Port Phillip Estate, 2001 Notley Gorge, 2001 Seville Estate, 2001 Tarrington Vineyards, 2001 Tinderbox Vineyard, 2001 Wedgetail Estate.

shiraz

Last year 19 wines at 95 points and above, this year 32, although there are slightly fewer on 94 points than last year. Here, too, there is an alphabet soup of regions. (Those on 94 points are listed in abbreviated form in alphabetical running text format.)

1998 Penfolds Grange	97
1998 Seppelt St Peters Shiraz	97
1998 Henschke Hill of Grace	96
2000 Houghton Frankland Shiraz	96
2000 Houghton Gladstones Shiraz	96
1999 Houghton Gladstones Shiraz	96
2000 Kilikanoon Oracle Shiraz	96
2000 Wirra Wirra RSW Shiraz	96
1999 Annie's Lane Copper Trail Shiraz	95
2001 Bannockburn Shiraz	95
2001 Cape Grace Shiraz	95
2000 Craiglee Shiraz	95
2001 Fairview Shiraz	95
2001 Gemtree Vineyards Uncut Shiraz	95
2000 Haan Shiraz Prestige	95
2000 Hanging Rock Winery Heathcote Shiraz	95
1999 Hardys Eileen Hardy Shiraz	95
2001 Howard Park Leston Shiraz	95
2001 Kaesler Old Bastard Shiraz	95
2000 Kaesler Old Vine Shiraz	95
1999 Leasingham Classic Clare Shiraz	95
2000 Majella Shiraz	95
2001 Merum Shiraz	95
1997 Orlando Lawson's Padthaway Shiraz	95
2001 Penna Lane The Willsmore Shiraz	95
1998 Peter Lehmann Stonewell Shiraz	95
2000 Scotchmans Hill Shiraz	95
1999 Settlers Ridge Shiraz	95
2000 Tatachilla Foundation Shiraz	95
2001 Tim Gramp McLaren Vale Reserve Shiraz	95
2000 Torbreck The Factor	95
2000 Wirra Wirra McLaren Vale Shiraz	95

2001 Ada River Heathcote, 2001 Alkoomi Frankland River, 2000 Alkoomi Jarrah, 2001 Armstrong Vineyards, 2001 Balgownie Estate, 1997 Baptista The Graytown Heathcote, 2000 Bowen Estate, 2001 Brindabella Hills, 1998 Browns of Padthaway T-Trellis, 2001 Capel Vale Kinnaird, 2001 Carbunup Crest Cella Rage, 2001 Clarendon Hills Piggott Range Vineyard Syrah, 2001 Clayfield, 2000 Dalwhinnie Eagle Series Pyrenees, 2000 d'Arenberg Dead Arm, 1999 Driftwood Estate, 2001 Evans & Tate Margaret River, 2001 Fox Creek Reserve, 2001 Gralyn Estate Old Vine, 1999 Hamilton's

Ewell Vineyards Fuller's Barn, 2001 Hare's Chase, 2001 Hewitson Ned & Henry's, 2001 Howard Park Scotsdale, 2000 Jim Barry The Armagh, 1999 Katnook Estate Prodigy, 2000 Kay Bros Amery Block 6, 2000 Kilikanoon Covenant, 2000 Langmeil The Freedom, 2000 Leeuwin Estate Art Series, 2000 McGuigan Personal Reserve Hunter Valley, 1999 McWilliam's Mount Pleasant Old Paddock and Old Hill, 2001 Mitolo Savitar McLaren Vale, 2000 Peerick Vineyard, 1997 Penfolds Grange, 1999 Penfolds RWT, 1998 Penfolds St Henri, 2001 Preveli, 1998 Reynell Basket Pressed, 2000 Rosemount Estate Rose Label Orange Vineyard, 2001 Sanguine Estate Heathcote, 2001 Scorpo, 2001 Summerfield Reserve, 2001 Torbreck The Struie, 2001 Twelve Staves Old Vine, 2001 Two Hands Ares Barossa Valley, 2001 Viking Grand, 2001 Voyager Estate, 2001 Western Range, 2001 Zema Estate, 2000 Zema Estate Family Selection.

shiraz blends and other varieties

A short list, but the wines are impressive.

2001 Clonakilla Shiraz Viognier	96
2001 Torbreck Descendant	96
2001 Gralyn Estate Shiraz Cabernet	94
2000 Metier Manytrees Vineyard Shiraz Viognier	94
2000 Mitchelton Crescent Shiraz Mourvedre Grenache	94
1998 Orlando Jacob's Creek Limited Release Shiraz Cabernet	94
2000 Stanton & Killeen Durif	94

cabernet sauvignon

A very slight increase on last year, up to 28 from 23, with newcomers part of the mix. (Those on 94 points are listed in abbreviated form in alphabetical running text format.)

2000 Wolf Blass Platinum Label Clare Valley Cabernet Sauvignon	97
1999 Leasingham Classic Clare Cabernet Sauvignon	96
2000 The Yarra Yarra	96
2000 Henschke Cyril Henschke Cabernet	95
1999 Houghton Gladstones Cabernet Sauvignon	95
2000 Houghton Margaret River Cabernet Sauvignon	95
1998 Katnook Estate Odyssey Cabernet Sauvignon	95
2000 Nepenthe Vineyards Hungry Ground Cabernet Sauvignon	95
1998 Orlando Jacaranda Ridge Cabernet Sauvignon	95
2000 Zema Estate Cabernet Sauvignon	95

2000 Brown Brothers Patricia, 2001 Cape Grace, 1999 Casas, 2001 Clairault Estate, 2001 De Bortoli Yarra Valley, 2001 Edwards Vineyard, 2001 Howard Park Leston, 2001 Howard Park Scotsdale, 2000 Katnook Estate, 2000 Lenton Brae Margaret River,

2000 Majella, 2000 Mildara Coonawarra, 2002 Mitolo Serpico McLaren Vale, 2000 Murdock, 2000 Pepper Tree Reserve Coonawarra, 2000 Phillip Island Vineyard, 2001 Summerfield Reserve Cabernet, 2000 Tatachilla.

cabernet blends, and other bordeaux varieties

Significantly more wines this year, the contribution of the Margaret River and Great Southern regions being as important this time around as it was last year. (Those on 94 points are listed in abbreviated form in alphabetical running text format.)

1999 Houghton Jack Mann	97
1998 De Bortoli Melba	96
2000 Houghton Jack Mann	96
2000 Jamiesons Run Reserve	96
2001 Cullen Cabernet Sauvignon Merlot	95
1999 De Bortoli Melba	95
2000 Haan Wilhemus	95
2000 Houghton Crofters Cabernet Merlot	95
2000 Majella The Malleea	95
1999 McWilliam's 1877 Cabernet Sauvignon Shiraz	95
2000 Petaluma Coonawarra	95
1999 Wolf Blass Black Label Cabernet Sauvignon Shiraz	95

2001 Arlewood Estate Cabernet Merlot, 2001 Chalice Bridge Estate Cabernet Shiraz, 2000 Devil's Lair Margaret River, 2001 Fire Gully Cabernet Sauvignon Merlot, 2001 Gilberts Cabernet Shiraz, 2000 Henschke Abbott's Prayer, 2001 Kulkunbulla Hilltops Cabernet Merlot, 2001 Lillydale Estate Cabernet Merlot, 2001 Moores Hill Estate Cabernet Merlot, 2000 Parker Coonawarra Estate First Growth, 2000 Vasse Felix Heytesbury, 2000 Warrenmang Grand Pyrenees, 2000 Woodside Valley Estate The Baudin Cabernet Merlot, 1998 Yalumba Signature Cabernet Shiraz.

fortified wines

It is high time for an update of Australia's great fortified wines. The notable omissions are Chambers Rosewood Muscats and Tokays (Bill Chambers doesn't submit samples to anyone, fearing it will stimulate demand he cannot meet), and Seppelt 1903 Para, released this year (2003), which would top the list.

NV All Saints Rare Rutherglen Muscat	97
NV All Saints Rare Rutherglen Tokay	97
NV Campbells Isabella Rare Rutherglen Tokay	97
NV Campbells Merchant Prince Rare Rutherglen Muscat	97
NV Morris Old Premium Liqueur Muscat	97
NV Morris Old Premium Liqueur Tokay	97
NV Seppelt Show Tawny Port DP90	97

NV Campbells Grand Rutherglen Muscat	96
NV Campbells Grand Rutherglen Tokay	96
NV Seppelt Show Reserve Muscat	96
NV Bullers Calliope Rare Liqueur Muscat	95
NV Seppelt Oloroso Sherry DP118	95
NV Seppelt Show Oloroso Sherry DP38	95
NV Westfield Liqueur Muscat	95
NV All Saints Grand Rutherglen Tokay	94
NV Bullers Calliope Rare Liqueur Tokay	94
NV Seppelt Amontillado Sherry DP116	94
NV Seppelt Para Liqueur Port	94
NV Seppelt Rutherglen Show Tokay DP57	94
1998 Stanton & Killeen Vintage Port	94

special value wines

I have selected ten of the best value wines in various self-explanatory groups. Correlating price and points is not easy at the best of times, and in some instances there were 30 or 40 wines with near-equal credentials. For any number of reasons, including all of them was out of the question, so I was compelled to make some fairly arbitrary choices. So it is that the title is 'Ten of the Best', not 'The Best Ten' for each group. It is, I am afraid, the usual suspects in the under $10 brackets, but a far broader spectrum once one goes over $10.

ten of the best value whites under $10

2002 De Bortoli Sacred Hill Colombard Chardonnay	84	$5.50
2002 De Bortoli Sacred Hill Traminer Riesling	86	$6.50
2002 Angove's Butterfly Ridge Colombard Chardonnay	85	$7
2002 Yalumba Oxford Landing Sauvignon Blanc	87	$7.95
2002 Yokain Vineyard Estate Unwooded Chardonnay	88	$8
2002 Orlando Jacob's Creek Semillon Sauvignon Blanc	89	$8.95
2002 Lindemans Bin 75 Riesling	92	$8.99
2002 Lindemans Bin 65 Chardonnay	88	$9
2002 Jindalee Estate Chardonnay	87	$9.50
2002 Eaglehawk Riesling	89	$9.99

best value reds under $10

2001 De Bortoli Sacred Hill Cabernet Merlot	86	$6
2002 De Bortoli Montage Cabernet Merlot	84	$8
2002 Lindemans Bin 40 Merlot	85	$8.99
2002 Zilzie Buloke Reserve Sangiovese	84	$8.99
2002 Zilzie Buloke Reserve Petit Verdot	85	$8.99
2002 Yalumba Y Series Merlot	86	$9.10
2002 Penfolds Rawson's Retreat Cabernet Shiraz	88	$9.99

| 2001 Toorak Willandra Estate Shiraz | 83 | $9.99 |
| 2001 De Bortoli Deen Durif | 84 | $9.99 |

ten of the best value whites $10–$15

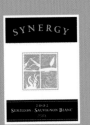

2002 Hamilton Synergy Semillon Sauvignon Blanc	92	$10.95
2002 Turkey Flat Semillon Marsanne	92	$12
2002 Mondah Brook Semillon Sauvignon Blanc	94	$13.99
2000 Cosham Chardonnay	94	$14
2001 James Estate Semillon	93	$14
2002 Xanadu Secession	94	$14
2002 Garlands Riesling	92	$15
2002 Leo Buring Clare Valley Riesling	94	$15
2002 McLeish Estate Semillon	94	$15
2001 Montrose Stony Creek Chardonnay	94	$15

ten of the best value reds $10–$15

2001 Carbunup Crest Cella Rage Shiraz	94	$12
2001 Stonehaven Stepping Stone Coonawarra Cabernet Sauvignon	91	$12
2002 Taylors Promised Land Cabernet Merlot	91	$13
2001 De Bortoli Black Creek Shiraz	91	$13.85
2001 Lindemans Reserve South Australia Shiraz	90	$13.99
2001 Pycnantha Hill Estate Shiraz	93	$15
2001 Western Range Shiraz	94	$15
2002 Judds Warby Range Estate Durif	91	$15
2001 Island Brook Estate Jakes Red	92	$15
2000 Orlando Jacob's Creek Reserve Cabernet Sauvignon	92	$15

ten of the best value whites $15–$20

2002 St Hallett Eden Valley Riesling	95	$16
2001 Chalkers Crossing Tumbarumba Chardonnay	96	$17.50
2002 Kilikanoon Morts Block Riesling	96	$18
2002 Ralph Fowler Limestone Coast Sauvignon Blanc	95	$18
2002 Sevenhill Cellars Riesling	95	$19
2002 Jim Barry Lodge Hill Riesling	95	$19.95
2002 Molly Morgan Semillon Sauvignon Blanc	95	$19.95
2002 Ferngrove Vineyards Cossack Riesling	96	$19.99
2000 Geoff Weaver Lenswood Riesling	95	$20
2002 O'Leary Walker Polish Hill River Riesling	95	$20

ten of the best value reds $15–$20

| 2000 Seppelt Victorian Premium Reserve Cabernet Sauvignon | 93 | $16 |
| 2001 Amberton Shiraz | 93 | $16.50 |

2000 Banks Thargo Merlot	93	$18.50
2000 Jimbour Station Shiraz	93	$19
2001 Witchmount Estate Cabernet Sauvignon	93	$19.50
2001 Evans & Tate Margaret River Shiraz	94	$19.99
2001 Alkoomi Frankland River Shiraz	94	$20
2001 MadFish Shiraz	93	$20
2001 Cardinham Estate Cabernet Merlot	93	$20
2001 Gilberts Cabernet Shiraz	94	$20

ten of the best
new wineries

My heading for this piece has been chosen with particular care. This is not the ten best new wineries, simply because I do not have the wisdom of Solomon, and in a field of 241 new wineries I doubt that even Solomon could come up with a fail-safe list. I have tried to provide a spread of regions, but beyond that, it all becomes very difficult.

Bay of Fires [page 36] Northern Tasmania
The flames have come from the ashes of Rochecombe, then the Ninth Island winery, purchased by BRL Hardy as its Tasmanian base of operations. Highly focused crisp and zesty wines.

Cape Grace [page 79] Margaret River
Self-taught viticulturist and winemaker Robert Karri-Davies and sales and marketing partner Karen Karri-Davies have wasted no time, with outstanding Shiraz and Cabernet Sauvignon from both 2000 and 2001.

Clayfield Wines [page110] Grampians
Simon and Kaye Clayfield have developed their own brand, building on the many years of experience gained by Simon as Best's former winemaker. Two hectares of shiraz planted between 1997 and 1999 are already providing great Shiraz; refusing to be bowed by a grass fire which destroyed the 2002 vintage.

Farr Rising [page 168] Geelong
Nicholas Farr is Gary Farr's son, and with the full encouragement of his father he has established his own brand while doubling up as winemaker at Innisfail Vineyards. Pinot Noir, sourced both from Geelong and the Mornington Peninsula, is, naturally enough, the heart of the business.

Hare's Chase [page 211] Barossa Valley
A partnership between two families, one owning a 100-year-old vineyard in the Maranaga Valley subregion, and the other providing the winemaking in the form of Southcorp senior red winemaker Peter Taylor. Shiraz is the cornerstone, coming from the centurion vines; Merlot is a side-light.

Higher Plane [page 223] Margaret River
An object lesson in planning and in researching the wine business from the ground up, by Perth-based surgeon Dr Craig Smith and wife Cathie; so much so that high-order success was inevitable.

Michael Unwin [page 318] Grampians
Michael Unwin, a Flying Winemaker of 16 years' standing, and his wife and business partner, Catherine Clark, are building a multi-faceted business, including contract winemaking and consulting, while making excellent wines under the Michael Unwin brand.

Mitolo Wines [page 326] McLaren Vale
Another new winery predestined for success, as Frank Mitolo has methodically covered every aspect of high-quality winemaking, from vineyard sources to very competent contract winemaking and highly sophisticated labelling and packaging.

Robert Channon Wines [page 421] Granite Belt
English-born former corporate lawyer Robert Channon and wife Peggie have established a permanently netted and immaculately maintained vineyard in a relatively remote part of the Granite Belt. With South African-trained Mark Ravenscroft as winemaker, they have achieved the seemingly impossible with Verdelho, not to mention outstanding Shiraz Cabernet Sauvignon.

Setanta Wines [page 453] Adelaide Hills
A family-owned business of the Sullivan family, first-generation Australians and of Irish parentage. Brilliant packaging is based on Gaelic mythology, and the wines are of the highest quality.

ten dark horses

Like the best new wineries list, this is a highly subjective list of wineries which have either shown recent but impressive improvement in their wines or simply deserve greater recognition.

Cardinham Estate [page 85] Clare Valley
The Cardinham wines are but the tip of the iceberg of the Smith family and Stephen John joint venture, the large vineyards dating

back to 1980, and Stephen John's winemaking career starting earlier still.

Chatsfield [page 102] Great Southern

Ken Lynch, an Irish-born doctor, has quite obviously secured an excellent winemaker (Dionne Miller) to realise the sometimes-lost quality of the grapes from the 25-year-old estate vineyard.

Cobaw Ridge [page 113] Macedon Ranges

After coming close to selling the business, the Coopers have added a stellar Pinot Noir and a Shiraz Viognier to a small portfolio of fascinating wines. Long may they continue.

Curlewis Winery [page 126] Geelong

Rainer Brett and Wendy Oliver live, eat and breathe Pinot Noir, which they make au naturel from 18-year-old vines. The price is high, the quality even higher.

Garlands [page 183] Great Southern

Having taken a couple of years to find his feet, Mike Garland has produced a full suite of quite lovely wines at bargain prices for the Garland/Drummond partnership.

James Estate [page 242] Upper Hunter Valley

It's not often that a substantial increase in volume is accompanied by a corresponding lift in quality, but that is precisely James Estate's achievement. What is more, the wines are very well priced.

Kilikanoon [page 262] Clare Valley

While seldom wide of the mark, hit a purple patch in 2002, whitewashing the competition at the Clare Valley Wine Show, taking six of the seven trophies awarded for Riesling, Shiraz and Cabernet Sauvignon.

McLeish Estate [page 301] Lower Hunter Valley

The McLeish family has progressively planted a 10-hectare vineyard since 1985, and uses the abundant skills and experience of contract winemaker Wayne Thomas to full advantage.

Peerick [page 376] Pyrenees

Chris and Meryl Jessup trialled many varieties in their vineyard before moving towards the present mix of high-quality white and red varietals, doing the region proud.

Pycnantha Hill Estate [page 407] Clare Valley

A formidable name inspired by the golden wattle (*Acacia pycnantha*) on the Howarth farm, but when you make wines as good as these, spelling and pronunciation problems become blissfully irrelevant.

australian vintage charts

Each number represents a mark out of ten for the quality of vintages in each region. NR denotes no rating.

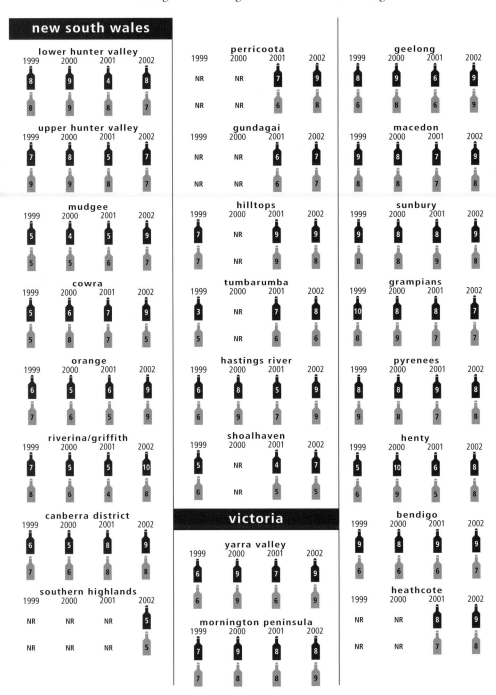

new south wales

lower hunter valley

1999	2000	2001	2002
8	9	4	8
8	9	8	7

upper hunter valley

1999	2000	2001	2002
7	8	5	7
9	9	8	7

mudgee

1999	2000	2001	2002
5	4	5	9
5	5	6	7

cowra

1999	2000	2001	2002
5	6	7	9
5	8	7	5

orange

1999	2000	2001	2002
6	5	6	9
7	6	5	9

riverina/griffith

1999	2000	2001	2002
7	5	5	10
8	6	4	8

canberra district

1999	2000	2001	2002
6	5	8	9
7	6	8	8

southern highlands

1999	2000	2001	2002
NR	NR	NR	5
NR	NR	NR	5

perricoota

1999	2000	2001	2002
NR	NR	7	9
NR	NR	6	8

gundagai

1999	2000	2001	2002
NR	NR	6	7
NR	NR	6	7

hilltops

1999	2000	2001	2002
7	NR	9	9
7	NR	9	8

tumbarumba

1999	2000	2001	2002
3	NR	7	8
5	NR	6	6

hastings river

1999	2000	2001	2002
6	8	5	9
6	9	7	9

shoalhaven

1999	2000	2001	2002
5	NR	4	7
6	NR	5	5

victoria

yarra valley

1999	2000	2001	2002
6	9	7	9
6	9	6	9

mornington peninsula

1999	2000	2001	2002
7	9	8	8
7	8	8	9

geelong

1999	2000	2001	2002
8	9	6	9
6	8	6	9

macedon

1999	2000	2001	2002
9	8	7	9
8	8	7	8

sunbury

1999	2000	2001	2002
9	8	8	9
8	8	9	8

grampians

1999	2000	2001	2002
10	8	8	7
8	9	7	7

pyrenees

1999	2000	2001	2002
8	8	9	8
9	8	7	8

henty

1999	2000	2001	2002
5	10	6	8
6	9	5	8

bendigo

1999	2000	2001	2002
9	8	9	9
6	6	6	7

heathcote

1999	2000	2001	2002
NR	NR	8	9
NR	NR	7	8

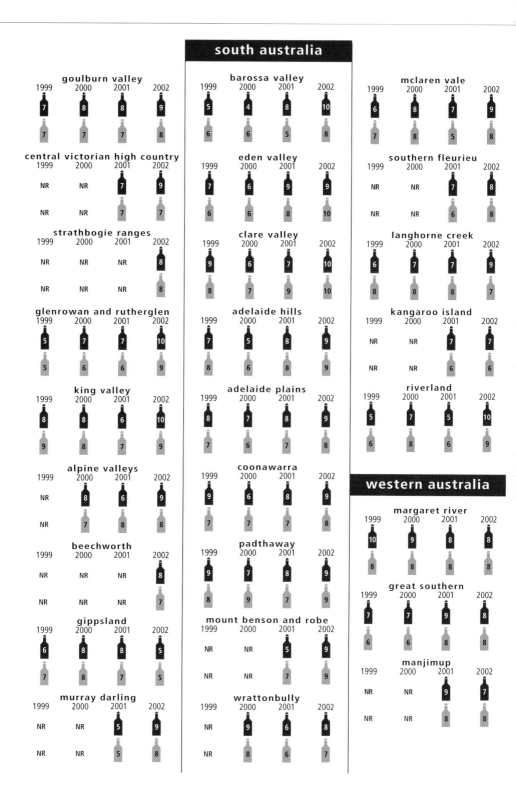

south australia

goulburn valley
1999	2000	2001	2002
7	8	8	9
7	7	7	8

central victorian high country
1999	2000	2001	2002
NR	NR	7	9
NR	NR	7	7

strathbogie ranges
1999	2000	2001	2002
NR	NR	NR	8
NR	NR	NR	8

glenrowan and rutherglen
1999	2000	2001	2002
5	7	7	10
5	6	6	9

king valley
1999	2000	2001	2002
8	8	6	10
9	8	7	9

alpine valleys
1999	2000	2001	2002
NR	8	6	9
NR	7	8	8

beechworth
1999	2000	2001	2002
NR	NR	NR	8
NR	NR	NR	7

gippsland
1999	2000	2001	2002
6	8	8	5
7	8	7	5

murray darling
1999	2000	2001	2002
NR	NR	5	9
NR	NR	5	8

barossa valley
1999	2000	2001	2002
5	4	8	10
6	6	5	8

eden valley
1999	2000	2001	2002
7	6	9	9
6	6	8	10

clare valley
1999	2000	2001	2002
9	6	7	10
8	7	9	10

adelaide hills
1999	2000	2001	2002
7	5	8	9
8	8	8	9

adelaide plains
1999	2000	2001	2002
8	7	8	9
7	6	7	8

coonawarra
1999	2000	2001	2002
9	6	8	9
7	7	7	8

padthaway
1999	2000	2001	2002
9	7	8	9
8	9	7	9

mount benson and robe
1999	2000	2001	2002
NR	NR	5	9
NR	NR	7	9

wrattonbully
1999	2000	2001	2002
NR	9	6	8
NR	8	6	7

mclaren vale
1999	2000	2001	2002
6	8	7	9
7	8	5	8

southern fleurieu
1999	2000	2001	2002
NR	NR	7	8
NR	NR	6	8

langhorne creek
1999	2000	2001	2002
6	7	7	9
8	8	8	7

kangaroo island
1999	2000	2001	2002
NR	NR	7	7
NR	NR	6	6

riverland
1999	2000	2001	2002
5	7	5	10
6	8	6	9

western australia

margaret river
1999	2000	2001	2002
10	9	8	8
8	8	8	8

great southern
1999	2000	2001	2002
7	7	9	8
6	6	8	8

manjimup
1999	2000	2001	2002
NR	NR	9	7
NR	NR	8	8

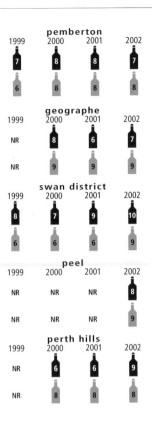

pemberton

1999	2000	2001	2002
7	8	8	7
6	8	8	8

geographe

1999	2000	2001	2002
NR	8	6	7
NR	9	9	9

swan district

1999	2000	2001	2002
8	7	9	10
6	6	6	9

peel

1999	2000	2001	2002
NR	NR	NR	8
NR	NR	NR	9

perth hills

1999	2000	2001	2002
NR	6	6	9
NR	8	8	8

queensland

granite belt

1999	2000	2001	2002
8	10	8	9
6	9	7	8

south burnett

1999	2000	2001	2002
NR	8	7	8
NR	7	6	8

tasmania

northern tasmania

1999	2000	2001	2002
9	9	8	9
9	9	8	9

southern tasmania

1999	2000	2001	2002
8	10	8	9
7	9	8	9

australian vintage 2003: a snapshot

there was one unifying force which gripped all but Western Australia in 2003: the drought, which in many parts of central and eastern Australia was the worst for 100 years. As always, the final figures from the Australian Bureau of Statistics won't be released until January 2004, but the preliminary outcome started to appear by the end of April 2003 – earlier than usual, thanks to that self-same drought.

Notwithstanding a 6 per cent increase in the area of vines in bearing, the average vineyard yield decreased by 21 per cent compared with 2002. This resulted in a crush of around 1.37 million tonnes, 14 per cent down on 2002. (Again, I must emphasise that these are estimates; there will be some variation in the final figures.)

Droughts have a nasty habit of ending with floods, as the winemakers of the **Barossa Valley** were forcibly reminded in 1983. For a brief time (20 to 21 February 2003) it looked as if history would repeat itself as tumultuous rain lashed the parched regions of South Australia, with particular impact on the **Barossa Valley**. (**Mudgee** was to have a similar experience the following month, with serious flooding in parts.)

Despite problems as the small berries soaked up the sudden moisture, particularly on the old, dry-grown vines, which led to berry splitting and the potential for disease, the weather then turned dry and warm, and humidity became the only threat. Indeed, the weather from this point on – through the end of February and the whole of March – was benign, if not ideal. The main problem confronting vignerons in South Australia and Victoria was the simultaneous (and relatively early) ripening of all varieties.

The east coast, from the **Hunter Valley** north, had its earliest vintage on record. Picking of white varieties began on 20 January, and was widespread within a few days. Yields were below average, but – particularly with the red grapes, which were also early – quality was high. Similar outcomes were experienced in Queensland, and **South Burnett** in particular. The growing season was milder and drier than 2002, with the two significant periods of rain (at budburst and around Christmas) perfectly timed. The sugar and acidity levels at harvest were ideal, and there was no disease.

This pattern of early ripening was as widespread in the coolest parts of eastern Australia as it was in the warmest. Thus **Tumbarumba**, in the Snowy Mountains, saw its grapes ripen four weeks earlier than usual, chardonnay being picked in the latter part of February, compared with April in cooler vintages.

Southern Victoria (the **Port Phillip Zone**) had an excellent vintage, with the growing season climate returning to normal (in terms of temperature, though not rainfall) after a series of abnormally warm or freakishly cool seasons since 1998. Yields were mostly below average (though much larger than 2002), and flavour developed very early, well before chemical ripeness – always a sign of high quality. Here, too, it was a very early vintage, finishing a month early.

Central Victoria is shiraz country first and foremost, and the drought conditions meant low yields but intensely coloured and flavoured red wines, picked up to three weeks early. The occasional bursts of heavy rain (which bypassed southern Victoria) did more good than harm overall.

Northeast Victoria experienced a very warm growing season, which benefited the **King** and **Alpine Valleys** in particular. The **Rutherglen** and **Glenrowan** areas experienced chemical ripening running more quickly than sensory/physiological ripening, so picking had to be delayed, resulting in a further diminution in yield.

Coonawarra more or less shrugged off the 21 to 22 February and 19 March (48 mm in five to six hours) rainfall episodes. Below average yields (20 to 30 per cent) of white wines had good varietal fruit definition; the cool to mild conditions before and after the March rainfall allowed ripening to proceed at a normal pace, notwithstanding the below-average yields.

Langhorne Creek is virtually drought-proof, thanks to the unlimited water available for irrigation, and vintage was close to normal in terms of both time and yield. Shiraz came in by late March/early April. Colour is exceptional, the flavour of the Shiraz a standout.

McLaren Vale yields were down around 20 per cent overall, with normal amounts of the best chardonnay for many years, cabernet sauvignon down 5 to 10 per cent and deeply coloured shiraz down 30 to 40 per cent. The yields, coupled with ideal ripening conditions, meant the vintage ran one to two weeks early.

The **Adelaide Hills**, in common with other cool regions, welcomed the very dry and warm growing conditions. Both flavour and acidity levels were excellent, flavour developing early in much the same way as in southern Victoria; its key white varieties of chardonnay and sauvignon blanc promise much.

The **Barossa** and **Eden Valleys**' red grapes were affected by the February rainfall, and yields below the long-term average did not fully compensate. In a theme which may occur to a lesser or greater degree in other South Australian regions, there will likely be some red wines with high baume/alcohol levels yet showing some green, unripe streaks, a situation which occurred in 2001. The specific cause this year has been rapid sugar accumulation and berry shrivel in the wake of the rain and the berry splitting. But it would be entirely wrong to take this as the rule rather than the exception.

The **Clare Valley**, chronically short of water, felt the full impact of the drought, with yields 30 to 40 per cent down on the long-term average. The conditions were warm and dry, accelerating ripening, and the miracle of the 2002 riesling quality (the highest since 1980) was not repeated. However, quality will be good, with pronounced aromas and balancing acidity. The small-berried red grapes will provide excellent colour and plenty of tannin; how much mid-palate flavour there is remains to be seen.

Like the Clare Valley, the **Riverland** and **Riverina** regions could not be expected to repeat the amazing 2002 vintage, which combined high yields with very high quality. Yields were down in 2003, and quality across the board is sound rather than outstanding, although red wine colour is a strong point.

As always, Western Australia marched to the tune of its own drum. The **Perth Hills** had one of its best years on record, the cooler than normal conditions and complete absence of disease providing grapes with great colour and flavour.

Following a very dry winter, most vineyards in the **Great Southern** region entered the 2003 growing season with lower than normal water reserves and low soil moisture levels. Budburst and flowering were good, with warm temperatures and low wind, conditions that would normally lead to good fruit set. However, many vineyards were already in water stress at this stage; this led to compromised set in some varieties (especially chardonnay, sauvignon blanc and merlot, 10 to 15 per cent down on estimates). The early part of the season, November through January, was very good: mild and dry. Intermittent rain in February saw botrytis infections in most whites, but a very hot spell dried out all infections, resulting in generally clean, sound whites. Rainfalls increased through March, with cool nights that triggered early leaf senescence; this meant that later varieties such as cabernet sauvignon struggled to achieve full ripeness. As always in such conditions, the best-managed vineyards and best sites came through the difficulties with good wines. Chardonnay, Sauvignon Blanc, Merlot and Shiraz are likely to emerge on top.

Margaret River shared much of the curate's egg with the Great Southern region. As ever, winter rainfall was good, and moderately warm weather from veraison set the scene for an outstanding vintage. But then rain fell at the end of February, followed by warm humid weather, which led to some botrytis outbreaks. Hot weather at the start of March led to rapid maturation of the white wine grapes, which, as for much of Australia, came off in a rush, the chardonnay doing best. From here on the reds matured slowly, harassed first by birds, and then (in early April) by more rain and cold weather. By this time most of the reds had been picked, but there will be considerable variation from one vineyard to the next, and also between the southern part of Margaret River and the middle/north.

Finally, **Tasmania** also followed much the same pattern as the Great Southern region. An absolutely textbook summer ended with rain prior to and during vintage. The early-ripening pinot noir and chardonnay varietals did best, but botrytis impacted on riesling and sauvignon blanc.

grape variety plantings

the following tables show the dramatic increase in Australia's vineyards over the past 7 years. I have elected to use the official Australian Bureau of Statistics (ABS) figures rather than those collected by the Winemakers' Federation of Australia (WFA). There has always been a discrepancy between the two, with the ABS figures lower than those of the WFA, not because the WFA figures are puffed up, but simply because they cast a broader net than does the ABS. Normally the difference has not been overly significant, but in 2002 there was a large discrepancy, largely attributable to shiraz. WFA figures showed a shiraz crush of 445 000 tonnes (and a total crush of 1.65 million tones), whereas the ABS shows a shiraz crush of 362 564 tonnes (and a total of 1 514 000 tonnes). A post mortem on the discrepancy was held, and unofficial agreement reached: the ABS figures understated the crush, but the WFA overstated them, due to some double counting.

Statistical hiccups to one side, riesling has at long last started to show the increase in plantings and crush reflecting the renewed interest in this category. The other figure requiring special comment is pinot noir: notwithstanding an increase in the number of hectares planted, the crush declined by 25 per cent compared with 2001. The reason was the extremely low yield of pinot noir in southern Victoria and Tasmania, two of its strongholds; this was a reflection of the cool and cloudy flowering conditions.

The split between white grape and red grape crush seems to have stabilised at around 45 per cent white and 55 per cent red, compared with 68 per cent white and 32 per cent red only 7 years ago.

wine	1996	1997	1998
Chardonnay			
hectares	11,721	13,713	14,662
tonnes	92,258	119,678	148,515
Riesling			
hectares	3,412	3,423	3,345
tonnes	37,135	32,907	33,811
Sauvignon Blanc			
hectares	1,538	1,725	1,904
tonnes	15,009	13,328	18,405
Semillon			
hectares	4,079	4,803	5,287
tonnes	45,062	52,829	57,112
Other White			
hectares	26,372	27,047	25,566
tonnes	326,894	265,288	271,620
TOTAL WHITE			
hectares	47,122	50,711	50,764
tonnes	516,358	484,030	529,463
Cabernet Sauvignon			
hectares	8,752	11,219	14,695
tonnes	68,839	67,015	91,876
Grenache			
hectares	1,940	2,014	1,988
tonnes	26,212	24,198	23,842
Mourvedre			
hectares	583	614	696
tonnes	8,821	7,629	8,238
Merlot			
hectares	1,246	2,461	3,802
tonnes	9,227	10,331	13,881
Pinot Noir			
hectares	1,748	1,896	2,192
tonnes	14,801	13,924	19,123
Shiraz			
hectares	10,389	13,410	17,930
tonnes	81,674	94,848	131,427
Other Red			
hectares	5,902	6,149	6,372
tonnes	36,469	34,503	38,224
TOTAL RED			
hectares	30,560	37,763	47,675
tonnes	246,043	252,448	326,611
TOTAL GRAPES			
hectares	77,682	88,474	98,439
tonnes	762,401	736,478	856,074
PERCENTAGE (tonnes)			
White	67.73%	65.73%	61.85%
Red	32.27%	34.27%	38.15%

wine	1999	2000	2001	2002
Chardonnay				
hectares	16,855	18,526	18,434	21,724
tonnes	210,770	201,248	245,199	256,328
Riesling				
hectares	3,347	3,658	3,558	3,962
tonnes	30,144	26,800	26,980	27,838
Sauvignon Blanc				
hectares	2,413	2,706	2,766	2,914
tonnes	22,834	21,487	25,326	28,567
Semillon				
hectares	6,044	6,832	6,803	6,610
tonnes	80,191	77,506	88,427	100,785
Other White				
hectares	26,331	27,873	25,781	26,215
tonnes	282,459	265,196	232,334	255,253
TOTAL WHITE				
hectares	54,990	59,595	57,342	61,425
tonnes	626,398	592,237	618,266	666,771
Cabernet Sauvignon				
hectares	21,169	26,674	28,609	29,573
tonnes	127,494	159,358	249,288	257,223
Grenache				
hectares	2,255	2,756	2,427	2,528
tonnes	24,196	23,998	22,563	26,260
Mourvedre				
hectares	866	1,147	1,128	1,238
tonnes	9,217	10,496	11,624	12,452
Merlot				
hectares	6,387	8,575	9,330	10,101
tonnes	31,801	51,269	80,142	104,423
Pinot Noir				
hectares	2,996	3,756	4,142	4,414
tonnes	19,668	19,578	29,514	21,341
Shiraz				
hectares	25,596	32,327	33,676	37,031
tonnes	192,330	224,394	311,045	326,564
Other Red				
hectares	8,656	11,347	11,621	12,284
tonnes	45,103	57,255	68,640	99,467
TOTAL RED				
hectares	67,925	86,582	90,933	97,169
tonnes	449,809	546,348	772,816	847,730
TOTAL GRAPES				
hectares	122,915	146,177	148,275	158,594
tonnes	1,076,207	1,138,585	1,391,082	1,514,501
PERCENTAGE (tonnes)				
White	59.21%	52.02%	44.45%	44.02%
Red	41.79%	47.98%	55.55%	55.98%

🐝 abbey rock   NR

67 Payneham Road, College Park, SA 5069 (postal) **region** Murray Darling
phone (08) 8362 0677 **fax** (08) 8362 9218 **open** Not
winemaker Les Sampson **est.** 2001
product range ($15 R) The basic wines, a Chardonnay, Shiraz and Cabernet Merlot, are made from contract-grown grapes in the Murray Darling and Wrattonbully regions. More extensive wines at various higher price points are being made from a mix of estate-owned vineyards and contract vineyards in the Adelaide Hills, Clare Valley and elsewhere. These wines, including Pinot Noir, Chardonnay and Cabernet Sauvignon, will be progressively brought onto the market over the next 12 months.
summary A new but rapidly expanding business with wines sourced from a number of regions spread across South Australia. The premium wines will be made from pinot noir (2.2 ha) and chardonnay (3.5 ha) near Hahndorf in the Adelaide Hills, and from chardonnay (2 ha), semillon (6.5 ha), shiraz (8 ha) and grenache (2 ha) in the Clare Valley. Plans are afoot to increase both the Adelaide Hills and the Clare Valley plantings.

abercorn   ★★★★

Cassilis Road, Mudgee, NSW 2850 **region** Mudgee
phone 1800 000 959 **fax** (02) 6373 3108 **open** Thurs–Mon 10.30–4.30
winemaker Tim Stevens **production** 7000 cases **est.** 1996
product range ($14.95–34.95 R) Chardonnay, Unwooded Chardonnay, Reserve Chardonnay, Shiraz, A Reserve Shiraz, Shiraz Cabernet; Barons Court is second label, comprising Chardonnay and Shiraz.
summary Tim and Connie Stevens acquired the 25-year-old Abercorn Vineyard in 1996. While admirably located next door to Huntington Estate, it had become somewhat run-down. Rejuvenation of the vineyard is largely complete, and the tasting room, opened in January 2001, has proved a major success. National distribution through National Wine & Beer Distributors; exports to the UK.

ada river   ★★★☆

2330 Main Road, Neerim South, Vic 3831 **region** Gippsland
phone (03) 5628 1661 **fax** (03) 5628 1661 **open** 10–6 weekends and public holidays
winemaker Peter Kelliher, Chris Kelliher **production** 2000 cases **est.** 1983
product range ($14–27 CD) From Gippsland-grown grapes Chardonnay, Pinot Noir, Merlot, Cabernet Sauvignon, Cabernets; from Yarra Valley grapes Traminer, Chardonnay, Pinot Noir; Heathcote Shiraz, Baw Baw Port.
summary The Kelliher family first planted vines on their dairy farm at Neerim South in 1983, extending the original Millstream Vineyard in 1989 and increasing plantings even further by establishing the nearby Manilla Vineyard in 1994. Until 2000, Ada River leased a Yarra Valley vineyard; it has since relinquished that lease and in its place has established a vineyard at Heathcote in conjunction with a local grower.

Ada River Gippsland Pinot Noir
YYYY 2001 Medium red, with just a touch of purple remaining; clean dark cherry and plum aromas are followed by a clean, direct cherry and plum-flavoured palate; not complex, but a pretty wine.   **rating:** 86
best drinking Now–2005 **drink with** Smoked quail • $18

Ada River Heathcote Shiraz
YYYYY 2001 Dense, inky purple-red; the bouquet ranges through dark berries, dark chocolate, licorice and subtle oak, the palate with full, rich and ripe dark berries and spices. Carries its alcohol without heat. **rating:** 94
best drinking 2006–2016 **best vintages** '00, '01 **drink with** Beef casserole • $27

Ada River Gippsland Merlot
YYYY 2001 Medium red-purple; the spicy, cedary, leafy, tobacco aromas are not too green; the oak sweetening on the palate is quite strong, but does not obscure the spicy varietal character of the fruit.   **rating:** 86
best drinking 2004–2008 **drink with** Braised rabbit • $18

affleck   NR

154 Millynn Road off Bungendore Road, Bungendore, NSW 2621 **region** Canberra District
phone (02) 6236 9276 **fax** (02) 6236 9090 **open** 7 days 9–5
winemaker Ian Hendry **production** 500 cases **est.** 1976
product range ($14–25 CD) Chardonnay, Late Picked Sauvignon Blanc, Sweet White, Pinot Noir, Cabernet Shiraz, Muscat, Vintage Port.

summary The cellar-door and mail-order price list says that the wines are 'grown, produced and bottled on the estate by Ian and Susie Hendry with much dedicated help from family and friends'. The original 2.5-hectare vineyard has been expanded to 7 hectares, and a new tasting room (offering light lunches) opened in 1999.

ainsworth estate ★★★☆

110 Ducks Lane, Seville, Vic 3139 **region** Yarra Valley
phone (03) 5964 4711 **fax** (03) 5964 4311 **open** Thurs–Mon 10.30–5
winemaker Denis Craig **production** 3000 cases **est.** 1994
product range ($18–35 CD) Unoaked Chardonnay, Chardonnay, Pinot Noir, Shiraz, Reserve Shiraz, Cabernet Sauvignon Cabernet Franc, Cabernet Sauvignon.
summary Denis Craig and wife Kerri planted their first 2 hectares of chardonnay and shiraz near Healesville in 1994. The grapes from this vineyard were sold until the 2000 vintage, when the first wines were made under the Ainsworth Estate label. In the intervening period they established a second vineyard at Ducks Lane, Seville, with another 2 hectares of vines, here planted to shiraz and pinot noir. They have also turned from selling to purchasing grapes, with a total of just under 3 hectares of chardonnay, shiraz and cabernet sauvignon grown for them under contract. Their cellar-door and barbecue area at Ducks Lane opened in March 2001; for the time being, at least, Denis Craig and Al Fencaros make the wines at Fencaros' Allinda Winery in Dixons Creek. Three executive apartments overlooking the vineyard are also available.

Ainsworth Estate Chardonnay
▼▼▼▽ 2001 Light to medium yellow-green; the bouquet is clean, with subtle oak and not overmuch fruit; the light-bodied palate is fresh though lacking fruit intensity; well handled in the winery. **rating:** 84
best drinking Now **drink with** Vegetarian antipasto • $21.50

Ainsworth Estate Shiraz
▼▼▼▼ 2001 Youthful red-purple; the firm bouquet is yet to open up and display varietal character, but the firm palate does offer dark cherry fruit on which to build with time in bottle. **rating:** 85
best drinking Now–2006 **drink with** Braised beef • $22

Ainsworth Estate Reserve Shiraz
▼▼▼▼ 2001 Medium red-purple, more advanced than the varietal version from the same year. The bouquet is solid, with greater complexity to the dark berry fruit, the palate likewise having slightly more weight and texture to the dark berry fruit flavours. Reasonable length; good result from a challenging vintage. **rating:** 86
best drinking Now–2007 **drink with** Porterhouse steak • $35

albert river wines ★★★☆

1–117 Mundoolun Connection Road, Tamborine, Qld 4270 **region** Queensland Coastal
phone (07) 5543 6622 **fax** (07) 5543 6627 **open** 7 days 10–4
winemaker Peter Scudamore-Smith MW (Consultant) **production** 5000 cases **est.** 1998
product range ($15–32 CD) Jacaranda Semillon, Unwooded Chardonnay, Chardonnay, Sparkling White, Sparkling Red, Roundelay (Shiraz Merlot Cabernet blend), Grand Masters Shiraz, Merlot, Shiraz Cabernet Merlot, Red Belly Black Port.
summary Albert River is yet another high-profile winery to open on the Gold Coast hinterland, with all of its distribution through cellar door, mail order and local restaurants. The proprietors are David and Janette Bladin, with a combined 30 years' experience in tourism and hospitality, who have acquired and relocated two of Queensland's most historic buildings, Tamborine House and Auchenflower House. The winery itself is housed in a newly constructed annex to Auchenflower House; the Bladins have established 10 hectares of vineyards on the property, and have another 50 hectares under contract.

Albert River Merlot
▼▼▼▽ 2001 Crimson-purple; the clean, fresh, light bouquet is followed, logically enough, by a light-bodied palate with enjoyable sweet berry fruit, fine tannins and minimal oak. **rating:** 84
best drinking Now–2005 **drink with** Lamb cutlets • $24

Albert River Cabernet Shiraz Merlot
▼▼▼▼▽ 2000 Medium to full red-purple; the bouquet offers plenty of ripe cassis/berry fruit with well-integrated oak, a theme which continues on the quite rich palate. A gold medal winner at the 2002 Cowra Wine Show, and deserved the award. **rating:** 90
best drinking Now–2008 **best vintages** '00 **drink with** Spring lamb • $22

aldgate ridge ★★★☆

23 Nation Ridge Road, Aldgate, SA 5154 **region** Adelaide Hills
phone (08) 8388 5225 **fax** (08) 8388 5856 **open** By appointment
winemaker David Powell (Contract) **production** 400 cases **est.** 1992
product range ($31 CD) Pinot Noir.
summary Jill and Chris Whisson acquired their vineyard property in 1988, when the land was still being used as a market garden. The 2.5 hectares of pinot noir now established were planted in two stages, in 1992 and 1997, the first block with some of the first of the new Burgundian clones to be propagated in Australia. Further plantings of pinot noir and a small block of sauvignon blanc have been added. The vineyard is typical of the Adelaide Hills region, on a rolling to steep southeast-facing hillside at the 440-metre altitude line. The wine is contract-made by the celebrated David Powell of Torbreck Wines in the Barossa Valley, and apart from mail order, has limited fine wine retail distribution.

Aldgate Ridge Pinot Noir

TTTT 2001 The colour is slightly dull or hazy, presumably because the wine is unfiltered. A complex earthy/foresty bouquet with black plum fruit is followed by a big, powerful palate, with abundant tannins on the finish. Really needs more mid-palate fruit to carry the power. Very much in the style of the 1999 vintage.
rating: 87

best drinking 2004–2007 **drink with** Rich game • $31

aldinga bay winery ★★★

Main South Road, Aldinga, SA 5173 **region** McLaren Vale
phone (08) 8556 3179 **fax** (08) 8556 3350 **open** 7 days 10–5
winemaker Nick Girolamo **production** 8000 cases **est.** 1979
product range ($13–21 CD) Verdelho, Chardonnay, Shiraz, Sangiovese, Petit Verdot, Reserve Tawny Port.
summary The former Donolga Winery has had a name and image change since Nick Girolamo, the son of founders Don and Olga Girolamo, returned from Roseworthy College with a degree in oenology. Nick Girolamo has taken over both the winemaking and the marketing; prices remain modest, though not as low as they once were, reflecting an increase in the quality and an upgrade in packaging. Aldinga Bay also has some very interesting varietal plantings, 16 varieties in all, including petit verdot, nebbiolo, barbera and sangiovese.

alexandra bridge wines ★★★★☆

101 Brockman Highway, Karridale, WA 6288 **region** Margaret River
phone (08) 9758 5999 **fax** (08) 9758 5988 **open** 7 days 10–4.30
winemaker Philip Tubb, Julian Scott **production** 12000 cases **est.** 1999
product range ($19.50–24.50 R) Sauvignon Blanc, Semillon Sauvignon Blanc, Unwooded Chardonnay, Shiraz, Cabernet Merlot; Reserve range of Semillon, Chardonnay, Shiraz, Cabernet Sauvignon.
summary To say that in the first few years of this decade Alexandra Bridge had a complicated and convoluted history is to put it mildly. However, it is the outcome which matters. Since July 2002 it has become the operating arm of Australian Wine Holdings, with the 800-tonne winery commissioned in February 2000, the first built in the Karridale area at the southern end of the Margaret River. The Brockman Vineyard, planted in three stages commencing in 1995, is estate-owned and has a total of 30 hectares of semillon, sauvignon blanc, chardonnay, shiraz and cabernet sauvignon. The grapes coming from the Brockman Vineyard are supplemented by long-term supply agreements with other Margaret River growers. The quality of the wines has not suffered during the period of corporate turmoil. The wines are exported to Europe and South-East Asia.

Alexandra Bridge Reserve Semillon

TTTT 2001 Light green-yellow; full, barrel-ferment spicy oak dominates the bouquet and the palate, although the length of the fruit does come through on the finish. Great for oak lovers, and for the judges at the 2002 Margaret River Wine Show, who gave the wine a top gold medal. **rating:** 88
best drinking Now–2006 **drink with** Pan-fried chicken breast

Alexandra Bridge Estate Sauvignon Blanc

TTTT 2002 Very pale, almost water-white; crisp, clean mineral aromas with a hint of gooseberry lead into a crisp, tangy and fresh, bone-dry palate, with a tingling finish. **rating:** 88
best drinking Now **drink with** Cold seafood salad • $19.50

Alexandra Bridge Estate Semillon Sauvignon Blanc

▼▼▼▼ 2002 Very pale straw-green; the bouquet is slightly fuzzy, with a hint of reduction, but the palate is altogether brighter and firmer, with good length and acid balance. **rating:** 85

best drinking Now drink with Poached mussels • $19.50

Alexandra Bridge Reserve Chardonnay

▼▼▼▼▽ 2001 Bright yellow-green; complex barrel-ferment aromas are in balance with the tangy stone fruit of the bouquet; a very powerful wine in the mouth, with considerable alcohol evident; rich peach fruit and good length. **rating:** 90

best drinking Now–2007 drink with Seafood risotto

Alexandra Bridge Estate Shiraz

▼▼▼▼▽ 2001 Medium to full red-purple; fresh black cherry with some white and black pepper nuances on the bouquet is followed by a fresh, red berry-fruited palate; vibrant, but needing time. **rating:** 91

best drinking 2004–2009 drink with Beef in black bean sauce • $24.50

Alexandra Bridge Reserve Shiraz

▼▼▼▼▽ 2001 Deep, inky purple; concentrated dark plum and complex barrel-ferment inputs on the bouquet lead into a massive palate tailor-made for the US and Robert Parker; failing that, extreme patience needed. **rating:** 92

best drinking 2010–2020 best vintages '01 drink with Leave it in the cellar

Alexandra Bridge Reserve Cabernet Sauvignon

▼▼▼▼▽ 2001 Medium to full red-purple; the moderately intense bouquet has blackcurrant/cassis fruit neatly tied in by French oak; focused varietal fruit on the palate, supported by fine tannins and balanced oak, attests to the winemaking skills used to produce this wine. **rating:** 93

best drinking 2006–2016 best vintages '01 drink with Kangaroo fillet

alkoomi ★★★★★

Wingebellup Road, Frankland, WA 6396 **region** Great Southern
phone (08) 9855 2229 **fax** (08) 9855 2284 **open** 7 days 10.30–5
winemaker Michael Staniford, Merv Lange **production** 80 000 cases **est.** 1971
product range ($17–59 R) Frankland River Riesling, Wandoo (Semillon), Sauvignon Blanc, Southlands Chenin Sauvignon Blanc, Chardonnay, Late Harvest, Sparkling Shiraz, Shiraz, Jarrah Shiraz, Southlands Cabernet Shiraz Merlot, Cabernet Sauvignon, Blackbutt, Pedro Ximinez Liqueur.
summary For those who see the wineries of Western Australia as suffering from the tyranny of distance, this most remote of all wineries shows there is no tyranny after all. It is a story of unqualified success due to sheer hard work, and no doubt to Merv and Judy Lange's aversion to borrowing a single dollar from the bank. The substantial production is entirely drawn from the ever-expanding estate vineyards, which by 2003 amounted to over 80 hectares. Wine quality across the range is impeccable, always with precisely defined varietal character. National retail distribution; exports to Hong Kong, Singapore, Japan, Thailand, the UK, the US, Canada, The Netherlands, Switzerland and France.

Alkoomi Frankland River Riesling

▼▼▼▼▽ 2002 Light straw-green; a clean, crisp, minerally bouquet, less pungently aromatic than is often the case with Alkoomi. The palate comes alive with fresh, lively lime and mineral flavours; the SO_2 and CO_2 evident now will stand the wine in good stead as it develops. **rating:** 90

best drinking 2005–2012 best vintages '94, '95, '96, '98, '99, '01 drink with Salad Niçoise • $19

Alkoomi Sauvignon Blanc

▼▼▼▼▽ 2002 Light green-yellow; a fragrant aromatic gooseberry bouquet with a faintly reductive edge is followed by a lively gooseberry and grass palate with abundant varietal character. **rating:** 90

best drinking Now best vintages '95, '96, '97, '98, '00, '01 drink with Ginger prawns • $19

Alkoomi Frankland River Shiraz

▼▼▼▼▼ 2001 Deep purple-red, bright and attractive; seductive raspberry and plum fruit aromas are supported by neatly handled oak; as the bouquet promises, the palate is powerful, yet elegant; raspberry and blackberry flavours plus fine, savoury tannins and restrained oak all contribute to a wine of great finesse in the typical Alkoomi style. **rating:** 94

best drinking 2006–2011 best vintages '90, '93, '94, '97, '98, '99, '01 drink with Lamb fillet • $20

Alkoomi Jarrah Shiraz

ŸŸŸŸŸ **2000** Medium purple-red; the fragrant and aromatic bouquet has fragrant red cherry/redcurrant and spice aromas, the oak subtle; the volume of fruit sweetness picks up markedly on the palate, which is almost entirely fruit-driven, although there are fine tannins and oak in support. **rating: 94**

best drinking 2004–2012 **best vintages** '99, '00 **drink with** Roast venison • $39

allandale ★★★★

Allandale Road, Allandale via Pokolbin, NSW 2321 **region** Lower Hunter Valley
phone (02) 4990 4526 **fax** (02) 4990 1714 **open** Mon–Sat 9–5, Sun 10–5
winemaker Bill Sneddon, Steve Langham **production** 18 000 cases **est.** 1978
product range ($15–24 CD) Semillon, Sauvignon Blanc, Verdelho, Chardonnay, William Methode Champenoise, Late Harvest Semillon Sauvignon Blanc, Fleur (dessert), Lombardo (light red), Hilltops Shiraz, Hilltops Cabernet Sauvignon, Orange Cabernet Sauvignon, Mudgee Cabernet Sauvignon.
summary Without ostentation, this medium-sized winery has been under the control of winemaker Bill Sneddon for well over a decade. Allandale has developed something of a reputation as a Chardonnay specialist, but does offer a broad range of wines of consistently good quality, with several red wines sourced from outside the Hunter Valley. The wines are exported to the UK, Switzerland, Singapore, Malaysia and Fiji.

Allandale Hunter River Chardonnay

ŸŸŸŸŸ **2002** Medium green-yellow, slightly developed given the age of the wine, but the hue is good. Complex barrel-ferment aromas do not feed too strongly into the palate, which has excellent intensity and length. **rating: 92**

best drinking Now–2007 **best vintages** '91, '94, '96, '98, '99, '00, '02 **drink with** Smoked salmon • $18

allinda NR

119 Lorimers Lane, Dixons Creek, Vic 3775 **region** Yarra Valley
phone (03) 5965 2450 **fax** (03) 5965 2467 **open** Weekends and public holidays 11–5
winemaker Al Fencaros **production** 2500 cases **est.** 1991
product range ($16.50–24.50 CD) Riesling, Sauvignon Blanc, Chardonnay, Late Harvest Riesling, Shiraz, Cabernets.
summary Winemaker Al Fencaros has a Bachelor of Wine Science (Charles Sturt University) and was formerly employed by De Bortoli in the Yarra Valley. All the Allinda wines are produced on-site; all except the Shiraz (from Heathcote) are estate-grown from a little over 3 hectares of vineyards. Limited retail distribution in Melbourne and Sydney.

all saints estate ★★★★★

All Saints Road, Wahgunyah, Vic 3687 **region** Rutherglen
phone (02) 6033 1922 **fax** (02) 6033 3515 **open** Mon–Sat 9–5.30, Sun 10–5.30
winemaker Dan Crane **production** 35 000 cases **est.** 1864
product range ($14–395 CD) At the top of the table wines come Carlyle Chardonnay, Sparkling Shiraz, Shiraz, Ruby Cabernet, Durif; then come All Saints Riesling, Marsanne, Images White, Angelina, Late Harvest Semillon, Images Rose, Images Shiraz, Shiraz, Merlot, Cabernet Sauvignon; The Keep Tawny Port. Tokays and muscats in the official Rutherglen three-tiered classification starting with Classic, then Grand, and finally, Rare.
summary The winery rating reflects the fortified wines, but the table wines are more than adequate. The Terrace restaurant (open 7 days for lunch and Saturday night for dinner) makes this a compulsory and most enjoyable stop for any visitor to the northeast. All Saints and St Leonards are now wholly owned by Peter Brown; the vast majority of the wines are sold through the cellar door and by mailing list. Exports to the US. The faux castle, modelled on a Scottish castle beloved of the founder, is now classified by the Historic Buildings Council.

All Saints Estate Carlyle Sparkling Shiraz

ŸŸŸŸ **2000** Medium purple-red, with good mousse; dark cherry and a touch of licorice on both bouquet and palate mark a well-balanced wine which is not too sweet, and which avoids overt oak in the base wine. **rating: 86**

best drinking Now–2006 **drink with** Cold meats • $25

All Saints Carlyle Durif

ŸŸŸŸ **2000** Medium to full red-purple; deep, ripe prune/plum jam/dark fruit aromas foretell a dense, powerful and concentrated palate full of similar flavours but needing to be approached with extreme caution. **rating: 89**

best drinking 2007–2017 **best vintages** '99 **drink with** Leave it in the cellar • $38

All Saints Classic Rutherglen Tokay (500 ml)

▼▼▼▼▽ NV Amber-brown; a clean bouquet with a mix of tea-leaf, toffee and butterscotch leads into a sweet, quite raisiny palate with very good balancing acidity on the finish.   **rating:** 91

best drinking Now **drink with** Espresso coffee and dark chocolate • $24

All Saints Grand Rutherglen Tokay (375 ml)

▼▼▼▼▼ NV Deep olive-amber brown; the bouquet is spicy and rich with some plum pudding aromas, the palate powerful and concentrated, less overtly sweet/raisiny than the Classic, but more complex and spicy; has excellent length and good acidity.   **rating:** 94

best drinking Now **drink with** Espresso coffee and dark chocolate • $32

All Saints Rare Rutherglen Tokay (375 ml)

▼▼▼▼▼ NV Deep olive; a rich, intense, complex and deep bouquet flows onto a palate with exceptional length and balance, having significantly more finesse than the Grand Tokay. The flavours are of tea-leaf and brown toffee, but no fish oil (a quite common varietal character for tokay). Fantastic length.   **rating:** 97

best drinking Now **drink with** Espresso coffee and dark chocolate • $65

All Saints Classic Rutherglen Muscat

▼▼▼▼▽ NV Some reddish tints to the medium tawny-brown colour are evidence of (relative) youth. A perfumed, grapey, raisiny bouquet leads into a lively, highly flavoured, grapey/raisiny palate. A very pure varietal expression of young Muscat.   **rating:** 90

best drinking Now **drink with** Espresso coffee and walnuts • $24

All Saints Grand Rutherglen Muscat

▼▼▼▼▽ NV Deeper brown than the Classic, and quite viscous when swirled in the glass. A rich and compelling bouquet is loaded with raisin and plum pudding aromas; the palate is intensely grapey and spicy, with fruit, not spirit, dominant.   **rating:** 93

best drinking Now **drink with** Espresso coffee and walnuts • $32

All Saints Rare Rutherglen Muscat

▼▼▼▼▼ NV Deep, dark brown with an olive rim; both the bouquet and palate are as complex and concentrated as one might expect, but, like the Rare Tokay, with remarkable finesse: this is not a raw expression of power or age. Once again, finishes with great acidity.   **rating:** 97

best drinking Now **drink with** Espresso coffee and walnuts • $65

allusion wines   NR

Smith Hill Road, Yankalilla, SA 5203 **region** Southern Fleurieu
phone (08) 8558 3333 **fax** (08) 8558 3333 **open** Thurs–Sun 11–5
winemaker Contract (previously Normans) **production** 750 cases **est.** 1996
product range ($17–35 CD) Semillon Sauvignon Blanc, Viognier, Shiraz Viognier, Cabernet Sauvignon.
summary Steve and Wendy Taylor purchased the property on which Allusion Wines is established in 1980, and have since planted 4 hectares of vines and 35 000 trees. Steve Taylor's 20 years as a chef has strongly influenced both the varietal plantings and the wine styles made, which (not altogether surprisingly) are designed to be consumed with good food. The wine is fermented off-site, then matured on-site before being contract-bottled.

allyn river wines   NR

Torryburn Road, East Gresford, NSW 2311 **region** Upper Hunter Valley
phone (02) 4938 9279 **fax** (02) 4938 9279 **open** Fri–Mon and public holidays 9–5, or by appointment
winemaker David Hook (Contract) **production** 650 cases **est.** 1996
product range ($14.50–16.50 CD) Semillon, Chardonnay Semillon, Dessert Semillon, Chambourcin.
summary Allyn River is situated on the alluvial soils on the banks of the stream which has given the vineyard its name. The plantings of 1.5 hectares each of semillon and chambourcin were in part inspired by the knowledge that Dr Henry Lindeman had established his famous Cawarra Vineyard in the locality, and since Allyn River's foundation in 1996, others have moved to the area to establish vineyards totalling more than 20 hectares within a 10-kilometre radius of Allyn River. As well as a wine tasting room and picnic facilities, self-contained cottage accommodation, known as the Maples Cottage, is available on the property.

🐝 amarillo vines · NR

27 Marlock Place, Karnup, WA 6176 **region** Peel
phone (08) 9537 1800 **open** 7 days, by appointment
winemaker Phil Franzone (Contract) **production** 665 cases **est.** 1995
product range ($12–16 CD) Verdelho, Chardonnay, Shiraz, Grenache, Merlot, Cabernet Sauvignon.
summary The Ashby family have market garden and landscaping backgrounds, and the establishment of a small vineyard on the block of land in which their house sits seemed a natural thing to do. What is unusual is the density of the planting, the utilisation of a lyre trellis, and the permanent netting erected around the vineyard. So it is that they do not speak of acres or hectares, but of the 2500 vines planted, and of the production as 8000 bottles.

🐝 amarok estate · ★★★☆

Lot 547 Caves Road, Wilyabrup, WA 6284 (postal) **region** Margaret River
phone (08) 9756 6888 **fax** (08) 9756 6555 **open** Not
winemaker Kevin McKay (Contract) **production** 1500 cases **est.** 1999
product range ($16–24 ML) Semillon Sauvignon Blanc, Sauvignon Blanc, Shiraz, Merlot, Cabernet Sauvignon.
summary John and Libby Staley, with their youngest daughter Megan, her husband Shane (and youngest grandson Lewis) have all had hands-on involvement in the establishment of 20 hectares of vineyards, clearing bushland, ripping, rock picking, stick picking and planting, etc. The soils are gravelly loam over a clay granite base, the vineyard having a western aspect 5 kilometres from the Indian Ocean. The Staleys senior have commenced building a home on the property, and Shane and Megan carry out all the viticultural tasks. Production will increase significantly in the years ahead as the vines come into full bearing.

Amarok Estate Sauvignon Blanc

♥♥♥♡ 2002 Light straw-green; the bouquet has a complex gooseberry/tropical mix, and a touch of slow-ferment character; the full-bodied palate has plenty of flavour, but is essentially soft, with a slightly spongy finish. **rating:** 84
best drinking Now **drink with** Breast of turkey • $17

Amarok Estate Shiraz

♥♥♥♥ 2002 Strong purple-red; sweet blackberry and plum fruit plus subtle oak on the bouquet lead into a powerful, slightly extractive palate, needing time to soften. Should repay patience. **rating:** 86
best drinking 2007–2012 **drink with** Leave it in the cellar • $24

Amarok Estate Merlot

♥♥♥♥ 2002 Solid, healthy red-purple; the rich bouquet has dark blackcurrant and olive varietal character, which comes through on the powerful, savoury palate, with notes of earth and olive surrounding the blackcurrant fruit. Positive varietal character, and well made. **rating:** 89
best drinking 2006–2011 **drink with** Butterfly leg of lamb • $22

Amarok Estate Cabernet Sauvignon

♥♥♥♥♡ 2002 Medium red-purple; the bouquet has very ripe black fruits, almost spicy, but not jammy; the palate has similar ripe, spicy/chocolatey/black fruit flavours supported by fine, ripe tannins and well-handled oak. Has a particularly nice finish and aftertaste. **rating:** 90
best drinking 2006–2013 **best vintages** '02 **drink with** Kangaroo fillet • $22.50

amberley estate · ★★★☆

Thornton Road, Yallingup, WA 6282 **region** Margaret River
phone (08) 9755 2288 **fax** (08) 9755 2171 **open** 7 days 10–4.30
winemaker Eddie Price, David Watson **production** 90 000 cases **est.** 1986
product range ($16–63 R) Semillon, Sauvignon Blanc, Semillon Sauvignon Blanc, Chenin Blanc, Chardonnay, Charlotte Street Chardonnay Semillon, Shiraz, First Selection Shiraz, Charlotte Street Shiraz Chardonnay Cabernet, Cabernet Merlot, Cabernet Sauvignon, Cabernet Reserve.
summary Based its initial growth on its ultra-commercial, fairly sweet Chenin Blanc, which continues to provide the volume for the brand, selling out well prior to the following release. However, the quality of all the other wines has risen markedly over recent years as the 31 hectares of estate plantings have become fully mature. Exports to the UK, France, Germany, Singapore, Japan, Hong Kong and the US.

Amberley Estate First Selection Chardonnay

YYYY 2001 Light to medium green-yellow; the wine has a distinctive herb and green metal bouquet, with allied leaf and mint flavours on the palate. The wine has been well made, but has all the hallmarks of unripe fruit. **rating: 86**

best drinking Now–2005 **drink with** Calamari • $36.85

🐌 ambrook wines NR

114 George Street, West Swan, WA 6055 **region** Swan Valley
phone (08) 9274 1003 **fax** (08) 9379 0334 **open** Wed–Fri 12–5, weekends and public holidays 10–5, or by appointment
winemaker Rob Marshal **production** 1200 cases **est.** 1990
product range ($13–16 CD) Semillon, Chenin, Classic White, Late Harvest Semillon, Sweet, Shiraz, Cabernet Sauvignon.
summary Michele Amonini established 4 hectares of chenin blanc, semillon, verdelho, shiraz, cabernet sauvignon and merlot and quietly went about producing a solid range of varietal, estate-based wines which have had their fair share of success at the various West Australian regional wine shows. Modest pricing increases the appeal.

Ambrook Shiraz

YYYY 2002 Inky purple-red; black fruits, prune and hints of earth come through on the very youthful bouquet and palate; as yet the wine is somewhat one-dimensional, but thanks to controlled tannins it has the balance to develop along the lines of the 2001. **rating: 85**

best drinking 2007–2012 **drink with** Beef spare ribs • $13

Ambrook Cabernet Sauvignon

YYYY 2001 Medium red-purple; the bouquet is driven by earthy, varietal blackcurrant fruit, with minimal oak input. On the palate blackcurrant flavours are joined by a touch of chocolate; still very youthful and as yet unshaped, but should get there. **rating: 84**

best drinking 2006–2011 **drink with** Braised lamb shanks • $16

amietta vineyard and winery ★★★☆

30 Steddy Road, Lethbridge, Vic 3332 **region** Geelong
phone (03) 5281 7407 **fax** (03) 5281 7427 **open** By appointment
winemaker Nicholas Clark, Janet Cockbill **production** 150 cases **est.** 1995
product range ($18–30 ML) Riesling, Chardonnay, Rose, Shiraz, Petit Verdot Shiraz, Cabernet Franc Merlot.
summary Janet Cockbill and Nicholas Clark are multi-talented. Both are archaeologists, but Janet manages to combine part-time archaeology, part-time radiography at Geelong Hospital and part-time organic viticulture. Nicholas Clark has nearly completed a viticulture degree at Charles Sturt University, and both he and Janet worked a vintage in France at Michel Chapoutier's biodynamic Domaine de Beates in Provence in 2001. Production is tiny, exacerbated by the couple's unwillingness to release wines which they consider to be not up to standard, and also by poor weather at flowering. Indeed, part of the minuscule production comes from locally grown, purchased grapes. All of that said, Amietta is producing cameo wines of some beauty.

Amietta Vineyard Riesling

YYYY 2001 Bright, light green-yellow; the bouquet has clean, sweet lime, passionfruit and herb aromas, the complex palate with some Germanic characters; slightly less residual sugar might have made an outstanding wine. As it is, exceptionally impressive given the total make of only 75 cases. **rating: 89**

best drinking Now–2007 **drink with** Asparagus and prosciutto • $20

Amietta Vineyard Rose

YYYY 2002 Salmon-pink; the clean bouquet once again shows appropriately protective winemaking; the dry, quite long palate makes no concession to cellar-door or other expectations. Here a mere 20 cases made.**rating: 85**

best drinking Now **drink with** Antipasto • $18

amulet vineyard ★★★☆

Wangaratta Road, Beechworth, Vic 3747 **region** Beechworth
phone (03) 5727 0420 **fax** (03) 5727 0421 **open** Fri–Mon, public and school holidays 10–5, or by appointment
winemaker Sue Thornton (Contract) **production** 1300 cases **est.** 1998

product range ($15–25 CD) Chardonnay Orange Muscat, Reserve Scintilla Rosso (Sparkling Sangiovese) Rosato, Shiraz, Sangiovese Shiraz, Barbera, Orange Muscat.

summary Sue and Eric Thornton have planted a patchwork quilt 4-hectare vineyard, with sangiovese taking 1 hectare, the other varieties 0.5 hectare or less each; in descending order of magnitude are barbera, shiraz, cabernet sauvignon, merlot, nebbiolo, orange muscat, pinot gris and pinot blanc. The vineyard (and cellar-door) is 11 kilometres west of Beechworth on the road to Wangaratta, with the vines planted on gentle slopes at an elevation of 300 metres. The cellar door enjoys panoramic views, and wine sales are both by the glass and by the bottle.

Amulet Vineyard Chardonnay Orange Muscat

♥♥♥♥ 2002 Light straw-green; the bouquet is quite aromatic, and the contribution of each variety is quite evident, with the orange blossom contribution of the muscat; the palate has an interesting flavour and structure, the fruit building on the aftertaste. The only reservation I have is the strange nature of the blend; that said, there is a so-called muscat clone of chardonnay in France. **rating:** 85

best drinking Now **drink with** Sugar-cured tuna • $15

Amulet Vineyard Rosato

♥♥♥♥ 2002 Pink, salmon-tinged; the clean, faintly spicy bouquet is followed by a clean, pleasant, well-made and nicely balanced palate, with touches of strawberry and a relatively dry finish. A blend of Shiraz, Sangiovese and Barbera. **rating:** 85

best drinking Now **drink with** Sun-dried tomatoes on bruschetta • $15

Amulet Vineyard Shiraz

♥♥♥♥♡ 2001 Medium red-purple; a clean, smooth bouquet with dark cherry and splashes of spice and licorice tied together with well-handled oak leads into a rich and powerful palate, needing a decade or more. Grapes grown in the Beechworth area; spends 18 months in French oak, 30 per cent new. **rating:** 92

best drinking 2007–2014 **drink with** Leave it in the cellar • $25

Amulet Vineyard Sangiovese Shiraz

♥♥♥♡ 2001 Typically light colour; a light, spicy/savoury bouquet is followed by a wine with pleasant mouthfeel, in a spicy/savoury/cherry spectrum. The back label is every bit as charming as the bicycling scarecrow on the front, arguably more so than the wine in the bottle. **rating:** 84

best drinking Now **drink with** Smoked beef • $18

anderson   NR

Lot 12 Chiltern Road, Rutherglen, Vic 3685 **region** Rutherglen
phone (02) 6032 8111 **fax** (02) 6032 9028 **open** 7 days 10–5
winemaker Howard Anderson **production** 1500 cases **est.** 1992
product range ($12.50–28 CD) Chenin Blanc, Doux Blanc, Unoaked Chardonnay, Chardonnay, Dulcette, Shiraz, Merlot, Durif, Cabernet Merlot, Cabernet Sauvignon, Late Harvest Tokay, Methode Champenoise range of Pinot Noir Chardonnay, Chenin Blanc, Doux Blanc, Shiraz.
summary Having notched up a winemaking career spanning over 30 years, including a stint at Seppelt Great Western, Howard Anderson and family started their own winery, initially with a particular focus on sparkling wine but now extending across all table wine styles.

Anderson Shiraz Methode Champenoise

♥♥♥♥ 1997 Medium to full red-purple; a complex bouquet with abundant spice, anise and licorice, then a palate with similar ripe fruit flavours, the touch of oak clogging up the finish a little. Somewhat surprisingly, Howard Anderson recommends the wine be drunk within 12 months of disgorgement (equated for this purpose with the date of purchase). **rating:** 87

best drinking Now–2007 **drink with** Borscht • $27

andraos bros   NR

Winilba Vineyard, 150 Vineyard Road, Sunbury, Vic 3429 **region** Sunbury
phone (03) 9740 9703 **fax** (03) 9740 9795 **open** Fri–Sun and public holidays 11–5, or by appointment
winemaker Fred Andraos, Mario Marson (Consultant) **production** 2500 cases **est.** 1989
product range ($18–70 CD) Released under the Olde Winilba label are Riesling, Semillon, Semillon Sauvignon Blanc, Chardonnay, Pinot Shiraz, Pinot Noir, Shiraz, Cabernet Shiraz, Cabernet Sauvignon.

summary The original Winilba Vineyard was first planted in 1863, and remained in production until 1889. Exactly 100 years later the Andraos brothers commenced replanting the vineyard on the property they had purchased 5 years earlier. Over the following years they built a winery from the ruins of the original bluestone cellar, making the inaugural vintage in 1996. They have also established Estelle's Cellar Restaurant on the second floor of the building; it is open for dinner from Tuesday to Sunday and for lunch on Friday, Saturday, Sunday and public holidays.

andrew garrett/ingoldby ★★★☆

Ingoldby Road, McLaren Flat, SA 5171 **region** McLaren Vale
phone (08) 8383 0005 **fax** (08) 8383 0790 **open** 7 days 10–4
winemaker Charles Hargrave **production** 170 000 cases **est.** 1983
product range ($9–27 R) Andrew Garrett range of Sauvignon Blanc Semillon, Marsanne, Chardonnay, Cabernet Merlot, Bold Shiraz, Vintage Chardonnay Pinot Noir, Vintage Sparkling Shiraz, Pinot Noir Chardonnay, Sparkling Burgundy; Garrett range of Sauvignon Blanc, Chardonnay Semillon, Sparkling Chardonnay, Shiraz Cabernet. Under the Ingoldby label are Sauvignon Blanc, Chardonnay, Shiraz, Reserve Shiraz, Roadblock Grenache Shiraz, Tawny Port.
summary Andrew Garrett and Ingoldby are brands within the Beringer Blass wine group, with many of the wines now not having a sole McLaren Vale source but instead being drawn from regions across southeastern Australia. Over the past few years, winemaker Charles Hargrave has produced some excellent wines which provide great value for money.

Ingoldby Rose

▼▼▼▼ 2002 Bright, light purple; the clean, cherry fruit of the bouquet leads into a structured, quite grippy, palate, unusual for the style. Could strike a chord with the appropriate food. **rating:** 85
best drinking Now **drink with** Asian food • $17

andrew garrett vineyard estates ★★★☆

11 Biralee Road, Regency Park, SA 5010 (postal) **region** Yarra Valley
phone (08) 8364 0555 **fax** (08) 8364 5799 **open** at The Grand Hotel, Yarra Glen
winemaker Andrew Garrett **production** 100 000 cases **est.** 1986
product range ($10–52 R) There are two premium wine ranges: from the Yarra Valley in Victoria comes the Yarra Glen label, from the Adelaide Hills in South Australia the Springwood Park label. In a lower price category come the Kelly's Promise (previously McLarens on the Lake) wines of Chardonnay, Shiraz, Cabernet Merlot, Brut Cuvee and the Ironwood range of Chardonnay, Shiraz, Merlot, Cabernet Sauvignon.
summary The irrepressible Andrew Garrett has risen once again after 20 years in the wine industry as 'winemaker, innovator, entrepreneur, marketer and personality' (to use his own words). Andrew Garrett Vineyard Estates is now the umbrella for the Yarra Valley-based Yarra Glen label, the Adelaide Hills-based Springwood Park label, and for the Kelly's Promise range. The 117-hectare Yarra Valley vineyards are the fruit source for all the Yarra Glen wines. The wines are exported to the UK, Europe, Asia and the US.

Kelly's Promise Reserve Langhorne Creek Semillon

▼▼▼▼ 2002 Medium yellow-green; a potent and aromatic bouquet with abundant ripe citrus and tropical fruit leads into an equally flavoursome, faintly sweet, drink asap, palate. Clever winemaking. **rating:** 87
best drinking Now **drink with** Takeaway • $14.99

Yarra Glen Sauvignon Blanc

▼▼▼▼ 2001 Glowing yellow-green; the clean bouquet has abundant ripe, tropical overtones to the core fruit; the palate is too ripe and tropical for much varietal character to come through, but the wine is certainly flavoursome. **rating:** 86
best drinking Now **drink with** Smoked salmon • $14.99

Yarra Glen Chardonnay Brut

▼▼▼▼ Bright, light green-straw; the firm and citrussy bouquet leads into a palate with good length and nectarine/citrus flavour; well balanced, although not especially complex. No indication whatsoever is given on the age of the wine or the time it spent on lees. **rating:** 87
best drinking Now–2005 **drink with** Hors d'oeuvres • $14.99

Springwood Park Botrytis

TTTT **1999** Golden bronze; the complex bouquet has cumquat, dried apricot and honey aromas, and while the palate is not especially luscious or sweet, its balance is good, as is its intensity. A blend of Semillon and Chardonnay from Coonawarra and the Adelaide Hills, an unholy alliance if ever there was one.   **rating:** 86

best drinking Now **drink with** Fruit tart • $16.99

Kelly's Promise Shiraz

TTTT **2001** Medium red-purple; the moderately intense bouquet has a mix of savoury and light blackberry aromas; the light-bodied palate has good balance between savoury edges, and blackberry and spice fruit.

rating: 85

best drinking Now–2005 **drink with** Meat pie • $9.99

Yarra Glen Shiraz

TTTT **2001** Bright purple-red; the clean bouquet offers blackberry, black cherry and some spice, and the elegant, light to medium-bodied palate has a nice blend of flavours, finishing with fine tannins.   **rating:** 88

best drinking 2004–2008 **drink with** Osso buco • $14.99

andrew harris vineyards   ★★★☆

Sydney Road, Mudgee, NSW 2850 **region** Mudgee
phone (02) 6373 1213 **fax** (02) 6373 1296 **open** By appointment
winemaker Frank Newman **production** 42 000 cases **est.** 1991
product range ($15–45 R) Semillon, Semillon Sauvignon Blanc, Pinot Gris, Verdelho, Chardonnay, Shiraz, Merlot, Cabernet Sauvignon; Reserve range of Chardonnay, Shiraz, Cabernet Merlot, Cabernet Sauvignon; Limited Release Orange Chardonnay, Three Regions Special Blend Chardonnay; the Flagships The Vision (Shiraz Cabernet Sauvignon), Double Vision (sparkling Shiraz).
summary Andrew and Deb Harris lost no time after purchasing a 300-hectare sheep station southeast of Mudgee in 1991. The first 6 hectares of vineyard were planted in that year and have since been expanded to 106 hectares. A substantial portion of the production is sold to others, but production under the Andrew Harris label has risen significantly in recent years. There is now a spread of price and quality, with a string of difficult vintages also impacting, so some care is needed in choosing the wines. Exports to the US, Canada, Singapore, Malaysia, Japan and New Zealand.

Andrew Harris Semillon Sauvignon Blanc

TTTT **2002** Medium yellow-green; the bouquet is clean and solid, with not much life or zest, the palate much the same. However, it must be said that some years of bottle development may benefit the wine greatly; at the moment the two components are simply checkmating each other.   **rating:** 85

best drinking 2004–2008 **drink with** Pasta • $16

Andrew Harris Orange Chardonnay

TTTT **2002** Bright, light yellow-green; very strong, high toast barrel-ferment aromas utterly dominate the bouquet, and, inevitably enough, come through strongly on the palate, where tight citrussy fruit is just discernible in the forest of oak.   **rating:** 85

best drinking 2004–2007 **drink with** Rich pasta • $35

Andrew Harris Premium Chardonnay

Drawn from a little over 20 hectares of estate plantings; the oak handling is less flamboyant and opulent than in the Reserve range, with brief French and American oak maturation.
TTTT **2001** Bright yellow-green; both the bouquet and palate have abundant stone fruit/yellow peach aroma and flavour, the texture mouthfilling, the finish soft. Neither oak nor malolactic fermentation appear to have played any role in shaping the wine.   **rating:** 86

best drinking Now **drink with** Fillet of pork • $16

Andrew Harris Reserve Chardonnay

TTTT **2002** Glowing yellow-green; the bouquet is quite complex, with obvious barrel-ferment inputs on nectarine and peach fruit; the medium-bodied palate is smooth, the balance good, particularly for those who are oak-tolerant.   **rating:** 87

best drinking Now–2006 **best vintages** '95 **drink with** Roast pork • $28

Andrew Harris Three Regions Special Blend Chardonnay

ŸŸŸŸ 2002 Bright yellow-green; strong, toasty, charry barrel-ferment aromas are powerful, but not as aggressive as those of the Orange version; the palate is complex, and while oak-driven, there is considerable fruit in the back seat. **rating: 88**

best drinking Now–2007 **drink with** Grilled spatchcock • $35

Andrew Harris Reserve Shiraz

ŸŸŸŸŸ 2001 Medium red-purple; dark blackberry fruit with hints of spice and a whiff of oak on the bouquet leads into a medium-bodied palate, with well-integrated blackberry fruit and oak; well balanced, replete with silky tannins. **rating: 91**

best drinking 2006–2011 **best vintages** '97, '01 **drink with** Braised oxtail • $28

Andrew Harris The Vision

ŸŸŸŸ 2001 The fairly light red-purple colour is not entirely convincing; the clean, moderately intense bouquet has a mix of red and black fruits, the oak not aggressive. The medium-bodied palate has blackberry fruit, the oak more obvious, and the tannins somewhat chewy. **rating: 87**

best drinking 2005–2010 **best vintages** '96, '97, '98 **drink with** Steak and kidney pie • $45

Andrew Harris Reserve Cabernet Sauvignon

ŸŸŸŸ 2001 Medium red-purple; the moderately intense bouquet has blackcurrant fruit and positive oak leading into a light to medium-bodied palate, with smooth, supple blackcurrant fruit needing more concentration for higher points. **rating: 86**

best drinking 2004–2009 **best vintages** '94 **drink with** Stir-fried beef • $28

andrew peace wines   NR

Murray Valley Highway, Piangil, Vic 3597 **region** Swan Hill
phone (03) 5030 5291 **fax** (03) 5030 5605 **open** Mon–Fri 9–4.30, weekends by appointment
winemaker Andrew Peace, Bill Small **production** 300 000 cases **est.** 1995
product range ($9–15 CD) Mighty Murray White, Chardonnay, Mighty Murray Rose, Mighty Murray Red, Shiraz, Shiraz Reserve, Shiraz Malbec.
summary The Peace family has been a major Swan Hill grape grower since 1980 and moved into winemaking with the opening of a $3 million winery in 1997. The modestly priced wines are aimed at supermarket-type outlets in Australia and, in particular, at the export market in the major destinations for Australian wine. Unfortunately, no recent tastings.

angove's   ★★★☆

Bookmark Avenue, Renmark, SA 5341 **region** Riverland
phone (08) 8580 3100 **fax** (08) 8580 3155 **open** Mon–Fri 9–5
winemaker Warrick Billings, Shane Clohesy, Tony Ingle **production** 1.3 million cases **est.** 1886
product range ($4.50–15 CD) A range of new label designs and packaging for the six ranges. At the top comes Sarnia Farm with Chardonnay, Shiraz, Cabernet Sauvignon; Classic Reserve, covering virtually all varieties; Bear Crossing Chardonnay, Cabernet Merlot; Stonegate Verdelho, Chardonnay, Cabernet Shiraz; Butterfly Ridge Riesling, Colombard Chardonnay, Spatlese Lexia, Shiraz Cabernet; Misty Vineyards with Dry White, Fruity White, Late Harvest Sweet White, Traditional Dry Red; fortifieds.
summary Exemplifies the economies of scale achievable in the Australian Riverland without compromising potential quality. Very good technology provides wines which are never poor and which can sometimes exceed their theoretical station in life; the white varietals are best. Angove's expansion into Padthaway has resulted in estate-grown premium wines at the top of the range. As well as national distribution, Angove's is exported to virtually all the major markets in Europe, North America and Asia. For good measure, it also acts as a distributor of Perrier Jouet Champagne and several small Australian wineries.

Angove's Classic Reserve Sauvignon Blanc

ŸŸŸŸ 2002 Light straw-green; the clean, crisp bouquet has aromas of green peas, grass and herb in clear-cut varietal mode; the palate is quite intense and long, again with clear varietal flavour. Well balanced, and the best for many years, reflecting the excellent vintage. **rating: 87**

best drinking Now **drink with** Shellfish • $14

Angove's Butterfly Ridge Colombard Chardonnay

ΥΥΥΥ 2002 Light straw-green; the fresh and clean bouquet announces a tangy, citrussy palate with well above-average flavour and length, augmented by lingering acidity. Excellent value. **rating:** 85

best drinking Now **drink with** Cold seafood • $7

Angove's Classic Reserve Colombard

ΥΥΥΥ 2002 Light yellow-green; quite aromatic fruit salad aromas and a twist of lemon lead into a clean, well-made palate with good balance and length, finishing with crisp acidity. Good value; perhaps a sign of the excellent 2002 vintage in the Riverland. **rating:** 85

best drinking Now **drink with** Light pasta dishes • $10

Angove's Bear Crossing Chardonnay

ΥΥΥΥ 2002 Medium yellow-green; clean, ripe, yellow peach, stone fruit and melon is a promising opening, and the palate does not betray the wine, with good mouthfeel, nice peachy flavour, and the barest hint of oak. Excellent value, and another example of the 2002 vintage at work. **rating:** 84

best drinking Now **drink with** Anything you like • $9

Angove's Sarnia Farm Chardonnay

ΥΥΥΥ 2002 Medium yellow-green; the fruit is relatively closed on the bouquet, some oak spice generating the most interest; the spicy oak is again obvious on the clean palate; the mouthfeel is quite nice, and there are some faint grapefruit flavours which come through. Modestly priced; all signs are of over-generous yield. Padthaway can do better than this. **rating:** 85

best drinking Now **drink with** Creamy pasta • $14

Angove's Sarnia Farm Shiraz

ΥΥΥΥ 2000 Medium red, showing some development already; red berry and vanilla aromas on the bouquet are followed by a pleasant palate, with soft red berry/cherry fruit, a dash of chocolate and soft tannins. **rating:** 84

best drinking Now **drink with** Bratwurst • $15

angus wines ★★★★

Captain Sturt Road, Hindmarsh Island, SA 5214 **region** Southern Fleurieu
phone (08) 8555 2320 **fax** (08) 8555 2323 **open** By appointment
winemaker Mike Farmilo **production** 1000 cases **est.** 1995
product range ($13–21.50 ML) Semillon, Shiraz.
summary Susan and Alistair Angus are the pioneer viticulturists on Hindmarsh Island, an island which has never been far from the headlines, but for reasons entirely divorced from viticulture. If the Bridge has had problems to contend with, so have the Angus family as they have progressed from a test plot of vines planted in 1992 through to the first tiny commercial crop in 1998 and a far larger crop in 1999. They have established 4.5 hectares of shiraz and 1.5 hectares of semillon, the wine being contract-made for them by Mike Farmilo at The Fleurieu Winery in McLaren Vale. Part is bottled under the Angus Wines label, a larger amount being sold in bulk to other wineries. Every aspect of packaging and marketing the wine has a sophisticated touch.

🐚 annapurna wines NR

Simmonds Creek Road, Mount Beauty, Vic 3698 **region** Alpine Valleys
phone (03) 9739 1184 **fax** (03) 9739 1184 **open** Wed–Sun 10–5
winemaker Frank Minutello **est.** 1989
product range ($11.30–28.5 CD) Pinot Gris, Chardonnay, Methode Traditionelle, Pinot Noir, Pinot Noir Reserve, Reserve Alfresco (light red), Merlot.
summary Ezio and Wendy Minutello began the establishment of the 18-hectare vineyard at 550 metres on Mount Beauty in 1989, planting pinot noir, chardonnay and pinot gris. The decision to produce some wine under the Annapurna label was taken in 1995, and the following year Annapurna was named the Victorian Wines Show Vineyard of the Year (assessed purely on the viticulture, not the wines). Finally, in 1999, the first wines were released. Annapurna, the second-highest mountain after Mount Everest, is Nepalese for 'goddess of bountiful harvest and fertility'. Frank Minutello makes a small amount of wine each year in a small, on-site winery, but the lion's share of the grapes is sold to other makers.

annie's lane ★★★★☆

Quelltaler Road, Watervale, SA 5452 **region** Clare Valley
phone (08) 8843 0003 **fax** (08) 8843 0096 **open** Mon–Fri 8.30–5, weekends 11–4
winemaker Caroline Dunn **production** 120 000 cases **est.** 1851
product range ($12–45 CD) Riesling, Semillon, Reserve Semillon, Shiraz, Copper Trail Shiraz, Old Vine Shiraz, Grenache Mourvedre, Clare/Barossa Cabernet Merlot.
summary The Clare Valley portfolio of Beringer Blass formerly made at Quelltaler is now sold under the Annie's Lane label, the name coming from Annie Weyman, a turn-of-the-century local identity. Since 1996, a series of outstanding wines have appeared under the Annie's Lane label. The Quelltaler winery has been leased to some Clare Valley vignerons determined to keep it in going-concern condition, but that lease is due to expire soon.

Annie's Lane Riesling

TTTTY 2002 Striking green-yellow; an intense, rich and ripe bouquet of lime, citrus and pineapple is followed by a palate of great depth and structure, and is surprisingly developed, particularly given the Stelvin cap. **rating:** 92
best drinking Now–2008 **best vintages** '96, '97, '98, '01 **drink with** Summer salad • $16.99

Annie's Lane Copper Trail Riesling

TTTTT 2002 Glowing yellow-green; the complex and rich bouquet spanning mineral, lime and tropical aromas is followed by a powerful, long palate which is tighter than the bouquet, thanks in no small measure to minerally acidity which also provides balance. Top example of a great vintage. **rating:** 96
best drinking 2004–2014 **drink with** Salad Niçoise • $35

Annie's Lane Semillon

TTTT 2002 Light to medium yellow-green; the firm bouquet has lemon and faintly toasty aromas, the palate has good balance and structure, but shortens off somewhat on the finish. **rating:** 86
best drinking Now **best vintages** '94, '96, '00 **drink with** Rich seafood • $16

Annie's Lane Shiraz

TTTTY 2001 Medium to full purple-red; the blackberry fruit of the bouquet has hints of spice, part fruit and part oak-derived; the smooth, supple palate has typically abundant blackberry and plum flavours, with good control of oak and tannin extract. Smooth, effortless commercial style offering particularly good value. **rating:** 90
best drinking 2005–2010 **best vintages** '94, '96, '98, '99, '00, '01 **drink with** Grilled porterhouse • $17

Annie's Lane Copper Trail Shiraz

TTTTT 1999 Medium to full red-purple; a rich, concentrated, dense bouquet with dark berry fruit and spicy vanillin oak leads into a rich and complex palate with abundant blackberry, black cherry, mocha and chocolate, replete with ripe tannins. A multi gold medal winner. **rating:** 95
best drinking 2004–2014 **best vintages** '96, '97, '99 **drink with** Calf's liver Italian-style • $45

Annie's Lane Cabernet Merlot

TTTT 2001 Light to medium purple-red; a light but quite fragrant bouquet has a mix of berry, leaf and mint; the light to medium-bodied palate provides the same red berry fruit together with balanced tannins and oak. **rating:** 87

best drinking Now–2007 **best vintages** '94, '95, '97, '99, '00 **drink with** Devilled kidneys • $17

annvers wines ★★★★

Lot 10, Razorback Road, Kangarilla, SA 5157 **region** Adelaide Hills
phone (08) 8374 1787 **fax** (08) 8374 2102 **open** Not
winemaker Duane Coates **production** 4000 cases **est.** 1998
product range ($20–43 R) Shiraz, Cabernet Sauvignon, Tawny Reserve.
summary Myriam and Wayne Keoghan established Annvers Wines with the emphasis on quality rather than quantity. The first Cabernet Sauvignon was made in 1998, and volume has increased to the point where 4000 cases of Cabernet Sauvignon and Shiraz were produced in 2002. The grapes come from vineyards in Langhorne Creek, McLaren Vale and the Annvers Estate Vineyard in the Adelaide Hills. The quality of the 2000 Shiraz and 2000 Cabernet Sauvignon show that the Keoghans have indeed succeeded in their aim. Since the wine was first released, it has been sold in the US and Singapore and has limited retail distribution in South Australia, New South Wales and Queensland. Exports also to Canada, Belgium and Switzerland.

Annvers Shiraz
▼▼▼▼▽ **2001** Deep red-purple; luscious, ripe, almost essency dark plum fruit is supported by controlled American oak on the bouquet. The palate has dense, dark plum and blackberry, licorice and dark chocolate fruit; the tannins are soft and the oak controlled. **rating:** 90

best drinking 2006–2011 **best vintages** '01 **drink with** Braised oxtail • $30

Annvers Cabernet Sauvignon
▼▼▼▼▽ **2001** Medium red-purple; the moderately intense bouquet has a mix of redcurrant and cassis in pure varietal mode; there is plenty of flesh and fruit concentration on the palate, again with hints of chocolate; good fruit and oak balance are matched by supple, flowing tannins. Spends 14 months in a mix of French and American oak. **rating:** 90

best drinking 2006–2012 **best vintages** '01 **drink with** Roast saltbush lamb • $30

Annvers 22 Years Old Aged Tawny 375 ml
▼▼▼▼ **NV** Distinctly tawny hues on the rim of the colour; a clean and quite rich bouquet with good rancio is followed by a palate with good balance and style, the biscuity aftertaste being just within the parameters of the style. Generously priced. **rating:** 89

best drinking Now **drink with** Dried fruits, nuts • $43

antcliff's chase

RMB 4510, Caveat via Seymour, Vic 3660 **region** Strathbogie Ranges
phone (03) 5790 4333 **fax** (03) 5790 4333 **open** Weekends 10–5
winemaker Chris Bennett, Ian Leamon **production** 800 cases **est.** 1982
product range ($14–30 CD) Riesling, Chardonnay, Pinot Noir, Ultra Pinot Noir, Cabernet Merlot.
summary A small family enterprise which commenced planting the vineyards at an elevation of 600 metres in the Strathbogie Ranges in 1982; commenced wine production from the 4-hectare vineyard in the early 1990s. After an uncertain start, wine quality has picked up considerably.

anthony dale ★★★☆

Lot 202 Robe Road, Bray, SA 5276 (postal) **region** Mount Benson
phone (08) 8735 7255 **fax** (08) 8735 7255 **open** Not
winemaker John Bird (Contract) **production** 1750 cases **est.** 1994
product range ($38 R) Shiraz Cabernet Sauvignon.
summary Anthony Dale has meticulously planned every aspect and detail of the vineyard and winery which bears his name. The vineyard was planted from 1995 to 1998; situated on the leeward side of the Woakwine Range, the light sandy soil is heavily impregnated with limestone. The decision has been taken to limit the crop to 1 tonne per acre (2.5 tonnes per hectare). Only one wine is made: a blend of shiraz and cabernet sauvignon; the winemaker is John Bird, a former senior Penfolds red winemaker with experience in helping make all the Penfolds top red wines (including Grange). As well as limited local and Queensland distribution, the wines are exported to the US and Switzerland. On the market at the time of going to print.

Anthony Dale Limited Release Shiraz Cabernet
▼▼▼▼ **2001** Youthful, deep purple-red; in keeping with the style, the oak is immediately evident on the bouquet, but is well-integrated; the palate has attractive blackberry and redcurrant fruit, soft, persistent tannins running through to the finish providing good structure; the oak is under much better control than in preceding vintages. **rating:** 89

best drinking 2004–2010 **best vintages** '01 **drink with** Smoked beef • $38

apsley gorge vineyard ★★★★☆

The Gulch, Bicheno, Tas 7215 **region** Southern Tasmania
phone (03) 6375 1221 **fax** (03) 6375 1589 **open** 7 days in summer 11–6, or by appointment
winemaker Brian Franklin **production** 2000 cases **est.** 1988
product range ($21–36 CD) Chardonnay, Pinot Noir.
summary While nominally situated at Bicheno on the east coast, Apsley Gorge is in fact some distance inland, taking its name from a mountain pass. Clearly, it shares with the other east coast wineries the capacity to produce Chardonnay and Pinot Noir of excellent quality.

apthorpe estate   NR

Lot 1073 Lovedale Road, Lovedale, NSW 2321 **region** Lower Hunter Valley
phone (02) 4930 9177 **fax** (02) 4930 9188 **open** Fri and Mon 10–4, weekends 10–5
winemaker Mark Apthorpe, Jim Chatto (Contract) **production** 1200 cases **est.** 1996
product range ($13.50–22 CD) Chardonnay, Sparkling Chambourcin, Chambourcin, Cabernet Franc, The
Convict Vintage Port.
summary Samuel Apthorpe was sentenced to 14 years' imprisonment as a convict in Australia for stealing a
few teaspoons. In the mid-1850s, after he had completed his sentence, he established a vineyard in the Hunter
Valley at Bishops Bridge. In 1996 his great-great-great-grandson Mark Apthorpe continued the tradition when
he planted 2.5 hectares of cabernet franc and 2.5 hectares of chambourcin at nearby Lovedale. The wines are
made at Monarch under the direction of Jim Chatto, with input from Mark Apthorpe, and it can be safely
assumed that the quality is high.

aquila estate   ★★★☆

85 Carabooda Road, Carabooda, WA 6033 **region** Swan District
phone (08) 9561 8166 **fax** (08) 9561 8177 **open** Weekends and public holidays 11–5, Mon–Fri by
appointment
winemaker Andrew Spencer-Wright **production** 20 000 cases **est.** 1993
product range ($15–40 CD) Riesling, Chenin Blanc, Sauvignon Blanc, Reflections (white blend),
Chardonnay, Shiraz, Merlot, Flame (red blend), Cabernet Sauvignon.
summary As Aquila Estate has matured, so have its grape sources centred on the Margaret River (principally)
and Blackwood Valley. The competitively priced wines are in many instances a blend of Blackwood Valley and
Margaret River grapes. Exports to the US, Canada, Singapore, Mauritius and Japan.

Aquila Estate Blackwood Valley Chardonnay

♥♥♥♥ 2002 Light straw-green; spicy clove oak marries with tangy nectarine, and citrus fruit on both bouquet
and palate; the wine has good length and intensity, but the oak phenolics do loom large on the finish. Mind
you, at the price, such criticism seems rather petty.   **rating:** 88

best drinking Now–2006 **drink with** Smoked eel • $15

Aquila Estate Shiraz

♥♥♥♥ 2000 Medium red-purple; light, spicy, savoury black fruit aromas lead into a light to medium-bodied
palate with chocolatey/savoury edges to the berry fruit and the oak in balance.   **rating:** 85

best drinking 2004–2008 **drink with** Pasta with meat sauce • $15

arakoon   ★★★☆

229 Main Road, McLaren Vale, SA 5171 **region** McLaren Vale
phone (08) 8323 7339 **fax** (02) 6566 6288 **open** Fri–Sun 10–5 by appointment
winemaker Patrik Jones, Raymond Jones **production** 1500 cases **est.** 1999
product range ($12–44 R) Chardonnay, Pinot Black (Pinot Noir), Doyen Shiraz, Reserve Shiraz, Sellick
Beach Shiraz Grenache, The Lighthouse Cabernet Sauvignon Shiraz.
summary Ray and Patrik Jones' first venture into wine came to nothing: a 1990 proposal for a film about the
Australian wine industry with myself as anchorman. Five years too early, say the Joneses. In 1991 they opened
an agency for Australian wine in Stockholm, and they started exporting wine to that country, the UK,
Germany and Switzerland in 1994. (They now also export to the US, Denmark, Belgium and Malaysia.) In
1999 they took the plunge into making their own wine, and exporting it as well as the wines of others. Patrik
is the winemaker, having completed a degree at the Waite Campus of the University of Adelaide. The graphic
design of the labels, incidentally, is as outrageous as the names of the wines.

Arakoon Doyen Shiraz

♥♥♥♥♡ 2001 Dense, opaque purple-red; powerful blackberry and prune aromas are followed by a massive palate,
reflecting the 16.5° alcohol. Don't light a match near your mouth after swallowing or spitting; very consistent
with the 2000, and impossible to give rational points to. From a single vineyard at Willunga.   **rating:** 90

best drinking 2007–2021 **drink with** Game • $44

Arakoon Reserve Shiraz

♥♥♥♥♡ 2001 Medium purple-red; the bouquet has abundant black cherry and blackberry fruit, the 20 months
of maturation in new French oak coming through much more overtly on the palate, which finishes with fine,
savoury tannins. From two vineyards in McLaren Vale, and a modest 14° alcohol.   **rating:** 90

best drinking 2006–2011 **best vintages** '01 **drink with** Braised ox cheek • $32

Arakoon Sellicks Beach Shiraz Grenache

ŢŢŢŢ 2001 Medium purple-red; the leafy, slightly gamey, spicy overtones to the bouquet are a little unsettling, but are almost certainly varietal rather than bacterial. Regional dark chocolate comes to the rescue on the palate, which finishes with fine tannins.   **rating: 84**

best drinking Now–2007 **drink with** Ragout of lamb • $22

Arakoon The Lighthouse Fleurieu Peninsula Cabernet Sauvignon

ŢŢŢŢ 2001 Medium red-purple; the bouquet has distinct savoury, spicy, earthy cabernet varietal character; the palate is partly sweetened by oak and a touch of chocolate, which help balance the savoury tannins. **rating: 85**

best drinking 2005–2010 **drink with** Herbed rack of lamb • $28

arlewood estate ★★★★☆

Harmans Road South, Wilyabrup, WA 6284 **region** Margaret River
phone (08) 9755 6267 **fax** (08) 9755 6267 **open** Weekends 11–5
winemaker Voyager Estate (Contract) **production** 6000 cases **est.** 1988
product range ($19–35 CD) Semillon, Sauvignon Blanc, Reserve Chardonnay, Pinot Noir, Shiraz, Cabernet Merlot, Cabernet Reserve (Cabernet Sauvignon Merlot Cabernet Franc).
summary The Heydon and Gosatti families acquired Arlewood Estate in October 1999, having previously established a small vineyard in Cowaramup in 1995. George Heydon is a Perth dentist whose passion for wine has led him to study viticulture at the University of Western Australia; Garry Gosatti has been involved in the boutique brewing and hospitality industries for many years. The area under vine has now been expanded to 15 hectares, and Arlewood has entered into a long-term winemaking contract with Voyager Estate, with consultancy advice from Janice McDonald. The quality and consistency of the wines is now impeccable. Retail distribution in most states and exports to the US and the UK.

Arlewood Estate Semillon

With a vineyard as well sited as that of Arlewood, it makes sense to let the fruit quality do the talking, as it does here.

ŢŢŢŢ 2002 Light straw-green; the strongly herbal bouquet has some spicy notes in the background, and the palate has a powerful impact and dry finish. Archetypal food style.   **rating: 88**

best drinking Now–2007 **best vintages** '98 **drink with** Tempura • $19

Arlewood Estate Sauvignon Blanc

ŢŢŢŢŢ 2002 Light straw-green; the spotlessly clean bouquet has mineral characters, but not a lot of varietal fruit escaping; the pace changes on the palate, which has good mouthfeel, balance and flow to the gentle tropical/gooseberry fruit flavours.   **rating: 90**

best drinking Now **drink with** Margaret River abalone • $19

Arlewood Estate Reserve Chardonnay

ŢŢŢŢŢ 2001 Light to medium yellow-green; seamless nectarine fruit and oak aromas lead into an intense nectarine and citrus palate; long finish, the oak playing a pure support role. Should mature well.   **rating: 93**

best drinking 2004–2009 **best vintages** '01 **drink with** Sashimi • $29

Arlewood Estate Shiraz

ŢŢŢŢŢ 2001 Medium to full red-purple; dusty plum and blackberry fruit is followed by a fine, medium-bodied palate with delicious fruit and well-integrated oak.   **rating: 90**

best drinking 2004–2009 **drink with** Roast kid • $25

Arlewood Estate Cabernet Reserve

Made prior to a change in ownership and winemaking direction, but certainly merits the Reserve status.

ŢŢŢŢŢ 2000 Medium to full red-purple; complex earthy blackcurrant and spice aromas lead into a palate with considerable depth, texture and structure. Here blackcurrant and bitter chocolate are supported by fine but ripe tannins.   **rating: 92**

best drinking 2006–2011 **drink with** Osso buco • $35

Arlewood Estate Cabernet Merlot

ŢŢŢŢŢ 2001 Bright purple-red; the fruit-driven bouquet has clean, raspberry and blackcurrant fruit; the luscious palate is flooded with blackcurrant and cassis fruit, then perfect savoury tannins to balance the finish.

rating: 94

best drinking 2006–2011 **best vintages** '01 **drink with** Rack of lamb • $25

armstrong vineyards ★★★★★

Lot 1 Military Road, Armstrong, Vic 3381 **region** Grampians
phone (08) 8277 6073 **fax** (08) 8277 6035 **open** Not
winemaker Tony Royal **production** 800 cases **est.** 1989
product range ($47 R) Shiraz.
summary Armstrong Vineyards is the brain- or love-child of Tony Royal, the former Seppelt Great Western winemaker who now runs the Australian business of Seguin Moreau, the largest of the French coopers. Armstrong Vineyards has 5 hectares of shiraz, the first 2 hectares planted in 1989, the remainder in 1995–96. Low yields (4.5 to 5.5 tonnes per hectare) mean the wine will always be produced in limited quantities.

Armstrong Vineyards Shiraz

▼▼▼▼▼ **2001** Bright purple-red; clean blackberry and spice aromas, along with a touch of oak, are followed by an impressive palate, with good texture, weight, structure, and, above all else, length.   **rating:** 94
best drinking 2007–2017 **best vintages** '96, '98, '00, '01 **drink with** Yearling steak • $47

arranmore vineyard   NR

Rangeview Road, Carey Gully, SA 5144 **region** Adelaide Hills
phone (08) 8390 3034 **fax** (08) 8390 0005 **open** By appointment
winemaker John Venus **production** 250 cases **est.** 1998
product range ($18–28 CD) Chardonnay, Black Pinot Noir.
summary One of the tiny operations which are appearing all over the beautiful Adelaide Hills. At an altitude of around 550 metres, the 2-hectare vineyard is planted to clonally selected pinot noir, chardonnay and sauvignon blanc. The wines are distributed by Australian Premium Boutique Wines and sold by mail order. Exports to the UK.

arrowfield   ★★★☆

Denman Road, Jerry's Plains, NSW 2330 **region** Upper Hunter Valley
phone (02) 6576 4041 **fax** (02) 6576 4144 **open** 7 days 10–5
winemaker Blair Duncan **production** 70 000 cases **est.** 1968
product range ($12–21 R) Top-of-the-range Show Reserve range of Chardonnay, Semillon, Shiraz, Merlot, Cabernet Sauvignon, Late Harvest Botrytis Semillon; Hunter Valley Chardonnay, Semillon, Shiraz; Cowra Chardonnay, Merlot; Arrowfield varietals Chardonnay, Semillon Chardonnay, Sauvignon Blanc, Verdelho, Sauvignon Blanc, Shiraz, Cabernet Merlot.
summary After largely dropping the Arrowfield name in favour of Mountarrow and a plethora of other brands, this Japanese-owned company has come full circle, once again marketing the wines solely under the Arrowfield label. Its principal grape sources are Cowra and the Upper Hunter, but it does venture further afield from time to time. Exports to the US, the UK, New Zealand, Germany, Malaysia and Hong Kong.

Arrowfield Show Reserve McLaren Vale Shiraz

▼▼▼▼ **1998** Medium red-purple; the moderately intense bouquet has fresh red berry fruit and nicely integrated vanilla oak, the medium-bodied palate adding a touch of chocolate; good extract and tannin management. Not surprisingly, a consistent silver medal winner.   **rating:** 88
best drinking Now–2008 **drink with** Lamb kebabs • $21

artamus   ★★★★

PO Box 489, Margaret River, WA 6285 **region** Margaret River
phone (08) 9757 8131 **fax** (08) 9757 8131 **open** Not
winemaker Michael Gadd **production** 280 cases **est.** 1994
product range ($16.25 R) Chardonnay.
summary Ann Dewar and Ian Parmenter (the celebrated television food presenter) planted a hectare of chardonnay cuttings (from Cape Mentelle) at their property on the north bank of the Margaret River. Their first wine was produced in 1998, made for them by Michael Gadd, and the style of each succeeding vintage has been remarkably consistent.

Artamus Margaret River Chardonnay

▼▼▼▼▽ **2001** Light green-yellow; a clean and elegant bouquet with melon and stone fruit, backed by subtle oak, leads into a stylish, unforced palate, with ultra-smooth flow and line.   **rating:** 92
best drinking Now–2007 **best vintages** '99, '01 **drink with** Margaret River marron • $16.25

arthurs creek estate ★★★★☆

Strathewen Road, Arthurs Creek, Vic 3099 **region** Yarra Valley
phone (03) 9714 8202 **fax** (03) 9824 0252 **open** Not
winemaker Tom Carson (Contract), Gary Baldwin (Consultant) **production** 1500 cases **est.** 1975
product range ($28–46 R) Chardonnay, Cabernet Sauvignon.
summary A latter-day folly of leading Melbourne QC, SEK Hulme, who began the planting of 3 hectares of
chardonnay, 4.3 hectares of cabernet sauvignon and 0.7 hectare of merlot at Arthurs Creek in the mid-1970s,
and had wine made by various people for 15 years before deciding to sell any of it. A ruthless weeding-out
process followed, with only the best of the older vintages offered. The Cabernets from the 1990s are absolutely
outstanding, deeply fruited and marvellously structured. Exports to the UK, the US, Denmark and Japan.

Arthurs Creek Chardonnay

▼▼▼▼ 2001 Medium yellow-green; bready, cashew malolactic and barrel-ferment influences play a major role
on both bouquet and the pleasant, light to medium-bodied palate; flows well.   **rating:** 89
best drinking Now–2007 **best vintages** '90, '92, '93, '94, '95, '97, '99, '00 **drink with** Veal fricassee • $46

Arthurs Creek Cabernet Sauvignon

▼▼▼▼ 1999 Medium purple-red; initially showed curious leather and oyster shell aromas which dissipated after
a period in the glass; a firm, savoury palate with not overmuch sweet fruit, and the tannins slightly dry. If this is
a truly representative bottle, it is doubtful whether it will repay extended cellaring. 260 dozen made. **rating:** 86
best drinking 2004–2009 **best vintages** '82, '87, '89, '91, '92, '93, '94, '95, '96 **drink with** Lamb fillets • $28

arundel ★★★★

Arundel Farm Estate, Arundel Road, Keilor, Vic 3036 (postal) **region** Sunbury
phone (03) 9335 3422 **fax** (03) 9335 4912 **open** Not
winemaker Bianca Conwell **production** 200 cases **est.** 1995
product range ($25 R) Shiraz.
summary Arundel has been built around a single acre of cabernet and shiraz planted by a previous owner in
the 1970s, but abandoned for many years. When the Conwell family purchased the property in the early 1990s,
the vineyard was resurrected, the first vintage being made by Rick Kinzbrunner in 1995. Thereafter the
cabernet was grafted over to shiraz, the block being slowly increased to 1.6 hectares. After the 1999 vintage,
Bianca Conwell took over the responsibility for winemaking on-site. An additional 4 hectares of shiraz and 1.6
hectares of viognier and marsanne have been planted, which will lead to significantly increased production in
the future.

Arundel Shiraz

▼▼▼▼ 2001 Medium to full red-purple; spotlessly clean, sweet, ripe blackberry/raspberry fruit aromas are
followed by a very dense, luscious, fruit-driven palate, lengthened by tannins. This and the slightly lower-
alcohol, slightly more savoury 2000 vintage are the first made by Bianca Conwell without Rick Kinzbrunner's
direction.   **rating:** 89
best drinking 2006–2011 **drink with** Braised ox cheek • $25

ashbrook estate ★★★★☆

Harmans Road South, Wilyabrup via Cowaramup, WA 6284 **region** Margaret River
phone (08) 9755 6262 **fax** (08) 9755 6290 **open** 7 days 11–5
winemaker Tony Devitt, Brian Devitt **production** 9000 cases **est.** 1975
product range ($16–27 CD) Gold Label Riesling, Black Label Riesling, Semillon, Semillon Reserve,
Sauvignon Blanc, Verdelho, Chardonnay, Cabernet Merlot.
summary A fastidious maker of consistently outstanding estate-grown table wines but which shuns publicity
and the wine show system alike and is less well known than it deserves to be, selling much of its wine through
the cellar-door and to an understandably very loyal mailing list clientele. All the white wines are of the highest
quality, year in, year out. Small quantities of the wines now find their way to Canada, Japan, Singapore, Hong
Kong, Indonesia, Holland and the UK.

Ashbrook Estate Gold Label Riesling

▼▼▼▼▽ 2002 Light straw-green; a clean and crisp bouquet has faint lemon/citrus fruit aromas; the palate is
similarly fresh and delicate, needing time to build.   **rating:** 90
best drinking 2004–2009 **best vintages** '99, '02 **drink with** Asparagus and salmon terrine • $16

Ashbrook Estate Semillon

TTTTY 2002 Light to medium yellow-green; a complex and quite intense bouquet suggests the use of some oak (there is in fact none) or lees contact; the palate has good length and intensity, with sweet lemon and lime fruit. **rating:** 91

best drinking Now–2007 **best vintages** '93, '94, '95, '97, '99, '01, '02 **drink with** Blanquette of veal • $15

Ashbrook Estate Chardonnay

TTTTY 2001 Medium yellow-green; a complex bouquet with an array of fig and melon fruit, nutty/cashew malolactic influences and subtle oak, then a fruit-forward palate with fig and cashew flavours, closing with good acidity. Slightly less intense than the very best vintages, but as stylish as ever. **rating:** 91

best drinking Now–2006 **best vintages** '92, '93, '94, '95, '98, '99, '00 **drink with** Grilled spatchcock • $21

ashton hills ★★★★★

Tregarthen Road, Ashton, SA 5137 **region** Adelaide Hills
phone (08) 8390 1243 **fax** (08) 8390 1243 **open** Weekends 11–5.30
winemaker Stephen George **production** 1500 cases **est.** 1982
product range ($17.50–30 CD) Riesling, Chardonnay, Salmon Brut, Pinot Noir, Piccadilly Valley Pinot Noir, Burra Burra Lone Star Shiraz, Five (Merlot Cabernet Sauvignon Malbec Cabernet Franc Petit Verdot).
summary Stephen George wears three winemaker hats: one for Ashton Hills, drawing upon a 3.5-hectare estate vineyard high in the Adelaide Hills; one for Galah Wines; and one for Wendouree. It would be hard to imagine three wineries producing more diverse styles, with the elegance and finesse of Ashton Hills at one end of the spectrum, the awesome power of Wendouree at the other. The Riesling and Pinot Noir have moved into the highest echelon. The grapes for this wine come from a vineyard established and owned by Stephen George's father. Export markets have been developed in the UK and the US.

Ashton Hills Chardonnay

TTTTT 2001 Bright, light to medium yellow-green; fine stone fruit, citrus and melon intermingles with subtle barrel-ferment aromas on the bouquet; the palate is beautifully weighted and proportioned, with delectable nectarine fruit, the oak in a pure support role. **rating:** 94

best drinking 2004–2009 **best vintages** '95, '97, '98, '99, '00, '01 **drink with** Grilled lobster • $25

Ashton Hills Salmon Brut

TTTT 2001 Vivid pink; a fresh, clean, strawberry-accented bouquet leads into a delicate, very well-balanced palate with clear strawberry fruit; not the least bit complex, but that's what it's about. **rating:** 87

best drinking Now–2005 **drink with** Seafood antipasto • $25

Ashton Hills Pinot Noir

TTTT 2001 Light red-purple; spicy, savoury, foresty aromas lead into a finely structured palate, with light cherry fruit coming alongside the more savoury characters of the bouquet; while long, it lacks the intensity of the best Ashton Hills Pinots. **rating:** 89

best drinking Now **best vintages** '88, '91, '92, '93, '94, '97, '98, '99, '00 **drink with** Smoked duck • $30

Burra Burra Lone Star Shiraz

TTTTY 2000 Medium to full red-purple; complex black fruits, leather and spice aromas are followed by a medium-bodied, elegant style reflecting its relatively low alcohol (12°); the tannins are strictly controlled on a long finish. **rating:** 90

best drinking 2005–2010 **best vintages** '96, '98, '99, '00 **drink with** Venison • $30

ashworths hill NR

Ashworths Road, Lancefield, Vic 3435 **region** Macedon Ranges
phone (03) 5429 1689 **fax** (03) 5429 1689 **open** Thurs–Mon 10–6
winemaker Anne Manning, John Ellis **production** 100 cases **est.** 1982
product range ($15–25 CD) Victorian Riesling, Victorian Chardonnay, Macedon Ranges Pinot Noir, Macedon Ranges Cabernet Sauvignon, fortifieds.
summary Peg and Ken Reaburn offer light refreshments throughout the day, and the property has scenic views of the Macedon Ranges.

audrey wilkinson ★★★☆

Oakdale, De Beyers Road, Pokolbin, NSW 2320 **region** Lower Hunter Valley
phone (02) 4998 7411 **fax** (02) 4998 7303 **open** Mon–Fri 9–5, weekends 9.30–5
winemaker Chris Cameron **production** 2755 cases **est.** 1999
product range ($16–30 CD) Traminer, Semillon, Unwooded Chardonnay, Chardonnay, Shiraz, Reserve Shiraz, Reserve Coonawarra Cabernet Sauvignon.
summary One of the most historic properties in the Hunter Valley, with a particularly beautiful location. The four wines come from the old plantings on the property, which has a very attractive cellar door. It is part of the James Fairfax wine group (headed by Pepper Tree).

august hill estate NR

763 Woodbridge Hill Road, Gardners Bay, Tas 7112 **region** Southern Tasmania
phone (03) 6229 2316 **open** Not
winemaker David Masterton **production** 600 cases **est.** 1996
product range ($14–45 ML) Pinot Noir, Directors Reserve Pinot Noir, Fruit Liqueur.
summary A relatively new and equally small venture in the Huon Valley which elected to make its own wines rather than use the contract winemaking services of Andrew Hood or others in the field. It was a pinot noir specialist, with 3 hectares planted, but was on the market in March 2003.

auldstone ★★★☆

Booths Road, Taminick via Glenrowan, Vic 3675 **region** Glenrowan
phone (03) 5766 2237 **fax** (03) 5766 2131 **open** Thurs–Sat and school holidays 9–5, Sun 10–5
winemaker Michael Reid **production** 2000 cases **est.** 1987
product range ($12–26 CD) Riesling, Traminer Riesling, Chardonnay, Late Picked Riesling, Sparkling Shiraz, Shiraz, Merlot, Cabernet Merlot, Cabernet Sauvignon, Herceynia Tawny Port, Liqueur Muscat.
summary Michael and Nancy Reid have restored a century-old stone winery and have replanted the largely abandoned 26-hectare vineyard around it. All the Auldstone varietal and fortified wines have won a string of medals (usually bronze) in Australian wine shows. Gourmet lunches are available on weekends.

Auldstone Merlot

ΨΨΨΨ 2000 Medium red, the purple hues starting to fade; earthy, savoury, olive edges to the dark fruits of the bouquet are followed by a substantial, if rustic, palate, with honest flavour and a degree of varietal character.

rating: 85

best drinking 2005–2009 **drink with** Shepherd's pie • $20

Auldstone Liqueur Muscat

ΨΨΨΨΨ NV Some red tints in the otherwise tawny-brown colour indicate a blend of ages; the bouquet has intense, vibrant, raisiny fruit, the powerful and concentrated palate showing high-quality young muscat, which really deserves further barrel age, and is, of course, imprisoned by bottling.

rating: 90

best drinking Now–2005 **drink with** Winter aperitif or with coffee

austin's barrabool ★★★★

50 Lemins Road, Waurn Ponds, Vic 3221 **region** Geelong
phone (03) 5241 8114 **fax** (03) 5241 8122 **open** By appointment
winemaker John Ellis (Contract), Pamela Austin **production** 3000 cases **est.** 1982
product range ($20–40 CD) Riesling, Sauvignon Blanc, Chardonnay, Pinot Noir, Shiraz, Cabernet Sauvignon.
summary Pamela and Richard Austin have quietly built their business from a tiny base, but it is now poised for much bigger things. The vineyard has been progressively extended to 55 hectares, and production has risen from 700 cases in 1998 to 3000 cases in 2003. Exports to Asia.

Austin's Barrabool Riesling

ΨΨΨΨ 2002 Water white; a light bouquet with a faint spice, talc and apple skin aroma web; the palate is similarly very restrained, with lemon and apple flavours; in a distinctive fruit style, presumably reflecting the vintage.

rating: 86

best drinking Now–2005 **drink with** Marinated scallops • $18

Austin's Barrabool Chardonnay

▼▼▼▼ 2001 Light straw-green; the moderately intense bouquet has a mix of smoky barrel ferment and melon fruit; the palate builds intensity, with citrus and stone fruit supported by subtle oak. Maturing nicely. **rating:** 88

best drinking Now–2007 **best vintages** '97 **drink with** Pan-fried scallops • $22

Austin's Barrabool Pinot Noir

▼▼▼▼ 2001 Medium purple-red, bright and clear; the spotlessly clean bouquet has light plum and a dusting of spice in classic varietal mould; the palate has intense flavours precisely replicating the bouquet, and a long, lingering finish. Wonderful varietal character; in stark contrast to the weird, densely coloured black-hole-in-space 2000 vintage, which looked as if it might not have undergone malolactic fermentation. **rating:** 94

best drinking 2004–2009 **best vintages** '01 **drink with** Duck breast • $25

Austin's Barrabool Cabernet Sauvignon

▼▼▼▼▽ 2000 Medium to full red-purple; blackcurrant, blackberry and plum aromas and flavours drive a powerful and concentrated wine, with well-balanced and integrated tannins and oak. **rating:** 90

best drinking 2005–2010 **drink with** Ragout of lamb • $28

avalon vineyard   NR

RMB 9556, Whitfield Road, Wangaratta, Vic 3678 **region** King Valley
phone (03) 5729 3629 **fax** (03) 5729 3635 **open** 7 days 10–5
winemaker Doug Groom **production** 1000 cases **est.** 1981
product range ($12–20 CD) Riesling, Semillon, Sauvignon Blanc, Chardonnay, Late Harvest Semillon, Pinot Noir, Shiraz, Cabernet Sauvignon, Pinot Noir Methode Champenoise.
summary Avalon Vineyard is situated in the King Valley, 4 kilometres north of Whitfield. Much of the production from the 10-hectare vineyard is sold to other makers, with limited quantities made by Doug Groom, a graduate of Roseworthy, and one of the owners of the property. Exports to the US.

avalon wines   NR

1605 Bailey Road, Glen Forrest, WA 6071 **region** Perth Hills
phone (08) 9298 8049 **fax** (08) 9298 8049 **open** By appointment
winemaker Rob Marshall **production** 700 cases **est.** 1986
product range ($13–17 CD) Semillon, Chardonnay, Cane-Cut Semillon, Cabernet Merlot.
summary One of the smaller wineries in the Perth Hills, drawing upon 0.75 of a hectare each of chardonnay, semillon and cabernet sauvignon.

avenel park/hart wines   ★★★

24/25 Ewings Road, Avenel, Vic 3664 **region** Goulburn Valley
phone (03) 9347 5444 **fax** (03) 9349 3278 **open** Sunday 11–4, or by appointment
winemaker David Traeger, Sam Plunkett (Contract) **production** 1000 cases **est.** 1994
product range ($12–24 CD) Lovers Hill Unwooded Chardonnay, Lovers Hill Rose, Shiraz, Shiraz Cabernet Sauvignon, Cabernet Sauvignon; under the Hart label are Shiraz, Cabernet Sauvignon.
summary Jed and Sue Hart have in their words 'turned the rocky, ironstone soils of Lovers Hill into a 22-acre vineyard over some back-breaking years'. Seven of the 10 hectares are planted to shiraz and cabernet sauvignon, with a small amount each of merlot, semillon and chardonnay. Most of the grapes have been and will continue to be sold to Southcorp, but since 2000 the equivalent of 1000 cases of wine have been retained and contract-made by David Traeger. Nonetheless, the Harts' main viticultural business (Jed Hart is in aviation) will be grape growing.

Hart Shiraz

▼▼▼▼ 2001 Medium red-purple; the bouquet has earthy regional characters supported by subtle oak; the firm fruit on the palate has hints of leaf and mint, needing to soften, although unlikely to gain much weight in the process. **rating:** 85

best drinking 2005–2009 **drink with** Braised rabbit • $24

Avenel Park Shiraz Cabernet Sauvignon

▼▼▼▽ 2001 Medium purple-red; a firm earthy/savoury bouquet sets the tone for the palate, which is firm and fresh, but slightly unformed and, like the Shiraz, needs some time in bottle. **rating:** 84

best drinking 2005–2009 **drink with** Braised beef • $24

avonmore estate   ★★★☆

Mayreef–Avonmore Road, Avonmore, Vic 3558   **region** Bendigo
phone (03) 5432 6291   **fax** (03) 5432 6291   **open** Thurs–Sun and public holidays 11–5, or by appointment
winemaker Shaun Bryans, Don Buchanan (Contract)   **production** 1500 cases   **est.** 1996
product range ($20–25 CD) Shiraz, Shiraz Cabernet Sauvignon, Sangiovese, Cabernet Sauvignon.
summary Rob and Pauline Bryans own and operate a certified Grade A Bio-Dynamic farm, producing and selling beef, lamb and cereals as well as establishing 9 hectares of viognier, sangiovese, cabernet sauvignon, cabernet franc and shiraz, which produced its first crop in 2000. Most of the wine is contract-made by Don Buchanan at the Tisdall Winery at Echuca, but a small amount is made on the property. The wine will be marketed under the Avonmore Estate label, but with the worldwide Demeter logo. Several of the unbottled wines have been awarded medals at Victorian wine shows, and the Bryans' cellar door is now open.

Avonmore Estate Shiraz

TTTT **2001** Medium purple-red; the moderately intense bouquet is clean and fresh, with small red berry fruits flowing over into the fresh, clean palate with slightly pointed acidity; one of those wines that is at its best while the fruit is at its zenith.   **rating:** 89
TTTT **2000** Excellent purple-red, still bright and clear; the clean, youthful palate has red and black berry and plum fruit, the concentrated palate with quite pronounced tannins. At the other end of the style spectrum from the 2001, and should not be approached before 2006.   **rating:** 89
best drinking Now–2006   **drink with** Fillet of beef • $22.50

Avonmore Estate Shiraz Cabernet

TTTT **2001** Medium purple-red; the bouquet is quite complex, with some faintly gamey notes accompanying the dark berry fruit; a very rich, chewy, chunky palate with ripe fruit and persistent tannins.   **rating:** 87
best drinking 2005–2010   **drink with** Char-grilled rump • $22.50

bacchanalia estate   NR

Taverner Street, Bacchus Marsh, Vic 3340   **region** Sunbury
phone (03) 5367 6416   **fax** (03) 5367 6416   **open** Sundays, by appointment
winemaker Pat Carmody (Contract), John Reid   **production** 500 cases   **est.** 1994
product range ($15–25 R) Semillon, Shiraz.
summary Noted ABC broadcaster and journalist John Reid, and wife Val, established Bacchanalia Estate in 1994 on the fertile black soils of Bacchus Marsh, adjacent to the Werribee River. Consultancy viticultural advice from Dr Richard Smart pointed to the inevitably vigorous growth to be expected from the rich, black soil, so a Geneva Double Curtain (GDC) trellis and canopy was utilised from the outset. Two hectares of shiraz, 0.6 hectare semillon, 0.4 hectare cabernet sauvignon and 0.2 hectare viognier have been established. For several years now Pat Carmody (of Craiglee) has been making the wine, the only wine he makes other than for his own label. Apart from local distribution through Geelong and Ballarat, the wine is available at Nick's Wine Merchants throughout Melbourne.

badger's brook   ★★★

874 Maroondah Highway, Coldstream, Vic 3770   **region** Yarra Valley
phone (03) 5962 4130   **fax** (03) 5962 4238   **open** Thurs–Mon 11–5
winemaker Contract   **production** 5000 cases   **est.** 1993
product range ($16–25 CD) The Badger's Brook range, all of which are from the Yarra Valley, mostly said to be estate-grown, and the Storm Ridge range, coming from various regions, including the Mornington Peninsula and as far away as Margaret River, but also with some Yarra component.
summary Situated prominently on the Maroondah Highway next door to the well known Rochford's Eyton. Location is all, although not for all the wines. As is proper, the Badger's Brook-branded wines are significantly better than the Storm Ridge range. Domestic distribution within the east coast by The Wine Company. Exports to Europe and Asia.

Badger's Brook Storm Ridge Pinot Noir

TTTT **2001** Medium red-purple; forest and spice aromas come first, then plum; the palate has slightly sweeter fruit and less structure, being fruit-driven and ready right now. One hundred per cent Yarra Valley grapes, not estate-grown.
                                                                                                         rating: 87
best drinking Now–2005   **drink with** Smoked chicken • $17

Badger's Brook Yarra Valley Pinot Noir

▼▼▼▼ 2001 Good pinot colour; the light bouquet mixes plum and more savoury/foresty notes, the wine coming into its own on the palate, which has considerable presence, and a particularly long, savoury finish. What is best described as a dry fruit style, as opposed to opulent. One hundred per cent estate-grown.   **rating:** 88

best drinking Now–2006 **drink with** Quail • $25

bago vineyards   ★★★

Milligans Road, off Bago Road, Wauchope, NSW 2446 **region** Hastings River
phone (02) 6585 7099 **fax** (02) 6585 7099 **open** 7 days 11–5
winemaker John Steel, John Cassegrain (Contract) **production** 5000 cases **est.** 1985
product range ($10–21.50 CD) Chardonnay, Jazz White Classic, Verdelho, Chambourcin, Merlot Chambourcin, Jazz Red Classic, Sparkling Pinot Noir Chardonnay, Sparkling Chambourcin, Tawny Port.
summary Jim and Kay Mobs commenced planting the Broken Bago Vineyards in 1985 with 1 hectare of chardonnay and have now increased the total plantings to 12.5 hectares. Regional specialist John Cassegrain is contract winemaker.

baileys of glenrowan   ★★★★

Cnr Taminick Gap and Upper Taminick Roads, Glenrowan, Vic 3675 **region** Glenrowan
phone (03) 5766 2392 **fax** (03) 5766 2596 **open** Mon–Fri 9–5, weekends 10–5
winemaker Matt Steel **production** 15 000 cases **est.** 1870
product range ($16–40 R) Shiraz, 1904 Block Shiraz, 1920's Block Shiraz, Cabernet Sauvignon are the principal wines; Founder Tokay, Muscat, Port.
summary Now part of the sprawling Beringer Blass empire, inherited via the Rothbury takeover. Has made some excellent Shiraz in recent years, but its greatest strength lies in its fortified wines.

Baileys 1920's Block Shiraz

▼▼▼▼ 2000 Medium to full red-purple; the bouquet offers black cherry, licorice, plum and leather varietal fruit; the rich, ripe, dense fruit of the palate has a toasty oak background, finishing with good length. Very good value.   **rating:** 89

best drinking 2004–2010 **best vintages** '91, '92, '93, '96, '97, '99 **drink with** Rare rump steak, venison • $18

Baileys Founder Liqueur Tokay

▼▼▼▼ NV Medium golden brown; full, complex, sweeter style of Tokay, with clean spirit. The palate is rich, full and textured, with flavours of butterscotch and sweet biscuit and a chewy texture, but finishing long and clean.   **rating:** 89

best drinking Now **drink with** Winter aperitif; summer after dinner • $17.95

Baileys Founder Liqueur Muscat

▼▼▼▼ NV Medium red-brown; an arresting bouquet with hints of spice to the sweet, ripe, complex fruit. The same unusual spicy/cinnamon aspects are apparent on the rich and complex palate.   **rating:** 88

best drinking Now **drink with** After coffee; alternative to Cognac • $17.95

bainton family wines   NR

390 Milbrodale Road, Fordwich, NSW 2330 **region** Lower Hunter Valley
phone (02) 9968 1764 **fax** (02) 9960 3454 **open** Not
winemaker Tony Bainton **production** 10 000 cases **est.** 1998
product range ($11–30 ML) Wollemi Semillon, Unwooded Chardonnay, Shiraz; Q Shiraz Chambourcin; Wollemi Gold Botrytis Semillon, Wollemi Gold Shiraz.
summary The Bainton family, headed by eminent Sydney QC Russell Bainton, has 48 hectares of vineyard, currently selling most of the grapes but intending to steadily increase production in-house.

bald mountain   ★★★☆

Hickling Lane, Wallangarra, Qld 4383 **region** Granite Belt
phone (07) 4684 3186 **fax** (07) 4684 3433 **open** 7 days 10–5
winemaker Simon Gilbert (Contract) **production** 5000 cases **est.** 1985

product range ($11–22 CD) Classic Queenslander Dry White (in fact 100 per cent Sauvignon Blanc), Chardonnay, Reserve Chardonnay, Dancing Brolga (Sauvignon Blanc Verdelho), Late Harvest Sauvignon Blanc, Shiraz, Reserve Shiraz, Shiraz Cabernet, Reserve Shiraz Cabernet.

summary Denis Parsons is a self-taught but exceptionally competent vigneron who has turned Bald Mountain into the viticultural showpiece of the Granite Belt. In various regional and national shows since 1988, Bald Mountain has won over 70 show awards, placing it at the forefront of the Granite Belt wineries. The two Sauvignon Blanc-based wines, Classic Queenslander and the occasional non-vintage Late Harvest Sauvignon Blanc, are interesting alternatives to the mainstream wines. Future production will also see grapes coming from new vineyards near Tenterfield, just across the border in New South Wales. Significant exports to The Netherlands.

Bald Mountain Classic Queenslander Dry White

▼▼▼▽ 2001 Light straw-green; the clean and crisp bouquet is minerally rather than fruity, the palate fresh, clean and well made, the neutrality making it a useful all-purpose wine. **rating:** 84

best drinking Now **drink with** Seafood, vegetarian • $15.50

Bald Mountain Reserve Shiraz

▼▼▼▼ 2000 Medium purple-red; clean, fresh cherry/small berry fruit aromas are followed by a light to medium-bodied palate with pleasing black cherry fruit and fine tannins. Silver medal Royal Melbourne Wine Show 2001. **rating:** 87

best drinking Now–2007 **drink with** Fillet steak • $22

Bald Mountain Reserve Shiraz Cabernet

▼▼▼▼▽ 2000 Medium red-purple; the moderately intense bouquet has a mix of red berry fruit and more savoury/earthy notes sweetened by vanilla oak; on the palate, blackberry, cherry, chocolate and a hint of lemon (the last probably from the oak) all come together to provide good palate feel. An elegant wine, still developing, and a unanimous silver medal winner at the 2002 National Wine Show. **rating:** 90

best drinking Now–2007 **drink with** Lamb forequarter • $22

balgownie estate ★★★★☆

Hermitage Road, Maiden Gully, Vic 3551 **region** Bendigo
phone (03) 5449 6222 **fax** (03) 5449 6506 **open** 7 days 11–5
winemaker Tobias Ansted **production** 4500 cases **est.** 1969
product range ($14–30 CD) Chardonnay, Pinot Noir, Shiraz, Cabernet Sauvignon; Maiden Gully Chardonnay, Cabernet Shiraz.

summary Balgownie Estate continues to grow in the wake of its acquisition by the Forrester family. A $3 million upgrade of the winery coincided with a doubling of the size of the vineyard to 35 hectares, and in 2003 Balgownie Estate opened a separate cellar door in the Yarra Valley. As well as national distribution through Negociants, exports to the UK, Switzerland, Hong Kong, New Zealand, the US and Asia.

Balgownie Estate Shiraz

▼▼▼▼▼ 2001 Dense, deep, impenetrable red-purple; a powerful, deep black cherry and black pepper bouquet is followed by a mouthfilling, round and lush palate, not extractive, and with good oak and good length. However, needs a decade to show its best. Does have a touch of Viognier. **rating:** 94

best drinking 2010–2020 **best vintages** '91, '93, '96, '97, '98, '99, '01 **drink with** Beef in red wine • $30

Balgownie Estate Cabernet Sauvignon

▼▼▼▼ 2001 Medium to full red-purple, bright and clear; smooth, gently ripe blackcurrant fruit is supported by subtle French oak on the bouquet; the tangy, savoury palate has a distinct herbal, olive, herbaceous finish, which is well within varietal expectations. The surprise is the total contrast between the Cabernet and the Shiraz from this vintage. **rating:** 87

best drinking 2005–2011 **best vintages** '75, '76, '80, '94, '96, '97, '98, '00 **drink with** Beef casserole • $30

ballabourneen wines NR

Talga Road, Rothbury, NSW 2320 **region** Lower Hunter Valley
phone (02) 4930 7027 **fax** (02) 4930 9180 **open** Thurs–Sun 10–5, or by appointment
winemaker Alasdair Sutherland, Andrew Thomas **production** 1200 cases **est.** 1994
product range ($13–18 CD) Verdelho, Chardonnay Verdelho, Chardonnay, Shiraz.

summary Alex and Di Stuart planted their first vines, 1.6 hectares of chardonnay and 1.2 hectares of verdelho, in 1994. They followed up these plantings in 1998 with 1.6 hectares of shiraz; the viticulture uses natural sprays, fertilisers, mulches and compost, with a permanent sward maintained between the rows. Competent contract winemaking by Alasdair Sutherland has bought show success for every vintage of the Verdelho, the high point being a trophy at the 1999 Hunter Valley Wine Show, while the Chardonnay Verdelho, made by Greg Silkman, has also won several medals.

ballandean estate ★★★☆

Sundown Road, Ballandean, Qld 4382 **region** Granite Belt
phone (07) 4684 1226 **fax** (07) 4684 1288 **open** 7 days 9–5
winemaker Dylan Rhymer, Angelo Puglisi **production** 18 000 cases **est.** 1970
product range ($12–40 CD) Semillon, Semillon Sauvignon Blanc, Black Label Sauvignon Blanc, Black Label Viognier, Black Label Chardonnay, Classic White, Sylvaner Late Harvest, White Pearl (semi-sweet white), Lambrusco, Estate Shiraz, Black Label Shiraz, Black Label Cabernet Merlot, Cabernet Sauvignon, fortifieds.
summary The senior winery of the Granite Belt and by far the largest. The white wines are of diverse but interesting styles, the red wines smooth and usually well made. The estate specialty, Sylvaner Late Harvest, is a particularly interesting wine of great character and flavour if given 10 years' bottle age, but isn't made every year. Exports to the UK and the US.

Ballandean Estate Semillon
▼▼▼▼▽ **2001** Pale straw-green; attractive grassy varietal aromas lead into a palate with good length and balance, followed by a crisp, clean finish. Tasted alongside a 1985, an outstanding wine with toast, honey, lime and great acidity, still at its peak. The 2002 will go in the same direction. **rating:** 90
best drinking 2006–2016 **best vintages** '85, '01 **drink with** Calamari

Ballandean Estate Sauvignon Blanc
▼▼▼▽ **2001** Light to medium yellow-green; the clean and smooth bouquet has restrained fruit salad aromas; the clean and smooth palate lopes along, without overmuch character; nonetheless, it is well balanced. **rating:** 83
best drinking Now–2005 **drink with** Pasta marinara • $18

Ballandean Estate Sylvaner
▼▼▼▼▼ **1993** Glowing yellow-green; complex apricot and toffee aromas flow through into the palate, which has abundant flavour and length, balanced by delicate acidity on the finish. An unusual and great wine, it was tasted alongside the freakish 1991, which has gorgeous honey, lime and butter aromas and flavours, great balance and great length. Limited quantities of the '93 were still on sale early in 2003. **rating:** 94
best drinking Now–2007 **best vintages** '93 **drink with** Aperitif or cake • $40

Ballandean Estate Black Label Viognier
▼▼▼▼ **2001** Very youthful, with some CO_2, doubtless intentional, and doubtless to help sustain the freshness. Varietal character – touches of fruit pastille and musk – are present on both bouquet and palate, and while the wine is fractionally hard, it is not excessively phenolic. **rating:** 85
best drinking Now–2007 **drink with** Pasta carbonara

Ballandean Estate Shiraz
▼▼▼▼ **2002** Strong colour; the wine is well balanced, with good length, and excellent control of extract. A barrel sample, some months away from bottling, and therefore given nominal points only. There are some signs of brettanomyces in some of the slightly older red wines from Ballandean. **rating:** 85
best drinking 2006–2011 **drink with** Braised beef

ballast stone estate wines NR

Myrtle Grove Road, Currency Creek, SA 5214 **region** Currency Creek
phone (08) 8555 4215 **fax** (08) 8555 4216 **open** Mon–Fri 10–4.30, weekends and public holidays 12–5
winemaker F John Loxton **production** 5000 cases **est.** 2001
product range ($12–20 CD) Riesling, Sauvignon Blanc, Chardonnay, Sparkling Chardonnay, Sparkling Shiraz, Grenache, Cabernet Sauvignon.
summary The Shaw family had been grape growers in McLaren Vale for 25 years before deciding to establish a large vineyard in Currency Creek in 1994. Two hundred and fifty hectares have been planted, mainly cabernet sauvignon and shiraz, with much smaller quantities of eight other trendy varieties. A large on-site winery has been built, managed by Philip Shaw (no relation to Rosemount's Philip Shaw) and John Loxton

(formerly senior winemaker at Maglieri). It handled the 1500 tonnes of grapes crushed in 2001, a crush expected to rise to over 5000 tonnes by 2004. Only a small part of the production will be sold under the Ballast Stone Estate label; most will be sold in bulk. A cellar door is to be established on the main Strathalbyn to Victor Harbour Road, tapping into the tourism trade of the Southern Fleurieu Peninsula.

balnaves of coonawarra ★★★★★

Main Road, Coonawarra, SA 5263 **region** Coonawarra
phone (08) 8737 2946 **fax** (08) 8737 2945 **open** Mon–Fri 9–5, weekends 10–5
winemaker Peter Bissell **production** 10 000 cases **est.** 1975
product range ($19–80 R) Chardonnay, Sparkling Cabernet, Shiraz, The Blend (Merlot Cabernet Franc), Cabernet Merlot, The Tally Reserve Cabernet Sauvignon.
summary Former Hungerford Hill vineyard manager and now viticultural consultant-cum-grape grower Doug Balnaves established his vineyard in 1975 but did not launch into winemaking until 1990, with colleague Ralph Fowler as contract winemaker in the early years. A striking 300-tonne winery was built in 1996, with former Wynns Coonawarra Estate assistant winemaker Peter Bissell in charge. The expected leap in quality has indeed materialised and been maintained. The wines are exported to the UK, the US, Switzerland, The Netherlands and Japan.

Balnaves Chardonnay

▼▼▼▼▽ **2001** Medium yellow-green; fruit and oak are subtly interwoven on the bouquet and on the particularly well-balanced palate, where citrus fruit, malolactic influences and quality oak all contribute to the length of a stylish wine. **rating:** 92
best drinking Now–2007 **best vintages** '92, '93, '94, '96, '98, '99, '00, '01 **drink with** Robe crayfish • $28

🐾 bamajura NR

775 Woodbridge Hill Road, Gardners Bay, Tas 7112 **region** Southern Tasmania
phone (03) 6295 0294 **fax** (03) 6295 0294 **open** By appointment
winemaker Scott Polley **est.** 1987
product range Pinot Noir.
summary Bamajura's name is derived from the first two letters of the late Ray Polley and his sisters Barbara, Margaret and Judy. The vineyard was planted by Ray Polley, and son Scott took over in the early 1990s; having undertaken the TAFE Tasmania viticulture course, he converted the vineyard to the Scott Henry trellis. In 2002 he took over the winemaking mantle from Michael Vishacki.

🐾 banks thargo wines ★★★★☆

Racecourse Road, Penola, SA 5277 **region** Coonawarra
phone (08) 8737 2338 **fax** (08) 8737 3369 **open** Not
winemaker Banks Kidman, Jonathon Kidman **production** 1500 cases **est.** 1980
product range ($18.50 R) Merlot, Cabernet Sauvignon.
summary The unusual name comes directly from family history. One branch of the Kidman family moved to the Mount Gambier district in 1858, but Thomas Kidman (who had been in the foster care of the Banks family from the age of two to 13) moved to the Broken Hill/southwest Queensland region to work for the famous Kidman Bros pastoral interests. When he 'retired' from the outback, he bought the property presently owned by the family in Coonawarra, in 1919. His second son was named Banks Thargomindah Kidman, and it is he and wife Jenny who decided to diversity their grazing activities by planting vines in the 1980s. Sixteen and a half hectares are under contract, leaving 1.3 hectares each of merlot and cabernet sauvignon for the subsequently established Banks Thargo brand. It is available by mail order, and in Melbourne it is distributed by Richwood Agencies.

Banks Thargo Merlot

▼▼▼▼▽ **2001** Medium to full red-purple; the smooth bouquet shows dark fruits with plenty of concentration and oak well to the background; the palate is flooded with fruit at the sweet end of the varietal spectrum; good extract and balance. **rating:** 92
▼▼▼▼▽ **2000** Medium to full red-purple; the bouquet is complex, with plenty of bite to the mix of dark berry fruit and tangy oak. While showing lots of flavour, the palate has more elegance and varietal character than the 2001, even if it is less rich. Good length and soft tannins round off a truly classy wine. **rating:** 93
best drinking Now–2008 **best vintages** '00, '01 **drink with** Rack of veal • $18.50

bannockburn vineyards ★★★★★

Midland Highway, Bannockburn, Vic 3331 **region** Geelong
phone (03) 5281 1363 **fax** (03) 5281 1349 **open** Not
winemaker Gary Farr **production** 9000 cases **est.** 1974
product range ($21.25–110 R) Riesling, Sauvignon Blanc, Chardonnay, SRH Chardonnay, (named in honour of the late Stuart Reginald Hooper, founder of Bannockburn), Pinot Noir, Saignee (Rose), Serre, Shiraz, Cabernet Sauvignon Merlot.
summary With the qualified exception of the Cabernet Merlot, which can be a little leafy and gamey, produces outstanding wines across the range, all with individuality, style, great complexity and depth of flavour. The low-yielding estate vineyards play their role, but so does the French-influenced winemaking of Gary Farr. The Serre Pinot Noir, from a close-planted block, is absolutely outstanding. Export markets have been established in the UK, Brussels, the US, Hong Kong, New Zealand and Indonesia.

Bannockburn Sauvignon Blanc

♥♥♥♥♡ **2002** Light green-yellow; the clean but quite complex bouquet has guava and tropical fruit aromas which all come through on the concentrated, intense palate; finishes with pleasing acidity. **rating:** 90
best drinking Now–2005 **best vintages** '02 **drink with** Marinated calamari • $25

Bannockburn Chardonnay

♥♥♥♥♡ **2001** Glowing yellow-green; complex, toasty barrel-ferment oak is easily matched by the fig and melon fruit of the bouquet; a dense, concentrated, layered palate follows, the oak once again very much in evidence. **rating:** 91
best drinking Now–2007 **best vintages** '88, '90, '91, '92, '94, '96, '98, '01 **drink with** Rich white meat dishes • $47

Bannockburn Pinot Noir

♥♥♥♥♡ **2001** Strong red-purple; a powerful array of black plum, spice, forest and hay aromas lead into a palate which moves up yet another notch: it is super-powerful, concentrated and complex, with layers of plum fruit. **rating:** 93
best drinking 2005–2010 **best vintages** '84, '86, '88, '89, '90, '91, '92, '94, '97, '99, '00, '01 **drink with** Rare roast squab • $47

Bannockburn Shiraz

♥♥♥♥♥ **2001** Medium to full red-purple; as ever, a very complex bouquet with cool-grown Côte Rôtie-like spice, licorice and pepper overtones to the black fruits. An intensely focused yet sensual palate, with a wonderfully complex palette of flavours; long carry and finish. **rating:** 95
best drinking 2006–2016 **best vintages** '88, '91, '92, '94, '95, '98, '00, '01 **drink with** Roast marinated venison • $47

Bannockburn Cabernet Sauvignon Merlot

♥♥♥♥ **2000** Medium red-purple; the bouquet has a mix of blackcurrant, cedar, earth and olive aromas, the medium-bodied and rather restrained palate running down a similar track, the blackcurrant fruit accompanied by touches of herb, olive and mint. **rating:** 88
best drinking 2005–2010 **drink with** Braised lamb • $37

banrock station ★★★☆

Holmes Road, off Sturt Highway, Kingston-on-Murray, SA 5331 **region** Riverland
phone (08) 8583 0299 **fax** (08) 8583 0288 **open** 7 days 10–4, except public holidays
winemaker Glenn James **production** 2.75 million cases **est.** 1994
product range ($7.99–12.99 R) Semillon Chardonnay, Chardonnay, Shiraz Cabernet, Cabernet Merlot; Premium Range includes Wigley Reach Unwooded Chardonnay, Napper's Verdelho, Ball Island Shiraz, Cave Cliff Merlot, Sparkling Chardonnay and Shiraz; The Reserve range includes Chardonnay, Shiraz, Petit Verdot.
summary The $1 million visitors' centre at Banrock Station was opened in February 1999. Owned by BRL Hardy, the Banrock Station property covers over 1700 hectares, with 240 hectares of vineyard and the remainder being a major wildlife and wetland preservation area. The wines have consistently offered excellent value for money.

Banrock Station The Reserve Chardonnay

♥♥♥♥ **2002** Bright, light green-yellow; a clean, fresh lifted bouquet with a hint of crushed pineapple, then a lively and quite long palate with citrus, melon and pineapple fruit flavours; very good unwooded style. **rating:** 87
best drinking Now **drink with** Sugar-cured tuna • $12.99

Banrock Station The Reserve Shiraz
▼▼▼▽ **2001** Medium red; the bouquet is clean, with soft plummy fruit and vanilla oak, the light to medium-bodied palate in the same register, but without any particular excitement. **rating: 84**
best drinking Now **drink with** Takeaway • $12.99

Banrock Station The Reserve Petit Verdot
▼▼▼▽ **2001** Deep, vivid purple-red; a concentrated, ripe blackberry jam bouquet leads into a powerful and tannic palate, showing just why the variety should be the minor component of a Bordeaux-blend. **rating: 84**
best drinking 2004–2008 **drink with** Barbecued meat • $12.99

🦋 baptista ★★★★☆

139 High Street, Nagambie, Vic 3608 **region** Nagambie Lakes
phone (03) 5794 2514 **fax** (03) 5794 1776 **open** 7 days 10–5
winemaker David Traeger **production** 400 cases **est.** 1993
product range ($115 R) The Graytown Shiraz.
summary In 1993 David Traeger acquired a vineyard he had coveted for many years, and which had been planted by Baptista Governa in 1891. He has been buying grapes from the vineyard since 1988, but it was in a run-down condition, and required a number of years of rehabilitation before he felt the quality of the grapes was sufficient for a single vineyard release. Ownership of the business did not pass to Dromana Estate when that company acquired the David Traeger brand; it is jointly owned by David Traeger and the Wine Investment Fund, the latter a majority shareholder in Dromana Estate. Apart from cellar door, the wine is distributed by The Wine Company.

Baptista The Graytown Heathcote Shiraz
▼▼▼▼▼ **1997** Medium red-purple, showing some development; complex, savoury, bottle-developed fruit aromas range through earth, spice and leather; the multi-flavoured palate has excellent length and fine tannins; the fruit flavour is savoury yet satisfying. This is a seriously good wine, but the price is daunting, even if it does come from vines which are more than 110 years old. **rating: 94**
best drinking Now–2013 **drink with** Rare roast beef • $115

barak estate NR

Barak Road, Moorooduc, Vic 3933 **region** Mornington Peninsula
phone (03) 5978 8439 **fax** (03) 5978 8439 **open** Weekends and public holidays 11–5
winemaker James Williamson **production** 500 cases **est.** 1996
product range ($17–20 CD) Chardonnay, Shiraz, Cabernet Sauvignon.
summary When James Williamson decided to plant vines on his 4-hectare Moorooduc property and establish a micro-winery, he already knew it was far cheaper to buy wine by the bottle than to make it. Undeterred, he ventured into grape growing and winemaking, picking the first grapes in 1993 and opening Barak Estate in 1996. Old telegraph poles, railway sleepers, old palings and timber shingles have all been used in the construction of the picturesque winery.

barambah ridge NR

79 Goschnicks Road, Redgate via Murgon, Qld 4605 **region** South Burnett
phone (07) 4168 4766 **fax** (07) 4168 4770 **open** 7 days 10–5
winemaker Stuart Pierce **production** 12000 cases **est.** 1997
product range ($10–24.95 CD) Semillon, Chardonnay Semillon, Ridge White, Verdelho, Unwooded Chardonnay, Reserve Chardonnay, Barambah Bubbles, Sparkling Shiraz, Laura Rose, Ridge Red, Classic Dry Red, Reserve Shiraz, Cabernet Sauvignon, Old Feedlot Port, Mayoral Muscat, Honey Mead.
summary Barambah Ridge is owned by Tambarambah Limited, an unlisted public company, and is a major new entrant on the Queensland wine scene. Tambarambah also owns Mount Tamborine Winery, and Barambah Ridge has three outlets: 79 Goschnicks Road, Redgate; On the Boardwalk, Noosa Harbour Marine Village, Tewantin; and South Maryborough Travel Stop, Bruce Highway, Maryborough.

baratto's NR

Farm 678, Hanwood, NSW 2680 **region** Riverina
phone (02) 6963 0171 **fax** (02) 6963 0171 **open** 7 days 10–5
winemaker Peter Baratto **production** 6250 cases **est.** 1975

product range ($6–18 CD) Chardonnay, Trebbiano Semillon (Late Harvest), Botrytis Semillon, Shiraz Cabernet Sauvignon, Cabernet Sauvignon; also variety of casks and cleanskins.

summary Baratto's is in many ways a throwback to the old days. Peter Baratto has 15 hectares of vineyards and sells the wine in bulk or in 10- and 20-litre casks from the cellar door at old-time prices, from as little as $2 per litre.

barnadown run ★★★★

390 Cornella Road, Toolleen, Vic 3551 **region** Heathcote
phone (03) 5433 6376 **fax** (03) 5433 6386 **open** 7 days 10–5
winemaker Andrew Millis **production** 1500 cases **est.** 1995
product range ($35–45 CD) Shiraz, Merlot, Cabernet Sauvignon, Henry Bennett's Voluptuary.
summary Named after the original pastoral lease of which the vineyard forms part, and established on rich terra rossa soil for which the best Heathcote vineyards are famous. Owner Andrew Millis carries out both the viticulture and winemaking at the 5-hectare vineyard. Exports to the US.

Barnadown Run Shiraz
♥♥♥♡ **2001** Medium red-purple; there are some dusty, leafy overtones to the fruit of the bouquet; the firm bouquet again has hints of leaf and slightly edgy, herbal characters. Radically different from the 2000. **rating:** 84
best drinking Now–2007 **drink with** Leave it in the cellar • $35

Barnadown Run Henry Bennett's Voluptuary
♥♥♥♥ **2001** Medium to full red-purple; blackberry, plum, blackcurrant and cedar aromas lead into a round palate, with quite ripe plummy fruit, soft tannins and subtle oak. A blend of Shiraz, Cabernet Sauvignon and Malbec inspired by Barnadown Run founder Henry Bennett's appreciation of luxury and sensual pleasure. **rating:** 88
best drinking 2004–2009 **drink with** Venison • $45

Barnadown Run Merlot
♥♥♥♥ **2001** Light to medium red-purple; the juicy berry fruit of the bouquet has hints of chocolate, the palate veering sharply back to varietal character, with olive and savoury notes against a background of the ripe fruit of the bouquet. **rating:** 86
best drinking 2004–2008 **drink with** Lamb kidneys • $35

Barnadown Run Cabernet Sauvignon
♥♥♥♥♡ **2001** Medium red-purple; the moderately intense, clean bouquet has redcurrant, blackcurrant and subtle oak; the palate follows on with smooth, supple red fruit flavours providing excellent mouthfeel. An elegant and totally delicious wine. **rating:** 93
best drinking 2006–2016 **best vintages** '00, '01 **drink with** Rare beef • $35

barossa ridge wine estate NR

Light Pass Road, Tanunda, SA 5352 **region** Barossa Valley
phone (08) 8563 2811 **fax** (08) 8563 2811 **open** By appointment
winemaker Marco Litterini **production** 2000 cases **est.** 1987
product range ($25–27 CD) Valley of Vines (Classic red blend), Old Creek Shiraz, Mardia's Vineyard Cabernet Franc, Bamboo Creek Merlot, Rocky Valley Cabernet Sauvignon.
summary A grape grower turned winemaker with a small list of interesting red varietals, including the Valley of Vines blend of Merlot, Cabernet Franc, Cabernet Sauvignon and Petit Verdot, the only such wine produced in the Barossa Valley. Production has doubled, and the wines have retail distribution in New South Wales. All its wines are built in an impressively heroic style. Exports to Switzerland, Germany, Malaysia and Thailand.

barossa settlers ★★★

Trial Hill Road, Lyndoch, SA 5351 **region** Barossa Valley
phone (08) 8524 4017 **fax** (08) 8524 4519 **open** 7 days 11–3, or by appointment
winemaker Jane Haese **production** 500 cases **est.** 1983
product range ($17–30 CD) Semillon, Chardonnay, Pinot Chardonnay, Shiraz, Finale Hoffnungsthal Settlement Shiraz, Joan's Block Grenache, Cabernet Sauvignon, Finale Cabernet Sauvignon, Port, Sherry.
summary A superbly located cellar door (dating back to 1860) is the only outlet (other than mail order) for the wines from this excellent vineyard owned by the Haese family. Production has slowed in recent years, with the grapes from the 31-hectare vineyard being sold to others.

Barossa Settlers Semillon

TTTT 2002 Medium yellow-green; the full and potent bouquet has exemplary grass and herb aromas; the palate is tighter than the bouquet suggests, with touches of lemon and a slightly grippy finish. **rating:** 86

best drinking Now–2005 **drink with** Avocado salad • $17

Barossa Settlers Grenache

TTTY 2001 Light to medium red-purple; the clean, fairly light bouquet has typically juicy berry aromas, the juicy/minty palate a logical follow-on; balanced finish. **rating:** 84

best drinking Now **drink with** Meat salads • $21

barossavale wines NR

PO Box 482, Nuriootpa, SA 5355 **region** Barossa Valley
phone (08) 8562 3193 **fax** (08) 8562 4490 **open** Not
winemaker Rob Gibson **production** 3200 cases **est.** 1996
product range ($20–70 R) Old Vine Collection Shiraz, Merlot.
summary Rob Gibson spent much of his working life as a senior viticulturist for Penfolds. While at Penfolds he was involved in research tracing the characters that particular parcels of grapes give to a wine, which left him with a passion for identifying and protecting what is left of the original vineyard plantings in wine regions around Australia. His future plans are to release tiny quantities of wines from other regions, drawing upon old vineyards. These days his work as a viticultural consultant takes him all over Australia, and indeed all over the world, so his research contacts are maintained. His 2000 Australian Old Vine Collection Shiraz won a double-gold at the San Francisco International Wine Competition, getting the business off on the right foot.

BarossaVale Merlot

TTTT 2000 Medium red-purple; spicy fruit plus lots of oak (a mix of French and American) comes through on the bouquet; the palate is quite tangy, with savoury/leafy/lemony varietal characters and fine tannins; overall it is slightly green. **rating:** 85

best drinking 2004–2007 **drink with** Marinated veal • $20

barossa valley estate ★★★★

Seppeltsfield Road, Marananga, SA 5355 **region** Barossa Valley
phone (08) 8562 3599 **fax** (08) 8562 4255 **open** 7 days 10–4.30
winemaker Stuart Bourne **production** 75000 cases **est.** 1984
product range ($9.99–59.99 R) Spires Chardonnay Semillon, Shiraz Cabernet Sauvignon; Moculta Chardonnay, Shiraz, Grenache, Cabernet Merlot; Ebenezer Chardonnay, Shiraz, Cabernet Sauvignon Merlot; the premium E & E Sparkling Shiraz and Black Pepper Shiraz.
summary Barossa Valley Estate is part-owned by BRL Hardy, marking the end of a period during which it was one of the last significant co-operative-owned wineries in Australia. Across the board, the wines are full flavoured and honest. E & E Black Pepper Shiraz is an upmarket label with a strong reputation and following, the Ebenezer range likewise. Over-enthusiastic use of American oak (particularly with the red wines) has been the Achilles heel in the past. The wines are distributed in Australia and the UK by BRL Hardy, and by independent distributors in North America.

Barossa Valley Estate Moculta Chardonnay

TTTT 2002 Medium yellow-green; clean stone fruit and white peach aromas, plus a touch of oak, lead into a fresh, lively, well-balanced commercial style, with particularly good acidity on the finish. **rating:** 87

best drinking Now–2005 **drink with** Chinese prawns • $13.99

Barossa Valley Estate Ebenezer Shiraz

TTTT 1999 Medium to full red-purple; rich, dark berry fruit and scoops of vanilla oak on the bouquet, then a succulent palate with plummy/raspberry fruit, soft tannins and good length, the oak justified (just). **rating:** 89

best drinking 2004–2009 **best vintages** '90, '91, '94, '96, '98 **drink with** Hare • $28.99

Barossa Valley Estate Moculta Shiraz

TTTT 2001 Bright purple-red; red berry and plum aromas on the bouquet and a whisk of oak lead into a smooth, medium-bodied palate with good fruit, tannin and oak balance, worthy of several years in the cellar. **rating:** 87

best drinking 2004–2008 **best vintages** '01 **drink with** Shepherd's pie • $15.99

Barossa Valley Estate Ebenezer Cabernet Merlot

ŸŸŸŸ **2000** Medium red-purple; aromas of dark berry, earth and a touch of leaf lead into a light to medium-bodied palate with savoury overtones and lingering tannins; a blend of 70 per cent Cabernet Sauvignon and 30 per cent Merlot. **rating:** 86

best drinking Now–2007 **drink with** Veal goulash • $28.99

barratt ★★★★☆

PO Box 204, Summertown, SA 5141 **region** Adelaide Hills
phone (08) 8390 1788 **fax** (08) 8390 1788 **open** By appointment at Uley Vineyard, Cornish Road, Summertown
winemaker Lindsay Barratt, Jeffrey Grosset (Contract) **production** 1200 cases **est.** 1993
product range ($24–39.20 ML) Chardonnay, The Bonython Pinot Noir, The Reserve Pinot Noir, Merlot.
summary Former medical practitioner Lindsay and his wife Carolyn Barratt own two vineyards at Summertown: the Uley Vineyard purchased from the late Ian Wilson in August 1990 and the Bonython Vineyard. They have 8.4 hectares of vines, some coming into production, adding sauvignon blanc and merlot to the wine range from 2002. Part of the production from the vineyards is sold to other makers, with Jeffrey Grosset the maker of the Chardonnay and Pinot Noir. Arrangements were finalised for a winery facility at the Adelaide Hills Business and Tourism Centre at Lobethal in time for the 2003 vintage. Limited quantities are sold in the UK, the US and Canada.

Barratt Chardonnay

ŸŸŸŸŸ **2001** Bright, light yellow-green; the bouquet has a subtle but complex interplay between fruit, barrel-ferment and malolactic-ferment aromas, logically followed by the still-tight, stylish and elegant palate, with its smooth mouthfeel and flow. **rating:** 92

best drinking Now–2008 **best vintages** '97, '99, '01 **drink with** Trout mousse • $26

Barratt The Bonython Pinot Noir

ŸŸŸŸŸ **2001** Medium red-purple; distinctly deeper than the Reserve; the darker plummy fruit is likewise very different, and the wine makes a much more positive statement as it enters, with a mix of plum and forest, but has nowhere near the length of the Reserve, notwithstanding some tannins on the finish. The first vintage from the estate-owned Bonython Vineyard, planted in 1997. **rating:** 90

best drinking 2004–2008 **best vintages** '01 **drink with** Braised venison • $26

Barratt The Reserve Pinot Noir

ŸŸŸŸŸ **2001** Light to medium red-purple; fragrant, tangy, savoury overtones to the strawberry and cherry fruit of the bouquet flow into an intense, elegant and relatively light-bodied palate. It has an extremely long finish and lingering aftertaste, and is one of those Pinot Noirs which creep up and take possession of you. From the original 18-year-old vines; spends 11 months in French oak. **rating:** 94

best drinking Now–2007 **best vintages** '01 **drink with** Roast squab • $39.20

Barratt Merlot

ŸŸŸŸ **2001** Medium red-purple; the spicy, cedary, gently savoury bouquet has good varietal character, with some sweet fruit in attendance; the berry flavours of the palate have a touch of mint; good texture, full of promise. The first vintage from the Bonython Vineyard. **rating:** 89

best drinking 2004–2008 **drink with** Lamb kidneys • $24

barretts wines ★★★★

Portland–Nelson Highway, Portland, Vic 3305 **region** Henty
phone (03) 5526 5251 **open** 7 days 11–5
winemaker Rod Barrett **production** 1000 cases **est.** 1983
product range ($15–18 CD) Riesling, Traminer, Late Harvest Riesling, Pinot Noir, Cabernet Sauvignon.
summary Has a low profile, selling its wines locally. The initial releases were made at Best's, but since 1992 all wines have been made on the property by Rod Barrett. The 5.5-hectare vineyard is planted to riesling, pinot noir and cabernet sauvignon.

Barretts Pinot Noir

ŸŸŸŸŸ **2000** Medium to full red, with a touch of purple; the ripe plum and black coffee aromas of the bouquet show bell-clear varietal character; the medium-bodied palate has spicy plum flavour, silky texture and great line and focus. A very good wine at any price, and outstanding value at the price which it is offered. **rating:** 92

best drinking Now–2007 **best vintages** '97, '00 **drink with** Peking duck • $18

🐝 barringwood park   NR

60 Gillams Road, Lower Barrington, Tas 7306 **region** Northern Tasmania
phone (03) 6492 3140 **fax** (03) 6492 3360 **open** Wed–Sun and public holidays 10–5
winemaker Tamar Ridge (Contract) **production** 1000 cases **est.** 1993
product range ($20–24 CD) Pinot Gris, Chardonnay, Pinot Noir, Mill Block Pinot Noir.
summary Judy and Ian Robinson operate a sawmill at Lower Barrington, 15 minutes south of Devonport on the main tourist trail to Cradle Mountain, and when they planted 500 vines in 1993 the aim was to do a bit of home winemaking for themselves and a few friends. In a thoroughly familiar story, the urge to expand the vineyard and make wine on a commercial scale came almost immediately, and they embarked on a 6-year plan, planting 1 hectare a year for the first 4 years (doing all the work themselves while also running their sawmill) and then building the cellar and tasting rooms during the following 2 years. They have planted pinot noir, chardonnay, pinot gris, schonburger and pinot meunier, and all the wines available at cellar door in early 2003 have won show medals.

barrymore estate   ★★★☆

76 Tuerong Rod, Tuerong, Vic 3933 **region** Mornington Peninsula
phone (03) 5974 8999 **fax** (03) 9789 0821 **open** Most days 11–5
winemaker Peter J Cotter, Richard McIntyre (Consultant) **production** 1800 cases **est.** 1998
product range ($17.50–26 CD) Sauvignon Blanc, Pinot Gris, Chardonnay, Pinot Noir; associated brands are Tuerong Station, Peninsula Pinot Noir, Tuerong Valley.
summary Barrymore Estate is part of a much larger property first settled in the 1840s; the abundance of water and wetlands, with the confluence of the Devil Bend and Balcombe Creeks nearby, has sustained grazing and farming since the first settlement. Peter Cotter has planted 8.5 hectares of pinot noir, 1 hectare each of chardonnay and sauvignon blanc, and 0.5 hectare of pinot gris, selling part of the grapes and making part under the Barrymore label.

Barrymore Estate Sauvignon Blanc
▼▼▼▼ 2002 Pale straw-green; the lively bouquet has a mix of grassy, capsicum and gooseberry aromas; the palate is fresh, light and pure, more restrained than the bouquet. Well made.   **rating:** 89
best drinking Now **drink with** Sautéed scallops • $17.50

Barrymore Estate Chardonnay
▼▼▼▼ 2002 Light green-straw; the wine was tank-fermented, but matured in 30 per cent new, 70 per cent older French oak, hence both the barrel-ferment and malolactic-ferment influences are very subtle, particularly on the bouquet. The light to medium-bodied palate has nectarine and citrus fruit, with the oak minimal, but the wine does have surprising length.   **rating:** 87
best drinking Now–2006 **drink with** Tempura • $22

barwang vineyard   ★★★★☆

Barwang Road, Young, NSW 2594 **region** Hilltops
phone (02) 6382 3594 **fax** (02) 6382 2594 **open** Not
winemaker Jim Brayne, Russell Cody, Scott Zrna **production** NFP **est.** 1969
product range ($15.95–31.50 R) Chardonnay, Semillon, Shiraz, Merlot, Cabernet Sauvignon.
summary Peter Robertson pioneered viticulture in the Young region when he planted his first vines in 1969 as part of a diversification programme for his 400-hectare grazing property. When McWilliam's acquired Barwang in 1989, the vineyard amounted to 13 hectares; today the plantings exceed 100 hectares. Wine quality has been exemplary from the word go; wines are always elegant, restrained and deliberately understated, repaying extended cellaring.

Barwang Vineyard Chardonnay
▼▼▼▼▽ 2000 Medium yellow-green; a soft and complex bouquet has some toasty/buttery overtones to the white peach fruit; the fruit flavours on the palate have nuances of citrus and melon as well as the white peach, all held together by fine acidity on the finish.   **rating:** 90
best drinking Now–2006 **best vintages** '94, '98 **drink with** Calamari • $19.95

Barwang Vineyard Show Chardonnay
▼▼▼▼▽ 1996 Full yellow-gold; the bouquet has a complex array of yellow peach, nut and honey aromas, with the palate a rich reflection of the bouquet, and certainly not broken. Excellent acidity on the finish ties the package together, but I have to wonder about its relevance as a style.   **rating:** 90
best drinking Now–2005 **drink with** Roast pork • $28

Barwang Vineyard Merlot

▼▼▼▼▽ **2001** Medium red-purple; savoury olive, blackcurrant and spice aromas feed into a generous palate with ripe blackcurrant fruit on entry, and the tannins and extract on the finish fine and appropriately savoury.

rating: 90

best drinking 2005–2010 **best vintages** '00, '01 **drink with** Braised veal • $31.50

Barwang Vineyard Cabernet Sauvignon

▼▼▼▼▽ **2001** Bright, full purple-red; clean blackcurrant and blackberry fruit is supported by quality French oak on the bouquet; the palate has sweet, luscious blackcurrant fruit balanced by fine, gently savoury tannins.

rating: 92

best drinking 2006–2011 **best vintages** '89, '91, '92, '93, '96, '97, '98, '00, '01 **drink with** Beef Wellington • $24

barwick wines ★★★☆

Level 1, 256 Georges Terrace, Perth, WA 6000 **region** South West Australia Zone
phone (08) 9765 1216 **fax** (08) 9765 1836 **open** By appointment
winemaker John Griffiths, Mark Lane (Contract) **production** 80 000 cases **est.** 1997
product range ($10–12 ML) Chardonnay, St John's Brook Shiraz, Dwalganup Shiraz Cabernet, Dwalganup Cabernet Sauvignon.
summary The production of 80 000 cases, rising in stages to over 100 000 cases, gives some guide to the size of the operation. Since 1997 Barwick Wines has been supplying grapes and bulk wine to some of the best known names in Western Australia and the eastern states from three very large vineyards. The first is the 83-hectare Dwalganup Vineyard in the Blackwood Valley region, the second the 38-hectare St John's Brook Vineyard in the Margaret River, and the third the 73-hectare Treenbrook Vineyard in Pemberton. The wines are contract-made at two locations, and sell for thoroughly old-fashioned prices. The owners of the business are four syndicates which have established the vineyards, and the business plan envisages that 80 per cent of production will be exported to over 10 countries, with local sales coming from what the owners describe as 'friends of Barwick'.

Barwick St John's Brook Margaret River Shiraz

▼▼▼▼ **2001** Medium purple-red; youthful but complex spice, berry, leaf and mint aromas are followed by a bright red and black cherry-flavoured palate, the oak subtle; slightly unformed, but should get there. **rating:** 87
best drinking 2004–2008 **drink with** Beef spare ribs • $11

Barwick Dwalganup Blackwood Valley Cabernet Sauvignon

▼▼▼▼ **2001** Medium red-purple; the moderately intense bouquet has dark berry fruit, a touch of spice and an airbrush of oak; the medium-bodied palate has plenty of ripe blackberry/cassis fruit, but does have a somewhat hard finish.

rating: 86

best drinking 2005–2009 **drink with** Lamb casserole • $11

basedow ★★★☆

161–165 Murray Street, Tanunda, SA 5352 **region** Barossa Valley
phone (08) 8563 3666 **fax** (08) 8563 3597 **open** Mon–Fri 10–5, weekends and public holidays 11–5
winemaker Peter Orr **production** 75 000 cases **est.** 1896
product range ($6.95–65 CD) Eden Valley Riesling, Barossa Valley Semillon, Sauvignon Blanc Semillon, Unwooded Chardonnay, Barossa Valley Chardonnay, Late Harvest, Bush Vine Grenache, Barossa Valley Shiraz, Mistella, Old Tawny Port; Barossa Valley Riesling, Semillon, Chardonnay; Johannes Barossa Shiraz is the flagship wine.
summary An old and proud label, particularly well known for its oak-matured Semillon (once called White Burgundy on the Australian market), which underwent a number of changes of ownership during the 1990s. Overall, a reliable producer of solidly flavoured wines, although the appointment of a receiver to owner Hill International in February 2002 threw a shadow over the business. Exports to the US and the UK.

basket range wines NR

c/- PO, Basket Range, SA 5138 **region** Adelaide Hills
phone (08) 8390 1515 **fax** (08) 8390 0499 **open** Not
winemaker Phillip Broderick **production** 500 cases **est.** 1980
product range ($20–22 ML) A single Bordeaux-blend of Cabernet Sauvignon, Cabernet Franc, Merlot, Malbec drawn from 3 hectares of estate plantings.
summary A tiny operation known to very few, run by civil and Aboriginal rights lawyer Phillip Broderick, a most engaging man with a disarmingly laid-back manner.

bass fine wines ★★★☆

Deviot Road, Gravelly Beach, Tas 7276 **region** Northern Tasmania
phone (03) 6231 6222 **fax** (03) 6231 6222 **open** Not
winemaker Guy Wagner **production** 2000 cases **est.** 1999
product range ($19–28 R) Strait Chardonnay, Block 1 Pinot Noir, Strait Pinot Noir.
summary Bass Fine Wines runs entirely counter to the usual Tasmanian pattern of tiny, estate-based businesses. Guy Wagner has set up Bass as a classic negociant operation, working backwards from the marketplace. He is currently completing a wine marketing degree at the University of Adelaide and intends to continue studies in oenology. The wines have been purchased from various vineyards in bottle and in barrel, but from the 2000 vintage he has also purchased grapes. The winery has been set up to focus on Pinot Noir, with three levels of Pinot in the business plan, commencing with Strait Pinot in the fighting sector of the market, then Bass as a premium brand, and ultimately there will be a super-premium Pinot, possibly to come from 30-year-old plantings which have been contracted.

bass phillip ★★★★★

Tosch's Road, Leongatha South, Vic 3953 **region** Gippsland
phone (03) 5664 3341 **fax** (03) 5664 3209 **open** By appointment
winemaker Phillip Jones **production** 1500 cases **est.** 1979
product range ($27–145) Tiny quantities of Pinot Noir in three categories: standard, Premium and an occasional barrel of Reserve. A hatful of Chardonnay also made; plus Pinot Rose and Gamay.
summary Phillip Jones has retired from the Melbourne rat-race to handcraft tiny quantities of superlative Pinot Noir which, at its best, has no equal in Australia. Painstaking site selection, ultra-close vine spacing and the very, very cool climate of South Gippsland are the keys to the magic of Bass Phillip and its eerily Burgundian Pinots.

Bass Phillip Pinot Noir

▼▼▼▼▽ **2001** Good colour; the fragrant and elegant bouquet is moderately intense, with spicy dark fruits and a hint of oak; the wine then really gets into stride, with a long, silky palate, lovely ripe tannins, and a nice touch of sous bois (forest floor). **rating:** 93

best drinking 2004–2007 **best vintages** '84, '85, '89, '91, '92, '93, '94, '95, '96 **drink with** Slow-cooked Tasmanian salmon

batista NR

Franklin Road, Middlesex, WA 6258 **region** Manjimup
phone (08) 9772 3530 **fax** (08) 9772 3530 **open** By appointment
winemaker Bob Peruch **production** 1200 cases **est.** 1993
product range ($19–28 CD) Pinot Noir, Shiraz, Shiraz Cabernet, Pinot Chardonnay Reserve Brut.
summary Batista is in fact the baptismal name of owner Bob Peruch, a Pinot Noir devotee whose father planted 1 hectare of vines back in the 1950s, although these have since gone. Between 1993 and 1996 Bob Peruch has planted 1.5 hectares of pinot noir, 1.85 hectares of shiraz and the cabernet family, and 0.5 hectare of chardonnay destined for sparkling wine. The estate has two vineyards, one selected for pinot noir and chardonnay, and the other, 2 kilometres away, for shiraz, cabernet sauvignon, cabernet franc and merlot. The well-drained soils are of quartz and ironstone gravel; yields are restricted to around 7 tonnes per hectare.

🐌 battely wines NR

Everton Ridge, PO Box 548, Beechworth, Vic 3747 **region** Beechworth
phone (03) 5727 0505 **fax** (03) 5727 0506 **open** Not
winemaker Russell Bourne **est.** 1998
product range ($16–28 ML) QED Beechworth range of Rose, Syrah, Merlot.
summary Dr Russell Bourne is an anaesthetist and former GP at Mount Beauty, and has always loved the food, wine and skiing of northeast Victoria. He is also completing his oenology degree at Charles Sturt University in consequence of his acquisition of the former Brown Brothers Everton Hills vineyard. Only days before writing these words I shared in a bottle of 1964 Everton Hills Cabernet Shiraz which had been entombed at Brown Brothers for over 35 years. The vineyard was sold by Brown Brothers many years ago (low yields made it uneconomic) and was overgrown and abandoned when Dr Bourne purchased it in 1998. In that year he planted 1.6 hectares of shiraz, and viognier in the spring of 2001, with further Rhône Valley varietal plantings planned, including counoise. Until the vineyard comes into production the wines are being made from purchased grapes grown in Beechworth.

✿ battunga vineyards   NR

RSD 25A, Tynan Road, Meadows, SA 5201 (postal)   **region** Adelaide Hills
phone (08) 8388 3866   **fax** (08) 8388 3877   **open** Not
winemaker Robert Mann, Simon White   **production** A few cases   **est.** 1997
product range Chardonnay.
summary The development of this substantial vineyard venture began in 1997 under the direction of David Eckert. The plantings extend to pinot noir (7 ha), merlot (3.6 ha), sauvignon blanc (3.4 ha), chardonnay (2.3 ha), shiraz (2 ha), pinot gris (1.8 ha) and viognier (1.8 ha), but only a limited amount of wine is to be made and released under the Battunga Vineyards brand.

✿ baudin rock wines   NR

RSD 109, Kingston SE, SA 5275 (postal)   **region** Mount Benson
phone (08) 8768 6217   **fax** (08) 8768 6217   **open** Not
winemaker Contract   **est.** 1997
product range Shiraz, Cabernet Sauvignon.
summary The Ling family, headed by Robin Ling, began the development of Baudin Rock Wines in 1997, and now have 40 hectares planted to sauvignon blanc, cabernet sauvignon, merlot and shiraz. The wines are made under contract, but with assistance from James Ling; the viticulturist is Paul Ling, and the production manager is Robin Ling. Only a small amount of the wine is made under the Baudin Rock label, with most of the production sold.

baxter stokes wines   NR

65 Memorial Avenue, Baskerville, WA 6065   **region** Swan Valley
phone (08) 9296 4831   **fax** (08) 9296 4831   **open** 9.30–5 weekends and public holidays
winemaker Greg Stokes   **production** 750 cases   **est.** 1988
product range ($10–14 CD) Chardonnay, Verdelho, Shiraz Pinot Noir, Shiraz Cabernet Sauvignon.
summary A weekend and holiday operation for Greg and Lucy Stokes, with the production sold by mail order and through the cellar door.

✿ bay of fires   ★★★★☆

40 Baxters Road, Pipers River, Tas 7252   **region** Northern Tasmania
phone (03) 6382 7622   **fax** (03) 6382 7225   **open** 7 days 10–5
winemaker Fran Austin   **production** 3500 cases   **est.** 2001
product range ($26.99 CD) Riesling, Sauvignon Blanc, Pinot Gris, Chardonnay, Pinot Noir, Pinot Chardonnay.
summary In 1994 BRL Hardy purchased its first grapes from Tasmania with the aim of further developing and refining its sparkling wines, a process which quickly gave birth to Arras. The next stage was the inclusion of various parcels of chardonnay from Tasmania in the 1998 Eileen Hardy, and then the development in 2001 of the Bay of Fires brand, offering wines sourced from various parts of Tasmania. As one would expect, there is great potential for the brand. The winery was originally that of Rochecombe, then Ninth Island, and now, of course, Bay of Fires.

Bay of Fires Riesling
ŸŸŸŸŸ 2001 Light yellow-green; the firm bouquet is at the minerally end of the spectrum, rather than the fruity end, with hints of lemon; the lively palate has good length and mouthfeel, sustained by typical Tasmanian acidity. It is sourced from the Pipers River region and will, of course, repay cellaring. Nonetheless, the line pricing with the other wines is interesting.   **rating:** 90
best drinking Now–2008   **drink with** Shellfish • $26.99

Bay of Fires Sauvignon Blanc
ŸŸŸŸŸ 2002 Bright straw-green; a spotlessly clean bouquet offers a mix of ripe gooseberry and more grassy herbal aromas, the palate following suit. Joins Meadowbank and Dalrymple as one of three Tasmanian producers able to invest Sauvignon Blanc with significant varietal flavour.   **rating:** 92
best drinking Now   **best vintages** '02   **drink with** Oysters • $26.99

Bay of Fires Pinot Gris
ŸŸŸŸ 2002 Very pale straw-green; a spotlessly clean bouquet with faint apple aromas leads into a nicely balanced palate; clever winemaking has made a virtue out of nothing.   **rating:** 88
best drinking Now–2005   **drink with** Seafood antipasto • $26.99

Bay of Fires Chardonnay

▼▼▼▼ 2001 Light to medium yellow-green; light, crisp citrus and mineral fruit has been sensitively supported on the bouquet by subtle oak; the palate is quite long, with citrus and stone fruit flavours, and that omnipresent Tasmanian acidity. Cool-fermented in new French oak, but I suspect (rightly) taken out of that oak earlier rather than later. **rating: 89**

best drinking Now–2007 **drink with** Chinese prawns • $26.99

Bay of Fires Pinot Chardonnay

▼▼▼▼▽ 1998 Light straw-green; quite fragrant white peach fruit with some bready/yeasty aromas is followed by a fine, delicate and highly focused palate, with citrus and nectarine flavours, fading slightly on the finish. A blend of Tasmanian and Yarra Valley base wine, which spends 4 years on lees. **rating: 91**

best drinking Now–2005 **best vintages** '98 **drink with** Steamed fish • $26.99

Bay of Fires Pinot Noir

▼▼▼▼▽ 2001 Bright purple-red; the moderately intense bouquet has clean plummy fruit, a dash of spice and neatly handled oak; the palate has excellent shape, mouthfeel and length, with a spicy, savoury finish. **rating: 92**

best drinking Now–2007 **best vintages** '01 **drink with** Roast quail • $26.99

Bay of Fires Cabernet Sauvignon

▼▼▼▼ 2001 Full red-purple; the powerful, albeit slightly closed, bouquet has a mix of blackberry and blackcurrant, the palate with massive extract and drying tannins. I have been fooled by Tasmanian cabernet tannins before, and am not prepared to say those tannins will never soften sufficiently, but at this point the wine ought to be left to its own devices. **rating: 85**

best drinking 2008–2015 **drink with** Leave it in the cellar • $26.99

🐦 bay of shoals   NR

19 Flinders Avenue, Kingscote, Kangaroo Island, SA 5223 (postal) **region** Kangaroo Island
phone (08) 8553 2229 **fax** (08) 8553 2229 **open** Not
winemaker Bethany Wines (Contract) **production** 500 cases **est.** 1994
product range ($18–27 R) Riesling, Chardonnay, Shiraz, Cabernet Sauvignon.
summary John Willoughby's vineyard overlooks the Bay of Shoals, which is the northern boundary of Kingscote, the island's main town. Planting of the vineyard began in 1994, and has now reached 10 hectares of riesling, chardonnay, sauvignon blanc, cabernet sauvignon and shiraz. In addition, 460 olive trees have been planted to produce table olives for sale at the cellar-door outlet, which is due to open in 2003.

bayview estate   NR

365 Purves Road, Main Ridge, Vic 3928 **region** Mornington Peninsula
phone (03) 5989 6130 **fax** (03) 5989 6373 **open** 7 days 12–5
winemaker Dean Burford **production** 6000 cases **est.** 1984
product range ($20–25 CD) Pinot Gris, Chardonnay, Pinot Noir, The Big Pig Red Cabernet Merlot, Cabernet Sauvignon Reserve.
summary Few enterprises have cast such a broad net over the tourist traffic in the Mornington Peninsula. The estate includes the Pig & Whistle Tavern, the cellar door, the five-star Views Restaurant, and an 80-seat beer garden (which serves 40 local and imported beers), a produce store, and rose and lavender gardens. Almost incidental are the 7 hectares of pinot gris, pinot noir and pinot grigio which produce 6000 cases of wine a year, sold through the cellar door, the Hilton Hotel and Crown Casino and several Mornington Peninsula restaurants.

Bayview Estate Pinot Gris

▼▼▼▼ 2000 Light to medium straw-green; aromas of apple, pear and a touch of citrus lead into an attractive palate, with sweet fruit on the mid-palate, then a quite dry finish. Some bottles suffer from cork taint. **rating: 86**

best drinking Now **drink with** Cold seafood • $24

🐦 b'darra estate   ★★★★

1415 Stumpy Gully Road, Moorooduc, Vic 3933 **region** Mornington Peninsula
phone 0418 310 638 **open** By appointment
winemaker Gavin Perry **production** 2000 cases **est.** 1998
product range ($24–28 ML) Chardonnay, Shiraz, Cabernet Sauvignon; fruit wine.

summary Gavin and Linda Perry fell in love with Bedarra Island (off the north Queensland coast) when they stayed there, hence the name of their property, which they acquired in 1998, planting just under 5 hectares of vines in 1999. They are progressively developing the 21-hectare holding, with a revegetation and wetland creation planned, of which a lake and two big dams form part. Gavin Perry made his first wine in 1993 from grapes grown in the Peninsula while completing a Winery Supplies course. Since that time he has won numerous trophies and gold medals, including Most Successful Exhibitor in 1997, 1999 and 2000 in the Amateur section of the Victorian Wines Show. Given the quality of the 2001 and 2002 B'darra Estate wines, I can only assume he will no longer be entering the Amateur wine section, which would be decidedly unfair, for these are very well-made wines.

B'darra Estate Chardonnay

TTTY 2002 Medium yellow-green; the clean bouquet has light citrus fruit, the oak (appropriately) barely perceptible; the palate provides more of the same, lacking fruit intensity, but well-made. Almost certainly no more or less than the function of young vines. **rating: 84**

best drinking Now–2005 **drink with** Shellfish • $24

B'darra Estate Shiraz

TTTTY 2001 Medium to full purple-red; the complex bouquet offers a range of fully ripe dark berry fruits with spicy/savoury overtones, characters which are wholly varietal; the similarly complex palate has abundant blackberry flavour, with good texture and mouthfeel. Impressive. **rating: 90**

best drinking 2006–2011 **best vintages** '01 **drink with** Rare roast beef • $28

B'darra Estate Cabernet Sauvignon

TTTT 2001 Medium to full red-purple; the moderately intense bouquet has clean, ripe cassis/blackcurrant fruit, the smooth and supple medium-bodied palate carried by the same cassis berry fruit; subtle oak treatment throughout. **rating: 89**

best drinking 2006–2011 **drink with** Rack of lamb • $28

beaumont estate ★★★☆

Lot 20, 155 Milbrodale Road, Broke, NSW 2330 (postal) **region** Lower Hunter Valley
phone 0419 616 461 **fax** (02) 5474 3722 **open** Not
winemaker Contract **production** 3400 cases **est.** 1998
product range ($21–25 ML) Hand Picked Semillon, Merlot.
summary The estate vineyards were planted in September 1999 on the river flats of Parson Creek, nestled between the Yengo and Wollemi National Parks. The soils were enhanced with organic preparations; after 17 months the 2.2 hectares of semillon and 1.3 hectares of merlot produced a substantial crop, the vine growth, so it is said, equivalent to 3 years under normal conditions. The intention is to continue the organic farming approach, and to eventually become certified Bio-Dynamic. Currently the wines are sold by phone, mail order and email, and future plans include a cellar door. Profits from wine sales will support a respite facility for limited-life children that is currently being constructed on the property.

Beaumont Estate Hand Picked Semillon

TTTT 2002 Light to medium yellow-green; the bouquet has light herb and hints of lanolin; the wine has already developed nice mouthfeel and some round fruit flavours on the light to medium-bodied palate, all suggesting, in Semillon terms at least, that this will be an early-developing style. **rating: 88**

best drinking Now–2007 **drink with** Balmain bugs • $20.85

beckett's flat ★★★☆

Beckett Road, Metricup, WA 6280 **region** Margaret River
phone (08) 9755 7402 **fax** (08) 9755 7344 **open** 7 days 10–6
winemaker Belizar Ilic **production** 5500 cases **est.** 1992
product range ($14–35 CD) Sauvignon Blanc Semillon, Verdelho, Chardonnay, Autumn Harvest, Liqueur Chardonnay, Crackling Rose, Shiraz, Reserve Shiraz, Merlot, Reserve Merlot, Cabernet Merlot, Cabernet Sauvignon.
summary Bill and Noni Ilic opened Beckett's Flat in September 1997. Situated just off the Bussell Highway, at Metricup, midway between Busselton and the Margaret River, it draws upon 14 hectares of estate vineyards, first planted in 1992. As from 1998 the wines have been made at the on-site winery. Accommodation is available.

Beckett's Flat Sauvignon Blanc Semillon

YYYY 2002 Pale straw-green; pristine and fine grass, lemon and mineral aromas come through in turn on the light-bodied palate; if only there were more intensity and weight on the mid-palate. **rating:** 85

best drinking Now **drink with** Delicate white-fleshed fish • $16

Beckett's Flat Shiraz

YYYYY 2001 Medium red-purple; the moderately intense bouquet has blackberry at its core, with spicy/savoury/briary overtones; the medium to full-bodied palate has good length and mouthfeel to the ripe fruit, savoury tannins and positive oak. **rating:** 91

best drinking 2005–2011 **best vintages** '01 **drink with** Pizza • $23

Beckett's Flat Cabernet Merlot

YYYY 2001 Light to medium red-purple; light minty, leafy, berry aromas on both bouquet and palate are supported by a touch of chocolate and soft tannins; like all the Beckett's Flat wines, elegance, rather than power, is the key word. **rating:** 86

best drinking 2004–2008 **drink with** Lamb chops • $21

beckingham wines NR

7/477 Warrigal Road, Moorabbin, Vic 3189 **region** Warehouse
phone (03) 9258 7352 **fax** (03) 9360 0713 **open** Weekends 10–5
winemaker Peter Beckingham **production** 2500 cases **est.** 1998
product range ($8–20 CD) Burnt Creek Riesling, Burnt Creek Riesling Pressings, Semillon, Edgehill Unwooded Chardonnay, Edgehill Chardonnay, Pas de Deux Sparkling, Sparkling, Botrytis Affected Riesling, Chardonnay Liqueur, Cabernet Pink, East Keilor Shiraz, Cornial Creek Shiraz, Strathbogie Shiraz, Strathbogie Merlot, Strathbogie Cabernet Franc Merlot, Strathbogie Cabernet, Cornelia Creek Cabernet, Pinot Noir Liqueur.
summary Peter Beckingham is a chemical engineer who has turned a hobby into a part-time business, moving operations from the driveway of his house to a warehouse in Moorabbin. The situation of the winery may not be romantic, but it is eminently practical, and more than a few winemakers in California have adopted the same solution. His friends grow the grapes, and he makes the wine, with the Mornington Peninsula, Echuca and the Strathbogie Ranges the prime source of grapes, other regions (such as the Yarra Valley) contributing from time to time. Peter Beckingham professes to be passionate about his wines, and is doubtless learning more as each vintage goes by.

Beckingham Edgehill Chardonnay

YYYY 2001 Light straw-green; clean, appealing melon/citrus fruit aromas lead into a lively, tangy and crisp palate, brisk acidity adding to its length. A good example of unoaked Chardonnay. **rating:** 85

best drinking Now–2005 **drink with** Light seafood • $15

beelgara estate ★★★

Farm 576, Beelbangera, NSW 2686 **region** Riverina
phone (02) 6966 0288 **fax** (02) 6966 0298 **open** Mon–Sat 10–5, Sun 11–3
winemaker James Ceccato, Belinda Morandin **production** 400 000 cases **est.** 1930
product range ($5–16 CD) Wattleglen Semillon Sauvignon Blanc Chardonnay and Shiraz Cabernet Sauvignon; the Silky Oak range (around $8) of Sauvignon Blanc, Verdelho, Chardonnay, Shiraz, Merlot, Cabernet Merlot, St Macaire; the Woorawa range (around $10) of Riesling, Chardonnay, Old Vine Shiraz, Cabernet Merlot; the Promenade range (around $15) of Semillon, Chardonnay, Botrytis Semillon, Old Vine Shiraz, Chambourcin, Cabernet Sauvignon; Sparkling, Dessert, Lambrusco, fortifieds.
summary Beelgara Estates was formed in 2001 after the purchase of the 60-year-old Rossetto family winery in the Riverina district of New South Wales by a group consisting of growers, distributors, wine industry funds and management. The name Beelgara is a contraction of the Beelbangera region, where the group is headquartered. The new management is placing far greater emphasis on bottled table wine (albeit at low prices), but continues to supply bulk, cleanskin and fully packaged product for both domestic and export markets.

belgenny vineyard ★★★☆

92 De Beyers Road, Pokolbin, NSW 2320 **region** Lower Hunter Valley
phone (02) 9247 5300 **fax** (02) 9247 7273 **open** Not
winemaker Monarch Winemaking Services (Contract) **production** 7000 cases **est.** 1990
product range ($12–30 R) Semillon, Unwooded Chardonnay, Partner's Reserve Chardonnay, Chardonnay, Proprietor's Reserve Chardonnay, Petit Rose, Merlot, Shiraz, Cabernet Sauvignon.

summary In 1999 partners Norman Seckold and Dudley Leitch realised a long-held ambition to establish a vineyard in the Hunter Valley with the acquisition of their 17-hectare site. Plantings have steadily increased and are presently chardonnay (5.7 ha), shiraz (4.9 ha), merlot (2 ha), semillon (1.2 ha) and a carefully thought out marketing strategy has been put in place. A cellar door and restaurant are planned. Exports to Hong Kong and Singapore.

bellarine estate ★★★☆

2270 Portarlington Road, Bellarine, Vic 3222 **region** Geelong
phone (03) 5259 3310 **fax** (03) 5259 3393 **open** 7 days 10–5
winemaker Robin Brockett **production** 5000 cases **est.** 1995
product range ($17.95–29.95 R) The premium range of Sauvignon Blanc, Unwooded Chardonnay, James' Paddock Chardonnay, Shiraz, Julian's Merlot is released under the Bellarine Estate label; the second range of Portarlington Ridge Sauvignon Blanc, The Pump Chardonnay, Pinot Noir, Shiraz, Merlot is, it would seem, a moveable feast, the back labels variously suggesting an estate origin (Pinot Noir and Shiraz) or southern Victorian origin (Sauvignon Blanc and Merlot).
summary A new arrival on the Bellarine Peninsula, but a substantial one, with 4 hectares each of chardonnay and pinot noir, 3 hectares of shiraz, 1 hectare of merlot and 0.5 hectare each of pinot gris and viognier. The wines are made by Robin Brockett at Scotchmans Hill. Bella's offers a seafood/Tuscan menu Friday–Sunday from 11 am for lunch and Friday and Saturday from 6 pm for dinner.

Bellarine Estate Cellar Reserve Sauvignon Blanc

▼▼▼▼ 2002 The colour is fractionally suspect, faintly grey, but the intense bouquet has plenty of tropical gooseberry fruit, albeit with a whisper of reduction; the palate is crisp, clean, bright, fresh and lively; only 80 cases made. **rating:** 88

best drinking Now **drink with** Cold seafood • $27.50

Portarlington Ridge Sauvignon Blanc

▼▼▼▼ 2002 Medium to full yellow-green, radically different from the Cellar Reserve; the bouquet is slightly diffuse, but clean, with tropical fruits, the ripe citrus/tropical/passionfruit-flavoured palate providing plenty to chew on. **rating:** 85

best drinking Now **drink with** Pasta marinara • $17.95

Bellarine Estate Unwooded Chardonnay

▼▼▼▼ 2001 Medium yellow-green; the moderately intense bouquet has straightforward nectarine and fig fruit, as one might expect, the palate has above-average weight, presence and length. **rating:** 85

best drinking Now **drink with** Quiche Lorraine • $19.95

Portarlington Ridge Pinot Noir

▼▼▼▼ 2001 Light to medium red-purple; clean, light, spiced plum fruit aromas are followed by a clean, fresh but rather light palate which lacks complexity but is undoubtedly varietal. **rating:** 85

best drinking Now–2005 **drink with** Chinese • $19.95

Bellarine Estate Shiraz

▼▼▼▼ 2000 Medium red-purple; the bouquet has sweet raspberry and plum fruit aromas to the forefront, oak in the background. The medium-bodied palate provides a replay of the bouquet, with touches of vanillin oak and chocolate together with ripe tannins. Spends 18 months in French and American oak. Far better value than the Portarlington Ridge Shiraz. **rating:** 88

best drinking 2004–2010 **drink with** Beef fillet • $21

Portarlington Ridge Merlot

▼▼▼▼ 2002 Medium red-purple; a clean bouquet with an array of minty/earthy/berry/leafy aromas; sweet red berry fruit makes its presence felt on the entirely fruit-driven palate; low tannins make the wine tailor-made for immediate consumption. **rating:** 85

best drinking Now–2005 **drink with** Lamb casserole • $18.95

🍂 bellendena   NR

240 Tinderbox Road, Tinderbox, Tas 7054 **region** Southern Tasmania
phone (03) 6229 8264 **fax** (03) 6229 8307 **open** By appointment
winemaker Andrew Hood **production** 35 cases **est.** 1995

product range ($20–25 ML) Chardonnay, Pinot Noir.
summary A typical micro operation only made possible by Andrew Hood's willingness to make one or two barrels for growers wanting to have their own wine. Andrew and Jane Elek, the former a consultant in international economic policy, the latter a biologist and entomologist, have established 0.5 hectare of vineyard, planted equally to chardonnay and pinot noir. The name Bellendena comes from the botanical name of a native Tasmanian plant, *Bellendena montana*, commonly known as Mountain Rocket. The label depicts the red seed capsules of the plant viewed from above. The wine is sold by mail order only.

benarra vineyards ★★★☆

PO Box 1081, Mt Gambier, SA 5290 **region** Mount Gambier
phone (08) 8738 9355 **fax** (08) 8738 9355 **open** Not
winemaker Martin Slocombe **production** 150 cases **est.** 1998
product range Flint Bed Pinot Noir.
summary Lisle Pudney has planted a substantial vineyard with the help of investors. In all there are over 26 hectares of pinot noir and 4 hectares each of sauvignon blanc and chardonnay, with another 40 hectares to be planted over the next 3 years. The vineyard is situated 20 kilometres from the Southern Ocean on ancient flint beds; a million-year-old mollusc found on the property by Lisle Pudney is depicted on the label of the Pinot Noir. Most of the grapes are sold; a small portion is contract-made for the Benarra label, and is of good quality and varietal character.

ben's run ★★★☆

71 Adams Peak Road, Broke, NSW 2330 (postal) **region** Lower Hunter Valley
phone (02) 6579 1310 **fax** (02) 6579 1370 **open** Not
winemaker Contract **production** 550 cases **est.** 1997
product range ($27 R) Shiraz.
summary Ben's Run has an interesting, almost schizophrenic, background. On the one hand, say the owners, 'it is named for our Kelpie dog for graciously allowing part of his retirement run to be converted into a showpiece shiraz-only vineyard'. On the other hand, patriarch Norman Marran was one of the pioneers of the Australian cotton industry, and has had a long and distinguished career as a director of both the Australian Wheat Board and the Grains Research Corporation, and is currently chairman of a leading food research company. The decision has been taken to produce only 500 cases of wine a year from the 3-hectare, low-yielding shiraz-only vineyard, the remainder being sold to Andrew Margan.

🦶 bent creek vineyards ★★★

Lot 10 Blewitt Springs Road, McLaren Flat, SA 5171 **region** McLaren Vale
phone (08) 8383 0414 **fax** (08) 8239 1538 **open** Sundays and public holidays 11–5
winemaker Michael Scarpantoni **production** 1250 cases **est.** 2001
product range ($17–25 CD) Chardonnay, Nero Sparkling Shiraz, Black Dog Shiraz, Reserve Shiraz.
summary Loretta and Peter Polson became wine drinkers and collectors a decade before they acquired a small patch of 40-year-old dry-grown chardonnay and shiraz at McLaren Flat, followed by the purchase of another small property at McLaren Vale planted to grenache, cabernet franc and chardonnay. Say the Polsons, 'Land barons? Hardly: 10 acres in all, but you will appreciate that it is enough for one man to look after and hand prune.' Until recently all the grapes were sold to d'Arenberg, but now a small proportion is kept back for the Bent Creek Vineyards.

Bent Creek Reserve Shiraz

 2001 Medium red-purple; the moderately intense bouquet has a mix of savoury, spicy, earthy fruit and gentle vanilla oak; the palate ranges through sweet red berry fruit to a touch of regional chocolate, finishing with soft tannins and gentle vanilla oak. 500 cases made. **rating:** 86
best drinking 2004–2010 **drink with** Smoked lamb • $25

beresford wines ★★★☆

49 Fraser Avenue, Happy Valley, SA 5159 **region** McLaren Vale
phone (08) 8322 3611 **fax** (08) 8322 3610 **open** Mon–Fri 9–5, weekends 11–5
winemaker Scott McIntosh **production** 120000 cases **est.** 1985
product range ($7.50–20 CD) At the bottom of the three-tier structure comes Beacon Hill Semillon Chardonnay, Sparkling Brut, Shiraz Cabernet; the second level is the Highwood range of Sauvignon Blanc,

Chardonnay, Shiraz, Merlot; then under the premium Beresford label are Clare Valley Riesling, Adelaide Hills Chardonnay, McLaren Vale Chardonnay, Clare Valley Shiraz, McLaren Vale Shiraz, McLaren Vale Cabernet Sauvignon.

summary The Beresford brand sits at the top of a range of labels primarily and successfully aimed at export markets in the UK, the US, Hong Kong and China. The intention is that ultimately most, if not all, of the wines will be sourced from grapes grown in McLaren Vale, with a new cellar door and boutique winery planned. Incidentally, it is run as an entirely separate operation from its sister winery, Step Road in Langhorne Creek.

Highwood Sauvignon Blanc

▼▼▼▼ **2002** Light green-yellow; the quite intense bouquet has slight traces of reduction, but abundant gooseberry and passionfruit more than compensate. The palate has positive flavour and good balance; excellent value at the price.   **rating:** 87

best drinking Now   **drink with** Blue swimmer crab • $12

Highwood McLaren Vale Shiraz

▼▼▼▼ **2001** Medium red-purple; the bouquet has some lifted prune and black fruits and a dash of vanilla oak; the palate has plenty of substance, with a range of savoury black fruits, the oak both balanced and appropriate to the flavours.   **rating:** 87

best drinking 2004–2008   **drink with** Takeaway • $13.50

Beresford McLaren Vale Shiraz

▼▼▼▼ **2001** Medium to full red-purple; the bouquet has a range of dark fruits including blackberry, and a hint of dark chocolate; the well-structured palate provides more of the same plus a hint of licorice; ripe tannins to close and nice American oak handling throughout.   **rating:** 89

best drinking 2005–2011   **drink with** Lamb cutlets • $20

berrys bridge   ★ ★ ★ ★

Forsters Road, Carapooee, St Arnaud, Vic 3478   **region** Pyrenees
phone (03) 5496 3220   **fax** (03) 5496 3322   **open** Weekends, by appointment
winemaker Jane Holt   **production** 1500 cases   **est.** 1990
product range ($42–45 CD) Shiraz, Merlot, Cabernet Sauvignon.
summary While the date of establishment is 1990, Roger Milner purchased the property in 1975, intending to plant a vineyard having worked for 3 years at Reynell winery in South Australia. In the mid-1980s he returned with Jane Holt, and together they began the construction of the stone house-cum-winery. Planting of existing 7 hectares of vineyard commenced in 1990, around the time that Jane commenced her viticultural studies at Charles Sturt University (completed in 1993, and a subsequent wine science degree course in 2000). Until 1997 the grapes were sold to others, the first vintage (from 1997) being released in November 1998, when Ian McDonald joined the business and became responsible for marketing and export. The wines are distributed in Victoria through Winestock to a number of well known retailers. Not surprisingly, the limited quantity sells out with great speed. Exports to the US, Germany and Switzerland.

Berrys Bridge Shiraz

▼▼▼▼ **2001** Dense red-purple; complex plum, black fruits, licorice, leather, earth and spice aromas are reflected in the array of flavours on the powerful palate. Would have merited higher points were it not for a slightly tough, aggressive mouthfeel which may, or may not, stem from a low level of aldehydes.   **rating:** 89

best drinking 2006–2016   **best vintages** '98, '00   **drink with** Flame-grilled rump steak • $42

Berrys Bridge Cabernet Sauvignon

▼▼▼▼▽ **2001** Medium red-purple; blackberry, blackcurrant and earth aromas foreshadow a ripe, full-bodied palate with abundant blackberry fruit and persistent tannins. Should richly repay extended cellaring. **rating:** 90

best drinking 2008–2018   **best vintages** '98   **drink with** Garlic and herb-studded leg of lamb • $42

best's wines   ★ ★ ★ ★

1 kilometre off Western Highway, Great Western, Vic 3377   **region** Grampians
phone (03) 5356 2250   **fax** (03) 5356 2430   **open** 7 days 10–5
winemaker Viv Thomson, Hamish Seabrook   **production** 30 000 cases   **est.** 1866
product range ($17–29 R) Great Western Riesling, Great Western Chardonnay, Concongella Chardonnay, Great Western Pinot Noir, Bin O Shiraz, Thomson Family Shiraz, Great Western Cabernet Sauvignon,

together with a large range of fortified wines sourced from St Andrews at Lake Boga. Some of these wines are available only at the cellar door.

summary An historic winery, owning some priceless vineyards planted as long ago as 1867 (other plantings are, of course, much more recent), which has consistently produced elegant, supple wines which deserve far greater recognition than they in fact receive. The Shiraz is a classic; the Thomson Family Shiraz magnificent. For some obscure reason, no tastings in the last 12 months. Exports to the UK, Canada, Holland, Belgium and Switzerland.

bethany wines ★★★☆

Bethany Road, Bethany via Tanunda, SA 5352 **region** Barossa Valley
phone (08) 8563 2086 **fax** (08) 8563 0046 **open** Mon–Sat 10–5, Sun 1–5
winemaker Geoff Schrapel, Robert Schrapel **production** 25 000 cases **est.** 1977
product range ($14.50–75 CD) Riesling, Eden Valley Riesling, Semillon, Chardonnay, Kangaroo Island Chardonnay, Steinbruch, Manse, Cuvee Chardonnay Pinot Noir Brut, Select Late Harvest Riesling, Shiraz, GR6 Reserve Shiraz, Shiraz Cabernet, Grenache, Cabernet Merlot, GR5 Reserve Cabernet Sauvignon, Old Quarry Barossa Tawny Port, Old Quarry Barossa Fronti (White Port).
summary The Schrapel family has been growing grapes in the Barossa Valley for over 140 years, but the winery has only been in operation since 1977. Nestling high on a hillside in the site of an old quarry, it is run by Geoff and Rob Schrapel, who produce a range of consistently well-made and attractively packaged wines. They have 36 hectares of vineyards in the Barossa Valley, 8 hectares in the Eden Valley and (recently and interestingly) 2 hectares each of chardonnay and cabernet sauvignon on Kangaroo Island. The wines enjoy national distribution in Australia, and are exported to the UK, New Zealand, Europe, Japan, Singapore and the US.

Bethany Trial Hill Eden Valley Riesling
▼▼▼▼ **2001** Light straw-green; the bouquet is still largely locked up, with tight mineral, apple and spice aromas in the background; the palate, while equally tight, moves more to citrus and mineral. A radically different style from the Barossa floor riesling. **rating:** 88
best drinking 2005–2010 **drink with** Blue swimmer crab • $26

Bethany Kangaroo Island Chardonnay
▼▼▼▼ **2001** Light green-yellow; the aromatic bouquet has a mix of stone fruit and grapefruit, oak not evident; the light to medium-bodied palate has good length, with a particularly attractive and fresh finish, doubtless due to the high natural acidity. From Dr Willoughby's tiny vineyard on Kangaroo Island. **rating:** 87
best drinking Now–2007 **drink with** Grilled whiting • $22

Bethany Select Late Harvest Cordon Cut Riesling
▼▼▼▼ **2002** Light green-yellow; rich, intense, tropical lime fruit on the bouquet leads into a palate with nicely balanced sweetness and acidity; plenty of length and flavour. Sold in a sensible 500 ml bottle. **rating:** 89
best drinking Now–2005 **best vintages** '89, '90, '92, '93 **drink with** Fresh fruit • $19.50

Bethany Shiraz
▼▼▼▼ **2000** Medium to full red-purple; ripe, dark berry fruits, earth and spice on the bouquet foreshadow a palate with an abundance of rich, ripe fruit, the oak subservient. Good length and development potential.
rating: 88
best drinking 2005–2012 **best vintages** '88, '90, '91, '92, '94, '96 **drink with** Mild curry • $27.80

Bethany Reserve Shiraz
▼▼▼▼ **1998** GR6. Medium red-purple; there are complex, gamey/meaty overtones to the dark berry fruit of the bouquet, with a replay of all these characters on the palate. The technocrats would no doubt suggest the wine has some brettanomyces. **rating:** 86
best drinking Now–2007 **best vintages** '95, '96 **drink with** Rack of lamb • $75

beyond broke vineyard NR

Cobcroft Road, Broke, NSW 2330 **region** Lower Hunter Valley
phone (02) 6026 2043 **fax** (02) 6026 2043 **open** Tastings available at Broke Village Store 10–4
winemaker Pete Howland (Contract) **production** 4000 cases **est.** 1996
product range ($14–22 R) Semillon, Verdelho, Chardonnay, Unwooded Chardonnay, Sparkling Semillon, Shiraz.
summary Beyond Broke Vineyard is the reincarnation of a former Lindemans vineyard purchased by Bob and Terry Kennedy in 1996. In a more than slightly ironical twist, the 1997 Beyond Broke Semillon won two

trophies at the Hunter Valley Wine Show of that year, the first for the Best Current Vintage Semillon and the second the Henry John Lindeman Memorial Trophy for the Best Current Vintage Dry White Wine. Subsequent shows have been less spectacularly kind, but there is nothing surprising in that, and its turn will come again when vintage conditions permit.

bianchet ★★★☆

187 Victoria Road, Lilydale, Vic 3140 **region** Yarra Valley
phone (03) 9739 1779 **fax** (03) 9739 1277 **open** Thurs–Sun 11–5
winemaker Gary Mills **production** 2500 cases **est.** 1976
product range ($15–25 CD) Copestone Semillon Sauvignon Blanc, Marsanne, Chardonnay, Chardonnay Cuvee, Duet (Gewurztraminer Semillon), Verduzzo, Pinot Noir, Shiraz, Merlot, Cabernet.
summary Owned by a small Melbourne-based syndicate, which acquired the business from the founding Bianchet family. One of the most unusual wines from the winery is Verduzzo Gold, a late-harvest sweet white wine made from the Italian grape variety. The wines are still basically sold through the cellar door.

Bianchet Chardonnay

TTTT 2001 Medium yellow-green; the moderately intense bouquet is clean, with melon fruit and just a touch of oak; the light to medium-bodied palate is well balanced, with gentle flavours, but has a Yarra Valley stamp of length to lift it out of the ruck. **rating:** 87

best drinking Now–2005 **best vintages** '97, '00 **drink with** Veal saltimbocca • $20

Bianchet Pinot Noir

TTTT 2001 Medium to full red-purple; the solid bouquet brings together plum, forest and spice in an overall savoury mode; a full-bodied and slightly old-fashioned palate with lots of extract and tannin, which needs time but will repay medium-term cellaring. **rating:** 89

best drinking Now–2006 **best vintages** '00 **drink with** Wild mushroom risotto • $25

bidgeebong wines ★★★☆

352 Byrnes Road, Bomen, NSW 2650 **region** Southern New South Wales Zone
phone (03) 9853 6207 **fax** (03) 9853 5499 **open** Mon–Fri 9–4
winemaker Andrew Birks **production** 15 000 cases **est.** 2000
product range ($16–20.50 R) Tumbarumba Chardonnay, Gundagai Shiraz, Tumbarumba Merlot.
summary Bidgeebong is a made-up name using a combination of Murrumbidgee and Billabong. It encompasses what the founders refer to as the Bidgeebong triangle lying between Young, Wagga Wagga, Tumbarumba and Gundagai, these being the four regions which will provide grapes for the Bidgeebong brand. Two of the partners in the venture are Andrew Birks, with a 30-year career as a lecturer and educator at Charles Sturt University, and Simon Robertson, who studied viticulture and wine science at Charles Sturt University, and after working in Europe and the Barwang Vineyard established by his father Peter in 1969, built a substantial viticultural management business in the area. A winery was completed for the 2002 vintage, and will eventually be capable of handling 2000 tonnes of grapes. As well as meeting Bidgeebong's own needs, it will process grapes for other local growers and larger producers who purchase grapes from the region. Exports to the UK.

Bidgeebong Gundagai Shiraz

TTTT 2001 Medium red-purple; the moderately intense bouquet has abundant clean dark cherry fruit, with appropriate oak in the background; the full-bodied palate has a mix of blackberry and black cherry with tannins to match. Needs time. **rating:** 88

best drinking 2006–2011 **drink with** Beef casserole • $20.50

Bidgeebong Tumbarumba Merlot

TTTT 2001 Medium to full red-purple; leaf, spice, bramble and berry aromas announce the variety; the palate opens well, with dark fruit flavours reflecting the bouquet, before finishing with a trace of bitterness. **rating:** 87

best drinking 2005–2009 **drink with** Lamb casserole • $20.50

big barrel vineyard and winery NR

787 Landsborough Road, Maleny, Qld 4551 **region** Queensland Coastal
phone (07) 5429 6300 **fax** (07) 5429 6331 **open** 7 days 10–5
winemaker Stuart Pierce **production** 1280 cases **est.** 2000

product range ($12.90–20 CD) Ridge White, Chardonnay Semillon, Verdelho, Unwooded Chardonnay, Chardonnay, Barambah Bubbles, Sparkling Shiraz, Ridge Red, Classic Dry Red, Reserve Shiraz, Durif, Merlot, Glasshouse Tawny Port.

summary The Pagano family's forebears made wine on the foothills of Mount Etna for many generations, and the family has been involved in the Australian wine industry for over 40 years. But it was not until 12 years ago that father Sebastian and wife Maria Pagano saw the Maleny area with its Glasshouse Mountain and surrounding Blackall Range, reminiscent of a scaled-down Mount Etna. They have now planted 4 hectares of chambourcin on-site, and opened a tasting room in the shape of a giant barrel: the chambourcin is yet to come into production, but there is a wide range of wines sourced from elsewhere in Australia. In the best Queensland tradition there are plenty of attractions for tourists, including vineyard tours, light foccacia lunches Monday to Saturday, and a continental buffet lunch on Sunday.

big hill vineyard ★★★☆

Cnr Calder Highway/Belvoir Park Road, Big Hill, Bendigo, Vic 3550 **region** Bendigo
phone (03) 5435 3366 **fax** (03) 5435 3311 **open** 7 days 10–5
winemaker John Ellis, Robert Fiumara (Contract) **production** 1200 cases **est.** 1998
product range ($11–30 CD) Granite White, Sauvignon Blanc, Verdelho, Chardonnay, Bendigo Chardonnay, Granite Botrytis, Granite Red, Bendigo Shiraz, Reserve Shiraz, Cabernet Sauvignon, Granite Port, Curly Port, Curly Muscat.

summary A partnership headed by Nick Cugura began the re-establishment of what is now called Big Hill Vineyard on a site which was first planted to grapes almost 150 years ago. That was in the height of the gold rush, and there was even a long-disappeared pub, the Granite Rock Hotel. The wheel has come full circle, for Big Hill Vineyard now has a cafe-restaurant overlooking the vineyard, with plans for bed and breakfast cottages. The restaurant specialises in wedding receptions, and provides limited conference facilities. The modern-day plantings began with 2 hectares of shiraz in 1998 (which provided the first wine in May 2000), followed by 1 hectare each of merlot and cabernet sauvignon.

Big Hill Vineyard Bendigo Shiraz

▼▼▼▼ 2000 Medium purple-red; the bouquet offers dark berry fruits, licorice and a touch of gamey complexity; the concentrated and powerful palate has generous flavour, supported by a firm finish. The touch of game to one side, it should repay cellaring. **rating:** 88

best drinking 2005–2012 **drink with** Venison • $30

Big Hill Vineyard Bendigo Reserve Shiraz

▼▼▼▼ 2001 Medium red-purple; ripe plum, spice, earth and vanilla aromas lead into a concentrated, very ripe palate with a mix of plummy fruit, vanilla oak and soft tannins. Aged in 100 per cent new American oak barrels. **rating:** 89

best drinking 2006–2016 **drink with** Game pie

🐚 big shed wines ★★★☆

1289 Malmsbury Road, Glenlyon, Vic 3461 **region** Macedon Ranges
phone (03) 5348 7825 **fax** (03) 5348 7825 **open** 7 days, winter 10–6, summer 10–7
winemaker Ken Jones **production** 900 cases **est.** 1999
product range ($15–45 CD) Intrigue (Spatlese Lexia), Chardonnay, Pinot Noir, Shiraz, Reserve Shiraz, Cabernet, Sticky Stuff (10-year-old Muscat).

summary Founder and winemaker Ken Jones was formerly a geneticist and molecular biologist at Edinburgh University, and the chemistry of winemaking comes easily. The estate-based wine comes from the 2 hectares of pinot noir; the other wines are made from purchased grapes grown in various parts of Central Victoria.

big shed Pinot Noir

▼▼▼▼ 2001 Medium red-purple; the light bouquet has plum and spice varietal aromas which carry through more or less precisely to the palate. Here somewhat sharp acidity detracts, and is unlikely to soften much.
rating: 85

best drinking Now **drink with** Spiced quail • $22

big shed Reserve Shiraz

▼▼▼▽ 2001 Medium purple-red; the bouquet is fruit-driven, but somewhat closed, with dark cherry peeping out; the light to medium-bodied palate has juicy berry flavours, but needed more barrel work, and is a trifle unbalanced by the high acidity. **rating:** 83

best drinking Now–2007 **drink with** Beef pie • $23

big shed Cabernet

ŦŦŦŦ 2001 Medium red-purple; clean, fresh blackberry/cassis fruit, together with a whisk of oak, leads into a round, mouthfilling palate with an abundance of that blackberry/cassis fruit, the acidity in balance. **rating:** 89

best drinking Now–2008 **drink with** Butterfly leg of lamb • $25

bimbadgen estate ★★★☆

Lot 21 McDonalds Road, Pokolbin, NSW 2321 **region** Lower Hunter Valley
phone (02) 4998 7585 **fax** (02) 4998 7732 **open** 7 days 9.30–5
winemaker Simon Thistlewood **production** 50 000 cases **est.** 1968
product range ($12.50–32 R) Semillon, Verdelho, Chardonnay, Botrytis Semillon, Sparkling Shiraz, Rose, Pinot Noir, Shiraz, Cabernet Franc Merlot; Signature range is the super-premium Semillon, Chardonnay, Sparkling Pinot Chardonnay, Shiraz; Grand Ridge Estate is the lower-priced label, with Semillon Chardonnay, Semillon Chardonnay Verdelho, Verdelho, Chardonnay, Sparkling Semillon, Shiraz, Shiraz Cabernet, Shiraz Cabernet Merlot, Cabernet Merlot.
summary Established as McPherson Wines, then successively Tamalee, then Sobels, then Parker Wines and now Bimbadgen, this substantial winery has had what might politely be termed a turbulent history. It has the great advantage of having 88.5 hectares of estate plantings, mostly with now relatively old vines, supplemented by a separate estate vineyard at Yenda for the lower-priced Grand Ridge series. The restaurant is open 7 days for lunch and from Wednesday to Saturday inclusive for dinner. Exports to Hong Kong, Japan, the UK and the US.

🐌 bindaree estate NR

Fish Fossil Drive, Canowindra, NSW 2804 **region** Cowra
phone (02) 6344 1214 **fax** (02) 6344 3217 **open** Wed–Fri 11–5, weekends 10–5
winemaker Contract **production** 2000 cases **est.** 1998
product range ($12–20 CD) Unwooded Chardonnay, Reserve Chardonnay, Shiraz, Reserve Shiraz, Dry Red, Cabernet Sauvignon, Reserve Cabernet Sauvignon.
summary The Workman family have established their property in the foothills of the Belubula River Valley, near Canowindra. They have planted 1 hectare of chardonnay, and 3 hectares each of cabernet sauvignon and shiraz. The first vintage (2001) was successful in the 2002 Cowra Wine Show, the Reserve Chardonnay winning silver and the Unwooded Chardonnay bronze.

bindi wine growers ★★★★★

343 Melton Road, Gisborne, Vic 3437 (postal) **region** Macedon Ranges
phone (03) 5428 2564 **fax** (03) 5428 2564 **open** Not
winemaker Michael Dhillon, Stuart Anderson (Consultant) **production** 1200 cases **est.** 1988
product range ($30–65 ML) Chardonnay, Quartz Chardonnay, Macedon Methode Champenoise Cuvee II, Original Vineyard Pinot Noir, Block 5 Pinot Noir.
summary One of the icons of Macedon, indeed Victoria. The Chardonnay is top-shelf, the Pinot Noir as remarkable (albeit in a very different idiom) as Bass Phillip, Giaconda or any of the other tiny-production, icon wines. Notwithstanding the tiny production, the wines are exported (in small quantities, of course) to the UK, The Netherlands, Italy, Singapore, Hong Kong, Canada and the US.

Bindi Chardonnay

ŦŦŦŦŦ 2001 Light to medium yellow-green; the clean, ultra-smooth, fruit-driven bouquet has ample melon and nectarine aromas; the elegant but intense palate has finely balanced and integrated oak to accompany the fruit; crisp acidity builds a long finish. 13.5° alcohol. **rating:** 94

best drinking Now–2008 **best vintages** '91, '94, '95, '96, '97, '01 **drink with** Corn-fed chicken • $30

Bindi Quartz Chardonnay

ŦŦŦŦŦ 2001 Medium yellow-green; a complex, rich and deep bouquet offers melon, fig and beautifully handled oak; the rich, round, smooth palate once again has an interplay between the melon, fig and peach on the one hand, and fine French oak on the other. 14° alcohol, and quite different in character from the sister wine. **rating:** 94

best drinking Now–2008 **best vintages** '00, '01 **drink with** Salmon risotto • $45

Bindi Macedon Chardonnay Pinot Noir

TTTTY **NV** Cuvee I. Light straw-yellow; the bouquet has obvious bready/savoury complexity, the powerful and intense palate showing the 6 years and 4 months the wine spent on lees, and the acidity is very much better balanced than that of the Cuvee III. A blend of 1993 to 1996 vintages. **rating:** 93

best drinking Now–2006 **drink with** Antipasto • $35

Bindi Block 5 Pinot Noir

TTTTT **2001** Strong, vibrant red-purple; the rich and intense bouquet ranges through deep, dark plum, spice and briar aromas, the concentrated palate with plush, dark plum, ripe tannins and perfectly managed oak. Just under 2 tonnes per acre. **rating:** 95

best drinking Now–2008 **best vintages** '97, '00, '01 **drink with** Rich game • $65

Bindi Original Vineyard Pinot Noir

TTTTT **2001** Vibrant purple-red; the smooth, rich, deep plummy fruit and sweet spices of the bouquet are followed by an intense, long and rich, yet elegant palate, with a quite different feel and profile from the Block 5; lingering, savoury finish. Yielded less than 1 tonne to the acre; the alcohol in the two wines is the same, at 14.5°. **rating:** 96

best drinking Now–2010 **best vintages** '93, '94, '96, '97, '98, '99, 00, '01 **drink with** Squab • $50

🐦 bird in hand ★★★★

Bird in Hand Road, Woodside, SA 5244 **region** Adelaide Hills
phone (08) 8232 9033 **fax** (08) 8232 9066 **open** Not
winemaker Andrew Nugent **production** 8000 cases **est.** 1997
product range ($20–70 R) Two in the Bush Sauvignon Blanc Semillon, Merlot Cabernet; Bird in Hand Sauvignon Blanc, Sauvignon Blanc Semillon, Sparkling Pinot Noir, Pinot Noir, Shiraz, Merlot, Cabernet Sauvignon; Nest Egg Cabernet Sauvignon.
summary It's not often a name as evocative as this presents itself ready-made. This substantial wine and olive oil-making property is situated on the Bird in Hand Road at Woodside, which in turn took its name from a 19th century gold mine called Bird in Hand. It is the venture of the Nugent family, headed by Dr Michael Nugent, who was formerly an owner and director of Tatachilla, and who acquired the property in 1997. Son Andrew Nugent is a Roseworthy graduate, and has had a successful career managing vineyards in various parts of South Australia. Andrew's wife Susie manages the olive oil side of the business; there are two large olive groves. Retail distribution is being set up throughout Australia, with exports to the UK underway, and planned for the US, Singapore and the Philippines. The family also has properties on the Fleurieu Peninsula and in the Clare Valley; the latter providing both riesling and shiraz (and olives from 100-year-old wild olive trees).

Bird in Hand Sauvignon Blanc

TTTT **2002** Light to medium yellow-green; clean mineral and citrus aromas have a slightly tropical edge, the rich, very flavoursome palate in mouthfilling, drink asap style. **rating:** 89

best drinking Now **drink with** Fish sautéed in lemongrass and ginger

Bird in Hand Sauvignon Blanc Semillon

TTTTT **2002** Medium yellow-green; the clean, powerful bouquet ranges through herb to tropical fruit aromas; the excellent fresh, tightly structured palate has abundant sweet citrus fruit, followed by a bright finish. **rating:** 94

best drinking Now–2005 **best vintages** '02 **drink with** Spicy Asian • $25

Bird in Hand Two in the Bush Sauvignon Blanc Semillon

TTTTY **2002** Light green-yellow; an intense, firm and powerful bouquet with classic green pea, grass and herb aromas is essentially replayed on the powerful palate, which has good length. **rating:** 91

best drinking Now–2005 **drink with** Grilled eggplant • $20

Bird in Hand Pinot Noir

TTTT **2002** Good purple-red hue; the highly aromatic bouquet has tangy, savoury aromas, with some minty notes which would be better not there; the strongly accented flavours of the palate track the bouquet, again suggesting that the grapes were not fully physiologically ripe. **rating:** 87

best drinking Now **drink with** Smoked quail • $40

Bird in Hand Shiraz

▼▼▼▼▽ **2001** Bright purple-red; the complex bouquet has a subtle interplay between blackberry, licorice and oak; on the rich and luscious palate, the American oak becomes that little bit more obvious, and less might have been even better. From the Fleurieu Peninsula. **rating:** 90

best drinking 2006–2011 **best vintages** '01 **drink with** Cassoulet • $35

Bird in Hand Cabernet Sauvignon

▼▼▼▼▽ **2001** Medium red-purple; there are very savoury, briary edges to the blackcurrant fruit of the bouquet; the palate is richer, with lush blackcurrant fruit and a touch of bitter chocolate; ripe tannins are also a feature. An impressive wine given its origins. **rating:** 91

best drinking 2005–2011 **best vintages** '01 **drink with** Lamb shoulder • $35

birdwood estate NR

Mannum Road, Birdwood, SA 5234 **region** Adelaide Hills
phone (08) 8263 0986 **fax** (08) 8263 0986 **open** Not
winemaker Oli Cucchiarelli **production** 600 cases **est.** 1990
product range ($14–23 ML) Chardonnay, Riesling, Merlot, Cabernet Sauvignon.
summary Birdwood Estate draws upon 7 hectares of estate vineyards progressively established since 1990. The quality of the white wines, and in particular the Chardonnay, has generally been good. The tiny production is principally sold through retail in Adelaide, with limited distribution in Sydney and Melbourne. No recent tastings.

birnam wood wines NR

Turanville Road, Scone, NSW 2337 **region** Upper Hunter Valley
phone (02) 6545 3286 **fax** (02) 6545 3431 **open** Weekends and public holidays 11–4
winemaker Monarch Wines (Contract) **production** 8000 cases **est.** 1994
product range ($7–20 R) Shakespeare Range: The Bards Tipple Hunter Valley Fruity, The Bards Tipple Hunter Valley Semillon, The Witches Brew Chardonnay, The Kings Cup Shiraz. Family Range: Semillon, Sauvignon Blanc, Semillon Sauvignon Blanc, Verdelho, Unwooded Chardonnay, Premium Reserve Chardonnay, Premium Reserve Shiraz.
summary Former Sydney car dealer Mike Eagan and wife Min moved to Scone to establish a horse stud; the vineyard came later (in 1994) but is now a major part of the business, with 32 hectares of vines. Most of the grapes are sold; part only is vinified for Birnam Wood. Exports to Switzerland, Canada and China. Son Matthew has now joined the business after working for 5 years for Tyrrell's in its export department.

black george NR

Black Georges Road, Manjimup, WA 6258 **region** Manjimup
phone (08) 9772 3569 **fax** (08) 9722 3102 **open** 7 days 10.30–4.45
winemaker Gregory Chinery **production** 3750 cases **est.** 1991
product range ($15–40 CD) Sauvignon Blanc, Sauvignon Blanc Chardonnay, Verdelho, Pinot Noir, Merlot Cabernet Franc, Cabernet Merlot, Cabernet Sauvignon, White Port.
summary Black George arrived with particular aspirations to make high-quality Pinot Noir. As with so much of the Manjimup region, it remains to be seen whether the combination of soil and climate will permit this; the quality of the Black George Merlot Cabernet Franc once again points in a different direction. No recent tastings. Retail distribution in New South Wales, Victoria, Western Australia and Queensland; exports to the UK and The Netherlands.

blackgum estate NR

166 Malmsbury Road, Metcalfe, Vic 3448 **region** Macedon Ranges
phone (03) 5423 2933 **fax** (03) 5423 2944 **open** Not
winemaker Simonette Sherman **production** 400 cases **est.** 1990
product range ($15–25 CD) Riesling, Chardonnay, Cabernet Sauvignon.
summary Simonette Sherman is the sole proprietor, executive winemaker and marketing manager of Blackgum Estate. It is situated 9 kilometres northeast of the historic village of Malmsbury, and 1.6 kilometres from the town of Metcalfe. The 4.5-hectare 10-year-old vineyard is planted to riesling, chardonnay, shiraz and cabernet sauvignon, with a planting of sagrantino (which sent me scuttling to Jancis Robinson's *Oxford Companion to Wine*) planned for the near future. It is a red variety grown strictly around the Italian university town of Perugia, and is said to produce wines of great concentration and, the USually, liveliness, with deep

ruby colour and some bitterness. So there; the varietal atlas of Australia continues to expand. Ms Sherman has retained Llew Knight of Granite Hills to make the 2001 Riesling, while the Cabernet Sauvignon and Chardonnay will be made on-site in consultation with Tom Gyorffy.

blackjack vineyards ★★★★

Cnr Blackjack Road and Calder Highway, Harcourt, Vic 3453 **region** Bendigo
phone (03) 5474 2355 **fax** (03) 5474 2355 **open** Weekends and public holidays 11–5, when stock available
winemaker Ian McKenzie, Ken Pollock **production** 2500 cases **est.** 1987
product range ($25–30 CD) Shiraz, Cabernet Merlot.
summary Established by the McKenzie and Pollock families on the site of an old apple and pear orchard in the Harcourt Valley. Best known for some very good Shirazs. Ian McKenzie, incidentally, is not to be confused with Ian McKenzie of Seppelt Great Western. Exports to New Zealand.

BlackJack Shiraz

♥♥♥♥♡ **2000** Medium red-purple; the bouquet offers attractive red fruits, a splash of spice, and subtle oak; the spotlessly clean palate flows with soft red berry fruit and silky, ripe tannins running through to a long finish.

rating: 90

best drinking 2004–2010 **best vintages** '93, '96, '97, '98, '00 **drink with** Barbecued T-bone • $30

BlackJack Cabernet Merlot

♥♥♥♥ **2000** Medium red-purple; the bouquet has clean, fresh red and blackcurrant aromas, the palate has clean, juicy blackcurrant and blackberry fruit, finishing with soft tannins. Not particularly complex, but easily approachable. A blend of 85 per cent Cabernet Sauvignon and 15 per cent Merlot. **rating:** 87
best drinking Now–2008 **best vintages** '98 **drink with** Lamb casserole • $25

blackwood crest wines NR

RMB 404A, Boyup Brook, WA 6244 **region** Blackwood Valley
phone (08) 9767 3029 **fax** (08) 9767 3029 **open** 7 days 10–6
winemaker Max Fairbrass **production** 1500 cases **est.** 1976
product range ($15–25 CD) Riesling, Sauvignon Blanc, Semillon Sauvignon Blanc, Chardonnay, Shiraz, Cabernet Sauvignon, Ruby Port, Liqueur Muscat.
summary A remote and small winery which has produced one or two notable red wines full of flavour and character; however, quality does fluctuate somewhat.

blackwood wines NR

Kearney Street, Nannup, WA 6275 **region** Blackwood Valley
phone (08) 9756 0088 **fax** (08) 9756 0089 **open** Thurs–Tues 10–4
winemaker Andrew Mountford (Contract) **production** 2000 cases **est.** 1998
product range ($17–29 CD) Blackwood White, Chenin Blanc, Unwooded Chardonnay, Late Harvest Verdelho, Pinot Noir, Merlot Cabernet Sauvignon, Merlot Cabernet Franc Malbec.
summary Blackwood Wines draws upon 1 hectare each of chardonnay, merlot and chenin blanc and 0.5 hectare of pinot noir, supplemented by contract-grown fruit which significantly broadens the product range. It also operates a Cellar Club with discounted prices for members, and a restaurant is open each day except Wednesday. Exports to the UK and Denmark.

Blackwood Clay Pit Late Harvest Verdelho

♥♥♥♥ **2001** Light straw-green; the bouquet is clean, with aromas of blossom, the palate with delicious fresh fruit salad and citrus flavours; well made, with balanced acidity. **rating:** 85
best drinking Now **drink with** Creamy pasta • $18

blanche barkly wines ★★★☆

Rheola Road, Kingower, Vic 3517 **region** Bendigo
phone (03) 5438 8223 **open** Weekends and public holidays 10–5, or by appointment
winemaker David Reimers, Arleen Reimers **production** 1000 cases **est.** 1972
product range ($25 CD) Mary Eileen Kingower Shiraz, Johann Kingower Cabernet Sauvignon.
summary After a long hiatus, tastings of the 2000 and 2001 vintage wines happily renewed my acquaintance with the winery. The tasting notes should speak for themselves.

Blanche Barkly Mary Eileen Shiraz

▼▼▼▼▽ 2001 Full, bright red-purple; rich dark berry, licorice and prune fruit aromas are replayed on the powerful palate which, however, does not err on the side of over-extraction, the tannins balanced.   **rating:** 90

best drinking 2005–2011 **best vintages** '01 **drink with** Lasagne • $25

Blanche Barkly Johann Cabernet Sauvignon

▼▼▼▼ 2001 Medium red-purple; dark berry/blackcurrant/blackberry on the bouquet, the palate opening with ripe cassis fruit before aggressive tannins take over.   **rating:** 85

best drinking 2005–2009 **drink with** Rack of lamb • $25

bleasdale vineyards   ★★★★

Wellington Road, Langhorne Creek, SA 5255 **region** Langhorne Creek
phone (08) 8537 3001 **fax** (08) 8537 3224 **open** Mon–Sat 9–5, Sun 11–5
winemaker Michael Potts, Renae Hirsch **production** 150 000 cases **est.** 1850
product range ($9–38 CD) Langhorne Crossing White and Red; Verdelho, Chardonnay, Late Picked Verdelho, Sparkling Shiraz, Shiraz Rose, Generations Shiraz, Bremerview Shiraz, Cabernet Shiraz, Malbec, Frank Potts Cabernet Malbec Merlot Petit Verdot, Mulberry Tree Cabernet Sauvignon, Fortified.
summary One of the most historic wineries in Australia, drawing upon vineyards that are flooded every winter by diversion of the Bremer River; this provides moisture throughout the dry, cool, growing season. The wines offer excellent value for money, all showing that particular softness which is the hallmark of the Langhorne Creek region. Production has soared; export markets established in the UK, the US, Canada, New Zealand and Germany.

Bleasdale Sparkling Shiraz

▼▼▼▼ NV Deep red-purple; ripe, earthy blackberry fruit on the bouquet is followed by a rich palate chock-full of berry fruit flavours, not oaky and not too sweet. Will repay cellaring.   **rating:** 88

best drinking 2006–2016 **drink with** Game terrine • $16.50

Bleasdale Generations Shiraz

▼▼▼▼▽ 2000 Medium red-purple; the smooth but complex ripe berry, plum, spice and earth fruit of the bouquet leads into a medium to full-bodied palate, again featuring ripe fruit flavours, and with tannin extension leading to a long finish.   **rating:** 90

best drinking 2005–2012 **best vintages** '97, '00 **drink with** Porterhouse steak • $38

Bleasdale Mulberry Tree Cabernet Sauvignon

▼▼▼▼ 2001 Medium red-purple; the clean, moderately intense bouquet has clear-cut savoury/spicy cabernet fruit; the fresh, fruit-driven palate is again focused on red berry fruit, finishing with soft tannins. Good value.

rating: 86

best drinking 2004–2007 **best vintages** '98 **drink with** Venison with juniper berry sauce • $16

Bleasdale Wood Matured Verdelho

▼▼▼▼ NV Light golden brown; the bouquet is clean and quite firm, with neutral spirit, the palate quite gentle, with an appealing touch of honeysnap biscuit, and a cleansing, well-balanced finish. If drunk in summer, should be slightly chilled.   **rating:** 88

best drinking Now–2005 **drink with** Aperitif • $13

bloodwood   ★★★★☆

4 Griffin Road, Orange, NSW 2800 **region** Orange
phone (02) 6362 5631 **fax** (02) 6361 1173 **open** By appointment
winemaker Stephen Doyle **production** 4000 cases **est.** 1983
product range ($12.50–28 ML) Riesling, Chardonnay, Schubert Chardonnay, Chirac (Pinot Chardonnay), Noble Riesling, Big Men in Tights (Rose), Rose of Malbec, Maurice (Bordeaux-blend), Merlot Noir, Cabernet Sauvignon.
summary Rhonda and Stephen Doyle are two of the pioneers of the burgeoning Orange district. The wines are sold mainly through the cellar door and an energetically and informatively run mailing list; the principal retail outlet is Ian Cook's Fiveways Cellar, Paddington, Sydney. Bloodwood has done best with elegant but intense Chardonnay and the intermittent releases of super-late-harvest Ice Riesling.

Bloodwood Riesling

♥♥♥♥♥ 2002 Bright green-yellow; a spotlessly clean and fragrant bouquet has lime and passionfruit aromas which come through strongly on the palate; a hint of CO_2 spritz adds rather than detracts; good balancing acidity finishes a stylish wine.

rating: 94

best drinking Now–2008 **best vintages** '88, '90, '92, '94, '95, '98, '01, '02 **drink with** Grilled scallops • $16.65

Bloodwood Chardonnay

♥♥♥♥ 2001 Light to medium yellow-green; the clean bouquet has melon fruit and well-integrated subtle, nutty oak; the generous palate has a sweeter profile than the Schubert, perhaps partly reflecting the still-high alcohol of 14°.

rating: 87

best drinking Now–2006 **drink with** White-fleshed fish • $22

Bloodwood Schubert

♥♥♥♥♥ 2001 Light to medium yellow-green; the bouquet offers melon, white peach and citrus chardonnay fruit, and the elegant palate is understated and stylish. One hundred per cent barrel fermented in new French oak, and 14.5° alcohol, yet retains finesse, a remarkable achievement.

rating: 90

best drinking Now–2007 **best vintages** '01 **drink with** Creamy pasta • $25

Bloodwood Big Men in Tights

♥♥♥♥ 2002 Light pink; the bouquet is not particularly aromatic, but there are some strawberry jam notes which come through on the palate, reflecting the malbec from which this Rose is made. Best served well chilled.

rating: 84

best drinking Now **drink with** Cold meats; ham • $12.50

Bloodwood Shiraz

♥♥♥♥♥ 2001 Medium red-purple; aromas of black cherry, spice and earth are joined by a touch of chocolate on the bouquet; dark fruit flavours fill the palate, surrounded by sweet spice and oak overtones. A most attractive style.

rating: 90

best drinking 2004–2010 **best vintages** '01 **drink with** Lamb casserole • $22

Bloodwood Maurice

♥♥♥♥ 2001 Light to medium red-purple; the light bouquet has very savoury, herb-like aromas, but sweet, juicy berry fruit comes through as a significant component of the mid-palate, followed by a more savoury finish.

rating: 87

best drinking 2005–2009 **drink with** Veal chops • $25

Bloodwood Cabernet Sauvignon

♥♥♥♥ 2001 Medium red-purple; the bouquet has a range of savoury, spicy, minty overtones to the berry fruit; on the palate, sweet blackcurrant and cedar flavours, together with nuances derived from the bouquet, plus fine tannins, all combine to create good mouthfeel.

rating: 89

best drinking 2004–2009 **drink with** Rib of veal • $23

blue pyrenees estate ★★★☆

Vinoca Road, Avoca, Vic 3467 **region** Pyrenees
phone (03) 5465 3202 **fax** (03) 5465 3529 **open** Mon–Fri 10–4.30, weekends and public holidays 10–5
winemaker Greg Dedman, Chris Smales **production** 90 000 cases **est.** 1963
product range ($12–34 CD) A four-tiered structure for the table wines sees Ghost Gum (sourced from southeast Australia) at the bottom; next Fiddlers Creek, sourced from Victoria but including estate-grown grapes; then Blue Pyrenees varietal range of Semillon, Sauvignon Blanc, Chardonnay, Pinot Noir, Shiraz, Merlot and Cabernet Sauvignon, sourced exclusively from the Pyrenees region; and at the top are the two Estate Reserve wines of Chardonnay and Red (a Bordeaux blend). Alongside are the two sparkling wines, Vintage Brut and Midnight Cuvee.
summary Forty years after Remy Cointreau established Blue Pyrenees Estate (then known as Chateau Remy), it sold the business to a small group of Sydney businessmen led by John Ellis (no relation to the John Ellis of Hanging Rock). The winemaking and marketing teams continue in place, although John Ellis has become involved in all areas of the business. The core of the business is the 180-hectare estate vineyard, much of it fully mature. Exports to all major markets.

Blue Pyrenees Estate Sauvignon Blanc

▼▼▼▼ 2002 Light straw-green; a crisp array of grass, asparagus and mineral aromas lead into a light to medium-bodied palate, precisely focused, and picking up the pace nicely towards the finish. One hundred per cent estate-grown.   **rating: 86**

best drinking Now   **drink with** Steamed fish • $17

Blue Pyrenees Estate Vintage Brut

▼▼▼▼ 1999 Light green-yellow; a fairly direct, fresh and citrussy bouquet is followed by a tangy, very lemony palate; neither bouquet nor palate shows much impact from lees contact, but it is doubtless somewhere there in the background.   **rating: 85**

best drinking Now–2007   **drink with** Aperitif • $24

Blue Pyrenees Estate Pinot Noir

▼▼▼▼ 2001 Strong red-purple; the bouquet shows fully ripe plum jam fruit; the solid palate borders on dry red, but does have surprising varietal character lurking in the depths; bottle age could spring an even greater surprise. Said to be 100 per cent estate-grown, from two elevated blocks.   **rating: 87**

best drinking Now–2007   **drink with** Seared tuna • $17

Blue Pyrenees Estate Shiraz

▼▼▼▼ 2001 Medium red-purple; the moderately intense bouquet has clean blackberry fruit, with spicy/earthy undertones; there is much more depth and concentration to the blackberry fruit of the palate, made more complex by a dash of spice and positive, quality oak.   **rating: 89**

best drinking 2006–2011   **drink with** Beef Bordelaise • $16.10

Blue Pyrenees Estate Cabernet Sauvignon

▼▼▼▽ 2001 Excellent purple-red; clean cassis and blackcurrant aromas are supported by nicely handled and balanced oak; the flavours of the palate are identical to those of the bouquet, the wine having good, ripe tannins and overall structure.   **rating: 90**

best drinking 2005–2011   **drink with** Hard cheese • $16.10

blue wren   ★★★★

1 Cassilis Road, Mudgee, NSW 2850   **region** Mudgee
phone (02) 6372 6205   **fax** (02) 6372 6206   **open** Wed–Sun 10.30–4.30
winemaker Various contract   **production** 3000 cases   **est.** 1985
product range ($15–26 CD) Semillon, Chardonnay, Cabernet Sauvignon.
summary James and Diana Anderson have two vineyards, the first called Stoney Creek, planted in 1985 and acquired from the Britten family in early 1999. It has 2 hectares each of chardonnay and semillon, 1.5 hectares of cabernet and 0.5 hectare of merlot, is situated 20 kilometres north of Mudgee, and the vines are dry-grown. The second vineyard has been planted to 2.4 hectares of shiraz and 1.4 hectares of verdelho, leaving more than 20 hectares as yet unplanted. The Bombira Vineyard, as it is known, is adjacent to the old Augustine vineyards owned by Beringer Blass. The capacious on-site restaurant is recommended – as are the wines.

boatshed vineyard   ★★★

703 Milbrodale Road, Broke, NSW 2330 (postal)   **region** Lower Hunter Valley
phone (02) 9876 5761   **fax** (02) 9876 5761   **open** Not
winemaker Tamburlaine (Contract)   **production** 3500 cases   **est.** 1989
product range ($14–18 ML) Verdelho, Estate Chardonnay, Botrytis Chardonnay, Chardonnay Pinot Noir, Chambourcin, Merlot, Cabernet Merlot, Cabernet Sauvignon.
summary Mark and wife Helen Hill acquired the property in June 1998. At that time it had 5 hectares of chardonnay, and in the spring of 1999 the plantings were extended with 2 hectares each of verdelho, merlot, chambourcin and cabernet sauvignon. As Mark Hill says, the new name of the vineyard has much more to do with his lifetime involvement with rowing, first as a schoolboy competitor and thereafter as a coach of his school's senior IVs. Sustainable viticultural practices are used, and no insecticides have been applied for the past 10 years. The wines are made under contract by Mark Davidson at Tamburlaine, with approximately 25 per cent of the wine made and bottled for Boatshed, the remainder being taken by Tamburlaine. There is no cellar door, and all sales are mail order or ex the vineyard on a wholesale basis to Sydney restaurants.

Boatshed Vineyard Wooded Chardonnay

▼▼▼▽ **2000** Developed yellow; the soft bouquet has buttery, yellow peach aromas, the oak in better restraint than the 1999 vintage; the palate follows the same track, being smooth, gently peachy and soft, with subtle French and American oak. **rating:** 84

best drinking Now **drink with** Gnocchi • $16

Boatshed Vineyard Botrytis Chardonnay

▼▼▼▼ **2001** Golden orange; the clean bouquet has a mix of cumquat and honey which are joined by a touch of mandarin on the palate; the wine is only moderately sweet, and the balance is good. **rating:** 85

best drinking Now **drink with** Light desserts • $18

Boatshed Vineyard Chambourcin

▼▼▼▼ **2001** Medium red-purple; the clean, moderately intense bouquet has attractive earthy/spicy edges, and the same earthy/savoury nuances accompany the red fruits of the palate; has better structure than most Chambourcins. **rating:** 85

best drinking Now–2005 **drink with** Grilled T-bone steak • $18

Boatshed Vineyard Cabernet Merlot

▼▼▼▽ **2001** Red-purple; a light, clean bouquet has leafy/stemmy fruit to the forefront, and the light to medium-bodied palate does not change the scene much, ranging through leafy/berry/earthy flavours, with the oak subtle. A blend of 52 per cent Cabernet Sauvignon, 48 per cent Merlot. **rating:** 84

best drinking Now–2006 **drink with** Lamb shanks • $18

🐚 bochara wines ★★★★

Glenelg Highway, Bochara, Vic 3300 **region** Henty
phone (03) 5571 9309 **fax** (03) 5570 8334 **open** Dec–Jan 7 days 11–5, Feb–Nov Thurs–Mon 11–5
winemaker Martin Slocombe **production** 1000 cases **est.** 1998
product range ($12–25 R) Sauvignon Blanc, Chardonnay, Arcadia Brut Cuvee, Picnic Train Rose, Pinot Noir, Merlot Cabernet Franc.
summary This is the small husband and wife business of experienced winemaker Martin Slocombe and former Yalumba viticulturist Kylie McIntyre. They have established 1 hectare each of pinot noir and sauvignon blanc, together with 0.5 hectare of pinot meunier, supplemented by grapes purchased from local grape growers. The modestly priced but well-made wines are principally sold through the cellar-door sales cottage on the property, which has been transformed from a decrepit weatherboard shanty with one cold tap to a fully functional two-room tasting area. The wines are also available through a number of local restaurants and bottle shops. The label design, incidentally, comes from a 1901 poster advertising the subdivision of the original Bochara property into smaller farms.

Bochara Sauvignon Blanc

▼▼▼▼▽ **2002** Light straw-green; a spotlessly clean and fragrant bouquet of passionfruit and gooseberry is repeated on the elegant, light to medium-bodied palate, fine and clear. **rating:** 91

best drinking Now **best vintages** '02 **drink with** Seafood • $15

Bochara Arcadia Brut Cuvee Blanc de Noirs

▼▼▼▼ **2001** Light, pale straw; the aromatic bouquet is driven by spice, herb and citrus-like aromas; the delicate fresh and crisp palate is not complex, but has considerable length. A blend of 60 per cent Pinot Noir and 40 per cent Pinot Meunier. **rating:** 87

best drinking Now–2005 **drink with** Antipasto • $22

Bochara Pinot Noir

▼▼▼▼ **2001** Light to medium red-purple; fragrant, ripe plum and subtle oak aromas lead into a moderately long palate, with direct, ripe plum and fruit spice flavours. Good varietal character and will develop more complexity in the medium term. **rating:** 89

best drinking Now–2006 **drink with** Coq au vin • $20

🐚 boggy creek vineyards NR

RMB 1780, Boggy Creek Road, Myrrhee, Vic 3732 **region** King Valley
phone (03) 5729 7587 **fax** (03) 5729 7600 **open** By appointment
winemaker Contract **est.** 1978

product range ($14–18 ML) Riesling, Sauvignon Blanc, Pinot Gris, Chardonnay, Unwooded Chardonnay, Shiraz, Barbera, Cabernet Sauvignon.

summary Graeme and Maggie Ray started their vineyard as a hobby in 1978, planting small quantities of riesling and chardonnay. Since then the vineyard has grown to over 30 hectares, and cabernet sauvignon, shiraz, barbera, pinot gris and other experimental lots have been planted. It is situated on northeast facing slopes at an altitude of 350 metres, with warm summer days and cool nights.

🐦 bogong estate   NR

Cnr Mountain Creek and Damms Roads, Mount Beauty, Vic 3699   **region** Alpine Valleys
phone 0419 567 588   **fax** (03) 5754 4946   **open** 7 days 10–5
winemaker Bill Tynan   **production** 2500 cases   **est.** 1997
product range ($15–20 CD) Pinotnoir.com.au Pinot Noir, Pinot Forte (Port).

summary In the flesh, Bill Tynan looks exactly as a tax partner for a large accounting firm should look: slim, quietly spoken and self-deprecating. His business card, featuring the imprint in vivid pink of an impression of Marilyn Monroe's lips, tells you that all is not what it seems. He has in fact given up accounting, and has wagered everything by planting 10 hectares of pinot noir in the upper reaches of Kiewa River Valley, with no near neighbours to keep him company. He goes on, 'Like all madmen, we like to make our own mistakes.' But he does take viticultural advice from Ben Rose of Performance Viticulture, and, in the shed-cum-winery, on winemaking from Brian Wilson. Winemaking is all about fermenting pinot noir in large plastic bags with gas valves, a system developed by the Hickinbotham family. Marketing the wine is no less lateral: Pinotnoir.com.au 2002 Pinot Noir is aimed at the young, fast movers of Melbourne and Sydney. The estate wine is directed towards the serious, probably older, market. There there is Bogong Estate Pinot Forte, a fortified Pinot Noir. These three wines all sell for $15–20, the aim being to create demand by overdelivery. Definitely, positively, all a bit mad.

Bogong Estate Pinot Noir
▼▼▼▼ 2000 Light to medium red; both the bouquet and palate are very much at the savoury/sappy end of the spectrum; the strength of the wine lies in its length and faintly spicy finish. Given all the circumstances of its making, a more than creditable first effort.   **rating:** 86
best drinking Now–2005   **drink with** Tea-smoked duck • $15

boireann   NR

Donnellys Castle Road, The Summit, Qld, 4377   **region** Granite Belt
phone (07) 4683 2194   **open** 7 days 10–4.30
winemaker Peter Stark   **production** 500 cases   **est.** 1998
product range ($18–27 CD) Grenache Mourvedre Shiraz, Reserve Shiraz Viognier, Petit Verdot, Merlot, Cabernet Merlot, Reserve Cabernet Sauvignon.

summary Peter and Therese Stark have a 10-hectare property set amongst the great granite boulders and trees which are so much part of the Granite Belt. They have established an acre and a half of vines planted to no less than 11 varieties, including the four Bordeaux varieties which go to make a Bordeaux blend; grenache and mourvedre provide a Rhône blend, and there will also be a straight Merlot. Tannat (French) and barbera and nebbiolo (Italian) make up the viticultural League of Nations.

bonneyview   NR

Sturt Highway, Barmera, SA 5345   **region** Riverland
phone (08) 8588 2279   **open** 7 days 9–5.30
winemaker Robert Minns   **production** 2500 cases   **est.** 1975
product range ($10–13 CD) Unoaked Chardonnay, Late Picked Frontignan, Shiraz Petit Verdot, Petit Verdot Merlot, Cabernet Blend.

summary The smallest Riverland winery selling exclusively through the cellar door, with an ex-Kent cricketer and Oxford University graduate as its owner/winemaker. The Shiraz Petit Verdot (unique to Bonneyview) and Cabernet Petit Verdot add a particular dimension of interest to the wine portfolio.

🐦 boora estate   NR

'Boora', Warrie Road, Dubbo, NSW 2830   **region** Western Plains Zone
phone (02) 6884 2600   **fax** (02) 6884 2600   **open** Sat–Tues 10–5, or by appointment
winemaker Frank Ramsay   **est.** 1984
product range ($15–22.50 CD) Semillon, Chardonnay, Shiraz, Merlot, Cabernet Sauvignon Cabernet Franc.

summary The wheel comes full circle with Boora Estate, where Frank Ramsay has established approximately 0.5 hectare each of chardonnay, semillon, cabernet franc, cabernet sauvignon, merlot, tempranillo and shiraz. In the 1870s and 1880s Dubbo supported a significant winemaking industry, with Eumalga Estate (owned and run by French-born JE Serisier) said (by the local newspaper of the time) to have the second-largest winery in Australia (which I doubt). Another highly successful winery was established by German-born Frederich Kurtz; Mount Olive won a number of awards in international exhibitions in the 1880s. That achievement was matched 120 years later by Boora Estate winning a silver medal at the 2001 Brisbane Wine Show with its 2000 Shiraz, competing against wines from all parts of Australia.

booth's taminick cellars NR

Taminick via Glenrowan, Vic 3675 **region** Glenrowan
phone (03) 5766 2282 **fax** (03) 5766 2151 **open** Mon–Sat 9–5, Sun 10–5
winemaker Peter Booth **production** 4000 cases **est.** 1904
product range ($6.50–12 CD) Trebbiano, Chardonnay, Late Harvest Trebbiano, Shiraz, Cabernet Merlot, Cabernet Sauvignon, Ports, Muscat.
summary Ultra-conservative producer of massively flavoured and concentrated red wines, some with more than a few rough edges which time may or may not smooth over.

borambola wines ★★★

Sturt Highway, Wagga Wagga, NSW 2650 **region** Gundagai
phone (02) 6928 4210 **fax** (02) 6928 4210 **open** 7 days 11–4
winemaker Greg Gallagher, Andrew Birks **production** 3000 cases **est.** 1995
product range ($14–16 CD) Chardonnay, Cabernet Merlot.
summary Borambola Homestead was built in the 1880s, and in the latter part of that century was the centre of a pastoral empire of 1.4 million hectares. Ownership passed to the McMullen family in 1992. It is situated in rolling foothills 25 kilometres east of Wagga Wagga in the newly declared Gundagai region. Just under 10 hectares of vines surround the homestead (4 ha shiraz, 3.5 ha cabernet sauvignon, 2.2 ha chardonnay) and the wines are made for Borambola at Charles Sturt University by the Charles Sturt winemakers Greg Gallagher and Andrew Birks.

Borambola Chardonnay

TTTT 2002 Medium yellow-green; the bouquet has clean, smooth nectarine fruit with subtle French oak in the background, the pace picking up on the palate with abundant sweet peachy fruit, subtle oak and a hint of residual sweetness, coming in part from the 14° alcohol. **rating:** 87

best drinking Now **drink with** Roast pork • $16

boston bay wines ★★★

Lincoln Highway, Port Lincoln, SA 5606 **region** Southern Eyre Peninsula
phone (08) 8684 3600 **fax** (08) 8684 3637 **open** Weekends, school/public holidays 11.30–4.30
winemaker David O'Leary, Nick Walker **production** 4500 cases **est.** 1984
product range ($11–24 CD) The Clare Riesling, Spatlese Riesling, The Oakbank Chardonnay, Riesling Mistelle, Shiraz, Baudin's Blend (Shiraz Cabernet Sauvignon Merlot), Merlot, Cabernet Sauvignon.
summary A strongly tourist-oriented operation which has extended the viticultural map in South Australia. It is situated at the same latitude as Adelaide, overlooking the Spencer Gulf at the southern tip of the Eyre Peninsula. Say proprietors Graham and Mary Ford, 'It is the only vineyard in the world to offer frequent sightings of whales at play in the waters at its foot.' No recent tastings.

botobolar ★★★☆

89 Botobolar Road, Mudgee, NSW 2850 **region** Mudgee
phone (02) 6373 3840 **fax** (02) 6373 3789 **open** Mon–Sat 10–5, Sun 10–3
winemaker Kevin Karstrom **production** 5000 cases **est.** 1971
product range ($8–22.50 CD) Sauvignon Blanc, Rain Goddess Dry White, Rain Goddess Sweet White, Marsanne, Chardonnay, Rain Goddess Red, Pinot Noir, Shiraz, R&B Shiraz, Cabernet Sauvignon; The King, The Saviour (both Cabernet Shiraz blends); Low Preservative Chardonnay and Preservative Free Shiraz.
summary One of the first organic vineyards in Australia, with present owner Kevin Karstrom continuing the practices established by founder Gil Wahlquist. Preservative Free Dry White and Dry Red extend the organic practice of the vineyard to the winery. Shiraz is consistently the best wine to appear under the Botobolar label. Exports to the UK, Denmark and Germany.

bowen estate ★★★★☆

Riddoch Highway, Coonawarra, SA 5263 **region** Coonawarra
phone (08) 8737 2229 **fax** (08) 8737 2173 **open** 7 days 10–5
winemaker Doug Bowen, Emma Bowen **production** 12 000 cases **est.** 1972
product range ($20.50–55 R) Chardonnay, Shiraz, Ampelon (Shiraz), The Blend, Cabernet Sauvignon.
summary One of the best known names among the smaller Coonawarra wineries, with a great track record of red winemaking. Full-bodied reds at the top end of the ripeness spectrum are the winery trademarks, and have a chewy richness uncommon in Coonawarra. Exports to the UK, Germany, Switzerland, Japan, Singapore, Indonesia, Vietnam, Hong Kong and New Zealand.

Bowen Estate Shiraz
▼▼▼▼▼ 2000 Medium to full red-purple; the bouquet is crammed with complex fruit and oak, swelling into dark plum, licorice and vanilla on the palate, finishing with plentiful, ripe tannins. A rich, traditional style. Gold medal Limestone Coast Wine Show 2002. **rating: 94**
best drinking 2004–2014 **best vintages** '86, '90, '91, '92, '94, '95, '97, '00 **drink with** Kangaroo fillet • $26.50

Bowen Estate The Blend
▼▼▼▼▽ 2000 Medium purple-red; ripe, rich blackcurrant and blackberry fruit drives the bouquet; a powerful, full-flavoured palate with touches of chocolate, and supple, ripe tannins. A mere 14° alcohol. **rating: 91**
best drinking 2004–2014 **best vintages** '95, '97 **drink with** Lasagne • $24.50

Bowen Estate Cabernet Sauvignon
▼▼▼▼▽ 2000 Medium red-purple; a savoury mix of oaky/earthy/berry aromas, followed by a powerful, complex and deep palate, exuding ripe fruit, ripe tannins and plenty of oak. **rating: 92**
best drinking 2006–2012 **best vintages** '86, '90, '91, '93, '94, '00 **drink with** Richly sauced beef casserole • $27.50

🐂 bowmans wines ★★★

RMB 543, Springs Road, Mount Barker, WA 6324 (postal) **region** Great Southern
phone (08) 9857 6083 **fax** (08) 9857 6083 **open** Not
winemaker Porongorup Winery (Contract) **production** 1000 cases **est.** 1998
product range ($14–16 R) Sauvignon Blanc, Shiraz.
summary Bowmans Wines is situated on a beef cattle farm owned by Gerald and Marion Jenkins. Six hectares of vines, planted on picturesque slopes, have been progressively established between 1998 and 2001. The first vintage of sauvignon blanc and shiraz came in 2001, and the wines have retail distribution in all the local towns, as well as through outlets in Perth.

Bowmans Shiraz
▼▼▼▼ 2001 Full purple-red; the clean bouquet ranges through plum, spice, prune and sundry dark berry aromas; a clean, medium to full-bodied palate adds a whisper of chocolate to the fruit mix of the bouquet, with the oak subtle; while fruit-driven, will develop nicely. Very impressive for a first-up vintage. **rating: 87**
best drinking 2004–2009 **drink with** Fillet of beef • $16

🐂 box stallion ★★★☆

64 Turrarubba Road, Merricks North, Vic 3926 **region** Mornington Peninsula
phone (03) 5989 7444 **fax** (03) 5989 7688 **open** 7 days 11–5
winemaker Alex White **production** 6000 cases **est.** 2001
product range ($16–27 CD) Sauvignon Blanc, Moscato, Arneis, Red Barn Chardonnay, The Enclosure Chardonnay, Blaze Rose, Dolcetto, Pinot Meunier, Shiraz.
summary Box Stallion is the joint venture of Stephen Wharton, John Gillies and Garry Zerbe, who have linked two vineyards, one at Bittern and one at Merricks North, with 20 hectares of vines planted between 1997 and 2003. What once was a thoroughbred stud has now become a vineyard, with the Red Barn (in their words) 'now home to a stable of fine wines'. Those wines are made at the jointly owned winery with Alex White as winemaker. The cafe is open daily from 11 am to 5 pm.

Box Stallion Arneis
▼▼▼▼ 2001 Light straw-green; the aromatic bouquet has lemon/lemon blossom/herb aromas, the palate flowing on logically, with a quite intense mix of herb and lemon; good length, and finishes crisp and dry. Another interesting example of this rapidly proliferating Italian variety. **rating: 86**
best drinking Now **drink with** Blue swimmer crab • $27

Box Stallion The Enclosure Chardonnay

ȲȲȲȲȲ 2001 Light to medium green; the clean, firm and fresh bouquet has melon enclosed with a faint web of smoky oak; the palate is all about finesse and delicacy, being long but fine, and maturing slowly.   **rating:** 91

best drinking Now–2008 **drink with** Grilled fish • $27

Box Stallion Shiraz

ȲȲȲȲ 2001 Bright purple-red; a clean and vibrant bouquet, with fresh berry and spicy fruit plus a hint of smoky oak, then a light to medium-bodied palate in distinctively cool-grown, peppery style.   **rating:** 89

best drinking Now–2007 **drink with** Braised beef • $27

Box Stallion Pinot Meunier

ȲȲȲȲ 2001 Medium red, bright and clear; the complex, strongly spicy, almost charry bouquet, with dark fruits, leads into a powerful palate that is slightly extractive, and needing to soften, which the variety is prone to do.   **rating:** 87

best drinking Now–2007 **drink with** Tea-smoked duck • $27

boynton's   NR

Great Alpine Road, Porepunkah, Vic 3741 **region** Alpine Valleys
phone (03) 5756 2356 **fax** (03) 5756 2610 **open** 7 days 10–5
winemaker Kel Boynton, Eleana Anderson **production** 11 000 cases **est.** 1987
product range ($14–60 CD) Riesling, Sauvignon Blanc, Chardonnay, Boynton's Gold (Noble Riesling Chardonnay blend), Pinots (Pinot Meunier Pinot Noir), Shiraz, Merlot, Cabernet Sauvignon, Alluvium (Cabernet Sauvignon Merlot Petit Verdot), Vintage Brut.
summary The original 12.5-hectare vineyard, expanded to almost 16 hectares by 1996 plantings of pinot gris, durif and sauvignon blanc, is situated in the Ovens Valley north of the township of Bright, under the lee of Mount Buffalo. In the early years a substantial part of the crop was sold, but virtually all is now vinified at the winery. Overall, the red wines have always outshone the whites, initially with very strong American oak input, but in more recent years with better fruit/oak balance. Striking, indeed strident, new labelling has led to a minor name change – the dropping of the words 'of Bright'. No recent tastings. The wines have distribution through the east coast of Australia; exports to Germany, Austria and the US.

🐦 bracken hill   NR

81 Tinderbox Road, Tinderbox, Tas 7052 **region** Southern Tasmania
phone (03) 6229 6475 **open** Annual open weekends in March and October
winemaker Contract **production** 120 cases **est.** 1993
product range ($20 ML) Gewurztraminer.
summary Max Thalmann came to Tasmania from Switzerland in 1961, retiring 30 years later, and took the decision to plant his 0.4-hectare vineyard entirely to gewurztraminer. As Tasmanian writer Phil Laing has pointed out, it is probably the only specialist gewurztraminer producer in the southern hemisphere, making Thalmann's decision all the more curious, because he prefers red wine to white wine. His logic, however, was impeccable: he could sell the grapes and/or the wine from his vineyard and use the money to buy red wines of his choice. Bracken Hill has its open weekend in October, and participates in the annual Tasmanian cellar door open weekend in March. The label, incidentally, comes from a painting by Max Thalmann himself, which proves he is a man of many talents.

braewattie   ★★★★

351 Rochford Road, Rochford, Vic 3442 **region** Macedon Ranges
phone (03) 9818 5742 **fax** (03) 9818 8361 **open** By appointment
winemaker John Flynn, John Ellis **production** 250 cases **est.** 1993
product range ($20–29 ML) Chardonnay, Pinot Noir, Macedon Brut (Pinot Noir Chardonnay).
summary Des and Maggi Ryan bought Braewattie in 1990; Maggi's great-grandfather, James McCarthy, had acquired the property in the 1880s, and it remained in the family until 1971. When the property came back on the market the Ryans seized the opportunity to reclaim it, complete with a small existing planting of 300 pinot noir and chardonnay vines. Those plantings now extend to 9.7 hectares, part of the production being sold as grapes, and a small amount contract-made. The Macedon Brut is a particularly good wine.

Braewattie Chardonnay

▼▼▼▼ 2001 Light straw-green; the bouquet is quite aromatic, albeit with faintly herbal/green edges to the fruit. A lively and bright palate with a mix of lemon, citrus and nectarine fruit, the oak entirely incidental; good length. Should be long-lived.   **rating:** 87

best drinking 3004–2009 **drink with** Sushi • $20

brahams creek winery   NR

Woods Point Road, East Warburton, Vic 3799 **region** Yarra Valley
phone (03) 9566 2802 **fax** (03) 9566 2802 **open** Weekends and public holidays 11–5
winemaker Geoff Richardson, Chris Young **production** 1200 cases **est.** 1990
product range ($11–13.50 CD) Chardonnay, Pinot Noir, Merlot, Cabernet Sauvignon, Tawny Port.
summary Owner Geoffrey Richardson did not start marketing his wines until 1994 and a string of older vintages are available for sale at the cellar door at an enticing price. Part of the grape production is sold to other Yarra Valley winemakers.

bramley wood   NR

RMB 205, Rosa Brook Road, Margaret River, WA 6285 (postal) **region** Margaret River
phone (08) 9757 9291 **fax** (08) 9757 9291 **open** Not
winemaker Cliff Royle, Mike Edwards (Voyager Estate) **production** 200 cases **est.** 1994
product range ($25 ML) Cabernet Sauvignon.
summary David and Rebecca McInerney planted 2 hectares of cabernet sauvignon in 1994, with an inaugural vintage in 1998, released in December 2000. Encouraged by the quality of that wine and, in particular, the 1999 which followed it, the McInerneys plan to one day expand their plantings. For the time being, the tiny production is sold by mail order and through the two self-contained chalets on the property, each capable of hosting 4–6 adults.

brand's of coonawarra   ★★★★☆

Riddoch Highway, Coonawarra, SA 5263 **region** Coonawarra
phone (08) 8736 3260 **fax** (08) 8736 3208 **open** Mon–Fri 8–5, weekends 10–4
winemaker Jim Brand, Jim Brayne **production** NFP **est.** 1966
product range ($19–66 R) Riesling, Chardonnay, Sparkling Cabernet Sauvignon, Cabernet Merlot, Shiraz, Stentiford's Reserve Shiraz, Merlot, Cabernet Sauvignon, Patron's Reserve.
summary Part of a very substantial investment in Coonawarra by McWilliam's, which first acquired a 50 per cent interest from the founding Brand family then moved to 100 per cent, and followed this with the purchase of 100 hectares of additional vineyard land. Significantly increased production of the smooth wines for which Brand's is known will follow.

Brand's of Coonawarra Shiraz

▼▼▼▼▽ 2000 Medium red-purple; spiced plum, black cherry and blackberry fruit is accompanied by the usual subtle oak on the bouquet; the medium-bodied palate follows precisely the same path, with fine tannins and good length. Elegant and unforced. 13.5° alcohol, and a total contrast to the style of neighbouring Bowen Estate of the same vintage.   **rating:** 91

best drinking 2004–2009 **best vintages** '90, '91, '96, '98, '99 **drink with** Braised lamb shanks • $24

Brand's of Coonawarra Stentiford's Reserve Shiraz

▼▼▼▼▽ 1999 Medium red-purple; clean, fresh, red and black cherry fruit is neatly balanced by French oak on the bouquet, but on the palate the oak becomes just a little intrusive. The wine spent 26 months in new French oak; 18 months might have been better.   **rating:** 93

best drinking 2004–2014 **best vintages** '96, '97, '98, '99 **drink with** Rack of lamb • $66

Brand's of Coonawarra Special Release Merlot

▼▼▼▼ 2000 Bright and youthful purple-red; the bouquet exudes sweet, ripe blueberry and blackberry aromas; the palate has abundant weight and flavour, adding touches of mint and herb, then fine-grained but assertive tannins on the finish. Has three gold medals to its credit.   **rating:** 89

best drinking 2004–2010 **drink with** Veal chops • $31

Brand's of Coonawarra Patron's Reserve

♥♥♥♥♥ 1999 Medium red-purple; the moderately intense bouquet has a range of cedary, savoury, blackberry aromas, which logically introduce the harmonious medium-bodied palate; fine tannins and controlled oak. A blend of Cabernet Sauvignon, Shiraz and Merlot, with three gold medals to its credit. **rating:** 91

best drinking 2004–2012 **best vintages** '98, '99 **drink with** Osso buco • $66

Brand's of Coonawarra Cabernet Sauvignon

♥♥♥♥♡ 2000 Medium red-purple; the moderately intense bouquet has smooth blackcurrant fruit together with hints of cedar and earth; the medium-bodied palate is well balanced, with attractive blackcurrant and blackberry fruit, fine tannins and subtle oak. Good value. **rating:** 91

best drinking 2004–2010 **best vintages** '86, '90, '91, '93, '94, '95, '98, '00 **drink with** Lamb Provençale • $24

brangayne of orange ★★★★

49 Pinnacle Road, Orange, NSW 2800 **region** Orange
phone (02) 6365 3229 **fax** (02) 6365 3170 **open** By appointment
winemaker Simon Gilbert (Contract), Richard Bateman **production** 3500 cases **est.** 1994
product range ($18–29 CD) Sauvignon Blanc, Chardonnay, Premium Chardonnay, Isolde Reserve Chardonnay, Pinot Noir, The Tristan (Cabernet blend).
summary Orchardists Don and Pamela Hoskins decided to diversify into grape growing in 1994 and have progressively established 25 hectares of high-quality vineyards. With viticultural consultancy advice from Dr Richard Smart and skilled contract winemaking by Simon Gilbert, Brangayne made an extraordinarily auspicious debut, underlining the potential of the Orange region. Daughter Nicola, having had experience at the marketing coal-face in Melbourne and Sydney, has returned to Orange and taken over responsibility for the day-to-day management of the business. Exports to the UK and Singapore.

Brangayne of Orange Sauvignon Blanc

♥♥♥♥ 2002 Very pale straw-green; potent, smoky, grassy/gooseberry varietal fruit has a faint touch of reduction lurking in the background of the bouquet, but the palate is crisp and lively, braced by minerally acidity. **rating:** 89

best drinking Now **drink with** Caesar salad • $20

Brangayne of Orange Isolde Reserve Chardonnay

♥♥♥♥♡ 2001 Light to medium yellow-green; the moderately intense bouquet has fresh melon and citrus fruit leading the way, and the oak in the background; an unforced, light to medium-bodied palate, with elegant citrus and melon fruit, the oak incidental. **rating:** 90

best drinking Now–2006 **best vintages** '97, '98, '01 **drink with** Flathead fillets • $24

bream creek ★★★☆

Marion Bay Road, Bream Creek, Tas 7175 **region** Southern Tasmania
phone (03) 6231 4646 **fax** (03) 6231 4646 **open** At Potters Croft, Dunally, telephone (03) 6253 5469
winemaker Steve Lubiana (Contract) **production** 3000 cases **est.** 1975
product range ($17–22 CD) Riesling, Traminer, Sauvignon Blanc, Schonburger, Chardonnay, Pinot Noir, Cabernet Sauvignon.
summary Until 1990 the Bream Creek fruit was sold to Moorilla Estate, but since that time the winery has been independently owned and managed under the control of Fred Peacock, legendary for the care he bestows on the vines under his direction. Peacock's skills have seen both an increase in production and also a vast lift in wine quality across the range, headed by the Pinot Noir. The 1996 acquisition of a second vineyard in the Tamar Valley has significantly strengthened the business base of the venture.

bremerton wines ★★★★☆

Strathalbyn Road, Langhorne Creek, SA 5255 **region** Langhorne Creek
phone (08) 8537 3093 **fax** (08) 8537 3109 **open** 7 days 10–5
winemaker Rebecca Willson **production** 22 000 cases **est.** 1988
product range ($15–30 CD) Sauvignon Blanc, Verdelho, Old Adam Shiraz, Selkirk Shiraz, Walter's Cabernet Sauvignon, Tamblyn (Cabernet Shiraz Malbec Merlot), Ciel Botrytised and Fortified Chenin Blanc.
summary The Willsons have been grape growers in the Langhorne Creek region for some considerable time, but their dual business as grape growers and winemakers has expanded significantly over the past few years. Their vineyards have more than doubled to over 100 hectares (predominantly cabernet sauvignon, shiraz and merlot),

as has their production of wine under the Bremerton label, no doubt in recognition of the quality of the wines. Strangely, no tastings in the past 12 months; rating is on prior releases. Wholesale distribution in all states of Australia; exports to the UK, the US, Canada, Singapore, Holland, Germany, Switzerland and New Zealand.

❧ bress   NR

Modesty Cottage, Church Street, Fryerstown, Vic 3451 (postal)   **region** Warehouse
phone 0409 566 773   **fax** 0409 435 465   **open** Not
winemaker Adam Marks   **production** 2000 cases   **est.** 2001
product range ($19.99–29.99 ML) There are two tiers, the Silver Label Margaret River Semillon Sauvignon Blanc and Yarra Valley Pinot Noir, and the Gold Label Heathcote Shiraz.
summary Adam Marks won the Ron Potter Scholarship in 1991 to work as assistant winemaker to Rodney Hooper at Charles Sturt University. Since that time he has made wine in all parts of the world, with extensive experience in France, interspersed with a period of time as chief winemaker for St Huberts, and more recently (1998 to 1999) making wine in California, Chile and Argentina for Beringer Blass. He came back to be winemaker at Dominion Wines for 2 years, then took the brave decision (during his honeymoon in 2000) to start his own business. He has selected Margaret River semillon and sauvignon blanc as the best source of white Bordeaux-style wine in Australia; Yarra Valley pinot noir as the best pinot noir region; and shiraz from Heathcote for precisely the same reason. The majority of the wine is sold to mailing list clients through the website, with some direct distribution to select restaurants and independent retailers.

Bress Yarra Valley Pinot Noir
ŸŸŸŸ 2002 Medium purple-red; the moderately intense bouquet has nice varietal, dark plum fruit supported by gentle oak; the light to medium-bodied palate offers dark plum fruit on entry, with positive varietal character and a touch of spice, before tailing off slightly on the finish. Quite likely comes from young vines. Stelvin closed.   **rating: 86**
best drinking Now–2005   **drink with** Braised rabbit with couscous • $20

brewery hill winery   NR

Olivers Road, McLaren Vale, SA 5171   **region** McLaren Vale
phone (08) 8323 7344   **fax** (08) 8323 7355   **open** Mon–Fri 9–5, weekends 10–5
winemaker Contract   **production** 12 000 cases   **est.** 1869
product range ($10–22.50 CD) Riesling, Classic Spatlese, Chardonnay, Classic Dry Red, Shiraz, Cabernet Sauvignon, Sparkling, fortifieds.
summary A change of name and of address for the former St Francis Winery, which has moved into the former Manning Park Winery and is now known as Brewery Hill Winery. Exports to Japan.

briagolong estate   ★★★★

Valencia–Briagolong Road, Briagolong, Vic 3860   **region** Gippsland
phone (03) 5147 2322   **fax** (03) 5147 2400   **open** By appointment
winemaker Gordon McIntosh   **production** 400 cases   **est.** 1979
product range ($35 ML) Chardonnay, Pinot Noir.
summary This is very much a weekend hobby for medical practitioner Gordon McIntosh, who tries hard to invest his wines with Burgundian complexity. Six years of continuous drought, with one break in 2002 when hail destroyed the crop, has meant no Chardonnay in 2000, 2001 or 2002, nor Pinot for 2002 (and the 2001 is in doubt). Given the quality of the 2000 Pinot, the loss is all the keener.

Briagolong Estate Pinot Noir
ŸŸŸŸŸ 2000 Medium red-purple; very ripe aromas with a complex array of plum and more spicy/savoury notes lead into an intense and powerful palate; has very good length, and grip to the finish, which will soften as the wine ages.   **rating: 91**
best drinking Now–2008   **best vintages** '00   **drink with** Braised duck • $35

brian barry wines   ★★★☆

PO Box 128, Stepney, SA 5069   **region** Clare Valley
phone (08) 8363 6211   **fax** (08) 8362 0498   **open** Not
winemaker Brian Barry, Judson Barry   **production** 4000 cases   **est.** 1977
product range ($18–35 R) Jud's Hill Handpicked Riesling, Handpicked Merlot, Handpicked Cabernet Sauvignon; Special Reserve Shiraz.

summary Brian Barry is an industry veteran with a wealth of winemaking and show-judging experience. His is nonetheless in reality a vineyard-only operation, with a substantial part of the output sold as grapes to other wineries and the wines made under contract at various wineries, albeit under Brian Barry's supervision. As one would expect, the quality is reliably good. Retail distribution through all states; exports to the UK and the US.

Brian Barry Jud's Hill Handpicked Riesling

▼▼▼▼ 2002 Light green-yellow; while somewhat closed, the bouquet does have some herb and spice aromas; the palate has a suite of lemon, herb and spice, but is not particularly long, which is surprising given the vintage and the age of the vines.   **rating:** 87

best drinking Now–2006 **best vintages** '91, '92, '94, '95, '00, '01 **drink with** Caesar salad • $18

Brian Barry Cabernet Sauvignon

▼▼▼▼ 2000 Light to medium red-purple; there are spicy/foresty/herb nuances to the black fruits of the bouquet; the palate sweetens up nicely, with blackberry and a hint of cassis; elegant and unforced; good length.
best drinking 2005–2011 **drink with** Beef Bordelaise • $25   **rating:** 89

briarose estate   NR

Bussell Highway, Augusta, WA 6290 **region** Margaret River
phone 0417 189 551 **fax** (08) 9479 1404 **open** 7 days 10–4.30
winemaker Cath Oates **production** 12 500 cases **est.** 1998
product range Semillon, Sauvignon Blanc, Semillon Sauvignon Blanc, Merlot, Cabernet Franc, Cabernet Merlot, Blackwood Cove (Cabernet Sauvignon Merlot Cabernet Franc), Cabernet Sauvignon Reserve.
summary Brian and Rosemary Webster began the development of the estate plantings in 1998. They now comprise sauvignon blanc (2.33 ha), semillon (1.33 ha), cabernet sauvignon (6.6 ha), merlot (2.2 ha) and cabernet franc (1.1 ha). The estate is situated at the southern end of the Margaret River region, 6 kilometres north of Augusta, and as Briarose and other new winery developments in the area have shown, the climate is distinctly cooler than that of the Margaret River proper. The quality of the wines so far released strongly suggests that this is a winery to watch.

Briarose Estate Sauvignon Blanc

▼▼▼▼▼ 2002 Pale straw; an exceedingly complex bouquet which initially had faint reductive characters, but which lost those characters the more the wine was aerated. It has great length, with an appealing balance between grass/citrus and riper flavours. Thoroughly deserved its gold medal at the Qantas Wine Show of Western Australia 2002.   **rating:** 94

best drinking Now **drink with** Tuna sashimi • $19

briar ridge   ★★★★☆

Mount View Road, Mount View, NSW 2325 **region** Lower Hunter Valley
phone (02) 4990 3670 **fax** (02) 4990 7802 **open** 7 days 10–5
winemaker Karl Stockhausen, Steven Dodd **production** 27 000 cases **est.** 1972
product range ($19.50–28.50 CD) Premium range of Early Harvest Semillon, Crop Thinned Verdelho, Hand Picked Chardonnay, Methode Champenoise, Old Vines Shiraz; Signature Release range of Stockhausen Semillon, Chardonnay, Stockhausen Shiraz.
summary Semillon and Hermitage, each in various guises, have been the most consistent performers, underlying the suitability of these varieties to the Hunter Valley. The Semillon, in particular, invariably shows intense fruit and cellars well. Briar Ridge has been a model of stability with the winemaking duo of Karl Stockhausen and Steven Dodd and also has the comfort of over 48 hectares of estate vineyards, from which it is able to select the best grapes. Exports to the US and Canada.

Briar Ridge Early Harvest Semillon

▼▼▼▼▽ 2002 Light green-yellow; an intense bouquet with classic herb, grass and mineral aromas is precisely reflected in the palate, with grassy herbal flavours and a nice twist of lemony acidity on the finish. 10.9° alcohol.   **rating:** 90

best drinking 2005–2012 **best vintages** '00, '01, '02 **drink with** Crab or shellfish • $19.50

Briar Ridge Karl Stockhausen Signature Release Semillon

▼▼▼▼▽ 2002 Light green-yellow; the bouquet is quite perfumed, with herb, spice and even blossom; the palate picks up on these characters, and is distinctly intense; curiously, however, it is not particularly long. A Curate's Egg, but perhaps the good parts are what matter.   **rating:** 92

best drinking 2006–2016 **best vintages** '01, '02 **drink with** Flathead fillets • $25

Briar Ridge Hand Picked Chardonnay

▼▼▼▼ **2002** Light to medium yellow-green; the moderately intense bouquet is clean and fresh, with tangy nectarine fruit; the palate follows logically, showing bright nectarine fruit building towards the finish; if oak has been used, it is very subtle. **rating:** 86

best drinking Now–2005 **best vintages** '87, '89, '91, '92, '97, '01 **drink with** Breast of chicken • $19.50

Briar Ridge Signature Release Adrian Lockhart Chardonnay

▼▼▼▼ **2002** Medium to full yellow-green; the bouquet is complex, with obvious toasty barrel-ferment inputs; the oak is well-integrated on the light to medium-bodied palate, even though it remains in the driver's seat; the crisp, tight underlying fruit does not show the 13.9° alcohol. Barrel fermented in new French oak and left there for 9 months. **rating:** 89

best drinking Now–2007 **drink with** Balmain bugs • $25

Briar Ridge Karl Stockhausen Shiraz

▼▼▼▼▽ **2001** Medium to full red-purple; the complex bouquet has blackberry fruit, a touch of regional earth and a lick of vanilla oak; the palate reflects the bouquet, with sweet fruit on the mid-palate and a noticeably smooth texture. Both this and the Old Vines Shiraz were picked at 12.5° baume, a welcome relief, and which will do nothing to shorten their longevity. **rating:** 91

best drinking 2006–2016 **best vintages** '86, '87, '89, '91, '93, '94, '96, '01 **drink with** Braised lamb shanks • $28.50

Briar Ridge Old Vines Shiraz

▼▼▼▼▽ **2001** Medium purple-red; the moderately intense, fruit-driven bouquet has clear cherry, plum and blackberry varietal fruit, as does the flavoursome, fresh, elegant, fruit-driven palate. **rating:** 92

best drinking 2006–2011 **best vintages** '01 **drink with** Beef casserole • $20

bridgeman downs　　　NR

Barambah Road, Moffatdale via Murgon, Qld 4605 **region** South Burnett
phone (07) 4168 4784 **fax** (07) 4168 4767 **open** Thurs–Mon 10–4
winemaker Bruce Humphery-Smith **est.** NA
product range ($12–18.50 CD) Cellar White and Red; Chardonnay, Verdelho, Shiraz, Merlot Cabernet.
summary A substantial, albeit new, vineyard with 4 hectares of vines, the major plantings being of verdelho, chardonnay and shiraz and lesser amounts of merlot and cabernet sauvignon. The perpetual-motion Bruce Humphery-Smith has been retained as consultant winemaker, which should ensure wine quality. However, no tastings.

bridgewater mill　　★★★★

Mount Barker Road, Bridgewater, SA 5155 **region** Adelaide Hills
phone (08) 8339 3422 **fax** (08) 8339 5311 **open** Mon–Fri 9.30–5, weekends 10–5
winemaker Brian Croser **production** 50 000 cases **est.** 1986
product range ($10–19 CD) 3 Districts Sauvignon Blanc, Chardonnay, Sparkling Riesling Brut, Millstone Shiraz.
summary The second label of Petaluma, which consistently provides wines most makers would love to have as their top label. The fruit sources are diverse, with the majority of the Sauvignon Blanc and Chardonnay coming from Petaluma-owned or managed vineyards, while the Shiraz is made from purchased grapes.

Bridgewater Mill Three Districts Sauvignon Blanc

▼▼▼▼ **2002** Very light straw-green; the bouquet is intense, but has a distinct edge of burnt match reduction; the crisp, crunchy, citrussy, minerally palate opens well, but that touch of reduction comes to haunt the finish. Others are much more tolerant of this character than I, and some expert tasters simply see it as part and parcel of varietal character. **rating:** 86

best drinking Now **best vintages** '92, '94, '95, '00, '01 **drink with** Mousseline of scallops • $19

brindabella hills　　★★★★☆

Woodgrove Close via Hall, ACT 2618 **region** Canberra District
phone (02) 6230 2583 **fax** (02) 6230 2023 **open** Weekends, public holidays 10–5
winemaker Dr Roger Harris **production** 2000 cases **est.** 1986
product range ($18–25 CD) Riesling, Sauvignon Blanc Semillon, Chardonnay, Reserve Chardonnay, Shiraz, Shiraz Cabernet Franc, Tumbarumba Merlot, Cabernets, Cabernet, Reserve Cabernet.

summary Distinguished research scientist Dr Roger Harris presides over Brindabella Hills, which increasingly relies on estate-produced grapes, with small plantings of cabernet sauvignon, cabernet franc, merlot, shiraz, chardonnay, sauvignon blanc, semillon and riesling. Wine quality has been consistently impressive. Limited retail distribution in New South Wales and the ACT.

Brindabella Hills Riesling
♥♥♥♥♥ 2002 Light green-yellow; a typically fragrant bouquet has gentle lime and passionfruit aromas, and considerable fruit weight on the palate; not heavy, simply generous. Good balance and length.　　**rating:** 93
best drinking Now–2010 **best vintages** '90, '92, '93, '95, '01, '02 **drink with** Grilled fish • $18

Brindabella Hills Sauvignon Blanc Semillon
♥♥♥♥ 2002 Light green-yellow; an intense mix of tropical, asparagus and grass aromas does not hide the faint touch of reduction behind the fruit, but the light to medium-bodied palate throws off such problems as exist with the bouquet; lively, fresh and crisp, the Semillon contributing significantly as always.　　**rating:** 89
best drinking Now–2006 **best vintages** '01 **drink with** Gravlax • $18

Brindabella Hills Shiraz
♥♥♥♥♥ 2001 Deep red-purple; rich, deep blackberry and dark plum aromas are built around quality oak; the very concentrated and powerful palate shows its cool-grown origins, yet is fully ripe, the oak in the back seat. Great future; deserved its Blue Gold medal at the Sydney International Wine Competition.　　**rating:** 94
best drinking 2006–2016 **best vintages** '92, '98, '01 **drink with** Lamb casserole • $25

Brindabella Hills Cabernets
♥♥♥♥ 2001 Medium red; both the bouquet and palate are stacked with savoury, tangy, earthy/leafy/minty aromas and flavours. A blend of Cabernet Sauvignon, Cabernet Franc and Merlot which, for whatever reason, did not achieve anything like the ripeness of the Shiraz.　　**rating:** 86
best drinking 2004–2009 **drink with** Moroccan lamb • $20

britannia creek wines　　NR

75 Britannia Creek Road, Wesburn, Vic 3799 **region** Yarra Valley
phone (03) 5967 1006 **fax** (03) 5780 1426 **open** Weekends 10–6
winemaker Charlie Brydon **production** 1600 cases **est.** 1982
product range ($12–24 CD) Semillon, Sauvignon Blanc, Cabernets, Cabernets Reserve.
summary The wines from Britannia Creek Wines are made under the Britannia Falls label from 4 hectares of estate-grown grapes. A range of vintages are available from the cellar door, with some interesting, full-flavoured Semillon.

broadview estate　　★★★★

Rowbottoms Road, Granton, Tas 7030 **region** Southern Tasmania
phone (03) 6263 6882 **fax** (03) 6263 6840 **open** Tues–Sun 10–5
winemaker Andrew Hood (Contract) **production** 250 cases **est.** 1996
product range ($16–18 CD) Stoney Ridge Riesling, Erin Vale Chardonnay.
summary David and Kaye O'Neil planted 0.5 hectare of chardonnay and 0.25 hectare each of riesling and pinot noir in the spring of 1996, producing limited quantities of Riesling and Chardonnay.

Broadview Estate Stoney Ridge Riesling
♥♥♥♥ 2002 Light straw-green; the bouquet is quite chalky and slatey, with some apple fruit also present. The precise and focused palate has clean, bright apple flavours balanced by a hint of sweetness on the finish. **rating:** 88
best drinking Now–2008 **drink with** Smoked eel

🐌 brockville wines　　★★★

15th Street Ext, Irymple South, Vic 3498 **region** Murray Darling
phone (03) 5024 5143 **open** By appointment
winemaker Contract **production** NFP **est.** 1999
product range ($14 CD) Cabernet Sauvignon.
summary Mark Bowring, a great-grandson of WB Chaffey (responsible for the design and implementation of the irrigation scheme in the Sunraysia district in the 1880s), and wife Leigh have been growing grapes since 1975. They have 10 hectares of chardonnay, 4.4 hectares of cabernet sauvignon and 1 hectare of shiraz. Most of

the grapes are sold to local wineries, but in 1999 the Bowrings decided to have a small portion of cabernet sauvignon vinified for their own label. They chose Brockville as the name, as it is (or was) the Canadian hometown of WB Chaffey. The wine is contract-made, and most of the small quantity produced is sold in local restaurants and liquor outlets.

Brockville Cabernet Sauvignon

▼▼▼♀ 2001 Medium red-purple, quite bright; the bouquet has fresh red fruit aromas, the oak very much in the background; the youthful, light to medium-bodied palate is well made in a simple, direct, fresh style. **rating:** 84

best drinking Now–2005 **drink with** Home-made pizza • $14

broke estate/ryan family wines ★★★☆

Wollombi Road, Broke, NSW 2330 **region** Lower Hunter Valley
phone (02) 9664 3000 **fax** (02) 9665 3303 **open** Weekends and public holidays 10–5, or by appointment
winemaker Matthew Ryan **production** 18 000 cases **est.** 1988
product range ($12–35 CD) Broke Estate is the premium label with Semillon, Chardonnay, Moussant Cabernets (sparkling), Lacrima Angelorum (sweet white), Cabernet Sauvignon; the second label is Ryan Free Run Chardonnay, Single Vineyard Cabernets.
summary With a high-profile consultant viticulturist (Dr Richard Smart) achieving some spectacular early results, Broke Estate was seldom far from the headlines. Some good wines were made in 2000 and 2001; most are now sold out.

Ryan Family Single Vineyard Cabernets

▼▼▼▼ 2000 Medium red-purple; the clean, light bouquet has cedary/savoury aromas; the light to medium-bodied palate is well balanced, with dark berry, cedar and a touch of earth; good value. **rating:** 86

best drinking Now–2007 **drink with** Pizza • $12

brokenwood ★★★★☆

McDonalds Road, Pokolbin, NSW 2321 **region** Lower Hunter Valley
phone (02) 4998 7559 **fax** (02) 4998 7893 **open** 7 days 10–5
winemaker Iain Riggs **production** 70 000 cases **est.** 1970
product range ($10–90 CD) Semillon, Cricket Pitch Sauvignon Blanc Semillon, ILR Reserve Semillon, Verdelho, Chardonnay, Graveyard Chardonnay, Harlequin White, Jelka Riesling (dessert), Cricket Pitch Red, Harlequin Red, Pinot Noir, Shiraz (regional blend and Hunter Dry Red), Rayner Vineyard Shiraz, Mistress Block Shiraz, Graveyard Shiraz, Cabernet Sauvignon Merlot.
summary Deservedly fashionable winery producing consistently excellent wines. Cricket Pitch Sauvignon Blanc Semillon has an especially strong following, as has Cabernet Sauvignon; the Graveyard Shiraz is one of the best Hunter reds available today, and the unwooded Semillon is a modern classic. In 1997 it acquired a controlling interest in Seville Estate (Yarra Valley), and has also been involved in the establishment of substantial vineyards in Cowra. National distribution in Australia; exports to the US, the UK, Canada and Sweden.

Brokenwood Semillon

▼▼▼▼♀ 2002 Shows semillon's ability to shrug off inclement vintage rain. Delicate but fragrant fresh grass, lemon zest and spice aromas lead into a crisp, mouth-tingling palate with a long, bright finish. Understated style. **rating:** 93

best drinking Now–2007 **best vintages** '85, '86, '89, '92, '94, '95, '96, '97, '98, '99, '00, '01, '02 **drink with** Balmain bugs • $17

Brokenwood ILR Reserve Semillon

▼▼▼▼▼ 1997 Glowing medium to full yellow-green; very complex toasty/grassy/herbal aromas on the bouquet come through strongly on the palate, where they are joined by some honey, and freshened on the finish by good acidity and the remnants of a touch of CO_2. Built for the long haul. **rating:** 95

best drinking Now–2013 **best vintages** '94, '96, '97 **drink with** Veal saltimbocca • $35

Brokenwood Chardonnay

▼▼▼▼ 2001 Medium yellow-green, showing some development; the complex bouquet exhibits strong oak inputs to the underlying stone fruit; on the palate, big and full-on, somewhat developed; may not necessarily be a typical bottle. A blend of Padthaway, McLaren Vale and Cowra fruit. **rating:** 86

best drinking Now **drink with** Quiche Lorraine • $19

Brokenwood Shiraz

▼▼▼▼ 2000 Medium red-purple; an aromatic bouquet with some gum leaf and red berry fruit; the firm palate is centred around similar red berry flavours; needs time to build complexity. **rating:** 87

best drinking 2004–2008 **best vintages** '91, '94, '95, '96 **drink with** Barbecued leg of lamb • $21

Brokenwood Cricket Pitch Red

▼▼▼▼ 2000 Light to medium red-purple; the light bouquet has aromas of leaf, earth and red berry, but the palate is rather sweeter and richer than the bouquet suggests, with blackcurrant and a touch of chocolate. **rating:** 86

best drinking Now **drink with** Any cheese or meat • $18

Brokenwood Cabernet Sauvignon Merlot

▼▼▼▼▽ 2000 Medium to full red-purple; a clean, moderately intense bouquet with ripe blackberry and cassis fruit; while firm, the palate has ripe cabernet fruit and lingering tannins; excellent for the region. The first single-region cabernet blend from Brokenwood after 16 prior vintages from the King Valley. Gold medal 2002 National Wine Show. **rating:** 92

best drinking 2004–2009 **drink with** Backstrap of lamb • $28

broke's promise wines ★★★☆

725 Milbrodale Road, Broke, NSW 2330 **region** Lower Hunter Valley
phone (02) 6579 1165 **fax** (02) 9438 4985 **open** By appointment
winemaker Andrew Margan (Contract) **production** 2000 cases **est.** 1996
product range ($17.50–20 R) Hunter Valley Semillon, Beholden Chardonnay, Hunter Valley Shiraz, Hunter Valley Barbera.
summary Jane Marquard and Dennis Karp (and their young children) have established Broke's Promise on the banks of the Wollombi Brook, adjacent to the Yengo National Park. They have followed tradition in planting shiraz, chardonnay and semillon, and broken with it by planting barbera and olive trees – the latter two inspired by a long stay in Italy. Exports to the UK and Asia.

brook eden vineyard ★★★★

Adams Road, Lebrina, Tas 7254 **region** Northern Tasmania
phone (03) 6395 6244 **fax** (03) 6395 6211 **open** 7 days 10–5
winemaker Mike Fogarty (Contract) **production** 500 cases **est.** 1988
product range ($17–28 CD) Riesling, Unwooded Chardonnay, Tribute Chardonnay, Pinot Noir, Pinot Noir Reserve.
summary Sheila and the late Jan Bezemer established a 2.2-hectare vineyard on the 60-hectare Angus beef property which they purchased in 1987. The vineyard site is beautiful, with viticultural advice from the noted Fred Peacock.

Brook Eden Vineyard Pinot Noir

▼▼▼▼ 2001 Good purple-red colour; the bouquet has counterpoints of plummy and foresty fruit, the same characters coming through on the concentrated and long palate, opening with plum flavours and finishing with forest. Like the 2000 vintage, split the judges at the 2003 Tasmanian Wines Show. **rating:** 88

best drinking Now–2007 **drink with** Saddle of hare • $22

Brook Eden Vineyard Pinot Noir Reserve

▼▼▼▼ 2001 Very deep colour; concentrated, ripe plum fruit aromas lead into a powerful, deep and ripe palate which is slightly extractive, but may well surprise with time in bottle. **rating:** 88

best drinking 2004–2009 **drink with** Jugged hare • $28

brookhampton estate ★★★☆

South West Highway, Donnybrook, WA 6239 **region** Geographe
phone (08) 9731 0400 **fax** (08) 9731 0500 **open** 7 days 10–4
winemaker Contract **production** 3000 cases **est.** 1998
product range ($18–21 CD) Sauvignon Blanc, Chardonnay, Shiraz, Cabernet Merlot, Cabernet Sauvignon.
summary Brookhampton Estate, situated 3 kilometres south of Donnybrook, has wasted no time since its establishment in 1998. One hundred and 27 hectares of vines have been established with three fashionable red varietals to the fore: cabernet sauvignon (34 ha), shiraz (29 ha) and merlot (22 ha). One hectare of tempranillo

and 3 hectares of grenache can safely be classed as experimental. The three white varieties planted are chardonnay, sauvignon blanc and semillon. The first contract-made vintage was in 2001, understandably in small quantities given the youth of the vineyard.

Brookhampton Estate Chardonnay

TTTT 2001 Medium yellow-green; the moderately intense but quite complex bouquet strikes a good balance between the nectarine fruit and nutty oak; similarly, the medium-bodied palate has some creamy/nutty malolactic complexity around fine nectarine fruit. **rating:** 89

best drinking Now–2005 **drink with** Gravlax • $18

Brookhampton Estate Shiraz

TTTT 2002 Light to medium red; juicy, raspberry fruit aromas utterly belie the 14.5° alcohol; the palate has more fruit weight and character, with raspberry and plum, but is very low in tannin extract. Tasted four weeks after it was bottled at the end of January 2003, but is unlikely to gain weight, raising the question whether this was ultra-gentle handling in the winery or the result of a large crop. **rating:** 87

TTTTY 2001 Medium to full red-purple; complex blackberry and spice aromas lead into a rich, mouthfilling palate of blackberry and spice; the tannins and extract are well controlled, and the wine carries its 14.3° alcohol. **rating:** 91

best drinking 2004–2008 **best vintages** '01 **drink with** Roast baby kid • $21

brookland valley ★★★★☆

Caves Road, Wilyabrup, WA 6284 **region** Margaret River
phone (08) 9755 6250 **fax** (08) 9755 6214 **open** 7 days 10–5
winemaker Larry Cherubino **production** 56 500 cases **est.** 1984
product range ($16.99–55 R) Sauvignon Blanc, Chardonnay, Merlot, Cabernet Merlot; Verse 1 Semillon Sauvignon Blanc, Chardonnay, Shiraz and Cabernet Sauvignon Merlot.
summary Brookland Valley has an idyllic setting, plus much enlarged Flutes Cafe (one of the best winery restaurants in the Margaret River region) and Gallery of Wine Arts, which houses an eclectic collection of wine and food-related art and wine accessories. In 1997 BRL Hardy acquired a 50 per cent interest in the venture and took responsibility for viticulture and winemaking. The move towards richer and more complex red wines evident before the takeover has continued; the white wines have an extra degree of finesse and elegance. Exports to the UK, Germany, Switzerland, Japan and Hong Kong.

Brookland Valley Verse 1 Semillon Sauvignon Blanc

TTTTY 2002 Light straw-green; an aromatic array of lemon, citrus and passionfruit moves into a lively and fresh palate with a similar mix of passionfruit and lemon, then crunchy acidity on the finish. **rating:** 92

best drinking Now–2005 **best vintages** '99, '02 **drink with** Avocado salad • $16.99

Brookland Valley Verse 1 Chardonnay

TTTT 2002 Light to medium yellow-green; the moderately intense bouquet has some oak-induced complexity, but on the palate it is the light, fresh grapefruit and melon flavours which take control, with the oak barely perceptible; good length. **rating:** 87

best drinking Now **best vintages** '99 **drink with** Lemon chicken • $17.99

Brookland Valley Verse 1 Shiraz

TTTT 2001 Bright purple-red; ripe black cherry, blackberry and plum with a twist of vanillin oak on the bouquet; good depth to the varietal fruit of the palate, which is replete with fine, ripe tannins. **rating:** 89

best drinking 2005–2011 **drink with** Beef shashlik • $19.99

Brookland Valley Cabernet Sauvignon Merlot

TTTTY 2000 Medium red-purple; attractive red and blackcurrant fruit aromas and a pleasing fruit/oak balance and integration on both bouquet and palate; the wine has soft, fine texture and tannins, again pointing to the sophisticated use of oak. **rating:** 91

best drinking 2005–2010 **best vintages** '90, '91, '92, '93, '95, '97, '99, '01 **drink with** Char-grilled steak • $39.99

Brookland Valley Verse 1 Cabernet Sauvignon Merlot

TTTT 2001 Youthful purple-red; solid blackberry and blackcurrant fruit aromas dominate the bouquet, the oak barely obvious; a powerful wine in the mouth, deep and quite tannic, but with plentiful rich blackcurrant and mulberry fruit. Could well develop, meriting higher points. **rating:** 89

best drinking 2006–2011 **best vintages** '98, '00 **drink with** Moroccan lamb • $19.99

Brookland Valley Reserve Cabernet Sauvignon

TTTT 2000 Medium purple-red; both the bouquet and palate are flooded with oak, even though the ripe cassis/berry fruit and ripe tannins fight the good fight. **rating:** 89

best drinking 2005–2015 **drink with** Leave it in the cellar • $55

brookside vineyard   NR

5 Loaring Road, Bickley Valley, WA 6076 **region** Perth Hills
phone (08) 9291 8705 **fax** (08) 9291 5316 **open** Weekends and public holidays 11–5
winemaker Darlington Estate (Contract) **production** 350 cases **est.** 1984
product range ($17–20 CD) Chardonnay, Cabernet Sauvignon, Cobbler's Leap Cabernet Sauvignon, Methode Champenoise.
summary Brookside is one of the many doll's house-scale vineyard operations which dot the Perth Hills. It has 0.25 hectare each of chardonnay and cabernet sauvignon, basically selling the wine through a mailing list. It does, however, offer bed and breakfast accommodation at the house, with attractive views of the Bickley Valley.

brookwood estate   ★★★☆

Treeton Road, Cowaramup, WA 6284 **region** Margaret River
phone (08) 9755 5604 **open** 7 days 10–6
winemaker Trevor Mann, Lyn Mann **production** 2500 cases **est.** 1999
product range ($13–24 R) Sauvignon Blanc, Semillon Sauvignon Blanc, Chenin Blanc, Shiraz, Cabernet Sauvignon.
summary Trevor and Lyn Mann began the development of their 50-hectare property in 1996, and now have 1.3 hectares each of shiraz, cabernet sauvignon, semillon, sauvignon blanc and chenin blanc planted. An on-site winery was constructed in 1999 to accommodate the first vintage. Viticultural consultants provide advice on management in the vineyard, and the Manns are in the course of establishing export markets.

🍂 brothers in arms   ★★★★

Lake Plains Road, Langhorne Creek, SA 5255 (postal) **region** Langhorne Creek
phone (08) 8537 3060 **fax** (08) 8537 3112 **open** Not
winemaker David Freschi **production** 8000 cases **est.** 1998
product range ($40 R) Shiraz.
summary The Adams family has been growing grapes at Langhorne Creek since 1891, when the first vines at the famed Metala vineyards were planted. Tom and Guy Adams are the fifth generation to own and work the vineyard, and over the past 20 years have both improved the viticulture and expanded the plantings to the present 40 hectares (shiraz and cabernet sauvignon). It was not until 1998 that they took the next step, deciding to hold back a small proportion of the production for vinification under the Brothers in Arms brand. The omnipresent Dan Phillips of The Grateful Palate imports the wine into the US, where it was rapturously received, selling out in 8 weeks after its release into the Australian market. The brothers' vision is to steadily raise production to around 16 000 cases, and to construct a 300-tonne winery to handle the crush. The winemaker is David Freschi, who has already made a name for himself with his brand Casa Freschi. Exports to the US, Canada, the UK and Singapore.

Brothers in Arms Shiraz

TTTT 2000 Medium red-purple; the solid bouquet has a mix of savoury, earthy and vanilla aromas on the one hand, and black fruits and spice on the other; ripe blackberry and chocolate flavours, soft tannins and sweet American oak drive the palate. **rating:** 89

best drinking 2005–2012 **drink with** Osso buco • $40

brown brothers   ★★★★

Snow Road, Milawa, Vic 3678 **region** King Valley
phone (03) 5720 5500 **fax** (03) 5720 5511 **open** 7 days 9–5
winemaker Terry Barnett, Wendy Cameron **production** 770 000 cases **est.** 1885
product range ($9.90–46.80 R) A kaleidoscopic array of varietal wines, with a cross-hatch of appellations, the broadest being Victorian (e.g. Victorian Shiraz), more specific being King Valley (e.g. NV Brut and Pinot Chardonnay) and Milawa (e.g. Noble Riesling), then the Limited Release, Family Selection (e.g. Very Old Tokay and King Valley Chardonnay) and the Family Reserve ranges. Dinning's Shiraz is a cellar-door special; other wines also exclusive to cellar door include Viognier, Tempranillo, Graciano and a range of Limited Release mainstream varietals. A new super-premium range of wines (released March 2003) under the Patricia

label (the matriarch of the family) includes Chardonnay, Pinot Chardonnay Brut, Shiraz, Merlot, Cabernet Sauvignon and Late Harvested Noble Riesling.

summary Brown Brothers draws upon a considerable number of vineyards spread throughout a range of site climates, ranging from very warm to very cool, with the climate varying according to altitude. It is also known for the diversity of varieties with which it works, and the wines always represent excellent value for money. Deservedly one of the most successful family wineries in Australia. The wines are exported to over 20 countries spread throughout Europe, the UK, Asia and the Far East. Conspicuously, Brown Brothers still remains out of the US market.

Brown Brothers King Valley Riesling

▼▼▼▼ 2002 Light green-yellow; the bouquet is clean, crisp and correct, although not particularly aromatic; the palate is fine and well structured, but, once again, not showing a lot of fruit. Should improve with time in bottle.   **rating: 85**

best drinking Now–2007 **drink with** Asparagus salad • $14.00

Brown Brothers Everton Chardonnay Sauvignon Blanc Pinot Grigio

▼▼▼▼ 2002 Light straw-green; a crisp and tangy bouquet in which the Sauvignon Blanc component is quite obvious, with grassy spicy elements; the lively, fresh and crisp palate has plenty of fruit, and a nice dry finish, Presumably a tripartite marriage of convenience, but works surprisingly well.   **rating: 87**

best drinking Now–2005 **drink with** Scampi • $13

Brown Brothers Roussanne

▼▼▼▼ 2001 Light to medium yellow-green; the clean, fresh bouquet has bright citrus/fruit salad aromas, which come through on the fresh, fruity but dry palate; wobbles fractionally on the finish, perhaps. A cellar-door release; it is not easy to find distinctive varietal character in the wine, but there is nothing new in that.   **rating: 86**

best drinking Now **drink with** Grilled fish • $15.40

Brown Brothers Pinot Grigio

▼▼▼▼ 2002 Distinctive, light pink-grey; gravelly pear aromas lead into a green pear and apple-flavoured palate, which, if nothing else, is certainly varietal.   **rating: 85**

best drinking Now–2005 **drink with** Salmon • $15.60

Brown Brothers Whitlands Pinot Chardonnay

▼▼▼▼ 1997 Medium yellow-green; an interesting and quite pungent lemon rind/lemon spice bouquet, then a long, intense palate with very lemony acidity. Treads perilously close to the edge.   **rating: 87**

best drinking Now–2005 **best vintages** '90, '91, '92, '93, '94, '96 **drink with** Shellfish • $39

Brown Brothers Noble Riesling

▼▼▼▼▽ 1999 Glowing gold; rich cumquat and toffee aromas lead into a very rich, luscious and mouthfilling palate, the flavours tracking the bouquet; in a style virtually unique to Brown Brothers.   **rating: 92**

best drinking Now–2007 **best vintages** '92, '94, '96, '98, '99 **drink with** Sticky date pudding • $26

Brown Brothers Patricia Shiraz

▼▼▼▼▽ 2000 Deep red-purple; vanilla, dark chocolate, black cherry all come through on the bouquet, the vanilla first and last. The palate is powerful and concentrated, with lashings of American oak and a warm finish from the 14.5° alcohol. Made in heroic style, and will appeal to many for precisely that reason.   **rating: 90**

best drinking 2006–2016 **best vintages** '00 **drink with** Char-grilled rump steak • $44.95

Brown Brothers Barbera

▼▼▼▽ 2001 Light to medium red-purple; the bouquet is clean, but with some faintly vegetal overtones to the red berry fruit; the palate opens with sweeter, darker, riper fruit, though still with a touch of herb and a slightly tart finish.   **rating: 84**

best drinking Now–2005 **drink with** Spiced Italian sausages • $15.50

Brown Brothers Cellar Door Release Tempranillo

▼▼▼▼ 2001 Light to medium red-purple; the clean and fresh bouquet does not have overmuch distinction, but the palate really opens up, intense and long, with spicy savoury flavours and obvious acid retention. Spent 16 months in new and 2-year-old American oak, which it has fully absorbed. Grown 20 kilometres east of Milawa.   **rating: 85**

best drinking Now–2006 **drink with** Air-dried Spanish ham • $18.80

Brown Brothers Patricia Merlot

▼▼▼▼ 2000 Medium red-purple; the bouquet has coffee, mocha and some savoury/olive aromas lurking in the background; the very big, rich, full, ripe and oaky palate says much more about red wine than it does about Merlot, with neither varietal character nor the appropriate texture. Spends between 12 and 15 months in 100 per cent new French oak; sourced from Brown Brothers' own Banksdale Vineyard in the King Valley.

rating: 88

best drinking 2006–2016 **drink with** Lamb shanks • $44.95

Brown Brothers Patricia Cabernet Sauvignon

▼▼▼▼▼ 2000 Very deep red-purple; lovely cassis berry aromas are married with but not swamped by French oak on the bouquet. The medium to full-bodied palate has excellent structure, with plenty of fruit, finishing with fine ripe tannins and positive but well-handled oak.

rating: 94

best drinking 2006–2016 **best vintages** '00 **drink with** Kangaroo fillet • $44.95

Brown Brothers Victorian Cabernet Sauvignon

▼▼▼▼ 2001 Medium purple-red; the moderately intense, clean bouquet ranges through blackberry, earth and olive, the medium-bodied palate with much the same flavours, plus some oak sweetening.

rating: 86

best drinking 2004–2010 **drink with** Roast beef • $18.60

Brown Brothers Very Old Tokay

▼▼▼▼▽ NV Medium mahogany-brown, with an olive rim; the bouquet is moderately sweet, with tangy tea-leaf and Christmas cake; the palate is distinctly less luscious than that of the Muscat, but is intense and long, the quality much the same. Both these wines appear to be better than prior blends.

rating: 92

best drinking Now–2010 **drink with** After coffee • $27.80

Brown Brothers Liqueur Muscat

▼▼▼▼▽ NV Deep brown-red, with some olive on the rim; a complex and rich bouquet with luscious raisiny plum pudding aromas; the palate has a wonderfully viscous mouthfeel, the flavours strongly varietal, raisiny and rich; shows the clever blending of very old and younger material.

rating: 93

best drinking Now–2010 **drink with** Nuts, dried fruits • $29.80

brown hill estate ★★★

Cnr Rosa Brook and Barrett Road, Rosa Brook, WA 6285 **region** Margaret River
phone (08) 9757 4003 **fax** (08) 9757 4004 **open** 7 days 10–5
winemaker Nathan Bailey **production** 1500 cases **est.** 1995
product range ($10–20 CD) Sauvignon Blanc, Semillon Sauvignon Blanc, Autumn Mist, Desert Rose, Shiraz, Cabernet Sauvignon.
summary The Bailey family's stated aim is to produce top-quality wines at affordable prices; this is to be achieved by uncompromising viticultural practices emphasising low yields per hectare, in conjunction with the family being involved in all stages of production with minimum outside help. They have established 7 hectares each of shiraz and cabernet sauvignon, 4 hectares of semillon and 2 hectares each of sauvignon blanc and merlot, and by the standards of the Margaret River, the prices are indeed affordable.

Brown Hill Estate Sauvignon Blanc

▼▼▼▽ 2002 Light straw-green; there is a faintly smoky background to the herb and grass bouquet, the light-bodied palate fleshed out by a touch of residual sugar.

rating: 84

best drinking Now **drink with** Shellfish • $14

Brown Hill Estate Shiraz

▼▼▼▼ 2001 Youthful red-purple; there is plenty of red berry and black cherry fruit, together with controlled oak, on the bouquet; the palate is youthful, and seems slightly underworked; needs time to settle down in bottle, but should repay patience.

rating: 87

best drinking 2005–2010 **drink with** Braised rabbit • $16

browns of padthaway ★★★★

Keith Road, Padthaway, SA 5271 **region** Padthaway
phone (08) 8765 6063 **fax** (08) 8765 6083 **open** At Padthaway Estate
winemaker Contract **production** 35 000 cases **est.** 1993

product range ($10–21 R) Classic Diamond, Riesling, Sauvignon Blanc, Non-Wooded Chardonnay, Verdelho, T-Trellis Shiraz, Ernest Shiraz, Redwood Cabernet Malbec, Myra Family Reserve Cabernet Sauvignon, Sparkling Shiraz.

summary The Brown family has for many years been the largest independent grape grower in Padthaway, a district in which most of the vineyards were established and owned by Wynns, Seppelt, Lindemans and Hardys, respectively. After a slow start, has produced some excellent wines since 1998.

Browns Of Padthaway T-Trellis Shiraz

♥♥♥♥♥ 1998 Medium to full red; a complex array of spice, earth, leather and licorice aromas lead into an attractively soft and ripe palate, with luscious (but not jammy) fruit and perfectly integrated oak. Gold medal Limestone Coast Wine Show 2002. **rating:** 94

best drinking Now–2012 **best vintages** '98 **drink with** Braised rabbit • $21

brush box vineyard NR

c/- 6 Grandview Parade, Mona Vale, NSW 2103 **region** Lower Hunter Valley
phone (02) 9979 4468 **fax** (02) 9999 5303 **open** Not
winemaker (Contract) **production** 1000 cases **est.** 1997
product range ($13–17 CD) Verdelho, Chardonnay, Cabernet Merlot.
summary Paul and Suzanne Mackay have established their 6.5-hectare Brushbox Vineyard at Broke. It is situated in a secluded part of the Fordwich Hills, with views across the Wollombi Valley to the northern perimeter of Yengo National Park. It is planted to chardonnay, verdelho, cabernet sauvignon and merlot and so far sold by mail order only.

☙ bulga wine estates ★★★☆

Bulga Road, Swan Hill, Vic 3585 **region** Swan Hill
phone (03) 5037 6685 **fax** (03) 5037 6992 **open** By appointment
winemaker Rod Bouchier **est.** 1999
product range ($15 R) Chardonnay, Shiraz.
summary Bulga Wine Estates draws on a little over 50 hectares: chardonnay (10 ha), cabernet sauvignon (10 ha), the remainder given over to shiraz and a little colombard. Only part of the wine is vinified under the Bulga Wine Estates label, and handsomely so.

Bulga Wine Estates Chardonnay

♥♥♥♥ 1999 Light to medium yellow-green; the gentle mix of melon and fig fruit of the bouquet is still fresh, the oak subtle. The palate provides a replay of the bouquet, with soft stone fruit and fig which has developed very well, and which will hold its form for some time yet. All in all, a surprise packet. **rating:** 88

best drinking Now–2005 **drink with** Steamed mussels • $15

Bulga Wine Estates Albert's Block Shiraz

♥♥♥♥ 2000 Bright and clear red-purple; the moderately intense bouquet has a complex array of leather, earth, spice and berry aromas, the palate following with rich red fruits plus good extract, tannin and oak management. Another surprise. **rating:** 88

best drinking Now–2008 **drink with** Venison sausages • $15

bullers beverford ★★★

Murray Valley Highway, Beverford, Vic 3590 **region** Swan Hill
phone (03) 5037 6305 **fax** (03) 5037 6803 **open** Mon–Sat 9–5
winemaker Richard Buller (Jnr) **production** 50 000 cases **est.** 1952
product range ($5.50–13 CD) Victoria Riesling, Victoria Spatlese Lexia, Semillon, Magee Semillon Chardonnay, Chenin Blanc, Sails Unwooded Chardonnay, Chardonnay, Victoria Chardonnay, Sparkling Spumante, Victoria Rose, Shiraz, Victoria Shiraz Grenache Mourvedre, Sails Shiraz Merlot Cabernet, Merlot, Magee Cabernet Sauvignon Shiraz, Cabernet Sauvignon; fortifieds include Port, Tokay, Muscat.
summary Traditional wines which in the final analysis reflect both their Riverland origin and a fairly low-key approach to style in the winery. It is, however, one of the few remaining sources of reasonable quality bulk fortified wine available to the public, provided in 22-litre Valorex barrels at $6.50 per litre.

bullers calliope ★★★★★

Three Chain Road, Rutherglen, Vic 3685 **region** Rutherglen
phone (02) 6032 9660 **fax** (02) 6032 8005 **open** Mon–Sat 9–5, Sun 10–5
winemaker Andrew Buller **production** 4000 cases **est.** 1921
product range ($14–65 CD) Limited Release range of Marsanne, Chardonnay, Shiraz, Merlot Cabernet Franc; Mondeuse Shiraz, Shiraz, Durif.
summary The Buller family is very well known and highly regarded in northeast Victoria, the business benefiting from vines now 80 years old. The rating is very much influenced by the superb releases of Museum fortified wines. Limited releases of Calliope Shiraz and Shiraz Mondeuse can also be very good. The rating is for the fortified wines.

Bullers Calliope Limited Release Shiraz

TTTTY 2000 Medium to full red-purple; the clean, moderately intense bouquet has blackberry and plum fruit and integrated oak; the lusciously sweet and smooth palate offers raspberry and blackberry fruit, the tannins fine and ripe. The wine spent 18 months in American oak, but the impact is barely perceptible. Made from dry-grown old vines and open fermented. Particularly good value. **rating:** 90
best drinking 2004–2014 **best vintages** '00 **drink with** Rich meat dishes • $19

Bullers Calliope Rare Liqueur Tokay

TTTTT NV Deep golden brown; a classic mix of sweet tea-leaf and Christmas cake aromas is followed by an outstanding palate showing the complexity which only age (and first-class base material) can bring; some nutty characters join the tea-leaf and Christmas cake of the bouquet. **rating:** 94
best drinking Now **drink with** Strictly unnecessary, a meal in itself • $65

Bullers Calliope Rare Liqueur Muscat

TTTTT NV Deep brown with a touch of olive on the rim; full and deep, almost into chocolate, with intense raisined fruit; richly textured, with great structure to the raisined/plum pudding fruit flavours, and obvious rancio age. Clean finish and aftertaste. **rating:** 95
best drinking Now **drink with** Strictly unnecessary, a meal in itself • $65

bulong estate ★★★☆

70 Summerhill Road, Yarra Junction, Vic 3797 (postal) **region** Yarra Valley
phone (03) 5967 2487 **fax** (03) 5967 2487 **open** Not
winemaker Contract **production** 2000 cases **est.** 1994
product range ($16–24 ML) Sauvignon Blanc, Pinot Gris, Chardonnay, Pinot Noir, Merlot, Cabernet Franc.
summary Judy and Howard Carter purchased their beautifully situated 45-hectare property in 1994, looking down into the valley below and across to the nearby ranges with Mount Donna Buang at their peak. Most of the grapes from the immaculately tended vineyard are sold, with limited quantities made for the Bulong Estate label.

Bulong Estate Sauvignon Blanc

TTTT 2002 Light straw-green; the fresh, light and crisp bouquet has mineral and slate aromas, but it is not until you get to the fine and delicate palate that the first hints of passionfruit and citrus appear; light-bodied, but has pure varietal character. **rating:** 88
best drinking Now **drink with** Fresh seafood • $16

Bulong Estate Chardonnay

TTTT 2002 Light straw-green; the light bouquet has stone fruit aromas and subtle oak; the clean palate is well balanced and well made, but surprisingly light given the tiny and concentrated 2002 vintage. **rating:** 85
best drinking Now–2005 **drink with** Light seafood • $24

Bulong Estate Pinot Noir

TTTY 2002 Light to medium red-purple; savoury, foresty earthy aromas and flavours lead the way; the plum fruit of the palate is slightly desiccated, suggesting some fruit shrivelling prior to harvest. **rating:** 84
best drinking Now–2005 **drink with** Light Asian • $24

🐌 bundaleera vineyard ★★★★

449 Glenwood Road, Relbia, Tas 7258 **region** Northern Tasmania
phone (03) 6343 1231 **fax** (03) 6343 1250 **open** Not
winemaker Rosevears Estate (contract) **production** 1000 cases **est.** 1996

product range ($16.50–27.50 CD) Riesling, Unwooded Chardonnay, Chardonnay, Pinot Noir.

summary David (a consultant metallurgist in the mining industry) and Jan Jenkinson have established 2.5 hectares of vines in a sunny, sheltered north to northeast position in the North Esk Valley. The 12-hectare property on which their house and vineyard are established give them some protection from the urban sprawl of Launceston. Jan is the full-time viticulturist and gardener for the immaculately tended property. The wines are on the wine list at La Notte in Lygon Street, Carlton, and can be purchased from David Jenkinson via his Melbourne office, phone (03) 9650 9547, fax (03) 9650 9548.

Bundaleera Vineyard Riesling

▼▼▼▼ 2001 Medium straw-green; the potent bouquet already shows some development, but desirably so; a big, bold wine in the mouth, with generous flavour and powerful structure.   **rating:** 89

best drinking Now–2006 **drink with** Salad Niçoise • $16.50

Bundaleera Vineyard Pinot Noir

▼▼▼▼▽ 2001 Medium red-purple; a clean and fresh bouquet offers dark plum and forest aromas; the powerful, concentrated and savoury palate has a slightly grippy, emphatic finish, which will probably sort itself out with a few more years in bottle. Certainly has abundant presence right now.   **rating:** 90

best drinking 2004–2008 **best vintages** '01 **drink with** Braised duck • $27.50

bungawarra   NR

Bents Road, Ballandean, Qld 4382 **region** Granite Belt
phone (07) 4684 1128 **fax** (07) 4684 1128 **open** 7 days 10–4.30
winemaker Jeff Harden **production** 1700 cases **est.** 1975
product range ($9–18 CD) Traminer, Thomas Semillon, Foundation Chardonnay, Reserve Chardonnay, Bliss, Festival Red, Shiraz, Cabernet Sauvignon, Liquid Amber, Paragon Liqueur, Liqueur Muscat.
summary Now owned by Jeff Harden. It draws upon 5 hectares of mature vineyards which over the years have shown themselves capable of producing red wines of considerable character.

bunnamagoo estate   ★★★☆

Bunnamagoo, Rockley, NSW 2795 **region** Southern New South Wales Zone
phone (02) 6377 5216 **fax** (02) 6377 5231 **open** Not
winemaker Jon Reynolds (Contract) **production** 2500 cases **est.** 1995
product range ($19–30 ML) Chardonnay, Cabernet Sauvignon.
summary Bunnamagoo Estate (on one of the first land grants in the region) is situated near the historic town of Rockley, which is as far south of Bathurst as it is west of Oberon. Here a 7-hectare vineyard planted to chardonnay, merlot and cabernet sauvignon has been established by Paspaley Pearls, a famous name in the pearl industry. The wines are contract-made under the direction of Jon Reynolds at the Cabonne Winery in Orange, and are sold by mail order and email. No tastings in the past year; rating for previous tastings.

burge family winemakers   ★★★★

Barossa Way, Lyndoch, SA 5351 **region** Barossa Valley
phone (08) 8524 4644 **fax** (08) 8524 4444 **open** Thurs–Mon 10–5
winemaker Rick Burge **production** 2700 cases **est.** 1928
product range ($15.80–38 CD) Olive Hill Riesling, Olive Hill Semillon, Olive Hill Shiraz Grenache Mourvedre, The Renoux (Shiraz Merlot Cabernet), Clochmerle (Grenache Cabernet), Garnacha Old Vine Grenache, A Nice Red (Merlot Cabernet), Draycott Shiraz.
summary Rick Burge and Burge Family Winemakers (not to be confused with Grant Burge, although the families are related) has established itself as an icon producer of exceptionally rich, lush and concentrated Barossa red wines. Rick Burge's sense of humour is evident with the Clochmerle Grenache Cabernet, and even more with the Merlot Cabernet blend made for those who come to cellar door and ask, 'Do you have a nice red?' Rick Burge is happy to provide precisely what they ask for.

Burge Family Olive Hill Riesling

▼▼▼▼ 2002 Light to medium yellow-green; a clean, crisp bouquet with flint and herb aromas is followed by a lively, full-flavoured palate with a mix of citrus, lime and mineral flavours. Well above average for the Barossa Valley floor.   **rating:** 89

best drinking Now–2008 **drink with** Honeyed chicken • $15.80

Burge Family Olive Hill Semillon

▼▼▼▼ 2002 Lovely green colour; a solid grassy/lemony bouquet; the palate has abundant, rich fruit flavour all suggesting drink as soon as possible, but on the other hand, keeping a bottle or two might provide you with a pleasant surprise. The wine has not been contaminated by oak, incidentally. **rating:** 87

best drinking Now **drink with** Kassler • $19.80

Burge Family Draycott Shiraz

▼▼▼▼▽ 2001 Medium to full red-purple; ripe, stewed plum, spice and prune aromas are followed by a very rich, ultra-ripe palate, replete with ripe tannins but subtle oak; USA here we come. As ever, 14.5° alcohol. **rating:** 90

best drinking 2005–2015 **best vintages** '88, '91, '94, '95, '98, '99, '00 **drink with** Wild duck; failing that, domestic duck • $38

Burge Family The Renoux Shiraz Merlot Cabernet

▼▼▼▼ 2001 Medium to full purple-red; fragrant berry and earth aromas are joined by hints of leaf and mint on the bouquet; the palate has very sweet raspberry and blackberry flavours; needs time to knit together. 45 per cent Shiraz, 38 per cent Merlot, 17 per cent Cabernet Sauvignon. **rating:** 87

best drinking 2006–2011 **drink with** Roast ox kidney • $27

Burge Family Olive Hill Shiraz Grenache Mourvedre

▼▼▼▼ 2001 Medium to full red-purple; a complex array of blackberry, anise, plum jam and spice, then a smooth, medium-bodied palate, with surprisingly soft tannins and a hint of chocolate on the farewell. **rating:** 89

best drinking 2004–2009 **drink with** Game • $29

Burge Family Garnacha Old Vine Grenache

▼▼▼▼ 2001 Medium to full red-purple; abundant prune, blackberry jam and spice aromas are followed by a voluptuously sweet and rich mid-palate, but the 15.5° alcohol really does burn the finish. **rating:** 87

best drinking 2004–2009 **best vintages** '00 **drink with** Game pie • $27

🍇 burke & hills   NR

Cargo Road, Lidster, NSW 2800 **region** Orange
phone (02) 6362 1101 **fax** (02) 6362 1101 **open** Fri–Mon 11–5 at Lakeside Cafe, Lake Canobolas
winemaker Christophe Derrez **production** 2800 cases **est.** 1999
product range ($18–23 CD) Sauvignon Blanc, Chardonnay; others in the pipeline including a Pinot Noir, Bordeaux-style red blend and sparkling.
summary This is an interesting venture: in an unofficial background response to my standard request for insight into motives and goals, founder Doug Burke wrote, 'I guess you would scream if you heard another new small vineyard/winery prattling on about small volumes, low yields, best practice ... in a quest for great quality, subtlety and complexity.' Very likely, but here the facts speak for themselves: a non-fatal search led to the selection of a steeply sloping, frost-free north-facing slope rising to an altitude of 940 metres on Mount Lidster; the planting of 10 hectares of classic varieties, but including an excellent mix of MV6, 114, 115 and 777 clones of pinot noir; the appointment of Brett Wilkins as viticulturist (with leading consultant Di Davidson in the background) and former Gevrey Chambertin-cum-Flying Winemaker Christophe Derrez; the erection of a 200-tonne capacity winery to supplement cash flow by undertaking contract winemaking; and the running of the Lakeside Cafe at Lake Canobolas, 2 kilometres from the winery ... All these things point to a carefully structured business plan with a simple objective: in Burke's words, 'Don't go broke.'

burnbrae   ★★★★

Hill End Road, Erudgere via Mudgee, NSW 2850 **region** Mudgee
phone (02) 6373 3504 **fax** (02) 6373 3601 **open** Wed–Mon 9–5
winemaker Alan Cox **production** NFP **est.** 1976
product range ($10–18 CD) Sauvignon Blanc, Chardonnay, Pinot Noir, Shiraz, Malbec, Cabernet Shiraz, Cabernet Sauvignon, Vintage Port, Liqueur Muscat.
summary The founding Mace family sold Burnbrae to Alan Cox in 1996. It continues as an estate-based operation with 23 hectares of vineyards. Since that time the Burnbrae wines have gone from strength to strength, improving beyond all recognition, attesting to the value of the old, dry-grown vines and the accumulation of winemaking experience by Alan Cox. Given the difficult vintages, the quality of the 2000 and 2001 unbottled red wines tasted at the 2002 Mudgee Wine show is quite remarkable.

burramurra ★★★☆

Barwood Park, High Street, Nagambie, Vic 3608 **region** Goulburn Valley
phone (03) 5794 2181 **fax** (03) 5794 2755 **open** Fri–Sun and public holidays 10–5, or by appointment
winemaker Mitchelton (Contract) **production** 1000 cases **est.** 1988
product range ($15–20 R) Sauvignon Blanc, Cabernet Sauvignon Merlot.
summary Burramurra is the relatively low-profile vineyard operation of the Honourable Pat McNamara. Most of the production is sold to Mitchelton; a small amount is contract-made for the Burramurra label. Glowing reviews in the US have led to brisk export business with that country and to the selection of Burramurra by various international airlines.

burrundulla NR

Sydney Road, Mudgee, NSW 2850 **region** Mudgee
phone (02) 6372 1620 **fax** (02) 6372 4058 **open** Not
winemaker Contract **est.** 1996
product range NA
summary A very substantial venture but one which is still in its infancy; the Cox family (Chris, Michael and Ted) are in the course of establishing 54 hectares of vineyards planted to chardonnay, shiraz and cabernet sauvignon.

🐦 burton premium wines ★★★★

248 Flinders Street, Adelaide, SA 5000 (postal) **region** Warehouse
phone (02) 9403 1012 **fax** (02) 9418 2197 **open** Not
winemaker Mike Farmilo, Pat Tocacui (Contract) **production** 5000 cases **est.** 1998
product range ($18–35 ML) McLaren Vale Chardonnay, McLaren Vale Shiraz, Limestone Coast Merlot, South East Australia Cabernet Merlot, Coonawarra Cabernet Sauvignon, Limestone Coast Cabernet Sauvignon.
summary Burton Premium Wines has neither vineyards nor winery, purchasing its grapes and having the wines made in various locations by contract winemakers. It brings together the marketing and financial skills of managing director Nigel Burton and the extensive wine industry experience (as a senior judge) of Dr Ray Healy, who is director in charge of all aspects of winemaking.

Burton Mclaren Vale Chardonnay

TTTT 2001 Light to medium yellow-green; smooth melon fruit and just the faintest touch of toast on the bouquet are reproduced on the smooth, medium-bodied palate; here the whisper of oak travels alongside the melon fruit; good balance and acidity. **rating:** 87
best drinking Now **drink with** Fish terrine • $22

Burton Mclaren Vale Shiraz

TTTTY 2000 Medium red-purple; the clean bouquet has dark plum fruit plus touches of chocolate and vanilla; the rich and supple palate presents similar flavours cradled in gentle oak. Good mouthfeel and balance.
rating: 90
best drinking 2004–2010 **best vintages** '00 **drink with** Game pie • $33

Burton Coonawarra Cabernet Sauvignon

TTTTY 2000 Medium to full red-purple; a solid blackberry and blackcurrant bouquet, with touches of earth, expresses both region and variety; the palate builds on the characters of the bouquet, with cedary, savoury touches to the blackberry fruit. **rating:** 90
best drinking 2005–2010 **drink with** Braised neck of lamb • $30

by farr ★★★★★

c/- Bannockburn, Midlands Highway, Bannockburn, Vic 3331 **region** Geelong
phone (03) 5281 1979 **fax** (03) 5281 1979 **open** Not
winemaker Gary Farr **production** 2000 cases **est.** 1999
product range ($45 R) Viognier, Chardonnay, Pinot Noir, Shiraz.
summary In 1994 Gary Farr and family planted just under 5 hectares of clonally selected viognier, chardonnay, pinot noir and shiraz on a north-facing hill which is directly opposite the Bannockburn Winery, having acquired the land from the late Stuart Hooper (Bannockburn's then owner). For a multiplicity of reasons, in 1999 Farr decided to establish his own label for some of the grapes coming from the vineyard; the

remainder go to Bannockburn. The quality of the wines is exemplary, their character subtly different from those of Bannockburn itself due, in Farr's view, to the interaction between the terroir of the hill and the clonal selection. As from 2000, the reference to Bannockburn was removed from the front label. Exports to the US, the UK, Japan, Denmark, Hong Kong, Singapore and Malaysia.

calais estate   NR

Palmers Lane, Pokolbin, NSW 2321 **region** Lower Hunter Valley
phone (02) 4998 7654 **fax** (02) 4998 7813 **open** 7 days 9–5
winemaker Adrian Sheridan **production** 11 000 cases **est.** 1987
product range ($14.50–40 CD) Semillon, Viognier, Shiraz, Chambourcin.
summary Richard and Susan Bradley purchased the substantial Calais Estate winery in April 2000. Long-serving winemaker Adrian Sheridan continues his role, and the estate offers a wide range of facilities for visitors, ranging from private function rooms to picnic spots to an undercover outdoor entertaining area. No recent tastings.

caledonia australis   NR

PO Box 54, Abbotsford, Vic 3067 **region** Gippsland
phone (03) 9416 4156 **fax** (03) 9416 4157 **open** Not
winemaker Tom Armstrong **est.** NA
product range ($18.65–40.50 ML) Chardonnay, Mount Macleod Pinot Noir, Pint Noir, Pinot Noir Reserve.
summary The reclusive Caledonia Australis is a Pinot Noir and Chardonnay specialist, with a total of 18 hectares planted to chardonnay and pinot noir in three separate vineyard locations. All the vineyards are in the Leongatha area, on red, free-draining, high-ironstone soils, on a limestone or marl base, and the slopes are east to northeast facing. Small-batch winemaking has resulted in consistently high-quality wines.

cambewarra estate   ★★★☆

520 Illaroo Road, Cambewarra, NSW 2540 **region** Shoalhaven Coast
phone (02) 4446 0170 **fax** (02) 4446 0170 **open** Thurs–Sun 10–5, public and school holidays
winemaker Tamburlaine (Contract) **production** 3500 cases **est.** 1991
product range ($15.50–36 CD) Verdelho, Unwooded Chardonnay, Wooded Chardonnay, Botrytis Chardonnay, Sparkling Chambourcin, Petit Rouge, Chambourcin, Cabernet Sauvignon, Vintage Port.
summary Geoffrey and Louise Cole founded Cambewarra Estate near the Shoalhaven River on the central southern coast of New South Wales, with contract winemaking competently carried out (a considerable distance away) at Tamburlaine Winery in the Hunter Valley. Cambewarra continues to produce attractive wines which have had significant success in wine shows.

Cambewarra Estate Chardonnay
▼▼▼▼▽ **2000** Bright yellow-green; the bouquet is clean but quite complex, marrying stone fruit with carefully measured French and American oak; the light to medium-bodied palate is supple and smooth, aging slowly and impressively.   **rating:** 90
best drinking Now–2006 **best vintages** '00 **drink with** Pan-fried veal • $20

Cambewarra Estate Chambourcin
▼▼▼▼ **2002** Typical, deep purple-red; a smooth dark berry bouquet with hints of leather and spice flows into a palate with good weight and depth, and well above-average structure. A top example of the variety, clean as a whistle.   **rating:** 89
best drinking Now–2005 **best vintages** '94, '97, '98, '02 **drink with** Italian cuisine • $21

camden estate vineyards   NR

172 Macarthur Road, Spring Farm, NSW 2570 **region** South Coast Zone
phone 0414 913 089 **fax** (02) 4568 0110 **open** Not
winemaker Evans Wine Company **production** 800 cases **est.** 1975
product range ($12–16 R) Chardonnay.
summary Camden Estate Vineyards was originally known as Bridge Farm Wines when it was established by Norman Hanckel. The 17 hectares of chardonnay he planted was one of the largest single plantings in Australia at the time, if not the largest. Over the years, most of the grapes were sold to other producers, various estate labels appearing and then disappearing in relatively short order. The grapes are now sold to the Evans Wine Company, which makes and distributes the wine from the vineyard under the Camden Park label.

campbells ★★★★★

Murray Valley Highway, Rutherglen, Vic 3685 **region** Rutherglen
phone (02) 6032 9458 **fax** (02) 6032 9870 **open** Mon–Sat 9–5, Sun 10–5
winemaker Colin Campbell **production** 60 000 cases **est.** 1870
product range ($9–94 CD) Riesling, Gewurztraminer, Semillon, Chardonnay Semillon, Cellar White, Pedro Ximinez, Trebbiano, Limited Release Chardonnay, Chardonnay, Autumn Harvest, Bobbie Burns Shiraz, Cellar Red, The Barkly Durif, Shiraz Durif Cabernet, Ruby Cabernet, Cabernets, Cabernet Sauvignon. Muscats and Tokays in Classic, Grand, Rare Rutherglen Classification hierarchy.
summary A wide range of table and fortified wines of ascending quality and price, which are always honest; as so often happens in this part of the world, the fortified wines are the best, with the extremely elegant Isabella Rare Tokay and Merchant Prince Rare Muscat at the top of the tree. For all that, the table wines are impressive in a full-bodied style; the winery rating is for the fortified wines. A feature of the cellar door is an extensive range of back vintage releases of small parcels of wine not available through any other outlet. National distribution through Red+White; exports to the UK, the US and Canada.

Campbells Rose

ŢŢŢŢ 2002 Bright, fresh fuchsia pink; flowery strawberry aromas set the scene for the flavours of the palate, which are joined by spice and appreciable residual sugar on the finish. Predominantly shiraz; a knock-down cellar-door style.   **rating:** 85

best drinking Now **drink with** Chinese • $14.10

Campbells Classic Rutherglen Tokay 500 ml

ŢŢŢŢŢ NV The colour is slightly deeper than that of the bottom tier wine; the pure bouquet has a mix of tea-leaf, toffee and Christmas cake; clean spirit. The palate has much more intensity, power and length, but still with pristine varietal character.   **rating:** 93

best drinking Now **drink with** Cake and coffee • $34.60

Campbells Grand Rutherglen Tokay

ŢŢŢŢŢ NV There is a dramatic colour shift to brown, with an olive rim; the complex bouquet has a mix of malt, tea-leaf and varietal fish oil aromas; the palate has great impact, exceptionally complex, with layer-upon-layer of flavour. As ever, the balancing acidity prevents the finish from cloying.   **rating:** 96

best drinking Now **drink with** Double espresso

Campbells Isabella Rare Rutherglen Tokay

ŢŢŢŢŢ NV The colour is an even deeper olive brown than the Grand Tokay; oriental spices inhabit the dark corners of the bouquet, which is marvellously fragrant; the incredibly complex, luscious and concentrated palate, with its flavours of spices, dried fruits, toffee and tea-leaf, finishes fresh and lively, the aftertaste lingering for many minutes. The freshness married with old material is the sign of master blending.   **rating:** 97

best drinking Now **drink with** As fine a winter aperitif as it is a digestif • $94

Campbells Classic Rutherglen Muscat 500 ml

ŢŢŢŢŢ NV Medium tawny, with the faintest hint of red; the bouquet is pure varietal muscat, ripe, raisiny and spicy; the potent palate has lots of character; the spirit comes through a little aggressively, but the muscat flavour is great.   **rating:** 91

best drinking Now **drink with** Walnuts and almonds • $34.60

Campbells Grand Rutherglen Muscat

ŢŢŢŢŢ NV Dark brown, with a typical olive rim; highly aromatic and intense, waves of raisiny fruit coming off on the bouquet with little or no swirling of the glass. A wonderfully rich and complex palate, with great raisiny typicity, and lively acidity helping prolong and dry the finish.   **rating:** 96

best drinking Now **drink with** Coffee

Campbells Merchant Prince Rare Rutherglen Muscat

ŢŢŢŢŢ NV Dark brown, with a deep olive rim; the bouquet is the essence of raisined complexity, with the huge power of the wine lying partially in wait. The wine floods every corner of the mouth, and sets every tactile and taste sensor ringing; a wine of ultimate richness.   **rating:** 97

best drinking Now **drink with** Just itself • $89

 **camyr allyn wines** ★★★☆

Camyr Allyn North, Allyn River Road, East Gresford, NSW 2311 **region** Upper Hunter Valley
phone (02) 4938 9576 **fax** (02) 4938 9576 **open** By appointment
winemaker Geoff Broadfield, James Evers **production** 2500 cases **est.** 1999
product range ($18–48 ML) Camyr Allyn Verdelho, Rose, Sparkling Shiraz, Shiraz, Merlot; the Chalk
Stream range under the Bredbo Collectors Series; the 'standard' Bredbo wine.
summary John and Judy Evers purchased the property known as Camyr Allyn North in 1997, and
immediately set about planting 1.7 hectares of verdelho, 1.4 hectares of merlot and 1.3 hectares of shiraz. John
Evers is a fly-fishing fanatic, which has led to the development of his Chalk Stream wine series, with the
Bredbo Collectors Pack at its head. The wines are made at the new Northern Hunter winery at East Gresford
by resident winemaker Geoff Broadfield and the owners' son James Evers, who worked for Mildara Blass in
Coonawarra for some time. The promotion and packaging of the wines is innovative and stylish.

Chalk Stream Bredbo Blend
▼▼▼▼ 2001 Bright and clear red–purple; the moderately intense bouquet has black and redcurrant fruit with
underlying hints of chocolate and spice; the clean, firm and fresh palate adds hints of leaf and mint, and finishes
with fairly brisk acidity. **rating:** 88
best drinking 2006–2011 **drink with** Rack of lamb • $48

Camyr Allyn Merlot
▼▼▼▼ 2001 Medium red–purple; the moderately intense bouquet has a mix of red berry fruit and slightly
earthy components; the palate is well weighted and textured; earth and olive flavours close with firm acidity.
Should improve with a few years' bottle age. **rating:** 86
best drinking 2004–2008 **drink with** Lamb shanks • $18.50

Camyr Allyn Chalk Stream Matuka Merlot
▼▼▼▼ 2001 Medium red–purple; solid blackcurrant/fruitcake aromas lead into a medium-bodied palate with
plenty of flavour; however, corrected acidity sharpens the finish unduly. The grapes come from Coonawarra.
rating: 85
best drinking 2005–2010 **drink with** Braised veal • $33

candlebark hill ★★★★

Fordes Lane, Kyneton, Vic 3444 **region** Macedon Ranges
phone (03) 9836 2712 **fax** (03) 9836 2712 **open** By appointment
winemaker David Forster, Vincent Lakey, Llew Knight (Consultant) **production** 600 cases **est.** 1987
product range ($25–49 CD) Chardonnay, Pinot Noir, Cabernet Merlot, Cabernet Shiraz; Reserve Pinot
Noir, Cabernet Merlot.
summary Candlebark Hill has been established by David Forster on the northern end of the Macedon
Ranges, and enjoys magnificent views over the central Victorian countryside north of the Great Dividing
Range. The 3.5-hectare vineyard is planted to pinot noir (1.5 ha) together with 1 hectare each of chardonnay
and the three main Bordeaux varieties, complete with 0.5 hectare of shiraz and malbec. The Reserve Pinot
Noir is especially meritorious.

cannibal creek vineyard ★★★☆

260 Tynong North Road, Tynong North, Vic 3813 **region** Gippsland
phone (03) 5942 8380 **fax** (03) 5942 8202 **open** Weekends and public holidays 10–5
winemaker Patrick Hardiker **production** 1800 cases **est.** 1997
product range ($16–28 CD) Sauvignon Blanc, Gilgai Chardonnay, Chardonnay, Pinot Noir, Merlot,
Cabernet Sauvignon.
summary The Hardiker family moved to Tynong North in 1988, initially only grazing beef cattle, but aware
of the viticultural potential of the sandy clay loam and bleached sub-surface soils weathered from the granite
foothills of Tynong North. Plantings began in 1997, using organically based cultivation methods, and by 1999
the vines were already producing grapes. The decision was taken to make their own wine, and a heritage-style
shed built from locally milled timber has been converted into a winery and small cellar-door facility.

Cannibal Creek Pinot Noir
▼▼▼▼▽ 2001 Medium to full red–purple; ultra-ripe cherry fruit is supported by subtle French oak on the
bouquet; the very powerful palate has a mix of ripe cherry, raspberry and spice fruit in abundance; a touch
more acidity would have lifted it into the highest class. **rating:** 91
best drinking Now–2007 **best vintages** '00, '01 **drink with** Coq au vin • $28

Cannibal Creek Merlot

ΨΨΨΨ **2001** Light to medium purple-red; light berry, earth and mint aromas are an equivocal opening, but the palate picks up the pace, with riper fruit, pleasing texture and fine tannins. **rating:** 86

best drinking 2004–2008 **drink with** Milk-fed lamb • $28

Cannibal Creek Cabernet Sauvignon

ΨΨΨΨ **2001** Medium red-purple; clean, smooth, bright blackcurrant/cassis aromas flow into a ripe and supple palate showing good varietal fruit; while a little simple, a great early-drinking style with plenty of flavour. **rating:** 89

best drinking Now–2008 **drink with** Moroccan lamb • $28

canobolas-smith ★★★

Boree Lane, off Cargo Road, Lidster via Orange, NSW 2800 **region** Orange
phone (02) 6365 6113 **fax** (02) 6365 6113 **open** Weekends and public holidays 11–5
winemaker Murray Smith **production** 2000 cases **est.** 1986
product range ($10–35 CD) Highland Chardonnay, Chardonnay, Shine Methode Champenoise, Shine Botrytis Chardonnay, Highland Red, Pinot Noir, Chambourcin Cabernet, Catombal Range, Alchemy (Cabernet blend), Cabernets.
summary Canobolas-Smith has established itself as one of the leading Orange district wineries with its distinctive blue wrap-around labels. Much of the wine is sold from the cellar door, which is well worth a visit. Exports to the US and Asia.

Canobolas-Smith Shine Botrytis Chardonnay

ΨΨΨΨ **1999** The brown tinges to the colour are a major worry, but once one passes through the obviously botrytised bouquet to the palate there is complex and quite concentrated mandarin, honey and cumquat fruit. **rating:** 85

best drinking Now–2005 **drink with** Home-made ice cream • $20

Canobolas-Smith Reserve Pinot Noir

ΨΨΨΨ **2001** Light to medium red-purple; the light fruit of the bouquet has distinctly sappy/stemmy aromas, characters which mark the savoury/tangy palate; the wine has length, if not overmuch flesh, finishing with elevated acidity. Should look good against appropriately chosen food. **rating:** 86

best drinking Now–2005 **drink with** Tea-smoked duck • $35

Canobolas-Smith Alchemy

ΨΨΨΨ **1999** Medium red-purple; the bouquet opens with some bottle-developed foresty/earthy/cedary aromas then moves into dark, spicy fruits; the palate has very ripe fruit, low in tannin and high in alcohol, the slightly hot finish pointing to the 15° alcohol. A 50/30/20 blend of Cabernet Sauvignon, Cabernet Franc and Shiraz. **rating:** 84

best drinking Now–2007 **best vintages** '98 **drink with** Milk-fed veal • $27

canonbah bridge NR

Merryanbone Station, Warren, NSW 2824 **region** Western Plains Zone
phone (02) 6833 9966 **fax** (02) 6833 9980 **open** Not
winemaker Simon Gilbert (Contract) **production** 3600 cases **est.** 1999
product range ($13–30 ML) Semillon, Semillon Sauvignon Blanc, Ram's Leap Semillon Sauvignon Blanc, Reserve Sparkling, Ram's Leap Shiraz, Reserve Shiraz, Shiraz Grenache Mourvedre.
summary The 29-hectare vineyard has been established by Shane McLaughlin on the very large Merryanbone Station, a grazing property. If you head out of Dubbo towards Bourke, you will pass by Warren to the northwest of Dubbo. The wine is made by Simon Gilbert in his new, large winery at Mudgee, and is sold by mail order, with exports to the US.

canungra valley vineyards NR

Lamington National Park Road, Canungra Valley, Qld 4275 **region** Queensland Coastal
phone (07) 5543 4011 **fax** (07) 5543 4162 **open** 7 days 10–5
winemaker Stuart Pierce, Mark Davidson (Contract) **production** NFP **est.** 1997
product range ($13.50–29 CD) Picnic range of White, Red, Semillon Chardonnay, Bubbles; Platypus Play Semillon, Unwooded Chardonnay, Chambourcin Shiraz, Port; Reserve range of Shane O'Reilly Shiraz, Viola

O'Reilly Cabernet, Bernard O'Reilly Chambourcin; Sparkling Argyle, Vince & Pete's Liqueur Muscat and Vintage Port, Golden Gleam.

summary Canungra Valley Vineyards has been established in the hinterland of the Gold Coast with a clear focus on broad-based tourism. Eight hectares of vines have been established around the 19th-century homestead (moved to the site from its original location in Warwick) but these provide only a small part of the wine offered for sale. In deference to the climate, 70 per cent of the estate planting is chambourcin, the rain and mildew-resistent hybrid, the remainder being semillon. As the product range makes perfectly obvious, all the wine being offered at this early stage has been purchased from other winemakers. On the other hand, Canungra Valley offers a great deal of natural beauty for the general tourist.

cape bouvard   NR

Mount John Road, Mandurah, WA 6210 **region** Peel
phone (08) 9739 1360 **fax** (08) 9739 1360 **open** 7 days 10–5
winemaker NA **production** 2000 cases **est.** 1990
product range ($13–20 CD) Chenin Blanc, Dry White, Tuart Shiraz, Cabernet Sauvignon, Port.
summary While it continues in operation after its sale in 2003, there have been recent changes, the details of which are currently unavailable.

 cape d'estaing   NR

North Coast Road, Wisanger, Kangaroo Island, SA 5222 (postal) **region** Kangaroo Island
phone (08) 8383 6299 **fax** (08) 8383 6299 **open** Not
winemaker Mike Farmilo (Contract), Robin Moody **est.** 1994
product range Shiraz, Cabernet Shiraz, Cabernet.
summary Graham and Jude Allison, Alan and Ann Byers, Marg and Wayne Conaghty and Robin and Heather Moody have established 10 hectares of cabernet sauvignon and shiraz near Wisanger on Kangaroo Island. Robin Moody was a long-serving senior employee of Southcorp, with a broad knowledge of all aspects of grape growing and winemaking. It's he who joins with contract winemaker Mark Farmilo each year. There is limited retail distribution in Adelaide, and exports to the US, Canada, Germany, Japan, Singapore, Austria and Switzerland. The wines are also available by mail order.

cape grace   ★★★★☆

Fifty One Road, Cowaramup, WA 6284 **region** Margaret River
phone (08) 9755 5669 **fax** (08) 9755 5668 **open** 7 days 10–5
winemaker Robert Karri-Davies, Mark Messenger (Consultant) **production** 1200 cases **est.** 1996
product range ($16–35 CD) Chenin Blanc, Chardonnay, Shiraz, Cabernet Sauvignon.
summary Cape Grace Wines can trace its history back to 1875, when timber baron MC Davies settled at Karridale, building the Leeuwin lighthouse and founding the township of Margaret River. One hundred and twenty years later, Robert and Karen Karri-Davies planted just under 6 hectares of vineyard to chardonnay, shiraz and cabernet sauvignon, with smaller amounts of merlot, semillon and chenin blanc. They make a good team: Robert is a self-taught viticulturist, keeping up to date through reading and field seminars. Karen Karri-Davies has over 15 years of international sales and marketing experience in the hospitality industry in Canada, Australia and Indonesia. Winemaking is carried out on the property under the direction of consultant Mark Messenger, a veteran of the Margaret River region, with over 9 years' experience at Cape Mentelle and 3 years at Juniper Estate. All the wines from the 2000 vintage have received recognition in one form or another, the 2000 Cabernet Sauvignon winning the very significant Chairman's Award for the Best Wine at the 2001 Sheraton/West Australian Wine Awards.

Cape Grace Chenin Blanc

♥♥♥♥ 2001 Light straw-green; the bouquet is clean, quite crisp but relatively neutral, but the palate picks up flavour, intensity, and – in particular – length. The fruit flavours are in the tropical spectrum; all in all, far better than the usual bland offerings of this variety.   **rating:** 86
best drinking Now **drink with** Quiche Lorraine • $16

Cape Grace Chardonnay

♥♥♥♥ 2001 Medium yellow-green; the complex bouquet shows strong barrel-ferment oak inputs; the palate is similarly dominated by oak, although the fruit fights bravely and may develop. The silver medal in the Chardonnay class at the Sheraton Wine Awards 2002. Terrific if you like lashings of oak.   **rating:** 88
best drinking Now **drink with** Brains in black butter • $28

Cape Grace Shiraz

ΥΥΥΥΥ **2001** Intense, dense purple-red; clean, powerful dark fruit aromas drive the bouquet, the palate exuding black plum and licorice and supple, ripe tannins. Should repay extended cellaring. Gold medal Qantas Wine Show of Western Australia 2002. **rating:** 95

best drinking 2005–2015 **best vintages** '01 **drink with** Steak • $28

Cape Grace Cabernet Sauvignon

ΥΥΥΥΥ **2001** Intense, inky purple-red; the dense blackcurrant fruit of the bouquet moves through into a powerful and long palate, replete with red and blackcurrant fruit and savoury tannins. Tied with the Cape Grace Shiraz of the same year as the top two gold medals in a class of 138 wines at the 2002 Qantas Wine Show of Western Australia. **rating:** 94

best drinking 2007–2017 **drink with** Leave it in the cellar • $35

cape horn vineyard   NR

Echuca–Picola Road, Kanyapella, Vic 3564 **region** Goulburn Valley
phone (03) 5480 6013 **fax** (03) 5480 6013 **open** 7 days 10.30–5
winemaker John Ellis (Contract) **production** 1000 cases **est.** 1993
product range ($17–29 CD) Marsanne, Chardonnay, Sparkling Durif Shiraz, Shiraz, Durif, Cabernet Sauvignon.
summary The unusual name comes from a bend in the Murray River which was considered by the riverboat owners of the 19th century to resemble Cape Horn, a resemblance now depicted on the wine label. The property was acquired by Echuca GP Dr Sue Harrison and her school teacher husband Ian in 1993. Ian Harrison has progressively established 1.5 hectares of chardonnay, shiraz, zinfandel and cabernet sauvignon, a hectare of marsanne and 0.5 hectare of durif.

cape jaffa wines   ★★★★

Limestone Coast Road, Cape Jaffa, SA 5276 **region** Mount Benson
phone (08) 8768 5053 **fax** (08) 8768 5040 **open** 7 days 10–5
winemaker Derek Hooper **production** 10000 cases **est.** 1993
product range ($15–35 CD) Unwooded Chardonnay (McLaren Vale), Semillon Sauvignon Blanc, Sauvignon Blanc, Barrel Fermented Chardonnay (Mount Benson and Padthaway), Shiraz (McLaren Vale), Siberia Shiraz, Cabernet Sauvignon (Mount Benson), Brocks Reef Cabernet Merlot.
summary Cape Jaffa is the first of the Mount Benson wineries to come into production, albeit with most of the initial releases coming from other regions. Ultimately all of the wines will come from the substantial estate plantings of 25 hectares, which include the four major Bordeaux red varieties: shiraz, chardonnay, sauvignon blanc and semillon. It is a joint venture between the Hooper and Fowler families, and the winery (built of local paddock rock) has been designed to allow eventual expansion to 1000 tonnes, or 70000 cases. Exports to the UK, the US, China and New Zealand.

Cape Jaffa Sauvignon Blanc

ΥΥΥΥ **2002** Pale straw-green; a classically firm and crisp bouquet, predominantly mineral, but with some tropical fruit behind, then a palate which follows a similar path, possessing both focus and length. **rating:** 89

best drinking Now **drink with** Steamed mussels • $16

capel vale   ★★★★

Lot 5 Stirling Estate, Mallokup Road, Capel, WA 6271 **region** Geographe
phone (08) 9727 1986 **fax** (08) 9727 1904 **open** Cellar door 7 days 10–4, Cafe Thurs–Mon 10–4
winemaker Nicole Esdaile **production** 150000 cases **est.** 1979
product range ($10–50 CD) CV Bistro range of Sauvignon Blanc, Chenin, Unwooded Chardonnay, Pinot Noir, Shiraz, Cabernet Merlot; Capel Vale Fine Dining range of Riesling, Semillon, Sauvignon Blanc, Sauvignon Blanc Semillon, Verdelho, Chardonnay, Late Harvest, Pinot Noir, Shiraz, Merlot, Cabernet Shiraz Merlot, Cabernet Sauvignon; Connoisseur range of Whispering Hill Riesling, Seven Day Road Sauvignon Blanc, Frederick Chardonnay, Kinnaird Shiraz, Howecroft Merlot; Sassy Sparkling Chardonnay, Botrytis Riesling, Duck Rose, Tawny Port.
summary Capel Vale continues to expand its viticultural empire, its contract-grape sources and its marketing, the last through the introduction of a series of vineyard, or similarly named, super-premium wines. Against the run of play, as it were, the most successful of these super-premiums are the red wines, for it was the Riesling which first captured attention. The strong marketing focus the company has always had is driven by its indefatigable owner, Dr Peter Pratten, who has developed export markets throughout Europe, Asia and the US.

Capel Vale Whispering Hill Riesling

▼▼▼▼▼ 2001 Excellent green-yellow; a highly aromatic bouquet in faintly old-fashioned style, with quasi-kerosene aromas is followed by a very powerful and intense palate; abundant character and grip. Gold medal Qantas Wine Show of Western Australia 2002. **rating:** 94

best drinking Now–2008 **best vintages** '97, '98, '01 **drink with** Thai cuisine • $22

Capel Vale Sauvignon Blanc

▼▼▼▼ 2002 Pale colour; a highly aromatic and fragrant bouquet is followed by a palate with complex fruit flavours occupying the full varietal spectrum; excellent length and intensity. **rating:** 89

best drinking Now **drink with** Shellfish • $15

Capel Vale Sauvignon Blanc Semillon

▼▼▼▼▽ 2001 Light straw-green; the clean bouquet has a mix of herbaceous and gooseberry fruit which achieves complexity without the use of perceptible oak. The palate is likewise complex, with excellent mouthfeel and balance; in the absence of oak, one suspects some lees contact and possibly other winemaking inputs. Top gold, Class 8, Western Australian Wine Show 2001. **rating:** 92

best drinking Now **drink with** Pan-fried fish • $16

Capel Vale Verdelho

▼▼▼▼ 2002 Light yellow-green; rich, ripe, rounded fruit on the bouquet then sustains a medium to full-bodied palate with strong varietal flavour and character, yet avoiding phenolic extraction and the dreaded sweetness often foisted on Verdelho. **rating:** 89

best drinking Now–2005 **best vintages** '02 **drink with** Takeaway • $16

Capel Vale Chardonnay

▼▼▼▼▽ 2000 Medium yellow-green; slightly smoky oak and tangy fruit make for a complex but restrained bouquet; there is much the same interplay on the palate, ranging through grapefruit, nectarine, cashew and spice, the last from the oak. **rating:** 90

best drinking Now–2007 **best vintages** '86, '87, '91, '92, '95, '99 **drink with** Marron • $21

Capel Vale Kinnaird Shiraz

▼▼▼▼▼ 2001 Full red-purple; smooth, clean, black cherry and plum fruit is supported by quality oak on the bouquet; the palate is powerful but not heavy, in typical Mount Barker style; cedar, spice, black cherry and blackberry fruit flavours are supported by fine oak. High quality. **rating:** 94

best drinking 2006–2016 **best vintages** '01 **drink with** Game pie • $50

Capel Vale Howecroft Merlot

▼▼▼▼▽ 2000 Medium red-purple; the bouquet has a subtle mix of savoury fruit and cedary oak, with some spicy notes; the palate has clearly pronounced varietal flavour; persistent but fine tannins will reward patience. From a single vineyard in the Geographe region. **rating:** 93

best drinking 2005–2015 **best vintages** '95, '97, '98, '00 **drink with** Rare eye fillet • $50

Capel Vale Cabernet Sauvignon

▼▼▼▼ 2001 Medium red-purple; the bouquet has soft blackberry fruit and subtle oak, and the palate offers a mix of blackcurrant and blackberry, and a touch of chocolate; tannins build on the finish. **rating:** 86

best drinking 2005–2010 **drink with** Grilled calf's liver • $21

cape mentelle ★★★★☆

Off Wallcliffe Road, Margaret River, WA 6285 **region** Margaret River
phone (08) 9757 3266 **fax** (08) 9757 3233 **open** 7 days 10–4.30
winemaker John Durham **production** 55 000 cases **est.** 1970
product range ($15.35–57.30 R) Semillon Sauvignon Blanc, Sauvignon Blanc Semillon Wallcliffe Reserve, Georgiana, Marmaduke, Chardonnay, Shiraz, Zinfandel, Cabernet Merlot Trinders Vineyard, Cabernet Sauvignon.
summary Notwithstanding ownership by Veuve Clicquot, David Hohnen remains in command of one of Australia's foremost medium-sized wineries. Exceptional marketing skills and wine of the highest quality, with the back-up of New Zealand's Cloudy Bay, are a potent combination. The Chardonnay and Semillon Sauvignon Blanc are among Australia's best, the potent Shiraz usually superb, and the berry/spicy Zinfandel makes one wonder why this grape is not as widespread in Australia as it is in California. Enlarged its business by the slightly quixotic acquisition of Mountadam in September 2000. Exports to the UK, Japan and Asia.

Cape Mentelle Wallcliffe Reserve Sauvignon Blanc Semillon

ŸŸŸŸŸ **2001** Medium yellow-green; the bouquet has an intense mix of grass, herb and gooseberry; the palate follows a similar track and, while not big, has great intensity, balance and length. Radically different from the 2000 vintage.   **rating:** 94

best drinking Now–2008 **best vintages** '01 **drink with** Sweetbreads • $31.50

Cape Mentelle Semillon Sauvignon Blanc

ŸŸŸŸŸ **2002** A 50/50 blend of the two varieties which is partially barrel fermented, and is one of the most reliable examples, year-in, year-out. The complex herb and spice fruit of the bouquet is followed by intense and powerful flavours of herb, citrus and gooseberry, the oak subtle throughout. Gold plated.   **rating:** 95

best drinking Now–2005 **best vintages** '85, '88, '91, '93, '95, '96, '97, '98, '99, '00, '01, '02 **drink with** Anything Asian • $22.30

Cape Mentelle Chardonnay

ŸŸŸŸŸ **2001** Medium yellow-green; the sophistication is typical, the restraint of the bouquet slightly less so, but there are certainly grapefruit, melon and fig aromas to be found; the very well-balanced and sculpted palate provides more of the same; it is simply that there is less overt fruit than in some prior vintages. Some bottles are oxidised.   **rating:** 91

best drinking Now–2010 **best vintages** '90, '91, '92, '93, '94, '95, '96, '97, '98, '99, '00 **drink with** Veal sweetbreads • $35

Cape Mentelle Shiraz

ŸŸŸŸŸ **2001** Full but bright red-purple; the bouquet has a complex array of dark fruits, roasted meat and spice, characters which come through on the very complex palate, completed with fine but persistent tannins.   **rating:** 92

best drinking 2006–2011 **best vintages** '90, '91, '93, '94, '96, '97, '98, '99, '00, '01 **drink with** Stir-fried Asian beef • $32.50

Cape Mentelle Zinfandel

ŸŸŸŸŸ **2001** Medium to full red-purple; an array of dark cherry, spice, licorice and chocolate aromas plus a dash of oak set the scene for a palate with complex texture and structure, the ripe juicy fruit balanced by some savoury, spicy notes and good tannins.   **rating:** 91

best drinking 2005–2010 **best vintages** '91, '92, '93, '94, '95, '97, '98, '99, '00, '01 **drink with** Rare char-grilled rump steak • $38

Cape Mentelle Trinders Vineyard Cabernet Merlot

ŸŸŸŸ **2001** Medium red-purple; the bouquet is solid, with some savoury/gamey edges to the dark berry fruit; the medium to full-bodied palate has ripe dark fruits with plenty of structure, then a savoury rejoinder on the finish.   **rating:** 87

best drinking 2005–2010 **best vintages** '00 **drink with** Butterfly leg of lamb • $28.25

Cape Mentelle Cabernet Sauvignon

ŸŸŸŸŸ **1999** Medium red-purple; an extremely complex bouquet with black fruits woven through more savoury/earthy/gamey characters; the powerful, masculine and sinewy palate is full of dark brooding fruits and tannins.   **rating:** 90

best drinking 2006–2016 **best vintages** '76, '78, '82, '83, '86, '90, '91, '93, '94, '95 **drink with** Loin of lamb • $57.20

capercaillie ★★★★

Londons Road, Lovedale, NSW 2325 **region** Lower Hunter Valley
phone (02) 4990 2904 **fax** (02) 4991 1886 **open** Mon–Sat 9–5, Sun 10–5
winemaker Alasdair Sutherland **production** 5500 cases **est.** 1995
product range ($17–40 CD) Watervale Riesling, Hunter Valley Gewurztraminer, Hunter Valley Semillon, Orange Highlands Sauvignon Blanc, Hunter Valley Chardonnay, Dessert Chardonnay, C Sparkling Red, Hunter Valley Rose, Hunter Valley Chambourcin, The Ghillie Shiraz, Ceilidh Shiraz, Hunter Valley Shiraz, Orange Highlands Merlot, The Clan (Cabernet Sauvignon Merlot Cabernet Franc).
summary The former Dawson Estate, now run by Hunter Valley veteran Alasdair Sutherland (no relation to Neil Sutherland of Sutherland Estate). The Capercaillie wines are very well made, with generous flavour. Following the example of Brokenwood, its fruit sources are spread across southeastern Australia. The wines are exported to the UK.

Capercaillie Hunter Valley Semillon

ϷϷϷϷϷ 2002 Light straw-green; a classic, clean and fresh bouquet with fragrant herb aromas is followed by an intense, piercing, long palate; top-quality young Semillon. **rating: 94**

best drinking 2005–2011 **best vintages** '98, '00, '01, '02 **drink with** Lemon chicken • $17

Capercaillie Hunter Valley Chardonnay

ϷϷϷϷ 2002 Light straw-green; the bouquet is clean, with subtle barrel ferment on somewhat subdued fruit; the white peach and nectarine fruit on the palate likewise lacks intensity; the winemaking has been right up to the mark. **rating: 85**

best drinking Now **best vintages** '01 **drink with** Rich fish dishes • $19

Capercaillie Hunter Valley Rose

ϷϷϷϷ 2002 Light, vivid purple-red; fresh, fragrant red cherry aromas are followed by a palate in clever cellar-door style, not too sweet, although it does finish abruptly. A blend of Chambourcin and Chardonnay. **rating: 85**

best drinking Now **drink with** Doesn't matter • $17

Capercaillie Ceilidh Shiraz

ϷϷϷϷϷ 2001 Medium to full red-purple; the attractive bouquet has dark plum, blackberry and subtle oak aromas, gaining pace on the smooth, rich palate with its nice blend of varietal fruit inputs in a broadly plummy spectrum; nice oak and soft tannins. A blend of McLaren Vale and Hunter Valley grapes. **rating: 93**

best drinking 2005–2011 **best vintages** '01 **drink with** Rack of veal • $25

Capercaillie Orange Highlands Merlot

ϷϷϷϷ 2001 Medium red-purple; a scented and fragrant bouquet with briary blackcurrant aromas; the elegant, light-bodied palate offers a mix of savoury olive and riper raspberry fruit. **rating: 87**

best drinking 2005–2010 **drink with** Lamb kidneys • $25

Capercaillie The Clan

ϷϷϷϷ 2001 Medium to full red-purple; the bouquet is as complex as the blend suggests (80 per cent Cabernet Sauvignon, 10 per cent Merlot and 10 per cent Petit Verdot, 60 per cent of the total coming from Coonawarra and the Barossa Valley, and 40 per cent from Orange), with a mix of blackberry, spice and blackcurrant aromas; on the palate, abundant dark berry fruit has some mint and savoury borders; the structure is not quite there. **rating: 89**

best drinking 2005–2010 **drink with** Lasagne • $25

capogreco winery estate   NR

Riverside Avenue, South Mildura, Vic 3500 **region** Murray Darling
phone (03) 5023 3060 **open** Mon–Sat 10–6
winemaker Bruno Capogreco **production** NFP **est.** 1976
product range ($8–12 CD) Riesling, Moselle, Shiraz Mataro, Cabernet Sauvignon, Claret, Rose, fortifieds.
summary Italian-owned and run, the wines are a blend of Italian and Australian Riverland influences. The estate has 13 hectares of chardonnay, 14 hectares of shiraz and 6 hectares of cabernet sauvignon, but also purchases other varieties.

✾ captains creek organic wines   NR

160 Mays Road, Blampied, Vic 3364 **region** Ballarat
phone (03) 5345 7408 **fax** (03) 5345 7408 **open** By appointment
winemaker Alan Cooper, Norman Latta **production** 500 cases **est.** 1994
product range ($20–25 ML) Unwooded Chardonnay, Chardonnay, Pinot Noir.
summary Doug and Carolyn May are the third generation farmers at the Captains Creek property, and have been conducting the business for over 20 years without using any chemicals. When they began their establishment of the vineyard in 1994, with 1 hectare each of chardonnay and pinot noir, they resolved to go down the same path, eschewing the use of insecticides or systematic fungicides, instead using preventive spray programmes of copper and sulphur. Thermal flame weeding and beneficial predatory insects control weeds and mites. There is also a neat historical connection, as Blampied takes its name from 20-year-old Anne-Marie Blampied and her 15-year-old brother Emile, who emigrated from Lorraine in France in 1853, lured by gold. Anne-Marie married Jean-Pierre Trouette, another Frenchman, and Trouette and Blampied were the first to plant vines in the Great Western region, in 1858.

captain's paddock   NR

18 Millers Road, Kingaroy, Qld 4610 **region** South Burnett
phone (07) 4162 4534 **fax** (07) 4162 4502 **open** 7 days 10–5
winemaker Ross Whitford **production** 2000 cases **est.** 1995
product range ($10–16 CD) Chardonnay, Captain's White, Shiraz, Shiraz Cabernet Sauvignon Merlot, Captain's Red (semi-sweet).
summary Don and Judy McCallum planted the first hectare of vineyard in 1995, followed by a further 3 hectares in 1996, focusing on shiraz and chardonnay. It is a family affair; the mudbrick cellar-door building was made with bricks crafted by Don McCallum and Judy's screenprinting adorns the tables and chairs and printed linen for sale to the public. Their two children are both sculptors, with works on display at the winery. Captain's Paddock is fully licensed, offering either light platters or full dishes incorporating local produce. Meals are served either inside or alfresco in the courtyard, which has views over the Booie Ranges.

carabooda estate   NR

297 Carabooda Road, Carabooda, WA 6033 **region** Swan District
phone (08) 9407 5283 **fax** (08) 9407 5283 **open** 7 days 10–6
winemaker Terry Ord **production** 1500 cases **est.** 1989
product range ($16–25 CD) Sauvignon Blanc, Semillon Sauvignon Blanc, Sweet Chenin, Shiraz, Cabernet Shiraz, Cabernet Sauvignon, Vintage Port.
summary 1989 is the year of establishment given by Terry Ord, but it might as well have been 1979 (when he made his first wine) or 1981 (when he and wife Simonne planted their first vines). It has been a slowly, slowly exercise, though, with production from the 3 hectares of estate plantings now supplemented by purchased grapes, and the first public release not being made until mid-1994. Since that time production has risen significantly.

🍂 carbunup crest vineyard   ★★★★

PO Box 235, Busselton, WA 6280 **region** Margaret River
phone (08) 9754 2618 **fax** (08) 9754 2618 **open** Not
winemaker Mark Lane (Contract, Flying Fish Cove) **production** 2000 cases **est.** 1998
product range ($7.50–12.50 ML) Cella Rage range of Classic White, Chardonnay Verdelho, Chardonnay, Shiraz, Merlot, Cabernet Merlot.
summary Carbunup Crest is operated by three local families, with Kris Meares managing the business. Initially it operated as a grapevine rootling nursery, but it has gradually converted to grape growing and winemaking. There are 6 hectares of vineyard, all of which are all now in production, but with plans to extend the plantings to 20 hectares in the years ahead (the property is 53 hectares in total). The contract-made wines are of excellent quality and simply sensational value, even if the names are kitschy. This is certainly a producer to watch.

Carbunup Crest Cella Rage Shiraz

▼▼▼▼▼ 2001 Strong red-purple; powerful, high-toned fruit and oak on the bouquet foreshadow a complex palate with full-on winemaking marrying fruit, oak and tannins.   **rating:** 94
best drinking 2005–2011 **best vintages** '01 **drink with** Roast venison • $12

Carbunup Crest Cella Rage Cabernet Sauvignon Merlot

▼▼▼▼ 2001 Similar bright red-purple; the dusty, cedary, spicy bouquet reflects the fruit on the palate, with a subliminal suggestion of slightly green fruit. Good wine, but not in the class of the Shiraz.   **rating:** 89
best drinking 2005–2010 **drink with** Herbed rack of lamb • $11.25

carbunup estate   NR

Bussel Highway, Carbunup, WA 6280 **region** Margaret River
phone (08) 9755 1111 **open** 7 days 10–5
winemaker Robert Credaro **production** NFP **est.** 1988
product range ($12–16 CD) Under the premium Vasse River Wines label: Chardonnay, Semillon, Sauvignon Blanc; under Carbunup Estate label: Verdelho, Shiraz.
summary Sells part of the grapes produced from the 18 hectares of vineyards but keeps part for release under the Carbunup Estate and Vasse River labels – strikingly different in design, and giving no clue that they emanate from the same winery. It had early success with its white wines, in particular its Chardonnay and Semillon. No recent tastings.

cardinham estate ★★★★☆

Main North Road, Stanley Flat, SA 5453 **region** Clare Valley
phone (08) 8842 1944 **fax** (08) 8842 1955 **open** 7 days 10–5
winemaker Smith John Wine Co. **production** 1000 cases **est.** 1980
product range ($17–30 CD) Clare Valley Riesling, Chardonnay, Sangiovese, Stradbrooke Shiraz, Cabernet Merlot, Cabernet Sauvignon.
summary The Smith family began the development of Cardinham Estate in 1980, over the years building the vineyard size up to its present level of 60 hectares, the largest plantings being of cabernet sauvignon (23 ha), shiraz (15 ha), and riesling (10.5 ha). It entered into a grape supply contract with Wolf Blass, which led to an association with then Quelltaler winemaker Stephen John. After 15 years supplying Wolf Blass and others, Stephen John and the Smiths formed the Smith John Wine Company in 1999. Its purpose is to provide contract winemaking services to small producers in the valley, and to supply bulk wine to others. The development of the Cardinham brand is a small but important part of the business. This has seen production rise to 1000 cases, with the three staples of Riesling, Cabernet Merlot and Stradbroke Shiraz available from the winery and through retail distribution, and additional wines made in small volume available only at the cellar door and by mail order.

Cardinham Estate Clare Valley Riesling

ŦŦŦŦŦ **2002** Light straw-green; a highly flowery bouquet, spotlessly clean, with a mix of citrus, passionfruit and apple blossom, leads into a palate with excellent balance, mouthfeel and length, the flavours precisely reflecting the bouquet.   **rating:** 94
best drinking Now–2013 **best vintages** '02 **drink with** Tuna sushi • $17

Cardinham Estate Stradbrooke Shiraz

ŦŦŦŦŸ **2001** Youthful red-purple; a rich, fully ripe but not jammy bouquet has dark berry to the fore, but with appealing oak in support. The palate has smooth, sweet, ripe berry fruit and supple tannins.   **rating:** 92
best drinking 2005–2010 **best vintages** '01 **drink with** Kangaroo fillet • $20

Cardinham Estate Sangiovese

ŦŦŦŦŸ **2002** Medium to full red-purple; amazing for Sangiovese; ripe, juicy berry with fruit spice and fragrance introduces a particularly interesting wine, with appealing structure, flavour and texture, but entirely at odds with all other Australian-grown and made Sangiovese.   **rating:** 90
best drinking 2004–2009 **drink with** Lasagne • $17

Cardinham Estate Cabernet Merlot

ŦŦŦŦŸ **2001** Medium red-purple; gently savoury, spicy fruit provides a harmonious bouquet, and the smooth, quite plush, palate has dark fruits and ripe tannins; a lovely, fruit-driven style. Outstanding value.   **rating:** 93
best drinking 2005–2012 **best vintages** '01 **drink with** Backstrap of lamb • $20

cargo road wines   NR

Cargo Road, Orange, NSW 2800 **region** Orange
phone (02) 6365 6100 **open** Weekends 11–5
winemaker James Sweetapple **production** 1800 cases **est.** 1983
product range ($14–22.50 CD) Riesling, Gewurztraminer, Sauvignon Blanc, Merlot, Zinfandel, Cabernet Merlot.
summary Originally called The Midas Tree, the vineyard was planted in 1984 by Roseworthy graduate John Swanson. He established a 2.5-hectare vineyard that included zinfandel 15 years ahead of his time. The property was acquired in 1997 by a syndicate, which is expanding the vineyard, particularly zinfandel.

carilley estate   ★★★☆

Lot 23 Hyem Road, Herne Hill, WA 6056 **region** Swan Valley
phone (08) 9296 6190 **fax** (08) 9296 6190 **open** Thurs–Mon 10.30–5.30
winemaker Rob Marshall **production** 1500 cases **est.** 1985
product range ($8.50–20 R) Chenin Blanc, Chardonnay, Shiraz, Titian Port.
summary Doctors Laura and Isavel Carija have 6 hectares of vineyard planted to shiraz, chenin blanc, chardonnay, viognier and merlot. Most of the grapes are sold, with only a small proportion made under the Carilley Estate label, with very limited retail or mail order distribution. The winery cafe supplies light Mediterranean food.

Carilley Estate Fortuniana Chenin Blanc

▼▼▼▼ 2001 Light straw-green; the moderately intense bouquet has quite firm, clean fruit salad aromas in typical varietal style; an attractive wine on the palate, with above-average length and intensity.   **rating: 85**
best drinking Now–2005 **drink with** Sugar-cured tuna • $15

Carilley Estate Sanguinea Shiraz

▼▼▼▼ 2002 Medium to full red-purple; a clean but complex bouquet has a mix of licorice and black fruits supported by subtle oak; the palate is softer and more developed than the bouquet, with spicy, savoury flavours and sweet tannins.   **rating: 89**
▼▼▼▼▼ 2001 Strong, deep and bright red purple; a powerful and complex array of dark berries, licorice and spice on the bouquet, then a medium to full-bodied palate with lots of dark berry fruit, fine tannins and well-controlled oak.   **rating: 92**
best drinking 2006–2012 **best vintages** '01 **drink with** Irish stew • $20

carindale wines   NR

Palmers Lane, Pokolbin, NSW 2321 **region** Lower Hunter Valley
phone (02) 4998 7665 **fax** (02) 4998 7065 **open** Fri–Mon 10–4.30
winemaker Brian Walsh (Contract) **production** 1000 cases **est.** 1996
product range ($21–26.50 CD) Chardonnay, Blackthorn (Cabernet blend).
summary Carindale draws upon 2 hectares of chardonnay, 1.2 hectares of cabernet franc and 0.2 hectare of merlot (together with few muscat vines). Exports to the US and Canada.

carosa   ★★★★

310 Houston Street, Mount Helena, WA 6082 **region** Perth Hills
phone (08) 9572 1603 **fax** (08) 9572 1604 **open** Weekends, holidays 11–5, or by appointment
winemaker James Elson **production** 800 cases **est.** 1984
product range ($15–19 CD) Jessica Semillon, Summer White, Classic Dry White, Chardonnay, Isabella Pinot Noir, Hannah Shiraz, Grenache Shiraz, Lucian Merlot, Cabernet Merlot, Cabernet Sauvignon.
summary Very limited production and small-scale winemaking result in wines which can only be described as rustic, but which sell readily enough into the local market. Winemaker Jim Elson had extensive eastern Australia winemaking experience (with Seppelt). The wines are sold through the cellar door and by mailing list.

Carosa Hannah

▼▼▼▼▼ 2001 Medium red-purple; an impressive bouquet with a rippling array of spicy, savoury, blackberry, licorice and chocolate aromas, all of which come through in the medium-bodied palate, finishing with sweet, fine tannins. By far the best Carosa red wine I have tasted. Shiraz is so much better suited to the Perth Hills than Pinot Noir that it is difficult to understand why growers persist with the latter.   **rating: 90**
best drinking 2006–2011 **best vintages** '01 **drink with** Braised oxtail • $19

🐌 carpinteri vineyards   NR

PO Box 61, Nyah, Vic 3594 **region** Swan Hill
phone (03) 5030 2569 **fax** (03) 5030 2680 **open** Not
winemaker Michael Kyberd (Contract) **production** 900 cases **est.** 1945
product range Unwooded Chardonnay, Medium Sweet White, Shiraz, Grenache Mataro, Shiraz Grenache Mataro.
summary Vince and Con Carpinteri are primarily grape growers, with 30 hectares planted to chardonnay, grenache, malbec, shiraz, mourvedre, black muscat and sultana. A small amount of wine is made under contract by Michael Kyberd at Red Hill Estate in the Mornington Peninsula, and the wines are sold by mail order for between $50 and $111 per dozen. The wines are also sold through East Melbourne Cellars.

casa fontana   NR

4 Cook Street, Lutana, Tas 7009 **region** Southern Tasmania
phone (03) 6272 3180 **open** Not
winemaker Mark Fontana, Steve Lubiana (Contract) **production** 250 cases **est.** 1994
product range ($22 ML) Chardonnay, Pinot Noir.

summary Mark Fontana and his Japanese wife Shige planted their first pinot noir in 1994, and over the following 2 years expanded the vineyard to its present level of 2.6 hectares, 1 hectare each of pinot noir and chardonnay, and 0.6 hectare of riesling. Mark Fontana is a metallurgist with Pasminco and came into grape growing through his love of fine wine.

casa freschi ★★★☆

30 Jackson Avenue, Strathalbyn, SA 5255 **region** Langhorne Creek
phone (08) 8536 4569 **fax** (08) 8536 4569 **open** Not
winemaker David Freschi **production** 800 cases **est.** 1998
product range ($34–54 R) Profondo, La Signora.
summary David Freschi graduated with a degree in oenology from Roseworthy in 1991, and spent most of the decade working overseas in California, Italy and New Zealand, culminating in a senior winemaking position with Corbans in New Zealand in 1997. In 1998 he and his wife decided to trade in the corporate world for a small family-owned winemaking business, with a core of 2.5 hectares of vines established by David Freschi's parents in 1972; an additional 2 hectares of nebbiolo have been planted adjacent to the original vineyard. Says David Freschi, 'The names of the wines were chosen to best express the personality of the wines grown in our vineyard, as well as to express our heritage.' I suspect some outstanding wines will come from Casa Freschi in good vintages; it is a pity they missed out on 1998. Exports to the US, Germany, Switzerland, Singapore and New Zealand.

casas vineyard and estate ★★★★

RMB 236D, Rosa Brook Road, Margaret River, WA 6285 **region** Margaret River
phone (08) 9757 4542 **fax** (08) 9757 4006 **open** By appointment
winemaker Janice MacDonald **production** 4000 cases **est.** 1992
product range ($16.50–34 CD) Sauvignon Blanc, Chardonnay, Shiraz, Cabernet Sauvignon.
summary John Casas has established 5 hectares of shiraz, 4 hectares of cabernet sauvignon and 1 hectare each of chardonnay and sauvignon blanc. The vineyard is managed to produce low yields, of 1–2 tonnes per acre, with the aim of making a wine of sufficient power and density to merit barrel maturation of 1¹/₂–2¹/₂ years. For the time being, the wines are sold direct from the winery and selected restaurants, and exported to the UK and the US, in the latter instance through Epicurean Wines of Seattle. The quality of the wines across the board is exemplary.

Casas Sauvignon Blanc

ΥΥΥΥ 2001 Medium yellow-green; a solid and ripe bouquet with gooseberry, herb and spice is followed by a palate with abundant flavour, but slightly losing its sharpness and focus, signalling that it is going into the transition phase. **rating:** 86
best drinking 2004–2006 **drink with** Salmon terrine • $19

Casas Chardonnay

ΥΥΥΥ 2001 Light green-yellow; a clean and smooth bouquet, with well-balanced and integrated oak, ranges through stone fruit, cashew and spice aromas; the light to medium-bodied palate is dominated by stone fruit, with just a touch of citrus, the oak trailing neatly behind, precisely where it should be. **rating:** 89
best drinking Now–2006 **drink with** Sushi • $18

Casas Shiraz

ΥΥΥΥ 2000 Medium red-purple; a solid, clean and smooth bouquet with blackberry and mulberry fruit supported by subtle oak leads into a medium-bodied palate, once again smooth, with fine texture and tannins; an elegant wine matured in new and used French oak for 12 months. **rating:** 89
best drinking Now–2009 **drink with** Ravioli • $25

Casas Cabernet Sauvignon

ΥΥΥΥ 2000 Medium red-purple; strong cedary/earthy bottle-developed overtones to the fruit of the bouquet; the palate is sweeter than the bouquet suggests, in no small measure thanks to the 14.8° alcohol; the structure and extract have been well handled. **rating:** 89
ΥΥΥΥΥ 1999 Dense red-purple; a powerful, deep blackcurrant and blackberry bouquet is followed by an ultra-powerful palate, complex and concentrated, with chocolate and black fruits; balanced, but needs a decade plus. **rating:** 94
best drinking 2005–2010 **drink with** Lamb shanks • $23

cascabel ★★★★☆

Rogers Road, Willunga, SA 5172 **region** McLaren Vale
phone (08) 8557 4434 **fax** (08) 8557 4435 **open** By appointment
winemaker Susana Fernandez, Duncan Ferguson **production** 2000 cases **est.** 1997
product range ($22–40 R) Eden Valley Riesling, Fleurieu Shiraz, McLaren Vale Grenache et al, Tempranillo Graciano, Monastrell.
summary Cascabel's proprietors, Duncan Ferguson and Susana Fernandez, established Cascabel when they purchased a property at Willunga on the Fleurieu Peninsula and planted it to roussanne, tempranillo, graciano, monastrel, grenache, shiraz and viognier. The choice of grapes reflects the winemaking experience of the proprietors in Australia, the Rhône Valley, Bordeaux, Italy, Germany and New Zealand – and also Susana Fernandez's birthplace, Spain. Both are fully qualified and intend to move the production base steadily towards the style of the Rhône Valley, Rioja and other parts of Spain. In the meantime, the 4000-case capacity winery which they erected on-site prior to the 1998 vintage is being kept busy with grapes sourced from areas throughout South Australia. The initial releases left no doubt that the proprietors know what they are doing, and it will be interesting to watch the development of the wines from the estate plantings. Exports to the US, the UK, Switzerland, New Zealand, Hong Kong, Singapore and Japan.

Cascabel Eden Valley Riesling

TTTTT 2002 An intensely aromatic lime/lime blossom bouquet is followed by a very intense and complex palate offering a marvellous mix of lime, apple and spice. Outstanding.   **rating:** 96
best drinking Now–2012 **best vintages** '99, '02 **drink with** Stir-fried prawns • $22

Cascabel Fleurieu Peninsula Shiraz

TTTTY 2001 Medium red-purple; dark plum and bitter chocolate aromas are woven through subtle oak on the bouquet; the palate has sweet, dark plum and blackberry in a dark chocolate coating; ripe tannins and good oak complete a delicious wine with years in front of it.   **rating:** 93
best drinking 2005–2015 **best vintages** '98, '99, '00, '01 **drink with** Ox cheek • $32

Cascabel Tempranillo Graciano

TTTTY 2001 Medium red-purple; the moderately intense bouquet has a mix of spicy and gently savoury aromas; the palate moves several notches, with surprisingly intense savoury, dark fruits; the complex structure is aided by ripe tannins. A very interesting wine, the first in Australia to flex the muscle of Tempranillo. **rating:** 92
best drinking 2004–2009 **best vintages** '01 **drink with** Braised ox cheek • $40

Cascabel Monastrell

TTTT 2001 Medium red-purple; the relatively light bouquet has some juicy varietal fruit aromas, backed by subtle oak. The palate is quite assertive, with somewhat grippy tannins; may or may not soften with time. Monastrell is the Spanish name for Mourvedre, which in this instance has 8 per cent grenache interplanted in the vineyard.   **rating:** 85
best drinking Now–2007 **drink with** Shepherd's pie • $40

Cascabel Grenache et al

TTTTY 2001 Light to medium red-purple; a typically fresh and juicy berry bouquet, the palate made more complex by attractively sweet cedary oak and fine, ripe tannins.   **rating:** 90
best drinking Now–2005 **best vintages** '01 **drink with** Beef stew • $25

casella ★★★

Wakely Road, Yenda, NSW 2681 **region** Riverina
phone (02) 6968 1346 **fax** (02) 6968 1196 **open** Not
winemaker Alan Kennett **production** 4 million cases **est.** 1969
product range ($4.95–19.50 R) Chardonnay, Shiraz, Cabernet Sauvignon; under the Carramar Estate label Semillon Sauvignon Blanc, Chardonnay, Unwooded Chardonnay, Botrytis Semillon, Merlot, Shiraz, Shiraz Cabernet, Cabernet Sauvignon; Yenda Vale Durif, Tempranillo, Cabernet Sauvignon Petit Verdot; also Cottlers Bridge at significantly lower prices. The yellow tail range of wines (Chardonnay, Shiraz, Merlot, Cabernet Shiraz, Cabernet Sauvignon) is for export.
summary Casella has been a large-volume producer for over 20 years, but sold most of its production in bulk. Its yellow tail range, with sales of over one million cases in the US, has changed all that, and propelled it into sixth place in Australia, with a crush of 50 000 tonnes in 2003, augmented by the purchase of the equivalent of another 12 000 tonnes.

cassegrain ★★★★

Hastings River Winery, Fernbank Creek Road, Port Macquarie, NSW 2444 **region** Hastings River
phone (02) 6583 7777 **fax** (02) 6584 0354 **open** 7 days 9–5
winemaker John Cassegrain **production** 45 000 cases **est.** 1980
product range ($12–28.10 CD) Gewurztraminer, Semillon, Verdelho, Unwooded Chardonnay, Chardonnay, Rose, Chambourcin, Shiraz, Sangiovese Grenache Shiraz, Cabernet Franc Cabernet Sauvignon; Five Mile Hollow Traminer Riesling, Chardonnay Semillon, Classic Red; Discovery Semillon, Chambourcin; The Premiere Collection series of Reserve Semillon, Reserve Fromenteau, Brut, Reserve Chambourcin, Reserve Shiraz, Reserve Cabernet Merlot; fortifieds.
summary A very substantial operation based in the Hastings Valley on the north coast of New South Wales. In earlier years it drew fruit from many parts of Australia, but it is now entirely supplied by the 154 hectares of estate plantings which offer 14 varieties, including the rare chambourcin, a French-bred cross. In February 2002 Cassegrain purchased Hungerford Hill from Southcorp, and secured the services of Phillip John as senior Hungerford Hill winemaker. The identity of Hungerford Hill as a separate venture will be preserved, and it is thus separately listed in this book. Exports to the UK, The Netherlands, Malaysia, Thailand, Philippines, Singapore and Japan.

Cassegrain Northern Slopes Semillon

♀♀♀♀ **2002** Light straw-green; clean, tight, minerally/stony aromas lead into a palate with touches of lemon, slate and talc; very closed, even for a young Semillon. Produced from grapes grown in the Northern Slopes Zone.   **rating:** 85
best drinking Now–2007 **drink with** Antipasto • $16.60

Cassegrain Fromenteau Reserve Chardonnay

♀♀♀♀ **2001** Medium yellow-green; the moderately intense bouquet has quite complex, ripe, yellow peach aromas backed by subtle oak; the peachy/nutty/creamy palate offers balanced acidity and similarly well-controlled oak.   **rating:** 88
best drinking Now–2005 **best vintages** '89, '91, '93, '95, '96 **drink with** Rich chicken or veal • $28.10

Cassegrain Shiraz

♀♀♀♀ **2001** Medium to full purple-red; fresh dark plum and blackberry fruit aromas are linked to spice and subtle oak; the powerful palate is fruit-driven but still angular, needing to round out. A blend of Hastings River, Northern Slopes and Cowra grapes.   **rating:** 87
best drinking 2004–2009 **drink with** Italian • $17.55

Cassegrain Hastings River Reserve Shiraz

♀♀♀♀ **2000** Medium red, the purple starting to fade; the bouquet has warm, regional savoury/earthy/sweet leather aromas, but on the palate gentle blackberry and plum fruits join in the savoury notes of the bouquet. The product of a good vintage in the Hastings River.   **rating:** 87
best drinking 2004–2009 **drink with** Beef pie • $26.60

Cassegrain Reserve Cabernet Sauvignon Merlot

♀♀♀♀ **2001** Medium to full red-purple; the moderately intense bouquet has ripe raspberry and blackberry fruit married with gentle oak; the palate fully reflects the bouquet, with no soapy or green characters whatsoever, and finishes with fine, cedary tannins. Grown on high-altitude vineyards in the New England area around Tenterfield and Inverell.   **rating:** 89
best drinking 2004–2009 **drink with** Lamb shanks • $26.60

castagna vineyard ★★★★☆

Ressom Lane, Beechworth, Vic 3747 **region** Beechworth
phone (03) 5728 2888 **fax** (03) 5728 2898 **open** By appointment
winemaker Julian Castagna **production** 2000 cases **est.** 1997
product range ($26–48 ML) Allegro, Genesis Syrah, La Chiave.
summary The elegantly labelled wines of Castagna will ultimately come from 4 hectares of estate shiraz and viognier that are in the course of establishment (the latter making up 15 per cent of the total). Winemaker Julian Castagna is intent on making wines which reflect the terroir as closely as possible, declining to use cultured yeast or filtration. Genesis Syrah deserves its icon status.

Castagna Allegro

YYYY 2001 Bright, light pink-salmon; the light spice and berry aromas of the bouquet lead into a fresh, crisp and lively palate with balanced acidity and good length. Good shiraz rose style, with above-average structure. **rating:** 86

best drinking Now **drink with** Antipasto • $26

Castagna Genesis Syrah

YYYYY 2001 Medium red-purple; the wonderfully complex and aromatic bouquet ranges through tobacco, spice, black pepper, plum and earth, the oak influence very much in the background; the remarkably intense and long palate has all the flavours promised by the bouquet, finishing with high natural acidity to underwrite its development in bottle. **rating:** 94

best drinking 2005–2015 **best vintages** '99, '01 **drink with** Braised rabbit • $48

castle rock estate ★★★★

Porongurup Road, Porongurup, WA 6324 **region** Great Southern
phone (08) 9853 1035 **fax** (08) 9853 1010 **open** Mon–Fri 10–4, weekends and public holidays 10–5
winemaker Robert Diletti **production** 5000 cases **est.** 1983
product range ($12–23 CD) Riesling, Robert Reserve White, Chardonnay, Late Harvest Riesling, Pinot Noir, Robert Reserve Red, Cabernet Sauvignon Merlot, Liqueur Muscat.
summary An exceptionally beautifully sited vineyard, winery and cellar-door sales area on a 55-hectare property with sweeping vistas from the Porongurups, operated by the Diletti family. The standard of viticulture is very high, and the site itself ideally situated (quite apart from its beauty). The two-level winery, set on the natural slope, was completed in time for the 2001 vintage, and maximises gravity flow, in particular for crushed must feeding into the press. The Rieslings have always been elegant, and have handsomely repaid time in bottle.

Castle Rock Estate Riesling

YYYYY 2002 Very pale straw-green; the classy, aromatic bouquet ranges through citrus, apple and passionfruit. The palate is long, with lingering, fine, lemony acidity running through to the finish. The best young Riesling from Castle Rock for some time (they usually take several years to express their quality). **rating:** 93

best drinking 2006–2012 **best vintages** '86, '89, '90, '91, '93, '94, '96, '97, '98, '00, '02 **drink with** Seafood salad • $18

Castle Rock Estate Pinot Noir

YYYY 2001 Light, bright red-purple; a fragrant bouquet of cherry and strawberry fruit is precisely repeated on the fresh, fractionally simple, palate. **rating:** 89

best drinking Now **drink with** Smoked quail • $21

cathcart ridge estate NR

Moyston Road, Cathcart via Ararat, Vic 3377 **region** Grampians
phone (03) 5352 1997 **fax** (03) 5352 1558 **open** 7 days 10–5
winemaker David Farnhill, Michael Unwin (Consultant) **production** 10 000 cases **est.** 1977
product range ($10–80 CD) Estate range of Shiraz, The Grampian Shiraz, Cabernet; Rhymney Reef Chardonnay, Shiraz, Cabernet Merlot, Old Tawny Port; at the bottom of the price range, Mount Ararat Classic Dry White, Shiraz, Merlot, Cabernet Merlot, Cabernet Sauvignon.
summary In recent years has raised capital to fund a significant expansion programme of both vineyards and the winery, but is still little known in the wider retail trade. Sporadic tastings haven't been particularly exciting. Exports to Ireland and the US.

Cathcart Ridge Rhymney Reef Cabernet Merlot

YYYY 1998 The colour shows obvious development, the bouquet likewise having soft, earthy bottle-developed aromas. The pace picks up on the palate, with quite rich berry fruit on the mid-palate, but the structure is slightly weak. A blend of 60 per cent Cabernet Sauvignon and 40 per cent Merlot. **rating:** 85

best drinking Now–2007 **drink with** Grilled chops • $15

cathedral lane wines ★★★☆

228 Cathedral Lane, Taggerty, Vic 3714 **region** Central Victorian High Country
phone (03) 5774 7305 **fax** (03) 5774 7305 **open** By appointment
winemaker Martin Williams MW **production** 400 cases **est.** 1997
product range ($24 ML) Pinot Noir.

summary Rod Needham and Heather Campbell formed the Acheron Valley Wine Company, which makes the Cathedral Lane wines, in 1997. The 3.2-hectare vineyard is situated on the lower slopes of Mount Cathedral at a height of 280 metres. A variant of the Scott Henry trellis system, with high-density 1-metre spacing between the vines, alternately trained up or down, has been employed. The vineyard planning was supervised by former Coldstream Hills viticulturist Bill Christophersen.

Cathedral Lane Pinot Noir

TTTT 2001 Medium to full red-purple; the bouquet offers a nice mix of black cherry and spice, but the powerful palate tends to grip somewhat; should soften with a little more bottle age, and, if it does so without compromising the fruit, would merit significantly higher points. **rating:** 86

best drinking 2004–2006 **drink with** Tea-smoked duck • $24

catherine vale vineyard ★★★☆

656 Milbrodale Road, Bulga, NSW 2330 **region** Lower Hunter Valley
phone (02) 6579 1334 **fax** (02) 6579 1334 **open** Weekends and public holidays 10–5, or by appointment
winemaker John Hordern (Contract) **production** 1500 cases **est.** 1994
product range ($12–16 CD) Semillon, Semillon Chardonnay, Chardonnay, Dolcetto.
summary Former schoolteachers Bill and Wendy Lawson have established Catherine Vale as a not-so-idle retirement venture. Both were involved in school athletics and sports programmes, handy training for do-it-yourself viticulturists. Most of the grapes from the 5.8-hectare vineyard are sold to contract winemaker John Hordern; a small proportion is vinified for the Catherine Vale label. A new cellar door is expected to be completed in 2003.

Catherine Vale Semillon

TTTTY 2001 Glowing yellow-green; a spotlessly clean bouquet with sweet lemony fruit emerging, honey to follow in due course; the palate is much tighter than the bouquet (reassuringly), with a well-balanced, long, dry finish. **rating:** 92

best drinking 2004–2015 **best vintages** '98, '00 **drink with** Shellfish • $14

Catherine Vale Semillon Chardonnay

TTTT 2001 Medium yellow-green; the moderately intense bouquet is clean, with gently ripe fruit, and the palate has good length and unexpected texture; the chardonnay adds a little to the mid-palate dimension, and the wine is well balanced. **rating:** 87

best drinking Now–2005 **drink with** Pasta carbonara • $12

Catherine Vale Chardonnay

TTTT 2001 Medium yellow-green; the bouquet is complex, but obvious barrel-ferment oak sits on top of the fruit; on the palate the delicate fruit struggles to carry its oak burden. **rating:** 85

best drinking Now **best vintages** '98 **drink with** Poached scallops • $15

catspaw farm NR

Texas Road, Stanthorpe, Qld 4380 **region** Granite Belt
phone (07) 4683 6229 **fax** (07) 4683 6386 **open** Thurs–Sun and public holidays 10–5, 7 days at Easter and June and September Queensland school holidays
winemaker Christopher Whitfort **production** 300 cases **est.** 1989
product range ($12–22 CD) Sauvignon Blanc Semillon, Chardonnay, Golden Queen, Shiraz Merlot, Chambourcin, Cabernet Shiraz, Cats Whiskers Liqueur Muscat, Gold Label Muscat.
summary The foundations for Catspaw Farm were laid back in 1989 when planting of the vineyard began with chardonnay, riesling, cabernet franc, cabernet sauvignon, merlot, chambourcin and shiraz, totalling 4.6 hectares. More recently, Catspaw has moved with the times in planting roussanne, semillon, barbera and sangiovese, lifting total plantings to just under 8 hectares. The newer plantings are yet to come into bearing and the wines are some time from release. In the meantime, a mixed bag of wines are available, some dating back to 1998. Catspaw, incidentally, also offers on-farm accommodation in a self-contained farmhouse (with disabled access) and picnic facilities.

cawdor wines ★★★★☆

Old Mount Barker Road, Echunga, SA 5153 **region** Adelaide Hills
phone (08) 8388 8456 **fax** (08) 8388 8807 **open** By appointment
winemaker Contract **production** 350 cases **est.** 1999
product range ($18 R) Sauvignon Blanc.

summary Jock Calder and his family began the establishment of Cawdor Wines with the purchase of 22 hectares near the township of Echunga. Five hectares of sauvignon blanc were planted in that year, with a further 2.6 hectares of sauvignon blanc, 7.9 hectares of shiraz and 2.7 hectares of riesling planted in the following year. The major part of the production is sold to Nepenthe Wines, but Cawdor nominates how much it wishes to have vinified under its own label each year. It has followed a softly, softly approach, with only small amounts being made; there is no cellar door, nor is one planned. The wine is sold via fax, email, phone, etc, with limited wholesale distribution through David Turner Agencies.

Cawdor Sauvignon Blanc

TTTTT 2002 Light straw-green; the powerful, spotlessly clean bouquet has a mix of gooseberry, herb, green pea and a touch of passionfruit; the long and intense palate sees the flavours move to gooseberry, with very good length. A most auspicious debut. **rating: 93**

best drinking Now–2005 **best vintages** '02 **drink with** Salmon terrine • $18

ceccanti kiewa valley wines   NR

Bay Creek Lane, Mongans Bridge, Vic 3691 **region** Alpine Valleys
phone (03) 5754 5236 **fax** (03) 5754 5353 **open** 7 days 11–5
winemaker Angelo Ceccanti, Moya Ceccanti, Danny Ceccanti **est.** 1988
product range ($13.90–18 CD) Riesling, Shiraz, Merlot, Cabernet Sauvignon.
summary Parents Angelo and Moya Ceccanti, with son Danny, have established 16 hectares of vines, and now use all of the production for their own wines, which are made on-site by the family. Angelo, raised in Tuscany, had extensive exposure to viticulture and winemaking, but it is Moya and Danny who have the technical knowledge.

cedar creek estate   NR

104–144 Hartley Road, Mt Tamborine, Qld 4272 **region** Queensland Coastal
phone (07) 5545 1666 **fax** (07) 5545 4762 **open** 7 days 10–5
winemaker Contract **est.** 2000
product range ($17.50 CD) Genesis Chardonnay Semillon.
summary Opened in November 2000, Cedar Creek Estate takes its name from the creek which flows through the property at an altitude of 550 metres on Tamborine Mountain. A small vineyard has been planted, but has yet to come into bearing, and the focus will always be on general tourism, with a host of facilities for visitors. It also offers Granite Belt wines made by Ballandean, Hidden Creek and Robinson Family. The single wine offered under the Cedar Creek Estate label at the present time is unambiguously directed to the cellar-door trade, being equally unambiguously sweet.

cellarmasters   ★★★★

Cnr Barossa Valley Way and Siegersdorf Road, Tanunda, SA 5352 **region** Barossa Valley
phone (08) 8561 2200 **fax** (08) 8561 2299 **open** Not
winemaker Simon Adams, Steve Chapman, Nick Badrice, John Schwartzkopff, Sally Blackwell, Mark Starick
production NFP **est.** 1982
product range ($16–40 ML) Produces a substantial number of wines under proprietary labels (Dorrien Estate, Rare Print, New Eden, Avon Brae) for the Cellarmaster Group; notable are Storton Hill, Di Fabio, Black Wattle Mount Benson, Wright's Bay, Amberton, Addison Selection 49, Bosworth Edge, Vasarelli and numerous others.
summary The Cellarmaster Group was acquired by Beringer Blass in 1997. Dorrien Estate is the physical base of the vast Cellarmaster network which, wearing its retailer's hat, is by far the largest direct-sale outlet in Australia. It buys substantial quantities of wine from other makers either in bulk or as cleanskin (i.e. unlabelled bottles), or with recognisable but subtly different labels of the producers concerned. It is also making increasing quantities of wine on its own account at Dorrien Estate, many of which are quite excellent, and of trophy quality. The labelling of these wines is becoming increasingly sophisticated, giving little or no clue to the Cellarmaster link. Chateau Dorrien is an entirely unrelated business.

Amberton Shiraz

TTTTT 2001 Striking and intense youthful purple colour; the bouquet is clean, exuding ripe black fruits. The palate is at once big, powerful and rich, yet with some velvety softness, all suggesting the use of micro-oxygenation. Trophy for Best Commercial Dry Red at the Liquorland National Wine Show 2002. **rating: 93**

best drinking 2005–2015 **best vintages** '01 **drink with** Leave it in the cellar • $16.50

Fowler Blair House Limestone Coast Shiraz

ŸŸŸŸŸ **2000** Medium red-purple; the clean bouquet has smoothly integrated fruit and oak. The medium-bodied palate is similarly well balanced, with nicely ripened black cherry fruit doing most of the work. **rating:** 92

best drinking 2004–2009 **drink with** Irish stew • $21.50

Langhorne Creek Area Red Blend

ŸŸŸŸŸ **1999** Medium to full red-purple; solid, dark berry and plum fruit mingles with generous slices of American oak on the bouquet; the palate plays the same tune, with a fleshy texture, fine tannins and plenty of well-integrated oak. A strange name for a blend of Cabernet Sauvignon, Shiraz, Merlot and Malbec made at Bleasdale from grapes supplied by 10 individual growers. Gold medals at Melbourne in 2000 and 2001, and trophy at 2002 Hobart Wine Show for Best Blended Dry Red of Show. **rating:** 90

best drinking Now–2008 **drink with** Backstrap of lamb • $31.50

Vasarelli Passito Amarone

ŸŸŸŸ **2001** Medium to full red-purple; authentic, ripe, dark prune and plum aromas lead into a concentrated palate, with savoury, lingering tannins. Packaged in an extraordinary, and doubtless extremely expensive, 500 ml bottle; a blend of Cabernet Sauvignon, Shiraz, Sangiovese, Merlot and Semillon, calculated to send the blood pressure of Italian Amarone producers soaring. **rating:** 87

best drinking 2004–2010 **drink with** Ragout of venison • $40

Black Wattle Cabernet Sauvignon

ŸŸŸŸŸ **2000** Medium to full red-purple; smooth, sweet blackberry and blackcurrant aromas mark the fruit-driven bouquet; the palate offers luscious fruit in the same flavour spectrum, sweet, but not heavy, with well-balanced tannins. **rating:** 91

best drinking 2004–2014 **best vintages** '98, '00 **drink with** Mature cheddar • $35.99

celtic farm ★★★★

39 Sweyn Street, North Balwyn, Vic 3104 (postal) **region** Warehouse
phone (03) 9857 3600 **fax** (03) 9857 3601 **open** Not
winemaker Gerry Taggert **production** 4000 cases **est.** 1997
product range ($18–28.50 R) South Block Riesling (Clare Valley), The Gridge Pinot Grigio (King Valley), Revenge Botrytis Semillon, Firkin Hall Yarra Valley Shiraz, Raisin Hell Rutherglen Muscat.
summary Yet another warehouse winery, these days owned and run by co-founder Gerry Taggert, joined by long-time friends Mark McNeill and Mike Shields – all fine Celts, according to Taggert. Taggert says, 'Celtic Farm is produced from classic varieties selected from Australia's premium wine regions and made with a total commitment to quality. While we have a desire to pay homage to our Celtic (drinking) heritage, we are also acutely aware that wine should be about enjoyment, fun and not taking yourself too seriously.' Not surprisingly, the team is negotiating with importers in Ireland, and in conjunction with the Celtic Farm brand, may develop an exclusive export label in addition to Celtic Farm.

Celtic Farm Revenge Botrytis Semillon

ŸŸŸŸŸ **2001** Deep gold; rich cumquat, apricot and peach aromas give a heady, exotic edge to the bouquet, in turn reflected by the complex marmalade and peach flavours of the palate, neatly balanced by acidity. **rating:** 92

best drinking Now–2006 **best vintages** '01 **drink with** Tarte Tatin • $26

Celtic Farm Firkin Hall Yarra Valley Shiraz

ŸŸŸŸ **2001** Medium purple-red; the aromatic bouquet initially shows unusual elements of fern and spice, the black cherry coming through thereafter. The attractive palate has sweet red and black cherry fruit coupled with fine tannins; subtle oak. **rating:** 89

best drinking Now–2008 **drink with** Cassoulet • $28

🍎 ceravolo st andrews estate ★★★☆

Suite 16, Tranmere Villate, 172 Glynburn Road, Tranmere, SA 5073 (postal) **region** Adelaide Plains
phone (08) 8336 4522 **fax** (08) 8365 0538 **open** Not
winemaker Collin Glaetzer, Ben Glaetzer (Contract) **est.** 1999
product range ($15–25 R) Chardonnay, Shiraz, Merlot.
summary The Ceravolo family has established a substantial business in the Adelaide Plains region, moving from contract grape growing to grape growing and winemaking under their St Andrews label. The principals

are parents Joe and Heather Ceravolo, and son Dr Joe Ceravolo, who still continues his dental practice, doubling up as vigneron and director of St Andrews Estate. In 1999 the label was launched, centred around shiraz, but with chardonnay and merlot in support. Conspicuous success at the London International Wine Challenge (bronze medals for the 1999 and 2001 Shiraz, gold for the 2000) led to containers of wine being exported to the UK, only to find that the Adelaide Plains region was not recognised by the EC. Thus the Ceravolos became centrally involved in obtaining the subsequently granted Geographical Indication; the place of origin (shown as South Australia for the 2000) has now reverted to Adelaide Plains, for in fact all the grapes are estate-grown.

Ceravolo St Andrews Estate Adelaide Plains Shiraz

▼▼▼▼ 2001 Medium red-purple; the rich and ripe bouquet is quite complex, with faintly gamey aromas in the background; the palate follows suit, with rich dark fruits, some chocolate and subtle oak; plenty of concentration, suggesting disciplined viticulture. **rating: 88**

▼▼▼▼▽ 2000 Medium red-purple; the complex bouquet has obvious American oak influence, but the fruit is there to sustain the oak, with a mix of ripe plum and prune running through to a chewy finish. Gold medal International Wine Challenge, London. **rating: 90**

best drinking Now–2007 **best vintages** '00 **drink with** Bistecca Fiorentina • $25

Ceravolo St Andrews Estate Adelaide Plains Merlot

▼▼▼▼ 2001 Medium red-purple; the moderately fragrant bouquet has a mix of spicy fruit and oak aromas leading through to a palate offering ripe red fruits but little or no varietal character, which is not altogether surprising. Bronze medal International Wine Challenge, London. **rating: 85**

best drinking 2004–2007 **drink with** Ravioli • $20

chain of ponds ★★★★

Adelaide Road, Gumeracha, SA 5233 **region** Adelaide Hills
phone (08) 8389 1415 **fax** (08) 8389 1877 **open** 7 days 10.30–4.30
winemaker Neville Falkenberg **production** 8000 cases **est.** 1993
product range ($10–29 CD) Purple Patch Riesling, Square Cut Semillon, Black Thursday Sauvignon Blanc Semillon, Special Release Sauvignon Blanc, Nether Hill Unwooded Chardonnay, The Morning Star Chardonnay, Corkscrew Road Chardonnay, Novello Rosso, Pinot Noir, Salem Pinot Noir, Ledge Shiraz, Grave's Gate Shiraz, Sangiovese, Amadeus Cabernet Sauvignon, Diva Pinot Chardonnay.
summary Caj and Genny Amadio are the largest growers in the Adelaide Hills, with 100 hectares of vineyards established on a Scott Henry trellis producing 1000 tonnes of grapes a year, almost all sold to Penfolds, but with a small amount made into wine for sale under the Chain of Ponds label. The full-flavoured wines have enjoyed consistent show success, and the brief tenure of energetic Adelaide man-about-town Zar Brooks as general manager enlivened the marketing of the brand and prompted the birth of a rash of new wine names and prolix back labels. The Vineyard Balcony restaurant provides lunches on weekends and public holidays.

Chain Of Ponds Purple Patch Riesling

▼▼▼▼ 2002 Light straw-yellow; a powerful but somewhat heavy and broad bouquet is replayed on the flavoursome, very broad palate. As ready now as it ever will be. **rating: 85**

best drinking Now **best vintages** '98 **drink with** Globe artichoke • $20

Chain of Ponds Black Thursday Sauvignon Blanc

▼▼▼▼▽ 2002 Light straw-green; a spotlessly clean bouquet but with somewhat unusual, sweet lime-accented fruit, which comes through quite strongly on the palate. The texture and weight is admirable; it is simply that the fruit character is left of centre. **rating: 90**

best drinking Now **best vintages** '02 **drink with** Shellfish • $20

Chain of Ponds Novello Nero

▼▼▼▼ 2002 Bright purple-red; the soft and clean bouquet has sweet, ripe, small berry fruit. The luscious, entirely fruit-driven palate ranges through raspberry, blackberry and cherry. A blend of 40 per cent Barbera, 32 per cent Grenache and 28 per cent Sangiovese. **rating: 89**

best drinking Now–2008 **drink with** Lasagne • $15

Chain of Ponds Jupiter's Blood Sangiovese

▼▼▼▼ 2001 Light to medium red, typical of the variety; the bouquet has juicy berry fruit mixed in with hints of tobacco leaf; the cedary, spicy fruit of the palate trails away into drying tannins on the finish. **rating: 85**

best drinking 2004–2007 **drink with** Italian • $27.50

🐌 chalice bridge estate   NR

Rosa Glen Road, Margaret River, WA 6285 **region** Margaret River
phone (08) 9388 6088 **fax** (08) 9382 1887 **open** By appointment
winemaker Tim Mortimer **production** 12 000 cases **est.** 1998
product range ($16–28 ML) Semillon Sauvignon Blanc, Chardonnay, Shiraz, Cabernet Shiraz, Cabernet Sauvignon.
summary Chalice Bridge Estate is a recent arrival in wine terms, but has a long history, dating back to 1924, when it was densely forested with jarrah and marri trees; a group of English settlers arrived with the aim of converting the forest to grazing land. Most gave up, but the Titterton family persevered, eventually selling the property in 1977. Planting of the vineyard began in 1987; there are now 47 hectares of cabernet sauvignon, 29 hectares of shiraz and 27 hectares of chardonnay, with lesser plantings of semillon, sauvignon blanc and merlot making up the total plantings of 121 hectares; this is the second-largest single vineyard in the Margaret River region. A cellar door and tea room is planned for late 2003.

Chalice Bridge Estate Semillon Sauvignon Blanc

▼▼▼▼ 2002 Light to medium yellow-green; the clean bouquet has a nice mix of herb and lemon, a background hint of oak adding complexity. The light to medium-bodied palate is smooth, with riper citrus fruit, and ever-so-subtle oak adding texture. The Sauvignon Blanc component was stainless steel fermented, the Semillon barrel fermented and matured. **rating:** 89

best drinking Now–2005 **drink with** Asian seafood • $16

Chalice Bridge Estate Chardonnay

▼▼▼▼ 2001 Medium yellow-green; the moderately complex bouquet with nutty/minerally overtones flows through into a restrained but crisp and well-balanced palate, with the light fruit not compromised by oak. Sensible winemaking. **rating:** 85

best drinking Now **drink with** Calamari • $20

Chalice Bridge Estate Shiraz

▼▼▼▼ 2000 Medium red-purple; the clean, direct and fresh bouquet ranges through cherry, raspberry and blackberry, the palate moving more into the blackberry/plum spectrum; seems slightly unfinished, needing to settle down with some bottle age. **rating:** 85

best drinking 2005–2010 **drink with** Steak and kidney pie • $24

Chalice Bridge Estate Cabernet Shiraz

▼▼▼▼▼ 2001 Deep purple-red; a complex, very powerful and dense bouquet, massively inky and rich, is followed by a similarly powerful palate, Cabernet-powered, with excellent tannins and a long finish. **rating:** 94

best drinking 2007–2017 **best vintages** '01 **drink with** Lamb rump • $28

Chalice Bridge Estate Cabernet Sauvignon

▼▼▼▼ 2001 Medium to full red-purple; the bouquet is quite complex, with abundant oak, blackcurrant fruit and a substrate of varietal earth. The palate has similar blackcurrant, earth and chocolate flavours plus somewhat raw tannins, giving the impression that the wine was rushed to bottle. **rating:** 85

best drinking 2004–2009 **drink with** Lamb shanks • $20

chalkers crossing   ★★★★☆

387 Grenfell Road, Young, NSW 2594 **region** Hilltops
phone (02) 6382 6900 **fax** (02) 6382 5068 **open** Mon–Fri 9–5, weekends 10–4
winemaker Celine Rousseau **production** 10 000 cases **est.** 2000
product range ($14–18 CD) Hilltops range of Riesling, Semillon, Shiraz, Shiraz Second Label, Cabernet Sauvignon Merlot, Cabernet Sauvignon; Tumbarumba range of Sauvignon Blanc, Chardonnay, Rose, Pinot Noir.
summary Owned and operated by Ted and Wendy Ambler, Chalkers Crossing is based near Young, where the first vines were planted at the Rockleigh vineyard in late 1997, with follow-up plantings in 1998 lifting the total to 10 hectares. It also purchases grapes from Tumbarumba and Gundagai to supplement the intake. A winery was opened for the 2000 vintage, with Celine Rousseau as winemaker. Born in France's Loire Valley and trained in Bordeaux, Celine has worked in Bordeaux, Champagne, Languedoc, Margaret River and in the Perth Hills, an eclectic mix of climates if ever there was one. This French Flying Winemaker (now an Australian citizen) has exceptional skills and dedication. Exports to France, Hong Kong and the UK.

Chalkers Crossing Hilltops Riesling

TTTTY 2002 Pale, almost water-white; an aromatic bouquet with lemon blossom and some free SO_2 evident. The palate has apple and passionfruit flavours, then moves into a tight, minerally finish; needs time, but is screwcap finished, which guarantees its cellaring potential. **rating:** 90

best drinking 2005–2010 **best vintages** '02 **drink with** Asparagus and salmon terrine • $16.50

Chalkers Crossing Hilltops Semillon

TTTTY 2002 Pale, almost water-white; the fresh bouquet has smoke, herb and grass aromas, and the palate is long, lively and fresh. Sixty per cent of the wine was barrel fermented and spends 4 months on lees, which mainly adds to the texture, but also (to a lesser degree) to the flavour; good persistence and aftertaste. Screwcap. **rating:** 92

best drinking 2004–2014 **best vintages** '00, '01, '02 **drink with** Caesar salad • $16.50

Chalkers Crossing Tumbarumba Sauvignon Blanc

TTTTY 2002 Light straw-green; a crisp, clean and fresh bouquet with herb and lemongrass aromas is followed by a bright palate in which the oak (40 per cent barrel fermented and 4 months on lees) impacts on the texture and structure, the fruit falling away fractionally on the finish. Screw-cap. **rating:** 90

best drinking Now **drink with** Marinated octopus • $16.50

Chalkers Crossing Tumbarumba Chardonnay

TTTTT 2001 Light straw-green; fragrant, citrus-accented aromas are almost into fruit blossom; an elegant, fine, long and intense palate marks a totally delicious cool-climate wine, cradled in an almost invisible web of oak. **rating:** 96

best drinking Now–2008 **best vintages** '01 **drink with** Gravlax • $17.50

Chalkers Crossing Tumbarumba Pinot Noir

TTTT 2002 Very light red-purple; the clean, light cherry/cherry stone/spice aromas of the bouquet are followed by a palate which moves decisively to the tangy/savoury end of the spectrum. Plenty of finesse, but not much flesh on the bones, despite 13.5° alcohol. **rating:** 88

best drinking Now–2006 **drink with** Squab • $18

Chalkers Crossing Hilltops Shiraz

TTTTY 2002 Medium purple-red; sweet blood plum aromas are matched by subtle, spicy oak on the bouquet; a complex palate, with fine-grained tannins running across its entire length, and a long finish. A wine which needs time, but carries its 15° alcohol impressively. **rating:** 90

best drinking 2006–2011 **best vintages** '02 **drink with** Lasagne • $18

Chalkers Crossing Hilltops Cabernet Sauvignon Merlot

TTTT 2001 Bright purple-red; aromatic berry, leaf and mint characters on the bouquet come through on the firm, slightly green, palate. Like the Hilltops Shiraz of the same vintage, seems to suggest early picking. **rating:** 86

best drinking 2004–2008 **drink with** Parmigiana • $18

Chalkers Crossing Hilltops Cabernet Sauvignon

TTTT 2002 Deep red-purple; clean, cassis/blackcurrant fruit aromas are followed by a palate anchored on blackcurrant fruit, but multi-faceted, with a tangy, savoury edge and well-worked oak. The components are all in balance, but need time to weld together. **rating:** 89

best drinking 2008–2013 **drink with** Braised ox cheek • $18

chalk hill ★★★★

Field Street, McLaren Vale, SA 5171 (postal) **region** McLaren Vale
phone (08) 8556 2121 **fax** (08) 8556 2221 **open** Not
winemaker Contract **production** 3000 cases **est.** 1973
product range ($15–25 CD) Unwooded Chardonnay, Shiraz, Cabernet Sauvignon.
summary Chalk Hill is in full flight again, drawing upon the 10 hectares of vineyards of grape-growing owners John and Di Harvey, who acquired the vineyard in 1995. There has been considerable work on the vineyard since its acquisition, part being re-trellised, and pre-existing riesling being replaced by new plantings of shiraz and cabernet sauvignon, plus small amounts of barbera and sangiovese. Domestic distribution is solely by mail order; a small portion is exported to Holland, Germany, Switzerland, Sweden, Malaysia and the US (under the Wits End label).

chambers rosewood ★★★★★

Barkly Street, Rutherglen, Vic 3685 **region** Rutherglen
phone (02) 6032 8641 **fax** (02) 6032 8101 **open** Mon–Sat 9–5, Sun 11–5
winemaker Bill Chambers, Stephen Chambers **production** 10 000 cases **est.** 1858
product range ($7–100 CD) A wide range of table wines, including such rarities as Gouias, Blue Imperial (which is in fact Cinsaut) and a wide range of fortified wines. The supremely great wines are the Rare Tokay and Rare Muscat, and the very good Special Muscat and Special Tokay. These are now offered in 375 ml bottles at prices which are starting to reflect their intrinsic value, and are rather higher than the prices for the same wines when last offered in 750 ml bottles.
summary The winery rating is given for the Special Muscat and Tokay (rated 'Grand' under the Rutherglen Classification system) and the Rare wines, which are on a level all of their own, somewhere higher than five stars. The chief virtue of the table wines is that they are cheap. Exports to the US, the UK and Belgium.

channybearup vineyard ★★★★

Lot 4, Channybearup Road, Pemberton, WA 6260 (postal) **region** Pemberton
phone (08) 9776 0042 **fax** (08) 9776 0043 **open** Not
winemaker Brenden Smith, Bruce Dukes **est.** 1999
product range ($18–20 R) Fly Brook range of Unwooded Chardonnay, Shiraz, Cabernet Sauvignon.
summary Channybearup has been established by a small group of Perth businessmen, who have been responsible for the establishment of 62 hectares of vineyards (the majority planted in 1999 and 2000). The principal varieties are chardonnay (22 ha), merlot (10 ha), shiraz (9 ha), cabernet sauvignon (7.5 ha), pinot noir (7 ha), with lesser amounts of verdelho and sauvignon blanc. While principally established as a grape supplier to other makers, limited amounts of Chardonnay, Shiraz and Cabernet Sauvignon have been made and released, with Pinot Noir, Merlot and Cabernet Merlot in the pipeline. Industry veteran Lionel Samson is a director, and the quality of the marketing material (for the mail list) is unimpeachable.

Channybearup Fly Brook Unwooded Chardonnay

???? 2002 Light to medium yellow-green; the clean bouquet has powerful varietal citrus and melon fruit, the light to medium-bodied palate nicely balanced and, while not quite delivering on the full promise of the bouquet, is an extremely good example of unwooded chardonnay.   **rating:** 89
best drinking Now **drink with** Smoked eel • $18

Channybearup Fly Brook Shiraz

????? 2001 Medium red-purple; the moderately intense bouquet has raspberry and plum aromas with background savoury/earthy hints; the palate moves emphatically towards dark cherry and dark chocolate, with a sprinkling of black pepper; ripe tannins and French oak complete the excellent wine.   **rating:** 91
best drinking 2005–2011 **best vintages** '01 **drink with** Kangaroo fillet • $20

Channybearup Fly Brook Cabernet Sauvignon

???? 2001 Bright purple-red; redcurrant/cassis/blackcurrant fruit on the bouquet is followed by a juicy berry palate, with some signs of overripe fruit with hints of hay and straw evident; subtle French oak and fine tannins help the finish.   **rating:** 85
best drinking 2005–2010 **drink with** Lamb shanks • $20

chanters ridge ★★★☆

440 Chanters Lane, Tylden, Vic 3444 **region** Macedon Ranges
phone 0427 511 341 **fax** (03) 9509 8046 **open** Weekends 10–4 by appointment
winemaker John Ellis **production** 250 cases **est.** 1995
product range ($25 CD) Pinot Noir.
summary Orthopedic surgeon Barry Elliott, as well as running the surgery unit at Melbourne's Alfred Hospital, became involved with the Kyneton Hospital 5 years ago. Through a convoluted series of events, he and his wife acquired the 24-hectare property without any clear idea of what they might do with it; later his lifelong interest in wine steered him towards the idea of establishing a vineyard. He retained local overlord John Ellis as his consultant, and this led to the planting of 2 hectares of pinot noir, and the first tiny make in 2000. Barry Elliott intends to retire from surgery and devote himself full-time to the challenge of making Pinot Noir in one of the more difficult parts of Australia, but one which will richly reward success.

Chanters Ridge Pinot Noir

TTTT **2001** Light to medium red-purple; a fragrant array of strawberry, cherry, fern and spice aromas are followed by a light-bodied palate, with delicate strawberry flavours; in this idiom, has good balance, flow and feel. A lovely lunch wine served slightly chilled. **rating: 88**

best drinking Now–2005 **drink with** Pot-roasted quail • $25

chapel hill ★★★★

Chapel Hill Road, McLaren Vale, SA 5171 **region** McLaren Vale
phone (08) 8323 8429 **fax** (08) 8323 9245 **open** 7 days 12–5
winemaker Pam Dunsford (Consultant), Angela Meaney **production** 50 000 cases **est.** 1979
product range ($14–29 CD) Verdelho, Unwooded Chardonnay, Reserve Chardonnay, McLaren Vale Shiraz, McLaren Vale/Coonawarra Cabernet Sauvignon, The Devil Tawny Port.
summary A leading medium-sized winery in the region; in the second half of 2000 Chapel Hill was sold to the diversified Swiss Thomas Schmidheiny group which owns the respected Cuvaison winery in California, as well as vineyards in Switzerland and Argentina. From my knowledge of Cuvaison stretching back 15 years or so, I am confident Chapel Hill is in safe hands. Exports to the UK, the US, Switzerland, Germany and Hong Kong.

Chapel Hill Reserve Chardonnay

TTTTY **2001** Medium yellow-green; the complexity builds progressively on a bouquet with cashew, melon, fig and citrus aromas which also shape the palate; a hint of creaminess comes on the mid-palate, braced by acidity on the finish. A most unusual blend of McLaren Vale, Denmark, Great Southern and Limestone Coast grapes barrel fermented in French oak. **rating: 93**

best drinking Now–2006 **best vintages** '91, '92, '93, '94, '97, '98, '01 **drink with** Slow-cooked fresh salmon • $24

Chapel Hill Shiraz

TTTT **2000** Medium purple-red; savoury berry fruit and some chocolate on the bouquet leads into a very sweet, slightly jammy palate, again with some regional chocolate flavours coming into play; restrained oak throughout. **rating: 86**

best drinking 2004–2008 **best vintages** '91, '94, '95, '96 **drink with** Grilled calf's liver • $29

Chapel Hill McLaren Vale/Coonawarra Cabernet Sauvignon

TTTT **2000** Medium red-purple; the bouquet has high-toned red berry fruit with lesser notes of mint and leaf, the medium-bodied palate fresh and lively, with a touch of regional chocolate also making its mark. A blend of 79 per cent McLaren Vale and 21 per cent Coonawarra grapes. **rating: 89**

best drinking 2004–2009 **best vintages** '88, '90, '91, '92, '95, '98, '99 **drink with** Marinated beef • $26

chapman's creek vineyard NR

RMS 447 Yelverton Road, Wilyabrup, WA 6280 **region** Margaret River
phone (08) 9755 7545 **fax** (08) 9755 7571 **open** 7 days 10.30–4.30
winemaker Various Contract **production** 5000 cases **est.** 1989
product range ($15–26 R) Chenin Blanc, Unoaked Chardonnay, Chardonnay, Merlot, Cabernet Merlot, Tawny Port.
summary Chapman's Creek was founded by the late Tony Lord, an extremely experienced wine journalist who for many years was editor and part-owner of Decanter magazine of the UK, one of the leaders in the field. Notwithstanding this, he was always reticent about seeking any publicity for Chapman's Creek; why, I do not know. Regrettably, it is now too late to find out, as he died in February 2002. Chapman's Creek will continue to be managed by his long-term pal, Chris Leach, who was one of those who kept an eye on him throughout his prolonged illness.

charles cimicky NR

Gomersal Road, Lyndoch, SA 5351 **region** Barossa Valley
phone (08) 8524 4025 **fax** (08) 8524 4772 **open** Tues–Sat 10.30–4.30
winemaker Charles Cimicky **production** 15 000 cases **est.** 1972
product range ($15–25 CD) Sauvignon Blanc, Chardonnay, Cabernet Franc, Classic Merlot, Cabernet Sauvignon, Signature Shiraz, Old Fireside Tawny Port.
summary These wines are of very good quality, thanks to the lavish (but sophisticated) use of new French oak in tandem with high-quality grapes. The intense, long-flavoured Sauvignon Blanc has been a

particularly consistent performer, as has the rich, voluptuous American-oaked Signature Shiraz. No tastings, regrettably; I am sure the wines would score well. Limited retail distribution in South Australia, Victoria, New South Wales and Western Australia, with exports to the UK, the US, Switzerland, Canada, Malaysia and Hong Kong.

charles melton ★★★★★

Krondorf Road, Tanunda, SA 5352 **region** Barossa Valley
phone (08) 8563 3606 **fax** (08) 8563 3422 **open** 7 days 11–5
winemaker Charlie Melton **production** 15 000 cases **est.** 1984
product range ($17.90–36.90 CD) Rose of Virginia, Pinot Meunier, Shiraz, Laura Shiraz, Nine Popes (Shiraz Grenache Mourvedre), Grenache, Cabernet Sauvignon, Sotto di Ferro (sweet white).
summary Charlie Melton, one of the Barossa Valley's great characters, with wife Virginia by his side, makes some of the most eagerly sought à la mode wines in Australia. Inevitably, the Melton empire grew in response to the insatiable demand, with a doubling of estate vineyards to 13 hectares (and the exclusive management and offtake of a further 10 ha) and the erection of a new barrel store in 1996. The expanded volume has had no adverse effect on the wonderfully rich, sweet and well-made wines. Exports to the UK, Ireland, Switzerland, France, the US and South-East Asia.

Charles Melton Rose Of Virginia

TTTTT 2002 Brilliant fuchsia; the bouquet offers an aromatic mix of raspberry, rosemary and spice, the palate with intense cherry and raspberry fruit. Great flavour; one of the best yet. **rating:** 94

best drinking Now **best vintages** '97, '98, '00, '01, '02 **drink with** Anything • $17.80

charles reuben estate NR

777 Middle Tea Tree Road, Tea Tree, Tas 7017 **region** Southern Tasmania
phone (03) 6268 1702 **fax** (03) 6231 3571 **open** Wed–Sun 10–5
winemaker Tim Krushka **production** 350 cases **est.** 1990
product range ($15–22 CD) Riesling, Chardonnay, Unwooded Chardonnay, Pinot Noir.
summary Charles Reuben Estate has 1.5 hectares of pinot noir, 0.5 hectare of chardonnay and a few rows of riesling in production. It has also planted 1.2 hectares of the four Bordeaux varieties, headed by cabernet sauvignon with a little cabernet franc, merlot and petit verdot, and 0.6 hectare of sauvignon blanc accompanied by a few rows of semillon. The principal wines will be Pinot Noir, Chardonnay, a Bordeaux-blend red and a Sauvignon Blanc Semillon, although there is an element of trial in the plantings to establish which varieties succeed best on the estate.

Charles Reuben Estate Pinot Noir

TTTT 2001 Medium red-purple; complex, dark berry aromas are followed by a long palate, with a savoury/foresty finish. Lots of character, although a highly contentious wine at the 2003 Tasmanian Wines Show. I have given it the benefit of the doubt. **rating:** 85

best drinking Now–2007 **drink with** Venison • $22

charles sturt university winery ★★★☆

McKeown Drive (off Coolamon Road), Wagga Wagga, NSW 2650 **region** Southern New South Wales Zone
phone (02) 6933 2435 **fax** (02) 6933 4072 **open** Mon–Fri 11–5, weekends 11–4
winemaker Greg Gallagher **production** 15 000 cases **est.** 1977
product range ($9–20 CD) The precise composition varies from one release to the next, but is divided into two sections: the top-of-the-range Limited Release Series (e.g. Pinot Gris, Chardonnay, Methode Champenoise, Cabernet Sauvignon, Botrytis Semillon, Liqueur Port and Liqueur Muscat) and a basic range of lower-priced varietals including Traminer Riesling, Sauvignon Blanc Semillon, Chardonnay, Shiraz and Cabernet Sauvignon Merlot.
summary A totally new $2.5 million commercial winery (replacing the 1977 winery) was opened on April 9, 2002, complementing the $1 million experimental winery opened in June 2001. The commercial winery has been funded through the sale of wines produced under the Charles Sturt University brand, wines which always offer the consumer good value. It seems reasonable to expect that the quality will rise in the wake of the opening of the two new facilities. Interestingly, this teaching facility is using screwcaps on all of its 2002 vintage wines, both white and red.

Charles Sturt Sauvignon Blanc Semillon

TTTY 2002 Light straw-green; the bouquet has a potent mix of herb and citrus, with a faintly reduced background; the light to medium-bodied palate is minerally and crisp, but without much mid-palate fruit, and has a fractionally grippy finish. From the Central Ranges and Big River Zones. The price is attractive. **rating:** 84

best drinking Now **drink with** Vegetarian • $13.10

Charles Sturt Limited Release Pinot Gris

TTTT 2002 Pale straw; a light but quite fragrant bouquet with green apple and mineral aromas are followed by a clean palate offering similarly flavoured fruit; has length, and the balance is good. **rating:** 85

best drinking Now **drink with** Light seafood • $18.15

Charles Sturt Limited Release Chardonnay

TTTT 2001 Medium yellow-green; melon, fig and fruit aromas are supported by a gentle touch of oak on the bouquet; the soft palate has plenty of weight with nuances of nuts and oak, but needed a touch more zip.

rating: 86

best drinking Now–2005 **best vintages** '93, '94, '96 **drink with** Prawns, creamy pasta • $19.80

charley brothers ★★☆

The Ruins Way, Inneslake, Port Macquarie, NSW 2444 **region** Hastings River
phone (02) 6581 1332 **fax** (02) 6581 0391 **open** Mon–Fri 11–5, weekends 10–5
winemaker John Cassegrain (Contract), Nick Charley **production** 1000 cases **est.** 1988
product range ($11–16 CD) Semillon, Chardonnay, Summer White, Pinot Noir, Shiraz, Cabernet Merlot, Cabernet Sauvignon, Inneslake Mist, Tawny Port.
summary The property upon which the Charley Brothers vineyard is established has been in the family's ownership since the turn of last century but in fact had been planted to vines by a Major Innes in the 1840s. After carrying on logging and fruit growing at various times, the Charley family planted vines in 1988 with the encouragement of John Cassegrain. Around 7.5 hectares of vines have been established.

charlotte plains NR

RMB 3180, Dooleys Road, Maryborough, Vic 3465 **region** Bendigo
phone (03) 5361 3137 **open** By appointment
winemaker Roland Kaval **production** 80 cases **est.** 1990
product range ($16 ML) Shiraz.
summary Charlotte Plains is a classic example of miniaturism. Production comes from a close-planted vineyard which is only 1.6 hectares, part being shiraz, the remainder sauvignon blanc. The minuscule production is sold solely through the mailing list and by phone.

charlotte's vineyard NR

Kentucky Road, Merricks North, Vic 3926 **region** Mornington Peninsula
phone (03) 5989 7266 **fax** (03) 5989 7500 **open** 7 days 11–5
winemaker Michael Wyles **production** NFP **est.** 1987
product range ($18–26 CD) Chardonnay, Shiraz, Cabernet Sauvignon.
summary Denise and Tony Aubrey-Slocock established a 3-hectare vineyard on the slopes of Merricks North. The vineyard was sold in 2002, and a new approach to both viticulture and winemaking has followed.

chateau champsaur NR

Wandang Lane, Forbes, NSW 2871 **region** Central Ranges Zone
phone (02) 6852 3908 **fax** (02) 6852 3902 **open** Saturday 10–5, or by appointment
winemaker Pierre Dalle, Andrew McEwin **production** 200 cases **est.** 1866
product range ($10–13 CD) Colombard Semillon, Chateau Dry White, Shiraz, Shiraz Cabernet, Fortified and Peach Wine.
summary No, the establishment date of 1866 is correct. In that year Frenchmen Joseph Bernard Raymond and Auguste Nicolas took up a 130-hectare selection and erected a large wooden winery and cellar, with production ranging up to 360,000 litres in a year in its heyday. They named it Champsaur after Raymond's native valley in France, and it is said to be the oldest French winery in the Southern Hemisphere. In recent years it traded as Lachlan Valley Wines, but under the ownership of Pierre Dalle has reverted to its traditional name and French ownership. Its business is in transition; most of the wines on offer at the moment are derived

from the Lachlan Valley days of the Chislett family, but with the new plantings and consultancy winemaking by Andrew McEwin, changes are almost certain.

chateau dore   NR

303 Mandurang Road, Mandurang near Bendigo, Vic 3551 **region** Bendigo
phone (03) 5439 5278 **open** 7 days 10–5
winemaker Ivan Grose **production** 1000 cases **est.** 1860
product range ($19–25 CD) Riesling, Shiraz, Cabernet Sauvignon, Tawny Port.
summary Has been in the ownership of the Grose family since 1860, with the winery buildings dating back respectively to 1860 and 1893. All wine is sold through cellar door and function centre.

chateau dorrien   NR

Cnr Seppeltsfield Road and Barossa Valley Way, Dorrien, SA 5352 **region** Barossa Valley
phone (08) 8562 2850 **fax** (08) 8562 1416 **open** 7 days 10–5
winemaker Fernando Martin **production** 2000 cases **est.** 1983
product range ($10–18 CD) Riesling, Semillon Chardonnay, Traminer, Frontignac Traminer, Frontignac Spatlese, Late Harvest Frontignac, Semillon Chardonnay Sparkling Brut, Prima Vera (light red), Limited Release Grenache, Shiraz, Cabernet Sauvignon, Tawny Port.
summary Unashamedly and successfully directed at the tourist trade.

chateau francois   NR

Broke Road, Pokolbin, NSW 2321 **region** Lower Hunter Valley
phone (02) 4998 7548 **fax** (02) 4998 7805 **open** Weekends 9–5, or by appointment
winemaker Don François **production** 700 cases **est.** 1969
product range Pokolbin Mallee Semillon, Chardonnay, Shiraz Pinot Noir.
summary The retirement hobby of former NSW Director of Fisheries, Don François. Soft-flavoured and structured wines which frequently show regional characters but which are modestly priced and are all sold through the cellar door and mailing list to a loyal following. The tasting room is available for private dinners for 12–16 people. Don François sailed through a quadruple-bypass followed by a mild stroke with his sense of humour intact, if not enhanced. A subsequent newsletter said (inter alia) '… my brush with destiny has changed my grizzly personality and I am now sweetness and light … Can you believe? Well, almost!' He even promises comfortable tasting facilities. No tastings for some years.

chateau hornsby   NR

Petrick Road, Alice Springs, NT 0870 **region** Alice Springs
phone (08) 8955 5133 **fax** (08) 8955 5133 **open** 7 days 11–4
winemaker Gordon Cook **production** 1000 cases **est.** 1976
product range ($12–17 CD) Riesling, Semillon, Chardonnay, Shiraz, Cabernet Sauvignon.
summary Draws in part upon 3 hectares of estate plantings, and in part from grapes and wines purchased from other regions. Very much a tourist-oriented operation, with numerous allied entertainments on offer.

chateau leamon   ★★★★

5528 Calder Highway, Bendigo, Vic 3550 **region** Bendigo
phone (03) 5447 7995 **fax** (03) 5447 0855 **open** Wed–Mon 10–5
winemaker Ian Leamon **production** 2500 cases **est.** 1973
product range ($17–38 CD) Riesling, Semillon, Chardonnay, Shiraz, Reserve Shiraz, Cabernet Sauvignon Cabernet Franc Merlot, Reserve Cabernet Sauvignon.
summary One of the longest-established wineries in the region, with estate and locally grown shiraz and cabernet family grapes providing the excellent red wines. It has to be said the white wines are of a lesser standard, but you can't win them all. Limited retail distribution in Victoria, New South Wales and Queensland; exports to Asia, the US, Canada, the UK and Germany.

Chateau Leamon Shiraz
▼▼▼▼▽ **2002** Medium to full red-purple; clean, gently ripe and sweet black cherry/black plum fruit on the bouquet leads into a luscious, ripe, but not jammy, palate; has lots of character, but you do need to accept the 15° alcohol.   **rating:** 90
best drinking 2005–2010 **best vintages** '02 **drink with** Deep-fried quail • $22

Chateau Leamon Reserve Shiraz

▼▼▼▼▽ 2001 Medium to full red-purple; complex but smooth blackberry and dark chocolate fruit aromas intermingle with quality oak; the intense, luscious palate has concentrated dark fruit flavours and lingering, fine tannins. **rating: 93**

best drinking 2004–2015 **best vintages** '97, '00 **drink with** Rich game • $38

Chateau Leamon Reserve Cabernet Sauvignon

▼▼▼▼▽ 2001 Medium to full red-purple; very attractive, clean, blackcurrant fruit and quality oak on the bouquet is followed by blackcurrant and dark chocolate fruit flavours in a supple and smooth palate. Quality oak is again apparent, as are fine tannins, and here the 15° alcohol does not spoil the party. **rating: 93**

best drinking 2006–2016 **best vintages** '01 **drink with** Leg of lamb • $38

chateau pato ★★★★☆

Thompson's Road, Pokolbin, NSW 2321 **region** Lower Hunter Valley
phone (02) 4998 7634 **fax** (02) 4998 7860 **open** By appointment
winemaker Nicholas Paterson **production** 300 cases **est.** 1980
product range ($36 CD) Shiraz.
summary Nicholas and Roger Paterson took over responsibility for this tiny winery following the death of their father David Paterson during the 1993 vintage. Two and a half hectares of shiraz, 1 hectare of chardonnay and 0.5 hectare of pinot noir; most of the grapes are sold, with a tiny quantity of shiraz being made into a marvellous wine. David Paterson's inheritance is being handsomely guarded.

Chateau Pato Shiraz

▼▼▼▼ 2001 Clear red-purple; a strongly regional bouquet with a mix of leafy, leathery, earthy overtones to the fruit leads into a medium-bodied palate, basically savoury in its flavour spectrum, and belies its 13.6° alcohol; needs a little more flesh on its bones, but that may come with time. **rating: 88**

best drinking 2006–2011 **best vintages** '86, '87, '90, '91, '94, '98, '99, '00 **drink with** Barbecued beef • $36

chateau tanunda NR

9 Basedow Road, Tanunda, SA 5352 **region** Barossa Valley
phone (08) 8563 3888 **fax** (08) 8563 1422 **open** 7 days 10–5
winemaker Simon Gilbert, Ralph Fowler (Contract) **production** 8000 cases **est.** 1890
product range ($14.50–38 CD) The Chateau Riesling, Botrytis Semillon, Shiraz, Merlot Cabernet; Chateau Cadet Semillon, Frontignac, Chardonnay, White Shiraz, Shiraz, Petit Verdot, Cabernet Sauvignon; Chateau Tanunda Shiraz, Cabernet Sauvignon.
summary This is one of the most imposing winery buildings in the Barossa Valley, built from stone quarried at nearby Bethany in the late 1880s. It started life as a winery, then became a specialist brandy distillery until the death of the Australian brandy industry, whereafter it was simply used as storage cellars. It has now been completely restored, and converted to a major convention facility catering for groups up to 400. The large complex also houses a cellar door where the Chateau Tanunda wines are sold; Chateau Bistro, gardens and a croquet lawn; the Barossa Small Winemakers Centre offering wines made by small independent winemakers in the region; and, finally, specialist support services for tour operators. It is a sister winery to Cowra Estate, both owned by the Geber family.

Chateau Tanunda The Chateau Riesling

▼▼▼▽ 2002 Light straw-green; tight, mineral and flowery, faintly cosmetic aromas lead into a crisp palate with crushed petal flavours, and a minerally finish. Well away from the usual. **rating: 84**

best drinking Now–2006 **drink with** Summer salads • $17.50

Chateau Tanunda The Chateau Shiraz

▼▼▼▼ 2000 Medium red-purple; the moderately intense bouquet is clean, but not particularly complex; however, the palate offers a great deal more, ranging through ripe, raspberry, chocolate and vanilla flavours; pleasing texture and subtle oak. **rating: 87**

best drinking 2005–2010 **drink with** Beef tongue • $28

chatsfield ★★★★☆

O'Neil Road, Mount Barker, WA 6324 **region** Great Southern
phone (08) 9851 1704 **fax** (08) 9851 1704 **open** Tues–Sun, public holidays 10.30–4.30
winemaker Dionne Miller **production** 7000 cases **est.** 1976

product range ($10–20 CD) Mount Barker Riesling, Sauvignon Blanc, Gewurztraminer, Chardonnay, Indulge (sweet white), Shiraz.

summary Irish-born medical practitioner Ken Lynch can be proud of his achievements at Chatsfield, as can most of the various contract-winemakers who have taken the high-quality estate-grown material and made some impressive wines, notably the Riesling, vibrant Cabernet Franc (as an unwooded nouveau style) and spicy licorice Shiraz. Exports to Ireland, the UK, the US, Japan, Hong Kong and Singapore.

Chatsfield Mount Barker Riesling

TTTTY 2002 Very pale straw-green; a spotlessly clean, flowery, lime blossom and mineral aromas lead into a crisp, lively palate, the flavours reflecting the bouquet and running through to a long finish. **rating:** 92

best drinking 2004–2011 **best vintages** '85, '87, '89, '90, '93, '94, '96, '01, '02 **drink with** Spring salads • $14

Chatsfield Sauvignon Blanc

TTTTY 2002 Light straw-green; another spotlessly clean bouquet with appealing gooseberry and tropical aromas lead into an elegant palate, delicate yet with quite intense fruit; good balance and length to a harmonious wine. **rating:** 91

best drinking Now **best vintages** '02 **drink with** Trout mousse • $16

Chatsfield Indulge 375 ml

TTTTY 2002 Bright, light straw-green; light, clean, lime juice aromas flow into intense lime juice flavours on the palate; good balancing acidity and length. As with all of the current release wines, excellent value. **rating:** 90

best drinking Now–2006 **drink with** Poached fruit • $10

Chatsfield Shiraz

TTTTY 2001 Strong, bright purple-red; classic black fruits with touches of spice and licorice lead into a medium-bodied, smooth, fruit-driven, blackberry and plum flavours. **rating:** 90

best drinking 2006–2011 **best vintages** '88, '89, '90, '94, '95, '98 **drink with** Mature cheddar, finer red meat dishes • $20

chatto wines ★★★★☆

57 Fleet Street, Branxton, NSW 2335 **region** Warehouse
phone 0417 109 794 **fax** (02) 4998 7294 **open** 7 days 9–5
winemaker Jim Chatto **production** 750 cases **est.** 2000
product range ($19.50–35 R) Hunter Valley Semillon; Tamar Valley Riesling and Pinot Noir.
summary Jim Chatto spent several years in Tasmania as the first winemaker at Rosevears Estate, and indeed helped design the Rosevears winery. He has since moved to the Hunter Valley to work for Monarch Winemaking Services, but has used his Tasmanian contacts to buy small parcels of riesling and pinot noir. Possessed of a particularly good palate, he has made wines of excellent quality under the Chatto label. Exports to Canada.

Chatto Pinot Noir

TTTTY 2001 Vivid red-purple; sweet red and black cherry aromas complexed by some notes of spice and stem introduce the wine; the palate is very complex and very powerful, with concentrated black cherry fruit, touches of earthy forest floor, brisk acidity and lingering tannins. May well merit higher points in the years ahead. **rating:** 92

TTTTT 2000 Medium red-purple; the bouquet is stylish and fragrant, with an array of black cherry, plum, spice and forest aromas; the long and intense palate has black cherry and plum fruit, finishing with fine, ripe tannins. The oak is well-integrated and balanced; another great Tasmanian Pinot from the 2000 vintage. **rating:** 94

best drinking Now–2008 **best vintages** '00, '01 **drink with** Venison • $35

chepstowe vineyard ★★★☆

Fitzpatricks Lane, Carngham, Vic 3351 **region** Ballarat
phone (03) 5344 9412 **fax** (03) 5344 9403 **open** 7 days 10–5
winemaker John Ellis (Contract) **production** 700 cases **est.** 1994
product range ($25–30 CD) Chardonnay, Pinot Noir.
summary Way back in 1983 Bill Wallace asked the then Yellowglen winemaker Dominique Landragin what he thought about the suitability of a block of steeply sloping grazing land on the side of the Chepstowe Hill, looking northeast across to the Grampians and its various mountains, including Mount

Misery. Landragin replied, 'it might be possible to grow grapes there', and Wallace subsequently acquired the property. It was not until November 1994 that 1 hectare each of pinot noir and chardonnay was planted, followed by an additional hectare of pinot noir in 1996. In the warmest of vintages it is possible to obtain full ripeness for table wines, but in normal years I suspect sparkling wine (of potentially high quality) might be the best option.

chestnut grove ★★★☆

Chestnut Grove Road, Manjimup, WA 6258 **region** Manjimup
phone (08) 9772 4345 **fax** (08) 9772 4543 **open** 7 days 10–4
winemaker Mark Aitken **production** 13 000 cases **est.** 1988
product range ($10–50 R) Platinum (Verdelho Sauvignon Blanc), Verdelho, Chardonnay, Autumn Harvest, Scintillement (Sparkling), Pinot Noir, Cabernet Merlot, Merlot, Vermilion (Shiraz Cabernet Sauvignon).
summary A substantial vineyard which is now reaching maturity and the erection of an on-site winery are the most obvious signs of change, but ownership, too, has been passed on by the late founder Vic Kordic to his sons Paul (a Perth lawyer) and Mark (who is the general manager of the wine business) and thence (in 2002) to Mike Calneggia's Australian Wine Holdings Limited group. Exports to Canada, Denmark, Germany, Hong Kong, Singapore and the UK.

Chestnut Grove Verdelho

▼▼▼▼ **2002** Medium yellow-green; a quite complex bouquet; both here and on the round, fleshy palate some attractive yellow peach flavours give the wine substance and interest. **rating:** 85

best drinking Now **best vintages** '97 **drink with** Pasta • $18

Chestnut Grove Merlot

▼▼▼▼▽ **2001** Medium to full red-purple; the clean bouquet has positive berry fruit with good olive and herb nuances; the medium to full-bodied palate has lots of flavour and structure in full varietal mode; serious Merlot by any standards. **rating:** 90

best drinking 2005–2010 **best vintages** '99, '01 **drink with** Milk-fed veal • $49.80

Chestnut Grove Cabernet Merlot

▼▼▼▽ **2000** Medium red-purple; spicy savoury overtones diminish the fruit on the bouquet; the very savoury palate has a mix of berry, cedar and spice flavours supported by fine tannins. Does not seem fully ripe. **rating:** 84

best drinking 2004–2007 **best vintages** '95 **drink with** Lamb's fry • $21.10

chestnut hill vineyard ★★★☆

1280 Pakenham Road, Mount Burnett, Vic 3781 **region** Gippsland
phone (03) 5942 7314 **fax** (03) 5942 7314 **open** Weekends and public holidays 10.30–5.30, or by appointment
winemaker Charlie Javor **production** 1200 cases **est.** 1995
product range ($23–27.50 CD) Sauvignon Blanc, Liberty Chardonnay, Pinot Noir.
summary Charlie and Ivka Javor started Chestnut Hill with small plantings of chardonnay and shiraz in 1985 and have slowly increased the vineyards to their present total of a little over 3 hectares. The first wines were made in 1995, and all distribution is through the cellar door and direct to a few restaurants. Situated less than one hour's drive from Melbourne, the picturesque vineyard is situated among the rolling hills in the southeast of the Dandenongs near Mount Burnett. The label explains 'Liberty is a gift we had never experienced in our homeland', which was Croatia, from which they emigrated in the late 1960s.

Chestnut Hill Vineyard Liberty Sauvignon Blanc

▼▼▼▼ **2000** Light straw-green; the bouquet is firm, still quite fresh, with a mix of herb, grass and mineral, characters which come through on the palate which has good depth and weight; holding impressively. **rating:** 88

best drinking Now **drink with** Grilled fish • $23

Chestnut Hill Vineyard Liberty Chardonnay

▼▼▼▼ **2000** Developed yellow-green; a developed nutty/buttery/oaky bouquet is followed by a concentrated and powerful palate from the big end of town, and needing to be drunk sooner rather than later. Complex winemaking techniques have been used. **rating:** 87

best drinking Now **drink with** Chicken pasta • $27.50

cheviot bridge ★★★★

10/499 St Kilda Road, Melbourne, Vic 3004 (postal) **region** Central Victorian High Country
phone (03) 9820 9080 **fax** (03) 9820 9070 **open** Not
winemaker Hugh Cuthbertson **production** 80 000 cases **est.** 1998
product range ($13–25 R) CB range from southeast Australia of Chardonnay, Shiraz and Cabernet Merlot, primarily destined for export; top drawer Yea Valley range of Chardonnay, Pinot Noir, Shiraz, Merlot, Cabernet Merlot.
summary After 15 years at Mildara Blass, Hugh Cuthbertson heads up a highly experienced group of wine professionals who own Cheviot Bridge, armed with a lifetime experience in sales and marketing. Murrindindi Vineyards, his parents' venture, continues as a totally separate entity; the top echelon Cheviot Bridge Yea Valley range comes from four large vineyards in the Yea Valley. The wines are made under the direction of Hugh Cuthbertson at Yering Station, and are distributed by T3 Fine Wines. The CB range is made under the direction of O'Leary Walker. The wines are sold domestically direct from the winery; exports to the US, Canada, the UK and New Zealand. By the time this book appears in print there may have been substantial changes for Cheviot Bridge.

Cheviot Bridge Yea Valley Chardonnay

♥♥♥♥ 2001 Medium yellow-green; the moderately intense and nicely complex bouquet has well-balanced fruit and oak, the palate likewise, with smooth cashew, melon and stone fruit flavours running through to a long finish. Much better than the preceding vintage. **rating: 88**

best drinking Now–2006 **drink with** Brains in black butter • $24

Cheviot Bridge Yea Valley Shiraz

♥♥♥♥♡ 2001 Medium red-purple; the clean and smooth bouquet has a mix of raspberry, mulberry and blackberry fruit, the oak in restraint; an appealing touch of dark chocolate joins the gently ripe fruit on the medium-bodied palate, the oak once again playing a support role. As with the Chardonnay, the oak far better handled than with prior releases. From the Larnoo and Jenbel Vineyards. **rating: 92**

best drinking 2006–2011 **best vintages** '01 **drink with** Leave it in the cellar • $24

Cheviot Bridge Yea Valley Merlot

♥♥♥♥ 2001 Light to medium red-purple; the bouquet is clean and fresh, with fairly light red berry fruit, the palate having somewhat greater length and varietal character than the bouquet suggests, and faintly olivaceous varietal character; fine tannins. **rating: 86**

best drinking Now–2006 **drink with** Veal chop • $25

 # chrismont wines ★★★☆

Upper King Valley Road, Cheshunt, Vic 3678 **region** King Valley
phone (03) 5729 8220 **fax** (03) 5729 8253 **open** 7 days 11–5
winemaker Warren Proft **est.** 1980
product range ($14–19 CD) Riesling, Chardonnay, Shiraz, Cabernet Merlot; La Zona range of Marzemino, Pinot Grigio, Barbera.
summary Arnold (Arnie) and Jo Pizzini have established 80 hectares of vineyards in the Whitfield area of the Upper King Valley. They have planted riesling, sauvignon blanc, chardonnay, pinot gris, cabernet sauvignon, merlot, shiraz, barbera, marzemino and arneis. The La Zona range ties in the Italian parentage of the Pizzinis, and is part of the intense interest in all things Italian.

Chrismont Riesling

♥♥♥♥♡ 2002 Light green-yellow; the fragrant bouquet has aromas of sage, herb, spice and lemon rind; there is plenty of sweet fruit on the mid-palate, and good length. Overall, a relatively soft, early drinking style with lots of appeal. **rating: 90**

best drinking Now–2005 **drink with** Prosciutto-wrapped asparagus • $14

Chrismont Cabernet Merlot

♥♥♥♡ 2000 Medium red-purple; a slightly vegetal, leafy berry bouquet is followed by a palate with a mix of savoury berry, leaf and mint; struggles to reach the ripeness barrier, but has flavour. **rating: 84**

best drinking Now–2007 **drink with** Parmigiana • $19

christmas hill   NR

RSD 25c, Meadows, SA 5201 (postal) **region** Adelaide Hills
phone (08) 8235 3000 **fax** (08) 332 2398 **open** Not
winemaker Peter Leske (Contract) **production** 750 cases **est.** 2000
product range ($14 ML) Sauvignon Blanc.
summary Christmas Hill is primarily a grape grower, selling all but a small part of its production of chardonnay (3.8 ha), sauvignon blanc (3.5 ha), shiraz (1.2 ha), cabernet sauvignon (2.6 ha) and pinot noir (1.4 ha), but keeping back the equivalent of 750 cases of Sauvignon Blanc which is made for Christmas Hill by Peter Leske at Nepenthe Wines. It is primarily sold to two leading Adelaide Clubs, a restaurant and through Christmas Hills' private mailing list, with a dribble finding its way onto the Adelaide retail market. It is offered only by the case to mail list customers.

ciavarella   ★★★

Evans Lane, Oxley, Vic 3678 **region** King Valley
phone (03) 5727 3384 **fax** (03) 5727 3384 **open** Mon–Sat 9–6, Sun 10–6
winemaker Cyril Ciavarella **production** 3000 cases **est.** 1978
product range ($10–28 CD) Aucerot, Chenin Blanc Aucerot, Semillon, Verdelho, Viognier, Unwooded Chardonnay, Chardonnay, Bianca (sweet white), Rosina, Durif, Dolcino (medium-bodied sweet red), Cabernet Sauvignon.
summary Cyril and Jan Ciavarella both entered the wine industry from other professions and have been producing wine since 1992. The vineyard was planted in 1978, with plantings and varieties being extended over the years. One variety, aucerot (first release in 375 ml bottles late 2001) was produced by Maurice O'Shea of McWilliam's Mount Pleasant in the Hunter Valley 50 or more years ago; the Ciavarella vines have been grown from cuttings collected from an old Glenrowan vineyard before the parent plants were removed in the mid-1980s.

clairault   ★★★★

Caves Road, Wilyabrup, WA 6280 **region** Margaret River
phone (08) 9755 6225 **fax** (08) 9755 6229 **open** 7 days 10–5
winemaker Will Shields **production** 40 000 cases **est.** 1976
product range ($14.50–50 CD) Riesling, Semillon, Sauvignon Blanc, Semillon Sauvignon Blanc, Chardonnay, Claireau (sweet white), Cape Pink, Cabernet Merlot, Cabernet Sauvignon, The Clairault Claddah Reserve; also Swagman's Kiss White, Chardonnay, Swagman's Kiss Red.
summary Bill and Ena Martin, with sons Conor, Brian and Shane acquired Clairault several years ago, which has led to a major expansion of the vineyards on the 120-hectare property. The 12 hectares of vines established by the Lewises, and up to 25 years old, are being supplemented by the development of another 70 hectares of vines on the property, with an end-point ratio of 70 per cent red varieties to 30 per cent white varieties. This will see continuing steep increases in production. A restaurant has been opened for lunch 7 days. Domestic distribution throughout all states; exports to the US, Canada, the UK and Germany.

Clairault Estate Riesling
▼▼▼▼ **2002** Light straw-green; a much richer bouquet than in prior vintages, with intense tropical lime aromas; the palate follows suit, ripe, rich and full of flavour; slightly broad, and early developing.   **rating:** 87
best drinking Now–2007 **best vintages** '85, '88, '91, '92, '93, '01 **drink with** Shellfish • $21

Clairault Estate Semillon
▼▼▼▼ **2002** Light to medium yellow-green; the complex bouquet has some oak woven through the ripe, lemon fruit; the palate provides more of the same, with well-balanced fruit and oak, but is definitely a food style wine.   **rating:** 88
best drinking Now–2006 **drink with** Smoked trout • $23

Clairault Sauvignon Blanc
▼▼▼▼♡ **2002** Pale straw-green; the clean, moderately intense bouquet ranges through grass, herb, redcurrant and mineral; the palate has plenty of flavour and mouthfeel; particularly on entry; well made.   **rating:** 90
best drinking Now **best vintages** '93, '95, '97, '02 **drink with** Shellfish • $18.50

Clairault Semillon Sauvignon Blanc
▼▼▼▼♡ **2002** Light straw-green; the bouquet is spotlessly clean with spice and mineral aromas. The palate has good balance and length, bringing touches of herb, grass and lemon into play.   **rating:** 90
best drinking Now–2005 **best vintages** '88, '91, '92, '93, '95, '97, '01 **drink with** Seafood salad • $18.50

Clairault Chardonnay

♥♥♥♥ 2002 Pale straw-green; the bouquet has a slight burnt match character, due either to a touch of reduction or charry barrel-ferment/solids inputs; the palate has citrus, nectarine and grapefruit flavours, the oak far less obvious. Fair length. **rating:** 87

best drinking Now–2006 **drink with** Sautéed chicken • $18.50

Clairault Swagman's Kiss Red

♥♥♥♥ 2001 Strong purple-red; blackberry, mint and spice aromas lead into a firm palate, with a mix of mint and blackberry providing plenty of flavour. The structure and depth aren't there, but this is excellent value for a Margaret River blend of Cabernet Sauvignon, Merlot and Cabernet Franc. **rating:** 86

best drinking 2004–2008 **drink with** Lamb backstrap • $14.50

Clairault Cabernet Merlot

♥♥♥♥ 2001 Medium red-purple; attractive, gently spicy/savoury edges to the red berry fruit of the bouquet is followed by a full-bodied palate, once again with a savoury/varietal grip to the deep blackcurrant fruit; needs time and will only go upwards from here. **rating:** 89

best drinking 2006–2011 **drink with** Braised lamb • $28

Clairault Cabernet Sauvignon

♥♥♥♥♡ 2001 Medium purple-red; the aromatic bouquet has blackcurrant, leaf and mint aromas, the palate swelling considerably, with luscious blackcurrant fruit at its core; appealing texture and structure. Good value. **rating:** 90

best drinking 2004–2009 **drink with** Game pie • $18.50

Clairault Estate Cabernet Sauvignon

♥♥♥♥♥ 2001 Medium purple-red; the complex bouquet has blackcurrant plus appealing touches of spice and sweet earth, the palate focusing on pure, sweet, ripe blackcurrant fruit; excellent tannin and oak balance. Lovely wine. **rating:** 94

best drinking 2006–2016 **best vintages** '00, '01 **drink with** Boned leg of lamb • $30

🐏 clancy's of conargo   NR

Killone Park, Conargo Road, Deniliquin, NSW 2710 **region** Riverina
phone (03) 5884 6684 **fax** (03) 5884 6779 **open** 7 days 10–6
winemaker Bernard Clancy, Jason Clancy **production** 1000 cases **est.** 1999
product range ($10–15 CD) Semillon Chardonnay, Verdelho, Tamingo, Mataro, Grenache, Shiraz, Cabernet Sauvignon
summary The Clancy family has been carrying on a mixed farming enterprise on their property north of Deniliquin for over 25 years, including lucerne growing, cropping and sheep production. A tiny planting of taminga was made in 1988, but it was not until 6 hectares were planted in 1997 that the Clancys ventured into commercial grape growing and winemaking. The predominant varieties are shiraz and semillon, all of the production being sold locally and through cellar door.

clarence hill   ★★★☆

PO Box 530, McLaren Vale, SA 5171 **region** McLaren Vale
phone (08) 8323 8946 **fax** (08) 8323 9644 **open** Not
winemaker Claudio Curtis, Brian Light (Contract) **est.** 1990
product range ($10–35 ML) Clarence Hill range of Riesling, Semillon, Sauvignon Blanc, Chardonnay, Shiraz, Grenache Shiraz, Cabernet Sauvignon Merlot, Cabernet Sauvignon, La Cavata Old Port; Landcross range of Sauvignon Blanc Semillon, Shiraz Cabernet Sauvignon.
summary This is indeed a complicated story, with the Curtis family as its core, encompassing a wine history dating back to the 15th century in Italy. In 1956 the family emigrated to Australia, purchasing its first vineyard land from one Clarence William Torrens Rivers, and renamed it Clarence Hill. Further land was acquired in the 1980s and 1990s, establishing the Landcross Farm and California Rise vineyards, which, together with Clarence Hill, now have over 100 hectares in production. In 1990 Claudio Curtis, having previously acquired a science degree from the University of Adelaide formed the Tiers Wine Co (Australia) Pty Ltd to undertake wine production and sales. That company, obviously enough, has nothing to do with Petaluma, and just to complicate matters yet further, a new winery adjacent to the company's vineyards, operational for the 2002 vintage, is called Landcross Estate Winery. Exports to the UK, Canada, Switzerland and Thailand.

Clarence Hill Sauvignon Blanc

♥♥♥♥ 2002 Light to medium yellow-green; the solid bouquet has varietal herb, capsicum and gooseberry aromas, the palate with plenty of depth in a big, bold style.　**rating:** 86

best drinking Now　**drink with** Grilled eggplant • $13

Clarence Hill Chardonnay

♥♥♥♥ 2002 Medium yellow-green; the solid bouquet is in typical Clarence Hill style, the palate with abundant ripe, soft peachy fruit providing ample mouthfeel. Any oak is incidental.　**rating:** 85

best drinking Now　**drink with** Takeaway • $14

Clarence Hill Shiraz

♥♥♥♥ 2000 Medium red-purple; the clean bouquet has a mix of blackberry (predominant) plus touches of chocolate, earth and oak; there is a balanced range of dark chocolate and black fruit flavours on the palate, supported by good tannins and extract.　**rating:** 89

best drinking 2005–2010　**best vintages** '98　**drink with** Char-grilled rump steak • $19.50

Clarence Hill Grenache Shiraz

♥♥♥♥ 2001 Light to medium red-purple; the bouquet has clear varietal character, with juicy, jammy berry aromas, the palate with sweet, spicy, juicy fruit and zero tannins.　**rating:** 86

best drinking Now　**drink with** Pasta with herbed tomato sauce • $15.50

Clarence Hill Cabernet Sauvignon

♥♥♥♥ 2000 Medium red-purple; the bouquet has savoury/earthy/vanilla overtones to the fruit; soft blackberry, chocolate and mint flavours are supported by soft tannins on the palate. A surprise gold from the 2003 Sydney International Wine Competition. Obviously the judges were looking for a particular style, and Clarence Hill fitted the bill exactly.　**rating:** 86

best drinking Now–2006　**drink with** Rack of lamb • $18.50

clarendon hills ★★★★☆

Brookmans Road, Blewitt Springs, SA 5171　**region** McLaren Vale
phone (08) 8364 1484　**fax** (08) 8364 1484　**open** By appointment
winemaker Roman Bratasiuk　**production** 12 000 cases　**est.** 1989
product range ($65–250 R) Individual vineyard releases of Pinot Noir, Syrah, Shiraz, Grenache and Cabernet Sauvignon.
summary Clarendon Hills produces some of the most startlingly concentrated, rich and full-bodied red wines to be found in Australia, rivalled in this respect only by Wendouree. Roman Bratasiuk is a larger-than-life figure who makes larger-than-life wines. Technocrats may quibble about this or that aspect, but influential judges such as Robert Parker have neither reservations about nor problems with the immense, brooding red wines which Bratasiuk regularly produces from small patches of old, low-yielding vines which he ferrets out. Moreover, even the technocrats have been silenced by the technical excellence of the wines since 1998. Exports to New Zealand, the US, Canada, Germany, Switzerland, Belgium, The Netherlands, Sweden, the UK and Japan.

Clarendon Hills Hickinbotham Vineyard Pinot Noir

♥♥♥♥ 2001 Medium to full red-purple; the bouquet is clean, without any suggestion of bacterial or other activity; spicy dark plum aromas lead into a fully-framed and bodied wine, with some varietal character, good oak and handling of extract. A well-made wine; the limitations lie in the vineyard, which will always provide fruit headed towards dry red.　**rating:** 87

best drinking 2004–2007　**drink with** Chinese deep-fried quail • $65

Clarendon Hills Brookman Shiraz

♥♥♥♥♡ 1999 Medium red-purple; a relatively discreet bouquet with wafts of spice, black cherry and leather is followed by a palate which is surprisingly light and elegant for Clarendon Hills; fine tannins and controlled oak. Jekyll and Hyde stuff.　**rating:** 90

best drinking 2004–2009　**best vintages** '98, '99　**drink with** Kangaroo fillet • $95

Clarendon Hills Piggott Range Vineyard Syrah

♥♥♥♥♥ 2001 Dense purple-red; the bouquet is spotlessly clean, with potent, powerful black fruit aromas which have absorbed the oak; the palate is crammed with blackberry fruit, the oak once again in the background, finishing with long, persistent tannins. A genuine 20-year proposition.　**rating:** 94

best drinking 2010–2020　**best vintages** '01　**drink with** Beef with bone marrow • $150

Clarendon Hills Brookman Merlot

ŸŸŸŸŸ **2001** Medium to full red-purple; deep, dark, briary, savoury, chocolatey aromas lead into a lavish, dark berry-fruited palate, mercifully not as tannic as expected, though still requiring patience, and – at best – a Robert Parker-type Merlot. **rating:** 90

best drinking 2007–2015 **best vintages** '01 **drink with** Tea-smoked lamb • $65

Clarendon Hills Old Vines Grenache

ŸŸŸŸ **2001** Medium red-purple; the bouquet is clean with juicy berry varietal character and subtle oak; the strongly varietal lush jammy red berry fruit of the palate has some tannins to give structure. **rating:** 88

best drinking 2005–2010 **drink with** Dinosaur rump • $65

Clarendon Hills Romas Vineyard Old Vines Grenache

ŸŸŸŸ **2001** Medium to full red-purple; the bouquet is more compact than that of the Clarendon Grenache of the same vintage, with clean, dark berry fruit; the palate, in turn, is very powerful, oozing tannins, and to be left strictly alone for a decade. **rating:** 89

best drinking 2011–2021 **best vintages** '99 **drink with** Leave it in the cellar • $85

Clarendon Hills Hickinbotham Vineyard Cabernet Sauvignon

ŸŸŸŸŸ **2001** Medium red-purple; an array of leafy/earthy/cedary/savoury aromas leads into a palate with good complexity and weight, a mix of blackberry and savoury fruit with definite overtones of Bordeaux; has considerable length and presence. **rating:** 92

best drinking 2006–2016 **best vintages** '98, '01 **drink with** Kangaroo fillet • $65

classic mclaren wines ★★★☆

Lot B, Coppermine Road, McLaren Vale, SA 5171 **region** McLaren Vale
phone (08) 8323 9551 **fax** (08) 8323 9551 **open** By appointment
winemaker Tony De Lisio **production** 7100 cases **est.** 1996
product range ($16.55–100 R) CMC range of Shiraz, Grenache, Cabernet Merlot; and La Testa range of Chardonnay, Shiraz, Blend (Shiraz Grenache Cabernet Sauvignon), Merlot, Grenache, Cabernet Sauvignon.
summary Tony and Krystina De Lisio have established a substantial business in a relatively short period of time. They have established vineyard plantings of shiraz (20.47 ha), merlot (11.34 ha), cabernet sauvignon (9.29 ha), semillon (3.9 ha) and chardonnay (0.41 ha), and are currently building a new winery and underground cellar storage for wine in barrel and packaged wine. When the new buildings are completed, there will be facilities for tastings, promotions and the possibility of limited cellar-door sales. The wines are distributed in Sydney and Melbourne by Ultimo Wine Centre, Adelaide being serviced direct from the winery. Exports to the UK, the US, Thailand, Germany, Belgium, Switzerland and New Zealand have been established at impressively high prices.

Classic McLaren Wines La Testa Chardonnay

ŸŸŸŸ **2001** Medium yellow-green; a rich, complex and powerful bouquet with obvious barrel-ferment and oak maturation inputs; some nectarine fruit comes through on the palate, but is still shackled by the abundance of oak. Some will doubtless love this style. **rating:** 87

best drinking Now–2005 **drink with** Pan-fried chicken breast • $29.80

Classic McLaren Wines Shiraz

ŸŸŸŸ **2000** Medium red-purple; the clean and smooth bouquet has moderately ripe red and black fruits coupled with nice oak; the light to medium-bodied palate brings a touch of regional chocolate to an easy-drinking style, finishing with soft tannins. **rating:** 87

best drinking Now–2006 **drink with** Gourmet sausages • $23.10

Classic McLaren Wines La Testa Blend

ŸŸŸŸ **2001** Medium to full red-purple; clean, dark fruit aromas dominate the bouquet; the palate gains weight and ripeness, with a lush, almost sweet array of prune, blackberry and chocolate, nice fine tannins and controlled oak. **rating:** 89

best drinking 2004–2011 **drink with** Bistecca Fiorentina • $46.35

Classic McLaren Wines Cabernet Merlot

ŸŸŸŸ **2000** Medium red-purple; the moderately intense bouquet has a complex array of earth, blackcurrant, dark chocolate and vanilla aromas, all of which are reflected in the ripe palate, which finishes with good tannins. **rating:** 87

best drinking 2004–2010 **drink with** Lamb casserole • $20

Classic McLaren Wines La Testa Cabernet Sauvignon

▼▼▼▼ 2000 Medium purple-red; the bouquet has sweet blackcurrant and blackberry fruit, the palate moving up a gear with extremely sweet fruit; an altogether curious wine, because the alcohol is only 13.5°, and yet the flavours are of hyper-ripe grapes.   **rating:** 87

best drinking 2005–2010 **best vintages** '98, '99 **drink with** Fillet of beef • $49.66

clayfield wines ★★★★☆

Wilde Lane, Moyston, Vic 3377 **region** Grampians
phone (03) 5354 2689 **open** 7 days 10–4; phone first if possible
winemaker Simon Clayfield **production** NFP **est.** 1997
product range ($45 CD) Shiraz.
summary Former long-serving Best's winemaker Simon Clayfield and wife Kaye are now doing their own thing. They have planted 2 hectares of shiraz between 1997 and 1999, and after early vintages from 1999 to 2001, would have produced a substantial crop in 2002 were it not for a grass fire a month before vintage which destroyed the entire crop and the inter-row cover crops of peas, strawberries, clover, oats and rye corn which had been laboriously established. Simon Clayfield takes what most would consider a sickening blow with the comment, 'considering the severity of the fires throughout other parts of Victoria and NSW lately, I don't think we have too much to complain about'. He is now busily retraining all of the regrowth in the vines. The volumes so far made are tiny, and the Clayfields expect to be producing more than 750 cases of Shiraz by 2005. The splendid Black Label Shiraz 2000 and 2001 sell for $45 at cellar door and are distributed through Woods Wines Pty Ltd (03) 9381 2263 and through retail at Armadale Cellars, High Street, Prahran. Currently one-third of the production is exported to the US.

Clayfield Shiraz

▼▼▼▼▼ 2001 Deep purple-red; the spotlessly clean, moderately intense bouquet has smooth blackberry and plum aromas which come through precisely on the palate. Here the silky, velvety texture provides excellent mouthfeel, and the structure is equally good, with a faint twist of acidity on the long finish. Somewhere in all of this a touch of chocolate also makes its appearance. Lovely wine.   **rating:** 94

▼▼▼▼ 2000 Medium to full red-purple; an array of dark fruit aromas of prune, plum and spice are followed by a palate with blackberry, faintly jammy plum, and soft, ripe tannins. Not as concentrated as the 2001; curiously, notwithstanding the ripe flavours, has 13° alcohol compared to the 13.5 for the 2001.   **rating:** 88

best drinking 2006–2016 **drink with** Braised oxtail • $45

claymore wines ★★★★☆

Leasingham Road, Leasingham, SA 5452 **region** Clare Valley
phone 0412 822 250 **fax** (08) 8284 2899 **open** Weekends and public holidays 10–5
winemaker Justin Ardill **production** 3000 cases **est.** 1998
product range ($16–30 CD) Joshua Tree Clare Valley Riesling, Joshua Tree Watervale Riesling, Duet Semillon Chardonnay, Duet Grenache Shiraz, Nocturne Shiraz, Dark Side of the Moon Shiraz, Merlot, Nocturne Cabernet.
summary Claymore Wines draws on various vineyards, some situated in the Clare Valley, others in McLaren Vale. The Kupu-Kupu vineyard at Penwortham has 9 hectares of shiraz and 2 of merlot planted in 1997; the Nocturne series of wines come from the Wilpena and Moray Park vineyards owned by the Trott family; while the Joshua Tree Watervale Riesling comes from old vines on the Leasingham to Mintaro road which are not, however, estate-owned (although the story is, I must admit, somewhat complex). It is the Joshua Tree Rieslings which have attracted high ratings from both magazines and at the Clare Valley Wine Show.

Claymore Joshua Tree Clare Valley Riesling

▼▼▼▼▼ 2002 Light straw-green; a clear, pure mineral and apple bouquet leads into a palate with great focus, intensity, and, above all else, length to the apple and lime flavours; minerally acidity to close. This falls in what I might call the 'classic' side of the divide of the 2002 Riesling wines.   **rating:** 94

best drinking 2007–2015 **best vintages** '02 **drink with** Grilled King George whiting • $18

Claymore Joshua Tree Watervale Riesling

▼▼▼▼▼ 2002 Light straw-green; more complex than the Clare Valley Riesling, with greater richness and ripeness; the palate has sweet lime, passionfruit, and even stone fruit; excellent length. Whereas the Clare Valley wine needs another 5 years to show its best, this wine is ready to roll right now.   **rating:** 94

best drinking Now–2010 **best vintages** '01, '02 **drink with** Salmon and asparagus terrine • $25

clearview estate mudgee ★★★

Cnr Sydney and Rocky Water Hole Road, Mudgee, NSW 2850 **region** Mudgee
phone (02) 6372 4546 **fax** (02) 6372 7577 **open** Fri–Mon 10–4, or by appointment
winemaker Letitia (Tish) Cecchini **production** 2200 cases **est.** 1995
product range ($14–19 CD) Church Creek Chardonnay (oaked and unoaked); Rocky Waterhole Red Shiraz and Cabernet Sauvignon.
summary No relationship with the famous Hawke's Bay winery, but doubtless John E Hickey and family would be delighted to achieve the same quality. They have progressively planted 4.16 hectares of shiraz, 2.16 hectares each of chardonnay and cabernet sauvignon, 1.5 hectare of merlot, and small amounts of cabernet franc, semillon, pinot grigio, barbera and sangiovese (yet to come into bearing) since 1995, and send the grapes to the Hunter Valley for contract-making. An 'Aussie Farm' style cellar door, with a timber deck looking out over the vineyard and surrounding vista was opened in September 2000. Exports to the US.

Clearview Estate Mudgee Church Creek Unwooded Chardonnay

▼▼▼▼ 2000 Bright, light yellow-green; clean, light nectarine fruit aromas are followed by tangy and lively palate, with some citrus as well as nectarine; developing very slowly, like the unwooded Chardonnays of Montrose many years ago; well above average for a normally boring wine. **rating:** 85
best drinking Now–2006 **drink with** Chinese baked fish • $15

Clearview Estate Mudgee Church Creek Chardonnay

▼▼▼▼ 2001 Light to medium yellow-green; the clean bouquet is fruit-driven, the oak barely perceptible; there is much the same play on the light to medium-bodied palate; developing slowly, but not a lot of fruit hiding in the basement. **rating:** 85
best drinking Now–2006 **best vintages** '00 **drink with** Pan-fried veal • $17

Clearview Estate Mudgee Rocky Waterhole Red Cabernet Sauvignon

▼▼▼▽ 2001 Light to medium red-purple; light, faintly jammy blackcurrant/berry fruit aromas fade somewhat on the light, savoury, cedary palate, holding in there by the skin of its teeth. **rating:** 84
best drinking Now–2005 **drink with** Pasta • $18

clemens hill ★★★★☆

686 Richmond Road, Cambridge, Tas 7170 **region** Southern Tasmania
phone (03) 6248 5985 **fax** (03) 6248 5985 **open** By appointment
winemaker Julian Alcorso (Contract) **production** 650 cases **est.** 1994
product range ($17.50–25 CD) Sauvignon Blanc, Chardonnay, Pinot Noir.
summary The Shepherd family acquired Clemens Hill in June 2001 after selling their Rosabrook winery in the Margaret River to Palandri Wines. They also have a shareholding in Winemaking Tasmania, the newly established contract winemaking facility run by Julian Alcorso, who will henceforth make the Clemens Hill wines. A trebling of the estate vineyards from 1 hectare to over 3 hectares (with 1.3 hectares of pinot noir) will occur in the spring of 2003.

Clemens Hill Pinot Noir

▼▼▼▼▼ 2001 Clear red-purple; a classy and complex bouquet features stylish oak handling, the ripe, plummy fruit coming through strongly on the similarly complex palate, rounded off with lovely savoury tannins. A top class act from go to whoa. Richly deserved gold medal 2003 Tasmanian Wines Show. **rating:** 95
best drinking Now–2007 **best vintages** '01 **drink with** Roast squab • $25

cleveland ★★★★

Shannons Road, Lancefield, Vic 3435 **region** Macedon Ranges
phone (03) 5429 1449 **fax** (03) 5429 2017 **open** 7 days 9–5
winemaker Keith Brien **production** 2500 cases **est.** 1985
product range ($10–45 CD) Chardonnay, Pinot Gris, Macedon Brut, Brut Rose, Pinot Noir, Heathcote Shiraz, Minus Five Cabernet Merlot; Brien Family Chardonnay Gordo, Muscat Gordo Blanco, Shiraz.
summary The Cleveland homestead was built in 1889 in the style of a Gothic Revival manor house but had been abandoned for 40 years when purchased by the Briens in 1983. It has since been painstakingly restored, and 3.8 hectares of surrounding vineyard established. In January 2002 a partnership was formed between Keith Brien and the Grange Group of Conference Centres which initiated fast-track development of The Grange at

Cleveland Winery, with 22 suites, plus a large conference room and facilities alongside the erection of a new winery and warehouse. The rating is for prior release tastings. Exports to the UK.

cliff house   NR

57 Camms Road, Kayena, Tas 7270 **region** Northern Tasmania
phone (03) 6394 7454 **fax** (03) 6394 7454 **open** By appointment
winemaker Julian Alcorso (Contract) **production** 2500 cases **est.** 1983
product range ($18–20 R) Riesling, Chardonnay, Pinot Noir, Devil's Elbow (Pinot Cabernet blend), Cabernet Sauvignon.
summary Cliff House has undergone a metamorphosis. In 1999 Geoff and Cheryl Hewitt sold the 4-hectare vineyard they established in the Tamar Valley area in 1983. They have now turned a two-hole golf course around their house into a second, new vineyard, planted to riesling and pinot noir. No recent tastings.

clonakilla   ★★★★★

Crisps Lane, Murrumbateman, NSW 2582 **region** Canberra District
phone (02) 6227 5877 **fax** (02) 6227 5871 **open** 7 days 11–5
winemaker Tim Kirk **production** 3500 cases **est.** 1971
product range ($16–55 CD) Riesling, Semillon Sauvignon Blanc, Viognier, Chardonnay, Shiraz Viognier, Hilltops Shiraz, Cabernet Merlot.
summary The indefatigable Tim Kirk, who has many of the same personality characteristics as Frank Tate (of Evans & Tate), has taken over the management of Clonakilla from father and scientist Dr John Kirk. The quality of the wines is excellent, none more so than the highly regarded Shiraz Viognier, which sells out quickly every year. Exports to the UK, the US, Canada, Singapore and Hong Kong.

Clonakilla Shiraz Viognier
ŸŸŸŸŸ 2001 Medium to full purple-red; a strikingly fragrant and exuberant, complex, multi-berry, licorice and leather bouquet is repeated on the palate, where there is an excellent balance between the spicy fruit and acidity, the oak positive but not dominant. **rating:** 96
best drinking 2005–2015 **best vintages** '90, '92, '93, '94, '95, '97, '98, '99, '00, '01 **drink with** Jugged hare • $55

clos clare   ★★★★

Old Road, Watervale, SA 5452 **region** Clare Valley
phone (08) 8843 0161 **fax** (08) 8843 0161 **open** Weekends and public holidays 10–5
winemaker Various Contract **production** 1000 cases **est.** 1993
product range ($18–23 CD) Riesling, Shiraz.
summary Clos Clare is based on a small (2 ha), unirrigated section of the original Florita Vineyard once owned by Leo Buring and which produces Riesling of extraordinary concentration and power. Exports to the US and Ireland.

clovely estate   NR

Steinhardts Road, Moffatdale via Murgon, Qld 4605 **region** South Burnett
phone (07) 3876 5200 **fax** (07) 3876 5200 **open** 7 days 10–5
winemaker David Lowe, Adam Chapman (Contract) **production** 15 000 cases **est.** 1998
product range ($12.95–14.95 CD) Left Field Semillon Chardonnay, Chardonnay, Merlot, Shiraz, Cabernet Merlot; Fifth Row Chardonnay, Shiraz Cabernet.
summary Although new-born, Clovely Estate has the largest vineyards in Queensland, having established 174 hectares of vines at two locations just to the east of Murgon in the Burnett Valley. There are 127 hectares of red grapes (including 74 hectares of shiraz) and 47 hectares of white grapes. The attractively packaged wines are sold in four tiers: Clovely Estate at the top end, and which will not be produced every year; Left Field, strongly fruity and designed to age; Fifth Row, for early drinking; and Outback, primarily designed for the export market.

clover hill   ★★★★☆

Clover Hill Road, Lebrina, Tas 7254 **region** Northern Tasmania
phone (03) 6395 6114 **fax** (03) 6395 6257 **open** 7 days 10–5, by appointment in winter
winemaker Peter Steer, Loic Le Calvez, Mark Laurence **production** 4000 cases **est.** 1986
product range ($33 R) Clover Hill (Sparkling).

summary Clover Hill was established by Taltarni in 1986 with the sole purpose of making a premium sparkling wine. Its 21 hectares of vineyards, comprising 12 hectares of chardonnay, 6.5 of pinot noir and 1.5 of pinot meunier, are now all in bearing, although extensive re-trellising took place in 2002. The sparkling wine quality is excellent, combining finesse with power and length.

🐦 clyde park vineyard   NR

2490 Midland Highway, Bannockburn, Vic 3331 **region** Geelong
phone (03) 5281 7274 **fax** (03) 5281 7274 **open** Weekends and public holidays 11–4
winemaker Ben Tyler **production** 3000 cases **est.** 1978
product range ($18–30 CD) Sauvignon Blanc, Pinot Gris, Chardonnay, Pinot Noir, Shiraz.
summary Clyde Park Vineyard was established by Gary Farr, but sold by him many years ago, then to pass through several changes of ownership. It is now owned by Terry Jongebloed and Sue Jongebloed-Dixon. It has significant, mature plantings of pinot noir (3.4 ha), chardonnay (3.1 ha), sauvignon blanc (1.5 ha), shiraz (1.2 ha) and pinot gris (0.9 ha).

coal valley vineyard   ★★★★☆

257 Richmond Road, Cambridge, Tas 7170 **region** Southern Tasmania
phone (03) 6248 5367 **fax** (03) 6248 4175 **open** Wed–Sun 10–4
winemaker Andrew Hood (Contract) **production** 450 cases **est.** 1991
product range ($18–35 CD) Riesling, Chardonnay, Pinot Noir, Cabernet Merlot.
summary Coal Valley Vineyard is the new name for Treehouse Vineyard and Wine Centre, the change brought about by the fact that Treehouse had been trade marked by the Pemberton winery, Salitage. The vineyard was purchased by Todd Goebel and wife Gillian Christian in 1999 who have set about doubling the size of the existing riesling vineyard, and establishing 1.5 hectares of another vineyard planted to pinot noir, with a few vines of cabernet. The Wine Centre now incorporates a full commercial kitchen and windows overlooking the existing vineyard and the Coal River Valley.

Coal Valley Vineyard Chardonnay
🍷🍷🍷🍷🍸 2002 Light straw-green; a clean and elegant wine with subtly interwoven stone fruit and oak on both bouquet and palate; crisp acidity adds to the length of a potentially very good wine.   **rating:** 90
best drinking Now–2006 **best vintages** '98, '99 **drink with** Grilled white-fleshed fish • $23

Coal Valley Vineyard Pinot Noir
🍷🍷🍷🍷🍷 2001 Medium red; a complex bouquet with earthy, spicy, foresty overtones to the plummy fruit at the centre; the palate is intense and complex, yet elegant and long. Excellent finish. Top gold 2003 Tasmanian Wines Show.   **rating:** 95
best drinking Now–2008 **best vintages** '01 **drink with** Rare breast of squab • $35

coalville vineyard   NR

RMB 4750 Moe South Road, Moe South, Vic 3825 **region** Gippsland
phone (03) 5127 4229 **fax** (03) 5127 2148 **open** 7 days 10–5
winemaker Peter Beasley **production** 3000 cases **est.** 1985
product range ($15–18 CD) Chardonnay, Malbec, Merlot, Cabernet Merlot, Cabernet Sauvignon.
summary This is the new name for Mair's Coalville, following the sale of the property by Dr Stewart Mair to Peter Beasley, who had significantly increased not only the volume but the range of wines available.

cobaw ridge   ★★★★☆

31 Perc Boyer's Lane, East Pastoria via Kyneton, Vic 3444 **region** Macedon Ranges
phone (03) 5423 5227 **fax** (03) 5423 5227 **open** 7 days 10–5
winemaker Alan Cooper **production** 1500 cases **est.** 1985
product range ($30–45 CD) Chardonnay, Lagrein, Pinot Noir, Shiraz Viognier.
summary Nelly and Alan Cooper established Cobaw Ridge's 6-hectare vineyard at an altitude of 610 metres in the hills above Kyneton complete with self-constructed pole-framed mudbrick house and winery. The plantings of cabernet sauvignon have been removed and partially replaced by lagrein, a variety which sent me scuttling to Jancis Robinson's seminal book on grape varieties, from which I learned it is a northeast Italian variety typically used to make delicate Rose, but at Cobaw Ridge it is made into an impressive full-bodied dry red. The planned sale of Cobaw Ridge did not proceed, and the Coopers now intend to stay, a sensible decision given the very high quality of the releases current in 2003.

Cobaw Ridge Chardonnay

▼▼▼▼▽ **2001** Light to medium yellow-green; the bouquet has attractive barrel-ferment oak inputs sitting alongside tangy, cool-grown, fruit; the light to medium-bodied palate is elegant but quite intense, with complex flavour dimensions, and the prior history of these wines virtually long-term improvement in bottle. **rating:** 93

best drinking Now–2008 **best vintages** '99, '01 **drink with** Honey chicken • $30

Cobaw Ridge Pinot Noir

▼▼▼▼▼ **2001** Medium to full purple-red, very deep for the variety; a complex bouquet of dark plum, spice and quality oak leads into an equivalently powerful, complex and rich palate, with great length. A bolt from the blue for me, and, so I gather, for Alan Cooper. The six-year-old pinot block was planted to a mix of MV6, 114 and 115 clones. **rating:** 94

best drinking Now–2008 **best vintages** '01 **drink with** Rare breast of duck • $35

Cobaw Ridge Shiraz Viognier

▼▼▼▼▽ **2001** Medium purple-red; a very high-toned bouquet with lots of complex, ripe dark cherry fruit and stylish oak is followed by a palate which has both flavour and texture complexity building progressively towards a savoury but stylish finish. The first Shiraz Viognier for Cobaw Ridge made with 100 per cent French oak. **rating:** 91

best drinking 2005–2011 **best vintages** '00, '01 **drink with** Salmon • $35

Cobaw Ridge Lagrein

▼▼▼▼ **2001** Medium purple-red; the fruity, fragrant raspberry and plum bouquet is followed by a medium-bodied, smooth and supple palate, but without distinctive fruit character. I suspect one is paying more for the label than for the wine, but so be it. **rating:** 89

best drinking 2006–2011 **best vintages** '99 **drink with** Braised ox cheek • $45

cobb's hill   NR

Oakwood Road, Oakbank, SA 5243 **region** Adelaide Hills
phone (08) 8388 4054 **fax** (08) 8388 4820 **open** Not
winemaker Martin Shaw, Willie Lunn **production** 700 cases **est.** 1997
product range ($15 ML) Riesling, Sauvignon Blanc, Chardonnay, Merlot.
summary Sally and Roger Cook have a 140-hectare property in the Adelaide Hills that takes its name from Cobb and Co, which used it as a staging post and resting place for 1000 horses. The Cooks now use the property to raise Angus cattle, grow cherries and, more recently, grow grapes. Three different sites on the property, amounting to just over 10 hectares, were planted to selected clones of sauvignon blanc, chardonnay, semillon and merlot, with riesling in the pipeline. Part of the production is sold to Shaw and Smith, who vinify the remainder for Cobb's Hill.

cockfighter's ghost vineyard   ★★★★

Lot 251 Milbrodale Road, Broke, NSW 2330 **region** Lower Hunter Valley
phone (02) 9667 1622 **fax** (02) 9667 1442 **open** By appointment
winemaker Patrick Auld **production** 7500 cases **est.** 1994
product range ($16.50–28.50 R) Semillon, Verdelho, Unwooded Chardonnay, Chardonnay, Pinot Noir, Shiraz, Merlot, Coonawarra Premium Reserve Cabernet Sauvignon.
summary Like Poole's Rock Vineyard, part of a rapidly-expanding wine empire owned by eminent Sydney merchant banker David Clarke, will be housed at the former Tulloch winery as from 2003. Accommodation is, however, available at the Milbrodale property. The wine has retail distribution throughout Australia and is exported to the UK and the US, Canada, New Zealand and Asia.

Cockfighter's Ghost Semillon

▼▼▼▽ **2002** Light green-yellow; a clean, crisp but somewhat closed bouquet is followed by an altogether unconvincing palate, with the suggestion of a touch of subliminal residual sugar. A disappointing sequel to the very good 2000 and 2001 vintages. **rating:** 84

best drinking Now–2006 **best vintages** '96, '98, '00, '01 **drink with** Fresh asparagus • $15

Cockfighter's Ghost Chardonnay

▼▼▼▼▽ **2000** Excellent bright green-yellow; the complex bouquet shows obvious barrel-ferment inputs, and slightly grainy oak, but on the palate, peachy fruit is the driver to a wine of good depth and length. Gold medal at the 2001 Hunter Valley Wine Show. **rating:** 92

best drinking Now–2005 **best vintages** '00 **drink with** Pasta • $16

Cockfighter's Ghost Shiraz

TTTT 2000 Excellent red-purple; the intense bouquet has a mix of dark blackberry and regional earthy aromas; the palate is super-concentrated, with very pronounced tannins; needs time and faith, but the price makes sense.　　　　　**rating: 88**

best drinking 2006–2016 **drink with** Ravioli • $21.95

Cockfighter's Ghost Merlot

TTTT 2001 Medium red-purple; solid, dark berry fruits and subtle oak on the bouquet is matched by the powerful beetroot and blackcurrant palate with its abundant tannin structure. Bordering on red wine rather than Merlot, but is not short of character. A blend of Limestone Coast, Langhorne Creek and McLaren Vale grapes.　　　　　**rating: 87**

best drinking 2005–2010 **drink with** Kangaroo fillet • $22.95

Cockfighter's Ghost Langhorne Creek Cabernet Sauvignon

TTTT 2001 Medium red-purple; red berry and mint aromas drive the bouquet, moving more to blackcurrant and chocolate on the medium-bodied palate; the tannins are soft and the French and American oak (15 months) barely impacts on the easy drinking palate.　　　　　**rating: 87**

best drinking 2004–2008 **drink with** Leg of lamb • $22.95

cofield wines　　★★★☆

Distillery Road, Wahgunyah, Vic 3687　**region** Rutherglen
phone (02) 6033 3798　**fax** (02) 6033 0798　**open** Mon–Sat 9–5, Sun 10–5
winemaker Max Cofield, Damien Cofield　**production** 11 000 cases　**est.** 1990
product range ($15–28 CD) Semillon, Semillon Sauvignon Blanc, Semillon Chardonnay, Chenin Blanc, Max's Blend White, Chardonnay, Late Harvest Muscadelle, Shiraz, Gramay, Merlot, Max's Blend Red, Cabernet Franc, Cabernet Sauvignon, Sparkling, Fortified; Quartz, Vein Shiraz, Durif are top of the range.
summary District veteran Max Cofield, together with wife Karen and sons Damien, Ben and Andrew, is developing a strong cellar-door sales base by staging in-winery functions with guest chefs, and also providing a large barbecue and picnic area. (The Pickled Sisters Cafe is open for lunch Wed–Mon; telephone (02) 6033 2377.) Limited retail distribution through Prime Wines in Melbourne, exports to the US.

Cofield Sauvignon Blanc Semillon

TTTY 2002 Very light yellow-green; the clean, light and fresh bouquet has grass and citrus aromas which come through on the light palate, refreshing and well made, but not particularly intense. For all that, a worthwhile addition to the range, replete with a smart new label design.　　　　　**rating: 84**

best drinking Now **drink with** Yabbies • $15

Cofield Quartz Vein Shiraz

TTTT 2000 Medium red; the moderately intense bouquet has dusty overtones to the ripe berry fruit, the palate with soft, gently ripe plummy fruit and subtle oak.　　　　　**rating: 85**

best drinking 2005–2010 **drink with** Ragout of beef • $28

Cofield Quartz Vein Durif

TTTT 2001 Medium to full red-purple; a typically powerful bouquet with spicy, savoury plum and prune aromas; the palate is dense and rich, with ripe prune/plum pudding flavours and equally ripe, lingering tannins. Durif is continuing to flex its muscles in northeast Victoria.　　　　　**rating: 88**

best drinking 2005–2012 **drink with** Braised duck • $28

coldstream hills　　NR

31 Maddens Lane, Coldstream, Vic 3770　**region** Yarra Valley
phone (03) 5964 9410　**fax** (03) 5964 9389　**open** 7 days 10–5
winemaker Andrew Fleming, Greg Jarratt, James Halliday (Consultant)　**production** 50 000 cases　**est.** 1985
product range ($20–57.50 CD) Pinot Gris, Sauvignon Blanc, Chardonnay, Reserve Chardonnay, Pinot Noir, Reserve Pinot Noir, Merlot, Reserve Merlot, Briarston (Cabernet Merlot), Reserve Cabernet Sauvignon, Pinot Noir Chardonnay Brut; occasional limited release wines sold chiefly through the cellar door.
summary Founded by the author, who continues to be involved with the winemaking, but acquired by Southcorp in mid-1996. Expansion plans already then underway have been maintained, with well in excess of 100 hectares of owned or managed estate vineyards as the base. Chardonnay and Pinot Noir continue to be the principal focus; Merlot came on-stream from the 1997 vintage. Vintage conditions permitting, these three wines are made in both varietal and Reserve form, the latter in restricted quantities.

Coldstream Hills Sauvignon Blanc

2002 Light straw-green; clean and crisp bouquet, with herb, gooseberry and mineral aromas. The palate is lively, well balanced and long, with a fresh finish. Flavours of gooseberry and apple reflect the cool vintage, and are less tropical than usual. **rating:** NR

best drinking Now **best vintages** '97, '98, '02 **drink with** Salad • $24.50

Coldstream Hills Limited Release Pinot Gris

2000 Straw-pink; the distinctly fruity bouquet has a range of aromas including almond. The palate is medium-bodied, flavours predominantly almond, marzipan and peach. Excellent acidity balances the sweetness, which is not the least cloying. **rating:** NR

best drinking Now **drink with** Aperitif • $27.50

Coldstream Hills Pinot Chardonnay

1998 Light to medium yellow-green, with good mousse; intense citrus fruit on the bouquet with touches of bready/yeasty character from the 4 years on lees prior to disgorgement. The wine has abundant flavour while retaining finesse, likewise has good balance. **rating:** NR

best drinking Now–2007 **drink with** Light hors d'oeuvres • $26.50

Coldstream Hills Pinot Noir

2002 Medium red-purple; a characteristic mix of plum and spice, still in its primary phase, the French oak subtle and well-integrated. The palate is intense and tight, with a long, lingering finish and excellent acidity. The spicy/savoury plum flavours are, like those of the bouquet, still in their infancy, and this wine will develop very well over the next 7–8 years. **rating:** NR

best drinking Now–2010 **best vintages** '87, '88, '91, '92, '94, '96, '97, '02 **drink with** Seared or slow-cooked salmon, Asian cuisine • $26.50

Coldstream Hills Merlot

2001 Strong and clear red-purple; the bouquet is strongly varietal, with a mix of dark berry/blackcurrant fruit, hints of spice and olive. Fruit intensity builds markedly on the palate, the blackcurrant fruit tinged with olive and hints of cedary, French oak. Good tannin structure, fine and supple. **rating:** NR

best drinking 2005–2011 **best vintages** '90, '97, '98, '00 **drink with** All red meats, cheeses and game • $27.50

Coldstream Hills Reserve Merlot

2000 Deep red-purple; an array of various red berry fruits, hints of chocolate, spice and a hint of vanilla mark the bouquet; the palate is soft, rich and textured throughout its entire length, with soft, fluffy tannins and supple mouthfeel. Particular mid-palate richness is a feature of the best Reserve Merlot made to date by Coldstream Hills. Winner of two trophies at the 2002 Royal Sydney Wine Show, for Best Merlot and Best 2000 Vintage Wine. **rating:** NR

best drinking 2005–2012 **best vintages** '00 **drink with** All red meats, cheeses and game • $55

Coldstream Hills Briarston

2000 Bright red-purple; a fragrant array of spice, cedar, olive, leaf and earthy/dusty cabernet on the bouquet. The palate is dominated by ripe, red berry fruit, with a fleshy mid-palate contributed by the Merlot, and a hint of bitter chocolate. Pronounced but fine tannins give the wine excellent texture and structure. 2000 was an outstanding vintage for the late-ripening red varieties due to the warmth of the growing season. This is the best Briarston produced to date. **rating:** NR

best drinking 2004–2010 **best vintages** '88, '90, '91, '92, '94, '97, '98, '99 **drink with** Lamb with redcurrant sauce • $25.50

Coldstream Hills Reserve Cabernet Sauvignon

2000 Full purple-red; a very fragrant and pure bouquet of cassis and earth varietal fruit, allied with cedary oak aromas, then a perfectly balanced palate with long, persistent flavours tracking those of the bouquet, finishing with fine, ripe tannins. By far the best Reserve Cabernet since 1992. Winner of eight trophies at the end of 2002, including Best Red Wine at the 2001 Liquorland National Wine Show, Canberra. **rating:** NR

best drinking 2005–2020 **best vintages** '92, '93, '94, '97, '00 **drink with** Rump steak • $57.50

collina wines NR

Princes Highway, Mogo, NSW 2536 **region** South Coast Zone
phone (02) 4474 0005 **open** 7 days 10–5
winemaker Nicola Collins **est.** 1999

product range ($15–22 CD) Chardonnay, Classic White, Gewurztraminer, Late Harvest Riesling Traminer, South Coast Cabernets, Rougon (semi-sweet red).

summary In the spring of 1980, Jim Collins planted the first vines on the south coast at Bega's Grevillea Estate. His daughter Nicola was winemaker from the outset and, having completed 16 vintages, encouraged her father to build a second winery at Mogo in the Eurobodalla region. The winery does not have vineyards of its own, sourcing grapes in part from Grevillea Estate and from the growing number of South Coast vineyards. As with Grevillea Estate, the operation is aimed at the general tourist rather than the wine connoisseur.

colmaur ★★★★

447 Native Corners Road, Campania, Tas 7026 **region** Southern Tasmania
phone (03) 6260 4312 **fax** (03) 6260 4580 **open** By appointment
winemaker Michael Vishacki (Contract) **production** 120 cases **est.** 1994
product range ($20 R) Chardonnay, Pinot Noir.
summary Colmaur is sufficiently small for the vines to be counted: presently 1100 chardonnay and 1700 pinot noir in production. In 2000/2001 a further 600 chardonnay, 1350 pinot noir and 250 cabernet sauvignon were planted, and that will be the total extent of the vineyard. Likewise, production will be limited to the five new French oak barrels purchased in 2000, producing 100 to 120 cases of wine per year; any surplus grapes will be sold. Likewise, there are 700 olive trees in production, and Colmaur has its own oil press. At the time of going to print, the 2002 wines had not been bottled.

Colmaur Chardonnay

♥♥♥♥♡ **2001** Medium yellow-green; citrus and melon fruit aromas are woven through subtle oak, the same balance neatly achieved on the palate, with obvious malolactic and barrel-ferment influences. **rating:** 90
best drinking Now **drink with** Shellfish • $20

Colmaur Pinot Noir

♥♥♥♥ **2000** Medium red; the bouquet is moderately intense, with plummy fruit in the background; that fruit comes through on the forepalate, but grippy tannins and acid need to soften on the finish. **rating:** 87
best drinking Now–2008 **drink with** Osso buco • $20

connor park winery NR

59 Connors Road, Leichardt, Vic 3516 **region** Bendigo
phone (03) 5437 5234 **fax** (03) 5437 5204 **open** 7 days 10–6
winemaker Ross Lougoon **production** 10 000 cases **est.** 1994
product range ($12–28 CD) Riesling, Semillon, Marsanne, Seanne, Sparkling Shiraz, Merlot, Shiraz, Cabernet, Port, Muscat.
summary The original planting of 2 hectares of vineyard dates back to the mid-1960s and to the uncle of the present owners, who had plans for designing an automatic grape harvester. The plans came to nothing, and when the present owners purchased the property in 1985 the vineyard had run wild. They resuscitated the vineyard (which formed part of a much larger mixed farming operation) and until 1994 were content to sell the grapes to other winemakers. Since then the vineyard has been expanded to 10 hectares. Production has risen from 2000 to 10 000 cases, with exports to the US and retail distribution in Melbourne, supplementing cellar door and mailing list sales.

constable & hershon ★★★☆

1 Gillards Road, Pokolbin, NSW 2320 **region** Lower Hunter Valley
phone (02) 4998 7887 **fax** (02) 4998 7887 **open** 7 days 10–5
winemaker Neil McGuigan (Contract) **production** 5000 cases **est.** 1981
product range ($20–24 CD) Semillon, Chardonnay, Unwooded Chardonnay, Vintage Collection Chardonnay, Shiraz, Merlot.
summary Features four spectacular formal gardens, the Rose, Knot and Herb, Secret and Sculpture; a free garden tour is conducted every Monday to Friday at 10.30 am lasting 30 minutes. The 9.75-hectare vineyard is itself spectacularly situated under the backdrop of the Brokenback Range. Typically offers a range of several vintages of each variety ex-cellar door or by mailing list. The quality is good, sometimes very good.

coolangatta estate ★★★☆

1335 Bolong Road, Shoalhaven Heads, NSW 2535 **region** Shoalhaven Coast
phone (02) 4448 7131 **fax** (02) 4448 7997 **open** 7 days 10–5
winemaker Tyrrell's (Contract) **production** 5000 cases **est.** 1988
product range ($16–22 CD) Semillon, Sauvignon Blanc Chardonnay, Classic Dry White, Alexander Berry Chardonnay, Verdelho, Chambourcin, Merlot Shiraz, Cabernet Sauvignon, Vintage Port.
summary Coolangatta Estate is part of a 150-hectare resort with accommodation, restaurants, golf course, etc, with some of the oldest buildings convict-built in 1822. It might be thought that the wines are tailored purely for the tourist market, but in fact the standard of viticulture is exceptionally high (immaculate Scott-Henry trellising), and the winemaking is wholly professional (contract by Tyrrell's).

Coolangatta Estate Alexander Berry Chardonnay

TTTT 2002 Light to medium yellow-green; the fruit and subtle oak of the bouquet have been well-integrated and balanced; the clean, light to medium-bodied palate has been well made, but does not have much varietal impact relatively early in its life. The track record of this wine shows it can develop excellently. **rating:** 85
best drinking Now–2007 **best vintages** '91, '94, '96, '97, '00 **drink with** Avocado and seafood • $22

Coolangatta Estate Eileen Chambourcin

TTTT 2002 Deep purple-red; ripe plummy aromas with a hint of varietal gamey character feed into lush, plummy fruit on entry to the mouth and mid-palate, then tailing off (as ever) on the finish. **rating:** 86
best drinking Now–2005 **best vintages** '99 **drink with** Pizza • $19

Coolangatta Estate Elizabeth Berry Cabernet Sauvignon

TTTT 2002 Youthful purple-red; clean and clear cassis and blackcurrant aromas lead into an appealing palate with bell-clear cabernet varietal character; the tannins are very soft, and there is not a great deal of structure. However, great early drinking style. **rating:** 88
best drinking 2004–2007 **drink with** Italian cuisine • $22

coombend estate ★★★★

Coombend via Swansea, Tas 7190 **region** Southern Tasmania
phone (03) 6257 8881 **fax** (03) 6257 8484 **open** 7 days 9–6
winemaker Andrew Hood (Contract) **production** 2500 cases **est.** 1985
product range ($19–26 CD) Riesling, Sauvignon Blanc, Late Harvest, Cabernet Sauvignon.
summary John Fenn Smith originally established 1.75 hectares of cabernet sauvignon, 2.25 hectares of sauvignon blanc and 0.3 hectare of riesling (together with a little cabernet franc) on his 2000-hectare sheep station, choosing that part of his property which is immediately adjacent to Freycinet. This slightly quixotic choice of variety has been justified by the success of the wine in limited show entries. In December 1998 Coombend opened a purpose-built cellar-door sales area and has also significantly expanded its plantings to include riesling and sauvignon blanc. Exports to Hong Kong and the UK.

Coombend Estate Sauvignon Blanc

TTTT 2002 Pale straw-green; the barrel-ferment oak is but part of a wine which is crammed with flavour from start to finish, and with some apparent sweetness, which may simply come from the fruit. The only criticism is that it is short on finesse. **rating:** 87
best drinking Now **drink with** Grilled eggplant and zucchini • $22

cooper wines NR

Lovedale Road, Lovedale, NSW 2321 **region** Lower Hunter Valley
phone (02) 4930 7387 **fax** (02) 4930 7900 **open** Mon–Fri 10–5, weekends 9.30–5
winemaker Greg Silkman (Contract) **production** 2000 cases **est.** 2001
product range ($17–25 CD) Semillon, Semillon Sauvignon Blanc, Verdelho, Chardonnay Semillon, Unoaked Chardonnay, Chardonnay, Chambourcin, Shiraz.
summary Max Cooper is a Qantas pilot who purchased the former Allanmere Winery and Vineyard, leasing the winery back to Allanmere but retaining the vineyards. The chardonnay is estate-grown; the other wines made from grapes purchased by growers in the region.

coorinja ★★☆

Toodyay Road, Toodyay, WA 6566 **region** Greater Perth Zone
phone (08) 9574 2280 **open** Mon–Sat 10–5
winemaker Michael Wood **production** 3200 cases **est.** 1870
product range ($8–10.50 CD) Dry White, Claret, Hermitage, Burgundy, fortifieds; the latter account for 50 per cent of Coorinja's production.
summary An evocative and historic winery nestling in a small gully which seems to be in a time-warp, begging to be used as a set for a film. A recent revamp of the packaging accompanied a more than respectable Hermitage, with lots of dark chocolate and sweet berry flavour, finishing with soft tannins.

cope-williams ★★★☆

Glenfern Road, Romsey, Vic 3434 **region** Macedon Ranges
phone (03) 5429 5428 **fax** (03) 5429 5655 **open** 7 days 11–5
winemaker David Cowburn **production** 7000 cases **est.** 1977
product range ($14–25 R) Chardonnay, Cabernet Merlot; d'Vine is second label, Riesling, Chardonnay and Cabernet Sauvignon; winery specialty sparkling wine Macedon R.O.M.S.E.Y.
summary One of the high country Macedon pioneers, specialising in sparkling wines which are full flavoured but also producing excellent Chardonnay and Pinot Noir table wines in the warmer vintages. A traditional 'English Green'-type cricket ground is available for hire and booked out most days of the week from spring through till autumn.

copper bull wines NR

19 Uplands Road, Chirnside Park, Vic 3116 **region** Yarra Valley
phone (03) 9726 7111 **open** Wed–Sun 11–6
winemaker David Schliefert **production** 800 cases **est.** 1982
product range Semillon, Sangiovese, Cabernet Sauvignon.
summary Copper Bull is the reincarnation of Halcyon Daze. The Rackleys, having gone into semi-retirement, have leased the vineyard, winery and cellar door to David and Janie Schliefert, who have produced the first wines under the Copper Bull label in 2003. David Schliefert spent 19 years at Lindemans Karadoc winery, becoming a cellar supervisor in the process, while wife Janie worked in quality management at Lindemans. The small production will be sold from the cellar door as and when it comes on stream.

copper country NR

Lot 6 Kingaroy Road, Nanango, Qld 4615 **region** South Burnett
phone (07) 4163 1011 **fax** (07) 4163 1122 **open** 7 days 9–5
winemaker Contract **production** 1000 cases **est.** 1995
product range ($10–16 CD) Shiraz.
summary The Winter family (Derek, Helena, Stephen and Justyne) were restaurateurs before venturing into grape growing and winemaking. The name of the vineyard and the restaurant is in recognition of the fact that copper was the first mineral mined in the region. As well as grape growing, the Winters make cheese, the principal outlet for their products being their restaurant and cellar door.

coriole ★★★★☆

Chaffeys Road, McLaren Vale, SA 5171 **region** McLaren Vale
phone (08) 8323 8305 **fax** (08) 8323 9136 **open** Mon–Fri 10–5, weekends and public holidays 11–5
winemaker Grant Harrison **production** 42000 cases **est.** 1967
product range ($15.25–75 R) Semillon, Lalla Rookh Semillon, Semillon Sauvignon Blanc, Chenin Blanc, Shiraz, Lloyd Reserve Shiraz, Redstone Shiraz Cabernet, Sangiovese, Nebbiolo, Mary Kathleen Cabernet Merlot, Cabernet Sauvignon.
summary Justifiably best known for its Shiraz, which – both in the rare Lloyd Reserve and standard forms – is extremely impressive. It has spread its wings in recent years, being one of the first wineries to catch onto the Italian fashion with its Sangiovese, but its white varietal wines lose nothing by comparison. It is also a producer of high-quality olive oil distributed commercially through all Australian States. The wines are exported to the UK, the US, Canada, Switzerland, Germany, The Netherlands, Sweden, Taiwan, Malaysia, Japan, Singapore and New Zealand.

Coriole Semillon

TTTT 2002 Very pale straw-green; classic herb, mineral and grass aromas and flavours may be less focused than top Hunter Valley wines, but has definite improvement in front of it. Estate-grown, 250 cases made. **rating:** 86

best drinking Now–2006 **drink with** Blue swimmer crab • $18.75

Coriole Semillon Sauvignon Blanc

TTTTY 2002 Light to medium yellow-green; the spotlessly clean bouquet has good varietal character definition in a gooseberry tropical spectrum, the palate with the expected flavour intensity promised by the bouquet, rich but not heavy. A very consistent producer of this style.   **rating:** 90

best drinking Now–2005 **best vintages** '02 **drink with** Deep-fried calamari • $17.95

Coriole Nebbiolo

TTTT 2001 Light to medium red; tangy, lemony, savoury varietal fruit aromas are not obscured by oak; the light to medium-bodied palate is quite piquant and lively; all in all, a particular style, and an extension of the Italian accent provided by the long-standing Sangiovese of Coriole. I remain to be convinced about the price, however.   **rating:** 85

best drinking 2004–2009 **drink with** Veal saltimbocca • $30.50

Coriole Cabernet Sauvignon

TTTT 2001 Medium red-purple; a fresh and youthful bouquet with blackcurrant and touches of leaf and mint; on the palate riper, more chocolatey fruit opens up a nice wine supported by neatly handled oak.   **rating:** 89

best drinking 2006–2011 **drink with** Rack of lamb • $27

cosham   ★★★★

101 Union Road, Carmel via Kalamunda, WA 6076 **region** Perth Hills
phone (08) 9293 5424 **fax** (08) 9293 5062 **open** Weekends and public holidays 10–5
winemaker Julie White (Jane Brook Estate) **production** 1000 cases **est.** 1989
product range ($14–22 CD) Chardonnay, Pinot Noir, Cabernet Merlot, Methode Champenoise Brut.
summary Has grown significantly over recent years, though admittedly from a small base. A complex Methode Champenoise and savoury/earth Cabernet Merlot are both creditable wines, the Chardonnay exceptional. The vineyard is planted on an old orchard, and consists of 2 hectares of cabernet sauvignon, merlot, shiraz, pinot noir, cabernet franc, chardonnay and petit verdot, established between 1990 and 1995. They grow in gravelly loam with some clay, but overall in a well-drained soil with good rainfall. Depending on the grape variety, vintage ranges from late February to early April.

Cosham Chardonnay

TTTTT 2000 Medium to full yellow-green; a massively and spectacularly intense bouquet and palate, with outstanding complexity. At its peak now, and, although it may hold it, there is surely nothing more to be found in the wine. Gold medal 2002 Qantas Wine Show of Western Australia.   **rating:** 94

best drinking Now **best vintages** '00 **drink with** Grilled spatchcock • $14

cowra estate   ★★★

Boorowa Road, Cowra, NSW 2794 **region** Cowra
phone (02) 6342 1136 **fax** (02) 6342 4286 **open** 7 days 9–6
winemaker Simon Gilbert (Contract) **production** 6000 cases **est.** 1973
product range ($12–19 CD) Chardonnay, Cabernet Rose, Cabernets; Eagle Rock Chardonnay and Classic Bat Cabernet Merlot are now at the head of the range.
summary Cowra Estate was purchased from the family of founder Tony Gray by South African-born food and beverage entrepreneur John Geber in 1995. A vigorous promotional campaign has gained a higher domestic profile for the once export-oriented brand. John Geber is actively involved in the promotional effort and rightly proud of the excellent value for money which the wines represent. The Quarry Wine Cellars and Restaurant offer visitors a full range of all of the Cowra Estate's wines but also wines from the other producers in the region, including Richmond Grove, Hungerford Hill, Arrowfield, Mulyan and Chiverton. The Geber family, incidentally, also owns Chateau Tanunda in the Barossa Valley.

Cowra Estate Cabernet Rose

TTTY 2002 Bright rose-pink; the clean and bright bouquet has spicy overtones, the similarly clean and fresh palate with light red fruits; well balanced, and, in particular, not sweet.   **rating:** 84

best drinking Now **drink with** Summer lunch • $12.30

Cowra Estate Cabernets

ŶŶŶŶ 2000 Medium red-purple; pleasant, ripe black berry fruits on the bouquet show neither green nor any other off character; the palate opens with very attractive fruit flavour, although does weaken towards the finish when the wine lacks tannin structure. Nonetheless, this is the best Cowra Estate Cabernets to date, and is well priced. **rating: 86**

best drinking Now–2005 **drink with** Lasagne • $12.30

crabtree of watervale ★★★★

North Terrace, Watervale SA 5452 **region** Clare Valley
phone (08) 8843 0069 **fax** (08) 8843 0144 **open** 7 days 11–5
winemaker Robert Crabtree **production** 5000 cases **est.** 1979
product range ($20 CD) Riesling, Semillon, Bay of Biscay Rose, Picnic Hill Vineyard Shiraz, Windmill Vineyard Cabernet Sauvignon, Zibibbo, Muscat of Alexandria, Windmill Tawny.
summary The gently mannered Robert Crabtree and wife Elizabeth are the drivers of the business, making full-flavoured, classic Clare Valley styles with outstanding success in some recent vintages. Exports to the UK and Kuala Lumpur.

Crabtree of Watervale Riesling

ŶŶŶŶŶ 2002 Pale straw-green; a very youthful bouquet with flinty, minerally/slatey aromas with an echo of apple are followed by a crisp, clean and balanced palate. In terms of flavour, the wine is too young to even crawl, let alone walk, and is difficult to point. Having moved to a Stelvin closure (and a label upgrade) there is every reason to suppose the wine will richly repay cellaring. **rating: 90**

best drinking 2005–2015 **best vintages** '99, '00, '01 **drink with** Ginger prawns • $20

Crabtree of Watervale Semillon

ŶŶŶŶ 1999 Medium yellow-green; high-toned, complex barrel-ferment aromas, with a touch of smoky bacon, are followed by a developed palate which seems to principally rely on the oak, the mid-palate being somewhat hollow. **rating: 85**

best drinking Now **drink with** Crumbed brains • $20

Crabtree of Watervale Picnic Hill Vineyard Shiraz

ŶŶŶŶ 2001 Medium red-purple; the moderately intense aromas of blackberry, spice and bramble lead into a medium-bodied palate, which is still quite tight, but which will open up and soften with time in bottle. **rating: 87**

best drinking 2004–2008 **drink with** Irish stew • $20

Crabtree of Watervale Windmill Vineyard Cabernet Sauvignon

ŶŶŶŶ 2001 Medium purple-red; the clean dark berry fruit of the bouquet has touches of earth, spice and a whiff of oak; the medium-bodied palate has an attractive mix of blackcurrant and chocolate; fine tannins to close. **rating: 89**

best drinking 2005–2010 **drink with** Roast lamb • $20

craig avon vineyard ★★★

Craig Avon Lane, Merricks North, Vic 3926 **region** Mornington Peninsula
phone (03) 5989 7465 **fax** (03) 5989 7615 **open** By appointment
winemaker Ken Lang **production** 1000 cases **est.** 1986
product range ($30–34 CD) Chardonnay, Pinot Noir, Cabernet.
summary The wines are competently made, clean and with pleasant fruit flavour. All of the wines are sold cellar door and by mailing list.

craigie knowe NR

80 Glen Gala Road, Cranbrook, Tas 7190 **region** Southern Tasmania
phone (03) 6259 8252 **fax** (03) 6259 8252 **open** 7 days, by appointment
winemaker Dr John Austwick **production** 500 cases **est.** 1979
product range ($25 CD) Cabernet Sauvignon, Pinot Noir.
summary John Austwick makes a small quantity of full-flavoured, robust Cabernet Sauvignon in a tiny winery as a weekend relief from a busy metropolitan dental practice. The Pinot Noir is made in a style which will appeal to confirmed Cabernet Sauvignon drinkers, and John Austwick had a couple of barrels of 1998 Cabernet Sauvignon which, had they been bottled separately, would have appealed to everyone who has ever lifted a wine glass. No recent tastings.

craiglee ★ ★ ★ ★ ★

Sunbury Road, Sunbury, Vic 3429 **region** Sunbury
phone (03) 9744 4489 **fax** (03) 9744 4489 **open** Sun, public holidays 10–5, or by appointment
winemaker Patrick Carmody **production** 3000 cases **est.** 1976
product range ($16–38 CD) Sauvignon Blanc, Chardonnay, Pinot Noir, Shiraz, Cabernet Sauvignon.
summary An historic winery with a proud 19th-century record which recommenced winemaking in 1976
after a prolonged hiatus. Produces one of the finest cool-climate Shirazs in Australia, redolent of cherry, licorice
and spice in the better (i.e. warmer) vintages, lighter-bodied in the cooler ones. Maturing vines and improved
viticulture have made the wines more consistent (and even better) over the past 10 years or so. Exports to the
UK, the US and New Zealand.

Craiglee Chardonnay

▼▼▼▼▽ 2001 Medium yellow-green; the multi-faceted bouquet offers melon, fig and nectarine woven
through some cashew malolactic characters and subtle oak; the smooth and stylish palate has all of the fruit of
the bouquet with creamy cashew wrapped around the fruit. **rating:** 93
best drinking Now–2006 **best vintages** '87, '90, '92, '96, '97 **drink with** Pan-fried veal • $30

Craiglee Pinot Noir

▼▼▼▼▽ 2001 Bright purple-red; the uncomplicated bouquet has dark cherry and plum fruit, the oak subtle;
the rich and full palate offers more of the same dark plum and cherry fruit, hovering on the edge of dry red.
Points for flavour rather than finesse, although it could develop more character as it ages. **rating:** 91
best drinking Now–2006 **best vintages** '01 **drink with** Roast baby kid • $32

Craiglee Shiraz

▼▼▼▼▼ 2000 A winery with a great 19th-century history, and an equally great 21st-century reputation for its
shiraz. Clean, bright red cherry fruit, a touch of spice and gentle oak on the bouquet, then (by Craiglee
standards) a voluptuously rich, ripe and supple palate. Seriously under priced, seriously good. **rating:** 95
best drinking 2005–2020 **best vintages** '84, '86, '88, '91, '92, '93, '94, '96, '97, '98, '00 **drink with** Italian
cuisine • $38

Craiglee Cabernet Sauvignon

▼▼▼▼ 2000 Medium red-purple; the bouquet has a mix of spicy/savoury/earthy aromas alongside red fruits, a
pattern which is repeated on the medium-bodied, savoury/briary palate, tweaked by a touch of oak. **rating:** 89
best drinking 2004–2010 **drink with** Loin of lamb • $30

craigow ★ ★ ★ ★ ☆

528 Richmond Road, Cambridge, Tas 7170 **region** Southern Tasmania
phone (03) 6248 4210 **fax** (03) 6248 5482 **open** Fri–Sun 10–5, or by appointment; 7 days Christmas to
Easter
winemaker Julian Alcorso (Contract) **production** 500 cases **est.** 1989
product range ($21–28 CD) Riesling, Gewurztraminer, Chardonnay, Botrytis Riesling, Pinot Noir.
summary Craigow has substantial vineyards, with 5 hectares of pinot noir and another 5 hectares divided
between riesling, chardonnay and gewurztraminer. Barry and Cathy Edwards have moved from being grape
growers with only one wine made for sale to a portfolio of four wines, while continuing to sell most of their
grapes. Their cellar door opened early in December 1999.

Craigow Gewurztraminer

▼▼▼▼▽ 2001 Light straw-green; the fragrant bouquet offers rose petal, spice and lychee aromas, the elegant
and delicate palate avoiding phenolics, but supporting the bouquet. One of the rare band of quality
Gewurztraminers. **rating:** 90
best drinking Now–2006 **best vintages** '01 **drink with** Asian • $24

Craigow Pinot Noir

▼▼▼▼▽ 2001 Light to medium red-purple; very ripe cherry fruit aromas, almost essency, lead into an intense
palate with a mix of cherry and spice on the one hand, and leaf and mint on the other. Something of a Curate's
Egg, but the good bits definitely outweigh the other bits. **rating:** 92
best drinking Now–2005 **best vintages** '01 **drink with** Roast baby kid • $28

craneford ★★★★

Moorundie Street, Truro, SA 5356 **region** Barossa Valley
phone (08) 8564 0003 **fax** (08) 8564 0008 **open** 7 days 10–5
winemaker John Zilm, Colin Forbes (Consultant) **production** 25 000 cases **est.** 1978
product range ($14–33 CD) Eden Valley Riesling, Barossa Semillon, Barossa Valley Chardonnay, Barossa Valley Unwooded Chardonnay, Shiraz, Quartet (Petit Verdot Cabernet Sauvignon Cabernet Franc Shiraz), Grenache, Coonawarra Cabernet Sauvignon, Mistelle (fortified), Sparkling Shiraz Petit Verdot.
summary The purchase of Craneford by owner/winemaker John Zilm has wrought many changes. It has moved to a new winery (and cafe) and is supported by contract-grown grapes, with the purchase price paid per hectare, not per tonne, giving Craneford total control over yield and (hopefully) quality. Colin Forbes continues to provide consultancy advice. Retail distribution in Sydney and Melbourne, and exports to Japan through Australian Prestige Wines.

crane winery NR

Haydens Road, Kingaroy, Qld 4610 **region** South Burnett
phone (07) 4162 7647 **fax** (07) 4162 8381 **open** 7 days 10–4
winemaker John Crane **production** 4000 cases **est.** 1996
product range ($12–25 CD) Semillon, Semillon Chardonnay, Verdelho, Marsanne, Hillside White, Chardonnay, Late Harvest Frontignac, Noble Chardonnay Botrytis, Sparkling Burgundy, Pinot Semillon Chardonnay Sparkling, Estate Sparkling Cuvee, Hillside Red, Pinot Noir, Shiraz, Chambourcin, Merlot, Liqueur Shiraz, Cream Sherry.
summary Established by John and Sue Crane, Crane Winery is one of several in the burgeoning Kingaroy (or South Burnett) region in Queensland, drawing upon 4 hectares of estate plantings but also purchasing grapes from 20 other growers in the region. Interestingly, Sue Crane's great-grandfather established a vineyard planted to shiraz 100 years ago (in 1898) and which remained in production until 1970.

cranswick estate ★★★

Walla Avenue, Griffith, NSW 2680 **region** Riverina
phone (02) 6962 4133 **fax** (02) 6962 2888 **open** 7 days 10–4
winemaker Andrew Schulz, Tim Pearce, Eddie Bonato, Sam Mittiga **production** 1.3 million cases **est.** 1976
product range ($6–25.50 CD) There are several ranges; at the top comes the Pioneer Old Vine Series comprising Semillon, Chardonnay, Shiraz, Cabernet Sauvignon; Autumn Gold Botrytis Semillon; then the Cocoparra range of Marsanne, Shiraz, Merlot, Cabernet Sauvignon; next is the volume-selling Vignette Range of Semillon, Verdelho, Chardonnay, Pinot Chardonnay, Unoaked Botrytis Semillon, Shiraz, Cabernet Merlot; also lower-priced ranges of The Masters, Kidman Way, Cedar Creek, Bond Blue and Barramundi Varietal.
summary Taking full advantage of the buoyant share market and the continuing export success of Australian wines, Cranswick Estate made a successful entry to the lists of the Australian Associated Stock Exchanges in 1997. The substantial capital raised has seen the further expansion of the business, firmly aimed at the export market in the UK and Europe, the US, Japan and Iceland, and South-East Asia. It did, however, make the headlines in 2002 when it offered some of its growers $100 per tonne to leave their grapes on the vine.

Cranswick Estate Autumn Gold Botrytis Semillon

♥♥♥♥♡ **1998** Very deep golden colour; complex, bottle-developed dried fruit and peach/apricot conserve aromas are joined by rich, honeyed/toffee flavours on the palate; finishes with good acidity. **rating:** 93
best drinking Now–2005 **best vintages** '94, '95, '96, '98 **drink with** Orange cake and King Island cream • $24

crawford river wines ★★★★★

Hotspur Upper Road, Condah, Vic 3303 **region** Henty
phone (03) 5578 2267 **fax** (03) 5578 2240 **open** 7 days 10–4 by appointment
winemaker John Thomson **production** 4000 cases **est.** 1975
product range ($20–35 CD) Riesling, Reserve Riesling, Semillon Sauvignon Blanc, Cabernet Merlot, Cabernet Sauvignon, Nektar.
summary Exemplary wines right across the range are made by part-time winemaker John Thomson, who clearly has the winemaker's equivalent of the gardener's green thumb. The Riesling is consistently outstanding, the Cabernet-based wines excellent in warmer vintages. The 2002 vintage resulted in a crush of 13 tonnes compared to the normal 100 tonnes. Exports to the UK, Germany, Denmark, Singapore, the US and Canada.

Crawford River Riesling

TTTTY 2002 Light green-yellow; as ever, a spotlessly clean and fresh bouquet, although the aromas are relatively subdued; the tight palate has crisp apple, mineral and lime flavours, the balance excellent, its whole life in front of it. **rating:** 92

best drinking Now–2013 **best vintages** '86, '88, '89, '91, '94, '96, '97, '98, '99, '00, '01 **drink with** Antipasto • $25

Crawford River Museum Release Riesling

TTTTT 1997 Light, vibrant green-yellow; the bouquet is still tight, with the first hint of toast starting to appear; a supremely elegant palate, with a fine, lingering, dry finish; great style, and still has years of life in front of it. A special cellar re-release. **rating:** 95

best drinking Now–2010 **best vintages** '97 **drink with** Tempura, vegetarian • $35

Crawford River Semillon Sauvignon Blanc

TTTTY 2002 Light yellow-green; clean grass and herb aromas with hints of fruit spice lead into a palate with intense fruit flavour reflecting the bouquet, and good length. **rating:** 90

best drinking Now–2005 **best vintages** '96, '97, '01, '02 **drink with** Crab or shellfish • $20

Crawford River Cabernet Merlot

TTTTY 2001 Light to medium red-purple; the fragrant bouquet has complex spice/anise overtones to the berry fruit; the palate is long and remarkably intense, with fine, dark fruits; very Bordeaux-like. **rating:** 93

best drinking 2005–2011 **best vintages** '01 **drink with** Rib of veal • $25

crisford winery   NR

556 Hermitage Road, Pokolbin, NSW 2022 **region** Lower Hunter Valley
phone (02) 9387 1100 **fax** (02) 9387 6688 **open** Not
winemaker Steve Dodd **production** 340 cases **est.** 1990
product range A single wine – Synergy (Merlot Cabernet Franc blend).
summary Carol and Neal Crisford have established 2.6 hectares of merlot and cabernet franc which go to produce Synergy (a name which I fancy has been trademarked by Hamilton). Neal Crisford produces educational videos on wine used in TAFE colleges and by the Australian Society of Wine Education. The wine is sold through the Hunter Valley Wine Society.

crooked river wines   NR

11 Willow Vale Road, Gerringong, NSW 2534 **region** Shoalhaven Coast
phone (02) 4234 0975 **fax** (02) 4234 4477 **open** 7 days 10.30–4.30
winemaker Bevan Wilson **production** 4000 cases **est.** 1998
product range ($15–20 CD) Verdelho, Chardonnay, Illawarra Flame, Shiraz, Chambourcin, Cabernet Merlot, Cabernet Sauvignon.
summary With 14 hectares of vineyard planted to chardonnay, verdelho, arneis, shiraz, cabernet sauvignon, merlot, ruby cabernet, sangiovese and chambourcin, Crooked River Wines has the largest vineyard on the south coast. Production is expected to increase to 10 000 cases by 2003 through a winery being constructed on-site. Cellar-door sales, craft shop and cafe opened in December 2001.

🍇 cross rivulet   NR

334 Richmond Road, Cambridge, Tas 7170 **region** Southern Tasmania
phone (03) 6228 5406 **open** First weekend March or by appointment
winemaker Lloyd Mathews **production** 350 cases **est.** 1980
product range ($7 ML) Riesling, Gewurztraminer, Muller Thurgau, Unwooded Chardonnay, Pinot Noir.
summary Geologist Lloyd Mathews is a self-taught viticulturist and winemaker, readily confessing that his main experience is learning from mistakes, a short adult education course on winemaking notwithstanding. The almost absurdly low price for the wines reflects the uncosted labour.

crosswinds vineyard   ★★★★

10 Vineyard Drive, Tea Tree, Tas 7017 **region** Southern Tasmania
phone (03) 6268 1091 **fax** (03) 6268 1091 **open** Mon–Fri 10–5
winemaker Andrew Vasiljuk **production** 650 cases **est.** 1990
product range ($18–60 CD) Non-Wooded Chardonnay, Barrel Fermented Chardonnay, Non-Wooded Pinot Noir, Barrel Matured Pinot Noir, Reserve Pinot Noir.

summary Crosswinds has two vineyards, with the 1-hectare Tea Tree Vineyard and the 2-hectare Margate Vineyard. As well as cellar-door sales, has retail distribution in Melbourne and small exports to the UK and South-East Asia. Both Chardonnay and Pinot Noir have excelled in recent years.

cruickshank callatoota estate ★★★

2656 Wybong Road, Wybong, NSW 2333 **region** Upper Hunter Valley
phone (02) 6547 8149 **fax** (02) 6547 8144 **open** 7 days 9–5
winemaker John Cruickshank, Laurie Nicholls, Andrew Thomas (Consultant) **production** 5000 cases
est. 1973
product range ($12–20 CD) Cabernet Rose, Shiraz, Cabernet Franc, Two Cabernets, Cabernet Sauvignon, Cabernet Sauvignon Carbonic Maceration, Cabernet Sauvignon Pressings, Show Reserve Cabernet Sauvignon, Old Tawny Port.
summary Owned by Sydney management consultant John Cruickshank and family. Wine quality definitely improved in the 1990s, although the wines still show strong regional, rather earthy, characters; the label itself likewise doggedly remains old-fashioned. The Cabernet Rose is typically delicate, clean and crisp and the most appealing of the range.

Cruickshank Callatoota Estate Cabernet Rose

TTTT 2002 Bright, light pink; clean and fresh small berry fruit aromas lead into a direct, fresh, light-bodied rose palate, well balanced and not sweet. **rating:** 85

best drinking Now **drink with** Meat salads • $12

Cruickshank Callatoota Estate Shiraz

TTTY 2001 Light to medium red; the moderately intense bouquet has raspberry and cherry fruit, the light-bodied palate with similar fruit flavours; the balance and extract are appropriate given the fruit weight. The second vintage from the vineyard planted in 1996. **rating:** 83

best drinking Now–2006 **drink with** Pasta • $15

cubbaroo cellars NR

Cubbaroo Station, Wee Waa, NSW 2388 **region** Western Plains Zone
phone (02) 6796 1741 **fax** (02) 6796 1751 **open** Thurs–Sun 12–10
winemaker Simon Gilbert (Contract) **est.** 1972
product range ($10–15 CD) Shiraz, Port.
summary Cubbaroo Cellars has lead a shadowy existence since the early 1970s in the heart of the Namoi Valley cotton country. For a while it seemed that it had ceased production under the Cubbaroo Cellars label, selling its grapes to wineries in the Hunter Valley. However, the 10.8 hectares of shiraz planted long ago has now been supplemented by 4 hectares of cabernet sauvignon, so its fortunes may be on the rise. The two wines presently available are sold only through the cellar door.

cullen wines ★★★★★

Caves Road, Cowaramup, WA 6284 **region** Margaret River
phone (08) 9755 5277 **fax** (08) 9755 5550 **open** 7 days 10–4
winemaker Vanya Cullen, Trevor Kent **production** 18 000 cases **est.** 1971
product range ($16.50–75 CD) Flagship wines: Semillon Sauvignon Blanc, Chardonnay, Pinot Noir, Mangan Malbec Petit Verdot Merlot, Reserve Cabernet Sauvignon Merlot; premium wines: Robinson's Riesling, Classic Dry White, Velvet Red, Autumn Harvest.
summary One of the pioneers of Margaret River which has always produced long-lived wines of highly individual style from the substantial and mature estate vineyards. Winemaking is now in the hands of Vanya Cullen, daughter of the founders; she is possessed of an extraordinarily good palate. The death of mother Di Cullen in early 2003 saddened the entire wine industry. The Chardonnay is superb, while the Cabernet Merlot goes from strength to strength; indeed, I would rate it Australia's best. The wines are distributed throughout Australia and also make their way to significant export markets in the UK, the US, Europe and Asia.

Cullen Sauvignon Blanc Semillon

TTTTT 2002 Light straw-green; a fragrant and complex bouquet with tangy fruit and perfectly balanced and integrated oak, then a palate which retains delicacy and crispness, through to a clean and lingering finish. 56 per cent barrel fermented in new French oak with 5 months lees stirring; 18 per cent wild yeast ferment. That is precision driving. **rating:** 94

best drinking Now–2007 **best vintages** '97, '98, '99, '00, '01, '02 **drink with** Margaret River marron • $30

Cullen Chardonnay

▼▼▼▼▽ 2001 Medium yellow-green; the clean bouquet interweaves melon fruit with nutty/spicy barrel-ferment notes; the palate is incredibly fresh and youthful; melon and citrus fruit is lengthened and accented by lingering acidity. Needs a decade to show its best. **rating: 91**

best drinking 2005–2015 **best vintages** '93, '94, '96, '98, '99, '00, '01 **drink with** Marron • $50

Cullen Cabernet Sauvignon Merlot

▼▼▼▼▼ 2001 Medium to full red-purple; deep, dark, blackberry and blackcurrant fruit, rich but not jammy floods the bouquet; the palate is surprisingly supple, notwithstanding the concentrated and powerful fruit; the tannins are finer-grained and softer than in some vintages; a wine of great balance, length and line. **rating: 95**

best drinking 2010–2020 **best vintages** '77, '84, '86, '90, '91, '92, '93, '95, '96, '97, '98, '99, '00, '01 **drink with** Braised ox tail • $75

curlewis winery ★★★★★

55 Navarre Road, Curlewis, Vic 3222 **region** Geelong
phone (03) 5250 4567 **fax** (03) 5250 4567 **open** By appointment
winemaker Rainer Breit **production** 1000 cases **est.** 1998
product range ($39–55 R) Chardonnay, Pinot Noir, Reserve Pinot Noir, Shiraz.
summary Rainer Breit and partner Wendy Oliver have achieved a great deal in a remarkably short period of time. In 1996 they purchased their property at Curlewis with 1.6 hectares of what were then 11-year-old pinot noir vines; previously, and until 1998 the grapes had been sold to Scotchmans Hill. They set to and established an on-site winery, making 800 cases of very good Pinot Noir in their first vintage of 1998. Rainer Breit is a self-taught winemaker, but the full bag of pinot noir winemaking tricks is used: cold-soaking, hot-fermentation, post-ferment maceration, part inoculated and partly wild yeast use, prolonged lees contact, and bottling the wine neither fined nor filtered. While Breit and Oliver are self-confessed 'pinotphiles', they have planted a little chardonnay and buy a little locally grown shiraz and chardonnay. The wines are sold into Australia's best restaurants or by mail order, and rarely hit retail shelves.

Curlewis Pinot Noir

▼▼▼▼▼ 2001 Medium red, the purple starting to fade; a wonderfully complex sappy, spicy, savoury, distinctly Burgundian bouquet feeds directly into the palate, with a scintillating array of the same characters, long savoury and foresty, but not the least bitter. The yield 1.5 tonnes to the acre; 500 cases made. **rating: 94**

best drinking Now–2007 **best vintages** '98, '00, '01 **drink with** Tea-smoked duck • $39

Curlewis Reserve Pinot Noir

▼▼▼▼▼ 2001 Medium red-purple; the bouquet is similar to the standard Pinot Noir, but with greater power and concentration to the fruit core of black plum; likewise, the palate offers another dimension to the fruit, with great depth and richness; will be long lived. Produced from 18-year-old estate vines yielding 0.75 tonne to the acre. 175 cases made. **rating: 96**

best drinking Now–2010 **best vintages** '01 **drink with** Marinated venison • $55

curly flat ★★★★

Collivers Road, Lancefield, Vic 3435 **region** Macedon Ranges
phone (03) 5429 1956 **fax** (03) 5429 2256 **open** First Sunday of each month, or by appointment
winemaker Phillip Moraghan and consultants **production** 3000 cases **est.** 1991
product range ($24–44 ML) Chardonnay, Lacuna Chardonnay (unwooded), Pinot Noir.
summary Phillip and Jeni Moraghan began the development of Curly Flat in 1992, drawing in part upon the inspiration Phillip Moraghan experienced when working in Switzerland in the late 1980s, and with a passing nod to Michael Leunig. With ceaseless help and guidance from the late Laurie Williams (who died unexpectedly in mid-2001) the Moraghans have painstakingly established 14 hectares of vineyard, principally pinot noir with lesser amounts of chardonnay and pinot gris. A multi-level, gravity flow winery was commissioned for the 2002 vintage. The quality of the 1999 wines on current release in March 2003 was excellent, the 2000 vintage rather weaker. Phillip Moraghan is very excited about the quality of the 2002 wines, made with advice from Gary Farr. Exports to the US.

Curly Flat Lacuna Chardonnay

▼▼▼▼ 2000 Medium yellow-green; some nutty, bottle-developed complexity drives the bouquet, but the palate still presents clean and clear nectarine and white peach fruit, with more than average flavour for unwooded Chardonnay. **rating: 85**

best drinking Now–2006 **drink with** Chinese prawns • $24

Curly Flat Chardonnay

❦❦❦❦❦ **1999** Vibrant yellow-green; the complex bouquet has tangy, bottle-developed, barrel-fermented inputs, but is still quite youthful overall; the tight, elegant palate marries citrus and honeydew with subtle oak. Most impressive. **rating:** 94

best drinking Now–2007 **best vintages** '98, '99 **drink with** Abalone • $35

Curly Flat Pinot Noir

❦❦❦❦ **2000** Light to medium red-purple; light, earthy, savoury aromas and flavours mark a wine which lacks depth, although it is well enough made. **rating:** 84

❦❦❦❦ **1999** Medium red-purple; with better depth than the 2000, and equally good hue; the complex bouquet has dark plum with some forest and game aromas; the rich and complex palate provides a replay, dark plum fruit on the mid-palate followed by a savoury finish; the presence of brettanomyces is quite possible, but doesn't spoil the enjoyment of the wine so far as I am concerned. **rating:** 89

❦❦❦❦❦ **1998** Excellent colour; the rich and complex bouquet oozes varietal fruit, the powerful, opulent and smooth palate with abundant dark plum flavour; very youthful still, and spotlessly clean. Remarkable wine. **rating:** 94

best drinking Now **drink with** Jugged hare • $44

currency creek estate ★★★☆

Winery Road, Currency Creek, SA 5214 **region** Currency Creek
phone (08) 8555 4069 **fax** (08) 8555 4100 **open** 7 days 10–5
winemaker John Loxton **production** 7000 cases **est.** 1969
product range ($9.95–25.95 CD) Sedgeland Sauvignon Blanc, The Creek Station Semillon Sauvignon Blanc, The Creek Station Semillon, Reserve Brut, Princess Alexandrina Noble Semillon, Ostrich Hill Shiraz, The Creek Station Grenache Shiraz, The Creek Station Cabernet Grenache, Cabernet Sauvignon; fortifieds.
summary Constant name changes early in the piece (Santa Rosa, Tonkins have also been tried) did not help the quest for identity or recognition in the marketplace, but the winery has nonetheless produced some outstanding wood-matured whites and pleasant, soft reds selling at attractive prices.

dalfarras ★★★☆

PO Box 123, Nagambie, Vic 3608 **region** Nagambie Lakes
phone (03) 5794 2637 **fax** (03) 5794 2360 **open** Not
winemaker Alister Purbrick, Alan George **production** 20 000 cases **est.** 1991
product range ($10.75–19.95 R) Sauvignon Blanc, Verdelho, Shiraz, Merlot.
summary The personal project of Alister Purbrick and artist-wife Rosa (nee) Dalfarra, whose paintings adorn the labels of the wines. Alister, of course, is best known as winemaker at Tahbilk, the family winery and home, but this range of wines is intended to (in Alister's words) 'allow me to expand my winemaking horizons and mould wines in styles different to Tahbilk'. It now draws upon 23 hectares of its own plantings in the Goulburn Valley, and the business continues to grow year by year.

Dalfarras Sauvignon Blanc

❦❦❦❦ **2002** Light to medium yellow-green; the fruit of the bouquet is largely tropical, with a hint of gooseberry also apparent. These flavours come through on the palate, which opens well, but finishes a fraction sweet and thick. **rating:** 85

best drinking Now **best vintages** '96 **drink with** Smoked eel • $10.75

Dalfarras Shiraz

❦❦❦❦ **1999** Light to medium red-purple; the light, juicy berry fruit of the bouquet is matched by a whisper of vanilla oak, the palate with the same characters, though with a little more tannin than expected. A mixture of McLaren Vale, Nagambie Lakes and Padthaway fruit which spent 18 months in American oak. **rating:** 84

best drinking Now **drink with** Grilled lamb chops • $19.95

Dalfarras Merlot

❦❦❦❦ **2001** Medium red-purple; the moderately intense bouquet has gentle slightly amorphous berry fruit, but with a savoury spice aspect hinting at the variety; the palate picks up where the bouquet leaves off, with olive/berry varietal fruit and minimal oak. The wine is sourced from vineyards across Australia, and comes with a completely new and very smart label design and package. **rating:** 84

best drinking Now–2006 **drink with** Pan-fried veal • $15.95

dalrymple ★★★★

1337 Pipers Brook Road, Pipers Brook, Tas 7254 **region** Northern Tasmania
phone (03) 6382 7222 **fax** (03) 6382 7222 **open** 7 days 10–5
winemaker Bertel Sundstrup **production** 4500 cases **est.** 1987
product range ($15–35 CD) Chardonnay, Unwooded Chardonnay, Sauvignon Blanc, Blanc de Blancs, Pinot Noir, Pinot Noir Special Bin.
summary A partnership between Jill Mitchell and her sister and brother-in-law, Anne and Bertel Sundstrup, inspired by father Bill Mitchell's establishment of the Tamarway Vineyard in the late 1960s. In 1991 Tamarway reverted to the Sundstrup and Mitchell families and it, too, will be producing wine in the future, probably under its own label but sold ex the Dalrymple cellar door. As production has grown (significantly), so has that of wine quality across the board, often led by its Sauvignon Blanc.

Dalrymple Sauvignon Blanc

▼▼▼▼▽ **2002** Light straw-green; a complex bouquet with well-integrated oak leads into a smooth, balanced palate, with ripe gooseberry flavours, and a long finish. **rating:** 90

best drinking Now **best vintages** '94, '96, '00 **drink with** Tartare of Atlantic salmon • $25

Dalrymple Blanc de Blanc

▼▼▼▼▽ **1998** Light green-yellow; a clean, firm, bright citrussy bouquet leads into a lively, fresh and crisp palate in archetypal Tasmanian style, but is well balanced and without the searing acidity which can be encountered. **rating:** 90

best drinking Now–2006 **best vintages** '98 **drink with** Aperitif • $25

Dalrymple Pinot Noir

▼▼▼▼ **2001** Light to medium red-purple; both bouquet and palate are on the lighter side, with touches of leaf and mint, quality oak helping build flavour. **rating:** 87

best drinking Now–2006 **best vintages** '98 **drink with** Roast rabbit • $25

dalwhinnie ★★★★☆

Taltarni Road, RMB 4378, Moonambel, Vic 3478 **region** Pyrenees
phone (03) 5467 2388 **fax** (03) 5467 2237 **open** 7 days 10–5
winemaker David Jones, Gary Baldwin (Consultant) **production** 5500 cases **est.** 1976
product range ($32–148 CD) Dalwhinnie Pinot Noir; Moonambel Chardonnay, Shiraz and Cabernet; Eagle Series Shiraz.
summary David and Jenny Jones have acquired full ownership of Dalwhinnie from Ewan Jones, and have three children of their own to ensure the future succession. In the meantime, Dalwhinnie goes from strength to strength, making outstanding wines right across the board. The wines all show tremendous depth of fruit flavour, reflecting the relatively low-yielding but very well-maintained vineyards. It is hard to say whether the Chardonnay, the Cabernet Sauvignon or the Shiraz is the more distinguished, the Pinot Noir a startling arrival from out of nowhere. A further 8 hectares of shiraz (with a little viognier) were planted in the spring of 1999 on a newly acquired block on Taltarni Road, permitting the further development of exports to the UK, Spain, Switzerland, the US, Canada, Switzerland, New Zealand and Hong Kong. A 50-tonne contemporary high-tech winery was built prior to the 2002 vintage allowing the Eagle Series Shiraz and Pinot Noir to be made on-site.

Dalwhinnie Moonambel Chardonnay

▼▼▼▼▽ **2001** Medium yellow-green; the smooth bouquet has melon and nectarine fruit interwoven with subtle barrel-ferment inputs; the medium-bodied palate is in typical understated mode, with barrel-ferment and malolactic-ferment cashew and melon flavours in seamless balance. **rating:** 91

best drinking Now–2007 **best vintages** '90, '92, '93, '94, '96, '98, '99, '00, '01 **drink with** Turkey • $32

Dalwhinnie Pinot Noir

▼▼▼▼▽ **2001** Light red-purple; fragrant and stylish tangy, savoury, spicy aromas lead into a palate with the same elegance and style, long, fine and lingering; the miracle continues. **rating:** 93

best drinking Now–2006 **best vintages** '00, '01 **drink with** Game • $35

Dalwhinnie Eagle Series Pyrenees Shiraz

▼▼▼▼▼ **2000** Medium to full red-purple; a dense and complex bouquet with spicy, savoury edges to the array of dark fruits; a powerful, savoury palate with blackberry fruit, and fine, lingering, squeaky tannins. **rating:** 94

best drinking 2006–2016 **best vintages** '98, '00 **drink with** Game • $148

Dalwhinnie Moonambel Shiraz

YYYY 2001 Medium red-purple, lighter than usual, although the hue is good; the moderately intense and clean bouquet has damson plum and cherry with a hint of spice and subtle oak; the palate is nicely balanced, but, like the bouquet, lighter than usual. **rating: 88**

best drinking 2006–2011 **best vintages** '86, '88, '90, '91, '92, '94, '95, '97, '98, '99, '00 **drink with** Potent cheeses, strong red meats • $46

Dalwhinnie Moonambel Cabernet Sauvignon

YYYY 2001 Medium red-purple; clean, fresh redcurrant and mulberry aromas, the palate with more length and intensity than the Shiraz, but with distinct herbal notes, and, once again, not as concentrated as usual. Lingering tannins are a plus. **rating: 89**

best drinking 2006–2011 **best vintages** '92, '93, '00 **drink with** Rare char-grilled rump steak • $42

dalyup river estate   NR

Murrays Road, Esperance, WA 6450 **region** South West Australia Zone
phone (08) 9076 5027 **fax** (08) 9076 5027 **open** Weekends 10–4 Oct-May
winemaker Tom Murray **production** 1000 cases **est.** 1987
product range ($13–17 CD) Hellfire White, Esperance Chardonnay (unwooded), Chardonnay, Esperance Shiraz, Esperance Cabernet Sauvignon, Rositter's Port.
summary Arguably the most remote winery in Australia other than Chateau Hornsby in Alice Springs, drawing upon 2.5 hectares of estate vineyards. The quantities are as small as the cellar-door prices are modest; this apart, the light but fragrant wines show the cool climate of this ocean-side vineyard. Came from out of the clouds to win the trophy for Best Wine of Show at the West Australian Show in 1999 with its Shiraz, but hasn't repeated that success.

dal zotto wines   ★★★★

Edi Road, Cheshunt, Vic 3678 **region** King Valley
phone (03) 5729 8321 **fax** (03) 5729 8490 **open** 7 days 11–5
winemaker Otto Dal Zotto, Michael Dal Zotto **production** 10 000 cases **est.** 1987
product range ($14–29 CD) Riesling, Chardonnay, Shiraz, Barbera, Merlot, Cabernet Merlot, Cabernet Sauvignon.
summary Dal Zotto Wines remains primarily a contract grape grower, with 48 hectares of vineyards (predominantly chardonnay, cabernet sauvignon and merlot, with smaller plantings of riesling, pinot gris, shiraz, sangiovese, barbera and marzemino). Increasing amounts are made under the Dal Zotto label, with retail distribution in New South Wales and exports to the US and Japan.

Dal Zotto Riesling

YYYYY 2002 Light straw-green; the crisp, clean, mineral and herb bouquet is followed by a long, tangy citrus and lime palate, with very good balance and line. A surprise packet; excellent value. **rating: 92**

best drinking Now–2010 **best vintages** '00, '02 **drink with** Grilled calamari • $15

Dal Zotto Chardonnay

YYYY 2001 bright yellow-green; the bouquet has well-balanced barrel-ferment inputs on the nutty, melon fruit; on the palate gentle melon and peach fruit runs through the length, the oak soft and well-integrated. **rating: 87**

best drinking Now **drink with** Seafood risotto • $19

Dal Zotto Shiraz

YYYY 2001 Strong purple-red; the moderately complex bouquet offers dark plum, spice and blackberry fruit, the palate with good fruit weight and shape to the sweet blackberry flavours and fine, savoury tannins. **rating: 88**

best drinking 2004–2008 **drink with** Beef shishkebabs • $29

Dal Zotto Cabernet Sauvignon

YYYY 2000 Medium red-purple; sundry herbs and spices intermingle with blackcurrant fruit on the bouquet; sweet, light, ripe cassis fruit drives the palate, which has only a little oak and few tannins to provide structure. What is there is good, in early drinking style. **rating: 85**

best drinking 2004–2007 **drink with** Wood-fired pizza • $19

danbury estate   NR

Billimari, NSW 2794 (PO Box 605, Cowra, NSW 2794) **region** Cowra
phone (02) 6341 2204 **fax** (02) 6341 4690 **open** Tues–Sun 10–4 at Chill Restaurant, Japanese Garden, Cowra
winemaker Hope Estate (Contract) **production** 6000 cases **est.** 1996
product range ($12.95–15.30 CD) Middleton Chardonnay, Middleton Sparkling, Reserve.
summary A specialist Chardonnay producer established by Jonathon Middleton, with 22 hectares in production
and the wines made under contract. The Quarry Restaurant at the winery is open Tuesday to Sunday 10–4.

d'arenberg   ★ ★ ★ ★ ☆

Osborn Road, McLaren Vale, SA 5171 **region** McLaren Vale
phone (08) 8323 8206 **fax** (08) 8323 8423 **open** 7 days 10–5
winemaker Chester Osborn, Phillip Dean **production** 180 000 cases **est.** 1912
product range ($11–60 R) Dry Dam Riesling, Broken Fishplate Sauvignon Blanc, Last Ditch Viognier,
Money Spider Roussanne, Stump Jump Sauvignon Blanc Chardonnay, Hermit Crab Marsanne Viognier, Olive
Grove Chardonnay, Other Side Chardonnay, Lucky Lizard Chardonnay, Noble Riesling, Noble Semillon,
Noble Traminer Riesling, Peppermint Paddock Sparkling Chambourcin, Feral Fox Pinot Noir, Dead Arm
Shiraz, Footbolt Old Vine Shiraz, Laughing Magpie Shiraz Viognier, Twenty Eight Road Mourvedre, d'Arry's
Original Shiraz Grenache, Stump Jump Grenache Shiraz, Ironstone Pressings Grenache Shiraz Mourvedre,
Custodian Grenache, Galvo Garage Cabernet Sauvignon Merlot Cabernet Franc, High Trellis Cabernet
Sauvignon, Coppermine Road Cabernet Sauvignon; Vintage Fortified Shiraz, Nostalgia Rare Tawny.
summary Originally a conservative, traditional business (albeit successful), d'Arenberg adopted a much higher
profile in the second half of the 1990s, with a cascade of volubly worded labels and the opening of a
spectacularly situated and high-quality restaurant, d'Arry's Verandah. Happily, wine quality has more than kept
pace with the label uplifts. An incredible number of export markets spread across Europe, North America and
Asia, with all of the major countries represented.

d'Arenberg The Broken Fishplate Sauvignon Blanc
♥♥♥♥♥ 2002 Light straw-green; the crisp bouquet offers a mix of herb, grass and gooseberry, the palate with
excellent balance, length and a particularly good aftertaste. A surprise packet.   **rating:** 93
best drinking Now **best vintages** '02 **drink with** Steamed fish • $17

d'Arenberg The Lucky Lizard Chardonnay
♥♥♥♥♥ 2001 Medium to full yellow-green; the complex and tangy bouquet has some Burgundian overtones,
the rich, sweet peachy fruit complexed by nutty malolactic and barrel-ferment oak inputs on the finish. The
fulsome back label will tell you all about the Lucky Lizard.   **rating:** 90
best drinking Now–2006 **best vintages** '01 **drink with** Grilled spatchcock • $19.95

d'Arenberg The Feral Fox Pinot Noir
♥♥♥♥♥ 2001 Medium red-purple; a complex bouquet with savoury, spicy plummy fruit, characters which
come through potently on the palate, which is at the big end of town.   **rating:** 90
best drinking Now–2006 **best vintages** '01 **drink with** Chicken liver ravioli • $24.95

d'Arenberg Dead Arm Shiraz
♥♥♥♥♥ 2000 Medium to full red-purple; masses of dark plum, prune and licorice fruit on the bouquet, then a
palate flooded with the same fruit characters plus a generous dash of bitter chocolate; lots of tannin and extract;
needs a decade.   **rating:** 94
best drinking 2006–2016 **best vintages** '94, '95, '96, '97, '98, '00 **drink with** Marinated beef • $60

d'Arenberg The Laughing Magpie Shiraz Viognier
♥♥♥♥♥ 2001 Strong purple-red; the fruit-driven bouquet has a range of rich plum, black cherry and sweet
spice aromas, the rich and mouthfilling palate exuding dark fruit flavours, finishing with slightly milky/furry
tannins which should settle down nicely with time.   **rating:** 93
best drinking Now–2009 **drink with** Marinated venison • $31

d'Arenberg The Coppermine Road Cabernet Sauvignon
♥♥♥♥ 2000 Medium red-purple; blackberry and blackcurrant fruit on the bouquet has some more savoury
characters in the background; there is more of the same on the palate, with fractionally edgy tannins running
from the back palate to the finish.   **rating:** 88
best drinking 2005–2010 **best vintages** '97, '99 **drink with** Leave it in the cellar • $60

d'Arenberg Nostalgia Rare Tawny

YYYY NV Golden tawny; honey, Christmas cake, nutty, rancio aromas lead into a quite fine Christmas cake palate, followed by a distinctly biscuity aftertaste. **rating:** 89

best drinking Now **drink with** Coffee • $30

dargo valley winery NR

Lower Dargo Road, Dargo, Vic 3682 **region** Gippsland
phone (03) 5140 1228 **fax** (03) 5140 1388 **open** Mon–Thurs 12–8, weekends, holidays 10–8 (closed Fridays)
winemaker Hermann Bila **production** 500 cases **est.** 1985
product range ($12.50–14.50 CD) Rhine Riesling, Sauvignon Blanc, Chardonnay, Pinot Noir, Cabernet Sauvignon, Port, Muscat.
summary Two and a half hectares are situated in mountain country north of Maffra and looking towards the Bogong National Park. Hermann Bila comes from a family of European winemakers; there is an on-site restaurant, and Devonshire teas and ploughman's lunches are served – very useful given the remote locality. The white wines tend to be rustic, the sappy/earthy/cherry Pinot Noir the pick of the red wines. Bed and breakfast accommodation is available.

darling estate ★★★

Whitfield Road, Cheshunt, Vic 3678 **region** King Valley
phone (03) 5729 8396 **fax** (03) 5729 8396 **open** By appointment
winemaker Guy Darling, Rick Kinzbrunner (Consultant) **production** 500 cases **est.** 1990
product range ($10–30 CD) Koombahla Riesling, Nambucca Chenin Blanc, Koombahla Chardonnay, Koombahla Pinot Noir, Nambucca Gamay, Koombahla Shiraz, Koombahla Cabernet Franc, Koombahla Cabernet Sauvignon.
summary Guy Darling was one of the pioneers of the King Valley when he planted his first vines in 1970. For many years the entire production was purchased by Brown Brothers, providing their well known Koombahla Estate label. Much of the production from the 23 hectares is still sold to Brown Brothers (and others), but since 1991 Guy Darling has had a fully functional winery established on the vineyard, making a small portion of the production into wine – which was, in fact, his original motivation for planting the first vines. All the wines on sale have considerable bottle age.

darling park ★★★★

232 Red Hill Road, Red Hill, Vic 3937 **region** Mornington Peninsula
phone (03) 5989 2324 **fax** (03) 5989 2324 **open** Weekends and public holidays 11–5, and throughout January
winemaker Rupert Loch, Winenet (Consultant) **production** 3000 cases **est.** 1986
product range ($17–30 CD) Sauvignon Blanc, Madhatters Sparkling, Querida (Rose), Te Quiero, Decadence, Pinot Noir, Estate Merlot, Cabernet Merlot, Estate Cabernet Sauvignon.
summary John Liberman (and wife Karen) and David Coe purchased Darling Park prior to the 2002 vintage. The Winenet consultancy group is providing advice on both the viticultural and winemaking side, and the product range has been revamped.

Darling Park Sauvignon Blanc

YYYYY 2002 Light straw-green; clear and precise varietal fruit aromas are midway between the grassy and gooseberry ends of the spectrum, the crisp and clean palate again nicely focused; good length. **rating:** 90

best drinking Now **best vintages** '02 **drink with** Scallops • $17

Darling Park Madhatters Sparkling

YYYYY 1996 Medium to full yellow-green; the bouquet is profoundly complex in genuine Champagne style; a big, complex wine on entry to the mouth, veering off slightly on the finish, but still of impressive quality and style. Pinot noir and chardonnay sourced from Macedon has spent 6 years on yeast lees. **rating:** 90

best drinking Now **drink with** Tempura or sushi • $30

Darling Park Querida Rose

YYYY 2002 Vivid fuchsia pink; a clean bouquet with gentle, small red fruit aromas is followed by a firm, crisp, dry palate which very much shows its red and white ancestry. A blend of Pinot Gris, Cabernet Sauvignon and Chardonnay. **rating:** 86

best drinking Now **drink with** Antipasto • $17

Darling Park Pinot Noir

TTTT **2001** Excellent red-purple colour; the bouquet offers gentle plum fruit with specks of spice, the big palate with slightly furry texture which lacks focus, but nonetheless has lots of soft, plummy flavour. **rating:** 87

best drinking Now–2006 **best vintages** '00 **drink with** Roast squab • $28

Darling Park Estate Merlot

TTTT **2000** Medium red-purple; the bouquet offers a mix of bright, fresh, small berry fruits and more savoury notes, the light to medium-bodied palate being direct and fresh, with touches of leaf and mint. **rating:** 87

best drinking Now–2006 **drink with** Braised lamb • $28

darlington estate ★★★☆

Lot 39 Nelson Road, Darlington, WA 6070 **region** Perth Hills
phone (08) 9299 6268 **fax** (08) 9299 7107 **open** Thurs–Sun and holidays 12–5
winemaker John Griffiths (Consultant) **production** 3000 cases **est.** 1983
product range ($13–30 CD) Sonata (Sauvignon Blanc), Semillon, Chardonnay, Symphony (Verdelho), Serenade (Chardonnay), Shiraz, Cabernet Sauvignon, Brut, Ruby Port; Darling Red (Grenache), Darling White (Unwooded Chardonnay), Darling Rose (Grenache).
summary Established by the van der Meer family, it is one of the oldest – and was once the largest – wineries in the Perth Hills, for a while setting the standard. With John Griffiths as consultant, the quality should once again be assured, although it will not challenge either Western Range or Millbrook in terms of size.

darlington vineyard ★★★☆

Holkam Court, Orford, Tas 7190 **region** Southern Tasmania
phone (03) 6257 1630 **fax** (03) 6257 1630 **open** By appointment
winemaker Andrew Hood **production** 350 cases **est.** 1993
product range ($15–18.50 CD) Riesling, Sauvignon Blanc, Chardonnay, Pinot Noir.
summary Peter and Margaret Hyland planted a little under 2 hectares of vineyard in 1993. The first wines were made from the 1999 vintage, forcing retired builder Peter Hyland to complete their home so the small building in which they had been living could be converted to a cellar door. The vineyard looks out over the settlement of Darlington on Maria Island, the site of Diego Bernacci's attempt to establish a vineyard and lure investors by attaching artificial bunches of grapes to his vines. The outline of Maria Island is depicted on the label.

Darlington Vineyard Riesling

TTTT **2001** Medium straw-green; a complex, fractionally old-fashioned bouquet leads into a very firm and focused palate, with tight acidity. Scored well on my sheet at the 2003 Tasmanian Wines Show. **rating:** 86

best drinking Now–2005 **drink with** Gazpacho • $15

Darlington Vineyard Chardonnay

TTTT **2002** Light to medium yellow-green; the oak influence is subtle throughout both bouquet and palate, with light cashew, peach and stone fruit flavours. Good balance and carry in a light-bodied mode. **rating:** 86

best drinking Now–2005 **drink with** Tempura • $17

david traeger ★★★☆

139 High Street, Nagambie, Vic 3608 **region** Nagambie Lakes
phone (03) 5794 2514 **fax** (03) 5794 1776 **open** 7 days 10–5
winemaker David Traeger **production** 10 000 cases **est.** 1986
product range ($11–29.50 R) Verdelho, Shiraz, Cabernet; Helvetia (available from cellar door only), Classic Dry (Riesling Semillon), Late Harvest (Riesling Verdelho), Cabernet Dolce, Cabernet Shiraz Merlot, Tawny Port.
summary David Traeger learned much during his years as assistant winemaker at Mitchelton, and knows central Victoria well. The red wines are solidly crafted, the Verdelho interesting but more variable in quality. In late 2002 the business was acquired by the Dromana Estate group, but David Traeger is staying on as winemaker. See also separate Baptista entry.

David Traeger Verdelho

TTTY **2002** Medium yellow-green; clean, gentle fruit salad aromas flow into a well-balanced light to medium-bodied palate, with equally gentle fruit salad flavours; will not frighten the horses. **rating:** 84

best drinking Now **best vintages** '91, '94, '95, '97 **drink with** Sweet and sour pork • $18.50

David Traeger Shiraz

TTTT **1999** Light to medium red-purple; a clean, savoury bouquet has modest fruit, although the palate comes up with more interest and intensity; savoury, earthy blackberry fruit and some tannins add structure. The wine was matured in a mix of new American and French oak, but the impact from that maturation (which may have been brief) is not apparent. **rating: 85**

best drinking 2004–2008 **best vintages** '88, '92, '97, '98 **drink with** Wild duck • $29.50

dawson estate   NR

Cnr of Old Naracoorte and Kangaroo Hill Roads, Robe, SA 5276 **region** Mount Benson
phone (08) 8768 2427 **fax** (08) 8768 2987 **open** Not
winemaker Derek Hooper (Contract) **production** 500 cases **est.** 1998
product range ($18–25 R) Shiraz, Cabernet Sauvignon.
summary Anthony Paul and Marian Dawson are busy people. In addition to establishing over 20 hectares of chardonnay, pinot noir, shiraz and cabernet sauvignon, they are in the process of opening a wine bar/restaurant in Robe, and intend to continue extending the vineyard on a further 16 hectares of plantable land. All of this is largely financed by the crayfishing boat which Anthony runs in the crayfish season.

dawson's patch valley   NR

71 Kallista-Emerald Road, The Patch, Vic 3792 (postal) **region** Yarra Valley
phone 0419 521 080 **open** Not
winemaker Paul Evans (Contract) **production** 400 cases **est.** 2000
product range ($15 R) Chardonnay.
summary In 1996 James and Jody Dawson planted 1.2 hectares of chardonnay on their vineyard at the southern end of the Yarra Valley. The climate here is particularly cool, and the grapes do not normally ripen until late April. Jody Dawson manages the vineyards, and is completing a degree in viticulture through Charles Sturt University. The tiny production is basically sold through local restaurants and cellars in the Olinda/Emerald/Belgrave area. So far only a barrel-fermented (French oak) wine has been produced, but it may be that an unoaked version will join the roster some time in the future.

deakin estate   ★★★☆

Kulkyne Way, via Red Cliffs, Vic 3496 **region** Murray Darling
phone (03) 5029 1666 **fax** (03) 5024 3316 **open** Not
winemaker Linda Jakubans **production** 550 000 cases **est.** 1980
product range ($10.50–15 R) Sauvignon Blanc, Colombard, Chardonnay, Brut, Shiraz, Merlot, Cabernet Sauvignon; Select range of Chardonnay, Sparkling Shiraz, Shiraz, Merlot.
summary Effectively replaces the Sunnycliff label in the Katnook Estate, Riddoch and (now) Deakin Estate triumvirate, which constitutes the Wingara Wine Group, now 60 per cent owned by Freixenet of Spain. Sunnycliff is still used for export purposes but does not appear on the domestic market any more. Deakin Estate draws on over 300 hectares of its own vineyards, making it largely self-sufficient, and produces competitively priced wines of consistent quality and impressive value. Exports to the UK, the US, Canada, New Zealand and Asia.

Deakin Estate Select Chardonnay

TTTT **2002** Light straw-green; the clean, very light, fruit-driven nectarine bouquet picks up somewhat on the palate, which has clean nectarine fruit, and good length. Well priced. **rating: 85**

best drinking Now **drink with** Takeaway • $15

Deakin Estate Shiraz

TTTT **2001** Medium red-purple; the bouquet has direct, fresh plum and cherry fruit with a subtle touch of oak; the palate delivers more of the same, smooth and supple, with attractive fruit flavours. This is commercial winemaking at its best; excellent value. **rating: 86**

best drinking Now **best vintages** '00 **drink with** One size fits all • $10.50

Deakin Estate Select Merlot

TTTY **2000** Medium purple-red; American oak is very evident on the bouquet, and while it also comes through on the palate (the wine is said to have spent 10 months in French and American oak) there is a fair volume of flavour at this price point. **rating: 84**

best drinking Now **drink with** Pizza • $15

de bortoli ★★★★

De Bortoli Road, Bilbul, NSW 2680 **region** Riverina
phone (02) 6966 0100 **fax** (02) 6966 0199 **open** Mon–Sat 9–5, Sun 9–4
winemaker Nick Guy, Ralph Graham, Julie Mortlock, Helen Foggo-Paschkow **production** 4.5 million cases **est.** 1928
product range ($4.90–42.50 CD) Noble One Botrytis Semillon is the flagship wine; Premium varietals under Deen De Bortoli label; mid-priced range of varietal and blended wines under the Montage and Wild Vine labels; low-priced range of varietal and generic wines under the Sacred Hill label; Sparkling, Fortified. Substantial exports in bulk.
summary Famous among the cognoscenti for its superb Botrytis Semillon, which in fact accounts for only a minute part of its total production, this winery turns around low-priced varietal and generic wines which are invariably competently made and equally invariably provide value for money. These come in part from 250 hectares of estate vineyards, but mostly from contract-grown grapes. Exports include Canada, Singapore, Japan, Hong Kong, Sweden and Thailand.

De Bortoli Sacred Hill Traminer Riesling

▼▼▼▼ 2002 Light to medium yellow-green; spicy, crushed lime leaves and lychee aromas introduce a palate with plenty of flavour and length; well balanced and not, as usual, sweet. Absolutely outstanding value at the price. **rating:** 86

best drinking Now **drink with** Thai green chicken curry • $6.50

De Bortoli Deen Sauvignon Blanc

▼▼▼▼ 2002 Light straw-green; the ripe gooseberry fruit of the bouquet shows obvious varietal character, although it has slightly blurry, reductive elements. The medium-bodied palate provides more of the same, with strong varietal fruit in a somewhat loose, broad frame. Well priced. **rating:** 86

best drinking Now **drink with** Fishcakes • $10

De Bortoli Sacred Hill Colombard Chardonnay

▼▼▼▽ 2002 Medium yellow-green; a clean, solid bouquet with faint peachy fruit, the generously flavoured palate benefitting from the crisp acidity provided by the colombard. **rating:** 84

best drinking Now **drink with** Takeaway • $5.50

De Bortoli Montage Semillon Sauvignon Blanc

▼▼▼▼ 2002 Light to medium yellow-green; the bouquet has light mineral, grass and herb aromas, the light to medium-bodied palate precisely toeing the line of the bouquet, the finish (mercifully) near dry. **rating:** 85

best drinking Now **drink with** Seafood • $7.50

De Bortoli Wild Vine White Zinfandel

▼▼▼▽ 2002 Pale pink; faint red berry fruit aromas lead into a palate which has gentle clean fruit, nice balance, and is not too sweet. Infinitely better than the oceans of Californian Blush made every year for the US market. **rating:** 83

best drinking Now **drink with** Anything • $7.50

De Bortoli Deen Durif

▼▼▼▽ 2001 Medium red-purple; the moderately intense bouquet offers a mix of blackberry and blackcurrant fruit, with similar dark fruit flavours coming through on the palate; slightly harsh acidity impacts, but the wine is well priced. **rating:** 84

best drinking Now–2006 **drink with** Takeaway • $9.99

De Bortoli Montage Cabernet Merlot

▼▼▼▽ 2002 Light to medium red-purple; fresh red berry aromas are followed by a palate with sweet berry fruit, virtually no tannins and a soft finish; drop-dead, easy drinking style. Very good value. **rating:** 84

best drinking Now **drink with** Pizza • $8

De Bortoli Sacred Hill Cabernet Merlot

▼▼▼▼ 2001 Medium purple-red; the moderately intense bouquet, spotlessly fresh and clean, has red juicy berry aromas; the palate is driven by abundant dark, juicy berry fruit with well above-average depth. Exceptional value for money. **rating:** 86

best drinking Now **drink with** Any red meat • $6

de bortoli (hunter valley) ★★★☆

Lot 1, Branxton Road, Pokolbin, NSW 2320 **region** Lower Hunter Valley
phone (02) 4993 8800 **fax** (02) 4993 8899 **open** 7 days 10–5
winemaker Scott Stephens **production** 40 000 cases **est.** 2002
product range ($13.85–18.90 CD) Hunter Valley range of Semillon, Chardonnay; Black Creek Range of Semillon Sauvignon Blanc, Shiraz, Cabernet Merlot; Wilderness range not yet available.
summary De Bortoli extended its wine empire in 2002 with the purchase of the former Wilderness Estate, giving it an immediate and substantial presence in the Hunter Valley courtesy of the 19 hectares of established vineyards, to be expanded significantly by the subsequent purchase of an adjoining 40-hectare property. The wines will be released in three price ranges: at the top the Hunter Valley Semillon and Chardonnay, made from Hunter Valley grapes; then the Black Creek range, utilising three region blends encompassing the Hunter, Yarra and King Valleys (Semillon Sauvignon Blanc and Cabernet Merlot) and Hunter Valley, Heathcote and Yarra Valley (Shiraz). The Wilderness range will come at the bottom of the pyramid with the mouthwatering price tag of $8 a bottle.

De Bortoli Black Creek Semillon Sauvignon Blanc

▼▼▼▽ 2002 Light straw-green; the Sauvignon Blanc is quite evident in the blend, adding a tropical edge to the fruit; the palate is very light, but has reasonable length and balance. A blend of Hunter Valley, Yarra Valley and King Valley material. **rating:** 84
best drinking Now **drink with** Poached scallops • $13.85

De Bortoli Hunter Valley Chardonnay

▼▼▼▼ 2000 Light to medium yellow-green; the clean, moderately intense bouquet has melon and stone fruit aromas, the light to medium-bodied palate with smooth mouthfeel and balance to the stone fruit flavour; a hint of French oak lingers in the background. **rating:** 87
best drinking Now **drink with** Avocado and prawn salad • $18.80

De Bortoli Black Creek Shiraz

▼▼▼▼▽ 2001 Medium red-purple; while light, the bouquet has some fragrant spice, leaf and berry, the palate with a ripple of red fruit flavours providing mouthfeel and balance; subliminal oak. A blend of Hunter Valley, Heathcote and Yarra Valley material. **rating:** 91
best drinking Now–2007 **best vintages** '01 **drink with** Spaghetti Bolognese • $13.85

De Bortoli Black Creek Cabernet Merlot

▼▼▼▼ 2001 Medium red-purple; the clean and fresh bouquet has light berry fruit with a hint of sweet minty characters underneath; the light-bodied palate is fresh, with easy fruit and barely perceptible tannins. Immediate drinking style. A blend of Hunter, Yarra and King Valley material. **rating:** 86
best drinking Now–2005 **drink with** Chump chops • $13.85

de bortoli (victoria) ★★★★★

Pinnacle Lane, Dixons Creek, Vic 3775 **region** Yarra Valley
phone (03) 5965 2271 **fax** (03) 5965 2442 **open** 7 days 10–5
winemaker Stephen Webber, David Slingsby-Smith, Ben Cane, Paul Bridgeman **production** 400 000 cases **est.** 1987
product range ($12–57.50 R) At the top comes the premium Melba (Cabernet blend), followed by Yarra Valley Gewurztraminer, Chardonnay, Pinot Noir, Shiraz, Cabernet Sauvignon; then comes the intermediate Gulf Station range of Riesling, Semillon Sauvignon Blanc, Chardonnay, Pinot Noir, Shiraz, Merlot, Cabernet Sauvignon; the Windy Peak range of Riesling, Spatlese Riesling, Sauvignon Blanc Semillon, Chardonnay, Prestige (Sparkling) Cabernet Rose, Pinot Noir, Cabernet Shiraz Merlot; Emeri Chardonnay Pinot Noir, Emeri Sparkling Durif.
summary The quality arm of the bustling De Bortoli group, run by Leanne De Bortoli and husband Stephen Webber, ex-Lindeman winemaker. The top label (De Bortoli), the second (Gulf Station) and the third label (Windy Peak) offer wines of consistently good quality and excellent value – the complex Chardonnay is of outstanding quality. Exports to the UK, Europe, Asia and the US.

De Bortoli Gulf Station Riesling

▼▼▼▼▽ 2002 Light straw-green; crisp mineral and apple aromas, plus a touch of lime. An elegant, fresh and lively palate continues the mix of mineral, apple and lime; good mouthfeel and balance. One of the relatively few rieslings from the Yarra Valley. **rating:** 92
best drinking Now–2008 **best vintages** '02 **drink with** Artichoke with hollandaise sauce • $15

De Bortoli Windy Peak Riesling

▼▼▼▼ 2002 Light to medium straw-green; the bouquet has solid fruit moving into the tropical spectrum, the palate in attractive, easy access style, offering a fruity mid-palate and dry finish. **rating:** 87

best drinking Now–2005 **best vintages** '90, '92, '94, '95, '96, '97, '99, '01 **drink with** Fresh asparagus • $12

De Bortoli Yarra Valley Gewurztraminer

▼▼▼▼ 2001 Medium to full yellow; strong, spicy Alsatian aromas come through strongly on the generously flavoured but soft palate, which avoids the phenolic trap. **rating:** 89

best drinking Now **best vintages** '99 **drink with** Chinese Szechuan-style food • $18

De Bortoli Gulf Station Semillon Sauvignon Blanc

▼▼▼▼ 2002 Medium yellow-green; the bouquet is clean, solid but not particularly expressive, but the palate has more flavour, offering a mix of citrus, gooseberry and tropical flavours; good length. **rating:** 89

best drinking Now–2005 **drink with** Summer seafood • $15

De Bortoli Gulf Station Chardonnay

▼▼▼▼♀ 2002 Light straw-green; the aromatic bouquet is driven by the nectarine and white peach fruit, the oak perfectly integrated; there is abundant fruit weight and length to the palate, the American oak (new and older) melding with the fruit in an impressive way. As with the Yarra Valley Chardonnay, a tribute to the low yields of the vintage. **rating:** 90

best drinking Now–2005 **best vintages** '95, '96, '97, '98 **drink with** Yabbies • $16

De Bortoli Windy Peak Chardonnay

▼▼▼▼ 2002 Light to medium yellow-green; peach and fig aromas are complemented by a wisp of oak, which likewise adds complexity to the palate. Good length and particularly good value. **rating:** 87

best drinking Now **best vintages** '90, '92, '93, '94, '97, '00, '02 **drink with** Sashimi • $12

De Bortoli Yarra Valley Chardonnay

▼▼▼▼▼ 2002 Pale straw-green; the bouquet is still very discreet, with restrained barrel-ferment and malolactic-ferment inputs giving a faintly nutty background; it is on the elegant palate that the nectarine and citrus fruit comes up and up as the wine is retasted; the oak remains subtle, but the wine has excellent length and intensity, with a long future in front of it. **rating:** 94

best drinking 2004–2009 **best vintages** '90, '92, '93, '94, '96, '97, '98, '99, '00, '01, '02 **drink with** Braised pork neck • $23

De Bortoli Yarra Valley Pinot Noir

▼▼▼▼▼ 2001 Medium red-purple; fragrant aromas of strawberry and cherry drive the bouquet; the palate has good structure and length, offering silky red fruits, finishing with fine tannins and an airbrush of oak. As ever, great value. **rating:** 94

best drinking Now–2006 **best vintages** '95, '96, '97, '00, '01 **drink with** Duck casserole • $29

De Bortoli GS Reserve Yarra Valley Shiraz

▼▼▼▼♀ 1999 Medium red-purple; complex, secondary blackberry and spice aromas are starting to develop, the palate showing an even more complex array of spicy, earthy, savoury, chocolate-tinged flavours. Good acidity and plenty of length. **rating:** 91

best drinking 2005–2010 **best vintages** '97, '98, '99 **drink with** Smoked quail • $57.50

De Bortoli Gulf Station Shiraz

▼▼▼▼ 2001 Medium purple-red; clear blackberry and black cherry fruit with a strong sprinkling of varietal spice aromatics flow into a light to medium-bodied palate, with fresh, bright fruit and subtle oak. A now-or-later special. **rating:** 89

best drinking Now–2008 **best vintages** '99, '00 **drink with** Osso buco • $15

De Bortoli Yarra Valley Shiraz

▼▼▼▼♀ 2001 Clear red-purple; the clean bouquet has a mix of raspberry, plum and blackberry fruit supported by the usual subtle oak; the excellent structure and mouthfeel of the palate comes from round berry fruit flavours, and supple tannins. **rating:** 92

best drinking 2005–2010 **best vintages** '88, '90, '91, '92, '94, '97, '98, '01 **drink with** Grilled calf's liver • $29

De Bortoli Melba

ȲȲȲȲȲ 1999 Medium to full red-purple; the smooth, clean bouquet has a lovely mix of blackcurrant, spice and mulberry; the medium-bodied palate is textured and satiny, with blackcurrant and touches of dark chocolate; a wine of great finesse and very good length. Spends 2 years in French oak, and typically 500–600 cases only are made. **rating: 95**

ȲȲȲȲȲ 1998 Medium red-purple; a fragrant blend of cedar and blackcurrant aromas flow into a beautifully balanced and framed palate, essentially fruit-driven, finishing with fine, lingering tannins. 500 cases made; trophy winner. **rating: 96**

best drinking 2004–2014 **best vintages** '93, '94, '95, '97, '98, '99 **drink with** Yarra Valley venison • $57.50

De Bortoli Windy Peak Cabernet Shiraz Merlot

ȲȲȲȲ 2001 Medium red-purple; the clean, moderately intense bouquet has fresh, red berry fruit aromas, the light to medium-bodied palate running down the same track, with sweet, soft, supple fruit. Great everyday drinking. **rating: 85**

best drinking Now–2005 **drink with** Braised lamb • $14

De Bortoli Yarra Valley Cabernet Sauvignon

ȲȲȲȲȲ 2001 Bright, deep purple-red; the bouquet has very pure cassis, blackcurrant fruit supported by generous yet subtle oak. The palate provides more of the same, with totally seductive, ripe, pure cabernet varietal fruit flavours, supported by soft but sufficient tannins, and impeccably handled French oak. **rating: 94**

best drinking 2006–2016 **best vintages** '88, '90, '91, '92, '94, '95, '97, '98, '01 **drink with** Beef casserole • $29

deep dene vineyard   NR

36 Glenisla Road, Bickley, WA 6076 **region** Perth Hills
phone (08) 9293 0077 **fax** (08) 9293 0077 **open** By appointment
winemaker Contract **production** 4000 cases **est.** 1994
product range ($25–28 R) Pinot Noir, Shiraz, Sparkling.
summary Improbably, was once one of the largest Perth Hills vineyards, but no more. It comprises 4 hectares of pinot noir and 0.5 hectare of shiraz, continuing the near obsession of the Perth Hills vignerons with pinot noir in a climate which, to put it mildly, is difficult for the variety, other than its use in sparkling wine.

deep woods estate   ★★★★

Lot 10 Commonage Road, Yallingup, WA 6282 **region** Margaret River
phone (08) 9756 6066 **fax** (08) 9756 6366 **open** Tues–Sun 11–5, 7 days during holidays
winemaker Ben Gould **production** 19 000 cases **est.** 1987
product range ($16–45 CD) Semillon, Semillon Sauvignon Blanc, Ivory (Semillon Sauvignon Blanc), Verdelho, Eden (Botrytis Semillon), Harmony (Rose), Shiraz, Ebony (Cabernet Sauvignon Shiraz), Cabernet Merlot, Cabernet Sauvignon, Cabernet Reserve.
summary The Gould family acquired Deep Woods Estate in 1991, 4 years after the commencement of the estate plantings. There are 15 hectares of estate vines planted to nine varieties, with the intake supplemented by extended family-grown grapes for the Ebony and Ivory wines. At the top of the tree are the occasional and tiny releases under the Boneyard label: the first such release was of 600 bottles of 2001 Cabernet Franc. These wines are only available to mail list customers, and are likely to be pre-sold to those on a waiting list, but overall production continues to steadily increase.

Deep Woods Estate Semillon Sauvignon Blanc

ȲȲȲȲ 2002 Light green-yellow; the bouquet is quite pungent, with a mix of herbal and earth, grass and mineral aromas, but the palate changes direction altogether, much lighter and with a subliminal touch of sweetness on the finish. **rating: 85**

best drinking Now **best vintages** '00, '01 **drink with** Margaret River abalone • $16

Deep Woods Estate Boneyard

ȲȲȲȲȲ 2001 Medium red-purple; the moderately intense bouquet is quite complex, offsetting mint and berry against more savoury/earthy aromas; the palate has an appealing array of berry, olive and earth flavours reflecting the varietal mix; it has good texture and balance, length and elegance. **rating: 90**

best drinking 2005–2012 **best vintages** '01 **drink with** Loin of lamb • $45

de iuliis   ★★★☆

21 Broke Road, Pokolbin, NSW 2320 **region** Lower Hunter Valley
phone (02) 4993 8000 **fax** (02) 4998 7168 **open** 7 days 10–5
winemaker Michael De Iuliis **production** 10 000 cases **est.** 1990
product range ($14–32 CD) Semillon, Verdelho, Chardonnay, Show Reserve Chardonnay, Pinot Chardonnay, Cordon Cut Semillon, Ruby Rose, Shiraz, McLaren Vale Shiraz.
summary Three generations of the De Iuliis family have been involved in the establishment of their 45-hectare vineyard at Keinbah in the Lower Hunter Valley. The family acquired the property in 1986 and planted the first vines in 1990, selling the grapes from the first few vintages to Tyrrell's but retaining small amounts of grapes for release under the De Iuliis label. Winemaker Michael De Iuliis, the third-generation family member, has completed postgraduate studies in oenology at the Roseworthy Campus of Adelaide University. The overall quality of the wines is good and the wines are available through cellar door and selected restaurants in the Hunter and Sydney, with small amounts coming to Melbourne.

De Iuliis Semillon

▼▼▼▼ **1998** Light straw-green; the bouquet is clean, and still developing, the palate in the same box; there is plenty of structure, but the wine is still in the mineral/herb stage of its development. An each way proposition for drinking or cellaring.   **rating:** 89
best drinking 2004–2010 **drink with** Pan-fried scallops • $14

De Iuliis Limited Release Chardonnay

▼▼▼▼ **2000** Medium yellow-straw; developed honey, toast, butter and peach aromas flow into a soft, peachy/buttery regional palate. Drink asap.   **rating:** 85
best drinking Now **drink with** Grilled spatchcock • $18

De Iuliis Limited Release McLaren Vale Shiraz

▼▼▼▼ **2000** Medium red-purple; moderately intense, smooth, gentle black fruits and subtle oak aromas flow into a fruit-driven palate, with supple blackberry and bitter chocolate flavours. Good balance and structure.   **rating:** 88
best drinking 2005–2009 **drink with** Grilled porterhouse • $32

De Iuliis Show Reserve Shiraz

▼▼▼▼▽ **2000** Medium red-purple; some regional savoury, spice and earth aromas on the bouquet lead into a medium-bodied palate, with a similar display of blackberry, earth and chocolate fruit. The tannins are ripe, and the wine has good length and balance.   **rating:** 90
best drinking 2005–2010 **best vintages** '00 **drink with** Braised rabbit • $20

delacolline estate   NR

Whillas Road, Port Lincoln, SA 5606 **region** Southern Eyre Peninsula
phone (08) 8682 5277 **fax** (08) 8682 4455 **open** Weekends 9–5
winemaker Andrew Mitchell (Contract) **production** 650 cases **est.** 1984
product range ($10–15 R) Riesling, Fume Blanc, Cabernet Sauvignon.
summary Joins Boston Bay as the second Port Lincoln producer; the white wines are made under contract in the Clare Valley. The 3-hectare vineyard, run under the direction of Tony Bassett, reflects the cool maritime influence, with ocean currents that sweep up from the Antarctic. No recent tastings.

delamere   ★★★☆

Bridport Road, Pipers Brook, Tas 7254 **region** Northern Tasmania
phone (03) 6382 7190 **fax** (03) 6382 7250 **open** 7 days 10–5
winemaker Richard Richardson **production** 2500 cases **est.** 1983
product range ($16–28.50 CD) Chardonnay, Chardonnay Reserve, Pinot Noir, Pinot Noir (Reserve), Sparkling Rose, Sparkling Cuvee.
summary Richie Richardson produces elegant, rather light-bodied wines that have a strong following. The Chardonnay has been most successful, with a textured, complex, malolactic-influenced wine with great, creamy feel in the mouth. The Pinots typically show pleasant varietal fruit, but seem to suffer from handling problems. Retail distribution through Prime Wines.

Delamere Cuvee

▼▼▼▼ **1997** Distinct bronze colour; the wine has plenty of biscuity aroma and flavour, the palate round and rich, even to the point of sweetness, but does not cloy.   **rating:** 88

best drinking Now–2005 **drink with** Duck consomme

delaney's creek winery   NR

70 Hennessey Road, Delaneys Creek, Qld 4514 **region** Queensland Coastal
phone (07) 5496 4925 **fax** (07) 5496 4926 **open** Mon–Fri 10–4, weekends and public holidays 10–5
winemaker Barry Leverett **production** 3000 cases **est.** 1997
product range ($10.50–16.50 CD) Verdelho, Chardonnay, Muscat Rose, Pinot Noir, Late Shiraz, fortifieds.
summary Barry and Judy Leverett established Delaney's Creek Winery in 1997 and by doing so has expanded the vineyard map of Queensland yet further. Delaney's Creek is situated near the town of Woodford, itself not far northwest of Caboolture. In 1998 they planted an exotic mix of 1 hectare each of shiraz, chardonnay, sangiovese, touriga nacional and verdelho. In the meantime they are obtaining their grapes from 4 hectares of contract grown fruit, including cabernet sauvignon, cabernet franc, merlot, shiraz, chardonnay, marsanne and verdelho.

delatite   ★★★★

Stoneys Road, Mansfield, Vic 3722 **region** Central Victorian High Country
phone (03) 5775 2922 **fax** (03) 5775 2911 **open** 7 days 10–4
winemaker Rosalind Ritchie **production** 12 000 cases **est.** 1982
product range ($15–35 CD) Riesling, Dead Man's Hill Gewurztraminer, Sauvignon Blanc, Pinot Gris, Unoaked Chardonnay, Chardonnay, Delmelza Pinot Chardonnay, Late Picked Riesling, Rose, Pinot Noir, Shiraz, Merlot, Malbec, Dungeon Gully, Devil's River (Cabernet Sauvignon Malbec Shiraz), Cabernet Sauvignon, fortifieds; V.S. Limited Edition Riesling, R.J. Limited Edition (Cabernet blend).
summary With its sweeping views across to the snow-clad alps, this is uncompromising cool-climate viticulture, and the wines naturally reflect the climate. Light but intense Riesling and spicy Traminer flower with a year or two in bottle, and in the warmer vintages the red wines achieve flavour and mouthfeel, albeit with a distinctive mintiness. In spring 2002 David Ritchie (the viticulturist in the family) embarked on a programme to adopt biodynamics, commencing with the sauvignon blanc and gewurztraminer. He says 'It will take time for us to convert the vineyard and change our mindset and practices but I am fully convinced it will lead to healthier soil and vines.' Exports to the UK, Switzerland, Malaysia and Singapore.

del rios vineyard   ★★★★

2320 Ballan Road, Anakie, Vic 3221 **region** Geelong
phone (03) 5284 1221 **fax** (03) 9497 4644 **open** Weekends 10–4, bus tours by appointment
winemaker Peter Flewellyn (Contract) **production** 5000 cases **est.** 1996
product range ($18–23 CD) Sauvignon Blanc, Chardonnay, Marsanne, Pinot Noir, Shiraz, Cabernet Merlot, Cabernet Sauvignon.
summary German del Rio was born in northern Spain (in 1920) where his family owned vineyards. After three generations in Australia, his family has established 15 hectares of vines on their 104-hectare property on the slopes of Mount Anakie, the principal focus being chardonnay, pinot noir and cabernet sauvignon (4 hectares each) then marsanne, sauvignon blanc, merlot and shiraz (1 hectare each). Planting commenced in 1996, and vintage 2000 was the first commercial release.

del Rios Sauvignon Blanc Anakie

▼▼▼▼ **2001** Light straw-green; an intensely aromatic bouquet with lots of tropical and gooseberry fruit sets the tone for the powerful palate, which almost inevitably thickens up a little on the finish, but nonetheless makes a powerful varietal statement.   **rating:** 89

best drinking Now **drink with** Delicate seafood • $18

del Rios Pinot Noir

▼▼▼▼ **2001** Medium red-purple; the complex savoury/spicy bouquet avoids jamminess; the big, powerful palate has stacks of character even if short on finesse.   **rating:** 85

best drinking Now–2005 **drink with** Smoked quail • $21

del Rios Shiraz

▼▼▼▼▽ 2001 Deep, youthful red-purple; the clean bouquet has licorice, prune and black fruit in abundance, the ultra-concentrated and powerful palate is neither excessively tannic nor over-extracted; simply needs a minimum of 10 years. **rating: 91**

best drinking 2007–2017 **best vintages** '00, '01 **drink with** Braised duck • $23

del Rios Cabernet Sauvignon Merlot

▼▼▼▼ 2001 Medium red-purple; the moderately intense bouquet has a mix of blackcurrant and more savoury/earthy/olive fruit; the palate is even more tilted to, or influenced by, Merlot, with a range of savoury, tangy, earthy flavours in a mix of olive, leaf and spice. **rating: 87**

best drinking 2004–2009 **drink with** Osso buco • $21

del Rios Reserve Cabernet Sauvignon El Pesca

▼▼▼▼▽ 2001 Medium to full red-purple; smooth, ripe cassis berry fruit drives the bouquet, with oak in the background; the full and fleshy palate has abundant, ripe cassis berry fruit, but is not over the top. Dedicated to 82-year-old German Del Rio. **rating: 92**

best drinking 2005–2015 **best vintages** '01 **drink with** Braised lamb shanks • $23

demondrille vineyards ★★★

RMB 97, Prunevale Road, Prunevale via Harden, NSW 2587 **region** Hilltops
phone (02) 6384 4272 **fax** (02) 6384 4292 **open** Weekends 10.30–5, or by appointment
winemaker George Makkas **production** 1500 cases **est.** 1979
product range ($12–22 CD) Riesling, Semillon, Semillon Sauvignon Blanc, Pinot Rose, Cabernet Sauvignon, Pinot Noir, The Raven (Shiraz).
summary Planted in 1979 and a totally dry land vineyard, Demondrille is set on a ridge between the towns of Harden and Young in NSW. In the past most of the wines were made under contract, however as from the 2002 vintage all wines will be made on-site. Greek-born and Australian-raised winemaker George Makkas will complete his degree in wine science at Charles Sturt University in 2003. Rob Provan runs the vineyard and cellar door. The Raven (Shiraz) has received several awards.

Demondrille Semillon Sauvignon Blanc

▼▼▼▽ 2002 Light straw-green; the clean and firm bouquet has mineral and herb aromas, driven by Semillon rather than Sauvignon Blanc; the palate is flavoursome, but unfortunately sweet. No doubt directed at the cellar door, but it does lead to an identity crisis. **rating: 83**

best drinking Now **drink with** Takeaway • $12

dennis ★★★

Kangarilla Road, McLaren Vale, SA 5171 **region** McLaren Vale
phone (08) 8323 8665 **fax** (08) 8323 9121 **open** Mon–Fri 10–5, weekends, holidays 11–5
winemaker Peter Dennis **production** 6000 cases **est.** 1970
product range ($16–40 CD) Sauvignon Blanc, Matilda (Semillon Sauvignon Blanc Chardonnay), Chardonnay, Shiraz, Matilda (Shiraz Merlot Cabernet), Merlot, Cabernet Sauvignon, Egerton Vintage Port, Old Tawny Port.
summary A low profile winery which has, from time to time, made some excellent wines, most notably typically full-blown, buttery/peachy Chardonnay. However, in 1998 the pendulum swung towards the Shiraz and Cabernet Sauvignon. Exports to the UK, New Zealand and Canada.

d'entrecasteaux NR

Boorara Road, Northcliffe, WA 6262 **region** Pemberton
phone (08) 9776 7232 **open** By appointment
winemaker Alkoomi (Contract) **production** 600 cases **est.** 1988
product range Chardonnay, Sauvignon Blanc, Pinot Noir, Cabernet Sauvignon.
summary Not to be confused with the now moribund Tasmanian winery of the same name but likewise taking its name from the French explorer Admiral Bruni D'Entrecasteaux, who visited both Tasmania and the southwest coast of Western Australia. Four hectares of estate vineyards, planted on rich Karri loam, produce grapes for the wines which are contract-made at Alkoomi.

derwent estate ★★★★☆

329 Lyell Highway, Granton, Tas 7070 **region** Southern Tasmania
phone (03) 6248 5073 **fax** (03) 6248 5073 **open** Not
winemaker Stefano Lubiana (Contract) **production** 300 cases **est.** 1993
product range ($17.50 ML) Riesling, Chardonnay, Pinot Noir.
summary The Hanigan family has established Derwent Estate as part of a diversification programme for their 400-hectare mixed farming property. Five hectares of vineyard have been progressively planted since 1993, initially to riesling, followed by chardonnay and pinot noir.

devil's lair ★★★★★

Rocky Road, Forest Grove via Margaret River, WA 6286 **region** Margaret River
phone (08) 9757 7573 **fax** (08) 9757 7533 **open** Not
winemaker Stuart Pym **production** 40 000 cases **est.** 1985
product range ($16–54 R) Chardonnay, Margaret River (Cabernet blend); Fifth Leg Dry White and Dry Red.
summary Having rapidly carved out a high reputation for itself through a combination of clever packaging and marketing allied with impressive wine quality, Devil's Lair was acquired by Southcorp Wine Group (Penfolds, etc) in December 1996, and production is projected to increase to over 50 000 cases.

Devil's Lair Fifth Leg White

♥♥♥♥♡ 2002 Aromatic fruit salad bouquet and well-structured palate offering tropical fruit salad balanced by lemony acidity running through to a long, cleansing finish. **rating:** 93
best drinking Now **best vintages** '96, '97, '02 **drink with** Brasserie food • $16

Devil's Lair Chardonnay

♥♥♥♥♥ 2000 Medium yellow-green; the spotlessly clean bouquet has perfect balance and seamless integration of fruit and oak, the long and intense palate with lingering nectarine and citrus fruit, again showing finely integrated oak. **rating:** 95
best drinking Now–2010 **best vintages** '92, '94, '96, '97, '99, '00 **drink with** Rich white meat • $40

Devil's Lair Fifth Leg Dry Red

♥♥♥♥♡ 2001 Bright red-purple, deep and clear; the bouquet has sweet blackcurrant, blackberry and plum fruit, the palate softer and richer than any prior vintage, with great, multi-layered flavours. French oak lurks in the background throughout. A blend of Cabernet Sauvignon, Shiraz and Merlot. **rating:** 92
best drinking 2004–2010 **best vintages** '99, '01 **drink with** Devilled kidneys • $20

Devil's Lair Margaret River

♥♥♥♥♥ 2000 Medium to full red-purple; complex, ripe blackcurrant/cassis/blackberry fruit is married with sweet French oak on the bouquet; then a powerful but polished palate with excellent balance of flavours, and supple, smooth tannins through to a long finish. **rating:** 94
best drinking 2005–2015 **best vintages** '97, '98, '99, '00 **drink with** Char-grilled rump • $40

diamond valley vineyards ★★★★☆

2130 Kinglake Road, St Andrews, Vic 3761 **region** Yarra Valley
phone (03) 9710 1484 **fax** (03) 9710 1369 **open** Not
winemaker David Lance, James Lance **production** 7000 cases **est.** 1976
product range ($17.50–65 R) Chardonnay, Pinot Noir, Cabernet; Yarra Valley (formerly Blue Label) Sauvignon Blanc, Chardonnay, Pinot Noir, Cabernet Merlot; Close Planted Pinot Noir.
summary One of the Yarra Valley's finest producers of Pinot Noir and an early pacesetter for the variety, making wines of tremendous style and crystal-clear varietal character. They are not Cabernet Sauvignon look-alikes but true Pinot Noir, fragrant and intense. The chardonnays show the same marriage of finesse and intensity, and the Cabernet family wines shine in the warmer vintages. Much of the wine is sold through an informative and well-presented mailing list, supplemented by national distribution through Red+White. Exports to the UK, Holland, Indonesia, Singapore and Malaysia.

Diamond Valley Yarra Valley Sauvignon Blanc

♥♥♥♥ 2002 Light to medium yellow-green; the aromas move from gooseberry into distinctly tropical fruit, the palate with plenty of concentration of flavour, but loses focus somewhat on the finish. **rating:** 88
best drinking Now **best vintages** '00 **drink with** Mussels • $17.50

Diamond Valley Estate Chardonnay

▼▼▼▼▽ **2001** Intense green-yellow; complex, rich barrel-ferment inputs to the ripe peach and melon fruit of the bouquet are followed by an intense and tight palate, with particularly good acidity, and the oak far less overt than it is on the bouquet. Certain to age well. **rating: 93**

best drinking Now–2007 **best vintages** '90, '92, '94, '96, '00, '01 **drink with** Cold smoked trout • $29.60

Diamond Valley Yarra Valley Chardonnay

▼▼▼▼▽ **2001** Bright, light to medium-yellow-green, with its typical brightness; complex, stylish barrel-ferment inputs on stone fruit and cashew make a strong opening statement. The medium-bodied palate has good length and balance, with appealing melon and stone fruit flavours. Good value. **rating: 92**

best drinking Now–2007 **best vintages** '99, '00, '00, '01 **drink with** Coquilles St Jacques • $19.95

Diamond Valley Estate Pinot Noir

▼▼▼▼▼ **2001** Medium purple-red; the bouquet is complex, with an obvious contribution from French oak, and some whole bunch maceration characters; the palate is unusually full-bodied for Diamond Valley, flooded with sweet plum and dark cherry fruit, soft and velvety throughout. **rating: 94**

best drinking Now–2008 **best vintages** '86, '90, '91, '92, '93, '94, '96, '98, '99, '01 **drink with** Wild duck • $59

Diamond Valley Estate Cabernet Merlot

▼▼▼▼ **1999** Light to medium red-purple; a light but fragrant bouquet with berry, mint and a touch of leaf is reflected in the fresh, light to medium-bodied palate following the same flavour track, closing with good acidity. **rating: 88**

best drinking Now–2008 **drink with** Risotto • $28.95

Diamond Valley Yarra Valley Cabernet Merlot

▼▼▼▼ **2001** Medium purple-red; scented, aromatic red and blackcurrant fruit are followed by an ultra-typical mint, berry and leaf-flavoured palate, with minimal tannins. **rating: 87**

best drinking Now–2007 **drink with** Yearling steak • $21.50

Diamond Valley Estate Cabernet Sauvignon

▼▼▼▼▽ **2000** Medium to full red-purple; ripe blackberry and blackcurrant fruit intermingle with cedary oak; the palate has sweet fruit and ripe tannins, the oak balanced and integrated. **rating: 90**

best drinking 2005–2010 **best vintages** '99, '00 **drink with** Marinated beef • $29.95

diggers rest   NR

205 Old Vineyard Road, Sunbury, Vic 3429 **region** Sunbury
phone (03) 9740 1660 **fax** (03) 9740 1660 **open** By appointment
winemaker Peter Dredge **production** 1000 cases **est.** 1987
product range ($16.50–22 CD) Chardonnay, Pinot Noir, Shiraz, Cabernet Sauvignon.
summary Diggers Rest was purchased from the founders Frank and Judith Hogan in July 1998; the new owners, Elias and Joseph Obeid, intend to expand the vineyard resources and, by that means, significantly increase production.

🐦 digiorgio family wines   ★★★☆

Riddoch Highway, Coonawarra, SA 5263 **region** Coonawarra
phone (08) 8736 3222 **fax** (08) 8736 3233 **open** 7 days 10–5
winemaker Pat Tocaciu **production** 6000 cases **est.** 1998
product range ($14–45 CD) Chardonnay, Chardonnay Pinot Noir Sparkling, Merlot, Cabernet Sauvignon.
summary Stefano DiGiorgio emigrated from Abbruzzi, Italy, arriving in Australia in July 1952. After 4 years working in various jobs, he purchased the first parcel of land at Lucindale. Over the years, he and his family gradually expanded their holdings. In 1989 the decision was taken to plant 2 hectares each of pinot noir and cabernet sauvignon, and when the vines flourished, the planting programme between then and 1998 resulted in the present holdings of cabernet sauvignon (99 ha), chardonnay (10 ha), merlot (9 ha), shiraz (6 ha) and pinot noir (2 ha). In 2002 the family purchased the historic Rouge Homme winery from Southcorp capable of crushing 10 000 tonnes of grapes a year, and its surrounding 13.5 hectares of vines. The Lucindale plantings are outside any existing region, and are simply part of the Limestone Coast Zone, with the likelihood that there will be two product ranges in the future. The enterprise is offering full winemaking services to vignerons in the Limestone Coast Zone. The newly-renovated cellar door is now open to the public. If the quality of the background material provided by the winery is any guide, this is an enterprise going places.

DiGiorgio Chardonnay

ￜￜￜￜ **2000** Light to medium yellow-green; the bouquet offers a mix of mineral, stone fruit and subtle oak; the light to medium-bodied palate has length, but not a great deal of depth. **rating:** 85

best drinking Now **drink with** Pasta • $18

DiGiorgio Merlot

ￜￜￜￜ **2000** Light to medium red-purple; a mix of herb, spice and leaf with some berry aromas lead into a light to medium-bodied palate which has quite sweet berry fruit, finishing with fine, soft tannins. **rating:** 86

best drinking Now–2005 **drink with** Braised rabbit • $25.50

DiGiorgio Cabernet Sauvignon

ￜￜￜￜ **2000** Medium red-purple; the bouquet has soft berry fruit and tobacco leaf merging with slightly dusty oak; the light to medium-bodied palate has berry, leaf and earth flavours; fine tannins. Simply needed a touch more fruit richness. **rating:** 85

best drinking Now–2007 **drink with** Shoulder of lamb • $22.50

DiGiorgio Francesco Cabernet Sauvignon

ￜￜￜￜￜ **1998** Medium red; the bouquet is voluptuous, bordering on the overripe, but the palate is much better, lush and ripe, but not jammy; good length and overall flavour. **rating:** 92

best drinking 2004–2013 **drink with** Beef Bordelaise • $45

 diloreto wines   ★★★★

45 Wilpena Terrace, Kilkenny, SA 5009 (postal) **region** Adelaide Plains
phone (08) 8345 0123 **open** Not
winemaker Tony Diloreto **production** 250 cases **est.** 2001
product range Shiraz.
summary The Diloreto family have been growing grapes since the 1960s, with 8 hectares of shiraz, cabernet sauvignon, mourvedre and grenache. The vineyard was founded by father Gesue Diloreto and, in common with so many Adelaide Plains grape growers, the family sold the grapes to South Australian winemakers. However, son Tony and wife Gabriell (herself with a winemaking background from the Rhine Valley in Germany) decided they would jointly undertake a short winemaking course at the end of the 1990s. The results were encouraging, and in 2001 Tony Diloreto entered two wines in the Australian Amateur Wine Show, competing against 700 vignerons from around Australia. Both were Shiraz from the 2001 vintage, one with new oak, the other not. Both won gold medals, and the judges strongly recommended that the wines be sold commercially. Great oaks from little acorns indeed.

Diloreto Reserve Shiraz

ￜￜￜￜￜ **2001** Full purple-red; the clean, dense blackberry fruit of the bouquet leads into an equally powerful and dense palate, with lots of new American oak, but the fruit to balance that oak. An exceptional achievement for a near-amateur. **rating:** 92

best drinking 2008–2018 **drink with** Kangaroo fillet

di lusso wines   NR

Eurunderee Lane, Mudgee, NSW 2850 **region** Mudgee
phone (02) 9905 8038 **fax** (02) 9939 5878 **open** Weekends 10–4 from August 2003
winemaker Drew Tuckwell (Contract) **production** 3000 cases **est.** 1998
product range ($15–25 CD) Pinot Grigio, Picolit (sweet white), Rosso (Barbera Nebbiolo Shiraz), Barbera, Sangiovese, Super T (Sangiovese Shiraz), Aleatico.
summary Rob Fairall and partner Luanne Hill have at last been able bring to fruition the vision they have had for some years to establish an Italian 'enoteca' operation, offering Italian varietal wines and foods. The plantings of 2 hectares each of barbera and sangiovese, 1 hectare of nebbiolo and 0.5 hectare of picolit, supplemented by the purchase of aleatico and sangiovese from the Mudgee region, and pinot grigio from Orange, set the tone for the wine which is made by contract winemaker Drew Tuckwell, a specialist in Italian varieties. The estate also produces olives for olive oil and table olives, and it is expected the range of both wine and food will increase over the years. An on-site winery came on-stream in early 2003, and the full cellar door will open in September.

di Lusso Aleatico

ￜￜￜￜ **2002** Light red; vibrant strawberry jam and mint aromas are followed by a fully sweet cellar-door-style palate. This is a legitimate style for Aleatico. **rating:** 83

best drinking Now **drink with** Picnic • $23

🦡 di stasio NR

Range Road, Coldstream, Vic 3770 **region** Yarra Valley
phone (03) 9525 3999 **fax** (03) 9525 3815 **open** By appointment, or at Cafe Di Stasio, 31 Fitzroy Street, St Kilda
winemaker Rob Dolan, Kate Goodman **production** 900 cases **est.** 1995
product range ($NFP) Chardonnay, Pinot Noir.
summary Famous Melbourne restaurateur Rinaldo (Ronnie) Di Stasio bought a virgin bushland 32-hectare hillside block in the Yarra Valley in 1994 adjacent to the Warramate Flora and Fauna Reserve. He has since established 2.8 hectares of vineyards, equally split between pinot noir and chardonnay, put in roads and dams, built a substantial house, and also an Allan Powell Monastery, complete with art gallery and tree-filled courtyard sitting like a church on top of the hill. Production has never been great, but did commence in 1999, the wines of that and subsequent vintages being initially sold through Cafe Di Stasio in St Kilda, a Melbourne icon. In 2003 he took the plunge and appointed Domaine Wine Shippers as his distributor, and the wines are now spread through the smartest restaurants in Melbourne and Sydney. The less said about the scrawled, handwritten labels, the better.

Di Stasio Chardonnay
▼▼▼▼ 2001 Medium yellow-green; the smooth, moderately intense bouquet has melon and fig aroma supported by subtle French oak; the oak is more obvious on the solid palate, the fruit less, but the total flavour is undiminished. **rating:** 89
▼▼▼▼⏀ 2000 Glowing yellow-green; complex bottle-developed, tangy, slightly funky aromas lead into a rich, ripe palate, with some alcohol sweetness to the peachy fruit; full bodied. **rating:** 92
best drinking Now–2006 **best vintages** '99, '00 **drink with** Grilled spatchcock

Di Stasio Pinot Noir
▼▼▼▼ 2001 Light red; clean, light strawberry and plum fruit aromas are followed by a palate which follows down the same track, neither concentrated nor complex; a pretty wine, but to be drunk sooner rather than later. **rating:** 85
▼▼▼▼ 2000 Good colour, hue and depth; clean, solid, plum and spice fruit aromas are supported by subtle oak; a big, firm-framed palate with lots of tannin and extract should benefit from further cellaring. **rating:** 88
best drinking Now–2006 **drink with** Braised duck

djinta djinta winery NR

10 Stevens Road, Kardella South, Vic 3950 **region** Gippsland
phone (03) 5658 1163 **open** Weekends and public holidays 10–5, or by appointment
winemaker Peter Harley **production** 200 cases **est.** 1991
product range ($15–20 CD) Semillon, Sauvignon Blanc, Marsanne, Cabernets Merlot.
summary Is one of a group of wineries situated between Leongatha and Korumburra, the most famous being Bass Phillip. Vines were first planted in 1986 but were largely neglected until Peter and Helen Harley acquired the property in 1991, set about reviving the 2 hectares of sauvignon blanc and a little cabernet sauvignon, planting an additional 3 hectares (in total) of merlot, cabernet franc, cabernet sauvignon, semillon, marsanne, roussane and viognier. The first vintage was 1995, during the time that Peter Harley was completing a Bachelor of Applied Science (Wine Science) at Charles Sturt University. They are deliberately adopting a low-technology approach to both vineyard and winery practices, using organic methods wherever possible.

domaine a ★★★★

Campania, Tas 7026 **region** Southern Tasmania
phone (03) 6260 4174 **fax** (03) 6260 4390 **open** Mon–Fri 9–4, weekends by appointment
winemaker Peter Althaus, Vetten Tieman **production** 5000 cases **est.** 1973
product range ($20–60 CD) Domaine A is the top label with Lady A Fume Blanc, Pinot Noir, Cabernet Sauvignon; second label is Stoney Vineyard with Aurora (wood-matured Sylvaner), Sauvignon Blanc, Cabernet Sauvignon.
summary The striking black label of the premium Domaine A wine, dominated by the single, multicoloured 'A', signified the change of ownership from George Park to Swiss businessman Peter Althaus many years ago. The wines are made without compromise, and reflect the low yields from the immaculately tended vineyards. They represent aspects of both Old World and New World philosophies, techniques and styles. Exports to the US, Singapore, Hong Kong, the UK, France and Switzerland.

Domaine A Stoney Vineyard Pinot Noir

TTTT **2001** Strong red-purple; powerful, complex, savoury dark fruit aromas flow into a massively powerful and complex palate, with strong dark fruit flavours; in its own style at 14.5°. **rating: 89**

TTTTY **2000** Healthy red-purple; rich plum, black cherry, spice and bramble aromas lead into a generously proportioned, super-rich palate which challenges many preconceptions about Tasmanian Pinot Noir. Whether this amount of power and flavour is desirable will depend on personal style perceptions, but you cannot doubt either the presence of the wine today nor its longevity. Thirteen and a half degrees alcohol, unfiltered; less than 100 cases made. **rating: 91**

best drinking 2004–2011 **best vintages** '00 **drink with** Ragout of venison • $32

Domaine A Cabernet Sauvignon

TTTTY **1999** Deep colour; very complex black fruits, tar and some sweet, French oak lead into a palate with an appealing balance of savoury and sweeter blackcurrant fruit; good oak handling and likewise tannin extract, all providing balance and length. **rating: 90**

best drinking 2006–2016 **best vintages** '86, '88, '90, '92, '94, '95, '97, '99 **drink with** Tasmanian venison • $55

domaine chandon ★★★★★

Green Point, Maroondah Highway, Coldstream, Vic 3770 **region** Yarra Valley
phone (03) 9739 1110 **fax** (03) 9739 1095 **open** 7 days 10.30–4.30
winemaker Dr Tony Jordan, Neville Rowe, James Gosper, John Harris **production** 150 000 cases **est.** 1986
product range ($22.95–38 CD) The most important sparkling wine is the Vintage Brut; then there is a range of special vintage cuvées, including Tasmanian Cuvee, Yarra Valley Brut, Blanc de Noirs, Blanc de Blancs and Brut Rose, together with a vintage Cuvee Prestige (the most expensive in the range), and given up to 6 years on lees prior to disgorgement. The sparkling range is rounded off with non-vintage Brut and a sparkling Pinot Shiraz. The table wines are released under the Green Point label, the Chardonnay and Pinot Noir appearing in both varietal and reserve mode; also a McLaren Vale Shiraz.
summary Wholly owned by Möet et Chandon, and one of the two most important wine facilities in the Yarra Valley, the Green Point tasting room having a national and international reputation and a number of major tourism awards in recent years. Not only has the sparkling wine product range evolved, but there has been increasing emphasis placed on the table wines. The return of Dr Tony Jordan, the first CEO of Domaine Chandon should further strengthen both the focus and quality of the brand. Exports to the UK, Asia and Japan.

Domaine Chandon Green Point Reserve Chardonnay

TTTTT **2001** Glowing yellow-green; a complex bouquet with subtle barrel-ferment and malolactic-ferment influences on the stone fruit and melon; an elegant, restrained palate with touches of cashew alongside the stone fruit, with good balance and length. **rating: 94**

best drinking 2004–2007 **best vintages** '98, '00, '01 **drink with** Grilled spatchcock • $35

Domaine Chandon Green Point Vineyards Chardonnay

TTTTY **2001** Having initially used the Green Point name only for its exported wines, Domaine Chandon is now introducing it domestically. Bright yellow-green; rich nectarine and melon fruit combines with neatly judged French oak on the bouquet, then a fresh, silky smooth, nectarine-accented, long palate. Stylish stuff. **rating: 93**

best drinking Now–2006 **best vintages** '92, '93, '96, '00, '01 **drink with** Free range chicken • $23

Domaine Chandon Blanc de Blancs

TTTTT **1999** Bright yellow, tinged with green; fresh stone fruit and cashew aromas are followed by a most attractive palate, light and crisp, well balanced and long, the flavours tracking those of the bouquet. **rating: 94**

best drinking Now–2006 **best vintages** '90, '92, '93, '95, '97 **drink with** Light seafood • $31.95

Domaine Chandon Blanc de Noirs

TTTTT **1997** Medium straw-yellow; a powerful and complex nutty/bready bouquet is followed by a well-structured palate, echoing the complexity of the bouquet, with brioche and strawberry, than a lively, crisp, dry finish. As the name implies, 100 per cent Pinot Noir. **rating: 94**

best drinking Now–2007 **best vintages** '90, '92, '94, '96 **drink with** Gougeres • $31.95

Domaine Chandon Vintage Brut

TTTTT **1999** Light straw-green, infinitely more reassuring than some of the earlier vintages; a fragrant and fresh citrus blossom bouquet is followed by a delicate palate, which has good line, length and balance, finishing appropriately dry. **rating: 94**

TTTTY **1998** Very deep straw-bronze; the full bouquet ranges through bread, yeast, nut and dried fruit aromas, the powerful palate fresher than the bouquet suggests, but scoring more on impact than finesse.   **rating:** 91
best drinking Now–2006 **best vintages** '88, '90, '91, '92, '93, '94, '95, '97, '99 **drink with** Ideal aperitif • $32.95

Domaine Chandon Tasmanian Cuvee

TTTTT **1999** Light straw-green; a clean, vibrant and fresh bouquet, but also showing quite complex autolysis characters; the long, clean, lively acidity of the palate is neatly balanced by the dosage. A 50 per cent Pinot Noir/50 per cent Chardonnay blend from the Tolpuddle Vineyard, with 3 years on yeast lees.   **rating:** 94
best drinking 2004–2007 **best vintages** '98, '99 **drink with** Aperitif • $32.95

Domaine Chandon Brut Rose

TTTTT **1998** Salmon pink; a typically complex spicy/nutty/strawberry bouquet, then a rich mid-palate, excellently balanced, moving through to a long, dry finish. Fifty-three per cent Pinot Noir, 45 per cent Chardonnay, 2 per cent Pinot Meunier, with 10 per cent Pinot Noir left on skins.   **rating:** 94
best drinking Now–2006 **best vintages** '90, '92, '93, '94, '97 **drink with** Poached salmon, Asian cuisine • $31.95

Domaine Chandon Green Point Reserve Pinot Noir

TTTT **2001** Light to medium red-purple; a clean, well-balanced bouquet with cherry, plum and well-integrated oak; the relatively austere and firm palate has plum at its core, swathed in savoury tannins. Like its predecessors, should repay cellaring.   **rating:** 89
best drinking 2004–2009 **best vintages** '00 **drink with** Jugged hare • $38

Domaine Chandon Green Point McLaren Vale Shiraz

TTTTY **2001** Medium purple-red; black cherry and blackberry, with a distinct touch of spice is supported by positive oak on the bouquet; the palate is rich, dense and ripe, with masses of black cherry/blackberry fruit running through to a long finish.   **rating:** 92
best drinking 2004–2011 **best vintages** '98, '01 **drink with** Kangaroo fillet • $26.95

dominion wines ★★★

Upton Road, Strathbogie Ranges via Avenel, Vic 3664 **region** Strathbogie Ranges
phone (03) 5796 2718 **fax** (03) 5796 2719 **open** By appointment
winemaker Travis Bush, Michael Clayden **production** 15 000 cases **est.** 1999
product range ($10–17 CD) Wines released in three tiers: the cheaper Vinus range of Muscat Gordo, Riesling, Chardonnay, Shiraz Cabernet, Sparkling Shiraz; followed by the Alexander Park label offering Riesling, Sauvignon Blanc, Unwooded Chardonnay, Chardonnay, Pinot Noir, Shiraz, Cabernet Sauvignon; then the Alexander Park Reserve Chardonnay and Shiraz.
summary Dominion is a major newcomer in the wine industry. Between December 1996 and September 1999, 91 hectares of vines were planted at Alexander Park with sauvignon blanc, chardonnay, pinot noir, shiraz and cabernet sauvignon the principal varieties, and smaller amounts of riesling, verdelho and merlot. Prior to the 2000 vintage a winery designed by award-winning architect Scott Shelton was erected at Alexander Park; at full capacity it will be able to process up to 7500 tonnes of fruit. It will have two functions: firstly, the production of the company's own brands of Dominion Estate, Alexander Park, Vinus and Saddle Mountain; secondly, contract winemaking services for other major Australian wine companies.

dominique portet ★★★★

870–872 Maroondah Highway, Coldstream, Vic 3770 **region** Yarra Valley
phone (03) 5962 5760 **fax** (03) 5962 4938 **open** 7 days 10–5
winemaker Dominique Portet, Marcus Satchell **production** 6000 cases **est.** 2000
product range ($16–40 CD) Sauvignon Blanc, Fontaine Rose, Fontaine (Cabernet Shiraz), Heathcote Shiraz, Merlot, Yarra Valley Cabernet Sauvignon.
summary Dominique Portet was bred in the purple. He spent his early years at Chateau Lafite (where his father was regisseur) and was one of the very first Flying Winemakers, commuting to Clos du Val in the Napa Valley where his brother is winemaker and helping with the initial vintages. Since 1976 he has lived in Australia, spending more than 20 years as managing director of Taltarni, and also developed the Clover Hill Vineyard in Tasmania. After retiring from Taltarni, he spent 6 months in Provence, with his family, making wine and setting up an international distribution network, but always intended to return to Australia and to set himself up in the Yarra Valley, a region he has been closely observing since the mid-1980s. In 2001 he found the perfect site he had long looked for, and in a twinkling of an eye, built his winery and cellar door, and planted a quixotic mix of viognier (0.9 ha) and merlot (0.7 ha) next to the winery (which, incidentally, can also be accessed from Maddens Lane). Exports to the UK, the US, Hong Kong, Japan, Malaysia and New Zealand.

Dominique Portet Yarra Sauvignon Blanc

ŶŶŶŶ 2002 Light straw-green; a spotlessly clean bouquet with a range of crisp grass, herb and more minerally aromas is followed by a palate with good intensity and length; the lift and grip no doubt comes from the small proportion of the wine barrel fermented in new French oak. **rating: 88**

best drinking Now–2005 **drink with** Shellfish • $22

Dominique Portet Fontaine Rose

ŶŶŶŶ 2002 Pale salmon-pink; some dried herb and spice aromas are followed by a crisp, dry palate, with a spicy/savoury aftertaste. A blend of shiraz and cabernet sauvignon both grown in the Christmas Hills sub-region of the Yarra Valley. **rating: 84**

best drinking Now **drink with** Yabby risotto • $18.50

Dominique Portet Heathcote Shiraz

ŶŶŶŶŶ 2001 Medium red-purple; clean, glossy cherry fruit is supported by subtle oak on the bouquet. The medium-bodied palate has complex texture to the cherry fruit, finishing with fine tannins and nicely balanced and integrated oak. **rating: 90**

best drinking 2006–2011 **best vintages** '00, '01 **drink with** Milk-fed veal • $40

Dominique Portet Yarra Valley Cabernet Sauvignon

ŶŶŶŶŶ 2001 Medium red-purple; distinctly savoury/earthy varietal character overlying berry fruit; the powerful blackberry and bitter chocolate palate has lots of depth and texture; a wine of distinction which really comes alive in the mouth. **rating: 92**

best drinking 2005–2011 **best vintages** '01 **drink with** Lamb shanks • $35

donnelly river wines   NR

Lot 159 Vasse Highway, Pemberton, WA 6260 **region** Pemberton
phone (08) 9776 2052 **fax** (08) 9776 2053 **open** 7 days 9.30–4.30
winemaker Blair Meiklejohn **production** 15 000 cases **est.** 1986
product range ($13–26 CD) Sauvignon Blanc, Chardonnay, Mist (white blend), Pinot Noir, Shiraz, Karri, Cabernet Sauvignon, Cascade, Mistella, Port, Liqueur Muscat.
summary Donnelly River Wines draws upon 16 hectares of estate vineyards, planted in 1986 and which produced the first wines in 1990. It has performed consistently well with its Chardonnay. Exports to the UK, Denmark, Germany, Singapore, Malaysia and Japan.

donnington   NR

Campbell's Corner, Pinnacle Road, Orange, NSW 2800 **region** Orange
phone (02) 6362 2947 **fax** (02) 6365 3517 **open** 7 days 11–4
winemaker John Hordern **production** 2000 cases **est.** 1991
product range ($16–19 CD) Sauvignon Blanc, Chardonnay, Pinot Noir, Cabernet Merlot, Cabernet Sauvignon.
summary Donnington vineyard has been established on the slopes of Mount Canobolas at an elevation of 960–990 metres, on the rich basaltic soils of the ancient volcano. Since 1991 10 hectares of chardonnay, sauvignon blanc, semillon, pinot noir, cabernet sauvignon and merlot have been planted, with plans to add riesling, shiraz and malbec. The cellar door has panoramic views of the vineyard and the rolling foothills of Mount Canobolas.

donnybrook estate   NR

Hacket Road, Donnybrook, WA **region** Geographe
phone (08) 9731 0707 **fax** (08) 9731 0707 **open** 7 days 10–5.30
winemaker Gary Greirson **production** 5000 cases **est.** 1997
product range ($10–30 CD) Semillon, Sauvignon Blanc, Verdelho, Unwooded Chardonnay, Chardonnay, Shiraz, Merlot, Tempranillo, Grenache, Graciano, Cinsault, Barbera, Zinfandel, Cabernet Sauvignon; Red and White Port.
summary Gary Greirson and wife Sally have completed the long-planned move to Donnybrook Estate from Cape Bouvard. The new winery was completed during the 2003 vintage, and Gary Greirson contract-makes a small amount of wine for others in the Donnybrook area. The wines are estate grown from 4.5 hectares of vineyards.

donovan wines NR

RMB 2017 Pomonal Road, Stawell, Vic 3380 **region** Grampians
phone (03) 5358 2727 **fax** (03) 5358 2727 **open** Mon–Sat 10–5, Sun 12–5
winemaker Simon Clayfield **production** 700 cases **est.** 1977
product range ($14–27 CD) Chardonnay, Shiraz, Cabernet Sauvignon, Sparkling.
summary Donovan quietly makes some concentrated, powerful Shiraz, with several vintages of the latter typically on offer. Limited distribution in Melbourne; otherwise most of the wine is sold via mail order with some bottle age. Has 5 hectares of estate plantings.

doonkuna estate ★★★☆

Barton Highway, Murrumbateman, NSW 2582 **region** Canberra District
phone (02) 6227 5811 **fax** (02) 6227 5085 **open** 7 days 11–4
winemaker Malcolm Burdett **production** 2000 cases **est.** 1973
product range ($12–26 CD) Riesling, Sauvignon Blanc Semillon, Chardonnay, Cian (Pinot Noir Chardonnay), Pinot Noir, Shiraz, Cabernet Sauvignon; Rising Ground Chardonnay, Shiraz, Cabernet Sauvignon Merlot.
summary Following the acquisition of Doonkuna by Barry and Maureen Moran in late 1996, the plantings have been increased from a little under 4 hectares to 20 hectares. The cellar-door prices remain modest, and increased production will follow in the wake of the new plantings.

Doonkuna Estate Riesling

TTTT 2002 Light straw-green; light mineral lemon aromas on the bouquet lead into a light, very soft palate, with a slightly fuzzy finish. Replete with a smart new label. **rating:** 84
best drinking Now–2006 **best vintages** '88, '90, '91, '92, '95, '97, '01 **drink with** Antipasto • $17

Doonkuna Estate Cian Pinot Chardonnay

TTTT 1998 Medium straw-green; complex, with nutty overtones, the palate full-flavoured and fruity, the acid just a little sharp on the finish – better, however, than being too sweet. **rating:** 84
best drinking Now–2005 **drink with** Oysters • $25

Doonkuna Estate Pinot Noir

TTTT 2001 Light to medium red-purple; clean but restrained fruit, with notes of spice and forest on the bouquet, but there is more happening on the palate, with some dried plum and savoury flavours improbably providing good texture. **rating:** 85
best drinking Now–2006 **drink with** Braised duck • $18

dowie doole ★★★★

Tatachilla Road, McLaren Vale, SA 5171 (postal) **region** McLaren Vale
phone (08) 8323 7428 **fax** (08) 8323 7305 **open** At Ingleburne, Willunga Road: Mon–Fri 10–5, weekends and public holidays 11–5
winemaker Brian Light (Contract) **production** 7000 cases **est.** 1996
product range ($15.50–40 CD) Semillon, Chenin Blanc, Shiraz, Reserve Shiraz, Merlot, Cabernet Sauvignon.
summary The imaginatively packaged and interestingly named Dowie Doole was a joint venture between two McLaren Vale grape growers: architect Drew Dowie and one-time international banker Norm Doole. Between them they have over 40 hectares of vineyards, and only a small proportion of their grapes are used to produce the Dowie Doole wines. In 1999 the partnership was expanded to include industry marketing veteran Leigh Gilligan, who returned to his native McLaren Vale after 5 years in Coonawarra (Gilligan is also involved with Boar's Rock). The wines have retail distribution in South Australia and the eastern States, and are exported to the US, Canada, Singapore and Germany.

drayton's family wines ★★★☆

Oakey Creek Road, Cessnock, NSW 2321 **region** Lower Hunter Valley
phone (02) 4998 7513 **fax** (02) 4998 7743 **open** Mon–Fri 8–5, weekends and public holidays 10–5
winemaker Trevor Drayton **production** 90 000 cases **est.** 1853
product range ($7–70 CD) Several label ranges including budget-priced Oakey Creek, New Generation and Hunter Valley; Vineyard Reserve Chardonnay, Semillon, Pinot Noir, Shiraz, Merlot; Sparkling and fortifieds; top-of-the-range Limited Release Chardonnay, Shiraz, Susanne Semillon, William Shiraz, Joseph Shiraz, Bin 5555 Shiraz, Botrytis Semillon, Old Vineyard Sherry and Liqueur Muscat.

summary A family-owned and run stalwart of the Hunter Valley, producing honest, full-flavoured wines which sometimes excel themselves and are invariably modestly priced. The size of the production will come as a surprise to many but it is a clear indication of the good standing of the brand, notwithstanding the low profile of recent years. It is not to be confused with Reg Drayton Wines; national retail distribution with exports to New Zealand, the US, Japan, Singapore, Taiwan, Samoa and Switzerland.

drews creek wines   NR

558 Wollombi Road, Broke, NSW 2330   **region** Lower Hunter Valley
phone (02) 6579 1062   **fax** (02) 6579 1062   **open** By appointment
winemaker David Lowe (Contract)   **production** 300 cases   **est.** 1993
product range ($10–16 R) Chardonnay, Unoaked Chardonnay, Merlot.
summary Graeme Gibson and his partners are developing Drews Creek step by step. The initial planting of 2 hectares of chardonnay and 3 hectares of merlot was made in 1991, and the first grapes produced in 1993. A further 2.5 hectares of sangiovese were planted in September 1999. Most of the grapes have been sold to contract-winemaker David Lowe, but a small quantity of wine has been made for sale to friends and through the mailing list. A cellar door has opened, and holiday cabins overlooking the vineyard and Wollombi Brook are planned.

driftwood estate   ★★★★

Lot 13 Caves Road, Yallingup, WA 6282   **region** Margaret River
phone (08) 9755 6323   **fax** (08) 9755 6343   **open** 7 days 11–4.30
winemaker Barney Mitchell, Mark Pizzuto   **production** 15 000 cases   **est.** 1989
product range ($15–29 CD) Classic White, Semillon, Sauvignon Blanc Semillon, Chardonnay, Cane Cut Semillon (dessert style), Shiraz, Shiraz Cabernet Sauvignon, Merlot, Cabernet Sauvignon, Tawny Port.
summary Driftwood Estate is now a well established landmark on the Margaret River scene. Quite apart from offering a brasserie restaurant capable of seating 200 people (open 7 days for lunch and dinner) and a mock Greek open-air theatre, its wines feature striking and stylish packaging (even if strongly reminiscent of that of Devil's Lair) and opulently flavoured wines. The winery architecture is, it must be said, opulent but not stylish. The wines are exported to Singapore.

Driftwood Estate Shiraz

▼▼▼▼▼ 1999 Very good, dense red-purple; the bouquet is flooded with licorice and black cherry fruit, as is the palate, joined by super-abundant tannins and oak somewhere in the background. A wine for the very long term future. Gold medal 2002 Qantas Wine Show of Western Australia.   **rating:** 94

best drinking 2007–2017 **best vintages** '98, '99 **drink with** Leave it in the cellar • $29

🐚 drinkmoor wines   ★★★

All Saints Road, Wahgunyah, Vic 3687   **region** Rutherglen
phone (02) 6033 5544   **fax** (02) 6033 5645   **open** 7 days 10–5
winemaker Damien Cofield   **production** 2500 cases   **est.** 2002
product range ($11.80–13.80 CD) Al Dente White, Chenin Blanc, Unoaked Chardonnay, Sticky (Late Harvest Muscadelle), Al Dente Red (Gamay), Shiraz, Cabernet Merlot, Cabernets, Traveller (Fortified White)
summary This is a separate venture of Max and Karen Cofield (who also own Cofield Wines) with a very clear vision and marketing plan. It is to encourage people to make wine their beverage of choice; in other words, don't drink beer or spirits, drink wine instead, or drink more wines. Thus the wines are made in an everyday, easy drinking style, with the cost kept as low as possible. The labelling, too, is designed to take the pretentiousness out of wine drinking, and to provide a bit of fun. Although the Cofields don't say so, this is the heartland of Generation X.

Drinkmoor Al Dente White

▼▼▼▽ NV Medium yellow-green; the bouquet is quite aromatic, with tropical fruit salad characters which provide the palate with good fruit depth; balanced by crisp acidity.   **rating:** 84

best drinking Now **drink with** Pasta • $11.80

Drinkmoor Unoaked Chardonnay

▼▼▼▽ NV Light straw-green; clean, very light, with some stone fruit to be found; the fresh, bright, light palate is not sweet; indeed, the corrected acidity is quite evident.   **rating:** 84

best drinking Now **drink with** Takeaway chicken • $11.80

Drinkmoor Sticky

▼▼▼▽ NV Medium yellow-green; clean pineapple/tropical fruit aromas lead into a soft, moderately sweet, palate with canned tropical fruit flavours. Well balanced. **rating:** 84

best drinking Now **drink with** Ice cream • $13.80

Drinkmoor Cabernet Merlot

▼▼▼▼ NV Light to medium red-purple; the bouquet has savoury, cedary, spicy edges to redcurrant fruit; the palate has good mouthfeel, with ripe blackcurrant fruit offset by soft tannins; an impressive wine, and by far the best of the group. **rating:** 87

best drinking Now–2006 **drink with** Lamb • $13.80

Drinkmoor Cabernets

▼▼▼▽ NV Light red-purple; spicy, earthy black fruit aromas lead into a tangy, savoury light to medium-bodied palate, finishing with fine tannins. **rating:** 84

best drinking Now **drink with** Pizza • $13.80

dromana estate

Cnr Harrisons Road and Bittern–Dromana Road, Dromana, Vic 3936 **region** Mornington Peninsula
phone (03) 5987 3800 **fax** (03) 5981 0714 **open** 7 days 11–4
winemaker Garry Crittenden, Rollo Crittenden **production** 30 000 cases **est.** 1982
product range ($15–54 CD) Dromana Estate Sauvignon Blanc Semillon, Chardonnay, Reserve Chardonnay, Pinot Noir, Reserve Pinot Noir, Shiraz, Cabernet Merlot; Second label Schinus range of Sauvignon Blanc, Chardonnay, Merlot; and a newly packaged range of Italian varietals Arneis, Barbera, Dolcetto, Sangiovese, Nebbiolo and Rosato under the Garry Crittenden 'i' label.
summary Since it was first established, Dromana Estate has always been near or at the cutting edge, both in marketing terms and in terms of development of new varietals, most obviously the Italian range under the i label. The Schinus range has likewise pushed the envelope. Rollo Crittenden has largely taken over winemaking responsibilities from Garry Crittenden, and the business is now majority-owned by outside investors. It is distributed domestically by Red+White in all states, and has exports to the UK and Singapore.

Dromana Estate Sauvignon Blanc Semillon

▼▼▼▼▽ 2002 Light straw-green; the gentle bouquet has aromas of gooseberry, herb and grass, the palate with good citrus and herb flavour and intensity; likewise good length and balance. **rating:** 90

best drinking Now **drink with** Seafood • $20

Garry Crittenden i Arneis

▼▼▼▽ 2002 Light straw-green; a hint of bottling SO_2 is evident, but the spicy pear fruit aromas are there and will grow in volume as the wine ages. The palate is well made, but it really is difficult to get too excited about a basically neutral variety. From the King Valley, and a small amount from the Mornington Peninsula. **rating:** 84

best drinking Now **best vintages** '00 **drink with** Vegetable terrine • $25

Dromana Estate Chardonnay

▼▼▼▼▼ 2001 Medium yellow-green; complex, tangy grapefruit aromas intermingle with barrel-ferment French oak, leading into a palate with plenty of depth and substance; once again barrel-ferment notes are evident but not dominant; good length to the tangy fruit. A particularly good outcome for the vintage. **rating:** 94

best drinking Now–2006 **best vintages** '91, '92, '97, '98, '99, '00, '01 **drink with** Crab • $30

Dromana Estate Reserve Chardonnay

▼▼▼▼▽ 2001 Light straw-green; as ever, a tight and elegant bouquet, clean and fresh; the palate is equally tight, with melon, citrus and stone fruit, and a touch of mlf cashew. **rating:** 92

best drinking Now–2007 **best vintages** '91, '94, '96, '97, '99, '00, '01 **drink with** Kassler • $43

Garry Crittenden i Rosato

▼▼▼▼ 2002 Light fuchsia pink; small berries, flowers and spice aromas lead into a clean, fresh, bright well-balanced palate, with a pleasingly dry finish. A blend of Sangiovese and Nebbiolo sourced from the King Valley and the Pyrenees. **rating:** 86

best drinking Now **drink with** Brasserie food • $15

Dromana Estate Pinot Noir

▼▼▼▼ 2001 Light to medium red-purple; a light, fresh, savoury bouquet with some strawberry notes leads into a fresh palate with light strawberry and mint flavours; pleasant, but without enough intensity and structure for higher points. **rating: 87**

best drinking Now **best vintages** '97, '00 **drink with** Grilled quail • $30

Dromana Estate Reserve Pinot Noir

▼▼▼▼▼ 2001 Medium red-purple; complex aromas of plum, spice, berry and forest are followed by a rich, full palate with abundant plum fruit offset by savoury tannins; very good structure; night and day compared to the varietal wine of the same vintage. **rating: 94**

best drinking Now–2006 **best vintages** '00, '01 **drink with** Braised duck

Garry Crittenden i Dolcetto

▼▼▼▼ 2002 Light to medium red-purple; fresh, juicy, spicy cherry fruit on the bouquet is followed by a quite firm palate, with black cherry and a sprinkling of spice. From the King Valley and Great Western. **rating: 88**

best drinking Now **drink with** Pizza • $25

Garry Crittenden i Sangiovese

▼▼▼▼ 2001 Light to medium red-purple; the light, clean bouquet has typical savoury, tobacco leaf overtones, the palate marching to the tune of the same drum, with spicy tobacco leaf flavours, but needing more red fruit generosity to quicken the pulse. **rating: 85**

best drinking Now–2005 **best vintages** '99 **drink with** Osso buco • $22

🍂 dudley partners NR

Porky Flat Vineyard, Penneshaw, Kangaroo Island, SA 5222 (postal) **region** Kangaroo Island
phone (08) 8553 1509 **fax** (08) 8553 1509 **open** Not
winemaker Wine Network (James Irvine) **est.** 1994
product range Peninsula Chardonnay, Porky Flat Shiraz, Shearing Shed Red (Shiraz Cabernet), Hog Bay River Cabernet.
summary Colin Hopkins, Jeff Howard, Alan Willson and Paul Mansfield have formed a partnership to bring together three vineyards on Kangaroo Island's Dudley Peninsula: the Porky Flat vineyard of 5 hectares, Hog Bay River of 2 hectares and Sawyers of 4 hectares. It is the quirky vineyard names which give the products there distinctive identities. The partners not only look after viticulture, but also join in the winemaking process. To date, most of the wines are sold through licensed outlets on Kangaroo Island, supplemented by retail sales in Adelaide.

🍂 duerden's wines NR

Lot 295 Waggon Road, Victor Harbor, SA 5211 **region** Southern Fleurieu
phone (08) 8552 8450 **fax** (08) 8552 8450 **open** 7 days 9–5
winemaker Harry Duerden **est.** 1996
product range ($14.75–39 CD) Sweet Frontignac, Cabernet Sauvignon Wildfire, Cabernet Sauvignon Bushfire, Waggon Road Cabernet Sauvignon First Press, Waggon Road Cabernet Sauvignon Show Reserve; Liqueurs.
summary Harry Duerden has established 2 hectares of vineyard (90 per cent cabernet sauvignon, 10 per cent frontignac) grown on the Italian pergola system. He cautiously says it is the only known commercial vineyard using this system in Australia, and you could be confident he is right. Deliberately and charmingly eccentric, he suggests the system is ahead of its time, rather than the ancient history others might describe it as. His one-line description of his First Press Cabernet Sauvignon follows down the same track, 'an alternative to alcoholic furniture polish'. If all this were not enough, he produces a range of liqueur-style products, including a quandong-flavoured wine product, with a fortified wine base.

🍂 duke's vineyard ★★★☆

Porongurup Road, Porongurup, WA 6324 **region** Great Southern
phone (08) 9853 1107 **fax** (08) 9853 1107 **open** 7 days 10–4.30
winemaker Rob Lee (Contract) **production** 2000 cases **est.** 1998
product range ($16–24 CD) Riesling, Autumn Riesling, Shiraz, Cabernet Sauvignon.
summary When Hilde and Ian (Duke) Ranson sold their clothing manufacturing business in 1998 they were able to fulfill a long-held dream of establishing a vineyard in the Porongurup subregion of Great Southern. It

took two abortive efforts before they became third-time-lucky with the acquisition of a 65-hectare farm at the foot of the Porongurup Range. They planted 3 hectares each of riesling and shiraz, and 3.5 hectares of cabernet sauvignon with 0.5 hectare of petit verdot to keep the cabernet company. Hilde Ranson is a successful artist, and it was she who designed the beautiful scalloped, glass-walled cellar door sale area with its mountain blue cladding. The wines are made by Rob Lee at the Porongurup Winery, and have limited New South Wales distribution through Lewis Fine Wines.

Duke's Vineyard Riesling

TTTT 2002 Light straw-green; the fragrant bouquet has a mix of mineral and apple blossom, the medium-bodied palate staying in the apple/apple blossom spectrum, but soft rather than minerally, making the wine accessible now. **rating:** 89

best drinking Now–2006 **drink with** Sashimi • $18

Duke's Vineyard Shiraz

TTTT 2001 Medium to full red-purple; the bouquet has a mix of plum, spice and blackberry, the oak subtle; the palate opens with spicy blackberry fruit bolstered by firm but fine tannins and crunchy acidity. **rating:** 88

best drinking 2006–2011 **drink with** Beef in red wine and olives • $24

Duke's Vineyard Cabernet Sauvignon

TTTT 2000 Medium red-purple; the moderately intense bouquet is clean, with redcurrant fruit to the fore, and oak very much in the background. The light to medium-bodied palate has a mix of red berry and more savoury characters, with gentle tannins adding to the overall feel of elegance. Perhaps fractionally short, however. **rating:** 86

best drinking Now–2007 **drink with** Lamb cutlets • $22

dulcinea   NR

Jubilee Road, Sulky, Ballarat, Vic 3352 **region** Ballarat
phone (03) 5334 6440 **fax** (03) 5334 6828 **open** 7 days 10–6
winemaker Rod Stott **production** 3000 cases **est.** 1983
product range Sauvignon Blanc, Chardonnay, Pinot Noir, Shiraz, Cabernet Sauvignon.
summary Rod Stott is passionate grape grower and winemaker (with 5 hectares of vineyard) who chose the name Dulcinea from 'The Man of La Mancha', where only a fool fights windmills. With winemaking help from various sources, he has produced a series of very interesting and often complex wines. Exports to Japan.

dusty hill vineyard   NR

Barambah Road, Moffatdale via Murgon, Qld 4605 **region** South Burnett
phone (07) 4168 4700 **fax** (07) 4168 4888 **open** 7 days 10–5
winemaker Stuart Pierce **production** 1500 cases **est.** 1996
product range ($15–20 R) Semillon, Verdelho, Rose (semi-sweet), Dusty Rose, Shiraz, Liqueur Muscat.
summary Joe Prendergast and family have established 2 hectares each of shiraz and cabernet sauvignon, 1 hectare of verdelho, and semillon and 0.5 hectare each of merlot and black muscat. The vines are crop-thinned to obtain maximum ripeness in the fruit and to maximise tannin extract, although the winery's specialty is the Dusty Rose, continuing a long tradition of rose/Beaujolais style wines from Queensland. The 2000 vintage of this wine came equal top at the 2000 Melbourne Royal Wine Show with a bronze medal.

dutschke wines   NR

Lyndoch Valley Road, Lyndoch, SA 5351 (postal) **region** Barossa Valley
phone (08) 8265 6567 **fax** (08) 8265 2635 **open** Not
winemaker Wayne Dutschke **production** 4000 cases **est.** 1990
product range ($20–38 R) Oscar Semmler Shiraz, St Jakobi Shiraz, Willowbend Merlot Shiraz Cabernet, The Tawny 22 Year Old Port.
summary Wayne Dutschke has had 10 years of winemaking experience with major wine companies in South Australia, Victoria and New South Wales but has returned to South Australia to join his uncle, Ken Semmler, a leading grape grower in the Barossa Valley and now in the Adelaide Hills. No recent tastings, simply because Dutschke sells out of wine in less than 6 months each year. Exports to the US, the UK, Germany and Singapore.

dyson wines   NR

Sherriff Road, Maslin Beach, SA 5170 **region** McLaren Vale
phone (08) 8386 1092 **fax** (08) 8327 0066 **open** 7 days 10–5
winemaker Allan Dyson **production** 2000 cases **est.** 1976
product range ($16–20 CD) Chardonnay, Viognier, Liqueur Chardonnay, Cabernet Sauvignon, Ambra Liqueur (White Port).
summary Allan Dyson, who describes himself as 'a young man of 50-odd years' has recently expanded his 1.5 hectares of viognier with 2 hectares each of chardonnay and cabernet sauvignon, and has absolutely no thoughts of slowing down or retiring. Some retail distribution in South Australia and New South Wales supplements direct sales from the cellar door.

east arm vineyard   ★★★★☆

111 Archers Road, Hillwood, Tas 7250 **region** Northern Tasmania
phone (03) 6334 0266 **fax** (03) 6334 1405 **open** Weekends and public holidays, or by appointment
winemaker Bert Sundstrup, Nicholas Butler (Contract) **production** 1200 cases **est.** 1993
product range ($17–23 CD) Riesling, Unwooded Chardonnay, Chardonnay, Pinot Noir.
summary East Arm Vineyard was established by Launceston gastroenterologist Dr John Wettenhall and partner Anita James, who also happens to have completed the Charles Sturt University Diploma in Applied Science (wine growing). The 2 hectares of vineyard which came into full production in 1998 are more or less equally divided between riesling, chardonnay and pinot noir. It is established on an historic block, part of a grant made to retired British soldiers of the Georgetown garrison in 1821, and slopes down to the Tamar River. The property is 25 hectares, and there are plans for further planting and, somewhere down the track, a winery. The Riesling is always excellent. Exports to Hong Kong.

East Arm Riesling

♀♀♀♀♀ **2002** Bright, light yellow-green; a fresh, lively lime, herb and mineral bouquet is followed by a fresh, long and intense palate, with a lingering finish and aftertaste. Back to its top form of 1998, '99 and '00.
rating: 94

best drinking Now–2013 **best vintages** '98, '99, '00, '02 **drink with** Scallops • $19.50

eastern peake   NR

Clunes Road, Coghills Creek, Vic 3364 **region** Ballarat
phone (03) 5343 4245 **fax** (03) 5343 4365 **open** 7 days 10–5
winemaker Norman Latta **production** 3000 cases **est.** 1983
product range ($17–30 CD) Reserve Chardonnay, Persuasion (Pinot Rose), Pinot Noir, Morillon Pinot Noir, Reserve Pinot Noir.
summary Norm Latta and Di Pym commenced the establishment of Eastern Peake, situated 25 kilometres northeast of Ballarat on a high plateau overlooking the Creswick Valley, almost 15 years ago. In the early years the grapes were sold to Trevor Mast of Mount Chalambar and Mount Langi Ghiran, but the 5 hectares of vines are now dedicated to the production of Eastern Peake wines. The Pinot Noir is on the minerally/stemmy side; earlier bottling might preserve more of the sweet fruit. Exports to the UK and Northern Ireland.

Eastern Peake Pinot Noir

♀♀♀♀ **2000** Medium red-purple; herb, forest and red berry aromas lead into a light to medium-bodied palate, with good texture and structure; in a slightly savoury, austere mode, but clearly varietal.   **rating: 87**
best drinking Now–2005 **drink with** Smoked quail • $25

🍇 echuca estate wines   NR

931 Murray Valley Highway, Echuca, Vic 3564 **region** Goulburn Valley
phone (03) 5480 7090 **fax** (03) 5480 7096 **open** 7 days 10–5
winemaker John Lake, Ellen Loiterton **production** 30 000 cases **est.** 2000
product range ($12–17 CD) Brands are: Echuca Wines, Jaengenya Vineyard, New Glory, Permitz Estate, Stevens Brook Estate and Tandarra Estate Wine.
summary Echuca Estate Wines has many strings to its bow. It brings together five vineyards, some on the New South Wales side of the Murray River, the others on the Victorian side, but all within a 20 kilometre radius of the winery. They are New Glory Vineyard (40 ha), Permitz Estate (25 ha), Jaengenya Vineyard (8 ha), Stevens Brook Estate (10 ha) and Tandarra Estate (16 ha). As well as making the wines for these vineyards for sale as

branded wines, Echuca Estate offers contract crushing, bulk storage of juices and wines, maturation programmes and the full gamut of wine management, marketing and sales. Contract-made wines include clean skins, bulk wines and juices, exclusive varieties for cellar-door sales, and exclusive wines developed for export markets. Its crush of around 1300 tonnes is planned to increase to 5000 tonnes by 2004.

eden springs   NR

Boehm Springs Road, Springton, SA 5235 **region** Eden Valley
phone (08) 8564 1166 **fax** (08) 8564 1265 **open** Not
winemaker Andrew Ewart (Contract) **production** 1000 cases **est.** 2000
product range ($15.50–24.50 ML) High Eden range of Riesling, Shiraz, Cabernet Sauvignon.
summary Richard Wiencke and Meredith Hodgson opened the Eden Springs wine doors on 1 July 2000, offering the first wines from the 19 hectares of vines made in 1999 (Shiraz and Cabernet Sauvignon) and the inaugural release of Riesling from 2000, contract-made by Andrew Ewart. It is a remote vineyard (6 kilometres by dirt road from Springton) and sells its wine through a high-quality newsletter to mail list customers, and a website which has brought export orders from the US, Denmark and Malaysia.

eden valley wines   NR

Main Street, Eden Valley, SA 5235 **region** Eden Valley
phone (08) 8564 1111 **fax** (08) 8564 1110 **open** 7 days 10–5
winemaker Peter Thompson **production** 1500 cases **est.** 1994
product range ($9–15 CD) Riesling, Spatlese Frontignac, Shiraz, Mourvedre, Golden Port.
summary Eden Valley Wines has waxed and waned over the years but seems now in the ascendant. The venture now has 30 hectares each of recently planted riesling, cabernet sauvignon and shiraz, with 5 hectares of much older mourvedre. A major part of the production is sold as grapes to others; the wines currently on sale have varied backgrounds, now moving to an estate-grown base. Exports to Malaysia.

edwards vineyard   ★★★★

Cnr Caves Road and Ellensbrook Road, Cowaramup, WA 6284 **region** Margaret River
phone (08) 9755 5999 **fax** (08) 9755 5988 **open** Thurs–Sun and public holidays 10.30–5.30 or by appointment
winemaker Michael Edwards, Stuart Pym (Contract) **production** 1200 cases **est.** 1994
product range ($19–26 CD) Semillon, Sauvignon Blanc, Chardonnay, Shiraz, Cabernet Sauvignon.
summary This is very much a family affair, headed by parents Brian and Jenny Edwards. Michael Edwards is the assistant winemaker at Voyager Estate, while overseeing the winemaking of the Edwards Vineyard wines; Chris Edwards is vineyard manager, while Fiona and Bianca Edwards are involved in sales and marketing. They have a substantial vineyard, planted to chardonnay (3 ha), semillon (2.5 ha), sauvignon blanc (2.1 ha), shiraz (4.8 ha) and cabernet sauvignon (7.6 ha) and have plans to build a winery in time for the 2004 vintage. One of the local attractions is the Tigermoth 'Matilda', flown from England to Australia in 1990 as a fundraiser, and which is now kept at the Edwards Vineyard and can be seen flying locally. Exports to Holland.

Edwards Vineyard Semillon Sauvignon Blanc
▼▼▼▼ 2002 Light straw-green; the moderately intense bouquet has some grassy, hay-like aromas which take the sauvignon blanc from the same vintage somewhere left of centre; the palate is predominantly in the grassy/herbal/stony spectrum, the small proportion fermented in new French oak adding complexity and structure, rather than flavour. **rating: 86**
best drinking Now–2005 **best vintages** '01 **drink with** Abalone • $19

Edwards Vineyard Shiraz
▼▼▼▼ 2001 Medium to full red-purple; solid blackberry, licorice and bitter chocolate aromas are followed by a medium to full-bodied palate, the ripe fruit and ripe tannins providing good mouthfeel and length. **rating: 89**
best drinking 2005–2010 **drink with** Smoked lamb • $24

Edwards Vineyard Cabernet Sauvignon
▼▼▼▼▼ 2001 Very good red-purple; well-balanced blackberry and earth fruit and cedary oak on the bouquet are precursors for an intense palate with classic cabernet varietal flavour and structure; classy, long, lingering finish. **rating: 94**
best drinking 2005–2015 **best vintages** '01 **drink with** Moroccan lamb • $26

elan vineyard ★★★☆

17 Turners Road, Bittern, Vic 3918 **region** Mornington Peninsula
phone (03) 5983 1858 **fax** (03) 5983 2821 **open** First weekend of month, public holidays 11–5, or by appointment
winemaker Selma Lowther **production** 400 cases **est.** 1980
product range ($14–17 CD) Chardonnay, Shiraz, Gamay, Cabernet Merlot.
summary Selma Lowther, then fresh from Charles Sturt University (as a mature-age student) made an impressive debut with her spicy, fresh, crisp Chardonnay, and has continued to make tiny quantities of appealing and sensibly priced wines. Most of the grapes from the 2.5 hectares of estate vineyards are sold; production remains minuscule.

Elan Vineyard Chardonnay

▼▼▼▼ **2001** Medium yellow-straw; a very complex bouquet with pronounced barrel-ferment inputs is followed by a palate with the fruit strength to partially carry the barrel-ferment oak; lots of character and very good value, particularly if you enjoy chardonnay with a strong barrel-ferment influence. **rating:** 88
best drinking Now–2006 **drink with** Brains in black butter • $16

Elan Vineyard Shiraz

▼▼▼▼▽ **2000** Medium red-purple, bright and clear; the bouquet has a range of blackberry and mulberry fruit with a dusting of black pepper; there is plenty of depth to the ripe fruit, the tannins fine but plentiful; overall, the texture is soft and thoroughly appealing. **rating:** 90
best drinking 2004–2009 **drink with** Osso buco • $17

Elan Vineyard Gamay

▼▼▼▽ **2002** Light to medium red-purple; the bouquet has light minty/leafy/berry aromas, the palate with spicy, dried leaf edges; devoid of tannins, but an interesting wine nonetheless. **rating:** 84
best drinking Now **drink with** Antipasto • $14

elderton ★★★★☆

3 Tanunda Road, Nuriootpa, SA 5355 **region** Barossa Valley
phone (08) 8568 7878 **fax** (08) 8568 7879 **open** Mon–Fri 8.30–5, weekends, holidays 11–4
winemaker Richard Sheedy, Allister Ashmead, James Irvine (Consultant) **production** 32 000 cases **est.** 1984
product range ($12.90–85 CD) Riesling, Sauvignon Blanc Verdelho, Unwooded Chardonnay, Chardonnay, Ashmead Family Reserve Sparkling Shiraz, Botrytis Semillon, Cabernet Rose, Shiraz, Friends Shiraz, Tantalus Shiraz Cabernet Sauvignon, Merlot, CSM, Cabernet Sauvignon, Friends Cabernet Sauvignon; Command Shiraz and Ashmead Single Vineyard Cabernet Sauvignon are flagbearers.
summary The wines are based on some old, high-quality Barossa floor estate vineyards, and all are driven to a lesser or greater degree by lashings of American oak; the Command Shiraz is at the baroque end of the spectrum and has to be given considerable respect within the parameters of its style. National retail distribution, with exports to the UK, the US, Europe and Asia.

Elderton Eden Valley Riesling

▼▼▼▼ **2002** Light to medium yellow-green; quite soft, gently sweet lime/tropical fruit aromas are repeated on the palate, made in a quick-developing style. **rating:** 87
best drinking Now **drink with** Pasta marinara • $14.50

Elderton Shiraz

Made in the no-holds-barred style for which Elderton has become well known, and which has been highly successful, both in domestic and export markets. I freely acknowledge that my sensitivity to American oak is not shared by the majority of consumers, or so it would seem.
▼▼▼▼ **2001** Medium to full red-purple; the bouquet offers a traditional mix of berry, plum, earth and vanilla oak; the solidly ripe palate responds with a similar array of earth, berry and vanilla; controlled tannins. **rating:** 87
best drinking 2006–2011 **best vintages** '86, '88, '90, '91, '92, '94 **drink with** Steak and kidney pie • $24.95

Elderton Command Shiraz

▼▼▼▼▽ **1999** Medium to full red-purple; ripe plum and well-balanced and integrated oak aromas are quite intense, leading logically to a concentrated, powerful but smooth palate, with good mouthfeel and flow; traditional Barossa. **rating:** 91
best drinking 2004–2009 **best vintages** '98 **drink with** Kangaroo • $85

Elderton CSM

▼▼▼▼ 1999 Medium red-purple; the moderately ripe fruit is threatened by the slightly sawdusty vanilla oak, but the wine comes together better on the palate, even though it is the American (rather than the French) oak which wins the war. **rating: 86**

best drinking 2004–2010 **best vintages** '95, '98 **drink with** Wild duck • $38

Elderton Ashmead Single Vineyard Cabernet Sauvignon

▼▼▼▼ 1999 Medium purple-red; complex bottle-developed and oak-influenced aromas are followed by a powerful palate with black fruit and chocolate flavours, plenty of French oak and pervasive tannins. Not easy to tell whether those tannins will soften, but the balance of probability is that they will. **rating: 88**

best drinking 2004–2009 **best vintages** '98 **drink with** Baby leg of lamb • $85

eldredge ★★★★☆

Spring Gully Road, Clare, SA 5453 **region** Clare Valley
phone (08) 8842 3086 **fax** (08) 8842 3086 **open** 7 days 11–5
winemaker Leigh Eldredge **production** 7000 cases **est.** 1993
product range ($13–40 CD) Watervale Riesling, Semillon Sauvignon Blanc, Hiltee Sparkling, Late Harvest Riesling, Blue Chip Shiraz, Gilt Edge Shiraz, M.S.G., Boundary (Sangiovese Cabernet Sauvignon), Cabernet Sauvignon, Tawny Port.
summary Leigh and Karen Eldredge have established their winery and cellar-door sales area in the Sevenhill Ranges at an altitude of 500 metres, above the town of Watervale. Hit a purple patch with its 2001 and 2002 white wines, complementing the very good Cabernet Sauvignon. The wines are distributed in Victoria and Queensland and exported to the UK, the US and Canada.

Eldredge Watervale Riesling

▼▼▼▼▽ 2002 Light to medium yellow-green; the soft and clean bouquet has flowery, lime blossom aromas predominant; the palate is very powerful, with lots of flavour, structure and depth. A total contrast in style early in its life to the 2001. **rating: 93**

best drinking Now–2013 **best vintages** '98, '01, '02 **drink with** Bruschetta • $16

Eldredge Semillon Sauvignon Blanc

▼▼▼▼▽ 2002 Light straw-green; a clean and fresh bouquet with herb and mineral aromas is followed by a lively, clean and fresh palate, finishing with nice acidity. The Semillon leads the way, but continues the surprising style and quality of this 60/40 blend. **rating: 90**

best drinking Now–2006 **best vintages** '01, '02 **drink with** Fishcakes • $16

Eldredge Boundary

▼▼▼▼ 2000 Medium to full red-purple; clean, deep, dark berry fruit with hints of spicy varietal character lead into a powerful, quite luscious and moderately tannic palate; I am far from sure about the varietal character, but there is certainly plenty of impact. A blend of 90 per cent Sangiovese and 10 per cent Cabernet Sauvignon. **rating: 89**

best drinking 2005–2010 **drink with** Game • $25

eldridge estate ★★★★☆

Red Hill Road, Red Hill, Vic 3937 **region** Mornington Peninsula
phone (03) 5989 2644 **fax** (03) 5989 2644 **open** Weekends, public holidays and January 1–26 11–5
winemaker David Lloyd **production** 1000 cases **est.** 1985
product range ($15–34 CD) Sauvignon Blanc Semillon, North Patch Chardonnay, Chardonnay, Pink Lloyd Rose, Gamay, West Patch Pinot Noir, Pinot Noir, Cabernet Merlot.
summary The Eldridge Estate vineyard, with 7 varieties included in its 3.5 hectares, was purchased by Wendy and David Lloyd in 1995. Major retrellising work has been undertaken, changing to Scott-Henry, and all of the wines will now be estate-grown and made. The wines are available at the Victorian Wine Centre and Tastings, Armadale, in Melbourne, and a few leading restaurants in Melbourne and Sydney.

Eldridge Estate Chardonnay

▼▼▼▼▽ 2001 Medium yellow-green; a clean, gently complex bouquet primarily driven by melon and stone fruit leads into a fine, restrained nectarine and stone fruit palate with malolactic and barrel-ferment inputs. **rating: 93**

best drinking Now–2007 **best vintages** '99, '00, '01 **drink with** Poached fish • $34

Eldridge Estate North Patch Chardonnay

TTTTY **2001** Medium yellow-green; clean, gently complex melon and cashew aromas are followed by a fruit-driven palate with citrus, melon and nectarine, longer but slightly lighter than the other Chardonnay release of the same vintage. Excellent value. **rating: 92**

best drinking Now–2006 **drink with** Calamari • $20

Eldridge Estate Pinot Noir

TTTTY **2001** Light to medium red, the purple starting to fade a little; the moderately intense bouquet is clean, with a mix of cherry, spice and more savoury aromas; the palate has good length, intensity and line, sustained by lingering, savoury tannins. **rating: 93**

best drinking Now–2007 **best vintages** '01 **drink with** Braised duck • $34

Eldridge Estate West Patch Pinot Noir

TTTT **2001** Light red; a light, sappy/savoury bouquet is quite stylish, the palate providing an instant replay of the bouquet. The fruit intensity of this wine seems distinctly lower than that of the main varietal release.

best drinking Now **drink with** Seared Tasmanian salmon • $20 **rating: 85**

elgee park ★★★★

Wallaces Road RMB 5560, Merricks North, Vic 3926 **region** Mornington Peninsula
phone (03) 5989 7338 **fax** (03) 5989 7338 **open** One day a year – Sunday of Queen's Birthday weekend
winemaker Contract **production** 1800 cases **est.** 1972
product range ($18–34 ML) Baillieu Myer Family Reserve Riesling, Viognier, Chardonnay, Pinot Noir, Merlot, Cabernet Merlot; Cuvee Brut
summary The pioneer of the Mornington Peninsula in its 20th-century rebirth, owned by Baillieu Myer and family. The wines are now made at Stonier and T'Gallant, Elgee Park's own winery having been closed, and the overall level of activity decreased. Melbourne retail distribution through Flinders Wholesale.

Elgee Park Family Reserve Riesling

TTTTY **2002** Light straw-green; the bouquet has a mix of crisp mineral and slate on the one hand, and fruit spice aromas on the other; the tight, crisp palate has well above-average length, finishing with minerally/lemony acidity. The effect of the microscopic yield is very obvious. **rating: 90**

best drinking Now–2008 **best vintages** '02 **drink with** Light seafood • $18

Elgee Park Family Reserve Viognier

TTTT **2001** Medium yellow-green; the bouquet is clean, as ever not particularly aromatic, but with some faint cosmetic/musk characters; the restrained palate follows on from the bouquet, its virtue being the good texture and mouthfeel. **rating: 87**

best drinking Now–2005 **drink with** Chinese prawns • $34

Elgee Park Family Reserve Chardonnay

TTTTY **2001** Light to medium straw-green; the clean and subtle bouquet shows very well-balanced barrel-ferment and malolactic-ferment inputs married with the melon fruit; the palate is, if anything, even more elegant. For some, there will not be quite enough emphasis. **rating: 90**

best drinking Now–2007 **best vintages** '00, '01 **drink with** Seafood risotto • $30

Elgee Park Family Reserve Pinot Noir

TTTT **2001** Light to medium red-purple; the moderately intense bouquet has clear spicy/foresty varietal character, the light-bodied palate following suit with plum, black cherry and a hint of mint. **rating: 88**

best drinking Now–2006 **best vintages** '97 **drink with** Quail • $30

Elgee Park Family Reserve Cabernet Merlot

TTTT **2000** Good colour; the moderately intense bouquet has lifted, blackberry, leaf and spice aromatics, and while ripeness comes through in the fruit expression of the palate, it is still in a savoury spectrum; good texture and fine tannins to close. **rating: 89**

best drinking 2004–2009 **drink with** Rack of lamb • $25

eling forest winery ★★★

Hume Highway, Sutton Forest, NSW 2577 **region** Southern New South Wales Zone
phone (02) 4878 9499 **fax** (02) 4878 9499 **open** 7 days 10–5
winemaker Leslie Fritz, Michelle Crockett **production** 3500 cases **est.** 1987

product range ($8–45 CD) Riesling, Tramini (Traminer), Furmint, Linden Leaf Harselvelu, Chardonnay, Lunel, Catherine Hill, Botrytis Riesling, Rose, Carla (Red), Cabernet Sauvignon, Peach Brandy, Peach Ambrosia, Cherry Port.

summary Eling Forest's mentally agile and innovative founder Leslie Fritz celebrated his 80th birthday not long after he planted the first vines at his Sutton Forest vineyard in 1987. He proceeded to celebrate his 88th birthday by expanding the vineyards from 3 hectares to 4, primarily with additional plantings of the Hungarian varieties. He has also developed a Cherry Port and is using the spinning cone technology to produce various peach-based liqueurs, utilising second-class peach waste. Right across the extensive range, the wines are increasingly technically well made, even if far more European than Australian in terms of fruit weight.

eljamar   NR

c/- Miramar Wines, Henry Lawson Drive, Mudgee, NSW 2850 **region** Mudgee
phone (02) 6373 3874 **fax** (02) 6373 3854 **open** Not
winemaker Ian MacRae **est.** 2000
product range Chardonnay, Shiraz, Cabernet Sauvignon.
summary Eljamar is owned by Ian and Carol MacRae, and is a sister operation to their main business, Miramar Wines. Eljamar has its own estate plantings of 10 hectares of shiraz and about 2 hectares each of cabernet sauvignon and chardonnay. The wines are made at Miramar but a cellar door will open on-site sometime in 2003. The property is only 5 kilometres from the town of Mudgee on Henry Lawson Drive and also fronts Craigmoor Road, giving it a prime position in the so-called 'golden triangle'. Update news on the opening of the cellar door and release of the first wines can be obtained through the Miramar newsletter.

ellender estate   ★★★☆

260 Green Gully Road, Glenlyon, Vic 3461 **region** Macedon Ranges
phone (03) 5348 7785 **fax** (03) 5348 4077 **open** Weekends and public holidays 11–5, or by appointment
winemaker Graham Ellender **production** 1000 cases **est.** 1996
product range ($16–35 CD) Chardonnay, Pinot Noir, Cabernet Franc, Shiraz, Merlot, Cabernet Sauvignon.
summary Former senior lecturer in dental science at the University of Melbourne, Graham Ellender, moved to Daylesford with wife Jenny with the twofold purpose of escaping academia and starting a vineyard and winery, simultaneously establishing dental practices at Daylesford and East Ivanhoe. The Ellenders have established 4 hectares of pinot noir, chardonnay, sauvignon blanc and pinot gris, and also source shiraz and sauvignon blanc from Cowra, cabernet sauvignon from Harcourt, cabernet franc from Macedon and pinot noir from Narre Warren. Formerly called Leura Glen Estate, marketplace confusion with other similar names, and other considerations, has led to the change of name to Ellender Estate.

Ellender Estate Macedon Ranges Chardonnay

♥♥♥♡ **2002** Medium yellow-green; the complex bouquet turns around stone fruit, the powerful and quite complex palate likewise, but the sharp finish. Could well surprise and merit far higher points in the years ahead.   **rating: 83**
best drinking 2004–2009 **drink with** Leave it in the cellar • $28

Ellender Estate Ballarat Pinot Noir

♥♥♥♥ **2001** Bright, light red-purple; clean, light and fresh strawberry fruit aromas come through on the light but clean palate. While more to rose in style, it is well balanced and Graham Ellender has resisted the temptation to over-extract the fruit.   **rating: 85**
best drinking Now–2005 **drink with** Braised duck • $28

elliot rocke estate   ★★★★

Craigmoor Road, Mudgee, NSW 2850 **region** Mudgee
phone (02) 6372 7722 **fax** (02) 6372 0680 **open** 7 days 9–4
winemaker Simon Gilbert **production** 6100 cases **est.** 1999
product range ($13–23 CD) Traminer, Semillon, Unwooded Chardonnay, Premium Chardonnay, Late Harvest, McLaren Vale Shiraz, Cabernet Sauvignon Merlot.
summary Elliot Rocke Estate is a new label for Mudgee, but planting of its 34 hectares of vineyards dates back to 1987, when the property was known as Seldom Seen. Twelve hectares of shiraz, 9 hectares of semillon, and 5 hectares each of chardonnay and cabernet sauvignon and 1 hectare of traminer are the main plantings, and contract winemaking by Simon Gilbert has resulted in an impressive range of wines which already have a strong show record. The wines are available through the cellar door, by mailing list, and through a number of Sydney retailers.

Elliot Rocke Estate Traminer

TTTT 2002 Very pale straw-green; clean, light spice and lychee aromas are followed by a delicate but precise and bone-dry palate; excellent varietal character throughout, and a major surprise, as well as great value.

best drinking Now **drink with** Thai • $12.95　　**rating:** 88

Elliot Rocke Estate Semillon

TTTT 2002 Light straw-green; quite complex herb, spice and lemon rind aromas lead into a palate with good length, balance and flavour, very much in the mould of the preceding three vintages.　　**rating:** 89

best drinking 2004–2011 **best vintages** '99, '00, '01, '02 **drink with** Light seafood • $14.95

Elliot Rocke Estate Premium Chardonnay

TTTTY 2000 Light straw-green; the clean, firm bouquet is, typically for the estate, developing slowly, with subtle fig and oak aromas. The elegant, nicely balanced palate has excellent length and finish.　　**rating:** 90

best drinking Now–2007 **best vintages** '00 **drink with** Deep-fried calamari • $17.95

elmslie　　★ ★ ☆

Upper McEwans Road, Legana, Tas 7277 **region** Northern Tasmania
phone (03) 6330 1225 **fax** (03) 6330 2161 **open** By appointment
winemaker Ralph Power **production** 600 cases **est.** 1972
product range ($18 ML) Pinot Noir, Cabernet Sauvignon.
summary A small, specialist red winemaker, from time to time blending Pinot Noir with Cabernet. The fruit from the now fully mature vineyard (0.5 hectare of pinot noir and 1.5 hectares of cabernet sauvignon) has depth and character, but operational constraints mean that the style of the wine is often somewhat rustic.

elmswood estate　　★ ★ ★ ☆

75 Monbulk-Seville Road, Wandin East, Vic 3139 **region** Yarra Valley
phone (03) 5964 3015 **fax** (03) 5964 3405 **open** Weekends 10–5 and by appointment
winemaker Contract **production** 2000 cases **est.** 1981
product range ($18–26 CD) Unoaked Chardonnay, Chardonnay, Cabernet Merlot, Cabernet Sauvignon, Barrel Select Cabernet.
summary Rod and Dianne Keller purchased their 9.5-hectare vineyard in June 1999; it had been planted in 1981 on the red volcanic soils of the far-southern side of the valley which stretch from Wandin to Warburton. Prior to their acquisition of the vineyard, the grapes had been sold to other Yarra Valley winemakers, but the Kellers immediately set about having their own wine made from the estate. The cellar door offers spectacular views across the Upper Yarra Valley to Mount Donna Buang and Warburton. The wines are sold chiefly through cellar door and mailing list, with limited restaurant listings.

elsewhere vineyard　　★ ★ ★ ★ ★

42 Dillons Hill Road, Glaziers Bay, Tas 7109 **region** Southern Tasmania
phone (03) 6295 1228 **fax** (03) 6295 1591 **open** Not
winemaker Andrew Hood (Contract), Steve Lubiana (Contract) **production** 4000 cases **est.** 1984
product range ($20–40 ML) Riesling, Chardonnay, Pinot Noir, Methode Champenoise.
summary Kylie and Andrew Cameron's evocatively named Elsewhere Vineyard used to jostle for space with a commercial flower farm. It is a mark of the success of the wines that in 1993 some of the long-established flowers made way for additional chardonnay and riesling, although it is Elsewhere's long-lived Pinot Noirs that are so stunning and declare the winery rating. The estate-produced range comes from 6 hectares of pinot noir, 3 hectares of chardonnay and 1 hectare of riesling which constitute the immaculately tended vineyard.

Elsewhere Vineyard Chardonnay

TTTT 2002 Bright, light green-yellow; a clean, fresh and tangy bouquet is followed by a similarly fresh and lively palate, the only reservation being slightly green fruit characters. The oak has been appropriately held in restraint throughout.　　**rating:** 87

best drinking Now–2005 **drink with** Marinated scallops • $25

Elsewhere Vineyard Pinot Noir

TTTTT 2001 The bouquet has a fragrant array of plum, spice and red berry aromas, but the long, silky and intense palate is even better, with a wonderfully delicate, gossamer-like, mouthfeel. To die for.　　**rating:** 94

best drinking Now–2007 **best vintages** '89, '91, '93, '95, '98, '99, '01 **drink with** Breast of duck with demi glaze • $30

Elsewhere Vineyard Bay of Eight Pinot Noir

▼▼▼▼▼ **2001** Medium purple-red; the bouquet has slightly more savoury/foresty overtones to the red berry, plum and spice fruit than does the 'standard' wine of the same year. Similarly, the palate has more structure and some savoury stem tannins; great intensity and character. **rating:** 95

best drinking Now–2008 **best vintages** '00, '01 **drink with** Braised duck • $40

Elsewhere Vineyard Footcrush Pinot Noir

▼▼▼▼▽ **2001** Light to medium red-purple; the spicy, savoury fragrance clearly shows whole bunch characters; the complex palate has less overt fruit than the other wines from the vintage, but does have lingering intensity on the finish. **rating:** 93

best drinking Now–2006 **best vintages** '01 **drink with** Pan-fried chicken livers • $30

elsmore's caprera grove   NR

657 Milbrodale Road, Broke, NSW 2330 **region** Lower Hunter Valley
phone (02) 6579 1344 **fax** (02) 6579 1355 **open** By appointment
winemaker Jim Chatto, Gary Reid (Contract) **production** 800 cases **est.** 1995
product range ($15–20 CD) Verdelho, Chardonnay, Peregrinus Methode Champenoise, Bartolomeo Botrytis Chardonnay, Shiraz.
summary Bindy and Chris Elsmore purchased their 16-hectare property at Broke in 1995, subsequently establishing a little over 4 hectares of chardonnay, verdelho and shiraz, with chardonnay taking the lion's share of the plantings. Their interest in wine came not from their professional lives – Chris is a retired commodore of the Royal Australian Navy and Bindy had a career in advertising, marketing and personnel – but from numerous trips to the wine regions of France, Italy and Spain.

Elsmore's Caprera Grove Verdelho

▼▼▼▼ **2002** Light straw-green; spotlessly clean, light fruit salad and citrus aromas lead into a fresh and seductive palate anchored on fruit salad/passionfruit flavours; delicate but has line; a major success. Striking packaging is another plus. **rating:** 88

best drinking Now **drink with** Fresh Tasmanian salmon • $16

eltham vineyards   NR

225 Shaws Road, Arthurs Creek, Vic 3099 **region** Yarra Valley
phone (03) 9439 4688 **fax** (03) 9439 5121 **open** By appointment
winemaker George Apted, John Graves **production** 700 cases **est.** 1990
product range Chardonnay, Pinot Noir, Cabernet Sauvignon.
summary Drawing upon vineyards at Arthurs Creek and Eltham, John Graves (brother of David Graves of the illustrious Californian Pinot producer Saintsbury) produces tiny quantities of quite stylish Chardonnay and Pinot Noir, the former showing nice barrel-ferment characters. No recent tastings.

elysium vineyard   NR

393 Milbrodale Road, Broke, NSW 2330 **region** Lower Hunter Valley
phone (02) 9664 2368 **fax** (02) 9664 2368 **open** Weekends 10–5, or by appointment
winemaker Wandin Valley Estate (Contract) **production** 500 cases **est.** 1990
product range ($20 R) Verdelho.
summary Elysium was once part of a much larger vineyard established by John Tulloch. John Tulloch (not part of the Tulloch operation previously owned by Southcorp) continues to look after the viticulture, with the 1 hectare of verdelho being vinified at Tyrrell's. The Elysium Cottage, large enough to accommodate six people, has won a number of tourism awards, and proprietor Victoria Foster conducts wine education weekends on request, with meals prepared by a chef brought in for the occasion. The cost for a gourmet weekend is $300–400 per person, depending on numbers.

🐚 empress vineyard   ★★★★

Drapers Road, Irrewarra via Colac, Vic 3249 **region** Western Victoria Zone
phone (03) 9427 9960 **fax** (03) 5352 1711 **open** Wed–Sat 11–5, or by appointment
winemaker Robin Brockett, Cate Looney **production** 1000 cases **est.** 1998
product range ($18–30 CD) Semillon Sauvignon Blanc, Chardonnay, Pinot Noir, Cabernet Sauvignon Merlot.

summary The background to the name of Empress Vineyard provides a fascinating insight into little-known history. It transpires that Napoleon Bonaparte applied to join the French scientific expedition to Australia in 1792, but ended up doing other things. The early French explorers named the Western District region Terre Napoleon in his honour, and the Empress Josephine followed Napoleon's interest in Australian flora and fauna, keeping kangaroos and emus at her home outside Paris in the early 1800s. Moreover, it was French settlers who planted vines near Lake Colac in the mid-1800s, only to see them destroyed by phylloxera 30 years later. Allistair Lindsay is hoping to lead a revival of plantings in the region, and has named his vineyard after Josephine. He has planted 1 hectare each of pinot noir, cabernet sauvignon and merlot, and 0.8 of chardonnay, supplemented by semillon, sauvignon blanc and chardonnay purchased from Geelong vineyards until the home plantings come into full production. The wines are very competently contract-made at Scotchmans Hill. The restaurant is open for lunch Thursday to Sunday and dinner Saturday evening.

Empress Vineyard Semillon Sauvignon Blanc

▼▼▼▼▽ **2001** Light to medium yellow-green; a firm, clear bouquet of grass, citrus and mineral is followed by a light to medium-bodied palate with lively lemony flavours, good mouthfeel and length. **rating:** 90

best drinking Now **best vintages** '01 **drink with** Deep-fried calamari • $18

Empress Vineyard Chardonnay

▼▼▼▼▽ **2000** Medium yellow-green; the bouquet is clean, still fresh, with melon/citrus fruit and perfectly integrated oak; the palate is stylish and elegant, showing the barrel-ferment and malolactic-ferment inputs, but retaining its varietal fruit. **rating:** 93

best drinking Now–2006 **best vintages** '00 **drink with** Mild-fed veal • $22

Empress Vineyard Irrewarra Pinot Noir

▼▼▼▼ **2001** Light to medium red-purple; the bouquet contrasts savoury/foresty aromas with delicate strawberry/small berry fruit, the light to medium-bodied palate following along similar lines, but with the savoury elements outweighing the sweet fruit. Drink sooner rather than later. **rating:** 88

best drinking Now **drink with** Veal kidneys • $20

Empress Vineyard Irrewarra Cabernet Merlot

▼▼▼▼ **2001** Medium red-purple; the bouquet offers a subtle mix of black olive, blackcurrant and earth; the primary fruit on the medium-bodied palate is still to soften, but is clearly articulated, adding hints of herb and chocolate. Subtle oak. **rating:** 89

best drinking 2006–2011 **drink with** Loin of lamb • $30

england's creek   NR

PO Box 6, Murrumbateman, NSW 2582 **region** Canberra District
phone (02) 6227 5550 **fax** (02) 6226 8898 **open** At Barrique Cafe, Murrumbateman Thurs–Sun
winemaker Ken Helm (Contract) **production** 250 cases **est.** 1995
product range ($17–20 ML) Riesling, Hand Picked Riesling, Shiraz, Hand Picked Shiraz.
summary The diminutive England's Creek was established in 1995 by Stephen Carney and Virginia Rawling with the planting of 1 hectare each of riesling and shiraz, subsequently doubling the size of each. The wines are available at selected Canberra restaurants and Vintage Cellars, Manuka or by contacting the winery on phone or fax.

ensay winery   NR

Great Alpine Road, Ensay, Vic 3895 **region** Gippsland
phone (03) 5157 3203 **fax** (03) 5157 3372 **open** Weekends, public and school holidays 11–5, or by appointment
winemaker David Coy **production** 1500 cases **est.** 1992
product range ($17–20 R) Chardonnay, Pinot Noir, Shiraz, Cabernet Sauvignon.
summary A weekend and holiday business for the Coy family, headed by David Coy, with 2.5 hectares of chardonnay, pinot noir, merlot, shiraz and cabernet sauvignon.

epis/epis & williams   ★★★★

Lot 16 Calder Highway, Woodend, Vic 3442 **region** Macedon Ranges
phone (03) 5427 1204 **fax** (03) 5427 1204 **open** By appointment
winemaker Stuart Anderson **production** 850 cases **est.** 1990
product range ($35–40 R) Epis Chardonnay, Pinot Noir; Epis & Williams Cabernet Sauvignon.

summary Three legends are involved in the Epis and Epis & Williams wines, two of them in their own lifetime. They are long-term Essendon guru and former player, Alec Epis, who owns the two quite separate vineyards and brands; Stuart Anderson, who makes the wines, with Alec Epis doing all the hard work; and the late Laurie Williams, the father of viticulture in the Macedon region and who established the Flynn & Williams vineyard in 1976. Alec Epis purchased that vineyard from Laurie Williams in 1999, and as a mark of respect (and with Laurie Williams' approval) continued to use his name in conjunction with that of Alec Epis. The cabernet sauvignon comes from this vineyard, the chardonnay and pinot noir from the vineyard at Woodend, where a small winery was completed prior to the 2002 vintage.

Epis Macedon Ranges Chardonnay
TTTT 2001 Medium yellow-straw, slightly ominous; complex mineral and malolactic-ferment aromas are followed by a tight palate with good length; obvious acidity helps, the barrel-ferment oak inputs under good control. **rating:** 89
best drinking Now–2007 **best vintages** '00 **drink with** Pan-fried veal • $35

Epis Macedon Ranges Pinot Noir
TTTTY 2001 Medium purple-red; the powerful dark plum and spice bouquet has swallowed up the oak; the palate is a replay, still largely in its primary phase; has all the requisites for development. **rating:** 93
best drinking Now–2007 **best vintages** '00, '01 **drink with** Smoked breast of duck • $40

Epis & Williams Cabernet Sauvignon
TTTT 2001 Medium to full red-purple; blackcurrant, leaf, mint and olive aromas lead into an exceedingly firm and taught palate; will need much time to soften, and the acidity will always be evident. **rating:** 88
best drinking 2005–2011 **best vintages** '00 **drink with** Leg of lamb • $35

eppalock ridge   NR
633 North Redesdale Road, Redesdale, Vic 3444 **region** Heathcote
phone (03) 5443 7841 **open** By appointment
winemaker Rod Hourigan **production** 1500 cases **est.** 1979
product range ($33 ML) Shiraz, Cabernet Merlot.
summary A low-key operation now focusing mainly on Shiraz produced from the 4 hectares of this variety, the other wine in the portfolio comes from the 2.7 hectares of cabernet sauvignon, merlot and cabernet franc. Exports to the US and New Zealand.

Eppalock Ridge Shiraz
TTTT 2000 Medium red-purple; the moderately intense bouquet has a mix of raspberry and plum aromas, moving to raspberry and chocolate on the palate; a trace of bitterness on the finish takes the edge off what is otherwise a very good wine. **rating:** 86
best drinking 2004–2009 **drink with** Light red meat dishes • $33

ermes estate   NR
2 Godings Road, Moorooduc, Vic 3933 **region** Mornington Peninsula
phone (03) 5978 8376 **fax** (03) 5978 8396 **open** Weekends and public holidays 11–5
winemaker Ermes Zucchet, Denise Zucchet **production** 700 cases **est.** 1989
product range ($10–20 CD) Riesling, Chardonnay, Pinot Grigio, Merlot, Cabernet Sauvignon.
summary Ermes and Denise Zucchet commenced planting of the 2.5-hectare estate in 1989 with chardonnay, riesling, cabernet sauvignon and merlot, adding pinot gris in 1991. In 1994 an existing piggery on the property was converted to a winery and cellar-door area (in the Zucchets' words, 'the pigs having been evicted'), and the modestly priced wines are on sale during the weekends. No recent tastings.

ese vineyards   ★★★★
1013 Tea Tree Road, Tea Tree, Tas 7017 **region** Southern Tasmania
phone 0417 319 875 **fax** (03) 6272 5398 **open** 7 days 10–5
winemaker Julian Alcorso (Contract) **production** 2600 cases **est.** 1994
product range ($24.50 CD) Chardonnay, Pinot Noir.
summary Elvio and Natalie Brianese are an architect and graphic designer couple whose extended family have centuries-old viticultural roots in the Veneto region of northern Italy. Ese has 2.5 hectares of vineyard and got off to a flying start with a gold and silver medal for its 1997 Pinot Noir. Subsequent vintages have been less exhilarating, but there is no question the potential is there, and there are plans to eventually double the size of the vineyard.

ese Vineyards Pinot Noir
▼▼▼▼▽ **2001** Full red-purple; a rich and complex bouquet, with dark plum, spice and a hint of forest; the powerful palate has rich, dark plum fruit with a strong savoury underground. Good length and balance; significantly better than the 2000 vintage for ese. **rating:** 90
best drinking Now–2006 **best vintages** '97, '01 **drink with** Rabbit casserole • $22

etain ★★★☆

Boodjidup Road, Margaret River, WA 6285 **region** Margaret River
phone 0407 445 570 **open** Not
winemaker Conor Lagan, Jurg Muggli **production** 5000 cases **est.** 2001
product range ($16–25 R) Riesling, Semillon Sauvignon Blanc, Merlot, Cabernet Merlot.
summary Etain is a private label of Conor Lagan, available only to trade through distributor Prime Wines. In Gaelic mythology Etain is the horse goddess, representing birth and rebirth. It is in turn linked to the fascinating story of Conor Lagan's life, which can be found on www.etainwines.com. The wines are sourced from vineyards in the Margaret and Frankland River regions.

Etain Frankland River Riesling
▼▼▼▼ **2001** Very light straw-green; the bouquet is firm and crisp, the fruit as yet subdued, and mineral notes dominate; there is more flavour on the palate with quite crunchy apple and nashi pear flavours. **rating:** 89
best drinking Now–2007 **drink with** Cold seafood • $19

Etain Margaret River Semillon Sauvignon Blanc
▼▼▼▼ **2001** Light to medium green-yellow; a pungent mix of grass, herbs and melon with a faintly reduced/smoky background. A truly interesting wine on the palate, with up-and-down flavours and mouthfeel. **rating:** 88
best drinking Now **drink with** Marron, yabbies • $19

Etain Margaret River Cabernet Merlot
▼▼▼▼ **2000** Bright red-purple; the bouquet is clean, with some cedary/savoury aspects to the fruit, but on the palate sweet fruit makes the play, with luscious berry and spice flavours and fine tannins. **rating:** 88
best drinking Now–2008 **drink with** Rack of lamb • $25

eumundi winery NR

2 Bruce Highway, Eumundi, Qld 4562 **region** Queensland Coastal
phone (07) 5442 7444 **fax** (07) 5442 7455 **open** 7 days 10–6
winemaker Andrew Hickinbotham (Contract) **production** 2500 cases **est.** 1996
product range ($12–15 R) Semillon Chardonnay, Taminga, Shiraz, Shiraz Cabernet, Shiraz Durif, Merlot, Chambourcin, Cabernet Sauvignon.
summary Eumundi Vineyard is set on 21 hectares of riverfront land in the beautiful Eumundi Valley, 12 kilometres inland from Noosa Heads. The climate is hot, wet, humid and maritime, the only saving grace being the regular afternoon northeast sea breeze. It is a challenging environment in which to grow grapes, and over 5 years the owners, Robyn and Gerry Humphrey, have trialled 14 different grape varieties and three different trellis systems. Currently they have tempranillo, shiraz, chambourcin, petit verdot, durif and mourvedre, and verdelho. Plantings in 2001 included tannat and others, which gives some idea of their eclectic approach. The establishment of the vineyard was financed by the sale of a 19-metre charter yacht which used to sail the oceans around northern Australia. Quite a change in lifestyle for the Humphreys.

evans & tate ★★★★

Metricup Road, Wilyabrup, WA 6280 **region** Margaret River
phone (08) 9755 6244 **fax** (08) 9755 6346 **open** 7 days 10.30–5
winemaker Steve Warne **production** 280 000 cases **est.** 1970
product range ($12–50 CD) Gnangara range of Sauvignon Blanc, Chenin Blanc, Unwooded Chardonnay, Shiraz, Cabernet Sauvignon; the Margaret River range of Margaret River Classic, Semillon, Sauvignon Blanc Semillon, Verdelho, Chardonnay, Cane Cut Semillon, Shiraz, Classic Shiraz Cabernet Merlot, Merlot, Cabernet Merlot; Redbrook Chardonnay, Cabernet Sauvignon.
summary From its Swan Valley base 30 years ago, Evans & Tate has grown to the point where it is the largest Margaret River winery and producer, with an uninterrupted pattern of growth. Having multiplied its estate vineyard holdings with the establishment of a large planting in the Jindong subregion, it raised substantial

capital by going public, successfully listing on the Stock Exchange. It then turned its attention eastwards, with the acquisition of Oakridge Estate in the Yarra Valley. Wine quality is always polished, and, within the Margaret River context, at the lighter end of the spectrum. National distribution and exports to all major wine markets.

Evans & Tate Margaret River Semillon

♥♥♥♥♥ **2001** Light straw-green; a striking wine, a highly aromatic and lifted bouquet followed by an intense and long palate with ripe, fresh fruit and very well handled oak. A return to form for a wine with a long pedigree. Gold medal 2002 Qantas Wine Show of Western Australia. **rating: 94**

best drinking Now–2006 **best vintages** '91, '92, '93, '94, '95, '00, '01 **drink with** Marron, yabbies • $18.99

Evans & Tate Margaret River Classic White

♥♥♥♥ **2002** Light straw-green; potent herb, grass and mineral aromas are reflected in the intense flavours of the palate; good length and persistence. A blend of Semillon and Sauvignon Blanc once again now entirely sourced from Margaret River. Impressive. **rating: 89**

best drinking Now–2005 **best vintages** '02 **drink with** Asian seafood • $17.99

Evans & Tate Margaret River Chardonnay

♥♥♥♥ **2002** Very pale; light citrus/peach fruit and some oak spice on the bouquet leads into a palate which is notably lacking in weight, albeit well made. Seems to be conforming to the style and perhaps the price. **rating: 85**

best drinking Now–2005 **drink with** Sugar-cured tuna • $20

Evans & Tate Redbrook Chardonnay

♥♥♥♥ **2000** Light to medium yellow-green; spicy barrel-ferment aromas pop up first, with melon fruit next on the bouquet. The clean, fresh, light to medium-bodied palate has a mix of melon, stone fruit and citrus, the oak less obvious. A good wine, but fully priced. **rating: 89**

best drinking Now–2007 **best vintages** '95, '96, '97, '00 **drink with** Marron or lobster • $40

Evans & Tate Margaret River Shiraz

♥♥♥♥♥ **2001** Strong colour; spice, black cherry and licorice aromas lead into a spicy, cedary medium-bodied palate, with considerable elegance; there is just a passing question on the amount of oak. **rating: 94**

best drinking 2006–2012 **best vintages** '86, '88, '90, '91, '92, '93, '95, '96, '00, '01 **drink with** Strong red meat dishes • $19.99

Evans & Tate Margaret River Merlot

♥♥♥♥♡ **1999** Medium to full red-purple; a solid, rich and quite complex bouquet with small red and blackberry fruit leads into a very powerful, strongly varietal wine which will repay extended cellaring. **rating: 91**

best drinking 2005–2015 **best vintages** '98, '99 **drink with** Osso buco • $40

evans family wines ★★★★☆

151 Palmers Lane, Pokolbin, NSW 2321 **region** Lower Hunter Valley
phone (02) 4998 7333 **fax** (02) 4998 7798 **open** 7 days 10–5
winemaker Nick Paterson (Contract) **production** 3500 cases **est.** 1979
product range ($11.50–24.50 CD) Semillon, Gamy, Pinot Noir, Shiraz; Lounge Lizard Sweet White, Rose, Lazy Red and Shiraz.
summary In the wake of the acquisition of Rothbury by Mildara Blass, Len Evans' wine interests now focus on Evans Family (estate-grown and produced from vineyards around the family home), the Evans Wine Company (a quite different, part-maker, part-negociant business) and, most recently, Tower Estate. Len Evans continues to persist with the notion that the Hunter Valley can produce Gamay and Pinot Noir of quality and, irritatingly, occasionally produces evidence to suggest he may be half right. There is, of course, no such reservation with the Semillon, the Chardonnay or the Shiraz. Exports to the US and the UK.

evelyn county estate ★★★★

55 Eltham-Yarra Glen Road, Kangaroo Ground, Vic 3097 **region** Yarra Valley
phone (03) 9437 2155 **fax** (03) 9437 2188 **open** Mon–Fri 9–5, weekends 8–6
winemaker James Lance, David Lance (Contract) **production** 2000 cases **est.** 1994
product range ($19–30 CD) Black Paddock range of Sauvignon Blanc, Chardonnay, Sticky, Pinot Noir, Merlot, Cabernet Sauvignon.

summary The 8-hectare Evelyn County Estate has been established by former Coopers & Lybrand managing partner Roger Male and his wife Robyn, who has completed a degree in Applied Science (Wine Science) at Charles Sturt University. David and James Lance (of Diamond Valley) are currently making the wines, and an architect-designed cellar-door sales, gallery and restaurant opened in April 2001. As one would expect, the quality of the wines is very good. A small planting of tempranillo will bear its first crop in 2004 and the wine will be made on-site by Robyn Male.

Evelyn County Estate Black Paddock Sauvignon Blanc
TTTT 2002 Light green-yellow; a clean, light, tight, minerally bouquet is followed by a crisp and tight palate, once again showing mineral characters, the fruit suppressed. Given the vintage, one can only assume the wine will burst free over the next year or so, and make the points look parsimonious. **rating:** 85
best drinking Now–2005 **best vintages** '01 **drink with** White-fleshed fish • $20

Evelyn County Estate Black Paddock Chardonnay
TTTTY 2001 Bright, light green-yellow; clean and fresh melon, nectarine and citrus fruit drives both the bouquet and the light to medium-bodied palate. The oak is subtle and well-integrated, the palate well balanced and long. **rating:** 91
best drinking Now–2006 **best vintages** '00, '01 **drink with** Yarra Valley trout • $25

Evelyn County Estate Black Paddock Sticky Botrytised Chardonnay 375 ml
TTTT 2001 Glowing yellow-green; a highly aromatic, tropical fruit salad and guava bouquet leads into a palate with moderate sweetness around that expected from a Spatlese; nicely balanced easy drinking style. **rating:** 88
best drinking Now–2005 **drink with** Poached pears • $26

Evelyn County Estate Black Paddock Pinot Noir
TTTTY 2001 Bright purple-red, amazing hue for a 2001 Pinot 2 years old when tasted; the aromatic and complex bouquet ranges through plum, spice, oak and shoe leather; the equally complex palate has forest, leather and spice overtones to the fruit. **rating:** 92
best drinking Now–2006 **drink with** Braised duck • $28

Evelyn County Estate Black Paddock Merlot
TTTTY 2001 Bright purple-red; ripe, sweet raspberry and redcurrant fruit is supported by subtle oak on the bouquet; the palate likewise has plenty of sweet fruit plus fine, sustained tannins; good oak handling and good length. **rating:** 90
best drinking 2004–2009 **best vintages** '99, '01 **drink with** Yearling steak • $30

Evelyn County Estate Black Paddock Cabernet Sauvignon
TTTT 2001 Medium red-purple; a fragrant bouquet of cassis, blackberry and subtle oak loses its way somewhat on the berry, mint and leaf palate, with a droopy finish. **rating:** 86
best drinking 2004–2007 **drink with** Roast veal • $28

excelsior peak   NR

PO Box 269, Tumbarumba, NSW 2653 **region** Tumbarumba
phone (02) 6948 5102 **fax** (02) 6948 5102 **open** Not
winemaker Contract **production** 700 cases **est.** 1980
product range ($18–22 ML) Chardonnay, Pinot Noir, Methode Champenoise.
summary Excelsior Peak proprietor Juliet Cullen established the first vineyard in Tumbarumba in 1980. That vineyard was thereafter sold to Southcorp, and Juliet Cullen subsequently established another vineyard, now releasing wines under the Excelsior Peak label. Plantings total over 10 hectares, with most of the grapes sold. Sales only by mail order.

faber vineyard   ★★★★

233 Hadrill Road, Baskerville, WA 6056 (postal) **region** Swan Valley
phone (08) 9296 0619 **fax** (08) 9296 0681 **open** Not
winemaker John Griffiths **production** 1000 cases **est.** 1997
product range ($12–35 ML) Verdelho, Chardonnay, Riche Shiraz, Shiraz, Reserve Shiraz, Shiraz Cabernet.
summary Former Houghton winemaker and now university lecturer and consultant John Griffiths has teamed with his wife Jane Micallef to found Faber Vineyard. Since 1997 they have established 1 hectare of shiraz, and

0.5 hectare each of chardonnay, verdelho, cabernet sauvignon, petit verdot and brown muscat. Says John Griffiths 'It may be somewhat quixotic, but I'm a great fan of traditional warm area Australia wine styles – those found in areas such as Rutherglen and the Barossa. Wines made in a relatively simple manner that reflect the concentrated ripe flavours one expects in these regions. And when one searches, some of these gems can be found from the Swan Valley.' Possessed of an excellent palate, and with an impeccable winemaking background, the quality of John Griffiths' wines is guaranteed.

Faber Vineyard Reserve Shiraz

▼▼▼▼▽ **2001** Dense, impenetrable purple; intense, deep plum, prune, chocolate and vanilla aromas lead into a massively powerful and complex palate, with great fruit depth and even more tannins. This needs more than a decade to show at its best.   **rating:** 93

best drinking 2011–2021 **drink with** Leave it in the cellar • $35

Faber Vineyard Riche Shiraz

▼▼▼▼ **2002** Impenetrable purple; complex, rich dark plum, prune and vanilla aromas are followed by a powerful palate with savoury overtones to the plum and black cherry fruit, the tannins certainly present but not aggressive. Despite all this, you have the slight feeling there is not quite enough flesh on the frame, but the price is certainly right.   **rating:** 88

best drinking 2005–2010 **best vintages** '01 **drink with** Beef pie • $16.50

Faber Vineyard Shiraz Cabernet

▼▼▼▽ **2002** Medium purple-red; the clean, firm, direct bouquet with red and black fruit aromas is basically repeated on the palate. A no-frills wine, but very well priced.   **rating:** 84

best drinking 2004–2007 **drink with** Takeaway • $12

fairview wines   ★★★★

422 Elderslie Road, Branxton, NSW 2335 **region** Lower Hunter Valley
phone (02) 4938 1116 **fax** (02) 4938 1116 **open** Weekends 10–5, or by appointment
winemaker Rhys Eather (Contract) **production** 1200 cases **est.** 1997
product range ($16–30 CD) Semillon, Verdelho, Saignée, Shiraz.
summary Greg and Elaine Searles purchased the property on which they have established Fairview Wines in 1997. For the previous 90 years it had sustained an orchard, but since that time 2 hectares of shiraz, 1 hectare of each of barbera, semillon and 0.5 hectare of chambourcin and verdelho have been established, using organic procedures wherever possible. The Searles operate the cellar door in person; retail distribution in Sydney and exports to the UK have also been established.

Fairview Semillon

▼▼▼▼▽ **2002** Light straw-green; the clean, restrained bouquet has hints of herb and lemon, the tangy palate with lemony citrus fruit, even flow, and good length. All it needs is time.   **rating:** 90

best drinking 2005–2012 **best vintages** '02 **drink with** Leave it in the cellar • $18

Fairview Shiraz

▼▼▼▼▼ **2001** Medium red-purple; the bouquet has perfectly balanced fruit and oak, the integration of that oak being equally impressive. The palate oozes blackberry and dark plum fruit with lovely satiny tannins woven through the fruit; exemplary structure, balance and length. Gold and trophy, Hunter Valley Wine Show 2002.   **rating:** 95

best drinking 2006–2016 **best vintages** '01 **drink with** Fillet of beef • $30

faisan estate   NR

Amaroo Road, Borenore, NSW 2800 **region** Orange
phone (02) 6365 2380 **open** Not
winemaker Col Walker **production** 500 cases **est.** 1992
product range Semillon, Chardonnay, Canobolas Classic White, Pinot Noir, Britton's Block Cabernet Sauvignon, Cabernet Sauvignon.
summary Faisan Estate, within sight of Mount Canobolas and 20 kilometres west of the city of Orange, has been established by Trish and Col Walker. They now have almost 10 hectares of vineyards coming into bearing and have purchased grapes from other growers in the region in the interim. No recent tastings.

 falls wines ★★★

Belubula Way, Canowindra, NSW 2804 **region** Cowra
phone (02) 6344 1293 **fax** (02) 6344 1290 **open** 7 days 10–4
winemaker Jon Reynolds (Contract) **production** 3200 cases **est.** 1997
product range ($14–22 CD) Classic Semillon, Fields of Gold Chardonnay, Squatter's Ghost Shiraz, Cabernet Merlot.
summary Peter and Zoe Kennedy have established Falls Vineyard and Retreat (to give it its full name) on the outskirts of Canowindra. They have planted chardonnay, semillon, merlot, cabernet sauvignon and shiraz, with luxury B&B accommodation retreat offering large, internal spa baths, exercise facilities, and a tennis court.

Falls Fields of Gold Chardonnay

▼▼▼▼ **2000** Light green-yellow; a clean, remarkably fresh bouquet with light nectarine and melon fruit is replayed on the palate, which has good length. Any oak used is incidental to the main action.   **rating:** 86
best drinking Now **drink with** Terrine of trout • $16

farmer's daughter wines ★★★☆

791 Cassilis Road, Mudgee, NSW 2850 **region** Mudgee
phone (02) 6373 3177 **fax** (02) 6373 3759 **open** 7 days 9–5
winemaker Joe Lesnik **production** 5000 cases **est.** 1995
product range ($17–22 CD) Reserve Semillon, Chardonnay, Shiraz, Merlot, Cabernet Sauvignon.
summary The intriguingly named Farmer's Daughter Wines is a family-owned vineyard, run by the daughters of a feed-lot farmer, with contract winemaking by Joe Lesnik. Much of the production from the substantial vineyard of 23 hectares, dominated by shiraz with 13 hectares, the rest taken up with chardonnay, merlot and cabernet sauvignon (3 ha each), and semillon (1 ha) is sold to other winemakers. However, a sufficient amount to produce 5000 cases is retained and contract-made. As well as local retail distribution (and 7-day cellar-door sales) the wines are available through Porters liquor outlets in Sydney. The first two vintages had outstanding (though somewhat controversial) show success.

Farmer's Daughter Chardonnay

▼▼▼▼ **2001** Light, bright yellow-green; clean, lively melon, peach and nectarine aromas lead into a subtle, understated palate, with good length and oak held in neat restraint.   **rating:** 88
best drinking Now–2005 **drink with** Mussels in creamy sauce • $17

Farmer's Daughter Shiraz

▼▼▼▼ **2000** Medium red-purple; a moderately complex bouquet with a mix of spicy/earthy secondary aromas is followed by a light to medium-bodied palate, with flavours all in a savoury spectrum; some tannins extend the finish.   **rating:** 85
best drinking 2004–2008 **best vintages** '99 **drink with** Shoulder of lamb • $22

 farosa estate NR

1157 Port Wakefield Road, Waterloo Corner, SA 5110 (postal) **region** Adelaide Plains
phone 0412 674 655 **fax** (08) 8280 6450 **open** Not
winemaker Frank Perre (Contract) **est.** 2000
product range Shiraz.
summary The family-owned Farosa Estate has 11 hectares of shiraz and 3.6 hectares of mourvedre (mataro) in production. The aim is to produce a full-bodied wine with the least amount of preservatives as possible, with open fermentation and oak maturation varying between 10 and 18 months. The first release of Farosa Estate Shiraz was in 2003, and the price has not yet been finally determined. To date, contract winemaking has taken place in the Barossa Valley, but the family is contemplating building its own winery.

Farosa Estate Shiraz

▼▼▼▼▽ **2002** Dense, youthful purple; clean, rich and ripe blackberry, prune and plum aromas, with some oak, are faithfully reflected in the rich, ripe, succulent and dense palate. A little more barrel work would have generated even higher points.   **rating:** 90
best drinking 2007–2012 **drink with** Beef casserole

farrell's limestone creek   NR

Mount View Road, Mount View, NSW 2325 **region** Lower Hunter Valley
phone (02) 4991 2808 **fax** (02) 4991 3414 **open** 7 days 10–5
winemaker Neil McGuigan (Contract) **production** 3500 cases **est.** 1980
product range Semillon, Chardonnay, Shiraz, Merlot, Cabernet Sauvignon Merlot.
summary The Farrell family purchased 20 hectares on Mount View in 1980 and gradually established 7.3 hectares of vineyards planted to semillon, verdelho, chardonnay, shiraz, cabernet sauvignon and merlot. Most of the grapes are sold to McWilliam's, a lesser amount made for cellar door and mail list orders. No recent tastings.

farr rising   ★★★★☆

27 Maddens Road, Bannockburn, Vic 3331 (postal) **region** Geelong
phone (03) 5281 1979 **fax** (03) 5281 1979 **open** Not
winemaker Nicholas Farr **production** 1000 cases **est.** 2001
product range ($22–33 R) Chardonnay, Saignée, Geelong Pinot Noir, Mornington Pinot Noir, Merlot.
summary Nicholas Farr is the son of Gary Farr, and with the full encouragement of his father, has launched his own brand. He has learnt his winemaking both in France and Australia, and has access to some excellent base material, so much can be expected.

Farr Rising Chardonnay
▼▼▼▼▽ **2001** Light to medium yellow-green; subtle but complex barrel-ferment French oak girdle tight nectarine fruit on the bouquet; the palate is similarly tightly knit, with hints of mineral, and still very youthful; should age with elegance in the French mode.   **rating:** 91
best drinking 2004–2010 **best vintages** '01 **drink with** Sushi • $32.99

Farr Rising Saignée
▼▼▼▼ **2001** Very light salmon; the clean bouquet has some earthy notes alongside red fruits, the fine, light palate with strawberry/lemony flavours.   **rating:** 86
best drinking Now **drink with** Gravlax • $21.99

Farr Rising Geelong Pinot Noir
▼▼▼▼▼ **2001** Excellent red-purple; a powerful, complex bouquet with dark plum and spice leads into a smooth but deep, round and mouthfilling palate; gobfuls (as one famous wine writer puts it) of dark plum and well-balanced oak.   **rating:** 94
best drinking 2004–2008 **best vintages** '01 **drink with** Squab • $32.99

Farr Rising Mornington Pinot Noir
▼▼▼▼▽ **2001** Medium red-purple, fractionally less deep than its Geelong sister; the bouquet is slightly more fragrant, with some savoury spice aromatics, then a palate with dark cherry and plum; quite different mouthfeel and structure.   **rating:** 92
best drinking Now–2007 **best vintages** '01 **drink with** Coq au vin • $32.99

felsberg winery   ★★★

Townsends Road, Glen Aplin, Qld 4381 **region** Granite Belt
phone (07) 4683 4332 **fax** (07) 4683 4377 **open** 7 days 9–5
winemaker Otto Haag **production** 2000 cases **est.** 1983
product range ($13–20 CD) Rhine Riesling, Traminer, Sylvaner, White Classic, Chardonnay, Shiraz, Merlot, Cabernet Shiraz, Cabernet Sauvignon, Mead, Ruby Mead.
summary Felsberg has a spectacular site, high on a rocky slope, the winery itself built on a single huge boulder. It has been offering wine for sale via the cellar door (and mail list) made by former master brewer Otto Haag for many years; the red wines are the winery strength.

Felsberg Shiraz
▼▼▼▽ **2001** Medium red-purple; the moderately intense bouquet is clean, with spicy, earthy overtones to the underlying red fruit; the light to medium-bodied palate does not have a great deal of depth to the fruit, but has been well made. A blend of 85 per cent Shiraz and 15 per cent Merlot.   **rating:** 84
best drinking 2004–2007 **drink with** Lasagne • $18

fenton views vineyard   NR

182 Fenton Hill Road, Clarkefield, Vic 3430 **region** Sunbury
phone (03) 5428 5429 **fax** (03) 5428 5304 **open** Weekends 11–5, or by appointment
winemaker David Spiteri **production** 500 cases **est.** 1994
product range ($16–20 R) Chardonnay, Pinot Noir, Shiraz.
summary Situated on the north-facing slopes of Fenton Hill at Clarkefield, just northeast of Sunbury, the Hume and Macedon Ranges providing a spectacular and tranquil setting. It is a small family operation, with plantings of shiraz and chardonnay, followed by pinot noir and cabernet sauvignon. Co-owner David Spiteri studied winemaking at Charles Sturt University, and has had vintage experience both in Australia and California.

ferguson falls estate   NR

Pile Road, Dardanup, WA 6236 **region** Geographe
phone (08) 9728 1083 **fax** (08) 9728 1616 **open** By appointment
winemaker Rob Bowen (Contract) **production** 1000 cases **est.** 1983
product range Chardonnay, Cabernet Sauvignon.
summary Peter Giumelli and family are dairy farmers in the lush Ferguson Valley, 180 kilometres south of Perth. In 1983 they planted 3 hectares of cabernet sauvignon, chardonnay and merlot, making their first wines for commercial release from the 1995 and 1996 vintages which confirmed the suitability of the region for the production of premium wine. No subsequent tastings.

fergusson   ★★★☆

Wills Road, Yarra Glen, Vic 3775 **region** Yarra Valley
phone (03) 5965 2237 **fax** (03) 5965 2405 **open** 7 days 11–5
winemaker Christopher Keyes, Peter Fergusson **production** 5000 cases **est.** 1968
product range ($16–30 CD) There are two basic ranges: the lower-priced Tartan Range sourced from grapes grown outside the Yarra Valley, with Chardonnay, Pinot Noir, Shiraz, Cabernet Sauvignon, Fine Old Tawny Port; and the Estate Range with Victoria Chardonnay, Victoria Reserve Chardonnay, Sparkling Pinot Noir Chardonnay, LJK Pinot Noir, Jeremy Shiraz, Benjamyn Cabernet Sauvignon.
summary One of the very first Yarra wineries to announce the rebirth of the Valley, now best known as a favoured tourist destination, particularly for tourist coaches, and offering hearty fare in comfortable surroundings accompanied by wines of both Yarra and non-Yarra Valley origin. For this reason the limited quantities of its estate wines are often ignored, but should not be. A promising 1999 Cabernet Sauvignon had not been bottled in February 2003, nor had the 2000 Chardonnay; both should reward if they make the transition safely. Exports to the UK and New Zealand.

Fergusson LJK Pinot Noir

TTTT 1999 Medium red-purple; the firm bouquet has earthy/foresty overtones to the black plum fruit, the palate springing no surprises, with a mix of dark plum, spice and a touch of game.   **rating:** 86
best drinking Now–2005 **drink with** Deep-fried quail • $30

fermoy estate   ★★★★

Metricup Road, Wilyabrup, WA 6280 **region** Margaret River
phone (08) 9755 6285 **fax** (08) 9755 6251 **open** 7 days 11–4.30
winemaker Michael Kelly **production** 20 000 cases **est.** 1985
product range ($17–45 CD) Semillon, Reserve Semillon, Sauvignon Blanc, Chardonnay, Merlot, Cabernet Sauvignon, Reserve Cabernet.
summary A long-established estate-based winery with 14 hectares of semillon, sauvignon blanc, chardonnay, cabernet sauvignon and merlot. A change of ownership several years ago seemed to coincide with a distinct shift in style – and improvement in – the wines, notwithstanding the continuation of Michael Kelly as winemaker. Exports to Singapore, Japan, The Netherlands, Switzerland and the UK.

Fermoy Estate Sauvignon Blanc

TTTT 2002 Water white, suggesting oxidative juice handling; the spotlessly clean bouquet has whispers of lemon and mineral, the palate opening light and crisp with a faint tropical background, then builds progressively through to the back palate and aftertaste.   **rating:** 88
best drinking Now **drink with** Sashimi

ferngrove vineyards estate ★★★★

Ferngrove Road, Frankland, WA 6396 **region** Great Southern
phone (08) 9855 2378 **fax** (08) 9855 2368 **open** 7 days 10–4
winemaker Kim Horton **production** 20 000 cases **est.** 1997
product range ($15–25 R) Cossack Riesling, Sauvignon Blanc, Semillon Sauvignon Blanc, Chardonnay, Shiraz, Dragon Shiraz, King Malbec, Merlot, Cabernet Merlot, Majestic Cabernet Sauvignon. Leaping Lizard is Ferngrove's second label.
summary After 90 years of family beef and dairy farming heritage, Murray Burton decided to venture into premium grape growing and winemaking in 1997. Since that time he has moved with exceptional speed, establishing 414 hectares of grapes on three vineyards in the Frankland River subregion, and a fourth at Mount Barker. The operation centres around the Ferngrove Vineyard, where a large rammed-earth winery and tourist complex was built in time for the 2000 vintage. Part of the vineyard production is sold as grapes; part sold as juice or must, part sold as finished wine; and part under the Ferngrove Vineyards own label. The 2002 Ferngrove Cossack Riesling is an outstanding wine, but all are well-made.

Ferngrove Vineyards Cossack Riesling

♥♥♥♥♥ 2002 Light green-yellow; a fragrant and diamond-clear bouquet of lime and mineral is followed by a fresh, fine, long palate, with the finesse and a Mosel-like delicacy to its limey fruit. Trophy for Best Wine of Show (and other trophies) at the 2002 Qantas Wine Show of Western Australia, and Best Wine of Show, Sydney Wine Show. **rating:** 96

best drinking Now–2010 **best vintages** '01 **drink with** Steamed crab • $19.99

Ferngrove Vineyards Sauvignon Blanc

♥♥♥♥ 2002 Light straw-green; the moderately intense bouquet is in a predominantly grassy/herbal spectrum, but the palate picks up weight, veering more towards medium-bodied, with a mix of grass and tropical fruit flavours. **rating:** 86

best drinking Now **drink with** Steamed fish • $17.99

Ferngrove Vineyards Shiraz

♥♥♥♥♡ 2001 Intense purple-red; the bouquet has abundant black fruits with a range of spice, briar, leather and licorice aromas; the very youthful palate has exceptional varietal fruit flavour, and will richly repay cellaring. Well priced into the bargain. **rating:** 90

best drinking 2005–2015 **best vintages** '01 **drink with** Braised duck • $17

Ferngrove Vineyards Merlot

♥♥♥♥ 2001 Youthful red-purple; the bouquet shows strong varietal character in a savoury/earthy/olive spectrum, the palate moving to riper, deeper fruit components on entry, then moving back to the characters of the bouquet towards the finish. An interesting wine. **rating:** 89

best drinking 2005–2011 **drink with** White Rocks veal • $17

fern gully winery NR

63 Princes Highway, Termeil, NSW 2539 **region** Shoalhaven Coast
phone (02) 4457 1124 **open** Weekends and holidays 11–5.30 (except Winter)
winemaker Max Staniford **production** 350 cases **est.** 1996
product range ($15–19 CD) Chardonnay, Shiraz, Chambourcin, Cabernet Sauvignon, Vintage Port.
summary Glenda and Max Staniford planted 0.25 hectare each of chardonnay, shiraz, cabernet sauvignon and chambourcin in the 1996 and 1997 planting seasons, producing the first grapes in 1998. The wines are all estate-grown (hence the limited production) and all of the winemaking takes place on-site. The vineyard is enclosed in permanent netting, and hand picking the grapes ensures the exclusion of diseased fruit. The wines have won a number of silver and bronze medals at (unspecified) shows.

fern hill estate ★★☆

Ingoldby Road, McLaren Flat, SA 5171 **region** McLaren Vale
phone (08) 8383 0167 **fax** (08) 8383 0107 **open** 7 days 10–5
winemaker Grant Burge (Contract) **production** 7000 cases **est.** 1975
product range ($15.95–19.95 CD) Semillon, Chardonnay, Brut, Shiraz, Cabernet Sauvignon.
summary One suspects there have been significant changes since Wayne Thomas sold Fern Hill to the Hill International Group, and not all for the better. Further changes will flow in the wake of Hill International's demise. Exports to the US, Brazil, the UK, Switzerland, Hong Kong, Japan, Fiji, Singapore and New Zealand.

fire gully ★★★★

Metricup Road, Wilyabrup, WA 6280 **region** Margaret River
phone (08) 9755 6220 **fax** (08) 9755 6308 **open** By appointment
winemaker Dr Michael Peterkin **production** 5000 cases **est.** 1988
product range ($19.80–39 R) Semillon, Sauvignon Blanc Semillon, Pinot Noir, Shiraz, Merlot, Cabernet Sauvignon Merlot, Cabernet Sauvignon.
summary The Fire Gully vineyard has been established on what was progressively a dairy and then a beef farm, with a 15-acre lake created in the gully ravaged by bushfires which gave the property its name, and which is stocked with marron; the vineyard was planted in 1988. In 1998 Mike Peterkin of Pierro purchased the property, and now manages the vineyard in conjunction with former owners Ellis and Margaret Butcher. He regards the Fire Gully wines as entirely separate to those of Pierro, being estate-grown, with just under 9 hectares planted to cabernet sauvignon, merlot, shiraz, semillon, sauvignon blanc, chardonnay and viognier. Exports to the US, Europe, Asia and Russia.

Fire Gully Semillon

▼▼▼▼▽ 2002 Light straw-green; a spotlessly clean and crisp bouquet with herbal fruit and the barest hint of oak is followed by a lively, fresh and appealing palate, with lemon bursting into stone fruit; good length and balance, the oak (from partial barrel ferment) mainly contributing to texture.   **rating:** 92
best drinking 2004–2009 **best vintages** '00, '01, '02 **drink with** Marinated baby octopus • $22.80

Fire Gully Sauvignon Blanc Semillon

▼▼▼▼▽ 2002 Light to medium green-yellow; a complex and intense array of aromas moving from herb, to gooseberry thence to peach logically introduces a rich, full-flavoured wine with abundant ripe fruit on the palate.   **rating:** 91
best drinking Now **best vintages** '00 **drink with** Grilled scampi • $19.80

Fire Gully Shiraz

▼▼▼▼ 2001 Youthful red-purple; the clean and fresh mix of cherry and raspberry fruit on the bouquet is followed by a decidedly brisk palate, not mouth-friendly as yet, but the sharp edges should round off with a little more bottle age.   **rating:** 87
best drinking 2004–2007 **drink with** Beef kebabs • $20.80

Fire Gully Cabernet Sauvignon Merlot

▼▼▼▼▼ 2001 Medium red-purple; a spotlessly clean bouquet has a cascade of sweet, small berry fruits and subtle oak; the palate has excellent balance, weight, structure and flavour, fine and supple, and a pleasure to taste even though its best years are in front of it.   **rating:** 94
best drinking 2005–2012 **best vintages** '01 **drink with** Yearling beef • $28.80

Fire Gully Cabernet Sauvignon

▼▼▼▼ 2000 Medium red-purple; the moderately intense bouquet has distinctly savoury/briary/earthy edges, characters which reappear on the palate, leavened by gentle touches of red berry fruit.   **rating:** 86
best drinking 2004–2008 **best vintages** '99 **drink with** Lamb shanks • $39

first creek wines ★★★★

Cnr McDonalds Road and Gillards Road, Pokolbin, NSW 2321 **region** Lower Hunter Valley
phone (02) 4998 7293 **fax** (02) 4998 7294 **open** 7 days 9.30–5
winemaker Greg Silkman **production** 25 000 cases **est.** 1984
product range ($15–20 CD) At the bottom of the range comes the Three Degrees Chardonnay, Verdelho, Shiraz and Cabernet Merlot, blends of various NSW regions. Next come the premium varietal range of Semillon, Verdelho, Chardonnay, Merlot and Shiraz which are single region wines; a limited range of single vineyard Allanmere wines will be released, and finally the Limited Release range of single vineyard wines with bottle age.
summary First Creek is the shop-front of Monarch Winemaking Services, which has acquired the former Allanmere wine business and offers a complex range of wines both under the First Creek and Allanmere labels. The quality is very reliable, although the wines are fully priced.

First Creek Semillon

▼▼▼▼ 2002 Pale straw-green; the clean, tight and correct bouquet has discreet herb and mineral aromas, the palate equally tight and restrained, with grass and citrus nuances peeping through. Absolutely demands time.   **rating:** 88
best drinking 2007–2012 **drink with** Leave it in the cellar • $17

First Creek Verdelho

TTTT 2002 Light straw-green; the clean and fresh bouquet brings touches of citrus to the mainstream fruit salad of the variety; the palate does not disappoint, with attractive, lively fruit salad flavours; a particularly good example of the variety. **rating:** 87

best drinking Now–2005 **drink with** Breast of turkey • $17

First Creek Chardonnay

TTTT 2001 Medium yellow-green; solid peachy fruit and obvious barrel-ferment oak on the bouquet is counterbalanced by a palate which is rather more elegant and tight than expected, but still presents a highly flavoured profile. **rating:** 87

best drinking Now **drink with** Avocado and smoked chicken • $20

First Creek Shiraz

TTTT 2000 Medium red-purple; the bouquet is in ultra-traditional Hunter Valley style, with leathery/earthy/savoury aromas, although much more blackberry and plum fruit come through on the mid-palate, before returning to the savoury characters of the bouquet on the finish. **rating:** 87

best drinking 2005–2012 **drink with** Braised rabbit • $25

First Creek Merlot

TTTTY 2001 Strong red-purple; the bouquet has a complex mix of savoury and dark berry fruits, but is clean, the oak subtle; a rich, ripe, but not jammy, palate has very good structure and oak handling. Pointed as a particularly good red wine, rather than a particularly good Merlot. **rating:** 91

best drinking 2005–2015 **best vintages** '01 **drink with** Braised oxtail • $25

5 corners wines ★★★☆

785 Henry Lawson Drive, Mudgee, NSW 2850 **region** Mudgee
phone (02) 6373 3745 **fax** (02) 6373 3749 **open** 7 days 9.30–5
winemaker Contract **est.** 2001
product range ($14–25 CD) Traminer, Sauvignon Blanc, Chardonnay, Shiraz.
summary 5 Corners Wines has come together in a hurry. Grant and Suzie Leonard came to Mudgee in 2001 for an overnight visit, and promptly fell in love with the region. So much so that they purchased a 40-hectare property with 5 hectares of established vineyard and a small cottage, which formed the basis for the venture. The property now includes the family's house (five children and six dogs come and go), the original cottage being occupied by the vineyard manager, and plantings having been increased by a further 3 hectares.

5 Corners Mudgee Sauvignon Blanc

TTTY 2002 Light to medium yellow-green; the bouquet is clean and fresh, with a nice touch of passionfruit, the light-bodied palate with an echo of the bouquet, and a minerally finish. Simply lacks intensity, but well made. **rating:** 83

best drinking Now **drink with** Cold seafood • $14

5 Corners Mudgee Chardonnay

TTTT 2002 Bright, light yellow-green; the clean, smooth, moderately intense bouquet matches melon fruit with gentle oak; the palate follows the same track, with pleasant flavour, a faint tangy cut, and good length. **rating:** 87

best drinking Now–2005 **drink with** Chinese prawns • $18

5 Corners Mudgee Shiraz

TTTT 2002 Exceptionally deep purple-red, almost opaque; deep blackberry, plum and chocolate fruit aromas all come through on the palate, which is flooded with fruit. The tannins are obvious but balanced; simply needs 10–20 years. **rating:** 89

best drinking 2010–2020 **drink with** Leave it in the cellar • $25

five oaks vineyard ★★★☆

60 Aitken Road, Seville, Vic 3139 **region** Yarra Valley
phone (03) 5964 3704 **fax** (03) 5964 3064 **open** Weekends and public holidays 10–5 and by appointment
winemaker Wally Zuk **production** 2000 cases **est.** 1997
product range ($19–45 CD) Riesling, Chardonnay, Merlot, Cabernet Sauvignon Merlot, Cabernet Sauvignon, SGS Cabernet Sauvignon.

summary Wally Zuk, together with wife Judy run all aspects of Five Oaks, far removed from Wally Zuk's background in nuclear physics. He has, however, completed his wine science degree at Charles Sturt University, and is thus more than qualified to make the Five Oaks wines.

Five Oaks Merlot

TTTT 2001 Medium red-purple; in vineyard style, the moderately intense bouquet is in the earthy, savoury, olive end of the spectrum, with a touch of mint joining in on the palate. Lingering tannins complete a wine with uncompromising, cool-grown varietal character. **rating: 86**

best drinking 2005–2009 **drink with** Braised veal • $26

Five Oaks Cabernet Merlot

TTTT 2001 Medium red, with a touch of purple; the clean, moderately intense bouquet has a mix of savoury briary mint and leaf aromas reminiscent of the Merlot, but more sweet blackcurrant fruit comes through on the light to medium-bodied palate, which has pleasing mouthfeel and smooth, ripe tannins. **rating: 88**

best drinking 2005–2010 **drink with** Steak and kidney pie • $25

572 richmond road ★★★★

572 Richmond Road, Cambridge, Tas 7170 (postal) **region** Southern Tasmania
phone 0419 878 023 **fax** (07) 3391 4565 **open** Not
winemaker Julian Alcorso (Contract) **production** 400 cases **est.** 1994
product range ($20–25 ML) Riesling, Gewurztraminer, Chardonnay, Pinot Noir.
summary It hardly need be said that 572 Richmond Road is both the address and the name of the vineyard. It is owned by John and Sue Carney, medical professionals, and is situated adjacent to Andrew Hood's winery, thus becoming part of a spectacular vineyard development with various ownerships but all situated close to the winery.

572 Richmond Road Riesling

TTTT 2002 Pale green-straw; a clean, fresh and delicate bouquet with lime, slate and mineral aromas; the palate is balanced, but then is unexpectedly somewhat short. Time may help, as it has with prior vintages. **rating: 87**

best drinking Now–2005 **drink with** Mussels • $20

572 Richmond Road Gewurztraminer

TTTT 2001 Straw-green; the bouquet is clean and fresh, with some lime aromas, the palate with good length and balance. There is both flavour and structure, but rather less distinctive varietal character. **rating: 87**

best drinking Now–2005 **best vintages** '00 **drink with** Chinese crystal prawns • $20

🐚 five sons estate NR

85 Harrison's Road, Dromana, Vic 3936 **region** Mornington Peninsula
phone (03) 5975 7121 **fax** (03) 5977 1759 **open** By appointment
winemaker Contract **production** 500 cases **est.** 1998
product range ($18–28 ML) The wines come in two ranges: the entry point is The Boyz Pinot Noir and Cabernet Shiraz, the premium wines under the Five Sons Estate label, the initial release being Pinot Noir.
summary Bob and Sue Peime purchased the most historically significant viticultural holding in the Mornington Peninsula in 1998. Development of the 68-hectare property began in the early 1930s, with the clearing of woodlands, and the planting of passionfruit. Then, in the 1940s it was sold to a member of the Seppelt family, who took out the passionfruit vines and planted riesling in 1948. Two years later the property was sold to the Broadhurst family, close relatives of Doug Seabrook, who persisted with growing and making riesling until a 1967 bushfire destroyed the vines. Since 1998 10 hectares of pinot noir, 5 hectares of chardonnay, 2.5 hectares of shiraz and 1.2 hectares each of pinot gris and cabernet sauvignon have been planted. The first vintage was made in 2001, and the size and scope of the business will grow rapidly as the vines come into full bearing.

Five Sons Estate The Boyz Cabernet Shiraz

TTTT 2001 Bright, light purple-red; leafy, spicy, earthy aromas lead into a fresh palate, where some oak sweetening helps the flavour balance; light bodied. **rating: 83**

best drinking Now–2005 **drink with** Ravioli • $18

flinders bay ★★★☆

Davis Road, Witchcliffe, WA 6286 **region** Margaret River
phone (08) 9757 6281 **fax** (08) 9757 6353 **open** Not
winemaker Contract **production** 15 000 cases **est.** 1995
product range ($15–20 R) Pericles Sauvignon Blanc Semillon, Dunsborough Hills Semillon Sauvignon Blanc, Verdelho, Chardonnay, Shiraz, Merlot, Merlot Cabernet Sauvignon, Agincourt Cabernet Malbec Merlot.
summary Flinders Bay is a joint venture between the Gillespie and Ireland families. The Gillespies have been grape growers and viticultural contractors in the Margaret River region for over 20 years, while Bill and Noel Ireland were very prominent retailers in Sydney from 1979 to 1996. All in all, a potent and synergistic combination. Fifty hectares of vines were planted between 1995 and 1998 at Karridale, an extremely cool subregion (possibly the coolest in Western Australia) with the climate influenced by both the Indian and Southern Oceans. The wines presently being produced are blends of grapes from the northern and central parts of the Margaret River with estate-grown grapes. Ultimately, all of the wines will be estate-produced. The white wines are contract-made at Vasse Felix, which also provides the cellar door facility for Flinders Bay. Exports to the UK and the US.

Flinders Bay Pericles Sauvignon Blanc Semillon

ŸŸŸŸ **2002** Light straw; the bouquet is somewhat subdued, the palate rather better with minerally flavours joined by citrus on the back palate, adding significantly to the length of the wine.　　　　**rating: 86**
best drinking Now **drink with** Margaret River marron • $18

Flinders Bay Dunsborough Hills Semillon Sauvignon Blanc

ŸŸŸŸ **2002** Light straw-green; the crisp, minerally bouquet is very typical of the 2002 vintage, with slightly suppressed fruit aromas; the lively, long lemon/mineral palate leaves the mouth fresh.　　　　**rating: 89**
best drinking Now **drink with** Fried oysters • $15

Flinders Bay Merlot

ŸŸŸŸ **2001** Deep red-purple; big fruit, lots of oak and quite gritty tannins all make for a wine which will utterly polarise opinion and, whatever else, is a very strange rendition of Merlot, however full of flavour and character it may be.　　　　**rating: 86**
best drinking 2005–2010 **drink with** Leave it in the cellar • $20

Flinders Bay Dunsborough Hills Merlot Cabernet Sauvignon

ŸŸŸŸ **2001** Medium red-purple; clean, youthful raspberry and redcurrant aromas show no hint of greenness; the similarly youthful but attractive palate has a mix of cassis and red berry fruit; minimal oak influence, and very good value. Possibly assisted by micro-oxygenation.　　　　**rating: 87**
best drinking Now–2008 **drink with** Milk-fed lamb • $15

🐚 flint wines　　NR

PO Box 8, Coonawarra, SA 5263 **region** Coonawarra
phone (08) 8736 5046 **fax** (08) 8736 5046 **open** Not
winemaker Bruce Gregory (Contract) **production** 700 cases **est.** 2000
product range Gammon Crossing Cabernet Sauvignon; Rostrevor Shiraz, Cabernet Sauvignon, Merlot.
summary Damian Flint and his family began the development of 21 hectares of cabernet sauvignon, shiraz and merlot in 1989, but it was not until 2000 that they decided to keep a small portion of cabernet sauvignon back and have it contract-made by Bruce Gregory at Majella, which is owned by their lifelong friends the Lynn brothers. Ten tonnes (around 700 cases) were vinified, and the wine had immediate show success in Melbourne; another 10 tonnes were diverted from the 2001 vintage, and the first wines are due for release in 2003.

fluted cape vineyard ★★★☆

28 Groombridge Road, Kettering, Tas 7155 **region** Southern Tasmania
phone (03) 6267 4262 **open** 7 days 10–5
winemaker Andrew Hood **production** 170 cases **est.** 1993
product range ($12–25 CD) Unwooded Chardonnay, Chardonnay, Pinot Noir.
summary For many years Val Dell was the senior wild life ranger on the central plateau of Tasmania, his wife Jan running the information centre at Liawenee. I met them there on trout fishing expeditions, staying in one of the park huts. They have now retired to the Huon Valley region, having established 0.25 hectare each of

pinot noir and chardonnay overlooking Kettering and Bruny Island, said to be a spectacularly beautiful site, which I wouldn't doubt. The high-quality wines are made for them by Andrew Hood and are sold from the cellar door, and through Hartzview Cellars in Gardners Bay. No recent tastings.

❦ flying fish cove ★★★★

Lot 125 Caves Road, Wilyabrup, WA 6284 (postal) **region** Margaret River
phone (08) 9755 6600 **fax** (08) 9755 6677 **open** Not
winemaker Mark Lane, Damon Eastaugh, Simon Burnell **est.** 2001
product range Semillon Sauvignon Blanc, Rose, Shiraz, Merlot, Cabernet Shiraz, Cabernet Sauvignon Merlot, Shareholders Reserve Cabernet Sauvignon.
summary Flying Fish Cove's major activity is that of a large contract winemaking facility for Margaret River (and other) vignerons. Given the rate of planting in the Margaret River, its services will be eagerly sought. Flying Fish Cove is also developing its own proprietary label, which will supplement the already significant sales of Buyers Own Brand products.

Flying Fish Cove Cabernet Sauvignon Merlot

♥♥♥♥♡ **2001** Full red-purple, deep but clear; rich, sweet blackcurrant/cassis fruit aromas are followed by a generous yet fine palate, with delicious fruit, subtle oak and fine tannins. **rating:** 92
best drinking 2005–2015 **best vintages** '01 **drink with** Yearling steak • $15.99

fonty's pool vineyards ★★★★

c/- Cape Mentelle Vineyards, PO Box 110, Margaret River, WA 6285 **region** Manjimup
phone (08) 9757 3266 **fax** (08) 9757 3233 **open** Not
winemaker Eloise Jarvis (Cape Mentelle) **production** 5000 cases **est.** 1998
product range ($20.75 R) Chardonnay, Pinot Noir, Shiraz.
summary The Fonty's Pool vineyards are part of the original farm owned by pioneer settler Archie Fontanini, who was granted land by the government in 1907. In the early 1920s a large dam was created to provide water for the intensive vegetable farming which was part of the farming activities. The dam became known as Fonty's Pool and to this day remains a famous local landmark and recreational facility. The first grapes were planted in 1989, and the vineyard is now one of the region's largest, supplying grapes to a number of leading West Australian wineries. Only a small part of the production is used for Fonty's Pool; the wines are made at Cape Mentelle by Eloise Jarvis, who is part of the Cape Mentelle winemaking team.

Fonty's Pool Chardonnay

♥♥♥♥♡ **2001** Light green-yellow; the bouquet is clean and crisp with direct citrus/stone fruit, the elegant, finely sculpted palate having good length and excellent finish. The best yet. **rating:** 91
best drinking 2004–2008 **best vintages** '01 **drink with** Oyster soup • $20.75

Fonty's Pool Pinot Noir

♥♥♥♥ **2001** Full red-purple; the bouquet has the nearly identical smoky bacon scent evident in the 2000, presumably coming from the oak; the medium-bodied palate has good structure and texture, with cherry/plum fruit and a savoury framework. Needs more intensity for higher points, but has been well made. **rating:** 86
best drinking Now–2005 **drink with** Coq au vin • $20.75

Fonty's Pool Shiraz

♥♥♥♥♡ **2001** Medium to full red-purple; the bouquet is clean, with abundant dark berry, licorice, plum and spice fruit, the oak playing a support role; the palate has very good texture and mouthfeel, following convincingly on from the 2000 vintage. Makes generalisations about Manjimup hazardous. **rating:** 92
best drinking 2005–2010 **best vintages** '00, '01 **drink with** Cassoulet • $20.75

forest hill vineyard ★★★★

Muirs Highway, Mt Barker, WA 6324 **region** Great Southern
phone (08) 9284 2825 **fax** (08) 9284 2835 **open** Not
winemaker Gordon Parker **production** 15 000 cases **est.** 1966
product range ($15–20 CD) Riesling, Sauvignon Blanc Semillon, Chardonnay, Shiraz, Cabernet Sauvignon.
summary This is one of the oldest 'new' winemaking operations in West Australia, and was the site for the first grape plantings for the Great Southern region in 1966 on a farming property owned by the Pearce family. The Forest Hill brand became well known, aided by the fact that a 1975 Riesling made by Sandalford from Forest

Hill grapes won nine trophies in national wine shows. In 1989 the property was acquired by Heytesbury Holdings (Janet Holmes à Court) as part of the Vasse Felix operation, and most of the grapes were used in the Vasse Felix wines. The only Forest Hill wines were a Riesling and a Cabernet Sauvignon, produced in small quantities and largely sold locally. In 1997 the property was acquired by interests associated with Perth stockbroker Tim Lyons, and a programme of renovation and expansion of the vineyards commenced. A new winery near Denmark was completed in time for the 2003 vintage.

fox creek wines ★★★★

Malpas Road, Willunga, SA 5172 **region** McLaren Vale
phone (08) 8556 2403 **fax** (08) 8556 2104 **open** 7 days 10–5
winemaker Daniel Hills, Tony Walker **production** 35 000 cases **est.** 1995
product range ($16–65 CD) Verdelho, Semillon Sauvignon Blanc, Sauvignon Blanc, Chardonnay, Vixen Sparkling Shiraz Cabernet Franc, Shadow's Run Shiraz Cabernet, Grenache Shiraz, Short Row Shiraz, Reserve Shiraz, Reserve Merlot, JSM Shiraz Cabernet Franc, Duet Cabernet Merlot, Reserve Cabernet Sauvignon.
summary Fox Creek has made a major impact since coming on-stream late in 1995. It is the venture of a group of distinguished Adelaide doctors (three of them professors), with particular input from the Watts family, which established the vineyard back in 1985. The Reserve red wines, and especially the Reserve Shiraz, are outstanding and have enjoyed considerable show success. As well as comprehensive distribution throughout Australia, the wines are exported to the UK, the US, Canada, Germany, Switzerland, Italy, France, New Zealand, Thailand and Hong Kong.

Fox Creek Reserve Shiraz

▼▼▼▼▼ 2001 Deep, bright purple-red; the smooth and luscious bouquet with blackberry and raspberry fruit supported by neatly judged oak is followed by a palate with excellent mouthfeel and balance; ripe blackberry and licorice flavours are accompanied by ripe tannins and more of the stylish oak of the bouquet. **rating:** 94

best drinking 2006–2016 **best vintages** '96, '98, '99, '01 **drink with** Grilled beef • $65

Fox Creek Short Row Shiraz

▼▼▼▼▽ 2001 Medium to full red-purple; the bouquet has rich, ripe blackberry/blackcurrant and chocolate fruit aromas supported by controlled oak. The powerful, complex, fruit-driven palate, with abundant ripe tannins, needs decades. **rating:** 91

best drinking 2008–2018 **best vintages** '01 **drink with** Beef spare ribs • $26

Fox Creek JSM

▼▼▼▼▽ 2001 Medium to full red-purple; solid, dark fruits and touches of dark chocolate and vanilla oak on the bouquet lead into a well-balanced, medium-bodied palate with sweet, chocolatey fruit and ripe tannins. Trophy and gold medal winner at the McLaren Vale Wine Show. **rating:** 90

best drinking 2005–2010 **best vintages** '99 **drink with** Rib of beef • $23

Fox Creek Reserve Merlot

▼▼▼▼ 2001 Medium red-purple; a solid bouquet with a mix of dark berry, earth and oak is followed by an ultra-powerful palate with the ubiquitous McLaren Vale chocolate and lashings of tannin; merlot on steroids. **rating:** 86

best drinking 2005–2010 **drink with** White Rocks veal • $36

Fox Creek Duet Cabernet Merlot

▼▼▼▼ 2001 Medium to full red-purple; complex dark berry/blackberry fruit leads the way, the round, smooth and supple palate continuing the trend of the last two vintages to better control of oak and tannins. **rating:** 89
best drinking 2005–2010 **drink with** Venison • $20

Fox Creek Reserve Cabernet Sauvignon

▼▼▼▼ 2001 Medium to full red-purple; ripe blackcurrant fruit floods the bouquet; the massive weight, extract and ripeness of the fruit on the palate does not work nearly as well as it does for the Shiraz. **rating:** 87

best drinking 2006–2016 **best vintages** '96, '97 **drink with** Game pie • $36

françois jacquard ★★★☆

14 Neil Street, Osborne Park, WA 6017 **region** Perth Hills
phone (08) 9380 9199 **fax** (08) 9380 9199 **open** Not
winemaker François Jacquard **production** 2000 cases **est.** 1997

product range ($17–42 R) Long Jetty Seafood Reserve Semillon Sauvignon Blanc; Terra Dura Millennium Collection Viognier, Reserve Collection Chardonnay, Millennium Collection Shiraz, De Beaux Vineyards Shiraz Viognier; Duyfken 1606 Replica Cabernet Sauvignon.

summary François (Franky) Jacquard graduated from Dijon University in 1983. He worked that vintage as a cellar hand at Domaine Dujac, then came to Australia for Bannockburn in 1985. Between then and 1992 he worked in both the northern and southern hemispheres, before moving back to become chief winemaker at Chittering Estate in the Perth Hills in 1992, a position he held until 1997 when he established his own brand. He does not have vineyards of his own, leasing one in the Chittering Valley, and having a long-term purchase arrangement with another. He now makes the wines at the new Sitella Winery in the Swan Valley. As Franky Jacquard himself recognises, the style of his wines is most definitely not mainstream Australian. He is much more interested in texture and longevity than primary fruit flavour, and is quite relaxed about a degree of controlled oxidation in his white wine making. The rating reflects previous extensive tastings.

frankland estate ★★★★

Frankland Road, Frankland, WA 6396 **region** Great Southern
phone (08) 9855 1544 **fax** (08) 9855 1549 **open** By appointment
winemaker Barrie Smith, Judi Cullam **production** 15 000 cases **est.** 1988
product range ($15–34.50 R) Under the Isolation Ridge label are Riesling, Chardonnay, Shiraz, Cabernet Sauvignon; Rivermist range of Riesling, Shiraz, Cabernets; Olmo's Reward (Bordeaux-blend) is the flagbearer; also Cooladerra Vineyard Riesling and Poison Hill Vineyard Riesling.

summary A significant Frankland River operation, situated on a large sheep property owned by Barrie Smith and Judi Cullam. The 29-hectare vineyard has been established progressively since 1988, and a winery was built on the site for the 1993 vintage. The recent introduction of an array of single vineyard Rieslings has been a highlight, and all the wines are energetically promoted and marketed by Judi Cullam, especially the Riesling. Frankland Estate has held several important International Riesling tastings and seminars over recent years. Exports to the US, Canada, the UK, Belgium, Switzerland, Denmark, Singapore and Japan.

Frankland Estate Cooladerra Vineyard Riesling

▼▼▼▼▽ **2002** Light straw-green; the intense bouquet has a faint whisper of reduction/slow ferment; the powerful, tightly knit palate has good length and aftertaste. **rating:** 90

best drinking Now–2008 **best vintages** '01, '02 **drink with** Asian seafood • $19

Frankland Estate Isolation Ridge Riesling

▼▼▼▼▼ **2002** Light straw-green; clean, mineral, lime and a hint of more tropical fruit on the bouquet leads into a palate with excellent balance and mouthfeel, line and length. **rating:** 94

best drinking 2005–2011 **best vintages** '92, '93, '94, '96, '98, '01, '02 **drink with** Antipasto • $22.50

Frankland Estate Poison Hill Vineyard Riesling

▼▼▼▼ **2002** Light straw-green; the bouquet is quite aromatic yet firm, with slate and hints of spice, but the palate heads off in a different direction, softer and shorter, without the length or intensity of the Isolation Ridge or Cooladerra wines. **rating:** 89

best drinking 2005–2010 **best vintages** '01 **drink with** Asian seafood • $19

Frankland Estate Rivermist Vineyard Riesling

▼▼▼▼ **2002** Light straw-green; lime, passionfruit and mineral aromas all make their appearance on the bouquet; the palate has unusual lime and nettle flavours, and finishes fractionally short, but very good value at the price. **rating:** 88

best drinking Now–2007 **drink with** Trout mousse • $15

Frankland Estate Isolation Ridge Chardonnay

▼▼▼▼ **2001** Medium yellow-green; the bouquet has complex, toasty, barrel-ferment oak to the fore; stone fruit, fig and peach flavours make their mark on entry to the mouth, the oak making a comeback on the finish. Less would have been better. **rating:** 87

best drinking Now–2006 **drink with** Fresh prawns • $21.50

Frankland Estate Rivermist Vineyard Shiraz

▼▼▼▼ **2001** Full, deep red-purple; the bouquet offers complex black fruits, spice, aniseed and a dash of gamey meat; the powerful and concentrated palate is somewhat derailed by persistent, drying tannins. There would appear to be exciting potential with this vineyard. **rating:** 86

best drinking 2004–2008 **drink with** Grilled calf's liver • $18

Frankland Estate Olmo's Reward

▼▼▼▼ **1999** Light to medium red-purple; the clean, savoury, earthy bouquet shows some old oak influence which slightly dulls the fruit; the complex, very savoury palate has spice, earth and lingering tannins, primary fruit playing little part in the shaping of the wine. A merlot-dominant blend. **rating: 88**

best drinking 2004–2009 **drink with** Veal chops • $34.50

Frankland Estate Rivermist Vineyard Cabernets

▼▼▼▼ **2001** Medium red-purple, bright and clear; the clean, moderately intense bouquet offers black and redcurrant fruit allied with a touch of earth. A powerful wine on the palate, with black fruits and dark chocolate, then persistent tannins needing to soften, but better balanced than the Shiraz. A blend of Cabernet Sauvignon, Merlot and Cabernet Franc. **rating: 88**

best drinking 2004–2010 **drink with** Lamb shanks • $18

freycinet ★★★★★

15919 Tasman Highway via Bicheno, Tas 7215 **region** Southern Tasmania
phone (03) 6257 8574 **fax** (03) 6257 8454 **open** 7 days 9.30–4.30
winemaker Claudio Radenti, Lindy Bull, Paula Kloosterman (Assistant) **production** 6000 cases **est.** 1980
product range ($18–50 CD) Riesling, Schonburger Riesling, Chardonnay, Radenti (Methode Champenoise), Pinot Noir, Cabernet Merlot.
summary The original 9-hectare Freycinet vineyards are beautifully situated on the sloping hillsides of a small valley. The soils are podsol and decaying granite with a friable clay subsoil, and the combination of aspect, slope, soil and heat summation produce red grapes of unusual depth of colour and ripe flavours. One of Australia's foremost producers of Pinot Noir, with a wholly enviable track record of consistency – rare with such a temperamental variety. Exports to the UK, Hong Kong and The Netherlands.

Freycinet Riesling

▼▼▼▼▽ **2002** Light yellow-green; the complex bouquet appears to have some botrytis or similar influence, the intense lime, lemon and apple palate imperious in its impact. **rating: 91**

best drinking Now–2012 **best vintages** '00, '01 **drink with** Seared scallops • $22

Freycinet Chardonnay

▼▼▼▼▽ **2001** Medium yellow-green; lively, expressive, citrus and nectarine fruit aromas are offset by a nice touch of barrel-ferment oak on the bouquet; the palate focuses primarily on clean, citrussy fruit, and has excellent line and length. **rating: 93**

best drinking Now–2008 **best vintages** '93, '94, '95, '96, '98, '99, '00 **drink with** Abalone • $32

Freycinet Radenti

▼▼▼▼▼ **1997** A blend of estate-grown chardonnay and pinot noir which spends 3 years on yeast lees, and named after Freycinet winemaker Claudio Radenti. Light straw-green; clear citrus and nectarine aromas and flavours drive a seductive wine with great harmony, mouthfeel and balance. **rating: 95**

best drinking Now **best vintages** '96, '97 **drink with** Oysters • $45

Freycinet Pinot Noir

▼▼▼▼▼ **2001** Arguably the most consistent producer of pinot noir in Tasmania, benefiting from a unique amphitheatre site and low yields. Strong purple-red; the complex bouquet opens with deep plum, then touches spice, forest and mint. The luscious and powerful palate has black plum/black cherry and spice, then background tannins. **rating: 95**

best drinking Now–2008 **best vintages** '91, '92, '94, '95, '96, '97, '98, '99, '00, '01 **drink with** Jugged hare • $50

✿ frogmore creek NR

Brinktop Road, Penna, Tas 7171 **region** Southern Tasmania
phone (03) 6224 6788 **fax** (03) 6224 6788 **open** Not
winemaker Andrew Hood (Contract) **est.** 1997
product range Riesling, Traminer, Chardonnay, Iced Riesling, Pinot Noir, Reserve Pinot Noir.
summary Frogmore Creek is Pacific rim joint venture, the two owners being Tony Scherer of Tasmania, and Jack Kidwiler of California. They have commenced the establishment of the only organically certified commercial vineyard in Tasmania, and plan to take the area under vine to 80 hectares over the next three to 5 years. An on-site winery will be constructed in three stages over the next 2 years, with Andrew Hood

undertaking the winemaking in the interim. When completed, the development will offer visitor centre and cellar-door sales area; an environmental centre with walking trails and lakeside picnic areas; an organic garden; and a restaurant, accommodation and event facilities. The name, incidentally, is taken from the creek which runs through the property. The first wines are due for release in March 2004.

frog rock ★★★☆

Cassilis Road, Mudgee, NSW 2850 **region** Mudgee
phone (02) 6372 2408 **fax** (02) 6372 6924 **open** 7 days 11–4
winemaker Simon Gilbert, David Lowe (Contract) **production** 13 000 cases **est.** 1973
product range ($14–25 CD) Creek Chardonnay, Premium Reserve Chardonnay, Chardonnay, Rose, Creek Shiraz, Old Vine Shiraz, Chambourcin, Merlot, Creek Cabernet, Old Vine Cabernet Sauvignon.
summary Frog Rock is the former Tallara Vineyard, established almost 30 years ago by leading Sydney chartered accountant Rick Turner. There are now 60 hectares of vineyard, with 22 hectares each of shiraz and cabernet sauvignon, and much smaller plantings of chardonnay, semillon, merlot, petit verdot and chambourcin. The wines are exported to the UK, the US, Canada, Singapore and Hong Kong.

Frog Rock Premium Chardonnay

▼▼▼▽ **2001** Light straw-green; interesting, ripe tropical/apricot aromas suggest there may have been some botrytis at work; similar flavours appear on the palate, which shortens slightly on the finish. **rating:** 84
best drinking Now **drink with** Pasta • $25

Frog Rock Merlot

▼▼▼▼ **2001** Light to medium red-purple; the clean, moderately intense bouquet has faintly herbal/spicy overtones, the palate offering more, with some small, sweet berry fruit at its core; finishes with a nice touch of oak and sweet tannins. **rating:** 87
best drinking Now–2007 **drink with** Milk-fed lamb • $20

🐸 frogspond NR

400 Arthurs Seat Road, Red Hill, Vic 3937 **region** Mornington Peninsula
phone (03) 5989 2941 **fax** (03) 9824 7659 **open** By appointment
winemaker David Lloyd **production** 200 cases **est.** 1994
product range ($32–35 R) Chardonnay, Pinot Noir.
summary The Nelson family has established 2 hectares of chardonnay and pinot noir on an ideal north-facing slope. The low yields produce grapes with intense fruit flavours, but only a tiny amount of wine is made, sold primarily by mail order.

fyffe field ★★★

1417 Murray Valley Highway, Yarrawonga, Vic 3730 **region** Goulburn Valley
phone (03) 5748 4282 **fax** (03) 5748 4284 **open** 7 days 10–5
winemaker Contract **production** 1300 cases **est.** 1993
product range ($11–15 CD) Verdelho, Late Harvest Semillon, Shiraz, Byramine Classic Red, Merlot, Cabernet Sauvignon, Tokay, Muscat, Tawny Snort.
summary Fyffe Field has been established by Graeme and Liz Diamond near the Murray River between Cobram and Yarrawonga in a mudbrick and leadlight tasting room opposite an historic homestead. They have 2 hectares of shiraz, 1 hectare each of semillon, verdelho, merlot and cabernet sauvignon, and 0.5 hectare each of touriga and petit verdot. A highlight is the ornamental pig collection, a display set up long before Babe was born.

Fyffe Field Verdelho

▼▼▼▽ **2002** Light to medium yellow-green; the bouquet is solid and clean, although not aromatic; the palate then springs a surprise with considerable fruit weight and richness, even if the finish is slightly congested. **rating:** 84
best drinking Now **drink with** Chicken nuggets • $12

Fyffe Field Merlot

▼▼▼▽ **2001** Medium red-purple; spicy, savoury, earthy, leafy berry aromas set the pattern for the palate, where a touch of mint joins the band; struggles towards the finish. **rating:** 83
best drinking Now **drink with** Weisswurst sausages • $15

gabriel's paddocks vineyard NR

Deasys Road, Pokolbin, NSW 2320 **region** Lower Hunter Valley
phone (02) 4998 7650 **fax** (02) 4998 7603 **open** Thurs–Mon 9–5
winemaker Contract **est.** 1979
product range Chenin Blanc, Chardonnay, Pinot Noir, Shiraz, Cabernet Merlot.
summary Formerly Sutherlands Wines, Gabriel's Paddocks is as much about general tourism and small conference accommodation as it is about wine production, with two separate buildings able to accommodate more than 20 people. The 13.6-hectare vineyards are planted to chardonnay, chenin blanc, pinot noir, merlot, shiraz and cabernet sauvignon; the wines from these varieties are all contract-made. No recent tastings.

galafrey ★★★☆

Quangellup Road, Mount Barker, WA 6324 **region** Great Southern
phone (08) 9851 2022 **fax** (08) 9851 2324 **open** 7 days 10–5
winemaker Ian Tyrer **production** 12 000 cases **est.** 1977
product range ($10–50 CD) Riesling, Muller, Art Label Semillon Sauvignon Blanc, Chardonnay, Unoaked Chardonnay, Art Label Premium Dry White, Reserve Botrytis Riesling, Pinot Noir, Shiraz, Art Label Shiraz, Merlot, Cabernet Sauvignon, Reserve Cabernet Sauvignon, Tawny Port.
summary Relocated to a new purpose-built but utilitarian winery after previously inhabiting the exotic surrounds of the old Albany wool store, Galafrey makes wines with plenty of robust, if not rustic, character, drawing grapes in the main from nearly 13 hectares of estate plantings at Mount Barker. Exports to the UK, Switzerland, Belgium, The Netherlands, Canada, New Zealand and Singapore.

Galafrey Rhine Riesling

▼▼▼▽ 2002 Developed, glowing yellow-green; the bouquet has subdued tropical fruit aromas, the palate generous but not focused. News travels slowly to the further reaches of the Great Southern region, and the wine is still labelled 'Rhine Riesling'. **rating:** 84
best drinking Now **best vintages** '90, '91, '97, '98, '99 **drink with** Sweet and sour pork • $14

Galafrey Merlot

▼▼▼▼ 2001 Healthy red-purple; the moderately intense bouquet has clean redcurrant/raspberry fruit, the light to medium-bodied palate with good varietal fruit aided by fine, persistent, savoury tannins. A keeper. **rating:** 88
best drinking 2004–2010 **drink with** Home-made pizza • $22

Galafrey Cabernet Sauvignon

▼▼▼▼ 1999 Medium red-purple; bottle-developed cedary/savoury/spicy overtones to the blackcurrant fruit of the bouquet are reflected in the blackcurrant/black olive palate; still needs time thanks to firmish tannins. **rating:** 86
best drinking 2004–2009 **drink with** Lamb shanks • $22

galah wine ★★★☆

Tregarthen Road, Ashton, SA 5137 **region** Adelaide Hills
phone (08) 8390 1243 **fax** (08) 8390 1243 **open** Available at Ashton Hills
winemaker Stephen George **production** 1500 cases **est.** 1986
product range ($7.50–35 ML) Unlabelled SA range of Semillon Chardonnay, Cabernet Shiraz, Cabernet Sauvignon; Brut, Clare Valley Sparkling Red, Adelaide Hills Three Sheds Red, Clare Valley Shiraz, Clare Valley Cabernet Malbec Shiraz, Clare Valley Cabernet Sauvignon.
summary Over the years, Stephen George has built up a network of contacts across South Australia from which he gains some very high-quality small parcels of grapes or wine for the Galah label. These are all sold direct at extremely low prices for the quality. Exports to the UK and the US.

Galah Three Sheds Red

▼▼▼▼ 2000 Medium red, the purple starting to fade; a range of light, savoury, spicy, earthy aromas lead into a cedary, brambly, blackberry palate with fine and soft tannins. A blend of Cabernet Sauvignon, Merlot, Shiraz and Cabernet Franc, all from the Adelaide Hills, and a new addition to the Galah range. **rating:** 87
best drinking Now–2006 **drink with** Rack of veal • $15

Galah Cabernet Merlot Shiraz

▼▼▼▼▽ 1998 Medium to full red-purple; sweet dark berry fruit is complemented by nice oak on the bouquet, then a typical deep, powerful and concentrated palate, with lingering tannins; needs a decade (ex Wendouree). **rating:** 90
best drinking 2008–2018 **drink with** Leave it in the cellar • $25

gallagher estate ★★★☆

Dog Trap Road, Murrumbateman, NSW 2582 **region** Canberra District
phone (02) 6254 9957 **fax** (02) 6254 9957 **open** Not
winemaker Greg Gallagher **production** 2500 cases **est.** 1995
product range ($14–20 R) Chardonnay, Shiraz.
summary Greg Gallagher was senior winemaker at Taltarni for 20 years, where he worked with Dominique Portet. He began planning a change of career at much the same time as did Dominique, and began the establishment of a small vineyard at Murrumbateman in 1995, planting a little over 1 hectare each of chardonnay and shiraz. He has now moved to the region with his family, his major job at the present time being winemaker at the Charles Sturt University Winery, playing a central role in training the winemakers of tomorrow. Retail distribution through Yarra Valley Wine Consultants in Victoria and New South Wales, and Oak Barrel Wines in Canberra. The rating reflects previous tastings.

galli estate ★★★★☆

1507 Melton Highway, Rockbank, Vic 3335 **region** Sunbury
phone (03) 9747 1444 **fax** (03) 9747 1481 **open** 7 days 11–5
winemaker Stephen Phillips **production** 10 000 cases **est.** 1997
product range ($16–36 R) Semillon, Sauvignon Blanc, Pinot Grigio, Chardonnay, Pinot Noir, Shiraz, Cabernet Sauvignon Franc Merlot, Sangiovese, Cabernet Sauvignon.
summary Galli Estate may be a newcomer to the scene, but it is a substantial one. Lorenzo and Pam Galli have planted 38 hectares of vineyard, the lion's share to cabernet sauvignon and shiraz, but with between 1.5–2.5 hectares of semillon, sauvignon blanc, pinot grigio, chardonnay, sangiovese and pinot noir. A large underground cellar has been constructed; already 50 metres long, it is to be extended in the future. A cellar-door sales, bistro and administration centre were completed in March 2002, with former Coldstream Hills winemaker Stephen Phillips now in charge. The quality is as high as the prices are low.

Galli Estate Sauvignon Blanc

▼▼▼▼ 2002 Light to medium yellow-green; the moderately intense bouquet has a complex array of asparagus, grass, gooseberry, tropical and smoke aromas, which all come through to a lesser or greater degree on the firm, clean palate with well-defined varietal character. **rating:** 87

best drinking Now **drink with** Poached scallops • $16

Galli Estate Pinot Grigio

▼▼▼▼ 2001 Pale straw-pink, typical of the variety; clear pear and apple aromas mix with more minerally, gravelly characters of the bouquet; the palate is quite intense and long, with minerally acidity and grip; pristine varietal character shown throughout. **rating:** 87

best drinking Now **drink with** Shellfish • $18

Galli Estate Chardonnay

▼▼▼▼▽ 2002 Light straw-green; fresh, vibrant, citrus fruit is married with subtle barrel-ferment and malolactic-ferment inputs on the bouquet; the same flavours come through on the palate, which has excellent proportion, balance and weight, with creamy, nutty nuances adding to the mouthfeel. Spends 8 months on lees in new and one-year-old French oak. **rating:** 91

best drinking 2004–2008 **best vintages** '02 **drink with** Sautéed chicken • $16

Galli Estate Pinot Noir

▼▼▼▼▽ 2002 Medium red-purple; vibrant spice, plum and cherry is supported by subtle oak on the bouquet; light but intense plummy varietal fruit plus spicy, savoury notes add to the complexity and to the length of the fine tannin finish. **rating:** 92

best drinking Now–2007 **drink with** Roast baby kid • $16

Galli Estate Shiraz

▼▼▼▼▽ 2001 Strong red-purple; attractive black cherry fruit is accompanied by splashes of spice on the bouquet, the palate showing similar cool-grown but fully ripened black cherry and spice fruit; good oak balance.

best drinking 2004–2011 **best vintages** '00 **drink with** Rich casserole • $22 **rating:** 90

Galli Estate Sangiovese

▼▼▼▼ 2001 Typical light red colour; a high-toned bouquet with savoury, spicy cherry aromas, then a palate with pleasant texture and balance, not overworked; a good example of the variety. Spends 9 months in French oak.

best drinking Now–2007 **drink with** Lasagne • $18 **rating:** 88

Galli Estate Cabernet Sauvignon Cabernet Franc Merlot

♥♥♥♥♡ **2001** Medium red-purple; a clean array of blackcurrant and blackberry fruit aromas announce an elegantly-proportioned and structured wine, replete with fine tannins and subtle oak running through the long finish. **rating:** 92

best drinking 2004–2012 **best vintages** '01 **drink with** Rack of lamb • $22

gapsted wines ★★★★

Great Alpine Road, Gapsted, Vic 3737 **region** Alpine Valleys
phone (03) 5751 1383 **fax** (03) 5751 1368 **open** 7 days 10–5
winemaker Michael Cope-Williams, Shayne Cunningham **production** 14 000 cases **est.** 1997
product range ($14–30 CD) Ballerina Canopy range of Sauvignon Blanc, Chardonnay, Shiraz, Durif, Merlot, Cabernet Franc, Cabernet Sauvignon; Limited Release Pinot Grigio, Late Harvest Riesling, Malbec, Petit Manseng and Saperavi; Tutu Chardonnay Verdelho, Cabernet Merlot.
summary Gapsted is the premier brand of the Victorian Alps Wine Co, the latter primarily a contract-crush facility which processes grapes for 48 growers in the King and Alpine Valleys. The estate plantings total 10 hectares of shiraz, cabernet sauvignon, petit verdot and merlot, but the Gapsted wines come both from these estate plantings and from contract-grown fruit. All incorporate the 'ballerina canopy' tag, a reference to the open nature of this particular training method which is ideally suited to these regions.

Gapsted Ballerina Canopy Chardonnay

♥♥♥♥♡ **2001** Bright straw-green; a spotlessly clean, fruit-driven bouquet with citrus/grapefruit aromas is supported by perfectly integrated oak; the elegant, light to medium-bodied palate has largely eaten up the new French oak in which the wine underwent fermentation and malolactic fermentation; good mouthfeel due to creamy malolactic inputs. **rating:** 90

best drinking Now–2006 **best vintages** '98, '99, '01 **drink with** Fettuccine à la pana • $20

Gapsted Limited Release Saperavi

♥♥♥♥ **2001** Medium red-purple; not as remarkable as the variety is wont to provide; black fruits and a touch of Christmas cake on the bouquet lead into a wine with black fruit flavours in a somewhat spare frame, lacking mid-palate flesh. Nonetheless, an interesting varietal which may well have an enduring place in the scheme of things. From the King and Alpine Valleys. **rating:** 85

best drinking Now–2006 **drink with** Lamb casserole • $25

Gapsted Ballerina Canopy Merlot

♥♥♥♥ **2000** Medium red-purple; the clean, relatively light bouquet is in typical form with spicy/savoury/leafy overtones; the light to medium-bodied palate has tight, savoury tannins running through its length, providing good texture. **rating:** 86

best drinking Now–2006 **best vintages** '98 **drink with** Grilled marinated lamb fillets • $22

garbin estate ★★★

209 Toodyay Road, Middle Swan, WA 6056 **region** Swan Valley
phone (08) 9274 1747 **fax** (08) 9274 1747 **open** 7 days 10.30–5.30
winemaker Peter Garbin **production** 3000 cases **est.** 1956
product range ($13–23 CD) Chenin Blanc, Chardonnay, Unwooded Chardonnay, Estate Shiraz, Shiraz, Merlot, Cabernet Merlot, Liqueur Muscat, Ruby Port.
summary Peter Garbin, winemaker by weekend and design draftsman by week, decided in 1990 that he would significantly upgrade the bulk fortified winemaking business commenced by his father in 1956. The 11-hectare vineyards have been replanted, the winery re-equipped, and the first of the new generation wines produced in 1994. The wines have since received significant critical acclaim, both locally and nationally. Exports to Hong Kong; otherwise sold direct from the winery.

Garbin Estate Shiraz

♥♥♥♥ **2001** Medium red-purple; the bouquet offers a nice mix of warm, earthy berry fruit and sweet oak; the medium to full-bodied palate exemplifies honest shiraz at its traditional best, with lots of varietal fruit. **rating:** 87

best drinking Now–2008 **drink with** Shepherd's pie • $23

garden gully vineyards ★★★★

Western Highway, Great Western, Vic 3377 **region** Grampians
phone (03) 5356 2400 **fax** (03) 5356 2400 **open** By appointment
winemaker Warren Randall **production** 2000 cases **est.** 1987
product range ($13–27 CD) Riesling, Shiraz, Sparkling Shiraz, Tokay.
summary Given the skills and local knowledge of the syndicate which owns Garden Gully, it is not surprising that the wines are typically good: an attractive stone cellar-door sales area is an additional reason to stop and pay a visit. Shiraz produced from the 100-year-old vines adjoining the cellar door is especially good. The 4 hectares of shiraz is complemented by 3 hectares of riesling, providing another good wine. Unfortunately, all wines were sold out in March 2003, and the cellar door will not reopen until newer vintages come on-stream. The rating reflects prior releases.

garlands ★★★★☆

Marmion Street off Mount Barker Hill Road, Mount Barker, WA 6324 **region** Great Southern
phone (08) 9851 2737 **fax** (08) 9851 2686 **open** Thurs–Sun and public holidays 10–4, or by appointment
winemaker Michael Garland **production** 3500 cases **est.** 1996
product range ($13–25 CD) Riesling, Reserve Chardonnay, Shiraz, Merlot, Saros; Barker Hill White and Red.
summary Garlands is a partnership between Michael and Julie Garland and their vigneron neighbours, Craig and Caroline Drummond. Michael Garland has come to grape growing and winemaking with a varied background in biological research, computer sales and retail clothing; he is now enrolled at Charles Sturt University for his degree in oenology, but already has significant practical experience behind him. A tiny but highly-functional winery was erected prior to the 2000 vintage, the earlier wines being made elsewhere. The winery has a capacity of 150 tonnes, and will continue contract-making for other small producers in the region as well as making the wine from the 6 hectares of estate vineyards planted to cabernet franc, sauvignon blanc, chardonnay, riesling, shiraz and cabernet sauvignon. Cabernet Franc is the winery specialty, but the quality of the wines has taken a giant leap forward. Exports to the UK.

Garlands Riesling

TTTTT 2002 Bright, light green-yellow; a spotlessly clean bouquet with fine apple, lime and mineral aromas leads into a palate with very good intensity and length, showing a faint CO_2 spritz on the finish which will simply assist the aging of the wine. Stelvin-finished. **rating:** 92
best drinking Now–2013 **best vintages** '02 **drink with** Fish terrine • $15

Garlands Barker Hill White

TTTT 2001 Light green-yellow; clean, light stone fruit and tropical fruit aromas lead into a crisp, lively and fresh palate with good length and finish. A puppy dog's tails blend of Chardonnay, Sauvignon Blanc, Semillon and Riesling. **rating:** 87
best drinking Now **drink with** Anything cold • $13

Garlands Reserve Chardonnay

TTTTT 2001 Medium yellow-green; the moderately intense bouquet has appealing nectarine fruit and nicely integrated and balanced oak; the fresh and lively palate has excellent fruit focus, good length and subtle oak. Whole bunch-pressed, and 100 per cent barrel-fermented in French oak puncheons; 11 months on lees and partial mlf. **rating:** 93
best drinking Now–2006 **drink with** Gravlax • $20

Garlands Shiraz

TTTTT 2001 Bright purple-red; clean, intense black cherry/blackberry/spice/licorice aromas lead into a medium to full-bodied palate, powered by smooth fruit, but with good extract of tannin and oak. **rating:** 92
best drinking 2006–2011 **best vintages** '01 **drink with** Game pie • $20

Garlands Barker Hill Red

TTTT 2001 Medium red-purple; clean and smooth dark berry fruit with good oak integration is followed by a palate with abundant ripe raspberry/blackberry flavours running through a long finish with fine tannins. Outstanding value. A blend of Cabernet Sauvignon, Merlot and Shiraz. **rating:** 89
best drinking Now–2006 **drink with** Osso buco • $13

Garlands Saros

▼▼▼▼▽ 2001 Medium but bright purple-red; rich, ripe, complex blackberry/blackcurrant/cassis fruit aromas are followed by a fruit-driven palate, with mouthfilling blackcurrant/cassis fruit and fine tannins. A blend of 88 per cent Cabernet Franc and 12 per cent Cabernet Sauvignon, and an outstanding example of Cabernet Franc.   **rating:** 93

best drinking 2005–2011 **best vintages** '96, '98, '01 **drink with** Venison pie • $25

gartelmann hunter estate ★★★★

Lovedale Road, Lovedale, NSW 2321 **region** Lower Hunter Valley
phone (02) 4930 7113 **fax** (02) 4930 7114 **open** 7 days 10–5
winemaker Monarch Winemaking Services (Contract) **production** 10 000 cases **est.** 1970
product range ($13–30 CD) Benjamin Semillon, Reserve Semillon, Chenin Blanc, Chardonnay, Semillon Chenin Blanc, Methode Champenoise, Botrytis Chenin Blanc, Diedrich Shiraz, Wilhelm Shiraz, Merlot.
summary In 1996 Jan and Jorg Gartelmann purchased what was previously the George Hunter Estate, established by Sydney restaurateur Oliver Shaul in 1970. They acquired 16 hectares of mature vineyards, producing a limited amount of wine under the Gartelmann label in 1997 and moving to full production in 1998. Diedrich Shiraz is the flagship, consistently good. Exports to the UK, Germany and Canada.

Gartelmann Benjamin Semillon

▼▼▼▼▽ 2002 Light straw-green; the bright and fresh bouquet has mineral, herb and lemon aromas; the light, lively and crisp palate follows suit, well balanced and closing with good acidity. Will reward cellaring. **rating:** 90
best drinking 2004–2010 **drink with** Blue swimmer crab • $16.10

Gartelmann Chardonnay

▼▼▼▼ 2002 Medium yellow-green; the moderately intense bouquet has excellent balance and integration of oak with the nectarine fruit; the intense peach and nectarine fruit drives the palate, the oak, in typical vineyard fashion, in restraint.   **rating:** 89
best drinking Now **drink with** Stir-fried abalone • $19

Gartelmann Wilhelm Shiraz

▼▼▼▼ 2001 Medium red-purple; the moderately intense bouquet has a range of tangy, savoury, spicy regional aromas, sweeter blackberry fruit coming through on the light to medium-bodied palate; fine tannins, but down on richness.   **rating:** 86
best drinking Now–2008 **drink with** Braised beef • $22

Gartelmann Merlot

▼▼▼▽ 2001 Light red-purple; the bouquet has a mix of dark berry and savoury/herbal varietal fruit, the palate initially presenting distinctly sweet dark fruit before rather pointed acidity takes over. A curate's egg which may settle down with time.   **rating:** 84
best drinking Now–2007 **drink with** Veal goulash • $23.30

gartner family vineyards NR

Sydney Road, Coonawarra, SA 5263 **region** Coonawarra
phone (08) 8736 5011 **fax** (08) 8736 5006 **open** 7 days 10–4
winemaker Peter Douglas **production** 15 000 cases **est.** 1997
product range ($14–28 CD) Limestone Coast Semillon Chardonnay, Padthaway Chardonnay, Padthaway Shiraz, Limestone Coast Shiraz Merlot, Coonawarra Cabernet Sauvignon.
summary Gartner Family Vineyards was a major entrant on the Australian winemaking scene. The family has been farming in Coonawarra since the 1930s, planting its first vineyard in 1988, and had more than 400 hectares of vines, including just under 330 hectares of cabernet sauvignon. In addition they were partners in 40 hectares of vineyard in Padthaway, 65 hectares in the Barossa Valley and 80 hectares in Central Victoria. The winery is being established in a disused quarry which forms part of the property, and is a spectacular sight, even when half built. Peter Douglas has returned to the region he knows so well, and has produced some outstanding first-up wines from good, but not great, vintages. All this, however, is in a state of flux following the appointment of receivers, and it seems almost certain there will be a sale of many of the vineyards.

gecko valley   NR

Bailiff Road, via 700 Glenlyon Road, Gladstone, Qld 4680 **region** Queensland Coastal
phone (07) 4979 0400 **fax** (07) 4979 0500 **open** 7 days 10–5
winemaker Bruce Humphery-Smith (Contract) **production** 1000 cases **est.** 1997
product range ($12.50–18.50 CD) Lightly Oaked Chardonnay, Special Reserve Chardonnay, Special Reserve Verdelho, Lazy Lizard White, Lazy Lizard Red, Special Reserve Shiraz, Liqueur Shiraz, Liqueur Mead.
summary Gecko Valley extends the viticultural map of Queensland yet further, situated little more than 50 kilometres off the tropic of Capricorn in an area better known for beef farming and mineral activities. The 3-hectare vineyard (1 hectare each of chardonnay, verdelho and shiraz) was established by Tony (an engineer) and Coleen McCray (an accountant) after taking consultancy advice from Garry Crittenden (of Dromana Estate). The coastal belt between Gladstone and Rockhampton has a unique climate, with lower rainfall than either the more northern or more southern coastal strips. The climate is hot, but the vineyard is only 1 kilometre from the tempering influence of the sea. It has been planted on free-draining, shallow soil, so excessive vigour is not a problem. The retention of Bruce Humphery-Smith underlines the serious aspirations of the McCrays to make 100 per cent Central Queensland wines of real quality, the levels of sweetness in some being imposed by the strong palate preferences of the all-important cellar door trade.

geebin wines   NR

3729 Channel Highway, Birchs Bay, Tas 7162 **region** Southern Tasmania
phone (03) 6267 4750 **fax** (03) 6267 5090 **open** 7 days 10–5
winemaker Andrew Hood (Contract) **production** 50 cases **est.** 1983
product range ($20–22 CD) Riesling, Chardonnay, Cabernet Sauvignon.
summary Although production is minuscule, quality has been consistently high. The Riesling is well made, but the interesting wine from this far southern vineyard is Cabernet Sauvignon – clearly, the vineyard enjoys favourable ripening conditions. With 0.7 hectare of vineyards. Geebin claims to be the smallest commercial producer in Australia, but isn't: Scarp Valley and (temporarily) Jollymont are smaller. The vineyard, incidentally, was once called Milnathort.

gehrig estate   ★★★☆

Cnr Murray Valley Highway and Howlong Road, Barnawartha, Vic 3688 **region** Rutherglen
phone (02) 6026 7296 **fax** (02) 6026 7424 **open** Mon–Sat 9–5, Sun 10–5
winemaker Brian Gehrig **production** 5000 cases **est.** 1858
product range ($13–32 CD) Chenin Blanc, Chardonnay, Autumn Riesling, Shiraz, Shiraz Cabernet, Durif, fortifieds.
summary An historic winery and adjacent house are superb legacies of the 19th century. Progressive modernisation of the winemaking facilities and operations has seen the quality of the white wines improve significantly, while the red wines now receive a percentage of new oak. Another recent innovation has been the introduction of the Gourmet Courtyard, serving lunch on weekends, public holidays and Victorian school holidays.

Gehrig Estate Shiraz
TTTT 2001 Full red-purple; an attractive, savoury bouquet has a mix of blackberry and plum pudding, with a trace of lift; the potent fruit on the palate again shows signs of some volatile lift, but within bounds; plenty of overall flavour.   **rating:** 86
best drinking 2005–2010 **drink with** Rump steak • $19.50

Gehrig Estate Durif
TTTT 2001 Deep red-purple; the bouquet has essence of prune plus blackberry and chocolate aromas; the intense and piquant palate has some of the VA (volatile acidity) lift of the Shiraz, but the wine has the density to carry that lift.   **rating:** 88
best drinking 2005–2012 **drink with** Venison • $23.50

Gehrig Estate Old Tawny Port
TTTT NV The colour is dark, with a few red hues still there indicating intermediate age. The bouquet is solid, with sweet fruit and some rancio; a big, rich Rutherglen style on the palate which, like the bouquet, does not show any signs of staleness.   **rating:** 86
best drinking Now **drink with** Coffee • $25

gembrook hill ★★★☆

Launching Place Road, Gembrook, Vic 3783 **region** Yarra Valley
phone (03) 5968 1622 **fax** (03) 5968 1699 **open** By appointment
winemaker Timo Mayer **production** 2000 cases **est.** 1983
product range ($18–35 R) Sauvignon Blanc, Chardonnay, Pinot Noir, Warrawong Pinot Noir.
summary The 6-hectare Gembrook Hill Vineyard is situated on rich, red volcanic soils 2 kilometres north of Gembrook in the coolest part of the Yarra Valley. The vines are not irrigated, with consequent natural vigour control., and naturally low yields. Harvest usually spans mid April, three weeks later than the traditional northern parts of the valley, and the style is consistently elegant. Exports to Denmark.

Gembrook Hill Sauvignon Blanc

▼▼▼▼ 2001 Light to medium green-yellow; clean, fresh herb and mineral aromas are followed by a similarly lively and fresh palate, with good length and a particularly good finish.   **rating:** 87
best drinking Now **best vintages** '90, '92, '93, '94, '95, '98 **drink with** Lobster bisque • $30

Gembrook Hill Chardonnay

▼▼▼▼ 2001 Medium yellow-green; soft nectarine fruit aromas, bolstered by tangy edges and subtle oak lead into the quite delicate palate, showing some malolactic-fermentation characters, and good length.   **rating:** 87
best drinking Now–2005 **best vintages** '90, '91, '93, '94, '97 **drink with** Crab, prawns • $30

Gembrook Hill Pinot Noir

▼▼▼▼ 2001 Light to medium red-purple; the clean and fresh bouquet has light cherry and plum fruit, the palate gaining some fruit weight and does have nice texture, thanks to fine-grained tannins and appropriate oak.   **rating:** 89
best drinking Now–2005 **best vintages** '97, '98 **drink with** Asian seafood dishes • $35

Gembrook Hill Warrawong Pinot Noir

▼▼▼▼ 2001 Medium to full red-purple; a complex bouquet with dark plum and spice aromas flows into a rich, full palate with abundant dark plum fruit and even more abundant tannins; at the opposite end of the spectrum to its sister wine from start to finish. An impromptu blending session established that 65 per cent of the estate pinot noir and 35 per cent of the Warrawong made by far the best wine; it must have been a great temptation to undertake the blend.   **rating:** 86
best drinking 2004–2009 **drink with** Roast Barbary duck • $18

gemtree vineyards ★★★★

Kangarilla Road, McLaren Flat, SA 5171 (postal) **region** McLaren Vale
phone (08) 8323 8199 **fax** (08) 8323 7889 **open** Not
winemaker Mike Brown **production** 6000 cases **est.** 1992
product range ($15–25 R) Chardonnay, Uncut Shiraz, Shiraz, Tatty Road (Cabernet blend).
summary The Buttery family, headed by Paul and Jill and with the active involvement of Melissa as viticulturist for Gemtree Vineyards, has been actively involved as grape growers in McLaren Vale since 1980, when they purchased their first vineyard. Today the family owns a little over 130 hectares of vines, the oldest block of 25 hectares on Tatachilla Road at McLaren Vale, planted in 1970. Exports to the US.

Gemtree McLaren Vale Shiraz

▼▼▼▼ 2000 Medium to full red-purple; a concentrated amalgam of dark fruits, chocolate and oak on the bouquet, then a palate which shows both the quality of the base material and good control of extract and oak in the winery.   **rating:** 89
best drinking 2004–2009 **best vintages** '98 **drink with** Rich casseroles • $25

Gemtree Uncut Shiraz

▼▼▼▼▼ 2001 Medium purple-red; rich, ripe blackberry, spice and chocolate aromas lead into a concentrated, rich but not extractive palate; delicious blackberry and plum fruit, soft tannins and exemplary oak throughout. Spends 20 months in French and American oak.   **rating:** 95
best drinking 2006–2011 **drink with** Braised beef • $25

geoff hardy wines ★★★☆

c/- Pertaringa Wines, Cnr Hunt and Rifle Range Roads, McLaren Vale, SA 5171 **region** Adelaide Hills
phone (08) 8323 8125 **fax** (08) 8323 7766 **open** At Pertaringa, Mon–Fri 9–5, weekends and public
holidays 11–5
winemaker Geoff Hardy, Ben Riggs **production** 2000 cases **est.** 1993
product range ($15–32 CD) Kuitpo Shiraz, Kuitpo Cabernet; Wirrega Vineyard Petit Verdot.
summary Geoff Hardy wines come from 20 hectares of vines, with a large percentage of the grape production
being sold to other makers. Retail distribution through South Australia, New South Wales, Victoria and
Queensland; exports to the UK, Denmark, Germany, Japan, Hong Kong, Canada and the US.

Geoff Hardy Kuitpo Shiraz

▼▼▼▼ **2000** Light to medium red-purple; the moderately intense bouquet is right in the mainstream of the
style of this wine, with savoury, spicy aromatics, berry and leaf intermingling. The palate follows down precisely
the same track, clearly showing the cool conditions of the vineyard, the flavours in a tangy, secondary, earthy
spicy spectrum. Utterly different to other South Australian Shiraz. **rating:** 87
best drinking 2005–2010 **best vintages** '93, '98 **drink with** Rich red meat dishes • $32

Geoff Hardy Wirrega Vineyard Petit Verdot

▼▼▼▽ **2000** Medium red-purple; the bouquet is more varietal and less minty than prior releases, with cedary
blackberry aromas; the light to medium-bodied palate is soft, and quite sweet, seemingly indicating generous
yields; a pleasant everyday wine which is a long way from the Petit Verdot of Bordeaux. **rating:** 84
best drinking Now–2005 **drink with** Designer sausages • $15

Geoff Hardy Kuitpo Cabernet

▼▼▼▼ **2000** Medium purple-red; the moderately intense, clean focused bouquet has clear-cut blackcurrant
fruit and a touch of cedary oak; the European-style palate has good structure, balance and texture, with gentle,
dark fruits at its heart. **rating:** 89
best drinking 2004–2009 **drink with** Lamb fillets • $32

geoff merrill wines ★★★★

291 Pimpala Road, Woodcroft, SA 5162 **region** McLaren Vale
phone (08) 8381 6877 **fax** (08) 8322 2244 **open** Mon–Fri 10–5, weekends 12–5
winemaker Geoff Merrill, Scott Heidrich **production** 80 000 cases **est.** 1980
product range ($17–150 R) A change in brand structure has resulted in the Geoff Merrill Wines having
Henley Shiraz at the top; the Reserve range representing the ultra-premium wines, the Regional range and the
Varietal range; Mount Hurtle wines are sold exclusively through Vintage Cellars/Liquorland.
summary If Geoff Merrill ever loses his impish sense of humour or his zest for life, high and not-so-high, we
shall all be the poorer. He is seeking to lift the profile of his wines on the domestic market; in 1998 the product
range was rearranged into three tiers: premium (in fact simply varietal); reserve, the latter being the older (and
best) wines, reflecting the desire for elegance and subtlety of this otherwise exuberant winemaker; and at the
top, Henley Shiraz. As well as national retail distribution, significant exports to the UK, Switzerland, Austria,
the US, Hong Kong, Malaysia and Singapore.

Geoff Merrill Sauvignon Blanc

▼▼▼▼ **2002** Light straw-green; the firm bouquet has a mix of mineral and a hint of herb, with gooseberry
joining in on the clean palate; fresh, firm finish. **rating:** 86
best drinking Now **drink with** Seafood • $17

Geoff Merrill Grenache Rose

▼▼▼▼▽ **2002** Light, bright purple-pink; clean, fresh small berry/strawberry aromas, then a delicious spicy
strawberry palate with very good fruit/acid balance. Dry finish. **rating:** 92
best drinking Now **drink with** Antipasto • $17

geoff weaver ★★★★★

2 Gilpin Lane, Mitcham, SA 5062 (postal) **region** Adelaide Hills
phone (08) 8272 2105 **fax** (08) 8271 0177 **open** Not
winemaker Geoff Weaver **production** 4500 cases **est.** 1982
product range ($18–35 ML) Riesling, Sauvignon Blanc, Chardonnay, Pinot Noir, Cabernet Merlot.

summary This is now the full-time business of former Hardy Group chief winemaker Geoff Weaver. He draws upon a little over 11 hectares of vineyard established between 1982 and 1988; for the time being, at least, the physical winemaking is carried out by Geoff Weaver at Petaluma. He produces invariably immaculate Riesling and Sauvignon Blanc, and one of the longest-lived Chardonnays to be found in Australia, which has intense grapefruit and melon flavour. The beauty of the labels ranks supreme with that of Pipers Brook. The wines are exported to the US, the UK and Singapore.

Geoff Weaver Lenswood Riesling

ŸŸŸŸŸ **2000** Each time I taste this wine it gets better, although the aging process is appropriately slow. The crisp aromas of mineral, toast, apple and lime are barely changed, and there is excellent intensity and balance to the gentle mix of lime, citrus and apple fruit of the palate. Stelvin capped. **rating:** 95

best drinking Now–2010 **best vintages** '90, '93, '94, '96, '98, '00, '01, '02 **drink with** Smoked salmon • $20

Geoff Weaver Lenswood Sauvignon Blanc

ŸŸŸŸŸ **2002** Stands alongside Shaw & Smith and Knappstein Lenswood as the foremost producers of sauvignon blanc in the Adelaide Hills, all revelling in the cool 2002 vintage. Typical delicate gooseberry aromatics lead into a palate with balanced and focused sweet gooseberry fruit, then a crisp, dry finish. Exemplary varietal character. **rating:** 94

best drinking Now **best vintages** '00, '01, '02 **drink with** Blue swimmer crab • $21

ghost rock vineyard NR

PO Box 311, Devonport, Tas 7310 **region** Northern Tasmania
phone (03) 6423 1246 **open** Due to open 2004
winemaker Tamar Ridge (Contract) **production** 500 cases **est.** 2001
product range Sauvignon Blanc, Chardonnay, Pinot Noir.
summary Cate and Colin Arnold purchased the former Patrick Creek Vineyard (itself planted in 1989) in August 2001. They run a printing and design business in Devonport, and were looking for a suitable site to establish a vineyard, when the opportunity to buy Patrick Creek came up. The 1-hectare vineyard comprises 0.5 chardonnay and 0.25 each of pinot noir and sauvignon blanc, planted on a northeasterly aspect on a sheltered slope.

Ghost Rock Vineyard Pinot Noir

ŸŸŸŸ **2001** Light to medium purple-red, the hues still good; a clean, fresh, direct bouquet and light, cherry/strawberry flavours on the palate. A simple, pretty wine, not subverted by excessive extract. **rating:** 84

best drinking Now–2005 **drink with** Grilled Tasmanian salmon

giaconda ★★★★★

McClay Road, Beechworth, Vic 3747 **region** Beechworth
phone (03) 5727 0246 **fax** (03) 5727 0246 **open** By appointment
winemaker Rick Kinzbrunner **production** 2000 cases **est.** 1985
product range ($50–90 R) Aeolia, Nantua Les Deux, Chardonnay, Pinot Noir, Warner Vineyard Shiraz, Cabernet Sauvignon.
summary Wines which have a super-cult status and which, given the tiny production, are extremely difficult to find, sold chiefly through restaurants and mail order. All have a cosmopolitan edge befitting Rick Kinzbrunner's international winemaking experience. The Chardonnay and Pinot Noir are made in contrasting styles: the Chardonnay tight and reserved, the Pinot Noir more variable, but usually opulent and ripe. The rating is based on extensive tastings over the years, and recent tastings in restaurants. Exports to the UK and the US.

giant steps NR

10–12 Briarty Road, Gruyere, Vic 3770 **region** Yarra Valley
phone (03) 5964 9555 **fax** (03) 5964 9551 **open** By appointment
winemaker Phil Sexton, Allison Sexton **production** 10000 cases **est.** 1998
product range ($19.95–24.50 R) The three basic releases will be Chardonnay, Pinot Noir and Merlot (all estate-grown) under the Giant Steps label; however, there will also be significantly smaller quantities of individual clonal selections of Pinot Noir and Chardonnay under the Sexton label, along with Sexton 'Harry's Monster' – a blend of the four Bordeaux varieties grown high on the north face of the main ridge.

summary Phil Sexton made his first fortune as a pioneer micro-brewer, and invested a substantial part of that fortune in establishing the ultra-premium Margaret River winery, Devil's Lair. Late in 1996 he sold Devil's Lair to Southcorp, which had purchased Coldstream Hills earlier that year. Two years later, whether or not coincidentally, Phil and Allison Sexton purchased a hillside property less than a kilometre away from Coldstream Hills and sharing the same geological structure and aspect. The name Giant Steps comes in part from their love of jazz and the 1960 release of John Coltrane's album under than name, and partly reflecting the rise and fall of the property across a series of ridges ranging from 120 metres (400 feet) to 360 metres (1200 feet) level. They have established a striking and substantial vineyard comprising almost 34 hectares, predominantly planted to clonal selections of pinot noir and chardonnay, but with significant quantities of cabernet sauvignon and merlot, plus small plantings of cabernet franc and petit verdot. The wines are distributed nationally through Tucker Seabrook and imported into the US by Old Bridge Cellars.

Giant Steps Chardonnay

YYYY 2001 Light to medium yellow-green; obvious barrel-ferment with quality, high toast oak invests both the bouquet and palate with complexity; the fruit on the palate is light to medium bodied, but does manage to carry that oak, and has good length.   **rating:** 87

best drinking Now–2005 **drink with** Brains in black butter • $19.95

Giant Steps Pinot Noir

YYYY 2001 Strong red-purple; the bouquet is generous and complex, with a mix of forest and plum supported by well-balanced oak; the overly powerful palate is, however, marred by excessive tannin extraction. Age may or may not tame the tannins.   **rating:** 84

best drinking Now–2006 **drink with** Venison and blood pudding • $19.95

Giant Steps Merlot

YYYY 2001 Bright red-purple; the bouquet offers soft, slightly amorphous dark fruit aromas, but varietal character comes through strongly on the tangy, olive-accented palate, the tannins trembling on the brink.   **rating:** 85

best drinking Now–2007 **drink with** Marinated veal chops • $23.50

gibraltar rock   ★★★★☆

Woodlands Road, Porongurup, WA 6324 **region** Great Southern
phone (08) 9481 2856 **fax** (08) 9481 2857 **open** Wed–Sun 10–5
winemaker Michael Garland (Contract) **production** 400 cases **est.** 1979
product range ($16–22 CD) Riesling, Shiraz.
summary A once-tiny Riesling specialist in the wilds of the Porongurups forced to change its name from Narang because Lindemans felt it could be confused with its (now defunct) Nyrang Shiraz brand; truly a strange world. This beautifully sited vineyard and its long-lived Riesling were acquired by Perth orthopaedic surgeon Dr Peter Honey prior to the 2001 vintage. The vineyard now has 26 hectares of riesling, sauvignon blanc, chardonnay, pinot noir, merlot, shiraz and cabernet franc, and most of the grapes are sold to Houghton under a ten-year contract. Dr Honey intends to slowly increase production from the older vines under the Gibraltar Rock label.

Gibraltar Rock Riesling

YYYYY 2001 Light straw-green; the clean and firm bouquet has a mix of apple with a hint of spice, the elegant and focused palate with apple, lime and mineral flavours running through to a long finish. A welcome reappearance after a five-year hiatus in my tastings.   **rating:** 94

best drinking Now–2010 **best vintages** '90, '91, '92, '94, '95, '01 **drink with** Cold tomato and basil soup • $16

Gibraltar Rock Shiraz

YYYYY 2001 Medium red-purple; a fragrant, cedary, savoury bouquet flows into a light to medium-bodied palate with gentle red berry fruit, fine tannins and subtle oak. Lovely wine.   **rating:** 92

best drinking 2004–2009 **drink with** Ragout of veal • $22

gidgee estate wines   NR

441 Weeroona Drive, Wamboin, NSW 2621 **region** Canberra District
phone (02) 6236 9506 **fax** (02) 6236 9070 **open** Weekends 12–4
winemaker David Madew, Andrew McEwin (Contract) **production** 500 cases **est.** 1996
product range ($15–16 CD) Janette Murray Riesling, Chardonnay, Ensemble (Cabernet blend).

summary Brett and Cheryl Lane purchased the 1-hectare vineyard in 1996; it had been planted to riesling, chardonnay, cabernet sauvignon, cabernet franc and merlot over a ten-year period prior to its acquisition, but had been allowed to run-down and needed to be rehabilitated. The Lanes intend to double the vineyard size over the next 2 years and have retained David Madew and Andrew McEwin as contract winemakers.

gilberts ★★★★☆

RMB 438 Albany Highway, Kendenup via Mount Barker, WA 6323 **region** Great Southern
phone (08) 9851 4028 **fax** (08) 9851 4021 **open** 7 days 10–5
winemaker Plantagenet (Contract) **production** 4000 cases **est.** 1980
product range ($14–21 CD) Riesling, Chardonnay, Cabernet Shiraz.
summary A part-time occupation for sheep and beef farmers Jim and Beverly Gilbert but a very successful one. The now mature vineyard, coupled with contract-winemaking at Plantagenet, has produced small quantities of high-quality Riesling and Chardonnay. The rating is for the Riesling which won the trophy for Best Wine of Show at the Qantas West Australian Wines Show in both 2000 and 2001. The wines sell out quickly each year, with retail distribution through New South Wales, Victoria, ACT and Western Australia, and exports to the US, the UK, Singapore and The Netherlands. A restaurant and function area opened in April 2003, and further plantings are planned for 2004.

Gilberts Riesling

▼▼▼▼ **2002** The colour comes as an early warning, for it is not, as it should be, pale green; the bouquet is, however, quite aromatic and intense, with a mix of mineral, slate and herb, but then the palate flattens off slightly, with fruit suppression, although the length is good. There has to have been some mischance with the wine somewhere between birth and bottle. **rating:** 86

best drinking 2004–2007 **best vintages** '91, '92, '94, '95, '96, '97, '00, '01 **drink with** Asparagus with prosciutto • $21

Gilberts Chardonnay

▼▼▼▼ **2001** Medium yellow-green; the moderately intense bouquet has nectarine and peach fruit swathed in subtle but evident oak; the mouthfilling, medium-bodied palate provides more of the white peach of the bouquet, the 14° alcohol poking its nose through on the finish. **rating:** 87

best drinking Now–2006 **best vintages** '90, '92, '94, '95, '97 **drink with** Grilled fish • $20

Gilberts Cabernet Shiraz

▼▼▼▼▼ **2001** Medium to full red-purple; the clean, rich blackberry and blackcurrant fruit of the bouquet is mirrored on the deep, ripe fruits of the palate; the tannins and oak are perfectly balanced and integrated with the superb fruit. More than makes up for the offbeat Riesling. **rating:** 94

best drinking 2006–2016 **best vintages** '01 **drink with** Braised lamb • $20

gilgai winery NR

Tingha Road, Gilgai, NSW 2360 **region** Northern Slopes Zone
phone (02) 6723 1204 **open** Mon–Sat 10–6, Sun 12–6
winemaker Keith Whish **production** 550 cases **est.** 1968
product range Pinot Noir, Malbec, fortifieds.
summary Inverell medical practitioner Dr Keith Whish has been quietly producing wines from his 6-hectare vineyard for almost 30 years. All of the production is sold through cellar door. No tastings for a decade or more.

glaetzer wines NR

34 Barossa Valley Way, Tanunda, SA 5352 **region** Barossa Valley
phone (08) 8563 0288 **fax** (08) 8563 0218 **open** Mon–Sat 10.30–4.30, public holidays 1–4.30
winemaker Colin Glaetzer, Ben Glaetzer **production** 3000 cases **est.** 1996
product range ($16.50–55 CD) Bush Vine Semillon, Semillon Ratafia, Grenache Mourvedre; Sparkling Pinot Noir, The Bishop Shiraz, Shiraz, Cabernet Sauvignon Malbec, Sparkling Shiraz.
summary Colin and Ben Glaetzer are almost as well known in South Australian wine circles as Wolf Blass winemaker John Glaetzer, and, needless to say, they are all related. Glaetzer Wines purchases its grapes from third and fourth-generation Barossa Valley growers and makes an array of traditional Barossa styles. The Shiraz comes predominantly from vines 80 years or more old. However, no recent tastings. National retail distribution; exports to the US, Canada, the UK, Belgium, Germany, Italy, The Netherlands, Switzerland, Singapore and Fiji.

🐚 glastonbury estate wines   NR

Gympie/Woolooga Road, Glastonbury, Qld 4570 (postal) **region** Queensland Coastal
phone (07) 5484 9106 **fax** (07) 5484 9111 **open** Not
winemaker Peter Scudamore-Smith MW (Consultant) **production** 4000 cases **est.** 2001
product range ($13–29 ML) Beach Series Unwooded Chardonnay, Emotions Cabernet Sauvignon.
summary Glastonbury Estate is situated in the hills of Glastonbury, high up in the Sunshine Coast hinterland, 50 minutes from Noosa. It is the vision of managing director Steve Davoren, who (in typical Queensland tradition) has established a combined wine and tourism venture. Six and a half hectares of chardonnay, merlot and cabernet sauvignon have been established on terraces cut into the hillsides, with further plantings underway. Peter Scudamore-Smith MW is the consultant winemaker, and the wines have already had significant success in wine competitions in Queensland. A large lodge comfortably sleeping three couples has been built, while Glastonbury Estate is intended to become one of the first developments in Queensland to offer building sites amongst the vines, with further details available from the website.

Glastonbury Estate Emotions Cabernet Sauvignon

▼▼▼▼ 2000 Medium to full red-purple; the solid, dark fruit of the bouquet is matched by lots of charry oak; the palate is highly extracted and heavily oaked, having spent 15 months in new French and American oak barriques. However, there is sufficient fruit to underwrite the future positive development of the wine.   **rating:** 85
best drinking 2005–2010 **drink with** Char-grilled rump steak • $29

glenalbyn   ★★★

84 Halls Road, Kingower, Vic 3517 **region** Bendigo
phone (03) 5438 8255 **fax** (03) 5438 8255 **open** 10.30–4.30 most days
winemaker Lee (Leila) Gillespie **production** 500 cases **est.** 1997
product range ($16–25 CD) Sauvignon Blanc, Pinot Noir, Cabernet Sauvignon.
summary When Leila Gillespie's great-grandfather applied for his land title in 1856, he had already established a vineyard on the property (in 1853). A survey plan of 1857 shows the cultivation paddocks, one marked the Grape Paddock, and a few of the original grape vines have survived in the garden which abuts the National Trust and Heritage homestead. In 1986 Leila and John Gillespie decided on a modest diversification of their sheep, wool and cereal crop farm, and began the establishment of 4 hectares of vineyards. Since 1997 Leila Gillespie has made the wine on a self-taught basis, with Cabernet Sauvignon, and more recently Pinot Noir and Sauvignon Blanc. In 2003 she commemorated 150 years of family ownership of the property.

Glenalbyn Sauvignon Blanc Gold

▼▼▼▼ 2002 Pale green-yellow; the spotlessly clean bouquet has light but clear varietal character, the crisp, tight palate with good length and feel. Well made.   **rating:** 87
best drinking Now–2005 **drink with** Antipasto • $16

glenayr   ★★★☆

Back Tea Tree Road, Richmond, Tas 7025 **region** Southern Tasmania
phone (03) 6260 2388 **fax** (03) 6260 2691 **open** Mon–Fri 8–5
winemaker Andrew Hood **production** 500 cases **est.** 1975
product range ($18–21 CD) Riesling, Chardonnay, Pinot Noir, Cabernet Shiraz Merlot; Tolpuddle Vineyards Chardonnay and Pinot Noir.
summary The principal occupation of Chris Harrington is as viticultural manager of the substantial Tolpuddle Vineyard, the grapes of which are sold to Domaine Chandon and BRL Hardy. Tiny quantities of wine are made from an adjacent 1-hectare vineyard for mailing list sales under the GlenAyr label; chardonnay and pinot noir grapes are also purchased from Tolpuddle Vineyards.

GlenAyr Pinot Noir

▼▼▼▼ 2001 Medium to full red, the purple starting to diminish; a complex bouquet, with tangy fruit and evident oak; the palate has abundant character, with tangy fruit and over-generous spicy oak. Without question, grabs the attention.   **rating:** 87
best drinking Now–2006 **best vintages** '91, '94, '96 **drink with** Braised duck • $21

🐦 glendonbrook ★★★☆

Lot 2 Park Street, East Gresford, NSW 2311 **region** Upper Hunter Valley
phone (02) 4938 9666 **fax** (02) 4938 9766 **open** Mon–Fri 9–5, weekends and public holidays 10.30–4.30
winemaker Geoff Broadfield **production** 12 000 cases **est.** 2000
product range ($18.40–22.50 CD) Semillon, Semillon Chardonnay, Verdelho, Chardonnay, Shiraz, Shiraz Cabernet Merlot, Merlot.
summary Highly successful Sydney businessman Tom Smith and wife Terese purchased the Bingleburra homestead at East Gresford in the mid-1990s. The 600-hectare property raises beef cattle, but in 1997 the decision was taken to plant 12.5 hectares of vines (8.3 ha shiraz, 4.2 ha verdelho), and this in turn led to the construction shortly prior to the 2001 vintage of a $2 million, 300-tonne capacity winery, lifting their total investment in the wine industry to $3 million. All of the winemaking equipment is new, and the Smiths employed the highly experienced Geoff Broadfield as winemaker (with 20 Hunter Valley vintages under his belt). The estate-grown grapes are supplemented by contract-grown grapes, and the winery has sufficient capacity to also offer contract winemaking facilities for others. It marks a major return to the Gresford area where Dr Henry Lindeman established his Cawarra vineyards in the mid-1800s.

Glendonbrook Verdelho

▼▼▼▽ **2001** Very pale colour; the clean, crisp bouquet has just a faint touch of fruit salad, the fresh and firm palate showing skilled winemaking, but also the inherent limitations of the variety. **rating:** 84
best drinking Now **drink with** Light pasta • $19.85

Glendonbrook Shiraz

▼▼▼▼ **2001** Medium red-purple; the solid bouquet offers a mix of ripe plum and earth fruit with a coating of vanilla oak; the well-structured palate has good weight and length, incipiently earthy and slightly gritty as young Hunter Valley shiraz so often is. **rating:** 85
best drinking 2004–2009 **drink with** Braised beef • $22.50

glen erin vineyard retreat   NR

Rochford Road, Lancefield, Vic 3435 **region** Macedon Ranges
phone (03) 5429 1041 **fax** (03) 5429 2053 **open** Weekends, public holidays 10–6
winemaker Brian Scales, John Ellis **production** 400 cases **est.** 1993
product range ($17–38 CD) Gewurztraminer, Chardonnay, Pinot Noir, Mystic Park Sparkling Macedon.
summary Brian Scales acquired the former Lancefield Winery and renamed it Glen Erin. Wines are contract-made from Macedon grapes and elsewhere and sold only through cellar door and restaurant; the conference and function facilities are supported by 24 accommodation rooms.

glenfinlass   NR

Elysian Farm, Parkes Road, Wellington, NSW 2820 **region** Central Ranges Zone
phone (02) 6845 2011 **fax** (02) 6845 3329 **open** Sat 9–5, or by appointment
winemaker Brian G Holmes **production** 500 cases **est.** 1971
product range ($15–25 CD) Sauvignon Blanc, Drought Drop (Shiraz, Cabernet Sauvignon, Sauvignon Blanc).
summary The weekend and holiday hobby of Wellington solicitor Brian Holmes, who has wisely decided to leave it at that. I have not tasted the wines for many years, but the last wines I did taste were competently made. Wines are in short supply owing to drought (1998), frost (1999) and flooding (2000), promptly followed by three more years of drought.

🐦 glengariff estate winery   NR

3234 Mount Mee Road, Dayboro Valley, Qld 4521 **region** Queensland Coastal
phone (07) 3425 1299 **fax** (07) 3425 1299 **open** Fri–Sun 10–3
winemaker Contract **production** 350 cases **est.** 1999
product range ($19.50–23.90 CD) Honorah's Semillon Chardonnay, Honorah's Chardonnay, Sparkling Celebrations, Wild Vine Red, Honorah's Shiraz Cabernet Merlot, Denny's Port.
summary The word historic is as much overused as the word passionate, but this is an historic property with a quite remarkable story. The twice-married Honorah Mullins, first to a Mr Doyle and later to a Mr Mullins, moved with her husband from County Cork, Ireland to Australia in 1875. In 1876 they moved to the Dayboro Valley and established the family dairy farm, now Glengariff Estate. At the age of 90 Honorah Mullins was still

milking a herd of 40 cows, and when 111 she continued to take her morning walk with one of her sons, Dennis Doyle. When she died on 1 May 1926, one day before her 115th birthday, she had lived through the reign of six English monarchs, from George III to George V. Tracey Wrightson, the great, great granddaughter of Honorah Mullins, together with husband Andrew and children, now own and run the 100-hectare Glengariff Estate. It operates as a tourist attraction, with a restaurant and wedding function venue and (since 1999) as a wine producer. Two hectares of shiraz, chardonnay, merlot and semillon have been planted, with the likelihood of a further 8 hectares of shiraz and chardonnay being planted in the near future.

glenguin ★★★☆

River Oaks Vineyard, Lot 8 Milbrodale Road, Broke, NSW 2330 **region** Lower Hunter Valley
phone (02) 6579 1009 **fax** (02) 6579 1009 **open** 7 days at Boutique Wine Centre, Broke Road, Pokolbin
winemaker Robin Tedder MW **production** 15 000 cases **est.** 1993
product range ($16.50–75 R) The Old Broke Block Semillon, Christina Semillon, River Terrace Vineyard Chardonnay, Griffith Vineyard Botrytised Semillon, Shiraz, Stonybroke Shiraz, School House Block Shiraz, Aristea Shiraz, Orange Vineyard Merlot.
summary Glenguin's vineyard has been established along the banks of the Wollombi Brook by Robin, Rita and Andrew Tedder, Robin and Andrew being the grandsons of Air Chief Marshal Tedder, made Baron of Glenguin by King George VI in recognition of his wartime deeds. (Glenguin is also the name of a Scottish distillery which continues to produce a single malt but which is otherwise unconnected.) Glenguin has 21 hectares of vineyard at Broke and another 3 hectares at Orange (cabernet and merlot). Exports to the UK, Germany and New Zealand.

Glenguin Stonybroke Shiraz
▼▼▼▼ **2000** Medium to full red-purple; ripe, smooth dark cherry fruit and minimal oak on the bouquet leads through to a medium-bodied palate in easy-flowing style, with more of that smooth, dark cherry fruit. Not complex, but then, why should it be? **rating:** 86
best drinking Now–2007 **drink with** Pasta bolognese • $22

🍂 glen isla estate ★★★☆

107 Glen Isla Road, Bickley, WA 6076 (postal) **region** Perth Hills
phone (08) 8357 1781 **fax** (08) 8357 1786 **open** Not
winemaker John Griffiths (Contract) **est.** 1998
product range ($16 ML) Shiraz, Merlot; Pinot Noir Methode Champenoise.
summary Jim Winterhalder has established 0.84 hectares each of merlot and pinot noir, and 2.38 hectares of shiraz, on slopes which straddle Piesse Brook, variously facing west, east and north. The wine is made by the highly-skilled John Griffiths, and, apart from a couple of retail outlets, is sold by mail order.

Glen Isla Estate Shiraz
▼▼▼▼ **2001** Strong, bright purple-red; clean black plum and blackberry fruit interplays with vanilla oak on the bouquet; the medium to full-bodied palate has good balance and structure, with savoury edges to the black fruits at the core; long finish. Spends 10 months in American oak. Full of promise. **rating:** 89
best drinking 2006–2011 **drink with** Beef spare ribs • $16

gloucester ridge vineyard ★★★★

Lot 7489 Burma Road, Pemberton, WA 6260 **region** Pemberton
phone (08) 9776 1035 **fax** (08) 9776 1390 **open** 7 days 10–5 (until late Saturday)
winemaker Brenden Smith **production** 12 000 cases **est.** 1985
product range ($12.50–30 CD) Sauvignon Blanc, Pemberton Classic White, Back Block White, Unwooded Chardonnay, Chardonnay, Reserve Chardonnay, Chimere (Sparkling), Late Harvest Riesling, Seduction (Rose style), Shiraz, Cabernet Merlot, Back Block Cabernet Sauvignon; Port.
summary Gloucester Ridge is the only vineyard located within the Pemberton town boundary, within easy walking distance. It is owned and operated by Don and Sue Hancock; some of the recent releases have been most impressive. Retail distribution in Queensland, New South Wales Victoria and WA.

Gloucester Ridge Unwooded Chardonnay
▼▼▼▼ **2002** Bright, light green-yellow; the clean and fresh bouquet has citrus fruit, joined on the light and fresh bouquet by some stone fruit flavours. Silver medal Perth Wine Show 2002. **rating:** 85
best drinking Now **drink with** Fish consomme • $16

Gloucester Ridge Premium Reserve Chardonnay

▼▼▼▼▼ 2001 Medium yellow-green; a very complex bouquet with some 'French funk' leads into a round, fleshy, well-balanced palate with a mix of yellow peach, nectarine and subtle oak, the funky characters of the bouquet absorbed by the fruit weight. Gold medal Sheraton Wine Awards 2002 and Blue Gold 2002 Sydney International Wine Competition. **rating: 94**

best drinking Now–2007 **drink with** Sweetbreads • $25

Gloucester Ridge Cabernet Merlot

▼▼▼▼ 2000 Medium red-purple; secondary, dusty, spicy, cedary aromas feed into a palate with unexpected chocolatey characters and nicely weighted, fine, sweet tannins. **rating: 87**

best drinking 2004–2009 **drink with** White Rocks veal • $20

gnadenfrei estate NR

Seppeltsfield Road, Maranga via Nuriootpa, SA 5355 **region** Barossa Valley
phone (08) 8562 2522 **fax** (08) 8562 3470 **open** Tues–Sun 10–5.30
winemaker Malcolm Seppelt **production** 1500 cases **est.** 1979
product range ($12–40 CD) Riesling, Semillon, Traminer Riesling, Shiraz Grenache, St Michael's Shiraz, Tawny Port, Sparkling.
summary A strictly cellar-door operation, which relies on a variety of sources for its wines but has a core of 2 hectares of estate shiraz and 1 hectare of grenache. A restaurant presided over by Joylene Seppelt is open for morning teas, lunches and afternoon teas. Small quantities of the wines make their way to Pennsylvania, the US.

Gnadenfrei Estate St Michael's Shiraz

▼▼▼▼▽ 2002 Dense, deep red-purple; aromas of dark plum, licorice, prune and blackberry are followed by a palate every bit as monumental as the colour and bouquet suggest, with volumes of black fruits balanced by strong, savoury tannins. The components are in balance, but the wine needs a minimum of 10 years to realise its full potential. The vines were planted in 1958, and have been dry-grown for the past 25 years. 15.3° alcohol. **rating: 93**

best drinking 2012–2020 **best vintages** '02 **drink with** Venison pie • $40

Gnadenfrei Estate Shiraz Grenache

▼▼▼▼▽ 2002 Strong red-purple; the bouquet has a complex mix of mocha, sweet leather and blackberry, the full and fleshy palate with excellent texture coming from fine-grained tannins; fruit-driven, although the oak contribution is evident. 15.2° alcohol, and a 50/50 blend of the two varieties. **rating: 90**

best drinking 2004–2009 **best vintages** '02 **drink with** Kangaroo fillet • $30

Gnadenfrei Estate Grenache

▼▼▼▼ 2002 Strong, bright red-purple; juicy black and redcurrant fruit, spice and chocolate aromas are followed by an abundantly flavoured palate, with above-average structure and, in particular, tannins. Not jammy. **rating: 88**

best drinking Now–2007 **drink with** Beef in black bean sauce • $20

gold dust wines NR

Southpark, Tallwood Road, Millthorpe, NSW 2798 **region** Orange
phone (02) 6366 5168 **fax** 902) 6361 9165 **open** By appointment
winemaker Jon Reynolds **production** 700 cases **est.** 1993
product range ($12–14.50 ML) Riesling, Chardonnay, Late Harvest Riesling.
summary John and Jacqui Corrie have established 3 hectares each of riesling and chardonnay, electing to sell two-thirds of the production, and have the remainder contract-made, since 2001 by Jon Reynolds. Most of the wine is sold by mail order.

golden grape estate NR

Oakey Creek Road, Pokolbin, NSW 2321 **region** Lower Hunter Valley
phone (02) 4998 7588 **fax** (02) 4998 7730 **open** 7 days 10–5
winemaker Neil McGuigan (Consultant) **production** NFP **est.** 1985
product range ($14.95–29.90 CD) Premier Semillon, Gewurztraminer, Sauvignon Blanc, Semillon Verdelho, Happy Valley Chardonnay, Five Star (light fruity), Frizzante Rose, Mount Leonard (Cabernet Sauvignon), Domaine Springton (Shiraz), Classic Red, fortifieds.

summary German-owned and unashamedly directed at the tourist, with a restaurant, barbecue and picnic areas, wine museum and separate tasting room for bus tours. The substantial range of wines are of diverse origins and style. The operation now has over 42 hectares of Hunter Valley plantings.

golden grove estate ★★★☆

Sundown Road, Ballandean, Qld 4382 **region** Granite Belt
phone (07) 4684 1291 **fax** (07) 4684 1247 **open** 7 days 9–5
winemaker Sam Costanzo **production** 10000 cases **est.** 1993
product range ($10–15 CD) Accommodation Creek Classic White and Classic Dry Red, Muscadean, Rose, Shiraz, Cabernet Merlot., Liqueur Muscat.
summary Golden Grove Estate was established by Mario and Sebastiana Costanzo in 1946, producing stone fruits and table grapes for the fresh fruit market. The first wine grapes (shiraz) were planted in 1972, but it was not until 1985, when ownership passed to son Sam Costanzo and wife Grace, that the use of the property started to change. In 1993 chardonnay and merlot joined the shiraz, followed by cabernet sauvignon, sauvignon blanc and semillon. Wine quality has steadily improved, with many medals in regional shows awarded up to 2002, leading to national (though limited) retail distribution.

golden gully wines NR

5900 Midwestern Highway, Mandurama, NSW 2792 **region** Orange
phone (02) 6367 5148 **fax** (02) 6367 4148 **open** Weekends 10–4, or by appointment
winemaker Jon Reynolds (Contract) **production** 1300 cases **est.** 1994
product range ($18–19 CD) Shiraz, Cabernet Merlot, Cabernet Sauvignon.
summary Kevin and Julie Bate have progressively established over 5 hectares of vineyard (2 ha cabernet sauvignon, 1.6 ha shiraz, 0.5 ha merlot and 0.5 ha each of semillon and sauvignon blanc). The first commercial crop came in 2001, but tiny makes in 1999 (Cabernet Shiraz) and 2000 Cabernet Sauvignon) have both won bronze medals at the Bathurst Cool Climate Wine Show.

golders vineyard ★★★★☆

Bridport Road, Pipers Brook, Tas 7254 **region** Northern Tasmania
phone (03) 6395 4142 **fax** (03) 6395 4142 **open** By appointment
winemaker Richard Crabtree **production** 500 cases **est.** 1991
product range ($20–32 R) Chardonnay, Pinot Noir, Reserve Pinot Noir.
summary The initial plantings of 1.5 hectares of pinot noir have been supplemented by a hectare of chardonnay. The quality of the Pinot Noir has been good from the initial vintage in 1995, hitting a high spot in 2000.

Golders Vineyard Reserve Pinot Noir

▼▼▼▼▽ 2001 Medium red-purple; a particularly complex and intense bouquet with a mix of spice, plum and stem aromas; the palate, likewise, is very intense and has great length, the only question being about the slightly hard finish, which should soften with time in bottle. **rating:** 92
best drinking 2005–2009 **drink with** Venison • $30

goona warra vineyard ★★★★☆

Sunbury Road, Sunbury, Vic 3429 **region** Sunbury
phone (03) 9740 7766 **fax** (03) 9744 7648 **open** 7 days 10–5
winemaker John Barnier, Nick Bickford **production** 3000 cases **est.** 1863
product range ($14–25 CD) Semillon Sauvignon Blanc, Chardonnay, Black Cygnet Chardonnay (unwooded), Pinot Noir, Shiraz, Black Cygnet Cabernet Shiraz, Cabernet Franc, Cabernet Merlot.
summary An historic stone winery, established under this name by a 19th-century Victorian premier. A capital infusion by a Melbourne-based venture capital group in early 2001 will result in a doubling of production. Excellent tasting facilities; an outstanding venue for weddings and receptions; Sunday lunch also served. Situated 30 minutes drive from Melbourne (10 minutes north of Tullamarine Airport). Berry Bros & Rudd import the wines into the UK.

Goona Warra Chardonnay

▼▼▼▼▽ 2001 Glowing green-yellow; the ultra-complex bouquet shows obvious barrel-ferment characters and some French solids nuances; the rich, intense and supple palate oozes nectarine and grapefruit, the oak well in the background. **rating:** 93
best drinking Now–2007 **best vintages** '01 **drink with** Pasta carbonara • $22

Goona Warra Pinot Noir

TTTTY 2001 Deep red-purple; the bouquet has very ripe, rich, dark plum fruit with echoes of spice and game; while the palate is very powerful, it has the balance and structure taking it away from dry red territory; nonetheless, needs years to show its best. **rating:** 92

best drinking 2004–2009 **drink with** Venison • $25

Goona Warra Cabernet Franc

TTTT 2000 Light to medium red-purple; moderately fragrant earthy/berry aromas are followed by a light to medium-bodied palate, offering soft, spicy tobacco leaf, earth and berry flavours; nice mouthfeel and clear varietal character. **rating:** 87

best drinking Now–2007 **best vintages** '88, '91, '92, '93 **drink with** Cannelloni • $25

Goona Warra Cabernet Merlot

TTTTY 2000 Medium red-purple; cedar, cigar, redcurrant, blackcurrant and spice aromas coalesce on the bouquet; the medium-bodied palate has sweet, supple red and blackcurrant fruit providing seductive mouthfeel and balance. **rating:** 93

best drinking Now–2009 **best vintages** '00 **drink with** Lamb casserole • $22

goundrey ★★★☆

Muir Highway, Mount Barker, WA 6324 **region** Great Southern
phone (08) 9851 1777 **fax** (08) 9851 1997 **open** 7 days 10–4.30
winemaker David Martin, Michael Perkins, Stephen Craig **production** 250 000 cases **est.** 1976
product range ($15.30–34 R) Windy Hill range of Chardonnay, Pinot Noir; Goundrey range of Riesling, Chenin Blanc, Classic White, Unwooded Chardonnay, Shiraz Cabernet, Cabernet Merlot; Reserve range of Riesling, Chardonnay, Pinot Noir, Shiraz, Cabernet Sauvignon; second label is Fox River, with Chenin Semillon Verdelho, Chardonnay, Pinot Noir, Shiraz, Shiraz Cabernet; also Langton Sauvignon Blanc Semillon.
summary Jack Bendat acquired Goundrey when it was on its knees; through significant expenditure on land, vineyards and winery capacity, it became the House that Jack Built. In late 2002 it was acquired by Vincorp, Canada's largest wine producer, for a price widely said to be more than $30 million, a sum which would have provided Bendat with a very satisfactory return on his investment. One suspects it will be more of the same with Vincorp, which will continue to expand the empire. National distribution; exports to the US, Canada, Asia, the UK and Europe.

Goundrey Riesling

TTTT 2002 Light to medium yellow-green; the bouquet and palate are quite forward and accessible, with an abundant mix of citrus and mineral; good balance, but drink sooner rather than later. **rating:** 88

best drinking Now **drink with** Asparagus • $17.85

Fox River Chenin Blanc Semillon Verdelho

TTTT 2002 Light straw-green; the clean tropical aromas of the bouquet flow through in the strong, fruit salad flavours of the palate; a relatively dry finish helps the overall feel. **rating:** 85

best drinking Now **drink with** Takeaway • $15.30

Goundrey Shiraz Cabernet Sauvignon

TTTT 2001 Medium purple-red; dark cherry, licorice and spice aromas on the bouquet flow into the full-flavoured palate, simply needing time for the slightly disjointed tannins to settle down. **rating:** 89

best drinking 2006–2011 **drink with** Braised beef • $16.15

governor robe selection NR

Waterhouse Range Vineyards, Lot 11, Old Naracoorte Road, Robe, SA 5276 **region** Limestone Coast Zone
phone (08) 8768 2083 **fax** (08) 8768 2190 **open** By appointment
winemaker Cape Jaffa Wines (Contract) **production** 750 cases **est.** 1998
product range ($17–24 R) Chardonnay, Shiraz.
summary Brothers Bill and Mick Quinlan-Watson, supported by a group of investors, began the development of Waterhouse Range Vineyards Pty Ltd in 1995, planting 15 hectares of vines that year, with further plantings over the following few years lifting the total area under vine to just under 60 hectares. The majority of the grapes are sold, with a lesser amount retained and contract-made at Cape Jaffa winery. The unusual name comes from the third Governor of South Australia, Frederick Holt Robe, who in 1845 selected the site for a port and personally put in the first survey peg at Robe. Next door is the Customs House, which is a National Trust building, and which is depicted on the label.

governor's choice winery NR

Berghofer Road, Westbrook via Toowoomba, Qld 4350 **region** Queensland Zone
phone (07) 4630 6101 **fax** (07) 4630 6701 **open** 7 days 9–5
winemaker James Yates **production** 1500 cases **est.** 1999
product range ($14–30 CD) Premium Semillon, Estate White, Verdelho, Chardonnay, Shiraz, Cabernet Shiraz, Cabernet Malbec, Cabernet Sauvignon, Tawny Port, White Port, Vintage Red Port.
summary This is a part winery, part premium guest house accommodation venture situated 18 kilometres from the town of Toowoomba. Three hectares of estate plantings produce chardonnay, shiraz, verdelho, cabernet sauvignon and malbec, made on-site and sold through the cellar door and to guests using the accommodation.

gowrie mountain estate NR

2 Warrego Highway, Kingsthorpe, Qld 4400 **region** Granite Belt
phone (07) 4630 0566 **fax** (07) 4630 0366 **open** Not
winemaker Peter Howland (Contract) **production** 4000 cases **est.** 1998
product range ($14–22 R) Semillon, Verdelho, Chardonnay, Shiraz, Gamay, Tempranillo, Chambourcin, Cabernet Sauvignon.
summary Situated northeast of Toowoomba, in the heart of the Darling Downs, this is a substantial new entrant, having already established 32 hectares to mainstream varieties, and to the new breed in the form of tempranillo (4 ha) and gamay (2 ha). Part of the production goes to Hope Estate in the Hunter Valley, which makes the red wines, and part to Preston Peak, where the white wines and Tempranillo are made. An underground barrel and bottled wine storage area has been completed, with a sales, restaurant and general tourist facility planned. All the Newberry family members, headed by father Ron, are involved in the venture.

grace burn estate ★★★☆

458 Maroondah Highway, Healesville, Vic 3777 **region** Yarra Valley
phone (03) 5962 4440 **fax** (03) 5962 1186 **open** 7 days 10–6 summer, weekends 10–6 winter
winemaker Rob Dolan, Kate Goodman (Contract) **production** 6000 cases **est.** 1998
product range ($18–24 CD) Sauvignon Blanc, Pinot Noir, Cabernet Sauvignon.
summary Planting on the 20-hectare Grace Burn property began in December 1998, and was completed in the spring of 1999. In all 13.6 hectares of vines have been established, including pinot noir (4.6 ha), cabernet sauvignon (2.6 ha), chardonnay (2.1 ha), sauvignon blanc and shiraz (2 ha each) and merlot (0.4 ha). A significant amount of the grape production has been sold, but the plan is to increase the amount made under the Grace Burn label. Situated 2.5 kilometres northeast of Healesville, it is one of the highest sites in the southern end of the Yarra Valley, the southern boundary of the sloping hillside being the Grace Burn, which gives the business its name.

Grace Burn Estate Sauvignon Blanc

♀♀♀♀♀ 2002 Light green-yellow; the spotlessly clean bouquet is at the grassy/herbal end of the spectrum, but on the lively, fresh palate gentle tropical and gooseberry flavours make their appearance. Excellent balance; skilled winemaking at work. **rating:** 92
best drinking Now **drink with** Gravlax • $20

Grace Burn Estate Pinot Noir

♀♀♀♀ 2001 Light red; light spicy/foresty/savoury aromas and flavours are certainly part and parcel of pinot noir, but the wine needs more sweet fruit for higher points. Drink sooner rather than later. **rating:** 84
best drinking Now **drink with** Chinese • $24

gracedale hills estate NR

770 Healesville–Kooweerup Road, Healesville, Vic 3777 **region** Yarra Valley
phone (03) 5967 3403 **fax** (03) 5967 3581 **open** Not
winemaker Gary Mills **production** 1300 cases **est.** 1997
product range Chardonnay, Shiraz.
summary Dr Richard Gutch has established 2 hectares of chardonnay and 2 hectares of shiraz at a time when most would be retiring from active business, but it represents the culmination of a life-long love of fine wine, and Richard Gutch showed no hard feelings towards me when I encouraged him in the mid-1990s to plant vines on the north-facing slopes of his property. Here, too, the grapes have been sold to others, but he is now retaining sufficient to make around 1300 cases a year.

✍ gralaine vineyard   NR

65 Feehan's Road, Mount Duneed, Vic 3216 (postal) **region** Geelong
phone 0429 009 973 **fax** (03) 9886 7377 **open** Available 7 days 10–5 at Hanging Rock Winery,
88 Jim Road, Newham
winemaker John Ellis (Contract) **est.** 1983
product range ($26 CD) Merlot.
summary Graeme and Elaine Carroll have gradually established 4 hectares of low-yielding merlot (with a few
cabernet sauvignon vines). There are no cellar-door sales, but the wine can be tasted at Hanging Rock Winery,
where it is contract-made by John Ellis.

gralyn estate   ★★★★★

Caves Road, Wilyabrup, WA 6280 **region** Margaret River
phone (08) 9755 6245 **fax** (08) 9755 6245 **open** 7 days 10.30–4.30
winemaker Graham Hutton, Merilyn Hutton, Bradley Hutton **production** 2500 cases **est.** 1975
product range ($16–90 CD) Premium Dry White, Late Harvest Riesling, Old Vine Shiraz, Late Harvest
Cabernet, Shiraz Cabernet, Unoaked Cabernet, Cabernet Sauvignon, and an extensive range of fortifieds
including Liqueur Riesling, White Port, Vintage Port and Ruby Port.
summary The move from primarily fortified wine to table wine production has been completed, and has
brought considerable success. The red wines are made in a distinctively different style from most of those from
the Margaret River region, with an opulence (in part from American oak) which is reminiscent of some of the
bigger wines from McLaren Vale. The age of the vines (25 years plus) and the site are also significant factors.
Exports to the US, Denmark and Singapore.

Gralyn Estate Old Vine Shiraz

�♦♦ 2001 Dense, opaque red-purple, staining the glass as it is swirled; the clean bouquet is extremely
powerful, with blackberry/black fruits dominant. The palate is equally compact and powerful, with the low-
yielding, 30-year-old vines doing all the work, American oak playing a pure support role.   **rating:** 94
best drinking 2006–2016 **best vintages** '94, '95, '96, '00 **drink with** Strong red meat dishes • $60

Gralyn Estate Shiraz Cabernet

♦♦♦♦♦ 2001 A similar dense, opaque purple-colour to that of the Old Vine Shiraz; powerful blackberry,
blackcurrant, oak and spice aromas flood the bouquet. An ultra-powerful palate, chunky and dense, with bitter
chocolate undertones and pronounced tannins, all make for a formidably long-lived wine.   **rating:** 94
best drinking 2010–2025 **best vintages** '95, '99, '00, '01 **drink with** Smoked lamb • $90

Gralyn Estate Cabernet Sauvignon

♦♦♦♦♡ 2001 Deep, dark inky purple; a dense and powerful bouquet with more of the blackcurrant/black
fruit aromas leads into a palate which floods the mouth with blackcurrant/cassis, and lingering, savoury tannins
on the finish and aftertaste.   **rating:** 93
best drinking 2010–2030 **best vintages** '99, '00, '01 **drink with** Marinated beef • $90

grampians estate   NR

Mafeking Road, Willaura, Vic 3379 **region** Grampians
phone (03) 5354 6245 **fax** (03) 5354 6257 **open** By appointment
winemaker Simon Clayfield **production** 1000 cases **est.** 1989
product range ($15.50–22 R) Mafeking Unwooded Chardonnay, Mafeking Gold Chardonnay, Mafeking
Shiraz.
summary Ten years ago local farmers and graziers Sarah and Tom Guthrie decided to diversify their activities,
while continuing to run their fat lamb and wool production. So they planted a little over 1.5 hectares each of
shiraz and chardonnay, and opened the Thermopylae Host Farm business. This offers two farm-stay buildings: a
five-bedroom shearer's cottage which sleeps 12 and a 5-room miner's cottage which sleeps ten. They also
secured the services of immensely experienced local winemaker Simon Clayfield to produce the Grampians
Estate wines. These are sold to those who stay on the farm, which is able to offer an unusually wide range of
activities; the wines are also available by direct mail order and at one or two local hotels, including the
Kookaburra Rest at Halls Gap.

🐌 grancari estate wines ★★★☆

50 Northumberland Road, Onkaparinga Hills, SA 5162 **region** McLaren Vale
phone (08) 8382 4465 **fax** (08) 8382 4465 **open** By appointment
winemaker Kevin O'Brien (Contract) **production** 800 cases **est.** 1999
product range ($25–32 CD) Shiraz, Old Vine Grenache, Old Vine Merlot.
summary In 1983 Rino and Greta Ozzella purchased a small vineyard in McLaren Vale which had been planted in the early 1940s to a little under 3 hectares of grenache. The grapes were sold to other winemakers, and in 1993 the Ozzellas purchased two properties at Loxton in the Riverland. After 3 years developing the vineyards there, the Ozzellas sold the blocks and returned to McLaren Vale, planting a further 2.5 hectares of shiraz on a westerly slope facing the sea, and took the decision to establish their own brand. The wines are contract-made by Kevin O'Brien at Kangarilla Road.

Grancari Estate Shiraz

YYYY 2001 Medium to full red-purple; the bouquet has a lifted and complex mix of herb, spice, black fruits and earth, the powerful, savoury palate adding dark chocolate as another flavour dimension. However, it does chop off fractionally on the finish – despite a towering 15.5° alcohol. **rating:** 89
best drinking 2005–2015 **drink with** Braised oxtail • $32

Grancari Estate Old Vine Merlot

YYYY 2002 Youthful purple-red; a clean and clear juicy, fruity varietal bouquet is followed by a palate with plenty of weight, strong varietal character and more structure than is sometimes encountered. **rating:** 87
best drinking Now–2006 **drink with** Game pie • $25

granite ridge wines NR

Sundown Road, Ballandean, Qld 4382 **region** Granite Belt
phone (07) 4684 1263 **fax** (07) 4684 1250 **open** 7 days 9–5
winemaker Dennis Ferguson, Juliane Ferguson **production** 1800 cases **est.** 1995
product range ($8–28 CD) Goldies Unwooded Chardonnay, First Oak Chardonnay, Citrine Semillon (sweet), il Bello Rosso (sparkling red), Topaz, Granite Garnet, Granite Rock Shiraz, Fergies Hill Merlot, The Ridge Merlot Cabernet Sauvignon, Millennium Cabernet Merlot, Bilby Red Cabernet Sauvignon, Granite Grange Cabernet Sauvignon, Granite Amber Liqueur Muscat, Pops Port, Surrender Cream Liqueur.
summary Formerly known as Denlana Ferguson Estate Wines, Granite Ridge had considerable success in the mid-1990s, with both the 1995 and 1996 Cabernet Sauvignon being judged Queensland's Best Cabernet (though quite by whom I am not sure); continues to be run by Dennis Ferguson. Its Goldies Unwooded Chardonnay was the first Queensland wine to be chosen as the official Parliamentary Wine of the Queensland government. Most of the production comes from its 5-hectare vineyard, which is planted to pinot gris, chardonnay, shiraz, petit verdot, tempranillo and cabernet sauvignon.

grant burge ★★★★

Barossa Vines, Krondorf Road, Tanunda, SA 5352 **region** Barossa Valley
phone (08) 8563 3700 **fax** (08) 8563 2807 **open** 7 days 10–5
winemaker Grant Burge **production** 108 000 cases **est.** 1988
product range ($10.50–100 R) Has moved to a series of vineyard-designated varietal wines including Thorn Vineyard Riesling, Zerk Vineyard Semillon, Kraft Vineyard Sauvignon Blanc, Barossa Ranges Chardonnay, Summers Chardonnay, Lily Farm Frontignac, Filsell Shiraz, Hillcott Merlot and Cameron Vale Cabernet Sauvignon. Top-of-the-range reds are Meshach Shiraz, The Holy Trinity (Grenache Shiraz Mourvedre), Reserve The Holy Trinity and Shadrach Cabernet Sauvignon; also Rubycind and Virtuoso; RBG Gewurztraminer, RBS1 Semillon, RBS2 Semillon, RSHZ Eden Valley Shiraz, MSJ1 Shiraz Cabernet, RBM1 Merlot; Sparkling, fortifieds. The budget-priced Barossa Vines range joined the band in late 1999, Miamba Shiraz in 2001.
summary As one might expect, this very experienced industry veteran makes consistently good, full-flavoured and smooth wines chosen from the pick of the crop of his extensive vineyard holdings, which total an impressive 200 hectares; the immaculately restored/rebuilt stone cellar-door sales buildings are another attraction. The provocatively named The Holy Trinity joins Shadrach and Meshach at the top of the range. In 1999 Grant Burge repurchased the farm from Mildara Blass by acquiring the Krondorf winery (not the brand) in which he made his first fortune. He has renamed it Barossa Vines and, taking advantage of the great views it offers, has opened a cellar door offering casual food, featuring local produce wherever possible. Exports to the UK, Europe, the US, Canada and Asia.

Grant Burge Thorn Vineyard Riesling

▼▼▼▼ 2002 Medium yellow-green; a clean, soft, ripe citrus/lime bouquet then plenty of mid-palate fruit before tightening up nicely on the finish. **rating:** 89

best drinking Now–2006 **best vintages** '88, '90, '92, '93, '94, '96, '98, '00 **drink with** Smoked trout mousse • $16.55

Grant Burge Barossa Vines Semillon Sauvignon Blanc

▼▼▼▼▽ 2002 The Barossa Valley is not the most likely source of a blend such as this, but Grant Burge does well. Rich, tropical aromas and a ripe semillon component underpin a palate with gooseberry and pineapple flavours; strongly structured and with good length. **rating:** 91

best drinking Now **best vintages** '02 **drink with** Pasta marinara • $11.50

Grant Burge Virtuoso

▼▼▼▼ 2002 Medium to full yellow-green; the solidly ripe bouquet is followed by a palate which has contrasting lemony flavours and fresh acidity. **rating:** 86

best drinking Now **best vintages** '98 **drink with** Brasserie food • $15.95

Grant Burge Pinot Noir Chardonnay

▼▼▼▼ NV Straw-pink; the bouquet has nutty, toasty lees contact aromas, and the palate has lots of strawberry and nuts to provide flavour; well-balanced dosage. **rating:** 87

best drinking Now–2006 **drink with** Chinese prawns • $21.50

Grant Burge Eden Valley Shiraz RSZ1

▼▼▼▼▽ 1999 Medium purple-red; the clean, moderately intense bouquet has dark cherry and plum fruit; an elegant medium-bodied palate follows, having good length, fine tannins and well-balanced and integrated French oak. **rating:** 92

best drinking 2004–2009 **best vintages** '99 **drink with** Roast kid • $45

Grant Burge Miamba Shiraz

▼▼▼▼ 2001 Good colour; the bouquet has an aromatic mix of red and black fruits with the obligatory sauce of vanilla oak; the medium-bodied palate has plenty of expressive fruit, nicely balanced tannins and controlled American oak. **rating:** 88

best drinking 2005–2010 **drink with** Steak and kidney pie • $20

Grant Burge The Holy Trinity Grenache Shiraz Mourvedre

▼▼▼▼ 1999 Medium red-purple; a clean and bright bouquet with hints of spice and jam to the sweet fruit, then a palate with good depth and structure, showing generous, sweet fruit throughout. **rating:** 89

best drinking Now–2006 **best vintages** '98 **drink with** Jugged hare • $33

greenock creek wines NR

Radford Road, Seppeltsfield, SA 5360 **region** Barossa Valley
phone (08) 8562 8103 **fax** (08) 8562 8259 **open** Wed–Mon 11–5 when wine available
winemaker Michael Waugh **production** 2500 cases **est.** 1978
product range ($25–160 CD) Alices Shiraz, Apricot Block Shiraz, Seven Acre Shiraz, Creek Block Shiraz, Roennfeldt Road Shiraz, Cornerstone Grenache, Cabernet Sauvignon, Roennfeldt Road Cabernet Sauvignon.
summary Michael and Annabelle Waugh are disciples of Rocky O'Callaghan of Rockford Wines and have deliberately accumulated a series of old dryland, low-yielding Barossa vineyards, aiming to produce wines of unusual depth of flavour and character. They have handsomely succeeded in this aim, achieving icon status and stratospheric prices in the US, making the opinions of Australian scribes irrelevant. They also offer superior accommodation in the ancient but beautifully restored two-bedroom cottage 'Miriam's'; Michael Waugh is a skilled stonemason.

green valley vineyard ★★★☆

3137 Sebbes Road, Forest Grove, WA 6286 **region** Margaret River
phone (08) 9757 7510 **fax** (08) 9757 7510 **open** 7 days 10–6
winemaker Moss Wood (Contract) **production** 3500 cases **est.** 1980
product range ($17.50–30 CD) Riesling, Chardonnay, Gelignite Block Shiraz, Cabernet Sauvignon.

summary Owners Ed and Eleanore Green commenced the development of Green Valley Vineyard in 1980. It is still a part-time operation, with the wines made by contract, but production has grown steadily from the 7.7 hectares of vines, and the Cabernet Sauvignon has been a consistent medal winner. Exports to Singapore and the US.

Green Valley Vineyard Riesling

♥♥♥♥ **2002** Light straw-green; the bouquet is clean with soft tropical lime aromas, quite different from the 2001; the palate has nicely balanced and easily accessible fruit. **rating:** 87

best drinking Now–2005 **drink with** Asparagus with hollandaise sauce • $17.50

Green Valley Vineyard Gelignite Block Shiraz

♥♥♥♥ **2001** Medium to full red-purple; the complex, dark fruits and gamey characters on both bouquet and palate are nearly identical to the previous vintage, and there has to be a question about the brettanomyces status of the wine. **rating:** 85

best drinking Now–2005 **drink with** Venison • $25

grevillea estate   NR

Buckajo Road, Bega, NSW 2550 **region** South Coast Zone
phone (02) 6492 3006 **fax** (02) 6492 5330 **open** 7 days 9–5
winemaker Nicola Collins **production** 3000 cases **est.** 1980
product range ($12–25 CD) Daisy Hill Riesling, Lunatic Hill Sauvignon Blanc, Unoaked Chardonnay, Peak Hill Chardonnay, Rose Hill Gewurztraminer, Traminer Riesling, Rougon, Grosse's Creek Merlot, Edmund Kirby Cabernet Sauvignon, Family Reserve Cabernet Sauvignon, Old Tawny Port.
summary A tourist-oriented winery which successfully sells all of its surprisingly large production through the cellar door and to local restaurants. All the wines have very attractive labels, and the quality has improved significantly in recent years.

grey sands   ★★★★

Cnr Kerrisons Road and Frankford Highway, Glengarry, Tas 7275 **region** Northern Tasmania
phone (03) 6396 1167 **fax** (03) 6396 1153 **open** Fourth Sunday of each month 10–5, or by appointment
winemaker Bob Richter **production** 300 cases **est.** 1989
product range ($22–35 CD) Pinot Gris, Merlot, Shiraz.
summary Bob and Rita Richter began the establishment of Grey Sands in 1988, slowly increasing the plantings over the ensuing 10 years to the present total of 2.5 hectares. The ultra-high density of 8900 vines per hectare reflects the experience gained by the Richters in their 3-year stay in England, during which time they visited many vineyards across Europe, and Bob Richter's graduate diploma in wine from Roseworthy Agricultural College.

Grey Sands Pinot Gris

♥♥♥♥♡ **2001** Light to medium yellow-green; the positively accented bouquet has distinct apple and spice aromas, and the palate has plenty of flavour, character and length. Shows that Pinot Gris does not have to be highly alcoholic to obtain flavour. 12.8° alcohol. **rating:** 90

best drinking Now–2006 **best vintages** '00, '01 **drink with** Bocconcini • $22

grosset   ★★★★★

King Street, Auburn, SA 5451 **region** Clare Valley
phone (08) 8849 2175 **fax** (08) 8849 2292 **open** Wed–Sun 10–5 from 1st week of September for approx 6 weeks
winemaker Jeffrey Grosset **production** 8500 cases **est.** 1981
product range ($24.50–58 CD) Watervale Riesling, Polish Hill Riesling, Semillon Sauvignon Blanc, Piccadilly Chardonnay, Gaia (a Cabernet blend), Reserve Pinot Noir.
summary Jeffrey Grosset served part of his apprenticeship at the vast Lindeman Karadoc winery, moving from the largest to one of the smallest when he established Grosset Wines in its old stone winery. He now crafts the wines with the utmost care from grapes grown to the most exacting standards; all need a certain amount of time in bottle to achieve their ultimate potential, not the least the Rieslings and Gaia, among Australia's best examples of their kind. At a Riesling Summit held in Hamburg in the latter part of 1998, Grosset was voted Riesling Winemaker of the Year. Exports to the US, Europe and Asia mean a continuous shortage of the wines in all markets.

Grosset Polish Hill Riesling

▼▼▼▼▼ **2002** Light straw-green; the toasty but discreet bouquet has crisp apple and mineral notes, but is far from flamboyant; the palate is already offering much more power than the bouquet, with flavours running through from apple to lime and a long finish. **rating:** 95

best drinking 2006–2016 **best vintages** '87, '90, '93, '94, '95, '96, '97, '98, '99, '00, '02 **drink with** Grilled South Australian whiting • $38

Grosset Watervale Riesling

▼▼▼▼▼ **2002** Light straw-green; the bouquet is intense, yet not exuberant, with some slate and spice aromas still in the course of the earliest stages of development; the long, clean and vibrant palate has crisp apple and lime flavours accompanied by excellent acidity. As often happens, is showing more in its youth than the Polish Hill, but in the course of time the positions will likely reverse. **rating:** 96

best drinking Now–2013 **best vintages** '81, '86, '90, '93, '94, '95, '96, '97, '98, '99, 00, '01, '02 **drink with** Fish terrine • $38

Grosset Semillon Sauvignon Blanc

▼▼▼▼▼ **2002** Lively, pristine aromas of gooseberry and green apple introduce a wine which literally dances on the tongue through to a long finish. All class. **rating:** 96

best drinking Now–2007 **best vintages** '93, '94, '95, '96, '97, '99, '00, '01, '02 **drink with** Antipasto • $29.50

Grosset Piccadilly Chardonnay

▼▼▼▼▼ **2001** Light to medium green-yellow; a distinctly Burgundian and very complex, tangy bouquet is followed by an equally complex palate in both texture and flavour; creamy/cashew characters marry neatly with the melon and stone fruit; subtle oak. **rating:** 95

best drinking Now–2005 **best vintages** '96, '97, '99, '00, '01 **drink with** Milk-fed veal • $47

Grosset Pinot Noir

▼▼▼▼▽ **2001** Light to medium red-purple; a complex and aromatic bouquet with forest, spice and mint, showing positive whole bunch characters; the lively, savoury, tangy palate has an almost citrussy finish; good length. Only 260 cases made. **rating:** 91

best drinking Now–2005 **best vintages** '00 **drink with** Braised duck • $58

Grosset Gaia

▼▼▼▼ **2000** Medium red-purple; a fragrant bouquet offering a mix of cedar, cassis, blackberry and herb leads into a light to medium-bodied palate with good texture and structure; some savoury notes, but not quite the fruit richness of the best vintages. **rating:** 89

best drinking 2005–2010 **best vintages** '90, '91, '92, '94, '95, '96, '98, '99 **drink with** Clare hare pie • $58

grove estate   NR

Murringo Road, Young, NSW 2594 **region** Hilltops
phone (02) 6382 6999 **fax** (02) 6382 4527 **open** Weekends 10–5, or by appointment
winemaker Monarch Winemaking Services (Contract) **production** 2000 cases **est.** 1989
product range ($14–21 CD) Hilltops Semillon, Murringo Way Chardonnay, The Cellar Block Shiraz, Hilltops Zinfandel, The Partners Cabernet Sauvignon.
summary A partnership headed by Brian Mullany has established a 30-hectare vineyard planted to semillon, chardonnay, merlot, shiraz, cabernet sauvignon and zinfandel. Most of the grapes are sold (principally to Southcorp), but a limited amount of wine is contract-made for the Grove Estate label. No recent tastings.

grove hill   ★★★★

120 Old Norton Summit Road, Norton Summit, SA 5136 **region** Adelaide Hills
phone (08) 8390 1437 **fax** (08) 8390 1437 **open** Sun 11–5
winemaker Contract **production** 500 cases **est.** 1978
product range ($35–40 CD) Chardonnay, Reserve Chardonnay, Sparkling Marguerite, Pinot Noir.
summary Grove Hill is a heritage property established in 1846 with the original homestead and outbuildings and held by the same family since that time. Winemaking by David Powell (of Torbreck) adds an extra degree of interest.

growlers gully ★★★☆

21a Shaws Road, Merton, Vic 3715 **region** Central Victorian High Country
phone (03) 5778 9615 **fax** (03) 5778 9615 **open** Fri 5–7, weekends and public holidays 12–6, or by appointment
winemaker Martin Williams MW, Daniel Crane MW (Contract) **production** 380 cases **est.** 1997
product range ($18–22 CD) Shiraz, Cabernet Sauvignon.
summary Les and Wendy Oates began the establishment of the Growlers Gully vineyard in 1997, extending it in 1998 to a total of 4 hectares of shiraz and 1 hectare of cabernet sauvignon. It sits at an elevation of 375 metres on fertile brown clay loam soil. Very competent contract winemaking by Martin Williams MW has led to richly flavoured and coloured wine. A rammed earth cellar-door sales outlet opened in early 2002, with the ambition of ultimately offering light meals and the opportunity for visitors to use the barbecue facilities on-site.

Growlers Gully Shiraz

▼▼▼▽ 2002 Medium red; fresh red fruit aromas and a light dusting of oak are followed by a pleasant, smooth, soft palate, medium-bodied, with red fruit flavours and light tannins. Doesn't really show its 13° alcohol. **rating:** 84
best drinking 2004–2007 **drink with** Braised ox cheek • $20

Growlers Gully Cabernet Sauvignon

▼▼▼▽ 2001 The colour is light, although the hue is quite good; light earthy/berry aromas and subtle French oak are followed by a palate with light, sweet redcurrant fruit; lacks depth and texture, and belies its 13.7° alcohol, but has been well made. Young vines are presumably part of the picture. **rating:** 84
best drinking 2004–2007 **drink with** Lamb cutlets • $18

haan wines ★★★★★

Siegersdorf Road, Tanunda, SA 5352 **region** Barossa Valley
phone (08) 8562 4590 **fax** (08) 8562 4590 **open** Not
winemaker James Irvine (Contract) **production** 4000 cases **est.** 1993
product range ($18–38 ML) Semillon, Viognier, Chanticleer Sparkling Rose, Wilhelmus (red blend), Shiraz Prestige, Merlot Prestige.
summary Hans and Fransien Haan established their business in 1993 when they acquired a 16-hectare vineyard near Tanunda (since extended to 36.7 ha). The primary focus was on Merlot and in particular on the luxury Merlot Prestige, and they understandably chose James Irvine as their contract winemaker; he has in fact produced sumptuous red wines across the range. There are no cellar-door sales; the wines are distributed in eastern Australia through Australian Prestige Wines and exported to the UK, the US, Switzerland, Germany, Malaysia, Singapore, Hong Kong and Japan.

Haan Viognier

▼▼▼▼▽ 2002 Light to medium yellow-green; the moderately intense bouquet shows clear varietal character with honeysuckle and blossom aromas, characters which come through on the palate, which has good length and grip yet avoids the phenolic trap. **rating:** 93
best drinking Now–2006 **best vintages** '99, '00, '01, '02 **drink with** Rich fish dishes • $24.95

Haan Shiraz Prestige

▼▼▼▼▼ 2000 Dark deep red; there are complex spicy/cedary overtones to the ripe plum of the bouquet, which unfolds into a luscious plum and prune-flavoured palate; expert winemaking has avoided over-extraction. **rating:** 95
best drinking Now–2013 **best vintages** '00 **drink with** Rump of lamb • $47.95

Haan Merlot Prestige

▼▼▼▼ 2000 Medium red-purple; concentrated and very ripe dark fruit aromas verge on plum pudding. The palate flows on with slightly jammy fruit, then potent tannins. Somewhat atypical for Haan. **rating:** 89
best drinking 2004–2010 **drink with** Game pie • $49.95

Haan Wilhelmus

▼▼▼▼▼ 2000 Strong, deep red-purple; the bouquet is redolent of ripe red and black fruits supported by positive oak; the palate has sweet blackcurrant, spice, anise and chocolate flavours within a mesh of fine, ripe tannins and good oak. Stylish wine; a blend of the five Bordeaux varieties which spends 20 months in French oak. **rating:** 95
best drinking 2005–2015 **best vintages** '00 **drink with** Braised lamb • $48.95

hackersley ★★★★

Ferguson Road, Dardanup, WA 6236 **region** Geographe
phone (08) 9384 6247 **fax** (08) 9383 3364 **open** Fri–Sun 10–4
winemaker Contract **production** 1000 cases **est.** 1997
product range ($18–23 CD) Semillon, Sauvignon Blanc Semillon, Verdelho, Shiraz, Cabernet Sauvignon.
summary Hackersley is a partnership between the Ovens, Stacey and Hewitt families, friends since their university days who had (so they say) the misguided belief that growing and making their own wine would be cheaper than buying it. They found what they describe as a 'little piece of paradise in the Ferguson Valley just south of Dardanup', and in September 1998 they planted a little under 8 hectares, extended in August 2000 to 9.5 hectares of the mainstream varieties (interestingly, they turned their backs on chardonnay). Most of the crop is sold to Houghton, but a small quantity of immaculately packaged wines have been made for release under the Hackersley label.

Hackersley Semillon

▼▼▼▼▽ **2002** Light to medium yellow-green; a complex mix of ripe lemon and subliminal spicy oak aromas move into a clean, fresh, long palate marked by lingering lemony fruit and acidity. **rating:** 92
best drinking Now–2006 **drink with** Saffron risotto • $18

Hackersley Verdelho

▼▼▼▼ **2002** Light straw-green; lively citrus-toned fruit salad and nectarine on the bouquet, then a palate with nectarine and, indeed, nougat. A Verdelho with attitude. **rating:** 87
best drinking Now **drink with** Pork spare ribs • $18

haig NR

Square Mile Road, Mount Gambier, SA 5290 **region** Mount Gambier
phone (08) 8725 5414 **fax** (08) 8725 5414 **open** 7 days 11–5
winemaker Martin Slocombe (Contract) **production** 1000 cases **est.** 1982
product range ($16–19 CD) Chardonnay, Late Harvest Chardonnay, Pinot Noir, Cabernet Sauvignon.
summary The 4 hectares of estate vineyards are planted on the rich volcanic soils near the slopes of the famous Blue Lake of Mount Gambier. I have neither seen nor tasted the wines.

hainault ★★★

255 Walnut Road, Bickley, WA 6076 **region** Perth Hills
phone (08) 9293 8339 **open** Weekends and public holidays 11–5, or by appointment
winemaker Tony Davis (Contract) **production** 4500 cases **est.** 1980
product range ($15–24 CD) Gewurztraminer, Talus (Sparkling Pinot Noir), Shiraz, Cabernet Sauvignon, Tawny Port.
summary Lyn and Michael Sykes became the owners of Hainault in 2002, after Bill Mackey and wife Vicki headed off elsewhere. The 11 hectares of close-planted vines are hand-pruned and hand-picked, and the pinot noir is very sensibly used to make a sparkling wine rather than a table wine. The plans are to open a restaurant when the necessary bureaucratic regulations have been dealt with.

hamelin bay ★★★★

McDonald Road, Karridale, WA 6288 **region** Margaret River
phone (08) 9758 6779 **fax** (08) 9758 6779 **open** 7 days 10–5
winemaker Philip Tubb, Julian Scott **production** 15 000 cases **est.** 1992
product range ($16–42 R) Sauvignon Blanc, Semillon Sauvignon Blanc, Chardonnay, Five Ashes Reserve Chardonnay, Rampant White, Rampant Red, Shiraz, Cabernet Merlot, Cabernet Sauvignon.
summary The 25-hectare Hamelin Bay vineyard was established by the Drake-Brockman family. The initial releases were contract-made, but a winery with a cellar-door sales facility was opened in 2000. In the meantime, production has increased from 5000 to 15 000 cases. Exports to the UK, Canada, Germany and Singapore.

Hamelin Bay Sauvignon Blanc

▼▼▼▼ **2002** Light straw-green; the positive, quite intense bouquet has clear savoury, herbaceous varietal character; the palate is firm, but not broad, making a robust impact. If ever there was a Sauvignon Blanc needing food, this is it. **rating:** 89
best drinking Now–2005 **drink with** Char-grilled octopus • $18.60

Hamelin Bay Semillon Sauvignon Blanc

▼▼▼▼▽ **2002** Light straw-green; the clean, crisp bouquet has a mix of mineral, spice and herb flavours. The bright and lively palate is intense and long; another positive wine from Hamelin Bay for this vintage. **rating:** 90

best drinking Now–2007 **drink with** Tempura • $18.60

Hamelin Bay Chardonnay

▼▼▼▼ **2001** Light to medium yellow-green; the bouquet has a subtle yet quite complex mix of melon and gentle oak; the palate has appealing flow and melon/cashew flavour; balanced finish. **rating:** 88

best drinking Now–2005 **best vintages** '00 **drink with** Lemon chicken • $25.30

Hamelin Bay Five Ashes Reserve Chardonnay

▼▼▼▼▼ **2001** Light to medium yellow-green; clean, intense nectarine and citrus fruit is supported by fine oak on the bouquet; the intense, long, elegant, fruit-driven palate is certain to age very well. A gold medal winner at the 2002 Margaret River Wine Show in what must be the most competitive Chardonnay class in the show system. **rating:** 94

best drinking 2004–2011 **best vintages** '01 **drink with** Salmon risotto • $42

Hamelin Bay Cabernet Sauvignon

▼▼▼▼ **2001** Strong red-purple; earthy blackberry fruit, with hints of herb à la Coonawarra, is followed by a very concentrated, herbal/herbaceous palate with lingering tannins. There are some very interesting dynamics going on with the Hamelin Bay red wines. **rating:** 89

best drinking 2006–2011 **drink with** Butterfly leg of lamb • $28.60

hamilton ★★★★☆

Main Road, Willunga, SA 5172 **region** McLaren Vale
phone (08) 8556 2288 **fax** (08) 8556 2868 **open** 7 days 10–5
winemaker Paul Gordon, Tim Bailey (Assistant) **production** 20 000 cases **est.** 1837
product range ($10.95–49.95 R) Slate Quarry Riesling, Synergy Semillon Sauvignon Blanc, Almond Grove Chardonnay, Colton Ruins GSM, Gumprs' Block Shiraz, Lot 148 Merlot, Synergy Cabernet Merlot, Hut Block Cabernet Sauvignon; Hamilton Reserve wines are Richard Hamilton Signature Chardonnay, Marion Vineyard Grenache Shiraz, Burton's Vineyard Grenache Shiraz, Centurion 100 Year Old Vines Shiraz, Egremont Reserve Merlot.
summary Hamilton has outstanding estate vineyards, some of great age, all fully mature, but I have often felt that the end products did not seem to do full justice to those vineyards. The arrival (in 2002) of former Rouge Homme winemaker Paul Gordon seems to have justified that feeling, for the overall quality has lifted significantly. Exports to Europe, the US, Canada, and Asia.

Hamilton Slate Quarry Riesling

▼▼▼▼▽ **2002** Light straw-green; a discreet mix of herb, spice, mineral and apple on the bouquet is largely repeated on the palate, which has good length and structure; an exceptionally good wine for a region unsuited to riesling. **rating:** 90

best drinking Now–2007 **best vintages** '02 **drink with** Summer salads • $14.95

Hamilton Synergy Semillon Sauvignon Blanc

▼▼▼▼▽ **2002** Medium yellow-green; a clean, aromatic mix of contrasting passionfruit and grass on the bouquet is followed by abundant mid-palate passionfruit and tropical fruit, tightened up by a crisp finish. **rating:** 92

best drinking Now–2005 **best vintages** '02 **drink with** King George whiting • $10.95

Hamilton Centurion Shiraz

▼▼▼▼▽ **2000** Medium red-purple; the clean, intense bouquet has an abundance of ripe plum and blackberry fruit; the powerful palate has ripe blackberry, dark chocolate, spice and licorice fruit in abundance, but not over-extracted; supported by good oak. The best for many years from these 100+-year-old vines. **rating:** 93

best drinking 2005–2015 **best vintages** '98, '00 **drink with** Braised ox cheek • $49.95

Hamilton Gumprs' Block Shiraz

▼▼▼▼ **2001** Medium red-purple; smooth blackberry, dark fruits and subtle vanilla oak on the bouquet flow into a medium-bodied palate with good balance and texture, a touch of dark chocolate and ripe tannins joining the fruit of the bouquet. **rating:** 88

best drinking 2006–2011 **best vintages** '00 **drink with** Kebabs • $22.95

Hamilton Burton's Vineyard Old Bush Vine Grenache Shiraz

▼▼▼▼ 1999 Medium red-purple; spicy/cedary, earthy/chocolatey aromas without any varietal jam, which does however appear to a certain degree on the generous, ripe palate. Since this is a clear indicator of varietal character, one can hardly complain, and the Shiraz has tempered the impact in any event. **rating:** 87

best drinking Now–2007 best vintages '91, '92, '94, '95, '98 drink with Cassoulet • $29.95

Hamilton Marion Vineyard Grenache Shiraz

▼▼▼▼ 2000 Medium red-purple; very ripe juicy/jammy fruit leads into a palate with lots of depth and some savoury/chocolatey notes to balance the sweetness. **rating:** 87

best drinking Now–2008 best vintages '98 drink with Spiced beef • $29.95

Hamilton Colton Ruins GSM

▼▼▼▼ 2001 Medium purple-red; sweet, clean, juicy blackberry fruit drives both the bouquet and palate, where sweet blackberry and blackcurrant fruit have much more structure than many Rhône blends; good balance and length. Colton was one of the first settlers in McLaren Vale, and the ruins of his house are adjacent to the vineyard which produces this wine. For the record, it is in fact Shiraz Grenache Mourvedre (SGM) even though it is labelled GSM. **rating:** 88

best drinking Now–2008 drink with Osso buco • $22.95

Hamilton Lot 148 Merlot

▼▼▼▼▽ 2001 Medium red-purple; a fragrant bouquet with earthy/olive aromas flows into a light to medium-bodied, well-balanced palate which has an attractive varietal mix of red berry and olive flavours; good length and fine tannins. **rating:** 90

best drinking 2004–2008 best vintages '01 drink with Grilled beef • $22.95

Hamilton Hut Block Cabernet Sauvignon

▼▼▼▼ 2001 Medium red-purple; the bouquet opens slightly uncertainly, with a mix of berry, leaf and mint, but the palate has more weight, concentration and grip to the mix of cassis, a touch of chocolate and persistent tannins. **rating:** 87

best drinking 2005–2011 best vintages '86, '90, '91, '93, '00 drink with Beef Provençale • $22.95

hamiltons bluff   NR

Longs Corner Road, Canowindra, NSW 2804 **region** Cowra
phone (02) 6344 2079 **fax** (02) 6344 2165 **open** Weekends and holidays 10–4, Mon–Fri by appointment
winemaker Andrew Margan (Contract) **production** 2000 cases **est.** 1995
product range ($14.50–22 CD) Canowindra Grossi Unwooded Chardonnay, Reserve Chardonnay, Chairman's Reserve Chardonnay, Sangiovese, Methode Champenoise.
summary Hamiltons Bluff is owned and operated by the Andrews family, which planted 45 hectares of vines in 1995. 1998 produced the first crop, and three different Chardonnays were contract-made by Andrew Margan. The Cowra Chardonnay and Canowindra Grossi Chardonnay received medals at the 1998 Cowra Wine Show. Cellar-door sales opened in early 1999, heralding a new stage of development for the Cowra region. Exports to the US.

hamilton's ewell vineyards   ★★★★

Siegersdorf Vineyard, Barossa Valley Way, Tanunda, SA 5352 **region** Barossa Valley
phone (08) 8231 0088 **fax** (08) 8231 0355 **open** Mon–Fri 10–5, weekends 11–5
winemaker Robert Hamilton, John Davey **production** 13 000 cases **est.** 1837
product range ($16–38 R) Limestone Quarry Chardonnay, Railway Chardonnay, Railway Shiraz, Fuller's Barn Shiraz, Stonegarden Grenache Shiraz, Ewell Cabernet Sauvignon.
summary Mark Hamilton, an Adelaide lawyer by profession, is a sixth-generation direct descendent of Richard Hamilton, who arrived in South Australia in 1838 (a year after the state was proclaimed) and made his first wine in 1841. Hamilton's Ewell Vineyards remained in the family until 1979, when it was acquired by Mildara Blass, much to Mark Hamilton's dismay. Since 1991 he has set about building yet another Hamilton wine business by making a series of astute vineyard acquisitions and buying back the name Hamilton's Ewell from Mildara. Most of the grapes are sold, but there is scope to very significantly increase production in the years ahead. Exports to the US, Canada, Hong Kong and the UK.

Hamilton's Ewell Fuller's Barn Shiraz

TTTTT 1999 Strong, bright red-purple; the very rich bouquet offers a mix of deep, sweet plum and blackberry fruit, joined by some bitter chocolate on the palate. This complex and high-quality wine has very good oak balance and integration to complete the picture. Only 200 cases made. **rating:** 94

best drinking 2004–2014 **best vintages** '98, '99 **drink with** Kangaroo fillet • $38

Hamilton's Ewell Limestone Quarry Shiraz

TTTT 2001 Bright, deep red-purple; complex blackberry, earth, hay and briar fruit drives the bouquet; the palate is very concentrated and slightly extractive, unusual for Wrattonbully, perhaps partly reflecting the alcohol of 14.2°. **rating:** 87

best drinking 2005–2012 **drink with** Beef casserole • $19

hanging rock winery ★★★★

88 Jim Road, Newham, Vic 3442 **region** Macedon Ranges
phone (03) 5427 0542 **fax** (03) 5427 0310 **open** 7 days 10–5
winemaker John Ellis **production** 40 000 cases **est.** 1982
product range ($12–55 CD) The wines are offered in four tiers: at the bottom the Rock range of Riesling, Chardonnay, Red (Shiraz blend), Merlot; next up the scale Victoria Chardonnay, Verdelho, S (sweet white); then the trio of Central Highlands Pinot Noir, Victoria Shiraz, Victoria Cabernet Merlot; at the top Jim Jim Sauvignon Blanc, Heathcote Shiraz, Macedon Cuvee, Gralaine Merlot.
summary The Macedon area has proved very marginal in spots, and the Hanging Rock vineyards, with their lovely vista towards the Rock, are no exception. John Ellis has thus elected to source additional grapes from various parts of Victoria to produce an interesting and diverse style of wines. The low-priced Rock series, with its bold packaging, has replaced the Picnic wines. Exports to the UK, Denmark, the US, Canada, New Zealand, Hong Kong, Malaysia, Taiwan and Japan.

Hanging Rock The Jim Jim Sauvignon Blanc

TTTTT 2002 Light to medium yellow-green; the bouquet has some lifted grassy/herbal aromas accompanied by some free SO$_2$, which will soon diminish. The palate has plenty of varietal character and definition, with a touch of passionfruit; well above-average intensity and length. **rating:** 92

best drinking Now **best vintages** '93, '95, '96, '99, '00, '01 **drink with** Oysters • $25

Hanging Rock Macedon Cuvee

TTTTT IX. The comparison with Bollinger is inevitable; both wines have a somewhat unorthodox, aldehyde-based background to their immense complexity, and both polarise opinion. Medium to full straw-gold; the very complex bouquet has abundant, spicy, bready, biscuity aromas, the rich palate providing more and more of the same. **rating:** 94

best drinking Now **best vintages** V, VI, VIII, IX **drink with** Oysters Kilpatrick • $40

Hanging Rock Central Highlands Pinot Noir

TTTT 2001 Medium red-purple; the moderately intense but complex bouquet has an array of strawberry, cherry and plum fruit aromas; the sweet fruit on entry to the mouth moves to a more savoury, tangy, slightly stemmy finish. Sourced from the Macedon Ranges, Bendigo, Ballarat and Sunbury; small wonder the wine is multi-flavoured. **rating:** 88

best drinking Now–2007 **best vintages** '98 **drink with** Braised rabbit • $18

Hanging Rock Heathcote Shiraz

TTTTT 2000 One of the gold medal winners at the 2002 Visy Board Great Australian Shiraz Challenge. Deeply coloured; abundant dark plum, black cherry and vanilla aromas swirl from the glass; the palate is rich in raspberry and plum fruit, the oak (very obvious at the start of the year) settling down impressively. **rating:** 95

best drinking 2005–2012 **best vintages** '97, '98, '00 **drink with** Roast venison • $55

Hanging Rock Victoria Shiraz

TTTT 2001 Bright red-purple; clean, smooth plum, blackberry and raspberry aromas are followed by a fruit-driven, light to medium-bodied palate; fresh, bright raspberry fruit makes for easy drinking. **rating:** 87

best drinking Now–2007 **best vintages** '90, '91, '92, '94, '00 **drink with** Marinated beef • $18

hangmans gully ★★★☆

St Ignatius Vineyard, Sunraysia Highway, Avoca, Vic 3467 **region** Pyrenees
phone (03) 5465 3542 **fax** (03) 5465 3542 **open** 7 days 10–5
winemaker Enrique Diaz **production** 1000 cases **est.** 1992
product range ($20–35 CD) Chardonnay, Shiraz, Cabernet Sauvignon.
summary Silvia and husband Enrique Diaz began the establishment of their vineyard, winery and restaurant complex in 1992. They have established shiraz (the major planting at 3.2 ha), chardonnay (1.6 ha), cabernet sauvignon (1 ha) and sauvignon blanc (0.4 ha) in bearing, with merlot (1.6 ha) and sangiovese (0.2 ha) planted but not yet in production. The vineyard has already received three primary production awards, and all the wine is made on-site by Enrique Diaz. Exports to the UK.

Hangmans Gully Shiraz

▼▼▼▼ 2001 Medium red-purple; complex licorice, spice and blackberry fruit aromas are followed by a lively, medium-bodied palate featuring ripe, not jammy, berry and spice flavours; ripe tannins complete the picture.
rating: 89

best drinking 2006–2011 **drink with** Gourmet sausages • $30

Hangmans Gully Cabernet Sauvignon

▼▼▼▼ 2001 Medium red-purple; fresh, youthful, dark fruit aromas and a hint of smoky oak lead into a palate with smooth, ripe blackberry/cassis on entry; the finish is still youthful and slightly tart; needs time. **rating:** 89
best drinking 2008–2013 **drink with** Leave it in the cellar • $35

hankin estate   NR

2 Johnsons Lane, Northwood via Seymour, Vic 3660 **region** Goulburn Valley
phone (03) 5792 2396 **fax** (03) 9353 2927 **open** Weekends and public holidays 10–5
winemaker Dr Max Hankin **production** 1700 cases **est.** 1975
product range ($8–28 CD) Semillon, Verdelho, Rose, Shiraz, Merlot, Merlot Cabernet Franc Malbec, Cabernets Malbec, Cabernet Sauvignon Merlot.
summary Hankin Estate is now the principal occupation of Dr Max Hankin, who has retired from full-time medical practice. He has to contend with phylloxera, which decimated the original plantings, but has successfully replanted most of the vineyard.

hansen hilltops   NR

Barwang Ridge, 1 Barwang Road, via Young, NSW 2594 **region** Hilltops
phone (02) 6382 6363 **fax** (02) 6382 6363 **open** 7 days 11–6
winemaker Charles Sturt University (Contract) **production** 2000 cases **est.** 1979
product range ($15.50–18 CD) Riesling, Chardonnay Semillon, Cabernet Sauvignon.
summary The vineyard has 5 hectares of vines, 1 hectare each of riesling, chardonnay, shiraz, cabernet sauvignon, and a further hectare roughly split between semillon, merlot and malbec. The plantings date back to 1979, but the first wines were not made until the late 1990s. Peter Hansen points out that there are only two vineyards at Barwang, both part of the original Barwang sheep station: McWilliam's and his. Perhaps a little cheekily, he goes on to point out that the difference is that his wines are produced solely from non-irrigated vines which are hand-picked and hand-pruned, and, into the bargain, are 10 years older than McWilliam's. No recent tastings.

hanson-tarrahill vineyard   NR

49 Cleveland Avenue, Lower Plenty, Vic 3093 (postal) **region** Yarra Valley
phone (03) 9439 7425 **fax** (03) 9439 4217 **open** Not
winemaker Dr Ian Hanson **production** 1000 cases **est.** 1983
product range ($21–30 R) Pinot Noir, Arundel (Cabernet blend), Tarra's Block Cabernets, Cabernet Sauvignon.
summary Dental surgeon Ian Hanson planted his first vines in the late 1960s, close to the junction of the Yarra and Plenty Rivers; in 1983 those plantings were extended (with 3000 vines), and in 1988 the Tarrahill property at Yarra Glen was established with a further 4 hectares. Hanson is the name which appears most prominently on the newly designed labels; Tarrahill Vineyard is in much smaller type. No recent tastings.

happs ★★★☆

571 Commonage Road, Dunsborough, WA 6281 **region** Margaret River
phone (08) 9755 3300 **fax** (08) 9755 3846 **open** 7 days 10–5
winemaker Erl Happ, Mark Warren, Anne-Coralie Fleury **production** 18 000 cases **est.** 1978
product range ($14–45 CD) Dry table wines are Semillon Chardonnay, Marrimee (Semillon Chenin Blanc), Viognier, Marsanne, PF White (Preservative Free), Verdelho, Chardonnay, PF Red (Preservative Free); Three Hills super premium range of Shiraz, Charles Andreas (Cabernet blend), Grenache, Merlot, Nebbiolo, Malbec, Cabernet Franc.
summary Former schoolteacher turned potter and winemaker Erl Happ is an iconoclast and compulsive experimenter. Many of the styles he makes are very unconventional, the future styles likely to be even more so: the Karridale vineyard planted in 1994 has no less than 28 different varieties established. Merlot has been a winery specialty for a decade. Limited retail distributed through New South Wales, Victoria and Queensland and, more recently, exports to the US.

Happs Chardonnay

TTTT 2001 Bright yellow-green; the moderately intense bouquet is clean and smooth, offering stone fruit and citrus, the light to medium-bodied palate fresh and elegant, with a clean, dry finish. Right in the mainstream of the Happs Chardonnay style, entirely fruit-driven. **rating:** 88

best drinking Now–2005 **best vintages** '91, '94 **drink with** Quiche • $18

Happs Three Hills Shiraz

TTTY 2000 Deep, dense colour; big, black cherry, licorice and plum fruit on both the bouquet and palate, the palate finishing with massively dry tannins. What a pity its claws were not cut. **rating:** 84

best drinking 2007–2012 **drink with** Ox • $45

Happs PF Red

TTTT 2001 Excellent colour; the bouquet offers dark, earthy fruits with no obvious aldehydes; the palate is soft and fruity, albeit somewhat short. It is really difficult to understand firstly the very unusual blend of Tempranillo and Tinta Cao, but, even more, how this wine is still on the market in 2003, without any sign of decay. PF, incidentally, stands for preservative-free. **rating:** 85

best drinking Now **drink with** Anything that takes your fancy • $17

Happs Three Hills Malbec

TTTT 2001 Purple-red, bright and strong; the bouquet is clean, with obvious juicy blackcurrant varietal fruit; the palate likewise has clear-cut varietal flavour and a touch of mint; as is so often the case with malbec, the wine is not over-endowed with structure. **rating:** 86

best drinking Now–2006 **drink with** Pasta • $22

harcourt valley vineyards ★★★★

3339 Calder Highway, Harcourt, Vic 3453 **region** Bendigo
phone (03) 5474 2223 **fax** (03) 5474 2293 **open** 7 days 11–5, 11–6 (during daylight saving)
winemaker John Livingstone **production** 1000 cases **est.** 1976
product range ($14–35 CD) Riesling, Barbara's Shiraz, Barbara's Reserve Shiraz, Cabernet Sauvignon.
summary John Livingstone (the winemaker) and wife Barbara (the viticulturist) acquired the 4-hectare vineyard many years ago. Shiraz remains the specialty; it has the rich, full-bodied style typical of the region.

Harcourt Valley Barbara's Shiraz

TTTT 2001 Youthful red-purple; a complex earthy/spicy/savoury web over dark/blackberry fruit on both bouquet and palate, with spice and mocha joining the blackberry fruit of the palate, all making for an appealing wine. **rating:** 89

best drinking 2004–2009 **drink with** Spicy designer sausages • $22

Harcourt Valley Barbara's Reserve Shiraz

TTTTY 2000 Medium red-purple; the moderately intense bouquet is clean, with mint, berry and spice aromas; the palate has good texture, structure and length, supported by fine tannins. A particularly elegant wine for this part of the world. **rating:** 91

best drinking 2005–2012 **best vintages** '00 **drink with** Rare roast beef • $35

hardys reynella ★★★★★

Reynell Road, Reynella, SA 5161 **region** McLaren Vale
phone (08) 8392 2222 **fax** (08) 8392 2202 **open** Mon–Fri 10–4, Sat 10–3.30, Sun 11–3.30, closed public holidays
winemaker Peter Dawson, Stephen Pannell, Ed Carr, Paul Lapsley **production** 4.5 million cases **est.** 1853
product range ($7–135 R) At the bottom comes the R&R range of all major varietals and blends; then Nottage Hill; Siegersdorf Riesling and Chardonnay; No Preservative Added range; next Sir James premium varietals; then Eileen Hardy Chardonnay and Shiraz and Thomas Hardy Cabernet Sauvignon; Sir James and Arras; also superior-quality Brandies and Ports including Australia's finest Vintage Port.
summary The 1992 merger of Thomas Hardy and the Berri Renmano group may well have had some of the elements of a forced marriage when it took place, but the merged group prospered mightily over the next 10 years. So successful was it that a further marriage followed in early 2003: Constellation Wines of the US was the groom, and BRL Hardy the bride. It has created the largest wine group in the world, but it does mean that the inevitable has happened: ownership and control of one of Australia's most dynamic and biggest companies has migrated to the US, even with senior BRL Hardy executives appointed to the top positions in the Constellation wine group.

Hardys Siegersdorf Riesling

▼▼▼▼ 2002 Light straw-green; the clean, crisp bouquet has mineral and citrus; the palate has good intensity, length and focus, again braced by minerally acidity for medium-term cellaring if you are so minded. Good value. **rating:** 88

best drinking Now–2008 **best vintages** '88, '90, '92, '93, '94, '96, '99 **drink with** Seafood • $10.99

Hardys Eileen Hardy Chardonnay

▼▼▼▼▼ 2000 Sourced from whichever cool regions of southern Australia provide the best material each year. A complex array of barrel-ferment and tangy fruit aromas literally leap from the glass, while the palate is still fresh, with tangy citrus and nectarine fruit to the fore, high-quality French oak in the background. **rating:** 95

best drinking Now–2008 **best vintages** '85, '87, '90, '91, '93, '94, '96, '99, '00 **drink with** Salmon pasta • $39.99

Hardys Nottage Hill Chardonnay

▼▼▼▼ 2001 Medium yellow-green; the clean and soft bouquet centres on peach and nectarine fruit, the oak influence incidental. The pleasant, easily accessed, medium-bodied palate has gentle peachy fruit, but a relatively short finish. How the International Wine Challenge in London decided this was the best Chardonnay in the competition, and best value wine, is, to my untutored palate, incomprehensible. **rating:** 87

best drinking Now **drink with** Chicken nuggets • $8.99

Hardys Sir James Chardonnay

▼▼▼▼ 2001 Light to medium yellow-green; the moderately intense bouquet has light citrus and nectarine fruit supported by balanced oak; while the palate is only light to medium-bodied, it has good length and line; fruit-driven. Predominantly from the Adelaide Hills and Padthaway. **rating:** 89

best drinking Now–2006 **drink with** Salmon terrine • $14.99

Hardys Arras

▼▼▼▼▽ 1998 Chardonnay Pinot. Very pale straw-green; the bouquet is still incredibly fresh, with pure mineral and citrus aromatics; the palate is super-fine and elegant, with citrus flavours driving the wine. Even after 4 years on yeast lees the emphasis is on finesse rather than complexity, and the wine falters fractionally on the finish. One hundred per cent Tasmania sourced. Highly probable that its best years are in front of it. **rating:** 93

best drinking Now–2008 **best vintages** '95, '97, '98 **drink with** Aperitif • $49.99

Hardys Sir James Vintage

▼▼▼▼▼ 1999 Pale straw-green; tight, slightly nutty/bready malolactic and lees aromas are followed by a gentle, quite delicate yet complex palate, with cashew and citrus playing counterpoints on the clean finish. **rating:** 94

best drinking Now–2007 **best vintages** '94, '97, '98 **drink with** Chinese dumplings • $25.99

Hardys Sir James Sparkling Shiraz NV

▼▼▼▼▽ NV Red-purple with good mousse; cherry, plum, spice and leather aromas lead into a strongly fruit-driven palate with abundant cherry and plum fruit, yet not phenolic; well balanced. No regional claims are made for the wine. **rating:** 91

best drinking Now–2007 **drink with** Prosciutto and melon • $25.99

Hardys Padthaway Noble Riesling

ΤΤΤΤΥ **2001** Medium to full yellow-green; intense lime botrytis and just a trace of the cuckoo's nest; the palate throws off that errant touch on the bouquet, with good limey flavour, length and acidity. **rating:** 92

best drinking Now–2007 **best vintages** '01 **drink with** Fruit tart • $19.99

Hardys Eileen Hardy Shiraz

ΤΤΤΤΤ **1999** Dense red-purple; the bouquet offers a rich amalgam of ripe black cherry fruit, dark chocolate and spicy French oak; the sumptuous and dense palate has a similar chewy mix of ripe fruit and spicy/toasty oak, sustained by ripe tannins. Irresistible Show style. **rating:** 95

best drinking 2004–2014 **best vintages** '70, '88, '91, '93, '95, '96, '97, '98, '99 **drink with** Game pie • $89.99

Hardys Sir James Cabernet Shiraz Merlot

ΤΤΤΤ **2001** Medium red-purple; the black fruit aromas are moderately intense, made complex by nuances of forest and spice; tannin grip on the medium to full-bodied palate adds length, but does not help fruit clarity overmuch. Matured in French and American oak; will soften with time. **rating:** 86

best drinking 2005–2009 **drink with** Rack of lamb • $14.99

Chateau Reynella Vintage Port

ΤΤΤΤΥ **1997** Dense purple-red; dark, spicy, blackberry and plum pudding aromas, with clean fortifying spirit, are followed by a powerful, spicy black fruit palate with some Christmas cake flavours; drier and longer than the traditional Reynella Vintage Port style. **rating:** 92

best drinking 2007–2027 **best vintages** '97 **drink with** Coffee and petit fours • $25.99

hardys tintara ★★★★

202 Main Road, McLaren Vale, SA 5171 **region** McLaren Vale
phone (08) 8392 4124 **fax** (08) 8392 4155 **open** 7 days 10–4.30
winemaker Simon White **production** 110 000 cases **est.** 1876
product range ($15–35 R) Limited Release Shiraz, Grenache; Tintara Cellars Chardonnay, Shiraz, Cabernet Sauvignon.
summary Hardys Tintara is run as a separate winemaking entity, although all the Hardys wines are offered at the cellar door. The Limited Release wines are first class; the Tintara Cellars appeal on the grounds of price. The rating is a compromise between the two ranges.

Tintara Cellars Chardonnay

ΤΤΤΤ **2001** Light to medium yellow-green; the bouquet is clean, the aromas basically underplayed and certainly subtle; gentle fruit drives the light to medium-bodied palate, the oak evident but no more. Predominantly sourced from McLaren Vales and the Adelaide Hills, and partially barrel fermented. **rating:** 86

ΤΤΤΤΥ **2000** Popped out of nowhere to win a gold medal at this year's Royal Sydney Wine Show. Partial barrel fermentation and maturation gives smoky overtones to the quite intense stone fruit of the bouquet; the fruit is still tight on the long palate, the French oak subtle. Aging impressively. **rating:** 92

best drinking Now **best vintages** '00 **drink with** Poached green-lipped mussels • $16

hare's chase ★★★★☆

PO Box 46, Melrose Park, SA 5039 **region** Barossa Valley
phone (08) 8277 3506 **fax** (08) 8277 3543 **open** Not
winemaker Peter Taylor **production** 2500 cases **est.** 1998
product range ($24–33 ML) Shiraz, Merlot.
summary Hare's Chase is the creation of two families who own the 100-year-old vineyard situated in the Marananga Valley subregion of the Barossa Valley. The simple, functional winery sits at the top of a rocky hill in the centre of the vineyard, which has some of the best red soil available for dry-grown viticulture. The winemaking arm of the partnership is provided by Peter Taylor, a senior red winemaker with Penfolds for over 20 years. The initial releases from the 8 hectares of estate shiraz and 2 hectares of estate merlot are, to put it mildly, impressive.

Hare's Chase Shiraz

ΤΤΤΤΤ **2001** Dense red-purple; a rich, complex, dense bouquet with blood plum, spice and vanilla oak aromas is followed by a velvety-textured palate, mouthfilling and rich, with excellent fruit and oak balance supported by ripe tannins. From Peter Taylor's own vineyard, finishing fermentation in American oak, where it spends 16 months. Neither filtered nor fined. **rating:** 94

best drinking 2006–2016 **best vintages** '01 **drink with** Kangaroo fillet • $33

Hare's Chase Merlot

TTTT **2001** Medium red-purple; the clean bouquet has some savoury edges to the core of redcurrant fruit, and the palate has nice weight and texture, even if it is varietally indistinct. Good oak handling and control of extract. **rating: 88**

best drinking 2005–2010 **drink with** Roast veal • $33

harewood estate ★★★☆

Scotsdale Road, Denmark, WA 6333 **region** Great Southern
phone (08) 9840 9078 **fax** (08) 9840 9053 **open** By appointment
winemaker Michael Kerrigan **production** 600 cases **est.** 1988
product range ($28–32.50 R) Chardonnay, Pinot Noir.
summary Keith and Margie Graham have established a showpiece vineyard at Binalong. The majority of the grapes are sold to Howard Park and Domaine Chandon, but gradually increasing amounts of wine are being made under the Harewood Estate label. The wines have retail distribution in Perth and are exported to the UK but are otherwise only available by mail order.

Harewood Estate Chardonnay

TTTT **2001** Medium yellow-green; a particularly complex bouquet pushes the envelope with the amount of oak influence, which also flows into the palate; however, citrus fruit goes part of the way to balancing the oak and giving length. **rating: 87**

best drinking Now **best vintages** '97, '98 **drink with** Seafood risotto • $28

Harewood Estate Pinot Noir C Block

TTTT **2001** Light to medium red; clean, fresh, light strawberry aromas are followed by a light to medium-bodied fruit-driven palate with clearly defined varietal character in a strawberry/cherry spectrum. An exceptional pretty wine, if not particularly complex. **rating: 88**

best drinking Now **drink with** Fresh Tasmanian salmon • $30

Harewood Estate Pinot Noir F Block

TTTTY **2001** Light to medium red, with some purple tinges; there is more depth to the fruit, consistent with the colour, and some plummy fruit. The palate is rounder, softer and riper, with more texture and feel, although the direct fruit appeal is still there, as is the length. Only after tasting did I realise this wine comes from the French Dijon clones. **rating: 92**

best drinking Now–2007 **drink with** Grilled quail • $30

🍇 harmans ridge estate NR

Cnr Bussell Highway and Harmans Mill Road, Wilyabrup, WA 6284 **region** Margaret River
phone (08) 9755 7444 **fax** (08) 755 7400 **open** Wed–Mon 10–4
winemaker Catherine Oates **production** 10 000 cases **est.** 1999
product range ($15–18 CD) Riesling, Sauvignon Blanc, Semillon Sauvignon Blanc, Marsanne, Chardonnay, Rose, Pinot Noir, Grenache, Shiraz, Cabernet Merlot, Cabernet Sauvignon.
summary Harmans Ridge Estate, with a crush capacity of 1600 tonnes, is primarily a contract winery for larger producers in the Margaret River region which do not have their own winery/winemaker. It does, however, have 2.5 hectares of shiraz, and does make wines under the Harmans Ridge Estate label from grapes grown in Margaret River. A cellar door opened in mid-2003. The wines are sold in Western Australia, and exported to the UK and Hong Kong.

🍇 harris estate NR

Paracombe Road, Paracombe, SA 5132 **region** Adelaide Hills
phone (08) 8380 5353 **fax** (08) 8380 5353 **open** By appointment
winemaker Trevor Harris **production** 1000 cases **est.** 1994
product range Shiraz, Cabernet Sauvignon.
summary Trevor and Sue Harris have established 2.5 hectares of chardonnay, shiraz and cabernet sauvignon at Paracombe in the Adelaide Hills. The wines are distributed by The Wine Group, Victoria, and Jonathan Tolley, South Australia, and by mail order.

hartz barn wines ★★★☆

1 Truro Road, Moculta, Barossa Valley, SA 5353 **region** Eden Valley
phone (08) 8563 9002 **fax** (08) 8563 9002 **open** By appointment
winemaker David Barnett **production** 1300 cases **est.** 1997
product range ($37–39 CD) General Store Shiraz, Mail Box Merlot, Carriages Cabernet Sauvignon.
summary Hartz Barn Wines was formed in 1997 by Penny Hart (operations director), David Barnett (winemaker/director), Katrina Barnett (marketing director) and Matthew Barnett (viticulture/cellar director), which may suggest that the operation is rather larger than it in fact is. The business name and label have an unexpectedly complex background, too. The 'z' was added to Hart to reflect early German settler heritage in the Barossa Valley; Barn is a shortened version of Barnett; the house depicted on the label is the north-facing wall of the family's home in Moculta, built in 1866; the heart logo comes from Penny's school days, when she used the heart symbol on her school books instead of writing Hart; the HBW symbol within the heart has dual heritage, including the sheep branding iron that David Barnett's father, Henry William Barnett, used in New Zealand. The grapes come from the estate vineyards, which are planted to riesling, lagrein, merlot, shiraz and cabernet sauvignon.

Hartz Barn General Store Barossa Valley Shiraz

ΨΨΨΨ 2001 Medium red-purple; ripe plum, prune and sundry black fruits dominate the bouquet, joined by touches of raspberry, mint and leaf on the palate, which has pleasing mouthfeel. The odd conjunction of differing fruit characters on bouquet and palate is not usual, but in no way detracts. **rating:** 89

best drinking 2006–2011 **drink with** Spaghetti bolognese • $39

Hartz Barn Mail Box Merlot

ΨΨΨΨ 2001 Medium red-purple; the bouquet is distinctly varietal, with an array of gamey/savoury characters, earth and olive becoming stronger on the palate. Barossa Valley Merlot doesn't often deliver such strongly accented Merlot. **rating:** 89

best drinking 2005–2010 **drink with** Braised veal • $37

hartzview wine centre NR

RSD 1034, Off Cross Road, Gardners Bay, Tas 7112 **region** Southern Tasmania
phone (03) 6295 1623 **open** 7 days 9–5
winemaker Andrew Hood (Contract), Robert Patterson **production** NFP **est.** 1988
product range ($18 CD) Chardonnay, Pinot Noir; also a range of Pig and Whistle Hill fruit wines.
summary A combined wine centre, offering wines from a number of local Huon Valley wineries, and also newly erected and very comfortable accommodation for six people in a separate, self-contained house. Hartzview table wines (produced from 3 hectares of estate plantings) are much to be preferred to the self-produced Pig and Whistle Hill fruit wines. No recent tastings.

haselgrove ★★★★

Foggo Road, McLaren Vale, SA 5171 **region** McLaren Vale
phone (08) 8323 8706 **fax** (08) 8323 8049 **open** Mon–Fri 9–5, weekends 10–5
winemaker Adrian Lockhart **production** NFP **est.** 1981
product range ($10–45 R) Lost Sheep range of Chardonnay, Shiraz, Cabernet Sauvignon; McLaren Vale Pictures Series Sauvignon Blanc, Chardonnay, Grenache, Shiraz, Cabernet Sauvignon; Futures Shiraz; Bentwing Chardonnay, Shiraz, Cabernet Sauvignon; premium releases under 'H' Reserve label and Limelight McLaren Vale Syrah; Sparkling, Port; lesser-priced varietals under Sovereign Series.
summary Haselgrove has been through a tumultuous period: first it was acquired by Barrington Estates, then Barrington collapsed. The underlying winemaking operations of Haselgrove have continued, and respected former Hunter winemaker Adrian Lockhart is senior winemaker.

hastwell & lightfoot ★★★☆

Foggo Road, McLaren Vale, SA 5171 (postal) **region** McLaren Vale
phone (08) 8323 8692 **fax** (08) 8323 8098 **open** Not
winemaker Goe DiFabio (Contract) **production** 1900 cases **est.** 1990
product range ($16.50–27.50 R) Viognier, Chardonnay, Shiraz, Tempranillo, Cabernet Franc, Cabernet.
summary Hastwell & Lightfoot is an offshoot of a rather larger grape-growing business, with the majority of the grapes from the 15 hectares of vineyard being sold to others; the vineyard was planted in 1988 and the first grapes were produced in 1990. Incidentally, the labels are once seen, never forgotten. Exports to the US, the UK, Germany, Singapore and New Zealand.

Hastwell & Lightfoot Viognier

ΨΨΨΨ 2002 Medium yellow-green; some honey and honeysuckle aromas introduce a big, solid wine with typical Viognier structure and texture profile. Bottled only a few days before being tasted, and may well show more once it has settled down. **rating:** 84

best drinking Now–2005 **drink with** Crumbed lamb's brains • $27.50

Hastwell & Lightfoot Shiraz

ΨΨΨΨΨ 2000 Medium to full red-purple; intense black plum, chocolate and spice aromas fold into a round and velvety palate; spice, chocolate and plum flavours are supported by ripe tannins and a subtle touch of oak. Shows that great flavour can be achieved in McLaren Vale at (only) 13° alcohol. **rating:** 91

best drinking 2004–2012 **best vintages** '98, '00 **drink with** Ravioli • $23.50

🐾 hawkers gate   NR

Lot 31 Foggo Road, McLaren Flat, SA 5171 **region** McLaren Vale
phone 0403 809 990 **fax** (08) 8323 9981 **open** By appointment
winemaker James Hastwell **production** 500 cases **est.** 2000
product range ($16 ML) Chardonnay, Shiraz.
summary James Hastwell (son of Mark and Wendy Hastwell of Hastwell & Lightfoot Wines) decided he would become a winemaker when he was 9 years old, and duly obtained his wine science degree from the University of Adelaide, working each vintage during his degree course at Haselgrove Wines and later Kay Bros. Most recently he joined the Kendall Jackson-owned Cardinale Winery in the Napa Valley for the 2002 vintage, where the cellar door prices start at US$120 a bottle. It is a long way from Hawkers Gate, which takes its name from the gate at the border of Australia's dog fence between South Australia and New South Wales, 250 kilometres north of Broken Hill. A small on-site winery in Foggo Road was completed in time for the 2003 vintage; as well as giving greater control over the making of the Hawkers Gate wines, it will act as a barrel storage facility for Hastwell & Lightfoot wines.

hawley vineyard   ★★★★

Hawley Beach, Hawley, Tas 7307 **region** Northern Tasmania
phone (03) 6428 6221 **fax** (03) 6428 6844 **open** 7 days
winemaker Julian Alcorso (Contract) **production** 1000 cases **est.** 1988
product range ($18–25 R) Rubicon Chardonnay, Unwooded Chardonnay, Rubicon Pinot Noir.
summary Hawley Vineyard overlooks Hawley Beach and thence northeast to Bass Strait. It is established on an historic 200-hectare farming property, with Hawley House offering dining and accommodation in a grand style. There are no other vineyards in what is a unique winegrowing region, and few hoteliers-cum-viticulturists as flamboyant as owner Simon Houghton. Limited distribution in Sydney. Rating is on the basis of previous tastings.

hay shed hill wines   ★★★★

RMB 398, Harmans Mill Road, Wilyabrup, WA 6280 **region** Margaret River
phone (08) 9755 6234 **fax** (08) 9755 6305 **open** 7 days 10.30–5
winemaker Simon Keall **production** 17 000 cases **est.** 1987
product range ($15–45 CD) Semillon, Sauvignon Blanc, Sauvignon Blanc Semillon, Chardonnay, Pinot Noir, Shiraz, Cabernet Franc, Cabernet Merlot, Cabernet Sauvignon; Pitchfork White, Pitchfork Pink (Rose), Pitchfork Red.
summary When erected in 1987, the winery was a landmark in the Margaret River region, and over the ensuing years the 'sold out' sign was often displayed. Quality wobbled in the lead-up to its ill-fated acquisition by Barrington Estate in 2000, but in November 2002 it joined Alexandra Bridge and Chestnut Grove as part of Mike Calneggia's Australian Wine Holdings Limited group, and a more settled future seems highly likely.

Hay Shed Hill Estate Chardonnay

ΨΨΨΨΨ 2000 Bright yellow-green; an elegant and intense bouquet with stone fruit and subtle oak is followed by a fine, satin-smooth, silky palate with stone fruit, cashew and subtle oak interwoven. Gold medal 2002 Qantas Wine Show of Western Australia. **rating:** 94

best drinking Now–2006 **best vintages** '00 **drink with** Margaret River abalone • $30

hayward's whitehead creek   NR

Lot 18A Hall Lane, Seymour, Vic 3660 **region** Goulburn Valley
phone (03) 5792 3050 **open** Mon–Sat 9–6, Sun 10–6
winemaker Sid Hayward, David Hayward **production** 700 cases **est.** 1975
product range Riesling, Shiraz, Cabernet Sauvignon.
summary The 4.5 hectares of low-yielding 25-year-old vines make powerful wines in a somewhat rustic mode, perhaps, but at low prices. No recent tastings.

heartland wines   NR

GPO Box 1243, Adelaide, SA 5001 **region** Warehouse
phone (08) 8357 9344 **fax** (08) 8357 9388 **open** Not
winemaker Ben Glaetzer **production** 10000 cases **est.** 2001
product range ($19–29R) Director's Cut Shiraz, Wirrega Limestone Coast Shiraz, Wirrega Limestone Coast Cabernet Merlot.
summary This is a joint venture between four industry veterans: winemakers Ben Glaetzer and Scott Collett, viticulturist Geoff Hardy and wine industry management specialist Grant Tilbrook. It draws upon grapes grown in the Limestone Coast, Barossa Valley and McLaren Vale, predominantly from vineyards owned by the partners. Its sights are firmly set on exports, and production is planned to increase from 10000 to 20000 cases with the introduction of Chardonnay, Viognier, Rose, Sangiovese and Cabernet Sauvignon to complement the existing releases. The wines are principally contract-made at Barossa Vintners, but there are no local or cellar-door sales facilities.

Heartland Director's Cut Shiraz

TTTT 2000 Strong red-purple; the bouquet has quite sweet, dark berry fruit with plenty of character. The palate similarly has good structure and density, ranging through dark/black berry and plum fruits with lingering tannins and controlled oak. From Blocks 1 & 2 of the Wirrega Vineyard.   **rating:** 89
best drinking 2004–2009 **drink with** Beef casserole • $29

heathcote winery   ★★★★

183–185 High Street, Heathcote, Vic 3523 **region** Heathcote
phone (03) 5433 2595 **fax** (03) 5433 3081 **open** 7 days 11–5
winemaker Jonathan Mepham **production** 10000 cases **est.** 1978
product range ($13.50–40.50 CD) Cellar door Thomas Craven range of MCV (Marsanne Chardonnay Viognier), Viognier, Chardonnay, Shiraz; premium range of Chardonnay, Cane Cut (Chenin Blanc), Violet (Rose style), Slaughterhouse Paddock Shiraz, Mail Coach Shiraz; super premium Curagee range of Viognier, Shiraz.
summary The Heathcote Winery is back in business with a vengeance. The wines are being produced predominantly from the 26 hectares of estate vineyard, with some grapes from local and other growers under long-term contracts, and the tasting room facilities have been restored and upgraded. Exports to the UK.

Heathcote Curagee Viognier

TTTT 2002 The colour is a little suspect, but there are no signs of oxidation. French barrel-ferment oak and complex fruit are equally balanced on both bouquet and palate; while this is a typically powerful and rich wine, with the varietal viscosity one expects, it manages to retain some finesse.   **rating:** 88
best drinking Now **best vintages** '00 **drink with** Leave it in the cellar • $35

Heathcote Mail Coach Chardonnay

TTTT 2001 Light to medium yellow-green; a clean and smooth bouquet with a subtle interplay between fruit and oak leads into a light to medium-bodied, understated palate; barrel ferment and 9 months in French oak have not suffocated the fruit, and the wine has some elegance.   **rating:** 86
best drinking Now–2005 **drink with** Avocado and prawn salad • $18.50

Heathcote Curagee Shiraz

TTTTY 2001 Bright red-purple; smooth and clean blackberry aromas are accompanied by hints of spice and subtle oak; the medium-bodied and smooth palate has a most attractive replay of the fruit of the bouquet, with plum adding an extra dimension. A blend of 96 per cent Shiraz and 4 per cent Viognier. Radically different from the '99.   **rating:** 92
best drinking 2006–2012 **best vintages** '98, '99, '01 **drink with** Venison • $40.50

Heathcote Mail Coach Shiraz

▼▼▼▼▽ 2001 Medium red-purple; quite complex and intense blackberry and spice aromas are followed by a powerful, deep and intense palate, the tannins fine and adding to the length. Has a dash of Viognier added. rating: 91

best drinking 2006–2012 best vintages '98, '99, '00 drink with Barbecued meat • $25

Heathcote Slaughterhouse Paddock Shiraz

▼▼▼▼▽ 2001 Medium red-purple; the bouquet offers a mix of black cherry, plum and blackberry, supported by subtle oak; the palate is concentrated and powerful, savoury tannins providing an interesting counterpoint to the fruit. It is hard to imagine that the name will have much appeal to women (who buy more than 50 per cent of Australian wine), but there you go. rating: 91

best drinking 2006–2012 drink with Barbecued gourmet sausages • $32

🐦 heathfield ridge wines   NR

PO Box 94, Kensington Park, SA 5068 region Limestone Coast Zone
phone (08) 8363 5800 fax (08) 8363 1980 open Not
winemaker Irvine Consultancy (Contract) production 20 000 cases est. 1997
product range ($10.50–45 ML) Super premium range of Jennifer Reserve Shiraz, Patrick Reserve Cabernet; premium range of Sauvignon Blanc, Reserve Chardonnay, Shiraz, Merlot, Cabernet Sauvignon; Wonambi Wines range of Chardonnay Sauvignon Blanc, Chardonnay, Shiraz and Caves Road range of Chardonnay Sauvignon Blanc, Chardonnay, Shiraz.
summary This is a different incarnation of Heathfield Ridge from that which appeared in my 2002 *Wine Companion*. The Heathfield Ridge Winery is now operated by Orlando Wyndham under what is described as a strategic alliance, and the Heathfield Ridge wines are no longer made at the winery, which is now called Russet Ridge. However, the Tidswell family have retained ownership of the two large vineyards, totalling 114 hectares, the lion's share planted to shiraz and cabernet sauvignon, with smaller plantings of merlot, chardonnay and sauvignon blanc. Part of the grape production is retained by the owners and vinified under the Heathfield Ridge label by the Irvine Consultancy group; the remainder is sold to Russet Ridge.

Heathfield Ridge Cabernet Sauvignon

▼▼▼▼ 1999 Medium red; both bouquet and palate are showing strongly regional, developed cabernet characters in a spice, chocolate and blackberry spectrum, with distinctly savoury notes throughout. rating: 86
best drinking 2004–2008 drink with Spiced lamb fillets • $19.30

heathvale   ★★★☆

Saw Pit Gully Road, via Keyneton, SA 5353 region Eden Valley
phone (08) 8564 8248 fax (08) 8564 8248 open By appointment
winemaker Jim Irvine (Contract) production 500 cases est. 1987
product range ($20–22 ML) Chardonnay, Shiraz.
summary The origins of Heathvale go back to 1865, when William Heath purchased a 60-hectare property, establishing a fruit orchard and 8 hectares of vineyard. The wine was made in the cellar of the house which stands on the property today, and is occupied by current owners Trevor and Faye March. Heath's vines disappeared in the early 1900s, but the Marches now have 3 hectares each of shiraz and cabernet sauvignon, and 2 hectares each of chardonnay and riesling in production. Trevor March is a trained viticulturist – he is completing his studies for a Master of Viticulture degree at the Waite Campus of the University of Adelaide – and is a TAFE lecturer. His son James is working on a six-language *Winemakers Phrasebook*, of which I am the general editor.

heggies vineyard   ★★★★☆

Heggies Range Road, Eden Valley, SA 5235 region Eden Valley
phone (08) 8565 3203 fax (08) 8565 3380 open At Yalumba
winemaker Peter Gambetta production 13 000 cases est. 1971
product range ($18–26 R) Riesling, Viognier, Chardonnay, Pinot Noir, Merlot.
summary Heggies was the second of the high-altitude (570 metres) vineyards established by S Smith & Sons (Yalumba), with plantings on the 120-hectare former grazing property commencing in 1973, now reaching 38 hectares. The once simple view of Heggies as a better white than red wine producer has become more complicated, with the pendulum swinging backwards and forwards according to vintage. Plantings of both chardonnay and viognier were increased in 2002. Exports to all major markets.

Heggies Riesling

YYYY 2002 Medium straw-yellow, puzzling given the Stelvin cap; the bouquet is quite powerful albeit slightly old-fashioned, with a hint of kerosene; abundant CO_2 on the palate needs to settle down, which it will do with time; the length is there. **rating:** 88

best drinking 2004–2010 **best vintages** '95, '96, '98, '99, '01 **drink with** Seafood salad • $18

Heggies Chardonnay

YYYYY 2001 Light to medium yellow-green; the bouquet is relatively subtle, with melon, stone fruit, fig and cashew. The palate offers a smooth interplay between malolactic and barrel-ferment inputs; has elegance and balance. **rating:** 93

best drinking Now–2005 **best vintages** '86, '91, '93, '97, '01 **drink with** Veal, turkey • $24.95

🐚 helen's hill estate   NR

PO Box 778, Lilydale, Vic 3140 **region** Yarra Valley
phone (03) 9739 1573 **fax** (03) 9739 0350 **open** Not
winemaker Master Winemakers (Contract) **est.** 1997
product range ($22.50–25 ML) Chardonnay, Pinot Noir.
summary Helen's Hill Estate is named in memory of the previous owner of the property, Helen Fraser, and has 41 hectares. Allan Nalder, Roma and Lewis Nalder and Andrew and Robyn McIntosh, with backgrounds in banking and finance, grazing and medicine respectively, are the five partners in the venture. A small planting of pinot noir and chardonnay dating from the mid-1980s is retained for the Helen's Hill Estate wines, but most of the output is sold to others, including Southcorp. The plantings now cover chardonnay, pinot noir, shiraz, merlot and cabernet sauvignon.

helm   ★★★★

Butt's Road, Murrumbateman, NSW 2582 **region** Canberra District
phone (02) 6227 5953 **fax** (02) 6227 0207 **open** Thurs–Mon 10–5
winemaker Ken Helm **production** 4000 cases **est.** 1973
product range ($14–25 CD) Riesling Classic Dry, Cowra Riesling Classic Dry, Gewurztraminer, Traminer Riesling, Unwooded Chardonnay, Chardonnay, Reserve Merlot, Cabernet Merlot, Cabernet Shiraz, Helm Reserve Blend.
summary Ken Helm is well known as one of the more stormy petrels of the wine industry, and is an energetic promoter of his wines and of the Canberra district generally. His wines have been consistent bronze medal winners, with silvers and the occasional gold dotted here and there. The wines have limited retail distribution in New South Wales, the ACT and Victoria. The rating is for the reliable Riesling.

Helm Riesling

YYYYY 2002 Bright straw-green; the floral bouquet has a mix of lime, spice, blossom and mineral. The palate has very good balance and mouthfeel thanks to sweet fruit on the mid-palate followed by a dry finish. **rating:** 92

best drinking Now–2007 **best vintages** '00, '02 **drink with** Asparagus terrine • $20

henke   NR

175 Henke Lane, Yarck, Vic 3719 **region** Central Victorian High Country
phone (03) 5797 6277 **fax** (03) 5797 6277 **open** By appointment
winemaker Tim Miller, Caroline Miller **production** 250 cases **est.** 1974
product range ($20–23 CD) Shiraz, Shiraz Cabernet.
summary Produces tiny quantities of deep-coloured, full-flavoured, minty red wines known only to a chosen few. Usually, a range of back vintages up to 5 years of age are available at the cellar door.

henkell wines   NR

Melba Highway, Dixons Creek, Vic 3775 **region** Yarra Valley
phone (03) 9417 4144 **open** Thurs and Sun 11–5, Fri–Sat 11–9
winemaker Contract **production** 500 cases **est.** 1988
product range ($13–29.50 CD) Under the Henkell label are Trocken, Trocken Piccolo, Trocken Magnum; under Henkell southeastern Australia are Riverland Riesling Spatlese, Botrytis Semillon, Riverland Cabernet Grenache, Port; under Henkell Yarra Valley are Riesling, Chardonnay, Pinot Noir, Shiraz, Cabernet Sauvignon.

summary Hans Henkell started with a 57-variety Heinz mix in the vineyard, but has now rationalised it to a total of 17.7 hectares of sauvignon blanc, chardonnay, pinot noir and cabernet sauvignon. Most of the grapes are sold, with small amounts contract-made each year. And yes, Hans Henkell is part of the family. A city cellar door, for case sales only, is open by appointment at 53 Victoria Parade, Collingwood, phone (03) 8415 1910.

henley park wines   NR

6 Swan Street, Henley Brook, WA 6055 **region** Swan Valley
phone (08) 9296 4328 **fax** (08) 9296 1313 **open** Tues–Sun 10–5
winemaker Claus Petersen, Lisbet Petersen **production** 5000 cases **est.** 1935
product range ($9.95–15.95 CD) Semillon, Chenin Blanc, Classic White, Chardonnay, Muscat Gordo Blanco (late picked), Mousse Rose Brut (Methode Champenoise), Pinot Noir, Merlot, Shiraz, Cabernet Sauvignon, Shiraz Cabernet Merlot, Vintage Port, Old Tawny.
summary Henley Park, like so many Swan Valley wineries, was founded by a Yugoslav family, but it is now jointly owned by Danish and Malaysian interests, a multicultural mix if ever there was one. Majority owner and winemaker Claus Petersen arrived in 1986 and had his moment of glory in 1990 when Henley Park was the Most Successful Exhibitor at the Mount Barker Wine Show. Much of the production is sold through the cellar door (and exported to Denmark and Japan).

henry's drive   ★★★★☆

PMB 182, Naracoorte, SA 5271 **region** Padthaway
phone (08) 8765 6057 **fax** (08) 8765 6090 **open** Not
winemaker Sparky Marquis, Sarah Marquis **production** 8000 cases **est.** 1998
product range ($25–45 ML) Sparkling Shiraz, Shiraz, Reserve Shiraz, Cabernet Sauvignon, Reserve Cabernet Sauvignon.
summary The Longbottom families have been farming in Padthaway since the 1940s, with a diverse operation, from sheep and cattle to growing crops and onions. In 1992 a decision was made to further diversify and plant a few vines. Now with almost 300 hectares, the vineyard is established, and is planted mainly to shiraz and cabernet sauvignon and other varieties such as chardonnay, merlot, verdelho and sauvignon blanc. Henry's Drive is owned and operated by Brian and Kay Longbottom. Exports to the US, Canada, South-East Asia, the UK, Japan, Germany and Switzerland. The rating is for previous tastings.

henschke   ★★★★★

Henschke Road, Keyneton, SA 5353 **region** Eden Valley
phone (08) 8564 8223 **fax** (08) 8564 8294 **open** Mon–Fri 9–4.30, Sat 9–12, public holidays 10–3
winemaker Stephen Henschke **production** 40000 cases **est.** 1868
product range ($14–243 CD) From the Henschke Eden Valley sources Julius Riesling, Joseph Hill Gewurztraminer, Louis Semillon, Sauvignon Blanc Semillon, Little Hampton Pinot Gris, Tilly's Vineyard, Cranes Chardonnay, Noble Rot Riesling, Johann's Garden Grenache Shiraz Mourvedre, Keyneton Estate, Mount Edelstone, Cyril Henschke Cabernet Sauvignon, Hill of Grace. From the Lenswood Vineyard in the Adelaide Hills Green's Hill Riesling, Coralinga Sauvignon Blanc, Croft Chardonnay, Giles Pinot Noir, Henry's Seven Shiraz Grenache Viognier, Abbott's Prayer Cabernet Merlot.
summary Henschke is regarded as the best medium-sized red wine producer in Australia, and has gone from strength to strength over the past two decades under the guidance of Stephen and Prue Henschke. The red wines fully capitalise on the very old, low-yielding, high-quality vines and are superbly made with sensitive but positive use of new small oak: Hill of Grace is second only to Penfolds Grange as Australia's red wine icon. Exports to the UK, Europe, Asia and the US.

Henschke Julius Eden Valley Riesling

ŶŶŶŶ 2002 Light to medium yellow-green; the bouquet shows the typical lime juice fruit of the Eden Valley, and the palate has rich, already accessible fruit on entry, then a complex structure with some grip to the finish.   **rating:** 92

best drinking 2004–2010 **best vintages** '02 **drink with** Barramundi • $23.50

Henschke Lenswood Green's Hill Riesling

ŶŶŶŶŶ 2002 Fragrant, flowery lime and passionfruit aromas are followed by a deliciously lingering, intense and silky palate tied up with a bow of minerally acidity to underwrite its future.   **rating:** 96

best drinking Now–2010 **best vintages** '94, '95, '02 **drink with** Smoked trout pâté • $24.80

Henschke Joseph Hill Gewurztraminer

▼▼▼▼▼ **2002** Light straw-green; concentrated spice and rose petal aromas are followed by a vivacious spice, pear and lychee-flavoured palate; excellent acidity and length. Gewurztraminers of this quality are a rarity in Australia. **rating:** 94

best drinking Now–2005 **best vintages** '02 **drink with** Delicate Asian • $27.80

Henschke Coralinga Sauvignon Blanc

▼▼▼▼ **2002** Very pale straw-green; the bouquet is slightly reduced, but (not surprisingly) has strong varietal character; the light to medium-bodied palate focuses on gooseberry fruit, finishing with good balance. **rating:** 88

best drinking Now **drink with** Shellfish • $21.80

Henschke Sauvignon Blanc Semillon

▼▼▼▼▽ **2002** Light green-yellow; quite pungent aromas of herb, grass, straw and spice are followed by a smooth and silky palate with far more sweet fruit apparent, building intensity towards the finish. 58 per cent Sauvignon Blanc, 42 per cent Semillon. **rating:** 93

best drinking Now–2006 **best vintages** '02 **drink with** Squid linguini • $20.80

Henschke Littlehampton Innes Vineyard Pinot Gris

▼▼▼▼ **2002** The faint straw tinge to the colour is quite acceptable given the variety; aromas of pear, pear skin and spice lead into a richly textured palate which avoids oiliness; well balanced, with the pear and spice flavours continuing to make their presence felt. **rating:** 88

best drinking Now **drink with** Salmon risotto • $24

Henschke Lenswood Giles Pinot Noir

▼▼▼▼▽ **2001** Light to medium red-purple; the complex aromas of the bouquet range through spicy/savoury/foresty/stemmy characters, but with a red fruit core; the palate focuses more on the fruit, but once again is complex, with a mix of red fruits, plum and small berry flavours. All in all, makes the biggest statement of any of the Giles Pinot Noirs to date. **rating:** 90

best drinking Now–2005 **best vintages** '01 **drink with** Confit of duck • $41

Henschke Hill Of Grace

▼▼▼▼▼ **1998** Medium to full purple-red; a clean and rich array of black berries, spice, licorice and compatible oak, then a palate with abundant dark berry and bitter chocolate flavour, with controlled tannins and oak. Has great length and great balance; fully reflects the outstanding vintage, and has an indefinite life in front of it if well cellared. **rating:** 96

best drinking 2005–2025 **best vintages** '59, '61, '62, '66, '78, '82, '85, '86, '88, '90, '91, '93, '96, '98 **drink with** Rich casserole dishes • $243

Henschke Mount Edelstone

▼▼▼▼ **2000** Medium red-purple; the moderately intense bouquet has berry, earth, vanilla and a touch of spice; it flows logically enough into the medium-bodied palate, with blackberry, plum and spice supported by light tannins and subtle oak. Tradesman-like rather than exhilarating. **rating:** 88

best drinking Now–2008 **best vintages** '52, '56, '61, '66, '67, '78, '82, '86, '88, '90, '92, '93, '94, '95, '96, '98 **drink with** Beef bourguignon • $66.50

Henschke Henry's Seven

▼▼▼▼▽ **2001** Tasted with both screwcap and cork closures. The light to medium red-purple of the Stelvin is already showing better hue, with more purple (March 2003). The palate seems riper, and certainly has more obvious juicy berry fruit; conversely, it is tighter and less evolved than the cork-finished wine. Closures apart, the wine has lots of varietal character and life, and the contribution of the viognier is significant. **rating:** 90

best drinking Now–2009 **drink with** Braised rabbit • $28

Henschke Johann's Garden Grenache Shiraz Mourvedre

▼▼▼▼ **2001** Medium red-purple; the aromatic tangy/juicy/jammy/spicy grenache aromas dominate the bouquet; the flavours come together well on the light to medium-bodied palate, which has good texture and structure. A blend of 50 per cent Grenache, 30 per cent Mourvedre and 20 per cent Shiraz which belies its 15 per cent alcohol. **rating:** 89

best drinking Now–2006 **best vintages** '98, '99 **drink with** Coq au vin • $32

Henschke Abbott's Prayer

▼▼▼▼▼ **2000** Medium red-purple; the moderately intense bouquet is fragrant, with an appropriate array of spicy, foresty, cedary aromas. The fine, light to medium-bodied palate has berry, cedar and olive flavours supported by fine, ripe tannins. Stylish and elegant. **rating:** 94

best drinking 2005–2010 **best vintages** '89, '90, '91, '92, '93, '94, '96, '97, '99, '00 **drink with** Guinea fowl in red wine sauce • $64

Henschke Cyril Henschke Cabernet

▼▼▼▼▼ **2000** Bright, deep red-purple; the bouquet offers clean, gently ripe blackcurrant and mulberry fruit together with a hint of cedar; the classy, sophisticated, ultra-smooth and supple palate has excellent flow and mouthfeel. For the record, the wine does have a percentage of Merlot and Cabernet Franc included. **rating:** 95

best drinking 2005–2020 **best vintages** '78, '80, '85, '86, '88, '90, '91, '92, '93, '94, '96, '98, '99, '00 **drink with** Roast lamb • $97.40

henty brook estate   NR

Box 49, Dardanup, WA 6236 **region** Geographe
phone (08) 9728 1459 **fax** (08) 9728 1459 **open** Weekends 10–4, Mon–Fri by appointment
winemaker James Pennington (Contract) **production** 400 cases **est.** 1994
product range ($10–15 CD) Sauvignon Blanc Semillon, Shiraz.
summary One hectare each of shiraz and sauvignon blanc and 0.5 hectare of semillon were planted in the spring of 1994. James Pennington is the contract winemaker; the first releases are now on the market.

heritage estate   ★★★★

Granite Belt Drive, Cottonvale, Qld 4375 **region** Granite Belt
phone (07) 4685 2197 **fax** (07) 4685 2112 **open** 7 days 9–5
winemaker Paola Carberaz Bono **production** 5000 cases **est.** 1992
product range ($9.50–35 CD) Semillon, Dry White, Semillon Chardonnay, Harvest Blend, Chardonnay, Club Red, Shiraz, Roswal Shiraz, Merlot, Cabernet Merlot, Fortified and flavoured wines.
summary Bryce and Paddy Kassulke operate a very successful winery, and have won many awards in recent years. The winery also showcases its wines through its cellar door at Mount Tambourine (cnr Bartle Road and The Shelf Road, phone (07) 5545 3144) in an old church converted into a tasting and sales area, with views over the Gold Coast hinterland. The cellar door also incorporates a restaurant, barbecue area and art gallery. The estate plantings, established in 1993, comprise chardonnay (2 ha), merlot (2 ha), shiraz (1 ha) and cabernet sauvignon (1 ha). The quality of the wines has been consistently good: in the top half dozen of the now innumerable Queensland wineries.

Heritage Estate Chardonnay

▼▼▼▼ **2002** Light to medium yellow-green; very strong charry/toasty barrel-ferment inputs dominate the bouquet, but stone fruit and peach make a partial comeback on the palate, with the oak better balanced. **rating:** 86

best drinking Now **drink with** Avocado and prawn salad • $15.50

Heritage Estate Botrytis Chardonnay

▼▼▼▼ **2002** Medium yellow-green; some dusty oak aromas on the bouquet are followed by bold, poached peach flavours on the palate; rich and luscious, balanced by good acidity. **rating:** 87

best drinking Now–2005 **drink with** Poached fruit

Heritage Estate Shiraz

▼▼▼▼ **2000** Medium red, with a hint of purple; a quite complex array of earthy, dusty, cedary aromas leads into a similar palate, with soft, cedary/leathery overtones to the red fruit flavours. **rating:** 87

best drinking 2004–2009 **drink with** Rib of beef • $18.50

Heritage Estate Private Reserve Shiraz

▼▼▼▼▽ **2000** Strong, deep red-purple; abundant, clean blackberry fruit drives the bouquet, with hints of licorice and oak; the palate has abundant flavour, excellent texture and good structure. A seriously good red wine; I cannot remember tasting a better Shiraz from Queensland (although the 2000 Jimbour Station gains equal points). **rating:** 93

best drinking 2005–2010 **best vintages** '99, '00 **drink with** Kangaroo fillet • $22.50

Heritage Estate Private Reserve Merlot

TTTT 2000 Medium red-purple; the clean, moderately intense, savoury/spicy bouquet leads into a medium-bodied palate with black fruits, some Christmas cake, and fine, savoury tannins. Another well-made and well-balanced wine. **rating: 87**

best drinking 2004–2009 **drink with** Rack of veal • $25

Heritage Estate Cabernet Sauvignon

TTTT 2000 Medium red-purple; clean, clear, ripe cassis cabernet varietal aromas raise the question of over-ripeness, but the palate rights the ship, with firm blackcurrant/cassis fruit; here the main issue is the lack of complexity. **rating: 85**

best drinking 2004–2009 **drink with** Leg of lamb • $18.50

heritage farm wines   NR

RMB 1005, Murray Valley Highway, Cobram, Vic 3655 **region** Goulburn Valley
phone (03) 5872 2376 **fax** (03) 5872 2376 **open** 7 days 9–5
winemaker Roy Armfield **production** 2000 cases **est.** 1987
product range ($5–12 CD) Riesling, Traminer Riesling, Moselle, Chardonnay are varietal releases; there are a considerable number of generic releases and fortified wines on sale at the cellar door.
summary Heritage Farm claims to be the only vineyard and orchard in Australia still using horsepower, with Clydesdales used for most of the general farm work. The winery and cellar-door area also boasts a large range of restored horse-drawn farm machinery and a bottle collection. All the wines are sold by mailing list and through the cellar door.

heritage wines   ★★★★

106a Seppeltsfield Road, Marananga, SA 5355 **region** Barossa Valley
phone (08) 8562 2880 **fax** (08) 8562 2692 **open** 7 days 11–5
winemaker Stephen Hoff **production** 6000 cases **est.** 1984
product range ($14–34 CD) Semillon, Barossa Shiraz, Rossco's Shiraz, Cabernet Malbec, Cabernet Sauvignon.
summary A little-known winery which deserves a far wider audience, for Stephen Hoff is apt to produce some startlingly good wines. At various times the Chardonnay, Riesling (from old Clare Valley vines) and Rossco's Shiraz (now the flag-bearer) have all excelled; at other times not. Exports to the UK and the US.

Heritage Wines Barossa Shiraz

TTTTY 2001 Bright purple-red; clean, rich and ripe dark cherry, plum and berry fruit leads into a fruit-driven, attractive and smooth palate with subtle oak and fine tannins. **rating: 90**

best drinking 2006–2011 **best vintages** '98, '99, '01 **drink with** Steak and kidney pie • $24

Heritage Wines Rossco's Shiraz

TTTTY 2001 Medium to full purple-red, bright and clear; dense, clean, dark berry/licorice fruit and integrated oak on the bouquet flows into a smooth and supple palate with almost creamy tannins and quality oak. **rating: 92**

best drinking 2006–2016 **best vintages** '98, '01 **drink with** Roast kid • $34

Heritage Wines Barossa Cabernet Malbec

TTTT 2000 Bright purple-red; powerful dark fruits with some spicy notes are enhanced by quality oak; juicy blackberry fruit and soft tannins complete the picture. Great value. **rating: 89**

best drinking 2004–2008 **drink with** Beef in red wine • $18

Heritage Wines Barossa Cabernet Sauvignon

TTTTY 2001 Medium to full red-purple; ripe blackcurrant/olive/earth/vanilla aromas, the wine coming through very well on the palate, supple and long, with ripe tannins and assured oak handling. **rating: 90**

best drinking 2006–2011 **best vintages** '98, '99, '01 **drink with** Barbecued beef • $24

herons rise vineyard   NR

Saddle Road, Kettering, Tas 7155 **region** Southern Tasmania
phone (03) 6267 4339 **fax** (03) 6267 4245 **open** By appointment
winemaker Andrew Hood **production** 250 cases **est.** 1984

product range ($17.50–25 CD) Muller Thurgau Riesling, Pinot Noir.

summary Sue and Gerry White run a small stone country guesthouse in the D'Entrecasteaux Channel area and basically sell the wines produced from the surrounding hectare of vineyard to those staying at the two self-contained cottages. The Pinot Noir is strongly recommended. The postal address for bookings is PO Box 271, Kettering, Tas 7155.

hesperos wines ★★★☆

PO Box 882, Margaret River, WA 6285 **region** Margaret River
phone (08) 9757 6565 **fax** (08) 9757 6565 **open** Not
winemaker Jurg Muggli **production** 2000 cases **est.** 1993
product range ($14.50–19.50 CD) Sauvignon Blanc, Syrah.
summary Hesperos is the venture of Jurg Muggli and Sandra Hancock. It supplies Jurg Muggli's winemaking skills to Xanadu, where Muggli has been resident winemaker for many years. It also has a 30-hectare property near Witchcliffe, between Cape Mentelle and Devil's Lair, with the potential of 15 hectares of vineyard; planting commenced in the winter of 1999. In the meantime the Hesperos wines are made from purchased grapes; Shiraz and Sauvignon Blanc have been produced in each vintage. Exports to Japan, Switzerland and Germany.

Hesperos Sauvignon Blanc

▼▼▼▼ 2002 Light straw-green; the fresh, clean, minerally bouquet is followed by a palate which opens in similar fashion, and it is not until the wine is swallowed that you realise the great extension on the finish. Whole bunch-pressed and barrel fermented in French oak, but the oak is barely perceptible, so well is it integrated. **rating:** 87

best drinking Now **drink with** Margaret River abalone • $14.50

Hesperos Syrah

▼▼▼▽ 2001 Youthful purple-red; a clean, fresh and direct berry-fruited bouquet is followed by a fresh, unevolved palate which really needed more winemaking to bring out the best in the fruit. **rating:** 84

best drinking Now–2006 **drink with** Pizza • $19.50

hewitson ★★★★☆

16 McGowan Avenue, Unley, SA 5061 **region** Warehouse
phone (08) 8271 5755 **fax** (08) 8271 5570 **open** By appointment, at 66 London Road, Mile End, SA 5000
winemaker Dean Hewitson **production** 10000 cases **est.** 1996
product range ($19–37 R) Eden Valley Riesling, L'Oizeau Shiraz, Old Garden Mourvedre, Ned & Henry's Barossa Shiraz, Miss Harry, Dry Grown and Ancient.
summary Dean Hewitson was a Petaluma winemaker for 10 years, and during that time managed to do three vintages in France and one in Oregon as well as undertaking his Masters at UC Davis, California. It is hardly surprising that the Hewitson wines are immaculately made from a technical viewpoint. However, he has also managed to source 30-year-old riesling from the Eden Valley and 70-year-old shiraz from McLaren Vale, following those with a Barossa Valley Mourvedre produced from 145-year-old vines at Rowland Flat and a Barossa Valley Shiraz and Grenache from 60-year-old vines at Tanunda. The vineyards are now under long-term contracts to Dean Hewitson. Exports to New Zealand, China, Japan, Malaysia, Singapore, the US, Canada, Finland, The Netherlands, Norway, Germany and the UK.

Hewitson Eden Valley Riesling

▼▼▼▼ 2002 Medium yellow-green; the abundant bouquet has potent lime aromas, almost to the point of heaviness; the medium-weight palate tightens up with a nice touch of mineral, and has good length. Minuscule production; only 650 cases made. **rating:** 89

best drinking Now–2008 **best vintages** '98, '99, '00 **drink with** Summer salads • $19

Hewitson L'Oizeau Shiraz

▼▼▼▼ 2000 Medium red-purple; the moderately intense bouquet offers plum, berry and a hint of chocolate alongside subtle oak. The palate has good balance and extraction of sweet fruit; the limitations of the wine lie with the vintage. **rating:** 87

best drinking Now–2009 **best vintages** '97, '98 **drink with** Hearty red meat dishes • $36

Hewitson Ned & Henry's Shiraz

▼▼▼▼▼ **2001** Bright purple-red; rich scents of blackberry, prune, chocolate and spice foreshadow a rich and delicious palate with supple mouthfeel and a similar range of flavours to the bouquet; French oak is in the background; classic Barossa with an extra twist from the excellent oak. **rating:** 94

best drinking 2006–2016 **drink with** Roast saltbush lamb • $25

hickinbotham NR

Nepean Highway (near Wallaces Road), Dromana, Vic 3936 **region** Mornington Peninsula
phone (03) 5981 0355 **fax** (03) 5981 0355 **open** 7 days
winemaker Andrew Hickinbotham **production** 3000 cases **est.** 1981
product range ($15–30 R) Chardonnay with Aligote, Taminga, Strawberry Kiss (sparkling), Pinot Noir, Luxuriance Shiraz, Merlot, Cabernet Merlot; Strawberry Elixir.
summary After a peripatetic period and a hiatus in winemaking, Hickinbotham established a permanent vineyard and winery base at Dromana. It now makes only Mornington Peninsula wines, drawing in part on 5 hectares of estate vineyards, and in part on contract-grown fruit. The wines are principally sold through the cellar door and by mail order.

hidden river estate NR

Mullineaux Road, Pemberton, WA 6260 **region** Pemberton
phone (08) 9776 1437 **fax** (08) 9776 0189 **open** 7 days 9–4
winemaker Brenden Smith, Phil Goldring **production** 2500 cases **est.** 1994
product range ($12.50–30 CD) Three Feathers Classic Dry White, Unwooded Chardonnay, Wooded Chardonnay, Sparkle Arse (Methode Champenoise), Late Picked Riesling, Pinot Noir, Authentic Basket Press Shiraz, Cabernet Sauvignon, Aged Cell Door Tawny Port, The Muskateer.
summary Phil and Sandy Goldring spent 10 years operating farm chalets in the Pemberton area before selling the business and retiring to become grape growers, with the intention of selling the grapes to others. However, they found old habits hard to kick, so opened a cellar-door sales and cafe/restaurant. It is a successful business with a very strong marketing push, a 1901 Kalgoorlie tram (the streetcar named Desire) having been purchased, renovated and installed on-site to provide more seating for the award-winning restaurant. I hope the Goldrings did not pay much for the tram.

highbank NR

Riddoch Highway, Coonawarra, SA 5263 **region** Coonawarra
phone (08) 8736 3311 **fax** (08) 8736 3122 **open** By appointment
winemaker Dennis Vice, Trevor Mast **production** 1000 cases **est.** 1986
product range ($40 CD) Chardonnay, Basket Pressed Cabernet Blend, Basket Pressed Cabernet Sauvignon.
summary Mount Gambier lecturer in viticulture Dennis Vice makes a tiny quantity of smooth, melon-accented Chardonnay and stylish Coonawarra Cabernet Blend of good quality which are sold through local restaurants and the cellar door, with limited Melbourne distribution. Intermittent exports to various countries.

higher plane wines ★★★★☆

Location 1077, Wintarru Rise via Warner Glen Road, Forrest Grove, WA 6286 (postal) **region** Margaret River
phone (08) 9336 7855 **fax** (08) 9336 7866 **open** Not
winemaker Keith Mugford (Contract) **production** 1600 cases **est.** 1997
product range ($20–28 ML) Chardonnay, Pinot Noir, Cabernet Merlot.
summary Plastic and hand surgeon Dr Craig Smith and wife Cathie left nothing to chance in planning and establishing Higher Plane. As a prelude, Cathie obtained a Master of Business in wine marketing from Edith Cowan University, and Craig began the wine marketing course at the University of Adelaide. Having read widely, and consulted Keith Mugford at Moss Wood and Dr Mike Peterkin at Pierro, the Smiths wrote to every real estate agent within the Margaret River region listing the criteria which had to be met for their proposed vineyard. Details of over 100 properties were faxed to the Smiths, and with consulting viticultural advice from Peter Gheradi and Keith Mugford, Craig Smith inspected 32 properties before hearing about the property they have in fact purchased, securing it only three days after it was first offered for sale. Its eastern and northern boundaries adjoin Devil's Lair, and it has similar gravelly, loamy, sandy soil. The same care was taken with sourcing vine material for the 6 hectares of vineyards now in production. The wines are sold through a mailing list with copious information; limited retail distribution through Perth, New South Wales and Queensland.

Higher Plane Chardonnay

▼▼▼▼♈ 2001 Medium yellow-green; the bouquet is driven by complex barrel-ferment and malolactic-ferment aromas, the fruit downplayed; on the palate, melon and stone fruit flavours come through strongly; good mouthfeel, length and finish. One hundred per cent new French oak; partial wild yeast fermentation; 100 per cent malolactic fermentation. **rating: 92**

best drinking Now–2007 best vintages '01 drink with Pan-fried veal • $24

Higher Plane Cabernet Merlot

▼▼▼▼♈ 2001 Medium red-purple; the clean, moderately intense bouquet offers fresh red and black fruit aromas; nicely judged oak in the background. The palate is no less clean and harmonious, with soft, gently sweet raspberry and blackcurrant fruit flavours, finishing with fine tannins. **rating: 91**

best drinking 2005–2012 drink with Rack of lamb • $25

highland heritage estate ★★★☆

Mitchell Highway, Orange, NSW 2800 **region** Orange
phone (02) 6361 3612 **fax** (02) 6361 3613 **open** Mon–Fri 9–3, weekends 9–5
winemaker John Hordern, Rex D'Aquino **production** 3500 cases **est.** 1984
product range ($10–30 CD) Under the Mount Canobolas label: Chardonnay, Sauvignon Blanc, Pinot Noir; Gosling Creek Chardonnay; and the newly released Wellwood Estate label.
summary The estate plantings have increased from 4 hectares to over 15 hectares, with plantings in 1995 and 1997 now in full production. The tasting facility is unusual: a converted railway carriage overlooking the vineyard.

high valley wines ★★★☆

Berowra Road, Dunedoo, NSW 2844 **region** Mudgee
phone (02) 6375 0292 **fax** (02) 6375 0228 **open** By appointment
winemaker Simon Gilbert, Ian MacRae (Contract) **production** 2300 cases **est.** 1995
product range ($13–18.50 CD) Chardonnay, Chardonnay Simon Gilbert, Premium Chardonnay, Shiraz, Reserve Shiraz.
summary The Francis family, headed by Ro and Grosvenor Francis, have operated a sheep, wheat and cattle property at Dunedoo for several generations. When they handed over the property to their sons in 1995, Ro and Grosvenor subdivided and retained a 40-hectare block on which they have since established 11 hectares of shiraz, 6 hectares of cabernet sauvignon and 5 hectares of chardonnay. A grape supply agreement was entered into with Rothbury Estate, but a decision was taken in 1998 to retain a portion of the grapes and develop the High Valley Wines label. While the property is only open by appointment, it does feature a gas and wood-fired working pottery, vineyard tours and farm tours.

hillbrook NR

639 Doust Road, Geary's Gap via Bungendore, NSW 2621 **region** Canberra District
phone (02) 6236 9455 **fax** (02) 6236 9455 **open** Weekends and public holidays 10–5
winemaker Contract **production** 2000 cases **est.** 1994
product range ($19–25 CD) Riesling, Chardonnay, Pinot Noir, Merlot, Tawny Port.
summary Adolf and Levina Zanzert began the establishment of 8.5 hectares of vines at Geary's Gap in 1994. The wines have good retail distribution in the ACT, Bungendore and Cooma, and are also available through the cellar door and by the mailing list.

🐌 hillbrook wines NR

Cnr Hillbrook and Wheatley Coast Roads, Quinninup, WA 6258 **region** Pemberton
phone (08) 9776 7202 **fax** (08) 9776 7202 **open** By appointment
winemaker Castle Rock Estate (Contract) **production** 350 cases **est.** 1996
product range ($8.50–13.50 ML) Sauvignon Blanc, Merlot.
summary Brian Ede and partner Anne Walsh have established 1 hectare of sauvignon blanc and 3 hectares of merlot, and have the wines made for them by Robert Diletti at Castle Rock Estate. They are sold through the cellar door and via a mailing list, and – increasingly – by word of mouth.

🐚 hillcrest vineyards ★★★★☆

31 Phillip Road, Woori Yallock, Vic 3139 **region** Yarra Valley
phone (03) 5964 6689 **fax** (03) 5961 5547 **open** By appointment
winemaker Contract **production** 200 cases **est.** 1971
product range ($30–45 ML) Chardonnay, Pinot Noir, Cabernet Sauvignon.
summary David and Tanya Bryant may or may not realise it, but my association with Hillcrest goes back to 1985, when Coldstream Hills first started purchasing grapes from the then owners Graeme and Joy Sweet. Although there was never a written contract, that arrangement continued until Hillcrest was sold, by which time the tiny amount of grapes coming from it was of no particular significance to Coldstream Hills. But the Sweets had stood by Coldstream Hills in the years of acute grape shortages, and we reciprocated further down the track. To say I am pleased that Hillcrest is in tender care, and receiving the attention it deserves, is putting it mildly. Incidentally, when (in my 2003 *Companion*) I gave 94 points to the 2000 Cabernet Sauvignon made by Shadowfax, I had no idea the grapes had come from Hillcrest Vineyard.

Hillcrest Chardonnay

♥♥♥♥♥ **2002** Light to medium yellow-green; the spotlessly clean bouquet has very good balance and integration of fruit and oak; the sophisticated, complex palate has both malolactic and barrel-ferment inputs giving a creamy feel to the fig and stone fruit flavours; good length, beautifully made.   **rating:** 94

best drinking Now–2008 **best vintages** '02 **drink with** Salmon risotto • $30

Hillcrest Pinot Noir

♥♥♥♥♡ **2001** Bright red-purple; the very complex bouquet has a mix of plum, spice and forest, all of which come through on the palate, which, while verging on austerity, has bell-clear varietal character; good length via fine tannins.   **rating:** 90

best drinking Now–2007 **best vintages** '01 **drink with** Roast quail • $45

hill smith estate ★★★★

Suite 1, 61 Parraween Street, Cremorne, NSW 2090 (postal) **region** Eden Valley
phone (08) 8561 3200 **fax** (08) 8561 3393 **open** At Yalumba
winemaker Louisa Rose **production** 5000 cases **est.** 1979
product range ($18.95 R) Sauvignon Blanc.
summary Part of the Yalumba stable, drawing upon its own estate plantings, which include 15 hectares of sauvignon blanc. Over the years has produced some excellent wines, but the style (and perhaps quality) does seem to vary significantly with vintage, and the winery rating is a compromise between the best and the least. Exports to all major markets.

Hill Smith Estate Sauvignon Blanc

♥♥♥♥ **2002** Light to medium yellow-green; ripe, tropical guava and gooseberry aromas are reflected in the abundant tropical flavours of the palate, gaining focus on a crisp finish.   **rating:** 89

best drinking Now **best vintages** '86, '92, '93, '94, '95, '96, '99 **drink with** Fresh mussels • $18.95

hills of plenty NR

370 Yan Yean Road, Yarrambat, Vic 3091 **region** Yarra Valley
phone (03) 9436 2264 **fax** (03) 9436 2264 **open** Last Sun of each month 12–5, or by appointment
winemaker Karen Coulston **production** 400 cases **est.** 1998
product range ($15–20 CD) Riesling, Sauvignon Blanc, Chardonnay, Pinot Noir, Shiraz, Cabernet Sauvignon.
summary Hills of Plenty has been established just outside the Melbourne metropolitan area, a few minutes' drive north of Greensborough. There is a tiny 0.2-hectare vineyard of riesling, chardonnay and cabernet sauvignon around the winery, but most of the fruit is purchased from other regions, notably Geelong, Gippsland and Swan Hill. The tiny production means that the cellar door only opens once a month, but it is turned into a festive occasion, with live music, and picnics or barbecues welcome.

hillstowe ★★★★

104 Main Road, Hahndorf, SA 5245 **region** Adelaide Hills
phone (08) 8388 1400 **fax** (08) 8388 1411 **open** 7 days 10–5
winemaker Justin McNamee **production** 12 000 cases **est.** 1980

product range ($16–46 R) A range of vineyard and varietal-designated wines of ascending price and quality, being Sauvignon Blanc, Scrub Block Pinot Gris, Buxton Chardonnay, Buxton Cabernet Merlot; at the top end, Adelaide Hills Udy's Mill Chardonnay, Udy's Mill Pinot Noir, Mary's Hundred Shiraz, The Pinch Row Lenswood Merlot.

summary Rapid-fire changes of ownership from founder Chris Lawrie to Banksia Wines then to Lion Nathan should (theoretically) not impact on the quality and style of the high-quality Hillstowe wines. Its principal vineyard, Udy's Mill at Lenswood, has 17 hectares planted, supplementing McLaren Vale grapes coming from the Buxton Vineyard. The wines are exported to the UK, Canada, the US, Europe and Asia.

Hillstowe Sauvignon Blanc

TTTTY 2002 Medium yellow-green; a complex and powerful bouquet ranging through mineral, herb and gooseberry aromas is followed by a concentrated palate, with good mouthfeel; sweet citrus and gooseberry flavours; good length. **rating:** 91

best drinking Now **best vintages** '90, '93, '94, '96, '02 **drink with** King George whiting • $17.95

Hillstowe The Scrub Block Lenswood Pinot Gris

TTTTT 2002 Pale straw-green; an attractively perfumed and highly floral bouquet leads into a palate with primary lemony fruit but a more complex underlay; good length and balance to an interesting wine showing both good fruit and skilled winemaking. **rating:** 94

best drinking Now–2005 **best vintages** '02 **drink with** Blue swimmer crab • $21.50

Hillstowe Buxton Chardonnay

TTTT 2002 Light to medium yellow-green; the aromas provide an interesting mix of lemon zest, spice and nectarine; the light to medium-bodied fruit-driven palate flows well across the tongue, with the barest touch of oak; well sculpted. **rating:** 88

best drinking Now–2005 **drink with** Trout risotto • $15.95

Hillstowe Udy's Mill Pinot Noir

TTTT 2001 Medium red-purple; a clean array of strawberry, cherry and plum fruit aromas are supported by subtle oak; the medium-bodied palate is neatly balanced and modulated, with smooth pinot varietal fruit. Just a little too domesticated, perhaps. **rating:** 89

best drinking Now–2006 **best vintages** '98 **drink with** Rich game • $29.95

Hillstowe Buxton Cabernet Merlot

TTTT 2000 Medium red, with the purple starting to diminish; the bouquet is slightly closed, but savoury dark fruit aromas are lurking in the background; the palate has much more weight and texture, with strong regional chocolate overtones to the fruit, and the wine comes together in convincing fashion. **rating:** 88

best drinking 2005–2010 **best vintages** '98 **drink with** Roast veal • $22.95

hills view vineyards ★★★☆

11 Main Avenue, Frewville, SA 5063 **region** McLaren Vale
phone (08) 8338 0666 **fax** (08) 8338 0666 **open** Not
winemaker Brett Howard **production** 12 000 cases **est.** 1998
product range ($10–30 R) Three ranges of wines produced: Blewitt Springs Semillon, Chardonnay, Shiraz and Cabernet Sauvignon; Howard Fleurieu Semillon and Coonawarra Shiraz; Hills View Chardonnay Verdelho, Shiraz Cabernet and Cabernet Merlot.
summary District veteran Brett Howard, with 20 years' winemaking experience, is now the winemaker for Hills View Vineyards, producing the Hills View Vineyards range of wines, the Blewitt Springs range and Howard label: a Fleurieu Semillon and a Coonawarra Shiraz are released only in the best vintages.

🍃 hillwood vineyard NR

55 Innocent Street, Kings Meadows, Tas 7249 (postal) **region** Northern Tasmania
phone 0418 500 672 **open** Not
winemaker Geoff Carr **est.** NA
product range Sauvignon Blanc, Pinot Gris, Chardonnay, Pinot Noir, Cabernet.
summary Geoff Carr, the owner, viticulturist and winemaker, has established his vineyard on the east bank of the Tamar River, looking out over the river. He supplements his estate-grown grapes by purchasing some chardonnay and pinot gris from local growers.

hochkirch wines   NR

Hamilton Highway, Tarrington, Vic 3301 **region** Henty
phone (03) 5573 5200 **fax** (03) 5573 5200 **open** 11–5 by appointment
winemaker John Nagorcka **production** 1500 cases **est.** 1997
product range ($11–24 ML) Riesling, Semillon, Pinot Noir, Shiraz, Cabernet Sauvignon.
summary Jennifer and John Nagorcka have developed Hochkirch in response to the very cool climate, which has growing season temperatures similar to those of Burgundy. A high-density planting pattern was implemented, with a low-fruiting wire to take advantage of soil warmth in the growing season, and the focus was placed on pinot noir (4.5 ha), with lesser quantities of riesling, cabernet sauvignon, semillon and shiraz. The vines are not irrigated and no synthetic fungicides, pesticides or fertilizers are used; currently the Nagorckas are trialling biodynamic practice. Wines with considerable complexity and interest are the result, the Pinot Noir having received critical acclaim in a number of quarters.

hoffmann's   ★★★

Ingoldby Road, McLaren Flat, SA 5171 **region** McLaren Vale
phone (08) 8383 0232 **fax** (08) 8383 0232 **open** 7 days 11–5
winemaker Nick Holmes (Consultant) **production** 2500 cases **est.** 1996
product range ($16–21 CD) Chardonnay, Shiraz, Cabernet Sauvignon.
summary Peter and Anthea Hoffmann have been growing grapes at their property in Ingoldby Road since 1978, and Peter Hoffmann has worked at various wineries in McLaren Vale since 1979. Both he and Anthea have undertaken courses at the Regency TAFE Institute in Adelaide, and (in Peter Hoffmann's words) 'in 1996 we decided that we knew a little about winemaking and opened a small cellar door'. Exports to the UK, Germany and Malaysia.

Hoffmann's Cabernet Sauvignon
♥♥♥♥ **2001** Medium red-purple; clean and fresh redcurrant and blackcurrant fruit aromas lead into a medium-bodied palate with smooth blackcurrant fruit, a whisk of chocolate, ripe tannins and subtle oak.   **rating:** 86
best drinking 2005–2010 **drink with** Boned leg of lamb • $21

hollick   ★★★★

Riddoch Highway, Coonawarra, SA 5263 **region** Coonawarra
phone (08) 8737 2318 **fax** (08) 8737 2952 **open** 7 days 9–5
winemaker Ian Hollick, David Norman **production** 40 000 cases **est.** 1983
product range ($17–60 R) A very disciplined array of products, with Riesling, Sauvignon Blanc Semillon, Wilgha Vineyard Unoaked Chardonnay, Pinot Noir, Tempranillo and Shiraz Cabernet Sauvignon at the lower end of the price range; Reserve Chardonnay, Cabernet Sauvignon Merlot, Pinot Noir Chardonnay, Sparkling Merlot are in the middle; Wilgha Shiraz, Neilson's Block Merlot and Ravenswood, the deluxe Cabernet Sauvignon, are at the top.
summary Winner of many trophies (including the most famous of all, the Jimmy Watson), its wines are well crafted and competitively priced, although sometimes a little on the light side. A $1 million cellar-door and restaurant complex opened in June 2002. National distribution in all states; exports to Europe and Asia.

Hollick Riesling
♥♥♥♥♡ **2002** Light straw-green; a bright, clean, flowery, nettle and lime bouquet leads into a palate with plenty of impact and presence; bright citrus fruit and lemony acidity make the wine an each-way proposition.
rating: 92
best drinking Now–2009 **best vintages** '99, '02 **drink with** Light seafood • $18.50

Hollick Sauvignon Blanc Semillon
♥♥♥♥ **2002** Light straw-green; firm mineral aromas with touches of lemon zest, spice and herb lead into a palate with abundant flavour and subliminal sweetness; well constructed, particularly for cellar-door trade. An 85/15 blend.   **rating:** 86
best drinking Now **drink with** Grilled seafood • $17

Hollick Reserve Chardonnay
♥♥♥♥ **2001** Medium yellow-green; the bouquet has a range of melon, nectarine and fig fruit supported by the usual subtle oak; the light to medium-bodied palate presents all the flavours promised by the bouquet in a soft, easy flow.   **rating:** 87
best drinking Now–2006 **best vintages** '00 **drink with** Steamed mud crab • $22

Hollick Wilgha Shiraz

▼▼▼▼▽ **2000** Strong red-purple; the bouquet is quite complex, with spicy, cedary overtones to the blackberry fruit; the rich palate has dense, ripe blackberry fruit counterpointed by gently savoury tannins on the finish; the oak is well balanced and integrated. **rating: 91**

best drinking 2006–2016 **best vintages** '00 **drink with** Braised beef • $43

Hollick Tempranillo Varietal Trial

▼▼▼▽ **2001** Light red, a disappointing start; scented, spicy red fruits on the bouquet are repeated on the light, spicy, sweetly savoury palate. Thirteen degrees alcohol; young vines or unripe? Hopefully there will be much more down the track. **rating: 83**

best drinking Now **drink with** Antipasto • $17.50

Hollick Cabernet Sauvignon

▼▼▼▼ **2000** Medium red; the bouquet shows some development, with the typical regional cabernet aromas in an earthy/chocolatey/savoury spectrum. The elegant, medium-bodied palate has fine tannins and balance; the question mark about the wine is its seemingly rapid development. **rating: 88**

best drinking Now–2006 **drink with** Spring lamb • $24

hollyclare   NR

940 Milbrodale Road, Broke, NSW 2330 **region** Lower Hunter Valley
phone (02) 6579 1193 **fax** (02) 6579 1269 **open** Weekends 10–5 by appointment
winemaker Tamburlaine (Contract) **production** 2000 cases **est.** 1987
product range Semillon, Unwooded Semillon, Chardonnay, Chardonnay Semillon, Shiraz.
summary John Holdsworth established the Hollyclare Vineyard (now totalling 3 hectares each of chardonnay, semillon, shiraz and 1 hectare of aleatico) 10 years ago, but the Hollyclare label is a relatively new one on the market. While the wines are made under contract at Tamburlaine, Hollyclare has its own dedicated wine tanks and all the wines are estate-grown.

holly folly   NR

649 Campersic Road, Baskerville, WA 6056 **region** Swan Valley
phone (08) 9296 2043 **fax** (08) 9296 2043 **open** By appointment
winemaker Peter Hollingworth **production** 400 cases **est.** 1995
product range ($5–15 ML) Dry White, Verdelho (Barrel Fermented and Barrel Aged), Marsanne, Methode Champenoise, Light Red, Merlot.
summary Peter Hollingworth clearly has a sense of humour and a sense of perspective. He began the establishment of the 11.5 hectares of vineyards (planted to chenin blanc, chardonnay, viognier, marsanne, verdelho, petit verdot, grenache and merlot) in 1995, but it was not until 2000 that the necessary producers licence was obtained, and in October of that year he embarked upon the limited release of the 400-case production, destined mainly for friends and acquaintances. Most of the grapes are sold to other producers.

holm oak   ★★★★

RSD 256, Rowella, West Tamar, Tas 7270 **region** Northern Tasmania
phone (03) 6394 7577 **fax** (03) 6394 7350 **open** 7 days 10–5
winemaker Nick Butler, Julian Alcorso **production** 3000 cases **est.** 1983
product range ($16–25 R) Riesling, Chardonnay, Reserve Chardonnay, Tyrian Rose Pinot Noir, Cabernet Sauvignon.
summary The Butler family produces tremendously rich and strongly flavoured red wines from the vineyard on the banks of the Tamar River. The winery takes its name from the grove of oak trees planted around the turn of the century and originally intended for the making of tennis racquets. The white wines, too, led by Riesling, have also impressed over the past few years. Rating based on previous tastings.

🍂 holtsbaum wines   NR

Mistletoe Lane, Pokolbin, NSW 2320 **region** Lower Hunter Valley
phone (02) 9252 5364 **fax** (02) 9252 5364 **open** Not
winemaker Greg Silkman (Contract) **production** 1300 cases **est.** 1994
product range ($17–21 R) Unwooded Chardonnay, Assheton Creek Chardonnay, Calf Pen Shiraz.

summary Robert and Jennie Holtsbaum began the development of their business when they purchased 40 hectares of open farmland from the Tyrrell family. Up to that point of time the rolling hills had been used solely for cattle grazing. Two and a half hectares each of chardonnay and shiraz were planted over the next 4 years, following the hillside contours. The first vintage was 1999, and it, and succeeding vintages, have been made by Greg Silkman at Monarch Winemaking Services. The wines are available by mailing list and are exported through Winex Corporation.

home hill ★★★★

38 Nairn Street, Ranelagh, Tas 7109 **region** Southern Tasmania
phone (03) 6264 1200 **fax** (03) 6264 1069 **open** 7 days 10–5
winemaker Peter Dunbaven, Jim Chatto (Consultant) **production** 2000 cases **est.** 1994
product range ($19–30 CD) Sauvignon Blanc, Kelly's Reserve Chardonnay, Kelly's Reserve Sticky, Kelly Cuvee, Pinot Noir, Kelly's Reserve Pinot Noir.
summary Terry and Rosemary Bennett planted their first 0.5 hectare of vines in 1994 on gentle slopes in the beautiful Huon Valley. The plantings were quickly extended to 3 hectares, with another hectare planted in 1999. A 70-seat restaurant is open for lunch Wednesday to Sunday and dinner on Saturday.

Home Hill Kelly's Reserve Chardonnay

▼▼▼▼▽ **2001** Bright yellow-green; a complex but elegant bouquet with citrus and nectarine fruit to the fore; the same fruit comes through on the palate, the oak influence under tight control. Classic sotto voce Tasmanian style. **rating:** 90

best drinking Now–2006 **best vintages** '01 **drink with** Gravlax • $23

Home Hill Pinot Noir

▼▼▼▼▽ **2001** Medium red-purple; a very tangy bouquet, almost into lemon/olive aromas, is followed by a lively, fresh palate with cherry fruit coming through strongly; an elegant and pretty wine. **rating:** 90

best drinking Now–2005 **best vintages** '00, '01 **drink with** Smoked quail • $30

honeytree estate ★★★★

16 Gillards Road, Pokolbin, NSW 2321 **region** Lower Hunter Valley
phone (02) 4998 7693 **fax** (02) 4998 7693 **open** Wed–Fri 11–4, weekends 10–5
winemaker Contract **production** 3600 cases **est.** 1970
product range ($15–25 CD) Semillon, Clairette, Dessert Semillon, Shiraz, Cabernet Sauvignon.
summary The Honeytree Estate vineyard was first planted in 1970, and for a period of time wines were produced under the Honeytree Estate label. It then disappeared, but the vineyard has since been revived by Dutch-born Henk Strengers and family. Its 10 hectares of vines are of shiraz, cabernet sauvignon, semillon and a little clairette, known in the Hunter Valley as blanquette, a variety which has been in existence there for well over a century. Jancis Robinson comments that the wine 'tends to be very high in alcohol, a little low in acid and to oxidise dangerously fast', but in a sign of the times, the first Honeytree Clairette sold out so quickly (in 4 weeks) that 2.2 hectares of vineyard has been grafted over to additional clairette. Exports to Holland.

Honeytree Estate Semillon

▼▼▼▼ **2001** Light to medium yellow-green; clean, gently ripe lemon, citrus and even a touch of peach aromas merge into a smooth, supple palate, moving easily into transition; nice flavour, in the typical Honeytree early developing style. **rating:** 89

best drinking Now–2007 **drink with** Thai chicken • $15

Honeytree Estate Clairette

▼▼▼▼ **2002** Light straw-green; the bouquet has tight, minerally aromas but next to no positive fruit; if varietal character is defined by the absence of any particular fruit aromatics, then the bouquet is certainly varietal. On the palate, very delicate lemon flavours are balanced by the clever use of a touch of residual sugar. A very surprising Blue Gold at the 2003 Sydney International Wine Competition. All very interesting. **rating:** 88

best drinking Now–2005 **drink with** Shellfish • $20

Honeytree Estate Dessert Semillon

▼▼▼▼ **NV** Glowing yellow-green; the pungent bouquet has a deal of oak, the sweet, peachy, rich palate needing more acidity to lift it into a higher class. **rating:** 87

best drinking Now **drink with** Rich tarts • $20

hope estate ★★★☆

Cobcroft Road, Broke, NSW 2330 **region** Lower Hunter Valley
phone (02) 6579 1161 **fax** (02) 6579 1373 **open** 7 days 10–4
winemaker Josh Steele **production** 30000 cases **est.** 1996
product range ($15–20 CD) Semillon, Verdelho, Chardonnay, Shiraz, Merlot.
summary Pharmacist Michael Hope has come a long way since acquiring his first vineyard in the Hunter Valley in 1994. The Hunter Valley empire now encompasses three substantial vineyards and the former Saxonvale Winery, acquired in 1996, renamed Hope Estate and refurbished at a cost of over $1 million. That, however, proved to be only the first step, for Hope has acquired most of the assets of the former public-listed Vincorp, including its Donnybrook Vineyard in Western Australia, and a $6 million acquisition of the Virgin Hills brand, its original 14-hectare vineyard, another nearby 32-hectare vineyard at Glenhope, a lease of the historic winery, and all Virgin Hills stocks. Exports to the US, the UK, Japan, Singapore and Hong Kong.

Hope Estate Semillon

♥♥♥♥♡ **2002** For those concerned about the booze bus, or the trend to high-alcohol reds, the 10° alcohol of this wine will come as a relief. It has considerable depth to the lemony/apply/grassy fruit of the bouquet, then a crisp and tight mouthfeel with both finesse and length. Good stuff. **rating:** 92
best drinking Now–2010 **best vintages** '02 **drink with** Tempura • $15

hoppers hill vineyards NR

Googodery Road, Cumnock, NSW 2867 **region** Central Ranges Zone
phone (02) 6367 7270 **open** By appointment
winemaker Robert Gilmore **production** NFP **est.** 1990
product range Chardonnay, Sauvignon Blanc, Dry White, Cabernet Franc Merlot, Cabernet Sauvignon.
summary The Gilmores planted their vineyard in 1980, using organic growing methods. They also use no preservatives or filtration in the winery, which was established in 1990. Not surprisingly, the wines cannot be judged or assessed against normal standards, but may have appeal in a niche market.

horseshoe vineyard NR

Horseshoe Road, Horseshoe Valley via Denman, NSW 2328 **region** Upper Hunter Valley
phone (02) 6547 3528 **open** Weekends 9–5
winemaker John Hordern **production** NFP **est.** 1986
product range ($13–18 CD) Classic Hunter Semillon, Chardonnay Semillon, Chardonnay, Pinot Noir.
summary Fell by the wayside after its wonderful start in 1986, with rich, full-flavoured, barrel-fermented Semillons and Chardonnays. The '87 Semillon was exhibited in the Museum Class at the 1996 Hunter Valley Wine Show and was still drinking beautifully, winning a strong silver medal. These days John Hordern's main occupation seems to be as a highly successful contract winemaker, particularly for Penmara.

houghton ★★★★★

Dale Road, Middle Swan, WA 6056 **region** Swan Valley
phone (08) 9274 5100 **fax** (08) 9274 5372 **open** 7 days 10–5
winemaker Larry Cherubino, Ross Pymment, Simon Osicka **production** 310000 cases **est.** 1836
product range ($9.90–90 R) Semillon Sauvignon Blanc, Chardonnay Verdelho, White Burgundy, Show Reserve White Burgundy, Chardonnay, Late Picked Verdelho, Cabernet Shiraz Merlot; Crofters Semillon Sauvignon Blanc, Chardonnay, Shiraz, Cabernet Merlot; the super-premiums Jack Mann (Cabernet blend) and Gladstones Shiraz.
summary The five-star rating was once partially justified by Houghton White Burgundy, one of Australia's largest-selling white wines – almost entirely consumed within days of purchase, but which is superlative with 7 or so years' bottle age. To borrow a phrase of the late Jack Mann, 'There are no bad wines here.' The Jack Mann red, Gladstones Shiraz, Houghton Reserve Shiraz, the Margaret River reds and Frankland Riesling are all of the highest quality, and simply serve to reinforce the rating.

Houghton Pemberton Sauvignon Blanc

♥♥♥♥♡ **2002** Light straw-green; the bouquet is aromatic, albeit with a hint of reduction over a groundswell of exotic, tropical fruit; as anticipated, the palate tightens up and throws off most of the reduction of the bouquet, with a long fruit carry across the tongue. **rating:** 90
best drinking Now **best vintages** '02 **drink with** Sugar-cured tuna • $21.99

Houghton Crofters Semillon Sauvignon Blanc

TTTTT 2002 Both this and its sister wine, 2002 Moondah Brook Semillon Sauvignon Blanc, are standouts of the vintage. Bright, light yellow-green, the complex bouquet has ripe gooseberry fruit and hints of lees contact and oak. The palate has great depth of ripe gooseberry and citrus fruit; a wine with attitude. **rating: 94**

best drinking Now **best vintages** '96, '01, '02 **drink with** Lemon chicken • $19

Houghton White Burgundy

TTTT 2002 Light straw-green; the bouquet is clean, with soft fruit salad aromas and no reduction or sweaty characters. The palate is fresh, with good length, the Semillon Sauvignon Blanc components a little more obvious than usual. Partial oak maturation is not obvious. Rated as it is today, not as it will be tomorrow, or in 5 years' time. **rating: 87**

best drinking Now–2008 **best vintages** '83, '87, '89, '91, '93, '95, '99, '00, '01 **drink with** Fish, chicken or veal • $11.99

Houghton Pemberton Chardonnay Pinot Noir

TTTTY 1999 Very light straw-green; a fresh, tangy, citrussy bouquet leads into a palate with almost gossamer-like delicacy to the white peach and citrus fruit; leaves the mouth as fresh as a daisy. **rating: 90**

best drinking Now–2006 **drink with** Aperitif • $26.99

Houghton Crofters Shiraz

TTTTY 2001 Medium to full red-purple; the bouquet is complex, with an obvious infusion of soft, toasted oak through the plum and spice fruit; the rich and powerful palate has abundant blackberry fruit, rippling tannins and well-handled oak. A blend of Mount Barker and Ferguson Valley material. **rating: 93**

best drinking 2006–2016 **drink with** Braised beef • $24.99

Houghton Frankland Shiraz

TTTTT 2000 Medium to full red-purple; a fragrant and complex bouquet with dark cherry, plum and spice flows into a medium-bodied palate with excellent texture, depth and mouthfeel; lots of licorice, black cherry and fine tannins, still fresh and flavoursome. **rating: 96**

best drinking 2004–2010 **best vintages** '95, '99, '00 **drink with** Aged beef • $29.95

Houghton Gladstones Shiraz

TTTTT 2000 Dense purple-red; dark plum, prune and berry fruit on the bouquet are followed by a palate with luscious fruit and harmoniously balanced oak and tannins. At the big end of town, to be sure, but beautifully handled. **rating: 96**

TTTTT 1999 Impenetrable purple; an ultra-complex bouquet of blackberry, plum, licorice and spice is followed by a commensurately rich, complex and powerful palate with blackberry, morello cherry, licorice, abundant tannins, good oak and quite possibly one of Gladstone's boots. Already a multiple gold medal winner, and sure to win many more before its show career ends. A marvellous testimonial to John Gladstones. **rating: 96**

best drinking 2008–2018 **best vintages** '00 **drink with** Leave it in the cellar • $59.99

Houghton Pemberton Merlot

TTTTY 2000 Medium to full red-purple; the bouquet shows neat integration of French oak and savoury berry fruit, following through into a palate with sweet, red berry/redcurrant fruit at its core, supported by well-balanced oak and tannins. Yet more proof that Pemberton is better suited to merlot than pinot noir. **rating: 90**

best drinking 2004–2009 **best vintages** '00 **drink with** Beef with olives • $29.95

Houghton Jack Mann

TTTTT 2000 Medium purple-red; scented, vibrant and lively fruit on the bouquet, then a palate flooded with cassis, blackberry, blackcurrant, and also juicy berry from the malbec component; beautifully balanced and structured. **rating: 96**

TTTTT 1999 A blend of cabernet sauvignon and malbec from Houghton's Frankland River Justin Vineyard, a true tribute to the wine style of the late Jack Mann. Dense purple-red; the rich and concentrated bouquet oozes sweet blackcurrant/cassis; the huge, ultra-concentrated fruit of the palate is balanced by appropriately firm tannins and lavish oak. **rating: 97**

best drinking 2008–2020 **best vintages** '94, '95, '96, '98, '99, '00 **drink with** Leave it in the cellar • $90

Houghton Crofters Cabernet Merlot

TTTTT 2000 Deep red-purple; a complex bouquet with fruit and sophisticated, spicy oak is followed by a palate with warm chocolate and dark berry fruit flavours, then lingering but soft tannins. High-class winemaking. **rating: 95**

best drinking 2004–2014 **best vintages** '94, '95, '97, '98, '99, '00 **drink with** Kangaroo • $22.99

Houghton Gladstones Cabernet Sauvignon

♥♥♥♥♥ 1999 Medium to full red-purple; a complex array of dark fruits and positive oak on the bouquet lead into a palate with lashings of luscious blackberry/blackcurrant fruit, once again supported by positive but balanced oak. **rating:** 95

best drinking 2005–2015 **drink with** Char-grilled rump

Houghton Margaret River Cabernet Sauvignon

♥♥♥♥♥ 2000 Full red-purple; the rich and deep bouquet is flooded with blackberry and blackcurrant fruit, which flows through into a really delicious palate, showing excellent texture, structure and balance. Ripe tannins and appropriate oak are all part of a wine which is still gathering pace. **rating:** 95

best drinking 2005–2015 **best vintages** '99, '00 **drink with** Braised ox tail • $29.95

house of certain views ★★★★

1238 Milbrodale Road, Broke, NSW 2330 **region** Lower Hunter Valley
phone (02) 6579 1317 **fax** (02) 6579 1317 **open** Not
winemaker Andrew Margan **production** 3000 cases **est.** 2001
product range ($20–38 R) Coonabarabran Sauvignon Blanc, Coonabarabran Chardonnay, Orange Shiraz, Mt Kaputar Merlot, Broke Fordwich Barbera, Coonabarabran Cabernet Sauvignon.
summary A stand-alone business owned by Andrew and Lisa Margan, with a fascinating portfolio of wines based on exclusive or fairly new wine-growing regions on the western side of the Great Dividing Range. The selection of the vineyard sites (via contract growers) involves a careful correlation of latitude, altitude, soil type and variety – the French catch it all in the single word 'terroir'. The packaging of the wines, incidentally, is brilliant.

House of Certain Views Orange Viognier

♥♥♥♥ 2002 Light to medium yellow-green; a floral array of sweet blossom and strong honeysuckle aromas leads into a palate which opens with similar characters, but finishes on the tough side; better with food, no doubt. **rating:** 88

best drinking Now–2005 **drink with** Veal in white sauce • $30

House of Certain Views Coonabarabran Chardonnay

♥♥♥♥ 2000 Medium to full yellow-green; a ripe, soft peachy bouquet with subtle oak leads into a soft palate with complex nutty/creamy flavours, the downside being the overall softness and the relatively high alcohol of 14.3°. Earlier picking might have made an even better wine. Fifty per cent barrel fermented in new French oak. **rating:** 86

best drinking Now–2005 **drink with** Smoked salmon pasta • $20

House of Certain Views Broke Fordwich Barbera

♥♥♥♥ 2001 Medium red-purple; the moderately intense bouquet is fruit-driven, with juicy, ripe, small berry fruit; a lemony note is added on the palate, which doesn't have a great deal of structure. All in all, an ambitious price for a wine made from a less than great variety. **rating:** 86

best drinking Now–2008 **drink with** Beef shashlik • $38

House of Certain Views Mt Kaputar Merlot

♥♥♥♥ 2001 Medium to full red-purple; ripe, sweet, small red berry aromas and subtle oak foretell a generously ripe palate moving more from red to dark berries, but still sweet; a nice wine, but very much the New World model of Merlot. **rating:** 89

best drinking Now–2009 **drink with** Moroccan lamb • $38

howard park (denmark) ★★★★★

Scotsdale Road, Denmark, WA 6333 **region** Great Southern
phone (08) 9848 2345 **fax** (08) 9848 2064 **open** 7 days 10–4
winemaker Michael Kerrigan, James Kellie **production** 100 000 cases **est.** 1986
product range ($22–35 R) Limited quantities of Howard Park Riesling, Howard Park Cabernet Sauvignon Merlot, Scotsdale Shiraz, Scotsdale Cabernet Sauvignon, all at the ultra-premium end; the MadFish Bay range of Premium White, Sauvignon Blanc Semillon, Chardonnay, Premium Red, Pinot Noir, Shiraz, Cabernet Sauvignon Merlot Cabernet Franc.

summary All the Howard Park wines are made here at the new, large winery. However, there are three groups of wines: those sourced from either Great Southern or Margaret River; the icon Howard Park Riesling and Cabernet Sauvignon Merlot; and the multi-regional Madfish range. Thus the Leston wines come from Margaret River, the Scotsdale from Great Southern. All are very impressive, MadFish having reached new heights in 2002/3. Exports to the UK and the US.

Howard Park Riesling

ㅜㅜㅜㅜ♈ **2002** Light green; a highly aromatic, floral, lime blossom and lime leaf bouquet leads into an intense and potent palate that has the acidity which has become part and parcel of the style over recent vintages. It is entirely natural acidity; moreover, on the basis of this (March 2003) tasting, it has to be freely acknowledged that while acid does not decrease in chemical analysis terms, the aging process does cause it to soften.   **rating: 91**

best drinking 2006–2016 **best vintages** '91, '93, '94, '95, '96, '97, '98, '99, '02 **drink with** Fresh asparagus, Asian seafood • $24

Howard Park Scotsdale Shiraz

ㅜㅜㅜㅜㅜ **2001** Excellent purple-red; clean, dark plum and blackberry fruit (quite different from that of the previous year) and subtle oak on the bouquet flow into a mouthfilling, rich, saturated palate with blackberry fruit and ripe tannins.   **rating: 94**

best drinking 2011–2021 **best vintages** '00, '01 **drink with** Spit-roasted baby lamb • $35

Howard Park Scotsdale Cabernet Sauvignon

ㅜㅜㅜㅜㅜ **2001** Clear, full purple-red; bright blackcurrant and redcurrant fruit aromas intermingle with classy French oak on the bouquet; the elegant medium-bodied palate is long and clean, the black fruits supported by fine tannins and balanced oak.   **rating: 94**

best drinking 2006–2016 **best vintages** '99, '00, '01 **drink with** Rare fillet steak • $35

howard park (margaret river)   ★★★★★

Miamup Road, Cowaramup, WA 6284 **region** Margaret River
phone (08) 9756 5200 **fax** (08) 9756 5222 **open** 7 days 10–5
winemaker Michael Kerrigan, James Kellie **production** 100 000 cases **est.** 1986
product range ($18–75 R) Limited quantities of Howard Park Riesling, Howard Park Cabernet Sauvignon Merlot, Scotsdale Shiraz, Scotsdale Cabernet Sauvignon, all at the ultra-premium end; the MadFish range of Premium White, Sauvignon Blanc Semillon, Chardonnay, Premium Red, Pinot Noir, Shiraz, Cabernet Sauvignon Merlot Cabernet Franc.
summary In the wake of its acquisition by the Burch family, and the construction of a large, state-of-the-art winery at Denmark, a capacious cellar door (incorporating Feng Shui principles) has been opened in the Margaret River, where there are also significant estate plantings. The Margaret River flagships are the Leston Shiraz and Leston Cabernet Sauvignon, but the Margaret River vineyards routinely contribute to all the wines in the range, from MadFish at the bottom to the icon Cabernet Sauvignon Merlot at the top. Exports to the UK and the US.

MadFish Premium White

ㅜㅜㅜㅜ♈ **2002** Bright, light yellow-green; an aromatic bouquet with some grapefruit and citrus, the palate quite intense, with good length and a pleasingly dry finish avoiding phenolics. In fact, 100 per cent unwooded chardonnay, and a particularly fine example.   **rating: 91**

best drinking Now **best vintages** '00, '01, '02 **drink with** Chicken • $17

Howard Park Chardonnay

ㅜㅜㅜㅜㅜ **2001** Winemaker Michael Kerrigan is hell-bent on moving to Stelvin for all Howard Park wines, and used it with this one. The fine, elegant, fruit-driven bouquet of citrus and nectarine is inevitably followed by a fine and perfectly modulated palate, with oak purely background support. Lingering delicacy.   **rating: 96**

best drinking Now–2010 **best vintages** '93, '94, '95, '96, '97, '99, '01 **drink with** Fish quenelles in white sauce • $35

MadFish Chardonnay

ㅜㅜㅜㅜㅜ **2001** Medium yellow-green; complex barrel-ferment oak inputs run alongside the nectarine and cashew of the bouquet; good though the bouquet is, the palate is even better, with masses of nectarine, melon and cashew fruit complemented by sure oak handling; perfect balance and length. From three vineyards in the Denmark, Porongurup and Margaret River regions.   **rating: 94**

best drinking Now–2006 **best vintages** '01 **drink with** Abalone • $20

Howard Park Leston Shiraz

❦❦❦❦❦ 2001 Medium to full red-purple; smooth, supple, ripe blackberry fruit plus hints of spicy, high-quality oak on the bouquet lead into a medium to full-bodied palate with outstanding texture and structure, thanks in no small measure to the fine, ripe, savoury tannins prolonging the length and aftertaste. The wine will be sold on the domestic market under a screwcap. **rating: 95**

best drinking 2008–2018 **best vintages** '99, '00, '01 **drink with** Spiced lamb with couscous • $35

MadFish Shiraz

❦❦❦❦❦ 2001 Deep, bright red-purple; smooth and ripe cherry and raspberry fruit with spicy/peppery undertones leads into a palate with excellent balance and texture; the French oak is controlled throughout, adding to the wine without taking away from the varietal fruit. **rating: 93**

best drinking 2004–2011 **best vintages** '01 **drink with** Venison pie • $20

Howard Park MadFish Premium Red

❦❦❦❦ 2001 Youthful purple-red; bright, fresh, dark fruit/dark berry aromas lead into a palate with abundant flavour and pleasing texture; extremely clever winemaking provides a drink-now or later style. Top value. A blend of 52 per cent Cabernet Sauvignon, 26 per cent Merlot and 22 per cent Cabernet Franc from the Great Southern, Pemberton and Margaret River regions. **rating: 89**

best drinking Now–2006 **best vintages** '95, '01 **drink with** Pasta, most Italian-accented dishes • $16

Howard Park Cabernet Sauvignon

❦❦❦❦❦ 2000 Medium red-purple; the fragrant bouquet has a sophisticated mix of savoury, spicy blackberry and blackcurrant aromas; the palate adds unexpected power and concentration to the richly layered dark fruit flavours, which are completed by lingering tannins on the finish. A blend of 76 per cent Margaret River and 24 per cent Frankland River material, 100 per cent Cabernet Sauvignon. **rating: 93**

best drinking 2006–2016 **best vintages** '86, '88, '89, '90, '92, '93, '94, '96, '98, '99, '00 **drink with** Lamb fillets, mature cheddar • $72

Howard Park Leston Cabernet Sauvignon

❦❦❦❦❦ 2001 A denser and deeper colour than the Scotsdale Cabernet of the same vintage; rich cassis/blackcurrant fruit is supported by complex oak on the bouquet; the palate is very concentrated and powerful, more austere than the bouquet suggests, in no small measure because of the lingering tannins. For very long-term cellaring. **rating: 94**

best drinking 2011–2021 **best vintages** '00, '01 **drink with** Saddle of lamb • $35

howards way vineyard   NR

Cobcroft Road, Broke, NSW 2330 **region** Lower Hunter Valley
phone (02) 4998 1336 **fax** (02) 4938 3775 **open** Not
winemaker Andrew Margan (Contract) **production** 3500 cases **est.** NA
product range ($15–20 ML) Semillon, Pinot Noir, Shiraz.
summary Yet another of the dozens of new vineyards and labels that have appeared in the Hunter Valley in the latter part of the 1990s. Eight hectares of shiraz, three of pinot noir and two of semillon provide a substantial base, and retail distribution began in 1999. No recent tastings.

hugh hamilton   ★★★☆

McMurtrie Road, McLaren Vale, SA 5171 **region** McLaren Vale
phone (08) 8323 8689 **fax** (08) 8323 9488 **open** Mon–Fri 10–5.30, weekends and public holidays 11–5.30
winemaker Hugh Hamilton **production** 5000 cases **est.** 1991
product range ($16.50–42 CD) Verdelho, Unwooded Chardonnay, Sparkling Merlot, The Rascal Shiraz, Menage à Trois Sangiovese Cabernet Shiraz, Merlot, Cabernet Merlot, Red Emperor Cabernet Sauvignon, Liqueur Muscat.
summary Hugh Hamilton is a member of the famous Hamilton winemaking family. There is an intensely (and well known) competitive spirit existing between family members – notably between Richard and Hugh – which can only be good for the consumer.

Hugh Hamilton The Rascal Shiraz

❦❦❦❦❦ 2000 Medium red-purple; the moderately intense bouquet has an array of berry, chocolate, earth and dusty aromas; on the palate, ripe, but not jammy, fruit sits in the driving seat, the pleasing mouthfeel assisted by fine, ripe tannins. Subtle use of oak throughout. **rating: 92**

best drinking 2005–2012 **best vintages** '00 **drink with** Beef casserole • $22

Hugh Hamilton Menage à Trois

▼▼▼▼ **2002** Medium red-purple; the bouquet has an array of ripe dark berry fruits, exotic spices and dried gum leaf aromas. The palate has abundant, soft, rich fruit, the feel suggesting the possibility of micro oxygenation. A blend of 77 per cent Sangiovese, 18 per cent Cabernet Sauvignon and 5 per cent Shiraz, which works very well. **rating:** 88

best drinking 2005–2010 **drink with** Ravioli • $19.50

Hugh Hamilton Red Emperor Cabernet Sauvignon

▼▼▼▼ **2000** Medium red-purple; the clean, fresh, moderately intense bouquet has berry fruit with touches of leaf and mint; the savoury/earthy blackcurrant flavours of the palate have a slightly pointed finish. **rating:** 85

best drinking 2005–2010 **drink with** Rack of lamb • $22

hugo ★★★★

Elliott Road, McLaren Flat, SA 5171 **region** McLaren Vale
phone (08) 8383 0098 **fax** (08) 8383 0446 **open** Mon–Fri 9–5, Sat 12–5, Sun 10.30–5
winemaker John Hugo **production** 12 000 cases **est.** 1982
product range ($15–38 R) Sauvignon Blanc, Unwooded Chardonnay, Chardonnay, Reserve Shiraz, Shiraz, Shiraz Grenache, Cabernet Sauvignon.
summary A winery which came from relative obscurity to prominence in the late 1980s with some lovely ripe, sweet reds which, while strongly American oak influenced, were quite outstanding. Has picked up the pace again after a dull period in the mid-1990s. There are 32 hectares of estate plantings, with part of the grape production sold to others. The wines are exported to the US, Canada, the UK, Germany and Singapore. The rating is on the basis of previous tastings.

🍇 hundred tree hill NR

c/- Redbank Winery, 1 Sallys Lane, Redbank, Vic 3478 **region** Pyrenees
phone (03) 5467 7255 **fax** (03) 5467 7248 **open** Not
winemaker Huw Robb, Scott Hutton, Sasha Robb **production** 6000 cases **est.** 1973
product range ($14.50–25 ML) Sauvignon Blanc, Chardonnay, Pinot Noir, Shiraz, Cabernet
summary The next generation of the Robb family (Emily, Huw and Sasha) have established their own vineyard, with 6 hectares each of shiraz, cabernet sauvignon and cabernet franc, plus 2 hectares of pinot noir. Hundred Tree Hill was so named to commemorate the hundred trees which went into the building of the Hundred Tree Homestead. For the time being, the focus is on export sales, but the Robbs intend to diversify into the domestic market in the near future.

hungerford hill ★★★★

1 Broke Road, Pokolbin, NSW 2321 **region** Lower Hunter Valley
phone 1800 187 666 **fax** (02) 4998 7375 **open** 7 days 10–5
winemaker Phillip John, Andrew Thomas **production** 15 000 cases **est.** 1967
product range ($12.50–27 CD) Clare Valley Riesling, Traminer Riesling, Hunter Valley Semillon, Tumbarumba Sauvignon Blanc, King Valley Pinot Gris, Cowra Verdelho, Cowra Chardonnay, Tumbarumba Chardonnay, Gundagai Chardonnay, Reserve Chardonnay, Dalliance Sparkling Chardonnay, Reserve Dalliance Sparkling Chardonnay, Cardinal Sparkling Shiraz, Griffith Botrytis Semillon, Tumbarumba Pinot Noir, Hilltops Shiraz, Cowra Shiraz, Central Ranges Shiraz, Merlot, Hilltops Cabernet Sauvignon, Liqueur Tokay, Liqueur Muscat, Liqueur Port.
summary Hungerford Hill, sold by Southcorp to Cassegrain Wines in 2002, has emerged with its home base at the impressive winery on the corner of Allandale and Broke Roads, previously known as One Broke Road. The development of the One Broke Road complex proved wildly uneconomic, and the rationalisation process has resulted in Hungerford Hill being the principal tenant, but with significant contract winemaking by Andrew Thomas for other Hunter Valley brands. Restaurant One and Cafe One continue under the direction of Giles Marx.

Hungerford Hill Clare Valley Riesling

▼▼▼▼ **2002** Light straw-green; the light, fresh bouquet has herbal aromas. The palate has much more appeal; here the hint of lime blossom, good acidity and length promise development as the wine ages in bottle. **rating:** 89

best drinking 2005–2012 **drink with** Grilled whiting • $20

Hungerford Hill Hunter Valley Semillon

▼▼▼▼ **2002** Light to medium yellow-green; spotlessly clean and attractive lemony fruit on the bouquet is followed by a lively palate, with a certain amount of CO_2 lifting the acidity and giving grip to the finish. Good outcome for a difficult vintage; patience will be rewarded. **rating:** 89

best drinking 2005–2015 **drink with** Shellfish • $20

Hungerford Hill Tumbarumba Sauvignon Blanc

▼▼▼▼▽ **2002** Light straw-green; the spotlessly clean mix of grass, herb and gooseberry aromas is followed by a bright, firm palate with a lively mix of the flavours promised by the bouquet, and a lingering, dry finish. **rating:** 90

best drinking Now **best vintages** '02 **drink with** Seafood risotto • $20

Hungerford Hill Reserve Chardonnay

▼▼▼▼▽ **1997** Bright, glowing yellow-green; another particularly complex bouquet with barrel-ferment aromas in a Burgundian mould, suggesting some unclarified juice in the ferment. A powerful palate follows, still surprisingly tight and youthful, and less advanced than the '98. **rating:** 93

best drinking Now–2005 **drink with** Tasmanian salmon grilled on rock salt • $27

Hungerford Hill Tumbarumba Chardonnay

▼▼▼▼▽ **1998** Glowing yellow-green; very complex, bottle-developed aromas showing strong barrel-ferment oak, cashew, fig and yellow peach. The light to medium-bodied palate is less effusive and more elegant, sustained by good acidity. **rating:** 91

best drinking Now **drink with** Mussels • $23

Hungerford Hill Merlot

▼▼▼▼ **2002** Medium purple-red; the light and clean bouquet has unmistakable varietal savoury/olive aromas; the palate is of appropriate weight and texture, once again showing clear varietal character. Grown on winemaker Phillip John's own vineyard near Karadoc. **rating:** 85

best drinking Now–2005 **drink with** Braised veal • $16.50

hunting lodge estate   NR

703 Mt Kilcoy Road, Mount Kilcoy, Qld 4515 **region** South Burnett
phone (07) 5498 1243 **fax** (07) 5498 1243 **open** Wed–Sun 10–5
winemaker Brian Wilson **production** 3300 cases **est.** 1999
product range ($14–25 CD) Mauritius Traminer Riesling, Serengeti Oaked Chardonnay, Kalahari Unoaked Chardonnay, Simpson Red, Zambezi Cabernet Merlot, Cape Cabernet Sauvignon, Hunters Cabernet Sauvignon, Nairobi Tawny Port, Estate Tawny Port.
summary Yet another new player in the rapidly expanding Queensland wine industry, established in 1999 with plantings of 1 hectare each of verdelho, merlot and cabernet sauvignon. However, is offering a range of wines ranging from 1997 to 1999, including 'our famous Nairobi Port'; the names of the table wines all cross-link both to hunting and South Africa, whence, one imagines, the owners originated.

huntington estate   ★★★★☆

Cassilis Road, Mudgee, NSW 2850 **region** Mudgee
phone (02) 6373 3825 **fax** (02) 6373 3730 **open** Mon–Fri 9–5, Sat 10–5, Sun 10–3
winemaker Susie Roberts **production** 20 000 cases **est.** 1969
product range ($13.50–30.50 CD) Semillon, Semillon Chardonnay, Chardonnay, Rose Dry, Rose, Sweet White Blend, Rose Sweet Fruity Style, Rose Pinot Noir Dry; red wines released under bin numbers (FB = full-bodied, MB = medium-bodied) are Shiraz, Dry Red Shiraz Cabernet, Cabernet Sauvignon.
summary The remarkable Roberts family members have a passion for wine which is equalled only by their passion for music, with the Huntington Music Festival a major annual event. The red wines of Huntington Estate are outstanding, and sell for relatively low prices. The wines are seldom exported; almost all are sold via cellar door and mailing list.

Huntington Estate Special Reserve Shiraz

▼▼▼▼▽ **2000** FB22. Medium red-purple; clean, smooth, ripe blackberry and plum fruit aromas with neatly handled vanilla oak lead into a rich, gently ripe and quite succulent palate finishing with smooth, soft tannins. **rating:** 92

best drinking 2005–2012 **best vintages** '93, '99, '00 **drink with** Venison • $30.50

Huntington Estate Special Reserve Cabernet Sauvignon

YYYYY 1999 FB31. Medium red-purple; solid black fruit aromas, supported by subtle oak, lead into an equally solid but smooth palate, with blackcurrant and chocolate nuances, excellent tannin management, and the oak characteristically subtle.   **rating:** 90

best drinking 2006–2016 **best vintages** '99, '99 **drink with** Rib of beef • $30.50

huntleigh vineyards ★★★☆

38 Tunnecliffes Lane, Heathcote, Vic 3523 **region** Heathcote
phone (03) 5433 2795 **fax** (03) 5433 2795 **open** 7 days 10–5.30
winemaker Leigh Hunt **production** 500 cases **est.** 1975
product range ($12–22 CD) Traminer, Shiraz, Cabernet Sauvignon.
summary The wines are all made at the winery by former stockbroker Leigh Hunt from 5 hectares of estate-grown grapes; the last-tasted Cabernet Sauvignon (1998) was of exemplary quality.

hunt's foxhaven estate   NR

Canal Rocks Road, Yallingup, WA 6282 **region** Margaret River
phone (08) 9755 2232 **fax** (08) 9255 2249 **open** Weekends, holidays 11–5, or by appointment
winemaker David Hunt **production** 800 cases **est.** 1978
product range ($12–20 CD) Riesling (dry and sweet), Semillon, Canal Rocks White, Yallingup Classic, Noble Riesling, Hunting Pink, Cabernet Sauvignon.
summary A low-profile operation, based on 4.5 hectares of vines progressively established, the oldest being 25-year-old riesling. It seems that some of the grapes are sold, some swapped for semillon and sauvignon blanc. All the wine is sold through the cellar door and by mail order.

hurley vineyard   NR

101 Balnarring Road, Balnarring, Vic 3926 **region** Mornington Peninsula
phone (03) 9608 8220 **fax** (03) 9608 7293 **open** Not
winemaker Contract **est.** 1998
product range Pinot Noir.
summary Hurley Vineyard has been established by Melbourne Queens Counsel, Kevin Bell. Four hectares of pinot noir were planted in 1998; no tastings to date.

hutton vale vineyard   NR

'Hutton Vale', Stone Jar Road, Angaston, SA 5353 **region** Eden Valley
phone (08) 8564 8270 **fax** (08) 8564 8385 **open** By appointment
winemaker David Powell, Chris Ringland, Caroline Dunn **production** 500 cases **est.** 1960
product range ($19–39 ML) Riesling, Shiraz, Grenache Mataro.
summary John Howard Angas (who arrived in South Australia in 1843, aged 19, charged with the responsibility of looking after the affairs of his father, George Fife Angas) named part of the family estate Hutton Vale. It is here that John Angas, John Howard's great-great-grandson, and wife Jan tend a little over 26 hectares of vines and produce (or, at least, Jan does) a range of jams, chutneys and preserves. Almost all the grapes are sold, a tiny quantity being made by the Who's Who of the Barossa Valley, notably David Powell of Torbreck, Chris Ringland of Rockford and Caroline Dunn of Beringer Blass. Most of the wine is sold by mail order, and what is left is exported. I haven't tasted the wines, but I'm prepared to wager they are of outstanding quality.

ibis wines   ★★★

239 Kearneys Drive, Orange, NSW 2800 **region** Orange
phone (02) 6362 3257 **fax** (02) 6362 5779 **open** Weekends and public holidays 11–5, or by appointment
winemaker Phil Stevenson **production** 1100 cases **est.** 1988
product range ($8–25 CD) Chardonnay, Pinot Blend, Cabernet Franc, Cabernet Sauvignon; Habitat Sauvignon Blanc, Pagan, Merlot; Kanjara Shiraz.
summary Ibis Wines is located just north of Orange (near the botanic gardens) on what was once a family orchard. Planting of the vineyard commenced in 1988, and after interim winemaking arrangements a new winery was completed on the property in 1998. The grapes are sourced from the home vineyards, which are at an altitude of 800 metres, from the Habitat Vineyard at 1100 metres on Mount Canobolas (pinot noir and merlot) and from the Kanjara Vineyard (shiraz). Wine quality has shown steady improvement over the past couple of years.

Habitat Sauvignon Blanc

TTTT 2001 Light green-yellow; the moderately intense and clean bouquet has a mix of grass, spice and gooseberry aromas; the well-crafted palate has good length and balance, and is a vast improvement over earlier vintages. **rating:** 88

best drinking Now **drink with** Vegetarian • $16

Ibis Chardonnay

TTTT 1999 Light to medium yellow-green; the moderately intense bouquet is clean, although not showing much varietal fruit expression; the very fresh and youthful palate doesn't have much fruit weight, but is well made and very fairly priced. Another big move in the right direction. **rating:** 85

best drinking Now **drink with** Avocado and prawn salad • $15

ilnam estate NR

750 Carool Road, Carool, NSW 2486 **region** Northern Rivers Zone
phone (07) 5590 7703 **fax** (07) 5590 7922 **open** Wed–Sun 10–5
winemaker Mark Quinn **production** 3500 cases **est.** 1998
product range ($8–33 CD) Blue Series of Semillon, Butterfly Kiss (rose style), Shiraz, Cabernet Sauvignon; Maroon Series of JMQ Chardonnay, Carool Chardonnay, Dryland Merlot, Dryland Cabernet Sauvignon.
summary This is the first vineyard and winery to be established in the Tweed Valley, 30 minutes from the Gold Coast. Two hectares each of chardonnay, cabernet sauvignon and shiraz, plus a small planting of chambourcin provide the basis for the estate-grown Carool wines. In addition, Ilnam Estate has a number of growers in the Stanthorpe area who supply grapes to complete the two series of wine. The first vintage (2000) included a Merlot which received a silver medal at the Australian Small Winemakers Show in 2001, a significant medal from a significant show.

immerse in the yarra valley NR

1548 Melba Highway, Yarra Glen, Vic 3775 **region** Yarra Valley
phone (03) 5965 2444 **fax** (03) 5965 2460 **open** 7 days 11–5, Fri and Sat evenings
winemaker Contract **production** 1200 cases **est.** 1989
product range ($22–24 CD) Sauvignon Blanc, Chardonnay, Pinot Noir.
summary Steve and Helen Miles have purchased the restaurant, accommodation and function complex previous known as Lovey's. A spa-based health farm has eight rooms, with a full range of services. I have to say that the name chosen both for the facility and for the wines is as far left of centre as it is possible to go. As previously, a substantial portion of the grapes produced is sold to other makers in the Yarra Valley, the 6.9-hectare vineyards having been rehabilitated.

inchiquin wines ★★★☆

PO Box 865, Clare, SA 5453 **region** Clare Valley
phone (08) 8843 4210 **open** Not
winemaker Stephen McInerney **production** 1000 cases **est.** 1998
product range ($12–17 ML) Riesling, Shiraz Cabernet.
summary Stephen McInerney learnt his trade on the winery floor in various parts of the world: his first experience came in 1985 at Jim Barry Wines, where he spent a number of years before moving to Pikes. In the intervening period he worked as a Flying Winemaker in France, Oregon, Spain and Argentina. He is now assistant winemaker at the large, new Kirribilly Winery in the Clare Valley. He established Inchiquin Wines with his partner Kate Strachan, who also has great industry credentials, primarily as the viticulturist for Taylor's (previously Southcorp), which has the largest vineyards in the Clare Valley. The wines, incidentally, are made by Stephen McInerney at Pikes. Exports to Ireland.

Inchiquin Shiraz Cabernet

TTTT 2001 Medium to full red-purple; a big, brawny, savoury bouquet with slightly gamey overtones leads into a big, rustic palate, with plenty of frame, but then a choppy finish. **rating:** 85

best drinking 2005–2010 **drink with** Leave it in the cellar • $17

indigo ridge ★★★

Icely Road, Orange, NSW 2800 **region** Orange
phone (02) 6362 1851 **fax** (02) 6362 1851 **open** First weekend of the month 12–5, or by appointment
winemaker Jon Reynolds (Contract) **production** 500 cases **est.** 1995

product range ($16–28 ML) Sauvignon Blanc, Cabernet Sauvignon, Ophir Gold.

summary Indigo Ridge has 4.5 hectares of vineyard planted to cabernet sauvignon, sauvignon blanc and merlot. Production is still very small, and almost all the wines are sold by cellar door and mail order; there is limited on- and off-premise distribution in Orange and Sydney.

Indigo Ridge Sauvignon Blanc

▼▼▼▽ **2001** Light straw-green; the bouquet is clean, with some gooseberry and herb aromas which are repeated on the very light-bodied palate. A clean finish helps, but the wine does lack fruit concentration ex the vineyard.   **rating:** 83

best drinking Now **drink with** Shellfish • $19

Indigo Ridge Cabernet Sauvignon

▼▼▼▽ **2001** Medium red-purple; the moderately intense bouquet has a mix of leafy and black fruit aromas. The palate has leafy, minty, berry flavours, crisp acidity and minimal tannins. Like the Sauvignon Blanc, well made, but does not have much concentration. Six per cent Merlot and maturation in new French oak for 18 months.   **rating:** 84

best drinking Now–2006 **drink with** Barbecued meat • $28

indijup point   NR

Caves Road, Wilyabrup, WA 6280 **region** Margaret River
phone 0408 955 770 **fax** (08) 9386 8352 **open** By appointment
winemaker Belinda Gould, Michael Standish **production** 1000 cases **est.** 1993
product range ($15–20 ML) Sauvignon Blanc, Semillon Sauvignon Blanc, Shiraz, Cabernets Merlot.
summary The development of the substantial Indijup Point vineyard began in 1993; the plantings now comprise 5 hectares of cabernet sauvignon, 3 hectares each of shiraz and cabernet franc, 2 hectares of merlot and 1 hectare each of sauvignon blanc, pinot noir and semillon. Most of the grapes are sold to other makers, with a small amount reserved for mail order sale and other local distribution. An extensive native garden surrounds the property, which has views to the adjacent Leeuwin–Naturaliste National Park.

☙ inghams skilly ridge wines   NR

Gillentown Road, Sevenhill via Clare, SA 5453 **region** Clare Valley
phone (08) 8843 4330 **fax** (08) 8843 4330 **open** Weekends 10–5
winemaker Clark Ingham, David O'Leary (Contract) **production** 2000 cases **est.** 1994
product range ($16–24 CD) Riesling, Shiraz, Tempranillo, Merlot, Cabernet Sauvignon Merlot, Cabernet Sauvignon.
summary Clark Ingham has established a substantial vineyard of shiraz (8 ha), cabernet sauvignon (7 ha), chardonnay (4 ha), riesling (3 ha), merlot (2 ha) and tempranillo and semillon (1 ha each). Part of the production is made by contract winemaker David O'Leary (with input from Clark Ingham), with the remaining grape production sold.

innisfail vineyards   ★★★★

Cross Street, Batesford, Vic 3221 **region** Geelong
phone (03) 5276 1258 **fax** (03) 5276 1258 **open** By appointment
winemaker Nick Farr **production** 2000 cases **est.** 1980
product range ($15–25 ML) Riesling, Chardonnay, Pinot Noir, Cabernet Sauvignon Merlot.
summary This 6-hectare estate-based producer released its first wines way back in 1988, but has had a very low profile, notwithstanding the quality of its early wines. Nick Farr, son of Gary Farr of Bannockburn, is now the winemaker and the profile has increased, as has the quality of the wines.

Innisfail Vineyards Riesling

▼▼▼▼ **2002** Light straw-green; the clean bouquet is minerally but the fruit is subdued; the palate opens quietly enough, but then quite sweet lime/passionfruit flavours build towards the finish.   **rating:** 86

best drinking Now–2007 **drink with** Mussels • $15

Innisfail Vineyards Chardonnay

▼▼▼▼▽ **2000** Medium yellow-green; complex barrel-ferment aromas surround ripe fig and melon fruit, which are well-integrated and balanced; the medium-bodied palate is equally smooth, with positive, sure oak handling running through to a long finish.   **rating:** 90

best drinking Now–2007 **drink with** Seared tuna • $20

Innisfail Vineyards Pinot Noir

▼▼▼▼ **2001** Light to medium red-purple; a light, fresh bouquet with cherry, strawberry and mint aromas then a tangy/savoury/foresty palate with good length, but not a lot of density or ripeness. **rating:** 86

best drinking Now–2005 **drink with** Mushroom risotto • $25

Innisfail Vineyards Cabernet Sauvignon Merlot

▼▼▼▼ **2001** Medium red-purple; clean but slightly subdued red berry/blackcurrant fruit on the bouquet develops rather more on the ripe palate, with touches of cedar and dark chocolate; fine tannins and appropriate oak. **rating:** 87

best drinking 2006–2011 **drink with** Butterfly leg of lamb • $20

ironbark ridge vineyard   NR

Middle Road Mail Service 825, Purga, Qld 4306 **region** Queensland Coastal
phone (07) 5464 6787 **fax** (07) 5464 6858 **open** By appointment
winemaker Contract **production** 250 cases **est.** 1984
product range ($15–28 ML) Chardonnay, Reserve Chardonnay, Shiraz, Vintage Port.
summary Ipswich is situated on the coastal side of the Great Dividing Range, and the high summer humidity and rainfall will inevitably provide challenges for viticulture here. On the evidence of the '98 Chardonnay, Ironbark Ridge is capable of producing Chardonnay equal to the best from Queensland.

iron pot bay wines   ★★★★

766 Deviot Road, Deviot, Tas 7275 **region** Northern Tasmania
phone (03) 6394 7320 **fax** (03) 6394 7346 **open** Thurs–Sun 11–5 Sept–May, June–Aug by appointment
winemaker Russell Cook **production** 2000 cases **est.** 1988
product range ($18–27 CD) Traminer, Semillon Sauvignon Blanc, Pinot Grigio, Unwooded Chardonnay, Kyra Sparkling Vintage.
summary Iron Pot Bay is now part of the syndicate which has established Rosevears Estate, with its large, state-of-the-art winery on the banks of the Tamar. The vineyard takes its name from a bay on the Tamar River and is strongly maritime-influenced, producing delicate but intensely flavoured unwooded white wines. The rating is on the basis of previous tastings.

ironwood estate   NR

RMB 1288, Porongurup, WA 6234 **region** Great Southern
phone (08) 9853 1126 **fax** (08) 9853 1172 **open** By appointment
winemaker Robert Lee, John Wade (Consultant) **production** 1000 cases **est.** 1996
product range ($14.50–19.50 CD) Riesling, Chardonnay, Reserve Chardonnay, Late Harvest, Rocky Rose, Shiraz, Merlot, Cabernet Merlot, Cabernet Sauvignon.
summary Ironwood Estate was established in 1996 when the first wines were made from purchased grapes. In the same year chardonnay, shiraz and cabernet sauvignon were planted on a northern slope of the Porongurup Range. The twin peaks of the Porongurups rise above the vineyard and provide the basis for the label design. The first estate-grown grapes were vinified at the new Porongurup Winery, erected for the 1999 vintage and jointly owned by Jingalla and Chatsfield Wines.

irvine   ★★★★

Roeslers Road, Eden Valley, SA 5235 (postal) **region** Eden Valley
phone (08) 8564 1046 **fax** (08) 8564 1314 **open** Not
winemaker James Irvine, Joanne Irvine **production** 4000 cases **est.** 1980
product range ($15–120 R) Under the cheaper Eden Crest label: Chardonnay, Pinot Gris, Merlot, Merlot Cabernet, Zinfandel Merlot, Meslier Brut; under the premium James Irvine label: The Baroness, Merlot Brut and (at the top of the tree) Grand Merlot.
summary Industry veteran Jim Irvine, who has successfully guided the destiny of so many South Australian wineries, quietly introduced his own label in 1991, although the vineyard from which the wines are sourced was commenced in 1983 and now comprises a patchwork quilt of a little over 12 hectares of vines. The flagship is the rich Grand Merlot. Much of the production is exported to the UK, Germany, Switzerland, the US, Japan, Taiwan, New Zealand, Hong Kong, the Philippines and Singapore. Rated on the basis of previous tastings.

irymple estate winery NR

2086 Karadoc Avenue, Irymple, Vic 3498 **region** Murray Darling
phone (03) 5024 5759 **fax** (03) 5024 5759 **open** Not
winemaker Contract **production** 1500 cases **est.** 1999
product range ($5.50 R) Chardonnay, Shiraz.
summary Irymple is a paradox. On the one hand, it is estate-based, with only 2 hectares each of chardonnay and shiraz, and less than 1 hectare of merlot and cabernet sauvignon. On the other hand, the contract-made wines are sold in the old-fashioned way at distinctly old-fashioned prices: on last advice, in the case of the Chardonnay, either cleanskin at under $5 a bottle; labelled at a little over $5 a bottle; or in a 10-litre cask costing $21.30. The Shiraz is offered only cleanskin or labelled, but at the same price as the Chardonnay. Wine quality is appropriate to the price.

island brook estate NR

817 Bussell Highway, Metricup, WA 6280 **region** Margaret River
phone (08) 9755 7501 **fax** (08) 9755 7008 **open** 7 days 10–5
winemaker Mark Shepherd **est.** 1985
product range Semillon, Chardonnay, Verdelho, Jakes Red, Merlot, Cabernet Sauvignon.
summary Linda and Peter Jenkins purchased Island Brook from Ken and Judy Brook in early 2001, and have undertaken major renovations, including extensive vineyard re-trellising, before opening their cellar door in November 2001, followed by luxurious accommodation set among 45 acres of forest.

Island Brook Estate Jakes Red

ϓϓϓϓϔ 2001 Medium purple-red; the clean and fresh bouquet has appealing cherry/plum fruit, and the palate has cedary overtones to the fruit; excellent length, finish and aftertaste. Great value. **rating: 92**
best drinking 2004–2008 **best vintages** '01 **drink with** Roast veal • $15

ivanhoe wines NR

Marrowbone Road, Pokolbin, NSW 2320 **region** Lower Hunter Valley
phone (02) 4998 7325 **fax** (02) 4998 7848 **open** 7 days 10–5
winemaker Stephen Drayton, Tracy Drayton **production** 7000 cases **est.** 1995
product range ($15–27 CD) Various varietal wines under the Ivanhoe and Stephen Drayton Signature Series, including Semillon, Verdelho, Chardonnay, Late Picked Gewurztraminer, Chambourcin, Shiraz, Cabernet Sauvignon.
summary Stephen Drayton is the son of the late Reg Drayton and, with wife Tracy, is the third branch of the family to be actively involved in winemaking in the Hunter Valley. The property on which the vineyard is situated has been called Ivanhoe for over 140 years, and 25 hectares of 30-year-old vines provide high-quality fruit for the label. The plans are to build a replica of the old homestead (burnt down, along with much of the winery, in the 1968 bushfires) to operate as a sales area.

jackson's hill vineyard ★★★☆

Mount View Road, Mount View, NSW 2321 **region** Lower Hunter Valley
phone (02) 4990 1273 **fax** (02) 4991 3233 **open** 7 days 10–5
winemaker Mike Winborne **production** 1200 cases **est.** 1983
product range ($14–20 CD) Semillon, Shiraz, Cabernet Franc, Cabernet Sauvignon.
summary One of the low-profile operations on the spectacularly scenic Mount View Road, making small quantities of estate-grown (3 ha) wine sold exclusively through the cellar door. Jackson's Hill also produces marvellous home-made chocolates.

jadran NR

445 Reservoir Road, Orange Grove, WA 6109 **region** Perth Hills
phone (08) 9459 1110 **open** Mon–Sat 10–8, Sun 11–5
winemaker Steve Radojkovich **production** NFP **est.** 1967
product range ($6–12 CD) Riesling, Hermitage, generic red and white table wines, Sparkling, fortifieds.
summary A quite substantial operation which basically services local clientele, occasionally producing wines of quite surprising quality from a variety of fruit sources.

james estate ★★★★☆

951 Bylong Valley Way, Baerami via Denman, NSW 2333 **region** Upper Hunter Valley
phone (02) 6547 5168 **fax** (02) 6547 5164 **open** 7 days 10–4.30
winemaker Peter Orr, Matthew Carter **production** 120 000 cases **est.** 1971
product range ($10–20 R) Semillon, Verdelho, Chardonnay, Late Harvest Sylvaner, Grand Cuvee, Shiraz, Merlot, Cabernet Sauvignon; Reserve Chardonnay, Shiraz; Sundara Semillon Chardonnay, Shiraz Cabernet.
summary A substantial viticultural enterprise with 98 hectares of vineyards planted to 10 varieties. Since a change of ownership in 1997 there have been many innovations, including the appointment of Peter Orr as winemaker (after a winemaking career with McWilliam's Mount Pleasant and thereafter Allandale Wines), and the complete revamping and repackaging of the wines. In December 2000 the company issued a prospectus seeking to raise just under $5 million to fund the development of over 80 hectares of new vineyards. This was successful, and has increased winery production. The quality of the wines is consistently good, and the brand deserves greater recognition than it in fact receives. Exports to the US and the UK.

James Estate Semillon

▼▼▼▼▽ **2001** Bright light to medium straw-green; the clean bouquet has positive lemony fruit and mineral backbone; the palate has excellent presence, with developing fruit on the mid-palate, then a long, crisp finish sustained by a touch of CO_2. Great value. **rating: 93**

best drinking Now–2009 **drink with** Grilled calamari salad • $14

James Estate Compass Verdelho

▼▼▼▼ **2001** Excellent green-yellow; clean, bright fruit salad aromas are followed by a palate with well above-average balance and length, the fruit salad flavour flowing evenly across the palate. Two gold medals, including Royal Sydney Wine Show. Good value. **rating: 89**

best drinking Now **drink with** Takeaway • $14

James Estate Chardonnay

▼▼▼▼▽ **2001** Impressive, bright green-yellow; the moderately intense bouquet is clean and fresh, with stone fruit and subtle but evident oak; the palate offers lively, tangy citrus and stone fruit supported by 12 months' maturation in new and 1-year-old French and American oak, which does not destroy or threaten the inherent delicacy of the wine. No direct claim of origin. **rating: 90**

best drinking Now–2005 **drink with** Chicken breast • $14

James Estate Reserve Chardonnay

▼▼▼▼▽ **2001** Bright and clear light to medium-yellow-green; the bouquet has complex barrel-ferment aromas well-integrated with the fruit; again, the palate is elegant, with fruit and oak well balanced and some appealing creamy cashew characters. Barrel fermented in new French and American oak. **rating: 92**

best drinking Now–2005 **drink with** Grilled spatchcock • $20

James Estate Reserve Shiraz

▼▼▼▼ **2001** Medium red-purple; clean, quite fresh, red berry fruit and minimal oak aromas lead into a light to medium-bodied palate offering red berry, a hint of chocolate and subtle oak. This year sourced from Langhorne Creek and McLaren Vale. **rating: 87**

best drinking 2004–2009 **drink with** Baked ham • $20

jamiesons run ★★★☆

Penola–Naracoorte Road, Coonawarra, SA 5263 **region** Coonawarra
phone (08) 8736 3380 **fax** (08) 8736 3307 **open** Mon–Fri 9–4.30, weekends 10–4
winemaker Andrew Hales **production** 160 000 cases **est.** 1955
product range ($13–50 R) Jamiesons Run Chardonnay, McShane's Block Shiraz, Coonawarra Red, Coonawarra Merlot, Coonawarra Reserve, Alexander Block Cabernet, O'Dea's Block Cabernet Sauvignon. Also made are Mildara Coonawarra Cabernet Sauvignon, Robertson's Well Shiraz and Cabernet Sauvignon, Jimmy Watson Chardonnay and Cabernet Shiraz and Greg Norman Estates Yarra Valley Chardonnay and Limestone Coast Cabernet Merlot.
summary Once the prized possession of a stand-alone Mildara, which spawned a child called Jamiesons Run to fill the need for a cost-effective second label. Now the name Mildara is very nearly part of ancient wine history, and the child has usurped the parent. Worldwide distribution via Beringer Blass.

Jamiesons Run Coonawarra Shiraz

TTTT 2001 Bright red-purple; the bouquet is moderately intense, with clean cherry fruit doing the talking, second and third-use American oak in the background. The light to medium-bodied palate is similarly fruit-driven, with black cherry, raspberry and some mocha and spice flavours in a no-frills but honest style. **rating:** 87

best drinking 2004–2008 **drink with** Lasagne • $16

Jamiesons Run McShane's Block Shiraz

TTTTY 2000 Full red-purple, bright and clear; the bouquet has rich, concentrated, ripe dark cherry fruit, with some plum and licorice in the background. The powerful palate has layers of chocolate, cherry and vanilla flavour, balanced tannins and controlled oak. **rating:** 92

best drinking 2005–2015 **best vintages** '98, '00 **drink with** Beef Bordelaise • $35

Jamiesons Run Coonawarra Merlot

TTTT 2001 Youthful red-purple; the bouquet has a mix of spice, olive, earth and black fruit aromas, the light to medium-bodied palate tracking the bouquet in terms of flavour, but not offering much structure. **rating:** 87

best drinking Now–2006 **drink with** Fillet of lamb • $15

Jamiesons Run Reserve

TTTTT 2000 Excellent deep and clear red-purple; rich blackberry/blackcurrant/cassis fruit on the bouquet leads into a beautifully balanced wine with intense cabernet sauvignon flavour, but also with great balance, the oak and extract in no way compromising pure varietal cabernet fruit. Multiple trophies, including Best Wine of Show, 2002 Limestone Coast Wine Show. For release mid-2003. **rating:** 96

best drinking 2005–2020 **best vintages** '95, '96, '98 **drink with** Porterhouse steak • $50

Jamiesons Run Coonawarra Cabernet Sauvignon

TTTTY 2001 Medium red-purple; clean cassis and blackcurrant fruit on the bouquet lead into a palate with quite clearly focused and pure cabernet varietal fruit, the oak inputs being well controlled, as are the tannins. Excellent value. Trophy for Best Red Wine Not Exceeding $20 at the 2003 Sydney Wine Show. **rating:** 92

best drinking 2004–2009 **drink with** Rack of lamb • $16

Mildara Coonawarra Cabernet Sauvignon

TTTTT 2000 Medium red-purple; attractive, lush blackcurrant and cassis aromas flow into a rich, plush chocolate and blackberry palate, balanced by pleasantly savoury tannins on the finish. **rating:** 94

best drinking 2004–2012 **best vintages** '63, '86, '88, '90, '91, '98, '00 **drink with** Beef casserole • $23

Jamiesons Run O'Dea's Block Cabernet Sauvignon

TTTTY 2000 Medium to full red-purple; solid blackberry/mulberry fruit on the bouquet flows into a palate led by blackberry and cassis with touches of earthy Coonawarra varietal cabernet characters; fine tannins and good length. **rating:** 91

best drinking 2005–2012 **drink with** Braised lamb • $35

jane brook estate ★★★☆

229 Toodyay Road, Middle Swan, WA 6056 **region** Swan Valley
phone (08) 9274 1432 **fax** (08) 9274 1211 **open** Mon–Fri 10–5, weekends and public holidays 12–5
winemaker Julie White, David Atkinson **production** 20 000 cases **est.** 1972
product range ($13.50–29.50 CD) Ferguson Valley Pemberton Semillon, Semillon Sauvignon Blanc, James Vineyard Verdelho, Plain Jane Chenin Chardonnay, James Vineyard Chardonnay, Atkinson Shiraz, Back Block Shiraz, Plain Jane Shiraz, Mountjoy Cabernet Merlot, Elizabeth Jane Methode Champenoise, Plain Jane Methode Champenoise, Benjamin David Methode Champenoise Shiraz; fortifieds.
summary An attractive winery which relies in part on substantial cellar-door trade and in part on varying export markets, with much work having been invested in the Japanese market in recent years. It has established a vineyard in the Margaret River and also is now sourcing fruit from Pemberton, Ferguson Valley and Arthur River. The appointment of Julie White as chief winemaker has led to a distinct improvement in wine quality and consistency. Exports to Japan, Singapore and Malaysia, with a gift service available to the UK.

Jane Brook James Vineyard Verdelho

TTTT 2002 Medium yellow-green; while there are some traces of reduction on the bouquet, there is abundant ripe tropical fruit salad to create plenty of presence. The palate has good length, with particularly pleasing lemony acidity to balance the ripe fruit flavours. High-quality Verdelho. **rating:** 88

best drinking Now **best vintages** '02 **drink with** Takeaway chicken • $18

Jane Brook Back Block Shiraz

❦❦❦❦ **2001** Medium purple-red; the clean bouquet has strong, warm-grown varietal fruit aromas with a slightly earthy edge; the juicy, blackberry fruit of the palate again has a slightly earthy edge, very similar to young Hunter Shiraz. Subtle American oak is well-integrated. **rating: 87**

best drinking 2005–2012 **best vintages** '89, '90, '92, '94, '95 **drink with** Oxtail • $20

❦ jansz ★★★★

1216b Pipers Brook Road, Pipers Brook, Tas 7254 **region** Northern Tasmania
phone (03) 6382 7066 **fax** (03) 6382 7088 **open** 7 days 10–5
winemaker Natalie Fryer **production** 15 000 cases **est.** 1985
product range ($18–40 CD) Premium, Non Vintage Cuvee, Premium Late Disgorged.
summary Jansz is part of the S Smith & Son/Yalumba group, and was one of the early sparkling wine labels in Tasmania, stemming from a short-lived relationship between Heemskerk and Louis Roederer. Its 15 hectares of chardonnay, 12 hectares of pinot noir and 3 hectares of pinot meunier correspond almost exactly to the blend composition of the Jansz wines. It is the only Tasmanian winery entirely devoted to the production of sparkling wine, which is of high quality.

Jansz Late Disgorged

❦❦❦❦❦ **1995** A blend of chardonnay and pinot noir, aged in magnums and then disgorged into 750 ml bottles. Brilliant green-yellow; tight, bright aromas of citrus, pear, apple and spice lead into an exceptionally fine and focused palate, citrus-dominated but not at all green. Great value. **rating: 96**

best drinking Now **best vintages** '95 **drink with** Oysters • $39

❦ jarretts of orange ★★★

Annangrove Park, Cargo Road, Orange, NSW 2800 (postal) **region** Orange
phone (02) 6364 3118 **fax** (02) 6364 3048 **open** Not
winemaker Mark Davidson, Chris Derrez **production** 2500 cases **est.** 1995
product range ($13–16 R) Sauvignon Blanc, Marsanne, Chardonnay, Cabernet Merlot.
summary Justin and Pip Jarrett have established a very substantial vineyard, planted to chardonnay (38.5 ha), cabernet sauvignon (29 ha), shiraz (26 ha), sauvignon blanc (19 ha), merlot (12 ha), pinot noir (7 ha), riesling (4 ha), marsanne (2 ha), cabernet franc (1.5 ha) and verdelho (1 ha), amounting to 140 hectares in total. As well as managing this vineyard, they provide management and development services to growers of another 120 hectares in the region. Most of the grapes are sold, with a limited amount produced for local distribution and by mail order, with exports to the US pending. The wines are modestly priced; the Marsanne is a bargain.

Jarretts of Orange Marsanne

❦❦❦❦ **2001** Light straw-green; faintly chalky/dusty/minerally aromatics are distinctly varietal, but give no hint of the lively palate, which has minerally/lemony cut and excellent length. **rating: 86**

best drinking Now **drink with** Shellfish • $13

Jarretts of Orange Chardonnay

❦❦❦❦ **2001** Light straw-green; citrus-tinged fruit and smoky/dusty oak on the bouquet lead into a very light, crisp and youthful palate, finishing with crunchy acidity, and belying its 13.5° alcohol. **rating: 85**

best drinking Now–2005 **drink with** Sushi • $15

Jarretts of Orange Cabernet Merlot

❦❦❦❦ **2001** Light to medium red-purple; the clean but light bouquet ranges through leaf, berry and earth aromas; the light-bodied palate has berry fruit, touches of mint, and savoury tannins to close. **rating: 84**

best drinking Now–2006 **drink with** Roast lamb • $16

jasper hill ★★★★★

Drummonds Lane, Heathcote, Vic 3523 **region** Heathcote
phone (03) 5433 2528 **fax** (03) 5433 3143 **open** By appointment
winemaker Ron Laughton, heading a team of four **production** 3500 cases **est.** 1975
product range ($24.50–82 ML) Georgia's Paddock Riesling, Georgia's Paddock Semillon, Georgia's Paddock Shiraz, Georgia's Paddock Nebbiolo, Emily's Paddock Shiraz Cabernet Franc.
summary The red wines of Jasper Hill are highly regarded and much sought after, invariably selling out at the cellar door and through the mailing list within a short time of release. These are wonderful wines in admittedly

Leviathan mould, reflecting the very low yields and the care and attention given to them by Ron Laughton. The oak is not overdone, and the fruit flavours show Central Victoria at its best. There has been comment (and some criticism) in recent years about the alcohol level of the wines. Laughton responds by saying he picks the grapes when he judges them to be at optimum ripeness, and is in no way chasing high alcohol, whether to suit the US market or otherwise.

Jasper Hill Georgia's Paddock Nebbiolo

▼▼▼▼▽ 2001 Medium red, with some purple hues remaining; a fragrant and distinctly varietal bouquet with tangy/spicy fruit aromas and subtle oak; the light to medium-bodied palate has lingering spicy/savoury flavours which are nonetheless sweet, with fine tannins running throughout and in no way compromising the mouthfeel or flavour. The best Australian wine I have yet tasted from an Italian grape variety, and Ron Laughton says the 2002 is better still. **rating:** 92

best drinking Now–2007 best vintages '01 drink with Osso buco • $51

jasper valley   NR

RMB 880, Croziers Road, Berry, NSW 2535 **region** Shoalhaven Coast
phone (02) 4464 1596 **fax** (02) 4464 1595 **open** 7 days 9.30–5.30
winemaker Contract **production** 1500 cases **est.** 1976
product range ($6.50–18 CD) Traminer Riesling, Verdelho, Chardonnay, Lambrusco, Shiraz, Shiraz Cabernet, Summer Red, Cabernet Sauvignon, Black Eagle Tawny Port; also non-alcoholic fruit wines.
summary A strongly tourist-oriented winery with most of its wine purchased as cleanskins from other makers, but with 2 hectares of estate shiraz planted in 1976 by former owner Sidney Mitchell; these are the oldest vines in the region. Features around 1 hectare of lawns and barbecue facilities, and has sweeping views.

jeanneret wines   ★★★★

Jeanneret Road, Sevenhill, SA 5453 **region** Clare Valley
phone (08) 8843 4308 **fax** (08) 8843 4251 **open** Mon–Fri 11–5, weekends and public holidays 10–5
winemaker Ben Jeanneret **production** 7500 cases **est.** 1992
product range ($17–55 CD) Riesling, Chardonnay, Sparkling Grenache, Grenache Shiraz, Shiraz, Denis Reserve Shiraz, Cabernet Sauvignon.
summary Jeanneret's fully self-contained winery has a most attractive outdoor tasting area and equally attractive picnic facilities situated on the edge of a small lake surrounded by bushland. While it did not open the business until October 1994, its first wine was in fact made in 1992 (Shiraz), and it has already established a loyal following. National wholesale distribution; exports to the US, Canada, Malaysia and Switzerland.

Jeanneret Riesling

▼▼▼▼▽ 2002 Bright, light straw-green; the clean bouquet opens with mineral and slate, with some lime coming through thereafter; the beautifully proportioned and balanced palate is silky and long, making for a highly accessible style. Has brought out the best of the great 2002 vintage, and is infinitely better than prior vintages. **rating:** 93

best drinking Now–2013 best vintages '02 drink with Shellfish • $17

Jeanneret Shiraz

▼▼▼▼ 2001 Medium red-purple; the bouquet has firm, earthy, herby edges to the core of dark berry fruit aromas; blackberry and black plum flavours on entry to the palate are followed by more savoury/earthy/chocolatey characters on the finish. **rating:** 89

best drinking 2005–2012 best vintages '00 drink with Beef stew with olives • $22

Jeanneret Denis Reserve Shiraz

▼▼▼▼ 2000 Medium red-purple; the bouquet has a range of earthy, savoury, herbal and spice aromas; the palate has entirely unexpected length and intensity. Tasted without any recollection of or reference to the '98 vintage, but has many features in common. Once again, a wine that shows that old vines do not necessarily produce blockbuster fruit. **rating:** 87

best drinking 2005–2015 drink with Rack of veal • $55

jeir creek   NR

Gooda Creek Road, Murrumbateman, NSW 2582 **region** Canberra District
phone (02) 6227 5999 **fax** (02) 6227 5900 **open** Fri–Sun, holidays 10–5
winemaker Rob Howell **production** 4000 cases **est.** 1984

product range ($16–22 CD) Riesling, Sauvignon Blanc, Chardonnay, Botrytis Semillon Sauvignon Blanc, Pinot Noir, Shiraz, Cabernet Merlot.

summary Rob Howell came to part-time winemaking through a love of drinking fine wine, and is intent on improving both the quality and consistency of his wines. It is now a substantial (and still growing) business, with the vineyard plantings increased to 11 hectares by the establishment of more cabernet sauvignon, shiraz and merlot. No recent tastings.

jenke vineyards ★★★☆

Barossa Valley Way, Rowland Flat, SA 5352 **region** Barossa Valley
phone (08) 8524 4154 **fax** (08) 8524 5044 **open** 7 days 11–5
winemaker Kym Jenke **production** 8000 cases **est.** 1989
product range ($15–40 CD) Semillon, Chardonnay, Sparkling Shiraz, Shiraz, Grenache, Mourvedre, Merlot, Cabernet Franc, Cabernet Sauvignon.
summary The Jenkes have been vignerons in the Barossa since 1854 and have over 45 hectares of vineyards; a small part of the production is now made and marketed through a charming restored stone cottage cellar door. Wholesale distribution in Victoria and New South Wales; exports to Singapore, Switzerland and New Zealand.

Jenke Chardonnay

▼▼▼▼ 2002 Light to medium yellow-green; the decidedly complex bouquet has tangy fruit and subtle, smoky barrel-ferment French oak inputs; the elegant, light to medium-bodied palate continues the theme; a real surprise packet. Excellent value. **rating:** 89
best drinking Now–2005 **drink with** Tempura • $15

Jenke Merlot

▼▼▼▼ 2000 Light to medium red, the purple starting to fade a little; the bouquet has a mix of savoury berry, earth and leaf aromas, and the medium-bodied palate has positive varietal fruit replicating the bouquet; soft texture and structure appropriate to the variety. **rating:** 87
best drinking Now–2007 **drink with** Braised pork • $20

jester hill wines NR

Mount Stirling Road, Glen Aplin, Qld 4381 **region** Granite Belt
phone (07) 4683 4380 **fax** (02) 6622 3190 **open** Fri–Mon 10–4
winemaker Contract **production** 1300 cases **est.** 1993
product range ($11–20 CD) Classic White, Chardonnay, Sparkling Shiraz, Summer Red, Shiraz, Cabernet Sauvignon, Fortified Shiraz.
summary A family-run vineyard situated in the pretty valley of Glen Aplin in the Granite Belt. The owners, John and Genevieve Ashwell, aim to concentrate on small quantities of premium-quality wines reflecting the full-bodied style of the region. Believing that good wine is made in the vineyard, John and Genevieve spent the first 7 years establishing healthy, strong vines on well-drained soil.

jim barry wines ★★★★☆

Main North Road, Clare, SA 5453 **region** Clare Valley
phone (08) 8842 2261 **fax** (08) 8842 3752 **open** Mon–Fri 9–5, weekends, holidays 9–4
winemaker Mark Barry **production** 60 000 cases **est.** 1959
product range ($12–130 CD) Watervale Riesling, Lodge Hill Riesling, Cellar Door Semillon, Clare Valley Chardonnay, Unwooded Chardonnay, Lavender Hill, Sparkling Pinot Chardonnay, Noble Riesling, Lodge Hill Shiraz, Shiraz Cabernet Sauvignon, McCrae Wood Shiraz, The Armagh (Shiraz), McCrae Wood Cabernet Sauvignon, Clare Valley Cabernet Sauvignon, Cabernet Sauvignon Shiraz.
summary The Armagh and the McCrae Wood range continue to stand out as the very best wines from Jim Barry, exceptionally concentrated and full flavoured. The remainder are seldom less than adequate but do vary somewhat from one vintage to the next. Has an exceptional viticultural resource base of 247 hectares of mature Clare Valley vineyards. Exports to the UK, much of Europe, North America, Japan and South-East Asia.

Jim Barry Lodge Hill Riesling

▼▼▼▼▼ 2002 Light straw-green; the spotlessly clean and crisp bouquet ranges through mineral, citrus and spice aromas; the palate moves onto an even higher plane, marvellously pure and fine, with great balance and length. A great wine from a great vintage. **rating:** 95
best drinking 2006–2016 **drink with** Leave it in the cellar • $19.95

Jim Barry Watervale Riesling Florita Vineyard

🍷🍷🍷🍷🍷 **2002** Very light straw-green; crisp, tight and unevolved, with some apple blossom aromas escaping, followed by a lean, unready palate; however, the balance and length are good, and it is perfectly certain that the wine will bloom in bottle, making the points seem miserable. From the most historic riesling vineyard in the Clare Valley. **rating: 90**

best drinking 2007–2017 **best vintages** '83, '86, '89, '91, '94, '95, '99, '01 **drink with** Salmon and asparagus terrine • $13

Jim Barry Late Picked Lavender Hill

🍷🍷🍷🍷 **2002** Light green-yellow; a tight mix of lime, lemon and mineral aromas is followed by a palate with very well-controlled sweetness which, while barely reaching spatlese level, lengthens the flavours, and augurs well for the future. **rating: 88**

best drinking 2005–2012 **drink with** Trout mousse • $12

Jim Barry The Armagh

🍷🍷🍷🍷🍷 **2000** Full red-purple; the powerful bouquet ranges through dark berry, leather and boot polish, with the oak restrained. A luscious, high-octane palate, oozing blackberry, plum and licorice; the oak and tannins both restrained – another great success. **rating: 94**

best drinking 2006–2016 **best vintages** '89, '90, '91, '92, '93, '95, '96, '98, '99, '00 **drink with** The richest game dish possible • $130

🐌 jimbour station ★★★★

Jimbour Station, Jimbour, Qld 4406 **region** Queensland Zone
phone (07) 4663 6221 **fax** (07) 4663 6194 **open** 7 days 10.30–5
winemaker Peter Scudamore-Smith MW **production** 10 000 cases **est.** 2000
product range ($14.25–19 CD) Verdelho, Chardonnay, Shiraz, Merlot, Cabernet Sauvignon.
summary Jimbour Station was one of the first properties opened in the Darling Downs; the heritage-listed homestead was built in 1876. The property has been owned by the Russell family since 1923, and has diversified by establishing a 20-hectare vineyard and opening a cellar door on the property. Its already substantial production, made under the direction of the well known Master of Wine Peter Scudamore-Smith, is an indication of its intention to become one of Queensland's major wine producers.

Jimbour Station Chardonnay

🍷🍷🍷🍷 **2001** Developed yellow-green; the bouquet is complex, with well-integrated and balanced oak plus nice stone fruit; on the palate the fruit struggles to express itself, and the strong cashew/biscuit aftertaste is slightly distracting. Barrel fermented and spends 10 months in a mix of French and American oak. **rating: 85**

best drinking Now **drink with** Avocado salad • $14.25

Jimbour Station Shiraz

🍷🍷🍷🍷🍷 **2000** Medium red-purple; the moderately intense bouquet has a mix of plum and blackberry fruit supported by subtle oak; on the palate, rich blackberry fruit is made complex by a touch of chocolate and cleverly handled American oak; ripe tannins give the wine excellent overall structure. Blue Gold at the 2003 Sydney International Wine Competition. Only 600 cases made. **rating: 93**

best drinking 2004–2009 **best vintages** '00 **drink with** Rare roast beef • $19

Jimbour Station Merlot

🍷🍷🍷🍷 **2001** Light to medium red-purple; a light array of leafy, minty, berry aromas lead into a light to medium-bodied palate with a distinctly savoury finish providing authentic varietal character. **rating: 86**

best drinking 2004–2008 **drink with** Rack of veal • $19

Jimbour Station Cabernet Sauvignon

🍷🍷🍷🍷 **2000** Medium red-purple; the bouquet has ripe cassis/berry fruit; the palate has good depth, weight and structure to the blackcurrant fruit and lingering tannins; a serious wine in similar class to the Shiraz. **rating: 89**

best drinking 2005–2010 **drink with** Butterfly leg of lamb • $19

jindalee estate ★★★★

265 Ballan Road, Moorabool, North Geelong, Vic 3221 **region** Geelong
phone (03) 5276 1280 **fax** (03) 5276 1537 **open** 7 days 10–5
winemaker Scott Ireland **production** 403 000 cases **est.** 1997

product range ($9.50–19.50 CD) Chardonnay, Shiraz, Merlot, Cabernet Sauvignon; under the Fettlers Rest label are Gewurztraminer, Chardonnay, Pinot Noir, Shiraz, Cabernet Shiraz.

summary Jindalee Wines made its debut with the 1997 vintage. It is part of the Littore Group, which currently has 500 hectares of premium-wine grapes in wine production and under development in the Riverland. Corporate offices are now at the former Idyll Vineyard, acquired by Jindalee in late 1997. Here 13 hectares of estate vineyards are being re-trellised and upgraded, and a premium Jindalee Estate range is now made. The Jindalee Estate Chardonnay can offer spectacular value, as it did in 2001. Retail distribution through Red+White and Options Wines (SA); exports to the UK, the US and Canada.

Fettlers Rest Gewurztraminer

▼▼▼▼ 2002 Light green-yellow; the bouquet has clean, clear, albeit light, varietal lychee and rose petal fruit, the palate can't quite deliver on the promise of the bouquet but is well made, and well above the average. **rating:** 86

best drinking Now–2005 **drink with** Lightly spiced Asian • $16

Jindalee Estate Chardonnay

▼▼▼▼ 2002 Light to medium yellow-green; as ever, there is an extra touch of complexity and interest to both the bouquet and the palate, which has multi-flavours and texture to the peachy fruit and light oak infusion. As always, excellent value. **rating:** 87

best drinking Now **best vintages** '01 **drink with** Takeaway chicken • $9.50

Fettlers Rest Chardonnay

▼▼▼▼ 2001 Bright, light straw-green; the tangy, citrussy, fruit-driven bouquet has some barrel-ferment oak adding to its appeal; the light to medium-bodied elegant palate is developing very slowly, with more to come. **rating:** 89

best drinking Now–2007 **drink with** Seafood risotto • $18

Fettlers Rest Pinot Noir

▼▼▼▼▽ 2001 Excellent purple-red; the bouquet has clean, pure varietal character, offering plum, a hint of raspberry and subtle oak. The palate has very good texture, mouthfeel and weight; fine rather than opulent. **rating:** 91

best drinking Now–2006 **best vintages** '00, '01 **drink with** Roast pigeon • $19.50

jindi creek   NR

426 Turner Road, Denmark, WA 6333 **region** Great Southern
phone (08) 9848 1113 **fax** (08) 9848 1844 **open** Thurs–Mon 11–4.30 Oct–July
winemaker Brendon Smith **production** 600 cases **est.** 1996
product range ($15–20 CD) Semillon Sauvignon Blanc, Semillon Wooded Chardonnay, Verdelho Chardonnay, Chardonnay, Pinot Noir, Shiraz, Cabernet Sauvignon.
summary The Ponsfords (Nick, Rosemary and son Andrew) used to run a stock fencing contract business, and Rosemary always had an interest in cooking and hospitality. They decided that moving into winemaking and running a restaurant would be an easier life, and now wryly admit, 'How wrong can you be!?' They have planted 5.5 hectares of chardonnay, semillon, sauvignon blanc, pinot noir, merlot and cabernet sauvignon, with a few rows of verdelho and marsanne, but till now have sold part of the crop to other wineries. They hope that in the future a newly formed co-operative will allow all the estate production to be vinified; at that stage they may need to look beyond the cellar door and restaurant through which all the present output is sold.

jingalla   ★★★☆

RMB 1316, Bolganup Dam Road, Porongurup, WA 6324 **region** Great Southern
phone (08) 9853 1023 **fax** (08) 9853 1023 **open** 7 days 10.30–5
winemaker Diane Miller, Gary Baldwin (Consultant) **production** 5000 cases **est.** 1979
product range ($13–25 CD) Great Southern White, Riesling, Riesling Reserve, Semillon Sauvignon Blanc, Verdelho, Late Harvest, Botrytis Riesling Verdelho, Shiraz, Shiraz Reserve, CabRouge, Cabernets Merlot, Cabernet Sauvignon, Tawny Port, Liqueur Muscat.
summary Jingalla is a family business, owned and run by Geoff and Nita Clarke and Barry and Shelley Coad, the latter the ever-energetic wine marketer of the business. The 8 hectares of hillside vineyards are low-yielding, with the white wines succeeding best, but it also produces some lovely red wines. A partner in the new Porongurup Winery, which means it no longer has to rely on contract winemaking. National distribution.

Jingalla Riesling Reserve

 TTTT 2002 Light straw-green; the bouquet is clean, with mineral, lime and a hint of passionfruit leading into a wine of moderate length and intensity, the flavours tracking those of the bouquet. **rating:** 88

best drinking Now–2008 **best vintages** '01 **drink with** Crayfish • $16

Jingalla Semillon Sauvignon Blanc

TTTT 2002 Light green-yellow; complex, ripe gooseberry and tropical fruit aromas make a dramatic start, and although the palate is much lighter than the bouquet suggests, this is still a pretty wine. **rating:** 86

best drinking Now **drink with** Char-grilled baby octopus • $13

Jingalla Verdelho

TTTT 2002 Light green-yellow; the clean, moderately intense bouquet has fruit salad aromas with a touch of lemon rind; the light to medium-bodied palate has gentle flavours and good balance. **rating:** 85

best drinking Now–2005 **best vintages** '90, '91, '94, '96 **drink with** Caesar salad • $18

Jingalla CabRouge

TTTY 2002 Medium red-purple, nothing to do with rose in colour; the bouquet is fresh, with sweet blackberry fruit, but the sweet palate is entirely unexpected; a schizophrenic in every respect, made from a blend of Cabernet Sauvignon and Riesling. Doubtless tailor-made for those who visit the cellar door and ask, 'Have you got anything a bit sweet?' **rating:** 83

best drinking Now **drink with** I can't imagine • $13

jinglers creek vineyard   NR

288 Relbia Road, Relbia, Tas 7258 (postal) **region** Northern Tasmania
phone (03) 6344 3966 **fax** (03) 6344 3966 **open** Not
winemaker Graham Wiltshire **est.** 1998
product range ($18–28 R) Pinot Noir.
summary One of the newer arrivals on the Tasmanian scene, with 2 hectares of pinot noir, pinot gris and chardonnay. Winemaking is done by industry veteran Graham Wiltshire, who knows more about growing grapes and making wine in Tasmania than any other active winemaker.

jinks creek winery   ★★★★

Tonimbuk Road, Tonimbuk, Vic 3815 **region** Gippsland
phone (03) 5629 8502 **fax** (03) 5629 8551 **open** By appointment
winemaker Andrew Clarke **production** 650 cases **est.** 1981
product range ($20–28 CD) Sauvignon Blanc, Pinot Noir, Heathcote Shiraz, Longford Shiraz, Yarra Shiraz.
summary Jinks Creek Winery is situated between Gembrook and Bunyip, bordering the evocatively named Bunyip State Park. While the winery was not built until 1992, planting of the 2.5-hectare vineyard started back in 1981 and all the wines are estate-grown. The 'sold out' sign goes up each year; small wonder in vintages such as 2000. Exports to the US and Singapore.

Jinks Creek Sauvignon Blanc

TTTT 2002 Very light straw-green; the aromatic bouquet has slight signs of reduction alongside the tropical gooseberry fruit; the same Jekyll and Hyde characteristics come into play on the palate. Others less intolerant of reduction would doubtless give the wine higher points. **rating:** 85

best drinking Now **drink with** Salads • $20

joadja vineyards   ★★★☆

Joadja Road, Berrima, NSW 2577 **region** Southern Highlands
phone (02) 4878 5236 **fax** (02) 4878 5236 **open** 7 days 10–5
winemaker Kim Moginie **production** 2000 cases **est.** 1983
product range ($15–28.50 CD) Classic Dry White, Sauvignon Blanc, Chardonnay, Botrytis Autumn Riesling, Cabernet Sangiovese, Cabernet Malbec, Cabernet Merlot, Mandemar, Christopher Tawny Port, Brambelini Liqueur.
summary The strikingly labelled Joadja Vineyards wines, first made in 1990, are principally drawn from 7 hectares of estate vineyards situated in the cool hills adjacent to Berrima. Mature vines and greater experience of this emerging region appears to have solved some of the early difficulties in securing full ripeness if the 2001 Cabernet Sangiovese is anything to go by.

Joadja Cabernet Sangiovese

▼▼▼▼ 2001 Light to medium red-purple; the bouquet is clean, spicy and savoury, but not minty; the palate has attractively sweet fruit, with spicy/savoury nuances appropriate to the Sangiovese; well made in early drinking style. **rating:** 87

best drinking Now–2006 **drink with** Pasta • $19

john gehrig wines ★★☆

Oxley–Milawa Road, Oxley, Vic 3678 **region** King Valley
phone (03) 5727 3395 **fax** (03) 5727 3699 **open** 7 days 9–5
winemaker John Gehrig **production** 5600 cases **est.** 1976
product range ($9–25 CD) Riesling, Oxley Dry White, Chenin Blanc, Chardonnay, Pinot Victoria, Late Harvest Riesling, Pinot Noir Brut, Oxley Rose, Pinot Noir, King River Red, Border Blend, Merlot, Cabernet Merlot, fortifieds.
summary Honest, if seldom exciting, wines; the occasional Chardonnay, Pinot Noir, Merlot and Cabernet Merlot have, however, risen above their station.

jollymont ★★★★

145 Pullens Road, Woodbridge, Tas 7162 (postal) **region** Southern Tasmania
phone (03) 6267 4594 **fax** (03) 6267 4594 **open** Not
winemaker Andrew Hood (Contract) **production** 60 cases **est.** 1988
product range ($24 R) Pinot Noir.
summary However briefly, Jollymont displaced Scarp Valley as the smallest producer in Australia, its 1998 vintage (the first) producing 10 cases, the next 20. The vines are not irrigated, nor will they be, and Peter and Heather Kreet do not intend to sell any wine younger than 3–4 years old. Their aim is to produce wines of maximum intensity and complexity.

Jollymont Pinot Noir

▼▼▼▼ 2001 Medium red-purple; a high-toned, intense, tangy bouquet sets the scene for a palate which shows many of the same characters – long, tangy and savoury. It is a style I particularly like. **rating:** 89

best drinking Now–2007 **drink with** Pasta • $24

jones winery & vineyard ★★★★

Jones Road, Rutherglen, Vic 3685 **region** Rutherglen
phone (02) 6032 8496 **fax** (02) 6032 8495 **open** Fri–Sun and public holidays 10–5
winemaker Mandy Jones **production** 600 cases **est.** 1864
product range ($15–40 CD) There are two labels; Jones The Winemaker is used for wines produced from contract-grown grapes (Sauvignon Blanc, Annie's White Marsanne, Chardonnay and Pinot Noir), while the Jones Winery & Vineyard label is used for wines made from estate-grown grapes (Shiraz and fortifieds).
summary Late in 1998 the winery was purchased from Les Jones by Leanne Schoen and Mandy and Arthur Jones (nieces and nephew of Les). The cellar-door sales area is situated in a building from the 1860s, still with the original bark ceiling and walls with handmade bricks fired on-site; it was completely renovated over 2002/03.

Jones Winery & Vineyard Shiraz

▼▼▼▼▽ 2001 Medium to full red-purple; ripe blackberry and prune fruit aromas have some savoury counterpoints; the medium-bodied palate has good structure, fine, ripe tannins, and a savoury finish to balance the core of rich, sweet fruit. **rating:** 91

best drinking 2006–2016 **best vintages** '01 **drink with** Beef spare ribs • $22

Jones Winery & Vineyard LJ Shiraz

LJ Shiraz is named to honour founder Les Jones. It is produced from the oldest vines on the vineyard, and is by far the best of the current releases.

▼▼▼▼▽ 2001 Medium to full red-purple; abundant blackberry, licorice and prune fruit has some oak somewhere in the background of the bouquet; the massively powerful and potent palate, reflecting its 15.5° alcohol, is tailor-made for Robert Parker's palate. **rating:** 90

best drinking 2011–2021 **best vintages** '99 **drink with** Char-grilled rump • $40

judds warby range estate ★★★★

Jones Road, Taminick via Glenrowan, Vic 3675 **region** Glenrowan
phone (03) 5765 2314 **open** Thurs–Mon 10–5, or by appointment
winemaker Ralph Judd **production** 500 cases **est.** 1989
product range ($10–15 CD) Shiraz, Durif.
summary Ralph and Margaret Judd began the development of their vineyard in 1989 as contract growers for Southcorp. They have gradually expanded the plantings to 4 hectares of shiraz and 0.5 hectare of durif; they also have 100 vines each of zinfandel, ruby cabernet, cabernet sauvignon, petit verdot, nebbiolo, tempranillo and sangiovese for evaluation. Up until 1995 all the grapes were fermented and then sent by tanker to Southcorp, but in 1996 the Judds made their first barrel of wine, and have now moved to opening a small cellar-door sales facility. The wines are monumental in flavour and depth, in best Glenrowan tradition, and will richly repay extended cellaring.

Judds Warby Range Estate Shiraz

▼▼▼▼ **2002** Dense red-purple; dense, rich, ripe almost essency fruit on the bouquet is followed by a palate flooded with rich, dense fruit, relatively low in tannin, and certainly not over-extracted. **rating:** 89
best drinking 2006–2016 **drink with** Braised beef with olives • $15

Judds Warby Range Estate Durif

▼▼▼▼▽ **2002** Deep, dark red-purple; rich blackberry, prune, licorice and spice aromas run through the bouquet; the wine predictably floods the mouth with dark berry fruit, and chewy (but not unbalanced) tannins come through on the finish. **rating:** 91
best drinking 2006–2016 **drink with** Rare rump • $15

juniper estate ★★★★☆

Harmans Road South, Cowaramup, WA 6284 **region** Margaret River
phone (08) 9755 9000 **fax** (08) 9755 9100 **open** 7 days 10–5
winemaker Mark Messenger **production** 10 000 cases **est.** 1998
product range ($14–32 CD) Under the Juniper Crossing label are Semillon Sauvignon Blanc, Chenin Blanc, Chardonnay, Late Harvest Riesling, Shiraz, Cabernet Merlot, Cabernet Sauvignon; Juniper Estate Riesling, Semillon, Shiraz, Cabernet Sauvignon; Wright's White Port.
summary This is the reincarnation of Wrights, which was sold by founders Henry and Maureen Wright in 1998. The 10-hectare vineyard has been re-trellised, and the last 1.5 hectares of plantable land has seen the key plantings of shiraz and cabernet sauvignon increase a little. A major building programme was completed in February 2000, giving Juniper Estate a new 250-tonne capacity winery, barrel hall and cellar-door facility. The Juniper family is a famous one in the Margaret River region, its strong artistic bent evident in the immaculate packaging and background material. Juniper Crossing wines use a mix of estate-grown and contract-purchased grapes from other Margaret River vineyards. The Juniper Estate releases are made only from the 28-year-old estate plantings. Exports to the US, the UK and Denmark.

Juniper Crossing Sauvignon Blanc

▼▼▼▼▽ **2002** Light green-yellow; clean, fresh, gently tropical aromas flow into a nicely flavoured and balanced palate, adding a touch of ripe apple to the mix. As good an example of the variety as one could wish for. **rating:** 90
best drinking Now **best vintages** '02 **drink with** Pasta • $16

Juniper Crossing Semillon Sauvignon Blanc

▼▼▼▼▽ **2002** Light straw-green; a highly aromatic bouquet with aromas of passionfruit and peach flows through into an appealing palate with tropical flavours running through to a well-balanced, long finish. **rating:** 90
best drinking Now **best vintages** '02 **drink with** Sugar-cured tuna • $16

Juniper Estate Shiraz

▼▼▼▼▽ **2000** Full purple-red; there is great fruit concentration on both the bouquet and palate, with powerful black cherry, licorice and ripe tannins. The only question is the exuberant use of oak; with any sort of luck, this should settle down as the wine ages. **rating:** 91
best drinking 2005–2015 **drink with** Beef in black bean sauce • $29

Juniper Crossing Cabernet Merlot

▼▼▼▼▽ **2001** Bright purple-red; fragrant berry and spice aromas are followed by a lively, tangy, juicy berry palate with a touch of leaf; fine tannins and subtle oak. **rating:** 91
best drinking 2004–2009 **drink with** Venison in red wine sauce • $19

Juniper Estate Cabernet Sauvignon

TTTT 2000 Medium red-purple; a stylish and complex bouquet features fine, dark berry fruit and integrated oak, leaving one entirely unprepared for the massively powerful and tannic palate. If the tannins soften and come back into balance the wine will handsomely repay those who are true believers, but right now it is hard to see how the tannins will soften sufficiently before the fruit fades. **rating: 88**

best drinking 2008–2018 **best vintages** '99 **drink with** Lamb shanks • $32

jyt wines NR

De Beyers Road, Pokolbin, NSW 2320 **region** Lower Hunter Valley
phone (02) 4998 7528 **fax** (02) 4998 7370 **open** Thurs–Tues 10–5
winemaker Jay Tulloch, Julie Tulloch **production** 2000 cases **est.** 1996
product range ($16.50 CD) Semillon, Verdelho, Chardonnay, Pink.
summary When Jay Tulloch left in 1996, it marked the end of a 100-year, multi-generational association with JY Tulloch and Sons (formerly part of the Southcorp wine group). However, it did not mark the end of the Tulloch family's involvement with the wine industry, for he and wife Julie have established a 3-hectare hillside vineyard on the picturesque De Beyers Road which (appropriately) overlooks the old Tulloch winery. Here they have planted 0.6 hectare each of semillon, chardonnay, verdelho, shiraz and sangiovese.

kaesler wines ★★★★☆

Barossa Valley Way, Nuriootpa, SA 5355 **region** Barossa Valley
phone (08) 8562 4488 **fax** (08) 8562 4499 **open** Mon–Sat 10–5, Sun and public holidays 11.30–4
winemaker Reid Bosward **production** 12 000 cases **est.** 1990
product range ($9.50–155 CD) Riesling, Home Block Semillon, Old Vine Semillon, Prestige Semillon, Stonehorse Late Harvest, Reid's Rasp, Stonehorse Gilt-Finish, Stonehorse Shiraz, Old Vine Shiraz, Old Bastard Shiraz, Old Vine Grenache, Single Wire Merlot, Cabernet Sauvignon, Tawny Port, Cottage Block Fortified White.
summary The Kaesler name dates back to 1845, when the first members of the family settled in the Barossa Valley. The Kaesler vineyards date back to 1893, but the Kaesler ownership ended in 1968. After several changes, the present, much expanded, Kaesler Wines was acquired by a Swiss banking family in conjunction with former Flying Winemaker Reid Bosward and wife Bindy. Bosward's vast experience in making wine in many different climates shows through in the wines, which now come from 24 hectares of estate vineyards. These vineyards, as well as the 1893 shiraz, grenache and mourvedre, have grenache and mourvedre that were planted in the 1930s. A new winery was completed in time for the 2002 vintage. Exports to the US, Canada, Switzerland, Denmark, Sweden, Japan, Hong Kong and New Zealand.

Kaesler Old Vine Semillon

TTTT 2002 Medium green-yellow, developed but with good hue; the ripe bouquet ranges through lemon, grass, herbs and flowers; the palate is generous and powerful right through to the finish. Unoaked; very good Barossa Semillon. **rating: 89**

best drinking Now–2005 **drink with** Fried chicken • $17.50

Kaesler Stonehorse Geelong Chardonnay

TTTTY 2001 Medium yellow-green; there is excellent fruit and oak balance and integration on both bouquet and palate; grapefruit, melon and stone fruit flavours nicely reflect the cool climate; good mouthfeel and balance to a well-made wine. **rating: 90**

best drinking Now–2007 **best vintages** '01 **drink with** Fresh Tasmanian salmon • $20

Kaesler Old Bastard Shiraz

TTTT 2001 Full red-purple; intense, concentrated dark fruit aromas lead into the expected intense and powerful palate; here blackberry, plum, prune and spice intermingle; happily, the wine has not been over-extracted and has good balance. It comes in a Dreadnought bottle with a wax seal and rather droll label design. I can actually imagine drinking my share of a bottle of this in my next life; the time remaining for me in this life is too short. **rating: 95**

best drinking 2010–2025 **best vintages** '99, '01 **drink with** Ten centimetre-thick rump steak • $155

Kaesler Old Vine Shiraz

TTTT 2000 Deep red-purple; the complex but smooth bouquet has seductive dark plum and blackberry fruit married with equally seductive French oak; the palate is flooded with flavour, and has very good texture, the fruit promised by the bouquet supported by ripe, fine tannins running through to a long finish. From 1893 and 1961 plantings; 2 years in French oak. **rating: 95**

best drinking 2005–2020 **best vintages** '98, '99 **drink with** Buffalo steak • $60

Kaesler Stonehorse Shiraz

▼▼▼▼▽ **2001** Medium purple-red; solid, smooth blackberry fruit aromas are followed by a dense and ripe palate with plum, prune and blackberry flavours; the wine has good tannins and is not over-extracted.　**rating:** 91

best drinking 2005–2015 **best vintages** '98, '01 **drink with** Beef casserole • $29

Kaesler Old Vine Avignon Shiraz Grenache Mourvedre

▼▼▼▼▽ **2001** Bright, youthful, light purple-red; there is a spicy edge to the sweet fruit of the bouquet; the rich palate altogether belies the colour, with a range of dark berry, dark chocolate and licorice fruit flavours; minimal oak influence; excellent, ripe tannins.　**rating:** 92

best drinking Now–2009 **drink with** Jugged hare • $30

Kaesler Cabernet Sauvignon

▼▼▼▼▽ **2001** Strong red-purple; voluminous blackcurrant and blackberry fruit, plus a touch of chocolate, drives the bouquet; a similarly powerful palate which is, however, not jammy; lingering tannins underwrite the structure.　**rating:** 90

best drinking 2006–2016 **best vintages** '01 **drink with** Grilled lamb chops • $22

kalari wines　NR

120 Carro Park Road, Cowra, NSW 2794 **region** Cowra
phone (02) 6342 1465 **fax** (02) 6342 1465 **open** Weekends and public holidays 9–5
winemaker Jill Lindsay, Jon Reynolds (Contract) **production** 1200 cases **est.** 1995
product range ($14–25 CD) Semillon, Verdelho, Chardonnay, Late Picked Verdelho, Shiraz, Fortelho (fortified Verdelho).
summary Kalari Vineyards is yet another of the new brands to appear in the Cowra region. Fourteen and a half hectares of vines have been established, with a Verdelho, Chardonnay and Shiraz being included in the initial release.

kamberra　★★★★

Cnr Northbourne Avenue and Fleminton Road, Lyneham, ACT 2602 **region** Canberra District
phone (02) 6262 2333 **fax** (02) 6262 2300 **open** 7 days 10–5
winemaker Alex McKay, Ed Carr, Glenn James, Stephen Pannell **production** 18 000 cases **est.** 2000
product range ($12–30 R) The wines come in two ranges: at the bottom the Meeting Place label of Riesling, Sauvignon Blanc, Chardonnay, Pinot Noir Chardonnay, Shiraz, Cabernet Sauvignon; the premium range is the Kamberra label, comprising Riesling, Chardonnay, Pinot Noir Chardonnay, Shiraz, Cabernet Sauvignon.
summary Kamberra is part of the BRL Hardy group, established in 2000 with the planting of 40 hectares of vines and a new winery within the Australian Capital Territory, only a few hundred metres away from the showground facilities where the national wine show is held every year. The two 100 per cent estate-grown wines are Riesling and Shiraz, but most of the wines have a Kamberra component.

Kamberra Riesling

▼▼▼▼▽ **2002** Pale straw-green; a spotlessly clean, light and flowery bouquet of apple blossom opens into a tangy and quite intense palate with layers of flavour on the tongue, and good length. A convincing blend of Canberra and Tumbarumba grapes.　**rating:** 92

best drinking Now–2009 **best vintages** '02 **drink with** Grilled scallops • $25

Kamberra Meeting Place Riesling

▼▼▼▼ **2002** Light straw-green; herb and mineral aromas intermingle with lime, grapefruit and more tropical fruit; the palate has good flavour depth and length, but not overmuch finesse.　**rating:** 87

best drinking Now–2007 **drink with** Artichoke with hollandaise sauce • $14.95

Kamberra Meeting Place Sauvignon Blanc

▼▼▼▼ **2002** Light straw-green; the clean, aromatic and strongly varietal bouquet has gooseberry, green pea and redcurrant aromas; the long, crisp and lively palate has tingling acidity, and the capacity for short-term development.　**rating:** 88

best drinking Now **drink with** Blue swimmer crab • $14.95

Kamberra Meeting Place Chardonnay

▼▼▼▼ **2001** Light to medium yellow-green; the fragrant bouquet offers citrussy fruit and just a hint of oak. The palate has pleasant nectarine and citrus flavours. No frills, but well made.　**rating:** 87

best drinking Now **drink with** Chicken ravioli • $14.95

Kamberra Pinot Noir Chardonnay

TTTT 1999 Medium yellow-green; a complex and rich nutty/bready bouquet is followed by a palate which opens as an extension of the bouquet, but then finishes firm, with crisp acidity. A blend of Tumbarumba and Canberra material; 100 per cent malolactic fermentation.   **rating:** 87

best drinking Now–2005 **drink with** Antipasto • $25

Kamberra Shiraz

TTTTY 2001 Medium red-purple; the bouquet has a complex mix of spicy, savoury blackberry and oak aromas; the palate builds on the bouquet with ripe blackberry fruit, soft, supple tannins, and restrained oak. Canberra District grapes.   **rating:** 90

best drinking 2006–2011 **best vintages** '01 **drink with** Beef shashlik • $25

Kamberra Meeting Place Shiraz

TTTT 2001 Medium red-purple; the bouquet has blackberry and hints of earth, spice and bitter chocolate; the light-bodied palate is well balanced, with more of the blackberry fruit, but not overmuch concentration. A mixture of Hilltops and Canberra District grapes.   **rating:** 85

best drinking 2004–2008 **drink with** Veal goulash • $15

kancoona valley wines   NR

123 Morgan's Creek Road, Kancoona South, Vic 3691 **region** Alpine Valleys
phone (02) 6028 9419 **fax** (02) 6028 9051 **open** Thurs–Sun 10–5, or by appointment
winemaker Joseph Birti **production** NFP **est.** 1989
product range ($20 CD) Pinot Noir, Pinot Noir Preservative Free, Cabernet Sauvignon, Cabernet Sauvignon Preservative Free.
summary Joseph and Lena Birti began planting their vineyard in 1989, situated in a natural amphitheatre 12 kilometres from the Kiewa River, halfway between Myrtleford and Mount Beauty. Thermal breezes rising from the Kiewa River valley help protect the vines from fungal disease, and the Birtis do not use any pesticides. They made their first wines in 1999, and from the word go have offered preservative-free alternatives.

kangarilla road vineyard & winery   ★★★☆

Kangarilla Road, McLaren Vale, SA 5171 **region** McLaren Vale
phone (08) 8383 0533 **fax** (08) 8383 0044 **open** Mon–Fri 9–5, weekends 11–5
winemaker Kevin O'Brien **production** 25 000 cases **est.** 1975
product range ($12–28 CD) Chardonnay, Viognier, Zinfandel, Shiraz, Cabernet Sauvignon, Tawny Port, Vintage Port.
summary Kangarilla Road Vineyard & Winery was formerly known as Stevens Cambrai. Long-time industry identity Kevin O'Brien and wife Helen purchased the property in July 1997, and have now fully established the strikingly labelled Kangarilla Road brand in place of Cambrai. Exports to the US, the UK, Singapore and Indonesia.

Kangarilla Road Shiraz

TTTT 2001 Medium red-purple; the bouquet has blackberry fruit plus hints of leaf and mint; a medium-bodied palate revolves around blackberry fruit, a repeat of the mint of the bouquet, finishing with fine tannins. Matured for 18 months in American oak barrels of varying age.   **rating:** 86

best drinking 2005–2009 **best vintages** '97, '99 **drink with** Barbecued beef • $20

kangaroo island vines   ★★★★

c/- 413 Payneham Road, Felixstow, SA 5070 **region** Kangaroo Island
phone (08) 8365 3411 **fax** (08) 8336 2462 **open** Not
winemaker Caj Amadio **production** 600 cases **est.** 1990
product range ($20–25 ML) Island Sting, Kate's Block Shiraz, Florance Cabernet Merlot, Special Reserve Cabernet Merlot.
summary Kangaroo Island is another venture of Caj and Genny Amadio, with the wines being sold through the Chain of Ponds cellar door. The Amadios have been the focal point of the development of vineyards on Kangaroo Island, producing the wines not only from their own tiny planting of 450 vines on 0.25 acre, but buying grapes from other vignerons on the island. The tiny quantities of wine so far produced strongly support the notion that Kangaroo Island has an excellent climate for Bordeaux-style reds, particularly the excellent Special Reserve Cabernet Merlot. Rated on the basis of previous tastings.

kangderaar vineyard   NR

Wehla–Kingower Road, Rheola, Vic 3517   **region** Bendigo
phone (03) 5438 8292   **fax** (03) 5438 8292   **open** Mon–Sat 9–5, Sun 10–5
winemaker James Nealy   **production** 800 cases   **est.** 1980
product range Riesling Traminer, Sauvignon Blanc, Chardonnay, Carmine, Cabernet Merlot, Rheola Gold (White Port), Vintage Port (Touriga).
summary The 4.5-hectare vineyard is situated at Rheola, near the Melville Caves, said to have been the hideout of the bushranger Captain Melville in the 1850s, and surrounded by the Kooyoora State Park. It is owned by James and Christine Nealy.

kanjara   NR

Cargo Road, Orange, NSW 2800   **region** Orange
phone (02) 6365 6148   **fax** (02) 6365 6148   **open** Not
winemaker Jan Carter, Mark Davidson (Contract)   **production** 130 cases   **est.** 1994
product range ($14.50–16 ML) Riesling, Chardonnay, Shiraz, Tiffin Cabernet Sauvignon.
summary Since 1994 Kanjara has progressively established 2.5 hectares of riesling, shiraz and cabernet sauvignon. Grapes have been produced on a commercial basis for 4 years, but the first wines (Riesling, Shiraz and Cabernet Sauvignon) were released at the 2001 October Winefest at Orange.

kara kara vineyard   ★★★☆

Sunraysia Highway, St Arnaud, Vic 3478 (10 km sth St Arnaud)   **region** Pyrenees
phone (03) 5496 3294   **fax** (03) 5496 3294   **open** Mon–Fri 10.30–6, weekends 9–6
winemaker John Ellis, Steve Zsigmond   **production** 2500 cases   **est.** 1977
product range ($20–29 CD) Sauvignon Blanc, Chardonnay, Shiraz, Cabernet Sauvignon.
summary Hungarian-born Steve Zsigmond comes from a long line of vignerons and sees Kara Kara as the eventual retirement occupation for himself and wife Marlene. He is a graduate of the Adelaide University Roseworthy campus wine marketing course, and worked for Yalumba and Negociants as a sales manager in Adelaide and Perth. He looks after sales and marketing from the Melbourne premises of Kara Kara, and the wine is contract-made by John Ellis, with consistent results. Draws upon 9 hectares of estate plantings.

Kara Kara Sauvignon Blanc
TTTT 2002 Light to medium yellow-green; the clean bouquet has neutral fruit with some latent power and mineral lurking; the medium-bodied palate tends to be broad and is not particularly well focused.   **rating:** 84
best drinking Now   **drink with** Seafood risotto • $20

Kara Kara Shiraz
TTTT 2001 Medium to full red-purple; clean, fresh red berry fruit aromas open up significantly on the ripe, multi-berry and plum palate; the structure is still linear, but will develop.   **rating:** 88
best drinking 2006–2012   **best vintages** '00   **drink with** Beef casserole • $27

Kara Kara Cabernet Sauvignon
TTTT 2001 Medium red-purple; the bouquet has smooth, ripe blackcurrant and mulberry fruit, largely untrammelled by oak; the medium-bodied palate has abundant red and black fruit flavours, simply needing more time for integration with the tannins, but with plenty of flavour.   **rating:** 87
best drinking 2006–2011   **drink with** T-bone steak • $27

karina vineyard   ★★★★

35 Harrisons Road, Dromana, Vic 3936   **region** Mornington Peninsula
phone (03) 5981 0137   **fax** (03) 5981 0137   **open** Weekends 11–5, 7 days in January
winemaker Gerard Terpstra   **production** 2000 cases   **est.** 1984
product range ($12–19 CD) Riesling, Sauvignon Blanc, Chardonnay, Pinot Noir, Cabernet Merlot.
summary A typical Mornington Peninsula vineyard, situated in the Dromana/Red Hill area on rising, north-facing slopes, just 3 kilometres from the shores of Port Phillip Bay, immaculately tended and with picturesque garden surrounds. Fragrant Riesling and cashew-accented Chardonnay are usually its best wines. Exports to Japan.

Karina Riesling

ΨΨΨΨ 2002 Light green-yellow; fresh and crisp apple and mineral aromas and flavours are utterly typical of the vineyard. The palate has good length and a firm finish; well made, as ever. **rating:** 89

best drinking Now–2008 **best vintages** '94, '97, '98, '01 **drink with** Crab, mussels • $15

karl seppelt ★★★☆

Ross Dewells Road, Springton, SA 5235 **region** Eden Valley
phone (08) 8568 2378 **fax** (08) 8568 2799 **open** 7 days 10–5
winemaker Karl Seppelt **production** 5000 cases **est.** 1981
product range ($14–20 CD) Rhine Riesling, Chardonnay, Chardonnay Brut, Brut Sauvage, Sparkling Shiraz, Shiraz, Merlot, Cabernet Sauvignon, Flor Fino Sherry, Vintage Port, Tawny Port, Liqueur Muscat.
summary After experimenting with various label designs and names, Karl Seppelt (former marketing director of Seppelt) has decided to discontinue the brand name Grand Cru (although retaining it as a business name) and henceforth market the wines from his estate vineyards under his own name; the wines are now made at a small winery constructed on the property. The quality is highly consistent across the range, and the wines are exported to Canada and Germany.

🐌 karri grove estate ★★★☆

PO Box 432, Margaret River, WA 6285 **region** Margaret River
phone (08) 9757 6281 **fax** (08) 9757 6353 **open** Not
winemaker Mark Lane (white), David O'Leary (red) (Contract) **production** 3000 cases **est.** 1991
product range ($14–18 ML) Sauvignon Blanc Semillon, Verdelho, Shiraz, Merlot, Cabernet Sauvignon.
summary Karri Grove Estate is loosely associated with Flinders Bay, from which it purchases most of its grapes. The white wines are made at Flying Fish Cove in the Margaret River region, but the grapes for the red wines are transported to South Australia, where they are contract-made by David O'Leary. Distribution is via wholesale distributors in New South Wales (Young and Rashleigh), Victoria (Sullivan Wine Agencies) and Queensland (Premier Small Vineyards). There is also limited availability by mail order.

Karri Grove Estate Shiraz

ΨΨΨΨ 2000 Bright purple-red; there are complex savoury, spicy overtones to the dark blackberry fruit of the bouquet; the palate has good fruit depth and intensity, albeit surprisingly undeveloped, with the French oak subtle. It almost makes one wonder whether it has not undergone malolactic fermentation. **rating:** 88

best drinking 2005–2010 **drink with** Rare roast beef • $18

Karri Grove Estate Merlot

ΨΨΨΩ 2001 Clear, medium red-purple; there are distinct leafy/savoury/earthy/tobacco aromas which are clearly varietal, but the acidic palate suggests the grapes were picked too early. **rating:** 84

best drinking 2005–2008 **drink with** Braised veal • $18

karriview ★★★★

Cnr Scotsdale and Roberts Roads, Denmark, WA 6333 **region** Great Southern
phone (08) 9840 9381 **fax** (08) 9855 1549 **open** Fri–Sun 11–4, school and public holidays 7 days 11–4
winemaker Elizabeth Smith **production** 550 cases **est.** 1986
product range ($25–32 R) Chardonnay, Pinot Noir.
summary One and a half hectares each of immaculately tended pinot noir and chardonnay on ultra-close spacing produce tiny quantities of two wines of at times remarkable intensity, quality and style. Available only from the winery, but worth the effort. There is some vintage variation; the winery rating is based on the successes, not the disappointments. Typically, back vintages are available; with age, the Pinot Noir acquires strong foresty characters which are quite Burgundian.

Karriview Chardonnay

ΨΨΨΩ 2001 Light to medium yellow-green; the bouquet is clean and relatively subdued, and the palate is tight, crisp and minerally, the oak influence restrained. May well flesh out with more bottle age. **rating:** 84

best drinking Now–2005 **best vintages** '90, '92, '93, '95, '98, '99 **drink with** Marron, yabbies • $25

Karriview Pinot Noir

ΨΨΨΩ 2001 Developed, light red-purple; the spicy, savoury, foresty bouquet is reflected in the light, very savoury/foresty palate, which needs more fruit intensity and sweetness. **rating:** 84

best drinking Now **best vintages** '90, '91, '92, '94 **drink with** Quail salad • $32

katnook estate ★★★★☆

Riddoch Highway, Coonawarra, SA 5263 **region** Coonawarra
phone (08) 8737 2394 **fax** (08) 8737 2397 **open** Mon–Fri 9–4.30, weekends 10–4.30
winemaker Wayne Stehbens **production** 120 000 cases **est.** 1979
product range ($17–80 R) Under the premium Katnook label: Riesling, Sauvignon Blanc, Chardonnay, Chardonnay Brut, Shiraz, Merlot, Cabernet Sauvignon, Odyssey (super-premium Cabernet), Prodigy (super-premium Shiraz); under the Riddoch label: Sauvignon Blanc, Chardonnay, Sparkling Shiraz, Shiraz, Cabernet Shiraz, Cabernet Merlot.
summary Still one of the largest contract grape growers and suppliers in Coonawarra, selling more than half of its grape production to others. The historic stone woolshed in which the second vintage in Coonawarra (1896) was made and which has served Katnook since 1980 is being restored. Together the 1997 launch of the flagship Odyssey and the 2000 follow-up Prodigy Shiraz point the way for a higher profile for the winemaking side of the venture. In a surprise (and not widely publicised) move, Freixenet, the Spanish cava producer, has recently acquired 60 per cent of Katnook. Exports to the UK, Europe, Asia and the US.

Katnook Estate Riesling

▼▼▼▼▽ 2002 Light straw-green; firm, flinty, flowery, lemony aromas lead into a palate with intense entry and big, powerful mid-palate flavour; after a heartbeat, the finish returns. In other words, there is a slight break in the line of the palate. **rating:** 90

best drinking 2005–2010 **best vintages** '00, '02 **drink with** Vegetable terrine • $20

Riddoch Chardonnay

▼▼▼▼▽ 2001 Brilliant yellow-green, the attractively smooth bouquet has nectarine fruit woven through subtle oak; the medium-bodied palate follows suit with fresh melon and nectarine fruit. Delicious. **rating:** 91

best drinking Now **best vintages** '01 **drink with** Pan-fried veal • $17

Katnook Estate Shiraz

▼▼▼▼▽ 2001 Medium red-purple; the complex bouquet has cedary, savoury spicy aromas in typical vineyard style; it is these characters which lead the palate, although black fruits do make their appearance; the wine scores principally on its satiny mouthfeel, fine tannins and extract. **rating:** 91

best drinking 2006–2012 **best vintages** '98, '00 **drink with** Rack of veal • $40

Katnook Estate Prodigy Shiraz

▼▼▼▼▼ 1999 Medium to full red-purple; complex, ripe mulberry, blackberry, bramble, spice and cedar aromas come rippling through the bouquet; a similarly complex and intense palate, with good balance and length. The oak has not been overplayed (this has been a problem in some vintages). **rating:** 94

best drinking 2004–2014 **best vintages** '97, '99 **drink with** Wild game • $80

Katnook Estate Merlot

▼▼▼▼▽ 2000 Medium red-purple; the fragrant bouquet has berry and olive varietal character supported by well-balanced and integrated oak; the sweet plummy fruit of the palate is similarly well supported by soft tannins and balanced oak. **rating:** 90

best drinking Now–2008 **best vintages** '00 **drink with** Roast wing rib of beef with mushrooms • $40

Riddoch Cabernet Merlot

▼▼▼▼ 2000 Medium red-purple; the bouquet is clean, the fruit ripe, but with some earthy regional notes; the underlying ripeness comes through on the sweet blackberry and blackcurrant palate, although here, too, there are touches of mint and earth. **rating:** 86

best drinking 2004–2008 **drink with** Lamb sausages • $20

Katnook Estate Cabernet Sauvignon

▼▼▼▼▼ 2000 Medium red, with the purple just starting to diminish; a bouquet of spice, bramble and blackberry woven through integrated French oak is followed by an altogether warmer palate, with chocolate, mocha and blackberry flavours, sweet oak and ripe tannins. **rating:** 94

best drinking 2005–2015 **best vintages** '90, '91, '92, '94, '97, '98, '00 **drink with** Prime rib of beef • $40

Katnook Estate Odyssey Cabernet Sauvignon

▼▼▼▼▼ 1998 Medium red-purple; the complex bouquet boasts a seamless marriage of oak (first) and fruit (second); the palate has very good texture and structure, blackcurrant fruit coming to the fore, leaving the tannins in an appropriate support role. **rating:** 95

best drinking 2004–2020 **best vintages** '91, '92, '94, '96, '97, '98 **drink with** Yearling beef • $80

kay bros amery ★★★★

Kay Road, McLaren Vale, SA 5171 **region** McLaren Vale
phone (08) 8323 8211 **fax** (08) 8323 9199 **open** Mon–Fri 9–5, weekends and public holidays 12–5
winemaker Colin Kay **production** 10 000 cases **est.** 1890
product range ($20–45 CD) Shiraz, Block 6 Shiraz, Hillside Shiraz, Shiraz Mourvedre Grenache, Merlot, Cabernet Sauvignon; Founders Very Old Tawny Solera, Liqueur Muscat.
summary A traditional winery with a rich history and nearly 20 hectares of priceless old vines; while the white wines have been variable, the red wines and fortified wines can be very good. Of particular interest is Block 6 Shiraz, made from 100-year-old vines; both vines and wine are going from strength to strength. Exports to New Zealand, Singapore, the US and Canada.

Kay Bros Amery Block 6 Shiraz

▼▼▼▼▼ **2000** Medium to full red-purple; rich, ripe dark plum, prune, chocolate and earth aromas lead into a soft and plush fruit-driven palate, ripe but by no means jammy, and with fine tannins aiding the excellent balance and length. From the 1.6 hectares of 108-year-old vines. 13.7° alcohol.   **rating:** 94
best drinking 2005–2020 **best vintages** '89, '91, '92, '93, '94, '00 **drink with** Jugged hare • $45

Kay Bros Amery Hillside Shiraz

▼▼▼▼▽ **2000** Medium red-purple; a mix of dark berry, blackberry, plum, earth and chocolate on the bouquet precede a medium-bodied palate with gently sweet fruit, excellent mouthfeel and texture; fine, savoury tannins.
                                                                                        rating: 90
best drinking 2005–2015 **best vintages** '98, '99, '00 **drink with** Braised beef • $35

Kay Bros Amery Shiraz Mourvedre Grenache

▼▼▼▼ **2000** Medium red-purple; a clean, smooth, direct juicy/spicy fruit-driven bouquet, then a palate in which the McLaren Vale chocolate comes through loud and clear, finishing with soft, fine tannins. Nice structure.   **rating:** 87
best drinking Now–2007 **drink with** Smoked beef • $22

Kay Bros Amery Merlot

▼▼▼▼ **2000** Strong and bright purple-red; distinctly ripe and sweet raspberry and blackberry aromas lead into a palate which is even riper than the bouquet suggests in terms of flavour, and a very long way from the right bank of Bordeaux. Interestingly, the alcohol is only 13°.   **rating:** 86
best drinking Now–2007 **drink with** Marinated beef • $22

Kay Bros Amery Cabernet Sauvignon

▼▼▼▼▽ **2000** Medium red-purple; solid blackberry/blackcurrant/chocolate fruit on the bouquet and palate are all in far better balance than the 1999, the ripe tannins particularly so. Subtle oak; good balance and length.
                                                                                        rating: 90
best drinking 2005–2010 **best vintages** '98, '00 **drink with** Herbed rack of lamb • $22

keith tulloch wine ★★★★★

Lilywood Farm, O'Connors Road, Pokolbin, NSW 2325 **region** Lower Hunter Valley
phone (02) 4990 7867 **fax** (02) 4990 7171 **open** Not
winemaker Keith Tulloch **production** 6500 cases **est.** 1997
product range ($16–44 R) Under the Keith Tulloch label: Semillon, Chardonnay, Kester Shiraz, Merlot, Forres Blend (Cabernet Sauvignon, Petit Verdot, Merlot); Perdiem label has Verdelho, Chardonnay, Shiraz, Cabernet Sauvignon.
summary Keith Tulloch is, of course, a member of the Tulloch family which has played such a leading role in the Hunter Valley for over a century. Formerly a winemaker at Lindemans and then Rothbury Estate, he is responsible for the production of Evans Family Wines as well as developing his own label since 1997. Currently moves are underway to centralise all the winemaking at Hunter Ridge Winery, where he will be permanently based. I cannot remember being more impressed with an initial release of wines than with those under the Keith Tulloch label. The only problem is the small scale of their production, like that of Jeffrey Grosset in his early days. There is the same almost obsessive attention to detail, the same almost ascetic intellectual approach, the same refusal to accept anything but the best.

Keith Tulloch Semillon

ŢŢŢŢŢ **2002** Light straw-green; a complex and intense bouquet shows herb and mineral, with just the barest hint of oak. The long palate builds intensity progressively, the oak contributing to the texture rather than the flavour. Every bit as impressive as the 2000. Only 400 cases made. **rating:** 95

best drinking Now–2013 **best vintages** '00, '02 **drink with** Teppanyaki seafood • $28

Keith Tulloch Chardonnay

ŢŢŢŢŢ **2002** Light to medium yellow-green; strong barrel-ferment aromas mark a complex bouquet, with the melon and fig fruit uncompromised. The components come into balance on the palate, which has excellent line and balance. **rating:** 93

best drinking Now–2006 **best vintages** '98, '01, '02 **drink with** Blue-eyed cod • $29

Keith Tulloch Kester Shiraz

ŢŢŢŢŢ **2001** Medium red-purple; the moderately intense bouquet has distinctly regional savoury, spice, hay and straw aromas, but on the palate blackberry and plum fruit come through strongly, with very fine, soft tannins; delicious texture. **rating:** 92

best drinking 2006–2016 **best vintages** '98, '99, '00, '01 **drink with** Rare fillet of beef • $44

kellermeister/trevor jones ★★★☆

Barossa Valley Highway, Lyndoch, SA 5351 **region** Barossa Valley
phone (08) 8524 4303 **fax** (08) 8524 4880 **open** 7 days 9–6
winemaker Trevor Jones **production** 25 000 cases **est.** 1996
product range ($14–72.50 CD) Kellermeister Sauvignon Blanc Semillon, Semillon, Colombard, Blue Moon Chardonnay, Frontignac Auslese, Sparkling, Red Cebo, Black Sash Shiraz, Shiraz Merlot, Merlot, Cabernet Sauvignon, Ports and Liqueurs. Under the Trevor Jones label: Riesling, Dry Grown Shiraz, Wild Witch Shiraz, Boots Grenache, SAFM Shiraz Cabernet, Cabernet Merlot.
summary Trevor Jones is an industry veteran, with vast experience in handling fruit from the Barossa Valley, Eden Valley and Adelaide Hills. He has finally taken the step of introducing his own strikingly designed label, using grapes purchased from various contract growers, with the first wines going on sale in 1996. Exports to the US (very successful) and Japan.

Trevor Jones Eden Valley Riesling

ŢŢŢŢ **2002** Light straw-green; clean, direct, crisp minerally aromas are followed by a palate with light fruit and some low-level residual sweetness. Unusually packaged in a white Bordeaux-shaped bottle (with a cork). **rating:** 84

best drinking Now–2005 **drink with** Fresh artichoke with hollandaise sauce • $17.50

Trevor Jones Dry Grown Barossa Shiraz

ŢŢŢŢ **1999** Medium to full red-purple; the bouquet is clean, with lifted, ripe raspberry and blackberry fruit supported by obvious oak; on the palate, the rich, powerful, compact dark fruit flavours have soaked up the oak; finishes with soft tannins. I found the '98 over the top; this is not. **rating:** 91

best drinking 2005–2015 **best vintages** '95, '96, '99 **drink with** Beef Wellington • $39

🐌 kells creek vineyards ★★★

Kells Creek Road, Mittagong, NSW 2575 **region** Southern New South Wales Zone
phone (02) 4878 5096 **fax** (02) 4878 5097 **open** Wed–Sun 10–4, public holidays 10–5, or by appointment
winemaker Eric Priebee **est.** 2001
product range ($13–25 CD) Riesling, Sauvignon Blanc, Chardonnay, Chloe's Red (Pinot Noir); Swifts Lane Maddie's White, Maddie's Red (on-premise only).
summary Kells Creek is one of the newer businesses to open in the rapidly expanding Southern Highlands region. It has been established by Eric Priebee and wife Gaby Barfield, and draws principally on other vineyards established in the Southern Highlands region around Mittagong, Moss Vale and Aylmerton. The one wine not to come from the Southern Highlands is a 2000 Pinot Noir, made before the establishment of Kells Creek, but which is of excellent quality. Kells Creek itself has 1 hectare of riesling planted, and operates an energetic marketing program under the direction of industry veteran Douglas Hamilton. Full details are available on the website and/or via email.

Kells Creek Chardonnay

TTTY 2001 Medium straw-green; the bouquet is clean, although the fruit aromas are somewhat neutral; the palate opens up rather more, with some citrus and nectarine fruit; balanced but subtle oak on a lightly framed wine. **rating:** 84

best drinking Now **drink with** Lemon chicken • $25

Kells Creek Chloe's Red

TTTT 2000 Strong red-purple, particularly for pinot noir; the clean bouquet has a mix of cherry and more spicy characters; the powerful palate has abundant plum and cherry fruit together with lingering tannins providing a solid textural base. Needs time; will develop. Made from pinot noir grown in Tumbarumba. **rating:** 89

best drinking Now–2007 **drink with** Squab • $25

kellybrook ★★★☆

Fulford Road, Wonga Park, Vic 3115 **region** Yarra Valley
phone (03) 9722 1304 **fax** (03) 9722 2092 **open** Mon 11–5, Tues–Sat 9–6, Sun 11–6
winemaker Darren Kelly, Philip Kelly **production** 3000 cases **est.** 1960
product range ($15–45 CD) Riesling, Gewurztraminer, Chardonnay, Pinot Noir, Shiraz, Cabernet Merlot, Brut Pinot Noir Chardonnay, Champagne Cider, Apple Brandy, Liqueur Muscat, Old Vintage Tawny Port.
summary The 8-hectare vineyard is situated at Wonga Park, the entrance to the principal wine-growing areas of the Yarra Valley, and has a picnic area and a full-scale restaurant. As well as table wine, a very competent producer of both cider and apple brandy (in Calvados style). A range of tank samples from the 2002 vintage all showed great promise; Kellybrook's bottling schedule and my writing schedule seem forever out of step. Retail distribution through Victoria, New South Wales and Queensland; exports to the UK.

Kellybrook Riesling

TTTT 2002 Light straw-green; the bouquet is clean, but rather muted and lacking expression; the story changes markedly on the palate, which is quite focused, with light lime, herb and slightly minerally flavours. **rating:** 86

best drinking Now–2006 **drink with** Ginger prawns • $18

kelly's creek ★★★★

RSD 226a, Lower Whitehills Road, Relbia, Tas 7258 **region** Northern Tasmania
phone (03) 6234 9696 **fax** (03) 6231 6222 **open** Not
winemaker Andrew Hood (Contract) **production** 650 cases **est.** 1992
product range ($15–18 R) Riesling, Chardonnay, Pinot Noir, Cabernet Sauvignon.
summary Kelly's Creek draws on 1 hectare of riesling and 0.2 hectare each of chardonnay, pinot noir and cabernet sauvignon. Its majority owner is Darryl Johnson, who runs the vineyard with help from Guy Wagner, who describes himself as 'merely a marketing minion'. Small quantities of Riesling are made for Kelly's Creek; all vintages have had notable success at the Tasmanian Wines Show.

Kelly's Creek Riesling

TTTT 2001 Medium yellow-green; there is abundant fruit on the slightly old-fashioned bouquet; the palate is very generous and very flavoursome; another wine for enjoyment over the next year or two. **rating:** 87

best drinking Now–2006 **best vintages** '96, '97 **drink with** Carpaccio of salmon • $15

Kelly's Creek Chardonnay

TTTTY 2001 Medium to full yellow-green; a complex and moderately rich bouquet with barrel-ferment inputs leads into a palate with ripe melon and fig; harmonious oak; well above-average total flavour. **rating:** 92

best drinking Now–2007 **best vintages** '01 **drink with** Chinese prawns • $18

kelman vineyards ★★★☆

Cnr Oakey Creek Road and Mount View Road, Pokolbin, NSW 2320 **region** Lower Hunter Valley
phone (02) 4991 5456 **fax** (02) 4991 7555 **open** 7 days 10–5
winemaker Simon Gilbert (Contract) **production** 3000 cases **est.** 1999
product range ($14.50–20 CD) Orchard Block Semillon, Pond Block Chardonnay, Lakeview Lane Shiraz.
summary Kelman Vineyards is a California-type development on the outskirts of Cessnock. A 40-hectare property has been subdivided into 80 residential development lots, but with 8 hectares of vines wending between the lots under common ownership. In a sign of the times, part of the chardonnay has already been

grafted across to shiraz before coming into full production, and the vineyard has the potential to ultimately produce 8000 cases a year. In the meantime, each owner will receive 12 cases a year of the wines produced by the vineyard, with the balance being available for sale via mail order (phone (02) 4991 5456 for details) and through a single Sydney retail outlet. The Chardonnay is a nice, fresh wine, with light melon fruit, free of the dreaded oak chips.

🐚 kelso   NR

Princes Highway, Narrawong, Vic 3285 **region** Henty
phone (03) 5529 2334 **open** By appointment
winemaker Contract **est.** NA
product range Riesling, Cabernet Sauvignon.
summary Howard and Glenda Simmonds have established their vineyard 11 kilometres east of Portland, and produce Riesling and Cabernet Sauvignon.

kenilworth bluff wines   NR

Lot 13 Bluff Road, Kenilworth, Qld 4574 **region** Queensland Coastal
phone (07) 5472 3723 **open** Fri–Sun 10–4, and by appointment
winemaker Bruce Humphery-Smith (Contract) **est.** 1993
product range ($13–16 CD) Semillon, Chardonnay, Shiraz, Merlot, Cabernet Sauvignon.
summary Brian and Colleen Marsh modestly describe themselves as 'little more than hobbyists', but also admit that 'our wines show tremendous promise'. They began planting the vineyards in 1993 in a hidden valley at the foot of Kenilworth Bluff, and now have 4 hectares (shiraz, cabernet sauvignon, merlot, semillon, chardonnay) coming into bearing. Presently the wines are made off-site, but one day the Marshes hope it will be feasible to establish an on-site winery.

kennedys keilor valley   NR

Lot 3 Overnewton Road, Keilor, Vic 3036 **region** Sunbury
phone (03) 9311 6246 **fax** (03) 9331 6246 **open** By appointment
winemaker Peter Dredge **production** 300 cases **est.** 1994
product range Chardonnay.
summary A small Chardonnay specialist, producing its only wine from 1.8 hectares of estate vineyards; half is sold as grapes, half is contract-made and sold by mail list and word of mouth.

kevin sobels wines   NR

Cnr Broke and Halls Roads, Pokolbin, NSW 2321 **region** Lower Hunter Valley
phone (02) 4998 7766 **fax** (02) 4998 7475 **open** 7 days (no fixed hours)
winemaker Kevin Sobels **production** 9000 cases **est.** 1992
product range ($15–25 CD) Gewurztraminer, Semillon, Verdelho, Chardonnay, Sparkling Burgundy, Traminer (Sticky), Rose, Pinot Noir, Shiraz, Cabernet Shiraz, Oak Aged Port.
summary Veteran winemaker Kevin Sobels has found yet another home, drawing upon 8 hectares of vineyards (originally planted by the Ross Jones family) to produce wines sold almost entirely through the cellar door and by mail order, with limited retail representation. The cellar door offers light meals and picnic and barbecue facilities.

kies family wines   ★★★☆

Barossa Valley Way, Lyndoch, SA 5381 **region** Barossa Valley
phone (08) 8524 4110 **fax** (08) 8524 4110 **open** 7 days 9.30–4.30
winemaker Jim Irvine **production** 2500 cases **est.** 1969
product range ($14–42 CD) Riesling, Unwooded Semillon, Wooded Semillon, White Barossa (sweet), Heysen Gold (sweet), Sparkling Heysen Gold (sweet sparkling), Gravel Road Sparkling Grenache Shiraz, Monkey Nut Tree Sparkling Merlot, Boutique Red, Klauber Block Shiraz, Dedication Shiraz, Lyndoch Creek Merlot, Chaff Mill Cabernet Sauvignon, Bastardo (Rose-style port), Tawny Port, White Muscat.
summary The Kies family has been resident in the Barossa Valley since 1857, with the present generation of winemakers being the fifth, their children the sixth. Until 1969 the family sold almost all the grapes to others, but in that year they launched their own brand, Karrawirra. The co-existence of Killawarra forced a name change in 1983 to Redgum Vineyard, and this business was in turn subsequently sold. Later still, Kies Family

Wines opened for business, drawing upon vineyards up to 100 years old which had remained in the family throughout the changes, and offering a wide range of wines through the 1880 vintage cellar door. Exports to the UK, the US, Canada and Singapore.

Kies Dedication Barossa Valley Shiraz

▼▼▼▼ 2000 Medium red-purple; the moderately intense bouquet offers nicely balanced earthy/leathery/berry shiraz with a traditional touch of vanilla oak. On the smooth palate milky fruit and oak tannins coalesce, abetted by touches of chocolate.   rating: 87

best drinking Now–2008 drink with Beef stroganoff • $42

kilgour estate   NR

85 McAdams Lane, Bellarine, Vic 3223 region Geelong
phone (03) 5251 2223 fax (03) 5251 2223 open Wed–Sun 10.30–6, 7 days in Jan
winemaker Karen Coulstone (Consultant) production 4000 cases est. 1989
product range Pinot Gris, Chardonnay, Pinot Noir, Cabernet Sauvignon, sparkling.
summary Kilgour Estate has 7 hectares of vines, and the wines are contract-made. Fruit-driven Pinot Noir and Chardonnay are winery specialties, the Pinot Noir having won at least one gold medal. The beautifully situated cellar door has a restaurant and barbecue facilities.

kilikanoon   ★★★★★

Penna Lane, Penwortham, SA 5453 region Clare Valley
phone (08) 8843 4377 fax (08) 8843 4377 open Weekends and public holidays 11–5
winemaker Kevin Mitchell production 15000 cases est. 1997
product range ($17–29 CD) Morts Block Riesling, Barrel Fermented Semillon, Sparkling Pinot Chardonnay, Second Fiddle Grenache Rose, Oracle Shiraz, Covenant Shiraz, Siblings (Shiraz Grenache), Prodigal Grenache, Blocks Road Cabernet Sauvignon, Reserve Muscat.
summary Kilikanoon has 20 hectares of estate vineyards at Leasingham and Penwortham. It had the once-in-a-lifetime experience of winning five of the six trophies awarded at the 2002 Clare Valley Wine Show, spanning Riesling, Shiraz and Cabernet, and including Best Wine of Show. Hardly surprising, then, that production has risen sharply. Wholesale distribution in South Australia, Victoria and Western Australia; exports to the US, Canada, the UK, Singapore and Hong Kong.

Kilikanoon Morts Block Riesling

▼▼▼▼▼ 2002 Light green-yellow; very fine, intense lime and mineral aromas are followed by an equally intense and particularly long palate, driven by fine, lime juice flavours; great aftertaste.   rating: 96

best drinking Now–2013 best vintages '02 drink with Sushi • $18

Kilikanoon Semillon

▼▼▼▼ 2001 Medium to full yellow-green; the oak is well balanced and integrated on the bouquet; on the palate, the oak adds to the flavour and structure equally; ripe, but not the least bit heavy. Clever winemaking.
                                                                                      rating: 89

best drinking Now–2006 drink with Vichysoisse • $17

Kilikanoon Second Fiddle Grenache Rose

▼▼▼▼ 2002 Light red-purple; the clean bouquet has a mix of black cherry, plum and spice; the light to medium-bodied palate is a halfway house between a conventional rose and a light-bodied red wine; notwithstanding the zero tannins, will stand up to food.   rating: 86

best drinking Now drink with Antipasto • $17

Kilikanoon Covenant Shiraz

▼▼▼▼▼ 2000 Medium to full purple-red; the complex bouquet has spice, fruitcake and blackberry aromas supported by subtle oak; the rich, deep blackberry fruit of the palate has some spicy/earthy notes adding to both structure and length. Estate-grown in the Leasingham region; matured in a mix of French and American oak.
                                                                                      rating: 94

best drinking 2005–2015 best vintages '00 drink with Eye fillet • $29

Kilikanoon Oracle Shiraz

▼▼▼▼▼ 2000 Medium to full purple-red; the clean, intense bouquet has blackberry and plum fruit, with excellent oak integration. The wonderfully intense and long palate brings some bitter chocolate into the equation, finishing with fine, ripe tannins. From the same vineyard as – and similar winemaking to – the Covenant Shiraz.   rating: 96

best drinking 2005–2015 best vintages '98, '00 drink with Roast shoulder of lamb • $29

Kilikanoon Prodigal Grenache

TTTT℔ **2000** Light to medium purple-red; the bouquet has rich spicy blackcurrant aromas; the palate lives up to the promise of the bouquet, with black fruits, a touch of chocolate and more texture and structure than one usually encounters with grenache. **rating:** 90

best drinking Now–2007 **drink with** Braised oxtail • $22

Kilikanoon Blocks Road Cabernet Sauvignon

TTTT℔ **2000** Medium to full red-purple; dense blackcurrant and blackberry fruit on the bouquet flow into the dense, fruit-driven black fruit and bitter chocolate palate; good control of extract. **rating:** 93

best drinking 2005–2015 **best vintages** '00 **drink with** Roast lamb • $24

killawarra ★★★☆

Tanunda Road, Nuriootpa, SA 5355 **region** Barossa Valley
phone (08) 8560 9389 **fax** (08) 8562 1669 **open** Not
winemaker Steve Goodwin **production** NFP **est.** 1975
product range ($9–15 R) Only sparkling wines: Brut, Brut Cremant, Premier Brut, Killawarra 'K' series Vintage Pinot Noir Chardonnay and Sparkling Shiraz Cabernet.
summary Purely a Southcorp brand dedicated to sparkling wine, without any particular presence in terms of either vineyards or winery, but increasingly styled in a mode different from the Seaview or Seppelt wines. As one would expect, the wines are competitively priced, and what is more, have performed well in national wine shows.

killerby ★★★★

Caves Road, Wilyabrup, WA 6280 **region** Margaret River
phone 1800 655 722 **fax** 1800 679 578 **open** Not
winemaker Mark Matthews **production** 15 000 cases **est.** 1973
product range ($19–30 CD) Semillon, Semillon Sauvignon Blanc, Sauvignon Blanc, Chardonnay, Shiraz, Cabernet Sauvignon and budget-priced April Class (Traminer Semillon Chardonnay).
summary Has moved from Geographe to the Margaret River following the acquisition of a long-established vineyard (with 23-year-old chardonnay vines) on Caves Road. It continues to own its substantial and mature vineyards in Geographe, where the wines are still made. Exports to the US and Denmark.

Killerby Semillon

TTTT **2001** Still water-white at 15 months of age; similarly, the bouquet is fresh, but with positive fruit characters yet to emerge; the commensurately tight palate opens with crisp mineral characters before touches of grass and citrus emerge on the aftertaste. The small percentage of barrel ferment in French oak has contributed more to the texture than the flavour. Unlimited development potential. **rating:** 88

best drinking 2004–2010 **best vintages** '99 **drink with** Grilled scampi • $19

Killerby Sauvignon Blanc

TTTT **2001** Light straw-green; obvious barrel-ferment aromas are the driving force of the bouquet and of the palate; less oak would have been better, but the wine does have good length. One hundred per cent barrel fermented in French oak, and matured in that oak for 5 months. **rating:** 86

best drinking Now–2006 **best vintages** '98 **drink with** Cold seafood • $19

Killerby Chardonnay

TTTT **2001** Light straw-green; typically restrained aromas with a mix of mineral and stone fruit are repeated on the palate; altogether belies its 14.5° alcohol, but still fails to excite even though the base material is better. **rating:** 86

best drinking Now–2006 **best vintages** '89, '92, '93, '94, '97, '98 **drink with** Chicken supreme • $30

Killerby Shiraz

TTTT℔ **2000** Bright and strong red-purple; the clean, lusciously rich bouquet has a mix of dark plum and blackberry which come through on the powerful palate with its rippling tannins and long finish. Impressive. **rating:** 90

best drinking 2004–2010 **best vintages** '91, '92, '94, '98, '99, '00 **drink with** Game pie • $24

Killerby Cabernet Sauvignon

TTTT **2000** Medium to full red-purple; an earthy/savoury bouquet matches austere Cabernet Sauvignon with well-integrated oak; the very powerful palate offers abundant dark fruits and (at this juncture) formidable tannins. Will take years to be easily approachable. **rating:** 89

best drinking 2006–2011 **best vintages** '87, '89, '92, '93, '94, '96, '99 **drink with** Mature cheddar • $24

kimbarra wines ★★★★

422 Barkly Street, Ararat, Vic 3377 **region** Grampians
phone (03) 5352 2238 **fax** (03) 5342 1950 **open** Mon–Fri 9–5
winemaker Peter Leeke, Ian McKenzie **production** 1000 cases **est.** 1990
product range ($14–22 CD) Riesling, Shiraz, Cabernet Sauvignon.
summary Peter and David Leeke have established 12 hectares of riesling, shiraz and cabernet sauvignon, the three varieties overall which have proved best suited to the Grampians region. The particularly well-made wines deserve a wider audience.

Kimbarra Riesling

▼▼▼▼♈ **2002** Light straw-green; a clean and fresh bouquet, with the aromatics still largely locked up, is followed by a palate with an attractive, minerally grip promising much for the future; well above-average length. Great value. **rating:** 91

best drinking 2005–2012 **best vintages** '02 **drink with** Sashimi • $14

Kimbarra Shiraz

▼▼▼▼♈ **2000** Medium to full red-purple, bright and clear; the clean, moderately intense bouquet mixes dark berry with earth, spice and cedar characters; the palate mirrors the bouquet, but with excellent mouthfeel and balance sustained by ripe tannins and positive oak. **rating:** 92

best drinking 2005–2012 **best vintages** '00 **drink with** Lasagne • $22

Kimbarra Cabernet Sauvignon

▼▼▼▼ **2000** Medium purple-red; focused, moderately intense, blackberry/blackcurrant fruit leads into an elegant medium-bodied palate with fine, savoury flavours and firm acidity to close. The points may well prove parsimonious. **rating:** 88

best drinking 2005–2010 **best vintages** '99 **drink with** Rack of lamb • $20

🐌 kimber wines NR

Chalk Hill Road, McLaren Vale, SA 5171 (PO Box 113, McLaren Vale) **region** McLaren Vale
phone (08) 8323 9773 **fax** (08) 8323 9773 **open** 7 days Dec–Apr 9–6, or by appointment
winemaker Reg Wilkinson **production** 300 cases **est.** 1996
product range ($11.50–16 CD) Unwooded Chardonnay, Cabernet Sauvignon.
summary Kimber Wines is primarily a grape grower, selling its production from 2.5 hectares each of chardonnay and cabernet sauvignon, and 0.6 hectare of petit verdot to other, larger producers. A very small amount of its grapes are retained and vinified under the Kimber Wines label, typically selling out within a few months of release through the cellar door (hence the restricted opening hours). An added attraction is pick-your-own fruit (peaches, apricots and plums) during the summer months.

Kimber Cabernet Sauvignon

▼▼▼▼ **2001** Medium purple-red; the bouquet has ripe, almost essency, blackberry and blackcurrant fruit, suggesting that the wine may be overripe. In fact the palate has good mouthfeel, with fine, satiny tannins and ripe fruit, but no alcohol burn. Nice wine. **rating:** 89

best drinking Now–2008 **drink with** Braised oxtail • $16

king river estate ★★★

RMB 9300, Wangaratta, Vic 3677 **region** King Valley
phone (03) 5729 3689 **fax** (03) 5729 3688 **open** Weekends, or by appointment
winemaker Trevor Knaggs **production** 2500 cases **est.** 1996
product range ($18–22 CD) Verdelho, Chardonnay, Nancy Shiraz, Merlot, Cabernet Sauvignon.
summary Trevor Knaggs, with the assistance of his father Collin (sic) began the establishment of King River Estate in 1990, making the first wines in 1996. The initial plantings were 3.3 hectares each of chardonnay and cabernet sauvignon, followed by 8 hectares of merlot and 3 hectares of shiraz. More recent plantings have extended the varietal range with verdelho, viognier, barbera and sangiovese, lifting the total plantings to a substantial 18 hectares. Home-stay accommodation is available in the farm-style guest house. Needless to say, bookings are essential.

kings creek winery NR

237 Myers Road, Bittern, Vic 3918 **region** Mornington Peninsula
phone (03) 5983 2102 **fax** (03) 5983 5153 **open** Not

winemaker NA **production** 3500 cases **est.** 1981
product range ($16–30 R) Sauvignon Blanc, Chardonnay, Reserve Chardonnay, Pinot Noir, Reserve Pinot Noir, Shiraz, Cabernet Sauvignon.
summary The implosion of Kings Creek, which started several years ago, and continued a year ago with the sale of the home vineyard block, has resulted in the dismemberment of the whole business; Graham and Dorothy Turner purchased the name Kings Creek and acquired the original home block, but are as yet not sure whether to rework the trellis system, changing it from lyre to vertical spur position, and whether, if they do that, they will be grape growers pure and simple, or part grape growers and part winemakers. The 2003 crop was sold to T'Gallant, which brought the wheel full circle, for it was Kevin and Kathleen McCarthy who were the original winemaker and vineyard managers. The other two parcels of land were sold at give-away prices; the intentions of the purchasers are unknown.

kingsley   NR

6 Kingsley Court, Portland, Vic 3305 **region** Henty
phone (03) 5523 1864 **fax** (03) 5523 1644 **open** 7 days 1–4
winemaker Contract **production** 500 cases **est.** 1983
product range ($14–16 CD) Riesling, Chardonnay, Botrytis Riesling, Cabernet Sauvignon.
summary Only a small part of the 10 hectares is made into wine under contract, the remainder being sold as grapes. Older vintages are sometimes available at the cellar door; tasting is strongly recommended, as there appears to be significant vintage variation.

kings of kangaroo ground   NR

15 Graham Road, Kangaroo Ground, Vic 3097 **region** Yarra Valley
phone (03) 9712 0666 **fax** (03) 9712 0566 **open** Mon–Sat 10–6, Sun 12–6
winemaker Ken King, Geoff Anson, Neil Johannesen **production** 600 cases **est.** 1990
product range ($16–45 CD) Chardonnay, Pinot Noir, Multi-vintage Pinot Noir, Shiraz, Yarra Valley Cabernet Merlot, Cabernet Sauvignon.
summary Ken King's involvement in wine began back in 1984, when he became an amateur member of the Eltham and District Winemakers Guild. Around that time, the Guild was asked to manage a tiny (0.1 ha) experimental vineyard planted on the rich volcanic soil of Kangaroo Ground. In 1988 Ken King purchased a little under 3 hectares of similar land, which he describes as 'chocolate cake', and established 1 hectare of chardonnay and 0.6 hectare of pinot noir in 1990. Until 2000, the grapes were sold to Diamond Valley, but each year King retained sufficient grapes to produce a barrel or two of Pinot Noir per vintage, and began experimenting with multi-vintage blends of pinot with up to 5 years of continuous aging in French barriques. The wines have been well received at amateur wine shows, and the planned cellar door has now opened.

kingston estate   ★★★

Sturt Highway, Kingston-on-Murray, SA 5331 **region** Riverland
phone (08) 8130 4500 **fax** (08) 8130 4511 **open** By appointment
winemaker Bill Moularadellis **production** 100 000 cases **est.** 1979
product range ($8–20 R) Empiric Selection Arneis, Verdelho, Chardonnay, Semillon Sauvignon Blanc, Tessera Chardonnay Viognier, Shiraz, Cabernet Sauvignon, Merlot; Tessera (Cabernet blend); Sarantos Soft Press Chardonnay, Merlot; Special Releases of Saprian NV, Durif, Zinfandel, Viognier; Reserve range of Chardonnay, Shiraz, Merlot, Petit Verdot; Ashwood Grove Chardonnay, Shiraz; Chambers Creek Chardonnay, Cabernet Sauvignon.
summary Kingston Estate is a substantial and successful Riverland winery, crushing 10 000 tonnes a year and exporting 80 per cent of its production. It is only in recent years that it has turned its attention to the domestic market, with national distribution. It has also set up long-term purchase contracts with growers in the Clare Valley, the Adelaide Hills, Langhorne Creek and Mount Benson, and embarked on a programme of expanding its varietal range. It seems also to have seized the opportunity to significantly increase its prices.

Kingston Estate Tessera Chardonnay Viognier

TTTT 2001 Medium yellow-green; the bouquet is quite rich and complex, with slightly oily fruit typical of viognier; there is plenty of fruit weight and flavour to the palate, which is at the big end of town. An 80/20 blend of Chardonnay and Viognier grown in the Adelaide Hills, with a small percentage of the Chardonnay barrel fermented. Drink soon, but excellent value.   **rating:** 87
best drinking Now **drink with** Rich fish dishes • $13.95

Kingston Estate Empiric Selection Arneis

TTTT 2001 Bright, light green-yellow; the clean and fresh bouquet has light aromatics offering hints of melon and honeydew. The similarly clean and fresh palate is sustained by quite pronounced acidity; an interesting wine, grown in the hot Riverland as opposed to the cool Italian hills around Alba. **rating:** 85

best drinking Now **drink with** Antipasto • $18

Kingston Estate Verdelho

TTTT 2002 Light to medium yellow-green; the clean bouquet has fruit salad and tropical aromas utterly typical of the variety; the light to medium-bodied palate is clean, well made, and nicely balanced. Good example of the variety. **rating:** 85

best drinking Now **drink with** Chinese pork • $13

Kingston Estate Chardonnay

TTTY 2002 Light to medium yellow-green; strong, sawdusty, chippy oak dominates the bouquet; the palate has fair fruit and length, but slightly green/raw notes come from the oak. An astonishing gold medal at the Royal Queensland Wine Show 2002. **rating:** 83

best drinking Now **drink with** Takeaway • $13

Kingston Estate Shiraz

TTTY 2001 Medium red-purple; the moderately intense bouquet mixes cherry and earth with a hint of oak; well made, with plenty of presence, but the tannins need to soften. **rating:** 84

best drinking 2004–2007 **drink with** Spaghetti bolognese • $13.50

Kingston Estate Merlot

TTTT 2000 Medium red-purple; distinctly tangy lemon and olive varietal aromas lead into a light to medium-bodied palate with a similar flavour spectrum, savoury and verging on green. Better this than varietal neutrality. Well priced. **rating:** 85

best drinking Now–2006 **drink with** Tortellini • $13.50

Kingston Estate Cabernet Sauvignon

TTTT 2000 Medium red-purple; soft red and blackcurrant fruit is supported by gently sweet oak on the bouquet; well put together, with quite generous fruit, and clever oak use. Excellent value. **rating:** 88

best drinking Now–2006 **best vintages** '00 **drink with** Spring lamb in filo pastry • $13.50

kingtree wines   NR

Kingtree Road, Wellington Mills via Dardanup, WA 6326 **region** Geographe
phone (08) 9728 3050 **fax** (08) 9728 3113 **open** 7 days 12–5.30
winemaker Contract **production** 1000 cases **est.** 1991
product range ($16–20 CD) Riesling, Sauvignon Blanc, Gerrasse White, Cabernet Merlot.
summary Kingtree Wines, with 2.5 hectares of estate plantings, is part of the Kingtree Lodge development, a four and a half-star luxury retreat in dense Jarrah forest.

🐌 kinloch wines   ★★★☆

Kainui, Wairere Road, Booroolite, Vic 3723 **region** Central Victorian High Country
phone (03) 5777 3447 **fax** (03) 5777 3449 **open** 7 days 10–4
winemaker Al Fencaros (Contract) **est.** 1996
product range ($20–35 CD) Chardonnay, Pinot Noir, Pinot Meunier; Kainui Estate Unwooded Chardonnay, Kainui Estate Chardonnay.
summary Susan and Malcolm Kinloch began the development of their vineyard in 1996, at an altitude of 400 metres on the northern slopes of the Great Dividing Range, 15 minutes' drive from Mansfield. One of the unusual varieties in the portfolio is Pinot Meunier. The grapes are hand-picked and taken to the Yarra Valley for contract making. As the tasting notes indicate, good levels of ripeness are achieved.

Kinloch Kainui Unwooded Chardonnay

TTTY 2001 Light straw-green; quite intense, faintly sweaty, grapefruit aromas roll into a light to medium-bodied palate, which gains weight towards the finish, and largely throws off the touch of reduction on the bouquet. Thirteen and a half degrees alcohol suggest ripeness is not a problem. **rating:** 84

best drinking Now–2005 **drink with** Cold prawns • $20

Kinloch Kainui Chardonnay

▼▼▼▼ **2001** Light to medium yellow-green; the fruit character is similar to that of the unwooded version, the oak subtle; the gentle, light to medium-bodied palate is clean and unforced; nice wine. **rating:** 85

best drinking Now–2005 **drink with** Fresh yabbies • $22

Kinloch Pinot Noir

▼▼▼▼ **2002** Light, bright red; savoury, spicy, strawberry and cherry aromas, free of any mint, lead into a fresh, lively, light-bodied palate with attractive cherry and strawberry fruit; almost no tannins, and to be enjoyed in its vibrant youth. **rating:** 88

best drinking Now **drink with** Grilled salmon on rock salt • $25

Kinloch Pinot Meunier

▼▼▼▼ **2002** Bright, light purple-red; clean, fresh, spicy raspberry aromas are followed by a light palate with supple, fine tannins; very well made. **rating:** 87

best drinking Now–2006 **drink with** Agnolotti • $25

kinvarra estate NR

RMB 5141, New Norfolk, Tas 7140 **region** Southern Tasmania
phone (03) 6286 1333 **fax** (03) 6286 2026 **open** Not
winemaker Andrew Hood **production** 90 cases **est.** 1990
product range ($13.50–15 ML) Riesling, Pinot Noir.
summary Kinvarra is the part-time occupation of David and Sue Bevan, with their wonderful 1827 homestead depicted on the label. There is only 1 hectare of vines, half riesling and half pinot noir, and most of the crop is sold to Wellington Wines.

kirkham estate NR

3 Argyle Street, Camden, NSW 2570 **region** South Coast Zone
phone (02) 4655 7722 **fax** (02) 4655 7722 **open** 7 days 11–5
winemaker Stan Aliprandi **production** 3000 cases **est.** 1993
product range ($6–15.50 CD) Estate range of Traminer Riesling, Semillon, Semillon Chardonnay, Chardonnay, Sparkling Pinot Noir White, Sparkling Pinot Noir Pink, Old Gold Botrytis Semillon, White Lambrusco, Lambrusco, Pinot Noir, Shiraz, Merlot, Cabernet Sauvignon, Port; Camden Vale range of Semillon Chardonnay, Classic Dry White, Classic Dry Red, Cabernet Shiraz.
summary Kirkham Estate is one of six or so wine producers near Camden, a far cry from the 18 producers of the mid-19th century but still indicative of the growth of vineyards and winemakers everywhere. It is the venture of Leif Karlsson and Stan Aliprandi, the latter a former Riverina winemaker with an interesting career going back over 30 years. The estate draws upon 9 hectares of vineyards, planted to chardonnay, semillon, verdelho, petit verdot, shiraz, merlot, pinot noir and cabernet sauvignon, supplemented, it would seem, by grapes (and wines) purchased elsewhere.

kirrihill estates ★★★★

Wendouree Road, Clare, SA 5453 **region** Clare Valley
phone (08) 8842 4087 **fax** (08) 8842 4089 **open** 7 days 10–4
winemaker Richard Rowe, David Mavor **production** 25 000 cases **est.** 1998
product range ($14.50–20 CD) Clare Valley Riesling, Clare Valley Semillon, Adelaide Hills Sauvignon Blanc, Adelaide Hills Chardonnay, Clare Valley Grenache Shiraz Mourvedre, Clare Valley Shiraz, Langhorne Creek Shiraz, Clare Valley Cabernet Sauvignon.
summary One of the larger vineyard and winery developments over the past 5 years, with a 7000-tonne, $10 million winery designed for modular expansion to 20 000 tonnes, currently storing 3 million litres of wine. It is associated with the Kirribilly Wine Group, which has developed and now manages 1300 hectares of vineyards through the Clare Valley, the Adelaide Hills and Langhorne Creek. Small parcels of its managed vineyards are taken for the Kirrihill Estates wine range, with a Cabernet Sauvignon from each of the Clare and Langhorne Creek, plus a Sauvignon Blanc from the Adelaide Hills to complete the range in the near future. Richard Rowe, the chief winemaker, was responsible for many years for the Leasingham Classic Clare range, while assistant David Mavor worked both in France and for Tyrrell's in the Hunter Valley. The quality of the wines is thus no surprise.

Kirrihill Estates Clare Valley Riesling

𝖸𝖸𝖸𝖸𝖸 **2002** Bright, light green-yellow; the bouquet is clean, with some mineral and citrus, although the aromatics are slightly suppressed at this early stage; the palate comes alive with lemony acidity extending the finish to a totally unexpected degree, and absolutely guaranteeing the future development o the wine. **rating:** 92

best drinking 2005–2013 **best vintages** '01, '02 **drink with** Leave it in the cellar • $17

Kirrihill Estates Clare Valley Semillon

𝖸𝖸𝖸𝖸 **2001** Light to medium yellow-green; the clean bouquet has faintly tropical but relatively subdued fruit, but the palate has abundant flavour and grip to the finish, providing positive mouthfeel. **rating:** 88

best drinking Now–2008 **drink with** Seafood pasta • $14.50

Kirrihill Estates Adelaide Hills Sauvignon Blanc

𝖸𝖸𝖸𝖸 **2002** Light green-yellow; the bouquet is clean and fresh, though, like the Riesling, not particularly aromatic, with hints of mineral and gooseberry; the clean, well-made palate is on the delicate side, notwithstanding the low yield. As with the Riesling, finished with a Stelvin cap. **rating:** 88

best drinking Now **drink with** Cold seafood • $16.50

Adelaide Hills Chardonnay

𝖸𝖸𝖸𝖸 **2001** Medium yellow-green, showing some development. A tangy, fruit-driven style with stone fruit, citrus and grapefruit on both bouquet and palate. Good length and tightly controlled oak. **rating:** 89

best drinking Now–2005 **drink with** Seafood risotto • $19.95

Kirrihill Estates Clare Valley Shiraz

𝖸𝖸𝖸𝖸𝖸 **2000** Medium red-purple; the complex and powerful bouquet is somewhat dominated by American oak, which continues on the palate, but is there met by abundant black cherry, blackberry and chocolate fruit plus ample, soft tannins. The big end of Clare Valley style, and none the worse for that. **rating:** 90

best drinking 2005–2010 **drink with** Braised beef • $19.50

kirwan's bridge wines   NR

Lobb's Lane/Kirwan's Bridge Road, Nagambie, Vic 3608 **region** Nagambie Lakes
phone (03) 5794 1777 **fax** (03) 5794 1993 **open** 7 days 10–5
winemaker Anna Hubbard **production** 1500 cases **est.** 1997
product range ($15–35 CD) Riesling, Marsanne, Shiraz, Merlot.
summary A major development, with over 35 hectares planted to a major emphasis on the Rhône varietals (7.9 ha marsanne, 2.7 ha viognier, with 1.3 ha of roussanne to be planted 2001; and 11.2 ha shiraz, 2.7 ha mourvedre and 2.5 ha grenache). A side bet on 4.8 hectares cabernet sauvignon, 2.4 hectares merlot and 1.3 hectares riesling rounds off the planting. The cellar-door complex includes a restaurant (open for lunch and dinner Thursday to Sunday – dinner bookings essential), conference facility and an art gallery.

knappstein lenswood vineyards   ★★★★★

Crofts Road, Lenswood, SA 5240 **region** Adelaide Hills
phone (08) 8389 8111 **fax** (08) 8389 8555 **open** By appointment
winemaker Tim Knappstein **production** 10 000 cases **est.** 1981
product range ($23–51 R) Semillon, Sauvignon Blanc, Chardonnay, Pinot Noir, The Palatine.
summary Knappstein Lenswood Vineyards is now the sole (and full-time) occupation of Tim and Annie Knappstein, Tim Knappstein having retired from the winery which bears his name in the Clare Valley, and having sold most of the Clare vineyards (along with the wine business) to Petaluma. With 25.5 hectares of close-planted, vertically trained vineyards maintained to Tim Knappstein's exacting standards, the business will undoubtedly add to the reputation of the Adelaide Hills as an ultra-premium area. Complex Chardonnay, intense Sauvignon Blanc and broodingly powerful yet stylish Pinot Noir are trailblazers. The wines are exported to the UK, the US, Canada, Japan, Belgium, Switzerland, Germany, Japan and Singapore.

Knappstein Lenswood Vineyards Sauvignon Blanc

𝖸𝖸𝖸𝖸𝖸 **2002** Light to medium yellow-green; intense, concentrated herb, snow pea and asparagus aromas, with no hint of reduction. The palate is mouthfilling and rich, but not phenolic; died-in-the-wool early drinking style. **rating:** 93

best drinking Now **best vintages** '94, '95, '97, '98, '01 **drink with** Shellfish • $23.15

knappstein wines ★★★★

2 Pioneer Avenue, Clare, SA 5453 **region** Clare Valley
phone (08) 8842 2600 **fax** (08) 8842 3831 **open** Mon–Fri 9–5, Sat 11–5, Sun and public holidays 11–4
winemaker Andrew Hardy **production** 45 000 cases **est.** 1976
product range ($17–39 R) Hand Picked Riesling, Dry Style Gewurztraminer, Semillon Sauvignon Blanc, Chardonnay, Shiraz, Chainsaw Shiraz, Enterprise Shiraz, Cabernet Merlot, Enterprise Cabernet Sauvignon.
summary Very much part of the Petaluma empire, with Andrew Hardy now a veteran of the region. The 90 hectares of mature estate vineyards in prime locations supply grapes both for the Knappstein brand and for wider Petaluma use. The wines are exported to the UK and much of Europe and Asia.

Knappstein Hand Picked Riesling

▼▼▼▼ 2002 Medium yellow-green; the slightly broad and certainly full and ripe bouquet is mirrored by the palate, which has abundant flavour but lacks focus. The 2002 Clare Rieslings do fall into distinct groups. **rating:** 88

best drinking Now–2007 **best vintages** '77, '78, '79, '80, '83, '86, '90, '93, '94, '96, '97 **drink with** Salads of all kinds • $21

Knappstein Clare Valley Chardonnay

▼▼▼▼ 2001 Medium to full yellow-green; the complex bouquet shows excellent barrel ferment and oak handling; an attractive wine in the mouth. It is entirely made in the winery, not in the vineyard; stirred every Monday for 7 months and matured in predominantly new French oak. About as good as the Clare Valley can every produce with this variety. **rating:** 89

best drinking Now–2006 **drink with** Takeaway • $19

Knappstein Cabernet Merlot

▼▼▼▼ 2000 Medium red-purple; the bouquet is somewhat closed, with savoury/earthy edges; the medium-bodied palate has well-balanced fruit, oak and tannins; it is just that the vibrant fruit of the 1999 vintage is lacking.
rating: 85

best drinking 2004–2009 **best vintages** '99 **drink with** Roast veal • $17.50

knight granite hills ★★★★☆

1481 Burke and Wills Track, Baynton, Kyneton, Vic 3444 **region** Macedon Ranges
phone (03) 5423 7264 **fax** (03) 5423 7288 **open** Mon–Sat 10–6, Sun 12–6
winemaker Llew Knight **production** 7000 cases **est.** 1970
product range ($13.90–55 R) Riesling, Chardonnay, Pinot Noir, Shiraz, Cabernet Sauvignon, Sparkling.
summary Knight Granite Hills is one of the enduring classics, pioneering the successful growing of riesling and shiraz in an uncompromisingly cool climate. It is based on 11 hectares of riesling, chardonnay, shiraz, cabernet sauvignon, merlot and pinot noir (the last used in its sparkling wine). After a quiet period in the 1990s, has been reinvigorated, its original two icons once again to the fore.

Knight Granite Hills Riesling

▼▼▼▼▽ 2002 Light straw-green; ultra-pure apple blossom, apple skin and mineral aromas lead into a tight, crisp and delicate palate, finishing with minerally acidity. Is simply crying out for time in bottle, even without the benefit of a screwcap. **rating:** 92

best drinking 2005–2015 **best vintages** '86, '90, '93, '94, '98, '00, '02 **drink with** Sugar-cured tuna • $18

Knight Granite Hills Reserve Shiraz

▼▼▼▼▽ 1999 Medium red-purple; the moderately intense bouquet is clean, smooth, with an attractive mix of cherry and spice; the medium-bodied palate flows faultlessly on from the bouquet, with similar berry/cherry/spice flavours, good balance and acidity. **rating:** 93

best drinking 2004–2014 **drink with** Beef bourgignon • $55

knights eurunderee flats NR

655 Henry Lawson Drive, Mudgee, NSW 2850 **region** Mudgee
phone (02) 6373 3954 **fax** (02) 6373 3750 **open** Wed–Fri and Sun 10–4, Sat 10–5
winemaker Peter Knights **production** 1350 cases **est.** 1985
product range ($12–20 CD) Riesling, Sauvignon Blanc, Shiraz, Merlin Rouge, Merlot, Cabernet Sauvignon, Round Table Tawny, Lancelot's Liqueur.
summary Sometimes called Knights Vines, although the wines are marketed under the Eurunderee Flats label. There are 5 hectares of vineyards producing white wines of variable quality, and rather better dry red table wines. Exports to Hong Kong.

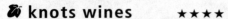 knots wines ★★★★

A8 Shurans Lane, Heathcote, Vic 3552 **region** Heathcote
phone (03) 5441 5429 **fax** (03) 5441 5429 **open** Select weekends, or by appointment
winemaker Lindsay Ross **production** 750 cases **est.** 2001
product range ($20–25 ML) Drummers Plait Semillon Sauvignon Blanc, Carrick Bend Chardonnay, Rose Lashing Rose, Sheep Shank Shiraz, Larks Head Cabernet Merlot, Capstan Cabernet Sauvignon.
summary This is the venture of erstwhile Balgownie winemaker Lindsay Ross and wife Noeline, and is part of a broader business known as Winedrops; Winedrops acts as a wine production and distribution network for the Bendigo wine industry. Knots wines are sourced from a number of long-established Heathcote and Bendigo vineyards, providing 0.5 hectare each of semillon and chardonnay, and 4 hectares each of shiraz and cabernets. The viticultural accent is on low-cropping vineyards with concentrated flavours; the winemaking emphasis is on flavour, finesse and varietal expression.

Knots Carrick Bend Chardonnay

▼▼▼▼ **2002** Light straw-green; the moderately intense bouquet has citrus and stone fruit in the driver's seat, a touch of French oak behind; the light to medium-bodied palate is well balanced and constructed, again showing subtle oak, and with a pleasant finish. **rating:** 87
best drinking Now–2005 **drink with** Smoked salmon • $20

Knots Capstan Cabernet Sauvignon

▼▼▼▼▽ **2001** Bright purple-red; the intense bouquet has pristine blackcurrant/blackberry fruit, and the oak is balanced and integrated; the palate springs no surprises, confidently following the bouquet with ripe blackcurrant and dark chocolate fruit, replete with ripe tannins. **rating:** 91
best drinking 2005–2010 **best vintages** '01 **drink with** Game pie • $25

knowland estate NR

Mount Vincent Road, Running Stream, NSW 2850 **region** Mudgee
phone (02) 6358 8420 **fax** (02) 6358 8423 **open** By appointment
winemaker Peter Knowland **production** 250 cases **est.** 1990
product range ($12.50–18 CD) Mt Vincent Semillon, Mt Vincent Sauvignon Blanc, Orange Pinot Noir, Mt Vincent Pinot Noir.
summary The former Mount Vincent Winery, at an altitude of 1080 metres, which sells much of its grape production from its 4 hectares of vineyards to other makers.

kominos wines NR

New England Highway, Severnlea, Qld 4352 **region** Granite Belt
phone (07) 4683 4311 **fax** (07) 4683 4291 **open** 7 days 9–5
winemaker Tony Comino **production** 4000 cases **est.** 1976
product range ($12–20 CD) Semillon, Sauvignon Blanc, Sauvignon Semillon, Chenin Blanc Semillon Sauvignon Blanc, Chardonnay, Vin Doux, Nouvelle, Shiraz, Shiraz Cabernet, Merlot, Cabernet Franc, Cabernet Sauvignon.
summary Tony Comino is a dedicated viticulturist and winemaker, and together with his father he has battled hard to prevent ACI obtaining a monopoly on glass production in Australia, foreseeing many of the things which have in fact occurred. However, Kominos keeps a very low profile, selling all its wine through the cellar door and by mailing list. No recent tastings.

kongwak hills winery NR

1030 Korumburra–Wonthaggi Road, Kongwak, Vic 3951 **region** Gippsland
phone (03) 5657 3267 **fax** (03) 5657 3267 **open** Weekends and public holidays 10–5
winemaker Peter Kimmer **production** 600 cases **est.** 1989
product range ($10–25 CD) Riesling, Pinot Noir, Shiraz, Cabernet Malbec.
summary Peter and Jenny Kimmer started the development of their vineyard in 1989 and now have 0.5 hectare each of cabernet sauvignon, shiraz and pinot noir, together with lesser quantities of malbec, merlot and riesling. Most of the wines are sold at the cellar door, with limited distribution in Melbourne through Woods Wines Pty Ltd of Fitzroy.

🐾 kooroomba vineyards ★★★

168 FM Bells Road, Mount Alford via Boonah, Qld 4310   **region** Queensland Zone
phone (07) 5463 0022 **fax** (07) 5463 0441 **open** Wed–Sun and public holidays 10–5
winemaker Ballandean Estate (Contract) **production** 2000 cases **est.** 1998
product range ($15–22 CD) Verdelho Marsanne, Alba, Chardonnay, Shiraz, Cabernet Merlot, Cabernet Sauvignon.
summary Kooroomba Vineyards is little more than one hour's drive from the Brisbane CBD, and offers cellar-door wine tasting and sales, a vineyard restaurant and a lavender farm. The 7.5-hectare vineyard is planted to verdelho, marsanne, merlot, shiraz and cabernet sauvignon, with chardonnay purchased from contract growers.

Kooroomba Vineyards Cabernet Merlot

▼▼▼▽ 2001 Light to medium red-purple; the light, fresh bouquet has leaf and mint overtones to the red berry fruit; the light-bodied palate is a faithful reflection of the bouquet; not much oak is evident at any time. The complex artwork and label printing certainly have appeal. **rating:** 83

best drinking Now–2005 **drink with** Delicate red meat dishes • $22

kooyong ★★★★

110 Hunts Road, Tuerong, Vic 3933 (postal)   **region** Mornington Peninsula
phone (03) 5989 7355 **fax** (03) 5989 7677 **open** Not
winemaker Sandro Mosele **production** 5000 cases **est.** 1996
product range ($36–45 R) Chardonnay, Pinot Noir.
summary Kooyong, owned by Chris and Gail Aylward, is one of the larger new entrants on the Mornington Peninsula scene, releasing its first wines in June 2001. Thirty-four hectares of vines are in bearing, 0.66 pinot noir, and 0.33 chardonnay. Winemaker Sandro Mosele is a graduate of Charles Sturt University, having previously gained a science degree. He has worked at Rochford and learnt from Sergio Carlei, of the Green Vineyards, and makes the wine at an on-site winery which also provides contract winemaking services for others. Production will eventually increase to 10 000 cases. The wines are distributed through Negociants Australia, and the quality is impressive. Exports to the US, the UK and Singapore.

Kooyong Chardonnay

▼▼▼▼ 2000 Light to medium yellow-green; the bouquet is still quite delicate and youthful. The fresh light to medium-bodied palate offers melon and white peach allied with some fruit sweetness; the French oak in which the wine was fermented is barely perceptible. **rating:** 87

best drinking Now–2006 **drink with** White-fleshed fish and beurre blanc • $36

Kooyong Pinot Noir

▼▼▼▼▼ 2000 Strong red-purple, holding its hue well; sultry dark plum and forest aromas are replayed on the powerful, long and complex palate; no over-extraction. An impressive wine with further development potential. **rating:** 94

best drinking Now–2007 **best vintages** '00 **drink with** Smoked quail • $41

koppamurra wines ★★★★

Joanna via Naracoorte, SA 5271   **region** Wrattonbully
phone (08) 8357 9533 **fax** (08) 8271 0726 **open** By appointment
winemaker John Greenshields **production** 3000 cases **est.** 1973
product range ($9–25 ML) Riesling, Chardonnay, Late Harvest Riesling, Dry Red, Pinot Meunier, Shiraz, Cabernet Merlot, Merlot, Cabernet Sauvignon, Barrel Selection Cabernet Sauvignon, Two Cabernets, McLaren Vale Muscat.
summary Which Hollywood actress was it who said, 'I don't care what they say about me, as long as they spell my name right'? This might be the motto for Koppamurra Wines, which became embroiled in a bitter argument over the use of the name Koppamurra for the region in which its vineyards are situated and which, through what seems to be sheer bloody-mindedness by various of the parties involved, is now known as Wrattonbully. The wines have limited retail distribution in the eastern states, and are exported to the US.

Koppamurra Cabernet Sauvignon

▼▼▼▼▽ 2000 Medium red-purple; a fragrant bouquet with blackberry, earth and chocolate aromas which are precisely repeated on the finely structured and balanced palate. Scores for elegance rather than outright power. **rating:** 90

best drinking 2004–2010 **best vintages** '90, '91, '96, '00 **drink with** Beef Bordelaise • $18.50

kopparossa wines ★★★★

PO Box 922, Naracoorte, SA 5271 **region** Wrattonbully
phone 1800 620 936 **fax** (08) 8762 0937 **open** Not
winemaker Gavin Hogg, Mike Press **production** 5000 cases **est.** 1996
product range ($15–27 CD) Coonawarra range of Chardonnay, Shiraz, Cabernet Sauvignon Merlot; Limestone Coast (Wrattonbully) range of Shiraz, Merlot, Cabernet Sauvignon.
summary Kopparossa has undergone several transformations since its establishment in 1996, but the partnership of Gavin Hogg and Mike Press, with more than 60 years' winemaking and grape growing experience between them, has continued throughout. The business is now based on two estate vineyards, one in the Adelaide Hills, the other in Coonawarra, plus contract-grown grapes from Wrattonbully. The Adelaide Hills property, developed by the Press family and known as Kenton Valley, has 24 hectares of pinot noir, merlot, shiraz, cabernet sauvignon and chardonnay planted throughout 1998 and 1999. The Coonawarra vineyard is (at first sight, controversially, but the vineyard is in fact on Stentiford Road) called Stentiford, and is, quite literally, Gavin and Julie Hogg's back yard. It was planted between 1992 and 1993 with cabernet sauvignon, merlot and chardonnay.

Kopparossa Coonawarra Shiraz

TTTTY 2000 Medium to full red-purple; the clean, fruit-driven bouquet has blackberry fruit and hints of herb, and the palate has plenty of depth and substance. Here sweet blackberry fruit has an appealing, spicy finish, part fruit-derived, part oak-derived. Infinitely better than the prior vintage. **rating:** 90
best drinking 2004–2009 **drink with** Slowly braised beef • $25

Kopparossa Wrattonbully Shiraz

TTTT 2000 Medium to full red-purple; very ripe prune, plum and berry fruit aromas flow through into the rich, similarly ripe palate with bitter chocolate and prune flavours; subtle oak. **rating:** 87
best drinking Now–2007 **drink with** Beef Provençale • $20

Kopparossa Wrattonbully Merlot

TTTTY 2000 Excellent, bright purple-red; complex blackcurrant, spice and earth aromas lead into a round, gently mouthfilling array of blackcurrant, chocolate and fruitcake flavours; while the overall impression is savoury, there is abundant sweet fruit at the core. Finishes with fine tannins. Great value. **rating:** 91
best drinking 2005–2010 **best vintages** '00 **drink with** Marinated lamb • $20

Kopparossa Coonawarra Cabernet Merlot

TTTT 1999 Medium red, with the purple hues starting to diminish; a mix of savoury, leafy, earthy berry aromas precede a richer and riper palate showing dark fruits and a touch of chocolate, and finishing with ripe tannins and neatly judged oak. A blend of 50 per cent of each variety. **rating:** 89
best drinking Now–2008 **drink with** Beef Bordelaise • $27

Kopparossa Wrattonbully Cabernet Sauvignon

TTTTY 2000 Strong red-purple; rich, ripe, concentrated blackcurrant fruit and neatly balanced oak on the bouquet lead into abundant blackcurrant and cassis fruit joined almost immediately by ripe tannins on the palate; the oak is very much in the background, fruit driving the flavour and providing the impact. Truly excellent value. **rating:** 92
best drinking 2006–2011 **best vintages** '00 **drink with** Lamb shanks • $20

kraanwood ★★★★☆

8 Woodies Place, Richmond, Tas 7025 **region** Southern Tasmania
phone (03) 6260 2540 **open** Not
winemaker Frank van der Kraan **production** 150 cases **est.** 1994
product range ($16–25 ML) Schonburger, Montage, Unwooded Chardonnay, Pinot Noir.
summary Frank van der Kraan and wife Barbara established their 0.5-hectare vineyard Kraanwood between 1994 and 1995, with approximately equal plantings of pinot noir, chardonnay and cabernet sauvignon. Frank van der Kraan also manages the 1-hectare Pembroke Vineyard, and procures from it small quantities of schonburger, chardonnay, riesling and sauvignon blanc.

Kraanwood Pinot Noir
TTTT 2001 Light to medium red; a light-bodied wine with pleasant fruit and a touch of sweet oak. Nowhere in the class of the 2000, simply because the fruit flavour and depth weren't there in the first place. Well handled in the winery, resisting the temptation to compensate by over-extraction. **rating:** 85

best drinking Now **best vintages** '00 **drink with** Jugged hare • $25

kreglinger estate NR

Limestone Coast Road, Mount Benson, SA 5265 (postal) **region** Mount Benson
phone (08) 8768 5080 **fax** (08) 8768 5083 **open** Not
winemaker Steve Grimley, Andrew Lanauze, Ralph Fowler **production** 85 000 cases **est.** 2000
product range Riesling, Sauvignon Blanc, Pinot Gris, Shiraz, Merlot, Cabernet Sauvignon.
summary This is by far the largest and most important development in the Mount Benson region. It is ultimately owned by a privately held Belgian company, G & C Kreglinger, established in 1797. Kreglinger Australia was established in 1893 as an agribusiness export company specialising in sheepskins. In early 2002 Kreglinger Australia acquired Pipers Brook Vineyard. The Mount Benson side commenced in 2000 with the development of a 160-hectare vineyard and 2000-tonne winery, primarily aimed at the export market. Kreglinger will maintain the separate brands of each venture

Kreglinger Estate Limestone Coast Sauvignon Blanc
TTTT 2002 Pale straw-green; soft gooseberry/tropical fruit aromas lead into a gently ripe palate with varietal fruit flavour in a relatively soft mode; fair balance. **rating:** 88

best drinking Now **drink with** Robe barramundi • $17.50

krinklewood ★★★★

712 Wollombi Road, Broke, NSW 2330 **region** Lower Hunter Valley
phone (02) 9969 1311 **fax** (02) 9968 3435 **open** Weekends, long weekends, and by appointment
winemaker Contract **production** 5000 cases **est.** 1981
product range ($16–22 ML) Semillon, Verdelho, Chardonnay, Francesca Rose, Botrytis Semillon.
summary Rod and Suzanne Windrim first ventured to the Hunter Valley in 1981, establishing Krinklewood Cottage at Pokolbin and a 1-hectare vineyard. In 1996 they sold that property and moved to the Broke/Fordwich region, where they planted 17.5 hectares with Dr Richard Smart as their viticultural consultant. They struck gold with their first vintage in 2000, the Chardonnay winning a Blue/Gold medal at the 2002 Sydney International Wine Competition, the 2001 Verdelho being similarly rewarded at the same show. Leading restaurant listings of the imaginatively packaged wines have followed, as have favourable reviews in various magazines.

Krinklewood Chardonnay
TTTTY 2002 Bright, light green-yellow; a complex and stylish bouquet, with melon fruit at its core and excellent oak balance and integration; the elegant, understated palate follows in the tracks of the bouquet, and, like the 2000, looks set to develop slowly, always a good thing with Hunter chardonnay. Barrel fermented in new French Vosges oak, lees contact, Champagne yeast, etc. **rating:** 90

best drinking Now–2007 **best vintages** '02 **drink with** Salmon risotto • $22

Krinklewood Botrytis Semillon
TTTT 2002 Light to medium yellow-green; a clean, quite tangy bouquet leads into a well-balanced fruit salad palate, without overmuch evidence of botrytis, although, given the vintage, it was no doubt there. Of only medium sweetness. **rating:** 86

best drinking Now–2005 **drink with** Fresh fruit • $22

Krinklewood Francesca Rose
TTTT 2002 Bright, light pink-purple; small red fruit and spice aromas lead into a clean, fresh palate with gentle acidity and a nice dry finish. Serious rose. **rating:** 87

best drinking Now **drink with** Summer salads • $16

kulkunbulla ★★★★☆

Brokenback Estate, Lot 1 Broke Road, Pokolbin, NSW 2320 **region** Lower Hunter Valley
phone (02) 4998 7140 **fax** (02) 4998 7142 **open** By appointment
winemaker Rhys Eather, Gavin Lennard **production** 5000 cases **est.** 1996

product range ($14–40 CD) Hunter Valley Semillon, Orion's Gate Semillon, The Glandore Semillon, Hunter Valley Chardonnay, Nullarbor Chardonnay, Orion's Gate Chardonnay, The Brokenback Chardonnay, Botrytis Semillon, Shiraz, Hilltops Shiraz, Petit Verdot, Cabernet Merlot.

summary Kulkunbulla is owned by a relatively small Sydney-based company (headed by Gavin Lennard) which has purchased part of the Brokenback Estate in the Hunter Valley formerly owned by Rothbury. For the time being all Kulkunbulla's wines are sold by mail order, with a sophisticated brochure entitled 'Vinsight'. Retail distribution in Victoria and Queensland.

Kulkunbulla Hunter Valley Semillon

ᵀᵀᵀᵀᵀ **2002** Light straw-green; the clean, fresh, delicate bouquet has faintly lemony overtones; the palate has very good balance, with more fruit evident than The Glandore, and will mature slightly more quickly, but is still a 10-year proposition.   **rating:** 92

best drinking 2006–2012 **best vintages** '02 **drink with** Seafood salad • $22.50

Kulkunbulla The Glandore Semillon

ᵀᵀᵀᵀᵀ **2002** Light straw-green; a spotlessly clean, fine and clear bouquet leads into a very delicate, fresh and fine, newborn palate. There is a lemony twist and tweak to the minerally finish, guaranteeing the future of the wine. The Stelvin screwcap underwrites that future; the wine comes from three rows of old vines.   **rating:** 93

best drinking 2007–2017 **best vintages** '98, '99, '00, '02 **drink with** Balmain bugs • $27.50

Kulkunbulla Hilltops Shiraz

ᵀᵀᵀᵀ **2001** Bright, full red-purple; the very ripe bouquet has prune, tobacco, cedar and spice aromas, with a trace of lift. The palate has interesting flavours and textures, with a mix of plum, prune and cedary oak, finishing with fine tannins. Stelvin-capped, and matured in French oak for 18 months. It is becoming clear that red wines take longer to settle down than white wines when Stelvin-capped.   **rating:** 88

best drinking 2005–2011 **drink with** Beef shashlik • $35

Kulkunbulla Hunter Valley Petit Verdot

ᵀᵀᵀᵀ **2001** Strong red-purple; earthy black fruits and savoury spice aromas lead into a palate with attractive dark fruit flavours; the wine has good structure thanks to fine tannins and, doubtless, to the open fermenters. Spent 15 months in used French oak. It was a Wyndham Cabernet Petit Verdot blend made in 1930 which led to Max Lake establishing Lake's Folly.   **rating:** 87

best drinking 2005–2012 **drink with** Saddle of lamb • $35

Kulkunbulla Hilltops Cabernet Merlot

ᵀᵀᵀᵀᵀ **2001** Medium to full red-purple; clean blackcurrant and blackberry fruit on the bouquet leads into a palate with ripe, black fruits and a dash of bitter chocolate. Good mouthfeel sustained by fine, ripe tannins. Open fermented and 18 months in French oak; Stelvin closed.   **rating:** 94

best drinking 2006–2020 **best vintages** '01 **drink with** Butterfly leg of lamb • 35

kyeema estate ★★★☆

43 Shumack Street, Weetangera, ACT 2614 (postal) **region** Canberra District
phone (02) 6254 7557 (AH) **fax** (02) 6254 7536 **open** Not
winemaker Andrew McEwin **production** 1200 cases **est.** 1986
product range ($8–27.50 ML) Chardonnay, Shiraz, Reserve Shiraz, Merlot, Cabernet Merlot; lower-priced Blue Gum Chardonnay, Shiraz Merlot Cabernet Sauvignon.
summary Part-time winemaker, part-time wine critic (with *Winewise* magazine) Andrew McEwin produces wines full of flavour and character; every wine released under the Kyeema Estate label has won a show award of some description. Limited retail distribution.

Kyeema Estate Shiraz

ᵀᵀᵀᵀ **2000** Medium red-purple; a traditional bouquet of earthy, dusty black fruits, characters which come through on the light to medium-bodied but well-balanced palate. From the Canberra District.   **rating:** 85

best drinking 2004–2008 **best vintages** '87, '88, '89, '90, '92, '94, '96, '97, '98 **drink with** Braised beef • $22

Kyeema Estate Reserve Shiraz

ᵀᵀᵀᵀᵀ **2001** Medium red-purple; the ripe bouquet has blackberry, licorice and spice set in neatly handled oak; the fruit-forward, medium-bodied palate has a similar mix of blackberry and sweet spices, the tannins ripe and fine. Nice wine.   **rating:** 90

best drinking 2006–2011 **drink with** Grilled sirloin • $27.50

Kyeema Estate Merlot

TTTT 2000 Medium red-purple; very ripe red and black fruit aromas on the bouquet are followed by a high-toned and flavoured palate with lots of mint alongside sweet, plummy fruit; soft tannins and subtle oak. Higher points without the mint. **rating:** 86

best drinking 2004–2009 **drink with** Lamb casserole • $25

🐂 kyneton ridge estate ★★★

90 Blackhill School Road, Kyneton, Vic 3444 **region** Macedon Ranges
phone (03) 5422 7377 **fax** (03) 5422 3747 **open** By appointment
winemaker John Boucher **production** 300 cases **est.** 1997
product range ($27 CD) Pinot Noir.
summary Kyneton Ridge Estate has been established by a family team of winemakers with winemaking roots going back four generations in the case of John and Ann Boucher. Together with Pauline Russell they found what they believe is a perfect pinot noir site near Kyneton, planting 2.5 hectares of pinot noir in 1997. Prior to the end of 2002, 1.5 hectares of chardonnay and 0.5 hectare of shiraz also went into the ground with high-density planting.

Kyneton Ridge Estate Pinot Noir

TTTT 2001 Medium red-purple; the clean bouquet is driven by sweet plummy fruit, with French oak in the background; the powerful palate is, however, overly extracted, and needed a lighter hand to realise the full potential of the underlying fruit. **rating:** 85

best drinking Now–2005 **drink with** Confit of duck • $27

laanecoorie NR

4834 Bendigo/Maryborough Road, Betley, Vic 3472 **region** Bendigo
phone (03) 5468 7260 **fax** (03) 5468 7388 **open** Weekends, and by appointment
winemaker John Ellis (Contract) **production** 1000 cases **est.** 1982
product range ($20 R) A single Bordeaux-blend dry red of Cabernet Franc, Cabernet Sauvignon and Merlot in roughly equal proportions.
summary John McQuilten's 7.5-hectare vineyard produces grapes of high quality, and competent contract winemaking by John Ellis at Hanging Rock has done the rest.

Laanecoorie Cabernet Sauvignon Cabernet Franc Merlot

TTTT 2000 Medium red-purple; the clean bouquet offers berry with touches of mint, earth, vanilla and spice, characters which come through on the light to medium-bodied palate; finishes with soft tannins. **rating:** 85

best drinking Now–2007 **drink with** Leg of lamb • $20

la cantina king valley NR

Honey's Lane, RMB 9460, King Valley, Vic 3678 **region** King Valley
phone (03) 5729 3615 **fax** (03) 5729 3613 **open** 7 days 10–5 (10–6 during daylight saving time)
winemaker Gino Corsini **production** 1500 cases **est.** 1996
product range ($10–14 CD) Riesling, Chardonnay, Dry Red, Shiraz, Barbera, Dolcetto, Nebbiolo, Sangiovese, Merlot, Cabernet Sauvignon.
summary Gino and Peter Corsini have 22 hectares of riesling, chardonnay, shiraz, merlot and cabernet sauvignon, selling most but making a small amount on-site in a winery 'made of Glenrowan granite stone in traditional Tuscan style'. The wines are made without the use of sulphur dioxide; in other words, they are organic.

🐂 ladbroke grove NR

Riddoch Highway, Coonawarra, SA 5263 **region** Coonawarra
phone (08) 8737 3777 **fax** (08) 8737 3268 **open** Wed–Sun 10–5
winemaker Contract **production** 5000 cases **est.** 1982
product range ($14–26 CD) Riesling, Sauvignon Blanc, Chardonnay Limited Release, Sparkling Cabernet Sauvignon, Township Block Shiraz, Wrattonbully Cabernet Merlot, Coonawarra Cabernet Sauvignon Reserve.
summary Having been established in 1982, Ladbroke Grove is a relatively old Coonawarra brand. However, while the vineyards remained, winemaking and marketing lapsed until the business was purchased by John Cox and Marie Valenzuela, who have quietly gone about the re-establishment and rejuvenation of the label,

rewarded by a string of wine show results in 2002 (the first year in which the new wines were entered in shows). It has extensive grape sources, including the Killian vineyard planted in 1990 to cabernet sauvignon (6 ha), merlot (2.4 ha) and chardonnay (1.6 ha). It also leases a little over 1 hectare of dry-grown shiraz planted in 1965 in the centre of the Coonawarra township. In the spring of 2002 it began the development of a further vineyard at the northern end of Coonawarra; this has been planted to 6 hectares of cabernet sauvignon, 4.5 hectares of shiraz and 1.6 hectares each of viognier, riesling and merlot.

Ladbroke Grove Limited Release Chardonnay

TTTT 2001 Medium yellow-green; the bouquet is clean but somewhat subdued, with nectarine and French oak peeping through; the light to medium-bodied palate is similarly understated, though well balanced; does show the impact of 10 months in new French oak, probably a good thing. Only 650 cases made.   **rating: 86**

best drinking Now–2006 drink with Chicken breast • $19

Ladbroke Grove Township Block Shiraz

TTTT 1999 Medium red, with a tinge of purple; the bouquet is moderately intense, but, like the Chardonnay, curiously closed and not particularly complex. However, the wine does have presence on the palate, with berry, earth and chocolate flavours in a positive savoury mode. Only 500 cases made, from the Coonawarra Township block.   **rating: 84**

best drinking 2004–2008 drink with Beef spare ribs • $23

Ladbroke Grove Wrattonbully Cabernet Merlot

TTTT 2000 Medium red-purple; the bouquet has abundant sweet, ripe plum, prune and licorice fruit aromas; these come through on the very plush, lush flavours of the palate, which finishes with soft tannins. A blend of predominantly Wrattonbully Cabernet Sauvignon and Coonawarra Merlot.   **rating: 88**

best drinking 2005–2012 drink with Beef Bordelaise • $24

Ladbroke Grove Cabernet Sauvignon

TTTT 2001 Medium red-purple; a leafy berry bouquet does not set the pulse racing, but the palate shows very clever winemaking; it is delicate, with the quite obvious sweetness balanced by the other flavours. Top-drawer cellar-door style.   **rating: 85**

best drinking Now–2005 drink with Braised lamb

Ladbroke Grove Reserve Cabernet Sauvignon

TTTT 2000 Medium purple-red; scented blackcurrant and spice aromas lead into a palate with abundant ripe fruit, spice and chocolate flavours, slightly diminished by coarse tannins.   **rating: 89**

best drinking 2005–2012 drink with Ox kidney • $26

lake barrington estate   ★★★★

1133–1136 West Kentish Road, West Kentish, Tas 7306 region Northern Tasmania
phone (03) 6491 1249 fax (03) 6334 2892 open Wed–Sun 10–5 (Nov–Apr)
winemaker Steve Lubiana (Sparkling), Andrew Hood (Table), both Contract production 500 cases est. 1986
product range ($18–35 CD) Riesling, Chardonnay, Pinot Noir, Alexandra (sparkling).
summary Lake Barrington Estate is owned by the vivacious and energetic Maree Taylor and takes its name from the adjacent Lake Barrington, 30 kilometres south of Devonport, which is on the northern coast of Tasmania. There are picnic facilities at the 3-hectare vineyard, and, needless to say, the scenery is very beautiful.

Lake Barrington Alexandra Methode Champenoise

TTTT 1998 Light green-yellow; the aromas are bright, fresh and lively; the palate is as crisp, clean and vibrant as a Tasmanian spring day.   **rating: 89**

best drinking Now–2006 best vintages '93, '94 drink with Shellfish • $35

lake breeze wines   ★★★★

Step Road, Langhorne Creek, SA 5255 region Langhorne Creek
phone (08) 8537 3017 fax (08) 8537 3267 open 7 days 10–5
winemaker Greg Follett production 12 000 cases est. 1987
product range ($15–40 CD) Chardonnay, Winemakers Selection Shiraz, Grenache, Cabernet Sauvignon, Bernoota (Cabernet Shiraz).

summary The Folletts have been farmers at Langhorne Creek since 1880, grape growers since the 1930s. Since 1987 a small proportion of their grapes has been made into wine, and a cellar-door sales facility was opened in early 1991. The quality of the releases has been exemplary; the red wines are particularly appealing. Retail distribution in Victoria, New South Wales, Queensland and Western Australia is now augmented by exports to the US, Canada, the UK and Switzerland.

Lake Breeze Winemaker's Selection Shiraz

♥♥♥♥♡ 2000 Medium purple-red; clean, moderately intense blackberry fruit and subtle oak on the bouquet lead into a round, smooth, medium-bodied palate with gently mouthfilling black fruit flavours, fine tannins and gentle acidity. The type of wine Australia should be making more of, not less. **rating:** 90

best drinking 2005–2010 best vintages '96, '98, '00 drink with Rib of beef • $40

Lake Breeze Bernoota

♥♥♥♥♡ 2001 Medium purple-red; clean, sweet blackberry and blackcurrant fruit aromas lead through to a palate with good texture and mouthfeel, a touch of bitter chocolate joining the sweet fruit of the bouquet; well-balanced and integrated tannins and oak. **rating:** 90

best drinking 2006–2011 best vintages '87, '88, '90, '92, '98, '00, '01 drink with Braised beef • $20

Lake Breeze Cabernet Sauvignon

♥♥♥♥♡ 2001 Bright, vibrant, purple-red; clean and fresh blackcurrant, mulberry and raspberry fruit aromas lead into a medium-bodied palate, opening with a similar array of bright fruits, and closing with distinctly savoury tannins on the finish. **rating:** 91

best drinking 2006–2011 best vintages '87, '88, '90, '95, '96, '98, '00, '01 drink with Smoked kangaroo fillet • $23

lake george winery ★★☆

Federal Highway, Collector, NSW 2581 **region** Canberra District
phone (02) 4848 0039 **fax** (02) 4848 0039 **open** By appointment
winemaker Angus Campbell **production** 750 cases **est.** 1971
product range ($25–48 CD) Semillon, Chardonnay, Botrytis Semillon, Pinot Noir, Merlot, Barrel Select Merlot, Cabernet Sauvignon.
summary Dr Edgar Riek was an inquisitive, iconoclastic winemaker who was not content with his role as Godfather and founder of the Canberra district; he was forever experimenting and innovating. His fortified wines, vintaged in northeastern Victoria but matured at Lake George, were very good. New owner and winemaker Angus Campbell is offering a range of table wines which would have been far better had they been sold 2 or 3 years ago, and consumed at that time.

Lake George Botrytis Semillon 375 ml

♥♥♥♥♡ 1999 Golden yellow; the bouquet is complex and rich, with good fruit and oak balance; the palate provides more of the same, and is well balanced and rich, with strong botrytised fruit flavours balanced by cleansing acidity on the finish. A marked exception to the other wines on offer in 2003. **rating:** 92

best drinking Now–2006 drink with Fruit tart • $45

lake moodemere vineyard NR

McDonalds Road, Rutherglen, Vic 3685 **region** Rutherglen
phone (02) 6032 9449 **fax** (02) 6032 9449 **open** Weekends and public holidays 10–5, Mon, Thurs, Fri 10–3.30
winemaker Michael Chambers **production** 30 cases **est.** 1995
product range ($12–25 CD) Riesling, Chardonnay, Late Harvest Biancone, Shiraz, Cabernet Sauvignon, Moodemere Muscat.
summary Michael, Belinda, Peter and Helen Chambers are all members of the famous Chambers family of Rutherglen. They have 30 hectares of vineyards (tended by Peter), and Lake Moodemere Homestead is in its 14th year as a bed and breakfast facility.

lake's folly ★★★★★

Broke Road, Pokolbin, NSW 2320 **region** Lower Hunter Valley
phone (02) 4998 7507 **fax** (02) 4998 7322 **open** Mon–Sat 10–4
winemaker Rodney Kempe **production** 4500 cases **est.** 1963
product range ($40 CD) Simplicity itself: Chardonnay and Cabernets.

summary The first of the weekend wineries to produce wines for commercial sale, long revered for its Cabernet Sauvignon and thereafter its Chardonnay. Very properly, terroir and climate produce a distinct regional influence and thereby a distinctive wine style. Some find this attractive, others are less tolerant. The winery continues to enjoy an incredibly loyal clientele, with much of each year's wine selling out quickly by mail order. Lake's Folly no longer has any connection with the Lake family, having been acquired some years ago by Perth businessman Peter Fogarty. Mr Fogarty's family company had previously established the Millbrook Winery in the Perth Hills, so is no stranger to the joys and agonies of running a small winery.

Lake's Folly Chardonnay

▼▼▼▼▽ 2001 Medium green-yellow; the moderately intense bouquet has subtle barrel-ferment oak running through ripe stone fruit and melon; the harmonious palate has excellent balance, the oak influence subtle but nonetheless evident throughout, the fruit pure and fresh.   **rating:** 93

best drinking 2004–2009 **best vintages** '81, '82, '83, '84, '86, '89, '92, '96, '97, '99, '00, '01 **drink with** Sweetbreads • $40

Lake's Folly Cabernets

▼▼▼▼▽ 2001 Medium red-purple; the clean, gently complex, savoury bouquet is fruit-driven, the oak diminuendo; a fine and elegant light to medium-bodied palate with a full array of red and black fruits, a touch of black olive, and fine tannins on the finish.   **rating:** 91

best drinking 2006–2015 **best vintages** '69, '75, '81, '87, '89, '91, '97, '98, '00 **drink with** Rabbit, hare • $40

lamont wines ★★★★

85 Bisdee Road, Millendon, WA 6056 **region** Swan Valley
phone (08) 9296 4485 **fax** (08) 9296 1663 **open** Wed–Sun 10–5
winemaker Keith Mugford (Consultant) **production** 12 000 cases **est.** 1978
product range ($10–25 CD) Riesling, Barrel Fermented Semillon, Quartet, Semillon Sauvignon Blanc, Chenin Blanc, Verdelho, Barrel Fermented Chardonnay, Methode Champenoise, Sweet White, Late Picked, Light Red Cabernet, Shiraz, Cabernet Merlot, Cabernet Sauvignon, Family Reserve; fortifieds, including Amontillado and Reserve Sherry (Oloroso style).
summary Corin Lamont is the daughter of the late Jack Mann, and, with the recent involvement of Keith Mugford as consultant, oversees the making of wines in a style which would have pleased her father. Lamont also boasts a superb restaurant run by granddaughter Kate Lamont. With a gallery for the sale and promotion of local arts. The wines are going from strength to strength, utilising both estate-grown and contract-grown (from southern regions) grapes. Exports to the US.

Lamont Riesling

▼▼▼▼▼ 2002 Light straw-green; spotlessly clean lime and mineral aromas are repeated on the palate, which has great length and intensity. Gold medal Qantas Wine Show of Western Australia 2002.   **rating:** 94

best drinking 2005–2010 **best vintages** '99, '02 **drink with** Bruschetta • $19.95

Lamont Semillon Sauvignon Blanc

▼▼▼▼ 2002 Light straw-green; a clean, crisp and moderately intense bouquet is followed by a well-balanced palate offering a mix of mineral and lemon flavours.   **rating:** 87

best drinking Now **drink with** Whitebait • $22

Lamont Barrel Fermented Chardonnay

▼▼▼▼▽ 2001 Medium yellow-green; the bouquet has complex barrel ferment and tangy fruit, well-integrated and well balanced. The palate follows in step, with appealing mouthfeel to the nectarine fruit and nicely judged oak. Swan Valley material; 100 per cent fermented in French oak.   **rating:** 90

best drinking Now–2005 **best vintages** '97, '99, '00 **drink with** Grilled Swan Valley marron • $22

Lamont Shiraz

▼▼▼▼ 2000 Medium red-purple; black cherry and spice aromas on the bouquet lead into a light to medium-bodied palate with soft cherry fruit, and much less oak than in prior vintages; a little short on the finish. **rating:** 85

best drinking 2005–2010 **drink with** Beef Bordelaise • $25

Lamont Vintage Port 500 ml

▼▼▼▼ 2000 Medium to full red-purple; complex blackberry and spice aromas, the spirit relatively neutral, flow into a palate with excellent structure and weight, not overly sweet. Some plum pudding and spice flavours are likewise consistent.   **rating:** 87

best drinking 2005–2015 **drink with** Coffee • $20

langanook wines ★★★

Faraday Road RSD 181, Castlemaine, Vic 3450 **region** Bendigo
phone (03) 5474 8250 **open** Weekends 11–5
winemaker Matt Hunter **production** 750 cases **est.** 1985
product range ($16.50–33.50 CD) Chardonnay, Syrah, Cabernet Sauvignon, Reserve Cabernet Sauvignon Blend.
summary The Langanook vineyard was established back in 1985 (the first wines coming much later), at an altitude of 450 metres on the slopes of Mount Alexander. The 2000 Langanook Reserve Cabernet Sauvignon Merlot Cabernet Franc is a pleasant wine; a little less oak would have helped its cause. Exports to Belgium and Canada.

langmeil winery ★★★★

Cnr Para and Langmeil Roads, Tanunda, SA 5352 **region** Barossa Valley
phone (08) 8563 2595 **fax** (08) 8563 3622 **open** 7 days 11–4.30
winemaker Paul Lindner **production** 15 000 cases **est.** 1996
product range ($12.50–55 CD) Eden Valley Riesling, White Frontignac, Semillon, Chardonnay, Bella Rouge Cabernet Sauvignon (Rose style), Valley Floor Shiraz, The Freedom Shiraz, Three Gardens Shiraz Grenache Mourvedre, The Fifth Wave Grenache, Cabernet Sauvignon, Liqueur Shiraz, Barossa Tawny.
summary Vines were first planted at Langmeil in the 1840s, and the first winery on the site, known as Paradale Wines, opened in 1932. In 1996 cousins Carl and Richard Lindner and brother-in-law Chris Bitter formed a partnership to acquire and refurbish the winery and its 5-hectare vineyard, which was planted to shiraz and included 2 hectares planted in 1846. This vineyard has now been supplemented by another vineyard acquired in 1998, taking total plantings to 14.5 hectares and including cabernet sauvignon and grenache. Distribution in New South Wales and Victoria; exports to the US, Canada. France, Russia, Holland, Malaysia, Hong Kong and New Zealand.

Langmeil The Freedom Shiraz

TTTTT **2000** Medium to full red-purple; complex, high-toned black fruits, spice and earth on the bouquet, then flowing, juicy berry fruit on the supple palate. Has great texture, tannins and length, the French oak playing a pure support role, yet adding to the appeal of the wine. **rating:** 94
best drinking 2006–2016 **best vintages** '98, '00 **drink with** Smoked Barossa sausage • $55

Langmeil Valley Floor Shiraz

TTTTY **2001** Medium red-purple; a complex but traditional mix of berry, vanilla and earth on the bouquet leads into a palate with ripe berry fruit, American oak and ripe tannins all in abundance. Guaranteed to cellar well. **rating:** 90
best drinking 2006–2016 **best vintages** '00, '01 **drink with** Ravioli • $22.50

Langmeil Cabernet Sauvignon

TTTT **2001** Medium red-purple; fully ripe blackcurrant fruit on the bouquet is the driving force on the medium to full-bodied palate, which has good line and continuity, closing with ripe tannins. Well priced. **rating:** 88
best drinking 2006–2011 **drink with** Barbecued sausages • $19.50

lark hill ★★★★☆

521 Bungendore Road, Bungendore, NSW 2621 **region** Canberra District
phone (02) 6238 1393 **fax** (02) 6238 1393 **open** Wed–Mon 10–5
winemaker Dr David Carpenter, Sue Carpenter **production** 4000 cases **est.** 1978
product range ($14–45 CD) Riesling, Sauvignon Blanc, Chardonnay, Late Harvest (dessert wine), Pinot Noir, Exaltation Pinot Noir, Shiraz, Exaltation Merlot, Cabernet Merlot, Exaltation Cabernet.
summary The Lark Hill vineyard is situated at an altitude of 860 meters, level with the observation deck on Black Mountain Tower, and offers splendid views of the Lake George Escarpment. Right from the outset, the Carpenters have made wines of real quality, style and elegance, but have defied all the odds (and conventional thinking) with the quality of their Pinot Noirs. Exports to the UK.

Lark Hill Riesling

TTTTY **2002** Light green-straw; clean, fresh lemon and lime aromas are followed by a well-modulated and balanced palate, the flavours precisely reflecting the bouquet. **rating:** 90
best drinking Now–2008 **best vintages** '88, '91, '92, '93, '94, '00, '01 **drink with** Gazpacho • $22

Lark Hill Chardonnay

▼▼▼▼▼ 2001 Light to medium yellow-green; a smooth, sophisticated bouquet with a subtle interplay of barrel-ferment characters, melon and stone fruit; the elegant palate has pure and seamless stone fruit and oak, and beguiling finish and length. **rating:** 95

best drinking Now–2007 **best vintages** '89, '91, '92, '93, '95, '00, '01 **drink with** Crispy chicken • $28

Lark Hill Pinot Noir

▼▼▼▽ 2001 Light to medium red-purple; the bouquet is distinctly minty, and the palate, too, has a minty overlay to the plummy fruit. The first time that Lark Hill has missed a beat with its Pinot Noir in many a year. **rating:** 84

best drinking Now–2005 **best vintages** '96, '97, '99, '00 **drink with** Venison • $33

Lark Hill Exaltation Pinot Noir

▼▼▼▼ 2001 Medium red-purple; the clean bouquet has moderately savoury aromas; the powerful palate delivers much more, with clear varietal character in a savoury/plummy/spicy spectrum, finishing with fairly grippy tannins. Needs a few years. **rating:** 89

best drinking 2005–2008 **best vintages** '00 **drink with** Breast of duck • $45

Lark Hill Exaltation Merlot

▼▼▼▼ 2000 Dense purple-red; a rich and concentrated bouquet with ripe, juicy, sweet mulberry and blackberry aromas moves into a massively concentrated, almost undrinkable palate. From very low yields, and should be left strictly alone for a minimum of 10 years. Robert Parker would love it. **rating:** 89

best drinking 2010–2020 **drink with** Leave it in the cellar • $45

Lark Hill Exaltation Cabernet

▼▼▼▼ 2001 Medium red-purple; the clean, intense bouquet has blackcurrant/dark berry fruit, the oak subtle; on the palate, a mix of blackcurrant, bitter chocolate and savoury flavours run into a long finish. Not for the fainthearted. **rating:** 89

best drinking 2006–2011 **drink with** Loin of lamb • $45

lashmar ★★★☆

c/- 24 Lindsay Terrace, Belair, SA 5052 **region** Warehouse
phone (08) 8278 3669 **fax** (08) 8278 3998 **open** Not
winemaker Colin Cooter (Contract) **production** 500 cases **est.** 1996
product range ($35 R) Kangaroo Island Cabernet Sauvignon, Three Valleys Shiraz (sourced from various regions in South Australia including Kangaroo Island, McLaren Vale and the Eden and Clare Valleys).
summary Colin and Bronwyn Cooter (who are also part of the Lengs & Cooter business) are the driving force behind Antechamber Bay Wines. The wines are in fact labelled and branded Lashmar; the Kangaroo Island Cabernet Sauvignon comes from vines planted in 1991 on the Lashmar family property situated on the extreme eastern end of Kangaroo Island overlooking Antechamber Bay. The first commercial wines were made in 1999 and released in October 2000. To give the business added volume, a second wine, known as Three Valleys Shiraz and coming from mainland regions of Eden Valley, Clare Valley and McLaren Vale, is also made. Exports to the US, Canada and Singapore.

Lashmar Kangaroo Island Cabernet

▼▼▼▼ 2000 Medium to full red-purple; the bouquet has ripe berry fruit with touches of chocolate and vanilla; a medium-bodied palate with slightly more savoury aspects adds complexity; has good length, tannins and oak handling. **rating:** 87

best drinking 2004–2008 **drink with** Kangaroo fillet • $35

latara NR

Cnr McDonalds and Deaseys Roads, Pokolbin, NSW 2320 **region** Lower Hunter Valley
phone (02) 4998 7320 **open** Sat 9–5, Sun 9–4
winemaker Iain Riggs (Contract) **production** 250 cases **est.** 1979
product range ($9.50–11 CD) Semillon.
summary The bulk of the grapes produced on the 6-hectare Latara vineyard, which was planted in 1979, are sold to Brokenwood. A small quantity is vinified for Latara and sold under its label. As one would expect, the wines are very competently made, and are of show medal standard.

laurel bank ★★★☆

130 Black Snake Lane, Granton, Tas 7030 **region** Southern Tasmania
phone (03) 6263 5977 **fax** (03) 6263 3117 **open** By appointment
winemaker Andrew Hood (Contract) **production** 1200 cases **est.** 1987
product range ($18–23 R) Sauvignon Blanc, Pinot Noir, Cabernet Sauvignon Merlot.
summary Laurel (hence Laurel Bank) and Kerry Carland began planting their 3-hectare vineyard in 1986. They delayed the first release of their wines for some years and (by virtue of the number of entries they were able to make) won the trophy for Most Successful Exhibitor at the 1995 Royal Hobart Wine Show. Things have settled down since; wine quality is solid and reliable.

Laurel Bank Sauvignon Blanc

▼▼▼▼ 2002 Light to medium straw-green; a complex and powerful bouquet is predominantly in the herbal spectrum, with some gooseberry fruit; the palate is, by Tasmanian standards at least, super-charged with flavour, teetering on the wild side. An interesting and compelling wine. **rating:** 88

best drinking Now **best vintages** '98, '99, '02 **drink with** Spring salad • $18

Laurel Bank Pinot Noir

▼▼▼▼ 2001 Light to medium red; the moderately intense bouquet has spicy edges, and the palate has a pleasant mix of cherry, raspberry, spice and stem. In the typically lighter style of Laurel Bank. **rating:** 85

best drinking Now–2006 **best vintages** '94, '95, '97 **drink with** Tasmanian venison • $21

lauren brook ★★★★

Eedle Terrace, Bridgetown, WA 6255 **region** Blackwood Valley
phone (08) 9761 2676 **fax** (08) 9761 1879 **open** Fri–Wed 11–4.30
winemaker Stephen Bullied **production** 500 cases **est.** 1993
product range ($17–35 CD) Chardonnay, Bridgetown Classic, Shiraz, Cabernet Sauvignon.
summary Lauren Brook is on the banks of the beautiful Blackwood River, and is the only commercial winery in the Bridgetown subregion of Mount Barker. An 80-year-old barn on the property has been renovated to contain a micro-winery and a small gallery. There is 1 hectare of estate chardonnay, supplemented by the purchase of local grapes.

Lauren Brook Shiraz

▼▼▼▼▽ 1999 Medium purple-red; dusty, cedary oak and spicy fruit intermingle on the bouquet; the palate provides more of the same around a core of sweet cherry fruit; fine, soft and ripe tannins to close. **rating:** 93

best drinking 2004–2009 **best vintages** '99 **drink with** Smoked lamb • $35

lawrence victor estate ★★★★

Arthur Street, Penola, SA, 5277 **region** Coonawarra
phone (08) 8737 3572 **fax** (08) 8737 3582 **open** 7 days 10–5
winemaker Contract **production** 2000 cases **est.** 1994
product range ($21–25 CD) Shiraz, Cabernet Sauvignon.
summary Lawrence Victor Estate is part of a large South Australian company principally engaged in the harvesting and transportation of softwood plantation logging. The company was established by Lawrence Victor Dohnt in 1932, and the estate has been named in his honour by the third generation of the family. Although a small part of the group's activities, the plantings (principally contracted to Southcorp) are substantial, with 11 hectares of shiraz and 20 hectares of cabernet sauvignon established between 1994 and 1999. An additional 12 hectares of cabernet sauvignon and 6 hectares of pinot noir were planted in 2000.

Lawrence Victor Shiraz

▼▼▼▼ 2000 Bright red-purple; complex savoury overtones to the blackberry fruit of the bouquet lead into a light to medium-bodied palate displaying all the characters of that bouquet, ranging through dark chocolate, spice and blackberry, and closing with savoury tannins. **rating:** 89

best drinking 2005–2012 **drink with** Shepherd's pie • $22

Lawrence Victor Cabernet Sauvignon

▼▼▼▼▽ 2000 Medium red-purple; moderately intense blackcurrant fruit, complemented by well-balanced integrated oak on the bouquet, is followed by a palate which gains richness and sweetness from strong cassis fruit; balanced, fine tannins to close. **rating:** 90

best drinking 2005–2013 **best vintages** '00 **drink with** Braised lamb • $25

lawson's hill ★★★

Henry Lawson Drive, Eurunderee, Mudgee, NSW 2850 **region** Mudgee
phone (02) 6373 3953 **fax** (02) 6373 3948 **open** Mon, Thurs, Fri, Sat 10–4.30, Sun 10–4
winemaker Various Contract and Jose Grace **production** 3500 cases **est.** 1985
product range ($11–39 CD) Chardonnay, Verdelho, Sauvignon Blanc, Riesling, Traminer Riesling, Louisa
Rose, Cabernet Merlot, Pinot Noir Gamay, Reserve Dryland Cabernet Sauvignon, Port.
summary Former music director and arranger (for musical acts in Sydney clubs) Jose Grace and wife June run
a strongly tourist-oriented operation situated next door to the Henry Lawson Memorial, offering a
kaleidoscopic array of wines, produced from 8 hectares of vineyard, and made under contract. The red wines
are richly representative of the deeply coloured, flavoursome Mudgee style.

lazy river estate NR

29R Old Dubbo Road, Dubbo, NSW 2830 **region** Western Plains Zone
phone (02) 6882 2111 **fax** (02) 6882 2111 **open** By appointment
winemaker Contract **production** 1400 cases **est.** 1997
product range ($15–35 ML) Hippo Beach Semillon, Squatters Chair Chardonnay, Hippo Beach Shiraz,
Squatters Chair Petit Verdot, Squatters Chair Cabernet Sauvignon.
summary The Scott family has planted 3 hectares each of chardonnay and semillon, 1 hectare of merlot, and
1.5 hectares each of petit verdot and cabernet sauvignon on their property, which is a little under 3 kilometres
from the end of the main street of Dubbo. The wines are made at Briar Ridge.

leabrook estate ★★★★

24 Tusmore Avenue, Leabrook, SA 5068 (postal) **region** Adelaide Hills
phone (08) 8331 7150 **fax** (08) 8364 1520 **open** Not
winemaker Colin Best **production** 1580 cases **est.** 1998
product range ($15–25 ML) Sauvignon Blanc, Chardonnay, Charleston Rose, Pinot Noir, Reserve Pinot
Noir, Cabernet Merlot.
summary With a background as an engineer, and having dabbled in home winemaking for 30 years, Colin Best
took the plunge and moved into commercial-scale winemaking in 1998. His wines are now to be found in a Who's
Who of restaurant wine lists, and some of the best independent wine retailers on the east coast. Best says, 'I consider
that my success is primarily due to the quality of my grapes, since they have been planted on a 1.2 x 1.2 metre
spacing and very low yields.' I won't argue with that; he has also done a fine job in converting the grapes into wine.

Leabrook Estate Sauvignon Blanc

TTTTT 2002 Light straw-green; the moderately aromatic bouquet runs at the tropical/passionfruit end of the
spectrum, and is free of any sweaty/reduced characters; a nicely balanced and particularly long palate follows,
with an intense finish and aftertaste. **rating:** 92
best drinking Now **best vintages** '02 **drink with** Fine seafood • $18

Leabrook Estate Chardonnay

TTTTT 2001 Light to medium yellow-green; a fresh and fragrant array of nectarine and citrus fruit is
supported by subtle French oak on the bouquet; a light to medium-bodied palate has lively, tangy fruit, well-
controlled oak, and good length and balance. **rating:** 90
best drinking Now–2006 **best vintages** '01 **drink with** Fresh Tasmanian salmon • $20

Leabrook Estate Pinot Noir

TTTT 2001 Light to medium red, quite developed; a light, faintly leafy/minty bouquet leads into a palate with
spicy/savoury varietal character and a long finish; needs a touch more sweet fruit flesh on the mid-palate. Pinot
can be picked too early, as well as too late. **rating:** 87
best drinking Now–2005 **drink with** Asian • $20

leasingham ★★★★☆

7 Dominic Street, Clare, SA 5453 **region** Clare Valley
phone (08) 8842 2555 **fax** (08) 8842 3293 **open** Mon–Fri 8.30–5.30, weekends 10–4
winemaker Kerri Thompson **production** 70 000 cases **est.** 1893
product range ($12.99–46 R) Classic Clare Riesling, Shiraz, Sparkling Shiraz, Cabernet Sauvignon at the top
end; mid-range Bin 7 Riesling, Bin 37 Chardonnay, Bin 23 Semillon, Bin 56 Cabernet Malbec, Bin 61 Shiraz;
low-priced Hutt Creek Riesling, Sauvignon Blanc, Shiraz Cabernet; also Bastion Shiraz Cabernet.

summary Successive big-company ownerships and various peregrinations in labelling and branding have not resulted in any permanent loss of identity or quality. With a core of high-quality, aged vineyards to draw on, Leasingham is in fact going from strength to strength under BRL Hardy's direction. The stentorian red wines take no prisoners, compacting densely rich fruit and layer upon layer of oak into every long-lived bottle; the Bin 7 Riesling also often excels.

Leasingham Bastion Riesling

▼▼▼▼ 2002 Light straw-green; a clean, firm bouquet with lime, spice, mineral and slate is followed by a medium-bodied palate; lime juice flavours have an even flow, but are very slightly broad. The first Riesling release under the Bastion label. **rating: 88**

best drinking Now–2007 **drink with** Ginger prawns • $12.95

Leasingham Bin 7 Riesling

▼▼▼▼▼ 2002 A classic wine from a classic region made in a classic vintage – sounds like pure hyperbole, but it happens to be true. A clean and crisp bouquet of light citrus, spice and mineral flows into an impeccably balanced palate with all the components required to repay extended cellaring. **rating: 94**

best drinking Now–2015 **best vintages** '97, '00, '02 **drink with** Vegetable terrine • $16

Leasingham Classic Clare Sparkling Shiraz

▼▼▼▼▽ 1995 Strong, deep red-purple; the complex blackberry and spice bouquet does not have as much obvious oak as prior releases, which is a thoroughly good thing; the luscious, rich and sweet mid-palate flavours are in typical style for this wine, which is the only credible challenger to the Seppelt Show Sparkling Shiraz. **rating: 92**

best drinking Now–2008 **best vintages** '94, '95 **drink with** Borscht • $45.99

Leasingham Bin 61 Shiraz

▼▼▼▼ 2000 Medium to full red-purple; archetypal Clare Shiraz, stuffed to the gills with earthy black fruits on the bouquet, although less spectacular on the palate; solid, middle of the road, but not particularly rich or luscious. **rating: 87**

best drinking 2005–2010 **best vintages** '88, '90, '91, '93, '94, '96, '99 **drink with** Spiced lamb kebabs • $21.95

Leasingham Classic Clare Shiraz

▼▼▼▼▼ 1999 Dense red-purple; powerful, intense dark berry fruit, vanilla and spice oak and a few savoury nuances to the bouquet lead into a dense, rich and powerful palate, with blackberry and black cherry fruit, balanced oak and ripe tannins. Exceedingly long-lived style. **rating: 95**

best drinking 2007–2019 **best vintages** '88, '90, '91, '92, '94, '95, '96, '97, '99 **drink with** Kangaroo, strong red meat, strong cheese • $45.99

Leasingham Bastion Clare Valley Shiraz Cabernet

▼▼▼▼ 2001 Vivid purple-red; a vibrant bouquet of blackberry, blackcurrant and a touch of mint leads into a sweet, juicy, fruit-driven palate; not complex, but has plenty of concentration. **rating: 87**

best drinking 2004–2010 **best vintages** '99, '00 **drink with** Roast saltbush lamb • $12.99

Leasingham Bin 56 Cabernet Malbec

▼▼▼▼▽ 2000 A wine with a great history (the 1971 is still superb) and a testament to the synergy of the cabernet malbec blend in the Clare Valley; spends 18 months in French and American oak. Blackcurrant and plum aromas are matched by the generous, mouthfilling mid-palate sweet fruit of the malbec; the cabernet adds authority to the finish. **rating: 93**

best drinking 2004–2014 **best vintages** '88, '90, '91, '94, '95, '96, '97, '00 **drink with** Jugged hare • $22

Leasingham Classic Clare Cabernet Sauvignon

▼▼▼▼▼ 1999 Festooned with trophies and gold medals from top shows, which comes as no surprise, for this is the big end of town. Dense red-purple, massively concentrated fruit has soaked up the new French oak on the bouquet. The palate has dense black fruits and chocolate, but remains well balanced. Monumental. **rating: 96**

best drinking 2004–2024 **best vintages** '88, '90, '91, '92, '93, '96, '99 **drink with** Rich red meat dishes • $46

leconfield ★★★★

Riddoch Highway, Coonawarra, SA 5263 **region** Coonawarra
phone (08) 8737 2326 **fax** (08) 8737 2385 **open** 7 days 10–5
winemaker Paul Gordon, Tim Bailey (Assistant) **production** 15 000 cases **est.** 1974

product range ($17.95–29.95 CD) Old Vines Riesling, Chardonnay, Noble Riesling, Shiraz, Merlot, Petit Verdot, Cabernet Sauvignon.

summary A distinguished estate with a proud, even if relatively short, history. Long renowned for its Cabernet Sauvignon, its repertoire has steadily grown with the emphasis on single varietal wines. The style overall is fruit-driven rather than oak-driven. Exports to Canada, the US, Asia, the UK and Europe.

Leconfield Old Vines Riesling

▼▼▼▼▼ **2002** A reminder that there were once large plantings of riesling in Coonawarra; Leconfield itself removed all but a few rows. In typical Coonawarra fashion, the floral bouquet has lime and passionfruit, the palate combining a crisp delicacy with intense and lively flavours which precisely track the bouquet. True elegance. **rating:** 94

best drinking Now–2007 **best vintages** '02 **drink with** Seafood salad • $18

Leconfield Chardonnay

▼▼▼▼▽ **2002** Medium yellow-green; an aromatic, lively and quite intense bouquet has ripe stone fruit aromas; the palate is elegant, fruit-driven, with a long, crisp finish. Has literally soaked up the new French oak in which it was barrel fermented and matured; nor is the malolactic influence overt. **rating:** 90

best drinking Now–2007 **best vintages** '98, '02 **drink with** Chicken pasta • $18.95

Leconfield Shiraz

▼▼▼▼▽ **2001** Medium red-purple; the clean blackberry and plum fruit of the bouquet has a nice touch of oak; the light to medium-bodied palate offers gently sweet blackberry and raspberry fruit, finishing with soft, ripe tannins. The wine is clean, and not gamey, and the fruit flavours are ripe. **rating:** 90

best drinking 2005–2010 **best vintages** '88, '90, '91, '94, '95, '96, '01 **drink with** Beef casserole • $27.95

Leconfield Petit Verdot

▼▼▼▼ **2001** Medium red-purple; the bouquet has tangy, herbal, olive, savoury nuances to the black fruits at its core; the palate sweetens up and softens noticeably, partly due to the oak handling. However, one has to question whether it is better used as part of a blend than as a straight varietal. **rating:** 86

best drinking 2005–2011 **drink with** Ox kidney • $27.95

Leconfield Merlot

▼▼▼▼ **2001** Light to medium red-purple; the elegant, light to medium-bodied palate is unashamedly varietal, with a range of savoury/secondary flavours, and without the sweet red fruits of the best vintages. **rating:** 87

best drinking 2005–2009 **best vintages** '97, '98, '00 **drink with** Duck casserole • $27.95

ledaswan ★★★

179 Memorial Avenue, Baskerville, WA 6065 **region** Swan Valley
phone (08) 9296 0216 **open** 7 days 11–4.30
winemaker Duncan Harris **production** 400 cases **est.** 1998
product range ($14–23 CD) Chenin Blanc, Verdelho, Shiraz, Pedro Ximinez, Muscat a Petits Grains.
summary LedaSwan claims to be the smallest winery in the Swan Valley. It uses organically grown grapes, partly coming from its own vineyard, and partly contract-grown, although the intention is to move to 100 per cent estate-grown in the future, utilising the 2 hectares of estate vineyards. Duncan Harris moved from the coast to Baskerville in 1998, and retired from engineering in 2001 to become a full-time vintner, winning several awards. Tours of the underground cellar are offered.

leeuwin estate ★★★★★

Stevens Road, Margaret River, WA 6285 **region** Margaret River
phone (08) 9759 0000 **fax** (08) 9759 0001 **open** 7 days 10–4.30, Saturday evening dinner
winemaker Bob Cartwright, Paul Atwood **production** 60 000 cases **est.** 1974
product range ($21–76 CD) Art Series Riesling, Sauvignon Blanc, Chardonnay, Pinot Noir, Shiraz, Cabernet Sauvignon; Brut; Prelude Vineyards Classic Dry White, Chardonnay, Cabernet Merlot and Siblings Sauvignon Blanc Semillon, Shiraz are lower-priced alternatives.
summary Leeuwin Estate's Chardonnay is, in my opinion, Australia's finest example based on the wines of the last 20 vintages, and it is this wine alone which demands a five-star rating for the winery. The Cabernet Sauvignon can be an excellent wine with great style and character in warmer vintages, and Shiraz has made an auspicious debut. Almost inevitably, the other wines in the portfolio are not in the same Olympian class, although the Prelude Chardonnay and Sauvignon Blanc are impressive at their lower price level. Exports to all major markets.

Leeuwin Estate Art Series Sauvignon Blanc

ŸŸŸŸŸ 2002 Bright, light green; a spotlessly fresh and clean bouquet has grass, mineral and faintly tropical aromas; the classic tightly focused palate provides more of the same, running through to a long finish. **rating:** 91

best drinking Now **best vintages** '95, '97, '99, '02 **drink with** Asian • $31

Leeuwin Estate Art Series Chardonnay

ŸŸŸŸŸ 2000 Bright, light straw-green; a tightly focused, fine, elegant and harmonious array of nectarine, grapefruit and oak aromas sets the scene for the palate, which has a purity of line particular to Leeuwin Estate. Very much in the style of the '99, even if a cat's whisker behind it in terms of absolute quality. **rating:** 95

best drinking 2005–2015 **best vintages** '90, '92, '94, '95, '96, '97, '98, '99, '00 **drink with** Tempura • $76

Leeuwin Estate Art Series Shiraz

ŸŸŸŸŸ 2000 Medium red-purple; an exceptionally complex and aromatic bouquet has spicy characters strongly reminiscent of Côte Rôtie; the palate has good texture, structure and weight; highly sophisticated winemaking techniques were employed, including 40 per cent whole bunches in open fermenters, and malolactic fermentation and maturation in 1-year-old French oak. Some will see these characters as deriving from brettanomyces; my belief is that they come from the fermentation techniques used. All in all, a very interesting and challenging extension to the Art Series portfolio. **rating:** 94

best drinking 2004–2010 **drink with** Venison • $34

Leeuwin Estate Art Series Cabernet Sauvignon

ŸŸŸŸ 1999 Medium red-purple; the bouquet has a complex array of cedary, spicy black fruit aromas; the medium-bodied palate is very much in the savoury, cedary end of the spectrum, but does have clean blackcurrant fruit underpinning the structure. The best for some years. **rating:** 88

best drinking 2005–2015 **best vintages** '79, '86, '87, '89, '90, '92, '93, '98 **drink with** Eye fillet of lamb • $54

legana vineyard   NR

24 Vale Street, Prospect Vale, Tas 7250 **region** Northern Tasmania
phone (03) 6344 8030 **fax** (03) 6343 2937 **open** By appointment
winemaker Richard Richardson (Contract) **production** 150 cases **est.** 1966
product range ($21–22 R) Pinot Noir, Cabernet Sauvignon.
summary The Legana vineyard was the first one established in the Tamar Valley, planted in 1966 by Graham Wiltshire, and provided the first Heemskerk wines. In 1983 Heemskerk moved to the Pipers River region, and Steven Hyde (Rotherhythe) leased the Legana vineyard until 1994. In May of that year Kurt and Kaye Beyer acquired the vineyard and began its rehabilitation, with rich dividends now being paid.

leland estate   ★★★★

PO Lenswood, SA 5240 **region** Adelaide Hills
phone (08) 8389 6928 **open** Not
winemaker Robb Cootes **production** 1250 cases **est.** 1986
product range ($19–27 R) Sauvignon Blanc, Pinot Noir, Adele (sparkling).
summary Former Yalumba senior winemaker Robb Cootes, with a Master of Science degree, deliberately opted out of mainstream life when he established Leland Estate, living in a split-level one-room house built from timber salvaged from trees killed in the Ash Wednesday bushfires. The Sauvignon Blanc is usually good. Retail distribution in Victoria, New South Wales and Queensland via Prime Wines; exports to Malaysia, Singapore, Hong Kong and the US.

Leland Estate Sauvignon Blanc

ŸŸŸŸŸ 2002 Light straw-green; the highly perfumed, aromatic, tropical bouquet almost inevitably has a background touch of reduction, which does not, however, impinge on the elegant, light to medium-bodied palate, which offers all the fruit flavours promised by the bouquet; has considerable length and is strongly varietal. **rating:** 90

best drinking Now–2005 **best vintages** '00, '02 **drink with** Angel hair pasta and salmon • $19

le 'mins winery   NR

40 Lemins Road, Waurn Ponds, Vic 3216 (postal) **region** Geelong
phone (03) 5241 8168 **open** Not
winemaker Steve Jones **production** 80 cases **est.** 1994
product range ($10 R) Pinot Noir.

summary Steve Jones presides over 0.5 hectare of pinot noir planted in 1998 to the MV6 clone, and 0.25 hectare of the same variety planted 4 years earlier to Burgundy clone 114. The tiny production is made for Le 'Mins at Prince Albert Vineyard, and the wine is basically sold by word of mouth.

lengs & cooter ★★★☆

24 Lindsay Terrace, Belair, SA 5042 **region** Warehouse
phone (08) 8278 3998 **fax** (08) 8278 3998 **open** Not
winemaker Contract **production** 2750 cases **est.** 1993
product range ($12–47 ML) Watervale Riesling, Clare Valley Semillon, Clare Valley Old Vines Shiraz, Reserve Shiraz, Victor (Grenache Shiraz), Swinton (Cabernet blend).
summary Carel Lengs and Colin Cooter began making wine as a hobby in the early 1980s. Each had (and has) a full-time occupation outside the wine industry, and it was all strictly for fun. One thing has led to another, and although they still possess neither vineyards nor what might truly be described as a winery, the wines have graduated to big boy status, winning gold medals at national wine shows and receiving critical acclaim from writers across Australia. However, no recent tastings. Exports to the UK, Canada and Singapore.

lenton brae wines ★★★★☆

Wilyabrup Valley, Margaret River, WA 6285 **region** Margaret River
phone (08) 9755 6255 **fax** (08) 9755 6268 **open** 7 days 10–6
winemaker Edward Tomlinson **production** 8000 cases **est.** 1983
product range ($14–29 CD) Semillon Sauvignon Blanc, Chardonnay, Late Harvest Semillon, Margaret River (Cabernet Sauvignon), Cabernet Merlot.
summary Former architect, town planner and political wine activist Bruce Tomlinson built a strikingly beautiful winery but would not stand for criticism of his wines or politics. Son Edward is more relaxed, and is in fact making wines which require no criticism. Retail distribution through all states, and exports to the UK, Singapore and Canada.

Lenton Brae Semillon Sauvignon Blanc

TTTTT 2002 Light straw-green; a spotlessly clean bouquet with lemon and citrus blossom aromas, the lively palate with good balance and length to the lemony fruit. Very much in the Lenton Brae style. **rating:** 92
best drinking Now–2005 **best vintages** '94, '95, '00, '02 **drink with** Asian dishes • $19

Lenton Brae Chardonnay

TTTTT 2001 Light to medium yellow-green; the bouquet offers a subtle but complex interplay of fig, citrus and melon fruit and barrel-ferment oak; the elegant and intense palate has nectarine, melon and citrus fruit running through to a long finish. Yet another classic Margaret River Chardonnay. Trophy winner Boutique Wine Show 2002. **rating:** 94
best drinking 2004–2009 **best vintages** '97, '99, '00, '01 **drink with** Smoked chicken • $29

Lenton Brae Margaret River

TTTTT 2000 Medium to full red-purple; complex dark berry/blackcurrant/cedar aromas move into a deep and concentrated palate with blackcurrant fruit supported by fine, ripe tannins; excellent balance and length. A blend of 82 per cent Cabernet Sauvignon and 18 per cent Merlot. **rating:** 94
best drinking 2005–2015 **best vintages** '98 **drink with** Grilled beef • $29

leo buring ★★★★☆

Tanunda Road, Nuriootpa, SA 5355 **region** Barossa Valley
phone (08) 8560 9408 **fax** (08) 8563 2804 **open** Not
winemaker Oliver Crawford **production** NFP **est.** 1931
product range ($10–35.50 R) A Riesling-only product range, headed by Leonay, with a changing bin number (for 2002 DWF18), and with Eden Valley Riesling and Clare Valley Riesling in support.
summary Earns its high rating by virtue of being Australia's foremost producer of Rieslings over a 35-year period, with a rich legacy left by former winemaker John Vickery. After veering away from its core business with other varietal wines, has now been refocused as a specialist Riesling producer.

Leo Buring Clare Valley Riesling

TTTTT 2002 Repackaged and repositioned in the market, but still the same gold medal (Adelaide Wine Show) quality, and a Stelvin cap to boot. Pale, bright colour, then aromas of herb, citrus and mineral are followed by a lively, long and well-balanced palate with ripe citrus and touches of CO_2 and toast. **rating:** 94
best drinking Now–2012 **best vintages** '02 **drink with** South Australian whiting • $15

Leo Buring Eden Valley Riesling

▼▼▼▼▽ **2002** Light to medium yellow-green; the fragrant, ripe tropical fruit bouquet leads into a palate with emphatic tropical fruit, even hints of pineapple and passionfruit; very flavoursome, in radically different style from the Clare Valley, and likely to develop a little more quickly. **rating:** 93

best drinking Now–2012 **best vintages** '02 **drink with** Shellfish

Leo Buring Leonay Riesling

▼▼▼▼▼ **2002** Light green-yellow; an intense yet superfine bouquet with ripe lime/citrus aromatics. The long and fine palate has great balance and excellent mouthfeel; intense, but not heavy. A touch of CO_2 is not overly distracting. **rating:** 94

best drinking 2004–2014 **best vintages** '70, '72, '75, '77, '79, '90, '91, '92, '94, '95, '97, '98, '02 **drink with** Baked fish, Chinese style • $35.50

lerida estate NR

The Wineries, Old Federal Highway, Collector, NSW 2581 **region** Canberra District
phone 0419 246 149 **fax** (02) 6295 6676 **open** By appointment
winemaker Greg Gallagher **production** 2000 cases **est.** 1999
product range ($15–20 CD) Unoaked Chardonnay, Pinot Noir, Merlot, Merlot Cabernet Franc; second label Gryphon made from purchased grapes.
summary Lerida Estate continues the planting of vineyards along the escarpment sloping down to Lake George. It is immediately to the south of the Lake George vineyard established by Edgar Riek 30 years ago. Inspired by Edgar Riek's success with pinot noir, Lerida founder Jim Lumbers has planted 6 hectares of pinot noir, 1 hectare each of chardonnay and merlot, and 0.5 hectare of pinot gris. The only Lerida wine so far released has been an unwooded Chardonnay; the other wines come from elsewhere. The intention is to ultimately rely entirely on estate-grown grapes for the Lerida label, with a second label (Gryphon) for wines made from purchased grapes. An open-air winery was put in place for the 2000 and 2001 vintages, and a Glen Murcott-designed tasting, barrel and function room is being erected on-site.

lethbridge wines ★★★★☆

74 Burrows Road, Lethbridge, Vic 3222 **region** Geelong
phone (03) 5281 7221 **fax** (03) 5281 7221 **open** Fri–Sun 10.30–5 first and third weekends of each month, or by appointment
winemaker Ray Nadeson, Maree Collis **production** 1500 cases **est.** 1996
product range ($19.95–38 CD) Sauvignon Blanc Semillon, Pinot Gris, Pinot Noir, Shiraz, Merlot, Old Vine Malbec.
summary Lethbridge has been established by three scientists, Ray Nadeson, Maree Collis and Adrian Thomas. In Ray Nadeson's words, 'Our belief is that the best wines express the unique character of special places. With this in mind our philosophy is to practise organic principles in the vineyard, complemented by traditional winemaking techniques, to allow the unique character of the site to be expressed in our fruit and captured in our wine.' As well as understanding the importance of terroir, the partners have built a unique load-bearing straw bale winery, designed for its ability to recreate the controlled environment of cellars and caves in Europe. Winemaking is no less ecologically sound: hand picking, indigenous yeast fermentations, small open fermenters, pigeage (treading the grapes) and minimal handling of the wine throughout the maturation process are all part and parcel of the highly successful Lethbridge approach.

Lethbridge Sauvignon Blanc Semillon

▼▼▼▼▽ **2002** Light straw-green; a clean, firm and fresh bouquet with lemony/citrussy aromas leads into a remarkably intense and very pure palate, once again showing citrus and lemon peel flavours; good length.

best drinking Now–2006 **best vintages** '02 **drink with** Calamari • $19.95 **rating:** 92

Lethbridge Pinot Noir

▼▼▼▼▽ **2001** Bright red-purple; the intense bouquet centres on dark plum fruit with well-handled oak in support; the very powerful and very concentrated palate borders on being over-extractive, but will reward patience, and is pointed accordingly. **rating:** 90

best drinking 2004–2009 **best vintages** '00, '01 **drink with** Duck risotto • $27.95

Lethbridge Shiraz

▼▼▼▼ **2001** Clear but full red-purple; there are distinct pepper, spice and licorice overtones to the red fruits of the bouquet; an elegant, medium-bodied palate with typical cool climate shiraz characteristics, the oak subtle.

best drinking 2004–2009 **drink with** Braised rabbit • $27.95 **rating:** 89

Lethbridge Merlot

♥♥♥♥♡ 2001 Medium red-purple; quite distinctive varietal character in the mix of red berry and olive aromas continues through to the well-structured and weighted palate, which finishes with fine, persistent tannins.

rating: 90

best drinking 2005–2010 **best vintages** '01 **drink with** Lamb Provençale • $38

liebich wein   ★★★☆

Steingarten Road, Rowland Flat, SA 5352 **region** Barossa Valley
phone (08) 8524 4543 **fax** (08) 8524 4543 **open** Weekends 11–5, Mon–Fri 11–5, appointments advisable
winemaker Ron Liebich **production** 1600 cases **est.** 1992
product range ($9–35 CD) Riesling of the Valleys (a blend of Barossa and Clare Valley Riesling), Riesling Traminer, Unwooded Chardonnay, Fortified Semillon, Leveret Shiraz, The Darkie Shiraz, The Potter's Merlot, The Lofty Cabernet Sauvignon, Tawny Port, Benno Port, Vintage Port, Muscat; bulk port constitutes major sales.
summary Liebich Wein is Barossa Deutsch for 'Love I wine'. The Liebich family have been grape growers and winemakers at Rowland Flat since 1919, with CW 'Darky' Liebich one of the great local characters. His nephew Ron Liebich commenced making wine in 1969, but it was not until 1992 that he and his wife Janet began selling wine under the Liebich Wein label. Exports to the US.

Liebich Wein The Darkie Shiraz

♥♥♥♥♡ 2001 Strong, deep red-purple; sweet, ripe blackberry and plum aromas lead into a rich, round, opulent and luscious palate with that mix of blackberry and peppermint unique to the Barossa Valley; 15° alcohol.

rating: 93

best drinking 2006–2016 **best vintages** '00, '01 **drink with** Charcoal-grilled rump • $35

lilac hill estate   ★★★

55 Benara Road, Caversham, WA 6055 **region** Swan Valley
phone (08) 9378 9945 **fax** (08) 9378 9946 **open** Tues–Sun 10.30–5.00
winemaker Stephen Murfit **production** 15 000 cases **est.** 1998
product range ($13–25 R) Chenin Blanc, Semillon, Semillon Sauvignon Blanc, Verdelho, Chardonnay Verdelho, Chardonnay, Late Picked Frontignan, Zinfandel, Shiraz, Merlot, Cabernet Merlot, White Port, Old Tawny Port.
summary Lilac Hill Estate is part of the renaissance which is sweeping the Swan Valley. Just when it seemed it would die a lingering death, supported only by Houghton, Sandalford and the remnants of the once Yugoslav-dominated cellar-door trade, wine tourism has changed the entire scene. Thus Lilac Hill Estate, drawing in part on 4 hectares of estate vineyards, has already built a substantial business, relying on cellar-door trade and limited retail distribution.

Lilac Hill Estate Chenin Blanc

♥♥♥♥ 2002 Light to medium yellow-green; clean, gentle fruit salad aromas lead into a smooth and quite rich palate, the flavour fleshed out by a touch of residual sugar which doesn't compromise the varietal fruit. **rating:** 85

best drinking Now **drink with** Creamy pasta • $14

Lilac Hill Estate Verdelho

♥♥♥♥♡ 2002 Light green-yellow; the bouquet is clean, with light fruit salad aromas; the palate is full flavoured and in appreciably sweet cellar-door mode.

rating: 84

best drinking Now **drink with** Crumbed brains • $17

Lilac Hill Estate Shiraz

♥♥♥♥ 2002 Strong purple-red; the clean, rich bouquet offers ripe black cherry and vanilla, which in turn translate into a similar array of flavours on the palate, finishing with soft, fine tannins.

rating: 87

best drinking 2004–2008 **drink with** Beef shashlik • $14

Lilac Hill Estate Cabernet Merlot

♥♥♥♥♡ 2002 Medium red; the moderately intense bouquet has lifted earthy/savoury characters with sweet berry underneath; those sweet berry characters appear strongly on the palate, which is bordering on being jammy.

rating: 84

best drinking 2004–2007 **drink with** Barbecued leg of lamb • $17

lillydale estate ★★★★

45 Davross Court, Seville, Vic 3139 **region** Yarra Valley
phone (03) 5964 2016 **fax** (03) 5964 3009 **open** 7 days 11–5
winemaker Jim Brayne, Max McWilliam **production** NFP **est.** 1975
product range ($14–23.50 R) Gewurztraminer, Sauvignon Blanc, Chardonnay, Pinot Noir, Shiraz, Cabernet Merlot.
summary Acquired by McWilliam's Wines in 1994; Max McWilliam is in charge of the business. With a number of other major developments, notably Coonawarra and Barwang, on its plate, McWilliam's has adopted a softly, softly approach to Lillydale Estate; a winery restaurant opened in February 1997.

Lillydale Sauvignon Blanc

ΨΨΨΨΥ 2002 Light straw-green; the bouquet has a crisp, clean mix of herb, grass and asparagus aromas; the spotlessly clean and lively palate, while light, has considerable length, its flavours tracking the bouquet. **rating:** 90
best drinking Now–2005 **best vintages** '98, '99, '02 **drink with** Delicate fish dishes • $18

Lillydale Chardonnay

ΨΨΨΨ 2001 The colour is quite developed, but the bouquet is more aromatic and fresher than the colour would suggest; the light to medium-bodied palate has pleasant stone fruit and citrus flavours supported by subtle oak. **rating:** 87
best drinking Now–2006 **best vintages** '86, '88, '90, '91, '97, '98, '00 **drink with** Avocado • $19

Lillydale Pinot Noir

ΨΨΨΨ 2001 Unusually deep colour for pinot noir from Lillydale Vineyards Estate; rich, ripe, dark plum dominates the bouquet and the palate; the wine is firm, with brisk acidity, and is not silky. It seems to me that the pH level is too low. **rating:** 87
best drinking Now–2007 **best vintages** '96 **drink with** Chinese seafood • $23.50

Lillydale Estate Shiraz

ΨΨΨΨ 2001 Medium red-purple; spotlessly clean, ripe plum, blackberry and black cherry aromas are reflected in the generously ripe fruit of the palate, showing strict control of extract and oak. Not spicy. **rating:** 89
best drinking 2006–2011 **drink with** Stir-fried Asian beef • $23.50

Lillydale Estate Cabernet Merlot

ΨΨΨΨΨ 2001 Strong, deep red-purple; the clean, firm and ripe blackcurrant fruit of the bouquet is not the least bit jammy; the palate has exceptional weight and structure, finishing with long, fine tannins. A spotlessly clean wine with strong overtones of Bordeaux. **rating:** 94
best drinking 2006–2016 **best vintages** '00, '01 **drink with** Veal • $23.50

lillypilly estate ★★★☆

Lillypilly Road, Leeton, NSW 2705 **region** Riverina
phone (02) 6953 4069 **fax** (02) 6953 4980 **open** Mon–Sat 10–5.30, Sun by appointment
winemaker Robert Fiumara **production** 15 000 cases **est.** 1982
product range ($10–16.50 CD) Semillon, Sauvignon Blanc, Chardonnay, Tramillon® (Traminer Semillon), Spatlese Lexia, Noble Riesling, Noble Muscat of Alexandria, Noble Harvest, Red Velvet® (medium-sweet red), Shiraz, Petit Verdot, Cabernet Sauvignon, Tawny Port, VP (fortified Shiraz).
summary Apart from occasional Vintage Ports, the best wines by far are the botrytised white wines, with the Noble Muscat of Alexandria unique to the winery; these wines have both style and intensity of flavour and can age well. The Noble Semillon and Noble Traminer add strings to the bow. Exports to the US and Canada.

Lillypilly Estate Sauvignon Blanc

ΨΨΨΨ 2002 Medium yellow-green; clear, albeit ripe, varietal tropical and gooseberry aromas lead into a clean, medium-bodied and well-balanced palate, with just a hint of residual sugar. Amply reflects the outstanding vintage and, I suspect, a one-in-ten-year event. **rating:** 86
best drinking Now **drink with** Local yabbies • $12.50

Lillypilly Estate Tramillon®

ΨΨΨΨ 2002 Light straw-green; an exotic and striking bouquet with perfumed, spicy traminer aromas is followed by a palate with inherently the same striking fruit, but with a relatively high level of residual sugar. Oh, for less sweetness, even though I recognise that it is part of this unique wine. **rating:** 87
best drinking Now **drink with** Gently spiced Asian dishes • $11.50

🐾 lilyvale wines ★★★

Riverton Road, via Texas, Qld 4385 **region** Granite Belt
phone (07) 4653 5280 **fax** (07) 5466 5409 **open** 7 days 10–4
winemaker John Hordern, Peter Scudamore-Smith (Contract) **est.** 1997
product range ($14–16 R) Semillon, Verdelho, Shiraz, Merlot.
summary Yet another new but substantial winery in Queensland. It has established 5 hectares each of shiraz and chardonnay, 3 hectares of cabernet sauvignon, around 2.5 hectares each of semillon and verdelho, and 1.5 hectares of merlot. The vineyard is situated near the Dumaresq River on the border between Queensland and New South Wales. Part of the wine is made under the direction of Peter Scudamore-Smith MW, and part goes all the way to New South Wales' Upper Hunter, where John Hordern is winemaker.

Lilyvale Semillon

▼▼▼▽ **2002** Light straw-green; the clean and faintly spicy bouquet is followed by a fresh palate with some mineral and lime fruit; well balanced, but not long. **rating:** 84
best drinking Now–2006 **drink with** Seafood basket • $14

Lilyvale Verdelho

▼▼▼▽ **2002** Light yellow-green; the bouquet is clean but not particularly aromatic; the well-made palate has nicely balanced, light, tropical fruit salad flavours. **rating:** 84
best drinking Now **drink with** Lemon chicken • $14

lindemans (coonawarra) ★★★★

Main Penola–Naracoorte Road, Coonawarra, SA 5263 **region** Coonawarra
phone (02) 4998 7684 **fax** (02) 4998 7682 **open** Not
winemaker Greg Clayfield **production** NFP **est.** 1908
product range ($10–50 R) Pyrus (Cabernet blend), Limestone Ridge (Shiraz Cabernet), St George (Cabernet Sauvignon).
summary Lindemans is clearly the strongest brand other than Penfolds (and perhaps Rosemount) in the Southcorp Group, with some great vineyards and a great history. The Coonawarra vineyards are of ever-increasing significance because of the move towards regional identity in the all-important export markets, which has led to the emergence of a new range of regional/varietal labels. Whether the fullest potential of the vineyards (from a viticultural viewpoint) is being realised is a matter of debate. Worldwide distribution.

Lindemans Limestone Ridge

▼▼▼▼ **1999** Medium red-purple; a complex mix of dark berry fruit and soft oak aromas leads into a palate with plenty of depth, but which seems to be lacking freshness. The track record of this wine strongly suggests that it may simply be going through an ugly phase of its development. **rating:** 89
best drinking 2004–2014 **best vintages** '86, '88, '90, '91, '93, '94, '96, '97, '98 **drink with** Beef casserole • $45

Lindemans Pyrus

▼▼▼▼▽ **1999** Medium red-purple; smooth blackberry, blackcurrant and redcurrant aromas have a gentle substrate of oak; the long, savoury palate shows the influence of merlot in the blend; finishes with lingering tannins. **rating:** 91
best drinking 2004–2012 **best vintages** '88, '90, '91, '96, '97, '98 **drink with** Entrecôte of beef • $45

Lindemans St George

▼▼▼▼ **1999** Medium red-purple; the bouquet is very dusty, with curiously ill-fitting oak; the palate has blackcurrant fruit before a very tannic finish. By far the least of the Lindemans trio this vintage. **rating:** 86
best drinking 2004–2008 **best vintages** '86, '88, '90, '91, '96, '97, '98 **drink with** Shoulder of lamb • $45

lindemans (hunter valley) ★★★☆

McDonalds Road, Pokolbin, NSW 2320 **region** Lower Hunter Valley
phone (02) 4998 7684 **fax** (02) 4998 7324 **open** 7 days 10–5
winemaker Various **production** NFP **est.** 1843
product range ($8–38 R) Hunter Valley Semillon, Chardonnay, Shiraz; Ben Ean Shiraz, Steven Shiraz.
summary One way or another, I have intersected with the Hunter Valley in general and Lindemans in particular for over 45 years. It is now but a shadow of its former self, no longer made in the Lower Hunter, its once mighty Semillon a mere shadow of its former self. However, the refurbished historic Ben Ean winery (while no longer making wine) is a must-see for the wine tourist.

lindemans (karadoc) ★★★☆

Edey Road, Karadoc via Red Cliffs, Vic 3496 **region** Murray Darling
phone (03) 5051 3333 **fax** (03) 5051 3390 **open** 7 days 10–4.60
winemaker Greg Clayfield, Wayne Falkenberg **production** 8 million cases **est.** 1974
product range ($7–13.99 R) Bin 23 Riesling, Bin 65 Chardonnay (one of the largest-selling Chardonnay brands in the world), Bin 95 Sauvignon Blanc, Bin 99 Pinot Noir, Bin 45 Cabernet Sauvignon, Bin 50 Shiraz, Bin 40 Merlot are the most important in terms of volume; Cawarra range of Colombard Chardonnay, Classic Dry White, Traminer Riesling, Shiraz Cabernet, Merlot; Karadoc also produces the group fortified wines.
summary Now the production centre for all of the Lindemans and Leo Buring wines, with the exception of special lines made in the Coonawarra and Hunter wineries. The biggest and most modern single facility in Australia, allowing all-important economies of scale, and the major processing centre for the beverage wine sector (casks, flagons and low-priced bottles) of the Southcorp empire. Its achievement in making several million cases of Bin 65 Chardonnay a year is extraordinary given the quality and consistency of the wines. Worldwide distribution.

Lindemans Bin 75 Riesling
▼▼▼▼♀ **2002** Light to medium yellow-green; a fine, intense and floral bouquet with some underlying mineral; the palate has very good length and balance, with a crisp finish. Entirely sourced from the Limestone Coast. Exceptional value. **rating:** 92
best drinking Now–2006 **best vintages** '02 **drink with** Calamari salad • $8.99

Lindemans Bin 65 Chardonnay
▼▼▼▼ **2002** Amazingly, has won gold medals at both the Brisbane and Adelaide Royal Wine Shows this year, against a myriad of much higher-priced contestants. The bouquet offers melon, stone fruit and the barest hint of oak; the palate is well balanced, with a touch of creaminess, and moderate fruit intensity. Clever winemaking. **rating:** 88
best drinking Now **best vintages** '02 **drink with** Virtually anything you choose • $9

Lindemans Reserve South Australia Shiraz
▼▼▼▼♀ **2001** Medium purple-red; complex fruit aromas of berry, licorice and herb lead directly into a palate with abundant blackberry/black cherry fruit; has length, and the French and American oak used is subtle. A great bargain. **rating:** 90
best drinking 2004–2008 **drink with** Roast beef • $13.99

Lindemans Bin 40 Merlot
▼▼▼▼ **2002** Medium purple-red; the bouquet has quite ripe red and blackberry fruit with a nice savoury streak; the light-bodied palate is soft and clean, uncomplicated, but with some recognisable varietal character. Great value for the variety. **rating:** 85
best drinking Now–2005 **drink with** Turkey • $8.99

lindemans (padthaway) ★★★★

Naracoorte Road, Padthaway, SA 5271 **region** Padthaway
phone (02) 4998 7684 **fax** (02) 4998 7682 **open** Not
winemaker Greg Clayfield **production** NFP **est.** 1908
product range ($11–15 R) Reserve Padthaway Chardonnay, Reserve Cabernet Merlot, plus the Limestone Coast varietal range.
summary Lindemans Padthaway Chardonnay is one of the better premium Chardonnays on the market in Australia, with an exceptional capacity to age. However, all the wines under the Padthaway label offer consistent quality and value for money.

Lindemans Padthaway Reserve Cabernet Sauvignon
▼▼▼▼ **2000** Medium red-purple; savoury, earthy cabernet varietal fruit comes through strongly on the bouquet, flowing through to the bright cassis/blackcurrant fruit of the palate, which has good length and structure. By far the best of the Reserve Padthaway releases from 1999 and 2000. **rating:** 88
best drinking 2005–2010 **drink with** Marinated beef

🐚 lindenderry at red hill ★★★★

142 Arthurs Seat Road, Red Hill, Vic 3937 **region** Mornington Peninsula
phone (03) 5989 2933 **fax** (03) 5989 2936 **open** By appointment
winemaker Lindsay McCall (Contract) **production** 1000 cases **est.** 1999

product range ($15–35 CD) Chardonnay, Pinot Blanc, Pinot Noir.

summary Lindenderry at Red Hill is a sister operation to Lancemore Hill in the Macedon Ranges and Lindenwarrah at Milawa. It offers a five-star country house hotel, conference facilities, a function area, an à la carte restaurant situated on 16 hectares of park-like gardens, but also includes a little over 3 hectares of vineyards, equally planted to pinot noir and chardonnay 10 years ago. The wines are made by Lindsay McCall of Paringa Estate fame, using techniques similar to those he uses for his estate wines.

Lindenderry at Red Hill Pinot Noir

▼▼▼▼ 2000 Light to medium red-purple; a fragrant sappy/spicy/foresty bouquet runs through into a potent palate which has some attractive, slightly stemmy, flavours and high acidity, belying its alcohol of 14°. One of those Pinots which demands food. **rating: 88**

best drinking Now–2007 **best vintages** '99 **drink with** Duck • $35

lindrum   NR

c/- Level 29, Chifley Tower, 2 Chifley Square, Sydney, NSW 2000 (postal) **region** Langhorne Creek
phone (02) 9375 2185 **fax** (02) 9375 2121 **open** Not
winemaker Michael Potts (Contract) **production** 12 000 cases **est.** 2001
product range ($17–99 ML) Premium range of Clara Semillon Chardonnay, Horace Cabernet Shiraz; Reserve range of Verdelho, Chardonnay, Shiraz, Cabernet Sauvignon.
summary The Lindrum story is a fascinating one; few Australians will not have heard of Walter Lindrum, who reigned as World Professional Billiards and Snooker Champion for over 30 years. What few would know is that his great-grandfather, Frederick Wilhelm von Lindrum, was a renowned vigneron in Norwood, South Australia, and also became Australia's first professional billiards champion, beating the English champion, John Roberts, in 1869. The wines are made from purchased grapes by contract winemaker Michael Potts at Potts' Bleasdale Winery; an active website helps the marketing effort, which is otherwise through retail sources.

lirralirra estate   ★★★☆

Paynes Road, Lilydale, Vic 3140 **region** Yarra Valley
phone (03) 9735 0224 **fax** (03) 9735 0224 **open** Weekends and holidays 10–6, Jan 7 days
winemaker Alan Smith **production** 300 cases **est.** 1981
product range ($17–30 CD) Sauvignon Blanc, Reserve Sauvignon Blanc, Fume Blanc, Semillon Sauvignon Blanc, Reserve Pinot Noir, Cabernets.
summary Twenty years ago I wrote that the Yarra Valley was a viticultural Garden of Eden; little did I know. The trials and tribulations of Lirralirra over the past 10 years have been awesome, yet Alan Smith retains a sense of proportion and faith in the future. All I can say is he deserves every success that comes his way.

Lirralirra Estate Fume Blanc

▼▼▼▼ 2001 Light to medium yellow-green; the firm bouquet has mineral and grass aromas with well-integrated and balanced oak; it is on the medium to full-bodied palate that the oak becomes a little too assertive.
rating: 85
best drinking Now **drink with** Smoked eel • $19

Lirralirra Sauvignon Blanc

▼▼▼▼ 2002 Light to medium yellow-green; a light but aromatic bouquet has plenty of passionfruit and gooseberry aromas, which come through on the palate; attractive flavour and good length. **rating: 88**
best drinking Now **best vintages** '94 **drink with** Shellfish • $19

Lirralirra Pinot Noir

▼▼▼▼▽ 2001 Exceptionally youthful and deep purple-red; full, ripe plum and a touch of spice on the bouquet flow through to the powerful and youthful palate, which has abundant flavour and development potential. Five days' cold maceration prior to fermentation has no doubt contributed to the colour and flavour. **rating: 90**
best drinking Now–2007 **best vintages** '01 **drink with** Smoked quail • $30

little river wines   NR

Cnr West Swan and Forest Roads, Henley Brook, WA 6055 **region** Swan Valley
phone (08) 9296 4462 **fax** (08) 9296 1022 **open** 7 days 10–5
winemaker Bruno de Tastes **production** 3000 cases **est.** 1934
product range ($15–28 CD) Chenin Blanc, Viognier, Chardonnay, Brut de Brut, Vin Doux Late Harvest, Noble Classic, Florial Dry Rose, Old Vines Shiraz, Cabernet Sauvignon Merlot.

summary Following several quick changes of ownership (and of consultant winemakers), the former Glenalwyn now has as its winemaker the eponymously named Count Bruno de Tastes. I, however, have had no recent tastes. The wines come from 4 hectares of estate vineyards. Exports to Hong Kong and Malaysia.

little's winery ★★★★

Cnr Palmers Lane and McDonalds Road, Pokolbin, NSW 2320 **region** Lower Hunter Valley
phone (02) 6579 1111 **fax** (02) 6579 1440 **open** 7 days 10–4
winemaker Ian Little, Suzanne Little **production** 11 000 cases **est.** 1984
product range ($15–24 R) Premium Hunter Valley range of Gewurztraminer, Semillon Chardonnay, Cabernet Shiraz Merlot; Olivine range of Verdelho, Merlot; Reserve range of Semillon, Chardonnay, Shiraz.
summary Little's Winery continues to flourish, having sold the old winery further down Palmers Lane, and moved into brand-new premises on the (busier) corner of McDonalds Road. There you find the same friendly service and friendly wines: aromatic, fresh white wines, light-bodied red wines in the premium range, and fuller, more structured wines in the Reserve range. Has grown steadily, with 41 hectares of estate vineyards; another 44 hectares of vineyards are leased. The wines are exported to the US, Canada and the UK.

Little's Gewurztraminer
▼▼▼▼ **2002** Light straw-green; distinctive rose petal and lychee varietal aromas lead into a light-bodied palate which retains the same distinctive varietal character in a delicate mode. A tour de force of winemaking given its Hunter Valley origins. **rating:** 88
best drinking Now **best vintages** '02 **drink with** Asian stir-fry • $16

Little's Reserve Semillon
▼▼▼▼ **2001** Light green-yellow; the clean bouquet has citrus, grass and herb aromas, and the palate provides pleasing flavour in a thoroughly unconventional style, more akin to that encountered in the Adelaide Hills or Margaret River. The wine has 12.5° alcohol, is given short skin contact and lees stirring. Patience not required. **rating:** 88
best drinking Now–2005 **best vintages** '00 **drink with** Summer salad • $18

Little's Olivine Verdelho
▼▼▼▼ **2002** Light straw-green; fresh, relatively delicate fruit salad and citrus aromas and flavours mark a quite fine wine which has intensity and length; well above average. Grown on a steep hillside in the Upper Hunter Valley. **rating:** 87
best drinking Now **drink with** Quiche Lorraine • $15

Little's Talga Chardonnay
▼▼▼▼ **2001** Medium yellow-green; the moderately intense bouquet is complex and aromatic, with well-balanced fruit and oak; the palate is in a slightly austere style, but does have length and persistence, with melon and stone fruit showing through. Will develop over the short term. **rating:** 88
best drinking Now–2007 **best vintages** '00 **drink with** Carpaccio of salmon • $24

Little's Reserve Shiraz
▼▼▼▼▽ **2000** Medium red-purple; fresh and lively spicy fruit with balanced/integrated oak on the bouquet leads into an elegant palate with a range of sweet leathery/savoury characters utterly typically of the Hunter Valley; the oak is particularly well-integrated, doubtless owing to the fact that the wine was actually fermented in barrels with the heads knocked out. For the record, a mixture of French and American. **rating:** 92
best drinking 2004–2014 **best vintages** '00 **drink with** Braised beef • $24

Little's Olivine Merlot
▼▼▼▼ **2001** Strong purple-red; solid, ripe dark fruit aromas and a hint of oak lead into a medium to full-bodied palate with little varietal character; a nicely made red wine. **rating:** 86
best drinking 2004–2009 **drink with** Beef spare ribs • $17

🍎 little valley ★★★★

RMB 6047, One Chain Road, Merricks North, Vic 3926 **region** Mornington Peninsula
phone (03) 5989 7564 **fax** (03) 5989 7564 **open** By appointment
winemaker Richard McIntyre (Contract) **production** 300 cases **est.** 1998
product range ($25 ML) Chardonnay, Pinot Noir.

summary Wesley College teacher Sue Taylor and her husband, part-time Anglican minister Brian, have planted 0.8 hectare each of chardonnay and pinot noir on their Little Valley property, simultaneously building their house on the property. They have Ian MacRae as consultant viticulturist, and Rick McIntyre (of Moorooduc Estate) makes the wines. Unfortunately, the 2002 vintage was so small that there will be no 2002 Chardonnay and less than 40 dozen bottles of Pinot Noir from the vintage. It is as well that the Mornington Peninsula is such a beautiful place; the Little Valley property itself is a prime example of that beauty, providing a return which is not measured in dollars and cents.

Little Valley Chardonnay

ΨΨΨΨ 2000 Developed yellow-straw colour, yet quite bright; lifted melon and citrus rind aromas and an airbrush of oak lead into a light to medium-bodied palate, with an interplay of crisp melon fruit, a touch of mineral and a touch of oak.   **rating:** 87

best drinking Now–2005 **drink with** Tempura calamari • $25

Little Valley Pinot Noir

ΨΨΨΨΨ 2001 Youthful, bright red-purple; fresh dark cherry and plum fruit aromas immediately set the scene for a palate with intense plum/cherry fruit, silky tannins and a long finish, oak playing a classic support role.

best drinking Now–2006 **best vintages** '01 **drink with** Rare roasted squab • $25   **rating:** 91

llangibby estate   NR

Old Mount Barker Road, Echunga, SA 5153 (postal) **region** Adelaide Hills
phone (08) 8338 5529 **fax** (08) 8338 7118 **open** Not
winemaker Ben Riggs (Contract) **production** 1200 cases **est.** 1998
product range ($10–17 ML) Sauvignon Blanc, Pinot Noir, Pinot Shiraz (Hermitage), Shiraz Cabernet, Tempranillo.
summary Chris Addams Williams and John Williamson have established a substantial vineyard cresting a ridge close to Echunga, at a height of 360 metres. The varietal choice is eclectic, the lion's share going to a little over 5 hectares each of shiraz and cabernet sauvignon, then 1.95 hectares of tempranillo, 1.4 hectares of sauvignon blanc and a tiny planting of pinot noir. Until 2002 this was used to provide a Pinot Hermitage blend, but from that year both a varietal Tempranillo and Pinot Noir have joined the product range alongside Sauvignon Blanc and Shiraz Cabernet.

logan wines   ★★★☆

Ground Floor, 160 Sailor's Bay Road, Northbridge, NSW 2063 **region** Orange
phone (02) 9958 6844 **fax** (02) 9958 1258 **open** Not
winemaker Peter Logan **production** 17 000 cases **est.** 1997
product range ($15–27 R) Sauvignon Blanc, Chardonnay, Reserve Chardonnay, Weemala Chardonnay, Shiraz, Weemala Shiraz, Weemala Merlot, Cabernet Merlot.
summary Logan wines is a family operation, founded by businessman Mal Logan assisted by three of his children: Peter, who just happens to be an oenology graduate from the University of Adelaide, Greg (advertising) and Kylie (office administrator). Retail distribution in all states; exports to the UK, the US, Canada, the Philippines and New Zealand.

Logan Sauvignon Blanc

ΨΨΨΨ 2002 Very light straw; the bouquet has obvious varietal character in a tropical, passionfruit spectrum and an underlying hint of sweatiness; the lively, fresh palate adds guava to the tropical fruit of the bouquet; freshened by a touch of CO_2, although that hint of reduction persists. I have not down-pointed the wine because of it.

best drinking Now **drink with** White asparagus • $18.95   **rating:** 88

Logan Shiraz

ΨΨΨΨ 1999 Light to medium red-purple; there are clean, spicy, cool-climate edges to fine black fruits on the bouquet; the light to medium-bodied palate has some sweet black fruits in the middle, surrounded by lighter, more savoury nuances.   **rating:** 85

best drinking 2004–2008 **best vintages** '97 **drink with** Game • $25

london lodge estate   NR

Muswellbrook Road, Gungal, NSW 2333 **region** Upper Hunter Valley
phone (02) 6547 6122 **fax** (02) 6547 6122 **open** 7 days 10–9
winemaker Gary Reed (Contract) **est.** 1988

summary The 16-hectare vineyard of Stephen and Joanne Horner is planted to chardonnay, pinot noir, shiraz and cabernet sauvignon, and sold through a cellar door (and restaurant) with a full array of tourist attractions, including arts and crafts.

long gully estate   NR

Long Gully Road, Healesville, Vic 3777 **region** Yarra Valley
phone (03) 9510 5798 **fax** (03) 9510 9859 **open** 7 days 11–5
winemaker Peter Florance, Luke Houlihan **production** 30 000 cases **est.** 1982
product range ($15–30 CD) Premium range of: Riesling, Sauvignon Blanc, Chardonnay, Reserve Ice Riesling, Pinot Noir, Shiraz, Reserve Merlot, Irma's Cabernet; Victoria Collection of Spatlese Riesling, Sauvignon Blanc Semillon Chardonnay, Chardonnay, Bunyarra Rose, Pinot Noir, Cabernet Sauvignon.
summary One of the larger (but by no means largest) of the Yarra Valley producers which have successfully established a number of export markets over recent years. Wine quality has risen, doubtless due to a core of mature vineyards; it is able to offer a range of wines with 2–3 years bottle age. Recent vineyard extensions underline the commercial success of Long Gully. Exports to the UK, Switzerland and Germany. No recent tastings.

longleat   ★★★☆

105 Old Weir Road, Murchison, Vic 3610 **region** Goulburn Valley
phone (03) 5826 2294 **fax** (03) 5826 2510 **open** Weekends and public holidays 10–5
winemaker David Traeger (Contract) **production** 3000 cases **est.** 1975
product range ($10–28 CD) River's Edge Riesling, Founder's Reserve Semillon, Semillon Sauvignon Blanc, Murchison Mill Shiraz, Old Weir Road Shiraz, Campbell's Bend Cabernet Sauvignon.
summary Longleat has a 7.5-hectare vineyard, largely planted over 25 years ago. This provides the riesling, semillon, shiraz and cabernet, with small amounts of sauvignon blanc brought in. All of the production goes to make the Longleat wines, which are now distributed nationally by Alepat Taylor, and exported to Malaysia and the US.

long point vineyard   ★★★

6 Cooinda Place, Lake Cathie, NSW 2445 **region** Hastings River
phone (02) 6585 4598 **fax** (02) 6584 8915 **open** Thurs–Sun and public holidays 10–6, or by appointment
winemaker Graeme Davies **production** 600 cases **est.** 1995
product range ($13–20 CD) Traminer, Chardonnay, Shiraz, Duet Cabernet Sauvignon Chambourcin. Also ginger beer, mead and orange liqueur.
summary In turning their dream into reality, Graeme (an educational psychologist) and Helen (chartered accountant) Davies took no chances. After becoming interested in wine as consumers through wine appreciation courses the Davies moved from Brisbane so that 36-year-old Graeme could begin his study for a post-graduate diploma in wine from Roseworthy. Late in 1993 they purchased a 5-hectare property near Lake Cathie, progressively establishing 2 hectares of chardonnay, shiraz, chambourcin, cabernet sauvignon and frontignac. As well as having a full-time job at Cassegrain and establishing the vineyard, Graeme Davies self-built the house designed by Helen with a pyramid shaped roof and an underground cellar. All of the wines are made on-site.

longview vineyard   NR

Pound Road, Macclesfield, SA 5153 **region** Adelaide Hills
phone (08) 8388 9694 **fax** (08) 8388 9693 **open** By appointment
winemaker Shaw & Smith, Kangarilla, d'Arenberg (Contract) **production** 1500 cases **est.** 1995
product range ($10–19 ML) Iron Knob Riesling, Beau Sea Viognier, Blue Cow Unwooded Chardonnay, Red Bucket Shiraz, Epitome Red, Nebbiolo, Zinfandel, Devils Elbow Cabernet.
summary In a strange twist of fate, Longview Vineyard came to be through the success of Two Dogs lemon-flavoured alcohol drink created by Duncan MacGillivray, sold in 1995 to the Pernod Ricard Groupe (also the owners of Orlando). Nearly 50 hectares have been planted, with shiraz and cabernet sauvignon accounting for more than half, followed by significant plantings of chardonnay and merlot, with smaller plantings of viognier, semillon, riesling, sauvignon blanc, zinfandel and nebbiolo. The majority of the production is sold to Rosemount, but $1.2 million has been invested in establishing a cellar door and function area, barrel rooms and an overall administration centre for the Group activities. All of the buildings enjoy a spectacular view over the Coorong and Lake Alexandrina.

lost lake vineyard & winery ★★★☆

Lot 3 Vasse Highway, Pemberton, WA 6260 **region** Pemberton
phone (08) 9776 1251 **fax** (08) 9776 1919 **open** By appointment
winemaker Contract **production** 3500 cases **est.** 1990
product range ($16–27 CD) Sauvignon Blanc, Semillon Chardonnay, Chardonnay, Pinot Noir, Shiraz.
summary Previously known as Eastbrook Estate, its origins go back to 1990 and to the acquisition of a 80-hectare farming property which was subdivided into three portions: 16 hectares, now known as Picardy, were acquired by Dr Bill Pannell; 18 hectares became the base for Lost Lake; and the remainder was sold. The initial plantings in 1990 were of pinot noir and chardonnay, followed by shiraz, sauvignon blanc, merlot and cabernet sauvignon between 1996 and 1998. Just under 8 hectares are now planted. A jarrah pole and cedar winery with a crush capacity of 300 tonnes was built in 1995, together with a restaurant which seats 150 people; it is open six days a week for lunch and for dinner on Friday and Saturday nights. In 1999 the business was acquired by four Perth investors.

Lost Lake Shiraz

▼▼▼▼ **2000** Medium red-purple; spice, sweet cedar and savoury aromas are followed by a palate with dark cherry fruit surrounded by lots of oak and oak tannins. **rating:** 87
best drinking 2004–2009 **drink with** Spiced beef • $17.95

lost valley winery ★★★☆

Strath Creek, Vic 3658 (postal) **region** Central Victorian High Country
phone (03) 9592 3531 **fax** (03) 9592 6396 **open** Not
winemaker Alex White (Contract) **production** 2200 cases **est.** 1995
product range ($30–33 R) Shiraz, Merlot, Cortese.
summary Dr Robert Ippaso planted the Lost Valley vineyard at an elevation of 450 metres on the slopes of Mount Tallarook, with 1.5 hectares of shiraz, merlot and cortese. The cortese is the only such planting in Australia. It pays homage to Dr Ippaso's birthplace in Savoie in the Franco-Italian Alps, where cortese flourishes. Exports to the UK and Singapore.

Lost Valley Cortese

▼▼▼▼ **2002** Light straw-green; an aromatic and crisp bouquet with aromas of herb, spicy mustard seed and lemon leads into a palate with lemony fruit, good mouthfeel, balance and length. **rating:** 88
best drinking Now–2007 **drink with** Light seafood • $30

Lost Valley Shiraz

▼▼▼▼ **2001** Medium red-purple; the moderately intense bouquet has spicy, leafy, earthy edges to the red fruits, the light to medium-bodied palate following down the same track, with a gently savoury, European feel. Despite its 14° alcohol, seems very much lighter and easier to access than the 2000. **rating:** 86
best drinking Now–2006 **drink with** Leave it in the cellar • $33

Lost Valley Merlot

▼▼▼▼ **2001** Medium red-purple; the bouquet has distinct savoury/earthy varietal overtones to the berry fruit; the powerful, quite sweet palate has dark fruits on entry, then olive and savoury notes towards the finish. Has good varietal presence, and should develop nicely. **rating:** 89
best drinking 2005–2010 **drink with** Saltimbocca • $33

louis-laval wines NR

160 Cobcroft Road, Broke, NSW 2330 **region** Lower Hunter Valley
phone (02) 6579 1105 **fax** (02) 6579 1105 **open** By appointment
winemaker Roy Meyer **production** 600 cases **est.** 1987
product range ($25 CD) Shiraz, Cabernet Sauvignon.
summary It is ironic that the winery name should have eponymous associations with Alfa Laval, the giant Swiss food and wine machinery firm. Roy Meyer runs an organic vineyard (using only sulphur and copper sprays) and is proud of the fact that the winery has no refrigeration and no stainless steel. The wines produced from the 2.5-hectare vineyard are fermented in open barrels or cement tanks, and maturation is handled entirely in oak. At its first entry into the Hunter Valley Small Winemakers Show, the 1998 Cabernet Sauvignon won a silver medal, and the 1998 Shiraz a bronze medal.

lovegrove vineyard and winery ★★★☆

1420 Heidelberg-Kinglake Road, Cottles Bridge, Vic 3099 **region** Yarra Valley
phone (03) 9718 1569 **fax** (03) 9718 1028 **open** Weekends and public holidays 11–6, Mon–Fri by appointment
winemaker Stephen Bennett **production** 1500 cases **est.** 1983
product range ($15–32 CD) Sauvignon Blanc, Chardonnay, Quest Chardonnay, Paradis, Petillant Methode Champenoise, Pinot Noir, Merlot, Cabernet Merlot.
summary Lovegrove is a long-established winery in the Diamond Valley sub-region, and while production is limited, offers the visitor much to enjoy, with picturesque gardens overlooking the Kinglake Ranges; antipasto, soup and cheese lunch; barbecue and picnic tables; and live music on the second Sunday of the month. Intermittent art exhibitions are staged, and the winery caters for private functions. The wines are produced from 4 hectares of estate plantings which are now fully mature, and a range of vintages is available.

lowe family wines ★★★★

Tinja Lane, Mudgee, NSW 2850 **region** Mudgee
phone (02) 6372 0800 **fax** (02) 6372 0811 **open** Fri–Mon 10–5, or by appointment
winemaker David Lowe, Jane Wilson **production** 6000 cases **est.** 1987
product range ($15–35 CD) Semillon, Chardonnay, Botrytis Semillon, Shiraz, Merlot, Orange Red (Cabernet blend); also Tinja Chardonnay, Merlot Rose, Sangiovese blend.
summary Former Rothbury winemaker David Lowe and Jane Wilson make the Lowe Family Wines at two locations, principally at their purpose-built winery at Mudgee, but also with a shop-front in the Hunter Valley via the former Peppers Creek. Exports to the UK, Germany and Canada.

Lowe Family Botrytis Semillon

▼▼▼▼▽ 2001 Glowing yellow; the complex bouquet has strong cumquat and honey aromas which come through strongly on the rich and very honeyed palate; nice balancing acidity and a flick of oak complete the palate. A mix of cordon-cut and botrytised material from 75-year-old vines matured in French oak. **rating:** 90
best drinking Now–2007 **best vintages** '99 **drink with** Fruit tart and King Island cream • $21

Lowe Family Shiraz

▼▼▼▼ 2001 Medium red-purple; a smooth, quite ripe bouquet has dusty berry, chocolate and a hint of vanilla; the light to medium-bodied palate repeats the exercise, with sweet plum and berry fruit, then soft, ripe tannins to close. **rating:** 87
best drinking 2004–2008 **drink with** Cheese • $28

Lowe Family Tinja

▼▼▼▼ 2002 Light to medium red-purple; fragrant, spicy edges to the light, small berry red fruit aromas of the bouquet make an interesting start; the light to medium-bodied palate is nicely balanced, once again focusing on the interesting blend of Sangiovese, Merlot and Barbera. **rating:** 87
best drinking Now–2006 **drink with** Lasagne • $15

Lowe Family Mudgee Merlot

▼▼▼▼▽ 2001 Medium red-purple; the clean bouquet offers sweet blackcurrant and redcurrant fruit, which also comes through strongly on the opening of the palate; then an attractive and varietal range of spice, cedar and savoury notes provide good texture and weight. **rating:** 90
best drinking 2004–2009 **best vintages** '01 **drink with** Braised veal • $25

lowe family wines (hunter valley) ★★★★

Cnr Broke Road/Ekerts Lane, Pokolbin, NSW 2321 **region** Lower Hunter Valley
phone (02) 4998 7121 **fax** (02) 4998 7121 **open** Wed–Mon 10–5
winemaker David Lowe, Jane Wilson **production** 2500 cases **est.** 1987
product range ($15–25 CD) Semillon, Chardonnay, Shiraz, Merlot, Orange Red (Cabernet blend), Yacht Club Port; also Peppers Creek wines (Hunter Valley) Rose, Merlot and Shiraz.
summary The former Peppers Creek winery has been acquired by David Lowe and Jane Wilson, and is now the Hunter Valley base for Lowe Family Wines. For the time being the Peppers Creek brand is being maintained.

loxley vineyard   NR

362 Pastoria East Road, Pipers Creek near Kyneton, Vic 3444 **region** Macedon Ranges
phone (03) 9616 6598 **fax** (03) 9614 2249 **open** Not
winemaker John Ellis, Llew Knight (Contract) **est.** 1999
product range Riesling, Sparkling, Pinot Noir, Merlot.
summary A partnership is developing a vineyard/resort/entertainment complex at Loxley. Seventeen hectares of vineyard have been planted, and contract winemaking arranged through John Ellis and Llew Knight. Wines will be produced under two labels, as part of the crop is being sold to John Ellis of Hanging Rock. The first commercial releases are expected in 2003–4.

lucas estate wines   NR

Donges Road, Severnlea, Qld 4352 **region** Granite Belt
phone (07) 4683 6365 **fax** (07) 4683 6356 **open** 7 days 10–5
winemaker Peter Lucas **production** 250 cases **est.** 1999
product range ($10–20 CD) Chardonnay, Rose, Shiraz, Merlot, Oaked Merlot, Cabernet Merlot, Cabernet Shiraz, Cabernet Sauvignon, Muscat, Vintage Port.
summary Peter and Robyn Lucas purchased the property on which their vineyard and winery is now established in 1994 in the wake of Peter's redundancy from his former occupation. Establishing the vineyard has been both slow and difficult, with drought-retarded growth, rabbit and wallaby attacks, and then drought-breaking rain-promoted fungal diseases inside the shields which had been put around the vines to stop rabbit and wallaby attack. Then, as everywhere, there are the birds. However, 2.5 hectares of chardonnay, merlot, shiraz, cabernet sauvignon, verdelho and muscat hamburg have been established, and the first good vintage came in 2000.

lyre bird hill   ★★★

370 Inverloch Road, Koonwarra, Vic 3954 **region** Gippsland
phone (03) 5664 3204 **fax** (03) 5664 3206 **open** Weekends and public holidays 10–5, or by appointment
winemaker Owen Schmidt **production** 2000 cases **est.** 1986
product range ($12–30 CD) Riesling, Riesling Cellar Reserve, Traminer, Sauvignon Blanc, Bowers Bouquet (white blend), Chardonnay, Shiraz Rose, Pinot Noir, Pinot Noir Cellar Reserve, Shiraz, Cabernet Sauvignon, Salut! (Cabernet Sauvignon Shiraz Merlot), Rhapsody (Sparkling), Phantasy (Sparkling), Golden Nectar (Dessert).
summary Former Melbourne professionals Owen and Robyn Schmidt make small quantities of estate-grown wine (the vineyard is 2.4 hectares in size), offering accommodation for three couples (RACV four-star rating) in their spacious guest house and self-contained cottage. Various weather-related viticulture problems have seen the Schmidts supplement their estate-grown intake with grapes from contract growers in Gippsland and the Yarra Valley.

🐌 mabrook estate   ★★★☆

258 Inlet Road, Bulga, NSW 2330 **region** Lower Hunter Valley
phone (02) 9971 9994 **fax** (02) 9971 9924 **open** By appointment
winemaker Larissa Kalt **production** 800 cases **est.** 1996
product range ($13.75–18 CD) Semillon, Apricot Paddock Semillon, Verdelho, Verdelho Wombat Creek Paddock, Shiraz.
summary The Swiss-born Kalt family began the establishment of Mabrook Estate in 1996, planting 3 hectares of semillon, 2 hectares of shiraz and 1 hectare of verdelho. Parents Mona and Tony Kalt decided to use organic growing methods from the word go, and the vineyard is now certified organic by NASAA (National Association Sustainable Agriculture Australia). Daughter Larissa, having obtained an Honours degree in Medical Science at the University of Sydney, decided to pursue winemaking by working as a 'lab rat' and cellar hand at Margan Family, and visited Switzerland and Italy to observe small-scale family winemaking in those countries. Wines from all three vintages (2000, 2001, 2002) have won show medals, and in 2002 the wines were made on-site at the small modern winery by Larissa Kalt; prior to that time they were contract-made.

Mabrook Estate Apricot Paddock Semillon

▼▼▼▼ **2002** Light straw-green; the clean, crisp, discreet bouquet is followed by a palate which, while light, has good mouthfeel and balance, the flavours moving from lemon to a hint of tropical fruit.   **rating:** 88
best drinking 2004–2009 **drink with** Asparagus salad • $15

mcalister vineyards NR

Golden Beach Road, Longford, Vic 3851 **region** Gippsland
phone (03) 5149 7229 **fax** (03) 5149 7229 **open** By appointment
winemaker Peter Edwards **production** 550 cases **est.** 1975
product range A single wine, The McAlister, a blend of Cabernet Sauvignon, Cabernet Franc and Merlot.
summary The McAlister Vineyards actively shun publicity or exposure which, on the basis of prior tastings, is a pity. Exports to the US and the UK.

macaw creek wines NR

Macaw Creek Road, Riverton, SA 5412 **region** Mount Lofty Ranges Zone
phone (08) 8847 2237 **fax** (08) 8847 2237 **open** Sun and public holidays 11–4
winemaker Rodney Hooper **production** 3000 cases **est.** 1992
product range ($13–35 CD) Riesling, Sauvignon Blanc Semillon, Pedro Ximinez (sweet white), Yoolang Preservative Free Shiraz, Shiraz, Reserve Shiraz Cabernet, Grenache Shiraz, Tawny Port.
summary The property on which Macaw Creek Wines is established has been owned by the Hooper family since the 1850s, but development of the estate vineyards did not begin until 1995; 10 hectares have been planted since that time, with a further 20 hectares planted in the winter/spring of 1999. Rodney and Miriam Hooper established the Macaw Creek brand previously (in 1992) with wines made from grapes from other regions, including the Preservative Free Yoolang Cabernet Shiraz. Rodney Hooper is a highly qualified and skilled winemaker with experience in many parts of Australia and internationally in Germany, France and the US. Exports to the UK, the US and Malaysia.

mcgee wines NR

1710 Wattlevale Road, Nagambie, Vic 3608 **region** Nagambie Lakes
phone (03) 5794 1530 **fax** (03) 5794 1530 **open** By appointment
winemaker Don Lewis (Contract) **production** 750 cases **est.** 1995
product range ($15.95 R) Chardonnay, Shiraz, Cabernet Sauvignon.
summary Andrew McGee and partner Kerry Smith (the latter the viticulturist) have established 12 hectares of vines on the banks of the Goulburn River, the majority planted to shiraz, with lesser quantities of grenache, viognier and mourvedre. Currently, 95 per cent of the production is sold to Mitchelton, where the McGee wines are presently made, but the plan is for the partners to make the wine for themselves in the future, and to increase production. The wines are distributed through Woods Wines, 35 Greeves Street, Fitzroy.

mcguigan wines ★★★★

Cnr Broke Road/McDonald Road, Pokolbin, NSW 2321 **region** Lower Hunter Valley
phone (02) 4998 7700 **fax** (02) 4998 7401 **open** 7 days 10–5
winemaker Brian McGuigan, Peter Hall, Thomas Jung, Brod Vallance **production** 1.4 million cases **est.** 1992
product range ($10–49.50 CD) The wines are sold in several price brackets: the Black Label range of Traminer Riesling, Verdelho Chardonnay, Chardonnay, Sparkling Chardonnay, Sparkling Shiraz and Black Label Red; the Bin range of 2000 Shiraz, 3000 Merlot, 4000 Cabernet Sauvignon, 6000 Verdelho, 7000 Chardonnay, 8000 Sauvignon Blanc, 9000 Semillon; Vineyard Selection Gewurztraminer, Chardonnay, Late Picked Semillon, Chambourcin, Grenache, Cabernet Merlot; Shareholder range of Lisa (sparkling), Late Picked Traminer, Shiraz; Superior Verdelho and Superior Verdot; the Personal Reserve range with Chardonnay, Louis (sparkling), Botrytis Semillon, Shiraz, Cabernet Sauvignon and Port; Genus 4 Old Vine Chardonnay, Shiraz and Cabernet Sauvignon; also Howcroft Estate Shiraz, Cabernet.
summary A public-listed company which is the ultimate logical expression of Brian McGuigan's marketing drive and vision, on a par with that of Wolf Blass in his heyday. Highly successful in its chosen niche market notwithstanding some labels which are garish. Has been particularly active in export markets, notably the US and more recently in China. There has been public discussion in the press and on the Internet of the difference between samples of McGuigan Genus 4 Old Vine Shiraz 2000 entered into a show and the wine later released for public sale. One of these days, the labelling laws may more effectively govern such practices, which by no means were confined to McGuigan Wines alone.

McGuigan Bin 9000 Semillon

▼▼▼▼▽ **2002** Pale straw-green; a classically clean, crisp and pure mineral and herb-accented bouquet is followed by a long, clean and pure palate, with subliminal residual sugar providing seductive balance; clever making.

rating: 91

best drinking Now–2010 **best vintages** '99, '00, '02 **drink with** Balmain bugs • $13.50

McGuigan Bin 7000 Chardonnay

▼▼▼▼♀ **2002** Medium to full yellow-green; the complex bouquet has deep peach and fig fruit accompanied by plenty of barrel-ferment oak; the palate has excellent balance to the rich, peachy fruit and the same, well-handled, oak. Gold medal Hunter Valley Wine Show 2002. **rating:** 90

best drinking Now **best vintages** '00, '02 **drink with** Breast of chicken • $13.50

McGuigan Genus 4 Old Vine Shiraz

▼▼▼▼♀ **2001** Medium red-purple; unusual five spice aromas run alongside ripe plum and blackberry fruit, the complex palate with plum, blackberry and cherry fruit, plus sweet spicy flavours. Two trophies at the 2002 Hunter Valley Wine Show, but I am less generous. **rating:** 90

best drinking 2006–2011 **best vintages** '00 **drink with** Jugged hare • $25

McGuigan Personal Reserve Hunter Valley Shiraz

▼▼▼▼▼ **2000** Medium red-purple; smooth and clean plum and blackberry fruit is accompanied by excellent oak balance and integration on the bouquet; the supple palate marries plum and blackberry fruit, smooth fine tannins, and gentle oak. Two trophies Hunter Valley Wine Show 2001 including Best Red Wine of Show. **rating:** 94

best drinking 2005–2015 **best vintages** '00 **drink with** Slow-braised beef • $49.50

McGuigan Genus 4 Old Vine Cabernet Sauvignon

▼▼▼▼ **2001** Medium red-purple; the clean, ripe bouquet has faintly jammy berry fruit; the powerful palate has ripe black fruits and tannins to match. The wine does indeed come from the Barossa Valley, not the Hunter Valley. **rating:** 87

best drinking 2004–2009 **best vintages** '00 **drink with** Lamb shoulder with garlic and rosemary • $25

McGuigan Personal Reserve Hunter Valley Cabernet Sauvignon

▼▼▼▼♀ **2000** Medium red-purple; earthy, blackcurrant bouquet is quite regional; moderately rich black fruits, nicely ripened and with plenty of depth and texture, are accompanied by cedary oak and ripe tannins on the palate. **rating:** 90

best drinking 2005–2012 **best vintages** '00 **drink with** Steak and kidney pie • $49.50

mcivor creek   NR

Costerfield Road, Heathcote, Vic 3523 **region** Heathcote
phone (03) 5433 3000 **fax** (03) 5433 3456 **open** 7 days 10–5.30
winemaker Peter Turley **production** 5000 cases **est.** 1973
product range ($12.50–27.50 CD) Chardonnay, Shiraz, Cabernet Shiraz, Fine Old Tawny Port.
summary The beautifully situated McIvor Creek winery is well worth a visit and does offer wines in diverse styles of which the red wines are the most regional. Peter Turley has 5 hectares of cabernet sauvignon together with 2.5 hectares of cabernet franc and merlot and supplements his intake with grapes from other growers. No recent tastings.

mclaren vale iii associates   ★★★★

130 Main Road, McLaren Vale, SA 5171 **region** McLaren Vale
phone 1800 501 513 **fax** (08) 8323 7422 **open** Mon–Fri 9–5, tasting by appointment
winemaker Brian Light **production** 12 000 cases **est.** 1999
product range ($16.80–40 R) Barrel Fermented Semillon, Three-D Sauvignon Blanc Semillon, Chenin Blanc, Chardonnay, Sparkling Chardonnay Pinot, The Third Degree (Merlot Cabernet Shiraz), Shiraz, Three Score & 10 Grenache, Merlot Elite.
summary The three associates in question all have a decade or more of wine industry experience; Mary Greer is managing partner, Reginald Wymond chairing partner, and Christopher Fox partner. The partnership owns 34 hectares of vines spanning two vineyards, one owned by Mary and John Greer, the other by Reg and Sue Wymond. The label was first introduced in 1999, the aim being to produce affordable quality wine. Exports to the US.

McLaren Vale III Associates Semillon Sauvignon Blanc

▼▼▼▼ **2002** Light to medium yellow-green; the bouquet is aromatic, albeit with a distinct matchstick reduction; the palate has plenty of flavour and length and the points are a cowardly compromise, for the wine won a trophy and gold medal at the highly respected McLaren Vale Wine Show in 2002. **rating:** 88

best drinking Now **drink with** Fish and chips • $16.80

McLaren Vale III Associates The Third Degree

♥♥♥♥♀ **2001** Medium red-purple; the bouquet a complex range of aromas, savoury/earthy, then dark chocolate, then cedar; the regional chocolate comes through very strongly on the palate which has a spectrum of red fruit flavours around that chocolate; good balance, length and oak handling. A blend of Merlot, Cabernet Sauvignon and Shiraz. **rating:** 92

best drinking 2005–2010 **best vintages** '01 **drink with** Adelaide pie floater • $21.80

mcleish estate ★★★★☆

Lot 3 De Beyers Road, Pokolbin, NSW 2320 **region** Lower Hunter Valley
phone (02) 4998 7754 **fax** (02) 4998 7754 **open** 7 days 10–5, or by appointment
winemaker Andrew Thomas **production** 3000 cases **est.** 1985
product range ($14–45 CD) Semillon, Semillon Chardonnay, Verdelho, Verdelho Chardonnay, Chardonnay, Botrytis Semillon, Shiraz, Merlot, Cabernet Sauvignon.
summary Bob and Maryanne McLeish commenced the establishment of their vineyard in 1985, and have progressively planted over 10 hectares. They have now moved to opening up their cellar door to the public, having accumulated a number of gold medals for their wines.

McLeish Estate Semillon

♥♥♥♥♥ **2002** Light to medium green-yellow; intense grass, herb and lemon aromas and flavours are lengthened and focused on the palate by the very good acidity. Follows directly on the outstanding 2001; like it, a gold medal winner at the Hunter Valley Wine Show in the year of its vintage. Already drinking well. **rating:** 94

best drinking Now–2008 **best vintages** '01, '02 **drink with** Raw tuna • $15

McLeish Estate Semillon Chardonnay

♥♥♥♥♀ **2002** Light green-yellow; the complex bouquet shows the sophisticated use of oak, the palate driven by semillon, providing both length and crisp acidity on the finish. Gold medal for best blended white wine at the Hunter Valley Wine Show 2002. **rating:** 90

best drinking Now–2008 **best vintages** '02 **drink with** Japanese • $14

McLeish Estate Chardonnay

♥♥♥♥♀ **2002** Light to medium yellow-green; a complex bouquet with smoky/toasty cashew and melon aromas; attractive, fresh melon, stone fruit and citrus flavours on the palate complemented by skilled oak handling. Spends 8 months in new and one-year-old; 40 per cent malolactic fermentation. **rating:** 90

best drinking Now–2007 **best vintages** '02 **drink with** Grilled spatchcock • $15

McLeish Estate Shiraz

♥♥♥♥♀ **2001** Bright red-purple; the intense bouquet has a range of smooth dark cherry, raspberry and subtle oak inputs; the medium-bodied palate is smooth and supple, with sweet fruit rather than oak providing the flavour. As with all of the McLeish wines, great value. **rating:** 90

best drinking 2005–2010 **drink with** Grilled porterhouse • $18

McLeish Estate Merlot

♥♥♥♥ **2001** Light to medium red-purple; bright, fresh, raspberry fruit aromas are precisely reflected in the supple, sweet fruit of the palate; minimal oak influence, and fine tannins. **rating:** 87

best drinking Now–2007 **drink with** Veal roulade • $18

mcpherson wines ★★★

PO Box 529, Artarmon, NSW 1570 **region** Nagambie Lakes
phone (02) 9436 1644 **fax** (02) 9436 3144 **open** Not
winemaker Guido Vazzoler, Andrew Dean, Andrew McPherson **production** 500 000 cases **est.** 1993
product range ($8–19 R) Murray Darling range of Semillon Chardonnay, Verdelho, Chardonnay, Shiraz, Shiraz Cabernet, Merlot, Cabernet Merlot, Cabernet Sauvignon; Goulburn Valley range of Reserve Chardonnay, Reserve Shiraz.
summary McPherson Wines is little known in Australia but is, by any standards, a substantial business. Its wines are almost entirely produced for the export market, with sales in Australia through the Woolworths group, including Safeway and First Estate. The wines are made at various locations from contract-grown grapes and represent good value at their price point. For the record, McPherson Wines is a joint venture between Andrew McPherson and Alister Purbrick of Tahbilk. Both have had a lifetime of experience in the industry. Exports to the US, Canada, the UK, Europe and Asia.

McPherson Reserve Goulburn Valley Chardonnay

TTTT 2001 Medium yellow-green; the clean, moderately intense bouquet has balanced fruit and oak, the light to medium-bodied palate well put together, with gentle white peach, cashew and a dash of oak. **rating:** 85

best drinking Now **drink with** Grilled spatchcock • $17.99

McPherson Reserve Goulburn Valley Shiraz

TTTT 2001 Medium red-purple; the bouquet has some complexity, with a mix of savoury cherry, raspberry and blackcurrant fruits; the medium-bodied palate follows on with quite good texture and weight; ripe tannins.

rating: 85

best drinking 2004–2008 **drink with** Grilled chump chops • $18.99

macquariedale estate   NR

170 Sweetwater Road, Rothbury, NSW 2335 **region** Lower Hunter Valley
phone (02) 6574 7012 **fax** (02) 6574 7013 **open** By appointment
winemaker Ross McDonald **production** 6000 cases **est.** 1993
product range ($12–22.80 ML) Old Vine Semillon, Premium Blend Semillon Chardonnay, Four Winds Chardonnay, Macqblush (Rose), Thomas Shiraz, Matthew Merlot, Cabernet Sauvignon.
summary Macquariedale is an acorn to oak story, beginning with a small hobby vineyard in Branxton many years ago, and now extending to three vineyards around the Lower Hunter with a total 15 hectares of semillon, chardonnay, shiraz, merlot and cabernet sauvignon. This has led to Ross McDonald and his family leaving a busy Sydney life for that of a full-time grape grower and winemaker. The wines are sold by mailing list, through the Boutique Wine Centre in Pokolbin or via the 30 or so restaurants that list the wines. Those restaurants have included such icons as Banc and Bathers Pavilion. Limited exports to the US and Canada.

🐚 mcvitty grove   ★★★

Wombeyan Caves Road, Mittagong, NSW 2575 **region** Southern New South Wales Zone
phone (02) 4878 5044 **fax** (02) 9702 5371 **open** From late 2003
winemaker Contract **production** 1000 cases **est.** 1998
product range ($22.50 R) Pinot Gris, Pinot Noir.
summary Notwithstanding his 20-year career in finance, Mark Phillips also had 6 years of tertiary qualifications in horticulture when he and wife Jane began the search for a southern highlands site suited to premium grape growing and olive cultivation. In 1998 their search culminated in the acquisition of 42 hectares of farm land on the Wombeyan Caves Road, just out of Mittagong. They have now established 5.5 hectares of pinot noir and pinot gris on deep, fertile soils at the front of the property. In addition, a 1.5-hectare olive grove has been planted, which will provide the backdrop for the cellar door and cafe due to be completed by late 2003.

McVitty Grove Pinot Gris

TTTT 2002 Light straw-green; a clean and correct bouquet with a mix of pear and apple, accompanied by a faint touch of oak spice is followed by a palate with a similar array of flavours; very well made, but does show some young vine character. **rating:** 85

best drinking Now **drink with** Seafood antipasto • $22.50

mcwilliam's   ★★★★☆

Jack McWilliam Road, Hanwood, NSW 2680 **region** Riverina
phone (02) 6963 0001 **fax** (02) 6963 0002 **open** Mon–Sat 9–5
winemaker Jim Brayne, Simon Crook **production** NFP **est.** 1916
product range ($6–80 R) A disciplined and easy-to-follow product range (all varietally identified) commencing with Hillside casks; Inheritance Range; Hanwood; Charles King; JJ McWilliam (first released 1996); Winemaker's Reserve Chardonnay and Cabernet Shiraz; and Regional Collection Limited Release Hunter Valley Chardonnay, Eden Valley Riesling and JJ McWilliam Riverina Botrytis Semillon. Also superb fortified wines including MCW11 Liqueur Muscat and 10-Year-Old Hanwood Tawny Port heading a much larger range of Sherries which still form an important part of the business.
summary The best wines to emanate from the Hanwood winery are from other regions, notably the Barwang Vineyard at Hilltops in New South Wales, Coonawarra and Eden Valley; as McWilliam's viticultural resources have expanded, so have they been able to produce regional blends from across southeastern Australia under the Hanwood label which, in the last few years, have been startlingly good. Exports to many countries, the most important being the UK, the US (via a major distribution joint venture with Gallo), Germany and New Zealand.

McWilliam's Hanwood Sauvignon Blanc

▼▼▼▼ 2002 Very pale, almost water white; the crisp, moderately intense bouquet offers herb, nettle and green pea aromas, the very crisp palate with lingering acidity; a surprise packet which is a reflection of the 2002 vintage, but which likely has some cool-grown fruit as a component. **rating:** 87

best drinking Now **drink with** Blue swimmer crab • $11

McWilliam's Margaret River Semillon Sauvignon Blanc

▼▼▼▼ 2002 Light straw-green; a crisp, clean, grass, mineral and herb bouquet is followed by a lively, bright and fresh palate; has gently ripe fruit, but doesn't have quite enough concentration for top points. **rating:** 87

best drinking Now **drink with** Asian seafood • $15.95

McWilliam's Hanwood Chardonnay

▼▼▼▼ 2002 Medium yellow-green; already showing some development; the moderately intense and quite complex bouquet is driven by peachy fruit, and just a hint of oak in the background. The light to medium-bodied palate is well balanced, with some stone fruit and that hint of oak. How it won the trophy for Best Current Vintage White Wine of Show at the 2002 Royal Queensland Wine Show, is anyone's guess, but it's great value. **rating:** 89

best drinking Now **best vintages** '99, '00, '01 **drink with** Fresh pasta • $11

McWilliam's Limited Release Botrytis Semillon

▼▼▼▼ 2000 Yellow-gold; a sweet, smooth honey and citrus mix of aromas is followed by a palate which seems to show as much late harvest character as botrytis; very sweet, and suggests a little more acidity might have made an even better wine. **rating:** 88

best drinking Now–2005 **best vintages** '98 **drink with** Rich dessert • $21

McWilliam's Hanwood Shiraz

▼▼▼▼ 2001 Light to medium red-purple; the clean, fruit-driven bouquet has a range of raspberry, cherry and mulberry aromas; the well-balanced medium-bodied palate again puts the emphasis on fruit, the oak incidental and the tannins fine. Excellent value. **rating:** 87

best drinking Now–2005 **drink with** Pizza • $11

McWilliam's Hanwood Merlot

▼▼▼▼ 2001 Medium red-purple; spicy, savoury, leafy varietal aromas are followed by a palate with an interesting core of riper fruit to counterbalance the more savoury characters of the bouquet; good texture and mouthfeel. Good value. **rating:** 85

best drinking Now–2005 **drink with** Takeaway • $11

McWilliam's 1877 Cabernet Sauvignon Shiraz

▼▼▼▼▼ 1999 Medium to full red-purple; rich, very complex, dark berry fruit and high-quality oak synergise on the bouquet; rich, generous yet not jammy fruit provides a luscious and layered palate, tied together by fine, ripe, positive tannins. Like the '98 before it, an exceptional wine. **rating:** 95

best drinking 2007–2017 **best vintages** '98, '99 **drink with** Slow-cooked rib of beef • $80

mcwilliam's mount pleasant ★★★★☆

Marrowbone Road, Pokolbin, NSW 2320 **region** Lower Hunter Valley
phone (02) 4998 7505 **fax** (02) 4998 7761 **open** 7 days 10–5
winemaker Phillip Ryan, Andrew Leembruggen **production** NFP **est.** 1921
product range ($10–45 R) Much simplified and rationalised over the past year. The base range now comprises Mount Pleasant Elizabeth, Philip, Late Harvest Dessert Wine, Semillon Sauvignon Blanc, Verdelho, Chardonnay, Unwooded Chardonnay, Pinot Chardonnay, Sparkling Pinot Noir, Merlot; then individual vineyard wines, Rosehill Shiraz, Old Paddock & Old Hill Shiraz, Lovedale Semillon (previously known as Anne), then Maurice O'Shea Chardonnay, Shiraz; finally Museum releases of Elizabeth, Lovedale Semillon, Late Harvest Reserve.
summary McWilliam's Elizabeth and the glorious Lovedale Semillon are generally commercially available with four to 5 years of bottle age and are undervalued treasures with a consistently superb show record. The three individual vineyard wines, together with the Maurice O'Shea memorial wines, add to the lustre of this proud name. Exports to many countries, the most important being the UK, the US, Germany and New Zealand.

McWilliam's Mount Pleasant Elizabeth

▼▼▼▼♀ 1999 Medium yellow-green; the bouquet is clean, with a mix of grassy and incipiently toasty aromas; though still fresh and entering the transition phase, the palate is well balanced, and the aftertaste is reassuring. Will certainly merit higher points in the years ahead. **rating: 90**

best drinking 2004–2009 **best vintages** '75, '81, '82, '83, '86, '89, '90, '91, '93, '94, '95, '96, '97, '98 **drink with** Pan-fried veal • $18

McWilliam's Mount Pleasant Lovedale Semillon

▼▼▼▼▼ 1998 Bright, light to medium yellow-green; the clean, intense, lemon-accented bouquet leads into a palate still relatively tight in structure, with the first signs of mature flavours just starting to emerge. Immaculately balanced, the touch of CO_2 simply underwriting the next 10–20 years of development. **rating: 96**

best drinking 2006–2020 **best vintages** '69, '72, '74, '75, '79, '84, '86, '95, '96, '97, '98 **drink with** Fine fish dishes • $44

McWilliam's Mount Pleasant Hunter Valley Chardonnay

▼▼▼▼ 2002 Medium yellow-green; the clean, moderately intense bouquet has a mix of cashew and melon, the light to medium-bodied palate with a similar melon and stone fruit base, the oak influence minimal. Fermented in French oak, partial malolactic and lees contact – all this for $15. **rating: 86**

best drinking Now **best vintages** '98 **drink with** Char-grilled calamari • $15

McWilliam's Mount Pleasant Maurice O'Shea Chardonnay

▼▼▼▼♀ 2000 Bright, full yellow-green; clear, clean melon and stone fruit is supported by obvious but balanced oak on the bouquet; the harmonious full-bodied palate has peach, nectarine and tropical fruit, the barrel-ferment oak in support. **rating: 90**

best drinking Now **best vintages** '98, '99, '00 **drink with** Roast pork • $33

McWilliam's Mount Pleasant Maurice O'Shea Shiraz

▼▼▼▼♀ 1999 Medium red-purple; the moderately intense and fragrant bouquet ranges through dark cherry, licorice and savoury/earthy regional aromas, augmented by attractive oak; the palate is unexpectedly powerful and quite tannic; for the very long haul. **rating: 91**

best drinking 2009–2024 **best vintages** '98 **drink with** Ragout of veal • $36

McWilliam's Mount Pleasant Old Paddock and Old Hill Shiraz

▼▼▼▼▼ 1999 A Hunter classic, the grapes coming from two estate vineyards planted in the 1880s and 1920s. The fragrant bouquet has dark cherry and regional nuances of leather and earth, the elegant and silky palate with finely balanced savour cherry fruit, tannins and oak. Will outlive many, myself included. **rating: 94**

best drinking 2004–2024 **best vintages** '65, '66, '67, '79, '85, '87, '90, '91, '94, '95, '96, '98, '99 **drink with** Roast veal • $35

madew wines ★★★☆

Westering, Federal Highway, Lake George, NSW 2581 **region** Canberra District
phone (02) 4848 0026 **fax** (02) 4848 0026 **open** Weekends, public holidays 11–5
winemaker David Madew **production** 2500 cases **est.** 1984
product range ($13–30 CD) Riesling, Belle Riesling, Reserve Riesling, Semillon, Pinot Gris, Belle Pinot Gris, Chardonnay, Phoenix (Botrytis Chardonnay), Dry Red, Merlot, Cabernets.
summary Madew Wines bowed to the urban pressure of Queanbeyan and purchased the Westering Vineyard from Captain G P Hood some years ago. Plantings there have now increased to 9.5 hectares, with 1 hectare each of shiraz and pinot gris coming into bearing. Madew's restaurant, grapefoodwine, which is open Friday to Saturday for lunch and dinner and Sunday for breakfast and lunch, won the Best Restaurant in a Winery award in 2001, and also hosts monthly music concerts.

Madew Riesling

▼▼▼▼ 2002 Light straw-green; the clean, fresh and crisp bouquet has more mineral than fruit at this stage, but the latter comes out with attractive lime blossom flavours on the palate, finishing with lingering acidity. **rating: 88**

best drinking Now–2008 **best vintages** '93, '94 **drink with** Antipasto • $20

Madew Belle Riesling

▼▼▼▼ 2002 Light straw-green; the mineral, slate and spice bouquet leads into a flavoursome palate, with distinct residual sugar offset by acidity. Its not easy to see why so much sweetness was left in this special selection from the Westering Vineyard. **rating: 86**

best drinking Now–2005 **drink with** Carpaccio of tuna • $25

Madew Pinot Gris

ŦŦŦŦ 2002 Light straw-green; the light bouquet has some interesting spicy complexity with some underlying mineral; the firm, dry palate has soaked up the Croatian oak in which the wine was barrel fermented and in which it spent 3 months thereafter. **rating:** 86

best drinking Now **drink with** Chinese prawns • $25

Madew Belle Pinot Gris

ŦŦŦŦ 2002 Light straw-green; the bouquet is quite complex, showing pear and spice varietal character, and the barest whisper of oak. The palate has good length and intensity to the pear and lemon fruit, supported in turn by subtle barrel-ferment French oak inputs. **rating:** 89

best drinking Now–2006 **drink with** Calamari salad • $30

Madew Chardonnay

ŦŦŦŦ? 2001 Glowing yellow-green; a rich and complex bouquet has ripe nectarine fruit and exuberant oak, but the palate, though flavoursome, is more restrained, with a long, clean finish. As with all of the new release Madew wines, uses a Stelvin closure which will guarantee cellaring. **rating:** 90

best drinking Now–2005 **drink with** Veal scallopine • $25

maglieri of mclaren vale ★★★☆

Douglas Gully Road, McLaren Flat, SA 5171 **region** McLaren Vale
phone (08) 8383 0177 **fax** (08) 8383 0735 **open** Mon–Sat 9–4, Sun 12–4
winemaker Charles Hargrave **production** 14000 cases **est.** 1972
product range ($5.50–40R) Produces a range of Italian-derived styles for specialty markets within Australia, is increasingly known for the quality of its varietal table wines, spearheaded by Semillon, Chardonnay, Merlot, Cabernet Sauvignon and Shiraz, the last released in two guises: as a simple varietal, and the top-end Steve Maglieri. Typically several vintages available at any one time.
summary Was one of the better-kept secrets among the wine cognoscenti but not among the many customers who drink thousands of cases of white and red Lambrusco every year, an example of niche marketing at its profitable best. It was a formula which proved irresistible to Beringer Blass, which acquired Maglieri in 1999. Its dry red wines are invariably generously proportioned and full of character, the Shiraz particularly so.

Maglieri Semillon

ŦŦŦŦ 2002 Light straw-green; the clean, light and fresh bouquet is fairly closed, but will doubtless develop; the palate is clean, fresh and light, with grass and lemon flavours; not phenolic and not cluttered up with oak. Will improve. **rating:** 85

best drinking Now–2005 **best vintages** '00 **drink with** Smoked eel • $14

main ridge estate ★★★★☆

80 William Road, Red Hill, Vic 3937 **region** Mornington Peninsula
phone (03) 5989 2686 **fax** (03) 5931 0000 **open** Mon–Fri 12–4, weekends 12–5
winemaker Nat White **production** 1100 cases **est.** 1975
product range ($36–45 CD) Chardonnay, Pinot Noir, Half Acre Pinot Noir.
summary Nat White gives meticulous attention to every aspect of his viticulture and winemaking, doing annual battle with one of the coolest sites on the Peninsula. The same attention to detail extends to the winery and the winemaking. Incidentally, with such minuscule production, domestic sales through cellar door and mail order, exports to the UK and Singapore.

Main Ridge Chardonnay

ŦŦŦŦ? 2001 Bright green-yellow; the citrus and melon fruit has attractive smoky barrel-ferment edges, the fine and elegant palate with gentle cashew malolactic inputs in classic Mornington style. **rating:** 91

best drinking Now–2008 **best vintages** '91, '92, '94, '96, '97 '98, '99, '00, '01 **drink with** Sweetbreads • $44

Main Ridge Half Acre Pinot Noir

ŦŦŦŦ? 2001 Bright purple-red; the clean and fresh bouquet is still bursting with primary cherry/strawberry fruit, a wisp of oak in the background; a fine, very stylish and lingering palate adds savoury/foresty nuances to the fruit of the bouquet. **rating:** 93

best drinking Now–2008 **best vintages** '97, '99, '00, '01 **drink with** Grilled salmon • $45

maiolo wines ★★★☆

Bussell Highway, Carbunup River, WA 6282 **region** Margaret River
phone (08) 9755 1060 **fax** (08) 9755 1060 **open** 7 days 10–5
winemaker Charles Maiolo **production** 3700 cases **est.** 1999
product range ($14.50–26 CD) Semillon Sauvignon Blanc, Chardonnay, Pinot Noir, Shiraz, Cabernet Sauvignon.
summary Charles Maiolo has established a 28-hectare vineyard planted to semillon, sauvignon blanc, chardonnay, pinot noir, shiraz, merlot and cabernet sauvignon. He has a wine science degree from Charles Sturt, and presides over a winery with a capacity of 250 to 300 tonnes. As the vines are still coming into bearing, production will increase from the present level of around 50 tonnes to over 200 tonnes, with the option of selling surplus grapes. The red wines, in particular, show great promise, with Shiraz and Cabernet Sauvignon to the fore. The white wines have a constant thread of reduction and are less appealing. The wines are distributed in Western Australia and New South Wales.

Maiolo Shiraz

▼▼▼▼ 2001 Medium to full purple-red; the rich and ripe bouquet has a mix of black plum, earth, game, prune and spice, all of which come through to a lesser or greater degree in the abundant dark fruit flavours of the palate, set within a quite savoury frame; good oak. **rating:** 89

best drinking 2006–2011 **drink with** Lamb shanks • $22

Maiolo Cabernet Sauvignon

▼▼▼▼ 2001 Medium to full red-purple; the firm, relatively austere bouquet has blackberry/blackcurrant fruit with background notes of earth and olive; the palate has good texture and structure, although the fruit remains on the austere side. **rating:** 88

best drinking 2005–2011 **drink with** Char-grilled steak • $26

majella ★★★★★

Lynn Road, Coonawarra, SA 5263 **region** Coonawarra
phone (08) 8736 3055 **fax** (08) 8736 3057 **open** 7 days 10–4.30
winemaker Bruce Gregory **production** 12 000 cases **est.** 1969
product range ($16–72 CD) Riesling, Sparkling Shiraz, Shiraz, The Malleea Shiraz Cabernet, Cabernet Sauvignon.
summary Majella is one of the more important contract grape growers in Coonawarra, with 61 hectares of vineyard, principally shiraz and cabernet sauvignon, and with a little riesling and merlot in production and now fully mature. Common gossip has it that part finds its way into the Wynns John Riddoch Cabernet Sauvignon and Michael Shiraz, or their equivalent within the Southcorp Group. Production under the Majella label is increasing as long-term supply contracts expire. Production under the Majella label has increased substantially over the past few years, rising from 2000 to 12 000 cases, with exports to the US, Canada, Singapore, Malaysia and Hong Kong.

Majella Shiraz

▼▼▼▼▼ 2000 Excellent, deep red-purple; sweet blackberry, plum, redcurrant and licorice aromas flow through into a palate with excellent intensity, weight and concentration; well-handled extract throughout provides good structure and length, and guarantees the long term future of the wine. Top gold medal Limestone Coast Wine Show 2002. **rating:** 95

best drinking 2005–2013 **best vintages** '97, '98, '99, '00 **drink with** Lamb chops • $32

Majella The Malleea

▼▼▼▼▼ 2000 Deep purple-red; abundant sweet berry fruit and high-quality oak swirl from the glass, the palate with equally generous cassis and blackberry fruit supported by balanced oak and tannins. As always, a wine of the highest quality. Gold medal winner 2002 National Wine Show. **rating:** 95

best drinking 2005–2015 **best vintages** '96, '97, '98, '99, '00 **drink with** Marinated beef • $72

Majella Cabernet Sauvignon

▼▼▼▼▼ 2000 Dense purple-red; rich, ripe and luscious cassis/blackcurrant aromas lead into a palate offering a mix of power and restraint: blackberry and blackcurrant fruit on the mid-palate, followed by a tight, finely structured finish. **rating:** 94

best drinking 2005–2015 **best vintages** '93, '94, '96, '98, '00 **drink with** Rack of lamb • $32

malcolm creek vineyard ★★★★

Bonython Road, Kersbrook, SA 5231 **region** Adelaide Hills
phone (08) 8389 3235 **fax** (08) 8389 3235 **open** Weekends and public holidays 11–5, or by appointment
winemaker Reg Tolley **production** 700 cases **est.** 1982
product range ($19–22 R) Chardonnay, Cabernet Sauvignon.
summary Malcolm Creek is the retirement venture of Reg Tolley, and keeps a low profile. However, the wines are invariably well made and develop gracefully; they are worth seeking out, and are usually available with some extra bottle age at a very modest price. Exports to the UK.

Malcolm Creek Vineyard Chardonnay

▼▼▼▼ **2001** Medium yellow-green; the intense bouquet has an appealing mix of nectarine, fig and integrated oak, the smooth and rounded palate following suit with honey, nectarine and fig flavours in a nicely weighted frame. One of those wines that creeps up on you. **rating:** 89

best drinking Now–2005 **best vintages** '88, '90, '91, '94, '95, '96, '98 **drink with** South Australian whiting • $19

Malcolm Creek Vineyard Cabernet Sauvignon

▼▼▼▼♀ **2000** Medium red-purple; the fragrant, cedary, olive-accented bouquet proclaims its cool-grown origins, but blackcurrant fruit comes through strongly on the palate, along with a touch of chocolate; appealing savoury tannins sustain a long finish. **rating:** 90

best drinking 2005–2011 **best vintages** '86, '88, '93, '96, '00 **drink with** Yearling beef • $22

maling family estate ★★★☆

Waverley-Honour, Palmers Lane, Pokolbin, NSW 2320 **region** Lower Hunter Valley
phone (02) 4998 7953 **fax** (02) 4998 7952 **open** 7 days 10–5
winemaker Gary Reed (Contract) **production** 4500 cases **est.** 1989
product range ($35–72 CD) Waverley Estate Semillon, Chardonnay, Sparkling, Hermitage, Cabernet Sauvignon.
summary The word unique is in the same category as passion: a grossly overused cliché. Nonetheless, unique is the only word to describe the Maling Family Estate operation, which dates back at the very least to 1989 and arguably to 1971 when the core of the existing vineyard was planted. In 1989 Terry Maling and family acquired the vineyard, which has since been increased to 21.5 hectares of shiraz, semillon, chardonnay and cabernet sauvignon. The large house-cum-cellar-door-restaurant-bed-and-breakfast complex has been constructed with materials from damaged heritage buildings from the 1989 Newcastle earthquake. Building materials include huge grey sandstone blocks, some blazed with convict tally markings, the big doors and roof trusses coming from Newcastle bond stores built c1860. 1989 not only marked the Newcastle earthquake, but the first vintage of Maling Estate Wines which, from that year onwards, have been made by Gary Reed. Remarkably, none of the wines were offered for sale until the end of 1999, and since 2000 a range of vintages have been on sale.

mandurang valley wines NR

77 Fadersons Lane, Mandurang, Vic 3551 **region** Bendigo
phone (03) 5439 5367 **fax** (03) 5439 3850 **open** Weekends 11–5
winemaker Wes Vine **production** 1200 cases **est.** 1994
product range ($13–18 CD) Riesling, Pinot Noir, Shiraz, Cabernet Sauvignon.
summary The eponymously-named Wes and Pamela Vine have slowly build Mandurang Valley Wines, utilising 2.5 hectares of estate vines and a further 6 hectares of estate-grown grapes. As from Easter 2001 they have been offering cafe lunches to complement the outdoor seating and barbecue facilities already in existence. The wines are chiefly sold cellar door and by mailing list, with limited Melbourne distribution through Bacchus Wines, Armadale.

mann NR

105 Memorial Avenue, Baskerville, WA 6056 **region** Swan Valley
phone (08) 9296 4348 **fax** (08) 9296 4348 **open** Weekends 10–5 and by appointment from 1 Aug until sold out
winemaker Dorham Mann **production** 600 cases **est.** 1988
product range ($18–30 CD) Methode Champenoise Cygne Blanc, Methode Champenoise (Cabernet).
summary Industry veteran Dorham Mann has established a one-wine label for what must be Australia's most unusual wine: a dry, only faintly pink, sparkling wine made exclusively from cabernet sauvignon grown on the 2.5-hectare estate surrounding the cellar door. Dorham Mann explains, 'Our family has made and enjoyed the style for more than 30 years, although just in a private capacity until recently.'

mansfield wines   NR

204 Eurunderee Lane, Mudgee, NSW 2850   **region** Mudgee
phone (02) 6373 3871   **fax** (02) 6373 3708   **open** Thurs–Mon and public holidays 10–5, or by appointment
winemaker Bob Heslop   **production** 3000 cases   **est.** 1975
product range ($8–32 CD) Sauvignon Blanc, Frontignac, Chardonnay, Spectabilis White (semi-sweet), Sparkling Muscat, Spectabilis Red, Shiraz, Touriga, Zinfandel, Cabernet Sauvignon Merlot, Cabernet Sauvignon, and a selection of fortified wines.
summary Mansfield Wines has moved with the times, taking the emphasis off fortified wines and on to table wines (though still offering some fortifieds) and expanding the product range to take in cutting edge varietal reds such as Touriga and Zinfandel. No recent tastings.

mantons creek vineyard   NR

Tucks Road, Main Ridge, Vic 3928   **region** Mornington Peninsula
phone (03) 5989 6264   **fax** (03) 5959 6060   **open** 7 days 10–5
winemaker Alex White (Contract)   **production** 5000 cases   **est.** 1998
product range ($15–25 CD) Sauvignon Blanc, Muscat, Pinot Gris, Chardonnay, Tempranillo, Pinot Noir.
summary The substantial Mantons Creek Vineyard was established in the early 1990s, with the grapes from the first 5 years' production being sold to other makers. Since that time events have moved quickly: the label was launched in 1998 and a restaurant-cum-tasting room was opened in December 1998 boasting two chefs with impeccable credentials. The 14-hectare vineyard includes 3 hectares of tempranillo, which John Williams says grows well in the cool climate of the Mornington Peninsula, making a very rich style of wine with great flavour. I am yet to taste it.

margan family winegrowers   ★★★★

1238 Milbrodale Road, Broke, NSW 2330   **region** Lower Hunter Valley
phone (02) 6579 1317   **fax** (02) 6579 1317   **open** 7 days 10–5
winemaker Andrew Margan   **production** 40 000 cases   **est.** 1997
product range ($15–27 CD) Semillon, Verdelho, Chardonnay, Botrytis Semillon, Shiraz, Shiraz Saignée, Merlot, Cabernet Sauvignon.
summary Andrew Margan followed in his father's footsteps by entering the wine industry 20 years ago and has covered a great deal of territory since, working as a Flying Winemaker in Europe, then for Tyrrell's, first as a winemaker then as marketing manager. His wife Lisa, too, has had many years of experience in restaurants and marketing. They now have 46 hectares of fully yielding vines at their 50-hectare Ceres Hill homestead property at Broke and lease the nearby Vere Vineyard of 13 hectares. The first stage of a 700-tonne on-site winery was completed in 1998, the first wines having been made elsewhere in 1997. Wine quality (and the packaging) is consistently good. Cafe Beltree is open for light meals and coffee. Exports to the UK, the US, Canada and The Netherlands.

Margan Family Semillon
▼▼▼▼ 2002 Medium to full yellow-green; a big, full, slightly broad bouquet, then a full, flavoured, rich, early drinking style.   **rating:** 86
best drinking Now   **best vintages** '99, '00   **drink with** Rich seafood • $17

Margan Family Botrytis Semillon
▼▼▼▼♡ 2001 Medium to full yellow-green; a complex bouquet offering mandarin, peach and a hint of nougat leads into a palate with excellent balance and length, particularly the acidity.   **rating:** 93
best drinking Now–2007   **best vintages** '00, '01   **drink with** Fruit tart • $25

Margan Family Shiraz
▼▼▼▼ 2001 Youthful red-purple; clean, ripe black cherry aromas are accompanied by touches of earth and spice; the clean, firm palate, with still-simple cherry and plum fruit, needs time to open up and start building complexity.   **rating:** 86
best drinking 2004–2010   **best vintages** '99   **drink with** Braised lamb shanks • $19.50

Margan Family Cabernet Sauvignon
▼▼▼▼ 2001 Medium red-purple; the moderately intense bouquet has blackcurrant fruit and subtle oak; the medium-bodied palate provides savoury characters adding complexity to the core of sweet blackcurrant fruit; good oak and extract.   **rating:** 89
best drinking 2004–2010   **best vintages** '00, '01   **drink with** Braised ox cheek • $19.50

marienberg ★★★

2 Chalk Hill Road, McLaren Vale, SA 5171 **region** McLaren Vale
phone (08) 8323 9666 **fax** (08) 8323 9600 **open** 7 days 10–5
winemaker Grant Burge (Contract) **production** 30 000 cases **est.** 1966
product range ($11.95–19.95 R) Cottage Classic range of Riesling, Sauvignon Blanc Semillon, Unwooded Chardonnay, Cabernet Grenache Mourvedre; Reserve Chardonnay, Shiraz and Cabernet Sauvignon; also Late Picked Frontignac, Nicolle Methode Traditionale and Tawny Port.
summary The Marienberg brand was purchased by the Hill International group of companies in late 1991 following the retirement of founder and Australia's first female winemaker, Ursula Pridham. Releases under the new regime have been honest, if unashamedly commercial, wines. The Reserve wines do offer a significant lift in quality above the basic range, reflecting the recent acquisition of the 33-hectare Douglas Gully Vineyard (up to 40 years old) in the foothills of McLaren Vale. The financial problems of Hill International may lead to an ownership change. The wines are exported to the US, Canada, Brazil, the UK, Denmark, Germany, Switzerland, Hong Kong, Indonesia, Fiji, Singapore, Thailand and New Zealand.

🐌 marinda park vineyard ★★★★

238 Myers Road, Balnarring, Vic 3926 **region** Mornington Peninsula
phone (03) 5989 7613 **fax** (03) 5989 7613 **open** By appointment
winemaker Sandro Mosele (Contract) **production** 3000 cases **est.** 1999
product range ($19–26 CD) Sauvignon Blanc, Chardonnay, Pinot Noir, Merlot.
summary Mark and Belinda Rodman have established 10 hectares of chardonnay, sauvignon blanc, pinot noir and merlot on their vineyard on the outskirts of Balnarring. They operate the business in conjunction with American partners Norm and Fanny Winton, who are involved in the sale and distribution of the wines in the US and Singapore. The wines are principally sold overseas, but are available locally by mail order, and will be sold at the cellar door at a small French Provincial-style cafe from October 2003.

Marinda Park Sauvignon Blanc

▼▼▼▼▽ 2002 Light to medium yellow-green; a spotlessly clean and restrained bouquet has a mix of herb and some green pea aromas, the palate delicate, but quite firm; good texture on the finish. **rating:** 90
best drinking Now–2005 **drink with** Trout mousse • $19

mariners rest NR

Jamakarri Farm, Roberts Road, Denmark, WA 6333 **region** Great Southern
phone (08) 9840 9324 **fax** (08) 9840 9321 **open** 7 days 11–5
winemaker Brenden Smith **production** 750 cases **est.** 1996
product range ($15–22.50 R) Chardonnay, Southern White, Autumn Gold, Autumn Red, Southern Red, Pinot Noir, Nelson's Blood (Tawny Port).
summary Mariners Rest is the reincarnation of the now defunct Golden Rise winery. A new 2.5-hectare vineyard was planted in the spring of 1997, and a slightly odd selection of replacement wines are being marketed.

Mariners Rest Autumn Gold

▼▼▼▼ 2002 Light to medium yellow-green; the bouquet is clean, but somewhat subdued, the palate barely off-dry and not particularly intense, but does have good balance to its lime flavours, and a degree of length. **rating:** 86
best drinking Now **best vintages** '00 **drink with** Prosciutto and melon • $15.50

maritime estate ★★★☆

Tucks Road, Red Hill, Vic 3937 **region** Mornington Peninsula
phone (03) 9848 2926 **fax** (03) 9848 2926 **open** Weekends and public holidays 11–5, 7 days Dec 27–Jan 26
winemaker Clare Halloran **production** 2000 cases **est.** 1988
product range ($16–28 CD) Pinot Gris, Unwooded Chardonnay, Chardonnay, Pinot Noir.
summary John and Linda Ruljancich and Kevin Ruljancich have enjoyed great success since their first vintage in 1994, no doubt due in part to skilled contract-winemaking but also to the situation of their vineyard, looking across the hills and valleys of the Red Hill subregion.

Maritime Estate Chardonnay

▼▼▼▼ 2001 JDR. Medium yellow-green; the clean and intense bouquet has nectarine, grapefruit and a subtle touch of barrel-ferment oak; the palate is in long, linear fruit-driven style, all the components in good balance.
rating: 89
best drinking Now–2006 **best vintages** '95 **drink with** Calamari • $26

309

Maritime Estate Pinot Noir

▼▼▼▼ 2001 PJR. Light red; light, spicy, savoury, earthy, strawberry aromas are all reflected on the palate, which has length, but not depth.   **rating:** 85

best drinking Now–2005 **best vintages** '00 **drink with** Breast of squab • $28

marius wines   NR

PO Box 45, Willunga, SA 5172 **region** McLaren Vale
phone 0402 344 340 **fax** (08) 8557 1034 **open** Not
winemaker Contract **production** 300 cases **est.** 1994
product range ($22.80 ML) Shiraz.
summary Roger Pike says he has loved wine for over 30 years; that for 15 years he has had the desire to add a little bit to the world of wine; and that 8 years ago he decided to do something about it, ripping the front paddock and planting 1.6 hectares of shiraz in 1994. He sold the grapes from the 1997–99 vintages, but when the 1998 vintage became a single vineyard wine (made by the purchaser of the grapes) selling in the US at $40, the temptation to have his own wine became irresistible. So in 2000 he sold half the crop, and retained half, which has now been released as the 2000 Marius Shiraz. There will be no wine from 2001 (the vintage was not a good one) but the 2002 is highly rated by Roger Pike. The wines are available by ordering through mail order and via www.mariuswines.com.au.

Marius Shiraz

▼▼▼▼ 2000 Medium red-purple; the moderately intense bouquet has gently spicy/savoury overtones, the similarly light to medium-bodied palate offering a mix of raspberry and blackberry fruit; a smooth finish with subtle oak. Spends 15 months in new and one-year-old French oak.   **rating:** 86

best drinking 2004–2008 **drink with** Braised rabbit • $22.80

markwood estate   NR

Morris Lane, Markwood, Vic 3678 **region** King Valley
phone (03) 5727 0361 **fax** (03) 5727 0361 **open** 7 days 9–5
winemaker Rick Morris **production** 100 cases **est.** 1971
product range ($15–30 CD) Riesling, Cabernet Sauvignon, White Port, Old Tawny Port.
summary A member of the famous Morris family, Rick Morris shuns publicity and relies virtually exclusively on cellar-door sales for what is a small output. Of a range of table and fortified wines tasted some years ago, the Old Tawny Port (a cross between Port and Muscat, showing more of the character of the latter than the former) and a White Port (seemingly made from Muscadelle) were the best.

marribrook   ★★★★

Albany Highway, Kendenup, WA 6323 **region** Great Southern
phone (08) 9851 4651 **fax** (08) 9851 4652 **open** Wed–Sun and public holidays 10.30–4.30
winemaker Gavin Berry, Richard Robson **production** 2200 cases **est.** 1990
product range ($14–25 CD) Semillon Sauvignon Blanc, Stirling White (Semillon), Botanica Chardonnay, Reserve Chardonnay, Marsanne, Marsanne Oaked, Marri Gold (Marsanne), Cabernet Malbec Merlot.
summary The Brooks family purchased the former Marron View 5.6-hectare vineyard from Kim Hart in 1994 and renamed the venture Marribrook Wines. Those wines are now made by Gavin Berry at Plantagenet, having been made at Alkoomi up to 1994. The Brooks have purchased an additional property on the Albany Highway north of Mount Barker and immediately south of Gilberts Wines. Cellar-door sales have moved to this location, and a dedicated cellar-door sales building encompassing a small restaurant and gallery was completed in 2000, with great views out to the Stirling Range. Retail distribution in Western Australia, and Victoria, exports to the US.

Marribrook Semillon Sauvignon Blanc

▼▼▼▼ 2002 Light straw-green; a spotlessly clean and fresh bouquet has primarily mineral aromas, backed up by some herb. The light to medium-bodied palate has good balance, line and flow, with an appealing spicy grip to the finish.   **rating:** 89

best drinking Now **drink with** Shellfish • $15

Marribrook Marsanne

▼▼▼▽ 2002 Pale straw-green; the clean bouquet has some honeysuckle sweetness, the palate likewise, seemingly partly fruit-derived, and partly residual sugar. Intelligent handling of a variety which is often neutral in its youth.   **rating:** 84

best drinking Now–2007 **best vintages** '97 **drink with** Antipasto • $15

Marribrook Marri Gold

▼▼▼▼ 2002 Pale green-yellow; scented, floral, peachy aromas are followed by a smooth, clean, well-balanced palate with dried apricot and almond flavours. Made from late-picked Marsanne, and 14.5° alcohol. An altogether interesting wine, although I am not sure how it will develop. **rating:** 87

best drinking Now–2005 **drink with** Fresh fruit • $17

Marribrook Cabernet Malbec Merlot

▼▼▼▼▽ 2000 Good colour; a gentle array of cedar, earth, berry and violets on the bouquet are followed by a wine with excellent, soft texture to the berry fruit and ripe tannins. Positive but not aggressive use of oak. **rating:** 90

best drinking 2005–2010 **best vintages** '99, '00 **drink with** Venison • $25

marsh estate NR

Deasy's Road, Pokolbin, NSW 2321 **region** Lower Hunter Valley
phone (02) 4998 7587 **fax** (02) 4998 7884 **open** Mon–Fri 10–4.30, weekends 10–5
winemaker Andrew Marsh **production** 7000 cases **est.** 1971
product range ($18–25 CD) Semillon, Private Bin Semillon, Chardonnay (oaked and unoaked), Semillon Sauternes, Shiraz (Private Bin, Vat S and Vat R), Cabernet Sauvignon, Cremant Brut.
summary Through sheer consistency, value-for-money and unrelenting hard work, the Marsh family (who purchased the former Quentin Estate in 1978) has built up a sufficiently loyal cellar-door and mailing list clientele to allow all of the considerable production to be sold direct. Wine style is always direct, with oak playing a minimal role, and prolonged cellaring paying handsome dividends. No recent tastings, but Marsh Estate has moved ahead with production rising to 7000 cases and Andrew Marsh succeeding Peter Marsh as winemaker.

martins hill wines ★★★☆

Sydney Road, Mudgee, NSW 2850 **region** Mudgee
phone (02) 6373 1248 **fax** (02) 6373 1248 **open** Not
winemaker Pieter Van Gent (Contract) **production** 700 cases **est.** 1985
product range ($13–16 R) Sauvignon Blanc, Pinot Noir.
summary Janette Kenworthy and Michael Sweeny are committed organic grape growers and are members of the Organic Vignerons Association. It is a tiny operation at the moment, with only 0.5 hectare each of sauvignon blanc and pinot noir, 0.5 hectare of cabernet sauvignon and 1.5 hectares of shiraz in production. While there is no cellar door (only a mailing list), organic vineyard tours and talks can be arranged by appointment.

marybrook vineyards NR

Vasse–Yallingup Road, Marybrook, WA 6280 **region** Margaret River
phone (08) 9755 1143 **fax** (08) 9755 1112 **open** Fri–Mon 10–5, 7 days 10–5 school holidays
winemaker Aub House **production** 2000 cases **est.** 1986
product range ($11–26.50 CD) Verdelho, Chardonnay, Classic White, Nectosia (sweet), Grenache, Cabernet, Cabernet Franc, Temptation (sweet red), Ruby Jetty Port, Liqueur Muscat.
summary Marybrook Vineyards is owned by Aub and Jan House. Eight hectares of vineyards are in production, with back vintages often available.

mary byrnes wine NR

Rees Road, Ballandean, Qld 4382 **region** Granite Belt
phone (07) 4684 1111 **fax** (07) 4684 1312 **open** Weekends and public holidays 10–5, or by appointment
winemaker Mary Byrnes **production** 2000 cases **est.** 1991
product range ($15–22 CD) Viognier, Marsanne, Chardonnay, Rose, Sweet Ayla Red, Shiraz, Liqueur Muscat.
summary Mary Byrnes, who has a wine science degree, acquired her property in 1991, subsequently planting 4 hectares of shiraz, and 1 hectare each of marsanne, viognier, roussane and mourvedre, topping the planting off with 0.5 hectare of grenache and 0.5 hectare of black hamburg muscat. She has deliberately grown the vines without irrigation, thereby limiting yield and (in her words) ensuring a distinctive regional quality and flavour. The wines are sold via mail order and the cellar door.

massoni wines   NR

Elmhurst-Landsborough Road, Landsborough, Vic 3384 **region** Pyrenees
phone 1300 131 174 **fax** 1300 133 185 **open** By appointment
winemaker Alex White **production** 10 000 cases **est.** 1984
product range ($17–35 R) Under the Massoni Homes label Chardonnay, Pinot Noir, Shiraz, Merlot, Cabernet Merlot; under the Massoni Red Hill label Chardonnay and Pinot Noir; under the Massoni Pyrenees label Shiraz, Cabernet Merlot, Cabernet Sauvignon; also Massoni Lectus Cuvee.
summary In 2003 Massoni Wines underwent the biggest of many transformations since it was founded by Leon Massoni back in 1984. It was purchased by Stanford Financial Services and now has tripartheid citizenship, its wines coming variously from Langhorne Creek, the Mornington Peninsula and the Pyrenees. No tastings yet.

matilda's meadow   ★★★☆

Eladon Brook Estate, RMB 654 Hamilton Road, Denmark, WA 6333 **region** Great Southern
phone (08) 9848 1951 **fax** (08) 9848 1957 **open** Tues–Sun and public holidays 10–5
winemaker Brenden Smith **production** 1500 cases **est.** 1990
product range ($12–25 CD) Semillon Sauvignon Blanc, Unwooded Chardonnay, Sparkling White, Sparkling Red, Late Picked Riesling, Autumn Amethyst (light red), Pinot Noir, Cabernet Sauvignon Shiraz, Cabernet Sauvignon Cabernet Franc, Tawny Port Muscat blend.
summary In September 2002 the founders of Matilda's Meadow, Don Turnbull and Pamela Meldrum sold the business to former citizen of the world, Steve Hall. It is a thriving business based on 6 hectares of estate plantings, with a restaurant offering morning and afternoon tea, lunch Tuesday to Sunday and dinner Thursday to Saturday.

Matilda's Meadow Semillon Sauvignon Blanc
▼▼▼▽ **2002** Developed yellow-green; there is plenty of tropical/gooseberry fruit on the bouquet, the full, soft palate with plenty of flavour in an early-developing style.   **rating:** 84
best drinking Now **drink with** Crab cakes • $16.50

mawarra winery   ★★★☆

69 Short Road, Gisborne, Vic 3437 **region** Macedon Ranges
phone (03) 5428 2228 **fax** (03) 9621 1413 **open** 7 days 10–5
winemaker John Ellis (Contract) **production** 1000 cases **est.** 1978
product range ($18–30 CD) Mt Gisborne Estate range of Semillon, Allegro Semillon, Duet (Chardonnay Semillon), Chardonnay, Pinot Noir.
summary Bob Nixon began the development of Mawarra way back in 1978, planting his dream vineyard row-by-row, then acre-by-acre. The early years were difficult, but he persevered, and has now established chardonnay, semillon and pinot noir. Once the vineyard was in full bearing, a cellar door was always part of the scheme, but he just happens to be married to Barbara Nixon, founder of Victoria Winery Tours, and who has been in and out of cellar doors around Australia with greater frequency than any other living person. So it is that the tasting room has eight-foot wide shaded verandahs, plenty of windows and sweeping views of the Chardonnay Bowl and Semillon Flats. Deli-style foods are offered, all pre-packaged, featuring deli meats, cheese, antipasto and biscuits.

Mawarra Mt Gisborne Estate Semillon
▼▼▼▼ **1999** Bright, light yellow-green; a powdery, slatey, mineral bouquet leads into a palate which is developing very slowly, with hints of dry hay and lemon rind. The dry finish is far preferable to the off-dry finish of the 2001 Allegro Semillon.   **rating:** 87
best drinking Now–2006 **drink with** Shellfish • $18

Mawarra Mt Gisborne Estate Chardonnay
▼▼▼▼▽ **2001** Light to medium yellow-green; the clean and fresh bouquet has citrus and nectarine fruit, the oak subtle. The palate has good mouthfeel thanks to fresh nectarine fruit and a long, clean finish.   **rating:** 90
best drinking Now–2007 **best vintages** '01 **drink with** Fresh Tasmanian salmon • $25

Mawarra Mt Gisborne Estate Pinot Noir
▼▼▼▼ **2001** Light to medium purple-red; the fragrant bouquet has strawberry, leaf, mint and earth aromas, the palate opening with strawberry, but then moving to green leaf flavours on the finish.   **rating:** 85
best drinking Now **drink with** Smoked quail • $30

mawson ridge   NR

24–28 Main Road, Hahndorf, SA 5066   **region** Adelaide Hills
phone (08) 8338 0828   **fax** (08) 8338 0828   **open** Summer Tues–Sat 11–5, Winter Wed–Sat 11–5, Sun 12–5
winemaker Michael Scarpantoni   **production** 400 cases   **est.** 1998
product range ($13–20 CD) Sauvignon Blanc, Pinot Gris, Unoaked Chardonnay, Chardonnay, Pinot Noir, Stringybark Cutter Merlot Cabernets, Flinder's Reef Cabernet Sauvignon; then the lower-priced range of Blend One (Barossa Cabernet Shiraz), Blend Two (McLaren Vale Grenache Shiraz), Blend Three (Clare Valley Grenache Cabernet).
summary You might be forgiven for thinking the winery name carries the cool-climate association a little bit too far. In fact, Sir Douglas Mawson, also a conservationist and forester, arrived in the Lenswood region in the early 1930s, harvesting the native stringy-barks for hardwood and replanting the cleared land with pine trees. A hut that Mawson built on the property still stands today on Mawson Road, the road to which the vineyard fronts. Here Raymond and Madeline Marin have established 5.5 hectares of vines, having added 2 hectares of pinot gris in 2002, with contract winemaking by Michael Scarpantoni.

maximilian's vineyard   NR

Main Road, Verdun, SA 5245   **region** Adelaide Hills
phone (08) 8388 7777   **fax** (08) 8388 1371   **open** Wed, Fri–Sun 10–5
winemaker Contract   **production** 1500 cases   **est.** 1994
product range ($14.50–25 CD) Unwooded Chardonnay, Chardonnay, Methode Champenoise, Cabernet Sauvignon.
summary Maximilian and Louise Hruska opened Maximilian's Restaurant in 1976, accommodated in a homestead built in 1851. Two hectares of chardonnay and 6 hectares of cabernet sauvignon were planted in 1994, and surround the restaurant. The Cabernet Sauvignon is made by Grant Burge, the Chardonnay at Scarpantoni Estate under the direction of the Hruska's eldest son Paul. Since graduating from Roseworthy, Paul Hruska has completed vintages in Burgundy, Spain, Margaret River and the Clare Valley, and when he finally decides to come home, an on-site winery will be developed. No recent tastings.

maxwell wines   ★★★☆

Olivers Road, McLaren Vale, SA 5171   **region** McLaren Vale
phone (08) 8323 8200   **fax** (08) 8323 8900   **open** 7 days 10–5
winemaker Mark Day, Mark Maxwell   **production** 16 000 cases   **est.** 1979
product range ($9–29 CD) Under the Maxwell Wines brand Old Vines Semillon, Verdelho, Frontignac Spatlese, Chardonnay, Cabernet Merlot; Ellen Street Shiraz, Four Roads Shiraz, Lime Cave Cabernet Sauvignon; and excellent Honey Mead, Spiced Mead and Liqueur Mead, Old Tawny Port, Liqueur Muscat.
summary Maxwell Wines has come a long way since opening for business in 1979 using an amazing array of Heath Robinson equipment in cramped surroundings. A state-of-the-art and infinitely larger winery was built on a new site in time for the 1997 vintage, appropriate for a brand which has produced some excellent white and red wines in recent years. Exports to the US, Canada, the UK, Switzerland, Austria, Germany, Belgium, Hong Kong, Singapore, Thailand and New Zealand.

Maxwell Ellen Street Shiraz
▼▼▼▼▽ 2000 Dense red-purple; very ripe, almost essency, cherry and chocolate aromas come through strongly on the lusciously rich and ripe palate, with its abundant sweet cherry fruit and ripe tannins; oak is somewhere there in the mix. A redeeming feature is that the wine is (only) 14°.   **rating:** 91
best drinking 2005–2012 **best vintages** '82, '88, '91, '92, '94, '98, '00 **drink with** Kangaroo • $29

m. chapoutier australia   ★★★★☆

PO Box 437, Robe, SA 5276   **region** Mount Benson
phone (08) 8768 5076   **fax** (08) 8768 5073   **open** Not
winemaker Olivier Antoine, Anna Hogarth   **production** 4000 cases   **est.** 1998
product range ($21.95 R) Shiraz, Cabernet Sauvignon.
summary This is one of several winemaking ventures the famous Rhône Valley firm of M Chapoutier is establishing in Australia. The large biodynamic vineyard comprises 16.5 hectares of shiraz, 10 hectares of cabernet sauvignon, 4 hectares each of marsanne and viognier, with 2 hectares of sauvignon blanc in the course of establishment. For the time being the wines are made at nearby Cape Jaffa; exports to Europe, Asia, the US, New Zealand, Kong Kong, Japan, Singapore and Indonesia.

M. Chapoutier Mount Benson Shiraz

▼▼▼▼▽ **2001** Medium purple-red; clean black plum and dark cherry fruit intermingles with aromas of black pepper and cedar; the palate has much more weight and substance than earlier wines, quite rich and ripe. Whether this extra weight will ultimately lead to a better wine remains to be seen. **rating:** 90

best drinking 2005–2012 **best vintages** '99, '00, '01 **drink with** Osso buco • $21.95

M. Chapoutier Mount Benson Cabernet Sauvignon

▼▼▼▼▽ **2001** Full red-purple; the bouquet has concentrated, dense blackcurrant, chocolate and oak aromas, the palate following down the same track; it is not over-extracted, and the tannins are fine; all the wine needs is time.
rating: 91

best drinking 2005–2011 **best vintages** '01 **drink with** Roast lamb • $21.95

meadowbank estate ★★★★☆

699 Richmond Road, Cambridge, Tas 7170 **region** Southern Tasmania
phone (03) 6248 4484 **fax** (03) 6248 4485 **open** 7 days 10–5
winemaker Andrew Hood (Contract) **production** 4795 cases **est.** 1974
product range ($24–37 CD) Riesling, Sauvignon Blanc, Unwooded Chardonnay, Grace Elizabeth Chardonnay, Mardi Methode Champenoise, Pinot Noir, Henry James Pinot Noir, Cabernet Sauvignon.
summary Now an important part of the Ellis family business on what was once (but is no more) a large grazing property on the banks of the Derwent. Increased plantings are being established under contract to BRL Hardy, and a splendid new winery has been built to handle the increased production, with wine quality consistently excellent. The winery has expansive entertainment and function facilities, capable of handling up to 1000 people, and offering an ongoing arts and music programme throughout the year, plus a large restaurant open 7 days.

Meadowbank Riesling

▼▼▼▼▽ **2002** Light green-yellow; the clean bouquet has considerable intensity, predominantly lime, but with some tropical fruit and a subliminal touch of toast; the powerful palate is particularly well balanced, offering citrus and baked apple flavours, then minerally acidity to close. **rating:** 93

best drinking 2004–2012 **best vintages** '99, '00, '02 **drink with** Asparagus • $24

Meadowbank Sauvignon Blanc

▼▼▼▼▽ **2002** Light straw-green; a powerful bouquet with sweet gooseberry, passionfruit redcurrant and herb aromatics, the lively and vibrant palate with good flavour and sweet fruit. One of the best Sauvignon Blancs to come from Tasmania. **rating:** 92

best drinking Now **best vintages** '01, '02 **drink with** Tuna sashimi • $27

Meadowbank Henry James Pinot Noir

▼▼▼▼▽ **2001** Medium purple-red; the clean, direct bouquet has a pleasing mix of red plum, raspberry and strawberry fruit, the palate with highly focused fruit flavours, but yet to break out into complexity. When it does, should merit even higher points. **rating:** 91

best drinking Now–2007 **best vintages** '94, '98, '99, '00, '01 **drink with** Rabbit casserole • $37

meerea park ★★★★

Lot 3, Palmers Lane, Pokolbin, NSW 2320 **region** Lower Hunter Valley
phone (02) 4998 7474 **fax** (02) 4930 7100 **open** At The Boutique Wine Centre, Broke Road, Pokolbin 9–5
winemaker Rhys Eather **production** 10 000 cases **est.** 1991
product range ($18.50–60 R) Epoch Semillon, Lindsay Hill Viognier, Lindsay Hill Verdelho, Chardonnay, Alexander Munro Chardonnay, Late Harvest Viognier, The Aunts Shiraz, Alexander Munro Shiraz, Terracotta Shiraz, Shiraz Viognier, Cabernet Merlot.
summary All of the wines are produced from grapes purchased from growers, primarily in the Pokolbin, Broke-Fordwich and Upper Hunter regions, but also from as far afield as Orange and Young. It is the brainchild of Rhys Eather, a great-grandson of Alexander Munro, a leading vignerons in the mid-19th century, and who makes the wine at the former Little's Winery on Palmer's Lane in Pokolbin. Retail distribution through the principal states, and the wines are exported to the UK, Switzerland, Germany, the US, New Zealand and Asia.

Meerea Park Alexander Munro Semillon

▼▼▼▼▽ **1998** Glowing medium to full yellow-green; a complex and rich array of toasty/limey/buttery aromas are repeated on the palate, balanced by penetrating, lingering acidity. The grapes come from the old Tallawanta Vineyard; tragically, the 40–50 year-old vines have been subsequently pulled out. **rating:** 90

best drinking Now–2007 **drink with** Truffled pheasant • $25

Meerea Park The Aunts Shiraz

▼▼▼▼ **2001** Medium red–purple; aromas of blackberry, earth, leather and spice are followed by a palate which offers quite sweet fruit on entry, then by more savoury characters; a little callow. **rating:** 87

best drinking 2004–2010 **drink with** Braised beef • $26

Meerea Park Shiraz Viognier

▼▼▼▼ **2001** Medium red–purple; direct earthy, dark berry fruit aromas are followed by raspberry and other red fruit flavours on the palate; the texture is good, the oak subtle. Contains 8 per cent Viognier; open-fermented; older French and American oak. **rating:** 88

best drinking Now–2008 **drink with** Braised ox tail • $18.50

melaleuca grove NR

8 Melaleuca Court, Rowville, Vic 3178 (postal) **region** Central Victorian High Country
phone (03) 9752 7928 **fax** (03) 9752 7928 **open** Not
winemaker Jeff Wright **production** 800 cases **est.** 1999
product range ($18 ML) Chardonnay, Shiraz, Merlot, Cabernet Sauvignon.
summary Jeff and Anne Wright are both honours graduates in biochemistry who have succumbed to the lure of winemaking after lengthy careers elsewhere, in the case of Jeff represented by 20 years in research and hospital science. He commenced his winemaking apprenticeship in 1997 at Green Vineyards, backed up by further vintage work in 1999 and 2000 at Bianchet and Yarra Valley Hills, both in the Yarra Valley. At the same time he began the external Bachelor of Applied Science (Wine Science) course at Charles Sturt University, while continuing to work in biochemistry in the public hospital system. They purchase grapes from various cool climate regions, including Yea and the Yarra Valley. Wines are available through selected Melbourne retailers and restaurants, and by mailing list.

mermerus vineyard ★★★★

60 Soho Road, Drysdale, Vic 3222 **region** Geelong
phone (03) 5253 2718 **fax** (03) 5226 1683 **open** First Sunday of each month and every Sunday in January
winemaker Paul Champion **production** 600 cases **est.** 2000
product range ($10–16 CD) Chardonnay, Pinot Noir, Pope's Eye Pinot Noir, Shiraz.
summary Commencing in 1996, Paul Champion has established 1.5 hectares of pinot noir, 1 hectare of chardonnay and 0.2 hectare of riesling at Mermerus, making the wine on-site at the winery built in 2000, also acting as contract winemaker for small growers in the region. The first commercial wines were made in the following year, and are sold through the cellar door/mailing list and selected restaurants.

Mermerus Vineyard Chardonnay

▼▼▼▼ **2001** Bright green–yellow; typical cool-grown nectarine and melon fruit aromas are set within subtle oak on the bouquet; the palate opens quietly, but the fruit weight builds substantially into sweet, white peach flavours, the oak again subtle. **rating:** 88

best drinking Now–2007 **drink with** Tuna tartare • $14

Mermerus Vineyard Pinot Noir

▼▼▼▼ **2001** Excellent pinot colour, bright and clear; although the alcohol is only 13°, the bouquet has very ripe, plummy fruit, which translates into rich, ripe plum flavours on the palate. However, the texture and weight are entirely appropriate, so the wine avoids the 'dry red' trap. **rating:** 88

best drinking Now–2006 **drink with** Breast of squab • $16

merrebee estate NR

Lot 3339 St Werburghs Road, Mount Barker, WA 6234 **region** Great Southern
phone (08) 9851 2424 **fax** (08) 9851 2425 **open** By appointment
winemaker Brenden Smith (Contract) **production** 1500 cases **est.** 1986
product range ($15–23 CD) Riesling, Chardonnay, Mount Barker Chardonnay, Shiraz; Giles Point Sauvignon Blanc Chardonnay and Unwooded Chardonnay.
summary Planting of the Merrebee Estate vineyards commenced in 1986 and have now reached a little under 9 hectares. The wines are available from selected retailers in Western Australia and from Rathdowne Cellars, Melbourne, and Ultimo Wine Centre, Sydney, exports to the UK, the US and Canada.

🥀 merricks creek wines ★★★★★

44 Merricks Road, cnr Yal Yal Road, Merricks, Vic 3916 **region** Mornington Peninsula
phone (03) 5989 8868 **fax** (03) 9827 2220 **open** By appointment
winemaker Nick Farr, Peter Parker **production** 330 cases **est.** 1998
product range ($22–45 CD) Sparkling Pinot Noir, Young Vines Pinot Noir, Merricks Pinot Noir, Close Planted Pinot Noir, Nick Farr Pinot Noir.
summary Peter and Georgina Parker retained Gary Farr (of Bannockburn) as viticultural consultant before they commenced establishment of their 2-hectare pinot noir vineyard. They say, 'He has been an extraordinarily helpful and stern taskmaster from day 1. He advised on clonal selection, trellis design and planting density, and visits the vineyard regularly to monitor canopy management.' (Son Nick Farr completes the circle as contract winemaker.) The vineyard is planted to a sophisticated and rare collection of new pinot noir clones, and is being planted at the ultra-high density of 500 mm spacing on 1-metre high trellising.

Merricks Creek Pinot Noir

▼▼▼▼▼ 2001 Very good, bright colour, similar to the Close Planted version of the same vintage. The aromatic bouquet has ripe plum, with touches of spice and forest; the palate is smooth, linear and intense, with great style and finesse; a long, fruit-driven aftertaste. **rating:** 95

best drinking Now–2008 **best vintages** '01 **drink with** Breast of squab • $34

Merricks Creek Close Planted Pinot Noir

▼▼▼▼▼ 2001 Excellent purple-red, bright and clear; the spotlessly clean bouquet has plum, a splash of spice, and neatly controlled oak. The very pure and intense fruit of the long palate sustains the promise of the bouquet; while ripe, there is no hint of raisined, dead fruit. **rating:** 94

best drinking Now–2008 **best vintages** '01 **drink with** Jugged hare • $43

Merricks Creek Nick Farr Pinot Noir

▼▼▼▼▼ 2001 Wonderful purple-red colour, great depth and hut; complex, dark plum fruit is supported by beautifully integrated oak on the bouquet; a supple but rich mid-palate is balanced by a savoury finish and aftertaste which is pure class. Has 13.5° alcohol compared to the 14° for the Close Planted and Merricks wines. **rating:** 96

best drinking Now–2010 **drink with** Roast baby kid • $45

Merricks Creek Young Vines Pinot Noir

▼▼▼▼ 2001 Light red-purple; a clean, fresh bouquet offers strawberry and a touch of mint, the fresh and lively palate with strawberry fruit before a tangy finish. Lacks the body and complexity of the other wines, which is hardly surprising. 12.5° alcohol. **rating:** 88

best drinking Now–2005 **drink with** Antipasto • $22

merricks estate ★★★☆

Thompsons Lane, Merricks, Vic 3916 **region** Mornington Peninsula
phone (03) 5989 8416 **fax** (03) 9606 9090 **open** First weekend of each month, each weekend in Jan and public holiday weekends 12–5
winemaker Paul Evans **production** 2500 cases **est.** 1977
product range ($28–33 CD) Chardonnay, Pinot Noir, Shiraz, Cabernet Sauvignon.
summary Melbourne solicitor George Kefford, together with wife Jacquie, runs Merricks Estate as a weekend and holiday enterprise as a relief from professional practice. Right from the outset it has produced distinctive, spicy, cool-climate Shiraz which has accumulated an impressive array of show trophies and gold medals.

merum ★★★★☆

Hillbrook Road, Quinninup, WA 6258 **region** Pemberton
phone (08) 9776 6011 **fax** (08) 9776 6022 **open** By appointment
winemaker Jan Davies (Contract) **production** 1000 cases **est.** 1996
product range ($20–28 ML) Semillon, Shiraz.
summary Merum was founded by the late Maria Melsom (formerly winemaker at Driftwood Estate) and Michael Melsom (former vineyard manager for Voyager Estate, both in the Margaret River region). The 6.3 hectares of vineyard (3.3 ha shiraz, 2 ha semillon, 1 ha chardonnay) was planted in 1996, and the first wine made in 1999. The quality of the wines so far released has been truly excellent. The tragic death of Maria Melsom through a car accident in 2001 left Michael with a tough job, but he has carried on the work. (In the first printing of my 2003 Wine Companion I incorrectly write that it was Michael who died, and I wish to publicly apologise for the undoubted hurt and embarrassment this error caused.)

Merum Semillon

▼▼▼▼♈ **2002** Light straw-green; the complex and potent bouquet has characters well beyond simple fruit, including, it must be admitted, the faintest touch of reduction. The rich and ripe palate again has an array of flavours above and beyond the normal, perhaps due to the subtle blending of 10 per cent Chardonnay. Merum regards this as the best Semillon it has made to date, and its easy to see why. **rating:** 90

best drinking 2004–2010 **best vintages** '02 **drink with** Eggplant terrine • $20

Merum Shiraz

▼▼▼▼▼ **2001** Medium to full red-purple; the clean bouquet exudes rich, ripe black cherry and black pepper fruit; luscious, round fruit on the palate, not the least bit jammy, provides great mouthfeel, the flavours augmented by excellent oak and fine, ripe tannins. A beautiful wine, and yet another to show that Pemberton (whatever else) can produce Shiraz out of the ordinary. **rating:** 95

best drinking 2005–2015 **best vintages** '99, '01 **drink with** Braised beef in red wine • $25

metcalfe valley NR

283 Metcalfe-Malmsbury Road, Metcalfe, Vic 3448 **region** Macedon Ranges
phone NA **open** Mon–Fri 9–5
winemaker John Frederiksen **production** 100 cases **est.** 1994
product range ($25 R) Shiraz.
summary John Frederiksen (a social worker in the drug and alcohol area) and wife Marilyn (a children's literacy consultant) began the development of their 6-hectare vineyard 7 years ago. It is situated in the far northeast corner of the Macedon Ranges, hard-up against the Heathcote/Bendigo boundaries. Shiraz is typically harvested in the last week of April, underlining the unambiguously cool nature of the region. Most of the production is sold to Virgin Hills, but over the 2000 and 2001 vintages, a tiny amount was kept back and made into wine by John Frederiksen. Refined but spicy and complex, it is worth pursuing. Available from cellar door, and local restaurants and outlets.

metier wines ★★★★★

Tarraford Vineyard, 440 Healesville Road, Yarra Glen, Vic 3775 (postal) **region** Yarra Valley
phone (03) 5962 2461 **fax** (03) 5962 2194 **open** Not
winemaker Martin Williams MW **production** 2000 cases **est.** 1995
product range ($19.95–37.50 R) Tarraford Vineyard Chardonnay, Schoolhouse Vineyard Chardonnay, Manytrees Vineyard Shiraz Viognier; new lower-priced Milkwood range of Semillon Sauvignon Blanc, Pinot Gris, Pinot Noir, Shiraz.
summary Metier is the French word for craft, trade or profession; the business is that of Yarra Valley-based winemaker Martin Williams, MW, who has notched up an array of degrees and winemaking stints in France, California and Australia which are, not to put too fine a word on it, extraordinary. The focus of Metier is to produce individual vineyard wines, initially based on grapes from the Tarraford and Schoolhouse Vineyards, both in the Yarra Valley. The quality of the Viognier, Pinot Noir, Shiraz and Chardonnay is extremely high. Exports to the UK.

Metier Schoolhouse Vineyard Chardonnay

▼▼▼▼♈ **2000** Medium to full yellow-green; a smooth and solid bouquet of cashew, melon and fig flows through to the medium-bodied palate, repeating the flavours of the bouquet; flows easily across the mouth, thanks to good acidity and balance. **rating:** 92

best drinking Now–2006 **best vintages** '98 **drink with** Veal scaloppine • $32

Metier Tarraford Vineyard Chardonnay

▼▼▼▼♈ **1999** Full yellow; a complex amalgam of nuts, honey and spicy/charry oak on the bouquet, moving into a rich opening on the palate before tightening up with good acidity on the finish. Excellent outcome for an indifferent vintage. **rating:** 93

best drinking Now–2006 **best vintages** '97, '99 **drink with** Milk-fed veal • $37.50

Metier Manytrees Vineyard Shiraz Viognier

▼▼▼▼▼ **2000** Medium to full red-purple; a scented spice and herb lift to black cherry fruit on the bouquet; the palate is medium-bodied, but with good length to the array of lively cherry, mint and savoury flavours. **rating:** 94

best drinking 2005–2012 **best vintages** '00 **drink with** Lamb • $37.50

🍷 meure's wines NR

16 Fleurtys Lane, Birchs Bay, Tas 7162 **region** Southern Tasmania
phone (03) 6267 4483 **fax** (03) 6267 4483 **open** By appointment
winemaker Michael Vishacki (Contract) **production** 500 cases **est.** 1991
product range ($25–40 ML) Sauvignon Blanc, Pinot Gris, Chardonnay, Pinot Noir.
summary Dirk Meure has established 1 hectare of vineyard on the shores of D'Entrecasteaux Channel, overlooking Bruny Island. The Huon Valley is the southernmost wine region in Australia, and it was here that Dirk Meure's parents settled on their arrival from The Netherlands in 1950. He says he has been heavily influenced by his mentors, Steve and Monique Lubiana, and uses Michael Vishacki as his consultant winemaker. The philosophy is to produce low yields from balanced vines and to interfere as little as possible in the winemaking and maturation process.

miceli ★★★★☆

60 Main Creek Road, Arthurs Seat, Vic 3936 **region** Mornington Peninsula
phone (03) 5989 2755 **fax** (03) 5989 2755 **open** First weekend each month 12–5, public holidays, and also every weekend and by appointment in Jan
winemaker Anthony Miceli **production** 2000 cases **est.** 1991
product range ($19–28 CD) Iolanda Pinot Grigio, Unwooded Chardonnay, Olivia's Chardonnay, Pinot Noir, Lucy's Choice Pinot Noir.
summary This may be a part-time labour of love for general practitioner Dr Anthony Miceli, but this hasn't prevented him taking the whole venture very seriously. He acquired the property in 1989 specifically for the purpose of establishing a vineyard, carrying out the first plantings of 1.8 hectares in November 1991, followed by a further hectare of Pinot Gris in 1997. Ultimately the vineyard will be increased to 5 hectares, with a projected production of 2500–3000 cases a year. Between 1991 and 1997 Dr Miceli enrolled in and thereafter graduated from the Wine Science course at Charles Sturt University, and thus manages both vineyard and winery. Retail distribution through fine wine outlets and restaurants in Melbourne.

Miceli Iolanda Pinot Grigio

♥♥♥♥♡ 2001 Light straw-green; lemon blossom and pear aromas lead into a palate with excellent balance and mouthfeel; positive lemon, pear and honeysuckle flavours all add up to a top-flight example of the variety.
rating: 90

best drinking 2004–2006 **best vintages** '01 **drink with** Shellfish • $21

Miceli Unwooded Chardonnay

♥♥♥♥ 2000 Bright green-yellow; quite complex, tangy bottled-developed grapefruit aromas are followed by a clean, nicely developed palate, with medium length and a positive finish. Should continue on for a few years yet.
rating: 87

best drinking Now–2005 **drink with** Quiche Lorraine • $26

Miceli Olivia's Chardonnay

♥♥♥♥♡ 2000 Glowing yellow-green; complex but subtle barrel-ferment oak on attractive melon and citrus fruit; the stylish, medium-bodied, silky smooth palate is holding well, and like its unwooded sister, has plenty of life left in front of it.
rating: 92

best drinking Now–2007 **best vintages** '99, '00 **drink with** Grilled fish • $26

Miceli Pinot Noir

♥♥♥♥ 2001 Very developed light red; the light, savoury spicy bouquet is followed by a palate with surprising intensity and length, albeit in savoury mode. Really needed more mid-palate sweetness early in its life to sustain it for much longer; at its best now.
rating: 88

best drinking Now **drink with** Wild mushroom risotto • $19

Miceli Lucy's Choice Pinot Noir

♥♥♥♥♥ 2000 Medium red-purple; tangy, spicy plum and black cherry fruit aromas are followed by a stylish, intense and long palate; the multi-flavours are set in a silky texture; very good wine.
rating: 94

best drinking Now–2007 **best vintages** '00 **drink with** Duck confit • $28

🍷 michael unwin wines ★★★★☆

49 Lambert Street, Ararat, Vic 3377 **region** Grampians
phone (03) 5352 5077 **fax** (03) 5352 4437 **open** Not
winemaker Michael Unwin **production** 1000 cases **est.** 2000

product range ($8.90–40 R) Acrobat Collection range of Riesling, Chardonnay, Botrytis Riesling, Shiraz, Cabernet Sauvignon; Wine Station Chardonnay, Muscat of Alexandria; Tattooed Lady Shiraz and Cabernet Sauvignon.

summary Michael Unwin Wines was established at Ararat, Victoria by winemaker Michael Unwin and wife and business partner, Catherine Clark. His track record as a winemaker is extensive, spanning 16 years and including extended winemaking experience in France, New Zealand and Australia, finding time in between to obtain a post graduate degree in oenology and viticulture at Lincoln University, Canterbury, New Zealand. He carries on a multiple business, including contract winemaking and consulting; the winemaking takes place in a converted textile factory. Prior to the end of 2003 calendar year it is planned to relocate to new premises at Beaufort on the Western Highway, whereafter the cellar door will be open.

Michael Unwin Acrobat Riesling
▼▼▼▼▽ **2000** Light to medium yellow-green; the spotlessly clean and quite intense bouquet ranges through mineral and lime; the palate has plenty of weight, starting to enter the secondary phase of its development. Nice punctuation to the finish.   **rating:** 90

best drinking Now–2008 **best vintages** '00 **drink with** Caesar salad • $16

Michael Unwin Acrobat Chardonnay
▼▼▼▼ **2001** Medium straw-yellow; the clean, moderately intense bouquet mixes subtle barrel-ferment characters with melon and fig fruit; barrel ferment, malolactic ferment and lees contact all drive the complex palate.   **rating:** 89

best drinking Now–2007 **drink with** Grilled spatchcock • $13.50

Michael Unwin Acrobat Botrytised Riesling
▼▼▼▼▼ **1997** Bright gold; a very rich and complex bouquet of dried fruit aromas is reflected in the similarly complex and rich palate; mandarin and cumquat flavours have great length, and perfect balancing acidity. A freakish wine to come from the Grampians.   **rating:** 94

best drinking Now–2006 **drink with** Rich desserts • $9.10

Michael Unwin Acrobat Shiraz
▼▼▼▼▽ **2001** Bright red-purple; ripe, sweet blackberry and plum fruit and well-balanced oak are a promising opening, and the palate does not disappoint. Here concentrated blackberry and bitter chocolate flavours have good texture and weight, coupled with an impressive finish and length.   **rating:** 91

best drinking 2006–2016 **drink with** Braised ox cheek • $15.40

Michael Unwin Tattooed Lady Shiraz
▼▼▼▼▽ **2001** Medium red-purple; complex blackberry and spice aromas have some savoury notes lurking underneath; the very powerful palate has a mix of concentrated dark fruits and more savoury characters; balanced extract and tannins.   **rating:** 93

best drinking 2007–2017 **drink with** Beef spare ribs • $40

Michael Unwin Tattooed Lady Cabernet Sauvignon
▼▼▼▼ **2001** Light to medium red-purple; clean cassis and redcurrant fruit, plus a touch of oak on the bouquet lead into a light to medium-bodied palate, savoury, but with more grip and length than the Acrobat wine of the same vintage.   **rating:** 88

best drinking 2006–2011 **drink with** Lamb casserole • $40

michelini wines   ★★★

Great Alpine Road, Myrtleford, Vic 3737 **region** Alpine Valleys
phone (03) 5751 1990 **fax** (03) 5751 1410 **open** 7 days 10–5
winemaker Greg O'Keefe **production** 2500 cases **est.** 1982
product range ($13.50–20 CD) Riesling, Unwooded Chardonnay, Chardonnay, Fizz Pinot Chardonnay, Fizz Merlot, Pinot Noir, Marzemino, Shiraz, Merlot, Cabernet Sauvignon, Fragolino.
summary The Michelini family are among the best known grape growers in the Buckland Valley of northeast Victoria. Having migrated from Italy in 1949, the Michelinis originally grew tobacco, diversifying into vineyards in 1982. A little over 42 hectares of vineyard have been established on terra rossa soil at an altitude of 300 metres, mostly with frontage to the Buckland River. The major part of the production is sold (to Orlando and others), but since 1996 an on-site winery has permitted the Michelinis to vinify part of their production. The winery in fact has capacity to handle 1000 tonnes of fruit, thereby eliminating the problem of moving grapes out of a declared phylloxera area.

middlebrook NR

RSD 43, Sand Road, McLaren Vale, SA 5171 **region** McLaren Vale
phone (08) 8383 0600 **fax** (08) 8383 0557 **open** Mon–Fri 9–5, weekends 10–5
winemaker Joseph Cogno **production** 12 000 cases **est.** 1947
product range ($14–20 CD) At the top come Middlebrook Pinot Chardonnay, Unwooded Semillon, Sauvignon Blanc, Chardonnay, Frontignac, Shiraz and Cabernet Sauvignon; then cheaper wines under the Cogno label.
summary After a brief period of ownership by industry veteran Bill Clappis (who renovated and reopened the winery) ownership has now passed to the Cogno Brothers Family, which has been winemaking at Cobbity, near Camden, NSW, since 1964. Through Middlebrook the family has become one of the largest producers of Lambrusco in Australia, available Australia-wide through Liquorland stores. Many other wines (18 in all) are produced under the Cogno Brothers label, while the Middlebrook cask hall has been given over to production of the Medlow chocolate range. The top wines are still sold under the Middlebrook label.

middleton estate NR

Flagstaff Hill Road, Middleton, SA 5213 **region** Currency Creek
phone (08) 8555 4136 **fax** (08) 8555 4108 **open** Fri–Sun 11–5
winemaker Nigel Catt **production** 3000 cases **est.** 1979
product range ($9–16 CD) Riesling, Sauvignon Blanc, Semillon Sauvignon Blanc, Cabernet Hermitage.
summary Nigel Catt has demonstrated his winemaking skills at Andrew Garrett and elsewhere, so wine quality should be good; despite its decade of production, I have never seen or tasted its wines, which come from 20 hectares of estate plantings. Less than half the grapes are used for the Middleton label, the remainder sold. A winery restaurant helps the business turnover.

milburn park ★★★

Campbell Avenue, Irymple, Vic 3498 **region** Murray Darling
phone (03) 5024 6800 **fax** (03) 5024 6605 **open** Mon–Sat 10–4.30
winemaker Krister Jonsson, Gary Magilton **production** 2 million cases **est.** 1977
product range ($4–15 R) Top-end wines under the Milburn Park label are Chardonnay, Pinot Noir Chardonnay, Shiraz and Cabernet Sauvignon; then comes the standard Salisbury Estate range of Riesling Dry, Sauvignon Blanc, Chardonnay, Shiraz, Merlot, Grenache, Cabernet Sauvignon, Cabernet Merlot; then the Castle Ridge range consisting of Colombard Chardonnay, Shiraz Malbec Mourvedre; Acacia Ridge non-vintage generics bring up the rear, with two wines in the Tennyson Vineyard off to one side.
summary Part of a widespread group of companies owned by Cranswick Premium Wines Limited, with a strong export focus.

milford vineyard ★★★★★

Tasman Highway, Cambridge, Tas 7170 **region** Southern Tasmania
phone (03) 6248 5029 **fax** (03) 6248 5076 **open** Not
winemaker Andrew Hood (Contract) **production** 200 cases **est.** 1984
product range ($22 R) Pinot Noir.
summary Given the tiny production, Milford is understandably not open to the public, the excellent Pinot Noir being quickly sold by word of mouth. The 150-hectare grazing property (the oldest Southdown sheep stud in Australia) has been in Charlie Lewis's family since 1830. Only 15 minutes from Hobart, and with an absolute water frontage to the tidal estuary of the Coal River, it is a striking site. The vineyard is established on a patch of 1.5-metre-deep sand over a clay base with lots of lime impregnation.

Milford Vineyard Pinot Noir

TTTTT 2001 Excellent bright purple-red; a complex bouquet of plum, forest and spice aromas is followed by a palate with great intensity, power and length, the flavours tracking the bouquet. **rating: 94**
best drinking Now–2007 **best vintages** '96, '98, '01 **drink with** Ravioli • $22

milimani estate NR

92 The Forest Road, Bungendore, NSW 2621 **region** Canberra District
phone (02) 6238 1421 **fax** (02) 6238 1424 **open** Weekends and public holidays 10–5
winemaker Lark Hill, Kyeema Estate (Contract) **production** 1400 cases **est.** 1989
product range ($15.40–19 R) Sauvignon Blanc, Chardonnay, Pinot Noir, Cabernet Franc Merlot.

summary The Preston family (Mary, David and Rosemary) have established a 3-hectare vineyard at Bungendore planted to sauvignon blanc, chardonnay, pinot noir, merlot and cabernet franc. Contract winemaking at Lark Hill guarantees the quality of the wine.

🍂 millbrook winery ★★★★

Old Chestnut Lane, Jarrahdale, WA 6124 **region** Perth Hills
phone (08) 9525 5796 **fax** (08) 9525 5672 **open** 7 days 10–5, lunches Wed–Sun 12–3
winemaker Tony Davis **production** NFP **est.** 1996
product range ($16.50–35 CD) Sauvignon Blanc, Chardonnay, Viognier, Shiraz, Cabernet Sauvignon Merlot; under the Barking Owl label Semillon Sauvignon Blanc, Viognier, Chardonnay, Late Harvest, Grenache Rose, Shiraz, Cabernet Sauvignon Merlot, Cabernet Plus.
summary The strikingly situated Millbrook Winery, opened in December 2001, is owned by the highly successful, Perth-based entrepreneur Peter Fogarty and wife Lee. They also own Lakes Folly in the Hunter Valley, and have made a major commitment to the quality end of Australian wine. Millbrook draws on 7.5 hectares of vineyards in the Perth Hills, planted to sauvignon blanc, semillon, chardonnay, viognier, cabernet sauvignon, merlot, shiraz and petit verdot. It also purchases grapes from both the Perth Hills and Geographe regions. The wines under both the Millbrook and second label, Barking Owl, are of consistently high quality. The wines are distributed by WA Vintners in Western Australia and Fesq & Co in New South Wales; exports to England and the US.

Barking Owl Semillon Sauvignon Blanc

ΨΨΨΨ 2002 Pale straw-green; a fresh, crisp bouquet with light passionfruit blossom aromas leads into a palate with good length and balance; the small percentage barrel fermented adds to texture, rather than flavour; predominantly semillon. **rating:** 89
best drinking Now–2006 **drink with** Scampi • $16.50

Barking Owl Chardonnay

ΨΨΨΨ 2001 Pale but bright straw-green; the bouquet is fragrant, with tinned clingstone peach aromas, the light-bodied palate fresh, and complexed with some creamy/spicy malolactic and barrel-ferment influences. Sophisticated winemaking. **rating:** 88
best drinking Now–2006 **drink with** Pan-fried veal • $16.50

Barking Owl Shiraz

ΨΨΨΨ 2001 Medium red-purple; spice, cedar and plum aromas introduce an elegant palate, with a spicy/cedary echo of the bouquet, finishing with fine, filigreed tannins. **rating:** 89
best drinking 2004–2009 **drink with** Smoked beef • $18

Barking Owl Cabernet Sauvignon Merlot

ΨΨΨΨΨ 2001 Bright although relatively light red-purple; a fresh and clean bouquet has spice, berry and earth aromas; the palate has very good structure, with red berry flavours supported by fine, ripe tannins. Shows the same elegance as the Shiraz. **rating:** 90
best drinking 2006–2011 **best vintages** '01 **drink with** Loin of lamb • $18

millers samphire NR

Watts Gully Road, Cnr Robertson Road, Kersbrook, SA 5231 **region** Adelaide Hills
phone (08) 8389 3183 **fax** (03) 8389 3183 **open** 7 days 9–5 by appointment
winemaker Tom Miller **production** 80 cases **est.** 1982
product range ($9 CD) Riesling.
summary Next after Scarp Valley, one of the smallest wineries in Australia offering wine for sale; pottery also helps. Tom Miller has one of the more interesting and diverse CVs, with an early interest in matters alcoholic leading to the premature but happy death of a laboratory rat at Adelaide University and his enforced switch from biochemistry to mechanical engineering. The Riesling is a high-flavoured wine with crushed herb and lime aromas and flavours.

millfield ★★★☆

Lot 341, Mount View Road, Millfield, NSW 2325 **region** Lower Hunter Valley
phone (02) 4998 1571 **fax** (02) 4998 0172 **open** Fri–Sun 10–4
winemaker David Lowe **production** 5000 cases **est.** 1997
product range ($20–25 CD) Semillon, Chardonnay, Shiraz.

summary Situated on the picturesque Mount View Road, Millfield made its market debut in June 2000. The neatly labelled and packaged wines have won gold medals and trophies right from the first vintage in 1998, and praise from winewriters and critics both in Australia and the UK. The wines are sold both through the cellar door and mailing list, and through a limited number of fine wine retail and top-quality restaurants. Exports to the UK through Corney & Barrow.

Millfield Shiraz

TTTT 2001 Medium red-purple; the bouquet has an earthy/dusty regional overlay on red fruits, the light to medium-bodied palate following along much the same track, but with a faint hint of game and what seems to be late-adjusted acidity. Very different to the 2000. **rating:** 85

best drinking 2004–2007 **drink with** Beef stroganoff • $25

millinup estate ★★★★

RMB 1280 Porongurup Road, Porongurup, WA 6324 **region** Great Southern
phone (08) 9853 1105 **fax** (08) 9853 1105 **open** Weekends 10–5
winemaker Mike Garland (Red), Rob Lee (White) **production** 250 cases **est.** 1989
product range ($15–20 CD) Twin Peaks Riesling, Old Cottage Riesling, Cabernet Sauvignon Cabernet Franc Merlot.
summary The Millinup Estate vineyard was planted in 1978, when it was called Point Creek. Owners Peter and Lesley Thorn purchased it in 1989, renaming it and having the limited production (from 0.5 hectare of riesling, supplemented by purchased red grapes) vinified at Garlands and the Porongurup winery.

minot vineyard ★★★☆

PO Box 683, Margaret River, WA 6285 **region** Margaret River
phone (08) 9757 3579 **fax** (08) 9757 2361 **open** By appointment
winemaker Cathy Oats **production** 1800 cases **est.** 1986
product range ($14–25 ML) Semillon, Semillon Sauvignon Blanc, Cabernet Sauvignon.
summary Minot, which takes its name from a small chateau in the Loire Valley in France, is the husband and wife venture of the Miles family, producing just two wines from the 4.5-hectare plantings of semillon, sauvignon blanc and cabernet sauvignon.

Minot Vineyard Semillon Sauvignon Blanc

TTTT 2002 Light straw-green; the bouquet is somewhat restrained, but the complex, grassy palate builds character through to the finish. **rating:** 87

best drinking Now **drink with** Cold seafood • $14

Minot Vineyard Cabernet Sauvignon

TTTT 2000 Medium red, the purple starting to diminish; spicy, earthy, blackcurrant varietal fruit aromas flow into a light to medium-bodied palate, with similar fruit at the core, but also showing some oak sweetness, closing with soft tannins. **rating:** 86

best drinking 2004–2008 **drink with** Lamb cutlets • $25

mintaro wines ★★★☆

Leasingham Road, Mintaro, SA 5415 **region** Clare Valley
phone (08) 8843 9046 **fax** (08) 8843 9050 **open** 7 days 9–5
winemaker Peter Houldsworth **production** 5000 cases **est.** 1984
product range ($16–24 CD) Riesling, Semillon Chardonnay, Late Picked Riesling, Anastasia's Sparkling Cabernet Shiraz, Shiraz, Reserve Shiraz, Cabernet Sauvignon, Cabernet.
summary Has produced some very good Riesling over the years, developing well in bottle. The red wines are formidable, massive in body and extract, built for the long haul.

miramar ★★★★

Henry Lawson Drive, Mudgee, NSW 2850 **region** Mudgee
phone (02) 6373 3874 **fax** (02) 6373 3854 **open** 7 days 9–5
winemaker Ian MacRae **production** 8000 cases **est.** 1977
product range ($10–33 CD) Riesling, Semillon, Fume Blanc, Chardonnay, Eurunderee Rose, Shiraz, Eljamar Shiraz, Cabernet Sauvignon; Doux Blanc (sweet white), Encore and Encore Rouge (Sparkling).

summary Industry veteran Ian MacRae has demonstrated his skill with every type of wine over the decades, ranging through Rose to Chardonnay to full-bodied reds. All have shone under the Miramar label at one time or another, although the Ides of March are pointing more to the red than the white wines these days. A substantial part of the production from the 35 hectares of estate vineyard is sold to others, the best being retained for Miramar's own use. As from 2002 all wines, including reds, have been or will be sealed with Stelvin.

Miramar Riesling

TTTT 2002 Light straw-green; a clean, crisp, focused bouquet with a tight mix of lime, citrus and mineral leads into a similarly crisp, focused, minerally palate, almost to the point of hardness; however, excellent value. Stelvin-capped in a light Bordeaux bottle looks a bit strange.   **rating:** 88

best drinking 2005–2012 **drink with** Fish in lemon sauce • $12

Miramar Semillon

TTTT 2002 Light green-yellow; the bouquet is spotlessly clean but very closed, and the palate is likewise extremely shy. However, the wine has the length and balance to repay cellaring and develop an amazing array of mature semillon like buttered toast with a smear of honey. Bottled and capped as is the Riesling.   **rating:** 87

best drinking 2006–2016 **drink with** Pasta • $12

Miramar Shiraz

TTTTY 2001 Youthful crimson-purple; the fresh, red berry fruit of the bouquet has minimal oak; the same fruit comes through on the firm palate which is nicely balanced, has good length, good acidity and a fine finish. From 28-year-old vines; finished with a Stelvin cap which will underwrite the undoubted cellaring potential of the wine.   **rating:** 90

best drinking 2006–2016 **best vintages** '86, '90, '94, '95, '97 **drink with** Braised oxtail or, better still, the ox • $19

Miramar Eljamar Shiraz

TTTTY 2001 Bright, deep red-purple; powerful red and black fruit aromas are followed by a complex and stylish palate, where vibrant fruit is neatly balanced with French and American oak; excellent finish. Once again shows what a first crop can produce.   **rating:** 92

best drinking 2005–2012 **best vintages** '01 **drink with** Grilled T-bone • $19

miranda wines – barossa   ★★★★

Barossa Highway, Rowland Flat, SA 5352 **region** Barossa Valley
phone (08) 8524 4537 **fax** (08) 8524 4066 **open** Mon–Fri 10–4.30, weekends 11–4
winemaker Garry Wall, Richard Langford **production** NFP **est.** 1919
product range ($14.95–33 R) Riesling, Sauvignon Blanc, Chardonnay, Shiraz, Cabernet Sauvignon; followed by Family Reserve range of Chardonnay, Old Vine Shiraz, Shiraz Cabernet, Grenache; The Drainings (Shiraz Cabernet blend).
summary Increasingly absorbed into the Miranda Wine Group since its acquisition, drawing on grapes produced both in the Barossa Valley and throughout other parts of southeast Australia. The accent is on value for money, with consistent show success underlining the quality. Exports to the UK, Europe, New Zealand and the US.

Miranda Eden Valley Riesling

TTTT 2002 Light straw-green; the bouquet offers quite full fruit, but is fractionally bready; the wine perks up on entry, but then wanders off with a slightly blurred finish.   **rating:** 85

best drinking Now **best vintages** '01 **drink with** Salmon roulade • $14.95

Miranda Family Reserve Barossa Old Vine Shiraz

TTTT 2000 Medium red-purple; the very ripe, juicy, jammy bouquet has fruit conserve aromas which come through with a dusting of spice on the palate; submitted in February 2003 and said to be a tank sample. **rating:** 85

best drinking 2004–2009 **drink with** Beef casserole • $23

Miranda Family Reserve Shiraz Cabernet

TTTTY 1998 Light to medium red-purple; as expected, some bottle development starting to show, with slightly dusty/pencilly oak alongside earthy, spicy fruit. The palate is intense and long, flavours of chocolate and red berry balancing (more or less) the oak. The wine spent 24 months in a mix of French and American oak. From the Eden Valley.   **rating:** 91

best drinking Now–2008 **best vintages** '98 **drink with** Beef Bordelaise • $22.95

miranda wines – griffith ★★★

57 Jondaryan Avenue, Griffith, NSW 2680 **region** Riverina
phone (02) 6960 3000 **fax** (02) 6962 6944 **open** 7 days 9–5
winemaker Sam F Miranda, Garry Wall, Hope Golding, Luis E Simian **production** 2.5 million cases **est.** 1939
product range ($6–18 R) Golden Botrytis; Mirool Creek range of Semillon Sauvignon Blanc, Chardonnay, Brut Reserve, Red Brut, Shiraz, Merlot, Durif, Cabernet Shiraz; Somerton Semillon Chardonnay, Unoaked Chardonnay, Shiraz Cabernet Merlot, Merlot; also lower-priced Christy's Land and assorted varietals, generics, sparkling and ports.
summary Miranda Wines continues its aggressive and successful growth strategy, having opened a new winery in the King Valley in 1998 and previously expanded winemaking operations into the Barossa Valley. A veritable cascade of wines now appear under the various brand names, the majority representing good value for money. Exports to the UK, Europe, New Zealand and the US.

Miranda Golden Botrytis

▼▼▼▼ 2001 Yellow-gold; rich, butterscotch, honey and citrus aromas are reflected in the very rich palate, of Beerenauslese sweetness; good acidity to balance. **rating:** 89
best drinking Now–2006 **best vintages** '93, '94, '96, '97, '00 **drink with** Fruit ice-cream, sweet pastries • $15

Miranda Reserve Golden Botrytis

▼▼▼▼▽ 2001 Full yellow-gold; the bouquet has the same fruit characters as the varietal release of the same year, but more oak is evident on the bouquet. The rich, multilayered and complex palate has good balance and impressive flavour. **rating:** 92
best drinking Now–2007 **drink with** Cake • $18

miranda wines – king valley ★★★

Cnr Snow and Whitfield Roads, Oxley, Vic 3768 **region** King Valley
phone (03) 5727 3399 **fax** (03) 5727 3851 **open** 7 days 10–5
winemaker Bruce Holm, Garry Wall **production** NFP **est.** 1998
product range ($12.95–13.95 R) The High Country series of Riesling, Sauvignon Blanc, Chardonnay, Sparkling Chardonnay, Merlot, Shiraz, Cabernet Sauvignon.
summary Miranda now has three quite separate winemaking entities: the original (and largest) in Griffith; the next in the Barossa Valley; and the most recent in the King Valley. It is at the latter winery that the High Country range is made, using 37 hectares of estate vineyards, supplemented by grapes purchased from elsewhere, including the Kiewa Valley. Exports to the UK, Europe, New Zealand and the US.

Miranda High Country Sauvignon Blanc

▼▼▼▼ 2002 Pale straw-green; the light bouquet shows clear varietal character in a gentle gooseberry and herb spectrum, the light, direct and fresh palate carrying on where the bouquet leaves off; not complex, but then few Sauvignon Blancs are. **rating:** 86
best drinking Now **drink with** Shellfish • $12.95

Miranda High Country Chardonnay

▼▼▼▼ 2001 Medium yellow-green; nutty/melon is supported by pleasantly balanced and integrated oak on the bouquet; the light to medium-bodied palate features lively stone fruit and melon flavours with good length, the oak in the background. Barrel fermented in a mix of French and American oak, and good value. **rating:** 87
best drinking Now **best vintages** '01 **drink with** Pizza • $13.95

Miranda High Country Cabernet Sauvignon

▼▼▼▼ 2000 Medium red, with just a touch of purple; blackcurrant, leaf and spice intermingle on the bouquet and on the medium-bodied palate, which has good length and balance. **rating:** 86
best drinking Now–2006 **drink with** Braised lamb • $13.95

mistletoe wines ★★★☆

771 Hermitage Road, Pokolbin, NSW 2320 **region** Lower Hunter Valley
phone (02) 4998 7770 **fax** (02) 4998 7792 **open** 7 days 10–6
winemaker John Cassegrain (Contract) **production** 2500 cases **est.** 1989
product range ($16–20 CD) Semillon, Silvereye Semillon, Chardonnay, Reserve Chardonnay, The Rose, Shiraz.

summary Mistletoe Wines, owned by Ken and Gwen Sloan, can trace its history back to 1909, when a substantial vineyard was planted on what was then called Mistletoe Farm. The Mistletoe Farm brand made a brief appearance in the late1970s but disappeared and has now been revived under the Mistletoe Wines label by the Sloans, with contract-winemaking providing consistent results. No retail distribution, but worldwide delivery service available ex-winery. The art gallery features works by local artists.

mitchell ★★★★

Hughes Park Road, Sevenhill via Clare, SA 5453 **region** Clare Valley
phone (08) 8843 4258 **fax** (08) 8843 4340 **open** 7 days 10–4
winemaker Andrew Mitchell **production** 30 000 cases **est.** 1975
product range ($17–25 CD) Watervale Riesling, The Growers Semillon, Noble Semillon, Sparkling Peppertree, The Growers Grenache, Peppertree Vineyard Shiraz, Sevenhill Cabernet Sauvignon.
summary For long one of the stalwarts of the Clare Valley, producing long-lived Rieslings and Cabernet Sauvignons in classic regional style but having extended the range with very creditable Semillon and Shiraz. A lovely old stone apple shed provides the cellar door and upper section of the compact winery. Production has increased by 50 per cent over the past few years and as well as national retail distribution, the wines are exported to the US.

Mitchell Watervale Riesling

▼▼▼▼ 2002 Light straw-green; a very powerful and intense bouquet, but obvious reduction spoils the picture; the palate is the same frustrating mix of excellent underlying fruit, but the impact of the reduction is just too strong. **rating:** 85
best drinking Now **best vintages** '78, '84, '90, '92, '93, '94, '95, '00, '01 **drink with** Grilled fish • $18

Mitchell Peppertree Vineyard Shiraz

▼▼▼▼ 2001 Medium purple-red; the clean, fresh bouquet has fresh plum, blackberry and black cherry fruit, the palate offering the same in even greater abundance; early in its life, the tannins are disjointed, and need to marry, but will do so given time. **rating:** 88
best drinking 2005–2011 **best vintages** '84, '86, '87, '94, '95, '96, '99 **drink with** Devilled kidneys • $25

mitchelton ★★★★

Mitchellstown via Nagambie, Vic 3608 **region** Nagambie Lakes
phone (03) 5736 2222 **fax** (03) 5736 2266 **open** 7 days 10–5
winemaker Don Lewis, Toby Barlow **production** 200 000 cases **est.** 1969
product range ($12–50 CD) Top-of-the-range is Print Shiraz; then come Chardonnay, Viognier, Airstrip Marsanne Roussanne Viognier, Shiraz, Crescent Shiraz Mourvedre Grenache, Cabernet Sauvignon; next Blackwood Park range of Riesling, Late Harvested Riesling, Botrytis Riesling; Preece range of Sauvignon Blanc, Chardonnay, Sparkling Chardonnay Pinot Noir, Shiraz, Merlot, Cabernet Sauvignon; and finally Thomas Mitchell range of Marsanne, Chardonnay, Shiraz, Cabernet Sauvignon Shiraz.
summary Acquired by Petaluma in 1994, having already put the runs on the board in no uncertain fashion with the gifted winemaker Don Lewis. Boasts an impressive array of wines across a broad spectrum of style and price, but each carefully aimed at a market niche. The wines are exported to throughout Europe, the UK, Asia and the US.

Mitchelton Blackwood Park Riesling

▼▼▼▼ 2002 Medium yellow-green; the bouquet is clean, but not particularly expressive, the palate thin and crisp, with good structure, but similar fruit suppression. Needs time, but not in the usually reliable class of its predecessors. **rating:** 86
best drinking 2004–2008 **best vintages** '85, '90, '91, '92, '94, '95, '96, '98, '99, '00, '01 **drink with** Sashimi • $15

Mitchelton Preece Sauvignon Blanc

▼▼▼▼ 2002 Light to medium yellow-green; a highly aromatic bouquet with rich, tropical fruit comes through strongly on the rich, ripe and sweet fruit of the palate. Generous and honest. **rating:** 88
best drinking Now **drink with** Dolmades and bocconcini • $16

Mitchelton Marsanne Roussanne Viognier

▼▼▼▼▽ 2001 Straw-yellow; the powerful bouquet ranges through hay, mineral and apple, the complex, full-bodied, palate befitting the blend, offering splashes of spice and tobacco; avoids phenolics on the finish. **rating:** 91
best drinking Now–2006 **best vintages** '01 **drink with** Rich pasta • $26

Mitchelton Print Shiraz

ŢŢŢŢỲ **1998** Dense red-purple; a concentrated bouquet of dark berry, chocolate, prune and oak is followed by a very powerful and concentrated palate with mouth-puckering tannins. Needs a decade. **rating:** 92

best drinking 2008–2015 **best vintages** '81, '82, '90, '91, '92, '95, '96, '97, '98 **drink with** Marinated venison • $50

Mitchelton Crescent Shiraz Mourvedre Grenache

ŢŢŢŢŢ **2000** Medium red-purple; the moderately intense bouquet offers a range of aromatic red fruits and spices; the wine fills the mouth with sweet, but not jammy, fruit, supported by soft, ripe tannins and just a hint of oak. Good value. **rating:** 94

best drinking 2004–2010 **best vintages** '00 **drink with** Barbecued lamb cutlets • $26

Mitchelton Cabernet Sauvignon

ŢŢŢŢỲ **1998** Medium red-purple; the clean, gently sweet and moderately intense bouquet centres on red berry and cassis fruit; the palate comes through well, adding a touch of chocolate, closing with well-balanced tannins.

best drinking Now–2008 **best vintages** '96 **drink with** Lamb casserole • $22 **rating:** 90

Mitchelton Preece Cabernet Sauvignon

ŢŢŢŢ **2001** Medium red-purple; the bouquet offers a mix of savoury, blackberry, earth and vanilla notes, the medium-bodied palate with plenty of fruit flavour, but a slightly rough texture. Could well settle down over the next couple of years. **rating:** 85

best drinking 2004–2008 **drink with** Spaghetti with pesto • $16

mitolo wines ★★★★☆

34 Barossa Valley Way, Tanunda, SA 5352 (postal) **region** McLaren Vale
phone (08) 8282 9000 **fax** (08) 8380 8312 **open** Not
winemaker Ben Glaetzer **production** 4000 cases **est.** 1999
product range ($22–65 R) Jester Tarlton Shiraz, GAM McLaren Vale Shiraz, Reiver Shiraz Barossa Valley, Savitar Shiraz McLaren Vale, Serpico McLaren Vale Cabernet Sauvignon.
summary Frank Mitolo began making wine in 1995 as a hobby, and soon progressed to undertaking formal studies in winemaking. His interest grew year by year, but it was not until 2000 that he took the plunge into the commercial end of the business, retaining Ben Glaetzer to make the wines for him. The first release of 2000 GAM McLaren Vale Shiraz (named after Mitolo's children Gemma, Alex and Marco) was launched at the Australia Day tasting in London, and the entire European allocation sold out in less than three hours. Since that time, a remarkably good series of wines have been released. Imitation being the sincerest form of flattery, part of the complicated story behind each label name is pure Torbreck, but Mitolo then adds a Latin proverb or saying to the label name. A natty little loosely tied explanation/translation booklet tied to the neck of each bottle would be useful.

Mitolo GAM McLaren Vale Shiraz

ŢŢŢŢỲ **2001** Bright purple-red; the complex bouquet has a range of black fruits, spices, earth and vanilla; the palate has excellent mouthfeel, with no hint of overripe fruit, the blackberry and bitter chocolate fruit set against well-balanced, savoury tannins. Excellent oak handling. **rating:** 93

best drinking 2006–2016 **best vintages** '01 **drink with** Char-grilled rump steak • $52

Mitolo Jester Tarlton Shiraz

ŢŢŢŢ **2001** Medium red-purple; the fresh bouquet has abundant blackberry, earth and spice aromas offset by vanillin oak; the vibrant palate has attractive blackberry and bitter chocolate flavours, the oak restrained and the tannins fine. **rating:** 89

best drinking 2006–2011 **drink with** Beef casserole • $26

Mitolo Reiver Barossa Shiraz

ŢŢŢŢỲ **2001** Medium red-purple, not particularly deep; blackberry, redcurrant and sweet leather aromas are followed by a palate with the complex structure which has already established itself as part of the Mitolo house style. Savoury black fruits are balanced by fine, long tannins, and quality French oak. **rating:** 90

best drinking 2006–2012 **best vintages** '01 **drink with** Osso buco • $48

Mitolo Savitar McLaren Vale Shiraz

ŢŢŢŢŢ **2001** Medium purple-red; the complex bouquet has a quite different range of aromatics, with edges of game, leather and spice; the palate is once again true to the Mitolo style, with multi-layered dark berry fruits, and fine-grained tannins suggesting long maceration. Presented in one of those Dreadnought bottles. **rating:** 94

best drinking 2006–2016 **best vintages** '01 **drink with** Roast venison • $65

Mitolo Serpico McLaren Vale Cabernet Sauvignon

❡❡❡❡❡ 2002 Bright, deep red-purple; spotlessly clean, welcoming blackcurrant, dark chocolate and sympathetic and balanced oak aromas are followed by a palate with excellent structure, mouthfeel and balance, those layered flavours again coming to the fore. Made in full-on Amarone style, with the grapes being allowed to dehydrate on racks for five weeks, leaving the wine with 15° alcohol by volume. As in the case of high class Amarones, the alcohol does not burn. **rating: 94**

best drinking 2007–2017 **best vintages** '02 **drink with** Braised ox cheek • $65

molly morgan vineyard ★★★★

Talga Road, Lovedale, NSW 2321 **region** Lower Hunter Valley
phone (02) 9816 4088 **fax** (02) 9816 2680 **open** By appointment
winemaker Sarah-Kate Wilson (Contract) **production** 4500 cases **est.** 1963
product range ($18–35 ML) Joe's Block Semillon, Old Vines Semillon, Semillon Sauvignon Blanc, Chardonnay, Shiraz.
summary Molly Morgan has been acquired by Andrew and Hady Simon, who established the Camperdown Cellars Group in 1971, becoming the largest retailer in Australia before passing on to other pursuits, and John Baker, one of Australia's best known fine wine retailers, who owned or managed Quaffers, Double Bay Cellars, the Newport Bottler and Grape Fellas (Epping) at various times. The property is planted to 5.5 hectares of 25-year-old unirrigated semillon, which goes to make the Old Vines Semillon, 0.8 hectare for Joe's Block Semillon, 2.5 hectares of chardonnay and 1.2 hectares of shiraz. The wines are contract-made (as has always been the case, in fact, but to a high standard). Exports to the US.

Molly Morgan Semillon Sauvignon Blanc

❡❡❡❡❡ 2002 Light green-yellow; a clean, fragrant and fresh bouquet with a mix of grass and lemon leads into a spotless palate, with excellent balance and length; the 10 per cent Sauvignon Blanc simply adds flavour interest without detracting from the classic structure of the Semillon. Trophy and gold medal Hunter Valley Wine Show 2002. The Sauvignon Blanc comes from grapes grown at Orange. **rating: 95**

best drinking Now–2010 **best vintages** '02 **drink with** Shellfish • $19.95

Molly Morgan Chardonnay

❡❡❡❡ 2000 Bright yellow-green; the solid bouquet has peach, melon and honey aromas, the palate fresher than the bouquet, and suggesting a slight lack of concentration. However, well made. **rating: 86**

best drinking Now–2005 **drink with** Lighter pasta dishes • $23

Molly Morgan Partner's Reserve Chardonnay

❡❡❡❡ 2002 Medium yellow-green; very obvious barrel-ferment aromas dominate the bouquet; tangy/citrussy fruit makes a partial comeback on the palate, but much less oak would have been better. **rating: 85**

best drinking Now–2005 **drink with** Pan-fried chicken breast • $35

Molly Morgan Partner's Reserve Shiraz

❡❡❡❡ 2000 Medium purple-red; the moderately intense bouquet is clean, with a mix of black cherry and plum fruit supported by subtle oak; savoury dark fruit flavours intensified by dark chocolate are balanced by a touch of oak and fine tannins on the finish of the palate. The back label claims regarding the occasional sale of Partner's Reserve wines to the public will bring a smile to the face of cynical readers. **rating: 87**

best drinking Now–2008 **drink with** Kangaroo fillet • $25

monahan estate ★★★★

Lot 1, Wilderness Road, Rothbury, NSW 2320 **region** Lower Hunter Valley
phone (02) 4930 9070 **fax** (02) 4930 7679 **open** Thurs–Sun 10–5
winemaker Monarch Winemaking Services **production** 2000 cases **est.** 1997
product range ($13–14 CD) Semillon, Old Bridge Semillon, Old Bridge Unwooded Chardonnay.
summary Having become partners with founder Matthew Monahan in 1999, John and Patricia Graham now own the estate outright. It is bordered by Black Creek in the Lovedale district, an area noted for its high-quality semillon; the old bridge adjoining the property is displayed on the wine label; the wines themselves have been consistent silver and bronze medal winners at the Hunter Valley Wine Show.

Monahan Estate Semillon

❡❡❡❡❡ 1999 Medium yellow-green; a firm, classic semillon bouquet with a mix of herb and a hint of lanolin; the palate has good weight and length, and a classic dry finish. **rating: 91**

best drinking Now–2009 **best vintages** '99, '01 **drink with** Summer salads • $14

Monahan Estate Old Bridge Semillon

▼▼▼▼ 2000 Bright, light to medium yellow-green; the clean bouquet has distinct herbs and citrus aromas; the palate is still quite youthful, with pleasing flavours, albeit fractionally short. **rating: 88**

best drinking Now–2007 drink with Barramundi • $13

Monahan Estate Old Bridge Chardonnay

▼▼▼▼ 2000 Excellent yellow-green; the clean bouquet has melon and white peach fruit supported by the barest hint of oak; the palate is still very fresh and lively, driven by its tangy fruit; good length. Both this wine and the 1999 Semillon are re-releases after the 2001 wines. **rating: 89**

best drinking Now–2005 drink with Tempura fish • $13

monichino wines   NR

1820 Berrys Road, Katunga, Vic 3640 **region** Goulburn Valley
phone (03) 5864 6452 **fax** (03) 5864 6538 **open** Mon–Sat 9–5, Sun 10–5
winemaker Carlo Monichino, Terry Monichino **production** 16 000 cases **est.** 1962
product range ($10–25 CD) Riesling, Semillon Sauvignon Blanc, Sauvignon Blanc, Chardonnay, Botrytis Semillon, Orange Muscat, Golden Lexia, Rose Petals Spatlese, Rosso Dolce, Shiraz, Merlot, Carlo's Pressings, Cabernet Sauvignon; various Ports and fortifieds; bulk sales also available.
summary A winery which has quietly made some clean, fresh wines in which the fruit character is carefully preserved, and has shown a deft touch with its Botrytis Semillon. No recent tastings.

montalto vineyards   ★★★★

33 Shoreham Road, Red Hill South, Vic 3937 **region** Mornington Peninsula
phone (03) 5989 8412 **fax** (03) 5989 8417 **open** 7 days 12–5
winemaker Robin Brockett **production** 3000 cases **est.** 1998
product range ($16.50–35 CD) Chardonnay, Rose, Pinot Noir; second label Pennon Riesling, Semillon Sauvignon Blanc, Chardonnay, Cuvee One, Rose, Pinot Noir, Shiraz.
summary John Mitchell and family established Montalto Vineyards in 1998, although the core of the vineyard goes back to 1986. There are 3 hectares of chardonnay and 5.6 hectares of pinot noir, with 0.5 hectare each of semillon, riesling and pinot meunier. Intensive vineyard work opens up the canopy, with yields ranging between 1.5 and 2.5 tonnes per acre, with the majority of the fruit hand-harvested. Wines are released under two labels, the flagship Montalto and Pennon, the latter effectively a lower-priced, second label. The restaurant, open daily for lunch on Friday and Saturday evenings, also features guest chefs and cooking classes. A winery to watch.

Montalto Pennon Riesling

▼▼▼▼ 2002 Very light green-yellow; the clean, light bouquet has mineral and faint blossom aromas, the crisp and lively palate picking up the pace with focused, fine, lime fruit. **rating: 88**

best drinking Now–2007 drink with Sushi • $17.50

Montalto Chardonnay

▼▼▼▼▽ 2001 Light to medium yellow-green; the bouquet has attractive nectarine and citrus fruit allied with cashew and spicy oak; the bright, crisp, fruit-driven palate has tangy fruit and good length, the oak in the background. **rating: 90**

best drinking Now–2006 drink with Sautéed scallops • $25

Montalto Pennon Chardonnay

▼▼▼▼ 2001 Light to medium yellow-green; clear, clean citrus and melon fruit on the bouquet feeds into a palate which is elegant and unforced, with good mouthfeel; if oak has been used, it is imperceptible. **rating: 87**

best drinking Now–2005 drink with Shellfish • $16.50

Montalto Pennon Rose

▼▼▼▼ 2002 Light, bright pink; spice, herb and berry aromas lead into a fresh, crisp and lively palate, with a bone-dry finish. A blend of Pinot Meunier and Pinot Noir, with only 100 cases made. **rating: 87**

best drinking Now drink with Antipasto • $17.50

Montalto Pinot Noir

▼▼▼▼▽ 2001 Medium red-purple; a fragrant and fruit-driven bouquet with plum and cherry fruit, then a similarly fruit-driven and smooth palate, with clean line and a fresh finish. Less than 300 cases made; doesn't have quite the richness of the 2000. **rating: 90**

best drinking Now–2007 best vintages '00, '01 drink with Breast of squab • $35

Montalto Pennon Pinot Noir

▼▼▼▼ 2001 Medium red-purple; ripe plum and some earthy notes on the bouquet are followed by a powerful palate, with slightly grainy tannins and extract. May well have enough in the tank to benefit from short to medium-term cellaring. **rating: 88**

best drinking Now–2006 best vintages '00 drink with Wild mushroom risotto • $23

montara ★★★☆

Chalambar Road, Ararat, Vic 3377 **region** Grampians
phone (03) 5352 3868 **fax** (03) 5352 4968 **open** Mon–Sat 10–5, Sun 12–4
winemaker Mike McRae **production** NFP **est.** 1970
product range ($13.50–27 CD) Riesling, Chardonnay, Pinot Noir, Shiraz, Merlot, Cabernet Sauvignon, Shiraz Port; 'M' range of Chardonnay, Pinot Noir Shiraz.
summary Achieved considerable attention for its Pinot Noirs during the 1980s, but other regions (and other makers) have come along since. It continues to produce wines of distinctive style, and smart new label designs do help. Limited national distribution; exports to the UK, Switzerland, Canada and Hong Kong.

Montara Chardonnay

▼▼▼▼ 2000 Medium yellow-green; the moderately intense bouquet has citrus and melon fruit, the oak somewhat raw and pencilly; however, the palate focuses on clean melon and cashew fruit, with quite good length; the oak less abrasive. **rating: 86**

best drinking Now–2005 drink with Deep-fried calamari • $21

Montara Merlot

▼▼▼▼ 2001 Light to medium red-purple; the bouquet has an array of minty berry, spice and leaf aromas, the flavours coalescing well in a sweetly spicy/savoury mode, giving the palate good length. **rating: 89**

best drinking 2004–2009 drink with Roast veal • $27

montgomery's hill ★★★☆

Hassell Highway, Upper Kalgan, Albany, WA 6330 **region** Great Southern
phone (08) 9844 3715 **fax** (08) 9844 1104 **open** 7 days 11–5
winemaker Robert Lee (Porongurup Winery), John Wade (Consultant) **production** 2000 cases **est.** 1996
product range ($15–22.50 R) Sauvignon Blanc, Chardonnay, Unwooded Chardonnay, Cabernet Franc, Cabernets.
summary Montgomery's Hill is situated 16 kilometres northeast of Albany on a north-facing slope on the banks of the Kalgan River. The vineyard is situated on an area which was previously an apple orchard and is a diversification for the third generation of the Montgomery family which owns the property. Chardonnay, cabernet sauvignon and cabernet franc were planted in 1996, followed by sauvignon blanc, shiraz and merlot in 1997. Since 1999 Montgomery's Hill has been made at the new Porongurup Winery.

monument vineyard NR

Cnr Escort Way and Manildra Road, Cudal, NSW 2864 **region** Central Ranges Zone
phone (02) 6364 2294 **fax** (02) 6364 2069 **open** By appointment
winemaker Alison Eisermann **production** 1000 cases **est.** 1998
product range ($12–18 CD) Riesling, Semillon Sauvignon Blanc, Pinot Gris, Marsanne, Rose, Pinot Noir, Shiraz, Hospital Hill Shiraz, Sangiovese, Cabernet Sauvignon Shiraz Merlot, Cabernet Sauvignon.
summary In the early 1990s five mature-age students at Charles Sturt University, successful in their own professions, decided to form a partnership to develop a substantial vineyard and winery development on a scale that they could not individually afford, but could do so collectively. After a lengthy search, a large property at Cudal was identified, with ideal terra rossa basalt-derived soil over a limestone base. The property now has 110 hectares under vine, as a result of planting in the spring of 1998 and 1999. The 2001 Cabernet Sauvignon was a trophy winner at the New South Wales Small Winemaker Show 2002; I much preferred the Shiraz.

Monument Vineyard Hospital Hill Shiraz

▼▼▼▼ 2001 Full red-purple; the ripe and juicy bouquet has dark plum, blackberry and cherry fruit aromas which come through on the ripe and juicy palate; subtle oak and soft tannins. The wine spent 12 months in a mix of French and American barrels. A bit more structure and texture would have generated higher points. **rating: 86**

best drinking Now–2006 drink with Lasagne • $18

moonbark estate vineyard NR

Lot 11, Moonambel-Natte Yallock Road, Moonambel, Vic 3478 (postal) **region** Pyrenees
phone 0439 952 263 **fax** (03) 9870 6116 **open** Not
winemaker Kim Hart (Contract) **production** 300 cases **est.** 1998
product range ($18 R) Shiraz.
summary Rod Chivers and his family have been slowly establishing their vineyard over the past 6 years, with
0.5 hectare of shiraz in bearing. A further hectare-plus of cabernet sauvignon and merlot are due to be planted
over the next few years on the red clay and quartz soils typical of the region. The wines are made at
Warrenmang Estate by Kim Hart, and are sold through local restaurants and retailers.

moondah brook ★★★★

c/- Houghton, Dale Road, Middle Swan, WA 6056 **region** Swan Valley
phone (08) 9274 5372 **fax** (08) 9274 5372 **open** Not
winemaker Larry Cherubino **production** 80 000 cases **est.** 1968
product range ($10–17 R) Chardonnay, Chenin Blanc, Verdelho, Sauvignon Blanc, Shiraz, Cabernet
Sauvignon, Maritime (Sparkling); also occasional Show Reserve releases of Chenin Blanc and Verdelho.
summary Part of the BRL Hardy wine group which has its own special character as it draws part of its fruit
from the large Gingin vineyard, 70 kilometres north of the Swan Valley, and part from the Margaret River and
Great Southern. In recent times it has excelled even its own reputation for reliability with some quite lovely
wines, in particular honeyed, aged Chenin Blanc and finely structured Cabernet Sauvignon.

Moondah Brook Semillon Sauvignon Blanc

▼▼▼▼▼ 2002 Bright, pale green-yellow; the spotlessly clean and fragrant bouquet has great varietal character,
the complex and long palate likewise, with a mix of citrus, lemon and gooseberry fruit. **rating:** 94
best drinking Now–2005 **best vintages** '02 **drink with** Mussels • $13.99

Moondah Brook Chardonnay

A wine which is sometimes plain, sometimes quite brilliant, sourced from vineyards all over Western Australia.
▼▼▼▼ 2002 Light to medium yellow-green; the bouquet has surprisingly obvious oak influence, and also
complexity; the palate swings solidly to sweet, peachy fruit, finishing a fraction hot. The only appellation
claimed is Western Australia. **rating:** 87
best drinking Now–2005 **best vintages** '95 **drink with** Marron • $13.99

Moondah Brook Cabernet Rose

▼▼▼▼ 2002 Light, bright purple; excellent fresh raspberry and cherry aromas and flavours on both bouquet
and palate; avoids the sweetness trap, and continues the great tradition of Cabernet Sauvignon Roses from the
Houghton stable. The Stelvin cap should prolong the life of the wine, but there is in fact nothing to be gained
from cellaring it. **rating:** 88
best drinking Now **drink with** Turkey with cranberry sauce • $12.95

moondarra NR

Browns Road, Moondarra, Vic 3825 (postal) **region** Gippsland
phone (03) 9598 3049 **fax** (03) 9598 0677 **open** Not
winemaker Neil Prentice **est.** 1991
product range ($41.50–91.50) Samba Side Pinot Noir, Conception Pinot Noir, Holly's Garden Pinot Noir.
summary In 1991 Neil Prentice and family established their Moondarra Vineyard in Gippsland, planted to
11 low-yielding clones of pinot noir. The vines are not irrigated, and vineyard management is predicated on
the minimum use of any sprays with the aim of ultimately moving to biodynamic/Pagan farming methods. The
winemaking techniques are strongly influenced by the practices of controversial Lebanese-born Burgundy
consultant Guy Accad, with 10 days pre-fermentation maceration and whole bunches added prior to
fermentation. The wines are distributed in Melbourne and Sydney by Select Vineyards, go to Japan via Vintage
Cellars, and to Hong Kong and Belgium.

moonrakers NR

321 Raymond Road, Gunns Plains, Tas 7315 **region** Northern Tasmania
phone (03) 6429 1186 **open** 7 days 9–5
winemaker Richard Richardson (Contract) **production** 300 cases **est.** 1997
product range ($15–25 CD) Chardonnay, Pinot Noir.

summary Stephen and Diana Usher came from Wiltshire in England, where a local legend was told of illegal smuggling of kegs of brandy which were thrown into a pond to avoid detection. Later that night, when the coast was clear, the smugglers began the job of raking the kegs out of the pond, only to be surprised by the customs officers. Asked what they were doing, the smugglers replied they were trying to rake the moon reflected in the water. Taking them to be idiot fools from the village, the excise men rode off. The Ushers should have no such problem, having planted only 0.5 hectare each of chardonnay and pinot noir on a north-facing slope above the picturesque valley of Gunns Plains. The deep loam over limestone soil holds much promise.

moonshine valley winery   NR

374 Mons Road, Forest Glen, Buderim, Qld 4556 **region** Queensland Coastal
phone (07) 5445 1198 **fax** (07) 5445 1799 **open** Mon–Fri 10–4, weekends 10–5
winemaker Tom Weidmann **production** 3000 cases **est.** 1985
product range ($10–30 CD) A kaleidoscopic array of basically fruit-based wines, including White Moon, Red Moon; Chardonnay, Shiraz, Shiraz Cabernet Merlot. Liqueurs are Limoncello, Almondo, Espresso; Old Buderim Ginger, Strawberry Port, Old Ned (spirit), Porto Rubino, Ruby Moon Port (Shiraz Durif Sangiovese).
summary Frederick Houweling brings a European background to his making of these fruit-based wines. The winery is situated on a large property among natural lakes and forest, and also offers a restaurant, cafeteria, and souvenir shop.

moorebank vineyard   NR

Palmers Lane, Pokolbin, NSW 2320 **region** Lower Hunter Valley
phone (02) 4998 7610 **fax** (02) 4998 7367 **open** Fri–Mon 10–5, or by appointment
winemaker Iain Riggs (Contract) **production** 2000 cases **est.** 1977
product range ($21.50–29.50 CD) Gewurztraminer, Summar Semillon, Charlton Chardonnay, Trueman Traminer Late Harvest, The Son's Sparkling Merlot, Merlot, now sold in the narrow 500-ml Italian glass bottle known as Bellissima.
summary Ian Burgess and Debra Moore own a mature 6-hectare vineyard with a small cellar-door operation offering immaculately packaged wines in avant-garde style. The peachy Chardonnay has been a medal winner at Hunter Valley Wine Shows.

moores hill estate   ★★★★

3343 West Tamar Highway, Sidmouth, Tas 7270 **region** Northern Tasmania
phone (03) 6394 7649 **fax** (03) 6394 7649 **open** 7 days 10–5 in summer
winemaker Julian Alcorso (Contract) **production** 2000 cases **est.** 1997
product range ($18–25 CD) Riesling, Chardonnay, Unwooded Chardonnay, Pinot Noir, Cabernet Merlot.
summary Karen and Rod Thorpe, the latter with a background in catering, have established their vineyard on the gentle slopes of the west Tamar Valley. They have planted 2.2 hectares of riesling, chardonnay, pinot noir, merlot and cabernet sauvignon, with additional newly planted riesling. It represents a full circle for the Thorpes, because when they purchased the property a little over 20 years ago there was an old vineyard which they pulled out. A wine tasting and sales area made from Tasmanian timber opened at the end of 2002.

Moores Hill Estate Riesling

♥♥♥♥♡ 2002 Light straw-green; aromas of mineral, herb and apple lead into a particularly harmonious palate, with the flavour extending throughout its length; clean, fresh and bright aftertaste. Gold medal 2003 Tasmanian Wines Show. **rating:** 93
best drinking 2004–2010 **best vintages** '02 **drink with** Asparagus terrine • $19

Moores Hill Estate Unwooded Chardonnay

♥♥♥♥ 2002 Light straw-green; aromas of citrus and a hint of mineral lead into a clean, fresh palate with lemony stone fruit flavours, good length and bright acidity in typical Tasmanian fashion, but retaining balance.
rating: 86
best drinking Now–2005 **drink with** Slow-cooked Tasmanian salmon • $19

Moores Hill Estate Cabernet Merlot

♥♥♥♥♥ 2001 Medium to full purple-red; savoury olive and berry fruit aromas lead into a palate with red and black berry fruit flavours, good balance and structure. Really does show sweet fruit, without losing finesse.
rating: 94
best drinking 2005–2011 **best vintages** '01 **drink with** Rack of lamb • $25

moorilla estate ★★★★☆

655 Main Road, Berriedale, Tas 7011 **region** Southern Tasmania
phone (03) 6277 9900 **fax** (03) 6249 4093 **open** 7 days 10–5
winemaker Michael Glover **production** 15 000 cases **est.** 1958
product range ($19.50–65 CD) White Label range of Riesling, Gewurztraminer, Unwooded Chardonnay, Pinot Noir, Cabernet Sauvignon; Black Label range of Sauvignon Blanc, Chardonnay, Pinot Noir, Cabernet Merlot; Reserve wines include Chardonnay, Botrytis Sauvignon Blanc, Pinot Noir, Winter Collection Merlot, Cabernet Sauvignon, Winter Collection Cabernet Sauvignon Merlot; Vintage Brut.
summary Moorilla Estate is an icon in the Tasmanian wine industry and is thriving. Wine quality continues to be unimpeachable, while the opening of the museum in the marvellous Alcorso house designed by Sir Roy Grounds adds even more attraction for visitors to the estate, a mere 15–20 minutes from Hobart. Five-star self-contained chalets are available, with a restaurant open for lunch 7 days a week. Exports to Hong Kong.

Moorilla Estate Riesling

▼▼▼▼▽ 2002 Light green-straw, with some CO_2. The bouquet is distinctly Germanic, with lime and lime blossom aromas; the palate is loaded with lime juice flavour and character, all adding up to some sweetness which is as much to do with the fruit as it is to residual sugar. **rating:** 90
best drinking Now–2006 **best vintages** '81, '82, '90, '91, '93, '94, '95, '97, '98, '99, '01, '02 **drink with** Asparagus • $22.50

Moorilla Estate Gewurztraminer

▼▼▼▼▼ 2001 Light straw-yellow; an exceptionally pungent and floral bouquet with an abundance of rose petal and spice is supported by a palate redolent with flavour; here there is a mix of lemon juice, rose petal and a touch of lychee. Quite outstanding. **rating:** 94
best drinking Now–2005 **best vintages** '01 **drink with** Chinese stir-fried prawns • $28.50

Moorilla Estate White Label Chardonnay

▼▼▼▼▽ 2000 Light to medium yellow-green; the clean, moderately intense and fresh bouquet has touches of citrus and melon woven through with gentle oak; the well-balanced palate shows similar fruit flavours; there is good length to an altogether stylish wine. **rating:** 92
best drinking Now–2005 **best vintages** '99, '00 **drink with** Lobster • $26.50

Moorilla Estate Black Label Pinot Noir

▼▼▼▼▼ 2001 The 2001 vintage in Tasmania may yet rival the great 2000; global warming has its upsides for some parts of the world. Sumptuous dark plum fruit aromas, sweet and intense, flow into a palate overflowing with ripe (but not jammy) fruit, held together by good structure and fine tannins. Top drawer. **rating:** 94
best drinking Now–2009 **best vintages** '00, '01 **drink with** Duck confit • $29.50

Moorilla Estate Reserve Pinot Noir

▼▼▼▼▼ 2001 Strikingly deep purple-red; a very complex and concentrated bouquet with abundant black plum fruit and spice, compounded by positive oak. The palate is voluptuously ripe and concentrated; an Australian answer to the style of the famous Burgundian producer Domaine Leroy. **rating:** 96
▼▼▼▼▽ 2000 Medium to full purple-red; the bouquet has rich plum, plum cake and spice fruit; the palate follows suit, crammed to the gills with plummy fruit, oak somewhere in the background. **rating:** 93
best drinking Now–2010 **best vintages** '96, '97, '99, '00, '01 **drink with** Marinated venison • $65

Moorilla Estate Cabernet Merlot

▼▼▼▼▽ 2000 Medium to full red-purple; the moderately complex bouquet has dark berry fruit, with hints of mint and game; the palate has plenty of depth of flavour, with some cassis fruit, although it does not quite have the finish and aftertaste of its Reserve brother. Gold medal 2003 Tasmanian Wines Show. **rating:** 92
best drinking 2005–2010 **best vintages** '00 **drink with** Rack of lamb • $27

Moorilla Estate Reserve Cabernet Merlot

▼▼▼▼▽ 2000 Deep red-purple; fully ripe cassis/blackcurrant fruit aromas are threaded through subtle oak on the bouquet; the palate is similarly ripe, a tribute to the Tamar Valley in the 2000 vintage. The tannins, initially formidable, have softened to a surprising degree, although still leaving the wine with great power and depth. Top gold and trophy winner 2003 Tasmanian Wines Show. **rating:** 93
best drinking 2005–2015 **best vintages** '98, '00 **drink with** Venison • $39

Moorilla Estate White Label Cabernet Sauvignon

▼▼▼▼ **2001** Medium red-purple; blackcurrant fruit is supported by appealing oak and a touch of chocolate on both bouquet and the light to medium-bodied, well-balanced palate. Not over-extracted and has style. **rating:** 89

best drinking 2005–2011 **best vintages** '98, '99 **drink with** Marinated venison • $31

moorooduc estate ★★★★★

501 Derril Road, Moorooduc, Vic 3936 **region** Mornington Peninsula
phone (03) 5971 8506 **fax** (03) 5971 8550 **open** Weekends 11–5
winemaker Dr Richard McIntyre **production** 4600 cases **est.** 1983
product range ($23–60 R) Pinot Gris, Chardonnay, The Moorooduc Chardonnay, Devil Bend Creek Chardonnay, Pinot Noir, The Moorooduc Pinot Noir, Devil Bend Pinot Noir, Shiraz, Robinson Vineyard Shiraz, Cabernet.
summary Dr Richard McIntyre regularly produces one of the richest and most complex Chardonnays in the region, with melon/fig/peach fruit set against sumptuous spicy oak, and that hallmark soft nutty/creamy/regional texture. As well as retail distribution, the wines are exported through Trembath and Taylor.

Moorooduc Estate Chardonnay

▼▼▼▼▽ **2001** Medium straw-yellow; a complex bouquet offering restrained barrel-ferment and malolactic-ferment influences on melon fruit, then a palate with good mouthfeel built around sweet melon and fig fruit, the oak restrained. **rating:** 93

best drinking Now–2006 **best vintages** '88, '90, '91, '92, '93, '94, '95, '97, '98, '99, '01 **drink with** Grilled spatchcock • $30

Moorooduc Estate The Moorooduc Chardonnay

▼▼▼▼▽ **2001** Medium straw-yellow; the bouquet is particularly complex, with strong cashew/nutty inputs onto the discreet fruit; the palate, while powerful and rich, is a fraction hot on the finish. Made using indigenous/wild yeast and the full kit and caboodle; 13.5° alcohol. **rating:** 93

best drinking Now–2006 **best vintages** '98, '01 **drink with** Grilled spatchcock • $60

The Moorooduc Pinot Noir

▼▼▼▼▼ **2001** Medium to full red-purple; dark plum fruit has complex savoury edges on the bouquet; cherry, plum and the faintest touch of mint run through the well-structured and long palate, which finishes with gentle tannins. Immeasurably better than the standard varietal wine of the same year. **rating:** 94

best drinking Now–2006 **best vintages** '01 **drink with** Breast of squab • $60

morgan simpson ★★★★

PO Box 39, Kensington Park, SA 5068 **region** McLaren Vale
phone (08) 8364 3645 **fax** (08) 8364 3645 **open** Not
winemaker Richard Simpson **production** 1200 cases **est.** 1998
product range ($15–17.50 R) Chardonnay, Stone Hill Shiraz, Row 42 Cabernet Sauvignon.
summary Morgan Simpson was founded by South Australian businessman George Morgan (since retired) and winemaker Richard Simpson, who is a wine science graduate from Charles Sturt University. The grapes are sourced from the Clos Robert Vineyard (where the wine is made) established by Robert Allen Simpson in 1972. The aim was – and is – to provide drinkable wines at a reasonable price. Prices have risen, but the rise in quality has been even greater.

Morgan Simpson Chardonnay

▼▼▼▼ **2001** Light to medium yellow-green; light peach and melon fruit shows the influence of gentle barrel ferment in older barrels; the light to medium-bodied palate is well made, with a touch of cashew joining the party; developing slowly. **rating:** 86

best drinking Now **drink with** Pasta • $15

Morgan Simpson Stone Hill Shiraz

▼▼▼▼▽ **2001** Medium to full red-purple; the bouquet has solid dark cherry fruit and subtle oak, the palate with plenty of richness and depth; obvious chocolate adds to the flavour complexity, the ripe tannins to the texture. Honest McLaren Vale style carrying its 15° alcohol very well. **rating:** 90

best drinking 2004–2009 **best vintages** '01 **drink with** Italian sausages • $17.50

Morgan Simpson Row 42 Cabernet Sauvignon

ŸŸŸŸŸ **2001** Medium red-purple; ripe, mainstream, blackcurrant cabernet sauvignon aromas lead into a palate with full-on flavour and ripeness. While exceptionally accessible, it does not go over the top, the finish aided by well-balanced, soft tannins. Outstanding value. **rating:** 91

best drinking 2005–2009 **best vintages** '01 **drink with** Braised ox cheek • $17.50

🐦 morgan vineyards   NR

30 Davross Court, Seville, Vic 3139 **region** Yarra Valley
phone (03) 5964 4807 **open** Mon–Fri 11–4, weekends and public holidays 11–5
winemaker Roger Morgan **production** 700 cases **est.** 1987
product range ($19–25 CD) Chardonnay, Pinot Noir, Merlot, Cabernet Merlot, Cabernet Sauvignon.
summary Roger and wife Ally Morgan have brought Morgan Vineyards along slowly. In 1987 they purchased a small 1.6-hectare vineyard of cabernet sauvignon and pinot noir which had been planted in 1971. They extended the plantings in 1989 with more pinot, again in 1991 (more cabernet sauvignon plus merlot) and finally in 1995 (chardonnay) bringing the total area under vine to 5.66 hectares. In 1997 Roger Morgan completed all the academic requirements of the wine science degree course at Charles Sturt University, and finally embarked on making the wines under the Morgan Vineyards label. An on-site winery and elegant tasting room has been established, Roger Morgan's aim being to build a reputation for making elegant wines at reasonable prices.

morialta vineyard   NR

195 Norton Summit Road, Norton Summit, SA 5136 **region** Adelaide Hills
phone (08) 8390 1061 **fax** (08) 8390 1585 **open** By appointment
winemaker Jeffrey Grosset (Contract) **production** 500 cases **est.** 1989
product range ($15–23 R) Sauvignon Blanc, Unwooded Chardonnay, Chardonnay, Rose, Pinot Noir.
summary Morialta Vineyard was planted in 1989 on a site first planted to vines in the 1860s by John Baker, who named his property Morialta Farm. The Bunya pine depicted on the label is one of the few surviving trees from that era, and indeed one of the few surviving trees of that genus. The 20-hectare property has 11 hectares under vine planted to chardonnay, pinot noir, cabernet sauvignon, sauvignon blanc, shiraz and merlot. Most of the grapes are sold to Southcorp. Given the age of the vineyard and contract winemaking by Jeffrey Grosset, it is not surprising the wines have done well in the Adelaide Hills Wine Show. They are sold through selected restaurants in Adelaide as well as by mail order.

morningside wines   ★★★★

711 Middle Tea Tree Road, Tea Tree, Tas 7017 **region** Southern Tasmania
phone (03) 6268 1748 **fax** (03) 6268 1748 **open** By appointment
winemaker Peter Bosworth **production** 500 cases **est.** 1980
product range ($19–34 ML) Riesling, Chardonnay, Pinot Noir, Cabernet Sauvignon.
summary The name 'Morningside' was given to the old property on which the vineyard stands because it gets the morning sun first – the property on the other side of the valley was known as 'Eveningside' – and, consistently with the observation of the early settlers, the Morningside grapes achieve full maturity with good colour and varietal flavour. Production is as yet tiny but will increase as the 2.5-hectare vineyard matures. Retail distribution through Sutherland Cellars, Melbourne and Tasmanian Wine Centre.

Morningside Cabernet Sauvignon

ŸŸŸŸŸ **2000** Medium to full red-purple; sweet and ripe blackcurrant/cassis fruit on the bouquet leads into a powerful palate, with touches of cedar, and tannins which tend to become more assertive the more the wine is tasted. Needs food. **rating:** 90

best drinking 2004–2009 **drink with** Stuffed shoulder of lamb • $25

🐦 morning star estate   NR

1 Sunnyside Road, Mount Eliza, Vic 3930 **region** Mornington Peninsula
phone (03) 9787 7760 **fax** (03) 9787 7160 **open** 7 days 10–5
winemaker Sandro Mosele (Contract) **production** 4000 cases **est.** 1992
product range ($12–34 CD) Chardonnay, Pinot Noir, Shiraz, Cabernet; Sunnyside range of Sauvignon Blanc, Pinot Gris, Chardonnay, Pinot Noir, Cabernet Sauvignon.

summary In 1992 Judy Barrett purchased this historic property, the house built in 1867, and (with her family) spent the next 10 years repairing years of neglect. Over the same timeframe, 10 hectares each of pinot gris, chardonnay and pinot noir were planted, and the wines – all sold through the Estate's accommodation, conference and function centre and cellar door – are made by Sandro Mosele at Kooyong Estate. Most of the grapes are sold, a lesser amount going to make the Morning Star wines.

mornington estate ★★★☆

c/- Dromana Estate, Harrison's Road and Bittern–Dromana Road, Dromana, Vic 3936 **region** Mornington Peninsula
phone (03) 5987 3800 **fax** (03) 5981 0714 **open** at Dromana Estate 7 days 11–4
winemaker Gary Crittenden, Rollo Crittenden **production** 8000 cases **est.** 1989
product range ($17–21.50 CD) Sauvignon Blanc, Chardonnay, Pinot Noir, Shiraz.
summary As with so many Mornington Peninsula vineyards, a high degree of viticultural expertise, care and attention is needed to get to first base. With a little over 20 hectares in production, it is one of the larger vineyards on the Peninsula and is an important part of the public-listed Dromana Estate group. The larger portion of the grapes are sold to others.

Mornington Estate Sauvignon Blanc

▼▼▼▼ **2002** Pale straw-green; a light, crisp, minerally bouquet with some lemon/citrus aromas is followed by a light-bodied palate, crisp and correct, with moderate length. **rating:** 87
best drinking Now **drink with** Seafood • $17

morris ★★★★★

Mia Mia Vineyard, Rutherglen, Vic 3685 **region** Rutherglen
phone (02) 6026 7303 **fax** (02) 6026 7445 **open** Mon–Sat 9–5, Sun 10–5
winemaker David Morris **production** NFP **est.** 1859
product range ($11–46 R) Table wines include Chardonnay, Sparkling Shiraz Durif, Shiraz, Rutherglen Durif, Rutherglen Blue Imperial Cinsaut, Cabernet Sauvignon; then fortified wines comprising Black Label Liqueur Muscat, Liqueur Muscat, Premium Liqueur Muscat, Liqueur Tokay, Premium Liqueur Tokay, Premium Amontillado, Black Label Tawny Port, Old Tawny Port; tiny quantities of Show Reserve are released from time to time, mainly ex-winery.
summary One of the greatest of the fortified winemakers, ranking with Chambers Rosewood. If you wish to test that view, try the Old Premium Muscat and Old Premium Tokay, which are absolute bargains given their age and quality and which give rise to the winery rating. The Durif table wine is a winery specialty, the others dependable, the white wines all being made by owner Orlando.

Morris Sparkling Shiraz Durif

▼▼▼▼ **NV** Medium red-purple; a solid bouquet with a range of dark fruit, plum and spice aromas is followed by equally abundant flavours of plum and leather on the palate; well balanced, and not too sweet. Once you have base wine such as this my inclination would be to give it the longest possible cork age, i.e. maturation in bottle.
best drinking 2007–2012 **drink with** Leave it in the cellar • $18 **rating:** 87

Morris Durif

▼▼▼▼▽ **1999** Medium red-purple; a complex bouquet ranging through dark fruits, spice and chocolate, then the expected powerful palate, with attractive dark chocolate and blackberry flavours; the tannins, extract and alcohol (only 14°) are all under control. **rating:** 90
best drinking 2005–2015 **best vintages** '70, '72, '74, '80, '83, '86, '88, '90, '92, '94, '96, '97, '98, '99 **drink with** Biltong • $20

Morris Liqueur Tokay

▼▼▼▼▽ **NV** Pale golden brown; a classic, fragrant tea-leaf, malt and cake aromas repeated on the very pure and varietally articulate palate; well balanced, for drinking as much as for sipping. **rating:** 91
best drinking Now–2013 **drink with** Either aperitif or at the end of the meal • $15.50

Morris Old Premium Liqueur Tokay 500 ml

▼▼▼▼▼ **NV** Dense, aged olive-brown; the olive rim a sure sign of age and quality. The bouquet is intensely complex, rich and luscious, the palate, if possible, even more so. It has great concentration of Christmas cake, spices and tea-leaf, balanced by cleansing acidity on the finish. **rating:** 97
best drinking Now–2013 **drink with** Coffee • $45

Morris Liqueur Muscat

▼▼▼▼ NV Distinct reddish hues indicate the inclusion of some quite young muscat in the solera blend; a strongly grapey, raisiny bouquet is reflected in the palate, which has vibrant, raisiny varietal character, but not the quality of the Tokay. **rating:** 89

best drinking Now–2010 **drink with** Aperitif or digestif • $15.50

Morris Old Premium Liqueur Muscat

▼▼▼▼▼ NV Deep mahogany brown with an olive rim; the ultra-rich bouquet has a complex mix of plum pudding, spice, toffee and coffee; the almost explosive flavour of the palate is intensely raisiny/dried raisin, then a cleansing finish investing the wine with enormous length. **rating:** 97

best drinking Now–2010 **drink with** Coffee, petits fours • $45

morrisons riverview winery   NR

Lot 2, Merool Lane, Moama, NSW 2731 **region** Perricoota
phone (03) 5480 0126 **fax** (03) 5480 7144 **open** 7 days 10–5
winemaker John Ellis **production** 2500 cases **est.** 1996
product range ($14–25 CD) Semillon, Sauvignon Blanc, Sauvignon Blanc Semillon, Pink Fronti, Adonis (late harvest Sauvignon Blanc), Shiraz, Cabernet Sauvignon Shiraz, Cabernet Sauvignon, Isaac White Port, Muscat; with Chardonnay coming next vintage.
summary Alistair and Leslie Morrison purchased this historic piece of land in 1995. Plantings began in 1996 with shiraz and cabernet sauvignon, followed in 1997 by sauvignon blanc, frontignac, and grenache in 1998, totalling 6 hectares. The cellar door and restaurant opened in spring 2000, serving light lunches, platters, picnic baskets, coffee and gourmet cakes; wines are sold by the glass, bottle or box and tastings are free of charge.

🍎 mortimers of orange   NR

'Chestnut Garth', 786 Burrendong Way, Orange, NSW 2800 **region** Orange
phone (02) 6365 8689 **fax** (02) 6365 8689 **open** 7 days 10–4
winemaker Simon Gilbert, Jim Chatto (Contract) **production** 2250 cases **est.** 1996
product range ($21–25 R) Chardonnay, with Pinot Noir, Shiraz and Cabernet Sauvignon due for the 2003 release.
summary Peter and Julie Mortimer began the establishment of their vineyard (named after a quiet street in the Humberside village of Burton Pidsea in the UK), in 1996. They now have just over 4 hectares of chardonnay, shiraz, cabernet sauvignon, merlot and pinot noir; the 2001 Chardonnay won a bronze medal at the Royal Brisbane Wine Show only a month after being bottled.

moss brothers   ★★★★

Caves Road, Wilyabrup, WA 6280 **region** Margaret River
phone (08) 9755 6270 **fax** (08) 9755 6298 **open** 7 days 10–5
winemaker David Moss **production** 15 000 cases **est.** 1984
product range ($15.90–37 CD) Semillon, Sauvignon Blanc, Jane Moss Semillon Sauvignon Blanc, Verdelho, Oaked Chardonnay, Non-Wooded Chardonnay, Moses Rock White, Jane Moss Pinot Noir, Shiraz, Cabernet Merlot, Cellar Door Red, Moses Rock Red (the last two unusual blends, Moses Rock including Merlot, Pinot Noir, Grenache, and Cabernet Franc); Drummond Hill range of Semillon, Sauvignon Blanc, Unwooded Chardonnay.
summary Established by long-term viticulturist Jeff Moss and his family, notably sons Peter and David and Roseworthy graduate daughter Jane. A 100-tonne rammed-earth winery was constructed in 1992 and draws upon both estate-grown and purchased grapes. Wine quality has improved dramatically, first the white wines, and more recently the reds. National wholesale distribution; exports to the US, Canada, Europe and Asia.

Moss Brothers Sauvignon Blanc

▼▼▼▼▽ 2002 Light straw-green; the clean, fresh and crisp bouquet marries grass from one end of the spectrum, and passionfruit/gooseberry from the other; the bright and lively palate has excellent length, finishing with an appealing lemony bite. **rating:** 93

best drinking Now **best vintages** '99, '02 **drink with** Calamari • $20

Moss Brothers Drummond Hill Sauvignon Blanc

▼▼▼▼ 2001 Light straw-green; a clean and fresh bouquet has light lemon and gooseberry aromas, the crisp and lively palate with a mix of lemon and mineral flavours; a clean, bright finish. **rating:** 87

best drinking Now **drink with** Steamed mussels • $15.90

Moss Brothers Dry Verdelho

▼▼▼▼ 2002 Light straw-green; the bouquet offers tropical pineapple, mango and fruit salad aromas, accompanied by a faint whiff of reduction. The palate opens strongly, but then thickens somewhat on the finish. It is, however, as the name indicates, dry rather than off-dry, which is a blessing.   **rating: 86**

best drinking Now **drink with** Chicken salad • $21.95

moss wood   ★★★★☆

Metricup Road, Wilyabrup, WA 6280 **region** Margaret River
phone (08) 9755 6266 **fax** (08) 9755 6303 **open** By appointment
winemaker Keith Mugford **production** 11 000 cases **est.** 1969
product range ($22–77 R) Semillon, Chardonnay, Lefroy Brook Vineyard Chardonnay, Pinot Noir, Lefroy Brook Pinot Noir, Cabernet Sauvignon, Glenmore Vineyard Cabernet Sauvignon; Ribbon Vale Semillon Sauvignon Blanc, Merlot, Cabernet Sauvignon Merlot Cabernet Franc.
summary Widely regarded as one of the best wineries in the region, capable of producing glorious Semillon (the best outside the Hunter Valley) in both oaked and unoaked forms, unctuous Chardonnay and elegant, gently herbaceous, superfine Cabernet Sauvignon which lives for many years. In 2002 Moss Wood acquired the Ribbon Vale Estate, which is now merged within its own business, the Ribbon Vale wines now being treated as vineyard-designated within the Moss Wood umbrella. Exports to the UK, the US, Switzerland, Germany, Denmark, Belgium, France, Japan, Hong Kong, Indonesia, Malaysia, Singapore and New Zealand.

Moss Wood Semillon

▼▼▼▼ 2002 Light to medium yellow-green; the quite complex tangy, grass and herb bouquet is in typical vineyard style, as is the complex and powerful palate, the 14.5° alcohol heating up the finish.   **rating: 88**

best drinking 2004–2008 **best vintages** '81, '82, '83, '84, '86, '87, '92, '94, '95, '97, '98, '99 **drink with** Crab, lobster • $28

Ribbon Vale Estate Semillon Sauvignon Blanc

▼▼▼▼▽ 2002 Light straw-green; the clean but complex bouquet has dried herb, grass and spice aromas which lead into a well-balanced and long palate; the flavours are quite soft, almost sweet on the mid-palate, then a crisp, dry finish. Cellar door release only.   **rating: 90**

best drinking Now–2005 **drink with** Sushi • $22

Moss Wood Chardonnay

▼▼▼▼▽ 2001 Medium yellow-green; the smooth, complex bouquet has nutty/oaky overtones to the underlying nectarine fruit; the generous, full-flavoured palate is at the big end of town, with peach and nectarine fruit together with lashings of oak.   **rating: 90**

best drinking Now–2006 **best vintages** '90, '91, '95, '98, '99, '00 **drink with** Smoked chicken • $47

Ribbon Vale Cabernet Merlot

▼▼▼▼▽ 2000 Medium red-purple; the clean, moderately intense bouquet has a mix of red berry and blackberry fruit, the medium-bodied palate focusing on red fruit flavours and a nice touch of new oak; fine tannins. Attractive wine.   **rating: 90**

best drinking 2004–2010 **best vintages** '00 **drink with** Ragout of lamb • $28

Moss Wood Glenmore Vineyard Cabernet Sauvignon

▼▼▼▼▽ 2001 Medium red-purple; a fragrant mix of raspberry and redcurrant fruit plus a touch of spice on the bouquet lead into a luscious mid-palate, followed by a more savoury finish; controlled tannins.   **rating: 91**

best drinking 2005–2012 **best vintages** '99, '00, '01 **drink with** Roast venison • $35

mountadam   ★★★★

High Eden Road, Eden Valley, SA 5235 **region** Eden Valley
phone (08) 8564 1900 **fax** (08) 8564 1999 **open** 7 days 11–4
winemaker Andrew Ewart, Adam Wynn **production** 25 000 cases **est.** 1972
product range ($13–52 CD) Under the premium Mountadam label is Riesling, Chardonnay, Pinot Noir Chardonnay, Pinot Noir, The Red (50 per cent Merlot, 50 per cent Cabernet), Merlot, Cabernet Sauvignon; under the David Wynn label is Chardonnay, Shiraz, Patriarch Shiraz; under organically grown Eden Ridge label is Sauvignon Blanc, Cabernet Sauvignon; also Ratafia Chardonnay and Pinot Noir.
summary One of the leading small wineries, founded by David Wynn and run by winemaker son Adam Wynn, initially offering only the Mountadam range at relatively high prices. The subsequent development of

the three ranges of wines has been very successful, judged both by the winemaking and wine-marketing viewpoint. Mountadam has built up an extensive export network over many years, with the US, Canada, Hong Kong, Japan and the UK being the major markets, but extending across the breadth of Europe and most Asian markets. This will doubtless be strengthened following the acquisition of Mountadam by Cape Mentelle in 2000.

Mountadam Chardonnay

▼▼▼▼ 1999 Developed medium to full yellow; the bouquet has ripe, yellow peach, fig and some bottle-developed buttery/nutty notes, the palate with similar peachy/nutty flavours, and sustained by a particularly clear finish, not cluttered up. Random bottle oxidation has badly affected some bottles of the wine. rating: 89

best drinking Now–2005 best vintages '86, '89, '90, '91, '92, '93, '94, '97, '98 drink with Salmon terrine • $36

Mountadam Patriarch Shiraz

▼▼▼▼▽ 1999 Medium red-purple; clean, dark small berry fruits, licorice and spice aromas lead into a medium-bodied palate with savoury aspects to the dark fruit at its core; good structure. rating: 90

best drinking 2004–2009 best vintages '90, '91, '93, '94, '96, '97 drink with Barbecued beef • $42

Mountadam Cabernet Sauvignon

▼▼▼▼ 1998 Medium red-purple; the complex bouquet has a mix of cedary, earthy aromas plus some dusty oak. The structure and flavour of the palate is quite European in cast, with cedar, earth, olive and blackberry. The upgrade of the label, incidentally, is outstanding; quite the best example of updating and enhancing I have encountered. rating: 87

best drinking Now–2008 best vintages '90, '91, '95, '96 drink with Lamb cutlets • $42

mount alexander vineyard ★★☆

Calder Highway, North Harcourt, Vic 3453 region Bendigo
phone (03) 5474 2262 fax (03) 5474 2553 open 7 days 10–5.30
winemaker Keith Walkden production 6000 cases est. 1984
product range ($10–14 CD) A wide range of various table wines, sparkling, fortifieds, meads and liqueurs.
summary A substantial operation with large vineyards with 17 hectares planted to all the right varieties. It is several years since I have tasted the wines, but a recent report gives me no reason to suppose they have changed much.

mount anakie wines ★★☆

130 Staughton Vale Road, Anakie, Vic 3221 region Geelong
phone (03) 5284 1256 fax (03) 5284 1405 open 7 days 11–5
winemaker Otto Zambelli production 6000 cases est. 1968
product range ($12–18 CD) Biancone, Riesling, Lexia, Semillon, Chardonnay, Vic Classic Red, Shiraz, Cabernet Shiraz, Cabernet Sauvignon, Tawny Port.
summary Also known as Zambelli Estate and once produced some excellent wines (under its various ownerships and winemakers), all distinguished by their depth and intensity of flavour. No recent tastings; prior to that, the wines tasted were but a shadow of their former quality. The level of activity seems relatively low.

mount avoca vineyard ★★★☆

Moates Lane, Avoca, Vic 3467 region Pyrenees
phone (03) 5465 3282 fax (03) 5465 3544 open Mon–Fri 9–5, weekends 10–5
winemaker Matthew Barry production 17 000 cases est. 1970
product range ($11–45 CD) Sauvignon Blanc, Chardonnay, Rhapsody, Trioss White, Trioss Red, Shiraz, Cabernet; Reserve range of Noble Semillon Sauvignon Blanc, Merlot, Shiraz, Cabernet, Arda's Choice (Cabernet Sauvignon Cabernet Franc Merlot).
summary A substantial winery which has for long been one of the stalwarts of the Pyrenees region, and is steadily growing, with 23.7 hectares of vineyards. There has been a significant refinement in the style and flavour of the red wines over the past few years. I suspect a lot of worthwhile work has gone into barrel selection and maintenance. Acquired by Barrington Estates in 2002, which promptly went into receivership. As at April 2003, the receiver was still seeking to dispose of the winery.

Mount Avoca Shiraz

ΤΤΤΤ **2000** Medium red-purple; the ripe and slightly jammy bouquet mixes plum and hints of earth, the medium-bodied palate again offering a blend of berry and earthy flavours; restrained oak inputs throughout. **rating:** 85

best drinking 2004–2009 **drink with** Marinated beef • $20

Mount Avoca Cabernet

ΤΤΤΤ **1999** Medium red; the bouquet is quite complex, ranging through earth, cedar, berry and mint aromas, the moderately intense and long palate following track, with distinct leafy/minty overtones. A blend of Cabernet Sauvignon, Merlot and Cabernet Franc. **rating:** 86

best drinking 2005–2009 **best vintages** '88, '90, '91, '92, '93, '95, '97 **drink with** Char-grilled steak • $20

mount beckworth NR

RMB 915 Learmonth Road, Tourello via Ballarat, Vic 3363 **region** Ballarat
phone (03) 5343 4207 **fax** (03) 5343 4207 **open** Weekends 10–6 and by appointment
winemaker Paul Lesock **production** 1000 cases **est.** 1984
product range ($16–20 CD) Unwooded Chardonnay, Wooded Chardonnay, Pinot Noir, Shiraz, Cabernet Merlot.
summary The 4-hectare Mount Beckworth vineyard was planted between 1984 and 1985, but it was not until 1995 that the full range of wines under the Mount Beckworth label appeared. Until that time much of the production was sold to Seppelt Great Western for sparkling wine use. It is owned and managed by Paul Lesock, who studied viticulture at Charles Sturt University, and his wife Jane. The wines reflect the very cool climate except in years such as 2000. Limited Victorian retail distribution.

mount broke wines ★★★☆

Adams Peak Road, Broke, NSW 2330 **region** Lower Hunter Valley
phone (02) 6579 1314 **fax** (02) 6579 1313 **open** Mon–Fri 11–2, Sat and public holidays 11–5, Sun 9.30–5
winemaker Contract **production** 1400 cases **est.** 1997
product range ($15–20 CD) Quince Tree Paddock Semillon, River Bank Verdelho, Adam's Peak Chardonnay, River Bank Shiraz, Black Pine Ridge Merlot, Quince Tree Paddock Barbera, Harrowby Cabernet Merlot.
summary Phil and Jo McNamara began planting 9.6-hectare vineyard to shiraz, merlot, verdelho, barbera, semillon, chardonnay and cabernet sauvignon in 1997 on the west side of Wollombi Brook. It is early days, but they have already established a wine club and have opened The Cow Cafe, with wine tasting and wine function capacity. While the 2001 Shiraz was not submitted for tasting, the two previous vintages were good.

Mount Broke Quince Tree Paddock Semillon

ΤΤΤΤΥ **2002** Light straw-green; a clean, fresh bouquet with a classic mix of grass and mineral aromas, then a delicate and elegant palate, well balanced and long; crisp finish. **rating:** 90

best drinking 2005–2015 **best vintages** '02 **drink with** Shellfish • $15

Mount Broke Quince Tree Paddock Barbera

ΤΤΤΤ **2001** Light to medium red, with just a touch of purple; the bouquet is light, with faint spicy, jammy aromas; the palate has interesting allspice plum pudding flavours, and almost no tannins. Not at all bad. **rating:** 85

best drinking Now–2005 **drink with** Spiced Asian • $16.50

mount cathedral vineyards ★★★☆

125 Knafl Road, Taggerty, Vic 3714 **region** Central Victorian High Country
phone 0409 354 069 **fax** (03) 9354 0994 **open** By appointment
winemaker Oscar Rosa, Nick Arena **production** 400 cases **est.** 1995
product range ($20–35 ML) Chardonnay, Merlot, Cabernet Sauvignon Merlot.
summary The Rosa and Arena families established Mount Cathedral Vineyards 1995, the vines being planted at an elevation of 300 metres on the north face of Mount Cathedral. The first plantings were of 1.2 hectares of merlot and 0.8 hectare of chardonnay, followed by 2.5 hectares of cabernet sauvignon and 0.5 hectare of cabernet franc in 1996. Oscar Rosa, chief winemaker, has completed two TAFE courses in viticulture and winemaking, and is currently in his fifth year of the Bachelor of Wine Science course at Charles Sturt University. He gained practical experience working at Yering Station during 1998 and 1999.

Mount Cathedral Vineyards Chardonnay

TTTT 2001 Medium yellow-green; in the style of the winery, the bouquet is tight, with discreet fruit and minerally aspects; the palate is likewise on the lean side, with touches of mineral and citrus running through to a clean finish. You just wish there was a little more fruit expression. **rating: 85**

best drinking Now–2007 **drink with** Deep-fried calamari • $20

Mount Cathedral Vineyards Merlot

TTTT 2001 Medium red-purple; the moderately intense bouquet, with berry, leaf and mint aromas, the oak in restraint, is followed by a strongly varietal palate with earthy/savoury/olive fruit. Does not have the depth of the 2000, but certainly makes a statement. **rating: 85**

best drinking 2004–2010 **drink with** Lamb Provençale • $35

mount charlie winery ★★★☆

228 Mount Charlie Road, Riddells Creek, Vic 3431 **region** Macedon Ranges
phone (03) 5428 6946 **fax** (03) 5428 6946 **open** Weekends by appointment
winemaker Trefor Morgan **production** 700 cases **est.** 1991
product range ($19–22 CD) Sauvignon Blanc, Chardonnay, Red (Shiraz Merlot Cabernet blend).
summary Mount Charlie's wines are sold principally through mail order and through selected restaurants. A futures programme encourages mailing list sales with a discount of over 25 per cent on the ultimate release price. Owner/winemaker Trefor Morgan is perhaps better known as a Professor of Physiology at Melbourne University.

Mount Charlie Chardonnay

TTTT 2001 Medium yellow-green; the clean bouquet has tight fruit and subtle oak, the wine opening up on the attractive palate, with citrus and stone fruit flavours; good length and mouthfeel for a fruit-driven, elegant style. Barrel fermented (older oak) with partial malolactic fermentation. **rating: 88**

best drinking Now–2007 **drink with** Summer salad • $22

mount coghill vineyard NR

Clunes-Learmonth Road, Coghills Creek, Vic 3364 **region** Ballarat
phone (03) 5343 4329 **open** Weekends 10–5
winemaker Norman Latta **production** 250 cases **est.** 1993
product range ($17–20 CD) Chardonnay, Pinot Noir.
summary Ian and Margaret Pym began the development of their tiny vineyard in 1995 with the planting of 1280 pinot noir rootlings, adding 450 chardonnay rootlings the next year. The first harvest in 2000 produced 0.5 tonne pinot noir and a 0.33 tonne of chardonnay (sold) but when production leapt to 4 tonnes of pinot noir and 1.5 tonnes of chardonnay in 2001, the decision was taken to have the wine made and released under the Mount Coghill Vineyard label.

Mount Coghill Vineyard Pinot Noir

TTTT 2001 Medium red-purple; aromas of dark plum, spice and briar on the bouquet lead into a palate suggesting low pH, quite intense and slightly grippy. The synthetic corks are a real worry for a wine which actually needs some time in bottle, and which have already betrayed the Chardonnay of the same vintage. **rating: 86**

best drinking Now **drink with** The utmost speed • $20

mount duneed NR

Feehan's Road, Mount Duneed, Vic 3216 **region** Geelong
phone (03) 5264 1281 **fax** (03) 5264 1281 **open** Public holidays and weekends 11–5, or by appointment
winemaker Ken Campbell, John Darling **production** 1000 cases **est.** 1970
product range ($10–18 CD) Semillon, Sauvignon Blanc, Riesling, Botrytis Semillon, Malbec, Cabernet Malbec, Cabernet Sauvignon.
summary Rather idiosyncratic wines are the order of the day, some of which can develop surprisingly well in bottle; the Botrytis Noble Rot Semillon has, from time to time, been of very high quality. A significant part of the production from the 7.5 hectares of vineyards is sold to others. No recent tastings.

mount eliza estate ★★★☆

Cnr Sunnyside Road and Nepean Highway, Mt Eliza, Vic 3930 **region** Mornington Peninsula
phone (03) 9787 0663 **fax** (03) 9708 8355 **open** 7 days 11–5
winemaker Scott Ireland (Contract) **production** 8500 cases **est.** 1997

product range ($16–35 CD) Riesling, Sauvignon Blanc, Chardonnay, Pinot Noir, Magnus Maximus Pinot Noir, Shiraz, Astrid Elizabeth Pinot Noir Chardonnay.

summary Robert and Jenny Thurley planted the 7.84-hectare vineyard at Mount Eliza Estate in 1997; the varieties are riesling, chardonnay, sauvignon blanc, shiraz, pinot noir and cabernet sauvignon. Son James, presently studying viticulture, has worked at the vineyard since day one under the direction of viticulturist Graeme Harrip, making the business a family affair. The cellar door, which has great views across Port Phillip Bay to the Melbourne city skyline, was opened in November 2000. The contract winemaker is Scott Ireland, of Provenance, who has had many years' experience in making wines from the Port Phillip Zone.

Mount Eliza Estate Riesling

▼▼▼▼ 2002 Medium yellow-green; the bouquet is rich and full, with tropical lime and pineapple aromas, the palate similarly rich, opulent and ripe; an interesting style, the ripe fruit flavours almost certainly due to tiny crops, for the vintage was in fact very cool.   **rating:** 89

best drinking Now–2006 **drink with** Asian • $19

Mount Eliza Estate Sauvignon Blanc

▼▼▼▼ 2002 Light green-yellow; the clean bouquet has gooseberry and some faintly tropical aromas, the light to medium-bodied palate clean and ripe, with good mouthfeel and balance. An easy going wine, but lacks distinctive varietal character.   **rating:** 85

best drinking Now **drink with** Avocado salad • $16

Mount Eliza Estate Pinot Noir

▼▼▼▼ 2001 Light to medium red-purple; the bouquet has a mix of strawberry and plum fruit on the one hand, and tangy/stemmy/earthy aromas on the other. The palate has strawberry and julep/garden mint flavours which suggest incomplete physiological ripeness. Nonetheless, the flavours are fresh.   **rating:** 86

best drinking Now **drink with** Mushroom risotto • $21

mount eyre vineyard ★★★☆

1325 Broke Road, Broke, NSW 2330 **region** Lower Hunter Valley
phone 0438 683 973 **fax** (02) 9744 3508 **open** By appointment
winemaker Stephen Hagan (Contract) **production** 9000 cases **est.** 1996
product range ($14–35 CD) Released under three labels: the Mount Eyre range of Semillon, Semillon Chardonnay, Unwooded Chardonnay; Three Ponds Semillon and Chardonnay, Shiraz; and Neptune (sparkling semillon).
summary Dr Aniello Inannuzzi's 24-hectare estate at Broke is planted to semillon, chardonnay, shiraz, cabernet franc and cabernet sauvignon, the wines being contract-made off-site.

mountford ★★★★

Bamess Road, West Pemberton, WA 6260 **region** Pemberton
phone (08) 9776 1345 **fax** (08) 9776 1345 **open** 7 days 10–4
winemaker Andrew Mountford, Saxon Mountford **production** 3000 cases **est.** 1987
product range ($14–30 CD) Sauvignon Blanc, Unwooded Chardonnay, Reserve Chardonnay, Pinot Noir, Merlot, Cabernet Merlot, Vintage Port, Sparkling.
summary English-born and trained Andrew Mountford and wife Sue migrated to Australia in 1983, first endeavouring to set up a winery at Mudgee and thereafter moving to Pemberton with far greater success. Their strikingly packaged wines are produced from 6 hectares of permanently netted, dry-grown vineyards.

Mountford Reserve Chardonnay

▼▼▼▼▼ 2001 Light straw-green; clean, lively citrus and nectarine fruit intermingles with oak on the bouquet; a long, citrussy, fine and pure palate is fruit-driven, the oak evident but not the least assertive.   **rating:** 90

best drinking Now–2006 **best vintages** '01 **drink with** Grilled spatchcock • $25

Mountford Merlot

▼▼▼▼▽ 2000 Light but bright red-purple; stylish cedar, olive and blackcurrant aromas lead into a light to medium-bodied palate with excellent varietal character; blackcurrant, olive-accented fruit is complexed by fine, cedary, savoury spices.   **rating:** 91

best drinking 2004–2011 **drink with** Ragout of lamb • $28.50

Mountford Cabernet Merlot

▼▼▼▼ 2001 Light to medium red-purple; the light, savoury, leafy, bramble aromas swell into much riper blackcurrant fruit on the palate with a lively finish thanks to crisp acidity; low tannins rob the wine of that extra degree of structure. A blend of 45 per cent Cabernet Franc, 35 per cent Cabernet Sauvignon and 20 per cent Merlot. **rating:** 86

best drinking 2004–2008 **drink with** Rack of veal • $25

mount gisborne wines ★★★☆

83 Waterson Road, Gisborne, Vic 3437 **region** Macedon Ranges
phone (03) 5428 2834 **fax** (03) 5428 2834 **open** Weekends 10–5
winemaker Stuart Anderson **production** 1500 cases **est.** 1986
product range ($14–25 CD) Chardonnay, Pinot Noir.
summary Mount Gisborne Wines is very much a weekend and holiday occupation for proprietor David Ell, who makes the wines from the 7-hectare vineyard under the watchful and skilled eye of industry veteran Stuart Anderson, now living in semi-retirement high in the Macedon Hills.

Mount Gisborne Chardonnay

▼▼▼▼ 2001 Light to medium green; there are minerally, tangy edges to the fruit of the bouquet, the oak input ultra-restrained; the light to medium-bodied palate is fresh and clean, direct and long. Available in a very useful 375 ml bottle. **rating:** 87

best drinking Now–2007 **best vintages** '94 **drink with** Yabbies • $14

Mount Gisborne Pinot Noir

▼▼▼▼ 2000 Light to medium red-purple; a highly savoury/tangy bouquet with overtones of olive and herb is followed by a palate with considerable savoury/tangy intensity, and good length. There is not a lot of flesh here; a cerebral Pinot Noir duly reflecting its growing conditions. **rating:** 88

best drinking Now–2006 **drink with** Quail salad • $25

mount horrocks ★★★★☆

The Old Railway Station, Curling Street, Auburn, SA 5451 **region** Clare Valley
phone (08) 8849 2243 **fax** (08) 8849 2265 **open** Weekends and public holidays 10–5
winemaker Stephanie Toole **production** 4500 cases **est.** 1982
product range ($23–38.95 CD) Watervale Riesling, Semillon, Chardonnay, Cordon Cut Riesling, Shiraz, Cabernet Merlot.
summary Mount Horrocks has well and truly established its own identity in recent years, aided by positive marketing and, equally importantly, wine quality which has resulted in both show success and critical acclaim. Exports to the UK, the US, Belgium, Switzerland, The Netherlands, Italy, New Zealand, Malaysia, Hong Kong, Singapore and Japan. Lunches available on weekends.

Mount Horrocks Watervale Riesling

▼▼▼▼▼ 2002 Light green-yellow; the intense bouquet is still largely locked in on itself, but some spice and ginger aromas dance in the background; the palate is very well proportioned, showing apple, spice and citrus flavours, again with that suggestion of ginger. As winemaker Stephanie Toole says, 'I nailed it'. **rating:** 94

best drinking 2004–2014 **best vintages** '86, '87, '90, '93, '94, '97, '01, '02 **drink with** Thai or Chinese soup • $27

Mount Horrocks Semillon

▼▼▼▼▼ 2001 Light to medium yellow-green; a potent bouquet dominated by grassy/herbal varietal fruit, but with a subtle push from barrel fermentation in French oak adding to the complexity of the wine. The palate has good mouthfeel, complex yet fine; the barrel fermentation has worked very well indeed, and the wine has excellent length. Stelvin-capped and sourced from a single, hand-picked vineyard. **rating:** 94

best drinking Now–2010 **best vintages** '97, '99, '00, '01 **drink with** Pan-fried fish • $26.50

Mount Horrocks Cordon Cut Riesling

▼▼▼▼ 2002 Light to medium yellow-green; strong lemon pastille aromas are followed by a palate with intense lemon and citrus fruit supported by well-balanced acidity; concentrated more than complex, and, while an interesting approach, cannot rival botrytised examples. **rating:** 89

best drinking Now–2009 **best vintages** '00, '01 **drink with** Pavlova • $32

Mount Horrocks Shiraz

▼▼▼▼▽ **2000** Light to medium red-purple; the moderately intense bouquet is clean and fresh, with tightly controlled oak; small, dark berry and plum fruit comes through precisely and elegantly on the palate, with lingering, savoury tannins to close. **rating: 90**

best drinking 2004–2009 **best vintages** '00 **drink with** Steak and kidney pie • $38.95

mount ida ★★★★

Northern Highway, Heathcote, Vic 3253 **region** Heathcote
phone (03) 8626 3340 **open** Not
winemaker Matt Steel **production** 2000 cases **est.** 1978
product range ($36 R) Shiraz.
summary Established by the famous artist Leonard French and Dr James Munro but purchased by Tisdall after the 1987 bushfires and thereafter by Beringer Blass when it acquired Tisdall. Up to the time of the fires, wonderfully smooth, rich red wines with almost voluptuous sweet, minty fruit were the hallmark. After a brief period during which the name was used as a simple brand (with various wines released) has returned to a single estate-grown wine.

mountilford NR

Mount Vincent Road, Ilford, NSW 2850 **region** Mudgee
phone (02) 6358 8544 **fax** (02) 6358 8544 **open** 7 days 10–4
winemaker Don Cumming **production** 1800 cases **est.** 1985
product range ($12–22 CD) Riesling, Highland White, Windamere, Sylvaner, Chardonnay, Pinot Noir, Pinot Shiraz, Cabernet Shiraz, Jubilation Cabernet Shiraz, Sir Alexander Port, Lady Alex.
summary Surprisingly large cellar-door operation which has grown significantly over the past few years, utilising 7 hectares of estate vineyards. Roughly half the production is sold to other winemakers. I have not, however, had the opportunity of tasting the wines.

mount langi ghiran vineyards ★★★★☆

Warrak Road, Buangor, Vic 3375 **region** Grampians
phone (03) 5354 3207 **fax** (03) 5354 3277 **open** Mon–Fri 9–5, weekends 12–5
winemaker Trevor Mast **production** 45 000 cases **est.** 1969
product range ($20–60 CD) Riesling, Pinot Gris, Botrytis Riesling, Cliff Edge Shiraz; under Langi label Shiraz and Cabernet Merlot.
summary A maker of outstanding cool-climate peppery Shiraz, crammed with flavour and vinosity, and very good Cabernet Sauvignon. The Shiraz points the way for cool-climate examples of the variety, for weight, texture and fruit richness all accompany the vibrant pepper-spice aroma and flavour. The business was acquired by the Rathbone family group in November 2002, and hence will be integrated with the Yering Station product range, a synergistic mix with no overlap. Trevor Mast will continue to run the Langi Ghiran operation, which has an export network throughout the US, Canada, New Zealand, Asia and Europe.

Langi Riesling

▼▼▼▼ **2002** Light to medium yellow-green; the citrus-driven bouquet is slightly pulpy and tending broad, the generous flavour and depth of the palate in similar territory, needing more focus and finesse. **rating: 85**

best drinking Now–2005 **drink with** Steamed asparagus • $20

Mount Langi Ghiran Pinot Gris

▼▼▼▼ **2002** A full-on pink colour is followed by a potent, powerful, complex spicy bouquet, the palate with a mix of citrus, spice and strawberry. Unquestionably, a Pinot Gris with attitude. **rating: 87**

best drinking Now **drink with** Antipasto • $22

Mount Langi Ghiran Cliff Edge Shiraz

▼▼▼▼▽ **2000** Medium red-purple; the clean bouquet has an attractive array of ripe plum/black cherry/spice aromas; in the mouth, lots of bitter, dark chocolate and a fleeting hint of mint join the red fruits of the bouquet, finishing with ripe tannins and gentle oak. High quality for a second label. **rating: 90**

best drinking 2004–2009 **best vintages** '00 **drink with** Spiced lamb • $29.95

Langi Shiraz

▼▼▼▼▽ **2000** Medium red-purple; perfumed cherry, raspberry and, plum aromas are the drivers of the elegant palate; raspberry, a touch of chocolate and fine, ripe tannins are all there. Less substantial than the '99 and will be ready sooner. **rating:** 91

best drinking 2004–2010 **best vintages** '86, '88, '90, '92, '93, '94, '96, '97, '98, '99 **drink with** Game • $55

Langi Cabernet Merlot

▼▼▼▼ **1999** Medium red-purple; there are pronounced foresty, stemmy, savoury overtones to the black fruits of the bouquet, which flow through into the palate, there joined by blackcurrant, a touch of mint and some cedar. Somewhat of a jumble at the moment, but should sort itself out with a little patience. **rating:** 87

best drinking 2004–2009 **best vintages** '97, '98 **drink with** Rare fillet of beef • $38

mount majura vineyard NR

RMB 314 Majura Road, Majura, ACT 2609 **region** Canberra District
phone 0403 355 682 **fax** (02) 6262 4288 **open** Not
winemaker Dr Frank van de Loo (Dr Roger Harris, Consultant) **production** 700 cases **est.** 1988
product range ($20–25 ML) Chardonnay, Pinot Noir, Cabernet Franc Merlot.
summary The first vines were planted in 1988 by Dinny Killen on a site on her family property which had been especially recommended by Dr Edgar Riek; its attractions were red soil of volcanic origin over limestone, the reasonably steep east and northeast slopes providing an element of frost protection. The 1-hectare vineyard was planted to pinot noir, chardonnay and merlot in equal quantities; the pinot noir grapes were sold to Lark Hill and used in their award-winning Pinot Noir, while the Chardonnay and Merlot were made for Mount Majura by Lark Hill, both wines enjoying show success. The syndicate which purchased the property in 1999 has extended the plantings, and Dr Frank van de Loo makes the wines in leased space at Brindabella Hills with consultancy advice from Dr Roger Harris.

🍂 mount markey NR

Swifts Creek-Omeo Road, Cassilis, Vic 3896 **region** Gippsland
phone (03) 5159 4264 **fax** (03) 5159 4599 **open** Wed–Mon 10–5
winemaker Howard Reddish **production** 750 cases **est.** 1991
product range ($13.50–18 CD) Morning Star Classic Dry White, Pinot Gris, Mountain Maid Chardonnay, The Howitt Pinot Noir, Cassilis Valley Dry Red, Lone Hand Cabernet Sauvignon; also Honey Meads, fruit wines.
summary Howard and Christine Reddish have established two vineyards, one of 2 hectares surrounding the winery, the other of 3 hectares on the slopes of Mount Markey, at an altitude of nearly 500 metres. The winery is appropriately built on the site of the Cassilis Wine Palace which served the local gold mining families for almost 70 years until the gold ran out in the 1940s. A sheltered BBQ spot is among the many attractions for the general and wine tourist alike.

mount mary ★★★★★

Coldstream West Road, Lilydale, Vic 3140 **region** Yarra Valley
phone (03) 9739 1761 **fax** (03) 9739 0137 **open** Not
winemaker Dr John Middleton **production** 3000 cases **est.** 1971
product range ($32–60 ML) Chardonnay, Triolet (Sauvignon Blanc, Semillon, Muscadelle), Pinot Noir, Cabernets Quintet (Bordeaux-blend).
summary Superbly refined, elegant and intense Cabernets and usually outstanding and long-lived Pinot Noirs fully justify Mount Mary's exalted reputation. The Triolet blend is very good, more recent vintages of Chardonnay even better. Limited quantities of the wines are sold through the wholesale/retail distribution system in Victoria, New South Wales, Queensland and South Australia.

mount moliagul ★★★☆

Clay Gully Lane, Moliagul, Vic 3472 **region** Bendigo
phone (03) 9809 2113 **open** By appointment, call 0427 221 641
winemaker Terry Flora **production** 400 cases **est.** 1991
product range ($16–22 ML) Unwooded Chardonnay, Pinot Noir, Shiraz, Shiraz Cabernet Sauvignon Merlot, Cabernet Sauvignon.

summary Terry and Bozenka Flora began the establishment of their tiny vineyard in 1991, gradually planting 0.5 hectare each of shiraz and cabernet sauvignon, and 0.2 hectare of chardonnay. Terry Flora has completed two winemaking courses, one with Winery Supplies and the other at Dookie College, and has learnt his craft very well. In 1998 and 2000, Mount Moliagul won the trophy for Best Red Wine of Show at the Victorian Wines Show. The cellar door opened in December 2001.

Mount Moliagul Unwooded Chardonnay

TTTT 2002 Medium yellow-green; the bouquet seems to show some lees-derived complexity to the tangy edges of the fruit; the palate has light citrus/melon/stone fruit flavours; well crafted. **rating:** 85

best drinking Now **drink with** Warm seafood • $16

Mount Moliagul Shiraz

TTTT 2001 Youthful, bright, purple-red; a complex array of plum, raspberry, spice and earth aromas flow into a palate with succulent raspberry and plum fruit supported by soft, fine tannins. Nicely balanced. **rating:** 87

best drinking 2005–2010 **drink with** Designer sausages • $18

mount prior vineyard ★★★☆

Gooramadda Road, Rutherglen, Vic 3685 **region** Rutherglen
phone (02) 6026 5591 **fax** (02) 6026 5590 **open** 7 days 9–5
winemaker James Ashe, Nick Henry **production** 15 000 cases **est.** 1860
product range ($13–40 CD) Chenin Blanc, Classic Ibis Dry White, Semillon Chardonnay, Chardonnay, Sparkling Shiraz Durif, Brut Cuvee, Late Picked Riesling, Noble Gold, Classic Ibis Dry Red, Shiraz, Durif, Merlot Limited Release, Cabernet Merlot, Port, Muscat, Tokay.
summary A full-scale tourist facility, with yet more in the pipeline. Full accommodation packages at the historic Mount Prior House; a restaurant operating weekends under the direction of Trish Hennessy (for groups of six or more), with four consecutive *Age* Good Food Guide awards to its credit; picnic and barbecue facilities; and a California-style gift shop. The wines are basically sold through cellar door and an active mailing list. The already substantial 40 hectares of vineyards were expanded by a further 5 hectares of durif planted in 1998, a mark both of the success of Mount Prior and of the interest in Durif.

Mount Prior Vineyard Director's Selection Muscat (375 ml)

TTTT NV Medium to full red; clean spirit, raisin and honey aromas, then a palate with greater density than the price would suggest, showing some older material with the predominantly fresh younger components; excellent value. **rating:** 86

best drinking Now **drink with** Chocolate • $13

Mount Prior Vineyard Reserve Port Museum Release

TTTT NV Medium to full red; Christmas cake, spice and aromas show the obvious wood age of the wine, those characters coming through on the palate but with special emphasis on chocolate, spice and biscuit. **rating:** 88

best drinking Now **drink with** Rich cakes, nuts • $40

🐍 mount surmon wines NR

Scarlatties Cellar Door Gallery, Basham Road, Stanley Flat, SA 5453 **region** Clare Valley
phone (08) 8842 1250 **fax** (08) 8842 4064 **open** Fri–Sun 10–4, or by appointment
winemaker Neil Paulett (Contract) **production** 200 cases **est.** 1995
product range ($16–19 CD) Riesling, Chardonnay, Sparkling Riesling, Shiraz, Cabernet Merlot.
summary The Surmon family has established just under 20 hectares of vineyard, half to shiraz, the remainder to cabernet sauvignon, nebbiolo, chardonnay, pinot gris and viognier. Most of the grapes are sold to other wineries (some on a swap basis for riesling and merlot), but small quantities are made under contract by Neil Paulett and are sold through Scarlatties Cellar Door Gallery, and a few local hotels. The first wines were made in 1999 (Cabernet Merlot and Shiraz) with white wines added in subsequent vintages.

mount tamborine winery NR

32 Hartley Road, Mount Tamborine, Qld 4272 **region** Queensland Coastal
phone (07) 5545 3981 **fax** (07) 5545 3311 **open** 7 days 10–4
winemaker Andrew Hickinbotham **production** 8000 cases **est.** 1993
product range ($12.90–34.90 CD) Hinterland range of Semillon, Late Harvest, Classic Dry Red, Sweet Red; Cedar Ridge range of Verdelho, Unwooded Chardonnay, Oaked Chardonnay, Blanc de Blanc, Shiraz Cabernet,

Cabernet Sauvignon; Tehembrin Reserve range of Imperial Reserve, Merlot; also Frontignac, Daisy, Emily Sparkling Merlot, Lily the Pink Rose, Black Shiraz, Bush Turkey Port, Mountain Muscat.

summary Mount Tamborine Winery draws upon 3 hectares of estate plantings adjacent to the winery, 30 hectares in Stanthorpe, and also purchases wine from the King Valley, Cowra and the Riverland to produce a wide range of wine styles. The Chardonnay and Merlot have both had success in Queensland wine shows and competitions, and the wines are sold both locally and exported to South-East Asia. It is a sister company to Barambah Ridge, both operations being owned by Tambarambah Limited.

mount trio vineyard ★★★★☆

Cnr Castle Rock and Porongurup Roads, Porongurup WA 6324 **region** Great Southern
phone (08) 9853 1136 **fax** (08) 9853 1120 **open** By appointment
winemaker Gavin Berry **production** 5000 cases **est.** 1989
product range ($14.90–22.50 R) Riesling, Sauvignon Blanc, Chardonnay, Pinot Noir, Shiraz, Cabernet Merlot.
summary Mount Trio was established by Gavin Berry and Gill Graham shortly after they moved to the Mount Barker district in late 1988. Gavin Berry was assistant winemaker to John Wade, and Gill managed the cellar-door sales. Gavin is now senior winemaker and managing director of Plantagenet, and Gill is the mother of two young children. In the meantime they have slowly built up the Mount Trio business, based in part upon estate plantings of 2 hectares of pinot noir and 0.5 hectare of chardonnay and in part on purchased grapes. An additional 6 hectares was planted in the spring of 1999, duly bringing production to its planned 5000-case level.

Mount Trio Sauvignon Blanc
▼▼▼▼▽ **2002** Light straw-green; the clean, crisp moderately intense bouquet has classic varietal aromas which flow into the palate, with a mix of tangy lemon and more tropical fruit. Good length and intensity. **rating:** 90
best drinking Now **best vintages** '02 **drink with** Asparagus mousse • $14.90

Mount Trio Chardonnay
▼▼▼▼▽ **2001** Medium yellow-green; the complex bouquet subtly integrates smoky barrel-ferment oak with melon, stone fruit and cashew; the tight bouquet adds a hint of grapefruit to the fruit characters of the bouquet, and is, indeed, the fruit which drives the wine. **rating:** 91
best drinking Now–2008 **best vintages** '98, '01 **drink with** Tempura • $17

Mount Trio Pinot Noir
▼▼▼▼▽ **2001** Medium red-purple; ripe plum, spice and more savoury/oaky aromas are followed by a powerful palate, where the plummy fruit has great intensity and length, offering far more focus and line than the bouquet. **rating:** 90
best drinking Now–2007 **drink with** Braised duck • $19

Mount Trio Shiraz
▼▼▼▼▽ **2001** Medium to full red-purple; there are complex overtones to the primary black fruit aromas of the bouquet, the palate (like the Pinot Noir) neatly collecting the pieces, offering licorice, black plum, blackberry and spice, closing with soft tannins. **rating:** 90
best drinking 2005–2010 **best vintages** '01 **drink with** Beef in red wine sauce • $22.50

Mount Trio Cabernet Merlot
▼▼▼▼ **2000** Medium red-purple; a fragrant, elegant fruit-driven bouquet is followed by a palate with striking flavour, atypical for the varieties, with hints of maraschino cherry. Restrained use of oak throughout. **rating:** 88
best drinking 2004–2009 **drink with** Yearling beef • $17.50

mount view estate ★★★★☆

Mount View Road, Mount View, NSW 2325 **region** Lower Hunter Valley
phone (02) 4990 3307 **fax** (02) 4991 1289 **open** 7 days 10–5
winemaker Andrew Thomas (Contract) **production** 3000 cases **est.** 1971
product range ($12–28 CD) Reserve Semillon, Reserve Verdelho, Chardonnay Semillon, Reserve Chardonnay, Pinot Noir, Reserve Shiraz, Basalt Hill Shiraz Pinot, Reserve Merlot, Cabernet Sauvignon, Reserve Cabernet Sauvignon.
summary The Tulloch family no longer owns nor has any interest in Mount View Estate following its sudden sale in 2000, but winemaking has passed to the capable hands of former Tyrrell's winemaker Andrew Thomas. The 30-year-old vines are paying big dividends.

Mount View Estate Reserve Semillon

♥♥♥♥♀ 2002 bright, light green-yellow, just as it should be; a classic, fresh and clean array of grassy/minerally aromas leads into a palate with excellent length, aided by perfectly balanced acidity. Notwithstanding the reputation of the two vintages, this is a better wine than the 2001, which was no slouch. **rating:** 93

best drinking 2005–2012 **best vintages** '01, '02 **drink with** Balmain bugs • $16

Mount View Estate Reserve Shiraz

♥♥♥♥♀ 2001 Medium purple-red; the complex bouquet has an array of blackberry, plum, herb and spice supported by a nice touch of vanilla oak; the palate moves strongly to plum, with good structure and weight, supported by fine, ripe tannins on the finish. **rating:** 90

best drinking 2006–2013 **best vintages** '97, '00, '01 **drink with** Fillet mignon • $20

Mount View Estate Reserve Merlot

♥♥♥♥♀ 2001 Medium to full red-purple; ripe, clean raspberry/redcurrant fruit aromas lead into a palate with abundant, intense, ripe fruit; controlled oak and tannins; outstanding for the Hunter Valley, but with a residual questionmark about the synergy (or lack thereof) between variety and region. **rating:** 91

best drinking 2004–2007 **best vintages** '01 **drink with** Braised oxtail • $28

Mount View Estate Reserve Cabernet Sauvignon

♥♥♥♥ 2001 Medium purple-red; there are earthy edges to the blackcurrant/berry fruit of the bouquet; the palate is well balanced, with good extract, showing sweet berry and chocolate fruit woven through with subtle oak. Sourced from McLaren Vale. Clever winemaking. **rating:** 89

best drinking 2006–2012 **drink with** Beef casserole • $20

mountview wines   NR

Mount Stirling Road, Glen Aplin, Qld 4381 **region** Granite Belt
phone (07) 4683 4316 **fax** (07) 4683 4111 **open** Fri–Mon 9.30–4.30, 7 days during school and public holidays
winemaker Phillipa Hambleton **production** 1250 cases **est.** 1990
product range ($10–18 CD) Chardonnay Semillon Sauvignon Blanc, First Pick (Chardonnay blend), Emu Swamp White, Chardonnay Royal (sparkling), Bianco Bubbles (sparkling), Blanc de Blancs, Sparkling Perry, Short Flat White (dessert), Cerise (light red), Short Flat Red (light red), Shiraz, Merlot, Cabernet Merlot, Shiraz Royal (sparkling).
summary Mountview Wines has changed hands and is now owned by Pauline Stewart. I have no reason to suppose the quality of the Shiraz (in particular) has diminished.

mount william winery   ★★★☆

Mount William Road, Tantaraboo, Vic 3764 **region** Macedon Ranges
phone (03) 5429 1595 **fax** (03) 5429 1998 **open** By appointment
winemaker Murray Cousins, John Ellis (Hanging Rock) **production** 2500 cases **est.** 1987
product range ($15–38 CD) Bedbur's Riesling, Stuart's Block Semillon, Chardonnay Semillon, Chardonnay, Macedon Sparkling Blanc de Blanc, Louise Clare (Sparkling red), Pinot Noir, Cabernets.
summary Adrienne and Murray Cousins established 5 hectares of vineyards between 1987 and 1999, planted to pinot noir, cabernet franc, merlot, semillon and chardonnay. The wines are made under contract (Hanging Rock) and are sold through a stone tasting room cellar-door facility which was completed in 1992, and also through a number of fine wine retailers around Melbourne.

Mount William Bedbur's Riesling

♥♥♥♥ 2001 Pale straw-green; the bouquet is clean, but slightly dull, with mineral rather than fruit on the bouquet; the light-bodied palate is clean, but the fruit expression is muted. The synthetic cork is almost certainly responsible for the loss of focus. **rating:** 85

best drinking Now **drink with** Fresh asparagus • $15

Mount William Stuart's Block Semillon

♥♥♥♥ 2001 Light to medium yellow-green; the moderately intense bouquet has grass, herb and fleeting mineral notes; the palate with good flavour, mouthfeel and balance, though not a lot of length. Once again, threatened by its synthetic cork and hence to be drunk as soon as possible. **rating:** 86

best drinking Now **drink with** Yabbies • $15

Mount William Chardonnay

▼▼▼▼ **2001** Light to medium yellow-green; the moderately intense bouquet is clean, with minimal oak influence; the wine comes alive on the fresh, tangy citrussy stone fruit palate, which finishes with lively acidity. Happily, a natural cork has been used.   **rating:** 87

best drinking Now–2007 **drink with** Chinese prawns • $26

Mount William Louise Clare

▼▼▼▼ **NV** Light to medium red; the bouquet is quite nutty and bready, suggesting lees autolysis; an unusual blend of pinot noir, cabernet sauvignon and shiraz made in a much lighter and more elegant mode than most sparkling reds. Distinct strawberry fruit flavours and well-balanced acidity.   **rating:** 85

best drinking Now **drink with** Hors d'oeuvres • $38

Mount William Pinot Noir

▼▼▼▼ **2001** Medium red-purple; the moderately intense bouquet has a mix of savoury spicy, cherry and plum aromas, the stylish and intense palate long and sappy; slightly piquant, and needs food.   **rating:** 89

best drinking Now–2006 **drink with** Smoked quail • $27

🌿 mr riggs wine company   NR

PO Box 584, McLaren Vale, SA 5171 **region** McLaren Vale
phone (08) 8556 4460 **fax** (08) 8556 4462 **open** Not
winemaker Ben Riggs **production** 2000 cases **est.** 2001
product range ($38 R) Shiraz.
summary After 14 years as winemaker at Wirra Wirra, and another six at various Australian wineries as well as northern hemisphere vintages in the Napa Valley, Bordeaux, Greece, Italy and the south of France, Ben Riggs has decided to establish his own business. His major activity is as consultant winemaker to Penny's Hill, Pertaringa, Coriole and Geoff Hardy, while keeping his hand in consulting for Cazal Viel in the south of France and for UK-based distributor, Western Wines. His domestic winemaking will also include sourcing grapes for and making commercial batches of wine for wholesale and retail entities in Australia, adopting a 'grape to plate' approach. Finally, and no less importantly, he will also make wine on his own behalf for the Mr Riggs label, initially buying select parcels of grapes from old vines in McLaren Vale, and in due course also utilising grapes from his own recently planted vineyard at Piebald Gully, where he has planted 4 hectares of shiraz, 1.5 hectares viognier and 1 hectare of petit verdot.

Mr Riggs Shiraz

▼▼▼▼▽ **2001** Medium to full red-purple; abundant black fruits, chocolate, earth and a dash of spice open proceedings; the medium to full-bodied palate takes all of these characters in a well-balanced framework, replete with ripe tannins. 450 dozen bottles made, packaged in a Dreadnought bottle, 14.5° alcohol. **rating:** 90

best drinking 2006–2016 **drink with** Beef fillet • $38

mt lofty ranges vineyard   ★★★★

Harris Road, Lenswood, SA 5240 **region** Adelaide Hills
phone (08) 8389 8339 **fax** (08) 8389 8349 **open** Weekends 11–5, or by appointment
winemaker Nepenthe (Contract) **production** 1000 cases **est.** 1992
product range ($16–20 CD) Five Vines Riesling, Sauvignon Blanc, Chardonnay, Old Pump Shed Pinot Noir.
summary Mt Lofty Ranges Vineyard is owned by Alan Herath and Jan Reed, who have been involved from the outset in planting, training and nurturing the 4.5-hectare vineyard. Both had professional careers but are now full-time vignerons. Skilled winemaking by Peter Leske at Nepenthe has already brought rewards and recognition to the vineyard. Victorian distribution through Colonial Wines; elsewhere direct from the winery.

Mt Lofty Ranges Vineyard Sauvignon Blanc

▼▼▼▼▽ **2002** Light green-yellow; a highly aromatic bouquet with passionfruit and gooseberry, then the faintest touch of reduction in the background, is followed by a vibrant and lively palate, with fresh fruit flavours replicating the bouquet.   **rating:** 93

best drinking Now **best vintages** '02 **drink with** Blue swimmer crab • $16

Mt Lofty Ranges Vineyard Chardonnay

▼▼▼▼▼ **2001** Light to medium green-yellow; a fresh, clean bouquet with light citrus, melon and cashew, then an intense and elegant, fruit-driven palate adding stone fruit to the mix and with great mouthfeel throughout.
best drinking Now–2007 **best vintages** '01 **drink with** Sweetbreads • $16   **rating:** 94

Mt Lofty Ranges Vineyard Old Pump Shed Pinot Noir

ŶŶŶŶ 2001 Bright but light red-purple; the clean and light bouquet ranges through strawberry and cherry, with spicy overtones; the light and fresh palate, with its crisp finish, is probably now at its best. **rating:** 88

best drinking Now **best vintages** '98, '00 **drink with** Braised ox cheek • $20

mudgee wines   NR

Henry Lawson Drive, Mudgee, NSW 2850 **region** Mudgee
phone (02) 6372 2258 **open** Thurs–Mon 10–5, holidays 7 days
winemaker David Conway **production** 600 cases **est.** 1963
product range ($9–15 CD) Chardonnay, Gewurztraminer, Trebbiano, Riesling, Rose, Shiraz, Pinot Noir, Cabernet Sauvignon.
summary Following the acquisition of Mudgee Wines by the Conway family, the organic winemaking practices of the former owner Jennifer Meek have been discontinued, with conventional viticultural and winemaking practices now adopted.

mulligan wongara vineyard   NR

603 Grenfell Road, Cowra, NSW 2794 **region** Cowra
phone (02) 6342 9334 **fax** (02) 9810 4697 **open** Weekends and public holidays 10–4 (10–6 in summer)
winemaker Jon Reynolds, David Carpenter (former), Sue Carpenter (former) **production** 2000 cases **est.** 1993
product range ($15–18 R) Chardonnay, Unwooded Chardonnay, Shiraz, Cabernet Sauvignon.
summary Andrew and Emma Mulligan began the establishment of their 16-hectare vineyard in 1993. Plantings now comprise chardonnay (14 ha), shiraz (2.5 ha), cabernet (3.5 ha) and sangiovese (1 ha); a significant part of the grapes are sold to others, the wines being made under contract by Jon Reynolds. A striking tower cellar door and cellar is now open, and the wines are sold direct to Sydney restaurants and retailers.

Mulligan Wongara Vineyard Shiraz

ŶŶŶŶ 2001 Light to medium red-purple; the light, spicy, leafy, earthy bouquet is reflected in the light to medium-bodied palate, with its savoury/spicy flavours; well made, but early developing. **rating:** 84

best drinking Now–2005 **drink with** Takeaway • $18

mulyan   ★★★

North Logan Road, Cowra, NSW 2794 **region** Cowra
phone (02) 6342 1289 **fax** (02) 6341 1015 **open** Sat–Mon and public holidays 10–5, or by appointment Mon–Fri (phone 02 6342 1336)
winemaker Simon Gilbert (Contract) **production** 2000 cases **est.** 1994
product range ($13–18 CD) Chardonnay, Bushrangers Bounty Chardonnay, Bushrangers Bounty Shiraz.
summary Mulyan is a 1350-hectare grazing property purchased by the Fagan family in 1886 from Dr William Redfern, a leading 19th century figure in Australian history. The current generation owners Peter and Jenni Fagan began the establishment of 45 hectares of shiraz in 1994, and intend increasing the vineyard area to 100 hectares. Presently there are 28.8 hectares of shiraz and 14.8 hectares of chardonnay, with an experimental plot of sangiovese. The label features a statue of the Roman God Mercury which has stood in the Mulyan homestead garden since being brought back from Italy in 1912 by Peter Fagan's grandmother. The wines have limited Sydney retail distribution and are also available through the Quarry Cellars in Cowra.

Mulyan Cowra Chardonnay

ŶŶŶŶ 2001 Light to medium green-yellow; both bouquet and palate are fresh and clean, with touches of melon and citrus; the problem is that the wine lacks weight and intensity. **rating:** 83

best drinking Now **drink with** Creamy pasta • $18

munari wines   ★★★★

1129 Northern Highway, Heathcote, Vic 3523 **region** Bendigo
phone (03) 5433 3366 **fax** (03) 5433 3095 **open** 7 days 10–5
winemaker Adrian Munari, Deborah Munari **production** 1500 cases **est.** 1993
product range ($25–45 CD) Chardonnay, Shiraz, Schoolhouse Red, Shiraz, Merlot, Malbec, Cabernet Sauvignon Cabernet Franc.

summary Adrian and Deborah Munari made a singularly impressive entry into the winemaking scene, with both their initial vintages winning an impressive array of show medals and have carried on in similar vein since then. With a little under 8 hectares of estate vines, production will be limited, but the wines are well worth seeking out. Exports to the US and Korea.

Munari Shiraz

ŸŸŸŸŸ **2001** Medium to full purple-red; a range of rich, ripe plum, blackberry and mulberry aromas lead into a palate with massive body and extract, although the tannins are not excessive, and the 14.5° alcohol does not burn. If ever there was a wine aimed at the American market, this is it. **rating:** 92

best drinking 2007–2017 **best vintages** '99, '00, '01 **drink with** Barbecued lamb • $45

Munari Schoolhouse Red

ŸŸŸŸ **2001** Medium to full red-purple; the solid, deep, dark berry fruits have a chocolatey edge; the wine has even higher alcohol than the Shiraz (15°) and while the mid-palate is fractionally hollow, it does carry the alcohol surprisingly well. A blend of 83 per cent Shiraz and 17 per cent Cabernet Sauvignon. **rating:** 88

best drinking 2004–2009 **drink with** Kangaroo fillet • $38

Munari Malbec

ŸŸŸŸ **2001** Medium purple-red; the clean, juicy, jammy berry bouquet exudes varietal character and the juicy berry palate does likewise; as ever, the problem with malbec as a single varietal is a lack of structure. **rating:** 87

best drinking 2005–2010 **best vintages** '98 **drink with** Game pie • $40

Munari Cabernet

ŸŸŸŸ **2001** Medium red-purple; ripe blackberry/cassis and regional mint drive the bouquet, with just a touch of oak coming through the abundance of fruit; the palate has similarly ripe, juicy blackberry fruit, but finishes with slightly soapy tannins. **rating:** 86

best drinking 2004–2008 **drink with** Lamb casserole • $35

mundrakoona estate   NR

Sir Charles Moses Lane, Old Hume Highway, Woodlands via Mittagong, NSW 2575 **region** Southern New South Wales Zone
phone (02) 4872 1311 **fax** (02) 4872 1322 **open** Weekends and public holidays 9–6
winemaker Anton Balog **production** 1800 cases **est.** 1997
product range ($18–32 CD) Riesling, Sauvignon Blanc, Reserve Chardonnay, Nouveau Rouge, Reserve Cabernet Sauvignon Merlot.
summary During 1998 and 1999 Anton Balog progressively planted 3.2 hectares of pinot noir, sauvignon blanc and tempranillo at an altitude of 680 metres. He is using wild yeast ferments, hand-plunging and other 'natural' winemaking techniques with the aim of producing Burgundian-style Pinot and Chardonnay and Bordeaux-style Sauvignon Blanc and Cabernet Sauvignon. For the foreseeable future, estate production will be supplemented by grapes grown from local Southern Highlands vineyards.

murdoch hill   NR

Mappinga Road, Woodside, SA 5244 **region** Adelaide Hills
phone (08) 8389 7081 **fax** (08) 8389 7991 **open** By appointment
winemaker Brian Light (Contract) **production** 1500 cases **est.** 1998
product range ($15–18 R) Sauvignon Blanc, Chardonnay, Cabernet Sauvignon.
summary A little over 21 hectares of vines have been established on the undulating, gum-studded countryside of the Erinka property, owned by the Downer family, 4 kilometres east of Oakbank. In descending order of importance the varieties established are sauvignon blanc, shiraz, cabernet sauvignon and chardonnay. The 2002 white wines and 2000 Cabernet Sauvignon were all pleasant, but very light, possibly due to the youth of the vines. The wines are distributed by Australian Prestige Wines in Melbourne and Sydney.

murdock   ★★★★★

Riddoch Highway, Coonawarra, SA 5263 **region** Coonawarra
phone (08) 8737 3700 **fax** (08) 8737 2107 **open** Not
winemaker Peter Bissell (Contract) **production** 2000 cases **est.** 1998
product range ($19–42 CD) Riesling, Merlot, Cabernet Sauvignon.

summary The Murdock family has established 10.4 hectares of cabernet sauvignon, 2 hectares of shiraz, 1 hectare of merlot, and 0.5 hectare each of chardonnay and riesling, and produces small quantities of an outstanding Cabernet Sauvignon, contract-made by Peter Bissell at Balnaves. The labels, incidentally, are ultra-minimalist; no flood of propaganda here.

Murdock Riesling

♥♥♥♥♥ **2001** Light straw-green; an aromatic and flowery bouquet of lime and passionfruit leads into a lively, lemon/citrus palate, with a long, intense finish sustained by good acidity. Just when you thought Murdock was all about Cabernet Sauvignon, this comes along. **rating:** 94

best drinking Now–2011 **best vintages** '01 **drink with** Gazpacho • $19

Murdock Merlot

♥♥♥♥♡ **2000** Strong purple-red, retaining its hue very well; the clean bouquet has ripe redcurrant fruit supported by subtle oak; the palate is distinctively and immediately varietal, with a display of olive, sage, blackcurrant and redcurrant flavours supported by perfectly judged tannins and oak. **rating:** 93

best drinking 2005–2015 **drink with** Braised veal • $24

Murdock Cabernet Sauvignon

♥♥♥♥♥ **2000** Strong red-purple; rich, ripe, dark berry fruits and positive oak on the bouquet lead into a palate loaded with massive, lush, ripe fruit flavours, held in check by savoury tannins on the finish. Not yet released; will become a classic in time. Due for release 2004. **rating:** 94

best drinking 2008–2018 **best vintages** '98, '99, '00 **drink with** Rack of lamb

murrindindi ★★★★

Cummins Lane, Murrindindi, Vic 3717 **region** Central Victorian High Country
phone (03) 5797 8217 **fax** (03) 5797 8422 **open** Not
winemaker Alan Cuthbertson **production** 2000 cases **est.** 1979
product range ($22 R) Chardonnay, Cabernets Merlot.
summary Situated in an unequivocally cool climate, which means that special care has to be taken with the viticulture to produce ripe fruit flavours. In more recent vintages, Murrindindi has succeeded handsomely in so doing. Limited Sydney and Melbourne distribution through Wine Source.

murrumbateman winery NR

Barton Highway, Murrumbateman, NSW 2582 **region** Canberra District
phone (02) 6227 5584 **open** Thurs–Mon 10–5
winemaker Duncan Leslie **production** 1500 cases **est.** 1972
product range ($14–30 CD) Riesling, Sauvignon Blanc, Sally's Sweet White, Rose, Shiraz, Cabernet Merlot, Mead, fortifieds and sparkling.
summary Revived after a change of ownership, the Murrumbateman Winery draws upon 4.5 hectares of vineyards, and also incorporates an à la carte restaurant and function room, together with picnic and barbecue areas.

🐚 myrtaceae NR

53 Main Creek Road, Red Hill, Vic 3937 **region** Mornington Peninsula
phone (03) 5989 2045 **fax** (03) 5989 2845 **open** First weekend of each month and public holidays
winemaker Julie Trueman **production** 150 cases **est.** 1985
product range ($18–22 CD) Chardonnay, Cabernet Sauvignon.
summary The development of the Myrtaceae vineyard began in 1985 with the planting of 0.66 hectare of cabernet sauvignon, cabernet franc and merlot intended for a Bordeaux-style red blend. Between 1988 and 1996 the grapes were sold, but it became evident that these late-ripening varieties were not well suited to the site, and between then and 2000 the vineyard was converted to 0.5 hectare each of pinot noir and chardonnay. The four vintages of Cabernet Sauvignon (1997 to 2000) will be sold progressively, and in the future the releases will be solely of Pinot Noir and Chardonnay. The viticulturist is John Trueman, the winemaker wife Julie Trueman, who are also the proprietors. Part of the property is devoted to the Land for Wildlife Scheme, with an extensive garden in the course of development, and a cellar-door sales area and courtyard opened in January 2003.

naked range wines ★★★☆

125 Rifle Range Road, Smiths Gully, Vic 3760 **region** Yarra Valley
phone (03) 9710 1575 **fax** (03) 9710 1655 **open** Weekends and public holidays 12–6 at Wellers Restaurant, 150 Eltham-Yarra Glen Road, Kangaroo Ground
winemaker Robert Dolan, Kate Goodman **production** 2000 cases **est.** 1996
product range ($19–22 CD) Naked Range of Sauvignon Blanc, Chardonnay, Pinot Noir, Merlot, Cabernet Merlot, Cabernet Sauvignon.
summary Mike Jansz began the establishment of the Jansz Estate vineyard in 1996 at Smiths Gully, in the Diamond Valley subregion of the Yarra Valley. He has established 7 hectares of vineyard, one-third planted to sauvignon blanc, a small patch to pinot noir and the remainder to cabernet sauvignon (predominant), merlot and cabernet franc. The wines are made at the Punt Road winery by former Yarra Ridge winemaker Rob Dolan, and marketed under the striking Naked Range label, one calculated to give the US BATF cardiac arrest if ever the wines were to be exported there. Limited retail distribution in all states, and exports to Indonesia and Vietnam supplement cellar door and mail list sales.

Naked Range Sauvignon Blanc

🍷🍷🍷🍷 2002 Light straw-green; distinct herb, spice and asparagus aromas are followed by a palate with excellent concentration, fully reflecting the very low yield of the vintage, and avoiding the phenolics of the 2001. **rating:** 90
best drinking Now **best vintages** '02 **drink with** Shellfish • $19

Naked Range Cabernet Sauvignon

🍷🍷🍷 2001 Medium purple-red; the bouquet quite leafy and earthy, the blackcurrant fruit of the bouquet similarly surrounded by savoury, earthy, leafy flavours. **rating:** 84
best drinking 2004–2007 **drink with** Spaghetti bolognese • $22

nandroya estate NR

262 Sandfly Road, Margate, Tas 7054 **region** Southern Tasmania
phone (03) 6267 2377 **open** By appointment
winemaker Andrew Hood (Contract) **production** 300 cases **est.** 1995
product range ($18–25 CD) Sauvignon Blanc, Pinot Noir.
summary John Rees and family have established 0.75 hectare each of sauvignon blanc and pinot noir, the wines being sold through the cellar door and to one or two local restaurants. The Reeses regard it as a holiday and retirement project and modestly wonder whether they deserve inclusion in this work. They certainly do, for wineries of this size are an indispensable part of the Tasmanian fabric.

narkoojee ★★★★

170 Francis Road, Glengarry, Vic 3854 **region** Gippsland
phone (03) 5192 4257 **fax** (03) 5192 4257 **open** 10–4 by appointment
winemaker Harry Friend, Axel Friend **production** 1500 cases **est.** 1981
product range ($14–29 CD) Chardonnay, Trafalgar Chardonnay, The Rose, Myrtle Point Shiraz, Cabernet Sauvignon.
summary Narkoojee Vineyard is within easy reach of the old gold mining town of Walhalla and looks out over the Strzelecki Ranges. The wines are produced from a little over 10 hectares of estate vineyards, with chardonnay accounting for half the total. Harry Friend was an amateur winemaker of note before turning to commercial winemaking with Narkoojee, his skills showing through with all the wines, none more so than the Chardonnay. Small amounts are exported; much is sold through the cellar door and mail list.

Narkoojee Chardonnay

🍷🍷🍷🍷🍷 2001 Bright yellow-green; a typically stylish bouquet with stone fruit and excellently balanced and integrated oak is followed by a harmonious stone fruit and cashew-flavoured palate; absolutely sure handling evident throughout. The wines are never flashy, just consistently immaculate. **rating:** 94
best drinking Now–2006 **best vintages** '87, '89, '92, '93, '94, '97, '99, '00, '01 **drink with** Salmon pizza • $27.50

Narkoojee Trafalgar Chardonnay

🍷🍷🍷🍷 2001 Medium yellow-green; the complex bouquet has tangy, citrus fruit and what appears to be barrel-ferment inputs; the light to medium-bodied palate is smooth and soft, with gently creamy/cashew flavours alongside the citrus. A second label of Narkoojee, and a very good one at that. **rating:** 88
best drinking Now–2006 **drink with** Smoked chicken • $17

Narkoojee Myrtle Point Shiraz

TTTT 2000 Light, limpid purple-red; the clean, fresh, light bouquet has cherry and raspberry aromas which come through without interference on the fresh and direct palate, with its flavours of spicy cherry. **rating:** 85

best drinking Now–2005 **drink with** Antipasto • $16

nashdale wines NR

Borenore Lane, Nashdale, NSW 2800 **region** Orange
phone (02) 6365 2463 **fax** (02) 6361 4495 **open** Weekends 2–6
winemaker Mark Davidson (Contract) **production** 1000 cases **est.** 1990
product range ($10–25 CD) Riesling, Sauvignon Blanc, Chardonnay, Pinot Noir, Cabernet Sauvignon.
summary Orange solicitor Edward Fardell commenced establishing the 10-hectare Nashdale Vineyard in 1990. At an elevation of 1000 metres, it offers panoramic views of Mount Canobolas and the Lidster Valley, with a restaurant-cafe open on weekends.

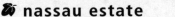

nassau estate ★★★☆

Fish Fossil Drive, Canowindra, NSW 2804 **region** Cowra
phone (02) 9267 4785 **fax** (02) 9267 3844 **open** Not
winemaker Andrew Margan (Contract) **production** 1500 cases **est.** 1996
product range ($19–22 R) Semillon, Chardonnay, Shiraz, Cabernet Sauvignon.
summary The Curran family established its 110-hectare vineyard adjacent to the Belubula River at Canowindra in 1996. The vineyard was named in honour of forebear Joseph Barbeler, who had been involved in a similar endeavour 140 years early in the Duchy of Nassau on the river Rhine near Frankfurt. A significant proportion of the grapes are contracted for sale to one of Australia's largest wineries, with selected amounts retained and contract-made for the Nassau Estate label by Andrew Margan.

Nassau Estate Semillon

TTTY 2000 Medium yellow-green; the bouquet is quite rich and full, suggesting some skin contact, but no oak; a generous, early developing palate which avoids phenolics but should really be drunk prior to the end of 2002. **rating:** 84

best drinking Now **drink with** Creamy pasta • $18.99

Nassau Estate Chardonnay

TTTY 2000 Medium yellow-green; very obvious American oak barrel-ferment characters dominate the bouquet, and are very evident on the palate. However, the wine does have nice structure and mouthfeel, the peachy fruit offset by a twist of acidity on the finish. **rating:** 83

best drinking Now **drink with** KFC • $18.99

neagles rock vineyards ★★★★

Lot 1 and 2 Main North Road, Clare, SA 5453 **region** Clare Valley
phone (08) 8843 4020 **fax** (08) 8843 4021 **open** 7 days 10–5
winemaker Neil Pike (Consultant), Steve Wiblin **production** 6000 cases **est.** 1997
product range ($18–21 CD) Riesling, Semillon Sauvignon Blanc, Shiraz, Grenache, Grenache Shiraz, Sangiovese, Cabernet Sauvignon.
summary Owner-partners Jane Willson and Steve Wiblin have taken the plunge in a major way, simultaneously raising a young family, and resuscitating two old vineyards, and – for good measure – stripping a dilapidated house to the barest of bones and turning it into a first-rate, airy restaurant-cum-cellar door (and which I wholeheartedly recommend from personal experience). They bring 35 years of industry experience to Neagles Rock. Jane Willson held a senior marketing position with Southcorp before heading up Negociants Australia's Sales and Marketing team in a 15-year career which brought her unqualified respect. Steve Wiblin's 20-year career spanned Guinness to Grange, public companies to small ones, marketing to finance. In 2003 Neagles Rock purchased the vineyards and winery of Duncan Estate, bringing its estate plantings to 25 hectares, two-thirds planted prior to 1980. Exports to the US and Singapore.

Neagles Rock Riesling

TTTTY 2002 Light straw-green; a clean, firm and crisp bouquet has regional powdery slate aromas; the fine, delicate but long palate, with some lime blossom fruit which simply needs time to come into full flower. **rating:** 90

best drinking 2004–2010 **drink with** Salad Niçoise • $18

Neagles Rock Semillon Sauvignon Blanc

♥♥♥♥ 2002 Light straw-green; the bouquet has dry mineral/apple aromas supported by a subtle touch of oak, the palate moving along the same track to a brisk, tangy finish. **rating:** 87

best drinking Now–2005 **drink with** Steamed mussels • $18

Neagles Rock Grenache Shiraz

♥♥♥♥ 2001 Medium red-purple; there is a mix of spice, juicy berry, and just a touch of earth on the bouquet; the medium-bodied palate is driven by fresh fruit and a touch of spice, the 14° alcohol showing on the finish. **rating:** 86

best drinking Now **drink with** Pizza • $18

Neagles Rock Cabernet Sauvignon

♥♥♥♥ 2001 Medium red-purple; the moderately intense bouquet has earthy varietal cabernet in a black olive/blackcurrant spectrum with well-integrated oak; the palate has abundant soft and ripe dark berry/blackcurrant fruit, finishing with supple tannins. **rating:** 88

best drinking 2004–2010 **drink with** Lamb shanks • $21

needham estate wines   NR

Ingoldby Road, McLaren Flat, SA 5171 **region** McLaren Vale
phone (08) 8383 0301 **fax** (08) 8383 0301 **open** Not
winemaker Contract **production** 2800 cases **est.** 1997
product range ($17–25 R) Albertus Shiraz, White House Shiraz.
summary Clive Needham has two vineyards; the first, of 4 hectares, is newly planted and will come into full production in 2001. The second has less than 0.5 hectare of 100-year-old shiraz vines, which go to produce the White House Shiraz, with an annual production of only 120 cases.

neighbours vineyards   NR

75 Fullarton Road, Kent Town, SA 5067 (postal) **region** McLaren Vale
phone (08) 8331 8656 **fax** (08) 8331 8443 **open** Not
winemaker Chester Osborn **production** 800 cases **est.** 1995
product range ($26 ML) Shiraz.
summary Esteemed (and dare I say now senior) journalist Bob Mayne planted 1.6 hectares of shiraz in McLaren Vale in 1995, without any clear objective in mind, and certainly not venturing into winemaking. However, one thing leads to another, and in 1998 he formed Neighbours Vineyards Pty Ltd, its 14 shareholders all being McLaren Vale grape growers. By 2001 their combined production had risen to 120 tonnes.

🍇 nelson touch   NR

Hamilton Road, Denmark, WA 6333 **region** Great Southern
phone (08) 9385 3552 **fax** (08) 9286 2060 **open** Not
winemaker Michael Staniforth (Contract) **production** 2000 cases **est.** 1990
product range ($20–25 R) Sauvignon Blanc, Pinot Noir, Cabernet Merlot.
summary Barbara and Brett Nelson began the development of their vineyard back in 1990, and until 1999, sold all of the grapes to other wineries, including Howard Park. While Howard Park continues to receive some grapes, the lion's share of the plantings of the 1.5 hectares each of sauvignon blanc, pinot noir and cabernet sauvignon, plus 0.5 hectare of merlot, is now used for the Nelson Touch label. The name comes from the saying that Admiral Nelson had the 'Nelson touch' when he defeated the French, because everything he did turned to naval gold.

Nelson Touch Sauvignon Blanc

♥♥♥♥ 2001 Very light straw-green; gooseberry, asparagus and herbs run through the bouquet, the crisp and lively palate providing a gentle repetition of the bouquet in classic no-frills fashion. **rating:** 89

best drinking Now **drink with** Shellfish

nepenthe vineyards   ★★★★☆

Jones Road, Balhannah, SA 5242 **region** Adelaide Hills
phone (08) 8431 7588 **fax** (08) 8431 7688 **open** 7 days 10–4
winemaker Peter Leske, Louise Brightman **production** 56 000 cases **est.** 1994

product range ($12.99–50 R) Riesling, Semillon, Sauvignon Blanc, Tryst White, Unwooded Chardonnay, Chardonnay, Pinot Gris, Pinot Noir, Tryst Red, Zinfandel, Tempranillo, The Rogue, The Fugue (Cabernet Merlot).

summary The Tweddell family has established a little over 160 hectares of close-planted vineyards at Lenswood since 1994, with an exotic array of varieties reflected in the wines. In late 1996 it obtained the second license to build a winery in the Adelaide Hills, Petaluma being the only other successful applicant back in 1978. A large winery has been constructed, with Peter Leske in charge of winemaking. Nepenthe has quickly established itself as one of the most exciting new wineries in Australia. Distribution through most states, and exports to the UK, the US, Switzerland, Belgium, Italy, Austria, Japan and Hong Kong.

Nepenthe Vineyards Adelaide Hills Riesling

▼▼▼▼▽ **2002** Light to medium yellow-green; the complex, rich bouquet has some distinct overtones of Alsace; the powerful palate has lots of depth, playing minerality off against a touch of sweet, almost peachy, soft fruit. Blue gold medal Sydney International Wine Competition 2003. **rating: 90**

best drinking Now–2012 **best vintages** '98, '99, '00, '01, '02 **drink with** Sashimi • $20

Nepenthe Vineyards Semillon

▼▼▼▼▼ **2001** Medium yellow-green; the bouquet is complex, the oak balanced and integrated, as it is on the palate, where appealing herb and ripe citrus fruit make their mark and support the oak inputs. Excellent barrel-fermented style. **rating: 94**

best drinking Now–2008 **best vintages** '97, '01 **drink with** Sautéed veal • $22

Nepenthe Vineyards Chardonnay

▼▼▼▼▼ **2001** Medium yellow-green; both bouquet and palate seem to rely more on fruit and less on winemaker inputs than previous vintages, but the quality is the same. Nectarine and grapefruit aromas lead into a light to medium-bodied palate, fruit-driven, with good mouthfeel and length; the barrel-ferment and malolactic influences sotto voce. **rating: 94**

best drinking Now–2006 **best vintages** '99, '00, '01 **drink with** Chinese steamed fish • $27

Nepenthe Vineyards Pinot Noir

▼▼▼▼▽ **2001** Light to medium red-purple; the clean and light bouquet has strawberry and spice aromas, the palate gathering more pace than the bouquet suggests, with good structure, length and lingering acidity. **rating: 92**

best drinking Now–2006 **best vintages** '99, '00, '01 **drink with** Confit of duck • $28

Nepenthe Vineyards Tempranillo

▼▼▼▼ **2001** Light to medium red-purple; an aromatic bouquet, the facets all in an earthy/savoury/leathery/spicy spectrum, the flavours of the palate a faithful reflection of the bouquet. There is enough sweet fruit here, but it is swathed in the other characters; an interesting wine, and the best result yet from a variety with great potential for Australia. **rating: 88**

best drinking 2004–2010 **drink with** Baby lamb • $26

Nepenthe Vineyards Lenswood Zinfandel

▼▼▼▼ **2001** Light to medium red-purple; the moderately intense aromas are in the sweet, juicy berry spectrum, the palate opening with juicy/jammy fruit before the 16.5° alcohol mounts a deadly attack. Best consumed near one's bedroom. **rating: 86**

best drinking Now **drink with** Salacious intent • $50

Nepenthe Vineyards Hungry Ground Cabernet Sauvignon

▼▼▼▼▼ **2000** Medium red-purple; a clean, elegant and fine bouquet with very pure blackcurrant cabernet sauvignon varietal character is supported by gentle oak; a similarly elegant, supple palate is the mark of a wine made with admirable restraint, fine tannins completing the picture. 400 magnums only were made; it represents the best wine from the 2000 vintage, and future limited releases will only be made if the quality of the varietal wine in question is outstanding. **rating: 95**

best drinking 2007–2017 **best vintages** '00 **drink with** Milk-fed lamb

🍷 new era vineyard   NR

PO Box 239, Woodside, SA 5244 **region** Adelaide Hills
phone (08) 8389 7562 **fax** (08) 8389 7562 **open** Not
winemaker Paracombe (Contract) **est.** 1988
product range Gold Cabernet Sauvignon.

summary Patricia Wark's 12.5-hectare vineyard, planted to chardonnay, cabernet sauvignon, merlot and shiraz is under long-term contract to Wolf Blass, providing the grapes for Wolf Blass Adelaide Hills Cabernet Merlot. A tiny proportion of cabernet sauvignon is retained and contract-made at Paracombe.

newstead winery   NR

Tivey Street, Newstead, Vic 3462 **region** Bendigo
phone (03) 5476 2733 **fax** (03) 5476 2536 **open** Weekends and public holidays 10–5
winemaker Ron Snep, Cliff Stubbs **production** 1500 cases **est.** 1994
product range ($15–16 CD) Welshman's Reef Semillon, Barrel Fermented Semillon, Unwooded Chardonnay, Cabernet Sauvignon; Burnt Acre Riesling, Shiraz.
summary Newstead Winery is established in the old Newstead Butter Factory, drawing upon two distinct vineyards at Welshman's Reef (near Maldon) and Burnt Acre Vineyard at Marong, west of Bendigo. Vineyard designations are used for each of the wines.

next generation wines   NR

Grants Gully Road, Clarendon, SA 5157 **region** Adelaide Hills
phone (08) 8383 5555 **fax** (08) 8383 5551 **open** By appointment
winemaker Natasha Mooney **production** 50 000 cases **est.** 2001
product range ($11–16 R) The wines have three levels. The Fifth Element is the flagship range of Barossa Valley Shiraz and Eden Valley Riesling. Next comes the Vin Five range, sourced from southeastern Australian and utilising cross-regional blends, all intended for current consumption. The third level is the budget-priced Stockman's Post range of Australian Dry Red and Dry White.
summary The trendily-named Next Generation was the brainchild of wine industry professionals Sam Atkins and David Cumming, with many years' experience between them working for some of Australia's largest companies. The appointment of Natasha Mooney, previously chief winemaker at Barossa Valley Estate, added significantly to the venture. In 2002 the business was acquired by Xanadu Wines which has now commenced domestic distribution to supplement the original business base established in the UK under the Phoenix brand.

nicholson river   ★★★☆

Liddells Road, Nicholson, Vic 3882 **region** Gippsland
phone (03) 5156 8241 **fax** (03) 5156 8433 **open** 7 days 10–4 for sales, tastings by appointment
winemaker Ken Eckersley **production** 2500 cases **est.** 1978
product range ($15–45 CD) Semillon, Chardonnay, Gippsland Chardonnay, Botrytis Semillon, Pinot Noir, Gippsland Pinot Noir, The Nicholson (Pinot Noir Merlot), Cabernet Merlot; second label Montview Chardonnay, Pinot Noir.
summary The fierce commitment to quality in the face of the temperamental Gippsland climate and the frustratingly small production has been handsomely repaid by some massive Chardonnays, mostly sold through cellar door; a little is exported to the UK, Thailand and the US. Ken Eckersley does not refer to his Chardonnays as white wines but as gold wines, and lists them accordingly in his newsletter.

Nicholson River Semillon

♥♥♥♥ **2001** Yellow-gold; massive, overwhelming charry barrel-ferment aromas and flavours completely dominate the wine. Indeed, I cannot remember a more oak-driven wine, and it certainly fits Ken Eckersley's description of a 'yellow' wine.   **rating:** 85
best drinking Now–2005 **drink with** Grilled eggplant • $25

Nicholson River Botrytis Semillon 375 ml

♥♥♥♥ **2000** Already gold in colour; mandarin peel and honey aromas flow into a palate which is not particularly sweet, but has plenty of character, and an assured finish.   **rating:** 86
best drinking Now–2005 **drink with** Cake or pastry desserts • $15

nightingale wines   NR

1239 Milbrodale Road, Broke, NSW 2330 **region** Lower Hunter Valley
phone (02) 6579 1499 **fax** (02) 6579 1477 **open** 7 days 10–4
winemaker Michael Caban, Nigel Robinson **production** 10 000 cases **est.** 1997
product range ($18–25 CD) Semillon, Verdelho, Unwooded Chardonnay, Chardonnay, Sparkling, Botrytis Semillon, Shiraz, Merlot, Cabernet Sauvignon, Port; Night Owl Selection Unwooded Chardonnay and Shiraz Cabernet Merlot.

summary Paul and Gail Nightingale have wasted no time since establishing their business in 1997. They have planted 3 hectares each of verdelho and merlot, 2 hectares of shiraz, 1.5 hectares each of chardonnay and cabernet sauvignon and 1 hectare of chambourcin. The wines are contract made, and are sold only through the cellar door and actively promoted wine club, and to selected local restaurants. Exports to the UK, Malaysia, Singapore and Canada.

noon winery ·· NR

Rifle Range Road, McLaren Vale, SA 5171 **region** McLaren Vale
phone (08) 8323 8290 **fax** (08) 8323 8290 **open** Weekends 10–5 from November (while stock is available)
winemaker Drew Noon **production** 2000 cases **est.** 1976
product range ($15–21 CD) One Night (Rose), Solaire Reserve Grenache, Eclipse (Grenache Shiraz), Reserve Shiraz, Vintage Port.
summary Drew Noon has returned to McLaren Vale and purchased Noon's from his parents (though father David still keeps an eye on things), having spent many years as a consultant oenologist and viticulturist in Victoria, thereafter as winemaker at Cassegrain. Some spectacular and unusual wines have followed, such as the 17.9° alcohol Solaire Grenache, styled like an Italian Amarone. Low prices mean each year's release sells out in four to five weeks. In 1998 Drew Noon gained the coveted Master of Wine (MW) award. Exports to the UK, the US, Canada, Germany, Switzerland, Belgium and New Zealand.

no regrets vineyard ·· NR

40 Dillons Hill Road, Glaziers Bay, Tas 7109 **region** Southern Tasmania
phone (03) 6295 1509 **fax** (03) 6295 1509 **open** By appointment, also at Salamanca Market, Hobart, most Saturdays
winemaker Andrew Hood (Contract), Eric Phillips **est.** 2000
product range ($20–25 CD) Riesling, Gewurztraminer, Chardonnay, Miss Otis (Sparkling), Pinot Noir.
summary Having sold Elsewhere Vineyard, Eric and Jette Phillips have turned around and planted another vineyard almost next door, called No Regrets. This is their 'retirement' vineyard because they will be producing only one wine from the 1 hectare of pinot noir newly planted. The first vintage came in 2003, in the meantime they were selling residual stock from their days at Elsewhere Vineyard. The last wines from the old venture were the 2000 Riesling, and the superb 2000 Pinot Noir. The wines are also available most Saturdays at Hobart's Salamanca Market.

nugan estate ·· ★★★☆

60 Banna Avenue, Griffith, NSW 2680 **region** Riverina
phone (02) 6962 1822 **fax** (02) 6962 6392 **open** Mon–Fri 9–5
winemaker John Quarisa, Darren Owers **production** 400 000 cases **est.** 1999
product range ($14.95–29.95 R) Sauvignon Blanc, Chardonnay, Durif, Cabernet Sauvignon; Cookoothama range of Sauvignon Blanc Semillon, Semillon Chardonnay, Chardonnay, Botrytis Semillon, Shiraz, Pigeage Merlot, Cabernet Merlot; Frasca's Lane Vineyard Sauvignon Blanc and Chardonnay, Manuka Grove Vineyard Durif, Saviours Rock Cabernet Sauvignon, Alcira Vineyard Cabernet Sauvignon.
summary Nugan Estate has arrived on the scene like a whirlwind. It is an offshoot of the Nugan group, a family company established over 60 years ago in Griffith as a broad-based agricultural business. It is headed by Michelle Nugan, inter alia the recipient of an Export Hero Award 2000. Eight years ago the company began developing vineyards, and is now a veritable giant, with 310 hectares at Darlington Point, 52 hectares at Hanwood and 120 hectares at Hillston (all in New South Wales), 100 hectares in the King Valley, Victoria, and 10 hectares in McLaren Vale. In addition, it has contracts in place to buy 1000 tonnes of grapes per year from Coonawarra. It sells part of the production as grapes, part as bulk wine and part under the Cookoothama and Nugan Estate labels. Ex McWilliam's winemaker John Quarisa is in charge of winemaking and the first wines from the estate have received both show success and highly favourable ratings in wine magazines. Exports to the US, Canada and New Zealand.

Nugan Estate Frasca's Lane Vineyard Sauvignon Blanc

▼▼▼▼ 2001 Light to medium yellow-green; a complex bouquet, built with a subtle touch of French oak; the palate is well balanced, without showing much varietal character, but nicely made. Drink asap. **rating:** 86
best drinking Now **drink with** Breast of turkey • $19.95

Cookoothama Chardonnay

▼▼▼▼ 2001 Glowing yellow-green; the clean stone fruit of the bouquet is matched with well-integrated and balanced oak, the medium-bodied palate providing an instant replay; good balance and feel. Barrel fermented and matured in oak for 12 months; notwithstanding its flavour, drink asap. Estate-grown, Darlington Point. **rating:** 87
best drinking Now **drink with** Pan-fried chicken • $14.95

Nugan Estate Frasca's Lane Vineyard Chardonnay

ŸŸŸŸ 2001 Light to medium yellow-green; the bouquet is clean, with nicely handled French oak, but not showing overmuch fruit. The palate is a different story, surprisingly elegant and well balanced, offering stone fruit and citrus through to a clean finish. Barrel fermented and 10 months maturation in new French oak.   **rating:** 89

best drinking Now–2005 **drink with** Avocado and prawn salad • $19.95

Cookoothama Botrytis Semillon

ŸŸŸŸŸ 2001 Golden yellow; the rich and complex bouquet shows intense botrytis influence producing apricot and peach aromas which in turn provide the flavour for the rich and luscious palate, offset by balanced acidity.   **rating:** 90

best drinking Now–2005 **best vintages** '01 **drink with** Rich desserts • $21.45

Nugan Estate Manuka Grove Vineyard Durif

ŸŸŸŸ 2001 Strong red-purple; clean, ripe black fruits and licorice aromas, then a full-on palate, with a huge extract of fruit, though not tannins. A head and shoulders wine. From the Manuka Grove Vineyard adjacent to the Nugan family home in the Riverina.   **rating:** 86

best drinking Now–2008 **drink with** Marinated venison • $23.95

Cookoothama Pigeage Merlot

ŸŸŸŸ 2001 Medium red-purple; distinctive clove/spice aromas run alongside some black fruit characters; the palate is astonishingly powerful, particularly for a wine foot-stamped and/or hand-plunged (pigeage). I can only imagine substantial quantities of free-run juice were taken off to concentrate the must.   **rating:** 85

best drinking Now–2007 **drink with** Osso buco • $29.95

Nugan Estate Alcira Vineyard Cabernet Sauvignon

ŸŸŸŸ 2000 Medium red-purple; the clean bouquet is moderately intense, offering a mix of berry, earth and light oak; the fresh and lively light to medium-bodied palate has a mixture of leaf, earth and cassis, which has swallowed up the 100 per cent new French oak barriques in which the wine was matured.   **rating:** 86

best drinking Now–2008 **drink with** Warm lamb fillet salad • $23.95

nuggetty vineyard   ★★★☆

280 Maldon-Shelbourne Road, Nuggetty, Vic 3463 **region** Bendigo
phone (03) 5475 1347 **fax** (03) 5475 1647 **open** Weekends and public holidays 10–4, or by appointment
winemaker Greg Dedman, Jackie Dedman **production** 1000 cases **est.** 1993
product range ($15–25 CD) Semillon, Shiraz, Cabernet Sauvignon.
summary The family-owned vineyard was established in 1994 by Greg and Jackie Dedman. Greg (a Charles Sturt University graduate) is also chief winemaker at Blue Pyrenees Estate, while Jackie (having spent 18 months at Bowen Estate between March 1997 and August 1998) has simultaneously undertaken the wine marketing degree at Charles Sturt University and the winemaking degree at the University of Adelaide. They share the vineyard and winery tasks which include 6.5 hectares of estate plantings (semillon, shiraz and cabernet sauvignon), with mailing list and cellar-door sales available while stocks last.

nursery ridge estate   ★★★

Calder Highway, Red Cliffs, Vic 3496 **region** Murray Darling
phone (03) 5024 3311 **fax** (03) 5024 3311 **open** By appointment
winemaker Donna Stephens **production** 1100 cases **est.** 1999
product range ($14–16 R) Sparkling Shiraz, Cassia Street Shiraz, Shiraz Cabernet, Petit Verdot, Cottrell's Hill Cabernet Sauvignon, Parb's Cabernet Sauvignon.
summary The estate takes its name from the fact that it is situated on the site of the original vine nursery at Red Cliffs. It is a family-owned and operated affair, with shiraz, cabernet sauvignon, chardonnay and petit verdot in production, and viognier planted in 2001. A cellar door and new winery site on the Calder Highway, Red Cliffs, opened prior to the end of 2001. The well-priced wines are usually well made, with greater richness and depth of fruit flavour than most other wines from the region, although I didn't know what to make of the incredibly dense and powerful 2001 Petit Verdot. Production is planned to rise from the 60 tonnes in 2002 to a total of 250 tonnes.

oakover estate   ★★★☆

14 Yukich Close, Middle Swan, WA 6056 **region** Swan Valley
phone (08) 9274 0777 **fax** (08) 9274 0788 **open** 7 days 11–5
winemaker Julie White (Contract) **production** 3500 cases **est.** 1990

product range ($16.50–22.50 CD) Verdelho, Chenin Blanc, S.V. Classic (Chardonnay Chenin Blanc), Chardonnay, Shiraz, Cabernet Sauvignon.

summary Owned by the Yukich family, part of the long-established Dalmatian Coast/Croatian cultural group in the Swan Valley, with its roots going back to the early 1900s. However, Oakover Estate is very much part of the new wave in the Swan Valley, with a very large vineyard holding of 64 hectares, planted predominantly to chardonnay, shiraz, chenin blanc and verdelho. Part of the production is sold to others, with the talented Julie White as contract winemaker for the 3500 cases sold through the cellar door and the large, new cafe/restaurant and function centre situated in the heart of the vineyard.

oakridge estate   ★★★☆

864 Maroondah Highway, Coldstream, Vic 3770 **region** Yarra Valley
phone (03) 9739 1920 **fax** (03) 9739 1923 **open** 7 days 10–5
winemaker David Bicknell **production** 17500 cases **est.** 1982
product range ($14–30 CD) Sauvignon Blanc, Chardonnay, Sparkling, Rose, Pinot Noir, Shiraz, Merlot, Cabernet Merlot, Cabernet Sauvignon.
summary The 1997 capital raising by Oakridge Vineyards Limited led to the opening of a new winery in 1998 on a prominent Maroondah Highway site. In 2001 the then struggling company was acquired by Evans & Tate. The appointment of David Bicknell (formerly for many years at De Bortoli) has revitalised the winemaking, and the unbottled samples of 2002 Sauvignon Blanc, Chardonnay and Pinot Noir, plus 2001 Cabernet Merlot and Cabernet Sauvignon were full of promise. The 2002 Pinot Noir, in particular should be outstanding.

Oakridge Estate Rose

▼▼▼▼ 2001 Bright, light fuchsia; fragrant cherry and redcurrant aromas, then a brisk, lively palate in stone-dry style, its Cabernet Sauvignon origins evident.   **rating:** 85

best drinking Now **drink with** Antipasto • $15

oakvale   ★★★★

Broke Road, Pokolbin, NSW 2320 **region** Lower Hunter Valley
phone (02) 4998 7088 **fax** (02) 4998 7077 **open** 7 days 10–5
winemaker Cameron Webster **production** 17000 cases **est.** 1893
product range ($17–30 CD) Gold Rock range of Semillon Chardonnay, Verdelho, Chardonnay, Shiraz; Reserve range of Elliott's Well Semillon, Peach Tree Chardonnay, Peppercorn Shiraz
summary All of the literature and promotional material emphasises the fact that Oakvale has been family-owned since 1893. What it does not mention is that three quite unrelated families have been the owners: first, and for much of the time, the Elliott family; then former Sydney solicitor Barry Shields; and, since 1999, Richard and Mary Owens, who also own the separately-run Milbrovale winery at Broke. Be that as it may, the original slab hut homestead of the Elliott family which is now a museum, and the atmospheric Oakvale winery, are in the 'must visit' category. The winery complex offers a delicatessen, espresso coffee shop, a book shop and has picnic and playground facilities. Live entertainment each weekend between 11 am and 3 pm. Exports to the UK, Ireland and the US.

Oakvale Gold Rock Semillon Chardonnay

▼▼▼▼ 2002 Pale straw-green; the clean and light bouquet is dominated by the Semillon component, as is the palate. There is the lightest imaginable touch of white peach from the Chardonnay, and surprising length from the Semillon. Will repay cellaring.   **rating:** 87

best drinking Now–2008 **drink with** Poached scallops • $16.99

Oakvale Gold Rock Verdelho

▼▼▼▼ 2002 Light green-yellow; light, clean fruit salad and citrus aromas lead into a tangy palate, again with a touch of citrus which gives extra length; nicely made.   **rating:** 85

best drinking Now **drink with** Takeaway • $16.99

Oakvale Gold Rock Chardonnay

▼▼▼▼ 2001 Medium yellow-green; the clean, peachy fruit of the bouquet is very regional, as is the full, smooth, peachy/nectarine fruit of the palate. Well made.   **rating:** 87

best drinking Now–2005 **drink with** Cassoulet • $16.99

Oakvale Peach Tree Chardonnay

ŦŦŦŦŸ **2001** Reserve. Bright, full yellow-green; the bouquet has a very good interplay between the peach and fig fruit and the oak balance and integration; the smooth, medium-bodied palate has soft but long peachy fruit and hints of honey; developing slowly and has some elegance.　　　**rating:** 90

best drinking Now–2006 **best vintages** '01 **drink with** Pan-fried veal • $29.99

☎ observatory hill vineyard　　NR

107 Centauri Drive, Mt Rumney, Tas 7170 **region** Southern Tasmania
phone (03) 6238 5380 **open** Not
winemaker Andrew Hood **production** 50 cases **est.** 1991
product range ($22–23 ML) Chardonnay, Cabernet Sauvignon.
summary Chris and Glenn Richardson have developed their vineyard slowly since acquiring the property in 1990. In 1991 50 vines were planted, another 300 in 1992, with further plantings over the intervening years lifting the total to 1.2 hectares in 2002. Whatever wine is not sold by mail order is sometimes available at the nearby Mornington Inn.

☎ occam's razor　　★★★★

c/- Jasper Hill, Drummonds Lane, Heathcote, Vic 3523 (postal) **region** Heathcote
phone (03) 5433 2528 **fax** (03) 5433 3143 **open** Not
winemaker Emily Laughton **production** 400 cases **est.** 2001
product range ($36 R) Shiraz.
summary Emily Laughton has decided to follow in her parents' footsteps after first seeing the world and having a range of casual jobs. Having grown up at Jasper Hill, winemaking was far from strange, but she decided to find her own way, buying the grapes from a small vineyard owned by Jasper Hill employee, Andrew Conforti, and his wife Melissa. She then made the wine 'with guidance and inspiration from my father, and with assistance from winemaker Mario Marson'. The name comes from William of Ockham (also spelt Occam) (1285–1349) a theologian and philosopher responsible for many sayings including that appearing on the back label of the wine 'what can be done with fewer is done in vain with more'. Only 400 cases are made, and the wine is being exclusively distributed in fine restaurants across Australia.

Occam's Razor Shiraz

ŦŦŦŦ **2001** Medium red-purple; the bouquet has a fragrant mix of spice, cedar, berry and a touch of warm oak; fine tannins run throughout the well-structured palate; some alcohol is present, but not to distraction. A thoroughly impressive first effort.　　　**rating:** 89

best drinking Now–2008 **drink with** Rare fillet steak • $36

old caves　　NR

New England Highway, Stanthorpe, Qld 4380 **region** Granite Belt
phone (07) 4681 1494 **fax** (07) 4681 2722 **open** Mon–Sat 9–5, Sun 10–4
winemaker David Zanatta **production** 3000 cases **est.** 1980
product range ($12–19.50 CD) Chardonnay, Light Red, Zinfandel, Merlot, Cabernet Merlot and a range of generic wines in both bottle and flagon, including fortifieds.
summary Old Caves is a family business run by David, his wife Shirley and their three sons, Tony, Jeremy and Nathan, drawing on 5 hectares of estate vineyards. The wines are sold locally, through the cellar door and by mail order.

old kent river　　★★★★☆

Turpin Road, Rocky Gully, WA 6397 **region** Great Southern
phone (08) 9855 1589 **fax** (08) 9855 1660 **open** At South Coast Highway, Kent River Wed–Sun 9–5 (extended hours during tourist season)
winemaker Alkoomi (Contract), Michael Staniford **production** 3000 cases **est.** 1985
product range ($19.50–65 CD) Sauvignon Blanc, Chardonnay, Pinot Noir, Reserve Pinot Noir, Shiraz, Diamontina (Sparkling).
summary Mark and Debbie Noack have done it tough all of their relatively young lives but have earned respect from their neighbours and from the other producers to whom they sell more than half the production from the 16.5-hectare vineyard established on their sheep property. More importantly still, the quality of their wines goes from strength to strength. Exports to Canada, the UK, The Netherlands, Hong Kong and Japan.

Old Kent River Sauvignon Blanc

♀♀♀♀ **2002** Pale straw-green; the complex bouquet has some spicy notes, possibly from fruit, possibly oak. The medium-bodied, well-balanced palate has length and grip, with mineral notes set against softer flavours, again suggesting the possibility of a percentage of barrel-fermented material. **rating:** 88

best drinking Now **drink with** Chinese dumplings • $18

Old Kent River Chardonnay

♀♀♀♀♀ **2001** Bright yellow-green; the clean bouquet is driven by nectarine, white peach and citrus, subtle barrel-ferment characters the incidental music. The lively, long and quite intense palate is focused on nectarine and citrus fruit running through to a lingering finish. **rating:** 92

best drinking Now–2007 **best vintages** '92, '95, '01 **drink with** Lemon chicken • $21

Old Kent River Diamontina

♀♀♀♀♀ **1998** Pale straw-green; the bouquet is quite aromatic and complex, but is still fruit-driven, notwithstanding the long time (4 years) on yeast lees prior to disgorgement. The palate is quite delicate and fine, citrussy flavours dominant, but well balanced. A blend of 70 per cent Pinot Noir and 30 per cent Chardonnay. **rating:** 90

best drinking Now–2007 **best vintages** '98 **drink with** Cold seafood

Old Kent River Pinot Noir

♀♀♀♀ **2001** Medium to full red-purple; a big, brooding bouquet of dark fruits, black plum and spice feeds into a massively-built palate, with similar dark fruits and a bootful of tannins. If nothing else, needs patience. **rating:** 89

best drinking 2004–2009 **best vintages** '99 **drink with** Pasta, cheese • $28

Old Kent River Reserve Pinot Noir

♀♀♀♀♀ **2001** Medium purple-red; the bouquet is powerful, showing more new oak, and complex, spicy fruits. Inevitably, the palate is powerful, with dark plum and sour cherry fruit, but has more finesse and length than the varietal version, the tannins finer and longer. A classic example proving that more is not necessarily better. **rating:** 93

best drinking 2004–2010 **best vintages** '01 **drink with** Game • $65

Old Kent River Shiraz

♀♀♀♀♀ **2001** Medium to full purple-red; a dense bouquet with blackberry, spice and a hint of game which some would regard with suspicion; whether it is of regional origin or bacterial is, so far as I am concerned, irrelevant given the total volume of aroma and flavour. The palate has rich blackberry fruit and soft, fine tannins. A worthy addition to the Old Kent River range. **rating:** 91

best drinking 2006–2016 **best vintages** '01 **drink with** Venison • $24

old loddon wines ★★★

5 Serpentine Road, Bridgewater, Vic 3516 **region** Bendigo
phone (03) 5437 3197 **fax** (03) 5438 3502 **open** Weekends 11–5, Mon–Fri by appointment
winemaker Russell Burdett **production** 5000 cases **est.** 1995
product range ($14–16 CD) Merlot, Merlot Cabernet Franc, Franc, Cabernet Blend, Cabernet Sauvignon.
summary Russell and Jill Burdett began planting 3 hectares of cabernet franc, merlot, cabernet sauvignon and shiraz in 1987 on the banks of the Loddon River at Bridgewater. Until 1995 all of the grapes were sold to other makers (including Passing Clouds), but in that year the Burdetts began to vinify part of the production, and have steadily increased their own wine production since that time with the assistance of their daughters Brooke and Lisa. All of the wine is sold through cellar door and mailing list.

Old Loddon Franc

♀♀♀♀ **2000** Medium to full red-purple; interesting tobacco leaf, cedar, spice and earth aromas are followed by a palate which moves more to raspberry, and a faint touch of mint. Nice mouthfeel; a particularly good example of a notoriously difficult grape (cabernet franc). **rating:** 88

best drinking 2004–2008 **drink with** Lamb casserole • $16

Old Loddon Merlot

♀♀♀♀ **2000** Medium red-purple; the bouquet is somewhat closed, with fractionally earthy/gamey overtones; olive, mint and berry come together on the palate to provide an curious sweet and sour effect, albeit with positive flavour and recognisable varietal character. **rating:** 84

best drinking Now–2007 **drink with** Vegetarian • $16

Old Loddon Merlot Franc

TTTT 2000 Medium red-purple; the bouquet has a mix of berry, spice, cedar and vanilla; the palate is deeper than the bouquet, with dark chocolate joining the flavour band. Well-integrated oak, but the wine has a fractionally sharp finish. A 50/50 blend of Merlot and Cabernet Franc said to be matured in new oak. **rating: 86**

best drinking 2004–2008 **drink with** Roast veal • $15

old station vineyard ★★★☆

St Vincent Street, Watervale, SA 5452 **region** Clare Valley
phone 0414 441 925 **fax** (02) 9144 1925 **open** Not
winemaker David O'Leary, Nick Walker **production** 2000 cases **est.** 1926
product range ($12–20 ML) Watervale Riesling, Watervale Free Run Rose, Grenache Shiraz, Shiraz.
summary When Bill and Noel Ireland decided to retire from the Sydney retail scene in 1996 to go all the way up (or down) the production stream and become grape growers and winemakers, they did not muck around. In 1995 they had purchased a 6-hectare, 70-year-old vineyard at Watervale and formed an even significantly larger joint venture in the Margaret River region, which has given birth to Flinders Bay wines. In their first year of shows the Old Station Vineyard wines won two gold, three silver and eight bronze medals, a reflection of the strength of old vines and the skills of contract winemaking at Quelltaler. Now, I just wonder what Bill Ireland feels about retailers who slash and burn the theoretical retail price of his wines.

Old Station Vineyard Shiraz

TTTT 2000 Medium red-purple; the bouquet opens up with earth and cedar, thereafter with slightly leafy characters; the palate moves to riper fruit, but overall the wine is somewhat angular. **rating: 85**

best drinking 2004–2008 **drink with** Braised beef • $18

old stornoway vineyard NR

370 Relbia Road, Relbia, Tas 7258 **region** Northern Tasmania
phone (03) 6343 4742 **fax** (03) 6343 4743 **open** 7 days 10–5
winemaker Julian Alcorso (Contract) **production** 2750 cases **est.** 1998
product range ($17–18 CD) Sauvignon Blanc, Unwooded Chardonnay, Chardonnay, Pinot Noir.
summary Old Stornoway Vineyard is headed for big things, having planted 10.6 hectares of vines in 1998 and 49.4 hectares in 1999. Pinot noir (33 ha), chardonnay (12 ha), pinot meunier (6.5 ha), riesling (3.5 ha), pinot gris (3.4 ha) and traminer (0.6 ha) will come into full bearing within a few years, and the recently completed cellar door facilities including a cafe/restaurant.

o'leary walker wines ★★★★☆

Main Road, Leasingham, SA 5452 (PO Box 49, Watervale, SA 5452) **region** Clare Valley
phone (08) 8271 1221 **fax** (08) 8357 1457 **open** Not
winemaker David O'Leary, Nick Walker **production** 14000 cases **est.** 2001
product range ($19–21 R) Riesling, Semillon, Chardonnay, Pinot Noir, Shiraz and Cabernet Merlot variously from the Clare and Eden Valleys, Adelaide Hills and McLaren Vale.
summary David O'Leary and Nick Walker have more than 30 years combined experience as winemakers working for some of the biggest Australian wine groups. They have taken the plunge, and have backed themselves to establish their own winery and brand. Their main vineyard is at Watervale in the Clare Valley, with over 36 hectares of riesling, shiraz, cabernet sauvignon, merlot and semillon. In the Adelaide Hills they have established 14 hectares of chardonnay, cabernet sauvignon, pinot noir, shiraz, sauvignon blanc and merlot. Winemaking skills are not in doubt, nor is the quality of the vineyards, and the wine prices are highly competitive. Exports to the US, Canada, Ireland and Singapore.

O'Leary Walker Polish Hill River Riesling

TTTTT 2002 Light to medium yellow-green; the bouquet has a classic mix of lime, apple, passionfruit and slate, the fine, but intense palate with a range of similar flavours running through to a long finish. Only 500 cases made.

best drinking Now–2012 **best vintages** '02 **drink with** Sashimi • $20 **rating: 95**

O'Leary Walker Watervale Riesling

TTTTT 2002 Light to medium yellow-green; the bouquet is more powerful than the Polish Hill River, but paradoxically is less aromatic. The palate has great flavour, passionfruit and lime flooding the mouth, balanced by good acidity. **rating: 94**

best drinking Now–2009 **best vintages** '01, '02 **drink with** Fresh asparagus • $20

O'Leary Walker Watervale Semillon

▼▼▼▼ 2002 Light to medium yellow-green; latent power lies behind the slightly closed mineral/lemon aromas of the bouquet; the palate provides a replay; once again, the power is there, but discreet, and the finish needs to fill out, as it is somewhat abrupt at the moment. **rating:** 88

best drinking 2004–2008 **drink with** Creamy pasta • $19.50

O'Leary Walker Adelaide Hills Pinot Noir

▼▼▼▼♈ 2001 Light to medium red-purple; the core of plum fruit on the bouquet has earthy, savoury, foresty overtones which are convincingly varietal. The palate has good mouthfeel, intensity and length to the savoury plum fruit. Stylish. **rating:** 90

best drinking Now–2006 **drink with** Veal kidneys • $20.75

O'Leary Walker Barossa Valley Shiraz

▼▼▼▼ 2000 Medium purple-red; ripe black plum and cherry fruit is augmented by a nice touch of oak on the bouquet; the palate, likewise, has abundant fruit, showing controlled extract, tannin and oak management. Well priced. **rating:** 89

best drinking 2004–2009 **drink with** Beef spare ribs • $21

O'Leary Walker Clare Valley McLaren Vale Shiraz

▼▼▼▼♈ 2001 Bright and deep red-purple; clean, concentrated black fruit aromas have well-integrated vanilla oak adding to the appeal; the full-bodied palate has smooth blackberry and plum fruit, with supple, ripe tannins and vanilla oak on the finish. **rating:** 91

best drinking 2006–2011 **best vintages** '01 **drink with** Char-grilled porterhouse • $20.75

olive farm   NR

77 Great Eastern Highway, South Guildford, WA 6055 **region** Swan Valley
phone (08) 9277 2989 **fax** (08) 9277 6828 **open** Wed–Sun 10–5.30 Cellar Sales, 11.30–2.30 Cafe
winemaker Ian Yurisich **production** 3500 cases **est.** 1829
product range ($11.50–35 CD) Traminer, Sauvignon Blanc Semillon, Chenin Blanc, Classic White, Verdelho, Unwooded Chardonnay, Chardonnay, Sauterne Style, Pinot Noir, Shiraz, Merlot, Cabernet Shiraz Merlot, Cabernet Sauvignon, fortifieds, Sparkling.
summary The oldest winery in Australia in use today, and arguably the least communicative. The ultra-low profile in no way inhibits flourishing cellar-door sales. The wines come from 14 hectares of estate plantings of 11 different varieties.

olivers taranga vineyards   ★★★★

Olivers Road, McLaren Vale, SA 5171 **region** McLaren Vale
phone (08) 8323 8498 **fax** (08) 8323 7498 **open** By appointment
winemaker Corrina Rayment **production** 2200 cases **est.** 1839
product range ($20–40 CD) Shiraz, HJ Reserve Shiraz.
summary 1839 was the year in which William and Elizabeth Oliver arrived from Scotland to settle at McLaren Vale. Six generations later, members of the family are still living on the Whitehill and Taranga farms, 2 kilometres north of McLaren Vale. The Taranga property has with 10 varieties planted on 62 hectares; historically, grapes from the property have been sold to up to five different wineries, but since 1994 some of the old vine shiraz has been made under the Oliver's Taranga label. From the 2000 vintage, the wine has been made by Corrina Rayment (the Oliver family's first winemaker and sixth generation family member). Exports to Belgium, Canada, Singapore, Germany, New Zealand, Switzerland, Thailand and the US.

Olivers Taranga Shiraz

▼▼▼▼♈ 2001 Medium purple-red; ripe, dark berry, plum, chocolate and vanilla oak aromas flow into a velvety, smooth palate on entry, with a slightly more savoury finish. Ripe tannins and well-integrated American oak result in a really attractive wine. **rating:** 91

best drinking 2005–2012 **best vintages** '99, '00, '01 **drink with** Rare roast beef • $20

Olivers Taranga HJ Reserve Shiraz

▼▼▼▼♈ 2000 Similar bright colour to the varietal shiraz; the smooth but complex bouquet ranges through spice, blackberry and chocolate, the rich and mouthfilling palate with dark chocolate and blackberry, the supple texture coming from ripe tannins and very well handled oak. Named in honour of HJ 'Bert' Oliver, who planted the vineyard in 1948. **rating:** 92

best drinking 2005–2015 **best vintages** '00 **drink with** Braised ox cheek • $40

olssens of watervale ★★★

Government Road, Watervale, SA 5452 **region** Clare Valley
phone (08) 8843 0065 **fax** (08) 8843 0065 **open** Fri–Mon and public holidays 11–5, or by appointment
winemaker Contract **production** 1000 cases **est.** 1994
product range ($19–26 CD) Riesling, Semillon, Botrytised Riesling, Merlot, Cabernet Sauvignon Cabernet Franc Merlot.
summary Kevin and Helen Olssen first visited the Clare Valley in December 1986. Within two weeks they and their family decided to sell their Adelaide home and purchased a property in a small, isolated valley 3 kilometres north of the township of Watervale. Between 1987 and 1993 production from the 5-hectare vineyard was sold to other makers, but in 1993 the decision was taken to produce wine under the Olssen label.

Olssens of Watervale Merlot

TTTT 2001 Light to medium red-purple; the light, spicy, savoury bouquet is reflected in the palate with its range of savoury, earthy, minty, leafy flavours, all varietal, but needing more flesh. **rating:** 84

best drinking Now–2005 **drink with** Veal goulash • $26

orani vineyard NR

Arthur Highway, Sorrel, Tas 7172 **region** Southern Tasmania
phone (03) 6225 0330 **fax** (03) 6225 0330 **open** Weekends and public holidays 9.30–6.30
winemaker Julian Alcorso (Contract) **est.** 1986
product range ($24–25 R) Riesling, Chardonnay, Pinot Noir.
summary The first commercial release from Orani was of a 1992 Pinot Noir, with Chardonnay and Riesling following in the years thereafter. Since that time Orani has continued to do well with its Pinot Noirs, including a ripe, plummy, highly flavoured wine from the 1999 vintage. Owned by Tony and Angela McDermott, the latter the President of the Royal Hobart Wine Show. All of the wines are released with some years bottle age.

orlando ★★★★★

Jacob's Creek Visitor Centre, Barossa Valley Way, Rowland Flat, SA 5352 **region** Barossa Valley
phone (08) 8521 3000 **fax** (08) 8521 3003 **open** 7 days 10–5
winemaker Philip Laffer, Bernard Hicken, Sam Kurtz **production** NFP **est.** 1847
product range ($8–60 R) The table wines are sold in four ranges: first the national and international best-selling Jacob's Creek Semillon Sauvignon Blanc, Semillon Chardonnay, Chardonnay, Riesling, Shiraz Cabernet and Grenache Shiraz and special Limited Releases; then the Gramp's range of Chardonnay, Botrytis Semillon, Grenache, Cabernet Merlot; next the Saint range, St Helga Eden Valley Riesling, St Hilary Padthaway Chardonnay, St Hugo Coonawarra Cabernet Sauvignon; finally the premium range of Steingarten Riesling, Jacaranda Ridge Cabernet Sauvignon and Lawsons Padthaway Shiraz; sparkling wines under the Trilogy and Carrington labels.
summary Jacob's Creek is one of the largest-selling brands in the world and is almost exclusively responsible for driving the fortunes of this French- (Pernod Ricard) owned company. A colossus in the export game, chiefly to the UK and Europe, but also to the US and Asia. Wine quality across the full spectrum from Jacob's Creek upwards has been exemplary, driven by the production skills of Philip Laffer. The global success of the basic Jacob's Creek range has had the perverse effect of prejudicing many critics and wine writers who fail (so it seems) to objectively look behind the label and taste what is in fact in the glass.

Orlando Jacob's Creek Riesling

TTTT 2002 Over many years, has consistently out-performed its price bracket, sometimes with gold medals. Light green-yellow, it has gently flowery lime blossom aromas leading into a well-balanced and structured palate with plenty of flavour. Against the trend, uses a conventional one-piece cork. **rating:** 89

best drinking Now **best vintages** '00, '02 **drink with** Summer salads • $9

Orlando St Helga Eden Valley Riesling

TTTTT 2001 Light straw-green; a discreet and fine bouquet, with some lime, the palate similarly fine and delicate; good structure and length; particularly ageworthy. **rating:** 90

best drinking Now–2007 **best vintages** '90, '92, '94, '95, '96, '01 **drink with** Asian cuisine • $16

Orlando Steingarten Riesling

TTTTT 2001 Light straw-green; clean, with gently sweet lime juice aromas are followed by a palate stacked with flavour, although the CO_2 is still intrusive; should evolve very well. Incidentally, Steingarten is now simply a brand rather than a vineyard-based wine. **rating:** 90

best drinking 2004–2011 **best vintages** '98 **drink with** Sautéed prawns • $25

Orlando Jacob's Creek Semillon Sauvignon Blanc

TTTT **2002** Light to medium yellow-green; the clean, moderately intense bouquet is dominated by the semillon component, the palate opening up with plenty of fruit in authentic style with grassy semillon mingling with ripe pear/tropical fruit salad flavours from the sauvignon blanc. Good balance and length. Great value. **rating:** 89

best drinking Now **drink with** Sugar-cured tuna • $8.95

Orlando Jacob's Creek Chardonnay

TTTT **2002** Light green-yellow; fresh apple, citrus and melon fruit aromas flow into a fresh palate with good length and intensity; altogether superior, and outstanding value. **rating:** 87

best drinking Now **best vintages** '00, '01, '02 **drink with** Whatever takes your fancy • $8.95

Orlando Jacob's Creek Limited Release Chardonnay

TTTTT **2001** Light to medium yellow-green; the fine and complex bouquet offers outstanding fruit and oak balance and integration, the palate with intense grapefruit and stone fruit flavours supported by subtle oak and malolactic influences through to a long, lingering finish. Lovely wine. **rating:** 95

best drinking Now–2007 **best vintages** '96, '98, '01 **drink with** Breast of guinea fowl • $30.95

Orlando Jacob's Creek Premium Chardonnay

TTTTT **2001** Medium yellow-green; a quite aromatic bouquet with fresh nectarine fruit and subtle fruit flows through into an elegant, unforced palate with malolactic cashew notes adding to the complexity of a very fine wine. Multiple trophy winner 2002 Limestone Coast Wine Show. **rating:** 94

best drinking Now **drink with** Grilled trout

Orlando Jacob's Creek Reserve Chardonnay

TTTTY **2001** Bright, light to medium yellow-green; grapefruit and melon aromas with gentle barrel-ferment inputs flow into a palate which, while quite fine and delicate, has intensity, and a long finish. **rating:** 90

best drinking Now–2006 **best vintages** '01 **drink with** Sautéed prawns

Orlando St Hilary Padthaway Chardonnay

TTTTY **2001** Light but bright yellow-green; the bouquet is complex, with obvious barrel-ferment French oak woven through grapefruit and melon; the fruit comes through with intensity and – in particular – length on the palate. Prior history suggests this wine will age with considerable grace. **rating:** 91

best drinking Now–2008 **best vintages** '96, '00, '01 **drink with** Veal • $18

Orlando Jacob's Creek Reserve Shiraz

TTTT **2000** Medium red-purple; the moderately intense bouquet has good ripe plum fruit and oak balance and integration, the clean, medium-bodied palate with gentle red fruit flavours and soft tannins. **rating:** 87

best drinking 2004–2009 **best vintages** '98, '99 **drink with** Rare roast beef • $14.95

Orlando Lawson's Padthaway Shiraz

TTTTT **1997** Medium to full purple-red; a smooth bouquet with perfectly integrated dark cherry, mint and oak is followed by a palate which is still well and truly on the upward track, powerful and tannic, but with more than enough fruit to sustain that structure. Winner of eight gold medals between 1998 and 2000, and more to come. **rating:** 95

best drinking 2007–2027 **best vintages** '88, '90, '91, '93, '94, '95, '96, '97 **drink with** Beef stroganoff • $60

Orlando Jacob's Creek Limited Release Shiraz Cabernet

TTTTT **1998** Medium red-purple; ripe, lush blackberry and blackcurrant fruit is married with well-balanced but evident oak on the bouquet; a powerful wine in the mouth, opening with fruit before ripe but persistent tannins move in on the back palate and finish. A distinguished wine with a great future. **rating:** 94

best drinking 2005–2020 **best vintages** '94, '96, '98 **drink with** Illabo lamb • $60

Orlando Trilogy

TTTT **2000** Light to medium red-purple; there is an aromatic mix of red berry, blackberry and mint aromas, together with a whisk of oak, leading into a light to medium-bodied palate where berry, mint, leaf and spice come together. A little less mint and leaf in the mix would have made an even better wine. **rating:** 87

best drinking Now–2006 **best vintages** '98, '00 **drink with** Roast shoulder of lamb • $13

Orlando Jacaranda Ridge Cabernet Sauvignon

TTTTT **1998** Medium red-purple; a clean, lush bouquet flooded with blackcurrant and mulberry fruit leads logically into the rich, full-bodied palate, featuring excellent balance, extract and oak handling. Due for release September 2003.   **rating: 95**

best drinking 2007–2017 **best vintages** '86, '88, '90, '94, '96, '97, '98 **drink with** Grilled beef • $58

Orlando Jacob's Creek Limited Release Cabernet Sauvignon

TTTTT **1998** Medium red-purple; a smooth bouquet with balanced fruit and oak inputs leads into a palate with considerable power to both the black fruit flavours and tannins, but the components are balanced. Matured for 20 months in new French oak, well-integrated into the wine. Patience will be rewarded.   **rating: 92**

best drinking 2005–2015 **best vintages** '98 **drink with** Barbecued leg of lamb • $30.95

Orlando Jacob's Creek Reserve Cabernet Sauvignon

TTTTT **2000** Has impressed every vintage since being added on to the basic Jacob's Creek range several years ago. Healthy red-purple; sweet cassis fruit, even a hint of jam, drives the bouquet, flowing logically into a palate with a great volume of ripe blackberry and blackcurrant fruit, controlled oak and tannins.   **rating: 92**

best drinking Now–2010 **best vintages** '98, '00 **drink with** Braised oxtail • $15

osborns   ★★★★

166 Foxeys Road, Merricks North, Vic 3926 **region** Mornington Peninsula
phone (03) 5989 7417 **fax** (03) 5989 7510 **open** First weekend of each month, holiday weekends, and by appointment
winemaker Richard McIntyre (Consultant), Frank Osborn **production** 1500 cases **est.** 1988
product range ($23–27 CD) Chardonnay, Pinot Noir, Cabernet Merlot, Cabernet Sauvignon.
summary Frank and Pamela Osborn are now Mornington Peninsula veterans, having purchased the vineyard land in Ellerina Road in 1988 and (with help from son Guy) planted the vineyard over the following 4 years. The first release of wines in 1997 offered six vintages each of Chardonnay and Pinot Noir and five vintages of Cabernet Sauvignon, quite a debut. Part of the production from the 5.5 hectares of vineyards is sold to others, but increasing amounts are made and marketed under the Osborns label.

Osborns Chardonnay

TTTT **2001** Medium yellow-green; toasty barrel-ferment and malolactic-ferment inputs combine with bottle development on the complex bouquet; all of these characters come through on the palate, where the fruit struggles to keep up the pace.   **rating: 86**

best drinking Now–2005 **best vintages** '97, '98, '99 **drink with** Sautéed scallops • $23

Osborns Pinot Noir

TTTT **2001** Light to medium red-purple; a light, savoury/earthy bouquet with strawberry and plum fruit, then a palate which picks up the pace, with moderately intense flavour and length. Almost inevitably, not in the same class as the 2000.   **rating: 87**

best drinking Now–2006 **best vintages** '97, '00 **drink with** Grilled quail • $25

Osborns Cabernet Sauvignon

TTTTT **2000** Outstanding, full red-purple; there is equally surprising depth to the blackberry/blackcurrant fruit of the bouquet, and the palate does not disappoint. Here ripe, rich dark chocolate and blackberry fruit have ripe tannins to provide texture and structure. An exceptional Cabernet Sauvignon for the Peninsula.   **rating: 92**

best drinking 2004–2009 **best vintages** '00 **drink with** Rack of lamb • $27

o'shea & murphy rosebery hill vineyard   NR

Rosebery Hill, Pastoria Road, Pipers Creek, Vic 3444 **region** Macedon Ranges
phone (03) 5423 5253 **fax** (03) 5424 5253 **open** By appointment
winemaker Barry Murphy, John O'Shea **production** 2000 cases **est.** 1984
product range ($24 R) Cabernet Sauvignon Cabernet Franc Merlot.
summary Planting of the 8-hectare vineyard began in 1984 on a north-facing slope of red basalt soil which runs at the 550 metre elevation line; it is believed the hill was the site of a volcanic eruption 7 million years ago. The vines were established without the aid of irrigation (and remain unirrigated), and produced the first small crop in 1990. No grapes were produced between 1993 and 1995 owing to mildew: Murphy and O'Shea say 'We tried to produce fruit with no sprays at all, and learned the hard way'. Part of the current production is made for the O'Shea & Murphy Rosebery Hill label, and part sold to others, all of whom attest to the quality of the fruit.

oyster cove vineyard   NR

134 Manuka Road, Oyster Cove, Tas 7054   **region** Southern Tasmania
phone (03) 6267 4512   **fax** (03) 6267 4635   **open** By appointment
winemaker Andrew Hood   **production** 100 cases   **est.** 1994
product range ($15–20 CD) Chardonnay, Pinot Noir.
summary The striking label of Oyster Cove, with a yacht reflected in mirror-calm water is wholly appropriate, for Jean and Rod Ledingham have been quietly growing tiny quantities of grapes from the 1 hectare of chardonnay and pinot noir since 1994.

padthaway estate   ★★★☆

Riddoch Highway, Padthaway, SA 5271   **region** Padthaway
phone (08) 8734 3148   **fax** (08) 8734 3188   **open** 7 days 10–4
winemaker Ulrich Grey-Smith   **production** 6000 cases   **est.** 1980
product range ($15–25 R) Unwooded Chardonnay, Chardonnay, Eliza Pinot Chardonnay, St Elgin Merlot, Cabernet Sauvignon.
summary For many years, until the opening of Stonehaven, the only functioning winery in Padthaway, set in the superb grounds of the Estate in a large and gracious old stone woolshed; the homestead is in the Relais et Chateaux mould, offering luxurious accommodation and fine food. Sparkling wines are the specialty of the Estate. Padthaway Estate also acts as a tasting centre for other Padthaway-region wines. National retail distribution; exports to the UK.

Padthaway Estate Unwooded Chardonnay
TTTT 2002 Light straw-green; clean, fresh citrus and grapefruit aromas are precisely reflected in the light to medium-bodied palate, with fresh, clean, direct citrussy fruit. Better than many.   **rating:** 85
best drinking Now–2005   **drink with** Seafood, shellfish • $15

Padthaway Estate Eliza Pinot Chardonnay
TTTT 2000 Light to medium straw-bronze; the aromatic and intense bouquet offers strawberry and a hint of peach, the palate more delicate, but again with Pinot Noir dominant; good acidity sustains the length. A blend of 87 per cent Pinot Noir, 12 per cent Chardonnay and 1 per cent Pinot Meunier.   **rating:** 87
best drinking Now–2005   **drink with** Aperitif • $25

palandri wines   ★★★☆

Bussell Highway, Cowaramup, WA 6284   **region** Margaret River
phone (08) 9755 5711   **fax** (08) 9755 5722   **open** 7 days 10–5
winemaker Tony Carapetis   **production** 240 000 cases   **est.** 1999
product range ($12–35 R) Baldivis Estate Classic Dry White and Cabernet Shiraz are the entry-point wines. Under the mid-priced Aurora label are Semillon Sauvignon Blanc, Semillon Chardonnay, Chardonnay, Shiraz, Merlot, Cabernet Shiraz; the flagship Palandri range consists of Riesling, Semillon, Sauvignon Blanc, Chardonnay, Shiraz, Cabernet Merlot, Cabernet Sauvignon.
summary A state-of-the-art winery completed just prior to the 2000 vintage, now has a capacity of 2500 tonnes. The vineyards which are scheduled to supply Palandri Wines with 50 per cent of its intake are situated in the Frankland River subregion of the Great Southern. 150 hectares of vines were planted at Frankland River in September 1999; the major varieties are shiraz, merlot, cabernet sauvignon, riesling, chardonnay and sauvignon blanc. A further 60 hectares were planted in early September 2000, making this the largest single vineyard developed in West Australia to this point of time. A second block has been purchased south of the Frankland River vineyard, and a further 140 hectares are being developed there. Palandri is a business driven by sales and marketing to a degree not hitherto seen in Australia.

Palandri Sauvignon Blanc
TTTT 2002 Light straw-green; a clean and fresh bouquet with flowery, blossom-accented gooseberry and passionfruit aromas is followed by a palate which, while reflecting the bouquet, is very delicate, and best consumed sooner rather than later. A blend of 85 per cent Margaret River, 15 per cent Great Southern fruit.
best drinking Now   **drink with** Shellfish • $19.95   **rating:** 87

Palandri Aurora Semillon Sauvignon Blanc
TTTT 2001 Light straw-green; light but fragrant gooseberry, herb and grass aromas then a lively repetition of the bouquet on the palate; while not particularly intense, is a nice wine at the price. A blend of 58 per cent Margaret River, 33 per cent Great Southern and 9 per cent Geographe grapes. Well priced.   **rating:** 87
best drinking Now   **best vintages** '00   **drink with** Lightly spiced seafood • $15

Palandri Shiraz

▼▼▼▼ 2001 Medium purple-red; the clean bouquet has a mix of raspberry and blueberry fruit supported by subtle oak; there is plenty of weight, depth and structure to the youthful palate, the fruit flavours ranging through raspberry to plum; the American oak has been particularly well-integrated. **rating:** 88

best drinking 2005–2011 **drink with** Stir-fried Asian beef • $24.95

Palandri Reserve Shiraz

▼▼▼▼ 2000 Light to medium red-purple; the bouquet is rather closed, with some light, spicy savoury aromas escaping; the light to medium-bodied palate has spicy overtones to the black and red berry fruits; subtle oak and minimal tannins to close. **rating:** 86

best drinking 2004–2008 **drink with** Grilled porterhouse • $35

Palandri Margaret River Cabernet Merlot

▼▼▼▼♡ 2001 Youthful, deep red-purple; ripe, dark berry fruit aromas on the bouquet are slightly simple, but the palate has an abundance of rich, dark berry fruit flavours, good tannins and well-handled oak. **rating:** 90

best drinking 2004–2009 **drink with** Rack of lamb • $21.95

Palandri Cabernet Sauvignon

▼▼▼▼ 2001 Youthful deep purple-red; juicy blackcurrant and blackberry fruit drives both the bouquet and palate, but the wine needed more barrel work to round it off; good base material. **rating:** 86

best drinking 2005–2010 **drink with** Lamb shanks • $27

Palandri Reserve Cabernet Sauvignon

▼▼▼▼ 2000 Medium red, the purple starting to diminish; clean, gently savoury earthy blackcurrant aromas lead into a palate opening with blackcurrant and blackberry fruit, moving through to a more savoury finish; the oak inputs are minimal. **rating:** 87

best drinking 2004–2009 **drink with** Lamb shanks • $35

palmara ★★★☆

1314 Richmond Road, Richmond, Tas 7025 **region** Southern Tasmania
phone (03) 6260 2462 **fax** (03) 6260 2462 **open** Sept–May 7 days 12–6
winemaker Allan Bird **production** 250 cases **est.** 1985
product range ($14.50–32.50 CD) Montage, Chardonnay, Exotica (Siegerrebe), Pinot Noir, Cabernet Sauvignon.
summary Allan Bird makes the Palmara wines in tiny quantities. (The vineyard is slightly less than 1 hectare in total.) The Pinot Noir has performed consistently well since 1990. The Exotica Siegerrebe blend is unchallenged as Australia's most exotic and unusual wine, with pungent jujube/lanolin aromas and flavours.

palmer wines ★★★☆

Caves Road, Wilyabrup, WA 6280 **region** Margaret River
phone (08) 9756 7388 **fax** (08) 9756 7399 **open** 7 days 10–5
winemaker Cathy Oates (Contract) **production** 6000 cases **est.** 1977
product range ($15–42 R) Sauvignon Blanc, Semillon Sauvignon Blanc, Chardonnay, Shiraz, Merlot, Shiraz Cabernet, Cabernet Sauvignon.
summary Stephen and Helen Palmer planted their first hectare of vines way back in 1977, but a series of events (including a cyclone and grasshopper plagues) caused them to lose interest and instead turn to thoroughbred horses. But with encouragement from Dr Michael Peterkin of Pierro, and after a gap of almost 10 years, they again turned to viticulture and now have 15 hectares planted to the classic varieties. A new cellar door opened in April 2002.

Palmer Semillon Sauvignon Blanc

▼▼▼▼ 2002 Medium straw-green; a complex and rich wine, bordering on the full-bodied, and showing the full gamut of winemaking tricks on both bouquet and palate; slightly sweetness detracts with this varietal mix.

rating: 86

best drinking Now **drink with** Beast of turkey • $14.95

pankhurst ★★★★

Old Woodgrove, Woodgrove Road, Hall, NSW 2618 **region** Canberra District
phone (02) 6230 2592 **fax** (02) 6230 2592 **open** Weekends, public holidays or by appointment
winemaker Dr David Carpenter, Sue Carpenter (Contract) **production** 4000 cases **est.** 1986

product range ($15–25 CD) Sauvignon Blanc Semillon, Chardonnay, Late Harvest Semillon, Pinot Noir, Cabernet Merlot, Cabernet Sauvignon.

summary Agricultural scientist and consultant Allan Pankhurst and wife Christine (with a degree in pharmaceutical science) have established a 5.7-hectare, split canopy vineyard. Tastings of the first wines produced showed considerable promise. In recent years Pankhurst has shared success with Lark Hill in the production of surprisingly good Pinot Noir – surprising given the climatic limitations. Says Christine Pankhurst, 'the result of good viticulture here and great winemaking at Lark Hill', and she may well be right.

Pankhurst Chardonnay

▼▼▼▼▽ **2001** Bright yellow-green; pleasing nectarine and white peach fruit on the bouquet has barrel-ferment oak in the background; the medium-bodied palate is nicely focused and balanced, the emphasis on attractive white peach fruit.   **rating:** 90

best drinking Now–2005 **best vintages** '00, '01 **drink with** Steamed mud crab • $18

Pankhurst Pinot Noir

▼▼▼▼▽ **2001** Medium red-purple; the complex and savoury bouquet has a mix of dark plum, spice and forest, the palate with good texture, weight and mouthfeel. Clear varietal character is evident throughout; well made.   **rating:** 93

best drinking Now–2007 **best vintages** '96, '97, '98, '01 **drink with** Tea-smoked duck • $25

Pankhurst Cabernet Merlot

▼▼▼▼ **2001** Medium to full red-purple; blackberry, leaf, earth, cedar, mint and spice aromas intermingle on the bouquet; the palate is much riper, with sweet blackcurrant fruit, a touch of raspberry, the tannins soft. Excellent value.   **rating:** 89

best drinking 2006–2011 **drink with** Leg of lamb • $18

panorama ★★★★☆

1848 Cygnet Coast Road, Cradoc, Tas 7109 **region** Southern Tasmania
phone (03) 6266 3409 **fax** (03) 6266 3482 **open** Wed–Mon days 10–5
winemaker Michael Vishacki **production** 210 cases **est.** 1974
product range ($10–160 CD) Sauvignon Blanc, Chardonnay, Reserve Chardonnay, Late Harvest, Rose, Pinot Noir, Reserve Pinot Noir, Cabernet Sauvignon, Ruby Port, Cherry Port, Pear Liqueur.
summary Michael and Sharon Vishacki purchased Panorama from Steve Ferencz in 1997, and have since spent considerable sums in building a brand new winery, an attractive cellar-door sales outlet, and in trebling the vineyard size.

Panorama Reserve Chardonnay

▼▼▼▼ **2001** Medium yellow-green; while the barrel-ferment aromas are complex, they are in fact well balanced with the fruit, which has good depth and concentration on the palate. The only reservation is a fractionally hard, phenolic finish.   **rating:** 88

best drinking Now–2006 **drink with** Shellfish • $28

Panorama Pinot Noir

▼▼▼▼▽ **2001** Good colour; the bouquet has solid plummy fruit as its foundation, the palate with abundant richness, and good structure. Built for medium-term cellaring, and very much in the Panorama style. **rating:** 90

best drinking Now–2008 **best vintages** '90, '91, '92, '93, '98, '01 **drink with** Venison • $37

Panorama Reserve Pinot Noir

▼▼▼▼ **2001** Dark, deep purple-red; a huge wine on both bouquet and palate, with massive flavour and extract; lacks light and shade, and if it is to ever come around, it will be in more than 5 years time. All of the judges and associates at the 2002 Tasmanian Wines Show gave it lesser points than the varietal version. **rating:** 86

best drinking 2008–2013 **drink with** Leave it in the cellar • $160

panton hill winery NR

145 Manuka Road, Panton Hill, Vic 3759 **region** Yarra Valley
phone (03) 9719 7342 **fax** (03) 9719 7362 **open** Weekends and public holidays 11–5, or by appointment
winemaker Dr Teunis AP Kwak **production** 400 cases **est.** 1988
product range ($18–30 CD) Chardonnay, Pinot Noir, Cabernet Franc, Cabernet Sauvignon Merlot, Autumn Muscat, Aromatica Fortified.

summary Melbourne academic Dr Teunis Kwak has a 4-hectare fully-mature vineyard, part planted in 1976, the remainder in 1988. Part of the production is sold to others, part retained for the Panton Hill label. The vineyard is a picturesque one, established on a fairly steep hillside, and there is a large stone hall available for functions.

paracombe wines ★★★★

Main Road, Paracombe, SA 5132 (postal) **region** Adelaide Hills
phone (08) 8380 5058 **fax** (08) 8380 5488 **open** Not
winemaker Paul Drogemuller **production** 3000 cases **est.** 1983
product range ($21–65 ML) Semillon, Sauvignon Blanc, Chardonnay, Shiraz, Somerville Shiraz Limited Release, Cabernet Franc, Cabernet Sauvignon.
summary The Drogemuller family have established 12 hectares of vineyards at Paracombe, reviving a famous name in South Australian wine history. The wines are ever-stylish and consistent, and are sold by mail order and through retailers in South Australia. Exports to the US, Malaysia, Sweden and the UK.

Paracombe Semillon

TTTTY **2002** Light green-yellow; ripe, citrus aromas with a faintly tropical overlay lead into a palate with considerable grip, texture and intensity, with some Sauvignon Blanc-like flavours. The low yield and cool vintage are obvious. **rating:** 91

best drinking Now–2007 **best vintages** '02 **drink with** Lemon-marinated fish • $21

Paracombe Sauvignon Blanc

TTTTY **2002** Pale straw-green; a zesty bouquet, with mineral, herb and a touch of capsicum lead into a palate with appealing mouthfeel and flow; green pea fruit and a long minerally finish in typical vineyard style. **rating:** 92

best drinking Now **best vintages** '95, '96, '97, '01, '02 **drink with** Trout mousse • $21

Paracombe Chardonnay

TTTT **2001** Medium yellow-green; the bouquet is fragrant and aromatic, with fresh melon fruit, and light barrel-ferment French oak inputs; the palate flows easily, with melon and white peach supported by neatly judged oak. **rating:** 88

best drinking Now–2005 **drink with** Seafood risotto • $25

Paracombe Cabernet Franc

TTTT **2001** Light to medium red-purple; the very ripe, juicy/jammy and spicy aromas of the bouquet make their presence felt on the palate, which, while less jammy, has distinct fruit/fruitcake flavours. All in all, curious varietal character, but, at the end of the day, in the style of the 2000. **rating:** 86

best drinking 2004–2008 **drink with** Pastrami • $27

paradise enough ★★★☆

Stewarts Road, Kongwak, Vic 3951 **region** Gippsland
phone (03) 5657 4241 **fax** (03) 5657 4229 **open** Sun, public holidays 12–5
winemaker John Bell, Sue Armstrong **production** 600 cases **est.** 1987
product range ($13–25 CD) Chardonnay, Reserve Chardonnay, Pinot Noir, Cabernet Merlot, Pinot Chardonnay.
summary Phillip Jones of Bass Phillip persuaded John Bell and Sue Armstrong to establish a small vineyard on a substantial dairy and beef cattle property.

paringa estate ★★★★★

44 Paringa Road, Red Hill South, Vic 3937 **region** Mornington Peninsula
phone (03) 5989 2669 **fax** (03) 5931 0135 **open** 7 days 11–5
winemaker Lindsay McCall **production** 6500 cases **est.** 1985
product range ($15–52 CD) Peninsula range of Chardonnay, Pinot Noir, Shiraz; Estate range of White Pinot, Pinot Gris, Chardonnay, Pinot Noir, Shiraz; Sparkling Shiraz, Cabernet Sauvignon.
summary No longer a rising star but a star shining more brightly in the Mornington Peninsula firmament than any other. As recent vintages have emphasised, the Red Hill district of the Mornington Peninsula region is sensitive to growing season conditions and Paringa shines most brightly in the warmer years. The restaurant is open 7 days 10–3.

Paringa Estate Pinot Noir

▼▼▼▼▼ **2001** Clear, bright red-purple; the bouquet and palate both have excellent intensity and focus, fine cherry/plum fruit backed by good acidity and fine tannins. Has the hallmark length of top-quality Pinot.**rating:** 94

best drinking Now–2008 **best vintages** '88, '90, '91, '92, '93, '95, '97, '99, '00 **drink with** Braised duck and wild mushrooms • $52

🐛 parish hill wines   NR

Parish Hill Road, Uraidla, SA 5142 (postal) **region** Adelaide Hills
phone (08) 8390 3927 **fax** (08) 8390 0394 **open** Not
winemaker Andrew Cottell **production** 500 cases **est.** 1998
product range ($25 ML) Arneis, Pinot Noir, Nebbiolo.
summary Andrew Cottell and Joy Carlisle only have a tiny 1.6-hectare vineyard adjacent to their house and micro-on-site winery (which has approval for a total crush of 15 tonnes) but have taken the venture very seriously. Andrew Cottell studied wine science and viticulture at Charles Sturt University, where he was introduced to the Italian varieties, and which led to the planting of 0.2 hectare of arneis and 0.5 hectare of nebbiolo. The other two varieties are mainstream Adelaide Hills chardonnay (0.7 ha) and pinot noir (0.2 ha). However, even here the new French clones selected by Professor Bernard at Dijon University have been grown, and the chardonnay sold as super-premium grapes. The vineyard is on a steep, sunny, exposed site at an altitude of 550 metres, harvest falling in April and May. An attempt to use an organic spray programme in 2002 was a complete failure, and while they adopt integrated pest management, soft environmental practices and beneficial insects, they have retreated to the safer ground of conventional vineyard management for the time being at least.

Parish Hill Arneis

▼▼▼▽ **2001** Light to medium yellow-green; the bouquet is complex and quite ripe, with spiced pear aromas; the full-bodied palate has similar spiced fruit flavours on entry, then heats up on the finish, the 14.8° alcohol being very obvious. I suspect the choice has been between a rock and a hard place.   **rating:** 84

best drinking Now–2005 **drink with** Antipasto • $25

Parish Hill Pinot Noir

▼▼▼▽ **2001** Light red, with a few purple hues remaining; the very light bouquet is in the spicy, foresty spectrum, without overmuch red fruit, and the palate provides a replay, well made, but lacking fruit intensity.   **rating:** 84

best drinking Now–2005 **drink with** Chicken livers • $25

parker coonawarra estate   ★★★★☆

Riddoch Highway, Coonawarra, SA 5263 **region** Coonawarra
phone (08) 8737 3525 **fax** (08) 8737 3527 **open** 7 days 10–4
winemaker Andrew Pirie, Peter Bissell (Contract) **production** 5000 cases **est.** 1985
product range ($30–81 R) Terra Rossa Merlot, Terra Rossa First Growth, Terra Rossa Cabernet Sauvignon.
summary While always a high profile brand, Parker Coonawarra Estate became headline news in March 2003 with the abrupt disappearance of Andrew Pirie from Pipers Brook Vineyards (which he had founded) and his equally rapid reappearance as chief executive of Parker Coonawarra Estate, responsible for every aspect of the business. The estate is now a 50/50 joint venture between the Parker family and interests associated with James Fairfax, the prior connection with Pepper Tree wines having been severed. While Andrew Pirie has ultimate winemaking responsibility, the wines are in fact contract-made by Peter Bissell at Balnaves. Exports to the US, the UK, Switzerland, Germany, Taiwan, Hong Kong, Singapore, Indonesia and Japan.

Parker Coonawarra Estate Terra Rossa Merlot

▼▼▼▼ **2000** Very good purple-red; the clean and powerful bouquet features cassis/red berry fruit, the intense palate opening with continued promise, but closing with a ragged, acid finish. A real curate's egg; it is just possible the good bits will prevail.   **rating:** 87

best drinking 2005–2010 **drink with** Spiced veal • $46

Parker Coonawarra Estate First Growth

▼▼▼▼▼ **2000** Dense red-purple; a complex bouquet of concentrated dark berry fruit and balanced oak, then a commensurately powerful and concentrated palate mixing blackberry and savoury flavours; lots of winemaking inputs.   **rating:** 94

best drinking 2008–2020 **best vintages** '91, '96, '98, '99, '00 **drink with** Prime rib of beef • $81

park wines NR

RMB 6291, Sanatorium Road, Allan's Flat, Yackandandah, Vic 3691 **region** Alpine Valleys
phone (02) 6027 1564 **fax** (02) 6027 1561 **open** Weekends and public holidays 10–5
winemaker Rod Park, Julia Park **est.** 1995
product range ($16–17 CD) Chardonnay, Cabernet Sauvignon.
summary Rod and Julia Park have a 6-hectare vineyard of riesling, chardonnay, merlot, cabernet franc and cabernet sauvignon, set in the beautiful hill country of the Ovens Valley. Part of the vineyard is still coming into bearing, and the business is still in its infancy.

passing clouds ★★★★

RMB 440 Kurting Road, Kingower, Vic 3517 **region** Bendigo
phone (03) 5438 8257 **fax** (03) 5438 8246 **open** Weekends 12–5, Mon–Fri by appointment
winemaker Graeme Leith **production** 4000 cases **est.** 1974
product range ($14–30 CD) Red wine specialist; principal wines include Pinot Noir, Grenache, Merlot, Graeme's Blend (Shiraz Cabernet), Angel Blend (Cabernet), Cabernets; Chardonnay and Sauvignon Blanc from the Goulburn Valley. Also available Three Wise Men Pinot Noir.
summary Graeme Leith is one of the great personalities of the industry, with a superb sense of humour, and makes lovely regional reds with cassis, berry and mint fruit. His smiling, bearded face adorned the front cover of many of the Victorian Tourist Bureau's excellent tourist publications for several years. Exports to the US.

Passing Clouds Graeme's Blend Shiraz Cabernet

▼▼▼▼ **2001** Medium purple-red; clean, sweet red and blackberry fruit drives the bouquet; the light to medium-bodied palate is smooth, with a mix of both red fruit and plum, the oak more obvious than on the bouquet; finishes with soft tannins. **rating:** 87

best drinking 2006–2011 **best vintages** '81, '82, '86, '90, '91, '92, '94, '97, '98 **drink with** Yearling steak or veal • $25

Passing Clouds Angel Blend

▼▼▼▼ **2001** Medium red-purple; the moderately intense bouquet has a range of berry, mint and leaf, together with a touch of spice, the oak subservient. A similar array of flavours comes through on the palate, once again accompanied by mint, but without dominating the wine. **rating:** 87

best drinking 2006–2011 **best vintages** '90, '91, '92, '94, '96, '97, '00 **drink with** Wild duck • $30

paternoster NR

17 Paternoster Road, Emerald, Vic 3782 **region** Yarra Valley
phone (03) 5968 3197 **fax** (03) 5968 3197 **open** Weekends 11–6
winemaker Philip Hession **production** 700 cases **est.** 1985
product range ($15–120 CD) Lily, Chardonnay, Jack of Hearts Chardonnay, Rosemary, Pinot Noir, Pinot Noir Reserve, Jack of Hearts Pinot Noir, Queen Jane Pinot Noir, Jack of Hearts Shiraz, Cabernets, Jack of Hearts Cabernets, Tawny Port.
summary The densely planted, non-irrigated vines (at a density of 5000 vines to the hectare) cascade down a steep hillside at Emerald in one of the coolest parts of the Yarra Valley. Pinot Noir is the specialty of the winery, producing intensely flavoured wines with a strong eucalypt mint overlay reminiscent of the wines of Delatite. No recent tastings; there also seems to be some dispute as to whether Paternoster falls within the Yarra Valley.

🍇 patrick's vineyard ★★★☆

Croziers Road, Cobaw via Mount Macedon, Vic 3441 (postal) **region** Macedon Ranges
phone 0419 598 401 **fax** (03) 9521 6266 **open** Not
winemaker Alan Cooper (Contract) **production** NFP **est.** 1996
product range ($17 ML) Patrick's Pinot.
summary Noell and John McNamara and Judy Doyle planted 2 hectares of pinot noir over the 1996 and 1997 planting seasons. The vineyard stands high on the southern slopes of the Cobaw Ranges with an 1862 settlers' cottage still standing and marking the first land use in the region. At an altitude of 600 metres, even pinot ripens very late in the season, typically at the end of April or early May, but in the right years, when the canopy has turned entirely from green to yellow-gold, the results can be impressive.

Patrick's Vineyard Pinot Noir

▼▼▼▼ **2001** Remarkably deep red-purple; rich, deep and ripe plum fruit drives the bouquet, with just a touch of French oak evident; the palate is equally rich, deep and powerful, amazing for the region, and equalled only by the power of Bindi. Given enough time in bottle, the points may be far too low. **rating:** 88

best drinking Now–2008 **drink with** Rich game • $17

patritti wines ★★☆

13–23 Clacton Road, Dover Gardens, SA 5048 **region** Adelaide Zone
phone (08) 8296 8261 **fax** (08) 8296 5088 **open** Mon–Sat 9–6
winemaker G Patritti, J Patritti **production** 100 000 cases **est.** 1926
product range ($3.70–25 CD) A kaleidoscopic array of table, sparkling, fortified and flavoured wines (and spirits) offered in bottle and flagon. The table wines are sold under the Blewitt Springs Estate, Patritti and Billabong Wines brands; the upper tier being the Dover Private Bin Wines.
summary A traditional, family-owned business offering wines at modest prices, but with impressive vineyard holdings of 10 hectares of shiraz in Blewitt Springs and 6 hectares of grenache at Aldinga North.

pattersons ★★★★

St Werburghs Road, Mount Barker, WA 6234 **region** Great Southern
phone (08) 9851 2063 **fax** (08) 9851 2063 **open** Sat–Wed 10–5, or by appointment
winemaker Plantagenet (Contract) **production** 1500 cases **est.** 1982
product range ($15–29 CD) Chardonnay, Unwooded Chardonnay, Pattersons Curse Chardonnay, Sparkling Shiraz, Pinot Noir, Shiraz, Pattersons Curse Shiraz.
summary Schoolteachers Sue and Arthur Patterson have grown chardonnay, shiraz and pinot noir and grazed cattle as a weekend relaxation for a decade. The cellar door is in a recently completed and very beautiful rammed-earth house, and a number of vintages are on sale at any one time. Good Chardonnay and Shiraz have been complemented by the occasional spectacular Pinot Noir. Retail distribution in New South Wales, Western Australia and Victoria. Rated on the basis of previous tastings.

paul conti wines ★★★★

529 Wanneroo Road, Woodvale, WA 6026 **region** Greater Perth Zone
phone (08) 9409 9160 **fax** (08) 9309 1634 **open** Mon–Sat 9.30–5.30, Sun by appointment
winemaker Paul Conti, Jason Conti **production** 8000 cases **est.** 1948
product range ($12–30 CD) The Tuarts Chenin Blanc, Unwooded Chardonnay, The Tuarts Chardonnay, Tuart Grove Chardonnay, Nero Sparkling Shiraz, Late Harvest Muscat Fronti, Medici Ridge Pinot Noir, Old Vine Grenache Shiraz, Medici Ridge Shiraz, Mariginiup Shiraz, Medici Ridge Merlot, The Tuarts Cabernet Sauvignon, White Port, Reserve Port, Reserve Muscat.
summary Third-generation winemaker Jason Conti has now assumed day-to-day control of winemaking, although father Paul (who succeeded his father in 1968) remains interested and involved in the business. Over the years Paul Conti challenged and redefined industry perceptions and standards; the challenge for Jason Conti (which he shows every sign of meeting) will be to achieve the same degree of success in a relentlessly and increasingly competitive market environment. Exports to the UK, Denmark, Singapore, Malaysia and Japan.

Paul Conti The Tuarts Chardonnay

▼▼▼▼ **2002** Light green-yellow; the moderately intense bouquet is complex, although the barrel-ferment inputs are subtle, simply giving a slightly toasty overlay to the melon fruit; the palate is very restrained, with its subtle mix of flavours, but will undoubtedly build with more time in bottle. Partially barrel fermented in a mix of aged and new French oak. **rating:** 86

best drinking 2004–2007 **best vintages** '01 **drink with** Calamari • $19.99

Paul Conti Medici Ridge Pinot Noir

▼▼▼▼ **2001** Light red; the light, spicy/foresty/brambly bouquet offers clear varietal character in a particular mode, as does the quite firm, savoury palate. The varietal character here, too, is clear, and unforced. **rating:** 87

best drinking Now–2006 **best vintages** '99 **drink with** Coq au vin • $23.99

Paul Conti Mariginiup Shiraz

▼▼▼▼ **2000** Medium to full red-purple; smooth black cherry, blackberry and mulberry fruit does the talking, oak a backdrop; the full-bodied palate has abundant warm, dark fruit and chocolate flavours, tannins aplenty. Patience is essential. **rating:** 88

best drinking 2006–2012 **best vintages** '98, '99 **drink with** Grilled steak • $30

Paul Conti Medici Ridge Shiraz

▼▼▼▼ 2000 Medium red-purple; the bouquet has savoury/spicy notes, touches of leather and fresh red fruits; an elegantly framed palate with savoury/cherry flavours, fine tannins, good balance and length. A blend of Pemberton and Carabooda (Swan District) grapes. **rating:** 88

best drinking Now–2008 **drink with** Spiced lamb kebabs • $20

Paul Conti Medici Ridge Merlot

▼▼▼▼▽ 2002 Medium red-purple; the clean and fresh bouquet has bright, red berry fruit, perfectly ripened, and the ripe, round palate, with its sweet red and dark berry fruits, provides more of the same. Spotlessly clean, the tannins fine. **rating:** 90

best drinking 2004–2010 **drink with** White Rocks veal • $14

paulett ★★★☆

Polish Hill Road, Polish Hill River, SA 5453 **region** Clare Valley
phone (08) 8843 4328 **fax** (08) 8843 4202 **open** 7 days 10–5
winemaker Neil Paulett **production** 13 000 cases **est.** 1983
product range ($13–42 CD) Polish Hill River Riesling, Unwooded Chardonnay, Late Harvest Riesling, Trillians Sparkling Riesling, Clare Blue Sparkling Shiraz, Shiraz, Andreas Shiraz, Cabernet Merlot; Stone Cutting Shiraz Cabernet Malbec.
summary The completion of the winery and cellar-door sales facility in 1992 marked the end of a development project which began back in 1982 when Neil and Alison Paulett purchased a 47-hectare property with a small patch of old vines (now extended to 14.4 ha) and a house in a grove of trees (which were almost immediately burnt by the 1983 bushfires). The beautifully situated winery is one of the features of the scenic Polish Hill River region, as is its Riesling and its Cabernet Merlot. Exports to the UK, Thailand and New Zealand.

Paulett Polish Hill River Riesling

▼▼▼▼ 2002 Faintly grey tinges to the basically light yellow-green colour are a worry; the firm but not aromatic bouquet leads into a palate with similar fruit suppression; just when all seems lost, the palate proceeds to build in body and intensity through to a long finish. Given the Stelvin cap, it is not easy to explain these contradictions. **rating:** 86

best drinking Now–2007 **best vintages** '84, '90, '92, '93, '95, '96, '98, '00 **drink with** Quiche Lorraine • $18

Paulett Cabernet Merlot

▼▼▼▼ 2000 Light to medium red-purple; the moderately intense bouquet has an array of red berry, cigar box and cigar aromas; fresh raspberry and red and blackcurrant fruit drive the nicely balanced palate; fine tannins and subtle oak. Elegant. **rating:** 88

best drinking Now–2007 **best vintages** '98 **drink with** Beef shashlik • $20

paul osicka ★★★★

Majors Creek Vineyard at Graytown, Vic 3608 **region** Heathcote
phone (03) 5794 9235 **fax** (03) 5794 9288 **open** Mon–Sat 10–5, Sun 12–5
winemaker Paul Osicka **production** NFP **est.** 1955
product range ($14–25 CD) Chardonnay, Riesling, Cabernet Sauvignon, Shiraz.
summary A low-profile producer but reliable, particularly when it comes to its smooth but rich Shiraz. The wines are distributed in Melbourne and Sydney by Australian Prestige Wines, with exports to the UK, Hong Kong and Japan.

paxton wines ★★★★

Sand Road, McLaren Vale, SA 5171 (postal) **region** McLaren Vale
phone (08) 8323 8645 **fax** (08) 8323 8903 **open** Not
winemaker Contract **production** 1000 cases **est.** 1997
product range ($38.50 R) Shiraz.
summary David Paxton is one of Australia's best known viticulturists and consultants. He founded Paxton Vineyards in McLaren Vale with his family in 1979, and has since been involved in various capacities in the establishment and management of vineyards in the Adelaide Hills, Coonawarra, Clare Valley, Yarra Valley, Margaret River and Great Southern. The family vineyards in McLaren Vale remain the centre of attention, and are still contract-growers for others. However, as a means of promoting the quality of the grapes produced by the vineyards, Paxton Wines has ventured into small-scale winemaking (via contract) with an initial release of

Shiraz. There are plans to increase the range in the future, but the volume of production of each wine will remain small. Exports to the US.

Paxton McLaren Vale Shiraz

ŸŸŸŸ 2001 Medium red-purple; the traditional, slightly earthy bouquet has ripe berry fruit and subtle American oak, the easy, user-friendly, medium-bodied palate with sweet, raspberry fruit and soft tannins. **rating:** 87

best drinking 2005–2010 **best vintages** '98, '99, '00 **drink with** Roast lamb • $38.50

peacock hill vineyard ★★★★

Cnr Branxton Road and Palmers Lane, Pokolbin, NSW 2320 **region** Lower Hunter Valley
phone (02) 4998 7661 **fax** (02) 4998 7661 **open** Thurs–Mon, public and school holidays 10–5, or by appointment
winemaker Bill Sneddon, Steve Langham (former) **production** 1500 cases **est.** 1969
product range ($18–35 CD) Top Block Chardonnay, Fond Memories, Jaan Shiraz, Faith Cabernet Sauvignon.
summary The Peacock Hill Vineyard was first planted in 1969 as part of the Rothbury Estate, originally being owned by a separate syndicate but then moving under the direct control and ownership of Rothbury. After several further changes of ownership as Rothbury sold many of its vineyards, George Tsiros and Silvi Laumets acquired the 8-hectare property in October 1995. Since that time they have rejuvenated the vineyard and built a small but attractive accommodation lodge for two people, and have a tennis court and petanque rink for their exclusive enjoyment. Over the years, Peacock Hill has been a consistent medal winner in local wine shows.

Peacock Hill Vineyard Top Block Chardonnay

ŸŸŸŸ 2002 Medium yellow-green; the bouquet is complex, with obvious barrel-ferment inputs, the oak slightly coarse; the oak is much less obvious on the palate with its light, crisp fruit; on the track record of the 2001, will develop with time in bottle. **rating:** 87

ŸŸŸŸŸ 2001 Glowing yellow-green; smooth nectarine/peach fruit with excellent oak balance and integration is followed by a flavoursome, but fine and elegant palate; good length and unforced. Gold medals Hunter Valley and Cowra Wine Shows 2002. **rating:** 94

best drinking Now–2006 **best vintages** '01 **drink with** Grilled spatchcock • $26

Peacock Hill Vineyard Jaan Shiraz

ŸŸŸŸ 2001 Bright but light purple-red; a spotlessly clean bouquet with raspberry and blackberry aromas is faithfully reflected in the clean, fresh, totally fruit-driven palate. **rating:** 85

best drinking 2004–2009 **drink with** Smoked beef • $25

pearson vineyards NR

Main North Road, Penwortham, SA 5453 **region** Clare Valley
phone (08) 8843 4234 **fax** (08) 8843 4141 **open** Mon–Fri 11–5, weekends 10–5
winemaker Jim Pearson **production** 800 cases **est.** 1993
product range ($13–18 CD) Riesling, Late Harvest Riesling, Cabernet Franc, Cabernet Sauvignon.
summary Jim Pearson makes the Pearson Vineyard wines at Mintaro Cellars. The 1.5-hectare estate vineyards surround the beautiful little stone house which acts as a cellar door and which appears on the cover of my book, *The Wines, The History, The Vignerons of the Clare Valley*.

peel estate ★★★★

Fletcher Road, Baldivis, WA 6171 **region** Peel
phone (08) 9524 1221 **fax** (08) 9524 1625 **open** 7 days 10–5
winemaker Will Nairn **production** 7000 cases **est.** 1974
product range ($16–30.90 CD) Wood Matured Chenin Blanc, Verdelho, Chardonnay, Pichet Premium Red, Shiraz, Cabernet Sauvignon.
summary The winery rating is given for its Shiraz, a wine of considerable finesse and with a remarkably consistent track record. Every year Will Nairn holds a Great Shiraz Tasting for six-year-old Australian Shirazs, and pits Peel Estate (in a blind tasting attended by 60 or so people) against Australia's best. It is never disgraced. The white wines are workmanlike, the wood-matured Chenin Blanc another winery specialty, although not achieving the excellence of the Shiraz. At 5 years of age it will typically show well, with black cherry and chocolate flavours, a strong dash of American oak, and surprising youth. There is limited retail distribution, and exports to the UK, Malaysia and Hong Kong. Rated on the basis of previous tastings.

peerick vineyard ★★★★☆

Wild Dog Track, Moonambel, Vic 3478 **region** Pyrenees
phone (03) 9817 1611 **fax** (03) 9817 1611 **open** Weekends 11–4
winemaker Contract **production** 2000 cases **est.** 1990
product range ($13–28 CD) Sauvignon Blanc, Semillon Sauvignon Blanc, Viognier, Pinot Noir, Shiraz, Merlot, Cabernet Sauvignon.
summary Peerick is the venture of Chris Jessup and wife Meryl. They have mildly trimmed their Joseph's coat vineyard by increasing the plantings to 5.6 hectares and eliminating the malbec and semillon, but still manage to grow cabernet sauvignon, shiraz, cabernet franc, merlot, sauvignon blanc, and viognier. Quality has improved year by year as the vines have approached maturity. Exports to New Zealand.

Peerick Vineyard Sauvignon Blanc

▼▼▼▼▽ 2002 Light green-yellow; the bouquet is fresh and clean, with a mix of herb, mineral and green pea aromas; the palate has good weight and mouthfeel, balancing mid-palate fruit sweetness against a dry-as-a-bone finish. Doubtless a product of a cool vintage ideal for sauvignon blanc. **rating:** 91
best drinking Now **best vintages** '02 **drink with** Mussels • $17

Peerick Vineyard Viognier

▼▼▼▼ 2002 Very light straw-green; the moderately light bouquet is clean, running in an apple blossom/orange blossom spectrum. Skilful winemaking has resulted in a wine of excellent proportion, feel and finish, all about texture, rather than flavour. Partial malolactic fermentation and part maturation in French oak has done the trick. **rating:** 87
best drinking Now–2005 **best vintages** '02 **drink with** Roast turkey • $25

Peerick Vineyard Shiraz

▼▼▼▼▼ 2000 Bright, full purple-red; clean, dense, complex blackberry, licorice and spice aromas lead into a mouthfilling palate, with lots of spicy blackberry fruit and fine, ripe tannins; easily carries its 14.5° alcohol. Matured in 35 per cent new French and American oak barriques for 18 months. **rating:** 94
best drinking 2006–2016 **best vintages** '00 **drink with** Braised venison • $25

Peerick Vineyard Merlot

▼▼▼▼ 2000 Medium red-purple; the clean, moderately intense bouquet has earthy, olivaceous overtones to the dark aromas; there is a similar range of flavours on the palate; the finish is good, as is the aftertaste. **rating:** 88
best drinking 2004–2009 **drink with** Rack of veal • $23

Peerick Vineyard Cabernet Sauvignon

▼▼▼▼▽ 2000 Medium red-purple; clean, moderately intense blackcurrant fruit has well-balanced oak on the bouquet; the medium-bodied palate brings similar dark fruits and fine savoury tannins to the party. Good oak handling throughout. Both the '99 and '98 Cabernets are also of similar style and quality. **rating:** 90
best drinking 2006–2012 **best vintages** '00 **drink with** Roast saltbush lamb • $20

pegeric vineyard NR

PO Box 227, Woodend, Vic 3442 **region** Macedon Ranges
phone (03) 9354 4961 **fax** (03) 9354 4961 **open** Not
winemaker Llew Knight, Ian Gunter, Chris Cormack **production** 100 cases **est.** 1991
product range ($75 ML) Pinot Noir, Tumbetin.
summary Owner and viticulturist Chris Cormack accumulated an oenological degree and experience in every facet of the wine industry here and overseas before beginning the establishment of the close-planted, non-irrigated, low-yielding Pegeric Vineyard at an altitude of 640 metres on red volcanic basalt soil. None of the wines have so far been released; the first vintage to be offered will be the 1998, due for release in December 2003. As a separate exercise, Chris Cormack has also made several vintages of a cross-regional blend of Cabernet Shiraz named Tumbetin.

pembroke NR

Richmond Road, Cambridge, Tas 7170 **region** Southern Tasmania
phone (03) 6248 5139 **fax** (03) 6234 5481 **open** By appointment
winemaker Andrew Hood (Contract) **production** 200 cases **est.** 1980
product range ($24 ML) Pinot Noir.

summary The 1-hectare Pembroke vineyard was established in 1980 by the McKay and Hawker families and is still owned by them. It is predominantly planted to pinot noir, with tiny quantities of chardonnay, riesling and sauvignon blanc.

penbro estate ★★★★

Cnr Melba Highway and Murrindindi Road, Glenburn, Vic 3717 **region** Central Victorian High Country
phone (03) 9215 2229 **fax** (03) 9215 2346 **open** Not
winemaker Martin Williams (Contract) **production** 3000 cases **est.** 1997
product range ($14.75–21.50 CD) Chardonnay, Unwooded Chardonnay, Pinot Noir, Shiraz, Merlot, Cabernet Sauvignon.
summary Since 1997 the Bertalli family has established 40 hectares of chardonnay, pinot noir, merlot, cabernet sauvignon and shiraz, the Unwooded Chardonnay from both 2000 and 2001 winning medals at the Victorian Wines Show in the year of making. Part of the grape production is sold, part vinified for the Penbro brand. Distribution in Victoria by The Wine Group.

Penbro Estate Chardonnay

▼▼▼▼▽ 2001 Medium yellow-green; classy melon, nectarine and citrus fruit drives the bouquet and the light to medium-bodied palate; the palate does have textural complexity without compromising its elegance. **rating:** 90
best drinking Now–2006 **drink with** Trout pâté • $19.95

Penbro Estate Shiraz

▼▼▼▼▽ 2001 Youthful purple-red; fresh, exuberant raspberry and plum fruit aromas are reflected in the medium-bodied palate, with ripe, but not jammy fruit, ripe tannins and subtle French oak. **rating:** 91
best drinking Now–2008 **best vintages** '01 **drink with** Braised oxtail • $21.50

pendarves estate ★★★☆

110 Old North Road, Belford, NSW 2335 **region** Lower Hunter Valley
phone (02) 6574 7222 **fax** (02) 9970 6152 **open** Weekends 11–5, Mon–Fri by appointment
winemaker Greg Silkman (Contract) **production** 12 000 cases **est.** 1986
product range ($18–25 CD) An unusual portfolio of Sauvignon Blanc, Verdelho, Unoaked Chardonnay, Chardonnay, Pinot Noir, Chambourcin, Shiraz, Merlot Malbec Cabernet.
summary The perpetual-motion general practitioner and founder of the Australian Medical Friends of Wine, Dr Philip Norrie, is a born communicator and marketer as well as a wine historian of note. He also happens to be a passionate advocate of the virtues of Verdelho, inspired in part by the high regard held for that variety by vignerons around the turn of the century. His ambassadorship for the cause of wine and health in both Australia and overseas has led to the development of a joint venture for the production and export distribution of a large volume brand 'The Wine Doctor', and to the establishment of export markets in Singapore, the UK, Germany, China and Malaysia (as well as national distribution).

penfolds ★★★★★

Tanunda Road, Nuriootpa, SA 5355 **region** Barossa Valley
phone (08) 8568 9290 **fax** (08) 8568 9493 **open** Mon–Fri 10–5, weekends and public holidays 11–5
winemaker Peter Gago **production** 1.4 million cases **est.** 1844
product range ($9–395 R) At the bottom of the price range is the Rawsons Retreat varietal white and red wines; next Koonunga Hill, then Thomas Hyland before moving into the bin range of Kalimna Bin 28 Shiraz, Bin 128 Coonawarra Shiraz, Old Vine Bin 138 Shiraz Grenache Mourvedre, Bin 407 Cabernet Sauvignon, Bin 389 Cabernet Shiraz and Bin 707 Cabernet Sauvignon. There are then the regional wines of Eden Valley Reserve Riesling, Adelaide Hills Chardonnay, Reserve Bin Chardonnay and Yattarna; and finally the top three red wines of St Henri Shiraz, RWT Shiraz and Grange. A range of tawny ports culminates in Great Grandfather.
summary Senior among the numerous wine companies or stand-alone brands in Southcorp Wines and undoubtedly one of the top wine companies in the world in terms of quality, product range and exports. The consistency of the quality of the red wines and their value for money is recognised worldwide, and – headed by the development of the ultra-premium Yattarna Chardonnay – it has steadily raised the quality of its white wines. Following the acquisition of Rosemount Estate by Southcorp in 2001, there has been even greater focus on the three leading brands of Penfolds, Lindemans and Rosemount, and the sale of some lesser brands and the deletion of others.

Penfolds Adelaide Hills Chardonnay

▼▼▼▼ 2000 Medium to full yellow-green; the moderately intense bouquet offers melon, stone fruit, cashew and controlled barrel-ferment inputs; the palate has similar balance and control, providing a wine of complexity but which, in the final analysis, needed a touch more brightness and focus. No doubt the hot vintage had something to do with that. **rating:** 90

best drinking Now–2006 **best vintages** '95, '98 **drink with** Marron • $25

Penfolds Koonunga Hill Chardonnay

▼▼▼▼ 2002 Medium yellow-green; ripe, tangy stone fruit and melon aromas, then a complex, medium-bodied palate which shows sophisticated winemaking inputs. **rating:** 87

best drinking Now **drink with** Avocado and prawn salad • $15

Penfolds Reserve Bin Chardonnay

▼▼▼▼ 2000 Bin 00A. Brilliant, bright light to medium green-yellow; the bouquet has complex barrel-ferment and malolactic-ferment inputs on intense citrus fruit; it is that combination of malolactic and ferment fruit which drives the long palate, anchored in nectarine and citrus, then a lingering finish and aftertaste. Seventy-five per cent from Tumbarumba and 25 per cent from the Adelaide Hills. I lost no time in acquiring half a case of the wine, which is only an eyelash behind Yattarna. **rating:** 96

best drinking Now–2010 **best vintages** '94, '95, '96, '98, '00 **drink with** Smoked chicken • $60

Penfolds Yattarna Chardonnay

▼▼▼▼ 1999 When first tasted in June 2002, the wine was superb, wonderfully youthful and promising to live for many years. When tasted by 7 judges in the March 2003 Divine State of Origin Challenge, the points ranged between 16.5 and 17.5 out of 20 – in other words, very consistently at high bronze to silver medal, looking full, peachy and slightly old-fashioned. Seven judges can't be wrong; the only possible culprit is random oxidation. **rating:** 88

▼▼▼▼ 2000 Light, bright green-gold; the piercingly intense bouquet is fruit-driven, as is the exceptionally long palate, where citrus and grapefruit come first, melon second. The oak is subtle, as is the impact of the malolactic fermentation. Largely sourced from Tumbarumba, and thus quite different to any of the preceding Yattarnas in terms of geographic base, but surely the best yet. **rating:** 97

best drinking 2004–2010 **best vintages** '95, '96, '97, '98, '00 **drink with** Rack of veal • $120

Penfolds Bin 128 Coonawarra Shiraz

▼▼▼▼ 2000 Medium red-purple; the bouquet is clean and smooth, with well-integrated fruit and oak. The smooth and supple palate has sweet blackberry and plum fruit, making for easy drinking without undue aspirations. **rating:** 88

best drinking 2004–2010 **best vintages** '63, '66, '80, '86, '89, '90, '91, '93, '94, '96, '98 **drink with** Veal; mild cheddar • $25

Penfolds St Henri Shiraz

▼▼▼▼ 1999 Medium to full purple-red; bramble, briar and spice aromas are followed by a palate with bitter chocolate, licorice and blackberry joining the background components of the bouquet. The tannins are very well handled; Penfolds is on top of this aspect of the game. **rating:** 93

best drinking 2005–2015 **best vintages** '66, '67, '76, '82, '85, '88, '90, '91, '93, '94, '96, '98, '99 **drink with** Braised lamb • $60

Penfolds Grange

▼▼▼▼ 1997 Medium to full red, with just a touch of purple remaining; powerful, complex dark fruits, chocolate and savoury lemon/vanilla oak on the bouquet, then a similarly powerful palate where earth and chocolate join the chorus of flavours promised by the bouquet; persistent tannins, of course. It's hard to suggest this will be regarded as a great Grange in 20 years or so, but it is nonetheless in the mainstream of Grange style. **rating:** 94

▼▼▼▼ 1998 Youthful purple-red, most impressive for a five-year-old wine; the bouquet oozes blackberry, blackcurrant and licorice fruit, leading into a palate saturated with plum, blackberry and licorice fruit. The wine has the hallmark fine, but ripe, tannins of the very best vintages of Grange. Needs to lose some of its fatness, and will richly reward those who wait. For the record, as it were, I do not see the 14.5° alcohol as a problem. **rating:** 97

best drinking 2010–2030 **best vintages** '80, '83, '86, '90, '91, '92, '94, '96, '98 **drink with** Aged fillet mignon • $395

Penfolds Kalimna Bin 28 Shiraz

ᵀᵀᵀᵀᵀ **2000** Medium purple-red; spotlessly clean black cherry and blackberry fruit on the bouquet is followed by largely fruit-driven palate, but with more weight and complexity than the Bin 128. Ripe tannins. The oak contribution is evident, but far from dramatic. **rating:** 90

best drinking 2004–2010 **best vintages** '64, '66, '71, '80, '81, '83, '86, '90, '91, '94, '95, '96, '98, '99 **drink with** Lamb or beef casserole • $25

Penfolds RWT Shiraz

ᵀᵀᵀᵀᵀ **1999** Medium to full red-purple; abundant ripe, sweet, dark berry fruit is married with French oak on the bouquet; the palate has excellent mouthfeel and structure with fine-grained but persistent tannins adding to the length of the wine. A particularly good outcome for the vintage. **rating:** 94

ᵀᵀᵀᵀᵀ **2000** Strong, deep purple-red; the bouquet offers a mix of blackberry (dominant), dark plum, chocolate, spice and cassis, all of which make their presence felt on the velvety palate. Ample but ripe tannins and controlled French oak round off an altogether superior wine. **rating:** 94

best drinking 2005–2020 **best vintages** '97, '99 '00 **drink with** Roast veal • $120

Penfolds St Henri Shiraz

ᵀᵀᵀᵀᵀ **1998** Medium red-purple; the moderately intense bouquet has, as one would expect, good fruit and oak balance and integration; strong blackberry fruit provides the ripe core of the palate, which has a quite savoury finish and tannins to provide ample structure. A great example of St Henri. **rating:** 94

best drinking 2005–2015 **best vintages** '66, '67, '76, '82, '85, '88, '90, '91, '93, '94, '96, '98 **drink with** Braised lamb • $50

Penfolds Thomas Hyland Shiraz

ᵀᵀᵀᵀ **2001** Medium purple-red; the smooth bouquet has a range of dark berry fruits, licorice and spice supported by well-balanced and integrated oak; the medium-bodied palate has the attractive fruit of the bouquet, but is unexpectedly immature, the tannins still with slightly sharp edges. Doubtless will settle down with a few more years in bottle. A new brand interposed between Koonunga Hill and the Bin range. **rating:** 87

best drinking 2004–2010 **drink with** Rare roast beef • $18.99

Penfolds Old Vine Barossa Valley Bin 138 Shiraz Mourvedre Grenache

ᵀᵀᵀᵀ **2001** Youthful red-purple; complex, ripe berry fruit and hallmark oak on the bouquet is followed by a palate which avoids confection flavours, has good structure and tannin support, all giving more power and interest than many of these Barossa-based Rhône-style blends. **rating:** 89

best drinking 2004–2009 **best vintages** '98 **drink with** Rich stews • $25

Penfolds Koonunga Hill Shiraz Cabernet

ᵀᵀᵀᵀᵀ **2001** The bouquet has good depth with dark berry fruits and a dash of sweet oak, a theme carried on through the generous plum and blackberry fruit of the palate, accompanied by supple tannins and controlled oak. If it ain't broke … **rating:** 90

best drinking Now–2008 **best vintages** '82, '87, '90, '91, '92, '94, '96, '98, '00, '01 **drink with** All red meat, cheese • $15

Penfolds Bin 389 Cabernet Shiraz

ᵀᵀᵀᵀᵀ **2000** Medium red-purple; clean, dark blackberry and blackcurrant fruit aromas are supported by the typical well-integrated oak; there is considerable depth to the black fruit and dark chocolate flavours of the palate, which finishes with fine tannins. **rating:** 92

best drinking 2005–2015 **best vintages** '66, '70, '71, '86, '90, '93, '94, '96, '98 **drink with** Double lamb loin chops • $41

Penfolds Rawson's Retreat Cabernet Shiraz

ᵀᵀᵀᵀ **2002** Youthful purple-red; a clean and lively bouquet with cherry, plum and mulberry fruit, then a soft, round, ripe, entirely fruit-driven palate; it is ever so easy to see the Rosemount influence, but that does not diminish the easy-drinking appeal of the wine. **rating:** 88

best drinking Now–2005 **drink with** Pizza • $9.99

Penfolds Bin 407 Cabernet Sauvignon

ᵀᵀᵀᵀᵀ **2000** Medium red-purple; the bouquet is clean, but somewhat closed, black fruits and subtle oak there but not demonstrative. The palate has reassuring substance, with earthy blackcurrant fruit, and subtle oak. The strongest point of the wine is the particularly good tannins on a long finish. **rating:** 90

best drinking 2005–2015 **best vintages** '90, '91, '92, '93, '94, '96, '98 **drink with** Venison, kangaroo fillet • $29

🐦 penfolds magill estate   NR

78 Penfold Road, Magill, SA 5072 **region** Adelaide Zone
phone (08) 8301 5569 **fax** (08) 8301 5588 **open** 7 days 9.30–4.30
winemaker Peter Gago **production** NFP **est.** 1844
product range ($60 R) Magill Estate Shiraz.
summary The birthplace of Penfolds, established by Dr Christopher Rawson Penfold in 1844, his house still part of the immaculately maintained property. It includes 6 hectares of precious shiraz used to make Magill Estate; the original and subsequent winery buildings, most still in operation or in museum condition; the Penfolds corporate headquarters; and the much-acclaimed Magill Restaurant, with panoramic views back to the city, a great wine list and fine dining. All this a 20-minute drive from Adelaide's CBD.

Penfolds Magill Estate Shiraz

▼▼▼▼▽ **1999** Medium red-purple; cedary/spicy/savoury aromas blossom into black cherry and plum flavours on the palate, supported by a greater level of tannins than is usual with this wine. Very good structure and length.   **rating:** 92

best drinking 2004–2014 **best vintages** '83, '86, '89, '90, '91, '93, '95, '96 **drink with** Rack of lamb • $60

penley estate   ★★★★☆

McLeans Road, Coonawarra, SA 5263 **region** Coonawarra
phone (08) 8736 3211 **fax** (08) 8736 3124 **open** 7 days 10–4
winemaker Kym Tolley **production** 28 000 cases **est.** 1988
product range ($19–75 CD) Chardonnay, Hyland Shiraz, Special Select Shiraz, Ausvetia Shiraz, Shiraz Cabernet Sauvignon, Merlot, Reserve Cabernet Sauvignon, Phoenix Cabernet Sauvignon.
summary Owner winemaker Kym Tolley describes himself as a fifth-generation winemaker, the family tree involving both the Penfolds and the Tolleys. He worked 17 years in the industry before establishing Penley Estate and has made every post a winner since, producing a succession of rich, complex, full-bodied red wines and stylish Chardonnays. Now ranks as one of the best wineries in Coonawarra, drawing upon 91 precious hectares of estate plantings. Exports to the US, Europe and Asia.

Penley Estate Chardonnay

▼▼▼▼ **2001** Medium yellow-green; attractive nectarine and melon fruit aromas lead into a medium-bodied palate, with good structure and balance; the oak sotto voce throughout.   **rating:** 88

best drinking Now **drink with** Pasta • $19.50

Penley Estate Ausvetia Shiraz

▼▼▼▼▽ **2000** Bright red-purple; quite complex dark berry, earth, spice and oak aromas on the bouquet are also reflected in the smooth and balanced palate. An export special which is now also available on the domestic market; doubtless the price slowed the stampede to buy the wine.   **rating:** 90

best drinking 2005–2010 **best vintages** '98, '00 **drink with** Baby lamb • $75

Penley Estate Hyland Shiraz

▼▼▼▼ **2001** Light to medium purple-red; clean raspberry and black cherry aromas lead into a light to medium-bodied palate driven by its fresh fruit; minimum oak and tannin inputs.   **rating:** 86

best drinking 2004–2007 **best vintages** '98 **drink with** Fillet mignon • $19

Penley Estate Special Select Shiraz

▼▼▼▼▽ **2000** Medium red-purple; the clean, smooth, moderately intense bouquet offers raspberry and some black fruits; the palate has good mouthfeel and structure, adding touches of dark chocolate to the suite of flavours, finishing with fine, savoury tannins.   **rating:** 90

best drinking 2005–2011 **best vintages** '00 **drink with** Pasta with meat sauce • $62

Penley Estate Shiraz Cabernet Sauvignon

▼▼▼▼▽ **2000** Medium red-purple; the clean bouquet has an attractive savoury berry and positive oak mix; the palate is well weighted and structured, seamlessly bringing together dark chocolate, blackberry and oak flavours. Matured in a mix of French and American oak; no regional claim is made for the wine.   **rating:** 90

best drinking 2004–2009 **best vintages** '88, '90, '91, '92, '94, '96, '98, '00 **drink with** Soft ripened cheese • $30

Penley Estate Merlot

▼▼▼▼▽ **2000** Medium red-purple; a complex and aromatic savoury mix of spice, leaf and red berry is followed by a palate with good balance and structure, the flavours in the olive/savoury end of the spectrum, but neither green nor herbal; fine tannins and good length. A prime example of the variety. **rating:** 92

best drinking 2004–2009 **best vintages** '96, '00 **drink with** Braised veal • $29

Penley Estate Phoenix Cabernet Sauvignon

▼▼▼▼ **2001** Medium red-purple; juicy blackcurrant fruit and slightly edgy, spicy oak on the bouquet is followed by a ripe, plush palate with lots of blackcurrant and cassis fruit, the edgy oak nowhere to be seen. **rating:** 88

best drinking 2004–2009 **best vintages** '98 **drink with** Aged parmesan cheese • $22

Penley Estate Reserve Cabernet Sauvignon

▼▼▼▼▽ **2000** Medium red-purple; the bouquet has a range of cedary, earthy, black fruit aromas plus integrated oak; the elegant, gently ripe, cedary palate is well made and well balanced, but needed greater fruit intensity for higher points. **rating:** 90

best drinking 2005–2010 **best vintages** '89, '90, '91, '92, '94, '96, '97, '98, '99 **drink with** Rare beef • $62

penmara ★★★

Bridge Street, Muswellbrook, NSW 2333 **region** Upper Hunter Valley
phone (02) 9362 5157 **fax** (02) 9362 5157 **open** Not
winemaker John Horden **production** 30 000 cases **est.** 2000
product range The wines are made in three levels: at the bottom the Five Families range; next in the ladder the Reserve range; and finally the Individual Vineyard range made only in exceptional vintages. The varieties offered including Semillon, Verdelho, Shiraz, Merlot, Cabernet Sauvignon.
summary Penmara was formed with the banner '5 Vineyards: 1 Vision'. In fact a sixth vineyard has already joined the group, the vineyards pooling most of their grapes, with a central processing facility, and marketing focused exclusively on exports. The members are Lilyvale Vineyards, in the Northern Slopes region near Tenterfield; Tangaratta Vineyards at Tamworth; Birnam Wood, Rothbury Ridge and Martindale Vineyards in the Hunter Valley; and Highland Heritage at Orange. In all these vineyards give Penmara access to 128 hectares of shiraz, chardonnay, cabernet sauvignon, semillon, verdelho and merlot. Exports to the US, Canada, Singapore and Japan.

Penmara The Five Families Orange Sauvignon Blanc

▼▼▼▽ **2002** Pale straw-green; the bouquet is clean and crisp, but does not show much fruit; the palate picks up the pace a little, with good length and balance, the fruit, once again, far from exuberant. On the other hand, modestly priced. **rating:** 84

best drinking Now **drink with** Grilled eggplant • $13.95

Penmara The Five Families Orange Pinot Noir

▼▼▼▼ **2001** Medium red, with the purple hues starting to fade; a soft, faintly spicy bouquet has hints of plum jam and forest; the palate has surprising structure and flavour, its varietal origin very evident, the fine, silky tannins the strong point. Bargain basement price for a good pinot, which well outperforms expectations. **rating:** 87

best drinking Now–2006 **drink with** Wild mushroom risotto • $13.95

penna lane wines ★★★★

Lot 51, Penna Lane, Penwortham via Clare, SA 5453 **region** Clare Valley
phone (08) 8843 4364 **fax** (08) 8843 4349 **open** Thurs–Sun and public holidays 11–5, or by appointment
winemaker Contract **production** 2500 cases **est.** 1998
product range ($16–35 CD) Riesling, Semillon, Shiraz, The Willsmore Reserve Shiraz, Cabernet Sauvignon.
summary Ray and Lynette Klavin, then living and working near Waikerie in the Riverland, purchased their 14-hectare property in the Skilly Hills in 1993. It was covered with rubbish, Salvation Jane, a derelict dairy and a tumbledown piggery, and every weekend they travelled from Waikerie to clean up the property, initially living in a tent and thereafter moving into the dairy which had more recently been used as a shearing shed. Planting began in 1996, and in 1997 the family moved to the region, Lynette to take up a teaching position and Ray to work at Knappstein Wines. Ray had enrolled at Roseworthy in 1991, and met Stephen Stafford-Brookes, another mature-age student, and both graduated from Roseworthy in 1993, having already formed a winemaking joint venture for Penna Lane. Picnic and barbecue facilities are available at the cellar door, and light lunches are served. Exports to the US.

Penna Lane Riesling

▼▼▼▼ **2002** The colour is showing early development, although the hue is good; rich, tropical lime fruit aromas are reflected in every detail on the palate; a very rich, flavoursome, drink-now style. Atypical, but none the worse for that.   **rating:** 89

best drinking Now–2007 **drink with** Fresh asparagus • $17

Penna Lane Semillon

▼▼▼▼ **2002** Light yellow-green; the complex bouquet interplays herb, citrus and subtle oak; the palate is texturally rich, the oak adding to the flavour of the tropical-accented fruit. Spends 5 months maturing in older French oak.   **rating:** 89

best drinking Now–2007 **drink with** Calamari • $16

Penna Lane The Willsmore Shiraz

▼▼▼▼▼ **2001** Dense purple-red; compact, powerful, ripe blackberry fruit is supported by good oak on the bouquet; the rich and ripe palate has delicious accents ranging through black cherry to blackberry; tannin and oak management is exemplary. A blend of Barossa Valley and Clare Valley material, matured in French and American oak.   **rating:** 95

best drinking 2006–2016 **best vintages** '01 **drink with** Braised ox cheek • $35

penny's hill ★★★★

Main Road, McLaren Vale, SA 5171 **region** McLaren Vale
phone (08) 8556 4460 **fax** (08) 8556 4462 **open** 7 days 10–5
winemaker Ben Riggs (Contract) **production** 7000 cases **est.** 1988
product range ($19–44 R) Goss Corner Semillon, Chardonnay, Nobilis Botrytis Semillon, Shiraz, Grenache, Specialized Shiraz Cabernet Merlot, Fortified Shiraz.
summary Penny's Hill is owned by Adelaide advertising agency businessman Tony Parkinson and wife Susie. The Penny's Hill vineyard is 43.5 hectares and, unusually for McLaren Vale, is close-planted with a thin vertical trellis/thin vertical canopy, the work of consultant viticulturist David Paxton. The innovative red dot packaging was the inspiration of Tony Parkinson, recalling the red dot sold sign on pictures in an art gallery and now giving rise to the Red Dot Art Galley opening at Penny's Hill. Exports to the US, Canada, the UK, Switzerland, Denmark and Singapore.

Penny's Hill Goss Corner Semillon

▼▼▼▼ **2001** Light to medium yellow-green; the clean, firm minerally herb and grass bouquet is followed by a light to medium-bodied palate with pleasing mouthfeel; ready now. Follows very much in the footprints of the 2000, but is a better wine.   **rating:** 87

best drinking Now–2005 **drink with** Rich fish dishes • $19

Penny's Hill Chardonnay

▼▼▼▼▽ **2001** Light to medium yellow-green; clean, smooth nicely ripened nectarine fruit is married with balanced and integrated oak on the bouquet; the palate has plenty of depth and length to the nectarine fruit, rounded off with neatly handled oak.   **rating:** 90

best drinking Now–2005 **best vintages** '01 **drink with** Smoked chicken • $20.50

Penny's Hill Shiraz

▼▼▼▼ **2000** Medium red-purple; the bouquet is absolutely in the slot for the Penny's Hill style with savoury, chocolate and small dark berry aromas, the palate with a range of spice, chocolate, cedar and plums, the oak speaking quietly.   **rating:** 88

best drinking 2004–2010 **best vintages** '97, '98 **drink with** Roast ox kidney • $29

Penny's Hill Specialized

▼▼▼▼▽ **2001** Medium to full red-purple; the appealing bouquet has a range of spicy/chocolatey/berry aromas, the fruit much more lush and ripe on the palate, complemented by good oak handling and soft tannins.   **rating:** 90

best drinking 2006–2011 **best vintages** '01 **drink with** Veal shanks • $27

Penny's Hill Vintage Fortified Shiraz 500 ml

▼▼▼▼ **2001** Strong, deep red-purple; dark berry fruits with clean spirit on the bouquet, then a powerful, traditional style, a little drier than most (a good thing); good length and finish. I'm not entirely convinced about the price, however.   **rating:** 88

best drinking 2009–2016 **drink with** Blue cheese; nuts • $44

pennyweight winery ★★★☆

Pennyweight Lane, Beechworth, Vic 3747 **region** Beechworth
phone (03) 5728 1747 **fax** (03) 5728 1704 **open** 7 days 10–5
winemaker Stephen Newton Morris **production** 1000 cases **est.** 1982
product range ($16–30 CD) The table wines include Beechworth Riesling, Semillon Sauvignon Blanc, Gamay (light red), Pinot Noir, Shiraz, Cabernet; also important is the range of Oloroso, Fino and Amontillado Sherries and a range of Ports from Old Tawny, Ruby, Gold and Muscat.
summary Pennyweight was established by Stephen Morris, great-grandson of GF Morris, founder of Morris Wines. The 4 hectares of vines are not irrigated and are organically grown. The business is run by Stephen, together with his wife Elizabeth and assisted by their three sons; Elizabeth Morris says, 'It's a perfect world', suggesting Pennyweight is more than happy with its lot in life.

Pennyweight Beechworth Shiraz

▼▼▼▼ **2001** Medium red-purple; the moderately intense, clean bouquet has a range of blackberry, leafy and savoury aromas, characters which are replayed on the elegant palate, marked by fine, silky tannins. **rating:** 88
best drinking 2006–2011 **drink with** Free range duck • $25

peos estate NR

Graphite Road, Manjimup, WA 6258 **region** Manjimup
phone (08) 9772 1378 **fax** (08) 9772 1372 **open** 7 days 10–4
winemaker Cathy Oats (Contract) **production** 2000 cases **est.** 1996
product range ($15–30 CD) Unwooded Chardonnay, Four Aces Shiraz, Cabernet Sauvignon.
summary The Peos family has farmed the West Manjimup district for 50 years, the third generation of four brothers commencing the development of a substantial vineyard in 1996. In all, little over 33 hectares of vines, with shiraz (10 ha), merlot (7 ha), chardonnay (6.5 ha), cabernet sauvignon (4 ha) and pinot noir, sauvignon blanc and verdelho (2 ha each).

pepper tree wines ★★★☆

Halls Road, Pokolbin, NSW 2321 **region** Lower Hunter Valley
phone (02) 4998 7539 **fax** (02) 4998 7746 **open** Mon–Fri 9–5, weekends 9.30–5
winemaker Chris Cameron **production** 60 000 cases **est.** 1993
product range ($16–70 CD) Gewurztraminer, Sauvignon Blanc, Unwooded Chardonnay, Chardonnay, The Lake Chardonnay, Semillon Cuvee, Shiraz, Shiraz Merlot, Merlot, Cabernet Merlot Franc; Reserve range of Semillon, Sauvignon Blanc, Verdelho Semillon, Verdelho, Viognier, Chardonnay, Shiraz, Merlot, Cabernet Franc, Malbec, Cabernet Sauvignon; fortifieds.
summary The Pepper Tree winery is situated in the complex which also contains The Convent guesthouse and Roberts Restaurant. In October 2002 it was acquired by a company controlled by Dr John Davis, who owns 50 per cent of Briar Ridge and has substantial vineyard interests throughout NSW and SA. Pepper Tree has made a determined, and quite successful, effort to establish its reputation as one of Australia's leading producers of Merlot. Exports to the US, the UK, Switzerland, Singapore and Indonesia.

Pepper Tree Reserve Coonawarra Merlot

▼▼▼▼▽ **2000** Bright and clear red-purple; clean, deep varietal redcurrant and blackcurrant fruit aromas lead into a palate with excellent texture, structure and weight. Has very clear varietal fruit definition, simply needing more time in the cellar. **rating:** 93
best drinking 2006–2012 **best vintages** '96, '00 **drink with** Smoked lamb • $70

Pepper Tree Reserve Coonawarra Cabernet Sauvignon

▼▼▼▼▼ **2000** Medium to full red-purple; the complex bouquet brings abundant oak and ripe blackcurrant fruit together; the medium to full-bodied palate is smooth, with ripe tannins running throughout the blackcurrant fruit, and sweeter notes provided by the oak. Winner of the Jimmy Watson Trophy in 2001. **rating:** 94
best drinking 2006–2016 **best vintages** '98, '99, '00 **drink with** Fillet steak • $50

perrini estate NR

Bower Road, Meadows, SA 5201 **region** Adelaide Hills
phone (08) 8388 3210 **fax** (08) 8388 3210 **open** Wed–Sun and public holidays 10–5
winemaker Antonio Perrini **production** 3500 cases **est.** 1997

product range ($13–21.50 CD) Semillon Sauvignon Blanc, Unwooded Chardonnay, Shiraz, Merlot, Cabernet Sauvignon, Tony's Blend, Tawny Port.

summary Perrini Estate is very much a family affair; Tony and Connie Perrini had spent their working life in the retail food business, and Tony purchased the land in 1988 as a hobby farm and retirement home (or so Tony told Connie). In 1990 Tony planted his first few grapevines, began to read everything he could about making wine, and thereafter obtained vintage experience at a local winery. Next came highly successful entries into amateur winemaker competitions, and that was that. Together the family established the 6 hectares of vineyard and built the winery and cellar door, culminating in the first commercial releases of the 1997 vintage, and steadily increasing production thereafter. Exports to Singapore.

pertaringa ★★★★

Cnr Hunt and Rifle Range Roads, McLaren Vale, SA 5171 **region** McLaren Vale
phone (08) 8323 8125 **fax** (08) 8323 7766 **open** Mon–Fri 9–5, weekends and public holidays 11–5
winemaker Geoff Hardy, Ben Riggs **production** 6000 cases **est.** 1980
product range ($10–28 CD) Semillon, Sauvignon Blanc, Shiraz, Undercover Shiraz, Cabernet Sauvignon, Liqueur Frontignac; Grandis Red (Merlot Shiraz Petit Verdot), Grandis White (Semillon).
summary The Pertaringa wines are made from part of the grapes grown by leading viticulturists Geoff Hardy and Ian Leask. The Pertaringa vineyard of 31 hectares was acquired in 1980 and rejuvenated; establishment of the ultra-cool Kuitpo vineyard in the Adelaide Hills began in 1987 and now supplies leading makers such as Southcorp and Petaluma. Retail distribution through South Australia, New South Wales, Victoria and Queensland; exports to the UK, the US, Canada, Denmark, Germany, Hong Kong, Japan and New Zealand.

Pertaringa Sauvignon Blanc

▼▼▼▼ **2002** Light straw-green; the bouquet is clean and crisp, with a hint of capsicum, but lacking ripe fruit; the palate follows track, sustained by the clever use of residual sugar.   **rating:** 85
best drinking Now **drink with** Sashimi • $14

Pertaringa Undercover Shiraz

▼▼▼▼▽ **2001** Medium red-purple; clean, ripe blackberry and blackcurrant fruit merge with positive oak on the bouquet; the palate has blackberry and abundant dark chocolate fruit rounded off by ripe tannins. A very attractive wine at the right price.   **rating:** 90
best drinking 2005–2011 **drink with** Beef pie • $18

peschar's NR

179 Wambo Road, Bulga, NSW 2330 **region** Lower Hunter Valley
phone (02) 4927 1588 **fax** (02) 4927 1589 **open** Not
winemaker Tyrrell's (Contract) **production** 8000 cases **est.** 1995
product range ($14–18.50 ML) Chardonnay, Shiraz, Cabernet Merlot.
summary In 1995 John and Mary Peschar purchased the historic Meerea Park property which had been in the ownership of the Eather family, the name of which continues to be used by the Eathers for a quite separate winemaking operation. The property acquired by the Peschars is situated at the foot of the Wollemi National Park which rises steeply behind the vineyard, the latter being planted on sandy alluvial soils. There are 16 hectares of chardonnay, the wine being contract-made by Tyrrell's. While the focus is on Chardonnay, the Peschars have sourced 6 hectares of vines in the Limestone Coast Zone of South Australia for the production of Shiraz and Cabernet Merlot.

petaluma ★★★★★

Spring Gully Road, Piccadilly, SA 5151 **region** Adelaide Hills
phone (08) 8339 4122 **fax** (08) 8339 5253 **open** At Bridgewater Mill
winemaker Brian Croser **production** 30 000 cases **est.** 1976
product range ($19–90 R) Riesling, Chardonnay, Coonawarra (Cabernet Blend), Croser (Sparkling); Second label Sharefarmers White and Red. Bridgewater Mill is another label – see separate entry.
summary The Petaluma empire comprises Knappstein Wines, Mitchelton, Stonier and Smithbrook. In late 2001 the Petaluma group was acquired by New Zealand brewer Lion Nathan, but left Brian Croser in place. Croser has never compromised his fierce commitment to quality, and doubtless never will. The Riesling is almost monotonously good; the Chardonnay is the big mover, going from strength to strength; the Merlot another marvellously succulent wine to buy without hesitation. The wines are exported to the UK and the US.

Petaluma Hanlin Hill Riesling

♥♥♥♥♥ **2002** Brian Croser believes this to be one of the best Petaluma Rieslings to date, and it's not hard to see why. Bright, light straw-green, the very pure and seductive lime/lime blossom aromas are followed by a palate of similar purity; perfect balance and acidity mark a great wine. Terrific value. **rating:** 96

best drinking Now–2015 **best vintages** '80, '86, '94, '96, '97, '98, '00, '01, '02 **drink with** Blue swimmer crab • $21

Petaluma Forreston Viognier

♥♥♥♥♡ **2001** Medium to full yellow-green; a scented mix of ripe apricot and honey aromas, then a smooth and rounded palate with a slightly hot finish from the alcohol which, by analysis, is not particularly high at 13.8°. **rating:** 91

best drinking Now **drink with** Quiche Lorraine • $32

Petaluma Piccadilly Vineyard Chardonnay

♥♥♥♥♥ **2000** Medium yellow-green; typically understated but tightly focused melon and nectarine aromas interwoven with quality oak on the bouquet; the elegance, finesse and balance of the palate are an understatement rather than the reverse; the wine also has excellent length. **rating:** 94

best drinking Now–2008 **best vintages** '87, '90, '91, '92, '95, '96, '99, '00 **drink with** Slow-roasted Tasmanian salmon • $40

Petaluma Merlot

♥♥♥♥♥ **1999** Medium red-purple; a fragrant and aromatic bouquet opens with spice, cedar and forest, then veering more to berry/cherry; the palate has a very good silky texture, supported by quite persistent tannins which are in balance, and add to the length. **rating:** 94

best drinking Now–2008 **best vintages** '94, '95, '96, '97 **drink with** Veal • $53

Petaluma Coonawarra

♥♥♥♥♥ **2000** An acknowledged classic, created with a clear but different vision to most top-end Coonawarra reds. Vivid purple-red, the bouquet is satin smooth, with perfectly integrated red currant/cassis fruit and French oak, the supple, round, medium-bodied palate again showing impeccable balance and integration of fruit and oak. Iron glove, velvet fist. **rating:** 95

best drinking 2005–2020 **best vintages** '79, '86, '88, '90, '91, '92, '95, '97, '98, '99, '00 **drink with** Saddle of lamb • $59

peter lehmann ★★★★

Para Road, Tanunda, SA 5352 **region** Barossa Valley
phone (08) 8563 2100 **fax** (08) 8563 3402 **open** Mon–Fri 9.30–5, weekends and public holidays 10.30–4.30
winemaker Andrew Wigan, Peter Scholz, Leonie Lange, Ian Hongell, Nathan Norman **production** 200 000 cases **est.** 1979
product range ($12–75 CD) Blue Eden Riesling, Barossa Semillon, Chenin Blanc, Semillon Chardonnay, Chardonnay, Noble Semillon, Seven Surveys Grenache Shiraz Mourvedre, Shiraz, Shiraz Grenache, Cabernet Franc, Cabernet Sauvignon, Clancy's Red. Premium wines are Eden Valley Reserve Riesling, Reserve Semillon, Mentor, Stonewell Shiraz, Eight Songs Shiraz, Black Queen Sparkling Shiraz.
summary Public listing on the stock exchange has not altered the essential nature of the company, resolutely and single-mindedly focused on Peter Lehmann's beloved Barossa Valley. Some of the top-of-the-range wines are seriously good, the base range highly rated by the *Wine Spectator* and the International Wine & Spirit Competition. Exports to the UK through its own subsidiary; also to New Zealand, Europe, Asia, the South Pacific and the US.

Peter Lehmann Blue Eden Riesling

♥♥♥♥♡ **2002** Bright, pale straw-green; a spotlessly clean bouquet with lovely, light, lime blossom aromas is followed by a palate with excellent length and pronounced minerally acidity. At the very start of a life which will richly repay cellaring. **rating:** 91

best drinking 2007–2017 **best vintages** '02 **drink with** Sashimi • $20

Peter Lehmann Eden Valley Reserve Riesling

♥♥♥♥♥ **1997** Glowing yellow-green; a very complex, classic mix of toast, lime and kerosene aromas leads into a powerful, intense, dry style, with very good length and aftertaste. Gives you a good idea where the Blue Eden will be in 5 years time. Winner of the English International Wine & Spirit Competition Trophy for Best Riesling in 2002. **rating:** 94

best drinking Now–2007 **best vintages** '93, '96, '97 **drink with** Prosciutto and melon • $24

Peter Lehmann Reserve Semillon

▼▼▼▼ **1998** Glowing green-yellow; a particularly complex toasty/nutty bouquet with quasi-oak aromas introduces a powerful wine with lots of presence and grip. I have to admit that it challenges some of my views about Semillon and the Barossa Valley, although it is at the height of its power now.   **rating:** 89
best drinking Now–2006 **drink with** Yabbies • $25

Peter Lehmann Black Queen Sparkling Shiraz

▼▼▼▼▽ **1996** Medium red, with some purple hues remaining; the plummy core of the bouquet has distinct secondary savoury, earthy, spicy edges; the moderately complex palate has good length, is not too sweet, and puts one and two-year-old sparkling reds to shame.   **rating:** 92
best drinking Now–2008 **best vintages** '94 **drink with** Anything you like • $35

Peter Lehmann Noble Semillon 375 ml

▼▼▼▼ **2001** Glowing yellow-green; intense blossom botrytis aromas plus background oak open proceedings; the palate is not as intense as the bouquet suggests, but is nicely balanced in a tropical fruit salad mode.   **rating:** 89
best drinking Now **drink with** Fruit tart • $16

Peter Lehmann Barossa Shiraz

▼▼▼▼ **2001** Medium red-purple; a light, unpretentious and straightforward bouquet is followed by a palate which picks up the pace, offering pleasantly soft plum and blackberry fruit.   **rating:** 85
best drinking Now–2008 **best vintages** '89, '90, '91, '92, '94 **drink with** Spiced Barossa sausage • $20

Peter Lehmann Eight Songs Shiraz

▼▼▼▼▽ **1999** Medium red-purple; the moderately intense bouquet is smooth, clean and with well-integrated and balanced oak; the palate opens up, showing deep and dense sweet blackberry fruit, soft oak and ripe tannins.   **rating:** 90
best drinking 2004–2009 **best vintages** '96, '97, '98, '99 **drink with** Four 'n' Twenty pie • $55

Peter Lehmann Stonewell Shiraz

▼▼▼▼▼ **1998** Medium to full red-purple; the potent, complex, powerhouse bouquet of prune, blackberry and earth, quality oak playing a support role, leads into a lush blackberry and licorice palate; exemplary structure, lingering ripe tannins and quality oak.   **rating:** 95
best drinking 2008–2018 **best vintages** '80, '89, '91, '92, '93, '94, '96, '97 **drink with** Kangaroo fillet • $75

Peter Lehmann Clancy's

▼▼▼▼ **2001** Medium red-purple; soft, ripe, stewed plum aromas lead into a soft and easy palate, with plum, prune and a dash of oak. A blend of Shiraz, Cabernet Sauvignon and Merlot; good value.   **rating:** 85
best drinking Now–2007 **best vintages** '91, '92, '94, '96, '98 **drink with** Pasta with tomato or meat sauce • $12

Peter Lehmann Seven Surveys Grenache Shiraz Mourvedre

▼▼▼▼ **1999** Medium red-purple; the bouquet opens with soft, spicy jammy fruit, then some tobacco; the surprisingly firm palate brings some blackberry and dark chocolate into play, finishing with firm, savoury tannins.   **rating:** 86
best drinking 2004–2008 **drink with** Shepherd's pie • $20

Peter Lehmann The Mentor

▼▼▼▼▽ **1999** Medium to full red-purple, particularly good given the age of the wine; a complex array of blackberry, blackcurrant and mint fruit aromas are matched by the tangy, olive, berry and spice palate; good persistence and length; savoury tannins.   **rating:** 90
best drinking 2004–2009 **best vintages** '80, '89, '91, '93, '94, '95, '96, '97, '98, '99 **drink with** Spiced beef • $40

peterson champagne house   NR

Cnr Broke and Branxton Roads, Pokolbin, NSW 2320 **region** Lower Hunter Valley
phone (02) 4998 7881 **fax** (02) 4998 7882 **open** 7 days 9–5
winemaker Contract **production** 7000 cases **est.** 1994
product range ($17–39 CD) Chardonnay, Shiraz; Sparkling wines including Peterson House Gateway, Botrytis Semillon, Semillon Pinot Noir, Chardonnay Pinot Noir, Pinot Chardonnay Meunier, Shiraz, Merlot, Chambourcin, Cabernet Sauvignon.
summary Prominently and provocatively situated on the corner of Broke and Branxton Roads as one enters the main vineyard and winery district in the Lower Hunter Valley. It is an extension of the Peterson family

empire and, no doubt, very deliberately aimed at the tourist. While the dreaded word 'Champagne' has been retained in the business name, the wine labels now simply say Peterson House, which is a big step in the right direction. Almost all of the wine is sold through cellar door and through the wine club mailing list.

petersons ★★★★

Mount View Road, Mount View, NSW 2325 **region** Lower Hunter Valley
phone (02) 4990 1704 **fax** (02) 4991 1344 **open** Mon–Sat 9–5, Sun 10–5
winemaker Colin Peterson, Gary Reed **production** 15 000 cases **est.** 1971
product range ($19–48 CD) Semillon, Shirley Semillon, Show Reserve Semillon, Verdelho, Chardonnay, Cuvee Chardonnay, Samantha Sparkling, Botrytis Semillon, Pinot Noir, Shiraz, Back Block Shiraz, Ian's Selection Shiraz, Cabernet Sauvignon, Back Block Cabernet Sauvignon, Muscat, Vintage Port.
summary Ian and Shirley Peterson were among the early followers in the footsteps of Max Lake, contributing to the Hunter Valley renaissance which has continued to this day. Grape growers since 1971 and winemakers since 1981, the second generation of the family, headed by Colin Peterson, now manages the business. It has been significantly expanded to include 16 hectares at Mount View, a 42-hectare vineyard in Mudgee (Glenesk), and an 8-hectare vineyard near Armidale (Palmerston). In 2002 the winery won nine gold medals and three trophies, mainly at lesser shows.

Petersons Show Reserve Semillon
▼▼▼▼▽ 1995 Glowing yellow-green; a clean and complex lemon butter bouquet is followed by a palate which is as fresh as a daisy, held together by brisk, lemony acidity. Has further improvement in front of it yet. **rating:** 90
best drinking Now–2008 **best vintages** '95 **drink with** Grilled spatchcock • $35

Petersons Chardonnay
▼▼▼▼▽ 2001 Bright, medium green-yellow; the complex bouquet is largely driven by strong, toasty barrel-ferment oak, but on the palate generous peach, nectarine and fig fruit stages a major comeback; good mouthfeel, and not phenolic. **rating:** 91
best drinking Now–2006 **best vintages** '86, '95 **drink with** Yabbies • $26

Petersons Botrytis Semillon
▼▼▼▼▽ 2002 Medium yellow-green; the very complex bouquet has obvious botrytis and a generous slather of new oak; the powerful and complex palate replays the fruit and the oak of the bouquet, but with good acidity and bite. **rating:** 92
best drinking Now–2007 **drink with** Crème brûlée • $28.50

Petersons Ian's Selection Shiraz
▼▼▼▼ 2001 Medium red-purple; the bouquet has a regional mix of earth, stone and blackberry fruit, the powerful palate precisely following suit, with regional savoury, almost stony, notes. It carries its 14.5° alcohol with relative ease. **rating:** 89
best drinking 2006–2016 **drink with** Lamb shanks • $48

🍇 petrene estate NR

Muirillup Road, Northcliffe, WA 6262 **region** Pemberton
phone (08) 9776 7145 **fax** (08) 9776 7145 **open** Weekends and holidays 10.30–4
winemaker Contract **est.** 1994
product range Sauvignon Blanc, Chardonnay, Pinot Noir.
summary Peter Hooker and Irene Wilson have established 2 hectares of chardonnay, sauvignon blanc and pinot noir, the tiny production being contract-made.

🍇 pettavel ★★★★

65 Pettavel Road, Waurn Ponds, Vic 3216 **region** Geelong
phone (03) 5266 1120 **fax** (03) 5266 1140 **open** 7 days 10–5.30
winemaker Peter Flewellyn **production** 25 000 cases **est.** 2000
product range ($14–40 CD) Evening Star range with Sauvignon Blanc Semillon, Chardonnay, Cabernet Sauvignon Merlot; Platina range of Chardonnay, Pinot Noir, Cabernet Sauvignon; Emigre Shiraz.
summary This is a major new landmark in the Geelong region. Mike and wife Sandi Fitzpatrick sold their large Riverland winery and vineyards, and moved to Geelong where, in 1990, they began developing vineyards at Sutherlands Creek. Here they have been joined by daughter Robyn (who overseas management of the

business) and son Reece (who coordinates the viticultural resources). A striking and substantial winery was opened in time for the 2002 vintage, prior to which time the wines were contract made at Mount Langi Ghiran. The development also includes a modern tasting area adjacent to a restaurant which is open 7 days a week for lunch. The size of the development is such that it can accommodate private functions and corporate events for up to 180 seated guests. The quality of the initial releases is thoroughly impressive.

Pettavel Evening Star Chardonnay

TTTT 2001 Light to medium yellow-green; striking and unusual guava/tropical/floral fruit aromas are reflected in the fruit-driven palate, oak pushed into the background. Pleasing notwithstanding the unusual fruit characters. **rating:** 87

best drinking Now **drink with** Saffron risotto • $16

Pettavel Platina Chardonnay

TTTT 2001 Light to medium yellow-green; the fruit is altogether more subtle and restrained than that of the Evening Star Chardonnay, complemented by delicate, smoky oak. The tight melon and citrus fruit of the palate has absorbed the new and one-year-old French oak which the wine was fermented and matured, and has obvious development potential. **rating:** 89

best drinking Now–2006 **drink with** Pan-fried garfish • $20

Pettavel Platina Pinot Noir

TTTTY 2000 Strong red-purple, deep for the variety; dark plum fruit, spice and attractive oak aromas lead into a deep and powerful palate, arguably a touch over-extracted, but promising development potential and already providing a lingering, savoury aftertaste. **rating:** 90

best drinking Now–2006 **drink with** Quail braised in red wine • $25

Pettavel Emigre Shiraz

TTTTY 2000 Full red-purple; a powerful and complex bouquet with five-spice, black fruits and vanilla is followed by a rich, strongly structured palate which has devoured the American oak in which it spent 18 months. Should be long-lived. **rating:** 93

best drinking 2005–2015 **best vintages** '00 **drink with** Lamb Provençale • $40

pewsey vale ★★★★☆

PO Box 10, Angaston, SA 5353 **region** Eden Valley
phone (08) 8561 3200 **fax** (08) 8561 3393 **open** At Yalumba
winemaker Louisa Rose **production** 18 000 cases **est.** 1961
product range ($13.50–20 CD) Riesling, The Contour Riesling.
summary Pewsey Vale was a famous vineyard established in 1847 by Joseph Gilbert, and it was appropriate that when S Smith & Son (Yalumba) began the renaissance of the high Adelaide Hills plantings in 1961, they should do so by purchasing Pewsey Vale and establishing 40 hectares of riesling. After a dip in form, Pewsey Vale has emphatically bounced back to its very best. The Riesling has also finally benefited from being the first wine to be bottled with a Stelvin screwcap in 1977. While public reaction forced the abandonment of the initiative for almost 20 years, Yalumba/Pewsey Vale never lost faith in the technical advantages of the closure. Exports to all major markets.

Pewsey Vale Riesling

TTTT 2002 Light to medium straw-green; a crisp, dry bouquet with aromas of spice, apple and mineral, the palate more generous and ripe than the bouquet suggests, with nice balance. **rating:** 89

best drinking Now–2006 **best vintages** '69, '99, '00, '01 **drink with** Vegetable terrine • $13.50

pfeiffer ★★★☆

Distillery Road, Wahgunyah, Vic 3687 **region** Rutherglen
phone (02) 6033 2805 **fax** (02) 6033 3158 **open** Mon–Sat 9–5, Sun 11–4
winemaker Christopher Pfeiffer **production** 27 500 cases **est.** 1984
product range ($11.50–46.50 R) Under the Pfeiffer label Riesling, Chardonnay Semillon, Chardonnay, Frontignac, Auslese Tokay, Ensemble (light Rose-style), Gamay, Pinot Noir, Shiraz, Merlot, Cabernet Sauvignon, Christopher's Vintage Port, Old Distillery Tawny, Old Distillery Classic Tokay, Old Distillery Classic Muscat, Old Distillery Liqueur Gold (all cellar door only); Vintage Reserve range of Chardonnay, Sparkling Brut, Sparkling Pinot Noir, The Piper; also the Carlyle range of Riesling, Chardonnay, Marsanne, Late Harvest Riesling, Shiraz, Cabernet Sauvignon and Classic Rutherglen Muscat, sold through retail and export.

summary Ex-Lindeman fortified winemaker Chris Pfeiffer occupies one of the historic wineries (built 1880) which abound in northeast Victoria and which is worth a visit on this score alone. The fortified wines are good, and the table wines have improved considerably over recent vintages, drawing upon 32 hectares of estate plantings. The winery offers barbecue facilities, children's playground, gourmet picnic hampers, and dinners (by arrangement). Exports to the UK, Canada, Singapore and Taiwan (under the Carlyle label).

Pfeiffer Riesling

▼▼▼▼ **2002** Very pale straw-green; the clean, correct bouquet has a minerally spine with touches of lime blossom; the palate has excellent length and intensity, with similar flavours to those of the bouquet; presumably grown in the Alpine areas. Well made and good value. **rating:** 89

best drinking Now–2007 **best vintages** '02 **drink with** Caesar salad • $13.50

pfitzner ★★★★☆

PO Box 1098, North Adelaide, SA 5006 **region** Adelaide Hills
phone (08) 8390 0188 **fax** (08) 8390 0188 **open** Not
winemaker Petaluma (Contract) **production** 1500 cases **est.** 1996
product range ($16.50–19.95 R) Sauvignon Blanc, Chardonnay, Pinot Noir, Merlot.
summary The subtitle to the Pfitzner name is Eric's Vineyard. The late Eric Pfitzner purchased and aggregated a number of small, subdivided farmlets to protect the beauty of the Piccadilly Valley from ugly rural development. His three sons inherited the vision, with a little under 6 hectares of vineyard planted principally to chardonnay and pinot noir, plus small amounts of sauvignon blanc and merlot. Half the total property has been planted, the remainder preserving the natural eucalypt forest. The wines are made by Petaluma, and roughly half the production is sold in the UK. The remainder is sold through single retail outlets in Adelaide, Sydney, Melbourne and Perth.

Pfitzner Eric's Vineyard Sauvignon Blanc

▼▼▼▼▼ **2001** Light green-yellow; an attractive, aromatic and fresh bouquet has a mix of herb and ripe, citrussy fruits; the palate follows down precisely the same path, elegant, supple and harmonious; sweet citrussy fruit, with a crystal-clear, dry finish. **rating:** 94

best drinking Now–2005 **best vintages** '01 **drink with** Shellfish • $16.50

Pfitzner Eric's Vineyard Chardonnay

▼▼▼▼▽ **2000** Medium to full yellow-green; the bouquet is complex and tangy, with some secondary bottle-developed aromas, the French oak in the background. A smooth and supple palate with nectarine and fig fruit has very good flow and line. **rating:** 93

best drinking Now–2006 **best vintages** '98, '99, '00 **drink with** Terrine of scallops • $19.95

phaedrus estate ★★★★

220 Mornington-Tyabb Road, Moorooduc, Vic 3933 **region** Mornington Peninsula
phone 903) 5978 8134 **fax** (03) 5978 8134 **open** Weekends and public holidays 11–5
winemaker Ewan Campbell, Maitena Zantvoort **production** 1000 cases **est.** 1997
product range ($18–20 R) Pinot Gris, Chardonnay, Pinot Noir, Shiraz.
summary Ewan Campbell and Maitena Zantvoort established Phaedrus Estate in 1997. At that time both had already had winemaking experience with large wine companies, and were at the point of finishing their wine science degrees at Adelaide University. They decided they wished to (in their words) 'produce ultra-premium wine with distinctive and unique varietal flavours, which offer serious (and lighthearted) wine drinkers an alternative to mainstream commercial styles'. Campbell and Zantvoort believe that quality wines are made in the process involving both art and science, and I don't have any argument with that.

Phaedrus Estate Pinot Gris

▼▼▼▼▽ **2001** Light straw-green; the spotlessly clean and fragrant bouquet has a range of lemon and apple blossom aromas; the lively and fresh palate has all of the flavours of the bouquet, and an excellent finish; top class for the variety. **rating:** 92

best drinking Now–2005 **best vintages** '01 **drink with** Sushi • $18

Phaedrus Estate Chardonnay

▼▼▼▼▽ **2001** Light to medium straw-green; the clean bouquet has a subtle mix of malolactic and barrel-ferment characters, welding cashew and melon together; the light to medium-bodied palate has good length and balance, maturing quietly but surely. Nice fruit and subtle oak. **rating:** 90

best drinking Now–2007 **best vintages** '01 **drink with** Fishcakes • $18

Phaedrus Estate Pinot Noir

▼▼▼▼ 2001 Bright and clear red-purple; the moderately intense bouquet has a mix of plum and savoury spices; the tight and tangy palate shows plum, stem and spice flavours, finishing with marked acidity, and demanding more time.　　　　　　　　　　　　　　　　　　　　　　　　　　**rating:** 88

best drinking Now–2007　**drink with** Smoked quail • $20

phillip island vineyard　　　★★★★☆

Berrys Beach Road, Phillip Island, Vic **region** Gippsland
phone (03) 5956 8465　**fax** (03) 5956 8465　**open** 7 days 11–7 (Nov–March) 11–5 (April–Oct)
winemaker David Lance, James Lance **production** 3500 cases **est.** 1993
product range ($17–36.50 CD) Sea Spray (Sparkling), Sauvignon Blanc, Cape Woolamai Semillon Sauvignon Blanc, Summerland (Chardonnay), Newhaven (Riesling Traminer), Botrytis Chardonnay, Pinot Noir, The Nobbies (Pinot Noir), Merlot, Berry's Beach (Cabernet Sauvignon), Western Port, Pyramid Rock (Shiraz).
summary 1997 marked the first harvest from the 2.5 hectares of the Phillip Island Vineyard, which is totally enclosed in the permanent silon net which acts both as a windbreak and protection against birds. The quality of the wines across the board make it clear; this is definitely not a tourist trap cellar door, rather a serious producer of quality wine. Withdrawn from the market having been offered for sale in 2002. Exports to South-East Asia.

Phillip Island Vineyard Sauvignon Blanc

▼▼▼▼ 2002 Light green-yellow; a clean and fresh bouquet with mineral, gooseberry and passionfruit is followed by a light to medium-bodied palate showing the same flavours; good length and a dry finish. Fully priced.　　　　　　　　　　　　　　　　　　　　　　　　　　　　　　**rating:** 88

best drinking Now　**best vintages** '97, '99, '00, '01　**drink with** Fresh crab • $28

Phillip Island Vineyard Chardonnay

▼▼▼▼▽ 2001 Light to medium green-yellow, brilliant and clear; fresh stone fruit, melon and citrus aromas are faithfully reproduced on the palate, where the oak is barely perceptible; the wine has nice flow and feel, but will be even better in a year or two.　　　　　　　　　　　　　　　　　**rating:** 90

best drinking Now–2006　**best vintages** '98, '00　**drink with** Sautéed prawns • $29.80

Phillip Island Vineyard Botrytis Chardonnay

▼▼▼▼ 2001 Medium yellow-green; the bouquet has intense botrytis, along with a curious edge to the aromas reminiscent of deep-fried nettle; the palate opens with luscious peachy fruit balanced by acidity, but once again those nettle/bee sting characters lurk in the background.　　　　　　　　　**rating:** 87

best drinking Now–2005　**drink with** Fresh fruit • $30

Phillip Island Vineyard Pyramid Rock Shiraz

▼▼▼▼ 2001 Youthful red-purple; the bright bouquet has fresh, red berry fruit and touches of spice and oak; the light to medium-bodied palate is typically elegant, with fresh cherry fruit and fine tannins; notwithstanding its relatively light body, it does need time.　　　　　　　　　　　　　　　**rating:** 89

best drinking 2004–2008　**drink with** Beef kebabs • $24

Phillip Island Vineyard Merlot

▼▼▼▼▽ 2001 Medium red-purple; the moderately intense bouquet offers a mix of berry, earth, spice and cedar, the palate following down the same track with savoury overtones to the berry fruit, fine tannins and a cedary finish. Classic Old World Merlot style.　　　　　　　　　　　　　**rating:** 91

best drinking Now–2008　**best vintages** '01　**drink with** Roast veal • $36.50

Phillip Island Vineyard Berry's Beach Merlot

▼▼▼▼▽ 2001 Medium red-purple; the bouquet has a positive mix of ripe berry, raspberry and olive aromas in positive varietal mode. The palate moves into an even riper spectrum, with dark berry fruit and solid, ripe tannins. Sourced from the Yarra Valley.　　　　　　　　　　　　　　**rating:** 90

best drinking 2004–2009　**best vintages** '01　**drink with** Wild mushroom risotto • $26

Phillip Island Vineyard Cabernet Sauvignon

▼▼▼▼▽ 2000 Medium purple-red; the focused bouquet has exemplary cabernet cassis/currant fruit with some herb and olive overtones befitting the climate. The palate has excellent fruit weight and style, with classic cool climate cabernet flavour and lingering but ripe tannins. A classy wine from a vintage made in heaven for the variety in this neck of the woods.　　　　　　　　　　　　　　　　　　　**rating:** 94

best drinking 2005–2012　**best vintages** '97, '00　**drink with** Roast veal • $29.80

🐚 phillips brook estate ★★★★

Lot 2, Redmond–Hay River Road, Redmond, WA 6332 (postal) **region** Great Southern
phone (08) 9845 3124 **fax** (08) 9845 3126 **open** Not
winemaker Rob Diletti (Contract) **production** 450 cases **est.** 1975
product range ($15–20 R) Riesling, Cabernet Sauvignon.
summary Bronwen and David Newbury first became viticulturists near the thoroughly unlikely town of Bourke, in western New South Wales. They were involved with Dr Richard Smart in setting up the First Light vineyard, with the aim of making the first wine in the world each calendar year. Whatever marketing appeal the idea may have had, the wine was never going to be great, so in May 2001 they moved back to Western Australian and the Great Southern region. The name comes from the adjoining Phillips Brook Nature Reserve, and the permanent creek in their property which they assume is the Phillips Brook. 2.2 hectares of riesling and 2.4 hectares of cabernet sauvignon had been planted in 1975, but thoroughly neglected in the intervening years. The Newburys have rehabilitated the old plantings, and have added 4.9 hectares of chardonnay, 1.15 hectares of merlot, 0.83 hectares of cabernet franc and 0.71 hectares of sauvignon blanc (complementing a single row of old vines).

Phillips Brook Estate Riesling
▼▼▼▼▽ **2002** Light straw-green; the spotlessly clean bouquet is very discreet and unevolved, but the palate comes alive with bracing, minerally fruit and lively acidity providing length. Absolutely demands cellaring. **rating:** 90
best drinking 2005–2012 **best vintages** '02 **drink with** Leave it in the cellar • $15.95

🐚 phillips estate NR

Lot 964a Channybearup Road, Pemberton, WA 6230 **region** Pemberton
phone (08) 9776 0381 **fax** (08) 9776 0381 **open** By appointment
winemaker Phillip Wilkinson **production** 3000 cases **est.** 1996
product range ($20–40 ML) Riesling, Sauvignon Blanc, Pinot Noir, Shiraz, Shiraz Merlot, Merlot Cabernet Sauvignon.
summary Phillip Wilkinson has developed 4.5 hectares of vines framed by an old-growth Karri forest on one side and a large lake on the other. As well as the expected varieties, he has planted 1 hectare of zinfandel; so far as I know, it is the only example of this variety in the Pemberton region. Sophisticated winemaking techniques are used at the fermentation stage, but fining and filtration are either not used at all, or employed to a minimum degree. Exports to the UK.

piano gully NR

Piano Gully Road, Manjimup, WA 6258 **region** Manjimup
phone (08) 9772 3140 **fax** (08) 9316 0336 **open** By appointment
winemaker Michael Staniford (Contract) **production** 4000 cases **est.** 1987
product range ($14–22 ML) Chardonnay Sauvignon Blanc, Chardonnay, Pinot Noir, Cabernet Sauvignon Shiraz, Cabernet Sauvignon.
summary The 5-hectare vineyard was established in 1987 on rich Karri loam, 10 kilometres south of Manjimup, with the first wine made from the 1991 vintage. A change of ownership and winemaker has seen a dramatic lift in wine quality. For the record, the name of the road (and hence the winery) commemorates the shipping of a piano from England by one of the first settlers in the region. The horse and cart carrying the piano on the last leg of the long journey were within sight of their destination when the piano fell from the cart and was destroyed. Prior tastings showed the skills of contract winemaker Michael Staniford.

picardy ★★★★

Cnr Vasse Highway and Eastbrook Road, Pemberton, WA 6260 **region** Pemberton
phone (08) 9776 0036 **fax** (08) 9776 0245 **open** By appointment
winemaker Bill Pannell, Dan Pannell **production** 5000 cases **est.** 1993
product range ($25–60 CD) Chardonnay, Pinot Noir, Tete de Cuvee Pinot Noir, Shiraz, Merlot Cabernet.
summary Picardy is owned by Dr Bill Pannell and his wife Sandra, who were the founders of Moss Wood winery in the Margaret River region (in 1969). Picardy reflects Bill Pannell's view that the Pemberton area will prove to be one of the best regions in Australia for Pinot Noir and Chardonnay, but it is perhaps significant that the wines to be released include a Shiraz, and a Bordeaux-blend of 50 per cent Merlot, 25 per cent Cabernet Franc and 25 per cent Cabernet Sauvignon. Time will tell whether Pemberton has more Burgundy, Rhône or Bordeaux in its veins. Picardy has lost no time in setting up national distribution, and exports to the US, Japan, Indonesia, Malaysia, Hong Kong and France.

Picardy Chardonnay

▼▼▼▼▼ 2001 Medium yellow-green; complex but finely balanced fruit and oak on the bouquet lead into a truly excellent palate, with citrussy/melon fruit, a long, lingering finish and great aftertaste. **rating:** 95

best drinking Now–2005 **best vintages** '01 **drink with** Seared tuna • $25

Picardy Tete de Cuvee Pinot Noir

▼▼▼▼ 2000 The colour is very light, but the hue good; a fresh, light, strawberry-accented bouquet leads into an elegant, light to medium-bodied palate with good balance and length; well made; the limitations lie in the terroir. Packaged in a wonderful replica of a very old French Burgundy bottle. **rating:** 87

best drinking Now–2005 **drink with** Ragout of veal kidneys • $60

Picardy Shiraz

▼▼▼▼ 2001 Medium red-purple; lifted berry, leaf, spice and earth proclaims its cool climate origins; similar flavours run through the light to medium-bodied palate, which has good length and balance. **rating:** 89

best drinking 2004–2009 **best vintages** '97, '00 **drink with** Moroccan lamb • $32

piccadilly fields   NR

185 Piccadilly Road, Piccadilly, SA 5151 **region** Adelaide Hills
phone (08) 8370 8800 **fax** (08) 8232 5395 **open** Not
winemaker Sam Virgara **production** 2000 cases **est.** 1989
product range Chardonnay, Merlot Cabernet Franc Cabernet Sauvignon.
summary Piccadilly Fields has only a passing resemblance to its original state. The Virgara family has joined with a syndicate of investors which jointly own 176 hectares of vineyards through various parts of the Adelaide Hills, producing up to 1000 tonnes per year. The lion's share is sold as grapes to other winemakers; a token 30 or so tonnes is held for the Piccadilly Fields label.

pierro   ★★★★☆

Caves Road, Wilyabrup via Cowaramup, WA 6284 **region** Margaret River
phone (08) 9755 6220 **fax** (08) 9755 6308 **open** 7 days 10–5
winemaker Dr Michael Peterkin **production** 10 000 cases **est.** 1979
product range ($22.90–65 CD) Chardonnay, Semillon Sauvignon Blanc LTC, Cabernet Merlot.
summary Dr Michael Peterkin is another of the legion of Margaret River medical practitioners who, for good measure, married into the Cullen family. Pierro is renowned for its stylish white wines, which often exhibit tremendous complexity. The Chardonnay can be monumental in its weight and complexity. The wines are exported to the UK, the US, Japan and Indonesia.

Pierro Semillon Sauvignon Blanc LTC

▼▼▼▼▼ 2002 Light straw-green; a complex array of fruit aromas ranging from herb to faintly tropical, then a powerful, intense and long palate; excellent acidity and grip. **rating:** 94

best drinking Now–2006 **best vintages** '87, '89, '90, '94, '95, '97, '01, '02 **drink with** Turkey breast • $24

Pierro Chardonnay

▼▼▼▼▽ 2001 Medium yellow-green; a powerful, complex and rich bouquet with intense fruit plus potent barrel-ferment and malolactic-ferment influences is followed by a massively ripe and powerful palate, offering a replay of the bouquet. In archetypal Pierro style, taking no prisoners. **rating:** 90

best drinking 2004–2008 **best vintages** '86, '87, '89, '90, '92, '94, '95, '96, '00 **drink with** Seafood pasta • $65

Pierro Cabernet Merlot

▼▼▼▼ 2000 Medium red-purple; savoury/earthy overtones to the berry fruit of the bouquet are faithfully repeated on the palate, with the addition of oak and tannins. An altogether austere style. **rating:** 87

best drinking 2005–2012 **best vintages** '98 **drink with** Lamb shoulder • $60

piesse brook   NR

226 Aldersyde Road, Bickley, WA 6076 **region** Perth Hills
phone (08) 9293 3309 **fax** (08) 9293 3309 **open** Sat 1–5, Sun, public holidays 10–5, and by appointment
winemaker Di Bray, Ray Boyanich (Michael Davies, Consultant) **production** 1200 cases **est.** 1974
product range ($10–17.50 CD) Chardonnay, Shiraz, Brian Murphy Reserve Shiraz, Merlot, Cabernet Sauvignon, Cabernet Merlot, Cabernet Shiraz, Cabernova (early-drinking style).

summary Surprisingly good red wines are made in tiny quantities; they have received consistent accolades over the years. The first Chardonnay was made in 1993; a trophy-winning Shiraz was produced in 1995. Now has 4 hectares of chardonnay, shiraz, merlot and cabernet sauvignon under vine. Exports to the UK.

pieter van gent ★★★☆

Black Springs Road, Mudgee, NSW 2850 **region** Mudgee
phone (02) 6373 3807 **fax** (02) 6373 3910 **open** Mon–Sat 9–5, Sun 11–4
winemaker Pieter van Gent, Philip van Gent **production** 15 000 cases **est.** 1978
product range ($11.50–24 CD) The dry wines are Verdelho, Chardonnay, Muller Thurgau, Matador Shiraz, Alba Crest Cabernet Merlot, Conquistador Cabernet Sauvignon; the Flower of Florence, Angelic White, Sundance White, Sundance Soft Red all have varying degrees of sweetness; fortified wines are the specialty, including Pipeclay Port, Mudgee White Port, Cornelius Port, Mudgee Oloroso, Mistella, Pipeclay Vermouth, Liqueur Muscat.
summary Many years ago Pieter van Gent worked for Lindemans, before joining Craigmoor then moving to his own winery in 1979. Here, he and his family have forged a strong following, initially for his fortified wines, but now also for the table wines. Visits to Duyfken Studio (Goldsmith Sabine van Gent's jewelry) are available, as is accommodation at the Bushman's Cottage.

piggs peake NR

697 Hermitage Road, Pokolbin, NSW 2321 **region** Lower Hunter Valley
phone (02) 6574 7000 **fax** (02) 6574 7070 **open** Mon–Sat 10–4, Sun 10–3
winemaker Steve Dodd, Lesley Minter **production** 5000 cases **est.** 1998
product range ($14–20 CD) Pokolbin Semillon, Lovedale Semillon, Pokolbin Verdelho, Rylstone Chardonnay, Lovedale Premium Chardonnay, Mudgee Botrytis Semillon, Hunter Valley Shiraz, Hunter Valley Merlot, Mudgee Tempranillo Cabernet.
summary The derivation of the name remains a mystery to me, and if it is a local landmark, I have not heard of it. Certain it is that it is one of the newest wineries to be constructed in the Hunter Valley, sourcing most of its grapes from other growers to complement the 1 hectare of estate plantings.

pikes ★★★☆

Polish Hill River Road, Sevenhill, SA 5453 **region** Clare Valley
phone (08) 8843 4370 **fax** (08) 8843 4353 **open** 7 days 10–4
winemaker Neil Pike, John Trotter **production** 35 000 cases **est.** 1984
product range ($14–24 CD) Riesling, Sauvignon Blanc Semillon, Viognier, Chardonnay, Shiraz, Shiraz Grenache Mourvedre, Premio Sangiovese, Merlot, Cabernet Sauvignon; Luccio.
summary Owned by the Pike brothers, one of whom (Andrew) was for many years the senior viticulturist with Southcorp; the other (Neil) is a former winemaker at Mitchell. Pikes now has its own winery, with Neil Pike presiding. Generously constructed and flavoured wines are the order of the day. The wines are exported to the UK, Switzerland, Ireland, Germany, Belgium, The Netherlands, Denmark, Japan, Hong Kong, Malaysia, New Zealand, the US and Canada.

Pikes Riesling
▼▼▼▼ 2002 Very light straw-green; the crisp bouquet has mineral, slate and earth aromas, together with a touch of lift; the palate has strong structure, the wine still locked up in itself. Paradoxically, one of the Clare Rieslings from 2002 to be released with a conventional cork closure. **rating:** 87
best drinking 2004–2009 **best vintages** '86, '90, '92, '93, '95, '97, '00 **drink with** Lightly spiced chicken salad • $21

Pikes Luccio (White)
▼▼▼▼ 2001 Light straw-green; firm mineral aromas are joined by touches of lemon citrus on the bouquet, all these characters coming together on the fresh palate, which has a pleasingly dry finish. An offbeat blend of Chardonnay, Sauvignon Blanc, Semillon and Pinot Gris, taking its name from the Italian word for pike. **rating:** 86
best drinking Now **drink with** Antipasto • $14

Pikes Shiraz
▼▼▼▼ 2000 Light to medium red-purple; moderately intense, direct and clean cherry/berry fruit on the bouquet leads into a palate with a mix of red berry, cherry and chocolate, finishing with smooth tannins and gentle oak. Good extract management provides the right texture and structure. **rating:** 88
best drinking 2004–2009 **best vintages** '85, '86, '90, '91, '93, '98 **drink with** Char-grilled rump • $24

Pikes Luccio (Red)

TTTT 2000 Medium red-purple; a tangy and lively bouquet of cherry and citrus is followed by a palate with interesting texture and mouthfeel, and slippery/rubbery tannins. A blend of Sangiovese, Merlot and Cabernet Sauvignon. **rating: 85**

best drinking Now–2005 **drink with** Pasta • $14

Pikes Merlot

TTTT 2000 Light to medium red-purple; savoury, spicy aromas and subtle oak on the bouquet are followed by similarly savoury/earthy flavours with fairly persistent tannins, all the component parts holding together well. **rating: 87**

best drinking 2004–2009 **drink with** Lamb Provençale • $24

pike & joyce   NR

Mawson Road, Lenswood, SA 5240 (postal)   **region** Adelaide Hills
phone (08) 8843 4370   **fax** (08) 8843 4353   **open** Not
winemaker Neil Pike, John Trotter   **production** 2000 cases   **est.** 1998
product range ($19–28 ML) Sauvignon Blanc, Pinot Gris, Chardonnay, Pinot Noir.
summary As the name suggests, this is a partnership between the Pike family (of Clare Valley fame) and the Joyce family, related to Andrew Pike's wife Cathy. The Joyce family have been orchardists at Lenswood for over 100 years, but also have extensive operations in the Riverland. Together with Andrew Pike (formerly chief viticulturist for the Southcorp group) they have established 18.5 hectares of vines, with the lion's share of the plantings going to pinot noir, sauvignon blanc and chardonnay, followed by merlot, pinot gris and semillon. The wines are made at Pikes Clare winery and are distributed nationally by Tucker Seabrook, with exports to the UK, the US and Japan.

pinelli   ★★★☆

30 Bennett Street, Caversham, WA 6055   **region** Swan Valley
phone (08) 9279 6818   **fax** (08) 9377 4259   **open** Mon–Fri 9–5.30, weekends 10–5
winemaker Robert Pinelli, Daniel Pinelli   **production** 7000 cases   **est.** 1979
product range ($10–14 CD) Chenin Blanc, Verdelho, Unwooded Chardonnay, Late Harvest Semillon, Scarlet (medium sweet red), Shiraz, Cabernet Sauvignon, Tawny Port.
summary Dominic Pinelli and son Robert – the latter a Roseworthy Agricultural College graduate – sell 75 per cent of their production in flagons but are seeking to place more emphasis on bottled wine sales in the wake of recent show successes with Chenin Blanc.

Pinelli Verdelho

TTTT 2002 Light straw-green; spice, mineral and passionfruit aromas flow into a palate with pleasing lime and passionfruit in a flavoursome duo; clean finish; impressive late-picked style. **rating: 88**

best drinking Now–2005 **drink with** Ginger prawns • $11

pinnacle wines   ★★★★

50 Pinnacle Road, Orange, NSW 2800   **region** Orange
phone (02) 6365 3316   **open** By appointment
winemaker David Lowe, Jane Wilson (Contract)   **production** 200 cases   **est.** 1999
product range ($22 ML) Pinot Gris.
summary Peter Gibson began the establishment of Pinnacle Wines with the planting of 2 hectares of pinot gris in 1999 on the slopes of Mount Canobolas at an elevation of around 1000 metres. The vineyard is close to Brangayne of Orange, and Peter Gibson says that Brangayne's success played a considerable part in his decision to plant the vineyard. One hectare of viognier is yet to come into production, and over 2002–2003 1 hectare of pinot noir using the new Burgundy clone 777 115 and 114 in conjunction with MV6, plus a little riesling, will bring the total to 4 hectares.

Pinnacle Pinot Gris

TTTTY 2002 Light straw-green; a spotlessly clean bouquet with pear and apple aromas is followed by an attractively tight wine, with bell-clear pear and apple fruit, good balance and length. Way above average. **rating: 90**

best drinking Now–2005 **best vintages** '02 **drink with** Grilled scampi • $22

pipers brook vineyard ★★★★☆

1216 Pipers Brook Road, Pipers Brook, Tas 7254 **region** Northern Tasmania
phone (03) 6382 7527 **fax** (03) 6382 7226 **open** 7 days 10–5
winemaker Rene Bezemer **production** 69 430 cases **est.** 1974
product range ($14.95–69.20 CD) The basic Estate varietals of Riesling, Gewurztraminer, Pinot Gris, Chardonnay, Pinot Noir; next Reserve Chardonnay and Pinot Noir; then Single Site Upper Slopes Riesling, Summit Chardonnay and The Lyre Pinot Noir; Opimian (Cabernet Blend). Also the Ninth Island range of Riesling, Sauvignon Blanc, Straits Dry White, Pinot Grigio, Frontignac, Chardonnay, Botrytis Riesling, Rose, Pinot Noir, Cuvee Tasmania, Tamar Cabernets; Wavecrest range of Riesling, Sauvignon Blanc Semillon, Chardonnay, Cabernet.
summary The Pipers Brook Tasmanian empire has over 220 hectares of vineyard supporting the Pipers Brook and Ninth Island labels, with the major focus, of course, being on Pipers Brook. As ever, fastidious viticulture and winemaking, immaculate packaging and enterprising marketing constitute a potent and effective blend. Pipers Brook operates two cellar-door outlets, one at headquarters, and one at Strathlyn (phone 03 6330 2388). In 2001 it became yet another company to fall prey to a takeover, in this instance by Belgian-owned sheepskin business Kreglinger, which has also established a large winery and vineyard at Mount Benson in South Australia. The wines are exported to the UK, Europe, the US, Japan, Canada and Singapore, and are distributed throughout Australia by S Smith & Son. In a seismic and utterly unexpected eruption in February 2003, Andrew Pirie's services were abruptly terminated.

Pipers Brook Vineyard Estate Riesling

▼▼▼▼▽ 2002 Light straw-green; a crystal-clear and fragrant bouquet with lime blossom aromas is followed by a beautifully balanced palate ranging through apple to lime, with a fine, filigreed finish and acidity. **rating:** 93
best drinking 2005–2015 **best vintages** '79, '82, '84, '85, '92, '93, '98, '99, '00, '02 **drink with** Pan-fried scallops • $25.35

Pipers Brook Vineyard Estate Gewurztraminer

▼▼▼▼ 2002 Light to medium green-yellow; the clean and fresh bouquet has somewhat muted varietal character; the palate has some spicy notes and the faintly phenolic grip which is often part and parcel of the variety. **rating:** 87
best drinking Now–2006 **best vintages** '99, '00, '01 **drink with** Duck liver pâté • $27.80

Pipers Brook Vineyard Estate Pinot Gris

▼▼▼▼ 2001 Medium straw-yellow; an array of tropical/pineapple, citrus and mineral aromas and flavours indicate a very ripe wine by Tasmanian standards; ends up a fraction loose, with the alcohol (13.2°) evident. **rating:** 89
best drinking Now **best vintages** '00 **drink with** Steamed fish, Chinese style • $23.65

Ninth Island Pinot Noir

▼▼▼▼ 2002 Medium to full red-purple; clean plummy fruit aromas lead into a palate with considerable richness and ripeness, the plummy fruit of the bouquet supported by sweet, soft tannins. Neither particularly complex, nor particularly long, but right now a pleasure to drink. **rating:** 89
best drinking Now **best vintages** '00, '01, '02 **drink with** Osso buco • $23.65

Pipers Brook Vineyard The Lyre Pinot Noir

▼▼▼▼▼ 2000 From a single site, chosen as the best of an exceptional vintage, oozing class but with its best years still in front of it. Bright purple-red, the clean, power-laden bouquet of complex dark plum is followed by a palate flooded with fruit, yet retaining finesse; very fine tannins. Ultimate quality. **rating:** 97
best drinking Now–2012 **best vintages** '99, '00 **drink with** Coq au vin • $69.20

piromit wines NR

113 Hanwood Avenue, Hanwood, NSW 2680 **region** Riverina
phone (02) 6963 0200 **fax** (02) 6963 0277 **open** Mon–Fri 9–5
winemaker Dom Piromalli, Pat Mittiga **production** 60 000 cases **est.** 1998
product range ($8–17 CD) Semillon, Old Briggie Semillon Chardonnay, Colombard Chardonnay, Chardonnay, Botrytis Semillon, Shiraz, Old Briggie Shiraz Cabernet, Cabernet Merlot, Cabernet Sauvignon.
summary I simply cannot resist quoting directly from the background information kindly supplied to me. 'Piromit Wines is a relatively new boutique winery situated in Hanwood, New South Wales. The winery complex, which crushed 1000 tonnes this season (2000), was built for the 1999 vintage on a 14-acre site which

was until recently used as a drive-in. Previous to this, wines were made on our 100-acre vineyard. The winery site is being developed into an innovative tourist attraction complete with an Italian restaurant and landscaped formal gardens.' It is safe to say that this extends the concept of a boutique winery into new territory, but then it is a big country. It is a family business run by Pat Mittiga, Dom Piromalli and Paul Hudson.

pirramimma ★★★★

Johnston Road, McLaren Vale, SA 5171 **region** McLaren Vale
phone (08) 8323 8205 **fax** (08) 8323 9224 **open** Mon–Fri 9–5, Sat 11–5, Sun, public holidays 11.30–4
winemaker Geoff Johnston, Simon Parker **production** 40 000 cases **est.** 1892
product range ($8.50–26.50 R) Stocks Hill Semillon Chardonnay, Adelaide Hills Semillon, McLaren Vale Semillon, Stocks Hill Semillon Chardonnay, Hillsview Chardonnay, Stocks Hill Shiraz, Petit Verdot, Hillsview Cabernet Merlot, Cabernet Sauvignon, Ports.
summary An operation with large vineyard holdings of very high quality and a winery which devotes much of its considerable capacity to contract-processing fruit for others. In terms of the brand, has been a consistent under-performer during the 1990s. The marketing of the brand does scant justice to the very considerable resources available to it, notably its gold medal-winning Petit Verdot and fine, elegant Chardonnay. Exports to the US, Canada, the UK, Germany, Switzerland, Malaysia, Singapore, Japan and New Zealand. Rated on the basis of previous tastings.

pizzini ★★★☆

King Valley Road, Wangaratta, Vic 3768 **region** King Valley
phone (03) 5729 8278 **fax** (03) 5729 8495 **open** 7 days 12–5
winemaker Alfred Pizzini, Joel Pizzini, Mark Walpole **production** 12 000 cases **est.** 1980
product range ($14–40 CD) Bianco, Riesling, Sauvignon Blanc, Arneis, Chardonnay, Verduzzo, Rosetta, Shiraz, Merlot, Sangiovese, Nebbiolo, Shiraz Cabernet, Cabernet.
summary Fred and Katrina Pizzini have been grape growers in the King Valley for over 20 years, and have 66 hectares of vineyard. Grape growing (rather than winemaking) still continues to be the major focus of activity, but their move into winemaking has been particularly successful, and I can personally vouch for their Italian cooking skills. It is not surprising, then, that their wines should span both Italian and traditional varieties. The rating is now perilously close to four stars. Exports to Hong Kong and China.

Pizzini Riesling
▼▼▼▼ 2002 Light straw-green; the crisp, delicate, flowery bouquet has faint blossom aromas; the palate has more weight, and heads off in another direction altogether, with slightly broad, ripe citrus fruit. **rating:** 85
best drinking Now–2005 **drink with** Deep-fried zucchini flowers • $14

Pizzini Sauvignon Blanc
▼▼▼▼ 2002 Light straw-green; the clean, minerally bouquet has herb and fruit spice aromatics; the fruit on the palate is crisp and delicate. The wine has surprising length, and has been well made. **rating:** 87
best drinking Now **drink with** Cold seafood • $14.50

Pizzini Bianco
▼▼▼▽ 2002 Light straw-green; the fresh bouquet is neutral in terms of fruit, as is the palate, although the components come together quite well on the bottom line. A blend of Chardonnay, Sauvignon Blanc and Verduzzo. **rating:** 84
best drinking Now **drink with** Lemon chicken • $14

Pizzini Verduzzo
▼▼▼▽ 2002 Light straw; spice and ripe fruit aromas precede a palate with ripe apple and hints of peach, thickening on the finish. Seems much higher in alcohol than the 12.5° it in fact has; more to do with texture than flavour. **rating:** 84
best drinking Now **drink with** Antipasto • $18

Pizzini Arneis
▼▼▼▼ 2002 Bright light green-yellow; a spotlessly clean and floral bouquet with a mix of lemon and apple blossom flows into a bright palate of apple and ripe pear, then an appealing bony/minerally finish. **rating:** 88
best drinking Now–2006 **drink with** Tempura • $20

Pizzini Chardonnay

▼▼▼▼ 2001 Pale straw-yellow; subtle fig, melon and creamy cashew aromas flow into a light to medium-bodied, elegant palate where the malolactic influence adds to the complexity without destroying the fruit.   **rating:** 87

best drinking Now **drink with** Chicken nuggets • $16

Pizzini Rosetta

▼▼▼▼ 2002 Bright pink; clean, spicy, fresh fruit aromas are followed by a focused and intense palate, not at all bitter, and with good length. A Rose made from Sangiovese.   **rating:** 88

best drinking Now–2005 **drink with** Antipasto • $14

Pizzini Shiraz

▼▼▼▼ 1999 Medium to full red-purple; the bouquet has a range of spice, licorice, earth and dark fruit aromas; the palate has plenty of flavour and concentration; ripe tannins and confident oak usage round off one of a number of impressive wines under the Pizzini label.   **rating:** 89

best drinking 2004–2009 **drink with** Ravioli • $20

Pizzini Shiraz Cabernet

▼▼▼▼ 2000 Medium red-purple; abundant blackberry fruit and oak in a support role, then a tight and savoury palate with good length and (once again) neatly handled, positive oak.   **rating:** 87

best drinking Now–2008 **drink with** Roast kid • $20

Pizzini Nebbiolo

▼▼▼▼ 1999 Full red, moving towards garnet; a fragrant mix of spice and crushed leaf on the bouquet is followed by a medium to full-bodied palate with savoury black fruits, and that pure acidity characteristic of the variety. Impressive.   **rating:** 89

best drinking 2004–2009 **drink with** Herbed rack of lamb • $40

Pizzini Cabernet Sauvignon

▼▼▼▼ 1999 Bright, clear red-purple; blackberry and mulberry fruit is supported by subtle oak on the bouquet; the medium-bodied palate opens with blackberry, then moves through to more gently earthy flavours, closing with well-balanced tannins.   **rating:** 86

best drinking 2004–2009 **drink with** Lamb backstrap • $20

plantagenet ★★★★

Albany Highway, Mount Barker, WA 6324 **region** Great Southern
phone (08) 9851 2150 **fax** (08) 9851 1839 **open** Mon–Fri 9–5, weekends 10–4
winemaker Gavin Berry **production** 55 000 cases **est.** 1974
product range ($11–38 CD) Riesling, Omrah Sauvignon Blanc, Omrah Chardonnay (unoaked), Mount Barker Chardonnay, Fronti, Fine White, Fine Red, Eros, Pinot Noir, Shiraz, Henry II, Cabernet Sauvignon, Mount Barker Brut; Breakaway Fine White, Fine Red.
summary The senior winery in the Mount Barker region, making superb wines across the full spectrum of variety and style – highly aromatic Riesling, tangy citrus-tinged Chardonnay, glorious Rhône-style Shiraz and ultra-stylish Cabernet Sauvignon. Exports to the US, the UK, Germany, Austria, Singapore, Japan, Switzerland and Hong Kong.

Plantagenet Mount Barker Riesling

▼▼▼▼▽ 2001 Light straw-green; strong kerosene characters are already emerging on the bouquet, and likewise on the powerful, grippy palate; in metamorphosis, but will age, albeit at the big end of town.   **rating:** 90

best drinking Now–2007 **best vintages** '81, '83, '86, '92, '94, '95, '96, '97, '00, '01 **drink with** Most Asian dishes • $16.50

Plantagenet Omrah Sauvignon Blanc

▼▼▼▼▽ 2002 A controversial wine which was a trophy winner at the 2002 Perth Wine Show, and a strong silver medal at the 2002 Qantas Wine Show of Western Australia. It is an exceptionally powerful and intense Sauvignon Blanc with great length and carry; the problem lies with the reduced/sweaty characters on the bouquet. Some are forgiving of this character, seeing it is a legitimate part of varietal expression; others are intolerant of it. This wine stands poised on the razor's edge, and is all the more interesting for that.   **rating:** 92

best drinking Now **best vintages** '00, '02 **drink with** Shellfish • $16

Plantagenet Hazard Hill Semillon Sauvignon Blanc

▼▼▼▼ 2002 A new second string for Plantagenet, attesting to the volume of these varieties from new plantings in Western Australia. Light straw-green; the clean and crisp aromas of lemon, gooseberry and grass flow into an easily accessed palate, the citrussy fruit neatly balanced by a subliminal hint of sweetness. **rating: 89**

best drinking Now best vintages '02 drink with Cold seafood • $11

Plantagenet Mount Barker Shiraz

▼▼▼▼▽ 2000 Medium red-purple; fragrant aromas of spice, cedar and blackberry lead into a palate with complex structure; black cherry and spice flavours provide the initial impact, then lingering tannins and a long, savoury finish. The wine incorporates some material from Geographe for the first time. **rating: 90**

best drinking 2004–2012 best vintages '82, '83, '85, '88, '89, '90, '91, '93, '94, '96, '98, '99 drink with Hare, squab • $38

Plantagenet Omrah Shiraz

▼▼▼▼ 2001 Medium purple-red; the moderately intense bouquet has blackberry, spice and neatly integrated oak; the fleshy, gently ripe and smooth palate has a nice touch of cedar and ripe tannins. Very good value. Produced from grapes grown in the Great Southern and Geographe regions. **rating: 88**

best drinking 2004–2007 best vintages '99 drink with Lamb shashlik • $17

Plantagenet Hazard Hill Shiraz Grenache

▼▼▼▼ 2001 Vivid, youthful purple-red; a complex, rich and concentrated bouquet with gamey aromas; a very big, concentrated palate, with lots of fruit and even more tannins; amazing for the price. Simply claims a 'Western Australia' appellation; it's likely that there is some northern material in it. **rating: 87**

best drinking 2004–2009 drink with Marinated beef • $12

Plantagenet Omrah Cabernet Merlot

▼▼▼▼ 2001 Medium red-purple; the bouquet has a mix of blackcurrant, mulberry and redcurrant aromas; the medium-bodied palate has authentic, if somewhat austere, fruit and savoury tannins to close. Sixty per cent Merlot and 40 per cent Cabernet Sauvignon from the Great Southern, Blackwood Valley and Geographe regions. **rating: 86**

best drinking 2004–2007 best vintages '99 drink with Fish with red wine sauce • $17

Plantagenet Mount Barker Cabernet Sauvignon

▼▼▼▼▽ 1999 Medium red-purple; a fragrant, savoury bouquet with red berry, earth and olive aromas is followed by a palate with excellent black and redcurrant fruit made more complex by the savoury characters of the bouquet. Lots of good things happening here. **rating: 92**

best drinking 2004–2009 best vintages '81, '83, '85, '86, '90, '91, '94, '98, '99 drink with Rack of lamb • $28

platt's   NR

Murray Valley Highway, Browns Plains via Rutherglen, Vic 3685 **region** Rutherglen
phone (02) 6032 9381 **fax** (02) 6372 1055 **open** 7 days 9–5
winemaker Barry Platt **production** 4000 cases **est.** 1983
product range ($9–12 CD) Chardonnay, Semillon, Gewurztraminer, Cabernet Sauvignon.
summary District veteran Barry Platt has moved the cellar door to the historic (but now renovated) Fairfield Winery, which was built in 1895. The 8 hectares of estate vineyards in Mudgee are supplemented by purchased grapes from other Mudgee growers, and the business has grown substantially. Platt's elects not to enter the Mudgee Wine Show, and it is many years since I have tasted the wines.

plunkett   ★★★★

Cnr Hume Highway and Lambing Gully Road, Avenel, Vic 3664 **region** Strathbogie Ranges
phone (03) 5796 2150 **fax** (03) 5796 2147 **open** 7 days 11–5 (cellar door), Thurs–Mon 11–5 (restaurant)
winemaker Sam Plunkett, Victor Nash **production** 15 000 cases **est.** 1980
product range ($16–35 CD) The top-of-the-range wines are released under the Strathbogie Ranges label: Riesling, Chardonnay, Reserve Shiraz, Merlot, Reserve Merlot, Cabernet Merlot, Tawny Port; standard wines are under the Blackwood Ridge brand: Gewurztraminer, Sauvignon Blanc, Unwooded Chardonnay, Pinot Noir, Shiraz.
summary The Plunkett family first planted grapes way back in 1968, establishing 1.2 hectares with 25 experimental varieties. Commercial plantings commenced in 1980, and 100 hectares are now under vine, with more coming. While holding a vigneron's licence since 1985, the Plunketts did not commence serious marketing of the wines until 1992, and have now settled down into producing an array of wines which are

pleasant and well priced; the Reserves are in another quality and price league. Wholesale distribution to all states; exports to Malaysia, Canada and Hong Kong.

Plunkett Strathbogie Ranges Riesling

ŶŶŶŶ **2002** Light straw-green; full and ripe lime and tropical fruit aromas and flavours make the wine ideal for early drinking. The palate is soft, rather than broad, and a touch of CO_2 helps lift the finish. **rating:** 88

best drinking Now–2007 **drink with** Stir-fried prawns • $16

Plunkett Strathbogie Ranges Reserve Shiraz

ŶŶŶŶŶ **2001** Full red-purple; the bouquet is replete with dark berry fruits, blackberry and spice; the palate is likewise flooded with sweet blackberry fruit nicely supported by sweet oak and ripe, fine tannins. **rating:** 90

best drinking 2005–2010 **best vintages** '98, '00, '01 **drink with** Rich Lebanese dishes • $35

Plunkett Strathbogie Ranges Reserve Merlot

ŶŶŶŶ **2000** Medium to full red-purple; the bouquet offers a mix of ripe, sweet berry, spice, herb and earth; the powerful and concentrated palate adds a distinct touch of mint to the mix, finishing with quite powerful tannins. Demands patience; perhaps more varietal character will emerge with time. **rating:** 89

best drinking 2005–2010 **drink with** Lamb Provençale • $35

poet's corner wines ★★★★☆

Craigmoor Road, Mudgee, NSW 2850 **region** Mudgee
phone (02) 6372 2208 **fax** (02) 6372 4464 **open** Mon–Fri 10–4.30, weekends and public holidays 10–4
winemaker James Manners **production** NFP **est.** 1858
product range ($10–22R) Semillon Sauvignon Blanc Chardonnay, Unwooded Chardonnay, Shiraz Cabernet Sauvignon Cabernet Franc; PC range of Chardonnay, Merlot, Pinot Chardonnay; Henry Lawson range of Semillon, Chardonnay, Shiraz, Cabernet Sauvignon; also home to the Craigmoor and Montrose labels.
summary Poet's Corner is located in one of the oldest wineries in Australia to remain in more or less continuous production: Craigmoor (as it was previously known) was built by Adam Roth in 1858/1860. His grandson Jack Roth ran the winery until the early 1960s. It is the public face for Poet's Corner, Montrose and Craigmoor wines, all of which are made at the more modern Montrose winery (which is not open to the public).

Henry Lawson Semillon

ŶŶŶŶŶ **2001** Pale straw-green; clean and crisp, ranging through mineral, grass and herb; the palate is a replay, but with the all-important length and balance. If you want flavour, simply wait for 5 years and it will all happen. **rating:** 90

best drinking 2006–2016 **best vintages** '00, '01 **drink with** Tempura • $17

Henry Lawson Chardonnay

ŶŶŶŶŶ **2001** Light to medium yellow-green; the complex bouquet shows obvious barrel-ferment French oak inputs alongside stone fruit and cashew; the oak is far less obvious on the palate, where citrus and stone fruit flavours predominate; good length, and developing slowly. Good value. **rating:** 90

best drinking Now **drink with** Breast of turkey • $17

Montrose Stony Creek Chardonnay

ŶŶŶŶŶ **2001** Light to medium yellow-green; a restrained and subtle bouquet and palate, as yet very light; as its history suggested it might, it has developed very well. It is still at the elegant, understated end of the spectrum, but with perfect fruit and oak balance. A great bargain, which starred in the 2003 *Divine* Magazine State of Origin Chardonnay Challenge. **rating:** 94

best drinking Now–2005 **best vintages** '01 **drink with** Veal fricassée • $15

pokolbin estate NR

McDonalds Road, Pokolbin, NSW 2321 **region** Lower Hunter Valley
phone (02) 4998 7524 **fax** (02) 4998 7765 **open** 7 days 10–6
winemaker Contract **production** 2500 cases **est.** 1980
product range ($14.50–40 CD) Riesling, Semillon, Chardonnay, Show Reserve Chardonnay, Late Harvest Riesling, Shiraz; Verdelho Solera, Tawny and Vintage Port.
summary An unusual outlet, offering its own label wines, made under contract by Trevor Drayton, together with other Hunter Valley wines; also cheap varietal 'cleanskins'. Wine quality under the Pokolbin Estate label has been very modest, although the 1997 Hunter Riesling (perversely, true Riesling, not Semillon) won a silver medal and was the top-pointed wine in its class at the 1997 Hunter Valley Wine Show. No recent news.

politini wines   NR

PO Box 27, Cheshunt, Vic 3678 **region** King Valley
phone (03) 5729 8277 **fax** (03) 5729 8373 **open** Not
winemaker Contract **est.** NA
product range ($14.50–21 ML) Sauvignon Blanc, Chardonnay, Shiraz, Merlot, Cabernet Sauvignon.
summary Another new venture in the King Valley region, by grape growers turned (partially) winemakers.

polleters   ★★★★

Polleters Road, Moonambel, Vic 3478 (postal) **region** Pyrenees
phone (03) 9569 5030 **open** Not
winemaker Mark Summerfield **production** 500 cases **est.** 1994
product range ($17.50–25 ML) Shiraz, Shiraz Merlot, Shiraz Cabernet, Merlot, Cabernet Franc.
summary Pauline and Peter Bicknell purchased the 60-hectare property on which their vineyard now stands in 1993, at which time it was part of a larger grazing property. The first vines were planted in spring 1994, and there are now 2 hectares each of shiraz and cabernet sauvignon, 1.25 hectares of cabernet franc and 0.75 hectare of merlot. In the first few years the grapes were sold, but as from 2001 part of the production has been taken for their own impressively rich and powerful wines. The grapes are hand-picked, fermented in open vats with hand plunging, and matured for 18 months in American oak. Since their first shows in 2002, all the entries have received silver medals.

Polleters Shiraz
▼▼▼▼ 2001 Dense purple-red; powerful blackberry, prune and licorice aromas precede a massive palate, the fruit having gobbled up the American oak in which it has been aged. A 15° alcohol special, tailor-made for the American market.   **rating:** 88
best drinking 2005–2015 **drink with** Rare rump steak • $25

Polleters Shiraz Merlot Cabernet Franc
▼▼▼▼▽ 2001 Deep purple-red; dense dark blackberry and blackcurrant aromas lead into another powerhouse palate, with blackberry and bitter chocolate flavours and balanced oak. 14.5° alcohol.   **rating:** 90
best drinking 2006–2016 **drink with** Braised ox cheek • $25

Polleters Shiraz Cabernet
▼▼▼▼ 2001 Full purple-red; complex touches of gum leaf and spice to the blackberry and blackcurrant fruit of the bouquet lead into a palate with less power but more elegance, reflecting the (near) 14° alcohol.   **rating:** 87
best drinking 2006–2011 **drink with** Irish stew • $17.50

Polleters Merlot
▼▼▼▼ 2001 Dense red-purple; powerful black fruit, plum and herb aromas are supported by well-balanced oak; the flavour-filled, rich, sweet and luscious palate says much about red wine and rather less about Merlot. 14.5° alcohol.   **rating:** 88
best drinking 2006–2012 **drink with** Roast veal chops • $25

pontville station   ★★★★

948 Midland Highway, Pontville, Tas 7030 **region** Southern Tasmania
phone (03) 6268 1635 **open** Not
winemaker Peter Rundle **production** 90 cases **est.** 1990
product range ($17–25 ML) Dessert Riesling, Pinot Noir.
summary Peter and Jane Rundle have a tiny vineyard of 0.5 hectare, mainly planted to pinot noir. Because the vineyard has been established in a frost-prone site, they have from time to time purchased small quantities of grapes from other growers, but in February 2002 they were able to make the first commercial vineyard release, hot on the heels of winning a silver medal with each wine at the 2002 Tasmanian Wines Show, the Pinot Noir in one of the strongest Pinot classes ever seen in Australia, and the Dessert Riesling coming second in its class.

Pontville Station Pinot Noir
▼▼▼▼ 2001 Bright purple-red; plum, spice, forest and oak aromas lead into a palate which opens with ripe, smooth plum fruit but is then swamped by oak. Split opinions at the 2003 Tasmanian Wines Show.   **rating:** 85
best drinking Now–2006 **best vintages** '00 **drink with** Braised quail • $25

poole's rock ★★★☆

De Beyers Road, Pokolbin, NSW 2321 **region** Lower Hunter Valley
phone (02) 9563 2500 **fax** (02) 9563 2555 **open** 7 days 10–5
winemaker Patrick Auld **production** 75 000 cases **est.** 1988
product range ($14.95–27.95 R) Chardonnay; Firestick Chardonnay, Shiraz Cabernet Sauvignon.
summary Sydney merchant banker David Clarke has had a long involvement with the wine industry. The 18-hectare Poole's Rock vineyard, planted purely to chardonnay, is his personal venture, the resource initially bolstered by the acquisition of the larger Simon Whitlam Vineyard (adjoining). However, the purchase of the 74-hectare Glen Elgin Estate upon which the 2500-tone former Tulloch winery is situated takes Poole's Rock (and its associated brand Cockfighter's Ghost) into another dimension. The wine has retail distribution throughout Australia and is exported to Europe, the US, Canada, New Zealand and Asia.

Poole's Rock Chardonnay
ŦŦŦŦ 2001 Glowing yellow-green, quite developed; the complex bouquet with yellow peach and toasty oak is followed by a rich, generously flavoured, peachy palate; drink asap. **rating:** 88
best drinking Now **best vintages** '92, '93, '95, '98, '99, '01 **drink with** Creamy pasta • $24.95

Poole's Rock Firestick Chardonnay
ŦŦŦŦ 2001 Light to medium yellow-green; quite complex smoky oak and melon fruit aromas mark the bouquet; the palate is more driven by gentle melon and white peach fruit than oak; well made, with good balance and length. From Mount Compass and Langhorne Creek. **rating:** 86
best drinking Now **drink with** Smoked eel • $14.95

pooley wines ★★★☆

Cooinda Vale Vineyard, Barton Vale Road, Campania, Tas 7026 **region** Southern Tasmania
phone (03) 6224 3591 **fax** (03) 6224 3591 **open** Tues–Sun 10–5
winemaker Mat Pooley, Andrew Hood (Contract) **production** 1500 cases **est.** 1985
product range ($16–40 CD) Coal River Riesling, Coal River Chardonnay, Nellie's Nest Pinot Noir, Cooinda Vale Pinot Noir, Coal River Pinot Noir; Reserve Range of Coal River Pinot Gris, Family Reserve Pinot Noir, Family Reserve Cabernet Merlot.
summary Three generations of the Pooley family have been involved in the development of the Cooinda Vale Estate; it was indeed under the Cooinda Vale label that the winery was previously known. After a tentative start on a small scale, plantings have now reached 8 hectares on a property which covers both sides of the Coal River in a region which is substantially warmer and drier than most people realise. The wines have limited retail distribution in Victoria (Sutherland Fine Wines) and of course in Tasmania. Limited exports to the UK and the US.

Pooley Coal River Riesling
ŦŦŦŦ 2001 Light to medium yellow-green; a rich and ripe bouquet with lime and pineapple aromas, suggesting the possibility of a small amount of botrytis, is followed by a palate with abundant flavour in the lime/tropical spectrum. At its best now and over the next few years. **rating:** 89
best drinking Now–2006 **drink with** Trout mousse • $20

Pooley Pinot Noir
ŦŦŦŦ 2001 Light to medium red-purple; a wine which is in every sense in stark contrast to the Family Reserve; has some finesse, with sappy, foresty offsets to the small dark fruit flavours. **rating:** 87
best drinking Now–2006 **drink with** Breast of duck • $24

Pooley Family Reserve Pinot Noir
ŦŦŦŦŸ 2001 Medium red, with some purple hues remaining; complex, ripe, stewed plum aromas lead into a powerful, complex and rich palate, the structure good and the fruit as ripe as the bouquet suggests it will be. Strangely, very nearly a top-class wine, but slightly over the top. **rating:** 91
best drinking Now–2007 **best vintages** '01 **drink with** Smoked quail • $40

Pooley Nellie's Nest Pinot Noir
ŦŦŦŦ 1998 Light red; light, savoury, secondary fruit aromas are now well in the ascendant; the palate has an attractive, light, fully mature style. **rating:** 85
best drinking Now **drink with** Spatchcock • $16

poplar bend   NR

RMB 8655, Main Creek Road, Main Ridge, Vic 3928 **region** Mornington Peninsula
phone (03) 5989 6046 **fax** (03) 5989 6460 **open** Weekends and public holidays 10–5, and by appointment
winemaker David Briggs **production** 350 cases **est.** 1988
product range ($16–28 CD) Pineau Chloe, Cabernet Chloe, Sparkling Chloe, Pinot Noir, Cellar Reserve Pinot Noir, Cabernet Shiraz.
summary Poplar Bend was the child of Melbourne journalist, author and raconteur Keith Dunstan and wife Marie, who moved into full-scale retirement in 1997, selling Poplar Bend to David Briggs. The changes are few; the label still depicts Chloe in all her glory, which could be calculated to send the worthy inhabitants of the Bureau of Alcohol, Tobacco and Firearms (of the US) into a state of cataleptic shock.

port phillip estate   ★★★★

261 Red Hill Road, Red Hill, Vic 3937 **region** Mornington Peninsula
phone (03) 5989 2708 **fax** (03) 5989 3017 **open** Weekends and public holidays 11–5
winemaker Lindsay McCall (Contract) **production** 4000 cases **est.** 1987
product range ($15–35 CD) Sauvignon Blanc, Chardonnay, Pinot Noir, Reserve Pinot Noir, Reserve Shiraz, Shiraz.
summary Established by leading Melbourne QC Jeffrey Sher, who, after some prevarication, sold the estate to Giorgio and Dianne Gjergja in February 2000. The Gjergjas are rightly more than content with the quality and style of the wines; the main changes are enhanced cellar-door facilities and redesigned labels.

Port Phillip Estate Chardonnay

YYYY 2001 Light to medium yellow-green; a clean, direct melon fruit and subtle oak bouquet; the medium-bodied palate mirrors the bouquet, and while not particularly complex, does have nice flavour.   **rating:** 87
best drinking Now–2006 **best vintages** '96, '97, '98 **drink with** Lobster, shellfish • $18

Port Phillip Estate Pinot Noir

YYYYY 2001 Medium purple-red; clean, fresh and bright strawberry/cherry aromas are joined by hints of leaf and mint; the palate moves more to strawberry and plum, and has good mouthfeel and fine tannins. Its elegance took it to top gold medal in class 10 at the 2002 National Wine Show.   **rating:** 94
best drinking Now–2007 **best vintages** '94, '01 **drink with** Quail • $30

Port Phillip Estate Shiraz

YYYY 2001 Medium red-purple; the moderately intense bouquet has a savoury mix of cherry, plum and spice aromas; the light to medium-bodied palate is gently complex, but needs more substance for higher points.
    rating: 86
best drinking 2004–2008 **drink with** Stewed oxtail • $30

portree   ★★★★

72 Powells Track via Mount William Road, Lancefield, Vic 3455 **region** Macedon Ranges
phone (03) 5429 1422 **fax** (03) 5429 2205 **open** Weekends and public holidays 11–5
winemaker Ken Murchison **production** 1000 cases **est.** 1983
product range ($15–38 CD) Chardonnay, Aged Release Chardonnay, Macedon (Blanc de Blanc, cellar door only), Pinot Noir, Damask (Cabernet Franc Rose), Quarry Red (Cabernet Franc Merlot).
summary Owner Ken Murchison selected his 5-hectare Macedon vineyard after studying viticulture at Charles Sturt University and being strongly influenced by Dr Andrew Pirie's doctoral thesis. All the wines show distinct cool-climate characteristics, the Quarry Red having clear similarities to the wines of Chinon in the Loire Valley. However, it is with Chardonnay that Portree has done best; it is its principal wine (in terms of volume). As from the 1998 vintage, the wines have been made at an on-site winery.

Portree Macedon Ranges Chardonnay

YYYY 2001 Light to medium yellow-green; the citrussy, minerally bouquet has minimal oak. The clean and direct palate has crisp acidity, all calling out for time in bottle. However, it will never approach the esoteric opulence of the 2000.   **rating:** 89
YYYYY 2000 Medium yellow-green; a complex and somewhat funky bouquet leads into a powerful, very intense, very long and very complex palate with a lingering aftertaste. An in-your-face style which will appeal to some but not others.   **rating:** 94
best drinking 2005–2010 **best vintages** '91, '93, '97, '98, '00 **drink with** Fish terrine • $28

port stephens winery   NR

69 Nelson Bay Road, Bobs Farm, NSW 2316 **region** Northern Rivers Zone
phone (02) 4982 6411 **fax** (02) 4982 6766 **open** 7 days 10–5
winemaker Contract **production** 3500 cases **est.** 1984
product range ($10.50–21.50 CD) Unwooded Chardonnay, Tri-Blend, Tomaree White, Golden Sands, Tomaree Red, Reserve Shiraz, Cabernet Merlot, Reserve Cabernet Sauvignon, sparkling, fortifieds.
summary Planting of the quite substantial Port Stephens Wines vineyard began in 1984, and there are now 4 hectares of vines in production. The wines are contract made in the Hunter Valley but are sold through the attractive Boutique Wine Centre on-site, which has recently been extended to offer over 100 wines from 30 wineries, including those as far afield as Manjimup in Western Australia.

pothana   ★★★☆

Pothana Lane, Belford, NSW 2335 **region** Lower Hunter Valley
phone (02) 6574 7164 **fax** (02) 6574 7209 **open** By appointment
winemaker David Hook **production** 5000 cases **est.** 1984
product range ($16–30 ML) Pothana Semillon, Chardonnay, Shiraz; also The Gorge range of Mosto (Semillon), Semillon, Semillon Sauvignon Blanc, Verdelho, Pinot Grigio, Unwooded Chardonnay, Chardonnay, Pinot Noir, Shiraz. All are estate-grown; the Pothana range is produced in tiny quantities (250 cases) and then only in the best vintages.
summary With over 20 years' experience, David Hook worked as a winemaker for Tyrrell's and Lake's Folly, also doing the full Flying Winemaker bit, with jobs in Bordeaux, the Rhône Valley, Spain, the US and Georgia. He and his family began the establishment of the vineyard in 1984 and the winery in 1990. The wines are available by mailing list, but have distribution by Grapelink in New South Wales and Victoria, Queensland and Tasmania by Prime Wines.

The Gorge Mosto
♥♥♥♥ **2002** Light green-gold; the bouquet wobbles around with lots of CO_2 and SO_2 obscuring the fruit; the palate is fresh, distinctly effervescent, and of spatlese sweetness. A totally deliberate style, with the fermentation stopped to provide both the sweetness and effervescence.   **rating:** 84
best drinking Now **drink with** A summer morning • $20

The Gorge Chardonnay
♥♥♥♥ **2002** Medium yellow-green; the moderately complex bouquet has slightly dusty oak, the soft peach and stone fruit flavours of the palate given a cursory lick of oak; marginally more interesting than the unwooded version.   **rating:** 85
best drinking Now **drink with** Salmon pizza • $16

The Gorge Shiraz
♥♥♥♥ **2001** Medium red-purple; a regional leather and spice overlay on a core of red fruits gives the bouquet complexity and typicity; there is a similar mix of cherry and more savoury flavours on the palate, which does, however, lighten off somewhat towards the finish.   **rating:** 87
best drinking Now–2006 **drink with** Rack of lamb • $16

potters clay vineyards   ★★★

Main Road, Willunga, SA 5172 **region** McLaren Vale
phone (08) 8556 2799 **fax** (08) 8556 2922 **open** Not
winemaker John Bruschi **production** 900 cases **est.** 1994
product range ($15.90–16.90 R) Chardonnay, Shiraz, Merlot Cabernet Franc.
summary John and Donna Bruschi are second-generation grape growers who assumed full ownership of the 16-hectare Potters Clay Vineyard in 1994 with the aim of establishing their own winery and label. In 1999 construction of stage one of a two-stage boutique winery was completed. Stage one is a winery production facility, stage two (at some future date) is to be cellar door, restaurant and garden/picnic area. At least this is in the correct order; all too often it is the cellar door and restaurant which come first. The clever packaging and high-quality promotional literature should do much to enhance sales.

powercourt vineyard   NR

2 McEwans Road, Legana, Tas 7277 **region** Northern Tasmania
phone (03) 6330 1225 **fax** (03) 6330 2161 **open** By appointment

powercourt vineyard

winemaker Ralph Power **production** 1000 cases **est.** 1972
product range ($18 CD) Pinot Noir, Cabernet Pinot, Cabernet Sauvignon.
summary A long-established but ultra-low profile winery with a mostly local clientele, but also retail distribution in Canberra.

preston peak ★★★

31 Preston Peak Lane, Toowoomba, Qld 4352 **region** Granite Belt
phone (07) 4630 9499 **fax** (07) 4630 9499 **open** Wed–Sun 10–5
winemaker Philippa Hambleton, Rod MacPherson **production** 17 500 cases **est.** 1994
product range ($12–27 CD) Leaf Series range of Semillon, Sauvignon Blanc, Verdelho, Chardonnay, Shiraz, Merlot, Cabernet Merlot; Wild Flower White, Wild Flower Red, Venus, Reserve Chardonnay, Reserve Shiraz, Cabernet Merlot; sparkling, fortified.
summary After faltering for a while, the ambitious growth plans of dentist owners Ashley Smith and Kym Thumpkin have been largely realised. The large, modern cellar door can accommodate functions of up to 150 people, and is often used for weddings and other events. It is situated less than 10 minutes' drive from the Toowoomba city centre, and has views of Table Top Mountain, the Lockyer Valley and the Darling Downs. There is no charge for tastings, but bookings for groups of more than 20 people are appreciated.

Preston Peak Verdelho
▼▼▼▼ 2002 Light straw-green; the pungent and aromatic bouquet is more reminiscent of Sauvignon Blanc than Verdelho, and the crisp and lively palate heads in much the same direction. All this simply makes for an interesting variation, and there is certainly no problem with the winemaking. Finished with a Stelvin cap. The grapes are 100 per cent Granite Belt. **rating:** 85
best drinking Now **drink with** Tempura • $17

Preston Peak Reserve Shiraz
▼▼▼▼ 2000 Medium to full red-purple; the clean bouquet ranges through raspberry, spice, leaf and mint. The pleasantly rounded palate has raspberry and blackberry fruit supported by well-balanced oak and tannins. Nice wine. **rating:** 87
best drinking Now–2008 **drink with** Spaghetti bolognese • $23

preveli wines ★★★★

Bessell Road, Rosa Brook, Margaret River, WA 6285 **region** Margaret River
phone (08) 9757 2374 **fax** (08) 9757 2374 **open** By appointment
winemaker Andrew Gamen Jnr, Frank Kittler (Contract) **production** 2000 cases **est.** 1995
product range ($16.45–29.95 R) Semillon, Semillon Sauvignon Blanc Reserve, Shiraz, Merlot, Cabernet Sauvignon.
summary Andrew and Greg Home have been the owner/operators of the caravan and camping ground at Prevelly Beach for over a decade. They also operate a liquor store, and have long been noted for the quality and diversity of the wines sold at the store. In 1995 they began planting a vineyard at Rosa Brook, where they have 1.6 hectares of cabernet sauvignon and 0.8 hectare each of semillon and merlot in production, with 0.6 hectare of pinot noir still to come into bearing. They supplement their estate production with purchases from the Jester Flats, Hayes and White vineyards at Rosa Brook. Their first releases, and in particular those from 2001, are excellent.

Preveli Semillon Sauvignon Blanc Reserve
▼▼▼▼ 2001 Light straw-green; the bouquet is complex, with obvious but well-integrated oak and soft tropical fruit underneath. The palate similarly shows a lot of oak influence which, while integrated, tends to drive the wine. Partially barrel fermented then matured in French oak for 8 months. **rating:** 88
best drinking Now–2005 **drink with** Crumbed brains

Preveli White
▼▼▼▼ 2001 Light straw-green; the bouquet has ripe fruit, complexed by subtle oak; a similar interplay occurs on the palate, with the ripe fruit (100 per cent estate-grown semillon), almost into the white peach spectrum, counterweighted with a touch of oak. **rating:** 88
best drinking Now–2006 **drink with** Caesar salad

Preveli Shiraz

▼▼▼▼▼ 2001 Bright, full purple-red; abundant, rich, dark fruit aromas are interwoven with well-integrated American oak; the palate has strong texture, structure and depth, with lush mid-palate blackberry and plum fruit, then fine tannins to close. Fermented and matured in new American oak, sourced from the Casas Vineyard near Rosabrook. Gold medal 2002 Sheraton Wine Awards.   **rating:** 94

best drinking 2004–2014 **best vintages** '01 **drink with** Rare roast beef

primo estate ★★★★☆

Old Port Wakefield Road, Virginia, SA 5120 **region** Adelaide Plains
phone (08) 8380 9442 **fax** (08) 8380 9696 **open** June–Aug Mon–Sat 10–4, Sep–May Mon–Fri 10–4
winemaker Joseph Grilli **production** 20 000 cases **est.** 1979
product range ($14–50 CD) La Biondina Colombard, Joseph d'Elena Pinot Grigio, Joseph La Magia Botrytis Riesling Traminer, Il Briccone Shiraz Sangiovese, Joseph Moda Amarone Cabernet Merlot, Joseph The Fronti, Joseph Sparkling Red.
summary Roseworthy dux Joe Grilli has risen way above the constraints of the hot Adelaide Plains to produce an innovative and always excellent range of wines. The biennial release of the Joseph Sparkling Red (in its tall Italian glass bottle) is eagerly awaited, the wine immediately selling out. Also unusual and highly regarded are the vintage-dated extra virgin olive oils. However, the core lies with the zingy, fresh Colombard, the velvet-smooth Adelaide Shiraz and the distinguished, complex Joseph Cabernet Merlot. National distribution through Negociants; exports to the UK, Asia and Europe.

Primo Estate La Biondina Colombard

▼▼▼▼ 2002 Light straw-green; the bouquet has distinct smoky/sweaty reduction, making it more Sauvignon Blanc-like than ever; some of the same characters come through on the palate, again with totally striking similarities to Sauvignon Blanc. Others will be more forgiving of the reduced aromas.   **rating:** 85

best drinking Now **best vintages** '99, '00, '01 **drink with** Shellfish • $14.90

Primo Estate Il Briccone Shiraz Sangiovese

▼▼▼▼▽ 2001 A thoroughly fashionable Italianate blend of predominantly shiraz and sangiovese with lesser amounts of barbera, nebbiolo and cabernet sauvignon. Scented, savoury, spicy dark berry aromas lead into a powerful palate with definite Italian overtones coming from its firm structure and lingering, savoury flavours and tannins. Go Joe.   **rating:** 92

best drinking Now–2008 **best vintages** '00, '01 **drink with** Bruschetta • $20

Primo Estate Joseph Moda Amarone Cabernet Merlot

▼▼▼▼▽ 2000 Medium to full red-purple; intense and powerful blackberry allied with touches of plum and leather mark the bouquet; there are rich and full dark fruit flavours on entry to the mouth, then lingering, savoury tannins through the mid-palate to the finish.   **rating:** 93

best drinking 2004–2011 **best vintages** '81, '84, '86, '90, '91, '93, '94, '95, '96, '97, '98, '00 **drink with** Bistecca Fiorentina • $47

prince albert ★★★★

100 Lemins Road, Waurn Ponds, Vic 3216 **region** Geelong
phone (03) 5241 8091 **fax** (03) 5241 8091 **open** By appointment
winemaker Bruce Hyett **production** 500 cases **est.** 1975
product range ($24.20 ML) Pinot Noir.
summary Australia's true Pinot Noir specialist (it has only ever made the one wine), which also made much of the early running with the variety: the wines always show good varietal character and have rebounded after a dull patch in the second half of the 1980s. In 1998 the vineyard and winery was certified organic by OVAA Inc. Apart from the mailing list, the wine is sold through fine wine retailers in Sydney and Melbourne, with a little finding its way to the UK.

Prince Albert Pinot Noir

▼▼▼▼ 2001 Light to medium red-purple, the hue bright and clear; the bouquet has a gently complex mix of cherry, strawberry and a savoury touch, all of which translate directly into the fine, elegant, light to medium-bodied palate. Deceptively effortless.   **rating:** 88

best drinking Now–2006 **best vintages** '97, '98, '00 **drink with** Game pie • $24.10

provenance wines ★★★★

Pollocksford Road, Barrabool, Vic 3221 **region** Geelong
phone (03) 5265 6055 **fax** (03) 5265 6077 **open** By appointment
winemaker Scott Ireland **production** 2000 cases **est.** 1995
product range ($23–29 R) Pinot Gris, Chardonnay, Pinot Noir, Shiraz.
summary Provenance is the reborn Melbourne Wine Company, with Scott Ireland its principal and sole winemaker. All the wines are sourced from the Geelong region, and are competently made, as one would expect from such an experienced winemaker, who also makes wine for others.

Provenance Geelong Pinot Gris

TTTTY 2002 Pale straw, with a faintly pink tinge, typical of the variety; the bouquet is highly aromatic and rich, almost into muscat, yet in no way coarse; the palate has well above-average total flavour, with a gentle hint of spicy biscuit from the French oak. Trophy for Best White Wine at the 2002 Geelong Wine Show. **rating:** 91
best drinking Now **best vintages** '02 **drink with** Sushi • $25

Provenance Geelong Pinot Noir

TTTT 2001 Medium red-purple; ripe plummy fruit, almost merging into prune on the bouquet; the strong, plummy fruit shows the hot vintage, with savoury, ripe tannins reinforcing the message. **rating:** 89
best drinking Now–2006 **best vintages** '99 **drink with** Smoked duck • $29

Provenance Geelong Shiraz

TTTT 2001 Medium red-purple; a cool-climate cornucopia of spice, licorice, game and black plum aromas leads into a finely structured palate with similar flavours; the one (minor) criticism is that the wine is fractionally short. **rating:** 88
best drinking 2005–2010 **drink with** Game pie • $29

providence vineyards ★★★★★

236 Lalla Road, Lalla, Tas 7267 **region** Northern Tasmania
phone (03) 6395 1290 **fax** (03) 6395 1290 **open** 7 days 10–5
winemaker Andrew Hood (Contract) **production** 600 cases **est.** 1956
product range ($17–35 CD) Riesling, Semillon, Botrytis Semillon, Chardonnay, Pinot Noir; in exceptional years may be released under the Miguet label.
summary Providence incorporates the pioneer vineyard of Frenchman Jean Miguet, now owned by the Bryce family, which purchased it in 1980. The original 1.3-hectare vineyard has been expanded to a little over 3 hectares, and has grafted over unsuitable grenache and cabernet (left from the original plantings) to chardonnay and pinot noir and semillon. Miguet in fact called the vineyard 'La Provence', reminding him of the part of France whence he came, but after 40 years the French authorities forced a name change to Providence. The rating reflects the consistent string of great Pinot Noirs from this vineyard.

punters corner ★★★★☆

Cnr Riddoch Highway and Racecourse Road, Coonawarra, SA 5263 **region** Coonawarra
phone (08) 8737 2007 **fax** (08) 8737 3138 **open** 7 days 10–5
winemaker Peter Bissell (Contract) **production** 10 000 cases **est.** 1988
product range ($17–59.50 CD) Chardonnay, Shiraz, Spartacus Reserve Shiraz, Cabernet Merlot, Cabernet Sauvignon, Cabernet.
summary The quaintly named Punters Corner started off life in 1975 as James Haselgrove, but in 1992 was acquired by a group of investors who quite evidently had few delusions about the uncertainties of viticulture and winemaking, even in a district as distinguished as Coonawarra. The arrival of Peter Bissell as winemaker at Balnaves paid immediate (and continuing) dividends. Sophisticated packaging and label design add to the appeal of the wines. National retail distribution; exports to the US, Hong Kong, Taiwan, Belgium and Switzerland. The rating is based on prior (consistent) tastings.

punt road ★★★★

10 St Huberts Road, Coldstream, Vic 3770 **region** Yarra Valley
phone (03) 9739 0666 **fax** (03) 9739 0633 **open** 7 days 10–5
winemaker Kate Goodman **production** 4000 cases **est.** 2000
product range ($18–25 R) Sauvignon Blanc, Pinot Gris, Chardonnay, Late Harvest Semillon, Pinot Noir, Shiraz, Merlot, Cabernet Sauvignon.

summary Punt Road was originally known as The Yarra Hill, a name abandoned because of the proliferation of wineries with the word 'Yarra' as part of their name. The situation of the vineyard and winery (opposite St Huberts) remains unchanged. The business is centred on a large, new winery which produces the Punt Road wines as well as undertaking substantial contract winemaking for others. The Punt Road wines are made from the best parcels of fruit grown on 100 hectares of vineyards owned by members of the Punt Road syndicate, and represent the tip of the iceberg.

Punt Road Sauvignon Blanc

ŶŶŶŶŶ **2002** Light straw-green; an aromatic and spotlessly clean bouquet of grass and gooseberry leads into a crisp and particularly long palate with a great aftertaste. **rating: 90**

best drinking Now **best vintages** '02 **drink with** Scampi • $18.50

Punt Road Pinot Gris

ŶŶŶŶ **2002** Light straw-green; the complex bouquet has pear/pear skin and spice aromas, the palate slightly chalky, veering more to grigio in style, then a dry finish. Complexed by a small portion of barrel ferment. **rating: 86**

best drinking Now **drink with** Antipasto • $18

Punt Road Late Harvest Semillon (500 ml)

ŶŶŶŶŶ **2001** Medium to full yellow-green; a rich and complex bouquet ranges through mandarin, peach and cumquat; the intense but nicely balanced palate follows those fruit characteristics; nicely weighted and good length. From the Nehme Vineyard in the Riverina. **rating: 93**

best drinking Now–2006 **best vintages** '01 **drink with** Dessert, the richer the better • $25

Punt Road Shiraz

ŶŶŶŶ **2001** Medium to full red-purple; blackberry/black cherry, prune, chocolate and spice aromas are followed by a firm, still relatively unyielding palate; will open up with time. **rating: 88**

best drinking 2005–2010 **drink with** Scotch fillet • $23

Punt Road Merlot

ŶŶŶŶ **2001** Medium red-purple; a typically varietal assemblage of leafy/savoury/earthy/berry aromas is followed by a quite ripe palate, offering a mix of dark berry and raspberry fruits, again showing savoury aspects. **rating: 87**

best drinking 2004–2008 **best vintages** '00 **drink with** Pot-roasted lamb rump • $23

Punt Road Cabernet Sauvignon

ŶŶŶŶ **2991** Medium red-purple; the bouquet has berry, earth, olive and leaf aromas; the light to medium-bodied palate has pleasant red berry fruit; nicely made, but needs a touch more intensity. **rating: 87**

best drinking 2005–2010 **best vintages** '00 **drink with** Kangaroo fillet • $23

pycnantha hill estate ★★★★☆

Benbournie Road, Clare, SA 5453 (postal) **region** Clare Valley
phone (08) 8842 2137 **fax** (08) 8842 2137 **open** Not
winemaker Jim Howarth **production** 1000 cases **est.** 1997
product range ($14–20 R) Riesling, Chardonnay, Shiraz, Reserve Shiraz, Cabernet Merlot.
summary The Howarth family progressively established 2.4 hectares of vineyard from 1987, making its first commercial vintage 10 years later in 1997. *Acacia pycnantha* is the botanical name for the golden wattle which grows wild over the hills of the Howarth farm, and they say it was 'a natural choice to name our vineyards Pycnantha Hill'. I am not too sure that marketing gurus would agree, but there you go. Moreover, the quality of the wines should speak for itself.

Pycnantha Hill Estate Riesling

ŶŶŶŶŶ **2002** Pale green-straw; delicate, scented, lime blossom aromas; intensity builds through the length of the palate, yet the wine is neither heavy nor broad. Excellent value. **rating: 91**

best drinking Now–2008 **drink with** Asparagus with hollandaise sauce • $14

Pycnantha Hill Estate Chardonnay

ŶŶŶŶ **2001** Light to medium yellow-green; the bouquet has melon, fig and stone fruit with nicely judged and integrated oak; the palate provides more of the same, and is as good as they come from the Clare Valley; well handled in the winery and with authentic varietal fruit. Principally barrel fermented, with a portion stainless steel fermented for fruit freshness. **rating: 89**

best drinking Now–2007 **drink with** Milk-fed veal • $16

Pycnantha Hill Estate Shiraz

ŢŢŢŢŢ 2001 Bright red-purple; clean, ripe, blackberry, dark plum and prune aromas lead into a succulent, fruit-driven, round and mouthfilling palate; excellent control of extract. Great value. Matured for 12 months in French and American oak. **rating: 93**

best drinking 2005–2015 **best vintages** '01 **drink with** Osso buco • $15

Pycnantha Hill Estate Reserve Shiraz

ŢŢŢŢŢ 2001 Medium to full red-purple; a much more complex bouquet than that of the varietal release, due to significantly greater new oak; the rich, complex and powerful palate is partially oak-driven; there is lots happening, and the wine will age well, but I still prefer the standard wine. Released mid-2003. **rating: 91**

best drinking 2006–2016 **drink with** Kangaroo fillet • $20

Pycnantha Hill Estate Cabernet Merlot

ŢŢŢŢ 2001 Medium red-purple; ripe blackcurrant, mint and earth aromas lead into ripe, juicy, blackcurrant flavours on entry, braced by finer, more savoury tannins on the finish. Spends 12 months in French oak. **rating: 88**

best drinking 2006–2011 **drink with** Herbed rack of lamb • $16

pyrenees ridge vineyard ★★★★

532 Caralulup Road, Lamplough via Avoca, Vic 3467 **region** Pyrenees
phone (03) 5465 3710 **fax** (03) 5465 3320 **open** Thurs–Mon and public holidays 10–5
winemaker Graeme Jukes **production** 700 cases **est.** 1998
product range ($19–39 R) Shiraz, Reserve Shiraz, Cabernet Shiraz, Cabernet Sauvignon, Vintage Port.
summary Notwithstanding the quite extensive winemaking experience (and formal training) of Graeme Jukes, this started life as a small-scale, winemaking in the raw version of the French garagiste winemaking approach. Together with wife Sally-Ann, Graeme Jukes has planted 2 hectares of cabernet sauvignon and 1 hectare of shiraz, with a further hectare of shiraz to be planted in 2002; the cabernet intake is supplemented by purchases from other growers within the region. The success of the wines has been such that prior to the 2004 vintage the winery size will be doubled, another 1.5 hectares of estate plantings will be completed, and contract purchases will be increased. Contract winemaking for others will also be expanded. Australian Prestige Wines distributes limited quantities of the wine in Melbourne, with a tiny percentage going overseas; the rest is sold by mail order and at the cellar door.

Pyrenees Ridge Vineyard Shiraz

ŢŢŢŢ 2001 Medium to full red-purple; a clean and smooth bouquet with cherry and plum fruit supported by subtle oak leads into a big, powerful palate with a mix of plum and blackberry; the tannins are still slightly grippy. **rating: 88**

best drinking 2006–2016 **drink with** Barbecued beef • $25

Pyrenees Ridge Vineyard Reserve Shiraz

ŢŢŢŢŢ 2001 Dense purple-red; a complex and rich bouquet with powerful fruit and obvious vanilla oak is followed by a massively rich and complex palate with sweet black cherry, plum and blackberry fruit, the vanillin oak firing a final salvo. Sixteen months in American oak. USA, here we come. **rating: 93**

best drinking 2008–2018 **best vintages** '01 **drink with** Leave it in the cellar • $39

Pyrenees Ridge Vineyard Shiraz Cabernet

ŢŢŢŢ 2001 Medium red-purple; ripe, dark fruits, spice and cigar box on the bouquet lead into a medium to full-bodied palate with powerful blackberry and plum fruit; it avoids being jammy, and the tannins are relatively soft. **rating: 87**

best drinking 2006–2011 **drink with** Braised ox cheek • $25

Pyrenees Ridge Vineyard Cabernet Sauvignon

ŢŢŢŢŢ 2001 Medium to full red-purple; there are strong chocolate/toffee overtones to the red berry fruits of the bouquet; ripe, but not jammy, cassis/blackcurrant fruit on the palate has soft tannins providing good balance and extract. **rating: 90**

best drinking 2006–2011 **drink with** Saddle of lamb • $25

queen adelaide ★★☆

Sturt Highway, Waikerie, SA 5330 **region** Barossa Valley
phone (08) 8541 2588 **fax** (08) 8541 3877 **open** Not
winemaker Various **production** NFP **est.** 1858
product range ($6–7 R) Rhine Riesling, Chenin Blanc, Semillon Chardonnay, Chardonnay, Spatlese Lexia, Sauvignon Blanc, Regency Red, Shiraz, Grenache Pinot Noir, Cabernet Sauvignon.

summary The famous brand established by Woodley Wines and some years ago subsumed into the Seppelt and now Southcorp Group. It is a pure brand, without any particular home either in terms of winemaking or fruit sources, but is hugely successful; Queen Adelaide Chardonnay is and has for some time been the largest-selling bottled white wine in Australia. The move away from agglomerate to Stelvin closures has ended the glue-taint problems of prior years.

raleigh winery   NR

Queen Street, Raleigh, NSW 2454 **region** Northern Rivers Zone
phone (02) 6655 4388 **fax** (02) 6655 4265 **open** 7 days 10–5
winemaker Lavinia Dingle **production** 600 cases **est.** 1982
product range ($14–27 CD) Fox Gully Dry White (Semillon Chardonnay), Late Harvest, Rouge (Rose), Riverbank Red (Shiraz Cabernet), Port.
summary Raleigh Winery lays claim to being Australia's most easterly vineyard. The vineyard was initiated in 1982 and was purchased by Lavinia and Neil Dingle in 1989, with the wine produced in part from 1 hectare of vines planted to no less than six varieties. The wines have won bronze medals at the Griffith Wine Show.

ralph fowler wines   ★★★★

Limestone Coast Road, Mount Benson, SA 5275 **region** Mount Benson
phone (08) 8365 6968 **fax** (08) 8365 2516 **open** 7 days 10–5
winemaker Ralph Fowler **production** 6000 cases **est.** 1999
product range ($14–27 CD) Sauvignon Blanc, Viognier, Botrytis Semillon, Shiraz, Cabernet Sauvignon.
summary Established in February 1999 by the Fowler family, headed by well known winemaker Ralph Fowler, with wife Deborah and children Sarah (currently studying wine science) and James all involved in the 40-hectare vineyard property at Mount Benson. Ralph Fowler began his winemaking career at Tyrrell's, rising to the position of chief winemaker before moving to Hungerford Hill, and then the Hamilton/Leconfield group. He thus brings great experience to the venture. He has, interestingly, planted two varieties to provide the flagship wines: shiraz and viognier. Exports to the US, Canada, the UK, Austria and Singapore.

Ralph Fowler Limestone Coast Sauvignon Blanc

♥♥♥♥♥ 2002 Fowler began his career in the Hunter Valley with Tyrrell's, thence to Coonawarra and now in Mount Benson. The delicate bouquet has a mix of tropical and gooseberry fruit, plus a subliminal touch of oak. The palate has much more intensity, the texture significantly enhanced by fermentation in French oak. Utterly seductive.   **rating:** 95
best drinking Now **best vintages** '02 **drink with** Pan-fried veal • $18

Ralph Fowler Limestone Coast Cabernet Sauvignon

♥♥♥♥ 2000 Medium red-purple; the moderately intense bouquet has a mix of blackberry, earth and olive. The palate adds blackcurrant to the mix; good tannin structure and subtle oak.   **rating:** 89
best drinking 2004–2009 **drink with** Rack of lamb • $27

ramsay's vin rose   ★★★

30 St Helier Road, The Gurdies, Vic 3984 **region** Gippsland
phone (03) 5997 6531 **fax** (03) 5997 6158 **open** Wed–Mon 12–5
winemaker Dianne Ramsay, Roger Cutler **production** 400 cases **est.** 1995
product range ($8–22 CD) Riesling, Chardonnay, Rose (dry), Satin Rose (sweet), Merlot, Cabernet Sauvignon.
summary The slightly curious name (which looks decidedly strange in conjunction with Riesling and Cabernet Sauvignon) stems from the original intention of Alan and Dianne Ramsay to grow roses on a commercial scale on their property. Frank Cutler, from Western Port Winery, persuaded them to plant wine grapes instead, establishing the first 2 hectares of vines in 1995. They opened their micro winery in 1999, and have four two-bedroom self-contained units set around their 800-bush rose garden. The pinot noir and chardonnay are sold to Diamond Valley, so for the time being the range of wines released is limited to Riesling, a Cabernet Franc-based Rose and Cabernet Sauvignon, with a Merlot maturing in barrel. Ultimately, the Ramsays hope to use all the estate grapes for their wines.

Ramsay's Vin Rose Cabernet Sauvignon

♥♥♥♥ 2000 Medium red-purple; savoury, leafy, berry aromas are followed by a light to medium-bodied palate, again with a herbaceous, minty edge to the berry fruit. No winemaking fault; indeed nicely put together.
                                                                rating: 85
best drinking Now–2006 **drink with** Veal chops • $22

ray-monde ★★★☆

250 Dalrymple Road, Sunbury, Vic 3429 **region** Sunbury
phone (03) 5428 2657 **fax** (03) 5428 3390 **open** Sundays, or by appointment
winemaker John Lakey **production** 700 cases **est.** 1988
product range ($25–30 CD) Rubina (Rose), Pinot Noir.
summary The Lakey family has established 5 hectares of pinot noir on their 230-hectare grazing property at
an altitude of 400 metres. Initially the grapes were sold to Domaine Chandon, but in 1994 son John Lakey
(who had gained experience at Tarrawarra, Rochford, Virgin Hills, Coonawarra plus a vintage in Burgundy)
commenced making the wine – and very competently.

Ray-Monde Wild Pinot Noir

♥♥♥♥ 2001 Light to medium purple-red; the complex bouquet has plum and strawberry fruit with more
foresty undercurrents; the powerful, savoury/foresty palate has good depth, and manages to carry its improbable
14.5° alcohol. Given that the 2000 Pinot Noir was 13.5° alcohol and showed unripe flavours, this high level of
alcohol (produced via wild yeast fermentation, incidentally) has to be accepted as necessary, however unusual.
best drinking Now–2008 **drink with** Marinated venison • $30 **rating:** 89

redbank winery ★★★★

Sunraysia Highway, Redbank, Vic 3467 **region** Pyrenees
phone (03) 5467 7255 **fax** (03) 5467 7248 **open** Mon–Sat 9–5, Sun 10–5
winemaker Neill Robb **production** 58 000 cases **est.** 1973
product range ($12–50 R) The range centres on a series of evocatively named red wines, with Sally's
Paddock the flagship; then Rising Chardonnay, Sunday Morning Pinot Gris, Frenchman's Pinot Noir, Fighting
Flat Shiraz, Percydale Cabernet Merlot. Long Paddock Shiraz Cabernet, Long Paddock Chardonnay and Emily
Pinot Chardonnay Brut Cuvee are cheaper, larger-volume second labels.
summary Neill Robb makes very concentrated wines, full of character; the levels of volatile acidity can
sometimes be intrusive but are probably of more concern to technical tasters than to the general public. Sally's
Paddock is the star, a single-vineyard block with an esoteric mix of Cabernet, Shiraz and Malbec and which
over the years has produced many great wines.

Redbank Sunday Morning Pinot Gris

♥♥♥♥♡ 2002 Light green-straw; citrus, apple, pear skin and spice aromas lead into a lively palate with a touch
of CO_2 spritz evident; 20 per cent of the wine was taken through malolactic fermentation in French oak and
matured in that oak for 3 months. This adds to the complexity but does take the edge off the varietal character.
A multiple gold medal winner, and well priced. Excellent packaging adds to the appeal. **rating:** 92
best drinking Now **best vintages** '02 **drink with** Creamy pasta • $20

red clay estate NR

269 Henry Lawson Drive, Mudgee, NSW 2850 **region** Mudgee
phone (02) 6372 4569 **fax** (02) 6372 4596 **open** Jan–Sept 7 days 10–5, Oct–Dec Mon–Fri 10–5, or by
appointment
winemaker Ken Heslop **est.** 1997
product range Cabernet Merlot.
summary Ken Heslop and Annette Bailey are among the recent arrivals in Mudgee, with a 2.5-hectare vineyard
planted to a diverse range of varieties. The wines are exclusively sold through the cellar door and by mail order.

🐌 red earth estate vineyard NR

18L Camp Road, Dubbo, NSW 2830 **region** Western Plains Zone
phone (02) 6885 6676 **fax** (02) 6882 8297 **open** 7 days 10–4, or by appointment
winemaker Ken Borchardt **production** 5000 cases **est.** 2000
product range ($12–16.50 CD) Riesling, Verdelho, Unwooded Chardonnay, Cuvee, Shiraz, Unwooded
Cabernet Sauvignon, Cabernet Sauvignon.
summary Ken and Christine Borchardt look set to be the focal point of wine growing and making in the future
Macquarie Valley region of the Western Plains Zone. They have planted 1.3 hectares each of riesling, verdelho,
frontignac, grenache, shiraz and cabernet sauvignon at the winery, with a further planting each of shiraz,
cabernet franc and cabernet sauvignon on another site. The winery has a maximum capacity of 14 000 cases, and
the Borchardts are offering contract winemaking facilities in addition to making and marketing their own brand.

red edge ★★★★★

Golden Gully Road, Heathcote, Vic 3523 **region** Heathcote
phone (03) 9337 5695 **fax** (03) 9337 7550 **open** By appointment
winemaker Peter Dredge, Judy Dredge **production** 500 cases **est.** 1971
product range ($37–40 ML) Shiraz, Cabernet Sauvignon.
summary Red Edge is a new name on the scene, but the vineyard dates back to 1971, at the renaissance of the Victorian wine industry. In the early 1980s it produced the wonderful wines of Flynn & Williams; it has now been rehabilitated by Peter and Judy Dredge, who produced two quite lovely wines in their inaugural 1997 vintage and have continued that form in succeeding vintages. They now have a little over 15 hectares under vine, and Red Edge has become a full-time occupation for Peter Dredge. Exports to the US and the UK.

Red Edge Shiraz

▼▼▼▼▽ **2001** The colour is as deep and dense as ever; powerful, concentrated black fruits on the bouquet, then the usual powerhouse palate offering dark cherry confit rounded off with fine, savoury tannins. **rating:** 93
best drinking 2005–2015 **best vintages** '97, '98, '99, '00, '01 **drink with** Leave it in the cellar • $40

Red Edge Cabernet Sauvignon

▼▼▼▼▽ **2001** Dense red-purple; aromas of blackberry essence, luscious and sweet; blackberry fruit on entry floods the mouth before giving way to long, lingering tannins on the finish. **rating:** 93
best drinking 2006–2016 **best vintages** '97, '98, '99, '01 **drink with** Leave it in the cellar • $38

redgate ★★★★

Boodjidup Road, Margaret River, WA 6285 **region** Margaret River
phone (08) 9757 6488 **fax** (08) 9757 6308 **open** 7 days 10–5
winemaker Andrew Forsell **production** 14 000 cases **est.** 1977
product range ($17–35 CD) OFS Semillon, Sauvignon Blanc Reserve, Sauvignon Blanc Semillon, Chenin, Chardonnay, Pinot Noir, Shiraz, Cabernet Franc, Cabernet Sauvignon Franc Merlot, Bin 588 (Cabernet blend), Cabernet Sauvignon, Anastasia's Delight (fortified Semillon), White Port.
summary Twenty hectares of vineyard provide the base for a substantial winery which probably has a lower profile than it deserves. The white wines are the winery's strength, even if the 2002 whites are not as impressive as were the 2001s. It is for the white wines (and for the two vintages) that the rating is given. The wines have limited distribution in the eastern states, and export markets in Singapore, Hong Kong, Canada, Japan, Denmark, Germany, Switzerland, the US and the UK have been established.

Redgate OFS Semillon

▼▼▼▼ **2002** Light straw-green, with lots of CO_2 evident; the fresh, crisp bouquet has subtle spice and herb aromas in inimitable Margaret River style; the medium-bodied palate has plenty of mid-palate flavour, but the alcohol does show on the finish. **rating:** 85
best drinking Now–2006 **best vintages** '00 **drink with** Salmon mousse • $22.50

Redgate Sauvignon Blanc Reserve

▼▼▼▼ **2002** Light straw-green; the very complex bouquet is driven by strong, spicy clove oak; the palate provides more of the same, which is great for oak lovers. It seems to me the oak is far more obvious than it was in the 2001 vintage wine. **rating:** 87
best drinking Now–2005 **best vintages** '99, '00, '01 **drink with** Creamy seafood pasta • $22.50

Redgate Sauvignon Blanc Semillon

▼▼▼▼▽ **2002** Pale straw-green; the spotlessly clean bouquet has fresh, zesty grass and green pea aromas; the light, lively and pure palate has mineral and green pea fruit; a wine of unusual clarity. **rating:** 90
best drinking Now–2006 **best vintages** '02 **drink with** Shellfish • $18.50

Redgate Chardonnay

▼▼▼▼ **2002** Light to medium yellow-green; the bouquet is complex, with obvious barrel-ferment inputs, but not over the top. A powerful wine on the palate, with concentration, but still curiously bound up. Its best years are to come. **rating:** 88
best drinking 2005–2009 **best vintages** '01 **drink with** Pan-fried veal • $25

red hill estate ★★★★

53 Redhill–Shoreham Road, Red Hill South, Vic 3937 **region** Mornington Peninsula
phone (03) 5989 2838 **fax** (03) 5989 2855 **open** 7 days 11–5
winemaker Michael Kyberd **production** 20 000 cases **est.** 1989
product range ($14–35 CD) Particular emphasis on Methode Champenoise, but also producing Pinot Grigio, Sauvignon Blanc, Chardonnay, Botrytis, Pinot Noir, Shiraz, Cabernet Merlot, Liqueur Muscat; Bimaris range of Sauvignon Blanc, Chardonnay, Rose, Pinot Noir; Classic Release Chardonnay, Pinot Noir.
summary Sir Peter Derham and family completed the construction of an on-site winery in time for the 1993 vintage, ending a period in which the wines were made at various wineries under contract arrangements. The 10-hectare vineyard is one of the larger estate plantings on the Mornington Peninsula, and the tasting room and ever-busy restaurant have a superb view across the vineyard to Westernport Bay and Phillip Island. Production continues to surge, and the winery goes from strength to strength.

Red Hill Estate Bimaris Sauvignon Blanc

▼▼▼▼ 2001 Light straw-green; a firm, complex bouquet with herb and faint onion weed aromas moves to riper, sweeter fruit on the mid-palate, but does shorten slightly on the finish. Bimaris, incidentally, means 'land between two waters'. **rating:** 87
best drinking Now **drink with** Cold seafood • $15

Red Hill Estate Bimaris Chardonnay

▼▼▼▼ 2001 Light to medium yellow-green; clean, tangy citrus, grapefruit and melon fruit aromas are followed by an entirely fruit-driven palate which has good length. Great value. **rating:** 88
best drinking Now–2006 **drink with** Salmon terrine • $15

Red Hill Estate Classic Release Chardonnay

▼▼▼▼▽ 2000 Medium yellow-green; a complex smoky/charry bouquet showing the influence of wild yeast barrel-ferment techniques; the palate is much tighter, with melon and stone fruit to the fore; good length, subtle oak. **rating:** 90
best drinking Now–2007 **best vintages** '00 **drink with** Tortellini • $30

Red Hill Estate Blanc de Blanc

▼▼▼▼▽ 2000 Bright, light green-yellow; the bouquet is quite intense and complex, with tangy, citrussy fruit. The long and intense palate has tingling acidity on the finish. High-quality sparkling wine. **rating:** 90
best drinking Now–2006 **best vintages** '00 **drink with** Aperitif • $26

Red Hill Estate Blanc de Noirs

▼▼▼▼▽ 2000 Pale salmon-pink; a fresh, lively strawberry-accented bouquet is followed by a palate with an interesting tangy, lemony and strawberry mix; better balanced than the Blanc de Blanc, but not as long. A blend of Pinot Noir and Pinot Meunier. **rating:** 90
best drinking Now–2006 **best vintages** '96, '00 **drink with** Delicate seafood • $30

Red Hill Estate Pinot Noir

▼▼▼▼ 2001 Light to medium red-purple; a light mix of savoury and plum aromas leads into a light to medium-bodied palate with a similar spread of flavours; needs more ripe fruit. **rating:** 86
best drinking Now–2006 **best vintages** '99 **drink with** Tea-smoked duck • $20

Red Hill Estate Classic Release Pinot Noir

▼▼▼▼▽ 2000 Light to medium red-purple; the moderately intense bouquet is in the foresty/savoury/spicy spectrum, pushed by a fair degree of oak. The palate moves up a gear: it is long and lingering, with well above-average intensity. **rating:** 90
best drinking Now–2006 **best vintages** '00 **drink with** Smoked quail • $35

redman ★★★☆

Riddoch Highway, Coonawarra, SA 5253 **region** Coonawarra
phone (08) 8736 3331 **fax** (08) 8736 3013 **open** Mon–Fri 9–5, weekends 10–4
winemaker Bruce Redman, Malcolm Redman **production** 18 000 cases **est.** 1966
product range ($13–27.99 R) Shiraz, Cabernet Sauvignon Merlot, Cabernet Sauvignon.
summary After a prolonged period of mediocrity, the Redman wines are showing sporadic signs of improvement, partly through the introduction of modest amounts of new oak, even if principally American. It would be nice to say that the wines now reflect the full potential of the vineyard, but there is still some way to go.

Redman Shiraz

♥♥♥♡ **2001** Medium red-purple; the bouquet is clean, the light to medium-bodied palate smooth, but as plain and disappointing as ever. **rating:** 84

♥♥♥♥ **2000** Medium red-purple; the clean, moderately intense bouquet has cherry, plum and spice; the palate has good depth and structure, the only question being the slightly firm, fractionally gritty tannins. However, has improved out of sight since first bottled. **rating:** 89

best drinking 2004–2008 **best vintages** '66, '69, '70, '90, '91, '93, '98 **drink with** Pasta • $16.99

Redman Cabernet Sauvignon Merlot

♥♥♥♥ **1999** Medium red-purple; clean blackcurrant and blackberry fruit are framed by subtle oak on the bouquet; the palate offers attractive, ripe blackcurrant fruit, fine tannins and good length. Just when you think all is lost with Redman, up comes a wine such as this. **rating:** 89

best drinking 2004–2009 **best vintages** '93, '94, '96, '97, '99 **drink with** Shoulder of lamb • $27.99

red rock winery   NR

Red Rock Reserve Road, Alvie, Vic 3249 **region** Geelong
phone (03) 5234 8382 **fax** (03) 5234 8382 **open** 7 days 10–5
winemaker Rohan Little **production** 5000 cases **est.** 1981
product range ($15–25 R) Semillon Sauvignon, Chardonnay, Pinot Noir, Shiraz, Cabernet Sauvignon Merlot.
summary The former Barongvale Estate, which has progressively established 10 hectares of sauvignon blanc, semillon, pinot noir, and shiraz; a part-time occupation for Rohan Little, with wines sold under both the Red Rock and Otway Vineyards labels. It takes its name from the now dormant Red Rock Volcano, which created the lakes and craters of the Western Districts when it last erupted, 8000 years ago. The winery cafe opened in early 2002.

red tail wines   NR

15 Pinnacle Place, Marlee, NSW 2429 **region** Northern Rivers Zone
phone (02) 6550 5084 **fax** (02) 6550 5084 **open** By appointment
winemaker Serenella Estate (Contract) **production** 300 cases **est.** 1992
product range ($11–15.50 ML) Marlee White, Semillon, Colombard, Semillon Colombard, Merlot.
summary Warren and Sue Stiff have planted 0.5 hectare each of colombard, semillon and verdelho, and 0.25-hectare of merlot, at their property in the Northern Rivers Zone, northwest of Taree. The vineyard takes its name from the red-tailed black cockatoo which inhabits the area; the very reasonably priced wines are available by phone, fax or mail order.

reedy creek vineyard   NR

Reedy Creek, via Tenterfield, NSW 2372 **region** Northern Slopes Zone
phone (02) 6737 5221 **fax** (02) 6737 5200 **open** 7 days 9–5
winemaker Contract **production** 2800 cases **est.** 1971
product range ($13–17 CD) Bianco Alpino, Chardonnay, Unwooded Chardonnay, Rosso Alpino, Shiraz Mourvedre, Old Vine Shiraz, Merlot, Durif, Liqueur Muscat, Red Deer Port.
summary Like so many Italian settlers in the Australian countryside, the De Stefani family has been growing grapes and making wine for its own consumption for over 30 years at its Reedy Creek property near Tenterfield, in the far north of New South Wales. What is more, like their compatriots in the King Valley, the family's principal activity until 1993 was growing tobacco; the continued rationalisation of the tobacco industry prompted the De Stefanis to turn a hobby into a commercial exercise. The vineyard has now been expanded to 6.1 hectares, and the first commercial vintage of Shiraz was made in 1995, with Chardonnay following in 1998. The wines are sold cellar door from the maturation cellar, which was opened in 1997.

rees miller estate   ★★★☆

5355 Goulbourn Highway, Yea, Vic 3717 **region** Central Victorian High Country
phone (03) 5797 2101 **fax** (03) 5797 3276 **open** Weekends and public holidays 10–5
winemaker David Miller **production** 1000 cases **est.** 1996
product range ($22–45 CD) Meadows Hill Chardonnay, Pinot Noir, Wilhemina Pinot Noir, Shiraz, Eildon Shiraz, Thousand Hills Reserve Shiraz, Manytrees Shiraz Viognier, Sier's Field Reserve (Cabernet blend).

summary Partners Sylke Rees and David Miller purchased the 64-hectare property in 1998, with 1 hectare of pinot noir (planted in 1996). They have since extended the plantings with another block of pinot noir, 3 hectares of cabernet sauvignon, 1 hectare each of merlot and shiraz and 0.5 hectare of cabernet franc, all of which came into production in 2002. They use integrated pest management (no insecticides) and deliberately irrigate sparingly, the upshot being yields of 1 ton to the acre. All the wines are made on-site, and the production will be limited to a Pinot Noir, a Shiraz and an Australian Bordeaux-style red, some named after the original owners of the property, Daniel Joseph and Wilhemina Therese Sier. Headed towards a four-star rating.

Rees Miller Estate Pinot Noir

TTTT 2000 Light to medium red-purple, the hue holding nicely; the aromatic bouquet is distinctly savoury/spicy/earthy. The light-bodied palate has black cherry fruit, with the structure slightly simple. The two Rees Miller Pinot Noirs are of consistent style. **rating: 86**

best drinking Now–2005 **drink with** Pastrami

Rees Miller Estate Wilhemina Pinot Noir

TTTT 2001 Medium red-purple; savoury, earthy, spicy aromas lead into a light to medium-bodied palate with some varietal black cherry fruit; the balance and finish are good. **rating: 86**

best drinking Now–2005 **drink with** Smoked quail • $26

Rees Miller Estate Shiraz

TTTT 2000 Medium to full red-purple; interesting briary, spicy aromas are quite appealing; the palate brings things together with a mix of blackberry and spicy raspberry fruit; good oak and tannin management. **rating: 89**

best drinking 2004–2009 **drink with** Ravioli • $22

Rees Miller Estate One Thousand Hills Shiraz

TTTT 2001 The colour is not 100 per cent bright, but the moderately intense bouquet has blackberry and spice aromas, while the palate gathers pace dramatically, offering sweet, ripe blackberry fruit rounded off by soft tannins. **rating: 88**

best drinking 2005–2010 **drink with** Beef in black bean sauce • $45

reg drayton wines ★★★☆

Cnr Pokolbin Mountain and McDonalds Roads, Pokolbin, NSW 2321 **region** Lower Hunter Valley
phone (02) 4998 7523 **fax** (02) 4998 7523 **open** 7 days 10–5
winemaker Tish Cecchini, Robyn Drayton **production** 6000 cases **est.** 1989
product range ($16–35 CD) Lambkin Semillon, Lambkin Verdelho, Pokolbin Hills Chardonnay, Pokolbin Hills Chardonnay Semillon, Pamela Robyn Sparkling Chardonnay, Botrytis Semillon, Rose, Three Sons Shiraz, Pokolbin Hills Shiraz, Pokolbin Hills Cabernet Shiraz, Hunter Classic Verdelho Liqueur, Tawny Port.
summary Reg and Pam Drayton were among the victims of the Seaview/Lord Howe Island air crash in October 1984, having established Reg Drayton Wines after selling their interest in the long-established Drayton Family Winery. Their daughter Robyn (a fifth-generation Drayton and billed as the Hunter's first female vigneron) and husband Craig continue the business, which draws chiefly upon the Pokolbin Hills Estate but also takes fruit from the historic Lambkin Estate vineyard.

Reg Drayton Lambkin Semillon

TTTT 2001 Medium yellow-green, starting to show some development; the bouquet is rather closed, and going into transition, but there is appealing fruit on the palate, with sweet lemon, herb and a touch of spice. **rating: 87**

best drinking 2004–2009 **drink with** Salmon roulade • $18

Reg Drayton After 7 pm Botrytis Semillon 375 ml

TTTT 2002 Deep gold; cumquat, mandarin and pineapple aromas, plus a touch of oak, are followed by an extremely luscious and exceedingly sweet palate. The back label reveals that the grapes were picked in the first week of May, and the appellation is South East Australia. In other words, the grapes come from Griffith, not the Hunter Valley. **rating: 86**

best drinking Now–2005 **drink with** Crème brûlée • $28

reilly's wines ★★★☆

Cnr Hill and Burra Streets, Mintaro, SA 5415 **region** Clare Valley
phone (08) 8843 9013 **fax** (08) 8843 9013 **open** 7 days 10–5, restaurant open for dinner Mon–Sat
winemaker Justin Ardill **production** 7000 cases **est.** 1994

product range ($16–27 CD) Watervale Riesling, Block 1919 Grenache Shiraz, Shiraz, Dry Land Shiraz, Cabernet Sauvignon.

summary Cardiologist Justin and Julie Ardill are relative newcomers in the Clare Valley, with half a dozen or so vintages under their belt. An unusual sideline of Reilly's Cottage is the production of Extra Virgin Olive Oil; unusual in that it is made from wild olives found in the Mintaro district of the Clare Valley. Exports to the US, the UK, Malaysia, Singapore and New Zealand.

Reilly's Watervale Riesling

▼▼▼▼▽ **2002** Light straw-green; a classic, clear bouquet with a balance between lime, mineral and slate aromas is followed by a palate with abundant flavour and richness provided by ripe citrus fruit. Drink sooner rather than later.

rating: 90

best drinking Now–2007 **best vintages** '94, '95, '02 **drink with** Antipasto • $16

Reilly's Dry Land Cabernet Sauvignon

▼▼▼▼ **2000** Medium red, the purple starting to fade; moderately intense and ripe blackcurrant fruit aromas translate into the driver of the powerful and ripe palate entry, balanced by savoury tannins on the finish. Not especially complex, but certainly has flavour. **rating: 86**

best drinking 2004–2009 **drink with** Pastrami • $27

renewan vineyard NR

Murray Valley Highway, Piangil, Vic 3597 **region** Swan Hill
phone (03) 5030 5525 **fax** (03) 5030 5695 **open** 7 days 10–5
winemaker John Ellis **est.** 1989
product range Riesling, Shiraz, Durif, Cabernet Sauvignon.
summary In 1990 former senior executive at Nylex Corporation in Melbourne, Jim Lewis, and artist wife Marg, retired to what is now Renewan Vineyard, set on the banks of the Murray River. It is a small business, based on 2.5 hectares of estate plantings, and all the production is sold through the cellar door and by mail order, with limited distribution to local hotels, bottle shops and restaurants.

reschke wines ★★★☆

'Rocky Castle', Rocky Castle Road, Coonawarra, SA 5263 **region** Coonawarra
phone (08) 8363 3343 **fax** (08) 8363 9949 **open** Not
winemaker Martin Williams MW (Contract) **production** 1500 cases **est.** 1998
product range ($100 ML) Taikurri (Cabernet blend), Empyrean Cabernet Sauvignon.
summary It's not often that the first release from a new winery is priced at $100 per bottle, but that is precisely what Reschke Wines has achieved. The family has been a landholder in the Coonawarra region for almost 100 years, with a large landholding which is partly terra rossa, part woodland; 15.5 hectares of merlot, 105 hectares of cabernet sauvignon, 0.5 hectare of cabernet franc and 2.5 hectares of shiraz are in production, with a further 26 hectares planted prior to the end of 2001, mostly to shiraz, but with a little petit verdot. The first release of 1998 Empyrean Cabernet Sauvignon, immaculately packaged, was an exceptionally good wine, the 1999 a return to earth, the 2000 better.

Reschke Taikurri

▼▼▼▼ **1999** Medium red-purple; a cedary, earthy, berry bouquet leads into a light to medium-bodied palate with a range of cedary, savoury, almost lemony flavours; well and truly into the secondary stage of flavour development, and without enough richness on the mid-palate to warrant higher points. A blend of 55 per cent Cabernet Sauvignon and 15 per cent each of Merlot, Malbec and Cabernet Franc. **rating: 85**

best drinking 2004–2008 **drink with** Braised veal

Reschke Empyrean Cabernet Sauvignon

▼▼▼▼ **2000** Medium red-purple; clean, briary/blackcurrant aromas are supported by subtle oak on the bouquet; the light to medium-bodied palate has blackcurrant, cedar and ripe tannins all contributing to pleasing flavour and feel. **rating: 89**

best drinking 2005–2010 **best vintages** '98 **drink with** Spit-roasted haunch of beef • $100

rex vineyard NR

Beaufort, WA 6315 **region** Central Western Australia Zone
phone (08) 9384 3210 **fax** (08) 9384 3210 **open** Not
winemaker Julie White (Contract) **production** 500 cases **est.** 1991

product range Unwooded Chardonnay, Elvira Methode Champenoise, Cabernet Sauvignon Shiraz Merlot.
summary Peter and Gillian Rex have established 2 hectares of chardonnay, cabernet sauvignon, merlot and shiraz. Approximately half of each year's production is sold as grapes; the remainder is contract made by the highly competent Julie White in the Swan Valley.

reynell ★★★★

Reynell Road, Reynella, SA 5161 **region** McLaren Vale
phone (08) 8392 2222 **fax** (08) 8392 2202 **open** 7 days 10–4, except public holidays
winemaker Stephen Pannell **production** 200 cases **est.** 1838
product range ($39.99 R) Basket Pressed Shiraz, Basket Pressed Merlot, Basket Pressed Cabernet Sauvignon.
summary Reynell is the name under which all wines from the historic Reynella winery (once called Chateau Reynella) are released. The range of wines was compressed and taken into the super-premium category with the introduction of the Basket Pressed range in 1997.

Reynell Basket Pressed Shiraz

TTTTT 1998 Impenetrable purple-red, amazing for a 5-year-old wine; the dense, complex black fruit, cedar and cigar aromas of the bouquet, and the equally concentrated, complex, rich and dense palate all suggest that the wine will live forever. Just for good measure, lingering tannins are there, but in balance. Spent 24 months in American oak. Released over 12 months after the 1999 vintage.   **rating: 94**

best drinking 2010–2020 **best vintages** '94, '95, '96, '98 **drink with** Barbecued rump steak • $39.99

reynolds vineyards ★★★★

'Quondong', Cargo Road, Cudal, NSW 2864 (postal) **region** Orange
phone (02) 6364 2330 **fax** (02) 6364 2388 **open** Not
winemaker Jon Reynolds, Nic Millichip, Tom Cleland, Robert Black **production** 250 000 cases **est.** 1994
product range ($12–29 CD) Moon Shadow Chardonnay, Marble Man Merlot, The Jezebel Cabernet Sauvignon (from Orange) at the top tier; then comes the Orange range of Chardonnay, Shiraz, Merlot, Cabernet Merlot, Cabernet Sauvignon; and finally the Little Boomey range (from the Central Ranges) of Sauvignon Blanc, Limited Release Chardonnay, Shiraz, Merlot, Cabernet Merlot, Cabernet Sauvignon.
summary In 2000 the Reynolds brand was acquired by Cabonne Limited. Later that year Cabonne Limited, which joined the stockmarket in 1999, announced a global alliance with Trinchero's Family Estates of the US, best known as the owner of America's biggest brand, Sutter Home. Cabonne is the ninth-largest vineyard operator in Australia, with 900 hectares of vineyards at Molong near Orange and a 20 000-tonne winery. The newly established three-tier range of wines has been put together by the winemaking team headed by Jon Reynolds, with exceptional skill. The labelling is clear, easy to understand, and attractive on the shelf, but it is the consistency of quality of the wines which is so impressive. Nonetheless, the group has not reached is (perhaps optimistic) initial sales targets, and had its shares suspended from trading from the Stock Exchange for a lengthy period.

Reynolds Little Boomey Limited Release Chardonnay

TTTT 2001 Excellent green-yellow; the clean, moderately intense bouquet marries stone fruit with a hint of oak; the well-balanced palate gains some complexity from some creamy notes although it is light-bodied. As with its more expensive brother, shortens slightly on the finish, but is very good value.   **rating: 86**

best drinking Now **drink with** Salmon pizza • $12

Reynolds Moon Shadow Chardonnay

TTTTY 2000 Medium yellow-green; complex bottle-developed aromas and the fusion of fruit and oak are followed by a palate with complex melon and fig flavours, excellent acidity and length, and balanced oak. Maturing impressively.   **rating: 92**

best drinking Now **best vintages** '99, '00 **drink with** Chinese-style steamed fish • $25

Reynolds Little Boomey Shiraz

TTTT 2001 Light to medium red-purple; light, fresh, direct cherry fruit aromas announce a skilfully assembled commercial red wine, with soft, gentle fruit and oak inputs; very good value. Stelvin finished.   **rating: 85**

best drinking Now–2005 **drink with** Lasagne • $12

Reynolds Orange Shiraz

TTTT 2001 Medium red-purple; the clean and moderately intense bouquet has a pleasant mix of raspberry and cherry fruit. The palate has good structure and balance, sustained by fine tannins and subtle oak.   **rating: 87**

best drinking 2004–2008 **drink with** Beef casserole • $17

Reynolds Marble Man Merlot

▼▼▼▼ **2000** Medium red-purple; the clean, moderately intense bouquet offers dark, small berry fruit aromas and subtle oak; the lively and firm palate moves down the same track, opening with savoury, dark fruit flavours and closing with brisk acidity. **rating:** 87

best drinking Now–2007 **drink with** Roast veal • $29

Reynolds Orange Merlot

▼▼▼▼ **2001** Medium red-purple; clearly defined savoury, sappy, olive, earth overtones to the raspberry fruit underneath open proceedings, and the light to medium-bodied palate has more or less precisely the same array of flavours running through to a smooth finish. **rating:** 86

best drinking 2004–2008 **best vintages** '98 **drink with** Stir-fried Asian beef • $17

Reynolds Little Boomey Cabernet Merlot

▼▼▼▼ **2001** Light to medium red-purple; the clean, straightforward bouquet of red berries and a hint of spice is followed by a palate which picks up the pace slightly, with fair depth of red and dark berry fruits supported by light, savoury tannins. Yet another cleverly crafted wine in this budget-priced Little Boomey range. **rating:** 86

best drinking 2004–2008 **drink with** Braised lamb shanks • $12

Reynolds Orange Cabernet Merlot

▼▼▼▼ **2001** Medium red-purple; a clean mix of raspberry and blackcurrant, plus the usual airbrush of oak on the bouquet, leads into smooth blackcurrant fruit, soft, fine tannins and good balance on the palate. **rating:** 87

best drinking 2004–2009 **drink with** Braised rabbit • $17

Reynolds Little Boomey Cabernet Sauvignon

▼▼▼▼ **2001** Medium red-purple; the clean and fresh bouquet has blackcurrant and spice aromas; yet again, very cleverly put together, with blackcurrant fruit and gently ripe tannins on the easy-drinking palate. The price needs no comment. **rating:** 87

best drinking 2004–2009 **drink with** Beef spare ribs • $12

Reynolds The Jezebel Cabernet Sauvignon

▼▼▼▼ **2000** Medium red-purple; the bouquet has a fragrant mix of cedar, earth and black fruits, but the powerful and aggressive palate demands patience, promising much if given time. **rating:** 87

best drinking 2005–2010 **drink with** Devilled kidneys • $29

ribarits estate wines   NR

Sturt Highway, Trentham Cliffs, NSW 2738 (postal) **region** Murray Darling
phone 0409 330 997 **fax** (03) 5024 0332 **open** Not
winemaker Contract **production** 4000 cases **est.** 1998
product range ($6.40–6.80 ML) Chardonnay, Shiraz, Merlot, Cabernet Sauvignon.
summary Adrian Ribarits has developed over 82 hectares of chardonnay, merlot, shiraz and cabernet sauvignon, primarily as a contract grape grower for Simeon Wines. A small part of the grape production is vinified for Ribarits Estate and sold by mail order at yesterday's prices; they have various bronze medals to their credit.

richfield vineyard   NR

Bruxner Highway, Tenterfield, NSW 2372 **region** Northern Slopes Zone
phone (02) 6737 5888 **fax** (02) 6737 5898 **open** Not
winemaker John Cassegrain **est.** 1997
product range Chardonnay, Shiraz, Merlot, Cabernet Sauvignon, with the first releases still in the pipeline.
summary Richfield is owned by Corporation Franco Asiatique, headquartered in Singapore. Bernard Forey is the majority shareholder of the company, and now lives in Brisbane. Denis Parsons, of Bald Mountain Vineyards, is a director and shareholder of the company, and is in charge of management of its operations, as it is only 20 minutes' drive south of Bald Mountain. It is located in a picturesque section of Tenterfield Creek, just to the west of the town of Tenterfield. A substantial vineyard has been established comprising shiraz (11.1 ha), cabernet sauvignon (4.3 ha), merlot (3.7 ha), ruby cabernet (3.1 ha), semillon (2.9 ha), chardonnay (2.6 ha) and verdelho (1.3 ha). The first vintage was made in 2000, and it is expected that the bulk of Richfield's sales will come from the export markets of South-East Asia.

🍏 richmond estate   NR

99 Gadds Lane, North Richmond, NSW 2754 **region** South Coast Zone
phone (02) 4573 1048 **open** Weekends 11–6
winemaker Tony Radanovic **production** 600 cases **est.** 1967
product range ($15–35 CD) Chardonnay, Shiraz, Malbec, Cabernet Sauvignon.
summary While this is the first time Richmond Estate has been listed in the *Wine Companion*, it was featured in a number of books I wrote between 1979 and 1984, as then proprietor Barry Bracken (a Sydney orthopaedic surgeon) was making excellent Shiraz and Cabernet Sauvignon. However, late in 1984 he sold the property, and it went through several owners before being purchased by Monica and Tony Radanovic in 1987. The Radanovics have restored the vineyard, which had been run-down in the years before their purchase, and while only 3 hectares are under vine, the vineyard is used by the University of Western Sydney as its field laboratory for undergraduate wine and wine production courses.

richmond grove   ★★★★

Para Road, Tanunda, SA 5352 **region** Barossa Valley
phone (08) 8563 7300 **fax** (08) 8563 2804 **open** Mon–Fri 10–5, weekends and public holidays 10.30–4.30
winemaker John Vickery **production** NFP **est.** 1977
product range ($12–18 R) Watervale Riesling, Barossa Riesling, Hunter Valley Semillon, Marlborough Sauvignon Blanc, Verdelho, McLaren Vale Chardonnay, French Cask Chardonnay, Chardonnay Pinot, Barossa Shiraz, Coonawarra Shiraz, Cabernet Merlot, Coonawarra Cabernet Sauvignon.
summary Richmond Grove now has two homes, including one in the Barossa Valley, where John Vickery presides. It is owned by Orlando Wyndham and draws its grapes from diverse sources. The Richmond Grove Barossa Valley and Watervale Rieslings made by John Vickery represent excellent value for money (for Riesling) year in, year out. If these were the only wines produced by Richmond Grove, it would have five-star rating. Exports to the UK.

Richmond Grove Watervale Riesling

▼▼▼▼▽ 2002 Light green-yellow; a classic bouquet of mineral, slate, apple and citrus, then smooth mid-palate fruit and a touch of CO_2 on the lingering finish. Has plenty of power.   **rating:** 93
best drinking 2004–2010 **best vintages** '94, '96, '97, '98, '99, '00 **drink with** Steamed fish, Chinese-style • $16

Richmond Grove Padthaway Chardonnay

▼▼▼▼ 2001 Light to medium yellow-green; a clean, essentially fruit-driven bouquet is enhanced by a light touch of oak; the palate likewise comes together well, with good intensity and length, the grapefruit nuances in good regional style. Well priced.   **rating:** 89
best drinking Now **drink with** Pan-fried fish • $16

Richmond Grove Coonawarra Cabernet Sauvignon

▼▼▼▼▽ 2000 Clear red-purple; the bouquet is spotlessly clean, with well-balanced fruit and oak; the palate has good texture, structure and depth to the blackberry fruit, rounded off with quite pronounced tannins which need time to settle, but should do so.   **rating:** 90
best drinking 2005–2012 **best vintages** '98, '00 **drink with** Lamb cutlets • $18

richmond park vineyard   ★★★★

Logie Road, Richmond, Tas 7025 (postal) **region** Southern Tasmania
phone (03) 6265 2949 **fax** (03) 6265 3166 **open** Not
winemaker Andrew Hood (Contract) **production** 250 cases **est.** 1989
product range ($15–22 ML) Chardonnay, Pinot Noir.
summary A small vineyard owned by Tony Park, which gives the clue to the clever name. It is 20 minutes' drive from Hobart, and a particular (and uncommon) attraction for mailing list clients is the availability of 375 ml bottles.

Richmond Park Chardonnay

▼▼▼▼ 2002 Light straw-green; an extremely complex, funky, Burgundian bouquet suggesting the use of some solids in the ferment; the palate is more conventional, fresh and long. An altogether interesting wine. **rating:** 87
best drinking Now–2005 **drink with** Seafood takeaway • $20

ridgeback wines ★★★★

New Chum Gully Estate, Howards Road, Panton Hill, Vic 3759 **region** Yarra Valley
phone (03) 9719 7687 **fax** (03) 9719 7667 **open** By appointment
winemaker Martin Williams MW **production** 1000 cases **est.** 2000
product range ($20–29 ML) Chardonnay, Pinot Noir, Merlot, Cabernet Sauvignon.
summary Ron and Lynne Collings purchased their Panton Hill property in March 1990, clearing the land and making it ready for the first vine planting in 1992. A little over 4 hectares is now planted on the hillside slopes beneath their house, and Ron Collings completed the degree in wine growing at Charles Sturt University in 1997, winning the Dean's Award for Academic Excellence. Most of the grapes were in the past sold to Coldstream Hills, but Ron Collings made small batches of wine himself each year, which ultimately led to the decision to establish the Ridgeback label, with contract winemaking, although Collings is never far from the scene at vintage. The name, incidentally, is intended to reflect in part the rolling hillside of Panton Hill, and to salute the Collings' Rhodesian Ridgeback dog. Exports to the UK.

Ridgeback Chardonnay
♥♥♥♥♡ **2001** Medium yellow-green; the bouquet offers a powerful interplay between intense nectarine and melon fruit on the one hand, and barrel ferment on the other; the palate is equally intense and tightly knit; should cellar well. **rating:** 90
best drinking Now–2005 **best vintages** '00 **drink with** Crumbed brains • $20

Ridgeback Pinot Noir
♥♥♥♥ **2001** Red-purple; the clean, firm bouquet has focused plum and black cherry fruit; the rich, deep and compact palate has precisely the same flavours. Should develop complexity over the next few years and merit even higher points. **rating:** 89
best drinking 2004–2008 **drink with** Braised duck • $24

Ridgeback Cabernet Sauvignon
♥♥♥♥♡ **2001** Bright purple-red; deep blackcurrant and blackberry fruit on the bouquet is followed by a powerful, focused palate with fruit in exactly the same register as the bouquet; very impressive for the vintage. **rating:** 90
best drinking 2005–2010 **best vintages** '01 **drink with** Roast kid • $23

🐾 rigel wines ★★★★

PO Box 18062, Collins Street East, Melbourne Vic 8004 **region** Mornington Peninsula
phone 1300 131 081 **fax** 1300 131 281 **open** From early 2004 at the General Store, Merricks
winemaker Richard McIntyre (Contract) **production** 1500 cases **est.** 1989
product range ($16.95–38 ML) The wines come under three labels: under Rigel Mornington Peninsula, Chardonnay, Pinot Noir and Shiraz; under Rigel Barooga Road, Chardonnay, Shiraz, Merlot and Cabernet Sauvignon; and under Rigel XLV, Sangiovese, Nebbiolo and Zinfandel.
summary Rigel Wine Company is owned by Dr Damian and Sue Ireland and Michael and Mary Calman; the Irelands own the Mornington Peninsula vineyard at Shoreham, which provides the grapes for the super-premium Rigel label. The second property is at Tocumwal, and has 80 hectares of vines and 6 kilometres of Murray River frontage. Most of the grapes are sold to other winemakers, but part of the production has been vinified for both the local and export markets. The 2003 and subsequent vintages will be made by Master Winemakers, and when the 2002 Rigel wines are released, they will bear a new label.

Rigel Chardonnay
♥♥♥♥♡ **2001** Medium yellow-green; the clean bouquet has good integration and balance between tangy fruit and oak; strong barrel-ferment/malolactic-ferment wild yeast characters are reflected in the nutty/creamy nuances of the palate. Works very well in typical Mornington fashion. **rating:** 90
best drinking Now–2007 **best vintages** '01 **drink with** Seafood risotto • $32

Rigel Pinot Noir
♥♥♥♥ **2001** Light but vivid purple-red; gently fragrant cherry, strawberry and slightly minty aromas lead into a palate which picks up the pace dramatically, with more texture to the strawberry/cherry fruit. However, traces of the fractionally unripe fruit (mint) are still evident. **rating:** 89
best drinking Now–2007 **drink with** Ragout of veal kidneys • $29

Rigel Shiraz

TTTT 2001 Light to medium red-purple; cedary, leafy, spicy, minty overtones to the blackberry fruit of the bouquet flow through into a palate offering a mix of savoury and blackberry fruit; good length and tannins and a lingering aftertaste. Amazing to see the 14.5° alcohol disclosed on the label; the wine does not show any late-picked characters. **rating:** 88

best drinking 2005–2010 **drink with** Rare roast beef • $35

rimfire vineyards ★★★

Bismarck Street, MacLagan, Qld 4352 **region** Queensland Zone
phone (07) 4692 1129 **fax** (07) 4692 1260 **open** 7 days 10–5
winemaker Tony Connellan **production** 6000 cases **est.** 1991
product range ($10–16 CD) Verdelho, Chardonnay, Marsanne Chardonnay, Pioneer White, Country Rose, Ruby Cabernet, Shiraz; fortifieds.
summary The Connellan family (parents Margaret and Tony and children Michelle, Peter and Louise) began planting the 12-hectare, 14-variety Rimfire Vineyards in 1991 as a means of diversification of their very large (1500-ha) cattle stud in the foothills of the Bunya Mountains, 45 minutes' drive northeast of Toowoomba. Increasingly producing a kaleidoscopic array of wines, the majority without any regional claim of origin. The Black Bull Cafe is open daily 10–5, blackboard menu and wine by the glass. Annual Jazz on the Lawn concert each spring.

rivendell NR

Lot 328 Wildwood Road, Yallingup, WA 6282 **region** Margaret River
phone (08) 9755 2235 **fax** (08) 9755 2301 **open** 7 days 10–5
winemaker Mark Standish, Michael Adderley **production** 3000 cases **est.** 1987
product range ($12.50–14.50 CD) Semillon Sauvignon Blanc, Honeysuckle Late Harvest Semillon, Verdelho, Shiraz Cabernet.
summary With 4 hectares of vineyards in bearing, production for Rivendell is supplemented by contract-grown grapes. The cellar-door sales facility is in a garden setting, complete with restaurant. An unusual sideline is the sale of 50 types of preserves, jams and chutneys. No recent tastings.

riverbank estate NR

126 Hamersley Road, Caversham, WA 6055 **region** Swan Valley
phone (08) 9377 1805 **fax** (08) 9377 2168 **open** Weekends and public holidays 10–5
winemaker Robert James Bond **production** 3500 cases **est.** 1993
product range ($12–16 CD) Semillon, Verdelho, Chenin, Chardonnay, Classic Sweet White, Pinot Noir, Grenache Shiraz, Shiraz, Cabernet, Fortified Muscat, Fortified Shiraz.
summary Robert Bond, a graduate of Charles Sturt University and a Swan Valley viticulturist for 20 years, established RiverBank Estate in 1993. He draws upon 11 hectares of estate plantings and, in his words, 'The wines are unashamedly full bodied, produced from ripe grapes in what is recognised as a hot grape growing region.' Wines extending back over many vintages are available at the cellar door.

riverina estate ★★★☆

700 Kidman Way, Griffith, NSW 2680 **region** Riverina
phone (02) 6963 8300 **fax** (02) 6962 4628 **open** Mon–Sat 9–5
winemaker Sam Trimboli **production** 650 000 cases **est.** 1969
product range ($5–25 CD) An extensive range of varietal wines with Warburn Estate, Ballingal Estate 3 Corners, Lizard Ridge and Kanga's Leap, Bushmans Gully, Kimberly Creek and Lombard Station all offering a kaleidoscopic range of varietals and varietal blends.
summary One of the large producers of the region, drawing upon 1000 hectares of estate plantings. While much of the wine is sold in bulk to other producers, selected parcels of the best of the grapes are made into table wines, with quite spectacular success. At the 1997 National Wine Show, Riverina Wines won an astonishing six gold medals, topping no less than four classes. That success has, it seems, given rise to the introduction of the Show Reserve wines, and while the 1997 success has not been equalled since, the top wines continue to impress. Exports to the US.

Warburn Estate Chardonnay

▼▼▼▽ **2002** Light to medium green-yellow; citrus, herb and stone fruit aromas and flavours are somewhat compromised by odd, bacony oak characters. A pity. **rating:** 84

best drinking Now **drink with** KFC • $11.10

riversands vineyards NR

Whytes Road, St George, Qld 4487 **region** Queensland Zone
phone (07) 4625 3643 **fax** (07) 4625 5043 **open** Mon–Sat 8–6, Sun 9–4
winemaker Ballandean Estate (Contract) **production** 4000 cases **est.** 1990
product range ($12–20 CD) Beardmore's Dry White, Explorers Chardonnay, Major Mitchell White, Western Rivers Run (dry red), Dr Seidel's Soft Red, Ellen Meacle Merlot, Stirlings Reserve, Golden Liqueur Muscat, Black Magic Port.
summary Riversands is situated on the banks of the Balonne River near St George in the southwest corner of Queensland. It is a mixed wine grape and table grape business, acquired by present owners Alison and David Blacket in 1996. The wines are very competently made under contract at Ballandean Estate and have already accumulated a number of silver and bronze medals. The Chardonnay is particularly meritorious.

🐌 robert channon wines ★★★★☆

Bradley Lane, Stanthorpe, Qld 4380 **region** Granite Belt
phone (07) 4683 3260 **fax** (07) 4683 3109 **open** Fri–Sun 10–5
winemaker Mark Ravenscroft **production** 3500 cases **est.** 1998
product range ($13–24.50 CD) Verdelho, Singing Lake White, Chardonnay, Singing Lake Rose, Light Horse Red, Singing Lake Dry Red, Merlot, Shiraz Cabernet Sauvignon, Casanova's Storm Liqueur Muscat.
summary Peggy and Robert Channon have established 1.6 hectares each of chardonnay, verdelho, merlot, shiraz and cabernet sauvignon under permanent bird protection netting. The initial cost of installing permanent netting is high, but in the long term it is well worth it. While primarily aimed at excluding birds, it also protects the grapes against hail damage. Finally, there is no pressure to pick the grapes before they are fully ripe. The strategy has already provided rewards with both the 2001 Verdelho and the 2000 Shiraz Cabernet Sauvignon winning gold medals at wine shows, the Verdelho winning the trophy for Best Queensland White Wine at the Queensland Wine Awards, the Shiraz Cabernet Sauvignon being runner up for Best Red Wine at the same show. The Shiraz Cabernet Sauvignon, incidentally, won its gold medal at the 2002 Small Winemakers Competition, which receives entries from all over Australia.

Robert Channon Verdelho

▼▼▼▼▼ **2002** Light straw-green; the highly aromatic bouquet is spotlessly clean, with some zesty citrussy characters reminiscent of the best Primo Estate Colombards. The palate is, if anything, even better, with intense, long, racy passionfruit-accented flavours and great acidity. The best Australian Verdelho to ever cross my palate. **rating:** 94

best drinking Now–2005 **best vintages** '02 **drink with** Seafood • $18.50

roberts estate ★★☆

Game Street, Merbein, Vic 3505 **region** Murray Darling
phone (03) 5024 2944 **fax** (03) 5024 2877 **open** Not
winemaker Ian McElhinney **production** 80 000 cases **est.** 1998
product range ($8–10 R) Chardonnay, Merlot, Shiraz, Cabernet Sauvignon; under the Denbeigh label Chardonnay, Semillon Chardonnay, Colombard Chardonnay, Shiraz, Cabernet Sauvignon, Shiraz Cabernet.
summary A very large winery acting as a processing point for grapes grown up and down the Murray River. Over 10 000 tonnes are crushed each vintage; much of the wine is sold in bulk to others, but some is exported under the Denbeigh and Kombacy labels.

robert stein vineyard ★★★☆

Pipeclay Lane, Mudgee, NSW 2850 **region** Mudgee
phone (02) 6373 3991 **fax** (02) 6373 3709 **open** 7 days 10–4.30
winemaker Robert Stein, Michael Slater **production** 5000 cases **est.** 1976
product range ($11–25 CD) Gewurztraminer, Semillon, Semillon Riesling, Semillon Chardonnay, Unwooded Chardonnay, Chardonnay, Cabernet Rose, Shiraz, Reserve Shiraz (cellar door only), Cabernet Sauvignon Shiraz, Cabernet Sauvignon and a range of muscats and ports.

summary The sweeping panorama from the winery is its own reward for cellar-door visitors. Right from the outset this has been a substantial operation, which has managed to sell the greater part of its production direct from the winery by mail order and through the cellar door, with retail distribution in Sydney, Victoria and South Australia. Wine quality, once variable, albeit with top wines from time to time, has become much more consistent. Exports to the UK.

Robert Stein Reserve Shiraz

TTTT 2001 Medium to full red-purple; spotlessly clean black fruits plus a hint of dark chocolate on the bouquet, then a well-balanced and modulated medium-bodied palate offering raspberry and blackberry fruit supported throughout by subtle oak. **rating: 89**

best drinking 2005–2015 **drink with** Grilled porterhouse • $25

Robert Stein Shiraz Cabernet

TTTT 2000 Youthful red-purple, particularly given its age; the moderately intense bouquet has blackberry and blackcurrant fruit; the light to medium-bodied palate has fair balance, but not particularly evocative; somewhat amorphous. Could well be in a development phase. **rating: 85**

best drinking 2004–2009 **drink with** Lamb casserole • $17

robinsons family vineyards ★★★

Curtin Road, Ballandean, Qld 4382 **region** Granite Belt
phone (07) 4684 1216 **fax** (07) 4684 1216 **open** 7 days 10–5
winemaker Craig Robinson **production** 3000 cases **est.** 1969
product range ($14–22 CD) Unwooded Chardonnay, Chardonnay, Vintage Brut, Shiraz, Shiraz Cabernet, Cabernet Sauvignon, Lyra Liqueur.
summary One of the pioneers of the Granite Belt, with the second generation of the family Robinson now in control. One thing has not changed: the strongly held belief of the Robinsons that the Granite Belt should be regarded as a cool, rather than warm, climate. It is a tricky debate, because some climatic measurements point one way, others in the opposite direction. Embedded in all this are semantic arguments about the meaning of the words 'cool' and 'warm'. Suffice it to say that shiraz and (conspicuously) cabernet sauvignon are the most suitable red varieties for that region; semillon, verdelho and chardonnay are the best white varieties.

Robinsons Family Chardonnay

TTTT 2000 Light to medium green-yellow, bright and clear; the clean, moderately intense bouquet offers light citrus and subtle oak; the light to medium-bodied palate follows with the same path, the neatly handled oak providing the complexity which the fruit lacks. Barrel fermented and aged in oak for 10 months. Bold and modern new labelling is another step in the right direction. The grapes are grown in the Granite Belt and King Valley. **rating: 86**

best drinking Now **best vintages** '83, '85, '89, '92, '93 **drink with** Calamari • $18

Robinsons Family Shiraz

TTT♀ 2000 Medium red-purple; the moderately intense bouquet has ripe fruit with hints of jam and game, but the medium-bodied palate veers away from over-ripeness towards berry and mint, with a slightly savoury finish. **rating: 84**

best drinking 2004–2007 **best vintages** '81, '82, '83, '85, '93 **drink with** Kangaroo fillet • $20

robinvale ★★★

Sea Lake Road, Robinvale, Vic 3549 **region** Murray Darling
phone (03) 5026 3955 **fax** (03) 5026 1123 **open** Mon–Fri 9–6, Sun 1–6
winemaker Bill Caracatsanoudis **production** 10 000 cases **est.** 1976
product range ($7.50–28 CD) A unique offering of white, red and fortified wines, the majority estate-grown under the internationally recognised Bio-Dynamic Demeter Grade A requirements, the highest level. In addition, a number are Kosher wines, and all are certified free of any genetically modified organisms.
summary Robinvale was one of the first Australian wineries to be fully accredited with the Biodynamic Agricultural Association of Australia. Most, but not all, of the wines are produced from organically grown grapes, with certain of the wines made preservative-free. Production has increased dramatically, no doubt reflecting the interest in organic and biodynamic viticulture and winemaking. Exports to the UK, Japan, Belgium, Canada and the US.

Robinvale Demeter Lexia

ΥΥΥΥ **2002** Light straw; the bouquet has obvious spicy, grapey varietal aromas. The palate is likewise, well balanced, not too sweet, just fruity. This preservative-free dry white wine is sealed with a Stelvin cap; this may prolong its life, but commonsense says it should be consumed well before the next vintage becomes available.

rating: 83

best drinking Now **drink with** Avocado salad • $15

Robinvale Demeter Reserve Kerner

ΥΥΥΥ **2002** Light straw-green; a hint of bottling SO_2 is evident, alongside the mineral and wild herb aromas; a crisp, tangy, minerally palate has lemony acidity on the finish, to give length and balance. No GMOs; vegan/vegetarian suitable; and, of course, biodynamic. Made from a rarely seen German cross, of which Robinvale has 1.5 hectares planted. **rating: 84**

best drinking Now–2006 **drink with** Seafood • $15

Robinvale Organic Origins

ΥΥΥΥ **2002** Bright purple-red; fresh, cherry plum and blackcurrant aromas are followed by a light to medium-bodied palate; well-balanced and refined tannins. A blend of Shiraz, Cabernet Sauvignon and Merlot. **rating: 84**

best drinking Now–2006 **drink with** Braised rabbit • $15

Robinvale Demeter Primitivo di Gioia

ΥΥΥΥ **2000** Medium red-purple; a mix of spice, plum and prune and more savoury aromas lead into a palate with attractive sweet fruit and a dry finish. There are surprisingly few tannins, which might have given the wine more structure. Primitivo is of course the Italian name for Zinfandel. **rating: 85**

best drinking Now–2005 **drink with** Home-made pasta • $12

Robinvale Demeter No Preservatives Cabernets

ΥΥΥΥ **2002** Vivid red-purple; the bouquet has dark, ripe fruit aromas, as yet with no hint of aldehydes. The palate has good depth and a soft, velvety structure. A particularly good example of a no preservative wine, although, once again, don't delay in drinking it. A blend of Cabernet Sauvignon, Cabernet Franc, Ruby Cabernet and Merlot. **rating: 87**

best drinking Now **drink with** Lamb casserole • $20

roche wines   NR

Broke Road, Pokolbin, NSW 2320 **region** Lower Hunter Valley
phone (02) 4998 7600 **fax** (02) 4998 7706 **open** 7 days 10–5
winemaker Sarah-Kate Wilson (Contract) **production** 8500 cases **est.** 1999
product range ($20–45 R) Tallawanta range of Semillon, Unwooded Chardonnay, Chardonnay, Shiraz.
summary Roche Wines, with its production of 8500 cases from 7 hectares each of semillon and shiraz and 5 hectares of chardonnay, is but the tip of the iceberg of the massive investment made by Bill Roche in the Pokolbin subregion. He has transformed the old Hungerford Hill development on the corner of Broke and McDonalds Roads, and built a luxurious resort hotel with extensive gardens and an Irish pub on the old Tallawanta Vineyard, as well as resuscitating the vines on Tallawanta. The wines are all sold on-site through the various outlets in the overall development.

rochford   ★★★★☆

Romsey Park, Rochford, Vic 3442 **region** Macedon Ranges
phone (03) 5962 2119 **fax** (03) 5962 5319 **open** By appointment
winemaker David Creed **production** 2000 cases **est.** 1983
product range ($13–35 R) Riesling, Chardonnay, Macedon Blanc de Blancs, Pinot Noir, Cabernet Sauvignon; Romsey Park label includes Riesling, Pinot Grigio, Chardonnay, Pinot Noir, Merlot, Cabernet Sauvignon.
summary Since acquiring Rochford in early 1998, Helmut Konecsny and Yvonne Lodoco-Konecsny have made a substantial investment in the estate vineyards, but have been more than content to leave the style unchanged, with David Creed continuing as winemaker. The emphasis is on Chardonnay and Pinot Noir, and as the new plantings come into bearing, so will production increase. Following the acquisition of Eyton-on-Yarra in late 2001, winemaking has moved to that site under the direction of David Creed.

rochford's eyton   NR

Cnr Maroondah Highway and Hill Road, Coldstream, Vic 3370 **region** Yarra Valley
phone (03) 5962 2119 **fax** (03) 5962 5319 **open** 7 days 10–5
winemaker David Creed **production** 12 000 cases **est.** 1993
product range ($22–40 R) There were three labels in the range: at the top NDC Reserve, a tribute to the late Newell Cowan, who effectively founded Eyton-on-Yarra; the main varietal range under the Eyton label; and the third label range of Dalry Road, the name of the second vineyard owned by Deidre Cowan. This range will change significantly once existing stocks are depleted.
summary Following the acquisition of Eyton-on-Yarra by Helmut and Yvonne Konecsny, major changes have followed. Most obvious is the renaming of the winery and brand, slightly less so the move of the winemaking operations of Rochford (which continues as an independent, estate-based brand) to Rochford's Eyton. The total production is 14 000 cases: 12 000 from the Yarra Valley and 2000 from the Macedon Ranges. No wines submitted for tasting since the acquisition.

rockbare wines   ★★★☆

9 Sandalwood Drive, Woodside, SA 5352 (postal) **region** McLaren Vale
phone (08) 8389 9584 **fax** (08) 8389 9587 **open** Not
winemaker Tim Burvill **production** 20 000 cases **est.** 2000
product range ($15–35 R) McLaren Vale Chardonnay, McLaren Vale Shiraz; then the higher-priced Elysian Fields range with Clare Valley Riesling, Adelaide Hills Chardonnay, Barossa Valley Shiraz.
summary A native of Western Australia, Tim Burvill moved to South Australia in 1993 to undertake the winemaking course at the University of Adelaide Roseworthy Campus. Having completed an honours degree in oenology he was recruited by Southcorp, and quickly found himself in a senior winemaking position, with responsibility for super-premium whites including Penfolds Yattarna. Knowing full well the cost of setting up a winery, he makes the wines under lend-lease arrangements with other wineries. They are distributed in Queensland, Victoria, the ACT and New South Wales by Wine Source, and in the other states by Red+White. Exports to the US and Canada.

RockBare Chardonnay
TTTT 2002 Light green-yellow; the bouquet is clean, light and tangy, the oak influence subliminal. The palate is light, fresh and well crafted; there simply isn't much depth to the fruit. Has modest aspirations to bottle development.   **rating:** 84
best drinking Now–2005 **drink with** Grilled whiting • $15

RockBare Shiraz
TTTT 2001 Medium red-purple; the bouquet offers a complex amalgam of earthy shiraz and well-handled oak; the palate has abundant sweet cherry flavour, but is neither heavy nor alcoholic; good length. Very good value.   **rating:** 89
best drinking Now–2008 **drink with** Braised beef • $15

rockfield estate vineyard   ★★★☆

Rosa Glen Road, Margaret River, WA 6285 **region** Margaret River
phone (08) 9757 5006 **fax** (08) 9757 5006 **open** 7 days 10.30–5
winemaker Mike Lemmes **production** 8000 cases **est.** 1997
product range ($13–30 CD) Semillon, Semillon Sauvignon Blanc, Unwooded Chardonnay, Chardonnay, Chardonnay Methode Champenoise, Autumn Harvest Semillon, Rosa (Rose), Shiraz, Cabernet Merlot.
summary Rockfield Estate Vineyard is very much a family affair. Dr Andrew Gaman wears the hats of chief executive officer, assistant winemaker and co-marketing manager; wife Anne Gaman is a Director; Alex Gaman and Nick McPherson are viticulturists, Andrew Gaman Jr is also an assistant winemaker and Anna Walter (née Gaman) helps Dr Andrew Gaman with the marketing. The Chapman Brook meanders through the property, the vines running from its banks up to the wooded slopes above the valley floor, and the winery offers light refreshments and food from the cafe throughout the day. Exports to the UK, Denmark, India, Thailand, Vietnam and Singapore.

Rockfield Estate Semillon
TTTT 2002 Light straw-green; the clean, attractive bouquet has ripe fruit with some similarities to Sauvignon Blanc; a powerful, tight, layered palate easily carries the 13.5° alcohol. In the inimitable Margaret River style.
best drinking Now–2007 **drink with** Lemon-marinated fish • $14.95   **rating:** 89

Rockfield Estate Semillon Sauvignon Blanc

❜❜❜❜ 2002 Light straw-green; the crisp, fresh bouquet has a range of mineral, herb and spice aromas; the palate has very good balance and mouthfeel; in a slightly sweeter fruit spectrum, but with an appropriately dry finish.

rating: 87

best drinking Now–2006 **drink with** Poached scallops in white wine sauce • $14.95

Rockfield Estate Unwooded Chardonnay

❜❜❜❜ 2002 Light green-yellow; a fresh, tangy bouquet with some grapefruit leads into a relatively light-bodied palate which does, however, have a clear expression of varietal fruit.

rating: 85

best drinking Now–2005 **drink with** Seafood risotto • $14.95

Rockfield Estate Chardonnay

❜❜❜❜ 2001 Light to medium yellow-green; strong, charry barrel-ferment aromas dominate the bouquet; the same characters come through on the palate; the stone fruit comes second, but isn't knocked out. **rating:** 85

best drinking Now–2006 **drink with** Brains in black butter sauce • $21.95

rockford ★★★★☆

Krondorf Road, Tanunda, SA 5352 **region** Barossa Valley
phone (08) 8563 2720 **fax** (08) 8563 3787 **open** Mon–Sat 11–5
winemaker Robert O'Callaghan, Chris Ringland **production** NFP **est.** 1984
product range ($10.50–53 CD) Eden Valley Riesling, Local Growers Semillon, White Frontignac, Alicante Bouchet, RD Pinot Chardonnay, Moppa Springs (Grenache Shiraz Mataro), Rod & Spur (Shiraz Cabernet), Basket Press Shiraz, Sparkling Black Shiraz, Cabernet Sauvignon, Marion Tawny Port.
summary The wines are sold through Adelaide retailers only (and the cellar door) and are unknown to most eastern Australian wine drinkers, which is a great pity, because these are some of the most individual, spectacularly flavoured wines made in the Barossa today, with an emphasis on old, low-yielding dryland vineyards. This South Australian slur on the palates of Victoria and New South Wales is exacerbated by the fact that the wines are exported to Switzerland, the UK and New Zealand; it all goes to show that we need proper authority to protect our living treasures.

Rockford Eden Valley Riesling

❜❜❜❜❜ 2000 Medium yellow-green; powerful bottle-developed lime aromas with a hint of underlying, traditional mineral and kerosene lead into a similarly powerful and classic palate with a bone-dry finish. **rating:** 90

best drinking Now–2010 **best vintages** '86, '88, '90, '94, '96, '00 **drink with** Kassler • $17.50

Rockford White Frontignac

❜❜❜❜ 2002 Pale straw-green; voluminous spicy/grapey varietal aromas lead to a palate stacked with flavour, the residual sugar well judged; drop-dead cellar-door style.

rating: 88

best drinking Now **drink with** Asian • $12.50

Rockford Black Shiraz

❜❜❜❜❜ NV Medium red, the purple starting to fade slightly; the moderately intense bouquet has the usual array of spice, earth, truffles and berries, moving into overdrive on the palate, which has exceptional finesse and length, a range of cedary truffly berry flavours, and an excellent dry finish. Disgorged August 2002. **rating:** 95

best drinking Now–2020 **drink with** Needs no accompaniment • $53

Rockford Alicante Bouchet Rose

❜❜❜❜ 2002 Vivid fuchsia; a bright, fresh and vibrant juicy/citrussy bouquet is followed by a palate with distinct sweetness; another cellar-door killer. The only maker of a varietal Alicante Bouchet in Australia. **rating:** 85

best drinking Now **drink with** Antipasto • $15

Rockford Basket Press Shiraz

❜❜❜❜ 2000 Medium red-purple; a very traditional style, with red and black fruit flavours merging into vanilla oak on the bouquet; riper, dark berry fruit comes through on the smooth but not particularly complex palate; for once, seems slightly off the pace.

rating: 87

best drinking 2004–2010 **best vintages** '86, '90, '91, '92, '95 **drink with** Smoked beef • $41

Rockford Moppa Springs

❜❜❜❜ 1999 Medium red-purple; light but fragrant juicy berry fruit aromas are followed by a light to medium-bodied palate which shows the Grenache first up, then gains structure from the Shiraz and Mataro in the blend.

rating: 85

best drinking Now–2006 **drink with** Pizza • $21.50

Rockford Cabernet Sauvignon

♥♥♥♥ 2000 Medium red-purple; the medium-bodied palate has gently sweet blackberry fruit swathed in equally gentle earth and vanilla, the tannins soft. **rating: 86**

best drinking 2005–2010 **drink with** Kangaroo fillet

Rockford PS Marion Tawny

♥♥♥♥ NV Bright, clear tawny; a clean and fresh bouquet with controlled rancio; the elegant and quite fresh (though not young) palate has exemplary light and clean biscuity/tangy flavours before a dry finish. **rating: 89**

best drinking Now **drink with** Coffee and biscuits • $25

🐌 rock house   NR

St Agnes Hill, Calder Highway, Kyneton, Vic 3444 (postal) **region** Macedon Ranges
phone (03) 5422 2205 **fax** (03) 9388 9355 **open** Not
winemaker Malcolm Stewart **production** 350 cases **est.** 1990
product range ($11–16.50 ML) Riesling, Kyneton Assemblage (red blend).
summary Ray Lacey and partners have established 6 hectares of riesling, cabernet sauvignon and merlot. By far the greatest percentage of the production is sold as grapes, with 5 tonnes being used for the Rock House wines. There are no cellar-door sales; all the wine is sold through local retail outlets and by mail order.

roehr   NR

Roehr Road, Ebenezer near Nuriootpa, SA 5355 **region** Barossa Valley
phone (08) 8565 6242 **fax** (08) 8565 6242 **open** Not
winemaker Contract **production** 300 cases **est.** 1995
product range Elmor's Ebenezer Old Vine Shiraz.
summary Karl Wilhelm Roehr arrived in Australia in 1841, and was amongst the earliest settlers at Ebenezer in the northern end of the Barossa Valley. His great great-grandson Elmor Roehr is the custodian of 20 hectares of shiraz, grenache, mataro and chardonnay on a vineyard passed down through the generations. In 1995 he decided to venture into winemaking and produced a Shiraz from 80-year-old vines which typically crop at less than 1.5 tonnes to the acre. It is sold exclusively in Germany and the US.

romavilla   NR

Northern Road, Roma, Qld 4455 **region** Queensland Zone
phone (07) 4622 1822 **fax** (07) 4622 1822 **open** Mon–Fri 8–5, Sat 9–12, 2–4
winemaker David Wall, Richard Wall **production** 2500 cases **est.** 1863
product range ($10–40 CD) An extensive range of varietal and generic table wines including Riesling, Crouchen, Chenin Blanc, Viognier, White Burgundy, Chardonnay, Reserve Chardonnay, Mist (sweet), Gold (sweet), Rose, Pinot Noir, Ruby Cabernet, Cellarman's Shiraz, Shiraz Cabernet and fortified wine styles, including Madeira and Tawny Port, are on sale at the winery; the Very Old Tawny Port is made from a blend of material ranging in age from 10 to 25 years.
summary An amazing historic relic, seemingly untouched since its 19th-century heyday, producing conventional table wines but still providing some extraordinary fortifieds, including a truly stylish Madeira made from Riesling and Syrian (the latter variety originating in Persia). David Wall has now been joined by son Richard in the business, which will hopefully ensure continuity for this important part of Australian wine history. Exports to Hong Kong.

rosabrook estate   ★★★★☆

Rosa Brook Road, Margaret River, WA 6285 **region** Margaret River
phone (08) 9757 2286 **fax** (08) 9757 3634 **open** 7 days 10–4
winemaker Simon Keall **production** 4000 cases **est.** 1980
product range ($15–22 CD) Semillon Sauvignon Blanc, Chardonnay, Autumn Harvest Riesling, Botrytis Riesling, Shiraz, Cabernet Merlot.
summary The 14-hectare Rosabrook Estate vineyards have been established progressively since 1980, with 7 varieties planted. The cellar-door facility is housed in what was Margaret River's first commercial abattoir, built in the early 1930s; a new winery was constructed in 1993. Its abortive acquisition by Palandri Wines should not divert attention from the quality of the wines.

Rosabrook Estate Chardonnay
🍷🍷🍷🍷🍷 **2002** Light straw-green; a very well-balanced amalgam of citrussy fruit and oak on the bouquet flows through into a palate with considerable length and style; fine oak again a feature. Well-deserved gold medal at the Qantas Wine Show of Western Australia 2002. **rating:** 94
best drinking Now–2005 **best vintages** '02 **drink with** Tempura

rosebrook estate   NR

1090 Maitlandvale Road, Rosebrook, NSW 2320 **region** Lower Hunter Valley
phone (02) 4930 1114 **fax** (02) 4930 1690 **open** By appointment
winemaker Graeme Levick **production** 1200 cases **est.** 2000
product range ($12–20 CD) Verdelho, Unwooded Chardonnay, Chardonnay, Shiraz, Muscat.
summary Graeme and Tania Levick run Rosebrook Estate and Hunter River Retreat as parallel operations. The retreat provides self-contained cottages, horse-riding, tennis, canoeing, swimming, bushwalking, fishing, a riverside picnic area, a recreation room and a minibus for winery tours and transport to functions or events in the area. Somewhere in the middle of all of this they have established 2.5 hectares each of chardonnay and verdelho, purchasing shiraz and muscat to complete the product range.

rosemount estate (hunter valley)   ★★★★

Rosemount Road, Denman, NSW 2328 **region** Upper Hunter Valley
phone (02) 6549 6450 **fax** (02) 6549 6499 **open** 7 days 10–4
winemaker Philip Shaw **production** NFP **est.** 1969
product range ($8.99–55.99 R) A very large range of wines which in almost all instances are varietally identified, sometimes with the conjunction of vineyards at the top end of the range; the lower-priced volume varietals increasingly come from all parts of southeast Australia. Names and label designs change regularly, but the emphasis remains on the classic varietals. Roxburgh Chardonnay is the white flag-bearer; Mountain Blue Shiraz Cabernet the real leader. Chardonnay, Shiraz and Cabernet Sauvignon under the labels are consistently excellent at the price. The regional range encompasses Coonawarra, Orange and Mudgee (Hill of Gold).
summary Rosemount Estate achieved a miraculous balancing act: maintaining wine quality while presiding over an ever-expanding empire and dramatically increasing production. The wines were consistently of excellent value; all had real character and individuality; not a few were startlingly good. The outcome was the merger with Southcorp in March 2001; while in financial terms Southcorp was the acquirer, all the key management positions within the merged group are held by Rosemount executives. However, the miracle ended in the first quarter of 2003 in no uncertain terms, with the forced departure of chief executive Keith Lambert, followed by the resignation of the chief financial officer, triggered by a distressingly poor financial performance throughout 2001/2002 and thereafter. Exports worldwide.

Rosemount Estate Diamond Label Semillon Sauvignon Blanc
🍷🍷🍷🍷 **2002** Light straw-green; a clean, light, fresh bouquet has hints of gooseberry and kiwi fruit; the light-bodied palate has the same fruit characters; well balanced and quite long. Good value. **rating:** 85
best drinking Now–2005 **drink with** Deep-fried fish • $10

Rosemount Estate Diamond Label Semillon Chardonnay
🍷🍷🍷🍷 **2002** Medium yellow-green, bright but quite developed for its age, doubtless reflecting 12 hours' skin contact; the bouquet has a pleasing mix of honey, stone fruit, and the barest suggestion of oak. The full-flavoured palate is fully developed and slightly sweet; a punter's special. **rating:** 85
best drinking Now **drink with** KFC • $10

Rosemount Estate Rose Label Orange Vineyard Chardonnay
🍷🍷🍷🍷🍷 **2001** Medium yellow-green; the bouquet is clean and complex, with good fruit and oak balance; an elegant palate opens with citrus and melon fruit, the barrel fermentation in French oak adding to the interest; good length and concentration. Starred in the 2003 Divine State of Origin Challenge. **rating:** 94
best drinking Now–2006 **best vintages** '92, '95, '96, '97, '99, '00, '01 **drink with** Oyster soup • $22.99

Rosemount Estate Roxburgh Chardonnay
🍷🍷🍷🍷🍷 **2001** Medium to full yellow-green; a big, complex and rich bouquet, with obvious barrel-ferment characters and the suggestion of some solids to add to complexity; the rich and concentrated palate has good length and intensity, with the oak controlled and the acidity good. The best for years under this label. **rating:** 94
best drinking Now–2007 **best vintages** '86, '87, '89, '91, '92, '93, '95, '97, '01 **drink with** Veal, pork • $54.99

Rosemount Estate Show Reserve Chardonnay

▼▼▼▼ 2001 Medium yellow-green; smooth, peachy fruit with well-integrated oak is followed by an equally peachy palate in good early-drinking style. Very different from the preceding vintage.　　**rating**: 89

best drinking Now　**best vintages** '97, '99　**drink with** Pan-fried veal • $22

Rosemount Estate Diamond Label Shiraz

▼▼▼▼ 2001 Medium purple-red; a quite complex bouquet has dark berry fruit and some savoury overtones, then a palate with good fruit weight, soft and rounded, softly sweet, and tied together by subtle oak. **rating**: 88

best drinking Now–2007　**best vintages** '88, '90, '91, '92, '94, '96, '98, '99, '00　**drink with** Lamb shanks • $15

Rosemount Estate Rose Label Orange Vineyard Shiraz

▼▼▼▼▼ 2000 Medium red-purple; the bouquet is clean, with dark berry fruit; the palate gathers pace and intensity with a mix of blackberry and spice; as yet, firm and spritely; will soften. Multiple trophy winner Liquorland National Wine Show 2002.　　**rating**: 94

best drinking 2005–2012　**best vintages** '97, '00　**drink with** Moroccan lamb • $31

Rosemount Estate Diamond Label Shiraz Cabernet

▼▼▼▼ 2002 Youthful purple-red; a clean and lively bouquet with an overlay of spice to the plum and blackberry/cherry fruit; the palate is quite rich, with more tannin and structure than the Penfolds Rawson's Retreat of the same vintage, a role-reversal if ever there was one.　　**rating**: 88

best drinking Now–2005　**best vintages** '96, '98, '99　**drink with** Lasagne • $10.99

Rosemount Estate Rose Label Orange Vineyard Merlot

▼▼▼▼▼ 2000 The high-altitude, cool-climate vineyards around Orange produce elegant wines, both white and red. This lovely example has fresh berry fruit plus hints of olive and herb on the bouquet; the palate shows the same focused varietal character, scoring for its length, balance and fine, savoury tannins.　　**rating**: 94

best drinking 2004–2009　**best vintages** '00　**drink with** Ragout of lamb • $31

Rosemount Estate Rose Label Orange Vineyard Cabernet Sauvignon

▼▼▼▼ 2000 Youthful purple-red; lifted, high-toned black fruit aromas together with a touch of spice precede a palate with penetrating, slightly sharp, fruit flavours. Shows its cool climate.　　**rating**: 87

best drinking 2004–2009　**best vintages** '96, '97　**drink with** Roast lamb shoulder • $38

rosemount estate (mclaren vale)　　★★★★☆

Ingoldby Road, McLaren Vale, SA 5171　**region** McLaren Vale
phone (08) 8383 0001　**fax** (08) 8383 0456　**open** Mon–Fri 10–4.30, weekends and public holidays 11–4.30
winemaker Charles Whish　**production** NFP　**est.** 1888
product range ($21.50–60.90 CD) Balmoral Syrah, Show Reserve Shiraz, GSM (Grenache Shiraz Mourvedre), Traditional (Cabernet blend).
summary The specialist red wine arm of Rosemount Estate, responsible for its prestigious Balmoral Syrah, Show Reserve Shiraz and GSM, as well as most of the other McLaren Vale-based Rosemount brands. These wines come in large measure from 325 hectares of estate plantings.

Rosemount Estate Show Reserve Shiraz

▼▼▼▼ 2000 Medium red-purple; the bouquet offers a mix of dark berry aromas with splashes of spice and licorice; the powerful fruit of the bouquet is still coming together; some licorice and cedar flavours, then slightly dusty tannins to close.　　**rating**: 89

best drinking 2004–2009　**best vintages** '90, '91, '93, '94, '95, '98, '99　**drink with** Braised ox cheek • $27

Rosemount Estate GSM

▼▼▼▼ 2000 Medium red-purple; clean, fresh, red berry fruits are supported by subtle oak on the bouquet, leading into a soft, round palate with red fruits, regional chocolate and soft tannins.　　**rating**: 89

best drinking Now–2008　**best vintages** '94, '95, '96, '99　**drink with** Beef with olives • $26

Rosemount Estate Traditional

▼▼▼▼ 2000 Medium red-purple; a particularly savoury/earthy bouquet has notes of chocolate before oak takes over; dark berry, chocolate and oak flavours open up promisingly on the palate, but then pervasive tannins take the wine out of balance. All is not lost, and it is quite possible that time will soften those tannins but leave the fruit relatively intact. A blend of Cabernet Sauvignon, Merlot and Petit Verdot.　　**rating**: 86

best drinking 2005–2012　**best vintages** '91, '94, '95, '96, '97, '98, '99　**drink with** Char-grilled beef • $23

Rosemount Estate Coonawarra Show Reserve Cabernet Sauvignon

▼▼▼▼ 2000 Medium red-purple; cassis and blackcurrant fruit are supported by positive oak on the bouquet, while on the palate attractive blackcurrant fruit contests tongue space with oak, resulting in a drawn match. The match spends 24 months in new and used French and American oak. **rating: 89**

best drinking 2005–2010 **best vintages** '98 **drink with** Steak with mushrooms • $27

rosenvale wines ★★★☆

Lot 385 Railway Terrace, Nuriootpa, SA 5355 **region** Barossa Valley
phone 0407 390 788 **fax** (08) 8565 7206 **open** By appointment
winemaker James Rosenzweig, John Zilm **production** 1000 cases **est.** 2000
product range ($10–26 ML) Semillon, Barrel Fermented Chardonnay, Shiraz, Shiraz Cabernet Sauvignon, Cabernet Sauvignon.
summary The Rosenzweig family has 80 hectares of vineyards, some old and some new, planted to riesling, semillon, semillon, pinot noir, grenache, shiraz and cabernet sauvignon. Most of the grapes are sold to other producers, but since 1999 select parcels have been retained and vinified for release under the Rosenvale label. The white wines are acceptable, the reds far more impressive. Exports through Australian Prestige Wines.

Rosenvale Semillon

▼▼▼▼ 1999 Deep, developed yellow, but with some green tinges; the bouquet is clean, still opening up, and showing some mineral and spice; the light to medium-bodied palate reflects the highly unusual 10° alcohol, typical for the Hunter Valley but very rare in the Barossa Valley; a brave attempt, slightly hollow, but far preferable to the other extreme. **rating: 86**

best drinking Now–2005 **drink with** Seafood risotto • $10

Rosenvale Barrel Fermented Chardonnay

▼▼▼▼ 2001 Glowing yellow-green; the bouquet shows some bottle development, but is still relatively closed and subtle; the nicely balanced palate has some length to the melon and citrus fruit, with the oak contribution negligible. **rating: 86**

best drinking Now **drink with** Smoked eel • $13.50

Rosenvale Shiraz Cabernet Sauvignon

▼▼▼▼ 2001 Medium to full red-purple; the moderately intense bouquet has dark berry fruits and touches of vanilla, chocolate and earth. The rich, plush, mouthfilling dark berry and plum fruit of the palate finishes with soft tannins. **rating: 89**

best drinking 2005–2010 **drink with** Ragout of lamb • $24

Rosenvale Cabernet Sauvignon

▼▼▼▼▽ 2001 Full red-purple; as the colour promises, concentrated blackcurrant fruit floods the bouquet; the palate is particularly rich, with luscious but not jammy dark fruits; very seductive. Controlled alcohol (13.5°) is a feature. **rating: 93**

best drinking 2005–2011 **best vintages** '01 **drink with** Braised lamb • $26

rosevears estate ★★★★

1a Waldhorn Drive, Rosevears, Tas 7277 **region** Northern Tasmania
phone (03) 6330 1800 **fax** (03) 6330 1810 **open** 7 days 10–4
winemaker Russell Cook **production** 8000 cases **est.** 1999
product range ($19–59 CD) Riesling, Winemakers Riesling, Sauvignon Blanc, Pinot Gris, Unwooded Chardonnay, Chardonnay, Reserve Chardonnay, Sparkling Brut, Sparkling Rose Brut, Rose, Pinot Noir, Reserve Pinot Noir, Cabernet Merlot, Cabernet Sauvignon; Notley Gorge range of Riesling, Chardonnay, Pinot Noir, Cabernet Merlot, Cabernet Sauvignon.
summary The multi-million dollar Rosevears Estate winery and restaurant complex was opened by the Tasmanian premier in November 1999. Built on a steep hillside overlooking the Tamar River, it is certain to make a lasting and important contribution to the Tasmanian wine industry. It is owned by a syndicate of investors headed by Dr Mike Beamish and incorporates both Notley Gorge and Ironpot Bay. Accommodation is currently under construction for a September 2003 opening.

Rosevears Estate Riesling

▼▼▼▼ 2001 Light yellow-green; dry, toasty/minerally aromas, with nuances of herb, lead into a palate which is, as usual, crisp and well balanced. **rating: 87**

best drinking Now–2006 **drink with** Seafood salad • $22

Notley Gorge Riesling

▼▼▼▼ 2001 Light straw-green; spotless citrus, lime and passionfruit aromas flow through into the palate, which has considerable weight and intensity, but also a slightly congested finish. Early-maturing style. **rating: 89**

best drinking Now–2008 **drink with** Summer salads • $19

Rosevears Estate Sauvignon Blanc

▼▼▼▽ 2002 Light green-yellow; the intense bouquet offers mineral and herb aromas, with a hint of capsicum; the palate opens up in similar fashion, but turns unexpectedly sweet on the finish. It's not altogether clear why the decision was taken to go down this route. **rating: 84**

best drinking Now **drink with** Gravlax • $25

Rosevears Estate Pinot Noir

▼▼▼▽ 2001 Deep colour; the bouquet exudes powerful oak and fruit. The palate is very extractive indeed; far less work in the winery would have produced a better wine. However, useful for those who prefer their Pinots to taste like Cabernets. **rating: 84**

best drinking 2005–2009 **drink with** Braised venison • $40

Notley Gorge Pinot Noir

▼▼▼▼▼ 2001 Bright, strong red-purple; rich, full dark plum spice and cherry aromas are accompanied by restrained oak on the bouquet. The palate is powerful and concentrated, with excellent length and persistence to the spice and plum flavours. Should mature particularly well in bottle. **rating: 94**

best drinking Now–2007 **best vintages** '01 **drink with** Braised duck • $30

rosily vineyard ★★★★

Yelveton Road, Wilyabrup, WA 6284 **region** Margaret River
phone (08) 9755 6336 **fax** (08) 9221 3309 **open** By appointment
winemaker Mike Lemmes, Dan Pannell (Consultant) **production** 5600 cases **est.** 1994
product range ($16–20ML) Semillon, Semillon Sauvignon Blanc, Sauvignon Blanc, Chardonnay, Shiraz, Cabernet Merlot, Cabernet Sauvignon.
summary The partnership of Mike and Barb Scott and Ken and Dot Allan acquired the Rosily Vineyard site in 1994. Under the direction of consultant Dan Pannell (of the Pannell family) 12 hectares of vineyard were planted over the next 3 years: first up sauvignon blanc, semillon, chardonnay and cabernet sauvignon, and thereafter merlot, shiraz and a little grenache and cabernet franc. The first crops were sold to other makers in the region, but in 1999 Rosily built a winery with a 120-tonne capacity, and is now moving to fully utilise that capacity.

Rosily Vineyard Semillon

▼▼▼▼ 2001 Light straw-green; firm grassy fruit is offset by subtle French oak on the bouquet; the elegant palate relies more on texture than flavour, with the oak particularly well handled. 400 cases made. **rating: 88**

best drinking Now–2005 **drink with** Swordfish • $20

Rosily Vineyard Sauvignon Blanc

▼▼▼▼▽ 2002 Light straw-green; a spotlessly clean bouquet with apple blossom and herb aromas, and not a trace of reduction, is followed by a palate with good length and balance. Pristine apple and gooseberry fruit flavours flow through to the finish. 880 cases made. **rating: 92**

best drinking Now **best vintages** '02 **drink with** Fresh crab • $16

Rosily Vineyard Semillon Sauvignon Blanc

▼▼▼▼ 2002 Very pale colour; the clean, moderately intense bouquet derives at least part of its complexity from French oak, as does the palate; moderate length and fresh finish. A blend of 60 per cent Semillon and 40 per cent Sauvignon Blanc, partly matured in French oak. 970 cases made. **rating: 86**

best drinking Now **drink with** Chinese steamed fish with ginger • $18

ross estate wines ★★★☆

Barossa Valley Way, Lyndoch, SA 5351 **region** Barossa Valley
phone (08) 8524 4033 **fax** (08) 8524 4533 **open** Mon–Sat 10–5, Sun 1–5
winemaker Rod Chapman **production** 10000 cases **est.** 1999
product range ($13–26 CD) Riesling, Semillon, Sauvignon Blanc, Chardonnay, Beekeeper's Blend (Late Harvest), Shiraz, Tempranillo Graciano (bi-annual cellar-door release only), Old Vine Grenache, Merlot, Lynedoch (Cabernet Sauvignon Cabernet Franc Merlot), Cabernet Sauvignon.
summary Darius and Pauline Ross laid the foundation for Ross Estate Wines when they purchased 43 hectares of vines which included two blocks of 75- and 90-year-old grenache. Also included were blocks of 30-year-old riesling and semillon, and 13-year-old merlot. The remaining vines were removed and planted with chardonnay, sauvignon blanc, cabernet sauvignon, cabernet franc and shiraz, which are now 7 years old. A winery was built in time for the 1998 vintage, and a tasting room was opened in 1999. The immensely experienced Rod Chapman, with 39 vintages under his belt, including 18 years as red winemaker with Southcorp/Penfolds, is in charge of winemaking. Exports to the US, Asia and Europe.

Ross Estate Riesling

▼▼▼▼ 2002 Light straw-green; the solid bouquet has ripe lime and pineapple aromas which come through on the big-framed palate, which, while having plenty of flavour, is not too broad. **rating:** 86

best drinking Now–2008 **drink with** Pasta marinara • $13

Ross Estate Shiraz

▼▼▼▼ 2001 Medium red-purple; clean, moderately intense blackberry, black cherry and plum fruit is supported by gentle American oak on the bouquet; the medium to full-bodied palate has abundant smooth blackberry fruit offset by fine savoury tannins, the oak far better integrated and balanced than in some prior vintages. **rating:** 89

best drinking 2006–2011 **drink with** Braised beef • $26

Ross Estate Lynedoch

▼▼▼▼▽ 2001 Medium purple-red; the clean, fragrant bouquet has blackcurrant, raspberry and mint aromas backed by gentle oak; the palate is somewhat richer than the bouquet, with cassis blackcurrant and a touch of chocolate; although Lyndoch is a relatively cool corner of the Barossa Valley, an impressive and unexpected outcome. Matured in French and American oak for 12 months. **rating:** 90

best drinking 2006–2011 **best vintages** '01 **drink with** Roast lamb • $25

ross hill vineyard NR

62 Griffin Road, via Ammerdown, Orange, NSW 2800 **region** Orange
phone (02) 6360 0175 **fax** (02) 6363 1674 **open** By appointment
winemaker David Lowe, Stephen Doyle (Contract) **production** 2000 cases **est.** 1994
product range ($15–24 CD) Sauvignon Blanc, Chardonnay, Rose, Mick's Lot Shiraz, Merlot, Cabernet Sauvignon.
summary Peter and Terri Robson began planting 12 hectares of vines in 1994. Chardonnay, sauvignon blanc, merlot, cabernet sauvignon, shiraz and cabernet franc have been established on north-facing, gentle slopes at an elevation of 800 metres. No insecticides are used in the vineyard, the grapes are hand-picked and the vines hand-pruned. Ross Hill also has an olive grove with Italian olive varieties and the Spanish variety manzanilla, which is also a popular table olive. Exports to the UK.

Ross Hill Vineyard Rose

▼▼▼▼ 2001 Salmon pink; clean small berry fruit aromas, then a savoury/minerally palate with a core of light cherry fruit. All in all a good example of Rose. A blend of merlot and cabernet sauvignon. **rating:** 85

best drinking Now **drink with** Hors d'oeuvres • $15

Ross Hill Vineyard Mick's Lot Shiraz

▼▼▼▼ 2001 Medium red-purple; while only moderately intense, the bouquet is quite complex, with a mix of spice, sweet leather and a touch of vanilla; red berry fruit comes through on the palate, balanced by well-handled tannins and oak; development potential. **rating:** 87

best drinking 2004–2008 **drink with** Roasted ox kidney • $24

Ross Hill Vineyard Merlot

YYYY 2001 Medium red-purple; the moderately intense bouquet has scented dusty/leafy/savoury varietal aromas; the light to medium-bodied palate is in the same groove; fine tannins and subtle French oak help, but it is a wine to appeal to the intellect rather than the stomach. **rating:** 86

best drinking 2004–2006 **drink with** Cassoulet • $22

rothbury ridge ★★★★

Talga Road, Rothbury, NSW 2320 **region** Lower Hunter Valley
phone (02) 4930 7122 **fax** (02) 4930 7198 **open** Mon–Sat 9–5, Sun 10–5
winemaker Peter Jorgensen **production** 10 000 cases **est.** 1998
product range ($15–55 CD) Stanleigh Park Reserve Semillon, Winemakers Semillon, Anne Chardonnay Semillon, Mary Unwooded Chardonnay (Chablis style), Steven Chardonnay, Mount Royal Reserve Durif, Edgar Chambourcin, Mount Royal Reserve Chambourcin, James Shiraz, Rose Chambourcin Traditional Methode Champenoise.
summary Rothbury Ridge has an extraordinarily eclectic choice of varieties planted, with between 1.2 hectares and 2.4 hectares each of chardonnay, semillon, verdelho, chambourcin, durif, shiraz and cabernet sauvignon. It is owned by a public company (not listed on the Stock Exchange) with an imposing array of directors, and actively markets its wines through a wine club.

Rothbury Ridge Stanleigh Park Vineyard Reserve Semillon

YYYYY 1999 Light to medium green-yellow; the clean and still youthful bouquet has intense, smooth fruit; the palate has similar seamless line and length. Very impressive; semillon is normally awkward at this intermediate stage. **rating:** 94

best drinking Now–2009 **best vintages** '99 **drink with** Lemon-marinated fish • $24

Rothbury Ridge Winemakers Selection Semillon

YYYY 1999 Medium yellow-green; a quite complex bouquet with smoky/toasty notes is followed by a palate with some of the same flavours, but without the length and fluidity of the Reserve. **rating:** 86

best drinking Now–2005 **drink with** Smoked eel • $15

Rothbury Ridge Anne Chardonnay Semillon

YYYY 1999 Medium to full yellow-green; a clean, relatively undeveloped bouquet, with the first hint of toast appearing, is followed by a fresh, light to medium-bodied palate driven by the semillon component, but with a touch of stone fruit from the chardonnay. **rating:** 87

best drinking Now–2005 **drink with** Deep-fried calamari • $17

Rothbury Ridge Steven Chardonnay

YYYY 1999 Medium yellow-green; complex barrel-ferment aromas on a peach/melon fruit base are followed by a nicely balanced and crafted palate, maturing quite slowly. **rating:** 88

best drinking Now–2006 **drink with** Grilled spatchcock • $18

Rothbury Ridge Edgar Chambourcin

YYYY 1998 Remarkably strong colour; spice, dark fruits and plum pudding aromas are followed by a rich and ripe palate with gamey varietal character which is not, as far as I can see, in any way affected by brettanomyces. Unusual for a Chambourcin to age as well as this wine has. **rating:** 87

best drinking Now–2005 **drink with** Irish stew • $25

rotherhythe NR

Hendersons Lane, Gravelly Beach, Exeter, Tas 7251 **region** Northern Tasmania
phone (03) 6394 4869 **open** By appointment
winemaker Steven Hyde **production** 1600 cases **est.** 1976
product range ($16–26.95 CD) Chardonnay, Pinot Noir, Cabernet Sauvignon, Pinot Chardonnay.
summary At the 1996 Tasmanian Wines Show Rotherhythe swept all before it, winning trophies galore. Ironically, two days later Dr Steven Hyde sold the vineyard, although he has retained all the existing wine stocks and will remain involved in the winemaking for some time to come. In both 1997 and 1998 Rotherhythe was awarded the trophy for Most Successful Exhibitor at the Tasmanian Wines Show. Since then the pace has slowed, with most of the grapes sold, one imagines at a substantial price.

rothvale vineyard ★★★★

Deasy's Road, Pokolbin NSW 2321 **region** Lower Hunter Valley
phone (02) 4998 7290 **fax** (02) 4998 7290 **open** 7 days 10–5
winemaker Max Patton, Luke Patton **production** 7000 cases **est.** 1978
product range ($14–28 CD) Vat 8 Semillon, Barrel Fermented Semillon, Sirens Lair Semillon, Semillon Muscat, Angus's Semillon Chardonnay, Unwooded Chardonnay, Reserve Chardonnay A (American Oak), Reserve Chardonnay F (French Oak), Annie's Dry Red, Tilda's Shiraz, Luke's Shiraz, Sirens Lair Shiraz, Cabernet Sauvignon.
summary Owned and operated by the Patton family, headed by Max Patton, who has the fascinating academic qualifications of BVSc, MSc London, BA Hons Canterbury – the scientific part has no doubt come in useful for his winemaking. The wines are sold only through the cellar door and direct to an imposing list of restaurants in the Hunter Valley and Sydney. Rothvale also has four vineyard cottages available for bed and breakfast accommodation. The wines have already accumulated an impressive array of medals, and are of commendably consistent style and quality, edging towards a 4.5-star rating. Exports to the UK and the US.

Rothvale Vineyard Barrel Fermented Semillon

▼▼▼▼♈ **2002** Bright yellow-green; the bouquet is complex, the barrel fermentation obvious but not excessive; thanks to a much lower alcohol level (10.5°) than prior vintages, the light to medium-bodied palate works well, with nice feel and flow; it is, needless to say, an alternative style, albeit pioneered by Rothbury in the mid-1970s. **rating:** 90
best drinking Now–2007 **best vintages** '02 **drink with** Roast chicken • $25

Rothvale Vineyard Sirens Lair Semillon

▼▼▼▼ **2002** The colour is not entirely convincing, but the bouquet has clean lemon and herb aromas. The fresh light-bodied palate has good length and a lemony twist; 9.5° alcohol points to early picking; the wine spent 7 months on lees. Has a truly dreadful label. **rating:** 87
best drinking Now–2008 **drink with** Shellfish • $14

Rothvale Vineyard Vat 8 Semillon

▼▼▼▼ **2002** Light green-yellow; a complex, powerful bouquet with slight solids characters is followed by a palate with weight and complexity; with 11° alcohol the wine is balanced. There is no question that Rothvale presents three very different styles of Semillon. **rating:** 88
best drinking Now–2008 **best vintages** '01 **drink with** KFC • $18

Rothvale Vineyard Reserve Chardonnay A

▼▼▼▼ **2002** Medium to full yellow-green; obvious charry barrel-ferment aromas dominate the bouquet and the opening stanza of the palate; light, tangy nectarine fruit makes a comeback on the finish. **rating:** 88
best drinking Now–2005 **drink with** Roast pork • $25

Rothvale Vineyard Reserve Chardonnay F

▼▼▼▼♈ **2002** Medium to full yellow-green; the oak is much less assertive than the American oak version, being here well-integrated and balanced. The palate is likewise quite seamless and elegant, with fresh citrus and nectarine fruit; medium length. Spends 9 months in a mix of new and old oak, corresponding in age to the American version. **rating:** 92
best drinking Now–2005 **best vintages** '99, '01, '02 **drink with** Pasta carbonara • $25

Rothvale Vineyard Luke's Shiraz

▼▼▼▼♈ **2001** Medium to full red-purple; complex blackberry, leather, earth and vanilla aromas come through in the rich and powerful palate, where blackberry and a touch of licorice are supported by good tannins. For the long term. **rating:** 91
best drinking 2006–2016 **best vintages** '01 **drink with** Barbecued rump steak • $25

Rothvale Vineyard Tilda's Shiraz

▼▼▼▼♈ **2002** Medium red-purple; raspberry and black cherry fruit aromas are supported by obvious oak on the bouquet; the rich but surprisingly elegant palate has a range of black cherry, vanilla, spice and sweet leather flavours; miraculously, achieved 14.5° alcohol in a vintage not noted for very ripe fruit, but the wine carries that alcohol level nicely enough. **rating:** 90
best drinking 2006–2011 **best vintages** '99, '00, '02 **drink with** Braised ox tail • $28

Rothvale Vineyard Cabernet Sauvignon

ΨΨΨΨ **2002** Medium red-purple; there is a distinctly regional earthy overlay to the bouquet, with the underlying chocolate and blackcurrant fruit coming through on the smooth, softly tannic palate. Has micro-ox made this wine so easy so young? **rating:** 88

best drinking 2005–2011 **best vintages** '98, '00 **drink with** Roast kid • $28

rouge homme ★★★☆

Riddoch Highway, Coonawarra, SA 5263 **region** Coonawarra
phone (08) 8736 3205 **fax** (08) 8736 3250 **open** Not
winemaker Brett Sharpe **production** NFP **est.** 1954
product range ($11–17 R) Semillon, Chardonnay, Unoaked Chardonnay, Pinot Noir, Reserve Pinot Noir, Shiraz Cabernet, Cabernet Merlot, Cabernet Sauvignon.
summary From time to time I have described Rouge Homme as the warrior brand of the Lindeman Group Coonawarra operations. In recent times it has proved a formidable warrior, particularly with its Cabernet and Cabernet blend wines benefiting from the 1996 and 1998 vintages. In March 2002 the winery was sold to DiGorgio, but the Rouge Homme brand and stock were retained.

Rouge Homme Shiraz Cabernet

ΨΨΨΨ **2000** Medium red-purple; a solid mix of blackberry, plum and chocolate on the bouquet shapes the firm palate, which has identical flavours and only a lick of oak. Nothing flash, but has improvement in front of it. **rating:** 87

best drinking 2005–2012 **best vintages** '88, '90, '91, '92, '94, '98 **drink with** King Island cheddar • $14.99

Rouge Homme Cabernet Merlot

ΨΨΨΨ **2000** Medium red-purple; a clean and smooth bouquet ranges through blackcurrant, blackberry and mulberry, setting the scene for the juicy berry fruit of the rich and quite luscious palate. Very good value. **rating:** 89

best drinking 2004–2009 **best vintages** '98 **drink with** Braised lamb • $14.99

roundstone winery & vineyard ★★★★

54 Willow Bend Drive, Yarra Glen, Vic 3775 **region** Yarra Valley
phone (03) 9730 1181 **fax** (03) 9730 1151 **open** Thurs–Sun and public holidays 10–5, or by appointment
winemaker John Derwin, Rob Dolan and Kate Goodman (Consultants) **production** 2000 cases **est.** 1998
product range ($17–35 CD) Chardonnay, Rose, Pinot Noir, Rubies Pinot Noir, Merlot, Shiraz Cabernet.
summary John and Lynne Derwin have moved quickly since establishing Roundstone, planting 8 hectares of vineyard (half to pinot noir with a mix of the best clones), building a small winery, and opening a cellar door and restaurant situated on the side of a dam. The Derwins prune the vineyard, enlist the aid of friends to pick the grapes, John makes the wine in conjunction with advice from Rob Dolan and Kate Goodman, Lynne is the chef and sommelier. Her pride and joy is a shearers' stove which was used at the Yarra Glen Grand Hotel for 100 years before being abandoned, and which is now at the centre of the kitchen. The restaurant opened in December 2001, and has established itself as one of the best winery restaurants in the valley.

Roundstone Chardonnay

ΨΨΨΨ♡ **2002** Medium yellow-green; the complex bouquet shows positive barrel-ferment oak inputs woven through intense melon and citrus fruit; the palate is smooth, long and very well balanced, the focus on melon fruit. **rating:** 92

best drinking Now–2006 **best vintages** '02 **drink with** Sushi • $20

Roundstone Charmed Chardonnay

ΨΨΨΨ **2002** Quite advanced yellow-green; the relatively developed bouquet has a complex mix of stone fruit, melon and mineral; the palate is even more developed, with a mix of stone fruit and honey, all pointing to early consumption. **rating:** 87

best drinking Now **drink with** Smoked chicken salad • $27

Roundstone Pinot Noir

ΨΨΨΨ **2001** Light to medium purple-red; the bright and fresh bouquet offers direct, fresh strawberry and plum fruit aromas; the palate has much more structure, courtesy of fine tannins, than expected, giving the wine an overall savoury, spicy feel. **rating:** 88

best drinking Now–2007 **drink with** Cold cuts • $20

Roundstone Rubies Pinot Noir

TTTTY **2001** Medium purple-red; the complex bouquet has distinct foresty/gamey aromas which are quite possibly partly due to brettanomyces; the medium-bodied palate has dark plum fruit of considerable depth supported by fine, lingering tannins. Not an easy wine to point; I have given it the benefit of the doubt.

rating: 91

best drinking Now–2007 **best vintages** '01 **drink with** Breast of duck • $35

Roundstone Merlot

TTTT **2001** Light to medium purple-red; the light leaf, mint and berry aromas appear clean, and are certainly varietal; the medium-bodied palate provides more of the same, but has nice, ripe, savoury tannins to carry the flavour.

rating: 86

best drinking 2004–2008 **drink with** Roast veal • $27

rumball sparkling wines   NR

55 Charles Street, Norwood, SA 5067 **region** Adelaide Zone
phone (08) 8332 2761 **fax** (08) 8364 0188 **open** Mon–Fri 9–5
winemaker Peter Rumball **production** 10 000 cases **est.** 1988
product range ($14–21 R) Vintage Brut, Sparkling Merlot, Sparkling Shiraz (also available in half bottles, magnums and jeroboams).
summary Peter Rumball has been making and selling sparkling wine for as long as I can remember, but has led a somewhat peripatetic life, starting in the Clare Valley but now operating one of the 12 Methode Champenoise lines in Australia, situated in the Adelaide suburb of Norwood. The grapes are purchased and the wines made under the supervision of Peter Rumball. His particular specialty has always been Sparkling Shiraz, and was so long before it became 'flavour of the month'. National retail distribution through Tucker Seabrook, and exports to the UK, the US and Japan.

rusden wines   NR

Magnolia Road, Tanunda, SA 5352 (postal) **region** Barossa Valley
phone (08) 8563 2976 **fax** (08) 8563 0885 **open** Not
winemaker Christian Canute **production** 900 cases **est.** 1998
product range Chenin Blanc, Shiraz, Grenache, Cabernet Sauvignon.
summary The Canute family (Dennis, Christine and Christian) have been long-term grape growers, with 14 hectares of sauvignon blanc, chenin blanc, grenache, cabernet sauvignon, merlot, shiraz, mourvedre and zinfandel. While only part of the production is vinified under the Rusden label, exports have been established to the US, Germany, England, Switzerland, Singapore and France.

russet ridge   ★★★★

Cnr Caves Road and Riddoch Highway, Naracoorte, SA 5271 **region** Wrattonbully
phone (08) 8762 0114 **fax** (08) 8762 0341 **open** Thurs–Mon 11–4.30
winemaker Philip Laffer, Sam Kurtz **production** NFP **est.** 2000
product range ($16 R) Coonawarra Chardonnay, Coonawarra Cabernet Shiraz Merlot.
summary This is the former Heathfield Ridge winery, built in 1998 as a contract crush and winemaking facility for multiple clients, but purchased by Orlando in 2000. It is the only winery in the large Wrattonbully region, and also receives Orlando's Coonawarra and Padthaway grapes, and other Limestone Coast fruit.

Russet Ridge Coonawarra Cabernet Shiraz Merlot

TTTT **1999** Medium red-purple; the bouquet offers quite obvious dusty oak and moderately ripe fruit, the fruit coming through more strongly on the palate, with a mix of black and red berry flavours supported by soft tannins.

rating: 86

best drinking Now–2008 **best vintages** '91, '92, '98 **drink with** Beef with olives • $16

rutherglen estates   ★★★☆

Cnr Great Northern Road and Murray Valley Highway, Rutherglen, Vic 3685 **region** Rutherglen
phone (02) 6032 8516 **fax** (02) 6032 8517 **open** Not
winemaker Nick Butler, David Valentine **production** 25 000 cases **est.** 2000
product range ($12–16 R) Chardonnay Marsanne, Shiraz, Shiraz Mourvedre, Durif, Sangiovese.

summary The Rutherglen Estates brand is an offshoot of a far larger contract crush and make business, with a winery capacity of 4000 tonnes (roughly equivalent to 280 000 cases). Rutherglen is in a declared phylloxera region, which means all the grapes grown within that region have to be vinified within it, itself a guarantee of business for ventures such as Rutherglen Estates. It also means that some of the best available material can be allocated for the brand, with an interesting mix of varieties.

Rutherglen Estates Shiraz

TTTT 2002 Dense, impenetrable inky purple; the bouquet is closed in on itself, a black hole in space. A massive, dense and impenetrable palate follows, almost impossible to point. I really have no idea where this wine will be in 20 years' time, but it could be an interesting ride for the young at heart. For the record, only 14° alcohol (rather than more).   **rating:** 87

best drinking 2010–2020 **drink with** Leave it in the cellar • $16

Rutherglen Estates Sangiovese

TTTY 2002 Medium red-purple; the delicacy of the wine comes as a total contrast after the Shiraz and Durif of the same vintage; the light to medium-bodied palate has some style and texture, with gentle sweetness and spice. Representative of the variety, and much more convincing than the Nebbiolo.   **rating:** 84

best drinking Now–2007 **drink with** Lasagne • $16

Rutherglen Estates Durif

TTTT 2002 Youthful, exuberant purple-red; clean, rich, ripe dark berry fruit aromas lead into a powerful and concentrated palate with abundant sweet, dark fruit flavours and abundant tannins. Needs a decade, but at least you can see through it.   **rating:** 88

best drinking 2007–2017 **drink with** Char-grilled rump • $16

ryland river   NR

RMB 8945 Main Creek Road, Main Ridge, Vic 3928 **region** Mornington Peninsula
phone (03) 5989 6098 **fax** (03) 9899 0184 **open** Weekends and public holidays 10–5, or by appointment
winemaker John W Bray **production** 2000 cases **est.** 1986
product range ($15–30 CD) Semillon Sauvignon Blanc, Chardonnay, Cabernet Sauvignon, Jack's Delight Tawny Port and Muscat.
summary John Bray has been operating Ryland River at Main Ridge on the Mornington Peninsula for a number of years, but not without a degree of controversy over the distinction between Ryland River wines produced from Mornington Peninsula grapes and those produced from grapes purchased from other regions. A large lake with catch-your-own trout and a cheese house are general tourist attractions.

rymill coonawarra   ★★★★

The Riddoch Run Vineyards, Riddoch Highway, Coonawarra, SA 5263 **region** Coonawarra
phone (08) 8736 5001 **fax** (08) 8736 5040 **open** 7 days 10–5
winemaker John Innes, Clemence Dournois (assistant) **production** 50 000 cases **est.** 1970
product range ($12–28.50 CD) Sauvignon Blanc, Pinot Noir Chardonnay, The Bees Knees Sparkling Red, June Traminer Late Harvest, Shiraz, MC2 (Merlot Cabernet Sauvignon Cabernet Franc), Cabernet Sauvignon.
summary The Rymills are descendants of John Riddoch and have long owned some of the finest Coonawarra soil, upon which they have grown grapes since 1970, with present plantings at 170 hectares. Peter Rymill made a small amount of Cabernet Sauvignon in 1987 but has long since plunged headlong into commercial production, with winemaker John Innes presiding over the striking winery portrayed on the label. Australian distribution is through Negociants Australia; exports go to all the major markets in Europe and Asia.

Rymill Sauvignon Blanc

TTTTY 2002 Light straw-green; the bouquet has a clean and flowery mix of passionfruit and gooseberry; the palate firms up considerably, moving more into a minerally mode, then a tight finish.   **rating:** 90

best drinking Now **best vintages** '02 **drink with** Yabbies • $15

saddlers creek   ★★★★

Marrowbone Road, Pokolbin, NSW 2320 **region** Lower Hunter Valley
phone (02) 4991 1770 **fax** (02) 4991 2482 **open** 7 days 9–5
winemaker John Johnstone **production** 15 000 cases **est.** 1989

product range ($21–58 CD) Classic Hunter Semillon, Verdelho, Marrowbone Chardonnay, Reserve Chardonnay, Classical Gas (Methode Champenoise), Botrytis Semillon, Equus Shiraz, Equus McLaren Vale Shiraz, Single Vineyard Hunter Shiraz, Reserve Shiraz, Reserve Merlot, Bluegrass Cabernet Sauvignon, Muscat Exclusif.

summary Made an impressive entrance to the district with consistently full-flavoured and rich wines, and has continued on in much the same vein, with good wines across the spectrum. Limited retail distribution in New South Wales, Queensland and Victoria. Exports to Canada, New Zealand and Mauritius.

Saddlers Creek Classic Hunter Semillon

▼▼▼▼ 2002 Light straw-green; restrained mineral and grass aromas with a faint hint of lanolin lead into a much more lively palate, the hint of residual sugar balanced by lively acidity. **rating:** 88

best drinking Now–2009 **best vintages** '01 **drink with** Shellfish • $21

Saddlers Creek Single Vineyard Hunter Shiraz

▼▼▼▼ 2000 Medium red-purple; the moderately intense bouquet has dark berry, earth and spice/licorice aromas; the medium-bodied palate is strongly regional, with a range of leathery, earthy, savoury notes around the mulberry fruit; finishes with fine tannins. From a dry-grown vineyard, and spends 18 months in French and American oak. **rating:** 85

best drinking 2004–2009 **drink with** Grilled porterhouse • $40

Saddlers Creek Langhorne Reserve Cabernet

▼▼▼▼ 2000 Medium red-purple; a moderately intense, clean bouquet has sappy/minty overtones to the berry fruit; the palate shows riper flavours, with blackberry, vanilla oak and chocolate all combining; finishes with fine, savoury tannins. Well made. **rating:** 89

best drinking 2004–2009 **drink with** Wood-fired oven pizza • $58

st anne's vineyards ★★★

Cnr Perricoota Road and 24 Lane, Moama, NSW 2731 **region** Perricoota
phone (03) 5480 0099 **fax** (03) 5480 0077 **open** 7 days 9–5
winemaker Richard McLean **production** 20 000 cases **est.** 1972
product range ($14–25 CD) Perricoota Semillon, Chardonnay, Grenache Shiraz Mourvedre, Shiraz, Cabernet Franc, Cabernet; Dulcet I (late-harvest Riesling), Dulcett II (dessert-style Semillon); Tawny Port, Belle Tawny, Liqueur Tawny.
summary St Anne's is by far the most active member of this newly registered (under the Geographic Indications Legislation) region in southern New South Wales. Richard McLean has established 80 hectares of estate vineyards, with another 120 hectares of grower vineyards to draw upon. Shiraz, cabernet sauvignon, grenache and mourvedre account for over 75 per cent of the plantings, but there is a spread of the usual white wines and few red exotics. The wines are all competently made.

st gregory's NR

Bringalbert South Road, Bringalbert South via Apsley, Vic 3319 **region** Henty
phone (03) 5586 5225 **open** By appointment
winemaker Gregory Flynn **production** NFP **est.** 1983
product range ($14 ML) Port.
summary Unique Port-only operation selling its limited production direct to enthusiasts (by mailing list).

st hallett ★★★★☆

St Hallett's Road, Tanunda, SA 5352 **region** Barossa Valley
phone (08) 8563 7000 **fax** (08) 8563 7001 **open** 7 days 10–5
winemaker Stuart Blackwell, Di Ferguson, Matt Gant **production** 100 000 cases **est.** 1944
product range ($13.95–59.95 R) Poacher's Blend (white), Eden Valley Riesling, Semillon Sauvignon Blanc, Blackwell Semillon, Black (Sparkling Shiraz), Gamekeeper's Reserve (red), Faith Shiraz, Blackwell Shiraz, Old Block Shiraz, Cabernet Shiraz, Cabernet Sauvignon.
summary Nothing succeeds like success. St Hallett merged with Tatachilla to form Banksia Wines, which was then acquired by New Zealand's thirsty Lion Nathan. St Hallett understandably continues to ride the Shiraz fashion wave, but all its wines are honest and well priced. It has established its own distribution network in the UK, and actively exports to Europe, the US, Canada and Asia.

St Hallett Eden Valley Riesling

▼▼▼▼▼ 2002 The trophy for Best White Wine at this year's Barossa Valley Wine Show (beating the great 1993 Peter Lehmann Riesling) puts this wine on the top shelf. Smooth, intense and seamless citrus, green apple and steely aromas come first, then a palate flooded with lime/citrus fruit providing great mouthfeel. Pure quality. **rating:** 95

best drinking Now–2010 **best vintages** '97, '01, '02 **drink with** Crab • $16

St Hallett Poacher's Blend

▼▼▼▼ 2002 Medium yellow-green; a delicious, fresh bouquet with gently sweet fruit flows through effortlessly to the light to medium-bodied, well-balanced palate, showing precisely the same characters as the bouquet. Made from the 'classic varieties', whatever that may mean. **rating:** 88

best drinking Now **drink with** Yabbies • $13.95

St Hallett Barossa Semillon Sauvignon Blanc

▼▼▼▼ 2002 Medium yellow-green; the solid, clean bouquet ranges through grass to tropical fruit aromas, and there is plenty of gently sweet fruit flavour and depth to the palate. Honest style. **rating:** 89

best drinking Now–2005 **drink with** Fish and chips • $15.95

St Hallett Black

▼▼▼▼▼ NV Medium red-purple; a savoury bouquet of berry, licorice, spice and vanilla translates into a similarly flavoured and complex palate; the finish is well balanced and not too sweet. Blended from base wines covering two decades, retrieved from old barrels in the corner of the winery. Given a minimum of 18 months on lees. **rating:** 94

best drinking Now–2006 **drink with** Yakitori • $49.50

St Hallett Blackwell Shiraz

▼▼▼▼ 1999 Medium red-purple; the bouquet offers an amalgam of vanilla, earth, spice and dark fruits; the medium-bodied palate has fruit in a generally savoury spectrum, finishing with fine tannins. **rating:** 87

best drinking 2004–2009 **best vintages** '96 **drink with** Lamb shanks • $29.95

St Hallett Faith Shiraz

▼▼▼▽ 2001 Medium purple-red; clean, fresh and direct dark cherry fruit aromas and a dash of oak lead into a medium-bodied palate with good balance and focus to the ripe cherry, plum and spice flavours. Classic Barossa style, well priced. **rating:** 90

best drinking 2004–2010 **best vintages** '01 **drink with** Italian • $21.50

St Hallett Old Block Shiraz

▼▼▼▼▽ 1999 Medium to full red-purple; smooth and intense dark plum and black cherry fruit marries with touches of chocolate and controlled oak on the bouquet; the medium-bodied palate lives up to the promise of the bouquet with the hallmark skilled handling of tannins and extract, the oak use judicious. **rating:** 92

best drinking 2004–2014 **best vintages** '80, '84, '86, '87, '88, '90, '91, '92, '93, '94, '96, '97, '98, '99 **drink with** Kangaroo, game • $59.95

st huberts ★★★★

Maroondah Highway, Coldstream, Vic 3770 **region** Yarra Valley
phone (03) 9739 1118 **fax** (03) 9739 1096 **open** Mon–Fri 9–5, weekends 10.30–5.30
winemaker Matt Steel **production** 15 000 cases **est.** 1966
product range ($19.50–43 R) Sauvignon Blanc, Roussanne, Chardonnay, Pinot Chardonnay, Pinot Noir, Cabernet Merlot, Cabernet Sauvignon, Reserve Cabernet Sauvignon.
summary The changes have come thick and fast at St Huberts, which is now part of the Beringer Blass group. It has produced some quite lovely wines, notably Chardonnay and Cabernet Sauvignon, but the brand seems to be slowly but surely losing its direction and meaning.

St Huberts Pinot Noir

▼▼▼▼ 2001 Medium red-purple; the plummy fruit of the bouquet is bordering on over-ripeness; similarly substantial dark plum fruit on the palate moves through to a slightly matty finish. Flavoursome, but ... **rating:** 88

best drinking Now–2005 **best vintages** '00 **drink with** Strong red meat dishes • $25.99

St Huberts Cabernet Merlot

YYYY **2000** Medium purple-red; aromatic red berry fruit and splashes of leaf, mint and spice; the redcurrant and blackberry fruit comes through strongly on the palate, nicely balanced by fine tannins and subtle oak. A good reflection of an excellent vintage. **rating:** 91

best drinking 2005–2015 **best vintages** '00 **drink with** Lamb kebabs • $25.99

st leonards ★★★

Wahgunyah, Vic 3687 **region** Rutherglen
phone (02) 6033 1004 **fax** (02) 6033 3636 **open** 7 days 10–5
winemaker Peter Brown, Dan Crane **production** NFP **est.** 1860
product range ($12–45 CD) Semillon, Chenin Blanc, Sauvignon Blanc, Sauvignon Blanc Semillon, Chardonnay, Orange Muscat, Wahgunyah Brut, Sparkling Shiraz, Kalara Rose, Pinot Noir, Shiraz, Wahgunyah Shiraz, Cabernet Franc, Heritage Cabernet Sauvignon, Heritage Release Tawny Port, Classic Rutherglen Muscat.
summary An old favourite, re-launched in late 1997 with a range of three premium wines cleverly marketed through a singularly attractive cellar door and bistro at the historic winery on the banks of the Murray. All Saints and St Leonards are now wholly owned by Peter Brown; the vast majority of the wines are sold through the cellar door and by the mailing list.

St Leonards Sauvignon Blanc Semillon

YYYY **2002** Light straw-green; the bouquet is clean, of light to moderate intensity, and it is not until the palate that the wine picks up pace, with a mix of grass and gooseberry; good acidity and balance. The sauvignon blanc is sourced from Lake Buffalo near Myrtleford, the semillon estate-grown. **rating:** 85

best drinking Now **drink with** Fried oysters • $16

St Leonards Orange Muscat

YYYY **2002** Light straw-green; a highly fragrant orange blossom bouquet is followed by a palate which is made dry and hence lighter, although the varietal character continues to be very obvious; for once, just a touch of residual sugar might have made an even more striking wine. From 25-year-old estate plantings. **rating:** 86

best drinking Now **drink with** Asian seafood • $14.50

St Leonards Shiraz

YYYY **2000** Medium red-purple; red berry, earth and vanilla aromas drive both the bouquet and the light to medium-bodied palate, all in thoroughly traditional style. **rating:** 84

best drinking Now–2007 **drink with** Steak and kidney pie • $22.50

st mary's NR

V & A Lane, via Coonawarra, SA 5277 **region** Limestone Coast Zone
phone (08) 8736 6070 **fax** (08) 8736 6045 **open** 7 days 10–4
winemaker Barry Mulligan **production** 4000 cases **est.** 1986
product range ($12–22 CD) Shiraz, Merlot, Cabernet Sauvignon.
summary The Mulligan family has lived in the Penola/Coonawarra region since 1909. In 1937 a 250-hectare property 15 km to the west of Penola, including an 80-hectare ridge of terra rossa over limestone, was purchased for grazing. The ridge was cleared; the remainder of the property was untouched and is now a private wildlife sanctuary. In 1986 Barry & Glenys Mulligan planted shiraz and cabernet sauvignon on the ridge, followed by merlot in the early 1990s. The first wines were made in 1990, and national distribution began in 1992, followed by exports in 1996. It remains a wholly estate-based operation.

st matthias ★★★☆

113 Rosevears Drive, Rosevears, Tas 7277 **region** Northern Tasmania
phone (03) 6330 1700 **fax** (03) 6330 1975 **open** 7 days 10–5
winemaker Michael Glover **production** 4000 cases **est.** 1983
product range ($9.35–24 CD) Riesling, Pinot Gris, Chardonnay, Brut, Pinot Noir, St Matthias (Cabernet blend).
summary After an uncomfortable period in the wilderness following the sale of the vineyard to Moorilla Estate, and the disposal of the wine made by the previous owners under the St Matthias label, Moorilla has re-introduced the label, and markets a full range of competitively priced wines which are in fact made at Moorilla Estate.

St Matthias Riesling

TTTT 2002 Light straw-green; a floral, aromatic bouquet with green lime aromas, then a punchy palate with lots of fruit, the acidity balanced by palpable residual sugar. **rating:** 89

best drinking Now–2010 **best vintages** '97, '99, '01 **drink with** Salmon mousse • $18.50

St Matthias Pinot Gris

TTTT 2002 Medium yellow, with some green tinges; the bouquet has some ripe apple aromas, and the palate has well above-average richness in a pear/apple spectrum. However, it really needs more texture to take it out of the white painting category. **rating:** 85

best drinking Now **drink with** Shellfish

St Matthias Cabernet Merlot

TTTT 2000 Medium red-purple; spicy, leafy, earthy, blackberry aromas in no way prepare you for the deeply structured and very tannic palate. In vintages like 2000, Tamar Valley-grown grapes throw the Tasmanian rule book out the window. Less would have been better. **rating:** 86

best drinking 2004–2009 **drink with** Barbecued beef • $24

salem bridge wines   NR

Salem Bridge Road, Lower Hermitage, SA 5131 **region** Adelaide Hills
phone (08) 8380 5240 **fax** (08) 8380 5240 **open** Not
winemaker Barry Miller **production** 300 cases **est.** 1989
product range ($NR) Cabernet Franc.
summary Barry Miller acquired the 45-hectare Salem Bridge property in the Adelaide Hills of South Australia in 1988. A little under 2 hectares of cabernet franc were planted in 1989, and cabernet franc has been the only commercial release prior to 1999. However, a further 14 hectares have been planted to cabernet sauvignon, shiraz and merlot, with a Shiraz and Cabernet Sauvignon release in the pipeline. The core business is contract growing, with only 10 per cent of the production vinified for the Salem Bridge label. The wine is made off-site by contract, with input from Barry Miller.

salena estate   NR

Bookpurnong Road, Loxton, SA 5343 **region** Riverland
phone (08) 8584 1333 **fax** (08) 8584 1388 **open** Mon–Fri 8.30–5
winemaker Grant Semmens **production** 130 000 cases **est.** 1998
product range ($13–31 CD) At the bottom is the Salena Estate range of Chardonnay, Shiraz, Merlot, Cabernet Sauvignon; next is Ellen Landing Shiraz, Petit Verdot, Cabernet Sauvignon; at the top is the Bookpurnong Hill range of Shiraz, Block 267 (blend of Cabernet Sauvignon, Petit Verdot, Merlot, Shiraz), Cabernet Sauvignon; Amore Fortified Chardonnay.
summary This business, established in 1998, encapsulates the hectic rate of growth across the entire Australian wine industry. Its 1998 crush was 300 tonnes, and by 2001 it was processing 7000 tonnes. This was produced from over 200 hectares of estate vineyards, supplemented by grapes purchased from other growers. It is the venture of Bob and Sylvia Franchitto, the estate being named after their daughter Salena. Export distribution to the US, the UK, Sweden, Malaysia, Hong Kong and Singapore has already been established to supplement local distribution; it is the export market which will take the lion's share.

salitage   ★★★★

Vasse Highway, Pemberton, WA 6260 **region** Pemberton
phone (08) 9776 1771 **fax** (08) 9776 1772 **open** 7 days 10–4
winemaker Patrick Coutts **production** 20 000 cases **est.** 1989
product range ($17–35 R) Sauvignon Blanc, Chardonnay, Unwooded Chardonnay, Pinot Noir, Pemberton (Cabernet blend); Treehouse range of Sauvignon Blanc, Chardonnay Verdelho, Pinot Noir, Shiraz, Cabernet Merlot.
summary Salitage is the showpiece of Pemberton. If it had failed to live up to expectations, it is a fair bet that the same fate would have befallen the whole of the Pemberton region. The quality and style of Salitage did vary substantially, presumably in response to vintage conditions and yields, but since 1999 it seems to have found its way, with a succession of attractive wines. Key retail distribution in all states, and exports to New Zealand, Singapore, Japan, Hong Kong, Malaysia, Germany, Switzerland, Canada, Denmark, the UK and the US.

Salitage Sauvignon Blanc

♥♥♥♥ 2002 Light straw-green; the moderately intense bouquet is clean (without the sweats), offering grass, gooseberry and snow pea aromas; the light to medium-bodied palate has exactly the same flavours, finishing with what seems to be a subliminal touch of sweetness. **rating:** 87

best drinking Now **drink with** Calamari • $20

Salitage Unwooded Chardonnay

♥♥♥♥ 2001 Medium yellow-green; a soft bouquet offers a mix of melon and cashew flowing through to the no less soft, almost sweet peach and melon fruit; integrated oak. In radically different style from the 2000. **rating:** 88

best drinking Now **best vintages** '97 **drink with** Vegetarian dishes • $30

Salitage Pinot Noir

♥♥♥♥♡ 2001 Medium red-purple; a clean, light, gently savoury/foresty bouquet leads into a palate with fruit on the light side, but well handled in the winery. Fine tannins and well balanced. **rating:** 90

best drinking Now–2005 **best vintages** '93, '94, '99, '00 **drink with** Barbecued quail • $34

Salitage Treehouse Shiraz

♥♥♥♥ 2001 Medium purple-red; the moderately intense bouquet ranges through fresh berry, licorice and earth aromatics; the long and powerful palate has textured red berry fruit and sustained tannins. Another sign of the lift in the Salitage quality. **rating:** 88

best drinking 2004–2009 **drink with** Spiced beef shashlik • $20

saltram ★★★★

Salters Gully, Nuriootpa, SA 5355 **region** Barossa Valley
phone (08) 8564 3355 **fax** (08) 8564 2209 **open** 7 days 10–5
winemaker Nigel Dolan **production** NFP **est.** 1859
product range ($10–49.95 R) At the top is No. 1 Shiraz; then Mamre Brook, now 100 per cent Barossa and comprising Chardonnay, Shiraz and Cabernet Sauvignon; Metala Black Label and White Label; and the Saltram Classic range, sourced from southeast Australia; also Pepperjack range, with Shiraz and Cabernet Sauvignon.
summary There is no doubt that Saltram has taken giant strides towards regaining the reputation it held 30 or so years ago. Under Nigel Dolan's stewardship, grape sourcing has come back to the Barossa Valley for the flagship wines, a fact of which he is rightly proud. The red wines, in particular, have enjoyed great show success over the past few years, with No. 1 Shiraz, Mamre Brook and Metala leading the charge.

Pepperjack Grenache Rose

♥♥♥♥ 2002 Bright, light pink-purple; the bouquet is fruity, with some spicy undertones; the palate has abundant fruit flavour, and a slightly sweet finish which will no doubt have market appeal. **rating:** 87

best drinking Now **drink with** Mediterranean food • $20

Saltram Mamre Brook Shiraz

♥♥♥♥♡ 2000 Medium red-purple; the moderately intense bouquet ranges through sweet leather, earth, dark berry and vanilla oak; the palate is richer, aided by lots of dark chocolate alongside dark berry fruit; neatly managed oak. **rating:** 90

best drinking 2004–2010 **best vintages** '98, '99 **drink with** Grilled calf's liver • $20

Metala Black Label Shiraz

♥♥♥♥♡ 2000 Medium red-purple; a rippling bouquet of dark cherry, plum, chocolate, licorice and vanilla determines the agenda for the medium to full-bodied palate, which is stacked with fruit and all the flavours promised by the bouquet; controlled tannin and oak. **rating:** 93

best drinking 2005–2015 **best vintages** '96, '98, '00 **drink with** Eye fillet of beef • $42

Pepperjack Barossa Shiraz

♥♥♥♥ 2000 Medium red-purple; the moderately intense bouquet has sweet cherry fruit supported by subtle oak; the palate has abundant richness and concentration in ripe fruit flavours, finishing with soft tannins. **rating:** 89

best drinking 2004–2009 **best vintages** '96 **drink with** Pepper steak • $21

Pepperjack Barossa Grenache Shiraz Mourvedre

♥♥♥♥ 2000 Medium red-purple; the moderately intense bouquet has sweet, gently juicy berry fruit and a waft of oak; the light to medium-bodied palate is entirely fruit-driven in a lively, drink-now style. **rating:** 88

best drinking Now **drink with** Pizza • $21

Metala Shiraz Cabernet

▼▼▼▼ 2000 Medium red-purple; the savoury bouquet has faintly lemony overtones to light, red berry fruit; the palate picks up more weight and moves more to the dark berry spectrum; neat oak and quite persistent, faintly rubbery, tannins on a long finish. The term 'rubbery', incidentally, denotes the mouthfeel/texture, not the flavour. **rating:** 88

best drinking Now–2008 **best vintages** '96 **drink with** Italian • $17

sandalford ★★★★

West Swan Road, Caversham, WA 6055 **region** Swan Valley
phone (08) 9374 9374 **fax** (08) 9274 2154 **open** 7 days 10–5
winemaker Paul Boulden **production** 80 000 cases **est.** 1840
product range ($12.95–35 R) At the bottom end, under the Caversham label, Chenin Verdelho, Late Harvest Cabernet Shiraz; then the 1840 Collection of Semillon Sauvignon Blanc, Chardonnay, Cabernet Merlot; under the premium range, Margaret River Mount Barker Riesling, Margaret River Verdelho, Mount Barker Margaret River Chardonnay, Mount Barker Margaret River Shiraz, Mount Barker Margaret River Cabernet Sauvignon; excellent fortifieds, notably Sandalera; also the new Element brand, including Chenin Verdelho, Chardonnay, Cabernet Shiraz.
summary The installation of a new winemaking team, headed by the energetic Paul Boulden, and continuing winery upgrading has meant that wine quality has continued to improve year by year, with good wines across the whole portfolio. The quality of the labelling and packaging has also taken a giant leap forward. Exports to the UK, Switzerland, the US, Japan, Singapore and Hong Kong.

Sandalford Semillon

▼▼▼▼ 2002 Light to medium green-yellow; the complex bouquet has dominant toasty oak followed by a palate which opens with the same dominant oak before the fruit comes through on the back palate and finish. Part barrel fermented and part stainless steel fermented; a bit less barrel work might have made an even better wine, but time in bottle should help. **rating:** 87

best drinking Now–2006 **drink with** Scallops • $25

Sandalford Semillon Sauvignon Blanc

▼▼▼▼ 2002 Light green-straw; a crisp and lively bouquet offers herb and grass, with just a hint of reduction; the medium-bodied palate has considerable length, the flavours tracking the bouquet in all respects. A blend of Frankland River and Margaret River grapes. **rating:** 88

best drinking Now–2006 **drink with** Crab soufflé • $22.50

Sandalford Margaret River Verdelho

▼▼▼▼ 2002 Light straw-green; a vibrant bouquet with citrus, tropical fruit salad and gooseberry aromas flows through into a palate which has well above-average flavour and length; produced from 30-year-old Margaret River vines. **rating:** 89

best drinking Now–2007 **best vintages** '87, '88, '91, '93, '94, '96 **drink with** Prosciutto and melon • $19.50

Sandalford Margaret River Chardonnay

▼▼▼▼▽ 2002 Light green-yellow; the clean and tangy bouquet is driven by its citrus/stone fruit, with the oak well-integrated and balanced. The medium-bodied palate has obvious development potential, the oak needing time to settle down. **rating:** 90

best drinking 2004–2009 **best vintages** '01 **drink with** Chicken salad • $29

Sandalford Element Late Harvest Verdelho

▼▼▼▼ 2002 Medium yellow-green; attractive aromatic, spicy aromas are followed by a palate with lime and spice flavours, lively acidity and freshness adding to the length. Unusual, but has real character and quality. **rating:** 89

best drinking Now–2005 **drink with** Prosciutto and melon • $13.75

Sandalford Mount Barker Margaret River Shiraz

▼▼▼▼ 2001 Excellent purple-red hue and clarity; bright red fruit on the bouquet marries with a gentle touch of vanilla oak; the firm, fresh, bright cherry fruit of the palate is balanced more by brisk acidity and oak (American) than by tannins. **rating:** 88

best drinking 2004–2009 **best vintages** '94, '95, '97 **drink with** Lamb chops • $24.50

Sandalford Element Merlot

🍷🍷🍷🍷 **2002** Light to medium red-purple; the moderately intense bouquet has bright, fragrant berry, leaf and mint aromas; the fresh, light to medium-bodied palate has red fruit flavours which are distinctly varietal; neatly priced. **rating:** 85

best drinking Now–2005 **drink with** Roast veal • $13

Sandalford Margaret River Cabernet Sauvignon

🍷🍷🍷🍷 **2000** Medium red-purple; the bouquet has subtle, gently earthy blackberry fruit allied with touches of cedar; the light to medium-bodied palate offers savoury blackberry fruit and fine tannins to close. **rating:** 86

best drinking Now–2008 **drink with** Lamb cutlets • $25

sandalyn wilderness estate   NR

Wilderness Road, Rothbury, NSW 2321 **region** Lower Hunter Valley
phone (02) 4930 7611 **fax** (02) 4930 7611 **open** 7 days 10–5
winemaker Adrian Sheridan (Contract) **production** 6000 cases **est.** 1988
product range ($16–25 CD) Semillon, Verdelho, Semillon Verdelho, Chardonnay, Semillon Late Harvest, Pinot Noir, Conservatory Shiraz, Sparkling.
summary Sandra and Lindsay Whaling preside over the picturesque cellar-door building of Sandalyn on the evocatively named Wilderness Road, where you will find a one-hole golf range and views to the Wattagan, Brokenback and Molly Morgan ranges. The estate has 8.85 hectares of vineyards. Exports to Ireland.

sand hills vineyard   NR

Sandhills Road, Forbes, NSW 2871 **region** Central Ranges Zone
phone (02) 6852 1437 **fax** (02) 6852 4401 **open** Mon–Sat 9–5, Sun 12–5
winemaker Jill Lindsay, John Saleh **production** 300 cases **est.** 1920
product range ($9–16 CD) Banderra The White, Colombard Semillon, Chardonnay, Banderra The Red, Vat 1 Dry Red, Dry Red, Pinot Noir, Shiraz Cabernet, Cabernet Shiraz, Lucien Tawny Port, Oloroso Cream Sherry.
summary Having purchased Sand Hills from long-term owner Jacques Genet, the Saleh family has replanted the vineyard to appropriate varieties, with over 6 hectares of premium varieties having been established. Winemaking is carried out by Jill Lindsay of Woodonga Hill.

sandhurst ridge   ★★★★

156 Forest Drive, Marong, Vic 3515 **region** Bendigo
phone (03) 5435 2534 **fax** (03) 5435 2548 **open** Mon–Fri 12–5, or by appointment
winemaker Paul Greblo, George Greblo **production** 2300 cases **est.** 1990
product range ($22–42 CD) Sauvignon Blanc, Chardonnay, Shiraz, Reserve Shiraz, Merlot, Cabernet Sauvignon.
summary The four Greblo brothers, with combined experience in business, agriculture, science and construction and development, began the establishment of Sandhurst Ridge in 1990 with the planting of the first 2 hectares of shiraz and cabernet sauvignon. Those plantings have now been increased to over 6 hectares, principally cabernet and shiraz, but with small amounts of merlot, sauvignon blanc and chardonnay. The fully equipped winery was completed in 1996 with a cellar capacity of 400 barriques. The winery rating is given for its red wines only, not for its whites. Exports to the US.

Sandhurst Ridge Shiraz

🍷🍷🍷🍷 **2001** Medium purple-red; dark plum, prune and spice aromas announce a full-bodied palate, with plum, prune and mint flavours warmed by the 14.9° alcohol; the American oak is subtle. **rating:** 88

best drinking 2006–2011 **drink with** Char-grilled rib of beef • $28

Sandhurst Ridge Reserve Shiraz

🍷🍷🍷🍷🍷 **2001** Excellent deep purple-red; powerful black plum, blackberry, spice and oak aromas come through strongly on the concentrated blackberry and bitter chocolate palate; good vanilla oak rounds off an archetypal big-bodied Australian red wine. Produced from the oldest vines on the property, open fermented, basket pressed, then spending 18 months in American oak. **rating:** 93

best drinking 2006–2016 **best vintages** '00, '01 **drink with** Aged venison • $42

443

Sandhurst Ridge Merlot

▼▼▼▼ 2001 Bright red-purple; the bouquet has moderately fragrant red berry fruit aromas. The palate is ripe and structured without losing varietal character; good oak and tannin extract. Open fermented, and completes fermentation in a mix of American and French oak plus 15 months' maturation. **rating: 87**

best drinking 2004–2009 **drink with** Lamb shanks • $28

Sandhurst Ridge Cabernet Sauvignon

▼▼▼▼ 2001 Medium red-purple, not dense; there are savoury, leafy, earthy overtones to the core of blackcurrant fruit on the bouquet; the palate is denser and slightly riper, with a distinct touch of dark chocolate; well-controlled tannins and extract. Made in the same way as the Merlot. **rating: 87**

best drinking 2005–2010 **drink with** Parmesan or aged cheddar • $28

sandstone   NR

Corner Johnson and Caves Road, Wilyabrup, WA 6280 **region** Margaret River
phone (08) 9755 6271 **fax** (08) 9755 6292 **open** Mon–Fri 11–4
winemaker Mike Davies, Jan Davies **production** 1500 cases **est.** 1988
product range ($12.50–31.50 CD) Semillon, Spindrift Semillon Sauvignon Blanc, Cabernet Sauvignon, Spindrift Cabernet Sauvignon.
summary The family operation of consultant winemakers Mike and Jan Davies, who also operate very successful mobile bottling plants. It will eventually be estate-based, following the planting of 6 hectares of semillon and 1 hectare of cabernet sauvignon in 2002. Strangely, no recent tastings.

sandy farm vineyard   NR

RMB 3734, Sandy Farm Road, Denver via Daylesford, Vic 3641 **region** Macedon Ranges
phone (03) 5348 7610 **open** Weekends 10–5, or by appointment
winemaker Peter Comisel **production** 800 cases **est.** 1988
product range ($19–28 CD) Preservative Free Pinot Noir and Cabernet Merlot.
summary Peter Comisel and Dot Hollow acquired Sandy Farm from founder Peter Covell. There are 1.5 hectares of cabernet sauvignon, cabernet franc, merlot and 0.5 hectare of pinot noir, with a small, basic winery in which they make preservative-free Cabernet Sauvignon, Merlot and Pinot Noir, attracting a loyal local following.

🐌 sanguine estate   ★★★★☆

77 Shurans Lane, Heathcote, Vic 3523 (postal) **region** Heathcote
phone (03) 9646 6661 **fax** (03) 9646 1746 **open** Not
winemaker Matt Hunter, Peter Dredge (Contract) **production** 450 cases **est.** 1997
product range ($35 R) Heathcote Shiraz.
summary The Hunter family, with parents Linda and Tony at the head, and their two children, Mark and Jodi with their respective partners Melissa and Brett, began the establishment of the vineyard in 1997. From a starting base of 4 hectares of shiraz planted that year, it has now grown to 13.4 hectares of shiraz, and 2 hectares of 8 different varieties, including chardonnay, viognier, merlot, tempranillo, zinfandel, petit verdot, cabernet sauvignon, merlot and cabernet franc. Yet another planting (in the spring of 2002) added another 7.3 hectares of shiraz. Low-yielding vines and the magic of the Heathcote region have produced Shiraz of exceptional intensity, which has received rave reviews in the US, and led to the 'sold out' sign being posted almost immediately upon release. With the ever-expanding vineyard, Mark Hunter has become full-time vigneron, and Jodi Marsh part-time marketer and business developer. For the foreseeable future the wines will continue to be contract-made. Exports to the US.

Sanguine Estate Heathcote Shiraz

▼▼▼▼▼ 2001 Medium to full red-purple; intensely aromatic, juicy raspberry and blackberry aromas are followed by blackberry, spice, fine and ripe tannins, and sweet oak on the palate. Carries the (relatively) modest 14.5° alcohol with ease. Definitely a wine to follow; it does, however, sell out very quickly. **rating: 94**

best drinking 2006–2016 **best vintages** '01 **drink with** Braised oxtail • $35

🐌 sanguine wines   ★★★★

18 North Terrace, Adelaide, SA 5000 (postal) **region** Wrattonbully
phone (08) 8212 1801 **fax** (08) 8212 4022 **open** Not
winemaker Steve Maglieri, Scott Rawlinson **production** 900 cases **est.** 1997
product range ($23.50 R) The Struggle Shiraz, The Commitment Cabernet Sauvignon.

summary There is a certain amount of (conscious or unconscious) irony in the name, for the development of the 33 hectares of cabernet sauvignon and 11 hectares of shiraz which constitute Sanguine vineyard was exceptionally difficult. It is situated on a terra rossa ridge top, but had unusually thick limestone slabs running through it, which had caused others to bypass the property. A 95-tonne bulldozer was hired to deep rip the limestone, but was unequal to the task, and ultimately explosives had to be used to create sufficient inroads to allow planting. Fifteen per cent of the production from the vineyard is used to make the Sanguine Wines under the direction of the immensely experienced Steve Maglieri.

Sanguine Wines The Struggle Shiraz

▼▼▼▼▽ **2001** Medium red-purple; the moderately intense bouquet has a mix of ripe dark plum, blackberry, chocolate and spice aromas supported by attractive oak; the stylish, medium-bodied palate is fruit-driven, still fresh and lively. **rating:** 90

best drinking 2005–2012 **best vintages** '01 **drink with** Irish stew • $23.50

Sanguine Wines The Commitment Cabernet Sauvignon

▼▼▼▼▽ **2001** Medium red-purple; the fragrant and stylish bouquet offers moderately ripe redcurrant and blackcurrant fruit; the palate follows precisely as expected, medium-bodied and elegant, with the cassis/blackcurrant fruit offset by a hint of savoury, black olive. **rating:** 90

best drinking 2005–2012 **best vintages** '01 **drink with** Roast saltbush lamb • $23.50

saracen estates ★★★☆

Caves Road, Wilyabrup, WA 6280 **region** Margaret River
phone (08) 9221 4955 **fax** (08) 9221 4966 **open** By appointment
winemaker Bill Crappsley **production** 20 000 cases **est.** 1998
product range ($12–28 R) Sauvignon Blanc, Classic Dry White, Chardonnay, Classic Dry Red, Shiraz, Cabernet Sauvignon; budget-priced Emu Springs range of Chardonnay, Shiraz, Cabernet Sauvignon.
summary The Cazzolli and Saraceni families have established 40 hectares of vines on their 80-hectare property at Metricup, with a restaurant and cellar door planned. The name not only echoes that of one of the founding families; it also pays tribute to the Saracens, one of the most advanced races in cultural and social terms at the time of the Crusades. The business has lost no time in securing eastern states distribution, with exports to the UK, Singapore, Malaysia, Papua New Guinea and Hong Kong.

Saracen Estates Sauvignon Blanc

▼▼▼▼ **2001** Light straw-green; a fresh, clean and delicate bouquet with passionfruit/gooseberry varietal fruit sets the tone; despite the light frame of the palate, it has good length and focus. **rating:** 89

best drinking Now **drink with** Marinated scallops • $24.99

Saracen Estates Chardonnay

▼▼▼▼ **2001** Light straw-green; the bouquet is clean, remarkably restrained and undeveloped; the light to medium-bodied palate has melon fruit and subtle oak; all in all, a Peter Pan style, and you wonder whether it will ever develop significant richness. **rating:** 86

best drinking Now–2008 **drink with** Green-lipped mussels • $24.99

Saracen Estates Shiraz

▼▼▼▼▽ **2001** Medium to full red-purple; masses of dark, ripe blackberry and prune fruit on the bouquet, matched by luscious, powerful black fruits and spice on the palate, both have abundant oak to add to the mix. **rating:** 91

best drinking 2006–2011 **drink with** Braised oxtail • $27.99

Saracen Estates Cabernet Sauvignon

▼▼▼▼ **2000** Bright red-purple; there are herbal overtones to the blackcurrant/blackberry fruit of the bouquet, then a savoury herb and sweet blackcurrant mix on the palate, with the oak well-integrated. The Achilles Heel is a slightly jumpy mouthfeel, which will hopefully settle down with age. **rating:** 86

best drinking 2005–2009 **best vintages** '99 **drink with** White Rocks veal • $27.99

sarsfield estate ★★★☆

345 Duncan Road, Sarsfield, Vic 3875 **region** Gippsland
phone (03) 5156 8962 **fax** (03) 5156 8970 **open** By appointment
winemaker Dr Suzanne Rutschmann **production** 1000 cases **est.** 1995

product range ($18.50–22 CD) Pinot Noir, Cabernets Shiraz Merlot.

summary The property is owned by Suzanne Rutschmann, who has a PhD in Chemistry, a Diploma in Horticulture and and a BSc (Wine Science) from Charles Sturt University, and by Swiss-born Peter Albrecht, a civil and structural engineer who has also undertaken various courses in agriculture and viticulture. For a part-time occupation, these are exceptionally impressive credentials. Their 2-hectare vineyard was planted between 1991 and 1998; the first vintage made at the winery was 1998, the grapes being sold to others in previous years. High-quality packaging is a plus.

Sarsfield Estate Pinot Noir

YYYY 2001 Light to medium red-purple; the bouquet has light, distinctly savoury/spicy notes, and the palate has a mix of savoury, cherry/strawberry fruit which is certainly varietal, but not as rich as the excellent 2000 vintage.   **rating:** 86

best drinking Now–2005 **best vintages** '00 **drink with** Braised duck • $22

Sarsfield Estate Cabernets Shiraz Merlot

YYYY 2001 Medium red-purple; there are earthy/savoury overtones to the olive and blackberry fruit of the bouquet; dark fruits build noticeably on the palate, with ripe blackcurrant and blackberry flavours supported by fine tannins. A blend of 44 per cent Cabernet Sauvignon, 20 per cent Cabernet Franc, 24 per cent Shiraz and 12 per cent Merlot. Well priced.   **rating:** 88

best drinking 2005–2010 **drink with** Shoulder of lamb • $18.50

scarborough ★★★★☆

Gillards Road, Pokolbin, NSW 2321 **region** Lower Hunter Valley
phone (02) 4998 7563 **fax** (02) 4998 7786 **open** 7 days 9–5
winemaker Ian Scarborough **production** 12 000 cases **est.** 1985
product range ($19–23 CD) Semillon, Chardonnay (Blue Label), Chardonnay (Traditional), Pinot Noir.
summary Ian Scarborough put his white winemaking skills beyond doubt during his years as a consultant, and has brought all those skills to his own label. He makes two radically different styles of Chardonnay, the Blue Silver Label in a light, elegant, Chablis style for the export market and a much richer, strongly barrel-fermented wine (with a mustard/gold label) for the Australian market. However, the real excitement lies with the future and the portion of the old Lindemans Sunshine Vineyard which he has purchased (after it lay fallow for 30 years) and planted with semillon and (quixotically) pinot noir. The first vintage from the Sunshine Vineyard will be in 2004; in the meantime, Ian Scarborough is practising with contract-grown semillon.

Scarborough Semillon

YYYY 2002 Light to medium yellow-green; the bouquet is surprisingly complex, with spicy and other aromas, possibly due to a touch of botrytis; the palate is already medium-bodied, and quite soft on the mid-palate, providing an easy-drinking, early-developing style.   **rating:** 88

best drinking Now–2006 **drink with** Rich fish dishes • $20

Scarborough Blue Silver Label Chardonnay

YYYYY 2001 Excellent green-yellow; fine melon and nectarine fruit drive the bouquet, which has great varietal character; the clean, long and intense palate mirrors the bouquet; as ever, there is little evidence of oak.   **rating:** 92

best drinking Now–2005 **best vintages** '01 **drink with** Grilled flathead • $19

Scarborough Gold Label Chardonnay

YYYY 2000 Similar bright green-yellow; the bouquet has nice bottle-developed aromas woven through the complex barrel-ferment oak The palate has generous nectarine and peach fruit, the oak neatly integrated; good balance and weight.   **rating:** 91

best drinking Now–2005 **best vintages** '87, '89, '91, '94, '96, '98, '99, '00 **drink with** Rich white meat dishes • $21

scarpantoni estate ★★★☆

Scarpantoni Drive, McLaren Flat, SA 5171 **region** McLaren Vale
phone (08) 8383 0186 **fax** (08) 8383 0490 **open** Mon–Fri 9–5, weekends and public holidays 11–5
winemaker Michael Scarpantoni, Filippo Scarpantoni **production** 25 000 cases **est.** 1979
product range ($6–36 CD) Block 1 Riesling, Sauvignon Blanc, Unwooded Chardonnay, Chardonnay, Cellared Release Chardonnay, Fleurieu Brut, Black Tempest (sparkling), Botrytis Riesling, Fiori, Ceres (Rose), School Block (Shiraz Cabernet Merlot), Block 3 Shiraz, Showcroft (Shiraz Grenache Gamay), Blue Tongue Cabernet Sauvignon, Estate Reserve, Tawny Port, Vintage Port, V.P. Shiraz.

summary With 14.5 hectares of shiraz, 5 hectares each of cabernet and chardonnay, 3 hectares of sauvignon blanc, 1 hectare each of merlot and gamay, and 0.5 hectare of petit verdot, Scarpantoni has come a long way since Domenico Scarpantoni purchased his first property of 5.6 hectares in 1958. At that time he was working for Thomas Hardy at its Tintara winery, and subsequently became vineyard manager for Seaview Wines, responsible for the contoured vineyards which were leading edge viticulture in the 1960s. In 1979 his two sons, Michael and Filippo, built the winery, which has now been extended to the point where all the grapes from the estate plantings are used to make wine under the Scarpantoni label. As the vines have matured, quality has gone from strength to strength, with distribution in all states and exports to the US, the UK, Switzerland, The Netherlands, Germany and New Zealand.

Scarpantoni Estate Sauvignon Blanc

▼▼▼▼ 2002 Light straw-green; a crisp and clean bouquet presents bright, fresh, grassy aromas which also come through on the palate, but are joined there by some softer, sweet fruit flavours; nice wine.   **rating:** 87

best drinking Now **drink with** Light seafood • $18

Scarpantoni Estate Block 3 Shiraz

▼▼▼▼▽ 2001 Medium red-purple; the clean, moderately intense bouquet has dark cherry fruit and background spicy characters supported by subtle oak; the wine gathers significant pace on the medium to full-bodied palate, where black cherry, chocolate, spice and licorice all combine; nice oak and well balanced.   **rating:** 90

best drinking 2006–2011 **best vintages** '96, '97, '98, '99 **drink with** Seared kangaroo fillet • $22

Scarpantoni Estate Reserve Shiraz Cabernet Sauvignon

▼▼▼▼ 1999 Medium to full red with some purple tinges remaining; the spotlessly clean bouquet has sweet berry, chocolate and warm oak aromas; the medium-bodied palate follows serenely on with plum, blackberry, licorice and spice fruit, and closing with fine tannins.   **rating:** 88

best drinking 2004–2009 **drink with** Beef Provençale • $36

Scarpantoni Estate Blanche Point Maslin Beach Vineyard

▼▼▼▼ 2000 Light to medium red-purple; there is not a lot of action on the bouquet, other than some briary, cedary notes; the palate, however, has much more power and substance, with concentrated, savoury blackberry/ blackcurrant fruit. From a new estate vineyard established almost on the edge of Maslin Beach. A blend of Cabernet Sauvignon, Shiraz and Merlot.   **rating:** 87

best drinking 2004–2008 **drink with** Braised rabbit • $25

Scarpantoni Estate Blue Tongue Cabernet Sauvignon

▼▼▼▼ 2001 Medium red-purple; the bouquet is quite complex, with a mix of blackcurrant, earth, leaf and savoury notes augmented by subtle French oak. The light to medium-bodied palate is marked by blackcurrant and raspberry fruit, with fine tannins to close. Elegant and unforced.   **rating:** 86

best drinking 2004–2008 **drink with** Roast lamb • $22

scarp valley vineyard   NR

8 Robertson Road, Gooseberry Hill, WA 6076 **region** Perth Hills
phone (08) 9454 5748 **open** By appointment
winemaker Contract **production** 25 cases **est.** 1978
product range ($20 ML) Darling Range Hermitage.
summary Owner Robert Duncan presides over what has to be one of the smallest producers in Australia, with 0.1 hectare of shiraz and 30 cabernet sauvignon vines producing a single cask of wine each year if the birds do not get the grapes first.

schild estate wines   ★★★☆

Cnr Barossa Valley Way and Lyndoch Valley Road, Lyndoch, SA 5351 **region** Barossa Valley
phone (08) 8524 5560 **fax** (08) 8524 4333 **open** 7 days 10–5
winemaker Ed Schild, Daniel Eggleton (Contract) **production** 6500 cases **est.** 1998
product range ($15–25 CD) Barossa Valley Riesling, Eden Valley Riesling, Semillon, Frontignac, Chardonnay, Shiraz, Merlot, Cabernet Sauvignon.
summary Ed Schild is a Barossa Valley grape grower who first planted a small vineyard at Rowland Flat in 1952, steadily increasing his vineyard holdings over the past 40 years to their present level of 126 hectares. Currently only 10 per cent of the production from these vineyards is used to produce Schild Estate Wines, but the plans are to steadily increase this percentage. The flagship wine will be made from 150-year-old shiraz vines

on the Moorooroo Block. The cellar-door sales facility is situated in what was the ANZ Bank at Lyndoch, and provides the sort of ambience which can only be found in the Barossa Valley. Exports to Malaysia, Belgium, Germany and the US.

Schild Estate Semillon

TTTT 2002 Light yellow-green; discreet, grassy varietal fruit on the bouquet is followed by a palate which once again shows strong grass/lemongrass/lemon varietal flavours. Its particular achievement is to turn 13.5 baume fruit into 12.5° alcohol. **rating:** 85

best drinking Now–2005 **best vintages** '00 **drink with** Smoked eel • $16

Schild Estate Frontignac

TTTT 2002 Water white; the bouquet is faintly grapey, otherwise spotlessly clean; the crisp, grapey palate is refreshing and almost dry, making it an ideal summer terrace wine. **rating:** 85

best drinking Now **drink with** Anything or nothing • $16

Schild Estate Merlot

TTTT 2001 Medium red-purple; an earthy, savoury, spicy mix of aromas is followed by a palate with pleasantly ripe raspberry and a touch of chocolate, finishing with fine tannins; attractive varietal character. **rating:** 88

best drinking 2004–2009 **drink with** Veal chops • $24

Schild Estate Cabernet Sauvignon

TTTT 2001 Light to medium red-purple; blackcurrant fruit is swathed by vanilla oak on the bouquet; a pleasant, light and softly textured wine in the mouth, once again with vanilla oak making a contribution. **rating:** 86

best drinking 2005–2010 **best vintages** '99 **drink with** Roast lamb • $24

schindler northway downs ★★★★

437 Stumpy Gully Road, Balnarring, Vic 3926 **region** Mornington Peninsula
phone (03) 5983 1945 **fax** (03) 9580 4262 **open** First weekend each month
winemaker Tammy Schindler-Hands **production** 450 cases **est.** 1996
product range ($18–22 ML) Chardonnay, Pinot Noir.
summary Establishment of the vineyard by the Schindler family began in 1996 with the planting of the first 2 hectares of pinot noir and chardonnay. A further 4 hectares of pinot noir were planted on an ideal north-facing slope in 1999, and the first vintage followed in 2000. The cellar door was subsequently established, and opens on the first weekend of each month, offering Austrian food and live Austrian music on the Sunday.

scorpo wines ★★★★

23 Old Bittern–Dromana Road, Merricks North, Vic 3926 **region** Mornington Peninsula
phone (03) 5989 7697 **fax** (03) 9813 3371 **open** By appointment
winemaker Paul Scorpo, Sandro Mosele **production** 2000 cases **est.** 1997
product range ($25–35 ML) Pinot Gris, Chardonnay, Pinot Noir, Shiraz.
summary Paul Scorpo has a 25-year background as a horticulturist and landscape architect involved in major projects varying from private gardens to golf courses in Australia, Europe and South-East Asia. His wife Caroline and daughters Emma, Sarah and Clare have a common love for food, wine and gardens, all of which led to the family buying a derelict apple and cherry orchard (originally planted in the early 1900s) on gentle rolling hills halfway between Port Phillip and Westernport Bay. It is part of a ridge system which climbs up to Red Hill, and offers north- and northeast-facing slopes on red-brown clay loam soils. Here they have established 2 hectares of pinot noir, 1.25 hectares of chardonnay, 0.75 hectare of pinot gris and 0.5 hectare of shiraz. The wines are made by Paul Scorpo and Sandro Mosele at Kooyong, and were first released in 2002. A cellar door, forming part of the original house on the property, is planned. It will have extensive ocean views from each side. The quality of the initial releases is very good, and the list of restaurants in Melbourne and Sydney with Scorpo on their wine lists is a veritable who's who of the best.

Scorpo Pinot Gris

TTTT 2001 Light straw-green; the clean, fresh bouquet has green apple; the palate has good weight, although the 14.5° alcohol heats up the finish somewhat; well made. **rating:** 85

best drinking Now **drink with** Antipasto • $25

Scorpo Chardonnay

▼▼▼▼ **2001** Medium yellow-green; the challenging bouquet hints at wild yeast and solids, along with charry barrel-ferment notes and some challenging edges; the complex barrel-ferment and malolactic-ferment inputs on the palate would seem to be beyond the capacity of the fruit to carry them. **rating:** 86

best drinking Now–2006 **drink with** Smoked salmon • $31

Scorpo Pinot Noir

▼▼▼▼ **2001** Particularly strong red-purple; the powerful bouquet has a range of deep plum, black cherry and spice aromas; the very powerful and concentrated palate has lingering tannins. More is not necessarily better with Pinot Noir; slightly over-extracted. **rating:** 89

best drinking Now–2008 **drink with** Duck breast • $35

Scorpo Shiraz

▼▼▼▼▼ **2001** Vivid, deep purple-red; very complex and intense spicy blackberry and pepper aromas are replayed on the powerfully compact palate, which has good structure and balance, despite all the muscle. **rating:** 94

best drinking 2006–2016 **best vintages** '01 **drink with** Haunch of beef • $31

scotchmans hill ★★★★

190 Scotchmans Road, Drysdale, Vic 3222 **region** Geelong
phone (03) 5251 3176 **fax** (03) 5253 1743 **open** 7 days 10.30–5.30
winemaker Robin Brockett **production** 50 000 cases **est.** 1982
product range ($12.50–75 CD) Riesling, Sauvignon Blanc, Chardonnay, Sutton Vineyard Chardonnay, Pinot Noir, Norfolk Pinot Noir, Shiraz, Cabernet Sauvignon Merlot; Swan Bay range of Sauvignon Blanc Semillon, Chardonnay, Pinot Noir, Shiraz; The Hill range of Chardonnay Sauvignon Blanc, Cabernet Sauvignon.
summary Situated on the Bellarine Peninsula, southeast of Geelong, with a well-equipped winery and first-class vineyards. It is a consistent performer with its Pinot Noir and has a strong following in both Melbourne and Sydney for its astutely priced, competently made wines. A doubling in production has seen the establishment of export markets to the UK, Holland, Switzerland, Hong Kong and Singapore. The second label of Spray Farm takes its name from a National Trust property with panoramic views of Port Phillip Bay and Melbourne, which has also been planted to vines by the Brown family and is run as a distinct vineyard and brand operation. The same four varieties are produced but at a lower price point across the range.

Scotchmans Hill Sauvignon Blanc

▼▼▼▼▽ **2002** Light green-yellow; the clean and fresh bouquet has a mix of grass and herb aromas; the fresh and lively palate follows down much the same track, minerally rather than tropical, but with good length and balance. **rating:** 90

best drinking Now–2005 **best vintages** '96, '02 **drink with** Light seafood • $22.50

Scotchmans Hill Chardonnay

▼▼▼▼ **2000** Medium to full yellow-green; the moderately complex bouquet has some interesting barrel-ferment characters along with the figgy fruit. The palate delivers ripe fig, peach and cashew flavours, with the oak use restrained. **rating:** 89

best drinking Now **best vintages** '91, '92, '94, '97 **drink with** Smoked salmon • $26.50

Swan Bay Chardonnay

▼▼▼▼ **2002** Light to medium green-yellow; the moderately intense bouquet is on the riper side, with nectarine and fig fruit; the palate has plenty of flavour, with slight sweetness adding to mass market appeal. **rating:** 86

best drinking Now **drink with** Takeaway • $16.50

Scotchmans Hill Pinot Noir

▼▼▼▼ **2001** Light to medium red-purple; a mix of grassy, gamey, spicy overtones to the cherry fruit of the bouquet is reflected in the light to medium-bodied palate, with firm cherry fruit, spice and a touch of game. **rating:** 86

best drinking Now **best vintages** '91, '92, '94, '97, '98, '00 **drink with** Squab • $29.50

Swan Bay Pinot Noir

▼▼▼▼ **2001** Medium red-purple; intriguingly, does not have the gamey characters of the higher-priced wine, although there is some dusty oak on the bouquet. The palate is very firm, with considerable length and grip, simply lacking the silky feel of the best Pinots. Good value. **rating:** 85

best drinking Now **drink with** Mushroom risotto • $20

Scotchmans Hill Shiraz

TTTTT 2000 A new arrival in the Scotchmans Hill portfolio, made from recent estate plantings at Geelong, and promising much for the riper vintages. An exotic array of licorice, spice, blackberry and cherry aromas and flavours are the fulcrum of a wine with excellent texture and structure, drawing on fine tannins and judiciously handled oak. **rating:** 95

best drinking Now–2008 **best vintages** '00 **drink with** Lasagne • $29.50

Swan Bay Shiraz

TTTT 2001 Medium red-purple; clean cherry/berry fruit aromas on the bouquet and similar direct fruit flavours on the palate provide a simple, uncomplicated wine for everyday drinking. **rating:** 85

best drinking Now–2005 **drink with** Anything which pleases • $19.99

Scotchmans Hill Cabernet Sauvignon Merlot

TTTT 2000 Medium red, showing some development; a complex array of aromas ranging through dark berry, earth, olive and some slightly dusty oak, the berry and olive palate speaking of the cool region from which it comes, albeit a warm vintage; good length. **rating:** 87

best drinking Now–2007 **drink with** Smoked lamb • $28

scotts brook NR

Scotts Brook Road, Boyup Brook, WA 6244 **region** Blackwood Valley
phone (08) 9765 3014 **fax** (08) 9765 3015 **open** Weekends, school holidays 10–5, or by appointment
winemaker Contract **production** 2000 cases **est.** 1987
product range ($10–18 CD) Riesling, Chardonnay, Cabernet Sauvignon.
summary The Scotts Brook winery at Boyup Brook (equidistant between the Margaret River and Great Southern regions) has been developed by local schoolteachers Brian Walker and wife Kerry – hence the opening hours during school holidays. There are 17 hectares of vineyards, but the majority of the production is sold to other winemakers, with limited quantities being made by contract.

scrubby creek wines NR

566 Crystal Creek Road, Alexandra, Vic 3714 **region** Central Victorian High Country
phone (03) 5772 2191 **fax** (03) 5772 1048 **open** 7 days 9–5
winemaker Martin Williams MW (Contract) **production** 700 cases **est.** 1995
product range ($20 CD) Chardonnay.
summary The Stastra and Napier families are next door neighbours, who have jointly planted 3.5 hectares of chardonnay, the wines being made by Martin Williams MW.

seaview ★★★★

Chaffey's Road, McLaren Vale, SA 5171 **region** McLaren Vale
phone (08) 8323 8250 **fax** (08) 8323 9308 **open** Not
winemaker Stephen Goodwin **production** NFP **est.** 1850
product range ($15–32 R) The table wines are no more, but Seaview's and Edwards & Chaffey's (E&C) sparkling range of Brut, Brut de Brut, Chardonnay, Blanc de Blancs, Grand Cuvee, Gull Rock, Pinot Noir Chardonnay Brut and Sparking Shiraz continues, although the wines are not produced from McLaren Vale grapes.
summary Now limited to sparkling wine production under the Seaview and Edwards & Chaffey labels.

seldom seen vineyard ★★★☆

Cnr Gulgong and Hill End Roads, Mudgee, NSW 2850 **region** Mudgee
phone (02) 6372 0839 **fax** (02) 6372 2806 **open** 7 days 9.30–5
winemaker Barry Platt, Marcus Platt **production** 3000 cases **est.** 1987
product range ($10–19 CD) Traminer, Unwooded Semillon, Semillon, Chardonnay Semillon, Unwooded Chardonnay, Chardonnay, Autumn Harvest (dessert), Cabernet Sauvignon Shiraz, Liqueur Muscat.
summary A substantial grape grower (with 18 hectares of vineyards) which reserves a proportion of its crop for making and release under its own label.

seppelt ★★★★★

1 Seppeltsfield Road, Seppeltsfield via Nuriootpa, SA 5355 **region** Barossa Valley
phone (08) 8568 6217 **fax** (08) 8562 8333 **open** Mon–Fri 10–5, weekends and public holidays 11–5
winemaker James Godfrey **production** NFP **est.** 1851
product range ($8–500 R) The great wines of Seppeltsfield are first and foremost Para Liqueur Port (bottling 121), Para Liqueur 21 year old, Vintage Tawny, Show Tawny Port DP90, Rutherglen Show Muscat, Rutherglen Show Tokay, Mount Rufus Finest Tawny Port DP4, Trafford DP30, Seppeltsfield Fino Sherry, Show Amontillado DP116, Show Fino DP117, Show Oloroso DP38, Seppelt Show Vintage Shiraz, Dorrien Cabernet Sauvignon. The 100 Year Old Para Liqueur Port is the $500 a bottle (375 ml) jewel in the crown, the current vintage being the 1903.
summary A multi-million-dollar expansion and renovation programme has seen the historic Seppeltsfield winery become the production centre for the Seppelt fortified and South Australian table wines, adding another dimension to what was already the most historic and beautiful major winery in Australia. It is now home to some of the world's unique fortified wines, nurtured and protected by the passionate James Godfrey. Worldwide distribution.

Seppelt Rutherglen Show Tokay DP57
♥♥♥♥♥ NV Mahogany gold; complex, sweet and rich tea-leaf, raisin and plum pudding aromas are followed by an equally complex, multiflavoured palate which leaves the mouth fresh, thanks to its perfect balance. **rating:** 94
best drinking Now–2019 **drink with** Fine, dark chocolate

Seppelt Show Reserve Muscat
♥♥♥♥♥ NV Deep mahogany brown, with a mix of gold and green on the rim. Rich, raisined, spicy plum pudding aromas are lifted by perfectly balanced and integrated spirit. The powerful, complex and rich palate – plum pudding and Christmas cake – has a very long, lingering finish. **rating:** 96
best drinking Now **drink with** Dried fruits

Seppelt Amontillado Sherry DP116
♥♥♥♥♥ NV Golden colour; the bouquet has enticing richness with brandysnap/biscuit aromas; a wine of great balance, with some sweetness on the mid-palate, then a long, dry, fresh finish. Now re-launched in an old-fashioned 750 ml bottle, selling at a price which is almost insultingly low. Don't be fooled; these are great wines. **rating:** 94
best drinking Now–2005 **drink with** A great winter aperitif • $19.95

Seppelt Oloroso Sherry DP118
♥♥♥♥♥ NV Golden brown; a very complex bouquet of nuts, dried fruits and rancio; the palate is intense, complex and very long, with acidity counterbalancing the sweetness, and outstanding rancio character preventing any chance of the wine cloying. **rating:** 95
best drinking Now–2005 **drink with** After dinner • $19.95

Seppelt Show Fino Sherry DP117
♥♥♥♥♡ NV Bright green-yellow; clean, vibrant, rancio aromas with some dried lemon skin lead into a fresh, bright palate, so bone-dry it almost disappears, but leaves a lingering, haunting aftertaste. **rating:** 93
best drinking Now–2005 **drink with** Olives, tapas • $19.95

Seppelt Show Oloroso Sherry DP38
♥♥♥♥♥ NV Golden brown; nutty rancio complexity, with just a hint of sweetness, introduces a finely balanced palate with a constant interplay between nutty, honeyed sweetness and drier, rancio characters. **rating:** 95
best drinking Now **drink with** Sweet biscuits

Seppelt Show Tawny Port DP90
♥♥♥♥♥ NV The tawny hues are rimmed with olive green, immediately proclaiming the age of the wine. The bouquet is fine, fragrant and penetrating, much closer to the Tawny Ports of Portugal than most Australian wines. The palate offers flavours of spice, butterscotch and more nutty characters, but it is the length of flavour and finish which is absolutely remarkable. Given its age, arguably the most undervalued wine on the Australian market today. **rating:** 97
best drinking Now **drink with** Dried fruits and nuts

Seppelt Para Liqueur Port

▼▼▼▼▼ **NV** Dark mahogany tinged with green; the bouquet is complex, and both richer and sweeter than DP90, with malt, butterscotch and strong rancio characters. The palate has complex structure and great power, yet paradoxically has an almost dry finish, and no biscuity aftertaste. **rating:** 94

best drinking Now **drink with** Coffee, chocolate

seppelt great western ★★★★★

Moyston Road, Great Western via Ararat, Vic 3377 **region** Grampians
phone (03) 5361 2222 **fax** (03) 5361 2200 **open** 7 days 10–5
winemaker Arthur O'Connor, Stephen Goodwin **production** NFP **est.** 1865
product range ($8–61 R) The table wine range has been rationalised with the Victorian portfolio of Sheoak Spring Riesling, Sunday Creek Pinot Noir, Chalambar Shiraz, Harpers Range Cabernet Sauvignon at the entry point; next up the range is the Premium Selection of Chardonnay, Shiraz, Cabernet Sauvignon; thence to the Winemaker's Selection of Jaluka Chardonnay, St Peters Great Western Shiraz. In addition there are occasional special releases from Seppelt's Drumborg Vineyard and of Great Western Riesling. Sparkling wines (from the bottom up) are Fleur de Lys non vintage and vintage; Original Sparkling Shiraz; Salinger and Show Sparkling Shiraz.
summary Australia's best known producer of sparkling wine, always immaculate in its given price range but also producing excellent Great Western-sourced table wines, especially long-lived Shiraz and Australia's best Sparkling Shirazs. The glitzy ever-changing labels have rightly been consigned to the rubbish bin, with a return to the classic feel of the 1960s, and the product range has been significantly rationalised.

Seppelt Jaluka Chardonnay

▼▼▼▼▼ **2000** Excellent bright, light yellow-green; the bouquet is at once intense yet subtle, thanks to the perfect integration of the fine oak with nectarine and citrus fruit; a wonderfully fine and elegant palate, with classic cool-climate length and subtle oak. Depending on whether you believe the front label or the back label, the wine comes from various parts of Victoria or from Drumborg. **rating:** 94

best drinking Now–2008 **best vintages** '00 **drink with** Smoked salmon • $27

Seppelt Victorian Premium Reserve Chardonnay

▼▼▼▼ **2002** Light to medium yellow-green; lively citrus and nectarine fruit is woven through subtle oak on the bouquet; the palate is framed by similar intense nectarine flavours, the oak evident but subservient. Good length.

best drinking Now–2006 **drink with** Seafood risotto • $16 **rating:** 89

Seppelt Salinger

▼▼▼▼▽ **2000** Light straw-green; the bouquet is quite fragrant, the complexity coming from the touch of aldehyde which accompanies the strawberry fruit. The palate is very youthful, with a mix of citrus, white peach and strawberry, still evolving and extending. **rating:** 90

best drinking 2004–2007 **best vintages** '88, '89, '90, '91, '93, '94, '95 **drink with** Aperitif, oysters, shellfish • $26.99

Seppelt Original Sparkling Shiraz

▼▼▼▼▽ **1998** Medium to full red, with strong and persistent mousse. The bouquet is surprisingly rich, with volumes of black cherry and anise; the palate has quite massive flavour, the typically high dosage intended to cover the tannins, and partially succeeding. Worthy of very extended cellaring; these wines do improve on cork. **rating:** 91

best drinking Now–2013 **best vintages** '93, '95 **drink with** Pâté and game • $18

Seppelt St Peters Shiraz

▼▼▼▼▼ **1998** From the vineyard adjacent to the Great Western winery, planted in the 1920s. Deep red-purple; rich blackberry, black cherry and spice aromas, matched by controlled French oak, flow into an opulently rich and luscious palate flooded with black cherry fruit; ripe tannins sustain the long finish. Eureka. **rating:** 97

best drinking Now–2025 **best vintages** '98 **drink with** Braised ox cheek • $41

Seppelt Victorian Premium Reserve Shiraz

▼▼▼▼▽ **2000** Time will tell whether yet another overhaul of the Seppelt brands and labels will achieve its aim; the quality of the wine deserves it. Dark berry, plum and dark chocolate aromas flow into a smooth, supple and rounded palate, with plum and cherry fruit, and fine, soft tannins. Excellent finish and aftertaste. Outstanding value.

best drinking Now–2010 **best vintages** '00 **drink with** Braised beef • $16 **rating:** 92

Seppelt Victorian Premium Reserve Cabernet Sauvignon
♥♥♥♥♡ **2000** Deep but bright red-purple; rich, ripe cassis varietal fruit and subtle oak on the bouquet are followed by a succulently ripe, fruit-driven palate. An irresistible bargain. **rating:** 93
best drinking Now–2012 **best vintages** '00 **drink with** Lamb shanks • $16

serafino wines ★★★☆

McLarens on the Lake, Kangarilla Road, McLaren Vale, SA 5171 **region** McLaren Vale
phone (08) 8323 0157 **fax** (08) 8323 0158 **open** Mon–Fri 10–5, weekends and public holidays 10–4.30
winemaker Scott Rawlinson **production** 17 000 cases **est.** 2000
product range ($12–20 CD) Serafino range of Semillon, Unwooded Chardonnay, Barrel Fermented Chardonnay, Shiraz, Cabernet Sauvignon; McLarens on the Lake range of Chardonnay, Reserve Chardonnay Pinot, Cabernet Shiraz Merlot, Old Tawny Port.
summary In the wake of the sale of Maglieri Wines to Beringer Blass in 1998, Maglieri founder Steve Maglieri acquired the McLarens on the Lake complex, which had originally been established by Andrew Garrett. The accommodation has been upgraded and a larger winery was commissioned before the 2002 vintage. The operation draws upon 40 hectares each of shiraz and cabernet sauvignon, 7 hectares of chardonnay, 2 hectares each of merlot, semillon, barbera, nebbiolo and sangiovese, and 1 hectare of grenache. Part of the grape production will be sold to others, the remainder will be used to produce wines under the Serafino and McLarens on the Lake labels. Exports to the UK, the US, Asia, Italy and New Zealand.

🐗 serenella NR

Lot 300 Hermitage Road, Pokolbin, NSW 2325 **region** Lower Hunter Valley
phone (02) 4998 7992 **fax** (02) 4998 7993 **open** 7 days 9.30–5
winemaker Letitia Cecchini **production** 6000 cases **est.** 1971
product range ($16–25 CD) Estate range of Reserve Semillon, Reserve Verdelho, Reserve Chardonnay, Botrytis Semillon, Late Picked Verdelho, Liqueur Verdelho, Cabernet Sauvignon; Arlecchino Semillon, Arlecchino Rose.
summary The establishment date of 1971 is that of the original incarnation of Serenella, which is now James Estate. It was in that year that Giancarlo and Maria Cecchini, who had immigrated from Italy 21 years earlier, established their first vineyard in the Upper Hunter. In 1997 the assets of Serenella Estate were sold, with a view to re-establishing the business in the Lower Hunter Valley. The following year they were able to buy a 43-hectare block of virgin land on Hermitage Road, Pokolbin, from Murray Tyrrell. The family lost no time in building a state-of-the-art winery, a restaurant (Arlecchino Trattoria), and a cellar-door sales and small function area, and planting 2 hectares of sangiovese. Daughter Tish Cecchini continues the senior winemaking role she had at the original Serenella Estate, with help from assistant winemaker Michael Hudson. The Serenella Estate range of wines are produced from Hunter Valley-grown grapes (the Semillon from a 40-year-old dryland vineyard) while the cheaper Arlecchino range is sourced variously from the Hunter Valley and Mudgee.

Serenella Arlecchino Semillon
♥♥♥♡ **2001** Medium straw-yellow; the bouquet is slightly closed, but the weight and flavour of the wine come through strongly on the palate. In a bigger and slightly broader style, likely to develop more quickly. **rating:** 83
best drinking Now–2006 **drink with** Seafood • $16

serventy organic wines ★★☆

Valley Home Vineyard, Rocky Road, Forest Grove, WA 6286 **region** Margaret River
phone (08) 9757 7534 **fax** (08) 9757 7534 **open** Fri–Sun, holidays 10–4
winemaker Peter Serventy **production** 1500 cases **est.** 1984
product range ($15 CD) Chardonnay, Pinot Noir, Shiraz.
summary Peter Serventy is nephew of the famous naturalist Vincent Serventy and son of ornithologist Dominic Serventy. It is hardly surprising, then, that Serventy should practise strict organic viticulture, using neither herbicides nor pesticides. The wines, too, are made with a minimum of sulphur dioxide, added late in the piece and never exceeding 30 parts per million.

🐗 setanta wines ★★★★★

RSD 43, Williamstown Road, Forreston, SA 5233 (postal) **region** Adelaide Hills
phone (08) 8380 5516 **fax** (08) 8380 5516 **open** Not
winemaker Rod Chapman, Rebecca Wilson **production** 1200 cases **est.** 1997

product range ($21–29 R) Speckled House Riesling, Emer Chardonnay, Cuchulain Shiraz, Black Sanglain Cabernet Sauvignon.

summary Setanta is a family-owned operation involving Sheilagh Sullivan, her husband Tony and brother Bernard; the latter is the viticulturist, while Tony and Sheilagh manage marketing, administration and so forth. Of Irish parentage (they are first-generation Australians) they chose Setanta, Ireland's most famous mythological hero, as the brand name. The beautiful and striking labels tell the individual stories, which in turn give rise to the names of each of the wines, immediately raising the question how much of *Lord of the Rings* was inspired by Celtic myth. The wines are distributed by Aria Wine Co. into selected wine retailers in Adelaide and the eastern states capital cities. They are well worth tracking down, not only for the outstanding quality of the wine, but also for those marvellous labels. Superb, hand-sorted corks of the highest quality.

Setanta Speckled House Riesling

▼▼▼▼▽ 2002 Light straw-green; a fragrant and flowery apple blossom and mineral bouquet flows into a delicate but quite intense palate; apple and a touch of lime run through to the well-balanced, long finish. 150 cases made. **rating:** 92

best drinking Now–2007 **best vintages** '02 **drink with** Sashimi • $21

Setanta Emer Chardonnay

▼▼▼▼▼ 2002 Medium yellow-green; the subtle but complex bouquet has a seamless marriage of melon fruit and subtle, faintly nutty, French oak. A beautifully made wine, all the winemaking inputs in harmony; a creamy yet fine palate, the alcohol (13.4°) spot on, the aftertaste excellent. Fermentation completed in barrel, and partial malolactic fermentation. 330 dozen made. **rating:** 94

best drinking Now–2007 **best vintages** '02 **drink with** Salmon risotto • $23

Setanta Cuchulain Shiraz

▼▼▼▼▽ 2001 Youthful purple-red; black cherry and blackberry fruit is welded with well-balanced and integrated French oak on the bouquet; the medium-bodied palate has black cherry to the fore, with splashes of spice; fine tannins complete a stylish and very elegant wine. 300 cases made. **rating:** 93

best drinking 2004–2009 **best vintages** '01 **drink with** Osso buco • $28

Setanta Black Sanglain Cabernet Sauvignon

▼▼▼▼▽ 2001 Medium red-purple; the bouquet has a mix of cedary, spicy, blackcurrant aromas leading into an elegant, medium-bodied palate, where ultra-fine tannins linger in the mouth, providing excellent length. Shows highly intelligent use of oak, a mixture of new French and aged American. 350 cases made. **rating:** 91

best drinking 2004–2011 **best vintages** '01 **drink with** Herbed rack of lamb • $29

settlers ridge ★★★★☆

54b Bussell Highway, Cowaramup, WA 6284 **region** Margaret River
phone (08) 9755 5883 **fax** (08) 9755 5883 **open** 7 days 10–5
winemaker Wayne Nobbs **production** 3200 cases **est.** 1994
product range ($15–27 CD) Chenin Blanc, Sauvignon Blanc, Shiraz, Merlot, Sangiovese Novello, Cabernet Sauvignon.

summary Wayne and Kaye Nobbs have established what they say is the only vineyard in Western Australia with organic certification and the only producer in Australia with dual classification from NASAA (National Association for Sustainable Agriculture Australia) and OVAA (Organic Vignerons Association of Australia Inc.). They have 7 hectares of vineyard, including shiraz, cabernet sauvignon, merlot, sangiovese, malbec, chenin blanc and sauvignon blanc. Exports to Germany.

Settlers Ridge Shiraz

▼▼▼▼▼ 1999 Very good colour; pristine plum and sweet red berry fruits on the bouquet; the palate has great richness and intensity of perfectly ripened fruit; ripe tannins and controlled oak add yet more to an excellent wine. **rating:** 95

best drinking 2005–2015 **drink with** Ox cheek • $27

Settlers Ridge Cabernet Sauvignon

▼▼▼▼▽ 1999 Medium to full red-purple; rich, dark berry fruits and positive charry oak on the bouquet are followed by a big and slightly chewy palate, with fruit and oak both contributing. Powerful and impressive, but not for the faint-hearted. **rating:** 90

best drinking 2006–2016 **drink with** Leg of lamb • $27

settlers rise montville ★★★

249 Western Avenue, Montville, Qld 4560 **region** Queensland Coastal
phone (07) 5478 5558 **fax** (07) 5478 5655 **open** 7 days 10–5
winemaker Peter Scudamore-Smith MW (Contract) **production** 1700 cases **est.** 1998
product range ($14.50–26.50 CD) Queensland Classic White, Blackall Range White, Verdelho, Chardonnay, Razorback Red, Reserve Shiraz, Shiraz Cabernet, Lake Baroon Cabernet Merlot, Tawny Port.
summary Settlers Rise is located in the beautiful highlands of the Blackall Range, 75 minutes' drive north of Brisbane and 20 minutes from the Sunshine Coast. A little over a hectare of chardonnay, verdelho, shiraz and cabernet sauvignon have been planted at an elevation of 450 metres on the deep basalt soils of the property. First settled in 1887, Montville has gradually become a tourist destination, with a substantial local arts and crafts industry and a flourishing bed and breakfast and lodge accommodation infrastructure.

Settlers Rise Montville Queensland Classic White

▼▼▼▼ 2002 Light yellow-green; the clean, crisp bouquet is dominated by the semillon component, as is the similarly structured palate, which has good balance and length. A blend of Semillon and Chardonnay coming from the Border Ranges and Inglewood Vineyards. **rating:** 85
best drinking Now **drink with** Tempura • $16

Settlers Rise Montville Verdelho

▼▼▼▼ 2002 Light green-yellow; the highly fruity bouquet has a mix of fruit salad and lime; the palate has abundant vibrant fruit; not too sweet, and has good length. From three vineyard areas in northern New South Wales. **rating:** 86
best drinking Now–2005 **drink with** Crab cakes • $16

Settlers Rise Montville Tawny Port

▼▼▼▼ NV Medium red, with some tawny hues; the spicy, raisiny bouquet shows some rancio; the palate has more tawny character than expected; spicy, well balanced and quite fresh. All is explained by the South Australian component in the wine alongside some Granite Belt material. **rating:** 85
best drinking Now **drink with** Coffee and biscuits • $20

sevenhill cellars ★★★★

College Road, Sevenhill, SA 5453 **region** Clare Valley
phone (08) 8843 4222 **fax** (08) 8843 4382 **open** 7 days 10–5
winemaker Brother John May, John Monten **production** 22 000 cases **est.** 1851
product range ($10–30 CD) Riesling, Gewurztraminer, St Aloysius (Chenin Blanc Chardonnay Verdelho), College White, Verdelho, Botrytis Semillon, Shiraz, STM (Shiraz Touriga Malbec), Shiraz Malbec, Grenache, Cabernet Sauvignon, Seven Brothers (Cabernet Shiraz), St Ignatius (Cabernet Sauvignon Merlot Malbec Cabernet Franc), fortifieds, sacramental wine.
summary One of the historical treasures of Australia; the oft-photographed stone wine cellars are the oldest in the Clare Valley, and winemaking is still carried out under the direction of the Jesuitical Manresa Society, and in particular Brother John May. Quality is very good, particularly of the powerful Shiraz; all the wines reflect the estate-grown grapes from old vines. Extensive retail distribution throughout all states; exports to New Zealand, Switzerland and the UK.

Sevenhill Cellars Riesling

▼▼▼▼▼ 2002 A new label design for this wine echoes its 150-year-old Jesuitical winery home. And boy, what a wine this is. The ultra-classic tight bouquet has a steely spine and lemon/lime fruit; the palate has deliciously full flavour while retaining finesse and a crunchy dry finish. Faith not required. **rating:** 95
best drinking Now–2012 **best vintages** '87, '89, '91, '92, '94, '97, '01, '02 **drink with** King George whiting • $19

Sevenhill Cellars Grenache

▼▼▼▼ 2002 Youthful, bright purple-red; abundant sweet, juicy fruit on both the bouquet and palate are quintessentially varietal; the palate is round and soft, ready to roll right now. **rating:** 85
best drinking Now–2005 **drink with** Pasta with meat sauce • $15

Sevenhill Cellars St Ignatius

▼▼▼▼▽ 2000 A Bordeaux-style blend of 44 per cent cabernet sauvignon, 26 per cent merlot, 17 per cent malbec and 13 per cent cabernet franc. Medium red-purple; an appealing blend of rich, ripe, dark fruits and gentle oak aromas, then a palate with great texture and mouthfeel, showing full, dark berry fruit, vanillin oak and tannins. Heavenly. **rating:** 93

best drinking 2004–2014 **best vintages** '80, '87, '89, '91, '92, '96, '98, '00 **drink with** Strong cheese or red meat • $24

🍇 seven mile vineyard   NR

84 Coolangatta Road, Coolangatta, NSW 2535 **region** Shoalhaven Coast
phone (02) 4448 5466 **fax** (02) 9357 3141 **open** Wed–Sun 10–6 (summer), Thurs–Sun 10–5 (winter)
winemaker Eric Swarbrick **production** 1500 cases **est.** 1998
product range ($15.80–17.55 CD) Verdelho, Chardonnay, Chambourcin, Petit Verdot, Cabernet Sauvignon.
summary The 1.8-hectare Seven Mile Vineyard was established by Joan and Eric Swarbrick in 1997. It is situated east of the town of Berry, and within the sound of the surf on the Seven Mile Beach. The vineyard overlooks Coomonderry Swamp, one of the largest coastal wetlands in New South Wales. The first three vintages (including 2003) used chambourcin, verdelho and cabernet sauvignon from the estate plantings; the petit verdot is due to come on-stream in 2004. In 2002 chardonnay juice was purchased from the adjacent Southern Highlands region, and was made and released in unoaked form. All the wines are made on-site by Eric Swarbrick.

sevenoaks wines   NR

304 Doyles Creek Road, Jerrys Plains, NSW 2330 **region** Lower Hunter Valley
phone (02) 6576 4285 **open** By appointment
winemaker John Hordern (Contract) **production** 1000 cases **est.** 1997
product range ($15–24 CD) Vino Estivo Sangiovese, Rows 1 to 26 Shiraz, Woodlands Shiraz.
summary Robert and Deborah Sharp established Sevenoaks Wines in 1997 with the original intention of selling the grapes to other winemakers. With only 2 hectares of shiraz, 1.5 hectares of sangiovese and 0.5 hectare of petit verdot, it was inevitable that the wine from their grapes would be blended with many others, so in 2000 the Sharps changed course, retaining John Hordern as contract winemaker. The vineyard is part of a 68-hectare property which abuts the Wollemi National Park at the bottom of the slopes that rise to be Mount Woodlands. Exports to the UK and Singapore.

severn brae estate   NR

Lot 2 Back Creek Road (Mount Tully Road), Severnlea, Qld 4352 **region** Granite Belt
phone (07) 4683 5292 **fax** (07) 3391 3821 **open** Mon–Fri 12–3, weekends 10–5, or by appointment
winemaker Bruce Humphery-Smith **production** 1400 cases **est.** 1987
product range ($14–16 CD) Murray Grey White, Unwooded Chardonnay, Estate Chardonnay, Light Fruity Red, Merlot Sangiovese, Reserve Shiraz; Liqueur Muscat and Chardonnay.
summary Patrick and Bruce Humphery-Smith have established 5.5 hectares of chardonnay with relatively close spacing and trained on a high two-tier trellis. Two-thirds of the production is sold, one-third used for the Severn Brae label.

seville estate   ★★★★★

65 Linwood Road, Seville, Vic 3139 **region** Yarra Valley
phone (03) 5964 2622 **fax** (03) 5964 2633 **open** Weekends and public holidays 10–5
winemaker Alistair Butt **production** 4000 cases **est.** 1970
product range ($23.50–60 CD) Chardonnay, Pinot Noir, Reserve Pinot Noir, Shiraz, Reserve Shiraz, Reserve Cabernet Sauvignon.
summary In February 1997 a controlling interest in Seville Estate was acquired by Brokenwood (of the Hunter Valley) and interests associated with Brokenwood. I was one of the founding partners of Brokenwood, and the acquisition meant that the wheel had turned full circle. This apart, Seville Estate has added significantly to the top end of the Brokenwood portfolio, without in any way competing with the existing styles. Hit a purple patch with its 2000 and 2001 vintage wines. Exports to the UK.

Seville Estate Pinot Noir
ŸŸŸŸŸ 2001 Trendily bottled unfiltered, not an easy task with pinot noir, but seen by some as a passport to authenticity. By the standards of pinot, the colour is quite deep; the bouquet has a complex array of smoky oak, plum and a touch of stem. The palate follows suit, with complex dark plum and a hint of game. **rating:** 94

best drinking Now–2007 **best vintages** '00, '01 **drink with** Rare breast of squab • $23.50

Seville Estate Reserve Pinot Noir

🍷🍷🍷🍷🍷 **2001** Quite deep red-purple; the bouquet has a complex mix of dark plum and cherry fruit with a spicy, savoury background, and the palate delivers more of the same; excellent depth and richness, a complex array of flavours, and good balance and length. **rating:** 95

best drinking Now–2009 **best vintages** '01 **drink with** Saddle of hare • $45

Seville Estate Reserve Cabernet Sauvignon

🍷🍷🍷🍷 **2000** Medium red-purple; the high-toned bouquet has a mix of leafy fruit and charry oak, changing into blackcurrant and cassis fruit on entry to the mouth, but then reverting with a slightly astringent finish. The parts are yet to come together. **rating:** 87

best drinking 2004–2009 **drink with** Spring lamb • $35

shadowfax vineyard and winery ★★★★☆

K Road, Werribee, Vic 3030 **region** Geelong
phone (03) 9731 4420 **fax** (03) 9731 4421 **open** 7 days 11–5
winemaker Matt Harrop **production** 15 000 cases **est.** 2000
product range ($19–35 CD) Sauvignon Blanc, Pinot Gris, Chardonnay, Pinot Noir, McLaren Vale Shiraz, K Road Sangiovese Merlot Shiraz, Yarra Valley Cabernet Sauvignon.
summary Shadowfax is part of an awesome development at Werribee Park, a mere 20 minutes from Melbourne towards Geelong. The truly striking winery, designed by Wood Marsh architects, was erected in time for the 2000 vintage crush, adjacent to the extraordinary 60-room private home built in the 1880s by the Chirnside family and known as The Mansion. It was then the centrepiece of a 40 000-hectare pastoral empire, and the appropriately magnificent gardens were part of the reason why the property was acquired by Parks Victoria in the early 1970s. The mansion is now The Mansion Hotel, with 92 rooms and suites, with the emphasis on conference bookings during the week and general tourism on the weekend. The striking packaging of the wines, and the quality of the first releases, all underline the thoroughly serious nature of this quite amazing venture. Exports to the UK, the US, Japan, Singapore and New Zealand.

Shadowfax Adelaide Hills Sauvignon Blanc

🍷🍷🍷🍷🍷 **2002** Light straw-green; a high-toned, flowery, aromatic bouquet with a mix of citrus, grass and passionfruit is followed by a palate with good flow and mouthfeel; protective winemaking throughout has maximised the flavour. **rating:** 92

best drinking Now **best vintages** '02 **drink with** Poached scallops in white wine sauce • $19

Shadowfax Adelaide Hills Geelong Pinot Gris

🍷🍷🍷🍷 **2002** Light straw-green; fresh, clean spice, pear, apple and almond aromas lead into a palate which builds flavour progressively through to the finish; the alcohol seems higher than 13.5°. Whole bunch-pressed, and fermented in older French oak. **rating:** 87

best drinking Now **drink with** Mediterranean food • $24

Shadowfax Chardonnay

🍷🍷🍷🍷 **2001** Light to medium yellow-green; the moderately intense bouquet has a web of ripe melon, stone fruit and subtle oak contributing to complexity; the powerful and concentrated palate has ripe peachy flavours, and seems a little higher in alcohol than the 13.5° attributed to the wine. A blend of 58 per cent Yarra Valley and 42 per cent Geelong material. **rating:** 89

best drinking Now **best vintages** '00 **drink with** Rock lobster • $30

Shadowfax Pinot Noir

🍷🍷🍷🍷 **2001** Light to medium red-purple; the light bouquet offers strawberry and plum fruit; the light to medium-bodied palate opens with similar flavours but finishes with slightly green, hard acidity. **rating:** 86

best drinking Now **best vintages** '00 **drink with** Braised duck Chinese-style • $33

Shadowfax McLaren Vale Shiraz

🍷🍷🍷🍷🍷 **2001** Deep but bright purple-red; the bouquet offers a mix of black cherry and dark chocolate fruit which swells into a towering palate; while the tannin and extract are not overdone, you cannot get away from the 15° alcohol. **rating:** 92

best drinking 2004–2011 **best vintages** '01 **drink with** Venison • $34

Shadowfax K Road Sangiovese Merlot Shiraz

🍷🍷🍷🍷 2001 Medium purple-red; there is an attractive mix of pleasantly ripe, dark, small berry fruit on the bouquet, joined on the palate with some savoury/spicy notes. A weird blend, but it works. A blend of Sangiovese and Merlot from the Adelaide Hills, and Shiraz from Geelong.　　**rating: 88**

best drinking Now–2006 **drink with** Italian • $24

shantell ★★★★

1974 Melba Highway, Dixons Creek, Vic 3775 **region** Yarra Valley
phone (03) 5965 2264 **fax** (03) 5965 2331 **open** 7 days 10.30–5
winemaker Shan Shanmugam, Turid Shanmugam **production** 2500 cases **est.** 1980
product range ($15–32 CD) Semillon, Chardonnay, Glenlea Chardonnay, Pinot Noir, Shiraz, Cabernet Sauvignon, Sparkling.
summary The substantial and now fully mature Shantell vineyards provide the winery with a high-quality fruit source; part is sold to other Yarra Valley makers, the remainder vinified at Shantell. In January 1998 Shantell opened a new cellar door at 1974 Melba Highway, 50 metres along a service road from the highway proper. Chardonnay, Semillon and Cabernet Sauvignon are its benchmark wines, sturdily reliable, sometimes outstanding (witness the 1997 and 2000 Chardonnay). An on-site cafe provides light lunches. Domestic and international distribution through Australian Prestige Wines.

Shantell Semillon

🍷🍷🍷🍷 2002 Medium yellow-green; tight, quite intense herb, grass and mineral aromas are repeated on the palate, with plenty of concentration, although it's fractionally short and (surprisingly) not quite where it should be given the vintage.　　**rating: 89**

best drinking Now–2007 **best vintages** '88, '90, '91, '92, '93, '97, '00 **drink with** Abalone • $15

Shantell Chardonnay

🍷🍷🍷🍷 2001 Medium yellow-green, quite developed; the ripe fig and melon fruit of the bouquet has well-integrated oak. The palate has solid, but not particularly bright, fruit; lacks the usual finesse of Shantell.　　**rating: 87**

best drinking Now–2005 **best vintages** '90, '92, '94, '97, '98, '99, '00 **drink with** Yarra Valley smoked trout • $24

Shantell Shiraz

🍷🍷🍷🍷 2000 Medium red-purple; the bouquet has gently ripe raspberry/cherry red fruits and subtle oak; the light to medium-bodied palate seems to wander around; the fruit lacks focus and concentration.　　**rating: 88**

best drinking 2004–2008 **drink with** Spiced lamb • $24

Shantell Cabernet Sauvignon

🍷🍷🍷🍷 2000 Medium red-purple; some savoury, cedary notes along with spice on the bouquet; the palate has blackberry, currant and cedar, and is quite long, with firm acidity. Nonetheless, like the Shiraz, somewhat dull (by the normal standards of Shantell) and one cannot help but question whether there might be a low level of bacterial activity (brett).　　**rating: 88**

best drinking 2005–2010 **best vintages** '90, '91, '92, '93, '95 **drink with** Shoulder of lamb • $24

sharmans ★★★★

Glenbothy, 175 Glenwood Road, Relbia, Tas 7258 **region** Northern Tasmania
phone (03) 6343 0773 **fax** (03) 6343 0773 **open** Weekends by appointment
winemaker James Chatto, Rosevears Estate (Contract) **production** 800 cases **est.** 1987
product range ($15–20 ML) Riesling, Sauvignon Blanc, Unoaked Chardonnay, Chardonnay, Pinot Noir.
summary Mike Sharman has very probably pioneered one of the more interesting wine regions of Tasmania, not far south of Launceston but with a distinctly warmer climate than (say) Pipers Brook. Ideal north-facing slopes are home to a vineyard now approaching 3 hectares, most still to come into bearing. The few wines produced in sufficient quantity to be sold promise much for the future.

Sharmans Chardonnay

🍷🍷🍷🍷🍷 2000 Bright yellow-green; the moderately intense bouquet is clean, balanced and smooth; the light to medium-bodied palate has fresh nectarine fruit, subtly integrated oak, pure varietal character and good length. An ultra-fine Chablis-ish style which really works.　　**rating: 94**

best drinking Now–2008 **drink with** Angel hair pasta • $18

shaw & smith ★★★★★

Lot 4 Jones Road, Balhannah, SA 5242 **region** Adelaide Hills
phone (08) 8398 0500 **fax** (08) 8398 0600 **open** Weekends 10–4
winemaker Martin Shaw **production** 30 000 cases **est.** 1989
product range ($18–39 CD) Riesling, Sauvignon Blanc, Unoaked Chardonnay, Reserve Chardonnay, M3 Vineyard Chardonnay, Elixir Shiraz, Merlot; also Incognito range of Eden Valley Riesling, Adelaide Hills Chardonnay, Adelaide Hills Merlot.
summary Has progressively moved from a contract grape base to estate production with the development of a 40-hectare vineyard at Balhannah in the Adelaide Hills, followed by the erection before the 2000 vintage of a state-of-the-art, beautifully designed and executed winery at Balhannah, ending the long period of tenancy at Petaluma. While wine quality has been exemplary, the perfectionism of Martin Shaw will now receive full play. The wines have wide international distribution including the UK, Japan, the US, Canada, Hong Kong, Japan and Singapore.

Shaw & Smith Riesling

▼▼▼▼♀ **2002** Light straw-green; the core of lime and mineral aromas has a faint tropical edge; there is a classic tight structure to the palate, presently driven and lengthened by mineral acidity, simply waiting for the fruit to develop. **rating:** 90

best drinking 2004–2009 **drink with** Grilled whiting • $20

Shaw & Smith Sauvignon Blanc

▼▼▼▼♀ **2002** Light straw-green; complex passionfruit and gooseberry aromas seem to have a faint hint of reduction lurking in the background; the palate shows no signs of any reduction, with good persistence to the complex fruit. **rating:** 91

best drinking Now **best vintages** '92, '93, '95, '97, '99, '00, '01 **drink with** Poached mussels • $20

Shaw & Smith M3 Vineyard Chardonnay

▼▼▼▼▼ **2001** Light straw-green; the clean and fresh bouquet is distinguished by the excellent balance and integration of the barrel-ferment oak inputs; the elegant and restrained palate focuses on melon and stone fruit; a superfine, cool-grown style with great aging potential. **rating:** 94

best drinking 2004–2010 **best vintages** '00, '01 **drink with** Lobster salad • $34

Shaw & Smith Elixir Shiraz

▼▼▼▼ **2000** Medium red-purple; the bouquet is subtle but complex, with excellent fruit and oak balance and integration; the medium-bodied palate has good texture, and savoury edges to the primary fruit flavour; fine tannins to close. Cellar-door sales only. **rating:** 89

best drinking 2005–2012 **drink with** Braised ox tail • $39

Shaw & Smith Merlot

▼▼▼▼♀ **2001** Medium red-purple; the moderately intense and clean bouquet shows distinctive varietal character with ripe, small berry fruit and touches of olive and herb; the palate has excellent structure and weight, with strong, savoury varietal character in evidence from start to finish. **rating:** 92

best drinking 2006–2011 **best vintages** '00, '01 **drink with** Veal saltimbocca • $30

🍇 shelmerdine vineyards ★★★★

PO Box 18152, Collins Street East, Melbourne, Vic 8001 **region** Yarra Valley
phone (03) 9207 3090 **fax** (03) 9207 3061 **open** Not
winemaker Kate Goodman (Contract) **est.** 1989
product range ($19–24.50 ML) Yarra Valley Sauvignon Blanc, Yarra Valley Pinot Noir, Heathcote Shiraz.
summary Stephen Shelmerdine has been a major figure in the wine industry for well over 20 years, like his family before him (who founded Mitchelton Winery), and has been honoured for his many services to the industry. The venture has 130 hectares of vineyards spread over three sites, Lusatia Park in the Yarra Valley and Merindoc Vineyard and Willoughby Bridge in the Heathcote region. Substantial quantities of the grapes produced are sold to others, with a small amount of high-quality wines contract-made by Kate Goodman at the Punt Road Winery.

Shelmerdine Vineyards Sauvignon Blanc

▼▼▼▼♀ **2002** Light straw-green; light and crisp herb and gooseberry aromas move into a light but lively palate with a mix of lemon and more tropical fruit flavours before a cleansing finish. Yarra Valley. **rating:** 90

best drinking Now **best vintages** '02 **drink with** Trout terrine • $19

Shelmerdine Vineyards Pinot Noir

▼▼▼▼ **2001** Light to medium red-purple; clean, light cherry and strawberry aromas precede a palate with more depth of flavour than expected, but, perhaps, slightly simple. Yarra Valley. **rating:** 88

best drinking Now–2005 **drink with** Magret of duck • $23

Shelmerdine Vineyards Shiraz

▼▼▼▼ **2001** Medium red-purple; soft, sweet, berry fruit is joined by spicy oak on the bouquet; the medium-bodied palate has good mouthfeel, with red fruits at the centre, but challenged by the French oak. Heathcote. **rating:** 89

best drinking Now–2008 **drink with** Rib of beef • $23

🐦 sherwood estate ★★★☆

1187 Gowings Hill Road, Sherwood, NSW 2440 **region** Hastings River
phone (02) 6581 4900 **fax** (02) 6581 4728 **open** Fri–Sun and public holidays 11–4, or by appointment
winemaker James Hilliard **production** 750 cases **est.** 1998
product range ($10–18 CD) Semillon, Gazebo White (Semillon Chardonnay), Verdelho, Chardonnay, Sherwood Frost (Dessert Semillon), Middle Paddock Chambourcin, Gazebo Red (Cabernet Merlot), Cabernet Merlot.
summary John and Helen Ross began planting the Sherwood Estate vineyard in 1998 with 2 hectares of chambourcin. Subsequently, verdelho, chardonnay, cabernet franc, semillon and (most recently) sangiovese have been planted, with 10 hectares now under vine. The vineyard is situated in the Macleay Valley, 15 minutes west of Kempsey on the New South Wales north coast, with a total of 43 hectares of undulating fertile soils, rich in limestone. The wines are also available from the Sherwood Wine Embassy, Pacific Highway, Port Macquarie, which is open 7 days. An impressive start, I must say.

Sherwood Estate Semillon

▼▼▼▼ **2001** Light straw-green; the bouquet shows classic young semillon character, fresh, light and crisp. The palate is similarly fresh and crisp, with a mix of mineral and lively, lemony flavours bolstered by some CO_2 yet to settle down. Good potential. **rating:** 87

best drinking 2004–2009 **drink with** Leave it in the cellar • $16

Sherwood Estate Chardonnay

▼▼▼▼ **2000** Light to medium yellow-green; a fresh and clean bouquet has a mix of tropical and citrus fruit aromas; the palate has well above-average weight, mouthfeel and flavour. A remarkably good example of an unoaked Chardonnay. **rating:** 88

best drinking Now–2005 **drink with** King prawns • $16

🐦 shingleback NR

Cnr Little and California Roads, McLaren Vale, SA 5171 (postal) **region** McLaren Vale
phone (08) 8556 4400 **fax** (08) 8556 4424 **open** Not
winemaker Contract **est.** 1995
product range Semillon, Chardonnay, Shiraz, Cabernet Sauvignon.
summary Shingleback has 75 hectares of vineyards in McLaren Vale, with part of the grape production vinified under the Shingleback label. It is a specialist export business with exports to Germany, Switzerland and the US, but the wines are also available by mail order locally. A 1998 Shiraz entered in the 2001 Great Australian Shiraz Challenge impressed me greatly, with its deep, lush fruit and positive but not excessive use of oak.

🐦 shirvington NR

PO Box 222, McLaren Vale, SA 5171 **region** McLaren Vale
phone (08) 8383 0554 **fax** (08) 8383 0556 **open** Not
winemaker Sarah Marquis, Sparky Marquis **production** 2500 cases **est.** 1996
product range ($40–50 R) Shiraz, Cabernet Sauvignon.
summary The Shirvington family began the development of their McLaren Vale vineyards in 1996 under the direction of viticulturist Peter Bolte, and now have 30 hectares under vine, the majority to shiraz and cabernet sauvignon, and with small additional plantings of merlot, cabernet franc and verdelho. A substantial part of the production is sold as grapes, a part (the best) being reserved for the Shirvington wines, which are made by the very well known team of Sarah and Sparky Marquis. Immediate success has come their way, the 2001 Cabernet Sauvignon winning the Bushing Prize for the Best Wine at the 2002 McLaren Vale Wine Show.

shottesbrooke ★★★☆

Bagshaws Road, McLaren Flat, SA 5171 **region** McLaren Vale
phone (08) 8383 0002 **fax** (08) 8383 0222 **open** Mon–Fri 10–4.30, weekends and public holidays 11–5
winemaker Nick Holmes, Hamish Maguire **production** 10 000 cases **est.** 1984
product range ($15–35 CD) Sauvignon Blanc, Chardonnay, Shiraz, Eliza Reserve Shiraz, Merlot, Cabernet Merlot Malbec, Cabernet Sauvignon, Bernesh Bray Liqueur Tawny.
summary Now the full-time business of former Ryecroft winemaker Nick Holmes; the grapes grown on his vineyard at Myoponga, at their best, show clear berry fruit, subtle oak and a touch of elegance. A compact, handsome new winery was erected before the 1997 vintage. Exports to the UK, the US, Canada, Thailand and Japan supplement distribution through all Australian states.

Shottesbrooke Fleurieu Sauvignon Blanc

▼▼▼▼ **2002** Light straw-green; faint blossom and gooseberry aromas build significant pace on the palate, which has both power and length, thanks to good acidity on the finish. **rating:** 86
best drinking Now **best vintages** '95, '98 **drink with** Baby octopus • $15

Shottesbrooke Shiraz

There is a remarkable consistency to the style of all the Shottesbrooke wines, white and red, an elegance which is in some ways at odds with the usually very rich McLaren Vale style. This is a good example of the Shottesbrooke approach.
▼▼▼▼ **2001** Medium red-purple; in typical Shottesbrooke style, the light bouquet has nuances of earth, spice and dark fruits, with the palate adding touches of dark chocolate; a light-bodied 'dry' style, the oak incidental. **rating:** 85
best drinking Now **drink with** Osso buco • $18

Shottesbrooke Eliza Shiraz

▼▼▼▼ **2000** Medium red-purple; the moderately intense bouquet is clean and smooth, with a range of raspberry and cherry red fruit aromas; the light to medium-bodied palate is smooth, with distinct savoury/spicy notes in typical Shottesbrooke style. **rating:** 87
best drinking 2004–2009 **best vintages** '98 **drink with** Roast leg of lamb • $35

Shottesbrooke Bernesh Bray Liqueur Tawny

▼▼▼▼ **NV** Reddish hues; some young material in the blend gives freshness to the bouquet, but the palate shows there are some nicely aged components, with spicy rancio notes aiding the length and balance. **rating:** 85
best drinking Now–2006 **drink with** Biscuits • $30

silk hill NR

324 Motor Road, Deviot, Tas 7275 **region** Northern Tasmania
phone (03) 6394 7385 **fax** (03) 6394 7392 **open** Thurs–Sun 9–5
winemaker Gavin Scott **production** 300 cases **est.** 1990
product range ($16–20 CD) Pinot's Rose, Pinot Noir.
summary Pharmacist Gavin Scott has been a weekend and holiday viticulturist for many years, having established the Glengarry Vineyard, which he sold, and then establishing the 1.5-hectare Silk Hill (formerly Silkwood Vineyard) in 1989, planted exclusively to pinot noir. Growing and making Pinot Noir and fishing will keep him occupied when he sells his pharmacy business.

simon gilbert wines ★★★☆

1220 Sydney Road, Mudgee, NSW 2850 (postal) **region** Mudgee
phone (02) 9958 1322 **fax** (02) 8920 1333 **open** Not
winemaker Simon Gilbert **production** 35 000 cases **est.** 1993
product range ($15–45 R) Card Series Semillon Sauvignon Blanc, Verdelho, Chardonnay, Shiraz, Cabernet Merlot; next Family Selection Orange Pinot Noir, Mudgee Shiraz, McLaren Vale Grenache Shiraz Mourvedre, Mudgee Sangiovese, Central Ranges Cabernet Merlot; and at the top, Wongalere McLaren Vale Shiraz, Abbaston Cabernet Sauvignon.
summary The transition from a converted butter factory at Muswellbrook to a spectacularly sited, state-of-the-art $10 million winery at Mudgee represents the culmination of a family winemaking history dating back to 1847, when forebear Captain Joseph Gilbert commenced the establishment of a splendid vineyard and winery at Pewsey Vale, in the East Barossa Ranges. Simon Gilbert Wines is now a significant public company,

listed on the Stock Exchange, with a primary base of large-scale contract winemaking for others, but with plans to rapidly develop a three-tiered range of proprietary wines sourced from grapes grown in premium regions around south east Australia and from the 42 hectares of hillside vineyards surrounding the winery. A spacious cellar door and restaurant overlooking the micro valley in which the winery is situated will open when turning lanes from the highway are completed. Exports to the UK, Canada and Singapore.

Simon Gilbert Mudgee Sangiovese

♥♥♥♥♡ **2002** Light to medium red-purple, good given the variety; clean, spicy, tangy fruit aromas are followed by a palate with excellent mouthfeel; here spicy berry fruit flavours intermingle with really delicious tannins; an outstanding Australian Sangiovese. **rating:** 91

best drinking 2004–2008 **best vintages** '02 **drink with** Duck ravioli • $22.95

simon hackett   ★★★☆

Budgens Road, McLaren Vale, SA 5171 **region** McLaren Vale
phone (08) 8323 7712 **fax** (08) 8323 7713 **open** Wed–Sun 11–5
winemaker Simon Hackett **production** 20 000 cases **est.** 1981
product range ($15–35 R) McLaren Vale Riesling, Barossa Valley Semillon, Barossa Valley Chardonnay, McLaren Vale Shiraz, McLaren Vale Anthony's Reserve Shiraz, McLaren Vale Old Vine Grenache, McLaren Vale Foggo Road Cabernet Sauvignon.
summary In 1998 Simon Hackett acquired the former Taranga winery in McLaren Vale, which has made his winemaking life a great deal easier. He also has 8 hectares of estate vines and has contract growers in McLaren Vale, the Adelaide Hills and the Barossa Valley, with another 32 hectares of vines.

Simon Hackett Riesling

♥♥♥♥ **2002** Light straw-green; the bouquet is clean, with some mineral aromas but neutral fruit; the palate follows the same track; well made, but inherently limited by the region, notwithstanding it has been hand-picked from a single vineyard. **rating:** 85

best drinking Now **drink with** Fish terrine • $15

Simon Hackett McLaren Vale Old Vine Grenache

♥♥♥♥ **2001** Medium red-purple; the bouquet has some appealing spicy notes on top of the usual varietal character, something which carries through, giving the palate an extra level of flavour complexity, although it is still light to medium-bodied in terms of extract. An attractive wine. **rating:** 87

best drinking Now–2006 **drink with** Ravioli • $15

Simon Hackett Foggo Road Cabernet Sauvignon

♥♥♥♥ **2000** Medium red-purple; the moderately intense bouquet is clean, with a nice marriage of blackcurrant and redcurrant fruit, the oak minimal. Savoury tannins run through the length of the palate, but don't overwhelm it. **rating:** 87

best drinking 2006–2011 **drink with** Roast lamb • $35

sinclair wines   NR

Graphite Road, Glenoran, WA 6258 **region** Manjimup
phone (08) 9421 1399 **fax** (08) 9421 1191 **open** By appointment
winemaker Brenden Smith (Contract) **production** 2500 cases **est.** 1994
product range ($15–25 CD) Sauvignon Blanc, Unwooded Chardonnay, Chardonnay, Chardonnay Manjimup, Rose of Glenoran, Cabernet Merlot Jezebel, Cabernet Sauvignon, Cabernet Sauvignon Giovanni.
summary Sinclair Wines is the child of Darelle Sinclair, a science teacher, wine educator and graduate viticulturist from Charles Sturt University, and John Healy, a lawyer, traditional jazz musician and graduand wine marketing student of Adelaide University, Roseworthy Campus. Five hectares of estate plantings are in production.

sirromet wines   ★★★★

850–938 Mount Cotton Road, Mount Cotton, Qld 4165 **region** Queensland Coastal
phone (07) 3206 2999 **fax** (07) 3206 0900 **open** 7 days 10–5
winemaker Adam Chapman, Alain Rousseau, Craig Stevenson **production** 80 000 cases **est.** 1998
product range ($12–30 CD) Perfect Day range of Semillon Verdelho Chardonnay, Harvest White, Chardonnay, Harvest Red, Shiraz Cabernet Merlot; Vineyard Selection range of Sauvignon Blanc Semillon, Chardonnay, Pinot Chardonnay Sparkling, Teewah, Chambourcin, Cabernet Sauvignon; Seven Scenes range of Chardonnay, Pinot Chardonnay Sparkling, Shiraz, Finito Muscat; and Private Bin TM at the top.

summary This is an unambiguously ambitious venture, with the professed aim of creating Queensland's premier winery. The Morris family, founders of Sirromet Wines, which owns Mount Cotton Estate, retained a leading architect to design the striking state-of-the-art winery with a 80 000-case production capacity; the state's foremost viticultural consultant to plant the three major vineyards which total 100 hectares; and the most skilled winemaker practising in Queensland, Adam Chapman, to make the wine. It has a 200-seat restaurant; a wine club offering all sorts of benefits to its members; and is firmly aimed at the domestic and international tourist market, taking advantage of its situation halfway between Brisbane and the Gold Coast. The intention is to move to a predominantly estate-based operation as quickly as the vineyards (planted to 14 varieties) come into production. Both the consistency and quality of the wines released so far and their modest pricing bodes well for the future.

Sirromet Vineyard Selection Queensland Verdelho
TTTT 2002 Medium yellow-green; the bouquet is rich and developed, suggesting some skin contact; the full-flavoured, honeyed, fruit salad palate reflects considerable care in making the wine. One hundred per cent Granite Belt. **rating:** 85

best drinking Now **drink with** Moreton Bay bugs • $16

Sirromet Queensland Chardonnay
TTTTY 2001 Medium yellow-green; complex barrel-ferment inputs into the bouquet have been well handled; the palate has very good melon and fig fruit, the oak handling again positive but in no way threatening the abundant flavour of the fruit. Very impressive. A blend of 56 per cent Granite Belt, 30 per cent South Burnett and 14 per cent Orange grapes. Fully fermented in French oak. **rating:** 90

best drinking Now–2007 **drink with** Calamari • $16

Sirromet Seven Scenes Shiraz
TTTT 2001 Medium to full red-purple; the intense bouquet has dark berry and plum aromas cradled in clean, subtle oak; the palate has plenty of depth, weight and extract; an altogether serious wine, fruit-driven, but with some oak, and good tannin management. **rating:** 89

best drinking 2005–2010 **drink with** Barbecued rib of beef • $25

Sirromet Vineyard Selection Shiraz
TTTT 2001 Medium red-purple; fully ripe plum, chocolate and blackberry fruit on the bouquet leads into a powerful palate with a big structure and frame; the tannins are a touch overplayed, but should come into balance in time; the wine offers excellent value. A blend of 65 per cent South Burnett and 35 per cent Granite Belt grapes. **rating:** 88

best drinking 2004–2009 **drink with** Grilled porterhouse • $16

Sirromet Teewah
TTTY 2001 Light to medium purple-red; a lightly scented bouquet is followed by a fresh, tangy palate with light-bodied fruit flavours, one step up from Rose. Mercifully, the wine has a dry finish. A highly original blend of Shiraz, Merlot and Cabernet Sauvignon plus 14 per cent Semillon and 10 per cent Sauvignon Blanc. Made for immediate drinking. **rating:** 84

best drinking Now **drink with** Light red meats • $16

sittella wines   NR

100 Barrett Road, Herne Hill, WA 6056 **region** Swan Valley
phone (08) 9296 2600 **fax** (08) 9296 2600 **open** Tues–Sun and public holidays 11–5
winemaker Julie White **production** 5000 cases **est.** 1998
product range ($11.95–22 CD) Frontignac, Silk, Chenin Blanc, Verdelho, Unwooded Chardonnay, Chardonnay, Sparkling Chenin, Sparkling Chardonnay, Shiraz, Cabernet Sauvignon.
summary Perth couple Simon and Maaike Berns acquired a 7-hectare block (with 2 hectares of vines) at Herne Hill, making the first wine in February 1998 and opening their most attractive cellar-door facility later in the year. They also own the 4-hectare Wildberry Springs Estate vineyard in the Margaret River region, which began to provide grapes from the 1999 vintage.

s kidman wines   ★★★

Riddoch Highway, Coonawarra, SA 5263 **region** Coonawarra
phone (08) 8736 5071 **fax** (08) 8736 5070 **open** 7 days 9–5
winemaker John Innes (Contract) **production** 8000 cases **est.** 1984
product range ($13–20 CD) Riesling, Sauvignon Blanc, Shiraz, Cabernet Sauvignon.

summary One of the district pioneers, with a 16-hectare estate vineyard which is now fully mature. Limited retail distribution in Melbourne and Adelaide.

S Kidman Shiraz

TTTT 2000 Medium red; the leathery, earthy bouquet runs in a savoury mould, but the palate offers much more, with pleasing licorice and plum fruit; well balanced, and gentle oak. **rating:** 86

best drinking Now–2007 **drink with** Barbecued lamb chops • $18

skillogalee ★★★★

Off Hughes Park Road, Sevenhill via Clare, SA 5453 **region** Clare Valley
phone (08) 8843 4311 **fax** (08) 8843 4343 **open** 7 days 10–5
winemaker Dave Palmer **production** 7000 cases **est.** 1970
product range ($12.50–35 CD) Riesling, Gewurztraminer, Chardonnay, Sparkling Riesling, Late Picked Riesling, Shiraz, The Cabernets, fortifieds.
summary David and Diana Palmer purchased the small hillside stone winery from the George family at the end of the 1980s and have capitalised to the full on the exceptional fruit quality of the Skillogalee vineyards. The winery also has a well-patronised lunchtime restaurant. All the wines are generous and full flavoured, particularly the reds. In July 2002 the Palmers purchased next door neighbour Waninga Vineyards, with 30 hectares of 30-year-old vines, allowing a substantial increase in production without any change in quality or style. Exports to the UK, Switzerland, Hong Kong and the US.

Skillogalee Riesling

TTTTY 2002 Light yellow-green; intense lime, lime blossom and touches of mineral highlight the bouquet; the palate is much richer and more powerful than usual, with abundant fruit, yet more evidence of the outstanding Clare vintage. **rating:** 91

best drinking Now–2007 **best vintages** '80, '84, '87, '90, '92, '97, '99, '01, '02 **drink with** Quiche Lorraine • $19.50

Skillogalee Shiraz

TTTT 2000 While the colour is on the light side, the hue is very good; minty, spicy, earthy, savoury aromas are followed by a medium-bodied palate offering a mix of red and black fruits with savoury/minty nuances; fine tannins to close. **rating:** 86

best drinking 2004–2008 **best vintages** '97, '98 **drink with** Rich game • $25.50

Skillogalee The Cabernets

TTTT 2000 Medium red-purple; aromatic blackcurrant fruit, with a touch of raspberry, leads into a fruit-driven, medium-bodied palate with a red fruit core and touches of spice and earth. Lighter framed than the '99. A blend of 70 per cent Cabernet Sauvignon, 25 per cent Cabernet Franc and 5 per cent Malbec. **rating:** 87

best drinking 2005–2010 **best vintages** '84, '87, '90, '93, '96, '97, '98 **drink with** Yearling steak • $25.50

🐌 small gully wines NR

Roenfeldt Road, Greenock, SA 5355 (postal) **region** Barossa Valley
phone 0411 690 047 **fax** (08) 8376 4276 **open** Not
winemaker Stephen Black **production** 2000 cases **est.** 2000
product range ($25–37 ML) Semillon, Shiraz, Gawler River Shiraz, Ringbark Red Shiraz Cabernet.
summary Stephen Black is producing a carefully positioned range of wines, from Barossa Valley Semillon ($7) and Gawler River Shiraz ($12) in cleanskin form, progressing upwards to $25 for the Ringbark Red Shiraz Cabernet blend and $37 for the flagship product, Small Gully Shiraz.

smithbrook ★★★★

Smith Brook Road, Middlesex via Manjimup, WA 6258 **region** Manjimup
phone (08) 9772 3557 **fax** (08) 9772 3579 **open** By appointment
winemaker Michael Symons, Jonathan Farrington **production** 15 000 cases **est.** 1988
product range ($16–37.50 R) Sauvignon Blanc, Chardonnay, Merlot, The Yilgarn, Cabernet Sauvignon.
summary Smithbrook is a major player in the Manjimup region, with 60 hectares of vines in production. A majority interest was acquired by Petaluma in 1997 but it will continue its role as a contract grower for other companies, as well as supplying Petaluma's needs and making relatively small amounts of wine under its own label. Perhaps the most significant change has been the removal of Pinot Noir from the current range of products, and the introduction of Merlot. National distribution through Negociants; exports to the UK, New Zealand and Japan.

Smithbrook The Yilgarn

TTTT **2000** Medium purple-red; a mix of ripe cassis and mulberry drives the bouquet; the palate has complex texture and structure, offering ripe tannins and clever oak use. 85 per cent Merlot and 7.5 per cent each of Cabernet Sauvignon and Petit Verdot. **rating: 89**

best drinking 2004–2009 **drink with** Braised ox cheek • $35

Smithbrook Merlot

TTTT **2000** Medium red-purple; clean, small red berry fruits have spicy/savoury/earthy undertones on the bouquet and palate; the wine has lingering, persistent tannins which are, however, well within the varietal spectrum. **rating: 88**

best drinking 2004–2009 **best vintages** '99 **drink with** Milk-fed veal • $24.50

smithleigh vineyard   NR

53 Osborne Road, Lane Cove, NSW 2066 **region** Lower Hunter Valley
phone 0418 484 565 **fax** (02) 9420 2014 **open** Not
winemaker Andrew Margan (Contract) **production** 3000 cases **est.** 1997
product range ($14–16 CD) Old Vine Hunter Semillon, Verdelho, Chardonnay, Shiraz.
summary As the name suggests, a partnership between Rod and Ivija Smith and John and Jan Leigh, which purchased the long-established vineyard from Southcorp in 1996. A lot of work in the vineyard, and skilled contract winemaking by Andrew Margan, has produced the right outcomes.

 # snowdon wines   ★★★☆

Bawden Road, Woodend, Vic 3442 **region** Macedon Ranges
phone (03) 5423 5252 **fax** (03) 5423 5272 **open** 7 days 10–5
winemaker Andrew Byers **production** 660 000 cases **est.** 1987
product range ($8.95–45 R) Koala Blue Chardonnay, Shiraz; Goldfields Semillon Sauvignon Blanc, Shiraz; Pipers Creek Chardonnay, Classic White, Dry Red, Shiraz; Five Mile Creek Colombard Chardonnay, Cabernet Merlot; Wood End Chardonnay, Shiraz; Mount Macedon Unwooded Chardonnay, Chardonnay, Pinot Noir, Shiraz, Cabernet Sauvignon Merlot; and at the top end Olivia (by Olivia Newton-John) Padthaway Chardonnay, Coonawarra Cabernet Sauvignon.
summary The Neylon family has built up a wide-ranging wine business, the principal winery of which just happens to be in the Macedon Ranges. It is their joint venture with Koala Blue which provides the business with its high volume; the Macedon Ranges (and the Olivia by Olivia Newton-John signature series) represent the quality end of the business. Happily, I have not been asked to taste the undoubtedly apt Koala Blue wines. Most of the wine is exported, the US being the principal market.

Mount Macedon Sauvignon Blanc

TTTT **2002** Very pale straw-green; the light, clean and crisp bouquet has herb and mineral aromas. The palate, like the bouquet, is spotlessly clean and well made, the principal problem being the lack of varietal punch. **rating: 85**

best drinking Now **drink with** Shellfish • $20

Mount Macedon Sauvignon Blanc

TTTY **2002** Light straw, with lots of CO_2 in the glass; the bouquet is clean, but low in fruit intensity, with hints of straw and citrus; the light-bodied palate is clean, citrus-driven, with the oak impact minimal. Part barrel fermented and part fermented in stainless steel. **rating: 84**

best drinking Now–2005 **drink with** Sushi • $35

Olivia Padthaway Chardonnay

TTTT **2001** Light to medium yellow-green; the gently complex bouquet has nutty barrel-ferment aromas; the pleasant, ever so slightly sweet palate has gently peachy fruit. The 'Olivia' is none other than Olivia Newton-John, although her exact role in all of this remains unclear. **rating: 87**

best drinking Now–2006 **drink with** Chicken pasta • $35

Olivia Coonawarra Cabernet Sauvignon

TTTTY **2000** Medium red-purple; clean, direct red and blackcurrant fruit aromas lead into a medium-bodied palate, with good texture and structure; blackcurrant, chocolate and positive oak come together well. **rating: 90**

best drinking 2005–2011 **best vintages** '00 **drink with** Kangaroo fillet • $45

snowy river winery   NR

Rockwell Road, Berridale, NSW 2628 **region** Southern New South Wales Zone
phone (02) 6456 5041 **fax** (02) 6456 5005 **open** Wed–Sun, 7 days during school holidays
winemaker Manfred Plumecke **production** 2500 cases **est.** 1984
product range ($10–20 CD) Snowy White, Alpine Dry White, Sauvignon Blanc Chardonnay, Sylvaner Muller Thurgau, Sieger Rebe [sic], Rhine Riesling Auslese, Noble Riesling, Snow Bruska, Snowy Port, Tawny Port.
summary An operation which relies entirely on the substantial tourist trade passing through or near Berridale on the way to the Snowy Mountains. The product range is, to put it mildly, eclectic; all the wines are said to be made on-site, and the grapes for all the white varietals are estate-grown.

somerset hill wines   ★★★☆

891 McLeod Road, Denmark, WA 6333 **region** Great Southern
phone (08) 9840 9388 **fax** (08) 9840 9394 **open** 7 days 11–5
winemaker Brenden Smith (Contract) **production** 3000 cases **est.** 1995
product range ($12.80–30 CD) Semillon, Sauvignon Blanc, Semillon Sauvignon Blanc, Chardonnay (unwooded), Constellation (sparkling), Harmony (sweet white blend), Pinot Noir, Merlot.
summary Graham Upson commenced planting 11 hectares of pinot noir, chardonnay, semillon, merlot and sauvignon blanc in 1995, and Somerset Hill Wines duly opened its limestone cellar-door sales area with sweeping views out over the ocean. Limited retail distribution in Melbourne and Sydney; exports to the UK.

Somerset Hill Pinot Noir
▼▼▼▼▽ **2001** Light to medium red, starting to shift to tawny; the aromatic bouquet is starting to show some equivalent shift away from primary fruit; the palate likewise has hints of forest and spice, finishing with fine tannins. Now at the peak of its form.   **rating: 90**
best drinking Now **best vintages** '01 **drink with** Mushroom risotto • $30

sorrenberg   NR

Alma Road, Beechworth, Vic 3747 **region** Beechworth
phone (03) 5728 2278 **fax** (03) 5728 2278 **open** Mon–Fri by appointment, most weekends 1–5 (by appointment)
winemaker Barry Morey **production** 1200 cases **est.** 1986
product range ($20–32 CD) Sauvignon Blanc Semillon, Chardonnay, Gamay, Cabernet Sauvignon, Havelock Hills Shiraz, Cabernet Merlot Franc.
summary Barry and Jan Morey made their first wines in 1989 from the 3-hectare vineyard on the outskirts of Beechworth. No recent tastings, but the wines have a good reputation and loyal clientele, selling out rapidly. The Gamay is a specialty, the Chardonnay likewise.

🦃 spring ridge wines   NR

880 Darbys Falls Road, Cowra, NSW 2794 **region** Cowra
phone (02) 6341 3820 **fax** (02) 6341 3820 **open** By appointment
winemaker Contract **est.** 1997
product range ($13–16 ML) Semillon, Chardonnay, Shiraz.
summary Peter and Anne Jeffery have established 5 hectares of shiraz, 2.5 hectares each of chardonnay and semillon, 1.7 hectares of cabernet sauvignon and 1 hectare of merlot. They sell by far the greatest part of the grape production, having only a small amount made under the Spring Ridge Wines label. The 2000 Shiraz had spectacular success, winning the Trophy for Best Red Wine at the Cowra Regional Judging 2001.

spring vale vineyards   ★★★★☆

130 Spring Vale Road, Cranbrook, Tas 7190 **region** Southern Tasmania
phone (03) 6257 8208 **fax** (03) 6257 8598 **open** Mon–Fri 10–5, or by appointment
winemaker Kristen Lyne **production** 3000 cases **est.** 1986
product range ($13.50–35 CD) Gewurztraminer, Chardonnay, Pinot Gris, Pinot Noir; Baudin Chardonnay and Pinot Noir.
summary Rodney Lyne has progressively established 1.5 hectares each of pinot noir and chardonnay and then added 0.5 hectare each of gewurztraminer and pinot gris; the latter produced a first crop in 1998. Frost has caused havoc from time to time; this is not only financially destructive, but also frustrating, for Spring Vale can, and does, produce first-class wines when the frost stays away. Exports to the UK.

springviews wine ★★★★

Woodlands Road, Porongurup, WA 6324 **region** Great Southern
phone (08) 9853 2088 **fax** (08) 9853 2098 **open** 7 days 10–5
winemaker Howard Park (Contract) **production** 500 cases **est.** 1994
product range ($16–20 CD) Riesling, Chardonnay, Cabernet Sauvignon.
summary Andy and Alice Colquhoun planted their 5-hectare vineyard (2 hectares each of chardonnay and cabernet sauvignon and 1 hectare of riesling) in 1994. The wine is contract-made and is sold through the cellar door and by the mailing list.

stanley brothers NR

Barossa Valley Way, Tanunda, SA 5352 **region** Barossa Valley
phone (08) 8563 3375 **fax** (08) 8563 3758 **open** 7 days 9–5
winemaker Lindsay Stanley **production** 12 000 cases **est.** 1994
product range ($11–25 CD) Sylvaner, Full Sister Semillon, Chardonnay, Premium Barossa Cuvee, John Hancock Shiraz, Thoroughbred Cabernet Sauvignon, Black Sheep, Fine Old Tawny Port.
summary Former Anglesey winemaker and industry veteran Lindsay Stanley established his own business in the Barossa Valley when he purchased (and renamed) the former Kroemer Estate in late 1994. As one would expect, the wines are competently made. Twenty-one hectares of estate plantings have provided virtually all the grapes for the business. Exports to Switzerland, Luxembourg, Japan and the US. No recent tastings.

stanton & killeen wines ★★★★★

Jacks Road, Murray Valley Highway, Rutherglen, Vic 3685 **region** Rutherglen
phone (02) 6032 9457 **fax** (02) 6032 8018 **open** Mon–Sat 9–5, Sun 10–5
winemaker Chris Killeen **production** 15 000 cases **est.** 1875
product range ($11–75 CD) A red wine and fortified wine specialist, though offering Chardonnay, Riesling, White Frontignac, Auslese Tokay and Parkview Dry White as well as Parkview Dry Red, Moodemere Shiraz, Cabernet Franc Merlot, Cabernet Shiraz, Shiraz, Durif; fortifieds include Rutherglen White Port, Rutherglen Ruby Port, Rutherglen Muscat; Classic Rutherglen Tawny, Tokay, Muscat; Grand Rutherglen Muscat; Rare Rutherglen Muscat.
summary Chris Killeen has skilfully expanded the portfolio of Stanton & Killeen but without in any way compromising its reputation as a traditional maker of smooth, rich reds, some of Australia's best Vintage Ports, and attractive, fruity muscats and tokays. All in all, deserves far greater recognition. Exports to the UK and the US.

Stanton & Killeen Moodemere Shiraz

♥♥♥♥ 2001 Medium red-purple; clean blackberry and plum fruit on the bouquet is supported by gentle vanilla oak; the palate has fine texture and balance, bolstered by ripe, savoury tannins. **rating:** 89
best drinking 2006–2011 **best vintages** '00 **drink with** Rump steak • $21

Stanton & Killeen Shiraz Durif

♥♥♥♥♡ 2001 Medium to full purple-red; rich dark plum, prune, licorice and blackberry aromas slide into abundant mid-palate fruit, with the tannins and overall extract well controlled; will build with time. A 50/50 blend of the two varieties. **rating:** 90
best drinking 2006–2016 **best vintages** '00, '01 **drink with** Whole roasted ox kidney • $17

Stanton & Killeen Durif

♥♥♥♥♥ 2000 Medium to full red-purple; dense, ripe, but not jammy, blackberry fruit floods the bouquet; mouth-coating blackberry and chocolate flavours repeat the job on the palate, sustained by remarkably fine tannins. Three gold and two silver medals independently attest to the quality of this wine. **rating:** 94
best drinking 2005–2015 **best vintages** '97, '98, '99, '00 **drink with** Two inch-thick rump steak • $30

Stanton & Killeen Tawny Port

♥♥♥♥♡ NV Medium red-tawny; the bouquet is clean with nice butterscotch overtones and, like the palate, shows positive but not aggressive rancio. **rating:** 93
best drinking Now **drink with** Aperitif or coffee

Stanton & Killeen Vintage Port

ŦŦŦŦŦ **1998** Medium to full red-purple; the bouquet shows excellent complexity and, in particular, subtle fortifying spirit. The long and complex palate has spicy plum cake flavours, with a pleasing long, dry finish taking it way outside the Australian mainstream and towards that of Portugal. A blend of Shiraz, Touriga, Durif, Tinta Cao and Tinta Barroca. Release November 2003. **rating:** 94

best drinking 2008–2018 **best vintages** '92, '93, '95, '98 **drink with** Walnuts • $25

🍇 stanton estate   NR

135 North Isis Road, Childers, Qld 4660 **region** Queensland Zone
phone (07) 4126 1255 **fax** (07) 4126 1823 **open** Weekends 10–5, or by appointment
winemaker Tom Wiedmann (Contract) **est.** 2000
product range ($13.50 CD) Organic range of Marsanne Verdelho, Verdelho, Marsanne, Cabernet Sauvignon Merlot; Chardonnay, Shiraz.
summary Keith and Joy Stanton have established 2 hectares of verdelho, marsanne, cabernet sauvignon and merlot using organic growing methods, and are seeking organic certification, making Stanton Estate the only organically grown wine in Queensland. The wines are also made to BFA standards, which permit the use of some SO_2, but within strictly controlled limits. The wines are contract-made at Moonshine Valley Winery near Nambour by Tom Wiedmann, and sell out rapidly through the cellar door and Woodgate Restaurant.

staughton vale vineyard   NR

20 Staughton Vale Road, Anakie, Vic 3221 **region** Geelong
phone (03) 5284 1477 **fax** (03) 5284 1229 **open** Fri–Mon and public holidays 10–5, or by appointment
winemaker Paul Chambers **production** 2000 cases **est.** 1986
product range Riesling, Pinot Noir, Staughton (Merlot blend), Tawny Port, Liqueur Shiraz.
summary Paul Chambers has 6 hectares of closely planted vines, with the accent on the classic Bordeaux mix of cabernet sauvignon, merlot, cabernet franc and petit verdot, although chardonnay and pinot noir are also planted. Weekend lunches are available at the Staughton Cottage Restaurant.

steels creek estate   NR

1 Sewell Road, Steels Creek, Vic 3775 **region** Yarra Valley
phone (03) 5965 2448 **fax** (03) 5965 2448 **open** Weekends and public holidays 10–6, or by appointment
winemaker Simon Peirce **production** 400 cases **est.** 1981
product range ($15–25 CD) Colombard, Chardonnay, Shiraz, Cabernet Sauvignon.
summary Established by brother and sister team Simon and Kerri Peirce. While only a tiny operation, with 1.7 hectares of vineyard planted at various times between 1981 and 1994, Steels Creek Estate has an on-site winery where the wines are made with assistance from consultants, but increasingly by Simon Peirce, who has completed his associate diploma in Applied Science (Winegrowing) at Charles Sturt University.

stefano lubiana   ★★★★☆

60 Rowbottoms Road, Granton, Tas 7030 **region** Southern Tasmania
phone (03) 6263 7457 **fax** (03) 6263 7430 **open** Sun–Thurs 11–3 (closed some public holidays)
winemaker Steve Lubiana **production** 6500 cases **est.** 1990
product range ($23–39 CD) Riesling, Sauvignon Blanc, Pinot Grigio, Sur Lie Chardonnay, Chardonnay, NV Brut, Pinot Noir, Primavera Pinot Noir, Merlot.
summary The charming, self-effacing Steve Lubiana has moved from one extreme to the other, having run Lubiana Wines at Moorook in the South Australian Riverland for many years before moving to Granton to set up a substantial winery. The estate-produced Stefano Lubiana wines come from 14 hectares of beautifully located vineyards sloping down to the Derwent River. All the Lubiana wines are immaculately crafted.

Stefano Lubiana Chardonnay

ŦŦŦŦŦ **2001** Medium yellow-green; while complex barrel-ferment oak is immediately obvious on the bouquet, it is well-integrated with the positive fruit. A wine with abundant character, great length and persistence, with pristine fruit the focus of the palate; Chablis style. **rating:** 94

best drinking Now–2007 **best vintages** '01 **drink with** Chinese prawns • $37

stellar ridge estate ★★★☆

Clews Road, Cowaramup, WA 6284 **region** Margaret River
phone (08) 9755 5635 **fax** (08) 9755 5636 **open** 7 days 10–5
winemaker Bernie Abbott **production** 1500 cases **est.** 1994
product range ($14–25 CD) Sauvignon Blanc, Verdelho, Unwooded Chardonnay, Late Harvest Sauvignon Blanc, Shiraz, Cabernet Sauvignon; also estate-grown varietally identified olive oil (Pendolino, Leccino, Frantolo, WA Mission).
summary Colin and Helene Hellier acquired a 49-hectare grazing property at Cowaramup in 1993 which included 2.5 hectares of chardonnay and sauvignon blanc planted in 1987. A large dam was constructed in 1994, and the following year 11 hectares of new vineyards and 4 hectares of olive trees were planted; 1.6 hectares of zinfandel followed in 1996, bringing total plantings to 15.1 hectares. The majority of the 100-tonne grape production is sold to other local wineries, with 14 to 15 tonnes being retained for the Stellar Ridge label. The wines are sold exclusively through the cellar door and by the mailing list.

Stellar Ridge Estate Sauvignon Blanc

▼▼▼▼▽ **2002** Pale straw-green; the moderately intense bouquet is spotlessly clean, with an attractive tropical/lemon mix, which also determines the flavours on the palate. **rating:** 90

best drinking Now **best vintages** '02 **drink with** Light seafood • $16

stephen john wines ★★★★

Government Road, Watervale, SA 5452 **region** Clare Valley
phone (08) 8843 0105 **fax** (08) 8843 0105 **open** 7 days 11–5
winemaker Stephen John **production** 7500 cases **est.** 1994
product range ($13–40 CD) Watervale Riesling, Semillon Sauvignon Blanc, Blanc de Blanc, Traugott Cuvee Sparkling Burgundy, Pinot Noir, Clare Valley Shiraz, Estate Reserve Shiraz, Merlot, Estate Reserve Cabernet Sauvignon.
summary The John family is one of the best known names in the Barossa Valley, with branches running Australia's best cooperage (AP John & Sons) and providing the chief winemaker of Lindemans (Philip John) and the former chief winemaker of Quelltaler (Stephen John). Stephen and Rita John have now formed their own family business in the Clare Valley, based on a 6-hectare vineyard overlooking the town of Watervale and supplemented by modest intake from a few local growers. The cellar-door sales area is housed in an 80-year-old stable which has been renovated and is full of rustic charm. The significantly increased production and good quality of the current releases has led to the appointment of distributors in each of the eastern states, and exports to the UK, the US, Malaysia and Singapore. Rated on the basis of tastings in 2002.

step road winery ★★★☆

Davidson Road, Langhorne Creek, SA 5255 (postal) **region** Langhorne Creek
phone (08) 8537 3342 **fax** (08) 8537 3357 **open** Not
winemaker Rob Dundon **production** 180 000 cases **est.** 1998
product range ($11.95–19.50 CD) The economy second label is Red Wing Chardonnay and Cabernet Sauvignon; under the Step Road label, Sauvignon Blanc (Adelaide Hills), Pinot Noir, Shiraz (McLaren Vale and Langhorne Creek), Sangiovese (Langhorne Creek), Cabernet Sauvignon (McLaren Vale and Langhorne Creek).
summary Step Road has 30 hectares of vineyard in Langhorne Creek, and 40 hectares in the Adelaide Hills, supplementing the production from those vineyards with cabernet sauvignon and shiraz purchased from McLaren Vale. It is an autonomous business, but operationally part of the Beresford Wines group. The wines are distributed nationally by Red+White; exports to the UK and the US.

Step Road Langhorne Creek Shiraz

▼▼▼▼▽ **2001** Bright, full red-purple; the solid bouquet has rich blackberry, licorice and oak aromas which feed into the medium to full-bodied palate, which has smooth blackberry, licorice and spice fruit, ripe tannins and good balance. **rating:** 90

best drinking 2005–2010 **best vintages** '01 **drink with** Beef Provençale • $19.50

Step Road Langhorne Creek Sangiovese

▼▼▼▼ **2001** Light to medium red, the purple hues starting to diminish; the clean, light, faintly spicy bouquet is an uncertain start, but the palate picks up the pace considerably, with sweet and savoury varietal fruit, fine tannins and subtle oak. **rating:** 86

best drinking 2004–2007 **drink with** Vitella tonnato • $16.95

sterling heights   NR

Faulkners Road, Winkleigh, Tas 7275 **region** Northern Tasmania
phone (03) 6396 3214 **fax** (03) 6396 3214 **open** By appointment
winemaker Moorilla Estate (Contract) **production** 400 cases **est.** 1988
product range ($14–16 CD) Riesling, Chardonnay, Breton Rose, Pinot Noir.
summary With 2 hectares of vines, Sterling Heights will always be a small fish in a small pond. However, the early releases had considerable success in wine shows, and the quality was all one could expect. The wines are also available through Hartzview Wine Centre. No recent tastings.

sticks   ★★★☆

886 St Huberts Road, Coldstream, Vic 3770 **region** Yarra Valley
phone (03) 9739 0666 **fax** (03) 9739 0633 **open** 7 days 10–5
winemaker Rob Dolan **production** 20 000 cases **est.** 2000
product range ($15–18 R) Sauvignon Blanc, Sauvignon Blanc Semillon, Chardonnay, Pinot Noir, Shiraz, Merlot, Cabernet Sauvignon.
summary Rob Dolan, the affable, towering (former) long-serving winemaker at Yarra Ridge, has always had the nickname Sticks, doubtless recognising his long legs. Since leaving Yarra Ridge several years ago he has made wine first at Dominion and now at The Punt Road winery. But he has also decided to produce his own range of wines, which he makes at The Yarra Hill, the grapes being chosen from 100 hectares spread across three Yarra Valley vineyards. The wines are keenly priced, the packaging excellent, and national distribution through Red+White should all contribute to rapid growth for the brand. A cellar door is under construction.

Sticks Sauvignon Blanc

▼▼▼▼ **2002** Light to medium green-yellow; a spotlessly clean and quite firm bouquet leads into tight, minerally palate with green fruits and a bright, dry finish.   **rating:** 88
best drinking Now **drink with** Shellfish • $15

Sticks Chardonnay

▼▼▼▽ **2002** Light straw-green; the clean, fresh, light bouquet with melon and stone fruit is precisely repeated on the palate, with the barest hint of oak. Made to a price.   **rating:** 84
best drinking Now **drink with** Wiener schnitzel • $15

Sticks Pinot Noir

▼▼▼▼▽ **2002** Medium red-purple; fresh plum and dark cherry fruit is not threatened by the oak on the bouquet; the palate is intense, long, yet not the least heavy, complexed by savoury nuances. Excellent wine.   **rating:** 90
best drinking Now–2006 **best vintages** '02 **drink with** Braised quail • $18

Sticks Merlot

▼▼▼▼ **2001** Medium red-purple; aromas of dark berry, olive, bramble and gentle oak open proceedings; the palate has redcurrant fruit and a hint of olive; good structure, length and varietal expression.   **rating:** 87
best drinking Now–2007 **drink with** Braised veal • $18

Sticks Cabernet Sauvignon

▼▼▼▼ **2001** Medium red-purple; the moderately intense bouquet has a mix of berry, olive, leaf and mint, the oak barely evident. The leafy berry palate has very subtle oak, the acidity a little on the high side.   **rating:** 85
best drinking Now–2006 **drink with** Yearling steak • $18

stone bridge estate   NR

RMB 189, Holleys Road, Manjimup, WA 6258 **region** Manjimup
phone (08) 9773 1371 **fax** (08) 9773 1309 **open** By appointment
winemaker Syd Hooker, Kate Hooker **production** 3000 cases **est.** 1991
product range ($20–30 R) Sauvignon Blanc Semillon, Methode Champenoise, Shiraz, Cabernet Merlot Malbec.
summary Syd and Sue Hooker purchased the property on which Stone Bridge Estate is established in 1990, and planted the first vines that year. A subsequent planting in 1996 has increased the vineyard size to 8 hectares, with shiraz (2 ha) a total of 1.7 hectares of pinot noir and chardonnay, 1.6 hectares of the four Bordeaux varieties, and 1 hectare each of semillon, sauvignon blanc and sangiovese. The pinot noir and chardonnay go to provide the Methode Champenoise, made (on-site, like all the other wines) by daughter Kate, a graduate winemaker and viticulturist from the Lycée Viticole d'Avize in Champagne.

🍇 stone chimney creek   NR

PO Box 401, Angaston, SA 5353 **region** Barossa Valley
phone (08) 8565 3339 **fax** (08) 8565 3339 **open** Not
winemaker Chris Ringland **production** 100 cases **est.** 1989
product range ($535 R) Three Rivers Shiraz.
summary Another tiny production wine produced by ringmaster Chris Ringland, and effectively sold only in the US through The Grateful Palate. Two hectares of old-vine shiraz produce between 60 and 100 cases per year of wine at a breathtaking price. Chris Ringland politely explains that due to the tiny production, he cannot routinely provide bottles for evaluation.

stonehaven   ★★★★

Riddoch Highway, Padthaway, SA 5271 **region** Padthaway
phone (08) 8765 6140 **fax** (08) 8765 6137 **open** 7 days 10–4
winemaker Tom Newton, Susanne Bell, Adrienne Cross **production** 75 000 cases **est.** 1998
product range ($12–35 R) Padthaway Unwooded Chardonnay, Cabernet Merlot, Chardonnay, Limestone Coast Chardonnay, Limestone Coast Viognier, Shiraz, Limestone Coast Shiraz, Padthaway Cabernet Sauvignon, Limited Release Chardonnay.
summary It is, to say the least, strange that it should have taken 30 years for a substantial winery to be built at Padthaway. However, when BRL Hardy took the decision, it was no half measure: $20 million has been invested in what is the largest greenfields winery built in Australia for more than 20 years. Exports to the US, Canada and the UK.

Stonehaven Limestone Coast Viognier

▼▼▼▼ 2002 Light straw-green; a moderately aromatic bouquet with mid-ripeness peach and apricot aromas is followed by a palate with undoubted varietal character, but which doesn't flow evenly across the mouth. Slightly disappointing given the vintage. **rating:** 86

best drinking Now **drink with** Rich seafood • $15.95

Stonehaven Limestone Coast Chardonnay

▼▼▼▼▽ 2001 Light to medium yellow-green; a striking, funky, wild ferment gives enormous complexity to the bouquet; while there is some fruit sweetness on the mid-palate, the same wild barrel-ferment characters come through strongly on the palate in a striking, Burgundian fashion. Nothing conventional about this wine.

best drinking Now–2006 **best vintages** '01 **drink with** Fresh crab cakes • $15.99 **rating:** 93

Stonehaven Limited Release Chardonnay

▼▼▼▼▽ 2001 Medium yellow-green; an intense and challenging bouquet and palate, with lifted characters giving some impression of volatility which in truth isn't there. The oak, too, is somewhat strident, but the wine has everything there to settle down with more time in bottle, and will probably rate higher points as it does so.

best drinking Now–2007 **best vintages** '99, '01 **drink with** Braised neck of pork • $26.99 **rating:** 90

Stonehaven Stepping Stone Padthaway Chardonnay

▼▼▼▼▽ 2002 Light to medium yellow-green; the clean bouquet is fruit-driven, with a rainbow of aromas running through nectarine, melon and tropical fruit, characters which come through on the light to medium-bodied palate; here the winemaking touches become evident, with 50 per cent taken through malolactic fermentation, and 5 per cent barrel fermented in older casks. Gold medal 2002 Limestone Coast Wine Show.

best drinking Now **drink with** Red Rooster • $12.95 **rating:** 90

Stonehaven Limited Release Shiraz

▼▼▼▼▽ 1999 Bright, deep, red-purple; a rich, dense bouquet flooded with dark plum leads into a palate with great texture, length and structure, the only passing question being the tannins, which need to soften, but will do so before the fruit fades. **rating:** 90

best drinking 2004–2014 **best vintages** '99 **drink with** Roast venison • $26.99

Stonehaven Stepping Stone Padthaway Shiraz

▼▼▼▼ 2001 Medium red-purple; the dark fruit aromas of the bouquet have touches of leather, spice, licorice and game; the light to medium-bodied palate has blackberry and mulberry fruit, with the tannins under total control. Excellent value. **rating:** 87

best drinking Now–2007 **drink with** Grilled steak • $12.95

Stonehaven Limestone Coast Cabernet Merlot

▼▼▼▼ 1999 Medium to full red-purple; intense dark fruits, dark chocolate and integrated oak on the bouquet promise much but, not for the first time for Stonehaven, the palate is marred by excessive tannins. At the price, it could be worth putting a few bottles in a dark corner of the cellar and leaving them there for 5 years before trying again. **rating: 86**

best drinking 2007–2012 drink with Barbecued sausages • $15.99

Stonehaven Padthaway/Coonawarra Cabernet Merlot

▼▼▼▼ 1999 Medium red-purple; clean blackcurrant and mint fruit drives the bouquet, with the oak influence minimal; sweet blackcurrant and chocolate on the medium-bodied palate are lengthened by persistent but fine tannins. **rating: 89**

best drinking 2004–2009 drink with Herbed rack of lamb • $15.99

Stonehaven Stepping Stone Coonawarra Cabernet Sauvignon

▼▼▼▼▽ 2001 Made at Hardys Stonehaven winery in Padthaway, and a remarkable bargain. Strong red-purple, its bouquet has abundant sweet cassis/blackcurrant fruit; the palate replicates this fruit spectrum. Oak has been used less lavishly than in many Hardy family reds, which is all to the good. **rating: 91**

best drinking Now–2010 best vintages '01 drink with Lamb casserole • $12

stonemont   NR

421 Rochford Road, Rochford, Vic 3442 **region** Macedon Ranges
phone (03) 5429 1540 **fax** (03) 5429 1878 **open** By appointment
winemaker Contract **production** 500 cases **est.** 1997
product range ($18 R) Chardonnay, Sparkling Macedon, Pinot Noir.
summary Ray and Gail Hicks began the establishment of their vineyard in 1993, extending plantings to a total of 1.5 hectares each of chardonnay and pinot noir in 1996. The tiny production of Chardonnay, Pinot Noir and Sparkling Macedon is contract-made by various Macedon Ranges winemakers, and the wines are sold by mail order and (by appointment) through the cellar door, which is situated in a heritage stone barn on the vineyard site.

stone ridge   NR

35 Limberlost Road, Glen Aplin, Qld 4381 **region** Granite Belt
phone (07) 4683 4211 **fax** (07) 4683 4211 **open** 7 days 10–5
winemaker Jim Lawrie, Anne Kennedy **production** 2100 cases **est.** 1981
product range ($10–60 CD) Semillon, Marsanne, Viognier, Chardonnay, Pinot Noir, Shiraz, Cabernet Malbec, Cabernet Sauvignon; Mount Sterling Dry Red Shiraz.
summary Spicy Shiraz is the specialty of the doll's-house-sized winery, but the portfolio has progressively expanded over recent years to include two whites and the only Stanthorpe region Cabernet Malbec (and occasionally a straight varietal Malbec).

stoney rise   ★★★☆

PO Box 185, Stepney, SA 5069 **region** Mount Benson
phone (08) 8332 3682 **fax** (08) 8332 3682 **open** Not
winemaker Joe Holyman **production** 2000 cases **est.** 2000
product range ($15–20 ML) Sauvignon Blanc, Hey Hey Rose, Cotes du Robe Shiraz.
summary Matt Lowe and Joe Holyman met as 14-year-old schoolboys in Tasmania, then headed off in different directions, Joe Holyman to establish a record for the most catches by a wicketkeeper on debut in first-class cricket, Matt Lowe to see the world. They came together once again at Roseworthy undertaking the marketing degree, leading to positions as sales representatives. Matt then trained to be a chef, while Joe set off for a series of vintages in Burgundy, Provence and the Douro Valley. Their paths crossed again when they both began working at Cape Jaffa Wines at Robe on the Limestone Coast, and led to the establishment of their own brand as a side interest. Exports to the US.

Stoney Rise Sauvignon Blanc

▼▼▼▼ 2002 Light straw-green; the clean, crisp, minerally bouquet is followed by a fine, delicate palate with herb and mineral flavours. Sauvignon Blanc does not have to be sweaty. **rating: 88**

best drinking Now drink with Seafood • $18

Stoney Rise Hey Hey Rose

ŦŦŦŦ 2002 Light crimson-purple; lively, juicy, tangy aromas flow through into the crisp palate, with a bone-dry finish. Made from McLaren Vale Grenache.　　　　**rating: 87**

best drinking Now **drink with** Antipasto • $16

Stoney Rise Cotes du Robe Shiraz

ŦŦŦŦ 2001 Strong purple-red; the clean bouquet has abundant ripe plum fruit which, however, stops well short of being porty or jammy, and has a distinct touch of spice. The deep and powerful palate has youthful, juicy, fruit-driven flavours, and will become more complex with bottle age.　　　　**rating: 89**

best drinking 2004–2009 **drink with** Game pie • $20

stonier wines　　★★★★☆

362 Frankston–Flinders Road, Merricks, Vic 3916 **region** Mornington Peninsula
phone (03) 5989 8300 **fax** (03) 5989 8709 **open** 7 days 12–5 (summer 11–5)
winemaker Tod Dexter, Geraldine McFaul **production** 25 000 cases **est.** 1978
product range ($19–45 CD) Chardonnay, Reserve Chardonnay, Pinot Noir, Reserve Pinot Noir.
summary Looked at across the range, Stonier and Paringa Estate are now the pre-eminent wineries in the Mornington Peninsula; Stonier's standing is based more or less equally on its Chardonnay and Pinot Noir under the Reserve label. Its acquisition by Petaluma in 1998 has given both Stonier (and the Mornington Peninsula as a whole) even greater credibility than hitherto. Exports to the UK, Canada, Belgium, Germany, Italy, The Netherlands, New Zealand, Malaysia, Hong Kong, Singapore and Japan.

Stonier Chardonnay

ŦŦŦŦ 2001 Light to medium yellow-green; the moderately intense and elegant bouquet has discreet melon and white peach fruit, the equivalently light to medium-bodied palate providing first-up citrus and melon, then a whiff of smoky oak.　　　　**rating: 87**

best drinking Now–2005 **best vintages** '91, '93, '94, '97, '98, '00 **drink with** Seafood pasta • $22

Stonier Reserve Chardonnay

ŦŦŦŦŸ 2001 Light to medium yellow-green; an elegant, fruit-driven bouquet offers intense melon and citrus fruit, with restrained oak; similar melon and citrus fruit drives the palate, tightened and lengthened by brisk acidity; the oak is very well-integrated.　　　　**rating: 91**

best drinking Now–2006 **best vintages** '86, '88, '91, '93, '94, '95, '96, '97, '98, '99, '00 **drink with** Milk-fed veal • $39

Stonier Pinot Noir

ŦŦŦŦŸ 2001 Medium red-purple, bright and clear; the bouquet has distinctive herb and sage edges together with a dash of spice; a stylish wine on the palate, well balanced and not extractive, centred on sweet cherry; good length and persistent, fine tannins.　　　　**rating: 90**

best drinking Now–2006 **best vintages** '92, '94, '95, '97, '00, '01 **drink with** Game of any kind • $23

Stonier Reserve Pinot Noir

ŦŦŦŦŸ 2001 Light to medium red-purple; clean, fresh cherry/strawberry aromas are reflected by the palate, with the accent on primary varietal fruit; will undoubtedly develop complexity with time.　　　　**rating: 92**

best drinking Now–2008 **best vintages** '90, '91, '92, '94, '95, '97, '99, '00, '01 **drink with** Coq au vin • $45

stratherne vale estate　　NR

Campbell Street, Caballing, WA 6312 **region** Central Western Australia Zone
phone (08) 9881 2148 **fax** (08) 9881 3129 **open** Not
winemaker Contract **production** 600 cases **est.** 1980
product range A single red wine made from a blend of Cabernet Sauvignon, Zinfandel, Merlot and Shiraz.
summary Stratherne Vale Estate stretches the viticultural map of Australia yet further. It is situated near Narrogin, which is north of the Great Southern region and south of the most generous extension of the Darling Ranges. The closest viticultural region of note is at Wandering, to the northeast.

strathewen hills　　NR

1090 Strathewen Road, Strathewen, Vic 3099 **region** Yarra Valley
phone (03) 9714 8464 **fax** (03) 9714 8464 **open** By appointment
winemaker William Christophersen **est.** 1991

product range ($32–75 R) Chardonnay, Pinot Noir, Merlot, Tribal Elder Shiraz, Merlot Cabernets.

summary Joan and William (whom, I have always called Bill) Christophersen began the slow process of establishing Strathewen Hills in 1991. The vineyard was established with ultra-close spacing, with 3 hectares planted predominantly to pinot noir, chardonnay, shiraz, merlot and small amounts of cabernet sauvignon, cabernet franc and a few bits and pieces, but frost caused persistent losses until protective sprinklers were installed. The first two commercial releases from the 2000 vintage are excellent wines, bearing testimony to both Bill Christophersen's undoubted skills as a winemaker and the ideal vintage. They also operate Sugar Loaf Cottage, a two-bedroom, self-contained bed and breakfast. No subsequent tastings.

strathkellar   NR

Murray Valley Highway, Cobram, Vic 3644 **region** Goulburn Valley
phone (03) 5873 5274 **fax** (03) 5873 5270 **open** 7 days 10–5
winemaker Tahbilk (Contract) **production** 2000 cases **est.** 1990
product range ($10–18 CD) Chenin Blanc, Chardonnay, Sparkling Brut Reserve, Sparkling Shiraz, Late Picked Chenin Blanc, Sweet Muscatel, Shiraz, Grenache Shiraz Mataro, Muscat, Tokay, Putters Port, Old Putters Port.
summary Dick Parkes planted his 6-hectare vineyard to chardonnay, shiraz and chenin blanc in 1990, and has the wine contract-made at Tahbilk by Alister Purbrick. The fact that the wines are made at Tahbilk is a sure guarantee of quality, and the prices are modest.

🐌 strath valley vineyard   NR

Strath Valley Road, Strath Creek, Vic 3658 **region** Central Victorian High Country
phone (03) 5784 9229 **fax** (03) 5784 9381 **open** Weekends 10–5, or by appointment
winemaker Contract **production** 1300 cases **est.** 1994
product range Sauvignon Blanc, Boundary Range Shiraz.
summary Chris and Robyn Steen have established 12.5 hectares of chardonnay, sauvignon blanc, cabernet sauvignon and shiraz. By far the largest part of the production is sold as grapes, with around 1300 cases of Sauvignon Blanc and Shiraz being sold through the cellar door.

straws lane   NR

1282 Mount Macedon Road, Hesket, Vic 3442 **region** Macedon Ranges
phone (03) 9654 9380 **fax** (03) 9663 6300 **open** Weekends and public holidays 10–4, or by appointment
winemaker Stuart Anderson, John Ellis **production** 1800 cases **est.** 1987
product range ($22–40 R) Gewurztraminer, Blanc de Noirs, Pinot Noir.
summary The Straws Lane vineyard was planted in 1987, but the Straws Lane label is a relatively new arrival on the scene; after a highly successful 1995 vintage, adverse weather in 1996 and 1997 meant that little or no wine was made in those years, but the pace picked up again with subsequent vintages. Stuart Anderson guides the making of the Pinot Noir, Hanging Rock Winery handles the Gewurztraminer and the sparkling wine base, and Cope-Williams looks after the tiraging and maturation of the sparkling wine. It's good to have co-operative neighbours.

stringy brae   ★★★★

Sawmill Road, Sevenhill, SA 5453 **region** Clare Valley
phone (08) 8843 4313 **fax** (08) 8843 4319 **open** Weekends and public holidays 10–5, Mon–Fri refer to road sign
winemaker Contract (Mitchell) **production** 2500 cases **est.** 1991
product range ($16–58 CD) Riesling, Sparkling Riesling, Shiraz, Mote Hill Reserve Black Knight Shiraz, Cabernet Sauvignon.
summary Donald and Sally Willson have established over 10 hectares of vineyards that since the 1996 vintage have produced all the grapes for their wines. (Previously grapes from Langhorne Creek were used.) The Australian domestic market is serviced direct by mail order, and the wines are exported to the UK and the US.

Stringy Brae Cabernet Sauvignon

🍷🍷🍷🍷♀ **2000** Medium red-purple; the moderately intense bouquet has some dusty/earthy overtones to the blackcurrant fruit, the wine shifting into top gear on the palate, which has silky and harmonious flavours, texture and mouthfeel.   **rating:** 91

best drinking 2005–2015 **best vintages** '00 **drink with** Chump chops • $20

stuart range estates ★★★

67 William Street, Kingaroy, Qld 4610 **region** South Burnett
phone (07) 4162 3711 **fax** (07) 4162 4811 **open** 7 days 9–5
winemaker Ross Whiteford **production** 15 000 cases **est.** 1997
product range ($9–18 CD) Semillon, Verdelho, SRE Chardonnay, Goodger Chardonnay, Range White and Range Red (both semi-sweet), Shiraz, Goodger Shiraz, Cabernet Merlot, Cabernet Sauvignon Shiraz Merlot, Cabernet Sauvignon, Blue Moon Liqueur, Explorer Port.
summary Stuart Range Estates is a prime example of the extent and pace of change in the Queensland wine industry, coming from nowhere in 1997 to crushing just under 120 tonnes of grapes in its inaugural vintage in 1998. The grapes are supplied by up to 7 growers in the South Burnett Valley with 52 hectares planted at the winery by 1996. A state-of-the-art winery has been established within an old butter factory building. The barrel-fermented Chardonnay won the trophy for the Best Queensland White Wine in the annual Courier-Mail Top 100 Wine Competition some years ago.

Stuart Range Estates Verdelho

TTTT 2002 Light straw-green; the aromatic bouquet has tropical fruit salad and citrus aromas; the light to medium-bodied palate is clean and within the limitations of the variety, well made. **rating:** 84
best drinking Now **drink with** Seafood salad • $15

Stuart Range Estates Cabernet Sauvignon Shiraz Merlot

TTTT 2001 Medium red-purple; the bouquet is clean but very light, with red berry fruit; the palate is clean, soft and fresh, not over-extracted, with light, minty red fruits. Simply lacks concentration and, to a degree, ripeness. **rating:** 83
best drinking Now–2005 **drink with** Veal • $14

🐚 studley park vineyard NR

5 Garden Terrace, Kew, Vic 3101 (postal) **region** Port Phillip Zone
phone (03) 9254 2777 **fax** (03) 9254 2535 **open** Not
winemaker Llew Knight (Contract) **production** 250 cases **est.** 1994
product range ($25 R) Cabernet.
summary Geoff Pryor's Studley Park Vineyard is one of Melbourne's best-kept secrets. It is situated on a bend of the Yarra River barely 4 kilometres from the Melbourne CBD on a 0.5-hectare block once planted to vines, but for a century used for market gardening. A spectacular aerial photograph shows how immediately across the river, and looking directly to the CBD, is the epicentre of Melbourne's light industrial development, while on the northern and eastern boundaries are suburban residential blocks. The vineyard is sheltered (and hidden) by groves of large elm and plane trees, although a glimpse of it can be seen from the Walmer Street footbridge which forms part of the main Yarra Trail. Because of zoning restrictions, cellar-door tastings and sales are not possible at the vineyard, and most sales take place over the internet from the website, www.studleypark.com.

Studley Park Vineyard Cabernet

TTTT 1998 Medium red-purple; the intense bouquet has berry fruit, with a strong earthy undertone, and a touch of mint; the light to medium-bodied palate focuses more on the mint and berry fruit, finishing with soft tannins. **rating:** 86
best drinking Now–2008 **drink with** Marinated beef • $25

stumpy gully ★★★☆

1247 Stumpy Gully Road, Moorooduc, Vic 3933 **region** Mornington Peninsula
phone (03) 5978 8429 **fax** (03) 5978 8419 **open** Weekends 11–5
winemaker Wendy Zantvoort, Maitena Zantvoort, Ewan Campbell **production** 3000 cases **est.** 1988
product range ($12–22 CD) Riesling, Sauvignon Blanc, Marsanne, Pinot Grigio, Chardonnay, Botrytis Riesling, Pinot Noir, Sangiovese, Shiraz, Merlot Cabernet, Cabernet Sauvignon, Fortified Sauvignon Blanc; Peninsula Panorama Chardonnay, Pinot Noir.
summary When Frank and Wendy Zantvoort began planting their first vineyard in 1989 there were no winemakers in the family; now there are three, plus two viticulturists. Mother Wendy was first to obtain her degree from Charles Sturt University, followed by daughter Maitena, who then married Ewan Campbell, another winemaker. Father Frank and son Michael look after the vineyards. The original vineyard has 9 hectares of vines, but in establishing the new 20-hectare Moorooduc vineyard (first harvest 2001) the Zantvoorts have deliberately gone against prevailing thinking, planting it solely to red varieties, predominately cabernet

sauvignon, merlot and shiraz. They believe they have one of the warmest sites on the Peninsula, and that ripening will in fact present no problems. In all they now have 10 varieties planted, producing a dozen different wines. Exports to the UK and Holland.

Stumpy Gully Riesling

TTTT 2002 Light green-yellow; the bouquet is clean, with a mix of mineral, apple and nashi pear; the palate is likewise crisp, tight and minerally, needing time to flower.   **rating:** 87

best drinking 2005–2010 **drink with** Seafood • $22

Stumpy Gully Chardonnay

TTTT 2001 Medium yellow-green; stone fruit and citrus marry with subtle oak on the bouquet; the light to medium-bodied palate has cashew flavours, and typical Mornington Peninsula subtle texture.   **rating:** 88

best drinking Now–2006 **drink with** Milk-fed veal • $16

Peninsula Panorama Chardonnay

TTTT 2001 Light green-yellow; clean, fresh and uncomplicated citrus/stone fruit aromas are reflected in the fresh, direct palate, which has quite intense fruit and good length. Just the stuff for early drinking.   **rating:** 87

best drinking Now **drink with** Takeaway • $12

Stumpy Gully Pinot Noir

TTTT 2001 Light red-purple; while light, the bouquet is quite aromatic, spicy and scented; the palate offers fresh strawberry and cherry fruit in a light-bodied frame. To be enjoyed as soon as possible.   **rating:** 86

best drinking Now **drink with** Light antipasto • $20

Stumpy Gully Merlot Cabernet

TTTT 2000 Medium red-purple; the moderately intense aromas of leaf, berry and earth are followed by rather sweeter and riper berry fruit on the palate; the oak influence is minimal, the tannins fine and soft. Reflects the excellent vintage for the late-ripening varieties.   **rating:** 88

best drinking 2004–2008 **drink with** Osso buco • $20

Stumpy Gully Cabernet Sauvignon

TTTT 2000 Medium red-purple; a mix of quite sweet mint and blackcurrant fruit, a touch of oak and a hint of earth on the bouquet lead into a light to medium-bodied palate, more to redcurrant/raspberry, finishing with fine tannins. Not quite as much mid-palate flavour as the Merlot Cabernet.   **rating:** 86

best drinking 2004–2008 **drink with** Roast lamb • $20

suckfizzle & stella bella   ★★★★☆

PO Box 403, Nedlands, WA 6909 **region** Margaret River
phone (08) 9389 6778 **fax** (08) 9389 6728 **open** Not
winemaker Janice McDonald **production** 15 000 cases **est.** 1997
product range ($17–45 R) Suckfizzle range of Sauvignon Blanc Semillon, Cabernet Sauvignon; Stella Bella range of Sauvignon Blanc, Semillon Sauvignon Blanc, Pink Muscat, Shiraz, Cabernet Merlot, Sangiovese Cabernet Sauvignon.
summary First things first. The back label explains: 'the name Suckfizzle has been snaffled from the 14th century monk and medico turned writer Rabelais and his infamous character the great Lord Suckfizzle'. Suckfizzle is the joint venture of two well known Margaret River winemakers who, in deference to their employers, do not identify themselves on any of the background material or the striking front and back labels of the wines. Exports to Singapore, Belgium and Canada.

Stella Bella Sauvignon Blanc

TTTTT 2002 An outrageous name and striking, avant garde (but beautiful) labelling gives a clue to the two semi-silent partners in the business. Striking straw-green, then a bouquet ranging through grass, herb, flint and a hint of smoke. The spotlessly clean palate leaves the mouth with a great aftertaste. Gulp, don't sip. **rating:** 94

best drinking Now **best vintages** '01, '02 **drink with** Margaret River abalone • $23

Stella Bella Semillon Sauvignon Blanc

TTTTY 2002 Light straw-green; a crisp and lively minerally bouquet leads into a wine with complex structure and mouthfeel, filling all the corners with an appealing blend of flavours.   **rating:** 92

best drinking Now–2006 **best vintages** '02 **drink with** Margaret River abalone • $20

Stella Bella Pink Muscat

ŸŸŸŸ 2002 Vivid pink; grapey/juicy aromas and flavours are cleverly balanced on the palate to provide a wholly seductive glass of fun.   **rating:** 88

best drinking Now **drink with** Nothing needed • $17

Stella Bella Shiraz

ŸŸŸŸŸ 2001 Dense purple-red; firm black cherry and plum aromas show the first signs of developing complexity. The powerful and concentrated palate has abundant ripe tannins and overall flavour, simply reinforcing the need for patience.   **rating:** 91

best drinking 2006–2011 **best vintages** '01 **drink with** Braised oxtail • $23

Stella Bella Sangiovese Cabernet Sauvignon

ŸŸŸŸŸ 2001 Medium to full purple-red; a fragrant bouquet with cassis, cherry and raspberry aromas which provide the fruit on the palate with its strong structure and persistent tannins. An interesting wine, which may develop into something special.   **rating:** 90

best drinking 2005–2010 **drink with** Bistecca Fiorentino • $27

Stella Bella Cabernet Sauvignon Merlot

ŸŸŸŸ 2000 Medium red-purple; an aromatic mix of dark berry, olive, leaf and mint is followed by a palate with good mouthfeel, thanks to a touch of oak sweetening and softer tannins.   **rating:** 89

best drinking 2004–2009 **drink with** Rack of lamb • $26

Suckfizzle Augusta Cabernet Sauvignon

ŸŸŸŸŸ 2000 Medium red-purple; a strongly varietal earthy/savoury/blackberry bouquet is followed by an intense and concentrated palate with an overall richness of texture, the flavours of the bouquet being joined by a touch of bitter chocolate and supported by quality French oak.   **rating:** 92

best drinking 2007–2017 **best vintages** '00 **drink with** Braised beef • $45

summerfield ★★★★☆

Main Road, Moonambel, Vic 3478 **region** Pyrenees
phone (03) 5467 2264 **fax** (03) 5467 2380 **open** 7 days 9–5.30
winemaker Ian Summerfield, Mark Summerfield **production** 3500 cases **est.** 1979
product range ($10–43 CD) Sauvignon Blanc, Trebbiano, Shiraz, Reserve Shiraz, Shiraz Cabernet, Cabernet Merlot, Cabernet Sauvignon, Reserve Cabernet.
summary A specialist red wine producer, the particular forte of which is Shiraz. The wines since 1988 have been consistently excellent: luscious and full-bodied and fruit-driven, but with a slice of vanillin oak to top them off. Exports to the US and the UK.

Summerfield Shiraz

ŸŸŸŸŸ 2001 Full red-purple; the bouquet is rich and dense but not jammy, with a mix of blackberry, plum and vanilla oak; there is commensurately abundant ripe fruit on the palate, but equally well-controlled extract; good balance and length at an appealing price.   **rating:** 91

best drinking 2005–2015 **best vintages** '79, '83, '88, '91, '92, '93, '94, '96, '97, '99, '00, '01 **drink with** Beef stew • $23

Summerfield Reserve Shiraz

ŸŸŸŸŸ 2001 Inky purple-red; dense, dark, blackberry/black cherry fruit, almost into cassis on the bouquet, then mouthfilling, ripe and luscious fruit, with hints of prune. The alcohol is evident without burning.   **rating:** 94

best drinking 2006–2016 **best vintages** '98, '99, '00, '01 **drink with** Venison pie • $42

Summerfield Merlot

ŸŸŸŸ 2001 Full red-purple; the solid bouquet exudes rich, ripe dark fruits; the palate follows closely with incredibly rich, ripe, mouthfilling chocolatey fruit; only Australia could produce a wine such as this from merlot.   **rating:** 89

best drinking 2006–2011 **drink with** Venison with blackcurrant jus • $35

Summerfield Cabernet Sauvignon

ŸŸŸŸŸ 2001 Medium to full red-purple; deep, dark blackcurrant/berry fruit on the bouquet flows into masses of sweet blackcurrant fruit on the palate; lingering but ripe tannins and subtle oak.   **rating:** 92

best drinking 2006–2016 **best vintages** '88, '90, '91, '92, '93, '94, '97, '01 **drink with** Rare beef • $23

Summerfield Reserve Cabernet

▼▼▼▼▼ **2001** Medium to full red-purple; deep blackcurrant/berry fruit on the bouquet, slightly less opulent but more focused than the varietal version; powerful, mouth-coating fruit on the palate, which has exemplary length; the overall extract and tannin management are outstanding. **rating: 94**

best drinking 2011–2021 **best vintages** '00, '01 **drink with** Osso buco • $43

summit estate ★★★

291 Granite Belt Drive, Thulimbah, Qld 4377 **region** Granite Belt
phone (07) 4683 2011 **fax** (07) 4683 2600 **open** 7 days 9–5
winemaker Paola Carberaz Bono **production** 2800 cases **est.** 1997
product range ($12–26 CD) Semillon Chardonnay, Verdelho, Chardonnay, Reserve Chardonnay, Sweet White, Sweet Red, Sparkling Pinot Noir, Emily Rose, Reserve Pinot Noir, Shiraz, Shiraz Cabernet Sauvignon, Reserve Merlot, Cabernets Merlot, Cabernet Sauvignon, Golden Gleam, Liqueur Muscat, Tawny Port.
summary Summit Estate is the public face of the Stanthorpe Wine Co., owned by a syndicate of 10 professionals who work in Brisbane, but who share a love of wine. They operate the Stanthorpe Wine Centre, which offers wine education as well as selling wines from other makers in the region and, of course, Summit Estate. They have established a vineyard with 3 hectares of shiraz, 2 hectares each of cabernet sauvignon and merlot, and 1 hectare each of petit verdot, tempranillo and verdelho, and have set up a small, specialised winemaking facility. Summit Estate wines received three bronze medals at the 2002 Australian Small Winemakers Show.

Summit Estate Reserve Chardonnay

▼▼▼▽ **2002** Light to medium green-yellow; very strong, charry barrel-ferment aromas, with American oak dominant, are followed by a palate where the oak is similarly overplayed, but certainly shows no shortage of effort. Made from Granite Belt grapes and barrel fermented in French and American oak. **rating: 84**

best drinking Now–2005 **drink with** Quiche Lorraine • $20

surveyor's hill winery NR

215 Brooklands Road, Wallaroo, NSW 2618 **region** Canberra District
phone (02) 6230 2046 **fax** (02) 6230 2048 **open** Weekends and public holidays or by appointment
winemaker Contract **production** 1000 cases **est.** 1986
product range ($10–22 R) Riesling, Sauvignon Blanc, Pinot Noir, Rosado Touriga, Shiraz, Cabernet Merlot.
summary Surveyor's Hill has 10 hectares of vineyard, but most of the grapes are sold to BRL Hardy Kamberra, which vinifies the remainder for Surveyor's Hill – which should guarantee the quality of the wines sold. Also offers bed and breakfast accommodation.

sutherland smith wines NR

Cnr Falkners Road and Murray Valley Highway, Rutherglen, Vic 3685 **region** Rutherglen
phone (02) 6032 8177 **fax** (02) 6032 8177 **open** Weekends, public and Victorian school holidays 10–5, other Fridays 11–5
winemaker George Sutherland-Smith **production** 1000 cases **est.** 1993
product range ($12.70–100 CD) Riesling, Josephine (Riesling Traminer), Chardonnay, George's Private Blend Shiraz Cabernet, George's Private Blend Merlot Cabernet Shiraz, Cabernet Shiraz, Cabernet Sauvignon, Port, Vintage Port.
summary George Sutherland-Smith, for decades managing director and winemaker at All Saints, has opened up his own small business at Rutherglen, making wine in the refurbished Emu Plains winery, which was constructed in the 1850s. He draws upon fruit grown in a leased vineyard at Glenrowan and also from grapes grown in the King Valley.

swanbrook estate wines ★★★☆

38 Swan Street, Henley Brook, WA 6055 **region** Swan Valley
phone (08) 9296 3100 **fax** (08) 9296 3099 **open** 7 days 10–5
winemaker Rob Marshall **production** 10 000 cases **est.** 1998
product range ($12–40 CD) Semillon, Classic Dry White, Chenin (wood aged), Verdelho, Chardonnay, Classic Shiraz, Estate Shiraz, Cabernet Merlot.

summary This is the reincarnation of Evans & Tate's Gnangara Winery. It secures most of its grapes from contract growers in the Perth Hills and Swan Valley, but also has the 60-year-old block of shiraz around the winery. A little under 40 per cent of the annual crush is for the Swanbrook label, the remainder being contract winemaking for others. Owner John Andreou (a Perth restaurateur) has invested $2 million in upgrading and expanding the facilities, and former Evans & Tate winemaker Rob Marshall has continued at Swanbrook, providing valuable continuity. Rated on the basis of previous tastings.

swan valley wines ★★★

261 Haddrill Road, Baskerville, WA 6065 **region** Swan Valley
phone (08) 9296 1501 **fax** (08) 9296 1733 **open** Fri–Sun and public holidays 10–5
winemaker Julie White (Contract) **production** 1000 cases **est.** 1999
product range ($13.50–16.50 CD) Semillon, Chenin Blanc, Chardonnay, Grenache Blush, Shiraz, Grenache, White Port, Tawny Port.
summary Peter and Paula Hoffman, together with sons Paul and Thomas, acquired their 6-hectare property in 1989. It had a long history of grape growing, and the prior owner had registered the name Swan Valley Wines back in 1983. In 1999 the family built a new winery to handle the grapes from 2.3 hectares of chenin blanc, 1.4 hectares of grenache, a little over 0.5 hectare each of semillon, malbec and cabernet sauvignon and a smaller amount of shiraz. South African-trained Julie White is contract winemaker. Exports to Japan. Rated on the basis of previous tastings.

sylvan springs estates ★★★☆

RSD 405, Blythmans Road, McLaren Flat, SA 5171 (postal) **region** McLaren Vale
phone (08) 8383 0500 **fax** (08) 8383 0499 **open** Not
winemaker Brian Light (Consultant) **production** 2000 cases **est.** 1974
product range ($12–17.60 ML) Chardonnay, Shiraz, Cabernet Sauvignon.
summary The Pridmore family has been involved in grape growing and winemaking in McLaren Vale for four generations, spanning over 100 years. The pioneer was Cyril Pridmore, who established The Wattles Winery in 1896 and purchased Sylvan Park, one of the original homesteads in the area, in 1901. The original family land in the township of McLaren Vale was sold in 1978, but not before third-generation Digby Pridmore had established new vineyards (in 1974) near Blewitt Springs. When he retired in 1990, his son David purchased the 45-hectare vineyard (planted to 11 different varieties) and, with sister Sally, ventured into winemaking in 1996, with Brian Light as consultant winemaker.

Sylvan Springs Estates Cabernet Sauvignon

▼▼▼▼ 2001 Medium red-purple; an earthy, savoury mix of blackberry, blackcurrant and chocolate on the bouquet comes together well on the medium-bodied, fruit-driven palate, which finishes with soft tannins.   **rating:** 87
best drinking 2005–2010 **drink with** Braised beef • $17.60

symphonia wines ★★★★

1699 Boggy Creek Road, Myrrhee, Vic 3732 **region** King Valley
phone (03) 5729 7519 **fax** (03) 5729 7519 **open** By appointment
winemaker Peter Read **production** 2000 cases **est.** 1998
product range ($15–30 CD) Riesling, Chardonnay Plus, Viognier Petit Manseng, Pinot Grigio, Pinot Chardonnay, Blanc de Blanc, Quintus, Merlot, Merlot Plus, Saperavi, Las Triadas.
summary Peter Read and his family are veterans of the King Valley, commencing the development of their vineyard in 1981 to supply Brown Brothers. As a result of extensive trips to both Western and Eastern Europe, Peter Read embarked on an ambitious project to trial a series of grape varieties little known in this country. The process of evaluation and experimentation continues, but since Symphonia released the first small quantities of wines in mid-1998 it has built on that start. A number of the wines have great interest and no less merit.

Symphonia Riesling

▼▼▼▼▽ 2002 Very pale straw-green; a clean, crisp, minerally bouquet leads into a lively mix of melon, citrus and mineral on the palate. Overall, very fresh and well balanced. King Valley Riesling doesn't come much better than this.   **rating:** 90
best drinking Now–2007 **drink with** Sashimi • $15

Symphonia Pinot Grigio

▼▼▼▼ 2002 Pale straw-green; spotlessly clean light apple, pear and mineral aromas; the crisp palate gains its length through the steely core of acidity, although the fruit does build somewhat. Well made.   **rating:** 85
best drinking Now–2005 **drink with** Vegetarian • $17.50

Symphonia Quintus

ΥΥΥΥ **2002** Medium purple-red; scented berry aromas with touches of mint and leaf lead into a well-structured and balanced medium to full-bodied palate. Here some earth and chocolate flavours join those promised by the bouquet; the oak is incidental, the acidity not.   **rating:** 87

best drinking 2006–2011 **best vintages** '99, '00 **drink with** Pasta with meat sauce • $20

Symphonia Las Triadas

ΥΥΥΥ **2002** Medium purple-red; the spicy, perfumed bouquet has some interesting crushed leaf aromas; the palate is potent, but not over-extracted. The fruit is intense, the brisk acidity likewise. Worth waiting for, but the end point is not easy to pick. Tempranillo/Cabernet Merlot blend.   **rating:** 87

best drinking 2004–2008 **drink with** Bratwurst • $20

Symphonia Saperavi

ΥΥΥΥ **2002** Dense purple-red, as its name ('dyer' in Russian) suggests. There is an array of powerful blackberry spice and pepper aromas, moving into a massively concentrated palate which is in balance, however formidable it may be at the moment. Needs 5 years at least, preferably ten.   **rating:** 89

best drinking 2007–2017 **drink with** Leave it in the cellar • $20

tahbilk ★★★★

Goulburn Valley Highway, Tabilk, Vic 3607 **region** Nagambie Lakes
phone (03) 5794 2555 **fax** (03) 5794 2360 **open** Mon–Sat 9–5, Sun 11–5
winemaker Alister Purbrick, Neil Larson, Alan George **production** 125 000 cases **est.** 1860
product range ($7.95–119.50 R) Riesling, Semillon, Sauvignon Blanc, Marsanne, Roussanne, Viognier, Verdelho, Chardonnay, Dulcet (sweet white), Brut Cuvee, Sparkling Lexia, Shiraz, 1933 Vines Reserve Shiraz, Cabernet Franc, Merlot, Malbec, Cabernet Merlot, Cabernet Sauvignon; 1860 Vines Shiraz is rare flagship, with a Reserve red released from each vintage; fortifieds.
summary A winery steeped in tradition (with high National Trust classification), which should be visited at least once by every wine-conscious Australian, and which makes wines – particularly red wines – utterly in keeping with that tradition. The essence of that heritage comes in the form of the tiny quantities of Shiraz made entirely from vines planted in 1860. As well as Australian national distribution through Tucker Seabrook, Tahbilk has agents in every principal wine market, including the UK, Europe, Asia and North America.

Tahbilk Viognier

ΥΥΥΥ **2002** Medium yellow-green; the full-blown bouquet offers dried fruit, pear and apricot aromas; the palate has similarly sturdy flavour, again showing some dried fruit characters, yet not phenolic. Thoroughly user-friendly.   **rating:** 88

best drinking Now–2005 **best vintages** '00 **drink with** Stacked eggplant • $14.95

Tahbilk Marsanne

ΥΥΥΥΥ **2001** Tried, true and trusty are the watch words both for Tahbilk and its marsanne, but don't underestimate the ability of the wine to blossom with age. The bouquet is showing the first signs of the honeysuckle and toast to come; the palate has good depth and a touch of sweet lime to lengthen the finish.   **rating:** 90

best drinking Now–2010 **best vintages** '53, '79, '80, '84, '87, '88, '89, '93, '95, '01 **drink with** Lighter Italian or Asian dishes • $12

Tahbilk Museum Release Marsanne

ΥΥΥΥΥ **1997** Glowing yellow-green; the bouquet offers an intense mix of toast, honey and honeysuckle; the palate has even weight and flow, and a fine and long finish. When first tasted back in October 1998 it was given 87 points, which simply serves to show the rewards for cellaring Marsanne in most (though not all) vintages.   **rating:** 92

best drinking Now–2007 **drink with** Sweetbreads • $16.95

Tahbilk Shiraz

ΥΥΥΥ **2000** Medium red-purple; the moderately intense bouquet has a mix of typically earthy/savoury aromas and red fruits at the centre. The palate is soft and quite supple, again showing savoury/briary characters, and finishes with fine tannins.   **rating:** 87

best drinking 2005–2015 **best vintages** '68, '71, '76, '78, '79, '81, '84, '86, '91, '98, '99 **drink with** Barbecued T-bone steak • $19.95

Tahbilk 1860 Vines Shiraz

TTTTY **1997** Medium red-purple; the moderately intense bouquet is smooth, with pleasingly sweet cherry/raspberry varietal fruit and the oak subdued. The palate, while driven by fruit, is very much the iron fist in velvet glove style, with excellent tannin and extract management. Reminiscent of the 1971 Tahbilk Shiraz tasted a few days previously in another context.   **rating:** 93

best drinking 2007–2017 **best vintages** '82, '84, '86, '91, '92, '95, '97 **drink with** Marinated venison • $119.50

Tahbilk Reserve Shiraz

TTTTY **1997** Red-purple, good for the age of the wine; the moderately intense bouquet has a complex earthy/savoury edge to the blackberry and spice fruit; the complex structure of the palate is sustained by fine tannins running throughout its length; in thoroughly traditional style for Tahbilk, although aged in French oak (rather than American) for 18 months.   **rating:** 90

best drinking 2004–2017 **best vintages** '94 **drink with** Lamb Provençale • $52.95

Tahbilk Cabernet Sauvignon

TTTT **2000** Medium red-purple; a mix of cedary, savoury berry aromas then a palate with red berry, mint and earth and fine, lingering tannins. Business-like and unpretentious.   **rating:** 87

best drinking 2004–2012 **best vintages** '65, '68, '71, '72, '76, '78, '79, '86, '90, '92, '97, '98, '99 **drink with** Strong mature cheddar, Stilton • $19.95

Tahbilk Reserve Cabernet Sauvignon

TTTTY **1997** Medium red-purple; a solid bouquet in traditional earthy/dusty varietal mode, backed by subtle oak, is followed by a palate which presents an altogether different picture: it is rich and sweet, with lots of blackcurrant fruit, balanced tannins and the usual downplayed oak.   **rating:** 91

best drinking 2007–2017 **best vintages** '62, '65, '68, '71, '75, '76, '80, '81, '82, '84, '85, '90, '94, '97 **drink with** Rich red meat dishes • $64.50

tait wines ★★★☆

Yaldara Drive, Lyndoch, SA 5351 **region** Barossa Valley
phone (08) 8524 5000 **fax** (08) 8524 5220 **open** Weekends and public holidays 11–5, or by appointment
winemaker Bruno Tait **production** 2000 cases **est.** 1994
product range ($15–30 CD) Chardonnay, Liquid Gold Fronti, Basket Pressed Shiraz, The Ball Buster (Shiraz Cabernet Merlot blend), Basket Pressed Cabernet Sauvignon.
summary The Tait family has been involved in the wine industry in the Barossa for over 100 years, making not wine but barrels. Their recent venture into winemaking was immediately successful; retail distribution through single outlets in Melbourne, Adelaide and Sydney; exports to the US, Germany, Malaysia and Singapore.

Tait Basket Pressed Shiraz

TTTT **2001** Medium red-purple; there is a curious leafy, spicy, foresty edge to the ripe berry aromas, but the palate comes back towards the mainstream, with blackberry and bitter chocolate flavours. Comes as a let-down after the marvellous '99.   **rating:** 86

best drinking 2006–2011 **best vintages** '99 **drink with** Rich game • $30

Tait The Ball Buster

TTTT **2001** Medium red-purple; the aromas dance around with minty, leafy, savoury, tobacco and pine all evident, the intense palate picking up all these characters in an aggressive framework. The alcohol is 14.9°, very hard to reconcile with some of the greener aspects of the wine. I'll go along with the name, however politically incorrect; for the record, it is a blend of Shiraz, Cabernet Sauvignon and Merlot.   **rating:** 85

best drinking 2007–2012 **drink with** Extreme caution • $15

Tait Basket Pressed Cabernet Sauvignon

TTTT **2001** Medium red-purple; clean blackberry and blackcurrant fruit is supported by a nice touch of oak on the bouquet; there is rich, quite lush fruit on entry into the mouth, then lingering tannins on the finish; plenty of character, and by far the most conventional of the Tait wines.   **rating:** 89

best drinking 2006–2012 **drink with** Beef spare ribs • $25

Tait Liquid Gold Fronti

TTTT **NV** Golden salmon; the bouquet is clean, with some biscuity/cake complexity, which is mirrored on the palate. A slightly hot, spirity finish detracts a little.   **rating:** 85

best drinking Now **drink with** Cake or pastry desserts • $20

talga ★★★★

824 Milbrodale Road, Broke, NSW 2330 **region** Canberra District
phone (02) 6579 1111 **fax** (02) 6579 1440 **open** At Little's Winery 7 days 10–4.30
winemaker Suzanne Little **production** 2000 cases **est.** 1998
product range ($24–26 CD) Chardonnay, Shiraz.
summary Talga is a partnership between two viticulturists – Anne and Anthony Richard – and their daughter and son-in-law, Suzanne and Ian Little, both winemakers at Little's Hunter Valley Winery. The vineyard was planted between 1980 and 1996 at an altitude of nearly 700 metres on the slopes of the Gundaroo Valley near Canberra. There are 2.1 hectares of shiraz and 0.9 hectare of chardonnay. The first commercial crop in 1998 was sent to Little's, originally with the intention of using it as part of a blend of other non-Hunter material. However, the quality was such that the parcels were kept separate and the partnership formed. Exports to the US.

talijancich NR

26 Hyem Road, Herne Hill, WA 6056 **region** Swan Valley
phone (08) 9296 4289 **fax** (08) 9296 1762 **open** Sun–Fri 11–5
winemaker James Talijancich **production** 10 000 cases **est.** 1932
product range ($17–135 CD) Verdelho, Voices Dry White, Grenache, Shiraz, Julian James White Liqueur, Julian James Red Liqueur, Liqueur Tokay 375 ml.
summary A former fortified wine specialist (with old Liqueur Tokay) now making a select range of table wines, with particular emphasis on Verdelho – on the third Saturday of August each year there is a tasting of fine 3-year-old Verdelho table wines from both Australia and overseas. Also runs an active wine club and exports to China, Japan and Hong Kong.

taliondal NR

270 Old North Road, Pokolbin, NSW 2320 **region** Lower Hunter Valley
phone (02) 9427 6812 **fax** (02) 9427 6812 **open** By appointment
winemaker Frank Brady **production** 240 cases **est.** 1974
product range ($8–15 ML) Traminer, Cab Fizz, Cabernet Sauvignon.
summary The Brady Bunch, headed by Frank Brady, acquired Taliondal in 1974 as a family hideaway. Says Frank Brady, 'When in the Hunter do as the Hunter does', so 1 hectare of cabernet sauvignon was planted in 1974, and 1.5 hectares of traminer the following year. For many years the family was content to sell the grapes to local vignerons, but now they take a small portion of the production and make wine on the property. The Cabernet Sauvignon has been a consistent medal winner at Hunter shows, the 1998 winning the trophy for Open Vintage Reds at the 1999 Boutique Winemakers Show. This has led to a decision to concentrate on red wine making, and while some Traminer remains for sale, future production will be of the Cabernet Sauvignon only.

tallarook ★★★★

Ennis Road, Tallarook, Vic 3659 **region** Central Victorian High Country
phone (03) 9818 3455 **fax** (03) 9818 3646 **open** Not
winemaker Martin Williams, Scott McCarthy **production** 11 000 cases **est.** 1987
product range ($15.95–32.50 R) Chardonnay, Marsanne, Rose, Pinot Noir, Shiraz; second label of Terra Felix with Chardonnay and Shiraz.
summary TallarooK has been established on a property between Broadford and Seymour at an elevation of 200–300 metres. Fourteen hectares of vines have been planted since 1987, the three principal varieties being chardonnay, shiraz and pinot noir. The retainer of Martin Williams as winemaker in the 1998 vintage brought a substantial change in emphasis, and the subsequent release of an impressive Chardonnay. The wines are mainly sold by mail order; also retail distribution in Melbourne and exports to the UK and Europe.

TallarooK Marsanne
▼▼▼▽ **2001** Medium yellow-green; there are some bottle-developed varietal touches of hay and chalk on the moderately intense bouquet; the texture of the light to medium-bodied palate is more interesting than the flavour, but, once again, is varietal. Will please those who do not like overt fruit in their wines; the 2000 was far more appealing overall. **rating:** 84
best drinking Now–2005 **drink with** Fish terrine • $27.50

TallarooK Chardonnay

▼▼▼▼▽ **2001** Medium yellow-green; the bouquet has a fine, complex web of barrel-ferment, malolactic-ferment and lees characters; the palate is subtle but very complex, with creamy/nutty edges to the tight fruit. Whole bunch pressed and fermented without the use of cultured yeasts.   **rating:** 93

best drinking Now–2007 **best vintages** '99, '01 **drink with** Pan-fried veal • $32.50

TallarooK Shiraz

▼▼▼▼ **2001** Medium red-purple; the light, leafy, spicy aromas of the bouquet are followed by a palate with much more substance and style, offering red fruits and well-balanced savoury tannins. Fermented incorporating the Marsanne pressings.   **rating:** 89

best drinking 2004–2009 **drink with** Ravioli • $27.50

🍂 tall poppy wines   NR

PO Box 4147, Mildura, Vic 3502 **region** Murray Darling
phone (03) 5022 7256 **fax** (03) 5022 7250 **open** Not
winemaker Barossa Vintners (Contract) **production** 20 000 cases **est.** 1997
product range ($13.95 R) Viognier, Unwooded Chardonnay, Chardonnay, Shiraz, Merlot, Petit Verdot, Sangiovese, Merlot Cabernet Sauvignon Shiraz, Cabernet Sauvignon.
summary Tall Poppy Wines is in its infancy as a wine brand, but it has lofty ambitions. It owns 4.5 hectares each of shiraz and viognier, but is able to draw upon grapes sourced from 170 hectares of vineyards owned by its directors, with a volume potential of 300 000 to 400 000 cases aimed at the export market.

taltarni   ★★★★

Taltarni Road, Moonambel, Vic 3478 **region** Pyrenees
phone (03) 5459 7900 **fax** (03) 5467 2306 **open** 7 days 10–5
winemaker Peter Steer, Loic Le Calvez, Mark Laurence **production** 80 000 cases **est.** 1972
product range ($12.50–45.70 R) Sauvignon Blanc, Fiddleback White, Brut, Brut Tache, Rose, Fiddleback Red, Shiraz, Cephas (Shiraz Cabernet), Merlot, Cabernet Merlot, Cabernet Sauvignon; Lalla Gully Sauvignon Blanc, Chardonnay.
summary After a hiatus of 2 years or so following the departure of long-serving winemaker and chief executive Dominique Portet, Taltarni has gathered new momentum and inspiration, with an executive and winemaking team headed by the multi-talented Peter Steer. Major changes in the approach to the vineyards; major upgrading of winery equipment and investment in new oak barrels; a long-term contract arrangement for the purchase of grapes from the Heathcote region; and the release of a new flagship wine, Cephas, are the visible signs of the repositioning of the business. It is still too early to say whether the portfolio of wines under Cephas will be (relative to their price) of similar quality, but there is every reason to guess that they will. Exports to all the major markets, including the UK, the US, Canada, Japan, Hong Kong, Switzerland, Sweden and extensively throughout South-East Asia and Western Europe.

Taltarni Sauvignon Blanc

▼▼▼▼ **2002** Light straw-green; clean, nicely ripened fruit with a mix of gentle gooseberry and grass aromas is precisely repeated on the palate, which is perhaps a tad more tropical; good varietal character and well made.   **rating:** 88

best drinking Now **best vintages** '96, '97, '98 **drink with** Calamari • $19.50

Lalla Gully Sauvignon Blanc

▼▼▼▼ **2002** Light straw-green; a clean and fresh bouquet with gentle gooseberry and grass aromas is precisely reflected in the light to medium-bodied palate, which has nice mouthfeel and fruit balance.   **rating:** 88

best drinking Now **drink with** Deep sea crab • $21.10

Taltarni Brut

▼▼▼▼ **2000** Light green-yellow, with excellent, fine mousse; the tangy, citrussy bouquet leads into a fine and elegant palate, with crisp citrussy acidity running through on a long finish. A blend of Pyrenees and Pipers River material which spends 18 months on yeast lees.   **rating:** 88

best drinking Now–2005 **drink with** Oysters, shellfish • $19.80

Taltarni Brut Tache

▼▼▼▼ **2000** Pale salmon-pink, with excellent mousse; the tangy citrus and small fruit aromas of the bouquet are followed by a fine, elegant, crisp palate, slightly less intense than the Brut, but very similar overall.   **rating:** 87

best drinking Now–2005 **drink with** Shellfish • $19.80

Taltarni Cephas

▼▼▼▼▽ 2000 Good, bright and deep colour; the bouquet is complex, with a lot more fruit evident than in any recent Taltarni red wine, and oak likewise more apparent. The good news continues on the palate, which is more supple and has more mid-palate fruit than hitherto; the length and balance are good. An estate-grown blend of 60 per cent Shiraz and 40 per cent Cabernet Sauvignon fermented in open fermenters, with components finishing their fermentation in new French and American oak, with 18–22 months' maturation.   **rating:** 92

best drinking 2007–2017 **best vintages** '00 **drink with** Roast eye fillet of beef • $45.70

talunga   NR

Adelaide to Mannum Road, Gumeracha, SA 5233 **region** Adelaide Hills
phone (08) 8389 1222 **fax** (08) 8389 1233 **open** Wed–Sun and public holidays 10.30–5
winemaker Vince Scaffidi **production** 6000 cases **est.** 1994
product range ($14.50–29.50 CD) Sauvignon Blanc, Chardonnay, Pinot Noir, Shiraz, Terrace Block Grenache, Sangiovese, Sangiovese Merlot, High Block Cabernet Sauvignon; Scaffidi Nebbiolo.
summary Talunga owners Vince and Tina Scaffidi have a one-third share of the 62-hectare Gumeracha Vineyards, and it is from these vineyards that the Talunga wines are sourced. In November 2002 the 2001 Sangiovese won the trophy for Best Red Wine of Show at the Australian Alternative Varieties Wine Show.

tamar ridge   ★★★★☆

Auburn Road, Kayena, Tas 7270 **region** Northern Tasmania
phone (03) 6394 7000 **fax** (03) 6394 7003 **open** 7 days 10–5
winemaker Michael Fogarty **production** 30 000 cases **est.** 1994
product range ($15–38 CD) Riesling, Sauvignon Blanc, Pinot Gris, Chardonnay, Josef Chromy Late Harvest Riesling, TRV Tasmania (Sparkling), Josef Chromy Blanc de Noir, Pinot Noir, Cabernet Sauvignon, Cellar Release Cabernet Sauvignon; second label Devil's Corner Riesling, Unwooded Chardonnay, Pinot Noir.
summary The bell has tolled once again for Joe Chromy with the sale of Tamar Ridge in April 2003 to Tasmanian timber and agribusiness company Gunns Limited. It is a lock, stock and barrel sale, incorporating the Tamar Ridge name, 63 hectares of estate vineyards, and a winery with a 1200-tonne capacity. All the management and winemaking staff will continue in place for the time being at least, and the understandable party line is that Tamar Ridge remains the largest Tasmanian wine business wholly owned by Tasmanians, and that Gunns Limited intends to make significant capital investments in Tamar Ridge, as well as providing export markets in Asia, where Gunns is already heavily involved.

Tamar Ridge Riesling

▼▼▼▼▽ 2002 Light straw-green; the crisp, minerally bouquet has very little fruit expression, and the palate is also tight, but there are lively touches of lime and mineral running through to a long finish. Initially tight, the wine developed dramatically in the 6 months following bottling, becoming thoroughly accessible.   **rating:** 92

best drinking Now–2007 **best vintages** '98, '99, '00, '01 **drink with** Blue-fin tuna • $20.95

Tamar Ridge Josef Chromy Selection Blanc de Noir

▼▼▼▼▽ 1996 The very fresh bouquet is more suggestive of Chardonnay than Pinot Noir, but that is not uncommon in very cool climates, including Champagne itself. The wine has good length and balance, sweet fruit on the mid-palate, and the dosage is perfectly weighted; lingering finish and aftertaste. The earlier disgorgements of this wine were tart and acidic; it has taken a considerable time for it to get its act together.

rating: 93

best drinking Now–2005 **best vintages** '96 **drink with** Oysters • $38

Tamar Ridge Josef Chromy Selection Late Harvest Riesling 375 ml

▼▼▼▼ 2000 Glowing yellow-green; a powerful and intense bouquet with lifted lime juice aromas directly translates into a very intense, limey, Germanic palate, notable as much for its high acidity as for its sweetness. Likely to develop into something quite special.   **rating:** 89

best drinking 2004–2010 **drink with** Fresh fruit if you must • $24

Tamar Ridge Pinot Noir

▼▼▼▼ 2001 Medium red-purple; fragrant, spicy, sappy notes to the small berry and plum fruit of the bouquet add interest and complexity; there is a similar spectrum of flavours on the palate, but an impression of slightly green tannins follows on the finish and aftertaste.   **rating:** 88

best drinking Now–2006 **best vintages** '00 **drink with** Venison pie • $24

Tamar Ridge Cabernet Sauvignon

♥♥♥♥♡ **2000** Medium purple-red; a complex bouquet, with dark berry fruit offset by touches of olive; the medium-bodied palate has excellent texture and balance, with black and redcurrant fruit offset by savoury tannins. Gold medal at the 2003 Tasmanian Wines Show. **rating:** 93

best drinking 2005–2011 **best vintages** '00 **drink with** Grass-fed beef • $24

tamburlaine ★★★☆

McDonalds Road, Pokolbin, NSW 2321 **region** Lower Hunter Valley
phone (02) 4998 7570 **fax** (02) 4998 7763 **open** 7 days 9.30–5
winemaker Mark Davidson, Michael McManus, Jon Heslop **production** 60 000 cases **est.** 1966
product range ($18–24 CD) Orange Reserve range of Riesling, Sauvignon Blanc, Chardonnay; Hunter Reserve range of Semillon, Verdelho, Chardonnay, Syrah; Natural Selection range of Shiraz, Chambourcin, Cabernet Sauvignon; Botrytis, Muscat Aged Liqueur.
summary A thriving business which, notwithstanding the fact that it has doubled its already substantial production in recent years, sells over 90 per cent of its wine through the cellar door and by the mailing list (with an active tasting club members' cellar programme offering wines which are held and matured at Tamburlaine). Unashamedly and deliberately focused on the tourist trade (and, of course, its wine club members).

Tamburlaine Natural Selection Shiraz

♥♥♥♡ **2001** Medium red-purple; berry, leaf, mint and spice aromas come through on the light to medium-bodied palate; a blend of Hunter Valley and Orange grapes, the Orange component dominating. **rating:** 84

best drinking Now–2008 **drink with** Spaghetti bolognese • $20

Tamburlaine Natural Selection Cabernet Sauvignon

♥♥♥♥ **2001** Medium red-purple; the bouquet has a complex array of leafy/earthy/herbaceous aromas on the one side, and mint and red berry on the other; the focus switches more to red and dark berry fruits on the palate, with fine tannins adding to the length. One hundred per cent Orange grapes. **rating:** 85

best drinking 2005–2010 **drink with** Lamb fillet • $20

tanglewood downs NR

Bulldog Creek Road, Merricks North, Vic 3926 **region** Mornington Peninsula
phone (03) 5974 3325 **fax** (03) 5974 4170 **open** Sun–Mon 12–5
winemaker Ken Bilham, Wendy Bilham **production** 1200 cases **est.** 1984
product range ($25 CD) Riesling, Gewurztraminer, Chardonnay, Pinot Noir, Cabernet Sauvignon, Cabernet Franc Merlot.
summary One of the smaller and lower-profile wineries on the Mornington Peninsula, with Ken Bilham quietly doing his own thing on 2.5 hectares of estate plantings. Winery lunches and dinners are available by arrangement.

🦡 tanglewood vines NR

RMB 383, Bridgetown, WA 6255 (postal) **region** Blackwood Valley
phone (08) 9764 4051 **open** Not
winemaker Contract **est.** 1999
product range Cabernet Sauvignon Merlot.
summary Tanglewood Vines has established 2.4 hectares of cabernet sauvignon and 2 hectares of merlot, with a planting of viognier in 2002. The wines should be coming onto the market in 2004.

tannery lane vineyard ★★★

174 Tannery Lane, Mandurang, Vic 3551 **region** Bendigo
phone (03) 5439 3227 **fax** (03) 5439 4003 **open** By appointment
winemaker Lindsay Ross (Contract) **production** 250 cases **est.** 1990
product range ($22–24 CD) Sangiovese, Shiraz.
summary In 1990 planting of the present total of 2 hectares of shiraz, cabernet sauvignon, cabernet franc, sangiovese, merlot and nebbiolo began. Their Sangiovese is one of two such wines coming from the Bendigo region at the present time. The micro-production is sold through the cellar door only, and then only while stocks last, which typically is not for very long. Now owned by the Williams family.

Tannery Lane Shiraz

▼▼▼▼ 2001 Medium purple-red; the bouquet ranges from sundry raspberry and red fruits through to dark plum and blackberry, an exciting opening; however, the palate is very youthful, with a rather grippy finish, and needed more work in the winery. Since it is too late for that, best left alone for 5 years. **rating:** 86

best drinking 2006–2011 **drink with** Leave it in the cellar • $22

Tannery Lane Sangiovese

▼▼▼▼ 2001 Good red-purple colour; the bouquet is very ripe, with distinctly jammy edges to the fruit; the similarly ripe palate has quasi-Amarone mid-palate fruit, but with savoury tannins as a sharp contrast on the finish. An interesting example, but earlier picking might have helped. **rating:** 85

best drinking 2005–2009 **drink with** Pasta with meat sauce • $24

tantemaggie   NR

Kemp Road, Pemberton, WA 6260 **region** Pemberton
phone (08) 9776 1164 **fax** (08) 9776 1810 **open** By appointment
winemaker Contract **production** 2000 cases **est.** 1987
product range ($18–55 CD) Verdelho, Cabernet Sauvignon.
summary Tantemaggie was established by the Pottinger family with the help of a bequest from a deceased aunt named Maggie. It is part of a mixed farming operation, and by far the greatest part of the 28 hectares is under long-term contract to Houghton. The bulk of the plantings are cabernet sauvignon, verdelho and chardonnay, the former producing the light-bodied style favoured by the Pottingers.

tapestry   NR

Olivers Road, McLaren Vale, SA 5171 **region** McLaren Vale
phone (08) 8323 9196 **fax** (08) 8323 9746 **open** 7 days 11–5
winemaker Jon Ketley **production** 10 000 cases **est.** 1971
product range ($10–18 CD) Riesling, Chardonnay, Spaetlese, Bin 338 Shiraz, Cabernet Shiraz, Cabernet Sauvignon, Muscat of Alexandria, Old Tawny Port.
summary After a relatively brief period of ownership by Brian Light and family, the property was acquired by the Gerard family, former owners of Chapel Hill, in 1997. It has 40 hectares of vineyards, 6.5 hectares in McLaren Vale and 33.5 hectares in Bakers Gully. Less than half the grapes are used for the Tapestry label.

☏ tarrangower estate   NR

17 Baldry Street, Malmsbury, Vic 3446 **region** Macedon Ranges
phone (03) 5423 2088 **fax** (03) 5423 2088 **open** Weekends 10–5, or by appointment
winemaker Tom Gyorffy **production** 200 cases **est.** 1993
product range ($23–29 CD) The Revolutionary's Chardonnay, Coliban Cabernet Shiraz.
summary Tarrangower Estate is situated on the northeastern edge of the township of Malmsbury, at the western end of the Macedon Ranges wine region. At an altitude of 470 metres, it is one of the warmest sites in the region, and overlooks the Coliban River Valley and up to Mount Alexander and Mount Macedon. The varieties planted are chardonnay and shiraz (0.8 ha each), cabernet sauvignon (0.4 ha) and merlot (0.1 ha). Tom Gyorffy is a Melbourne lawyer, but as a mature-age student he graduated with an associate degree in applied science (wine growing) from Charles Sturt University in 1997. He has also completed a number of other certificate courses in winemaking, and has accumulated five vintages at Tarrangower Estate. His philosophy is to make 'natural wines' and to deliberately oxidise (hyper-oxidation) the chardonnay. While some of the wines are decidedly unconventional, the 1998 Cabernet Franc (the first commercial release from Tarrangower) won a silver medal at the 2000 Cool Climate Wine Show.

tarrawarra estate   ★★★★☆

Healesville Road, Yarra Glen, Vic 3775 **region** Yarra Valley
phone (03) 5962 3311 **fax** (03) 5962 3887 **open** 7 days 10.30–4.30
winemaker Clare Halloran, Damian North **production** 25 000 cases **est.** 1983
product range ($23–48 R) Chardonnay and Pinot Noir; also Kidron Chardonnay and Shiraz (kosher).
summary Slowly developing Chardonnay of great structure and complexity is the winery specialty; robust Pinot Noir also needs time and evolves impressively if given it. National retail distribution; exports to the UK, Switzerland, Belgium, Singapore, Hong Kong and the US.

Tarrawarra Chardonnay

▼▼▼▼▽ **2001** Bright yellow-green; the bouquet offers a subtly complex interplay between barrel-ferment and malolactic-ferment characters on the one hand, and melon/fig fruit on the other. The palate provides more of the same, with a long, gently creamy, nutty mouthfeel and flow. Stylistically at the opposite end of the world from the related Tin Cows Chardonnay. **rating:** 93

best drinking 2004–2009 **best vintages** '87, '88, '90, '92, '93, '94, '97, '98, '01 **drink with** Pheasant, turkey • $40

Tarrawarra Pinot Noir

▼▼▼▼▽ **2001** Medium red-purple; smooth, gently spiced plum aromas lead into a harmonious palate with plenty of depth; spice, plum and a touch of briar; good length and outcome for the vintage. **rating:** 92

best drinking 2004–2008 **best vintages** '88, '90, '91, '92, '94, '95, '96, '98, '01 **drink with** Squab • $48

tarrington vineyards ★★★★★

Hamilton Highway, Tarrington, Vic 3301 **region** Henty
phone (03) 5572 4509 **fax** (03) 5572 4509 **open** By appointment
winemaker Tamara Irish **production** 300 cases **est.** 1993
product range ($27.50–35 R) Chardonnay, Pinot Noir, Cuvee Emilie Pinot Noir.
summary The grape growing and winemaking practices of Burgundy permeate every aspect of Tarrington Vineyards. While its establishment began in 1993, there has been no hurry to bring the vineyard into production. Two varieties only have been planted: pinot noir and chardonnay, with a planting density varying between 3333 and 8170 vines per hectare. There are no less than nine clones in the 2 hectares of pinot noir, and four clones in the 1 hectare of chardonnay. This approach to making the Pinot Noir is common in Burgundy; the unoaked Chardonnay is kept in tank on fine lees for 9 months, the traditional method of making Chablis. Everything about the operation speaks of a labour of love, with a high standard of packaging and presentation of all background material. The exemplary wines are to be found on a thoroughly impressive collection of Victoria's top restaurant wine lists.

Tarrington Vineyards Chardonnay

▼▼▼▼▽ **2001** Light straw-green; discreet but complex melon, spice, fig and mineral aromas lead into a graceful, light to medium-bodied palate, with the accent on melon and a touch of citrus. While the wine has been given extended lees contact, it is unoaked, the complexity reflecting the cool climate and low yield per vine. Only 80 dozen made, with Chablis (French) as the guide. **rating:** 90

best drinking Now–2007 **drink with** Grilled scampi • $30

Tarrington Vineyards Pinot Noir

▼▼▼▼▼ **2001** Medium to full red-purple; an intense and complex range of fruit aromas including mint, spice and dark plum; the palate has immaculate balance and structure, considerable length and neatly judged extract. Slightly less lush than the 2000 vintage, and more cerebral, but another very good wine from this outstanding Pinot producer. **rating:** 94

best drinking Now–2007 **best vintages** '00, '01 **drink with** Braised duck • $27.50

Tarrington Vineyards Cuvee Emilie Pinot Noir

▼▼▼▼▼ **2000** Medium to full red-purple; an ultra-complex bouquet with potent plum and spice aromas, almost into plum pudding; the very rich and intense palate has a tapestry of flavours centred around plum and spice; great length and balance and an outstanding Pinot. **rating:** 96

best drinking Now–2010 **best vintages** '99 **drink with** Wild duck • $35

tarwin ridge NR

Wintles Road, Leongatha South, Vic 3953 **region** Gippsland
phone (03) 5664 3211 **fax** (03) 5664 3211 **open** Weekends and holidays 10–5
winemaker Brian Anstee **production** 700 cases **est.** 1983
product range ($16–27 CD) Sauvignon Blanc, White Merlot, Pinot Noir, Pinot Noir Premium, Cabernet Merlot.
summary For the time being Brian Anstee is making his wines at Nicholson River under the gaze of fellow social worker Ken Eckersley; the wines come from 2 hectares of estate pinot and 0.5 hectare each of cabernet and sauvignon blanc.

tatachilla ★★★★

151 Main Road, McLaren Vale, SA 5171 **region** McLaren Vale
phone (08) 8323 8656 **fax** (08) 8323 9096 **open** Mon–Sat 10–5, Sun and public holidays 11–5
winemaker Michael Fragos, Justin McNamee **production** 250 000 cases **est.** 1901
product range ($11.95–60 CD) Adelaide Hills Sauvignon Blanc, Growers (Chenin Blanc Semillon Sauvignon Blanc), Adelaide Hills Chardonnay, McLaren Vale Chardonnay, Padthaway Chardonnay, Sparkling Pinot Noir, Sparkling Malbec, Foundation Shiraz, McLaren Vale Shiraz, Adelaide Hills Merlot, McLaren Vale Merlot, Clarendon Merlot, Keystone (Grenache Shiraz), Partners (Cabernet Sauvignon Shiraz), McLaren Vale Cabernet Sauvignon, Padthaway Cabernet Sauvignon, 1901 Cabernet Sauvignon, Tawny Port; also the lower-priced Breakneck Creek range of Chardonnay, Shiraz, Merlot, Cabernet Sauvignon.
summary Tatachilla was reborn in 1995 but has an at times tumultuous history going back to 1901. For most of the time between 1901 and 1961 the winery was owned by Penfolds, but it was closed in that year before being reopened in 1965 as the Southern Vales Co-operative. In the late 1980s it was purchased and renamed The Vales but did not flourish, and in 1993 it was purchased by local grower Vic Zerella and former Kaiser Stuhl chief executive Keith Smith. After extensive renovations, the winery was officially reopened in 1995 and won a number of tourist awards and accolades. The star turns are Keystone (Grenache Shiraz) and Foundation Shiraz, bursting with vibrant fruit. Became part of Banksia Wines in 2001, in turn acquired by Lion Nathan in 2002.

Tatachilla Adelaide Hills Sauvignon Blanc

ŸŸŸŸŸ 2002 Light straw-green; the aromatic, perfumed, apple blossom and passionfruit bouquet is sustained on the lively, tangy and come-hither palate. **rating:** 93
best drinking Now **best vintages** '02 **drink with** Calamari • $19.80

Tatachilla Adelaide Hills Chardonnay

ŸŸŸŸ 2001 Medium yellow-green; the bouquet has clean, gentle stone fruit supported by subtle oak; much the same play occurs on the light to medium-bodied palate, with its gentle fruit and good length. **rating:** 87
best drinking Now–2005 **drink with** Creamy pasta • $19

Tatachilla Sparkling Pinot Noir

ŸŸŸŸ NV Pale salmon rose; clean strawberry and citrus aromas are followed by an attractive, lively and fresh palate with pure strawberry fruit; simple, but well balanced; it is in fact a sparkling rose, rather than sparkling pinot noir, if you understand what I mean. **rating:** 88
best drinking Now–2006 **drink with** Antipasto • $19.50

Tatachilla Foundation Shiraz

ŸŸŸŸŸ 2000 Deep, dense red-purple; lush, rich and scented blackberry, plum and spice aromas are followed by a voluptuous, plush palate with blackberry fruit, lots of bitter chocolate, soft tannins and quality oak. **rating:** 95
best drinking 2005–2015 **best vintages** '95, '97, '98, '99, '00 **drink with** Kangaroo fillet • $49.95

Tatachilla McLaren Vale Shiraz

ŸŸŸŸ 2000 Medium red-purple; the bouquet has lush, ripe, dark plum confit and a touch of vanilla; some dark chocolate joins the fruit flavours on the palate, with somewhat assertive tannins running through from the mid-palate to the close; surprisingly, the wine regains balance with a good aftertaste. **rating:** 88
best drinking 2005–2010 **best vintages** '98, '99 **drink with** Rump steak • $22.95

Tatachilla Keystone

ŸŸŸŸ 2001 Medium red-purple; a vibrant bouquet with strong varietal cherry jam aromas is repeated on the palate, where Grenache seems to do almost all the work; typically soft tannins to close. **rating:** 89
best drinking Now–2006 **best vintages** '94, '96, '97, '99 **drink with** Roast pigeon breast • $17.95

Tatachilla Adelaide Hills Merlot

ŸŸŸŸŸ 2000 Medium red-purple; attractive, sweet red and black fruit aromas precede a powerful palate, with lots of ripe raspberry and blackberry fruit. Very much in the Tatachilla style, the overall softness being of particular appeal. **rating:** 90
best drinking Now–2008 **best vintages** '99 **drink with** Osso buco • $24.50

Tatachilla Clarendon Vineyard Merlot

ŸŸŸŸŸ 2000 Full red-purple; ripe, rich, dark berry fruit and restrained oak on the bouquet flows into a rich, plush, dark berry-flavoured palate. While a highly regarded wine, and, for that matter, style, I have given it points as a red wine, rather than as a varietal. **rating:** 90
best drinking 2004–2010 **best vintages** '00 **drink with** Yearling beef • $60

Tatachilla McLaren Vale Merlot

♥♥♥♥ 2001 Medium to full red-purple; ripe, sweet blackcurrant and blackberry aromas intermingle; the palate has abundant fruit in the same spectrum, plus regional chocolate. As ever, a richly flavoured dry red wine, the varietal character evident only in the controlled tannins. **rating:** 88

best drinking 2005–2010 **best vintages** '96, '97, '98, '99 **drink with** Rare rump steak • $22.95

Tatachilla 1901 Cabernet Sauvignon

♥♥♥♥♥ 2000 Full, bright red-purple; powerful, dense black fruits on the bouquet announce a palate with a mix of blackberry, blackcurrant and dark chocolate, medium to full-bodied. Supple, smooth tannins provide extra length for a particularly good wine. A blend of McLaren Vale and Padthaway material. **rating:** 94

best drinking 2006–2016 **best vintages** '98, '00 **drink with** Beef in black bean sauce • $41.95

Tatachilla McLaren Vale Cabernet Sauvignon

♥♥♥♥♡ 2000 Medium red-purple; the clean bouquet ranges through berry, olive and dark chocolate, and has a controlled touch of oak; the palate has good depth and mouthfeel, the flavours tracking the bouquet; good length, nice wine. **rating:** 90

best drinking 2005–2015 **best vintages** '97, '98, '00 **drink with** Rare roast baby lamb • $22.95

Tatachilla Padthaway Cabernet Sauvignon

♥♥♥♥ 2001 Medium to full red-purple; solid blackcurrant, blackberry and cassis aromas feed into an entirely fruit-driven palate, with soft tannins; definitely user-friendly. **rating:** 88

best drinking 2004–2009 **best vintages** '00 **drink with** Beef pie • $21.80

tatehams wines ★★★☆

Main North Road, Auburn, SA 5451 **region** Clare Valley
phone (08) 8849 2030 **fax** (08) 8849 2260 **open** Wed–Sun 10–5
winemaker Mike Jeandupeux **production** 500 cases **est.** 1998
product range ($15–21 CD) Riesling, Shiraz.
summary Mike and Isabel Jeandupeux left the French-speaking part of Switzerland in September 1997 to begin a new life in Australia. They now operate a restaurant and guest house at Auburn, in the southern end of the Clare Valley. The 1863 stone building, which originally operated as a general store and stables, has been completely refurbished, with several buildings offering a variety of upscale accommodation. The winemaking side of the business is effectively an add-on, with most of the wine sold through the restaurant and cellar door, but with a mailing list and limited distribution in Adelaide. The Riesling is particularly attractive.

tatler wines NR

Lot 15 Lovedale Road, Lovedale, NSW 2321 **region** Lower Hunter Valley
phone (02) 4930 9139 **fax** (02) 4930 9145 **open** 7 days 9.30–5.30
winemaker Jim Chatto (Contract) **production** 2000 cases **est.** 1998
product range ($14–24 CD) Nigel's Semillon, Whisper's Chardonnay Semillon Sauvignon Blanc, Dimitri's Paddock Chardonnay, Archie's Paddock Shiraz.
summary Planting of the vineyard began in 1998 with 2 hectares of chardonnay, and slightly less than 2 hectares of shiraz. One hectare of semillon was planted the following year, and the first small vintage came in 2000, demonstrating yet again that very young vines can produce excellent wine. Contract winemaking by Jim Chatto will ensure the maximum result is obtained from the available fruit. A cellar door complex is scheduled for completion in March 2003 with a cafe and three-bedroom self-contained unit on top of the cellar door.

tawonga vineyard NR

2 Drummond Street, Tawonga, Vic 3697 **region** Alpine Valleys
phone (03) 5754 4945 **open** By appointment
winemaker John Adams **production** 300 cases **est.** 1994
product range ($12.95–13.95 CD) Verdelho, Shiraz, Merlot.
summary Diz and John Adams made their first wine in 1995, but it was not until 1998 that they finally received their producer's licence entitling them to sell the wine they had made. With a planned maximum production of less than 1000 cases, Tawonga has been able to take advantage of the small business tax exemption. In the meantime their handcrafted wines (virtually all of which have won show medals) remain at magically low prices.

taylors ★★★★☆

Taylors Road, Auburn, SA 5451 **region** Clare Valley
phone (08) 8849 2008 **fax** (08) 8849 2240 **open** Mon–Fri 9–5, Sat and public holidays 10–5, Sun 10–4
winemaker Adam Eggins, Helen McCarthy **production** 250 000 cases **est.** 1972
product range ($9–55 R) At the top comes the super-premium St Andrews releases of Riesling, Chardonnay, Shiraz and Cabernet Sauvignon, then the premium range consists of Clare Valley Riesling, Gewurztraminer, Semillon, White Burgundy, Promised Land Unwooded Chardonnay, Chardonnay, Pinot Noir, Shiraz, Promised Land Shiraz Cabernet, Merlot and Cabernet Sauvignon; the lower-priced 80 Acres range consists of Dry White, Crouchen Riesling and Classic Dry Red; Wakefield Tawny Port.
summary The family founded and owned Taylors continues to flourish and expand, with yet further extensions to its vineyards, now totalling over 500 hectares, by far the largest holding in Clare Valley. There have also been substantial changes on the winemaking front, both in terms of the winemaking team and in terms of the wine style and quality, particularly through the outstanding St Andrews range. Widespread national distribution, with exports to the UK, Ireland, New Zealand and Malaysia.

Taylors Clare Riesling

▼▼▼▼ 2002 Light straw-green; the bouquet is clean, tight and unevolved, the palate with good depth and concentration, but, like the bouquet, somewhat locked up. Ripe lime flavours are waiting to express themselves; marginally disappointing from such a highly rated vintage. **rating:** 88
best drinking Now–2008 **best vintages** '82, '87, '92, '93, '94, '96, '99, '01 **drink with** Avocado • $16

Taylors St Andrews Riesling

▼▼▼▼▼ 1998 Medium yellow-green; the bouquet has a classic and complex mix of rich lime and toast; the full-flavoured palate builds richness on the mid-palate, followed by great finishing acidity. **rating:** 96
best drinking Now–2008 **best vintages** '96, '98 **drink with** Asparagus risotto • $35

Taylors Shiraz

▼▼▼▼ 2002 Medium to full red-purple; the moderately intense bouquet has slightly dusty vanilla oak as the first impression, sweet, dark fruits as the second; the powerful palate brings it all together, with dark plum and blackberry fruit supported by typical Clare Valley tannins. **rating:** 88
best drinking 2006–2012 **best vintages** '86, '89, '90, '92, '95, '01 **drink with** Carpaccio of beef • $16

Taylors Merlot

▼▼▼▼ 2002 Medium to full red-purple; the bouquet is clean, with abundant black fruits and a touch of chocolate; a dense, concentrated, imposing regional red wine, which will be long lived, but which (as with previous vintages) has little to do with the commonly accepted view of Merlot. **rating:** 89
best drinking 2007–2012 **best vintages** '99 **drink with** Veal saltimbocca • $16

Taylors Promised Land Cabernet Merlot

▼▼▼▼▽ 2002 Medium to full red-purple; the clean bouquet has abundant blackcurrant and cassis fruit, as does the plush, velvety, deep palate. One strongly suspects skilfully used micro-oxygenation; very good value. **rating:** 91
best drinking 2005–2009 **drink with** Shepherd's pie • $13

Taylors Cabernet Sauvignon

▼▼▼▼ 2001 Medium red-purple; well-balanced and integrated dark berry fruit and oak on the bouquet is followed by a palate with plenty of depth and structure; the fruit is ripe, and while the tannins tremble on the brink of over-extraction, they don't go over the top. Just be patient. **rating:** 88
best drinking 2006–2011 **best vintages** '86, '89, '90, '92, '94, '99, '00 **drink with** Mixed grill • $16

temple bruer ★★★☆

Milang Road, Strathalbyn, SA 5255 **region** Langhorne Creek
phone (08) 8537 0203 **fax** (08) 8537 0131 **open** Mon–Fri 9.30–4.30
winemaker Nick Bruer **production** 14 000 cases **est.** 1980
product range ($12.80–23.70 R) Riesling, Verdelho, Viognier, Chenin Blanc, Sauvignon Blanc, Botrytis Riesling, Cornucopia Grenache, Cabernet Merlot, Reserve Merlot, Shiraz Malbec, Sparkling Cabernet Merlot.
summary Always known for its eclectic range of wines, Temple Bruer (which also carries on a substantial business as a vine propagation nursery) has seen a sharp lift in wine quality. Clean, modern redesigned labels add to the appeal of a stimulatingly different range of red wines. Part of the production from the 24 hectares of estate vineyards is sold to others, the remainder being made under the Temple Bruer label. The vineyard is now certified organic.

Temple Bruer Sauvignon Blanc

TTTT 2002 Light to medium yellow-green; clean, gently ripe tropical passionfruit aromas lead into a palate with very attractive mouthfeel and balance, the flavours tracking the bouquet. A real bargain.   **rating:** 89

best drinking Now **drink with** Seafood risotto • $12.50

templer's mill   ★★★☆

The University of Sydney, Leeds Parade, Orange, NSW 2800 **region** Orange
phone (02) 6360 5570 **fax** (02) 6362 7625 **open** Mon–Fri 9–4.30 or by appointment
winemaker Reynolds Wines **production** 1500 cases **est.** 1997
product range ($12.50–16 CD) Sauvignon Blanc, Chardonnay, Shiraz, Merlot, Cabernet Sauvignon.
summary Templer's Mill was one of Australia's first flour mills, providing flour for early gold fields at Ophir near Orange. This historic mill is now a ruin on Narrambla, an adjacent property to the University of Sydney's Orange Campus farm and birthplace of AB (Banjo) Paterson. The 19.4-hectare vineyard is planted to cabernet sauvignon, chardonnay, shiraz, sauvignon blanc and merlot (in descending order of magnitude); part of the production is made under the Temper's Mill label, part sold as grapes, the operation overseen by viticulture lecturer Peter Hedberg.

tempus two wines   ★★★☆

Broke Road, Pokolbin, NSW 2321 **region** Lower Hunter Valley
phone (02) 9818 7222 **fax** (02) 9818 7333 **open** 7 days 9–5
winemaker Sarah-Kate Wilson **production** 50 000 cases **est.** 1997
product range ($16–28 CD) Varietal range of Eden Valley Riesling, Semillon Sauvignon Blanc, Verdelho, Cowra Chardonnay, Hunter Shiraz, Merlot, Cabernet Merlot; Pewter range of Sparkling Chardonnay, Botrytis Semillon, Vine Vale Shiraz, Hunter Merlot, Hollydene Cabernet Sauvignon.
summary Tempus Two is the name for what was once Hermitage Road Wines, a piece of doggerel akin to that of Rouge Homme, except that it is not Franglais, but a mix of Latin (Tempus means time) and English. I should not be too critical, however; the change was forced on the winery by the EU Wine Agreement and the prohibition of the use of the word 'hermitage' on Australian wine labels. Nor should the fracas over the labels disguise the fact that some very attractive wines have appeared so far, and will do so in the future, no doubt, particularly given the arrival of Sarah-Kate Wilson as winemaker. Exports to New Zealand and the Philippines.

Tempus Two Botrytis Semillon 250 ml

TTTT 2002 Glowing yellow-green; the quite fragrant bouquet has lemony/citrussy fruit aromas, the palate lively, with spatlese-level sweetness, and nice acidity on the finish. The bottle probably costs more than the wine inside it, hence the equivalent price of $54 for a normal 750 ml bottle.   **rating:** 85

best drinking Now–2006 **drink with** Home-made ice-cream • $18

Tempus Two Reserve Hollydene Cabernet Sauvignon

TTTT 2000 Medium purple-red; sweet, dark blackcurrant and blackberry fruit aromas are supported by positive French oak; the palate ranges through similar flavours, adding a touch of chocolate and, once again, spicy French oak; soft tannins to close. From the Hollydene Vineyard.   **rating:** 89

best drinking 2005–2012 **best vintages** '98 **drink with** Braised beef in olives • $28

ten minutes by tractor wine co   ★★★★☆

111 Roberts Road, Main Ridge, Vic 3928 **region** Mornington Peninsula
phone (03) 5989 6084 **fax** (03) 5989 6599 **open** Weekends and holidays 11–5
winemaker Richard McIntyre (Pinot Noir, Chardonnay), Alex White (Sauvignon Blanc, Pinot Gris)
production 3000 cases **est.** 1999
product range ($18.50–45 CD) Sauvignon Blanc, Pinot Gris, Chardonnay, Sweet Allis, Pinot Noir, Pinot Noir Reserve; Judd Vineyard Chardonnay, Pinot Noir; McCutcheon Vineyard Chardonnay, Pinot Noir; Wallis Vineyard Chardonnay, Pinot Noir.
summary This has to be one of the cleverest pieces of marketing I have ever come across, the unforgettable name reinforced by superb graphics. But it also has a particularly clever business plan, and some excellent wines to support the business. The company belongs to the Judd, McCutcheon and Wallis families, each of which established a 6-hectare vineyard a decade ago, but decided to merge the operations in 1999, realising that each of the three properties are only 10 minutes by tractor distant from each other. While most of the grapes were and are sold to other winemakers, in 2000 they began making limited quantities of wines under the 10X label (drawing on all three properties) and individual vineyard selection wines from each of the three properties. A

number of Melbourne restaurants list the wines, and exports to Hong Kong, San Francisco, New York and London are being developed. The cellar door serves light lunches.

10X Tractor Sauvignon Blanc

ŦŦŦŦ♀ **2002** Light straw-green; fragrant and spotlessly clean gooseberry, tropical, lychee aromas are followed by a delicate palate, providing the precise flavours promised by the bouquet; good flow and line.　**rating:** 91

best drinking Now **drink with** Fresh seafood • $18.50

10X Tractor Chardonnay

ŦŦŦŦ♀ **2001** Medium yellow-green; complex melon, peach and fig fruit combines with barrel-ferment oak on the bouquet, the generously flavoured, but not broad or coarse, palate providing an instant replay. Neatly balanced.　**rating:** 90

best drinking Now–2005 **best vintages** '01 **drink with** Lambs brains in black butter • $28

Ten Minutes by Tractor Sweet Allis

ŦŦŦŦ **2001** Light green-yellow; obvious botrytis tropical aromas flow into a complex palate with yellow peach and butterscotch flavours. The wine is sweet, but not oppressively so, the acid well balanced. A blend of botrytised chardonnay and sauvignon blanc.　**rating:** 89

best drinking Now **drink with** Fruit tart • $23.50

10X Tractor Pinot Noir

ŦŦŦŦ **2001** Light to medium red-purple; light spicy/savoury/stemmy aromas are joined by an unwelcome hint of mint on the bouquet; brisk red fruits (cherry and strawberry) are accompanied by a sappy finish.　**rating:** 89

best drinking Now–2006 **drink with** Grilled Atlantic salmon • $32.50

10X Tractor Reserve Pinot Noir

ŦŦŦŦ♀ **2001** Medium red-purple; the moderately intense bouquet has a complex mix of savoury notes and plummy fruit; the elegant, supple palate supports the plum fruit with fine, silky tannins running through to a long finish.　**rating:** 91

best drinking Now–2006 **drink with** Veal kidneys • $45

terrace vale　★★★★

Deasey's Lane, Pokolbin, NSW 2321 **region** Lower Hunter Valley
phone (02) 4998 7517 **fax** (02) 4998 7814 **open** 7 days 10–4
winemaker Alain Leprince **production** 8000 cases **est.** 1971
product range ($14.50–40 CD) Gewurztraminer, Semillon, Chardonnay, Unwooded Chardonnay, Fine Hunter White, Shiraz, Pinot Shiraz, Fine Hunter Red, Cabernet Merlot, Chardonnay Pinot Noir Brut, Elizabeth Sauvignon Blanc (dessert), Vintage Port; Family Reserve wines include Campbell's Orchard Semillon, Lachlan's Block Chardonnay and Alexanders Old Vine Shiraz.
summary In April 2001, the Batchelor family acquired Terrace Vale, but little else has change. Alain Leprince remains as winemaker, and the wines still come from the 30-year-old estate plantings.

Terrace Vale Campbell's Orchard Semillon

ŦŦŦŦ♀ **2001** Medium green-yellow, bright and strong; the clean bouquet has ripe semillon fruit, the aromas almost into peach; the palate has generous flavour, again showing ripe fruit, yet not broad or heavy. Gold medal 2001 Hunter Valley Boutique Winemakers Show.　**rating:** 90

best drinking Now–2007 **drink with** Seafood salad • $25

Terrace Vale Collector Series Cabernet Sauvignon

ŦŦŦŦ **2000** Light to medium red-purple; savoury aromas of the bouquet range through hay, earth and redcurrant; the light to medium-bodied palate focuses more on black and redcurrant fruit, finishing with fine tannins. Trophy 2001 Hunter Boutique Winemakers Show.　**rating:** 85

best drinking Now–2007 **drink with** Smoked lamb • $40

t'gallant　★★★★

1385 Mornington–Flinders Road, Main Ridge, Vic 3928 **region** Mornington Peninsula
phone (03) 5989 6565 **fax** (03) 5989 6577 **open** 7 days 10–5
winemaker Kathleen Quealy, Kevin McCarthy **production** 30 000 cases **est.** 1990
product range ($15–49 R) An ever-changing list of names (and avant-garde label designs), but with Unwooded Chardonnay and Pinot Gris at the centre. Labels include The T'Gallant Chardonnay, Pinot Grigio,

Tribute Pinot Gris, Imogen Pinot Gris, Celia's White Pinot, Cape Schanck Pinot Grigio Chardonnay, Io Botrytis Pinot Gris, Triumph Late Harvest Pinot Gris, Holystone, Romeo, Batch #1 Pinot Noir, Cape Schanck Pinot Noir, Juno Lyncroft Pinot Noir; TGQ Moscato and Sangiovese.

summary Husband and wife consultant winemakers Kathleen Quealy and Kevin McCarthy carved out an important niche market for the T'Gallant label, so much so that in April 2003, after protracted negotiations, it was acquired by Beringer Blass. The acquisition of a 15-hectare property, and the planting of 10 hectares of pinot gris gives the business a firm geographic base, as well as providing increased resources for its signature wine. The yearly parade of new (usually beautiful and striking, it is true) labels designed by Ken Cato do not make my life at all easy. No sooner is the database built up than it is discarded for next year's rash of labels. La Baracca Trattoria is open 7 days for lunch and for specially booked evening events. Exports to the UK and the US.

T'Gallant Pinot Grigio

ΨΨΨΨΨ **2002** Light to medium yellow-green; a concentrated array of fruit aromas moving from herbal/ mineral through to citrus, characters which come through on the long and intense palate, to the point of being a fraction grippy. For the followers of T'Gallant, 12.5° alcohol. **rating:** 91

best drinking Now–2005 **best vintages** '02 **drink with** Smoked salmon • $24

T'Gallant Unwooded Chardonnay

ΨΨΨΨΨ **2001** Bright green-yellow; an aromatic and perfumed bouquet of apple, citrus and nectarine is followed by a palate of great length and fruit intensity; remarkable for an unoaked chardonnay. **rating:** 93

best drinking Now–2006 **best vintages** '01 **drink with** Tempura • $24

thalgara estate NR

De Beyers Road, Pokolbin, NSW 2321 **region** Lower Hunter Valley
phone (02) 4998 7717 **fax** (02) 4998 7774 **open** 7 days 10–5
winemaker Steve Lamb **production** 3000 cases **est.** 1985
product range ($15–30 CD) Chardonnay, Show Reserve Chardonnay, Semillon Chardonnay, Shiraz, Show Reserve Shiraz, Shiraz Cabernet.
summary A low-profile winery which had its moment of glory at the 1997 Hunter Valley Wine Show when it won the Doug Seabrook Memorial Trophy for Best Dry Red of Show with its 1995 Show Reserve Shiraz.

the blok estate NR

Riddoch Highway, Coonawarra, SA 5263 **region** Coonawarra
phone (08) 8737 2734 **fax** (08) 8737 2994 **open** 7 days 10–4
winemaker Contract **production** 1200 cases **est.** 1999
product range ($16–28 CD) Riesling, Chardonnay, Pinot Chardonnay, Shiraz, Cabernet Sauvignon.
summary Di and John Blok have owned a tiny vineyard planted to cabernet sauvignon for the past 5 years. They have now decided to take the production from this and from contract-grown grapes elsewhere in Coonawarra for release under their own label. The cellar door is situated in an old stone home which has recently been renovated and surrounded by newly landscaped gardens.

🍷 the carriages vineyard ★★★

549 Kotta Road, Echuca, Vic 3564 **region** Goulburn Valley
phone (03) 5483 7767 **fax** (03) 5483 7767 **open** By appointment
winemaker Plunkett (Contract) **production** 600 cases **est.** 1996
product range ($17–19 R) Merlot, Cabernet Merlot.
summary David and Lyndall Johnson began the development of The Carriages in 1996, planting 2.5 hectares of merlot and a little over 1.5 hectares of cabernet sauvignon, the latter subsequently increased by a further 2 hectares. The wines are made at Plunkett's, where David Johnson was previously employed. The name and the extremely innovative packaging stems from the fact that the Johnsons bought four old railway carriages which they have parked side-by-side and painstakingly rehabilitated, now providing them with their house. Each bottle is identified with a cardboard rail ticket, printed by the company which provides the tickets for the Puffing Billy railway in the Dandenongs, and which is strikingly similar to the tickets of bygone years. Vertically bisected with brown on the left side, and yellow on the right side, the ticket manages to show the brand name, the vintage, the variety, the number of standard drinks, the alcohol and the bottle number (which is in fact the ticket number, or vice versa). Amazingly, all of this information appears on the ticket without cluttering it up. Finally, the ticket is fixed to the label with fine twine, so it can be removed either as a memento or for further orders.

The Carriages Vineyard Cabernet Merlot

▼▼▼▽ **2001** Medium to full red-purple; very ripe, indeed distinctly jammy, fruit on the bouquet is followed by an ultra-ripe, jammy palate. The generosity of the flavour will appeal to some, and it is easier to pull back than to build up. **rating: 84**

best drinking Now–2008 **drink with** Steak and kidney pie • $19

the falls vineyard NR

RMB 2750 Longwood–Gobur Road, Longwood East, Vic 3665 **region** Strathbogie Ranges
phone (03) 5798 5291 **fax** (03) 5798 5437 **open** By appointment 9–5
winemaker Andrew Cameron **production** 1000 cases **est.** 1969
product range ($10–16 CD) The Falls Riesling, The Falls Chardonnay, Longwood Shiraz, The Falls Shiraz, Longwood Reserve Shiraz.
summary The Falls Vineyard was planted by Andrew and Elly Cameron way back in 1969, as a minor diversification for their pastoral company. Two hectares of shiraz, originally established on a wide T-trellis, but now converted to vertical spur positioning, provides both the Longwood Shiraz and the Longwood Reserve Shiraz. The wines (showing pronounced cool climate characteristics) are made on-site, but are bottled at Mitchelton. With only 1000 cases per year, the wines are basically sold by word of mouth, and the cellar door is open only if you phone beforehand or take advantage of the bed and breakfast accommodation offered by the Camerons.

the fleurieu NR

Main Road, McLaren Vale, SA 5171 **region** McLaren Vale
phone (08) 8323 8999 **fax** (08) 323 9332 **open** 7 days 9–5
winemaker Mike Farmilo **production** 3500 cases **est.** 1994
product range ($18–35 R) Shiraz, released under the Fleurieu and Stump Hill labels.
summary A specialist Shiraz producer, with 6.5 hectares of estate vineyards and contract winemaking by the former long-serving Seaview/Edwards & Chaffey winemaker Mike Farmilo. Exports to the UK, the US, Singapore, Hong Kong, Japan, Philippines and Canada.

the gap vineyard ★★★

Pomonal Road, Halls Gap, Vic 3381 **region** Grampians
phone (03) 5356 4252 **fax** (03) 5356 4645 **open** Wed–Sun 10–5, 7 days school and public holidays
winemaker Trevor Mast **production** 1500 cases **est.** 1969
product range ($13–26 CD) Chardonnay, Reserve Chardonnay, Rose, Reserve Shiraz, Shiraz Grenache, Shiraz Cabernet Sauvignon, Cabernet Sauvignon, Cassel Port; Four Sisters Sauvignon Blanc Semillon and Shiraz; Billi Billi Creek Shiraz Grenache Cabernet
summary The Gap is the reincarnation of Boroka, a spectacularly situated vineyard 5 kilometres east of Halls Gap, with the slopes of the Mount William Range forming a backdrop. The vineyard was planted in 1969 but following its acquisition by Mount Langi Ghiran has been rehabilitated (including transplanted riesling vines), and extensive renovations have been made to the cellar-door sales area which offers estate-grown The Gap wines and a selection of Mount Langi Ghiran and Four Sisters wines. Exports to Germany and Singapore.

Four Sisters Sauvignon Blanc Semillon

▼▼▼▼ **2002** Light straw-green; clean, crisp herb/mineral aromas come through on the palate with a twist of lemon on the finish to add interest. **rating: 86**
best drinking Now **drink with** Shellfish • $13.95

the garden vineyard NR

174 Graydens Road, Moorooduc, Vic 3933 **region** Mornington Peninsula
phone (03) 5978 8336 **fax** (03) 5978 8343 **open** Weekends Nov–Mar and first weekend of Oct and Apr–Jun 11–5, or by appointment (closed July, Aug, Sept)
winemaker Richard McIntyre (Contract) **production** 130 cases **est.** 1995
product range ($20–25 CD) Pinot Gris, Pinot Noir.
summary This captures the delights of the Mornington Peninsula in so many ways. As the name suggests, it is as much a garden as it is a vineyard; Di and Doug Johnson began the establishment of a walled garden 7 years ago, at much the same time as they decided to increase the existing 0.5 hectare of pinot noir (planted in 1989) with an additional hectare of pinot noir and 0.5 hectare of pinot gris. The entrance fee to the garden is $8, but there is no charge for wine tasting. Most visitors end up enjoying both.

the green vineyards and carlei estate ★★★★☆

1 Albert Road, Upper Beaconsfield, Vic 3808 **region** Yarra Valley
phone (03) 5944 4599 **fax** (03) 5944 4599 **open** Weekends by appointment
winemaker Sergio Carlei **production** 10 000 cases **est.** 1994
product range ($16–59 ML) The Green Vineyards Organic range of Yarra Valley Sauvignon Blanc, Cardinia Ranges Chardonnay, Cardinia Ranges Pinot Noir, Heathcote Forties Old Block Shiraz, Bendigo Shiraz, Yarra Valley Cabernets; The Green Vineyards Non-Organic range of: Cardinia Ranges Sauvignon Blanc, Yarra Valley Chardonnay, Port Phillip Pinot Rose, Yarra Valley Pinot Noir, Heathcote Mt Camel Shiraz, Yarra Valley Cabernets; then the Carlei Estate range of: Halcyon Estate Yarra Valley Riesling, Woongarra Estate Cardinia Ranges Tre Bianchi, Halcyon Estate Yarra Valley Chardonnay, Karagola Estate Yarra Valley Pinot Noir, Jenmar Estate Geelong Shiraz, Halcyon Estate Yarra Valley Merlot, Karagola Estate Yarra Valley Cabernets, Yarra Valley Cabernets, The Forties Old Block Heathcote Tre Rossi (Shiraz Nebbiolo Marzemino).
summary The Green Vineyards and Carlei Estate has come a long way in a little time, with Sergio Carlei graduating from home winemaking in a suburban garage to his own (real) winery in Upper Beaconsfield, which happens to fall just within the boundaries of the Yarra Valley. Along the way Carlei acquired a Bachelor of Wine Science degree from Charles Sturt University, Wagga Wagga. He also established a 2.25-hectare vineyard organic and biodynamic accreditation adjacent to the Upper Beaconsfield winery. As each vintage has passed, more and more irresistible parcels of quality wine from here, there and everywhere have led to a bewildering but usually excellent array of wines made in quantities as little as 50 cases. To include tasting notes of all is out of the question; those given are for the best wines in the two portfolios (in the indicated vintages, the same pattern will not be followed year-in, year-out).

Carlei Riesling

▼▼▼▼▼ 2002 Light green-yellow; a clean, rich aromatic bouquet with tropical lime juice aromas is followed by a remarkably intense, powerful and rich palate, with very good length. A freakish wine which avoids the phenolic trap, produced from the 2002 yield of 0.5 tonne to the acre. **rating:** 95
best drinking 2004–2014 **best vintages** '02 **drink with** Rich shellfish, seafood • $24

Carlei Yarra Valley Pinot Noir

▼▼▼▼▽ 2000 Medium red-purple; warm spice and plum aromas combine with positive oak on the bouquet; the palate has excellent texture and mouthfeel, offering a complex mix of ripe fruit and more savoury characters. **rating:** 90
best drinking Now–2006 **best vintages** '00 **drink with** Coq au vin • $59

The Green Vineyards Biodynamic Bendigo Shiraz

▼▼▼▼▽ 2001 Medium red-purple; complex dark berry, chocolate and licorice aromas combine with positive oak on the bouquet; the palate has lots of textural play amid the complex dark fruit flavours and lingering tannins. One tonne to the acre; wild yeast; French oak for 18 months. **rating:** 91
best drinking 2005–2015 **drink with** Wild duck • $35

Carlei The Forties Old Block Tre Rossi

▼▼▼▼ 2000 Medium red-purple; the very ripe and spicy bouquet verges on being jammy, the palate again with very sweet, ripe fruit, punching well above its 13.5° alcohol. Produced from blocks yielding 1 tonne to the acre, and included as much for its varietal interest as anything else, for it is a blend of 85 per cent Shiraz, 10 per cent Marzemino and 5 per cent Nebbiolo. **rating:** 87
best drinking 2005–2015 **drink with** Well hung game • $59

Carlei Halcyon Estate Merlot

▼▼▼▼ 1998 Medium red-purple; fragrant raspberry and redcurrant fruit mingles with evident French oak on the bouquet; an intense and penetrating palate, long and lingering, explains why the wine spent 2 years in new French oak. **rating:** 89
best drinking Now–2013 **drink with** White Rocks veal • $49

The Green Vineyards Yarra Valley Cabernets

▼▼▼▼▽ 2000 Medium red-purple; a solid, dense, rich and ripe bouquet with redcurrant raspberry and blackcurrant dominant leads into a palate with abundant black and red fruit flavours, a touch of chocolate, ripe tannins and subtle oak. A blend of Cabernet Sauvignon, Cabernet Franc and Merlot. **rating:** 93
best drinking 2005–2015 **drink with** Butterfly leg of lamb • $26

🐌 the grove vineyard   NR

Cnr Metricup and Carter Roads, Wilyabrup, WA 6284   **region** Margaret River
phone (08) 9755 7458   **fax** (08) 9755 7458   **open** 7 days 9–4
winemaker Steven Hughes   **production** 2000 cases   **est.** 1995
product range ($10–25 CD) Sauvignon Blanc, Verdelho, Wood Matured Verdelho, Chardonnay, Sweet Reserve White, Country Rose, Tempranillon Graciano, The Shed Red, Cabernet Sauvignon, Vintage Port; Sparkling.
summary Steve and Val Hughes gave their vineyard its name to acknowledge their former residence in a street called The Grove, which was in turn part of an olive grove near Perth planted by the monks from the New Norcia monastery north of Perth. They have planted a fruit salad vineyard, the major varieties being sauvignon blanc (2.65 ha), chardonnay (1.5 ha), cabernet sauvignon (1.88 ha), with lesser but not insignificant plantings of semillon, pinot noir, shiraz, merlot, verdelho, tempranillo and graciano. They run a restaurant, provide accommodation, feature coffee roasting sales and tastings, a gourmet delicatessen, olive oil and, of course, cellar-door sales with a wide range of wines reflecting the fruit salad plantings.

the gurdies   NR

St Helier Road, The Gurdies, Vic 3984   **region** Gippsland
phone (03) 5997 6208   **fax** (03) 5997 6511   **open** 7 days 10–5, or by appointment
winemaker Peter Kozik   **production** 1500 cases   **est.** 1991
product range ($18–25 CD) Riesling, Gurdies Hill White (Chardonnay), Pinot Noir, Reserve Pinot Noir, Shiraz, Merlot, Cabernet Merlot, Gurdies Hill Red (Cabernet Sauvignon Shiraz), Cabernet Sauvignon.
summary The only winery in the southwest Gippsland region, established on the slopes of The Gurdies hills overlooking Westernport Bay and French Island. Plantings of the 3.5-hectare vineyard commenced in 1981, but no fruit was harvested until 1991 owing to bird attack. A winery has been partially completed, and it is intended to increase the vineyards to 8 hectares and ultimately build a restaurant on-site.

the lane   ★★★★☆

Ravenswood Lane, Hahndorf, SA 5245   **region** Adelaide Hills
phone (08) 8388 1250   **fax** (08) 8388 7233   **open** Not
winemaker Robert Mann, Stephen Pannell (Red), Glenn James (White) at Hardys   **production** 12 800 cases   **est.** 1993
product range ($18–49.95 R) Gathering Sauvignon Semillon, Beginning Chardonnay, Reunion Shiraz; Starvedog Lane Sauvignon Blanc, Chardonnay, Sparkling, Shiraz, Cabernet Sauvignon.
summary With their sales and marketing background, John and Helen Edwards opted for a major lifestyle change when they began the establishment of the first of the present 28.1 hectares of vineyards in 1993. Initially, part of the production was sold to BRL Hardy, but now some of the wine is made for release under The Lane label (until 2003, Ravenswood Lane). A joint venture with BRL Hardy is Starvedog Lane, producing wines from a patchwork of vineyards throughout the Adelaide Hills. Exports to the UK and Singapore.

Starvedog Lane Sauvignon Blanc
▼▼▼▼ **2002** Light straw-green; passionfruit and sweaty reduction characters dominate the bouquet, but the palate partly redeems the wine, crisp and lively, with some unusual but far from unpleasant crushed herb flavours. Simply a pity about the sweaty character which seems to affect so many (but not all) Sauvignon Blancs.   **rating:** 85
best drinking Now   **best vintages** '01   **drink with** Marinated fish • $19

The Lane The Gathering Sauvignon Semillon
▼▼▼▼▼ **2002** Light straw-green; spotlessly clean, moderately intense herb and lemon aromas lead into a lovely palate, with clean, long, lingering lemon and passionfruit flavours.   **rating:** 94
best drinking Now–2005   **best vintages** '99, '00, '02   **drink with** Coquilles St Jacques • $24.95

The Lane Reunion Shiraz
▼▼▼▼▽ **2000** Strong red-purple; rich, very complex black fruits with Côte Rôtie-like spice is followed by a powerful, complex palate with layers of flavour, but not overly extractive; good oak.   **rating:** 93
best drinking 2006–2016   **best vintages** '97, '98, '00   **drink with** Beef bourgignon • $49.95

Starvedog Lane Shiraz

YYYY 2000 Medium red-purple; the fragrant bouquet has a mix of spice, cherry, raspberry and plum; the palate opens with spicy/cedary flavours, but finishes with somewhat drying tannins; a pity. **rating:** 88

best drinking 2004–2010 **best vintages** '97, '98, '99 **drink with** Turkish lamb pizza • $27

The Lane 19th Meeting Cabernet Sauvignon

YYYY 2000 Medium to full red-purple; a powerful, highly accented wild herb and black fruit bouquet is magnified further by the palate; way out in left field, but certainly makes a statement. **rating:** 89

best drinking 2006–2011 **drink with** Herbed rack of lamb • $49.95

the mews   NR

84 Gibson Street, Kings Meadows, Tas 7249 **region** Northern Tasmania
phone (03) 6344 2780 **fax** (03) 6343 2076 **open** Not
winemaker Graham Wiltshire **production** 300 cases **est.** 1984
product range Chardonnay.
summary Robin and Anne Holyman have established 0.4 hectare of pinot noir and 9.2 hectares of chardonnay at Kings Meadows, only 4 kilometres from the centre of Launceston. Most of the grapes are sold; industry veteran Graham Wiltshire acts as winemaker for the remainder, and the wines are sold by direct contact with the Holymans.

the minya winery   NR

Minya Lane, Connewarre, Vic 3227 **region** Geelong
phone (03) 5264 1397 **fax** (03) 5264 1097 **open** Public holidays or by appointment
winemaker Susan Dans **production** 1400 cases **est.** 1974
product range ($15.50–18 CD) Gewurztraminer, Chardonnay, Shiraz, Grenache, Cabernet Sauvignon Merlot.
summary Geoff Dans first planted vines in 1974 on his family's dairy farm, followed by further plantings in 1982 and 1988 lifting the total to 4 hectares. I have not tasted any of the wines, but the concerts staged in summer sound appealing. Grenache is a highly unusual variety for this neck of the woods.

the natural wine company   ★★★

217 Copley Road, Upper Swan, WA 6069 **region** Swan Valley
phone (08) 9296 1436 **fax** (08) 9296 1436 **open** Wed–Sun and public holidays 10–5
winemaker Colin Evans **production** 1500 cases **est.** 1998
product range ($15 CD) Semillon, Chenin Semillon, Chenin Blanc, Verdelho, Unwooded Chardonnay, Chardonnay, Pinot Noir, Shiraz, Cabernet Sauvignon.
summary Owners Colin and Sandra Evans say the name of the business is intended to emphasise that no herbicides or systemic pesticides are used in the vineyard, which is situated on the western slopes of the Darling Range. Weed control is achieved through mulching, and Sandra does the vineyard work and helps with the night shift during vintage. She was also responsible for the koala emerging from the barrel on the unusual label. The vineyard is within a short walk of Bells Rapids and close to the Walunga National Park. Rated on the basis of previous tastings.

the oaks vineyard and winery   ★★★☆

31 Melba Highway, Yering, Vic 3770 **region** Yarra Valley
phone (03) 9739 0070 **fax** (03) 9739 0577 **open** Weekends 10.30–5, or by appointment
winemaker Karen Coulston (Contract) **production** 500 cases **est.** 2000
product range ($13.50–22.50 CD) Deschamps (Sauvignon Blanc Chardonnay Riesling), Chardonnay, Pinot Noir, Cabernet Sauvignon Merlot.
summary The Oaks has been established in what was originally a Presbyterian Manse, the change in use coming after a long period of neglect, and thus not incurring the wrath of the previous occupants. Owner Pauline Charlton spent 12 months restoring the Victorian homestead to its former glory prior to the opening. An on-site gallery features photographs by Pauline Charlton's daughter, Mackenzie, and fellow students of the Photography Studies College. The vineyard is close-planted, and the wine competently made by contract maker Karen Coulston. Rated on the basis of previous tastings.

the rothbury estate ★★★★

Broke Road, Pokolbin, NSW 2321 **region** Lower Hunter Valley
phone (02) 4998 7363 **fax** (02) 4993 3559 **open** 7 days 9.30–4.30
winemaker Neil McGuigan **production** 82 500 cases **est.** 1968
product range ($8.90–22 R) At the top comes the Individual Vineyard range of Hunter Valley Semillon, Chardonnay and Shiraz; next the Hunter Valley range of varietals; and finally varietals from Mudgee and Cowra.
summary Rothbury celebrated its 30th birthday in 1998, albeit not quite in the fashion that founder and previous chief executive Len Evans would have wished. After a protracted and at times bitter takeover battle, it became part of the Beringer Blass empire. Quality has bounced back dramatically since the advent of Neil McGuigan as winemaker.

Rothbury Estate Brokenback Semillon

♥♥♥♥♥ **2001** Bright medium green-yellow; the spotlessly clean and fragrant bouquet has a mix of gentle herb and citrus aromas; a lovely wine with a classic, tight structure and perfect balance; absolutely guaranteed to age. 10° alcohol. Right in the slot of the 2001 vintage. **rating:** 95

best drinking Now–2021 **best vintages** '97, '98, '00, '01 **drink with** Smoked eel • $21

Rothbury Estate Neil McGuigan Series Mudgee Chardonnay

♥♥♥♥ **2002** Light to medium yellow-green; the bouquet is fairly light, with some stone fruit and subtle oak; the light to medium-bodied palate clean and smooth, in unthreatening commercial mode. **rating:** 85

best drinking Now **drink with** Pasta • $18

Rothbury Estate Neil McGuigan Series Hunter Valley Shiraz

♥♥♥♥ **2001** Light to medium red-purple; a spotlessly clean bouquet offers cherry and just a touch of oak; the medium-bodied palate is still well and truly in the primary fruit phase, but is well balanced and will develop. **rating:** 88

best drinking 2005–2010 **drink with** Designer sausages • $20

Rothbury Estate Neil McGuigan Series Mudgee Cabernet Sauvignon

♥♥♥♥ **2001** Medium to full red-purple; solid blackberry and blackcurrant fruit on the bouquet is supported by subtle oak; the powerful palate is dominated by tannins, and I am left to wonder why it was not fined. **rating:** 85

best drinking 2006–2011 **drink with** Leave it in the cellar • $20

the settlement wine co NR

Cnr Olivers and Chalk Hill Roads, McLaren Vale, SA 5171 **region** McLaren Vale
phone (08) 8323 7344 **fax** (08) 8323 7355 **open** 7 days 10–5
winemaker Vincenzo Berlingieri **production** 3500 cases **est.** 1992
product range ($16–20 CD) Langhorne Creek wines with Pinot Noir, Shiraz, Cabernet Franc, Cabernet Sauvignon Cabernet Franc, Sparkling Shiraz; McLaren Vale Shiraz.
summary Vincenzo Berlingieri, one of the great characters of the wine industry, arrived in Sydney with beard flowing and arms waving in the 1970s and successfully gained considerable publicity for his then McLaren Vale winery. Fortune did not follow marketing success for this research scientist who had arrived to work in plant genetics at Melbourne University's Botany Department in 1964, armed with a doctorate in agricultural science from Perugia University, Italy. However, after various moves he is in business again with his children, Jason, John and Annika, sourcing most of the grapes from Langhorne Creek and McLaren Vale. Most of the business is in unlabelled cleanskin form at yesterday's prices, sold only through a mailing list/direct order system.

the silos estate NR

Princes Highway, Jaspers Brush, NSW 2535 **region** Shoalhaven Coast
phone (02) 4448 6082 **fax** (02) 4448 6246 **open** 7 days 10–5
winemaker Bevan Wilson **production** 1000 cases **est.** 1985
product range ($10–25 CD) Traminer Riesling, Semillon, Unoaked Chardonnay, Chardonnay, Simply Savvy, Wileys Creek Brut, Diva (Dessert), Coral Blush, Coral Crossing, Reserve Shiraz, Tawny Port, Liqueur Muscat.
summary Since 1995, Gaynor Sims and Kate Khoury, together with viticulturist Jovica Zecevic, have worked hard to improve the quality of the wine, starting with the 5 hectares of estate vineyards but also in the winery. The winery continues to rely on the tourist trade, however, and the wines do not appear in normal retail channels.

the warren vineyard   NR

Conte Road, Pemberton, WA 6260 **region** Pemberton
phone (08) 9776 1115 **fax** (08) 9776 1115 **open** 7 days 11–5
winemaker Bernard Abbott **production** 400 cases **est.** 1985
product range ($15–30 CD) Riesling, Cabernet Merlot, Cabernet Blanc.
summary The 1.5-hectare vineyard was established in 1985 and is one of the smallest in the Pemberton region, coming to public notice when its 1991 Cabernet Sauvignon won the award for the Best Red Table Wine from the Pemberton Region at the 1992 SGIO Western Australia Winemakers Exhibition. Bottle-aged Riesling has also had notable success, the 1994 winning the trophy for Best Aged White at the 1998 Qantas Wine Show of West Australia.

the willows vineyard   ★★★★

Light Pass Road, Light Pass, Barossa Valley, SA 5355 **region** Barossa Valley
phone (08) 8562 1080 **fax** (08) 8562 3447 **open** 7 days 10.30–4.30
winemaker Peter Scholz, Michael Scholz **production** 6000 cases **est.** 1989
product range ($13.50–25.50 R) Riesling, Semillon, Shiraz, Cabernet Sauvignon.
summary The Scholz family have been grape growers for generations and have almost 40 hectares of vineyards, selling part and retaining part of the crop. Current generation winemakers Peter and Michael Scholz could not resist the temptation to make smooth, well-balanced and flavoursome wines under their own label. These are all marketed with some years bottle age. Exports to the UK and New Zealand. Rated on the basis of previous tastings.

thistle hill   ★★★☆

McDonalds Road, Mudgee, NSW 2850 **region** Mudgee
phone (02) 6373 3546 **fax** (02) 6373 3540 **open** Mon–Sat 9.30–5, Sun and public holidays 9.30–4
winemaker Lesley Robertson, Ian MacRae **production** 3000 cases **est.** 1976
product range ($15–21 CD) Riesling, Semillon, Special Reserve Semillon, Chardonnay, Pinot Noir, Cabernet Shiraz, Cabernet Sauvignon, Liqueur Muscat.
summary The sudden death of Dave Robertson in September 2001 robbed Mudgee of one of its great characters and wife Lesley and daughters Lucy and Sally of a much-loved husband and father. They have vowed to continue Thistle Hill, selling the back vintages made by Dave until approximately 2004, when wines contract made by Ian MacRae (Miramar) from Thistle Hill grapes will come on-stream. With typical Aussie humour, they say they will not rename the property Feminist Hill.

Thistle Hill Riesling

▼▼▼▼ **2002** Pale straw-green, with some CO_2 spritz evident; the clean, flinty/spicy/slatey/citrus aromas lead into a well made, clean and balanced palate. Mudgee can produce surprisingly good riesling, even though the wines lack the finesse of the top Clare Valley/Eden counterparts. **rating:** 87
best drinking Now–2007 **drink with** Caesar salad • $15

Thistle Hill Chardonnay

▼▼▼▼ **2001** Medium yellow-green; attractive and quite complex bottle-developed aromas are starting to appear, the fruit and oak balance spot on; the palate has rich, ripe peachy fruit, the slightly assertive acid counterpoint on the finish needing to back off a little. **rating:** 88
best drinking Now–2008 **best vintages** '84, '86, '88, '92 **drink with** Creamy pasta • $17

Thistle Hill Cabernet Sauvignon

▼▼▼▼ **2000** Medium red; light, savoury, spicy aromas and flavours are anchored in blackberry fruit, the palate with fine, ripe tannins and good length. An excellent outcome for a pretty miserable vintage. **rating:** 86
best drinking 2004–2008 **best vintages** '85, '86, '88, '89, '90, '97 **drink with** Barbecued meat • $21

thomas wines   ★★★★

c/- The Small Winemakers Centre, McDonalds Road, Pokolbin, NSW 2321 **region** Lower Hunter Valley
phone (02) 4991 6801 **fax** (02) 4991 6801 **open** 7 days 10–5
winemaker Andrew Thomas **production** 1500 cases **est.** 1997
product range ($20–32 R) Semillon, Shiraz.

summary Andrew Thomas came to the Hunter Valley from McLaren Vale, to join the winemaking team at Tyrrell's. After 13 years with Tyrrell's, he left to undertake contract work and to continue the development of his own winery label, a family affair run by himself and his wife Jo. The Semillon is sourced from a single vineyard owned by local grower Ken Bray, renowned for its quality, while the Shiraz is a blend of 60 per cent Hunter Valley shiraz and 40 per cent McLaren Vale shiraz. The wines are virtually exclusively available at the Small Winemakers Centre, although they can be found on restaurant lists throughout the Hunter Valley. Rated on the basis of previous tastings.

🐦 thomson vintners   NR

5 O'Loughlin Street, Waikerie, SA 5330 (postal) **region** Riverland
phone (08) 8541 2168 **fax** (08) 8541 3369 **open** Not
winemaker Colin Glaetzer, Ben Glaetzer **production** 80 000 cases **est.** 1996
product range ($9.95 R) Woolpunda range of Chardonnay, Shiraz, Merlot, Cabernet; also Larra Pinta Sparkling Burgundy.
summary Although the year of establishment is shown as 1996, Thomson Vintners had been grape growers in the Riverland since 1961, among the first to plant cabernet sauvignon, and also (much later on) among the first to introduce regulated deficit irrigation (to reduce yield and improve quality). Most of the 7000–8000 tonnes of grapes produced from the 480 hectares of vineyards are sold to major wine companies, but the plan is to lift the amount used for the Thomson's Woolpunda label from its present level of about 8 to 9 per cent to 20 per cent, moving production upwards from 50 000 to 120 000 cases per annum. With the experienced winemaking team of Colin and Ben Glaetzer in charge, the under $10 price point for the wines is obviously attractive, and the wines are now distributed in most states, with exports to the UK, Canada, Germany, Denmark, China, Norway and Singapore.

🐦 thornborough estate   NR

PO Box 678, Virginia, SA 5120 **region** Adelaide Plains
phone (08) 8235 0419 **open** Not
winemaker George Girgolas **production** 2000 cases **est.** 2000
product range ($25–30 R) Shiraz.
summary George Girgolas has been a long-term grape grower near Virginia in the Adelaide Plains region, with 116 hectares of 38-year-old vines, the grapes all previously contract-sold to Yalumba. He was indeed Yalumba's Grower of the Year in 2000. Three years ago he and his family acquired the Thornborough property (5 kilometres away from the vineyard) which includes a two-storey stone house built in 1827, and straddles the Gawler River. The plans are to convert Thornborough into a guest house.

thorn-clarke wines   ★★★☆

Milton Park, Gawler Park Road, Angaston, SA 5353 **region** Barossa Valley
phone (08) 8564 3373 **fax** (08) 8564 3255 **open** Not
winemaker Jim Irvine (Consultant) **est.** 1997
product range SandPiper Eden Valley Riesling, SandPiper Barossa Shiraz, Shotfire Ridge Barossa Shiraz, Randell Barossa Shiraz, Shotfire Ridge Barossa Quartage, SandPiper Barossa Cabernet Sauvignon.
summary To say this is a substantial new venture is to put it mildly. Two hundred and sixty-four hectares of vineyard has been established, with shiraz (136 ha), cabernet sauvignon (59 ha) and merlot (28 ha) being the principal plantings, supported by lesser amounts of petit verdot, cabernet franc, chardonnay, riesling and pinot gris. The first wines were released in the Australian domestic market in August 2002, and one imagines that exports will also be the focus of attention, particularly given the role of Jim Irvine as consultant winemaker.

Thorn-Clarke SandPiper Eden Valley Riesling
🍷🍷🍷🍷 2002 Pale straw-green; a clean and crisp bouquet with lime blossom and mineral/slate aromas, then a palate with a mix of apple and tropical fruit, and a subliminal hint of sweetness.   **rating:** 86
best drinking Now–2006 **drink with** Gravlax • $14.95

Thorn-Clarke Shotfire Ridge Barossa Valley Shiraz
🍷🍷🍷🍷 1999 Bright red-purple; the complex bouquet has good fruit and oak balance and integration, but the American oak takes over on the palate; less would have been much better. The wine spent only 5 months in American oak, and 18 months in French, but, as ever, the American oak swamps the French.   **rating:** 85
best drinking Now–2007 **drink with** Smoked beef • $22.95

Thorn-Clarke William Randell Barossa Valley Shiraz

🍷🍷🍷🍷♀ **1999** Medium red-purple; the bouquet has a complex mix of dark fruits and vanillin oak; excellent shiraz fruit (particularly for 1999) stands up to the oak on the palate, with vanilla and black cherry coalescing, the length sustained by ripe tannins. **rating:** 93

best drinking 2004–2014 **best vintages** '99 **drink with** Beef in red wine sauce • $44.95

Thorn-Clarke Shotfire Ridge Barossa Valley Quartage

🍷🍷🍷🍷 **2000** Medium to full red-purple; red berry fruits are joined by abundant, dusty vanilla oak on the bouquet. The powerful, dense palate likewise brings jammy fruit and lashings of oak to the party. A blend of Cabernet Sauvignon, Cabernet Franc, Merlot and Petit Verdot. **rating:** 86

best drinking 2004–2009 **drink with** Steak and kidney pie • $22.95

three moon creek   NR

Waratah Vineyard, Gladstone Road, Mungungo via Monto, Qld 4630 **region** South Burnett
phone (07) 4166 5100 **fax** (07) 4166 5200 **open** Tues–Sun and public holidays 10–5
winemaker Peter Scudamore-Smith MW (Contract) **production** 1500 cases **est.** 1998
product range ($14–20 CD) White Blend, Gentle Annie White, Waratah Estate Verdelho, Rose, Gentle Annie Red, Shiraz, Monal Merlot, The Gorge (fortified dessert wine).
summary David Bray is one of the doyens of wine journalism in Brisbane, and, indeed, Australia. After decades of writing about wine he and wife Pamela have joined Max Lindsay (Pamela's brother) and partner Lynne Tucker in establishing the Waratah Vineyard and Winery joint venture at Mungungo, near Monto, at the top of the Burnett Valley. The wines are principally sourced from the 4 hectare Waratah Vineyard with 3.2 hectares of vineyard planted to chardonnay, verdelho, semillon, marsanne, viognier, shiraz, merlot and petit verdot, an exotic mix if ever there was one, supplemented by grapes grown at Inglewood and Murgon. The wines are made by the energetic Peter Scudamore-Smith MW.

Three Moon Creek The Gorge

🍷🍷🍷🍷 **NV** Tawny red; fruity raisiny berry aromas lead into a simple but well-balanced palate, the spirit clean. Infinitely better than expected, and, even more surprisingly, produced from Queensland-grown grapes and Burnett Valley spirit. **rating:** 85

best drinking Now **drink with** Whatever takes your fancy • $18

🌿 three wise men   ★★★★☆

RMB 440 Kurting Road, Kingower, Vic 3517 (Passing Clouds) **region** Port Phillip Zone
phone (03) 5438 8257 **fax** (03) 5438 8246 **open** Weekends 12–5, Mon–Fri by appointment
winemaker Graeme Leith **production** 800 cases **est.** 1994
product range ($27–50 CD) Pinot Noir, Reserve Pinot Noir, Shiraz.
summary The Three Wise Men are (or were) Graeme Leith (of Passing Clouds fame), Dr Bruce Jones (Woongarra vineyard owner and grape grower) and Dr Graham Ellender (a semi-retired dentist-turned-winemaker). It came about after a trial batch was made in 1998 by Bruce Jones' consultant Andrew Clarke. The 1999 and 2000 vintages were made at Graham Ellender's winery, but he thereafter retired from the venture as his own production grew, and there are now two wise men, Graham Leith as winemaker and Bruce Jones as grape grower. Each takes half of the resulting wine, and sells it through their respective wineries, Passing Clouds and Woongarra. The quality of the wines speaks for itself.

Three Wise Men Pinot Noir

🍷🍷🍷🍷♀ **2001** Light to medium red-purple; the cherry and strawberry fruit aromas of the bouquet are strongly and clearly varietal, and the palate follows down the same track, the strawberry and cherry fruit set among more spicy/savoury characters, It has exemplary length, line and style, the tannins fine, the balance perfect. **rating:** 93

best drinking Now–2006 **best vintages** '01 **drink with** Rare duck breast • $27

Three Wise Men Reserve Pinot Noir

🍷🍷🍷🍷🍷 **2001** Deeper in colour than the varietal of the same vintage, the bouquet has an added level of complexity, deriving chiefly from the new oak, although it is not the least bit assertive. On the palate, plummy nuances join the strawberry and cherry, and there is an added layer of complexity and of tannins. **rating:** 95

best drinking 2005–2009 **best vintages** '01 **drink with** Coq au vin • $50

Three Wise Men Shiraz

▼▼▼▼ 2001 Medium red-purple; the moderately intense bouquet has complex, cool-grown spice and berry aromas; the palate follows on with spice, leaf, berry and pepper flavours; has only just struggled across the ripeness threshold.   **rating:** 85

best drinking Now–2007 **drink with** Asian meat dishes

thumm estate wines   NR

87 Kriedeman Road, Upper Coomera, Qld 4209 **region** Queensland Coastal
phone (07) 5573 6990 **fax** (07) 5573 4099 **open** 7 days 9–5, 9–6 in summer
winemaker Robert Thumm **production** 1000 cases **est.** 2000
product range ($14–22.50 CD) Riesling, Semillon, Sauvignon Blanc, Unwooded Chardonnay, Chardonnay, Shiraz, Cabernet Sauvignon.
summary Robert Thumm, born in 1950, is the eldest son of Hermann Thumm, founder of Chateau Yaldara in the Barossa Valley, gaining his degree in oenology from the University of Geisenheim, Germany. In 1999, when the family business was sold, he and wife Janet decided to move to Queensland, establishing the new winery in a valley below the Tambourine Mountain Tourist Centre. Here they have planted cabernet sauvignon and petit verdot, but also have 1.5 hectares of riesling and 1.2 hectares of sauvignon blanc in production in the Adelaide Hills. The venture, and its associated wine club, is firmly aimed at the general tourist market, Thumm Estate being yet another such venture in this part of Australia which relies so heavily on tourism, and which offers so much to tourists.

tilba valley   NR

Lake Corunna Estate, 947 Old Highway, Narooma, NSW 2546 **region** South Coast Zone
phone (02) 4473 7308 **fax** (02) 4473 7484 **open** Oct–April 7 days 10–5, May–Sept Wed–Sun 11–4 (closed August)
winemaker Bevan Wilson **production** 600 cases **est.** 1978
product range ($16–18 CD) Traminer Riesling, Semillon, Semillon Chardonnay, Chambourcin, Cabernet Shiraz.
summary A strongly tourist-oriented operation, serving a ploughman's lunch daily from noon to 2 pm. Has 8 hectares of estate vineyards; no recent tastings.

tim adams   ★★★★

Warenda Road, Clare, SA 5453 **region** Clare Valley
phone (08) 8842 2429 **fax** (08) 8842 3550 **open** Mon–Fri 10.30–5, weekends 11–5
winemaker Tim Adams **production** 30 000 cases **est.** 1986
product range ($16–60 CD) Riesling, Semillon, Botrytis Riesling, The Fergus (Grenache), Shiraz, Aberfeldy Shiraz, Cabernet, Tawny Port.
summary Tim and Pam Adams have built a first-class business since Tim Adams left his position as winemaker at Leasingham in 1985. Eleven hectares of estate vineyards increasingly provide the wine for the business, supplemented by grapes from local growers. Tim Adams has consistently produced wines of exceptional depth of flavour and he also makes significant quantities of wine under contract for others in the district. Exports to the UK and the US.

Tim Adams Riesling

▼▼▼▼▼ 2002 Light to medium yellow-green; the aromas are tight, initially ranging through herb, mineral and lemon, then a touch of spice; the well-balanced palate is equally tight, lively and crisp, offering citrus, apple and lemon flavours. Very much the product of a great vintage.   **rating:** 94

best drinking Now–2013 **best vintages** '02 **drink with** Seafood salad • $16

Tim Adams Shiraz

▼▼▼▼ 2001 Bright, full purple-red; oak makes the first call on the bouquet, with blackberry and black cherry one step behind; the boots-and-all palate mixes fruit, tannins and oak in abundance; extreme patience should be well rewarded.   **rating:** 89

best drinking 2006–2016 **best vintages** '86, '88, '90, '92, '93, '96 **drink with** Leave it in the cellar • $19

Tim Adams Aberfeldy Shiraz

▼▼▼▼♀ 2000 Medium red-purple; a fragrant, high-toned bouquet with black cherry fruit, lemon/vanillin oak and touches of earth, then a palate with plenty of action; a rich core of fruit is surrounded and supported by ripe tannins and nice oak.   **rating:** 92

best drinking 2005–2015 **best vintages** '97, '98, '99, '00 **drink with** Ragout of venison • $50

Tim Adams The Fergus Grenache

TTTY 2001 Clear red-purple; aromas of jam, spice and herb on the bouquet are followed by a palate loaded with sweet, juicy, jammy varietal character. The blend may not be as haphazard as might appear, because the wine works better than some. The blend is 86 per cent Grenache, 10 per cent Cabernet Franc and 4 per cent Shiraz. **rating:** 84

best drinking Now **drink with** Marinated beef • $22

Tim Adams Cabernet

TTTT 2001 Medium red-purple; the complex bouquet is driven by earthy, blackberry fruit and nicely balanced and integrated French oak. The palate is in the mainstream of Tim Adams style, with blackberry, savoury and olive flavours in a powerful frame, girdled by strong but balanced tannins. **rating:** 88

best drinking 2006–2011 **best vintages** '86, '88, '90, '92, '94, '98 **drink with** Char-grilled rump steak • $19

tim gramp ★★★★

Mintaro Road, Watervale, SA 5452 **region** Clare Valley
phone (08) 8344 4079 **fax** (08) 8342 1379 **open** Weekends and holidays 10.30–4.30
winemaker Tim Gramp **production** 5000 cases **est.** 1990
product range ($16.50–36.50 R) Watervale Riesling, McLaren Vale Shiraz, McLaren Vale Reserve Shiraz, McLaren Vale Grenache, Watervale Cabernet Sauvignon.
summary Tim Gramp has quietly built up a very successful business with a limited product range, and – by keeping overheads to a minimum – provides good wines at modest prices. The operation is supported by 2 hectares of cabernet sauvignon around the cellar door. Exports to the UK, the US and New Zealand.

Tim Gramp Watervale Riesling

TTTT 2002 Light to medium yellow-green; full lime, plus a dash of pineapple/tropical aromas, immediately tell you which side of the divide (of 2002) it will fall; the palate opens with similar flavours but has a faint touch of bitterness on the finish. In all probability, that trace would not be apparent when the wine is being drunk with appropriate food. **rating:** 87

best drinking Now–2007 **best vintages** '97, '98 **drink with** Bouillabaisse • $19.80

Tim Gramp McLaren Vale Reserve Shiraz

TTTTT 2001 Strong, full red-purple; a clean but complex array of blackberry, chocolate, spice, savoury and vanilla aromas lead into a totally delicious palate, crammed with red and black fruit flavours; very good oak and extract; fine tannins. Monster bottle, not monster alcohol, only 13.5°. By far and away the best wine to date from Tim Gramp. **rating:** 95

best drinking 2006–2016 **best vintages** '01 **drink with** Kangaroo fillet • $36.50

Tim Gramp Watervale Cabernet Sauvignon

TTTT 2001 Medium red-purple; the relatively light bouquet has a range of earthy/leafy/berry aromas, characters which come through on the light to medium-bodied palate, where they are joined by touches of mint and chocolate. **rating:** 85

best drinking 2004–2009 **drink with** Barbecued beef • $19.80

tim smith wines NR

PO Box 446, Tanunda, SA 5352 **region** Barossa Valley
phone (08) 8563 0939 **open** Not
winemaker Tim Smith **production** 500 cases **est.** 2001
product range ($23–29 R) Shiraz, Grenache Mataro Shiraz.
summary Tim Smith aspires to make wines in the mould of the great producers of Côte Rôtie and Chateauneuf du Pape, but using a new world approach. It is a business in its infancy, with only two wines, a Shiraz and a Grenache Shiraz Mourvedre blend.

tin cows ★★★★

Tarrawarra Estate, Healesville Road, Yarra Glen, Vic 3775 **region** Yarra Valley
phone (03) 5962 3311 **fax** (03) 5962 3887 **open** 7 days 10.30–4.30
winemaker Clare Halloran, Damian North **production** 18 000 cases **est.** 1983
product range ($23–25 CD) Chardonnay, Pinot Noir, Shiraz, Merlot.

summary Tin Cows (formerly Tunnel Hill) is regarded by Tarrawarra as a separate business, drawing most of its grapes from the 21-hectare Tin Cows Vineyard adjacent to the Maroondah Highway. The wines are intended to be more accessible when young, and are significantly cheaper than the Tarrawarra wines.

Tin Cows Chardonnay

ŶŶŶŶ♡ 2001 Glowing yellow-green; a fragrant and vibrant bouquet of melon and nectarine fruit offset by gentle oak leads into a very good, fruit-driven palate; abundant length and texture. **rating:** 92

best drinking Now–2006 **best vintages** '01 **drink with** Fresh Tasmanian salmon • $23

Tin Cows Pinot Noir

ŶŶŶŶ 2001 Light to medium red-purple; the clean, fresh bouquet has plum and red cherry fruit aromas, the medium-bodied palate has good texture, length, and fine tannins, but really needs a touch more fruit flesh on the bones. **rating:** 88

best drinking Now–2006 **best vintages** '91, '92, '94, '96, '97, '00 **drink with** Game pie • $25

Tin Cows Shiraz

ŶŶŶŶ 2001 Medium red-purple; fresh red and black fruit aromas together with some oak lead into a far riper and richer palate, with lots of blackberry and plum fruit, reflecting the blend of Yarra Valley and Heathcote material. It is the latter which powers the wine. **rating:** 89

best drinking 2004–2009 **drink with** Braised oxtail • $25

Tin Cows Merlot

ŶŶŶŶ♡ 2000 Light to medium red-purple; a strongly varietal bouquet with a range of savoury, earthy, spicy, leafy aromas, all of which come through on the palate, finishing with fine tannins and subtle oak. Nicely handled, and reflects an excellent Yarra Valley vintage. **rating:** 90

best drinking Now–2007 **best vintages** '00 **drink with** Rack of veal • $24

tinderbox vineyard ★★★★☆

Tinderbox, Tas 7054 **region** Southern Tasmania
phone (03) 6229 2994 **fax** (03) 6229 2994 **open** By appointment
winemaker Andrew Hood (Contract) **production** 175 cases **est.** 1994
product range ($28 CD) Pinot Noir.
summary Liz McGown is a Hobart nurse who has established her 1-hectare vineyard on the slope beneath her house, overlooking the entrance to the Derwent River and the D'Entrecasteaux Channel. The attractive label was designed by Barry Tucker, who was so charmed by Liz McGown's request that he waived his usual (substantial) fee.

Tinderbox Vineyard Pinot Noir

ŶŶŶŶŶ 2001 Medium red-purple; the moderately intense bouquet has plum, spice and tangy aromas; the wine comes storming through on the long, intense and stylish palate, with its mix of red berries and more sappy flavours. Well deserved gold medal Tasmanian Wines Show 2003. **rating:** 94

best drinking Now–2007 **best vintages** '99, '01 **drink with** Duck casserole • $28

tingle-wood ★★★★☆

Glenrowan Road, Denmark, WA 6333 **region** Great Southern
phone (08) 9840 9218 **fax** (08) 9840 9218 **open** 7 days 9–5
winemaker Brenden Smith (Contract) **production** 1000 cases **est.** 1976
product range ($15–18 CD) Yellow Tingle Riesling, Tree Top Walk (late harvest), Red Tingle Cabernet Sauvignon Shiraz.
summary An intermittent producer of Riesling of extraordinary quality, although birds and other disasters do intervene and prevent production in some years. The rating is given for the Riesling, which remains a sentimental favourite of mine. Exports to the UK.

tinklers vineyard ★★★☆

Pokolbin Mountains Road, Pokolbin, NSW 2330 **region** Lower Hunter Valley
phone (02) 4998 7435 **fax** (02) 4998 7529 **open** 7 days 10–4
winemaker Ian Tinkler **production** 750 cases **est.** 1997
product range ($11–25 CD) School Block Semillon, Flemings Semillon, Pokolbin Mountains Semillon Verdelho, Lucerne Paddock Verdelho, Mt Bright Chardonnay, Eruptions Sparkling Shiraz, Volcanic Ash (sweet

white), Côte D'or Shiraz, Mt Bright Shiraz, U&I Shiraz, Mt Bright Merlot, Pokolbin Mountains Cabernet Merlot, Pokolbin Mountains Cabernet Sauvignon, Usher Gordon Muscat.

summary Brothers Ian and Usher Tinkler own a large (41.5-ha) vineyard on the slopes of the Pokolbin Mountain Road; most of the production is sold, a small amount being contract-made for cellar-door sales. The names of the wines are, if nothing else, highly imaginative.

tinlins   NR

Kangarilla Road, McLaren Flat, SA 5171 **region** McLaren Vale
phone (08) 8323 8649 **fax** (08) 8323 9747 **open** 7 days 9–5
winemaker Warren Randall **production** 30 000 cases **est.** 1977
product range ($1.50–3.40 CD) Generic table, fortified and flavoured wines priced from $3.70 for table wines and $4.50 for fortified wines.
summary A very interesting operation run by former Seppelt sparkling winemaker Warren Randall, drawing upon 100 hectares of estate vineyards, which specialises in bulk-wine sales to the major Australian wine companies. A small proportion of the production is sold direct through the cellar door at mouthwateringly low prices to customers who provide their own containers and purchase by the litre. McLaren Vale's only bulk-wine specialist.

tinonee vineyard   NR

Milbrodale Road, Broke, NSW 2330 **region** Lower Hunter Valley
phone (02) 6579 1308 **fax** (02) 9719 1833 **open** Weekends and public holidays 11–4
winemaker Andrew Margan, Ray Merger (Contract) **production** 384 cases **est.** 1997
product range ($15–18 CD) Verdelho, Chardonnay, Shiraz, Durif, Merlot, Chambourcin.
summary Ian Craig has established 14 hectares of vineyards on a mix of red volcanic and river flat soils at Broke. Part are in production, with the remainder coming into bearing, ultimately capable of producing 5000 cases of wine per year.

🍂 tin shed wines   ★★★★

PO Box 504, Tanunda, SA 5352 **region** Eden Valley
phone (08) 8563 3669 **fax** (08) 8563 3669 **open** Not
winemaker Andrew Wardlaw, Peter Clarke **production** 1500 cases **est.** 1998
product range ($15–40) Riesling, Rose, Shiraz, Three Vines MSG (Mourvedre Shiraz Grenache).
summary Tin Shed proprietors Andrew Wardlaw and Peter Clarke weave all sorts of mystique in producing and marketing the Tin Shed wines. They say 'our wines are hand-made so we can only produce small volumes; this means we can take more care at each step of the winemaking process ... most bizarre of all we use our nose, palette (sic) and commonsense as opposed to the safe and reliable formula preached by our Uni's and peers.' The Tin Shed newsletter continues with lots of gee-whizz, hay-seed-jollity, making one fear the worst, when the reality is the wines (even the Wild Bunch Riesling, wild-fermented without chemicals) are very good indeed. The retail stockists also tell you this is a quality producer: they include Ultimo Wines in Sydney; Burwood Cellars and Nicks in Melbourne; Melbourne Street Cellars, Edinburgh Cellars and East End in Adelaide; and Nedlands Hotel in Perth.

Tin Shed Wild Bunch Riesling

▼▼▼▼ 2002 Light straw-green; the bouquet is not particularly intense, but does have lime and soft, tropical echoes on the bouquet; the pleasant, mid-weight palate has plenty of flavour, and is built in easy access style.   **rating:** 86
best drinking Now–2005 **drink with** Deep-fried calamari • $24

Tin Shed Single Wire Shiraz

▼▼▼▼ 2001 Medium red-purple; the moderately intense bouquet has a traditional mix of earthy, red and black fruits and nicely handled French oak. The smooth and ripe, medium-bodied palate moves more towards the raspberry/plum spectrum, the oak once again well handled.   **rating:** 89
best drinking 2005–2011 **drink with** Rib of beef • $40

Tin Shed Three Vines Mourvedre Shiraz Grenache

▼▼▼▼▽ 2001 Medium to full red-purple; a rich and complex mix of dark berry and more savoury aromas is followed by a palate which lives up to the promise of the bouquet, with lots of texture and weight; the lush mid-palate is held together by ripe tannins on the finish.   **rating:** 92
best drinking 2004–2009 **drink with** Kangaroo fillet • $35

tintilla wines ★★★★

725 Hermitage Road, Pokolbin, NSW 2320 **region** Lower Hunter Valley
phone (02) 6574 7093 **fax** (02) 9767 6894 **open** Weekends 10.30–6, Mon–Fri afternoons by appointment
winemaker Greg Silkman, Monarch (Contract) **production** 4000 cases **est.** 1993
product range ($16.50–35 CD) Semillon, Rosato di Jupiter, Reserve Shiraz, James Shiraz, Saphira
Sangiovese, Catherine de'M Sangiovese Merlot, Shiraz, Justine Merlot, Merlot, Fortified Semillon (White
Port), Fortified Shiraz (Vintage Port).
summary The Lusby family has established a 7.5-hectare vineyard (including 1 hectare of sangiovese) on their
northeast facing vineyard, with its red clay and limestone soil. They have also planted an olive grove producing
four different types of olives, which are cured and sold on the estate.

Tintilla Hunter Semillon

TTTTY 2002 Light green-yellow; the moderately intense bouquet is strongly minerally/slatey, and has lots of
character; the clean, crisp and long palate has a bright, minerally finish. Absolutely in the heart of classic
Hunter Semillon style, which will richly reward cellaring. **rating:** 91
best drinking 2007–2017 **best vintages** '02 **drink with** Leave it in the cellar • $16.50

Tintilla James Shiraz

TTTT 2001 Medium red-purple; the clean bouquet has light red fruits with a slightly leafy edge; the palate
moves up a notch, still with some leafy tangy aspects, but has length, even if not a great deal of tannin structure.
rating: 85
best drinking 2005–2010 **drink with** Stir-fried beef • $22.50

Tintilla Catherine de'M Sangiovese Merlot

TTTTY 2000 Light to medium red-purple; the clean, moderately intense bouquet has spicy, savoury aromas;
the fine and supple palate is distinctly Tuscan in its weight and feel, with lingering, fine tannins. Blue Gold at
the 2003 Sydney International Wine Competition, and a blend of 70 per cent Sangiovese, 30 per cent Merlot.
Might as well be Machiavelli as Medici. **rating:** 90
best drinking 2004–2009 **drink with** Truffle risotto • $22.50

Tintilla Justine Merlot

TTTTY 2001 Medium purple-red; the spotlessly clean, moderately intense bouquet is entirely driven by its
ripe red fruits; there is plenty of richness and depth on the palate, and a surprising degree of varietal definition
comes through, thanks in part to the savoury, olive-accented finish. **rating:** 92
best drinking 2006–2011 **best vintages** '01 **drink with** Milk-fed veal • $25.60

tipperary hill estate NR

Alma–Bowendale Road, Alma via Maryborough, Vic 3465 **region** Bendigo
phone (03) 5461 3312 **fax** (03) 5461 3312 **open** Weekends 10–5, or by appointment
winemaker Paul Flowers **production** 500 cases **est.** 1986
product range ($16–24 CD) Pinot Shiraz, Cabernets, Tulkara.
summary All of the wine is sold through the cellar door and on-site restaurant, open on Sundays. Says Paul
Flowers, production depends 'on the frost, wind and birds', which perhaps explains why this is very much a
part-time venture. Situated 7 kilometres west of the city of Maryborough, Tipperary Hill Estate is the only
winery operating in the Central Goldfields Shire. Winemaker Paul Flowers built the rough-cut pine winery and
the bluestone residential cottage next door with the help of friends. Together with wife Margaret he also
operates a restaurant.

tizzana winery NR

518 Tizzana Road, Ebenezer, NSW 2756 **region** South Coast Zone
phone (02) 4579 1150 **fax** (02) 4579 1216 **open** Weekends, holidays 12–6, or by appointment
winemaker Peter Auld **production** 300 cases **est.** 1887
product range ($11.50–17 CD) From Tizzana vineyards Rosso di Tizzana (a light, dry Cabernet Sauvignon),
Waterloo Shiraz, Sackville Tawny, Vintage Port, Old Liqueur Sweet White and Mrs Fiaschi's Old Sweet Red;
the Tizzana Selection from other regions of Traminer Riesling, White Port, Sherry (the latter two from Stanton
& Killeen) and then two wines from South Australia under the Hawkesbury History Heritage 2001 Committee
(a strange combination), including Federation Semillon Chardonnay and Federation Tawny Port.

summary Tizzana has been a weekend and holiday occupation for Peter Auld for many years now, operating in one of the great historic wineries built (in 1887) by Australia's true renaissance man, Dr Thomas Fiaschi. The wines may not be great, but the ambiance is. Peter Auld has also developed Tizzana as a wine education centre.

tokar estate   NR

6 Maddens Lane, Coldstream, Vic 3770 **region** Yarra Valley
phone (03) 5964 9585 **fax** (03) 9706 4033 **open** Fri–Sun and long weekends 10–5
winemaker Paul Evans **production** 1500 cases **est.** 1996
product range ($19.50–25 CD) Pinot Noir, Shiraz, Tempranillo, Cabernet Sauvignon.
summary Leon Tokar is one of the number of new arrivals on Maddens Lane, having established over 5 hectares of pinot noir, 2.5 hectares of shiraz, and 2 hectares each of cabernet sauvignon and – interestingly – tempranillo. Part of the grape production is sold to Southcorp, the remainder contract-made. A new cellar door, barrel room and restaurant were opened in late 2002.

tollana   ★★★★

Tanunda Road, Nuriootpa, SA 5355 **region** Barossa Valley
phone (08) 8560 9408 **fax** (08) 8562 2494 **open** Not
winemaker Oliver Crawford **production** NFP **est.** 1888
product range ($13–22 R) Eden Valley Riesling, Adelaide Hills Sauvignon Blanc, Eden Valley Adelaide Hills Chardonnay, Botrytis Riesling, Shiraz Bin TR16, Cabernet Sauvignon Bin TR222.
summary As the Southcorp wine group moves to establish regional identity for its wines, Tollana is emphasising its Eden Valley base. Seemingly as a byproduct of Penfolds development of Yattarna and related wines, the Tollana Chardonnay style has become more elegant, now standing comfortably alongside the flavoursome Riesling and Shiraz. Rated on the basis of previous tastings.

tom's waterhole wines   NR

Felton, Longs Corner Road, Canowindra, NSW 2804 **region** Cowra
phone (02) 6344 1819 **fax** (02) 6344 2172 **open** Weekends 10–5
winemaker Graham Kerr **production** 800 cases **est.** 1997
product range ($8–14 CD) Waterhole Blend Dry White, Chardonnay, Waterhole Blend Dry Red, Cabernet Sauvignon, Humpers Port.
summary Graham Timms and Graham Kerr started the development of Tom's Waterhole Wines in 1997, progressively establishing 3 hectares of shiraz, 2 hectares of cabernet sauvignon, and 1 hectare of semillon, merlot, the planting programme completed in 2001. A decision has been taken to bypass the use of irrigation, and the yields will be low, with an expectation that the small on-site winery will crush around 20 tonnes per year.

🍇 toolangi vineyards   ★★★☆

2 Merriwee Crescent, Toorak, Vic 3142 (postal) **region** Yarra Valley
phone (03) 9804 3364 **fax** (03) 9804 3365 **open** Not
winemaker Contract **production** 2500 cases **est.** 1995
product range ($19–42.95 R) Chardonnay, Estate Chardonnay, Reserve Chardonnay, Pinot Noir, Shiraz, Cabernet.
summary Garry and Julie Hounsell acquired their property in the Dixons Creek sub-region of the Yarra Valley, adjoining the bottom edge of the Toolangi State Forest, in 1995. Plantings have taken place progressively since that year, with 8 hectares planted, and another 4 hectares to be planted in the future. The primary accent is on pinot noir, chardonnay and cabernet, accounting for all but 1 hectare which is predominantly shiraz, and a few rows of merlot. As only half the vineyards are in bearing, production is supplemented by chardonnay and pinot noir contract-grown in the Coldstream sub-region, cropped at 2 tonnes per acre. Winemaking is split between Tom Carson of Yering Station, Rick Kinzbrunner of Giaconda and Trevor Mast of Mount Langi Ghiran, as impressive a trio of contract winemakers as one could wish for. Exports to the UK.

Toolangi Vineyards Chardonnay
▼▼▼▼ 2001 Bright, light green-yellow; the bouquet is a little uncertain, with some fermentation solids/wet hessian aromas, the palate providing more focus, crisp and firm, but without a great deal of fruit intensity. **rating:** 85
best drinking Now **drink with** Stir-fried chicken • $19

Toolangi Vineyards Estate Chardonnay

ҮҮҮҮ 2001 Medium yellow-green; the bouquet features the subtle balance and integration of fruit and oak, the malolactic influence obvious on the palate, which (nonetheless) has brightness and length.   **rating:** 89

best drinking Now–2005 **drink with** Pan-fried scallops • $29.95

Toolangi Vineyards Reserve Chardonnay

ҮҮҮҮҮ 2001 Medium yellow-green; a strongly Burgundian, complex bouquet with obvious barrel-ferment/solids aromas, then a similarly powerful and complex palate, with the fingerprints of contract winemaker Rick Kinzbrunner everywhere.   **rating:** 91

best drinking Now–2007 **best vintages** '01 **drink with** Smoked salmon risotto • $42.95

Toolangi Vineyards Shiraz

ҮҮҮҮ 2001 Bright purple-red; a complex mix of red berry, spice and game is followed by a very firm palate, with high acidity, needing time to soften and come together.   **rating:** 85

best drinking 2004–2009 **drink with** Rib of beef • $29.95

toorak estate   NR

Toorak Road, Leeton, NSW 2705 **region** Riverina
phone (02) 6953 2333 **fax** (02) 6953 4454 **open** Mon–Sat 9–5
winemaker Robert Bruno **production** 100 000 cases **est.** 1965
product range ($4.40–30 CD) Leeton Selection range of Traminer, Semillon Chardonnay, Shiraz, Soft Shiraz, Cabernet Shiraz, Cabernet Merlot; Willandra Estate range of Semillon, Chardonnay, Botrytis Semillon, Shiraz, Cabernet Sauvignon, Muscat of Alexandria; Amesbury Estate range of Semillon Sauvignon Blanc, Lambrusco Red, Grenache Shiraz; Sparkling; fortifieds.
summary A traditional, long-established Riverina producer with a strong Italian-based clientele around Australia. Production has been increasing significantly, utilising 150 hectares of estate plantings and grapes purchased from other growers.

Toorak Willandra Estate Shiraz

ҮҮҮҮ 2001 Medium red-purple; very ripe, slightly jammy fruit on the bouquet is followed by a palate with surprising weight and complexity; the fruit is hyper-ripe and slightly jammy, but this is a great barbecue red at the price.   **rating:** 83

best drinking Now–2005 **drink with** Barbecue • $9.99

torbreck vintners   ★★★★★

Roennfeldt Road, Marananga, SA 5352 **region** Barossa Valley
phone (08) 8562 4155 **fax** (08) 8562 4195 **open** 7 days 10–6
winemaker David Powell, Dan Standish **production** 43 000 cases **est.** 1994
product range ($18.50–125 ML) VMR (Viognier Marsanne Rousanne), The Bothie (Dessert), The Steading (Grenache Shiraz), The Struie (Shiraz), The Juveniles (Grenache, Mourvedre, Shiraz), The Descendant (Shiraz Viognier), The Factor (Shiraz); Woodcutter's Red.
summary Between 1994 and early 2002 Torbreck was in the headlines for all the right reasons, and in particular the quality, style and branding of its outstanding red wines. For the next 12 months it was in the headlines for all the wrong reasons, as the marriage breakup between David Powell and his wife lead to a near-death experience for Torbreck. The outcome has been that the business is now owned by Jack Cowan and Colin Ryan, David Powell continuing as chief winemaker and general manager. The hope and expectation is that he will be able to progressively build back part-ownership of the business. It has great assets, including precious holdings of old, dry-grown vines and contacts second to none with external growers. The branding has always been of the highest order, and the wines have not lost their icon status.

Torbreck The Factor

ҮҮҮҮҮ 2000 Medium to full red-purple; a complex mix of dark, ripe plum, cherry, spice and oak on the bouquet, then a marvellously complex palate with multiple layers of flavour to the dark berry fruits, and exceptionally well handled tannin and extract.   **rating:** 95

best drinking 2007–2017 **best vintages** '98, '99, '00 **drink with** Braised ox cheek • $125

Torbreck The Struie

ҮҮҮҮҮ 2001 Medium to full red-purple; intense, pure blackberry varietal fruit aromas have first class oak in support; a beautifully crafted wine in every way, offering blackberry, a touch of chocolate, the same excellent oak of the bouquet, and fine, lingering tannins to complete the palate. A Barossa and Eden Valley Shiraz blend.

The name is derived via the view from Struie across the Dornoch Firth. As one expects with Torbreck wines, the wine lives up to the clever packaging. **rating:** 94

best drinking 2006–2016 **best vintages** '01 **drink with** Rare roast beef • $46

Torbreck Woodcutter's Red

♥♥♥♥ 2001 Light to medium red-purple; the moderately intense bouquet offers notes of earth, leather and spice, the firm and fresh palate with spice, vanilla and berry. Not convincing, and I am puzzled about Dave Powell's description of the colour as 'deep purple-black', and the suggestion that 2001 was equal to or better than 1998. For the record, 100 per cent hand-picked Barossa shiraz, open-fermented. **rating:** 85

best drinking Now–2007 **drink with** Lamb cutlets • $20

Torbreck The Descendant

♥♥♥♥♥ 2001 Full red-purple; opulently rich and scented blackberry and spice aromas feed into a mouthfilling, opulent palate with layers upon layers of flavour, sweet blackberry and blackcurrant providing continuity. 14.5° alcohol is carried easily on the long finish. **rating:** 96

best drinking 2006–2016 **best vintages** '00, '01 **drink with** Leave it in the cellar • $125

Torbreck The Juveniles

♥♥♥♥ 2002 Medium red-purple; fresh, juicy berry aromas are replicated on the palate, which has plenty of flavour yet is very soft and with ripe tannins. Micro-oxygenation may well have been used in this unoaked blend of Grenache, Mourvedre and Shiraz. **rating:** 88

best drinking Now–2005 **drink with** Rich pasta • $27.50

Torbreck The Steading

♥♥♥♥ 2001 The colour is slightly dull, but not distressingly so; earthy, spicy, savoury fruit aromas are followed by a medium-bodied palate with typical, slightly jammy fruit; not in the same class as the other top-flight wines from Torbreck, but good by any other standard. **rating:** 88

best drinking 2005–2011 **best vintages** '97, '98, '99 **drink with** Lamb Provençale • $32.50

touchwood wines ★★★★☆

PO Box 91, Battery Point, Tas 7004 **region** Southern Tasmania
phone (03) 6223 3996 **fax** (03) 6223 2384 **open** Not
winemaker Moorilla Estate (Contract) **production** 1500 cases **est.** 1992
product range ($27.50–30 R) Coal River Cuvee, Pinot Noir.
summary Peter and Tina Sexton planted 5 hectares of vineyard in the early 1990s; pinot noir and chardonnay are the principal varieties, with a small amount of cabernet sauvignon and merlot. While on a north-facing hill, with heavy black soil over a calcareous lime base, it has never been an easy site, frost claiming some vintages, and, lack of heat, others. A small quantity of 2002 Pinot Noir will be released at some point in 2003, and the quality of its sparkling wine, the 1998 Coal River Cuvee is outstanding.

Touchwood Coal River Cuvee

♥♥♥♥♥ 1998 Light straw-green; the clean and fresh bouquet has appealing citrussy aromas, the palate with great intensity, and hence length. Deserving trophy winner at the 2003 Tasmanian Wines Show. **rating:** 94

best drinking Now–2006 **drink with** Seafood antipasto • $30

tower estate ★★★★★

Cnr Broke Road/Hall Road, Pokolbin, NSW 2320 **region** Lower Hunter Valley
phone (02) 4998 7989 **fax** (02) 4998 7919 **open** 7 days 10–5
winemaker Dan Dineen **production** 10 000 cases **est.** 1999
product range ($19–40 CD) Clare Valley Riesling, Hunter Valley Semillon, Adelaide Hills Sauvignon Blanc, Hunter Valley Verdelho, Hunter Valley Chardonnay, Adelaide Hills Chardonnay, Yarra Valley Pinot Noir, Hunter Valley Shiraz, Barossa Valley Shiraz, Coonawarra Cabernet Sauvignon, Muscat.
summary Tower Estate is a joint venture headed by Len Evans, featuring a luxury conference centre and accommodation. It draws upon varieties and regions which have a particular synergy, coupled with the enormous knowledge of Len Evans and the winemaking skills of Dan Dineen.

Tower Estate Adelaide Hills Chardonnay

♥♥♥♥♡ 2001 Light straw-green; the bouquet offers a subtle interplay between stone fruit and gently nutty oak; the fresh and well-balanced palate follows on logically, good length and well handled oak. **rating:** 92

best drinking Now **best vintages** '01 **drink with** Crumbed lamb's brains • $26

509

Tower Estate Hunter Valley Chardonnay

ŸŸŸŸŸ 2001 Light straw-green; nectarine, fig and peach fruit is woven through subtle, nutty, oak on the bouquet. The light to medium-bodied palate features lively nectarine/stone fruit flavours and good acidity; reflects the strength of the 30-year-old vines at Maxwell's Maluna vineyard. **rating:** 94

best drinking Now–2006 **best vintages** '00, '01 **drink with** Sautéed veal • $26

Tower Estate Barossa Shiraz

ŸŸŸŸŸ 2001 Medium to full red-purple; the complex and aromatic bouquet has excellent integration of fruit and oak; the powerful, tightly knit and structured palate turns around blackberry fruit and spice; once again, assured oak handling. **rating:** 93

best drinking 2005–2015 **best vintages** '99, '00, '01 **drink with** Barbecued rump steak • $40

Tower Estate Coonawarra Cabernet Sauvignon

ŸŸŸŸŸ 2000 Medium red-purple; the moderately intense but quite aromatic bouquet has a mix of blackberry, blackcurrant and earth, the medium-bodied palate presenting equally pristine cabernet varietal character on the mid-palate, then soft, fine tannins to close. **rating:** 91

best drinking 2004–2010 **best vintages** '00 **drink with** Saddle of lamb • $35

towerhill estate NR

Albany Highway, Mount Barker, WA 6324 **region** Great Southern
phone (08) 9851 1488 **fax** (08) 9851 2982 **open** Fri–Sun 10–5 (7 days during school holidays)
winemaker Brenden Smith (Contract), Dave Cleary **production** 1000 cases **est.** 1993
product range ($13–20 CD) Unwooded Chardonnay, Sweet Riesling, Merlot.
summary The Williams family, headed by Alan and Diane began the establishment of Towerhill Estate in 1993, planting chardonnay (2.5 ha), cabernet sauvignon (2 ha), riesling (1 ha) and merlot (1 ha). Commencing in 1996, the grapes were sold to other producers, but since 1999 limited quantities have been made under contract by Brenden Smith at West Cape Howe Wines. These wines have had consistent show success at the Qantas Wine Show of Western Australia and sell out quickly through cellar door and local outlets. Exports to Singapore.

trafford hill vineyard NR

Lot 1 Bower Road, Normanville, SA 5204 **region** Southern Fleurieu
phone (08) 8558 3595 **open** Thurs–Mon and holidays 10.30–5
winemaker John Sanderson **production** 500 cases **est.** 1996
product range ($8–19 CD) Riesling, Sparkling Shiraz, Family Reserve Red, Sam-Jack Tawny Port, Parsons Ghost Liqueur Tawny Port.
summary Irene and John Sanderson have established 2 hectares of vineyard at Normanville, on the coast of the Fleurieu Peninsula near to its southern extremity. Irene carries out all the viticulture, and John Sanderson makes the wine with help from district veteran Allan Dyson. Distribution is through local restaurants, the remainder through mail order and cellar door.

train trak ★★★☆

957 Healesville–Yarra Glen Road, Yarra Glen, Vic 3775 **region** Yarra Valley
phone (03) 9429 4744 **fax** (03) 9427 1510 **open** By appointment
winemaker Yering Station (Contract) **production** 2000 cases **est.** 1995
product range ($19–26 R) Chardonnay, Pinot Noir, Shiraz.
summary The unusual name comes from the abandoned Yarra Glen to Healesville railroad, which was built in 1889 and remained in use until 1980. Part of it passes by the Train Trak vineyard, although I do not know why Trak has been spelt as it has. A total of 18.5 hectares of vines have been established, the oldest (2.3 ha of pinot noir, 1.1 ha of chardonnay and 1 ha of shiraz) dating back to 1995 and hence in bearing; the remaining 14.1 hectares yet to come into bearing. The first commercial releases from the 2000 vintage bode well for the future. Distribution by Pinot Now, Melbourne.

Train Trak Chardonnay

ŸŸŸŸ 2001 Medium yellow-green; the solid bouquet has stone fruit, some fig and subtle oak; the palate is in the same métier, smooth and deep, and subtle oak. Hampered by a fractionally short finish. **rating:** 86

best drinking Now–2005 **drink with** Seafood risotto • $19

Train Trak Pinot Noir

♥♥♥♥ **2001** Bright red-purple; the bouquet offers an appealing blend of fresh cherry and strawberry fruit, the clearly focused palate with identical flavours; uncomplicated but will develop some additional complexity over the next two or 3 years. **rating:** 89

best drinking Now–2006 **drink with** Smoked quail • $24

tranquil vale ★★★☆

325 Pywells Road, Luskintyre, NSW 2321 **region** Lower Hunter Valley
phone (02) 4930 6100 **fax** (02) 4930 6105 **open** Fri–Mon 10–4, or by appointment
winemaker Andrew Margan, David Hook **production** 3000 cases **est.** 1996
product range ($17–25 CD) Semillon, Chardonnay, Old Luskie (Dessert), Shiraz, Cabernet Franc Shiraz.
summary Phil and Lucy Griffiths purchased the property site unseen from a description in an old copy of the *Australian Weekend* found in the High Commission Office in London. The vineyard they established is situated on the banks of the Hunter River, opposite Wyndham Estate, on relatively fertile, sandy, clay loam. Irrigation has been installed, and what is known as VSP trellising. Within the blink of an eye, they have become experts, and find themselves 'in the amusing position that people ask us our opinion!' The three luxury, self-contained cottages on-site offer the extras of a swimming pool, tennis court, gymnasium, etc and sleep a family or two couples each. Finally, competent contract-winemaking has resulted in the production of good wines, some of which have already had show success.

Tranquil Vale Semillon

♥♥♥♥ **2002** Curiously developed yellow-green colour; powerful grass, herb and citrus aromas and flavours are not coarse, nor seemingly oxidised, simply developed. Perhaps some skin contact was used. Whatever be the case, it is in emphatic, early-drinking style. **rating:** 87

best drinking Now–2005 **drink with** Roast chicken • $17

Tranquil Vale Chardonnay

♥♥♥♥ **2002** Medium yellow-green; the bouquet is clean, with a subtle interplay of barrel-ferment and nectarine aromas, an interplay more or less precisely repeated on the palate; corrected acidity pokes its nose up on the end of the palate. **rating:** 87

best drinking Now **drink with** Roasted tomato and basil soup • $19

Tranquil Vale Cabernet Franc Shiraz

♥♥♥♥ **2002** Medium to full purple-red; the bouquet has a ripe mix of plum, mulberry and blackcurrant aromas, the nicely rounded palate with similar fruit, and subtle oak. A blend of Cabernet Franc and Shiraz. **rating:** 86

best drinking 2004–2009 **drink with** Roast beef • $17

🐾 trappers gully NR

Lot 6, Boyup Road, Mount Barker, WA 6324 **region** Great Southern
phone (08) 9851 2565 **open** By appointment
winemaker Michael Garland **production** 800 cases **est.** 1998
product range ($12–15 CD) Chenin Blanc.
summary The Lester and Candy families, with fascinating and varied backgrounds, began the development of Trappers Gully in 1998. Clea Candy has the most directly relevant CV as a qualified viticulturist and practised winemaker, and, according to the official history 'mother, daughter and wife, and pretty much the instigator of all heated discussions'. The families have progressively planted 1.2 hectares each of chenin blanc, sauvignon blanc and shiraz, and slightly less than 1 hectare of cabernet sauvignon. Only chenin blanc (the first in the Great Southern region) is so far in bearing, the other varieties coming though progressively from 2003 and onwards. Michael Garland is making the wines, but the Trappers Gully business plan calls for an on-site winery to be erected in time for the 2004 vintage.

treen ridge estate NR

Packer Road, Pemberton, WA 6260 **region** Pemberton
phone (08) 9776 1131 **fax** (08) 9776 0442 **open** Wed–Fri 11–5, weekends 10–5
winemaker Andrew Mountford (Contract) **production** 600 cases **est.** 1992
product range ($15–25 CD) Riesling, Sauvignon Blanc, Springfield Shiraz, Reserve Vintage Shiraz, Sparkling Shiraz.
summary The 1.7-hectare Treen Ridge vineyard and three-room accommodation is set between the Treen Brook State Forest and The Warren National Park and is operated by Mollie and Barry Scotman.

treeton estate NR

North Treeton Road, Cowaramup, WA 6284 **region** Margaret River
phone (08) 9755 5481 **fax** (08) 9755 5051 **open** 7 days 10–6
winemaker David McGowan **production** 3000 cases **est.** 1984
product range ($15–17 R) Chardonnay, Riesling, Estate White, Petit Rouge, Shiraz, Liqueur Muscat.
summary In 1982 David McGowan and wife Corinne purchased the 30-hectare property upon which
Treeton Estate is established, beginning to plant the vines 2 years later. David has done just about everything in
his life, and in the early years was working in Perth, which led to various setbacks for the vineyard. The wines
are light and fresh, sometimes rather too much so.

trentham estate ★★★★

Sturt Highway, Trentham Cliffs, NSW 2738 **region** Murray Darling
phone (03) 5024 8888 **fax** (03) 5024 8800 **open** Mon–Fri 9–5, weekends 9.30–5
winemaker Anthony Murphy, Shane Kerr **production** 55 000 cases **est.** 1988
product range ($9–20 CD) Riesling, Murphy's Lore Semillon Chardonnay, Sauvignon Blanc, Viognier,
Chardonnay, Noble Taminga, Sparkling Ruby, Pinot Noir, Shiraz, Cellar Reserve Shiraz, Murphy's Lore Shiraz
Cabernet, Nebbiolo, Merlot, Ruby Cabernet, Petit Verdot, Cabernet Sauvignon Merlot, Vintage Port, Burke
& Wills Tawny Port.
summary Remarkably consistent tasting notes across all wine styles from all vintages since 1989 attest to the
expertise of ex-Mildara winemaker Tony Murphy, now making the Trentham wines from his family vineyards.
All of the wines, whether at the bottom or top end of the price range, offer great value for money. The winery
restaurant is also recommended. National retail distribution; exports to the US, the UK, Belgium, The
Netherlands and New Zealand.

Trentham Estate Sauvignon Blanc

▼▼▼▼ 2002 Light straw-green; the bouquet is clean and crisp, tending neutral, with some minerally characters,
but on the palate there is clearly defined varietal fruit; gentle passionfruit and baked apple flavours, and good
balance and length. Great value. **rating:** 89
best drinking Now **drink with** Seafood salad • $12.50

Trentham Estate Viognier

▼▼▼▼ 2002 Light to medium yellow-green; the spotlessly clean bouquet has rather more fruit salad than
honeysuckle aromas, the peachy, lively and fresh palate showing (as always) immaculate winemaking. **rating:** 87
best drinking Now **drink with** Creamy pasta • $18.50

Trentham Estate Pinot Noir

▼▼▼▼ 2001 Medium red-purple; charry/toasty oak is more emphatic than the cherry fruit of the bouquet; the
palate is well put together, with silky tannins and mouthfeel; a tour de force to produce a pinot noir with this
amount of authenticity from such an unlikely region. Into the bargain, excellent value. Silver medal National
Wine Show 2002. **rating:** 88
best drinking Now **drink with** Roast duck • $12

Trentham Estate Cellar Reserve Shiraz

▼▼▼▼▽ 1999 Medium red-purple; the bouquet is starting to show some bottle-developed complexity with a
mix of dark fruit, oak and savoury/leather nuances; the smooth, medium-bodied palate has good oak balance
and length; with obvious wine show appeal, for it has won two gold medals (Adelaide and Hobart) in 2002.
Good value. **rating:** 90
best drinking Now–2008 **drink with** Barbecued beef • $20

Trentham Estate Nebbiolo

▼▼▼▽ 2001 Light to medium red-purple; the stridently earthy bouquet is somewhat forbidding; the very long,
lemony/savoury, lingering finish is the strong point of an altogether interesting wine. **rating:** 83
best drinking Now–2005 **drink with** Porcini risotto • $16

Trentham Estate Petit Verdot

▼▼▼▼ 2001 Medium to full red-purple; the earthy, savoury bouquet shows strong varietal character with
forest/smoky/charry edges. The palate offers much sweeter fruit, with blackberry jam coming through, neatly
supported (but not threatened) by tannins. **rating:** 87
best drinking 2004–2011 **drink with** Moroccan lamb • $18.50

Trentham Estate Merlot

▼▼▼▼ **2000** Light to medium red-purple; the bouquet has a mix of earth, berry, leaf and a hint of vanilla; the palate has very appealing mouthfeel, with gently soft and sweet fruit. **rating:** 89

best drinking Now–2005 **best vintages** '92, '93, '94 **drink with** Marinated rabbit • $15.50

trevelen farm ★★★★

Weir Road, Cranbrook, WA 6321 **region** Great Southern
phone (08) 9826 1052 **fax** (08) 9826 1209 **open** Thurs–Mon 10–4.30 or by appointment
winemaker Michael Staniford (Contract) **production** 2800 cases **est.** 1993
product range ($16–18 R) Riesling, Sauvignon Blanc Semillon, Chardonnay, Cabernet Sauvignon Merlot.
summary John and Katie Sprigg, together with their family, operate a 1300-hectare wool, meat and grain-producing farm, run on environmental principles with sustainable agriculture at its heart. As a minor, but highly successful, diversification they established 5 hectares of sauvignon blanc, riesling, chardonnay, cabernet sauvignon and merlot in 1993, adding 1.5 hectares of shiraz in 2000. Vines, it seems, are in the genes, for John Sprigg's great- great-grandparents established 20 hectares of vines at Happy Valley, South Australia, in the 1870s. The quality of the wines is as consistent as the prices are modest, and visitors to the cellar door have the added attraction of both garden and forest walks, the latter among 130 hectares of remnant bush which harbours many different orchids which flower from May to December. Exports to the UK, Europe, the US and Asia.

Trevelen Farm Riesling

▼▼▼▼ **2002** Light green-straw; the bouquet has some fruit obscuration, with slightly funky/tropical overtones; the palate has lots of flavour, some spritz, and arms and legs all over the place. Clearly, needs time in bottle to come to terms with itself. **rating:** 85

best drinking 2005–2009 **best vintages** '00 **drink with** Fresh asparagus • $17

Trevelen Farm Sauvignon Blanc Semillon

▼▼▼▼♡ **2002** Light straw-green; the clean, firm bouquet has mineral, gooseberry and a touch of herb, the palate with very attractive flavour and mouthfeel; gooseberry and tropical fruit flavours are thoroughly harmonious.
rating: 90

best drinking Now–2005 **best vintages** '02 **drink with** Sautéed scallops • $16

Trevelen Farm Chardonnay

▼▼▼▼ **2000** Developed yellow-green; complex, bottle-developed, tangy grapefruit and oak aromas are followed by a similarly complex palate round and weighty, the slightly funky characters adding to rather than detracting from the appeal. Apparently a re-release. **rating:** 89

best drinking Now–2005 **drink with** Sweetbreads • $17

Trevelen Farm Cabernet Merlot

▼▼▼▼ **2001** Medium purple-red; earthy/savoury/minty overtones to black fruits on the bouquet lead into a medium-bodied, well-balanced palate, driven by red and blackcurrant fruit, and very gentle tannins on the finish. **rating:** 88

best drinking 2005–2010 **drink with** Leg of lamb • $18

🌿 tuart ridge ★★★☆

344 Stakehill Road, Baldivis, WA 6171 **region** Peel
phone (08) 9524 1445 **fax** (08) 9524 1445 **open** Weekends 10–4
winemaker Phil Franzone **production** 2000 cases **est.** 1996
product range ($10–18 CD) Verdelho, Classic White, Chardonnay, Bianchino, Shiraz, Merlot, Cabernet Sauvignon.
summary Phil Franzone has established 5 hectares of chardonnay, verdelho, shiraz, cabernet sauvignon, grenache and merlot on the coastal tuart soils. 2001 was the first vintage, and production will peak at around 3000 cases. Phil Franzone also acts as contract winemaker for several of the many new ventures springing up in the Peel region.

Tuart Ridge Shiraz

▼▼▼▼ **2001** Strong red-purple; attractive black cherry and plum fruit, with well-integrated oak on the bouquet, leads into a smooth, medium-bodied palate with dark fruits and a touch of mint; fine, savoury tannins give the wine texture and balance. Picked at 12.8° baume, as opposed to the 12.4 of the Bin 262. Matured in French and American oak. **rating:** 88

best drinking 2004–2009 **drink with** Beef casserole • $14

Tuart Ridge Bin 262 Shiraz

TTTY 2001 Light to medium red-purple; the bouquet is quite aromatic, with gently spicy/savoury fruit, lightening off considerably on the palate, which has some green/herb notes on the finish. Made in a lighter style for immediate consumption. **rating: 83**

best drinking Now **drink with** Grilled steak • $18

tuck's ridge ★★★★

37 Shoreham Road, Red Hill South, Vic 3937 **region** Mornington Peninsula
phone (03) 5989 8660 **fax** (03) 5989 8579 **open** 7 days 12–5
winemaker Phillip Kittle **production** 14 000 cases **est.** 1988
product range ($15–35 CD) Riesling, Chardonnay, Callanans Road Chardonnay, Callanans Road Late Harvest Pinot Grigio, Vues, Pinot Noir, Altera Pinot Noir, Callanans Road Pinot Noir, Trial Selection Pinot Noir, Callanans Road Shiraz, Merlot; under the Prentice brand Whitfield Pinot Gris, Whitlands Pinot Noir.
summary After an initial burst of frenetic activity following its launch in July 1993, Tuck's Ridge has slowed down a little. Nonetheless, plantings have been increased to a little over 25 hectares, making it one of the largest vineyards in production on the Mornington Peninsula, with wine quality to match. Rumours of a sale in early 2002 turned out to be entirely wrong. Tuck's Ridge has sold its Red Hill vineyard for $2.4 million, and used the proceeds to retire debt and acquire the Prentice wine brand, which will henceforth be available both at retail and through the Tuck's Ridge cellar door. Exports to the US, Hong Kong and China.

Prentice Whitfield Pinot Gris

TTTT 2001 Light straw-green; clean, fresh and crisp apple/apple blossom aromas flow into a clean and correct palate, which has exceptional length and persistence. From grapes grown at Whitfield and Whitlands; 14° alcohol. **rating: 87**

best drinking Now–2005 **drink with** Fresh crab • $22

Tuck's Ridge Chardonnay

TTTTT 2002 Light to medium yellow-green; melon, stone fruit, citrus and mineral aromas intermingle with subtle oak on the bouquet; the palate has exceptional mouthfeel and weight, almost glossy, yet not heavy nor hot. A lovely, fruit-driven wine. **rating: 95**

best drinking Now–2008 **best vintages** '99, '02 **drink with** Thai cuisine • $23

Tuck's Ridge Callanans Road Chardonnay

TTTT 2001 Medium yellow-straw; the bouquet has bright citrus, nectarine and herb aromas, the tangy/citrussy fruit of the palate on the lean side. **rating: 85**

best drinking Now–2005 **drink with** Sautéed scallops • $16

Tuck's Ridge A Trial Selection Pinot Noir

TTTTY 2001 Bright, light purple-red; a complex and powerful bouquet, with dark plum, spice and forest floor aromas leads into a powerful, long and intense palate, with another dimension altogether to the standard Pinot Noir of the same vintage. **rating: 93**

best drinking Now–2008 **best vintages** '00, '01 **drink with** Pastrami • $35

Tuck's Ridge Callanans Road Pinot Noir

TTTT 2001 Clear, light to medium red-purple; the bouquet is clean and fresh, a mix of plum and a touch of spice; the light to medium-bodied palate is similarly direct and fresh, with cherry and plum fruit, but far less complex than one might expect at the end of 2002. Another year or so may well do the trick. **rating: 87**

best drinking Now–2005 **drink with** Guinea fowl or pheasant • $21

Tuck's Ridge Callanans Road Shiraz

TTTT 2001 Medium red-purple; the bouquet has spicy, cedary, black cherry and blackberry aromas, but the wine disappoints with its light to medium-bodied, spicy/leafy palate. Strange, after such an impressive opening. **rating: 86**

best drinking 2004–2007 **drink with** Beef shashlik • $20

tumbarumba wine estates ★★★☆

PO Box 190, Tumbarumba, NSW 2653 **region** Tumbarumba
phone (02) 6948 8326 **fax** (02) 6948 8326 **open** Not
winemaker Greg Silkman (Contract) **production** 2000 cases **est.** 1989

product range Mannus range of Sauvignon Blanc, Chardonnay, Pinot Noir Chardonnay, Merlot, Cabernet Merlot, Cabernet Shiraz.
summary Having established his vineyards progressively since 1982, Frank Minutello decided to seek to add value (and interest) to the enterprise by having a small proportion of his production vinified, commencing with the 1995 vintage. The wines are sold by mail order and from The Elms Restaurant in Tumbarumba.

Mannus Sauvignon Blanc

▼▼▼▼▽ **2002** Very pale straw-green; the clean, crisp and minerally bouquet also has some blossom aromas, characters which flow through into the light, bright and fresh palate with its mix of lemon and apple blossom; good mouthfeel; spotlessly clean. **rating:** 90
best drinking Now **drink with** Fresh calamari • $18

Mannus Pinot Noir Chardonnay

▼▼▼▼ **1997** Light to medium green-yellow; the tight, minerally bouquet is flecked with citrus, a very youthful palate with bright fruit flavours; intense, tangy citrus/grapefruit run through to a long finish. **rating:** 88
best drinking Now **drink with** Antipasto • $21

Mannus Merlot

▼▼▼▼ **2000** Medium red, with the purple starting to fade; there are some green leaf overtones to the fruit of the bouquet, and while the light to medium-bodied palate has good texture and undoubted varietal character, the slightly green/earthy flavours attest to the cool climate. **rating:** 86
best drinking Now–2007 **drink with** Veal chop • $21

Mannus Cabernet Shiraz

▼▼▼▼ **1998** Light to medium red-purple; the light bouquet ranges through leaf, mint and berry, but the palate is far riper than the bouquet suggests, offering dark berry fruit, a touch of chocolate and fine tannins. **rating:** 88
best drinking Now–2006 **drink with** Herbed rack of lamb • $20

tumbarumba wine growers   NR

Sunnyside, Albury Close, Tumbarumba, NSW 2653 **region** Tumbarumba
phone (02) 6948 3055 **fax** (02) 6948 3055 **open** Weekends and public holidays, or by appointment
winemaker Charles Sturt University (Contract) **production** 600 cases **est.** 1996
product range ($15–25) Chardonnay, Pinot Noir and Pinot Chardonnay sparkling wines under the Black Range label, with further individual labels likely for the future.
summary Tumbarumba Wine Growers has taken over the former George Martins Winery (itself established in 1990) to provide an outlet for wines made from Tumbarumba region grapes. It is essentially a co-operative venture, involving local growers and businessmen, and with modest aspirations to growth.

turkey flat   ★★★★☆

Bethany Road, Tanunda, SA 5352 **region** Barossa Valley
phone (08) 8563 2851 **fax** (08) 8563 3610 **open** 7 days 11–5
winemaker Peter Schell **production** 12000 cases **est.** 1990
product range ($12–32R) Semillon, Semillon Marsanne, Rose, Grenache, Butchers Block (Mataro Shiraz Grenache blend), Shiraz, Cabernet Sauvignon.
summary The establishment date of Turkey Flat is given as 1990 but it might equally well have been 1870 (or thereabouts), when the Schulz family purchased the Turkey Flat vineyard, or 1847, when the vineyard was first planted to the very shiraz which still grows today. In addition there are 8 hectares of very old grenache and 8 hectares of much younger semillon and cabernet sauvignon, together with a total of 7.3 hectares of mourvedre, dolcetto and (a recent arrival) marsanne. An on-site winery completed just prior to the 2001 vintage will give Turkey Flat even greater control over its wine production. Retail distribution in Adelaide, Melbourne and Sydney; exports to the US, the UK and Belgium.

Turkey Flat Semillon Marsanne

▼▼▼▼▽ **2002** Light green-yellow; the complex bouquet has an attractive mix of ripe lemon, some mineral, and background whispers of spice; the palate has great length and even greater power; the partial barrel fermentation certainly adds to the complexity, but in no way threatens the expression of the fruit. A touch hot, and really needs food to show its best. **rating:** 92
best drinking Now–2007 **best vintages** '02 **drink with** Roast turkey breast • $15.50

Turkey Flat Rose

TTTT 2002 Vivid fuchsia; a fragrant and vibrant bouquet with cherry citrus fruit and spice aromas is followed by a palate which flows on logically, with sweet fruit on the mid-palate, then a dry finish. A blend of Grenache, Cabernet Sauvignon, Shiraz and Dolcetto. **rating: 92**

best drinking Now **best vintages** '00, '01, '02 **drink with** Nothing or anything • $18

Turkey Flat Butchers Block

TTTT 2001 Youthful red-purple; clean, fresh juicy berry aromas are followed by a fruit-driven palate, with good length, and the prospect of pleasing medium-term development. **rating: 87**

best drinking Now–2008 **drink with** Mushroom risotto • $25

Turkey Flat Grenache

TTTT 2001 Light to medium red-purple; light, spicy jammy fruit aromas are followed by a palate with spicy, savoury flavours with pleasing texture and soft tannins. **rating: 87**

best drinking Now–2006 **best vintages** '91, '92, '93, '96, '98 **drink with** Maggie Beer's game pie • $24

Turkey Flat Pedro Ximinez 375 ml

TTTT NV Orange-red; the rich bouquet has clean spirit and a touch of rancio, the flavoursome palate in knock 'em dead cellar-door style, the clear glass bottle in the shape of a squared off bowling pin. The back label tells us this is a 'mellow sherry'. **rating: 85**

best drinking Now **drink with** Zest • $22.50

turramurra estate ★★★☆

RMB 4327 Wallaces Road, Dromana Vic 3926 **region** Mornington Peninsula
phone (03) 5987 1146 **fax** (03) 5987 1286 **open** 12–5 first weekend of the month or by appointment
winemaker David Leslie **production** 6000 cases **est.** 1989
product range ($24.95–36 CD) Sauvignon Blanc, Chardonnay, Pinot Noir, Shiraz, Cabernet Sauvignon.
summary Dr David Leslie gave up his job as a medical practitioner after completing the Bachelor of Applied Science (Wine Science) at Charles Sturt University to concentrate on developing the family's 10-hectare estate at Dromana. Wife Paula is the viticulturist. Limited retail distribution in Melbourne and Sydney; exports to the UK.

Turramurra Estate Chardonnay

TTTT 2000 Medium yellow-green; clean melon and cashew aromas are backed by gentle oak; the delicate palate has melon fruit and a well judged touch of oak; lacks intensity but nonetheless has appeal. **rating: 87**

best drinking Now–2006 **drink with** Brains in black butter sauce • $24.95

12 acres ★★★

Nagambie–Rushworth Road, Bailieston, Vic 3608 **region** Goulburn Valley
phone (03) 5794 2020 **fax** (03) 5794 2020 **open** Thurs–Mon 10–6, July weekends only
winemaker Peter Prygodicz, Jana Prygodicz **production** 700 cases **est.** 1994
product range ($16 CD) Shiraz, Merlot, Cabernet Franc, Cabernet Sauvignon.
summary The charmingly named 12 Acres is a red wine specialist, with Peter and Jana Prygodicz making the wines on-site in a tiny winery. The wines could benefit from renewal of the oak in which they are matured; the underlying fruit is good.

12 Acres Shiraz

TTTT 2000 Light to medium red, with just a touch of purple; the earthy/savoury bouquet is not concentrated, nor is the fruit on the palate. On the other hand, there has been no attempt to overly extract flavour or tannins. **rating: 83**

best drinking Now–2005 **drink with** Rack of lamb • $16

twelve staves wine company ★★★☆

Box 620, McLaren Vale, SA 5171 **region** McLaren Vale
phone (08) 8178 0900 **fax** (08) 8178 0900 **open** Not
winemaker Peter Dennis, Phil Christinson, Brian Light (Consultant) **production** 1300 cases **est.** 1997
product range ($17–38 R) Grenache, Old Vine Shiraz.
summary Twelve Staves has a single vineyard block of a little under 5 hectares of 70-year-old, bush-pruned grenache vines. The highly experienced team of Peter Dennis and Brian Light (in a consulting role) produce an

appealing Grenache in a lighter mode and a monumental Shiraz, and which has an eclectic range of retail outlets on the east coast, and limited exports to the US, Canada and the UK.

Twelve Staves Old Vine Shiraz

ＹＹＹＹＹ 2001 Opaque, impenetrable purple-red; the rich blackberry, licorice and spice fruit of the bouquet has well-balanced oak in support; a rich, luscious and voluptuous palate with archetypal, concentrated fruit, and a dusting of dark chocolate. A mere 14°. **rating:** 94

best drinking 2006–2016 **best vintages** '01 **drink with** Haunch of beef • $37.50

Twelve Staves Grenache

ＹＹＹＹ 2001 Bright red-purple; clean, fresh juicy fruit aromas is followed by a medium-bodied palate, driven by that juicy berry fruit. **rating:** 86

best drinking Now **drink with** Light red meat dishes • $20

twin bays   NR

Lot 1 Martin Road, Yankalilla, SA 5203 **region** Southern Fleurieu
phone (08) 8267 2844 **fax** (08) 8239 0877 **open** Weekends and holidays
winemaker Bruno Giorgio, Alan Dyson **production** 1000 cases **est.** 1989
product range ($11–23 CD) Riesling, Reserve Bin Riesling, Aged Riesling, Liqueur Riesling, Outrageous Sparkling Late Picked Pinot Noir, Rosado, Shiraz, Wild Grenache, Cabernet Shiraz, Cabernet Sauvignon, fortifieds.
summary Adelaide doctor and specialist Bruno Giorgio, together with wife Ginny, began the establishment of their vineyard back in 1989, but have opted to keep it small (and beautiful). The principal plantings are of cabernet sauvignon, with lesser amounts of shiraz and riesling, taking the total plantings to 2 hectares. It was the first vineyard to be established in the Yankalilla district of the Fleurieu Peninsula, and has spectacular views from the vineyard sited on the slopes above Normanville, taking in hills, valleys, the coastal plains, and the rugged Rapid Bay and more tranquil Lady Bay as the prime focus. The cellar door features the ocean views, the wines on sale being complemented by red and white wine vinegar, Fleurieu olive oil and other local souvenirs.

twin valley estate   NR

Hoffnungsthal Road, Lyndoch, SA 5351 **region** Barossa Valley
phone (08) 8524 4584 **fax** (08) 8524 4978 **open** Weekends 10–5
winemaker Fernando Martin, Kay Martin **production** 3500 cases **est.** 1990
product range ($9–18 CD) Traminer, Frontignac Spatlese, Eden Valley Riesling, Semillon Chardonnay, Cabernet Sauvignon Franc, Classic Burgundy, Pinot Cabernet, White Port, Martin's Mead.
summary While Fernando Martin has always had his sights set firmly on the tourist trade, the Twin Valley Estate wines are more than acceptable, the spicy, limey Frontignac Spatlese being a particularly good example of its kind. This is the site of the former Karrawirra Winery (the name and ownership change forced by Killawarra many years ago).

2 bud spur   ★★★★★

Unit 2, 8 Binney Court, Sandy Bay, Tas 7005 (postal) **region** Southern Tasmania
phone (03) 6225 0711 **fax** (03) 6233 3477 **open** Not
winemaker Michael Vishacki **production** 300 cases **est.** 1996
product range ($25 ML) Sauvignon Blanc, Chardonnay, Pinot Noir.
summary Phil Barker and Anne Lasala commenced establishing 2.2 hectares of vineyard in 1996. Phil Barker has the most extraordinary qualifications, having worked as a chef for over 10 years after acquiring a PhD in botany, and is now a botanist with the Tasmanian Parks and Wildlife Department. There was some agonising about the name; originally named Latitude, it has now become 2 Bud Spur, a term viticulturists are very familiar with, but which will intrigue the average wine drinker. The rating, incidentally, is given for its Pinot Noir.

2 Bud Spur Chardonnay

ＹＹＹＹＹ 2001 Medium yellow-green; an exceptionally complex, indeed slightly funky, bouquet and palate invest the wine with striking character, and would be disastrous were it not for the opulent, intense fruit which is of sufficient weight to carry the winemaking inputs. Trophy winner 2003 Tasmanian Wines Show. **rating:** 94

best drinking Now–2008 **best vintages** '01 **drink with** Seafood risotto • $25

two hands wines ★★★★

Seppeltsfield Road, Greenock, SA 5355 **region** Warehouse
phone 0412 824 453 **fax** (08) 8342 6375 **open** By appointment
winemaker Matt Wenk, Rolf Binder (Consultant) **production** 10 000 cases **est.** 2000
product range ($25–120 R) The Wolf Riesling, Shiraz (Angel's Share, Lily's Garden, Sophie's Garden, Bella's Garden, Bad Impersonator, Ares), Brave Faces Shiraz Grenache, The Bull and the Bear (Cabernet Sauvignon Shiraz).
summary The 'Hands' in question are those of South Australian businessmen Michael Twelftree and Richard Mintz, Twelftree in particular having extensive experience in marketing Australian wine in the US (for other producers) and now turning that experience to his own account (and that of Richard Mintz, of course). On the principle that if big is good, bigger is better, and biggest is best, the style of the wines has been aimed fairly and squarely at the palate of Robert Parker Jnr and that of the *Wine Spectator's* Harvey Steiman. The first wines were made by Sarah and Sparky Marquis at Fox Creek, thereafter by Rolf Binder at Veritas. The 2000 make of just 17 tonnes of shiraz rose to 150 tonnes in 2002, sourced from the Clare Valley, Padthaway, McLaren Vale and Barossa Valley, adding a little grenache and cabernet to the basic fare of shiraz. In 2003 a Heathcote-sourced shiraz will be added to the portfolio. Each of the individual wines is made in microscopic quantities (down to 50 dozen) and are exported to both the US and other countries, the policy being (one assumes) to keep demand well in excess of supply in any given market.

Two Hands The Wolf Riesling

TTTTT 2002 Light straw-green; the intense citrus and herb bouquet has excellent varietal fruit, the long, very intense and powerful palate, with a lemony/citrussy finish, lives up to the reputation of the vintage, although like all the wines under the Two Hands label, is certainly fully priced. **rating:** 94

best drinking 2004–2012 **best vintages** '02 **drink with** Caesar salad • $30

Two Hands Angel's Share McLaren Vale Shiraz

TTTTY 2002 Strong red-purple; a spotlessly clean mix of blackberry and dark chocolate aromas flow into a mouthfilling array of black fruits and dark chocolate, supported by excellent tannin and extract management; precisely judged oak inputs. Medium-bodied, and doubtless intended for early consumption. Stelvin closure. **rating:** 90

TTTT 2001 Deep red-purple; the clean bouquet has a mix of black plum, blackberry and earth aromas, with the barest touch of oak. The palate follows suit with attractive red fruit and regional chocolate flavours intermingling. Very youthful; needs time. Interestingly, closed with a Stelvin cap. **rating:** 87

best drinking 2004–2009 **best vintages** '02 **drink with** Braised beef • $25

Two Hands Ares Barossa Valley Shiraz

TTTTT 2001 Medium to full red-purple; the rich and complex bouquet has ripe, but not the least jammy, black fruits with hints of earth and vanilla; an extremely powerful, savoury palate has layers of blackberry fruit with built-in tannins; great length and cohesion; a minimum ten-year proposition. A trendy label where the front (meaningless except for its graphics) is the back, and vice versa. **rating:** 94

best drinking 2011–2021 **best vintages** '01 **drink with** Leave it in the cellar • $120

Two Hands Bad Impersonator Shiraz

TTTT 2001 Medium red-purple; the very spicy fruit of the bouquet leads into a palate with raspberry and plum fruit, followed by fairly high acidity. 300 cases made; one is left to guess whether the name is witting or unwitting. **rating:** 85

best drinking 2004–2009 **drink with** Grilled T-bone • $45

Two Hands Bella's Garden Shiraz

TTTT 2001 Bright, full red-purple; ripe blackberry and plum fruit on the bouquet is followed by a palate with abundant weight and concentration, the slightly gamey undertones providing a subject for discussion. Like the Bad Impersonator, 14.5° alcohol. **rating:** 85

best drinking 2005–2015 **drink with** Kangaroo fillet • $55

Two Hands Lily's Garden Shiraz

TTTTY 2001 Medium to full red-purple; the clean and ripe spice, plum and black chocolate aromas of the bouquet lead into a lush, juicy palate which does not, however, go over the top; nice wine. Sourced from McLaren Vale. **rating:** 91

best drinking 2005–2015 **best vintages** '01 **drink with** Braised oxtail • $55

Two Hands Sophie's Garden Shiraz

TTTT 2001 Excellent colour; a cascade of black cherry, earth, spice and mint aromas is followed by a very concentrated, almost soupy, palate which needs to resolve its contradictions. **rating: 88**

best drinking 2005–2015 **drink with** Beef Provençale • $55

Two Hands Brave Faces Barossa Valley Shiraz Grenache

TTTTY 2002 Youthful red-purple; sweet blackberry and redcurrant aromas marry with subtle oak on the bouquet; the rich, soft and round palate has no lolly/confection/jam characters, so often the Achilles heel of grenache. Overall, has excellent texture and structure, even if it does shorten fractionally on the finish. Stelvin capped. **rating: 92**

best drinking Now–2008 **best vintages** '02 **drink with** Steak and kidney pie • $32.50

Two Hands The Bull and the Bear

TTTT 2001 Medium red-purple; the earthy, leafy, spicy bouquet, with its subtle oak, gives relatively little hint of the very ripe plum, blackcurrant and chocolate fruit flavours of the palate, which finish with soft tannins. A blend of 60 per cent Barossa Valley Shiraz and 40 per cent McLaren Vale Cabernet Sauvignon. **rating: 87**

best drinking 2005–2011 **drink with** Ox kidney • $45

two rivers ★★★

Yarrawa Road, Denman, NSW 2328 (postal) **region** Upper Hunter Valley
phone (02) 6547 2556 **fax** (02) 6547 2546 **open** Not
winemaker Greg Silkman **production** 25 000 cases **est.** 1988
product range ($14.99–35 R) Stone's Throw Semillon, Shady Bank Verdelho Chardonnay, Hidden Hive Verdelho, Wild Fire Unwooded Chardonnay, Lightning Strike Chardonnay, Winters Mist Merlot, Golfer's Folly Cabernet Franc, Thunderbolt, Rocky Crossing Cabernet Sauvignon; Reserve Hunter Valley Semillon, Chardonnay, Shiraz and Cabernet Sauvignon; Rock End Cottage Port.
summary A significant addition to the viticultural scene in the Upper Hunter Valley, with almost 170 hectares of vineyards established, involving a total investment of around $7 million. Part of the fruit is sold under long-term contracts, but part is made under contract for the expanding winemaking and marketing operations of Two Rivers, the chief brand of Inglewood Vineyards. The emphasis is on Chardonnay and Semillon, and the wines have been medal winners in the wine show circuit. In early 2002 it acquired the Tulloch brand from Southcorp, and has taken the decision to separately market and distribute the Tulloch brand (through Angove's). The labels proudly bear gold medals for Hunter Valley Vigneron of the Year and Hunter Farmer of the Year.

Two Rivers Stone's Throw Semillon

TTTT 2002 Light straw-green; the bouquet has clear varietal character, with lemon and touches of spice and herb; the clean, light-bodied palate has a touch of residual sugar, broadening its appeal and making the wine immediately accessible. **rating: 85**

best drinking Now–2005 **drink with** Antipasto • $14.99

Tulloch Hector Shiraz

TTTT 1996 Medium red; the bouquet has a gently earthy/leathery cast typical of mature Hunter Valley Shiraz, and the palate follows precisely down the same track, with savoury, ripe tannins providing good length. Ready now, but will go on for another 10 years without losing direction. **rating: 89**

best drinking Now–2012 **drink with** Braised beef • $35

tyrrell's ★★★★★

Broke Road, Pokolbin, NSW 2321 **region** Lower Hunter Valley
phone (02) 4993 7000 **fax** (02) 4998 7723 **open** Mon–Sat 8–5
winemaker Andrew Spinaze, Mark Richardson **production** 800 000 cases **est.** 1858
product range ($8–95 R) At the bottom end the large-volume Long Flat White, Chardonnay and Red; next in price is Traditional Range of Traminer Riesling, Twin Wells Chardonnay, Twin Wells Shiraz Cabernet; then Old Winery Semillon, Semillon Sauvignon Blanc, Chardonnay Semillon, Verdelho, Chardonnay, Pinot Noir, Shiraz, Cabernet Merlot; Rufus Stone Heathcote Shiraz, Rufus Stone McLaren Shiraz, Rufus Stone McLaren Vale Merlot, Long Bow; next the Individual Vineyard range of wines including Lost Block Semillon, Shee-Oak Chardonnay, Moon Mountain Chardonnay, Eclipse Pinot Noir, Brokenback Shiraz; then Reserve Stevens range of Semillon, Shiraz; at the very top Vat 1 Semillon, Vat 47 Chardonnay, Vat 6 Pinot Noir, Vat 8 Shiraz Cabernet, Vat 9 Shiraz. Also Sparkling, fortifieds.

summary An extraordinary family winery which has grown up from an insignificant base in 1960 to become one of the most influential mid-sized companies, successfully competing with wines running all the way from cheap, volume-driven Long Flat White up to the super-premium Vat 47 Chardonnay and Vat 1 Semillon, a promiscuous gatherer of trophies and gold medals as it ages. There is a similar range of price and style with the red wines, and in recent years Tyrrell's has simply never faltered within the parameters of price and style. Exports to all of the major markets throughout North America, Europe and South-East Asia.

Tyrrell's Reserve HVD Semillon

ŸŸŸŸŸ **1995** Glowing yellow-green; a mesmerising mix of youthful and mature aromas, intense yet delicate, leads into a palate of equal complexity; here penetrating lemon and citrus fruit, still retaining a hint of CO_2, is slowly moving towards the honeyed/nutty phase of the wine. Deserves every one of the eight trophies it has collected including that for Best Wine at the National Wine Show in Canberra 2001. **rating:** 97

best drinking Now–2015 **best vintages** '95 **drink with** Grilled lobster • $95

Tyrrell's Old Winery Semillon Sauvignon Blanc

ŸŸŸŸŸ **2002** Light straw-green; a spotless but aromatic bouquet ranging through gooseberry to citrus to tropical fruit is an impressive opening which is sustained on the intense palate with a mix of lemon/citrus and tropical flavours; good length and acidity. Entirely sourced from Western Australia: Margaret River, Mount Barker, Geographe. **rating:** 91

best drinking Now **best vintages** '02 **drink with** Fried oysters • $14

Tyrrell's Reserve Brokenback Shiraz

ŸŸŸŸŸ **1998** Bright, strong red-purple, excellent for the age of the wine; ripe and clean black cherry and dark plum fruit drive the bouquet, with a nice touch of oak in support. The palate has abundant and fully ripened dark fruit flavours supported by soft, ripe tannins; an impressive wine developing well. **rating:** 93

best drinking Now–2013 **best vintages** '98 **drink with** Beef in red wine sauce • $35

Tyrrell's Rufus Stone Long Bow

ŸŸŸŸŸ **2000** Medium red-purple; the bouquet offers a pleasing mix of red and dark berry fruits with well-integrated French oak. Ripe, blackberry and blackcurrant fruit drive the palate; should cellar well. A blend of 62 per cent Cabernet Sauvignon, 28 per cent Merlot, 6 per cent Malbec and 4 per cent Petit Verdot, all sourced from the Limestone Coast. **rating:** 90

best drinking 2004–2010 **drink with** Lamb casserole • $29.95

uleybury wines ★★★★

Uley Road, Uleybury, SA 5114 **region** Mount Lofty Ranges Zone
phone (08) 8280 7335 **fax** (08) 8280 7925 **open** 7 days 10–4
winemaker Tony Pipicella **production** 5000 cases **est.** 1995
product range ($11.90–23 R) Semillon, Uley Chapel Shiraz, Grenache, Grenache Shiraz, Merlot, Sangiovese, Cabernet Sauvignon.
summary The Pipicella family – headed by Italian-born Tony – has established nearly 45 hectares of vineyard near the township of One Tree Hill in the Mt Lofty Ranges. Ten varieties have been planted, with more planned. Daughter Natalie Pipicella, who has completed the wine marketing course at the University of South Australia, was responsible for overseeing the design of labels, the promotion and advertising, and the creation of the website. The wines are currently being made off-site under the direction of Tony Pipicella, who seems able to invest the wines with great texture and mouthfeel. A cellar door opened in June 2002; an on-site winery will follow.

Uleybury Uley Chapel Shiraz

ŸŸŸŸŸ **2001** Medium to full red-purple; clean, luscious raspberry, and touches of mint and plum on the bouquet feed into a smooth, supple and round palate, with excellent silky texture and mouthfeel; fine tannins to close. **rating:** 93

best drinking Now–2008 **best vintages** '01 **drink with** Lasagne • $23

Uleybury Merlot

ŸŸŸŸŸ **2001** Youthful red-purple; clean, moderately intense black and redcurrant fruit is supported by subtle oak on the bouquet; a round, fleshy, sweet berry palate with soft tannins, and excellent structure/mouthfeel. **rating:** 90

best drinking 2004–2009 **best vintages** '01 **drink with** Veal roulade • $23

Uleybury Cabernet Sauvignon

▼▼▼▼ 2001 Medium red-purple; there is a spicy, leafy edge to the black fruits of the bouquet, but a touch of sweet chocolate adds to the appeal of the palate; long, fine tannins and good oak handling.　　　**rating: 88**

best drinking 2005–2010 **drink with** Rack of lamb • $23

undercliff　　　NR

Yango Creek Road, Wollombi, NSW 2325 **region** Lower Hunter Valley
phone (02) 4998 3322 **fax** (02) 4998 3322 **open** 7 days 10–5, or by appointment
winemaker David Carrick **production** 1500 cases **est.** 1990
product range ($17–35 CD) Semillon, Chardonnay, Azure Dessert Semillon, Sparkling Shiraz, Shiraz, Chambourcin.
summary Peter and Lesley Chase now own Undercliff, but it continues to function as both winery cellar door and art gallery. The wines, produced from 2.5 hectares of estate vineyards, have won a number of awards in recent years at the Hunter Valley Wine Show and the Hunter Valley Small Winemakers Show. All of the wine is sold through cellar door.

🐦 upper murray estate　　　NR

Murray River Road, Walwa, Vic 3709 **region** Northeast Victoria Zone
phone (02) 6037 1456 **fax** (03) 6037 1457 **open** 7 days 10–6
winemaker Howard Anderson (Contract) **production** 300 cases **est.** 1998
product range ($16.50–18.50 CD) Unwooded Chardonnay, Chardonnay, Pinot Noir, Shiraz, Merlot, Cabernet Merlot Shiraz, Cabernet Sauvignon.
summary The Upper Murray Estate vineyard has been established at a height of 400 metres roughly equidistant between Tumbarumba and Corryong. It is on the banks of what is a fast-flowing Murray River as it descends from the mountains. The estate is part of a much larger business offering the largest tourism and convention facilities in northeast Victoria, based on 16 single and double-storey cottages and four motel-type rooms. There are approximately 4 hectares each of chardonnay, pinot noir, merlot, shiraz and cabernet sauvignon, with 2.3 hectares of riesling. Industry veteran Howard Anderson makes the wines at his Rutherglen winery. The first two vintages – 2000 and 2001 – are, to put it mildly, interesting. It will be fascinating to see what emerges as the vines mature and weather patterns (presumably) cease to be so extreme.

Upper Murray Estate Pinot Noir

▼▼▼▽ 2001 Dark, dense impenetrable colour is utterly atypical for Pinot Noir. The bouquet exudes ripe, complex dark plum, chocolate and spice aromas, with some hint of the varietal origin; then a massive palate with very ripe plum, chocolate and masses of tannin. A freakish wine beyond anything I have ever seen from the variety. For the record, 14° alcohol.　　　**rating: 84**

best drinking Now–2005 **drink with** Rump steak • $18.50

Upper Murray Estate Shiraz

▼▼▼▼ 2001 Strong, deep red-purple; the complex bouquet has some interesting spicy characters reminiscent of Côte Rôtie; the palate has lively, dark, spicy fruit interwoven with tannins, and finishing with fresh acidity. A nice wine with plenty of character and interest.　　　**rating: 87**

best drinking 2004–2009 **drink with** Game pie • $16.50

Upper Murray Estate Cabernet Sauvignon

▼▼▼▼ 2000 Light to medium red-purple; the youthful, clean, light bouquet in an earthy/berry spectrum is followed by a fresh, direct berry and mint flavoured palate, lively and with some elegance. In very much the same mould as the following (2001) vintage.　　　**rating: 85**

best drinking Now–2007 **drink with** Rack of lamb • $18.50

upper reach vineyard　　　★★★★

77 Memorial Avenue, Baskerville, WA 6056 **region** Swan Valley
phone (08) 9296 0078 **fax** (08) 9296 0278 **open** Thurs–Sun and public holidays 11–5
winemaker Derek Pearse, John Griffiths **production** 2000 cases **est.** 1996
product range ($13–18 CD) Verdelho, Chenin Blanc, Unwooded Chardonnay, Reserve Chardonnay, Shiraz, Cabernet Sauvignon Shiraz, Cabernet Sauvignon.
summary The 10-hectare property, situated on the banks of the upper reaches of the Swan River, was purchased by Laura Rowe and Derek Pearse in 1996. Four hectares of 12-year-old chardonnay made up the

original vineyard, being expanded with 1.5 hectares of shiraz and 1 hectare of cabernet sauvignon, with plans for trials of merlot, zinfandel and barbera in the pipeline. The partners also own 4 hectares of vineyard in the Margaret River region planted to shiraz, cabernet sauvignon, merlot and semillon, but the releases so far have been drawn from the Swan Valley vineyards. The fish on the label, incidentally, is black bream, which can be found in the pools of the Swan River during the summer months.

Upper Reach Vineyard Verdelho

TTTT 2002 Light straw-green; the clean, fresh and crisp bouquet is yet to evolve fruit varietal character, the palate similarly crisp, lively and fresh, sustained by good acidity. Very well made, and should open up into citrus and honeysuckle over the next 12 months (and thereafter). 100 cases made. **rating: 87**

best drinking Now–2006 **best vintages** '00 **drink with** Avocado terrine • $15

Upper Reach Vineyard Reserve Chardonnay

TTTT 2001 Light green-yellow; the bouquet is restrained, but quite stylish, with nutty and stone fruit aromas; the medium-bodied palate has seamless flavours and what can only be described as sophisticated mouthfeel. 150 cases made. **rating: 89**

best drinking Now–2005 **drink with** White Rocks veal • $16

Upper Reach Vineyard Shiraz

TTTT 2001 Vivid purple-red; rich, ripe spiced plum and cherry fruit comes through strongly on both the bouquet and palate. The American oak used is not assertive; 170 cases made. **rating: 88**

best drinking Now–2008 **drink with** Yearling beef • $18

Upper Reach Vineyard Cabernet Sauvignon Shiraz

TTTT 2001 Medium red-purple; a clean, moderately intense bouquet offers a mix of blackberry and earth, supported by subliminal oak. The smooth palate moves on with dark berry, chocolate, mint and earth, weakening ever so slightly on the finish. 300 cases made. **rating: 87**

best drinking Now–2007 **drink with** Steak and kidney pie • $16

vale view wines NR

5 Berrys Road, Vale View, Qld 4352 **region** Queensland Zone
phone (07) 4696 2282 **fax** (07) 4696 2039 **open** Weekends and public holidays 10–5, 7 days during school holidays, or by appointment
winemaker Giovanni Chersini, Hazel Chersini **production** 320 cases **est.** 1999
product range ($15 CD) Semillon, Chardonnay, Wooded Chardonnay, Shiraz, Cabernet Sauvignon, Dolce Rosso, Muscat, fruit wines.
summary Giovanni (John) Chersini was born in Valle d'Isria (then in Italy but now part of Croatia) in a wine-growing region. Visits by John, wife Hazel and son Matthew to John's birthplace inspired the planting of a few experimental vines in 1991, and to the subsequent expansion of the vineyard to its present 2.4 hectares of cabernet sauvignon, shiraz, chardonnay, semillon and frontignac. A family affair it may be, but it is also a multicultural one in the fullest sense of the word: both Hazel and Matthew are nearing completion of the external course in wine science at Charles Sturt University, while John prefers to adhere to the philosophies and practices inherited from his forebears.

vale vineyard ★★★☆

2914 Frankston-Flinders Road, Balnarring, Vic 3926 (postal) **region** Mornington Peninsula
phone (03) 5983 1521 **fax** (03) 5983 1942 **open** Not
winemaker John Vale **production** 500 cases **est.** 1991
product range ($19.95–26.95 R) Chardonnay, Pinot Grigio, Cabernet Sauvignon, Cabernet Sauvignon Pressings.
summary After a lifetime in the retail liquor industry, John and Susan Vale took a busman's retirement by purchasing a grazing property at Balnarring in 1991. They planted a little under 0.5 hectare of cabernet sauvignon, and John Vale undertook what he describes as 'formal winemaking training' before building a 20-tonne winery in 1997 from stone and recycled materials. Their younger daughter Caroline is taking the winemaking course at Charles Sturt University, and is assistant winemaker at Blue Pyrenees Estate as well as assisting her parents at Vale Vineyard. In 2000 they extended the plantings with 1.4 hectares of tempranillo, riesling and durif, seeking to move outside the square with unusual varieties. In future they look forward to making Verduzzo, Lagrein and Arneis from a nearby vineyard, which will be exclusively sold through a local

restaurant. In the meantime the wine range has been extended by the purchase of chardonnay and pinot grigio from local growers.

Vale Vineyard Pinot Grigio

TTTT 2001 Full-on pink; a spotlessly clean bouquet offers a mix of ripe apple, pear and spice; the firm and crisp palate has good balance and length, again with hints of rose petal and spice. **rating:** 86

best drinking Now **drink with** Cold seafood • $19.95

Vale Vineyard Chardonnay

TTTT 2001 Light to medium yellow-green; attractive ripe melon fruit is married with subtle barrel-ferment oak on the bouquet; the elegant, light to medium-bodied palate is likewise built around the quite crisp melon and stone fruit flavours, the oak where it should be in the background. **rating:** 89

best drinking Now–2007 **drink with** Pan-fried veal • $26.95

van de scheur   NR

O'Connors Lane, Pokolbin, NSW 2321 **region** Lower Hunter Valley
phone (02) 4998 7789 **fax** (02) 4998 7789 **open** Weekends 10–5
winemaker Kees Van De Scheur **production** 2000 cases **est.** 1995
product range ($16.50 CD) Semillon, Chardonnay, Shiraz.
summary Kees Van De Scheur is a Hunter Valley veteran, having spent the last 25 years in the Hunter Valley, first with the Robson Vineyard and then Briar Ridge, before leaving in November 1993 to establish his own winery and label. He has purchased part of the historic Ingleside property established by vigneron Frederick Ingle in 1872. After a hiatus of 60 years, vines have returned, with an initial planting of a little over 1 hectare (semillon, chardonnay and shiraz) since increased to 5 hectares. Van De Scheur also provides viticultural consulting services.

varrenti wines   NR

'Glenheather', Blackwood Road, Dunkeld, Vic 3294 **region** Grampians
phone (03) 5577 2368 **fax** (03) 5577 2367 **open** 7 days 12–5
winemaker Ettore Varrenti **production** 500 cases **est.** 1999
product range ($15 CD) Grenache, Grenache Shiraz, Cabernet Shiraz.
summary Ettore Varrenti has established 4 hectares of pinot noir, malbec, shiraz and cabernet sauvignon at the extreme southern end of the Grampians National Park. It is remote from any other winery, and appears to be on the edge of the Grampians region.

vasse felix   ★★★★☆

Cnr Caves Road and Harmans Road South, Wilyabrup, WA 6284 **region** Margaret River
phone (08) 9756 5000 **fax** (08) 9755 5425 **open** 7 days 10–5
winemaker Clive Otto, David Dowden **production** 125 000 cases **est.** 1967
product range ($19–65 R) Classic Dry White, Semillon, Chardonnay, Heytesbury Chardonnay, NV Brut, Noble Riesling, Classic Dry Red, Shiraz, Cabernet Merlot, Cabernet Sauvignon, Heytesbury (Cabernet blend).
summary In 1999 the production of Vasse Felix wines moved to a new 2000-tonne winery; the old winery is dedicated entirely to the restaurant and tasting rooms. A relatively new 140-hectare vineyard at Jindong in the north of the Margaret River supplies a large part of the increased fruit intake. National Australian distribution; exports to the US, the UK, Europe and Asia.

Vasse Felix Semillon

TTTTY 2002 Medium yellow-green; the ultra-complex bouquet is driven by strong, spicy oak, with some fruit trailing along behind; tangy fruit comes through much better on the boldly styled palate, finishing with good acidity. Barrel-fermented in French and American oak for 4 months. **rating:** 92

best drinking Now–2006 **best vintages** '92, '93, '95, '96, '99, '02 **drink with** Coquilles St Jacques • $22.50

Vasse Felix Classic Dry White

TTTT 2002 Medium yellow-green; the bouquet is quite solid, with some ripe fruit, but otherwise not particularly expressive; the palate is livened and lengthened by tingling acidity, but the wine stops there. **rating:** 86

best drinking Now **best vintages** '95 **drink with** Summer salads • $19

Vasse Felix Chardonnay

🍷🍷🍷🍷 2001 Full yellow, quite advanced; complex barrel-ferment charry oak surrounds citrus and stone fruit on the bouquet, but on the palate powerful Margaret River chardonnay fruit comes back into the driving seat; good length and intensity. **rating:** 92

best drinking Now–2006 **best vintages** '99, '01 **drink with** Pork chops • $22.50

Vasse Felix Heytesbury Chardonnay

🍷🍷🍷🍷 2001 Light to medium yellow-green; very complex barrel-ferment aromas, with a touch of Burgundian funk is a racy start, but the wine tightens up on the powerful and long palate, with masses of flavour and good oak balance. Topped the aggregate judges' points at the 2003 Divine State of Origin Challenge, but I was a minor dissenter, simply because of the oak dominance. However, I don't doubt it will go on from there as it ages. **rating:** 91

best drinking 2005–2010 **best vintages** '97, '98, '99, '01 **drink with** Rich seafood • $35

Vasse Felix Noble Riesling 375 ml

🍷🍷🍷🍷 2002 Light straw-green; fragrant lime and lime blossom aromas lead into a fresh, zesty, tangy palate, with perfectly balanced acidity and sweetness. **rating:** 90

best drinking Now–2006 **best vintages** '98, '02 **drink with** Fresh fruit • $19

Vasse Felix Heytesbury

🍷🍷🍷🍷🍷 2000 Medium red-purple; the aromatic bouquet has a mix of slightly leafy/spicy overtones to the core of blackberry fruit; the palate, too, has a mix of blackberry and a touch of olive, giving it some Bordeaux characteristics. Gold medal 2002 Qantas Wine Show of Western Australia. **rating:** 94

best drinking 2005–2015 **best vintages** '95, '96, '97, '98, '99, '00 **drink with** Beef Bordelaise • $65

vasse river wines   NR

Bussell Highway, Carbunup, WA 6280 **region** Margaret River
phone (08) 9755 1111 **fax** (08) 9755 1111 **open** 7 days 10–5
winemaker Robert Credaro, Bernie Stanlake **production** 3500 cases **est.** 1993
product range ($14–20 CD) Semillon Sauvignon Blanc, Verdelho, Chardonnay, Shiraz, Ruby Red, Cabernet Merlot.
summary This is a major and rapidly growing business owned by the Credaro family. Forty-five hectares of chardonnay, semillon, verdelho, sauvignon blanc, cabernet sauvignon, merlot and shiraz have been established on the typical gravelly red loam soils of the region. These plantings will be in full production by 2005, and it is intended to build a new winery and cellar-door sales area prior to that time.

veritas   ★★★★

Cnr Seppeltsfield and Stelzer Roads, Tanunda, SA 5352 **region** Barossa Valley
phone (08) 8562 3300 **fax** (08) 8562 1177 **open** Mon–Fri 10–4.30, weekends 11–4
winemaker Rolf Binder, Christa Deans **production** 22 000 cases **est.** 1955
product range ($11–30 CD) Tramino, Christa Rolf Semillon, Chardonnay, Shiraz, Hanisch Shiraz, Binder's Bull's Blood Shiraz, Christa Rolf Shiraz Grenache, Henrich Shiraz Mataro Grenache, Mourvedre Pressings, Cabernet Sauvignon Merlot, Tawny Port, Oom Pah Pah Port, Special Liqueur Muscadelle.
summary The Hungarian influence is obvious in the naming of some of the wines, but Australian technology is paramount in shaping the generally very good quality. Veritas has 28 hectares of estate vineyards to draw on. A near-doubling of production has coincided with the establishment of export markets to the UK, Germany, Belgium, Austria and the US. The occasional tasting here and there fully justifies the rating.

verona vineyard   NR

Small Winemakers Centre, McDonalds Road, Pokolbin, NSW 2321 **region** Lower Hunter Valley
phone (02) 4998 7668 **fax** (02) 4998 7430 **open** 7 days 10–5
winemaker Greg Silkman, Gary Reed (Contract) **est.** 1972
product range ($15–18.50 CD) Produces two ranges, under the Verona label are Verdelho, Semillon and Shiraz; also Tallamurra Verdelho, Chardonnay and Shiraz.
summary Verona has had a chequered history, and is still a significant business acting, as it does, as a sales point for a number of other Hunter Valley winemakers from its premises in McDonalds Road, directly opposite Brokenwood. The Verona wines come from 22 hectares at Muswellbrook, and 5 hectares surrounding the winery.

versace wines ★★★

Lot 258 Heaslip Road, MacDonald Park, SA 5121 **region** Adelaide Plains
phone (08) 8379 7132 **fax** (08) 8338 0979 **open** By appointment
winemaker Dominic Versace, Armando Verdiglione **production** 2000 cases **est.** 2000
product range ($20–50 R) Shiraz, Casalingo Rosso (Shiraz Sangiovese Grenache), Sangiovese Ruspantino.
summary Dominic Versace and brother-in-law Armando Verdiglione have a long association with wine, through their families in Italy and in Australia since 1980. In that year Dominic Versace planted 4.5 hectares of shiraz, grenache and sangiovese (one of the earliest such plantings in Australia) selling the grapes to Joe Grilli of Primo Estate until 1999. Armando Verdiglione had in the meantime helped create the first commercial vineyard on Kangaroo Island, together with Caj Amadio and Michael von Berg. In 2000 the pair decided to pool their experience and resources, using the near-organically grown grapes from the Versace vineyard, and using deliberately rustic winemaking techniques, including open fermenters, a basket press, no filtration, no pumping and old barrels.

Versace Sangiovese Ruspantino

♥♥♥♡ **2002** Light red-purple; clean, strawberry/spicy/cherry aromas lead into a light, fresh palate with small red berry fruit flavours, and a lively, dry finish. **rating:** 83

best drinking Now **drink with** Antipasto • $20

Versace Sangiovese

♥♥♥♥ **2000** Light red; an unusual spice and mint bouquet, with smoky oak adding a dimension is essentially replayed on the light-bodied palate, which has some cedar and spice varietal character, but it has a challenging price. **rating:** 85

best drinking Now–2006 **drink with** Ravioli • $50

vicarys NR

Northern Road, Luddenham, NSW 2745 **region** South Coast Zone
phone (02) 4773 4161 **fax** (02) 4773 4411 **open** Mon–Fri 9–5, weekends 10–5
winemaker Chris Niccol **production** 3000 cases **est.** 1923
product range ($12–36 CD) Chardonnay, Semillon, Riesling, Gewurztraminer, Fume Blanc, Cabernet Sauvignon, Shiraz Cabernet Merlot, Sparkling, fortifieds. Also produces kosher wines.
summary Vicarys justifiably claims to be the Sydney region's oldest continuously operating winery, having been established in a very attractive, large, stone shearing shed built about 1890. Most of the wines come from other parts of Australia, but the winery does draw upon 1 hectare of estate traminer and 3 hectares of chardonnay for those wines, and has produced some good wines of all styles over the years.

viking wines ★★★★☆

RSD 108 Seppeltsfield Road, Marananga, SA 5355 **region** Barossa Valley
phone (08) 8562 3842 **fax** (08) 8562 4266 **open** 7 days 11–5
winemaker Rolf Binder (Contract) **production** 1000 cases **est.** 1995
product range ($45–50 CD) Grand Shiraz, Shiraz Cabernet.
summary Based upon 40-year-old, dry-grown and near-organic vineyards with a yield of only 1–1.5 tonnes per acre, Viking Wines has been 'discovered' by Robert Parker with inevitable consequences for the price of its top Shiraz. There are in 5 hectares of shiraz and 3 of cabernet sauvignon; quaffing white wines are made from purchased grapes. The immensely experienced Rolf Binder is contract winemaker for this operation which sells its wine through several retailers in Sydney and Melbourne, and exports to the US, Europe and Japan.

Viking Grand Shiraz

♥♥♥♥♥ **2001** Medium to full red-purple; the deeply accented bouquet covers the full spectrum from savoury/foresty aromas on the one side, and blackberry, prune and all-spice on the other; all of these characters are in abundance on the palate, plus a dash of bitter chocolate; a wine with great personality and good oak handling into the bargain. The big end of town to be sure, and you wouldn't want to drink the bottle without assistance from friends. **rating:** 94

best drinking 2006–2016 **best vintages** '01 **drink with** Barbecued ox • $50

Viking Grand Shiraz Cabernet

♥♥♥♥ **2001** Medium purple-red; the bouquet has a curious mix of spice, earth, olive and blackberry, the differing inputs coming through again on the sweet, lush palate, with its rich texture and mouthfeel. Seems much riper than the 14° disclosed on the label. A 50/50 blend. **rating:** 89

best drinking 2006–2011 **drink with** Rare rump steak • $45

villa primavera   NR

Mornington–Flinders Road, Red Hill, Vic 3937   **region** Mornington Peninsula
phone (03) 5989 2129   **fax** (03) 5931 0045   **open** Weekends, public holidays 10–5 and 7 days from Dec 26 to end January
winemaker Gennaro Mazzella   **production** 300 cases   **est.** 1984
product range ($18–30 CD) Chardonnay, Pinot Noir, Limoncello, Methode Champenoise.
summary A most unusual operation, which is in reality a family Italian-style restaurant at which the wine is principally sold and served, and which offers something totally different on the Mornington Peninsula. A consistent winner of tourism and food awards, it is praised by all who go there.

vinden estate   ★★★☆

17 Gillards Road, Pokolbin, NSW 2320   **region** Lower Hunter Valley
phone (02) 4998 7410   **fax** (02) 4998 7421   **open** 7 days 10–5
winemaker Guy Vinden, John Baruzzi (Consultant)   **production** 2000 cases   **est.** 1998
product range ($19.50–23 CD) Semillon, Unwooded Chardonnay, Chardonnay, Shiraz.
summary Sandra and Guy Vinden have bought their dream home with landscaped gardens in the foreground and 9 hectares of vineyard with the Brokenback mountain range in the distance. Much of the winemaking is now done on-site, and increasingly drawn from the estate vineyards. The wines are available through the cellar door and also via a wine club which offers buying advantages to members. The restaurant, Thai on Gillards Road, is open weekends and public holidays from 10.30 am to 4 pm.

Vinden Estate Semillon

TTTT 2002 Light straw-green; the aromatic bouquet has lively, sweet citrus/lemon aromas, the palate with plenty of presence, built around sweet lemony/citrus fruit. The style seems to vary somewhat from one year to the next.   **rating: 89**
best drinking Now–2007 **best vintages** '01 **drink with** Rich fish dishes • $19.50

Vinden Estate Unwooded Chardonnay

TTTT 2002 Light straw-green; the bouquet is quite complex, strongly suggesting some oak, when there is apparently none there; the palate has good length and intensity to the citrus and nectarine fruit; all up I strongly preferred it to the oaked Chardonnay of the same vintage.   **rating: 88**
best drinking Now–2005 **drink with** Avocado and prawn salad • $19

Vinden Estate Shiraz

TTTY 2001 Light to medium red-purple; light savoury, earthy, spicy aromas are the drivers on the light to medium-bodied palate, which, while well-made lacks concentration.   **rating: 84**
best drinking 2004–2007 **drink with** Yearling beef • $21

🐚 vinecrest   ★★★

Cnr Barossa Valley Way and Vine Vale Road, Tanunda, SA 5352   **region** Barossa Valley
phone (08) 8563 0111   **fax** (08) 8563 0444   **open** Fri–Mon 11–4, or by appointment
winemaker Mos Kaesler **production** 2000 cases **est.** 1999
product range ($10.95–28 CD) Semillon, Late Harvest, Shiraz, Connections Shiraz, Sparkling Shiraz.
summary The Mader family has a long connection with the Barossa Valley. Ian Mader is a fifth generation descendant of Gottfried and Maria Mader who immigrated to the Barossa Valley in the 1840s, while his wife Suzanne is the daughter of a former long-serving vineyard manager for Penfolds. In 1969 Ian and Suzanne established their 12-hectare Sandy Ridge Vineyard, and more recently a further 12 hectares on the Turrung Vineyard a few minutes from the township of Tanunda. Having been grape growers for 30 years, in 1999 they decided to establish Vinecrest, utilising a small portion of the production from their vineyards, establishing their cellar door on the Turrung Vineyard, adjacent to the tall gum trees of Kroemer's Reserve.

Vinecrest Sparkling Shiraz

TTTT 2001 Medium to full red-purple; the clean and rich bouquet offers a mix of blackberry and plum; an unusually dry style in the mouth, with dark blackberry fruit; could age well.   **rating: 85**
best drinking Now–2008 **drink with** Terrine, pâté • $22.50

Vinecrest Shiraz

 TTTT **2000** Red-purple, bright and healthy; clean, sweet plum and raspberry fruit aromas are followed by a juicy, rich raspberry and blackberry palate, entirely fruit-driven but with nice structure.   **rating:** 87

best drinking 2004–2009 **drink with** Lasagne • $24

vinifera wines   ★★★

194 Henry Lawson Drive, Mudgee, NSW 2850 **region** Mudgee
phone (02) 6372 2461 **fax** (02) 6372 6731 **open** 7 days 10–5.30
winemaker Phillip van Gent, Tony McKendry **production** 1500 cases **est.** 1997
product range ($14–23 CD) Riesling, Semillon, Chardonnay, Easter Semillon (sweet), Tempranillo, Cabernet Sauvignon.
summary Tony and Debbie McKendry have much in common with (the late) Dave and Leslie Robertson of Thistle Hill, the latter another Mudgee winery. Dave Robertson lost a leg in a motorcycle accident, and used the compensation proceeds to establish Thistle Hill, turning adversity into good fortune. The McKendry's tell a similar tale. Having lived in Mudgee for 15 years, Tony McKendry (a regional medical superintendent) and Debbie succumbed to the lure, and planted and tended their small (1.5-ha) vineyard in 1995. In Debbie's words, 'Tony, in his spare two minutes per day, also decided to start Wine Science at Charles Sturt University in 1992'. She continues, 'His trying to live 27 hours per day (plus our four kids!) fell to pieces when he was involved in a severe car smash in 1997. Two months in hospital stopped full-time medical work, and the winery dreams became inevitable'. Here, too, financial compensation finally came through and the small winery was built. The vineyard now extends to 11 hectares, including 2 hectares of tempranillo and 1 hectare of graciano.

Vinifera Riesling

TTTY **2002** Light straw-green; the crisp and minerally bouquet has some earthy, spicy notes, the palate moderately sweet in classic cellar-door style.   **rating:** 83

best drinking Now **drink with** Sweet and sour pork • $16

Vinifera Chardonnay

TTTT **2002** Medium yellow-green; the clean, smooth bouquet has nectarine fruit and subtle oak, the understated palate in the same vein, the balance and length good.   **rating:** 85

best drinking Now–2005 **drink with** Smoked pork • $16

Vinifera Easter Semillon

TTTT **2001** Glowing yellow-green; the clean, moderately intense bouquet has honey and cumquat aromas; a well-balanced palate has rich but not excessively sweet fruit; balanced acidity provides good length.   **rating:** 87

best drinking Now–2005 **drink with** Poached peaches • $19

Vinifera Tempranillo

TTTY **2001** Light red; the bouquet has light, spicy/earthy aromas, which are not particularly fruity. The light palate has gentle fruit sweetness, but little structure or depth. Hopefully, the vines will provide more concentrated grapes as they mature.   **rating:** 82

best drinking Now **drink with** Meat salads • $23

vintina estate   NR

1282 Nepean Highway, Mount Eliza, Vic 3930 **region** Mornington Peninsula
phone (03) 9787 8166 **fax** (03) 9775 2035 **open** 7 days 9–5
winemaker Jim Filippone, Kevin McCarthy (Consultant) **production** 400 cases **est.** 1985
product range ($12–14 CD) Chardonnay, Semillon, Pinot Gris, Pinot Noir, Cabernet Sauvignon.
summary The initial releases of Vintina from 1.6 hectares of estate plantings (the only wines tasted to date) were mediocre. With competent contract-winemaking, improvement might have been expected. However, no recent tastings.

virage   NR

13B Georgette Road, Gracetown, WA 6284 **region** Margaret River
phone (08) 9755 5318 **fax** (08) 9755 5318 **open** Not
winemaker Bernard Abbott **production** 1000 cases **est.** 1990
product range ($13–20 R) Sauvignon Blanc, Semillon Chardonnay, Traminer Riesling, Cabernet Shiraz Zinfandel, Cabernet Merlot.

summary Former Vasse Felix winemaker Bernard Abbott, together with wife Pascale, acquired (under long-term lease) the former government research station vineyard at Bramley Estate in 1990. Bernard Abbott makes the wines at a local Margaret River winery and sells them by mailing list and direct to retailer and restaurants in Perth, Melbourne and Sydney.

virgin hills ★★★★★

Salisbury Road, Lauriston West via Kyneton, Vic 3444 **region** Macedon Ranges
phone (03) 5422 7444 **fax** (03) 5422 7400 **open** By appointment
winemaker Josh Steele **production** 2500 cases **est.** 1968
product range ($55 R) A single Cabernet Sauvignon Shiraz Merlot Blend called Virgin Hills; occasional limited Reserve release.
summary Virgin Hills has passed through several ownership changes in a short period of time. It is now owned by Michael Hope, who presides over the fast-growing Hope Estate in the Hunter Valley. While there have been one or two raised eyebrows at some of the events in the Hunter Valley several years ago, the quality of the wines currently being made at Hope Estate cannot be questioned, any more than the quality of the 1998 Virgin Hills. So, after some prevarication, the five-star rating remains in place. Exports to the UK and the US.

voyager estate ★★★★★

Lot 1 Stevens Road, Margaret River, WA 6285 **region** Margaret River
phone (08) 9757 6354 **fax** (08) 9757 6494 **open** 7 days 10–5
winemaker Cliff Royle **production** 30 000 cases **est.** 1978
product range ($19.50–100 R) Semillon, Sauvignon Blanc Semillon, Tom Price Semillon Sauvignon Blanc, Chardonnay, Shiraz, Cabernet Sauvignon Merlot, Tom Price Cabernet Sauvignon.
summary Voyager Estate has come a long way since it was acquired by Michael Wright (of the mining family) in May 1991. It now has an important, high-quality 63.5-hectare vineyard which puts Voyager Estate in the position of being able to select only the best parcels of fruit for its own label, and to supply surplus (but high-quality) wine to others. The Cape Dutch-style tasting room and vast rose garden are a major tourist attraction, although the winery itself remains in strictly utilitarian form. Exports to the UK, The Netherlands, Switzerland, China, Malaysia, Singapore, Japan, New Zealand, Canada and the US.

Voyager Estate Semillon
ΨΨΨΨ 2001 Light green-yellow; the youthful, tight and spotlessly clean bouquet has citrus and herb aromas, the medium-bodied palate loosening up enough to provide good mouthfeel and attractive flavours. **rating:** 90
best drinking Now–2007 **best vintages** '95, '96, '00, '01 **drink with** Chicken • $24.50

Voyager Estate Sauvignon Blanc Semillon
ΨΨΨΨ 2002 Medium straw-green; an aromatic bouquet with a touch of passionfruit leads into a lively and fresh palate with a backbone of mineral to the tropical fruit flavours. **rating:** 88
best drinking Now–2005 **best vintages** '95, '97, '01 **drink with** Marinated octopus • $19.50

Voyager Estate Tom Price Semillon Sauvignon Blanc
ΨΨΨΨΨ 2001 Light to medium green-yellow; toasty, charry barrel-ferment oak dominates the bouquet; tight fruit, with racy acidity, makes a partial comeback on the palate, but the wine is too oaky for my taste. Others will doubtless profoundly disagree. **rating:** 90
ΨΨΨΨΨ 2000 Medium to full yellow-green; a rich and smooth bouquet, with excellent fruit and oak balance and integration; the palate has developed slowly and will age superbly like a top-flight white Bordeaux; beautifully balanced and made; an iron fist in the velvet glove. **rating:** 96
best drinking 2004–2008 **best vintages** '96, '99, '00 **drink with** Rich seafood • $38

Voyager Estate Chardonnay
ΨΨΨΨΨ 2001 Bright, light to medium green-yellow; the complex but elegant bouquet has a subtle interplay between melon/nectarine fruit and subtle barrel-ferment oak. The palate has very attractive mouthfeel and delicious flavour, bright, citrus and nectarine fruit walking the talk. A star at the 2003 Divine State of Origin Challenge. **rating:** 94
best drinking Now–2008 **best vintages** '92, '93, '95, '96, '97, '98, '99, '00, '01 **drink with** Braised pork neck • $35

Voyager Estate Shiraz

ŶŶŶŶŶ **2001** Deep, bright red-purple; the complex bouquet has deep, dark plum in the vanguard, together with touches of licorice, chocolate and oak. The powerful, ripe but not jammy palate lives up to the bouquet, the opulent fruit offset by excellent, ripe tannins.　　　　　　　　　　　　　　　　**rating:** 94

best drinking 2006–2013 **best vintages** '99, '00, '01 **drink with** Barbecued leg of lamb • $28.50

Voyager Estate Cabernet Sauvignon Merlot

ŶŶŶŶ♀ **2000** Medium to full red-purple; the solid bouquet has blackberry, blackcurrant and chocolate aromas, the oak positive but not aggressive. Excellent tannin balance and extract provides the cornerstones for an excellent wine, the flavours tracking the fruit of the bouquet.　　　　　　　　　　　　　**rating:** 93

best drinking 2008–2015 **best vintages** '91, '93, '97, '98, '99, '00 **drink with** Beef in red wine sauce • $39

wadjekanup river estate　　　NR

Flatrocks Road, Broomehill, WA 6318 **region** Great Southern
phone (08) 9825 3080 **fax** (08) 9825 3007 **open** By appointment
winemaker Michael Staniford (Alkoomi Contract) **production** 400 cases **est.** 1995
product range ($16–18 CD) Sauvignon Blanc, Shiraz.
summary The Witham family (Scott and Sue, Jim and Ann) began the development of Wadjekanup River Estate in 1995 as a minor diversification for a 3000-hectare wool, prime lamb, beef and cereal cropping enterprise worked by the family. They began with 1.2 hectares of shiraz and sauvignon blanc, since extended to 8 hectares including a 1-hectare block of merlot with its first production in 2001. The aims for the future include a purpose-built cellar for storage and sales, with a possibility of farm-stay accommodation also being considered. The present wine range of Sauvignon Blanc and Shiraz will be extended with a varietal Merlot, and the possibility of a Semillon or other white somewhere down the track.

Wadjekanup River Estate Sauvignon Blanc

ŶŶŶŶ **2002** Straw-green; voluminous/tropical/passionfruit aromas are matched by plenty of sweet, tropical fruit flavours, in turn balanced by good acidity.　　　　　　　　　　　　　　　**rating:** 88

best drinking Now **drink with** Sushi • $16

wallington wines　　　NR

Nyrang Creek Vineyard, Canowindra, NSW 2904 **region** Cowra
phone (02) 6344 7153 **fax** (02) 6344 7105 **open** By appointment
winemaker Blair Duncan, Murray Smith (Contract) **production** 1500 cases **est.** 1992
product range ($12–20 CD) Chardonnay, Shiraz, Cabernet Sauvignon.
summary Anthony and Margaret Wallington commenced the development of their Nyrang Creek Vineyard with 2 hectares of cabernet sauvignon in 1992, followed by 7 hectares of chardonnay in 1994, then shiraz (2 ha) and semillon (0.75 ha) in 1995, 0.75 hectare each of cabernet franc and pinot noir in 1998, thereafter adding a mix of grenache, mourvedre, tempranillo and viognier. Most of the production is sold, but Blair Duncan at Arrowfield makes the Wallington Chardonnay and Murray Smith of Canobolas-Smith Wines at Orange makes the Cabernet Sauvignon and Shiraz. The quality of the wines is such that exports to the US have already commenced.

walsh family winery　　　NR

90 Walnut Road, Bickley, WA 6076 **region** Perth Hills
phone (08) 9291 7341 **fax** (08) 9291 7341 **open** Weekends 10–5
winemaker Rob Marshall (Contract) **production** 200 cases **est.** 1995
product range ($12–17 CD) Gewurztraminer, Mary's Request Shiraz.
summary Walsh Family Winery is aptly named: it is a partnership of the Walshes and their eight children. One of those children has established 11 hectares of vines near Bridgetown in the Great Southern, the grapes from which form part of the Walsh Family winery intake.

wandering brook estate　　　NR

North Wandering Road, Wandering, WA 6308 **region** Peel
phone (08) 9884 1084 **fax** (08) 9884 1064 **open** Weekends 9.30–6
winemaker Steve Radojkovich **production** 1400 cases **est.** 1989
product range Verdelho, Chardonnay, Unwooded Chardonnay, Soft Red and White, Cabernet Sauvignon, Sparkling Verdelho, Port.

summary Laurie and Margaret White have planted 10 hectares of vines on their 130-year-old family property in a move to diversify. Up to 1994 the wines were made at Goundrey, currently at Jadran. Renamed Wandering Brook Estate late in 1994; up till then known as Red Hill Estate. Over half the annual production of grapes is sold.

wandin valley estate ★★★☆

Wilderness Road, Lovedale, NSW 2320 **region** Lower Hunter Valley
phone (02) 4930 7317 **fax** (02) 4930 7814 **open** 7 days 10–5
winemaker Nicholas Paterson, Karl Stockhausen (Consultant) **production** 15 000 cases **est.** 1973
product range ($15–28 CD) Pavilion range of Rose, Cabernet Malbec Shiraz; Estate Range of Verdelho, Chardonnay, Shiraz, Cabernet Merlot, Muscat; top of the range Sparkling Semillon, Reserve Semillon, Bridie's Shiraz, Riley's Reserve Cabernet Sauvignon.
summary The former Millstone vineyard, now owned by the producer of Australian television's classic 'A Country Practice'. Rapidly developing Chardonnays have been the focal point of Wandin Valley's considerable show success. The estate also boasts a Cope-Williams-type village cricket oval and extensive cottage accommodation. Exports to the US, Denmark, Malaysia and Japan. The Cafe Crocodile is open Wednesday–Sunday for lunch, and dinner Friday and Saturday.

Wandin Valley Estate Reserve Semillon

▼▼▼▼ 2002 Light straw-green; the bouquet is clean and bright, but (not surprisingly) still fairly neutral and unevolved. The palate has more expression, with a mix of grass, citrus and mineral flavours; certainly worth cellaring. **rating:** 89

best drinking Now–2007 **best vintages** '01 **drink with** Grilled white-fleshed fish and lemon • $18

Wandin Valley Estate Pavilion Rose

▼▼▼▽ 2002 Vivid fuchsia; fragrant cherry and mint aromas and flavours run through the bouquet and palate, which has good length and neatly balanced acidity and residual sugar. A cellar door special. **rating:** 84

best drinking Now **drink with** Takeaway • $15

wangolina station ★★★☆

Cnr Southern Ports Highway/Limestone Coast Road, Kingston SE, SA 5275 **region** Mount Benson
phone (08) 8768 6187 **fax** (08) 8768 6149 **open** 7 days 10–5
winemaker Anita Goode **production** 1500 cases **est.** 2001
product range ($15 CD) Semillon, Sauvignon Blanc, Cabernet Sauvignon Shiraz.
summary Four generations of the Goode family have been graziers at Wangolina Station, renowned for its shorthorn cattle stud. The family now has two connections with the wine industry: it sold the land to Kreglinger for its vineyard and winery, and also sold land to Ralph Fowler. The second connection is even more direct: fifth generation Anita Goode has become a vigneron, with 3.2 hectares of shiraz and 1.6 hectares each of cabernet sauvignon, sauvignon blanc and semillon established on the family property.

Wangolina Station Semillon

▼▼▼▼ 2002 Light straw-green; a fragrant bouquet of passionfruit and lemon is followed by a light to medium-bodied palate, with similar flavours, moderate length, and a faintly grippy finish. Shows considerable potential for this variety in the Mount Benson region. **rating:** 86

best drinking Now–2005 **drink with** Lobster mousse • $15

Wangolina Station Sauvignon Blanc

▼▼▼▼ 2002 Light to medium yellow-green; the clean and firm bouquet has a mix of mineral and herbs, the palate progressively building intensity and flavour towards the finish; good mouthfeel. **rating:** 88

best drinking Now **drink with** Grilled scallops • $15

Wangolina Station Cabernet Sauvignon Shiraz

▼▼▼▼ 2001 Medium red-purple; a fresh and lively bouquet with a mix of spicy, minty, red berry aromas leads into a palate which adds a touch of chocolate to the core of fresh, gently sweet red berry fruit, with no hint of green; has an appealing savoury, spicy finish. **rating:** 89

best drinking 2004–2009 **drink with** Lamb kebabs • $15

wansbrough wines NR

Richards Road, Ferguson, WA 6236 **region** Geographe
phone (08) 9728 3091 **fax** (08) 9728 3091 **open** Weekends 10–5
winemaker Willespie Wines (Contract) **production** 250 cases **est.** 1986
product range ($12–18 CD) Riesling, Semillon, Sauvignon Blanc, Constantia (late-picked Semillon), Shiraz Cabernet, Port.
summary Situated east of Dardanup in the picturesque Ferguson Valley, Wansbrough enjoys views of the distant Geographe Bay and the nearer State forest with the Bibblemun Track running along its northern and eastern borders. To taste the wine you need either to order by mail or visit the Wansbrough restaurant on weekends.

wantirna estate NR

Bushy Park Lane, Wantirna South, Vic 3152 (postal) **region** Yarra Valley
phone (03) 9801 2367 **fax** (03) 9887 0225 **open** Not
winemaker Maryann Egan, Reg Egan **production** 800 cases **est.** 1963
product range ($42–48 ML) Isabella Chardonnay, Lily Pinot Noir, Amelia Cabernet Sauvignon Merlot.
summary Situated well within the boundaries of the Melbourne metropolitan area, Wantirna Estate is an outpost of the Yarra Valley, and one of the first established in the rebirth of the Valley. In deference to Reg Egan's very firmly held views on the subject, neither the winery nor the wines are rated.

Wantirna Estate Lily Pinot Noir

2001 NV Bright and clear red-purple; the bouquet has a complex array of spice, dark plum and dark cherry, the palate with good depth, weight and extract, the tannins borderline, but underwriting the medium-term cellaring ability of the wine. **rating:** NR
best drinking 2004–2007 **drink with** Peking duck • $48

Wantirna Estate Amelia Cabernet Sauvignon Merlot

2000 NV Bright red-purple; the bouquet has firm, earthy blackberry and blackcurrant fruit, the fine and elegant palate with ripe berry fruit and cedary oak; long finish, fine wine. **rating:** NR
best drinking 2005–2012 **best vintages** '90, '91, '92, '93, '98 **drink with** Roast veal • $48

warrabilla ★★★★☆

Murray Valley Highway, Rutherglen, Vic 3685 **region** Rutherglen
phone (02) 6035 7242 **fax** (02) 6035 7298 **open** 7 days 10–5
winemaker Andrew Sutherland Smith **production** 10 000 cases **est.** 1986
product range ($12–28 CD) Chardonnay, KV Brut Rose, Brimin Shiraz, Reserve Shiraz, Merlot, Reserve Merlot, Reserve Durif, Reserve Cabernet, Vintage Port, Liqueur Muscat.
summary Former All Saints winemaker Andrew Sutherland Smith has leased a small winery at Corowa to make the Warrabilla wines from a 17-hectare vineyard developed by himself and Carol Smith in the Indigo Valley. The red wines are made in open fermenters, hand-plunged and basket-pressed, then matured in quality oak, mainly French. The quality of the Reserve wines has been uniformly high; the 2002 red wines arrived after the final (extended) deadline for this edition of the *Wine Companion*.

Warrabilla Liqueur Muscat

♀♀♀♀♀ NV Olive-brown colour attesting to some age. The rich raisin and plum pudding bouquet shows exemplary varietal character, and the palate does not disappoint; rich raisin, toffee and plum pudding flavours providing excellent value. **rating:** 90
best drinking Now **drink with** Nuts, dried fruits, biscuits • $15

warramate ★★★★

27 Maddens Lane, Gruyere, Vic 3770 **region** Yarra Valley
phone (03) 5964 9219 **fax** (03) 5964 9219 **open** 7 days 10–6
winemaker David Church **production** 900 cases **est.** 1970
product range ($20–35 CD) Riesling, Shiraz, Cabernet Merlot.
summary Wine quality has been variable in recent years; it would seem that the oak in some of the older barrels is questionable. At their best, the wines reflect the distinguished site on which the vineyard sits. The 2000/2001 extension of the 30-year-old vineyard will lead to greater production in the years ahead.

Warramate Shiraz

▼▼▼▼▽ **2000** Medium red-purple; the clean, fresh bouquet has plenty of black cherry fruit, with just a hint of spice in the background. An elegant, fruit-driven palate provides similar flavours; good mouthfeel and style. **rating:** 90

best drinking 2004–2009 **best vintages** '88, '92, '93, '97, '98, '00 **drink with** Spiced lamb • $35

Warramate Cabernet Merlot

▼▼▼▼▽ **2000** Medium red-purple; clean blackcurrant and raspberry fruit on the bouquet leads into a palate showing perfectly ripened fruit, sweet tannins and subtle oak; good balance and length, reflecting the exceptional vintage. **rating:** 90

best drinking 2005–2010 **best vintages** '00 **drink with** Butterfly leg of lamb • $25

warraroong estate ★★★★

Wilderness Road, Lovedale, NSW 2321 **region** Lower Hunter Valley
phone (02) 4930 7594 **fax** (02) 4930 7199 **open** Thurs–Mon 10–5
winemaker Andrew Thomas, Adam Rees **production** 2000 cases **est.** 1988
product range ($15–25 CD) Semillon, Sauvignon Blanc, Chenin Blanc, Chardonnay, Semillon Methode Champenoise, Ruby Cabernet Methode Champenoise, Malbec Rose, Shiraz, Malbec.
summary Warraroong Estate was formerly Fraser Vineyard and adopted its new name after it changed hands in 1997. The name 'Warraroong' is an Aboriginal word for hillside, reflecting the southwesterly aspect of the property looking back towards the Brokenback Range and Watagan Mountains. The label design is from a painting by local Aboriginal artist Kia Kiro who, while coming from the Northern Territory, is living and working in the Hunter Valley.

Warraroong Estate Semillon

▼▼▼▼▽ **2002** Light green-yellow; the intense, firm and clean bouquet has lemon and herb aromas in the foreground, mineral in the background; the palate has good grip, presence and length, and an even better finish. The aftertaste is as pure as mountain air. **rating:** 93

best drinking Now–2010 **drink with** Cold seafood • $18

Warraroong Estate Chenin Blanc

▼▼▼▼ **2002** Light green-yellow; the clean, light bouquet has fruit salad plus a hint of citrus aromatics; the palate has fresh mouthfeel, the fruit salad flavours with some length; skilled winemaking, the limitations lying with the variety. **rating:** 85

best drinking Now **drink with** Takeaway • $15

Warraroong Estate Chardonnay

▼▼▼▼ **2002** Light to medium yellow-green; the bouquet has a subtle interplay of tight fruit and subliminal oak; the light to medium-bodied palate has good length and, in particular, finish, and will develop well. Shows that new oak is not essential in creating mouthfeel and texture; this wine has been made with old oak and extended lees contact. **rating:** 88

best drinking Now–2006 **drink with** Trout pâté • $20

Warraroong Estate Malbec Rose

▼▼▼▼ **2002** Bright fuchsia; the bouquet has fresh berry fruit, not the least bit jammy; the palate is dry, and surprisingly long and intense; for serious rose drinkers. **rating:** 86

best drinking Now **drink with** Meat salads • $16

Warraroong Estate Shiraz

▼▼▼▼ **2001** Medium purple-red; the moderately intense bouquet has an archetypal Hunter mix of dark berry and earth, the medium-bodied and well-balanced palate following in precisely the same track; not forced to be something it isn't. **rating:** 87

best drinking 2005–2011 **best vintages** '98 **drink with** Roast beef • $20

warrego wines ★★★

9 Seminary Road, MS292, Marburg, Qld 4306 **region** Queensland Coastal
phone (07) 5464 4400 **fax** (07) 5464 4800 **open** 7 days 10–4
winemaker Kevin Watson **production** 12 000 cases **est.** 2000

product range ($9.95–28.95 CD) Cane Cutter's Riesling, Sawmill Sauvignon Blanc, Coalface Chardonnay, Sirois Chardonnay, Dance's Delight, Cane Cutter's Cuvee, Cane Cutter's Pinot Noir, Brigalow Shiraz, Seminary Shiraz, Cunningham's Coonawarra Cabernet Sauvignon, Rum Distillery Tawny Port.

summary Cathy and Kevin Watson have established their small winery in the historic Dances Bakery at Marburg, which is halfway between Toowoomba and Brisbane, attracted – like so many others – by the lifestyle opportunities and the tourism potential of southern Queensland. Kevin Watson has completed his wine science degree at Charles Sturt University, and the primary purpose of his business is custom winemaking for the many small growers in the region. In 2001 a company, Marburg Custom Crush, developed a state-of-the-art winery (as the cliché goes), cellar door and restaurant. $500 000 in government funding, local business investment and significant investment from China provided the funds, and the complex opened in April 2002. In 2003 Warrego crushed 230 tonnes, from the Granite Belt, coast regions, and far further afield.

Warrego Sirois Chardonnay

ΨΨΨΨ 2001 Medium to full yellow-green; clean, ripe peach and nectarine fruit is supported by subtle oak on the bouquet; the light to medium-bodied palate has ripe peach flavours; well made, even if it is rather short. A mix of Cowra and Harrisville (Queensland) grapes. **rating:** 86

best drinking Now **drink with** Roast chicken • $18.95

Warrego Seminary Shiraz

ΨΨΨΨ 2001 Medium red-purple; the relatively light bouquet has a range of spicy, cedary, leafy, blackberry aromas, the light-bodied palate in a spicy, cedary spectrum; not a lot of fruit weight, but has been well made. Improbably, the grapes come from Mornington Peninsula and brought to the winery in a refrigerated truck and crushed at the winery. Spends 16 months in French and American oak. **rating:** 85

best drinking 2004–2007 **drink with** Lasagne • $19.95

warrenmang vineyard & resort ★★★★

Mountain Creek Road, Moonambel, Vic 3478 **region** Pyrenees
phone (03) 5467 2233 **fax** (03) 5467 2309 **open** 7 days 10–5
winemaker Luigi Bazzani, Kim Hart **production** 12 000 cases **est.** 1974
product range ($16–120 R) The wines are released in two ranges: the lower-priced Bazzani white and red blends, Salute Methode Champenoise and Vintage Port; then a subtly differing range of wines under the Warrenmang label, predominantly estate-grown and including Sauvignon Blanc, Chardonnay, Late Harvest Traminer, Grand Pyrenees, Shiraz, Cabernet Sauvignon; and, at the top, a flagship wine which varies from time to time.

summary Warrenmang is now the focus of a superb accommodation and restaurant complex created by former restaurateur Luigi Bazzani and wife Athalie, which is in much demand as a conference centre as well as for weekend tourism. The striking black Bazzani label is partly responsible for the growth in the volume of production. However, the real quality comes from the estate-grown wines. Exports to Asia, Europe and the US.

Warrenmang Sauvignon Blanc

ΨΨΨΨ 2002 Light straw-green; a clean, correct and fresh bouquet with predominantly grass and mineral aromas, joined by a touch of gooseberry; then a light to medium-bodied palate, likewise fresh, well balanced and not aggressive. **rating:** 87

best drinking Now **drink with** Pyrenees yabbies • $25

Warrenmang Red Gold Reserve Shiraz

ΨΨΨΨ NV Medium red-purple; the clean and smooth bouquet ranges through ripe blackcurrant and plum aromas, but the palate seems utterly disjunctive, for reasons not self-apparent. The wine is in fact a blend of the best single barrel from each of the 1997, '98 and 2000 vintages put together for the 25th anniversary of Warrenmang. Each of the components has been highly rated. **rating:** 88

best drinking 2005–2015 **drink with** Leave it in the cellar • $120

Warrenmang Vinello

ΨΨΨΨ 2002 Light red-purple; a tangy, viney lemony, spicy bouquet is followed by a fruity and surprisingly smooth and well-balanced palate, the overall impression akin to a fleshy rose. A blend of Barbera, Nebbiolo, Sangiovese and Dolcetto which can be served slightly chilled. **rating:** 84

best drinking Now **drink with** Antipasto • $20

Warrenmang Grand Pyrenees

ΨΨΨΨΨ 2000 Medium red-purple; instantly attractive cedary, savoury, spicy edges to the blackberry fruit of the bouquet flow into a delicious palate with blackcurrant and blackberry fruit, soft, ripe tannins, and good oak.

best drinking 2005–2015 **best vintages** '97, '00 **drink with** Aged rump • $45 **rating:** 94

warrina wines NR

Back Road, Kootingal, NSW 2352 **region** Northern Slopes Zone
phone (02) 6760 3985 **fax** (02) 6765 5746 **open** Weekends 10–4
winemaker David Nicholls **production** 100 cases **est.** 1989
product range ($5–12 CD) Sauvignon Blanc, Chardonnay, Shiraz, Cabernet Sauvignon.
summary David and Susan Nicholls began the establishment of their 2.5-hectare vineyard all the way back in 1989, and were content to sell the grapes to other producers, making occasional forays into winemaking, until deciding to commence winemaking on a commercial basis in 2001.

waterton estate NR

Rowella, Tas 7270 **region** Northern Tasmania
phone (03) 6327 4170 **fax** (03) 6331 9982 **open** Not
winemaker Julian Alcorso, Nick Butler **production** 400 cases **est.** 1995
product range ($11 ML) Riesling, Chardonnay, Cabernet Sauvignon.
summary The near-invisible Waterton Estate is owned by a 7-member syndicate who doubtless consume much of the annual production themselves, selling the remainder by word of mouth to friends and acquaintances. Contract winemaking by Julian Alcorso and Nick Butler does the rest.

water wheel ★★★☆

Bridgewater-on-Loddon, Bridgewater, Vic 3516 **region** Bendigo
phone (03) 5437 3060 **fax** (03) 5437 3082 **open** Oct–Apr 7 days 11–5, May–Sept Mon–Fri 11–5, weekends and public holidays 1–4
winemaker Peter Cumming, Bill Trevaskis **production** 35 000 cases **est.** 1972
product range ($14–18 R) Bendigo Sauvignon Blanc, Bendigo Chardonnay, Bendigo Shiraz, Bendigo Cabernet Sauvignon.
summary Peter Cumming gained great respect as a winemaker during his four-year stint with Hickinbotham Winemakers, and his 1989 purchase of Water Wheel was greeted with enthusiasm by followers of his work. The wines are of remarkably consistent quality and modest price, being distributed throughout Australia and with export markets in New Zealand, Asia, the UK, Switzerland, Belgium, Austria, the US and Canada.

Water Wheel Bendigo Sauvignon Blanc

ŸŸŸŸ 2002 Light straw-green; the bouquet is clean, but relatively neutral and varietally indistinct; the palate picks up to a degree, having substance, but little or no varietal precision. Ideal for those who don't really like too much varietal flavour in their Sauvignon Blanc but want to keep away from low-priced wooded Chardonnay. **rating:** 83
best drinking Now **best vintages** '00 **drink with** Asian seafood • $14

Water Wheel Bendigo Shiraz

ŸŸŸŸ 2001 Light to medium red-purple; the clean bouquet has a mix of earth, spice and red berry fruit, the light to medium-bodied palate is fresh and direct, but lacks concentration. The jazzy new labels should help the market appeal. **rating:** 84
best drinking Now–2005 **best vintages** '94, '96, '97, '98, '99 **drink with** Rich meat dishes • $18

🌿 wattagan estate winery NR

'Wattagan', Oxley Highway, Coonabarabran, NSW 2357 **region** Western Plains Zone
phone (02) 6842 2456 **fax** (02) 6842 2656 **open** 7 days 10–5
winemaker Contract **production** NFP **est.** 1996
product range ($10.50–18 CD) Sauvignon Blanc, Chardonnay, Shiraz, Cabernet Merlot.
summary Coonabarabran is known for its sheep grazing, but most emphatically not for viticulture. As far north of Sydney as Port Macquarie, it is 440 kilometres west of that town, with the striking Warrumbungle Range on one side, and the national park on the other. The modest production is sold through three outlets in Coonabarabran, and 'exported' to Gunnedah and Boggabri.

🌿 waugoola wines NR

Cultowa Road, Canowindra, NSW 2804 **region** Cowra
phone (02) 6342 1435 **open** Weekends 10–6, or by appointment
winemaker Rodney Hooper (Contract) **production** 1300 cases **est.** 1996

product range Carro Park Chardonnay, Cuttowa Shiraz, Shiraz.

summary Casey and Laura Proctor have established two vineyards, Cultowa Road of 4 hectares, and Carro Park of 2.5 hectares. Part of the production is sold, and part contract-made by the talented Rodney Hooper.

waybourne   NR

60 Lemins Road, Waurn Ponds, Vic 3221 **region** Geelong
phone (03) 5241 8477 **fax** (03) 5241 8477 **open** By appointment
winemaker David Cowburn (Contract) **production** 730 cases **est.** 1980
product range ($12–16 ML) Riesling, Trebbiano, Pinot Gris, Cabernet Sauvignon.
summary Owned by Tony and Kay Volpato, who have relied upon external consultants to assist with the winemaking. No recent tastings.

wayne thomas wines   ★★★

26 Kangarilla Road, McLaren Vale, SA 5171 **region** McLaren Vale
phone (08) 8323 9737 **fax** (08) 8323 9737 **open** 7 days 12–5
winemaker Wayne Thomas **production** 5000 cases **est.** 1994
product range ($14–25 CD) Dry Riesling, Unwooded Chardonnay, Patricia Methode Champenoise, Shiraz, Cabernet Sauvignon.
summary Wayne Thomas is a McLaren Vale veteran, having commenced his winemaking career in 1961, working for Stonyfell, Ryecroft and Saltram before establishing Fern Hill with his late wife Pat in 1975. When they sold Fern Hill in April 1994 they started again, launching the Wayne Thomas Wines label, using grapes sourced from 10 growers throughout McLaren Vale. The wines are exported to the US, as well as enjoying limited retail distribution through all Australian States except WA.

Wayne Thomas Dry Riesling

▼▼▼▽ **2002** Light straw-green; some bottling SO$_2$ is evident, but the bouquet is otherwise crisp, with faint lime aromas; the wine has been well made, the problem being the uneasy relationship between McLaren Vale and the variety. **rating:** 84
best drinking Now **drink with** Light seafood • $15

Wayne Thomas McLaren Vale Shiraz

▼▼▼▼ **2001** Medium red-purple; the moderately intense, clean bouquet offers spiced plum, blackberry and chocolate aromas interwoven with vanillin oak; the palate has soft, gently ripe berry, chocolate and mocha flavours; pleasing, easy drinking style. **rating:** 87
best drinking 2004–2009 **best vintages** '99 **drink with** Wagu beef • $25

Wayne Thomas McLaren Vale Cabernet Sauvignon

▼▼▼▽ **2001** Medium red-purple; the ripe berry/blackcurrant bouquet sits uneasily with the American oak; the palate is slightly more cohesive, but the oak sweetness clashes with the varietal fruit characters. **rating:** 84
best drinking 2004–2008 **best vintages** '99 **drink with** Kangaroo fillet • $25

wedgetail estate   ★★★★☆

40 Hildebrand Road, Cottles Bridge, Vic 3099 **region** Yarra Valley
phone (03) 9714 8661 **fax** (03) 9714 8676 **open** Weekends and public holidays 11–5, or by appointment, closed 25 Dec–24 Jan
winemaker Guy Lamothe **production** 1500 cases **est.** 1994
product range ($17–65 CD) Semillon Sauvignon Blanc, Old Barrique Chardonnay, Chardonnay, Par 3 Pinot, Pinot Noir, Reserve Pinot Noir, Merlot, Cabernet.
summary Canadian-born photographer Guy Lamothe and partner Dena Ashbolt started making wine in the basement of their Carlton home in the 1980s. Insidiously, the idea of their own vineyard started to take hold, and the search for a property began. Then, in their words 'one Sunday, when we were 'just out for a drive', we drove past our current home. The slopes are amazing, true goat terrain, and it is on these steep slopes that in 1994 we planted our first block of pinot noir.' While the vines were growing – they now have 5.5 hectares in total – Lamothe enrolled in the winegrowing course at Charles Sturt University, having already gained practical experience working at Tarrawarra in the Yarra Valley, Mornington Peninsula and Meursault. The net result is truly excellent wine. Distributed in New South Wales and ACT by The Fine Wine Specialist; exports to Belgium, China and the UK.

Wedgetail Estate Chardonnay

▼▼▼▼▽ 2001 Medium yellow-green; the moderately complex palate has a complex blend of tangy grapefruit/stone fruit aromas, the palate fruit-driven with good length and intensity; subtle barrel-ferment/cashew characters add another dimension. **rating:** 92

best drinking Now–2007 **best vintages** '01 **drink with** Sweetbreads • $34

Wedgetail Estate Pinot Noir

▼▼▼▼▼ 2001 Light to medium purple-red; an aromatic and complex array of plum, spice and earth aromas are followed by a palate with silky texture, good length, and a lively finish. There was no Reserve Pinot made this vintage. **rating:** 94

best drinking Now–2007 **best vintages** '98, '99, '00, '01 **drink with** Roast quail • $38

Wedgetail Estate Par 3 Pinot Noir

▼▼▼▼ 2001 Light to medium red-purple; clean, savoury, spicy fruit has zest and lift, with a replay on the lively palate. Lots of varietal character, but clearly to be drunk asap. **rating:** 89

best drinking Now **best vintages** '99 **drink with** Lightly smoked cold meat • $22

Wedgetail Estate Cabernet

▼▼▼▼ 2001 Youthful red-purple; a mix of earth, berry, spice and leaf on the bouquet is repeated on the elegant palate which, however, is a little hard in the mouth, and needing time to settle down. **rating:** 86

best drinking 2004–2008 **best vintages** '99 **drink with** Kangaroo fillet • $32

🐛 wehl's mount benson vineyards   NR

Wrights Bay Road, Mount Benson, SA 5275 **region** Mount Benson
phone (08) 8768 6251 **fax** (08) 8678 6251 **open** 7 days 10–4
winemaker Contract **production** 1000 cases **est.** 1989
product range ($25 R) Shiraz, Cabernet Sauvignon.
summary Peter and Leah Wehl were the first to plant vines in the Mount Benson area, beginning the establishment of their 24-hectare vineyard, two-thirds shiraz and one-third cabernet sauvignon, in 1989. While primarily grape growers, they have moved into winemaking via contract makers, and plan to increase the range of wines available by grafting 1 hectare of merlot and 1.5 hectares of sauvignon blanc onto part of the existing plantings. They also intend to upgrade their cellar door facilities in the future.

wellington   ★★★★☆

Cnr Richmond and Denholms Roads, Cambridge, Tas 7170 **region** Southern Tasmania
phone (03) 6248 5844 **fax** (03) 6248 5855 **open** First Sunday of every month 12–4, or by appointment
winemaker Andrew Hood, Jeremy Dineen **production** 3000 cases **est.** 1990
product range ($19–28 CD) Riesling, Iced Riesling, Sauvignon Blanc, Chardonnay, Pinot Noir, Ruby Port.
summary Consultant-winemaker Andrew Hood (ex-Charles Sturt University) and wife Jenny have constructed a state-of-the-art winery on land leased from the University of Tasmania. The 3000-case production of Wellington is dwarfed by the 4500 cases contract-made for others, but all the wines are flawlessly crafted.

Wellington Sauvignon Blanc

▼▼▼▼▽ 2002 Light straw-green; intense gooseberry and passionfruit aromas announce a wine with real varietal character on the elegant, well-balanced palate. **rating:** 90

best drinking Now **best vintages** '02 **drink with** Steamed mussels • $19

Wellington Chardonnay

▼▼▼▼▽ 2001 Light to medium yellow-green; fine and fragrant nectarine and citrus fruit aromas are subtly complexed by barrel-ferment inputs; the palate is absolutely in the mainstream of the Wellington style, lean and elegant, crisp and tight, finishing with typically high acidity. **rating:** 90

best drinking Now–2011 **best vintages** '92, '95, '96, '97, '98, '99, '00, '01 **drink with** Salmon gravlax • $24

Wellington Iced Riesling 375 ml

▼▼▼▼▽ 2002 Brilliant green-yellow; intense lime juice and lime blossom aromas lead into a very pure palate, with identical varietal fruit characters, and balanced acidity. That sweetness is of spatlese, rather than auslese, level. **rating:** 93

best drinking 2007–2011 **best vintages** '97, '98, '99, '01 **drink with** Sorbet • $22

Wellington Pinot Noir

TTTT 2001 Light to medium red-purple; the bouquet offers an unusual array of rosemary and mint overtones to the primary fruit; the light to medium-bodied palate has more conventional plum and cherry fruit flavours, although the rosemary still makes its mark. **rating:** 88

best drinking Now–2005 **best vintages** '94, '98, '99, '00 **drink with** Venison fillet • $24

wells parish wines ★★★

Benerin Estate, Sydney Road, Kandos, NSW 2848 **region** Mudgee
phone (02) 6379 4168 **fax** (02) 6379 4996 **open** By appointment
winemaker Pieter Van Gent **production** 1000 cases **est.** 1995
product range ($25 CD) Chardonnay, Cabernet Sauvignon, Strayleaves Vintage Port.
summary Richard and Rachel Trounson, with help from father Barry Trounson, have established 17 hectares of vineyards at Benerin Estate since 1995. Most of the grapes are sold to Southcorp, but small quantities of wine are made for sale under the Wells Parish label. The vineyards are situated at the eastern extremity of the Mudgee region, near Rylstone, and both the soils and climate are distinctly different to those of the traditional Mudgee area.

Wells Parish Chardonnay

TTTT 2002 Medium yellow-green; a clean, solid bouquet with some stone fruit and fig flows through into the palate, with similar flavours complexed by the faintest flick of oak. **rating:** 85

best drinking Now–2007 **best vintages** '99 **drink with** Roast chicken • $25

wendouree ★★★★★

Wendouree Road, Clare, SA 5453 **region** Clare Valley
phone (08) 8842 2896 **open** By appointment
winemaker Tony Brady **production** 2500 cases **est.** 1895
product range ($18–40 ML) Shiraz, Shiraz Malbec, Shiraz Mataro, Cabernet Malbec, Cabernet Sauvignon, Muscat of Alexandria.
summary The iron fist in a velvet glove best describes these extraordinary wines. They are fashioned with passion and yet precision from the very old vineyard with its unique terroir by Tony and Lita Brady, who rightly see themselves as custodians of a priceless treasure. The 100-year-old stone winery is virtually unchanged from the day it was built; this is in every sense a treasure beyond price. For two reasons, neither Tony Brady nor I see any point in providing tasting notes for the most recently released vintage. Firstly, the wines will have sold out, and moreover, there is no room for newcomers on the mailing list for the next release. Second, all I will ever be able to say is wait for 20 years before drinking the wine.

🐌 we're wines ★★★★

Cnr Wildberry and Johnson Roads, Wilyabrup, WA 6280 **region** Margaret River
phone (08) 9389 9177 **fax** (08) 9389 9166 **open** Weekends and school holidays 10–5
winemaker Jan Davies (Contract) **production** 3600 cases **est.** 1998
product range ($17.95–27.95 CD) Sauvignon Blanc Semillon, Semillon Sauvignon Blanc, Shiraz, Cabernet Sauvignon.
summary Owners Diane and Gordon Davies say 'We are different. We're original, we're bold, we're innovative and we want to be.' This is all reflected in the bold, graphic design of the front labels; the even more unusual back labels, incorporating pictures of the innumerable pairs of braces which real estate agent Gordon Davies wears on his Perth job; in the early move to screwcaps for both white and red wines; and, for that matter, to the underground trickle irrigation system installed in their Margaret River vineyard which can be controlled from Perth. The wines, made by Jan Davies, are excellent.

We're Wines Sauvignon Blanc Semillon

TTTTY 2002 Light, bright straw-green; a fruit-driven, clean and fragrant bouquet of citrus and lemon is followed by a tangy, lemony palate, with plenty of concentration and length; well made. **rating:** 90

best drinking Now–2005 **drink with** Calamari • $17.95

We're Wines Shiraz

TTTT 2001 Bright purple-red; the moderately intense bouquet has well-integrated blackberry/plum fruit and savoury French oak; the light to medium-bodied palate is fruit-driven, clean and fresh, with well-balanced tannins. Still fairly callow, and needs a few years in bottle to settle down. Part of the freshness is undoubtedly due to the Stelvin screwcap, which will guarantee rewards to those who are patient. **rating:** 87

best drinking 2005–2010 **drink with** Beef spare ribs • $23.95

We're Wines Cabernet Sauvignon

TTTT 2001 Medium purple-red; the complex bouquet has some leather and game overtones to the ripe blackcurrant fruit; the palate has great depth to the blackcurrant and dark chocolate flavours, no doubt stemming from the 14.7° alcohol; the oak evident, but not over the top, the tannins fine. **rating:** 89

best drinking 2006–2011 **drink with** Braised lamb • $27.95

west cape howe wines ★★★★☆

Lot 42 South Coast Highway, Denmark, WA 6333 **region** Great Southern
phone (08) 9848 2959 **fax** (08) 9848 2903 **open** 7 days 10–5
winemaker Brenden Smith, Dave Cleary **production** 20 000 cases **est.** 1997
product range ($11.75–22 CD) Riesling, Semillon Sauvignon Blanc, Unwooded Chardonnay, Chardonnay, Late Picked Riesling, Shiraz, Cabernet Merlot, Cabernet Sauvignon, Muscat.
summary Brenden Smith was senior winemaker at Goundrey Wines for many years and has branched into business on his own with a contract-winemaking facility for growers throughout the Great Southern region. The overall quality and consistency of the wines is wholly admirable. West Cape Howe wines are exported to Hong Kong, Singapore, Japan and The Netherlands.

West Cape Howe Riesling

TTTTT 2002 Light to medium yellow-green; a powerful and potent bouquet with a mix of citrus, pineapple and tropical aromas, then a palate which tightens up nicely, with good length and excellent lemony acidity on the finish. **rating:** 90

best drinking 2005–2012 **best vintages** '02 **drink with** Shellfish • $18

West Cape Howe Semillon Sauvignon Blanc

TTTT 2002 Light straw-green; a lively bouquet with crushed herbs, spices and smoke, with a repeat of the same on the generously flavoured palate. A slightly congested finish takes the edge off an otherwise very good wine. **rating:** 86

best drinking Now **best vintages** '01 **drink with** Seafood risotto • $16.99

West Cape Howe Chardonnay

TTTT 2002 Medium green-yellow; the complex bouquet has an attractive mix of melon and smoky barrel-ferment characters, the palate focusing on the smooth, peach and melon fruit, the oak in relative restraint. **rating:** 89

best drinking Now–2007 **best vintages** '99 **drink with** Roast pork • $22

West Cape Howe Shiraz

TTTTT 2001 Medium to full red-purple; complex dark fruits with overtones of spice and licorice on the bouquet, then a palate with good texture and depth; attractive red berry fruits are rounded off by fine, sweet tannins. **rating:** 92

best drinking 2004–2014 **best vintages** '01 **drink with** Lamb fillets • $16.99

West Cape Howe Cabernet Merlot

TTTTT 2002 Medium purple-red; ripe, juicy blackcurrant fruit aromas are supported by a touch of oak; attractive, sweet blackcurrant, redcurrant and cassis fruit drives the palate, which finishes with ripe, fine tannins. Excellent value. **rating:** 90

best drinking 2006–2011 **best vintages** '02 **drink with** Venison with blackcurrant jus • $17

West Cape Howe Cabernet Sauvignon

TTTTT 2001 Medium purple-red; firm blackberry fruit drives the bouquet, the oak very much in the background; a clear, clean and focused palate, blackberry fruit again to the fore, then finishing with fine, gently savoury tannins. **rating:** 92

best drinking 2005–2010 **best vintages** '00, '01 **drink with** Game pie • $21

westend estate wines ★★★☆

1283 Brayne Road, Griffith, NSW 2680 **region** Riverina
phone (02) 6964 1506 **fax** (02) 6962 1673 **open** Mon–Fri 8.30–5, weekends 9.30–4
winemaker William Calabria, Bryan Currie **production** 80 000 cases **est.** 1945
product range ($5.95–19.95 CD) Sauvignon Blanc, Chardonnay, Shiraz, Cabernet Sauvignon; Outback Traminer Riesling, Semillon Sauvignon Blanc, Unwooded Chardonnay, Shiraz; Richland Sauvignon Blanc,

Chardonnay, Shiraz, Merlot, Cabernet Merlot, Cabernet Sauvignon; Port and Liqueur Muscat; are followed by 3 Bridges range of Chardonnay, Shiraz, Durif, Cabernet Sauvignon and Golden Mist Botrytis Semillon.

summary Along with a number of Riverina producers, West End is making a concerted move to lift both the quality and the packaging of its wines, spearheaded by the 3 Bridges range, which has an impressive array of gold medals to its credit since being first released in April 1997, anchored in part on 20 hectares of estate vineyards. It has also ventured into the export market, with distribution in the UK, Canada, New Zealand, Hong Kong, Malaysia, Fiji, Singapore and Switzerland.

Westend Richland Chardonnay

▼▼▼▼ **2002** Medium to full yellow-green, developed for its age; the bouquet has rich peachy fruit, with more of the same on the palate; seems to show prolonged skin contact characters; honest and full flavoured, but drink asap. **rating:** 85

best drinking Now **drink with** KFC • $10.95

Westend 3 Bridges Golden Mist Botrytis Semillon

▼▼▼▼▽ **2002** Full yellow-gold; a complex and rich bouquet showing obvious barrel-ferment oak inputs, then a palate ranging through tangy lime, lemon and honey flavours; good acidity, but is nonetheless at its best now. Two gold medals. **rating:** 90

best drinking Now–2005 **best vintages** '96, '99, '02 **drink with** Fruit tart • $19.95

Westend Estate Richland Shiraz

▼▼▼▼ **2002** Medium to full red-purple; generous fruit with quite complex berry aromas and flavours. The palate has good fruit weight, showing the marvellous 2002 vintage, although there is not much structure or tannin. **rating:** 85

best drinking Now–2005 **drink with** Steak and kidney pie • $10.95

Westend Estate 3 Bridges Durif

▼▼▼▼▽ **2001** Deep, intense red-purple; rich, ripe dark berry/plum fruit, the oak in restraint; a very rich, concentrated and ripe palate with a mix of chocolate and blackberry, the extract held under control (just). Four gold and four silver medals. **rating:** 92

best drinking Now–2008 **best vintages** '01 **drink with** Shepherd's pie • $19.95

western range wines ★★★★

Lot 88 Chittering Road, Lower Chittering, WA 6084 **region** Perth Hills
phone (08) 9571 8800 **fax** (08) 9571 8844 **open** Weekends 10–4
winemaker Steve Hagan (previous Mark Nairn) **production** 45 000 cases **est.** 2001
product range ($13–20 CD) The wines come in three ranges: the entry point is 8 Vineyard White, Red, Chenin Blanc, Chenin Blanc Verdelho, Shiraz Grenache, Cabernet Shiraz; the mid-range with Verdelho, Chardonnay, Viognier, Shiraz, Grenache, Cabernet Malbec; then the premium range consisting of Viognier, Accord Shiraz, Carnelian Shiraz, Organic Shiraz.
summary Between the mid-1990s and 2001 several prominent Western Australians, including Marilyn Corderory, Malcolm McCusker, Terry and Kevin Prindiville and Tony Rechner have established approximately 125 hectares of vines (under separate ownerships) in the Perth Hills, with a kaleidoscopic range of varietals. The next step was to join forces to build a substantial winery which is a separate venture to the growers individual vineyards, but which takes the grapes and then markets the wine under the Western Range brand. All in all, an impressive combination. Distribution through all mainland states, primarily by Australian Liquor Merchants.

Western Range Viognier

▼▼▼▼▽ **2002** Medium to full yellow, with a faint haze; the pastille richness of the bouquet gives the wine distinctive varietal character right from the outset; the generous palate fulfills the promise, with buttery/nutty peach and apricot flavours. **rating:** 90

best drinking Now **best vintages** '02 **drink with** Grilled eggplant and zucchini • $20

Western Range 8 Vineyard Chenin Blanc

▼▼▼▼ **2002** Light straw-green; clean, quite firm tropical fruit salad aromas do not deceive; the lively palate has remarkable intensity and length, with more of the same bright fruit salad flavours. Shows that Australian Chenin Blanc does not have to be boring. **rating:** 87

best drinking Now–2005 **drink with** Avocado and prawn salad • $13

Western Range Verdelho

▼▼▼▼ 2002 Light straw-green; a spotlessly clean bouquet has a mix of fruit salad and honeysuckle aromas which drive the well-made palate, closing with nice acidity. **rating:** 87

best drinking Now–2005 **drink with** Deep-fried calamari • $15

Western Range Chardonnay

▼▼▼▼ 2002 Light straw-green; the bouquet is clean, although the fruit aromatics are slightly subdued; the wine comes alive on the palate, with fresh, citrus and melon fruit supported by subtle oak. **rating:** 87

best drinking Now **drink with** Lemon chicken • $15

Western Range Shiraz

▼▼▼▼♀ 2002 Youthful purple-red; the clean, fresh and ripe raspberry and blackberry fruit of the bouquet spills over into the mouthfilling, smooth palate; the gently ripe fruit again shows excellent control of extract and tannin, the wine with years to go. **rating:** 90

▼▼▼▼▼ 2001 Medium to full red-purple; clean, solid and ripe dark berry, plum, chocolate and mint aromas flow into a sweet and ripe palate with a similar array of dark berry mint and plum fruit supported by nicely balanced tannins. Good oak, and considerable depth. Gold medal winner 2002 Great Australian Shiraz Challenge. **rating:** 94

best drinking 2004–2014 **best vintages** '02 **drink with** Braised rabbit • $15

Western Range Accord Shiraz

▼▼▼▼ 2001 Medium red-purple; a complex, scented Côte Rôtie-like bouquet is followed by a very youthful palate, still to fully settle down. There is a question whether the Rôtie characters come from fruit (97 per cent Shiraz, 3 per cent Viognier) or from some other source, but the wine recently won a gold medal at the Perth Hills Wine Show. **rating:** 87

best drinking Now–2007 **drink with** Stir-fried Asian beef • $20

Western Range Organic Shiraz

▼▼▼▼♀ 2002 Medium purple-red; ripe, dark plum and blackberry fruit has attractive spicy oak on the bouquet; the full, long, sustained palate has slightly more savoury characters overall than the varietal Shiraz; finishes with fine tannins. **rating:** 91

best drinking 2004–2014 **best vintages** '02 **drink with** Smoked beef • $20

Western Range 8 Vineyard Shiraz Grenache

▼▼▼▼ 2002 Medium purple-red; smooth, ripe plum, raspberry and blackberry aromas are followed by a palate with much more structure, the fruit less jammy than most South Australian Grenache; supple and seductive; exceptional value. **rating:** 87

best drinking 2005–2010 **drink with** Beef casserole • $13

Western Range 8 Vineyard Red

▼▼▼▼ 2001 Medium red-purple; solid, ripe black fruits with some chocolate tinges on the bouquet, then a palate with plentiful ripe and sweet fruit, the grenache component subtle. Particularly well-priced. **rating:** 86

best drinking Now–2006 **drink with** Wood-fired pizza • $13

Western Range Grenache

▼▼▼▼ 2002 Light to medium purple-red; as with all of the Western Range wines, spotlessly clean; spicy red berry fruit aromas are followed by a nicely balanced, fruit-driven palate; does not have a lot of weight or structure, but it is neither jammy nor forced. **rating:** 87

best drinking Now–2006 **drink with** Shepherd's pie • $15

Western Range Cabernet Malbec

▼▼▼▼ 2002 Bright purple-red; clean blackcurrant and raspberry aromas lead into a smooth, light to medium-bodied palate, with clean, juicy fruit flavours, but not a lot of structure. A blend of 65 per cent Cabernet Sauvignon and 35 per cent Malbec. **rating:** 87

best drinking Now–2008 **drink with** Beef spare ribs • $15

Western Range 8 Vineyard Cabernet Shiraz

▼▼▼▼ 2002 Medium to full red-purple; complex, ripe blackberry and blackcurrant fruit drives the bouquet, subtle oak in the back seat; the palate has rich, ripe and generous plushy fruit; yet another bargain. **rating:** 89

best drinking 2004–2008 **drink with** Spaghetti bolognese • $13

westfield ★★★☆

Cnr Memorial Ave and Great Northern Highway, Baskerville, WA 6056 **region** Swan Valley
phone (08) 9296 4356 **fax** (08) 9296 4356 **open** 7 days 10–5.30
winemaker John Kosovich **production** 11 000 cases **est.** 1922
product range ($14–75 CD) Chenin Blanc, Verdelho, Unwooded Chardonnay, Chardonnay, Bronze Wing Chardonnay, Sparkling Burgundy, Late Pick Verdelho, Autumn Harvest, Shiraz, Bronze Wing Shiraz, Bronze Wing Merlot, Cabernet Sauvignon, Liqueur Muscat, Liqueur Verdelho, Liqueur Shiraz, Vintage Port.
summary Consistent producer of a surprisingly elegant and complex Chardonnay; the other wines are more variable, but from time to time has made attractive Verdelho and excellent Cabernet Sauvignon. 1998 saw the first release of wines partly or wholly coming from the family's new planting at Pemberton, those being Swan/Pemberton blends released under the Bronze Wing label. Limited retail distribution in Perth, Melbourne and Brisbane, exports to Singapore.

Westfield Liqueur Muscat
▼▼▼▼▼ NV Dark tawny-brown; an intense raisiny bouquet with pronounced rancio is followed by an unctuously rich and sweet raisins-in-brandy palate, quite remarkable for its depth and intensity, and which in no way cloys. **rating:** 95
best drinking Now **drink with** Coffee and walnuts • $48

westgate vineyard NR

'Westgate', RMB 1124, Ararat, Vic 3377 **region** Grampians
phone (03) 5356 2394 **fax** (03) 5356 2594 **open** By appointment
winemaker Bruce Dalkin **production** 200 cases **est.** 1999
product range ($17–19 CD) Riesling, Cabernet Shiraz.
summary Westgate has been in the Dalkin family ownership since the 1860s, the present owners Bruce and Robyn Dalkin being the sixth generation owners of the property, which today focuses on grape production, a small winery, four and a half star accommodation, and wool production. Over 12 hectares of vineyards have been progressively established since 1969, including a key holding of 10 hectares of shiraz; most of the grapes are sold to Mount Langi Ghiran and Seppelt Great Western, but a vigneron's licence was obtained in 1999 and a small amount of wine is made under the Westgate Vineyard label.

wetherall NR

Naracoorte Road, Coonawarra, SA 5263 **region** Coonawarra
phone (08) 8737 2104 **fax** (08) 8737 2105 **open** 7 days 10–4
winemaker Michael Wetherall **production** 1500 cases **est.** 1991
product range ($20–22 CD) Shiraz, Cabernet Sauvignon.
summary The Wetherall family has been growing grapes in Coonawarra for more than 30 years with 115 hectares of mature vines, and Michael Wetherall (a Roseworthy graduate) has been responsible for overseeing wine production since Wetherall extended its operations into winemaking (in a small way) in 1991. Exports to Canada. No recent tastings.

wharncliffe NR

Summerleas Road, Kingston, Tas 7050 **region** Southern Tasmania
phone (03) 6229 7147 **fax** (03) 6229 2298 **open** Not
winemaker Andrew Hood (Contract) **production** 115 cases **est.** 1990
product range ($20 ML) Chardonnay.
summary With total plantings of 0.75 hectare, Wharncliffe could not exist without the type of contract-winemaking service offered by Andrew Hood, which would be a pity, because the vineyard is beautifully situated on the doorstep of Mount Wellington, the Huon Valley and the Channel regions of southern Tasmania.

whiskey gully wines NR

Beverley Road, Severnlea, Qld 4352 **region** Granite Belt
phone (07) 4683 5100 **fax** (07) 4683 5155 **open** 7 days 9–5
winemaker Philippa Hambleton, Rod MacPherson **production** 500 cases **est.** 1997
product range ($12–30 CD) Leaping Lizard Colombard, Hitching Rail Colombard Chardonnay, Opera House Unwooded Chardonnay, Beverley Chardonnay, Republic Red, Shiraz, Upper House Cabernet Sauvignon.

summary Close inspection of the winery letterhead discloses that The Media Mill Pty Ltd trades as Whiskey Gully Wines. It is no surprise, then, to find proprietor John Arlidge saying 'Wine and politics are a heady mix; I have already registered the 2000 Republic Red as a voter in 26 marginal electorates and we are considering nominating it for Liberal Party pre-selection in Bennelong'. Wit to one side, John Arlidge has big plans for Whiskey Gully Wines, with long-range plans to establish 40 hectares of vineyards, extending the varietal range with petit verdot, malbec, merlot, semillon and sauvignon blanc. At present the wines are made off-site, but if production and sales increase significantly, on-site winemaking will be progressively introduced.

Whiskey Gully Upper House Cabernet Sauvignon

▼▼▼▼ **2000** Medium red-purple; the moderately intense, clean bouquet has red and blackcurrant fruit to the fore; the light to medium-bodied palate follows on in the same fashion, with sweet cassis berry flavours and just a hint of oak; well balanced. From Granite Belt grapes, and has won a trophy at the Boutique Winemakers Show and various silver medals.   **rating:** 87

best drinking 2004–2009 **drink with** Lamb fillets • $22

whispering hills   NR

580 Warburton Highway, Seville, Vic 3139 **region** Yarra Valley
phone 0418 303 205 **open** By appointment, cellar door opening mid-2003
winemaker Murray Lyons, Martin Williams MW **production** 850 cases **est.** 1985
product range ($22.50 ML) Chardonnay, Pinot Noir, Shiraz, Cabernet Sauvignon.
summary The minuscule production of Whispering Hills from its 3.5-hectare vineyard is limited to four wines which are sold by mail order and word of mouth., as well as at 20 or so local restaurants. While no tastings, Whispering Hills starred at the 2002 Concours des Vins du Victoria.

whisson lake   NR

Lot 2, Gully Road, Carey Gully, SA 5144 **region** Adelaide Hills
phone (08) 8390 1303 **fax** (08) 8390 3822 **open** By appointment
winemaker Roman Bratasiuk (Contract) **production** 300 cases **est.** 1985
product range ($27.50–31.50 CD) Pinot Noir.
summary Mark Whisson is primarily a grape grower, with 4.5 hectares of close-planted, steep-sloped north-facing vineyard. A small quantity of the production is made for the Whisson Lake label by Roman Bratasiuk, best known as the owner/winemaker of Clarendon Hills. Tiny quantities are exported to the US and the UK.

whistler wines   ★★★☆

Seppeltsfield Road, Marananga, SA 5355 **region** Barossa Valley
phone (08) 8562 4942 **fax** (08) 8562 4943 **open** Weekends and public holidays 10.30–5, or by appointment
winemaker Rolf Binder, Christa Deans (Contract) **production** 3000 cases **est.** 1999
product range ($12–35 CD) Unwooded Semillon, Late Harvest Golden Semillon, Black Piper Sparkling Shiraz, Black Piper Sparkling Merlot, Shiraz, Merlot, Cabernet Merlot, Cabernet Sauvignon.
summary Whistler Wines had a dream start to its life at the 2000 Barossa Valley Wine Show when its 2000 Semillon won trophies for the Best Dry White Semillon and for the Most Outstanding Barossa White Table Wine. Add to that the distinguished US importer Weygandt-Metzler, and it is no surprise to find the sold out sign going up on the extremely attractive (modern) galvanised iron cellar door building. The operation is presently based on 5 hectares of shiraz and 2 hectares each of semillon, merlot and 1 hectare of cabernet sauvignon, with an additional 4 hectares of grenache, mourvedre and riesling planted in 2001. The hope is to have a restaurant on-site by 2004, and to gradually increase production to match already existing market demands.

whitehorse wines   NR

4 Reid Park Road, Mount Clear, Vic 3350 **region** Ballarat
phone (03) 5330 1719 **fax** (03) 5330 1288 **open** Weekends 11–5
winemaker Noel Myers **production** 900 cases **est.** 1981
product range ($10–18 CD) Riesling, Riesling Muller Thurgau, Chardonnay, Pinot Noir, Cabernet Shiraz.
summary The Myers family has moved from grape growing to winemaking, utilising the attractive site on its sloping hillside south of Ballarat. Four hectares of vines are in production, with pinot noir and chardonnay the principal varieties.

🐦 whitsend estate   ★★★

52 Boundary Road, Coldstream, Vic 3770   **region** Yarra Valley
phone (03) 9739 1917   **fax** (03) 9739 0217   **open** By appointment
winemaker Paul Evans   **production** 500 cases   **est.** 1998
product range ($19.20–20 CD) Chardonnay, Merlot, Cabernet Sauvignon.
summary The Baldwin family, headed by Ross and Simone, but with Trish, Tim and Jenny Baldwin all involved in one way or another, have established a 13-hectare vineyard planted to pinot noir, shiraz, merlot and cabernet sauvignon. The lion's share of the production is sold to local wineries, but a small amount is retained and made for the Baldwins by Paul Evans.

Whitsend Estate Merlot

▼▼▼▼ **2001** Medium red-purple; the ripe bouquet has sweet blackcurrant and blackberry aromas; on the palate, the fruit and oak stand apart, and need time to knit, but the wine has stacks of flavour.   **rating:** 87
best drinking 2006–2011   **drink with** Barbecued lamb • $20

Whitsend Estate Cabernet Sauvignon

▼▼▼▽ **2001** Medium red-purple; the moderately intense bouquet has a range of mint, leaf and berry aromas, while minty, leafy flavours come through strongly on the palate, which seemingly struggled to ripen; well-handled in the winery.   **rating:** 83
best drinking 2004–2008   **drink with** Veal casserole • $20

wignalls wines   ★★★★

Chester Pass Road (Highway 1), Albany, WA 6330   **region** Great Southern
phone (08) 9841 2848   **fax** (08) 9842 9003   **open** 7 days 12–4
winemaker Bill Wignall   **production** 6000 cases   **est.** 1982
product range ($10.80–30 CD) Sauvignon Blanc, Chardonnay, Late Harvest Frontignac, Pinot Noir, Shiraz, Cabernet Sauvignon, Tawny Port.
summary A noted producer of Pinot Noir which has extended the map for the variety in Australia. The Pinots have shown style and flair, but do age fairly quickly. The white wines are elegant, and show the cool climate to good advantage. A new winery was constructed and opened for the 1998 vintage, utilising the production from the 16 hectares of estate plantings. Exports to Japan, Malaysia, Indonesia, Singapore and the US.

Wignalls Chardonnay

▼▼▼▼ **2001** Light to medium yellow-green; in a typical Wignall style, the bouquet is light, clean and fresh, with appropriately subtle oak. The palate veers towards the nutty, minerally spectrum, the fruit somewhat subdued. Works well enough in a quasi-European mode.   **rating:** 86
best drinking Now   **best vintages** '85, '88, '91, '92, '96   **drink with** Milk-fed veal • $21

Wignalls Pinot Noir

▼▼▼▼▽ **2001** Medium red-purple, with more depth than recent vintages; the bouquet is clean, with some plum and hints of forest; the palate has much more substance and ripeness; the dark plum fruit is supported by evident tannins, and the wine has continued to develop well in bottle, with more in the tank.   **rating:** 90
best drinking Now–2005   **best vintages** '85, '86, '88, '91, '93, '95, '97, '00, '01   **drink with** Seared Tasmanian salmon • $21

wild broke wines   NR

Milbrodale Road, Broke, NSW 2330   **region** Lower Hunter Valley
phone (02) 6579 1065   **open** Not
winemaker Monarch Winemaking Services   **production** 400 cases   **est.** 1999
product range ($40 R) The Idlewild range of Wild Yeast Chardonnay, Succo Del Sol (dessert wine), Cabernet Shiraz, Barbera and Cabernet Franc.
summary Wild Broke Wines is a spin-off from Ryan Family Wines; it is a partnership between Matthew Ryan (who continues as viticulturist for Ryan Family Wines on Broke Estate and Minimbah Vineyards) and wife Tina Ryan who continues to run Wild Rhino PR Marketing and Events in Sydney. At the present time it draws on 2 hectares of shiraz and cabernet sauvignon, and 1 hectare each of merlot, barbera, chardonnay and tempranillo. A cellar door is due to open late in 2003.

Wild Broke Ildewild Wild Yeast Chardonnay

TTTTY 2002 Light to medium yellow-green; a subtle but complex bouquet with a mix of nutty cashew, melon and fig aromas is followed by a complex yet subtle palate; the numerous winemaking inputs (whole bunch pressing, wild yeast ferment, new French oak and 10 months maturation) have worked particularly well; good length and mouthfeel. **rating:** 93

best drinking Now–2006 **best vintages** '01, '02 **drink with** Fresh Tasmanian salmon • $40

Wild Broke Cabernet Franc

TTTT 2002 Light to medium purple-red; fresh, red berry aromas and subtle oak are a quiet opening, the wine picking up the pace significantly on the palate with a mix of sweet fruit, cedar and cigar box, the fine tannins providing grip and texture. Seldom a particularly rewarding variety on its own, but has been well made in this instance, with a 12-day fermentation in open fermenters and then matured in a mix of 50 per cent new French and 50 per cent used American barrels. **rating:** 87

best drinking 2004–2007 **drink with** Osso buco • $40

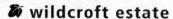 **wildcroft estate** ★★★☆

98 Stanleys Road, Red Hill South, Vic 3937 **region** Mornington Peninsula
phone (03) 5989 2646 **fax** (03) 9783 9469 **open** 7 days 10–5
winemaker Phillip Jones (Contract) **production** 650 cases **est.** 1988
product range ($26–59 CD) Black Sheep is the premium range of Shiraz and Cabernet Sauvignon; the second range is Wildcroft Chardonnay, Pinot Noir and Cabernet Sauvignon.
summary Wildcroft Estate is the brainchild of Devendra Singh, best known as the owner of Siddhartha, established in 1984 and one of Victoria's oldest Indian restaurants. In 1988 he purchased the land upon which 4 hectares of pinot noir, chardonnay, shiraz and cabernet sauvignon have been established, with the management and much of the physical work carried out by Devendra's wife Shashi Singh, who is currently undertaking a viticulture course. The vineyard is one of the few unirrigated vineyards on the Peninsula, and the wines are made by the renowned Phillip Jones (of Bass Phillip). The mud brick cellar door also has a restaurant – Cafe 98 – allowing Devendra Singh to explore the novel matching of Indian food with wine. Chef Lindsey Perry serves modern cuisine with Indian and middle eastern influences, using local produce wherever possible.

Wildcroft Estate Black Sheep Shiraz

TTTTY 2000 Medium red-purple; complex berry, spice and leaf aromas are supported by a nice touch of oak; the palate has good structure and particularly good mouthfeel, offering similar flavours in a medium-bodied frame. Made by Phillip Jones, but the price is challenging. **rating:** 90

best drinking Now–2008 **drink with** Ragout of kidneys • $59

Wildcroft Estate Black Sheep Cabernet Sauvignon

TTTT 2000 Medium to full red-purple; ripe, blackberry and blackcurrant fruit on the bouquet and palate, are joined by touches of leaf and earth; finishes with savoury fine tannins, with controlled, albeit positive, oak use.
rating: 87

best drinking 2004–2009 **drink with** Herbed rack of lamb • $45

wild dog NR

South Road, Warragul, Vic 3820 **region** Gippsland
phone (03) 5623 1117 **fax** (03) 5623 6402 **open** 7 days 10–5
winemaker John Farrington **production** 3300 cases **est.** 1982
product range ($12–22 CD) Riesling, Unwooded Chardonnay, Chardonnay, Wild Dog Sparkling, Rose, Pinot Noir, Shiraz, Cabernet Sauvignon.
summary An aptly named winery which produces somewhat rustic wines from the 12 hectares of estate vineyards; even the Farringtons say that the Shiraz comes 'with a bite', also pointing out that there is minimal handling, fining and filtration.

wild duck creek estate NR

Spring Flat Road, Heathcote, Vic 3523 **region** Heathcote
phone (03) 5433 3133 **fax** (03) 5433 3133 **open** By appointment
winemaker David Anderson **production** 4000 cases **est.** 1980
product range ($25–75 CD) Springflat Shiraz, Alan's Cabernets, Alan's Cabernets Pressings, The Blend, Duck Muck, Cabernet Sauvignon Reserve, Sparkling Duck 2.

summary The first release of Wild Duck Creek Estate from the 1991 vintage marked the end of 12 years of effort by David and Diana Anderson. They commenced planting the 4.5-hectare vineyard in 1980, made their first tiny quantities of wine in 1986, the first commercial quantities of wine in 1991, and built their winery and cellar-door facility in 1993. Exports to the US (where Duck Muck has become a cult wine), Canada, the UK, Singapore, Belgium and New Zealand.

wild soul   NR

Horans Gorge Road, Glen Aplin, Qld 4381 **region** Granite Belt
phone (07) 4683 4201 **fax** (07) 4683 4201 **open** Weekends and public holidays 10–4
winemaker Andy Boullier **production** 400 cases **est.** 1995
product range ($14–16 CD) Shiraz, Cabernet Sauvignon.
summary Andy and Beth Boullier have been on the land throughout their life, working in various capacities, before buying their small property at Glen Aplin. They have established a little over 1 hectare of vines, more or less equally split between cabernet sauvignon and shiraz, with a little merlot. They use organic principles in growing the fruit which provide challenges of themselves, challenges compounded by birds, drought and kangaroos. A small winery enables Andy Boullier to make the wine on-site; the Shiraz the better of the two wines.

wildwood   ★★★★

St John's Lane, Wildwood, Bulla, Vic 3428 **region** Sunbury
phone (03) 9307 1118 **fax** (03) 9331 1590 **open** 7 days 10–6
winemaker Dr Wayne Stott, Ben Sieber **production** 2000 cases **est.** 1983
product range ($20–30 CD) Chardonnay, Pinot Noir, Shiraz, Cabernets.
summary Wildwood is situated just 4 kilometres past Melbourne airport, at an altitude of 130 metres in the Oaklands Valley, which provides unexpected views back to Port Phillip Bay and the Melbourne skyline. Plastic surgeon Wayne Stott has taken what is very much a part-time activity rather more seriously than most by undertaking (and completing) the Wine Science degree at Charles Sturt University. Four years of drought has cut production and forced the early release of the red wines.

Wildwood Pinot Noir

TTTTY **2001** Bright, light red-purple; the stylish bouquet has a mix of savoury, cherry and strawberry fruit supported by subtle oak; while the palate is only light to medium-bodied, it is well balanced and focused, showing positive varietal character in savoury mode.   **rating:** 90
best drinking Now–2006 **best vintages** '98 **drink with** Duck breast • $25

wildwood of yallingup   ★★★★

Caves Road, Yallingup, WA 6282 **region** Margaret River
phone (08) 9755 2066 **fax** (08) 9754 1389 **open** 7 days 10–5
winemaker James Pennington **production** 3000 cases **est.** 1984
product range ($14–28 CD) Hotham Valley Semillon, Semillon Sauvignon Blanc, Sunrise White, Pennington Chardonnay, Sparkling Dawn, Sparkling Dusk, Pinot Noir, Sunset Red, Shiraz Cabernet, Pennington Cabernet Merlot, Tawny Port. The Hotham Valley Semillon will be sold as a six-vintage pack (1992–1997) at $95 for the six.
summary In the wake of the demise of the Hotham Valley wine group, and its subsequent restructuring and renaming, James Pennington acquired the 5.5-hectare Wildwood vineyard, planted in the mid-1980s, having been first cleared in the late 1940s. The vineyard was established without irrigation and remains dry-grown. All of the future releases will be released either under the Wildwood of Yallingup label or Pennington, but small stocks of previously bottled and labelled Hotham Valley Semillon were being sold in 2003.

Hotham Valley Semillon

TTTTY **1993** Strong, glowing yellow-green; a lovely, soft, developed wine at its peak, with honey, cream and nuts offset by typical Semillon acidity. The best of a vintage pack spanning the 1997 to 1990 vintages being sold at the winery in 2003.   **rating:** 90
best drinking Now **best vintages** '93 **drink with** Rich seafood dishes

Wildwood of Yallingup Semillon Sauvignon Blanc

TTTT **2001** Light to medium green-yellow; a potent array of gooseberry, tropical, passionfruit aromas is followed by a palate which softens somewhat, but has the flavour for short-term drinking.   **rating:** 87
best drinking Now **drink with** Sugar-cured tuna • $16

Wildwood of Yallingup Pennington Chardonnay

TTTTY 2001 Medium yellow-green; the complex bouquet has obvious barrel-ferment inputs to the stone fruit and fig at its core; the silky smooth palate has great mouthfeel and length, the flavours tracking those of the bouquet. **rating: 93**

best drinking Now–2006 **drink with** Sweetbreads • $28

willespie ★★★★

Harmans Mill Road, Wilyabrup via Cowaramup, WA 6284 **region** Margaret River
phone (08) 9755 6248 **fax** (08) 9755 6210 **open** 7 days 10.30–5
winemaker Kevin Squance **production** 10 000 cases **est.** 1976
product range ($16–60 R) Riesling, Semillon Sauvignon Blanc, Verdelho, Chardonnay, Shiraz, Cabernets, Cabernet Sauvignon, Cabernet Sauvignon Reserve; Harmans Mill White and Harmans Mill Red are cheaper second-label wines.
summary Willespie has produced many attractive white wines over the years, typically in brisk, herbaceous Margaret River style. All are fruit- rather than oak-driven; the newer Merlot also shows promise. The wines have had such success that the Squance family (which founded and owns Willespie) has substantially increased winery capacity, drawing upon an additional 26 hectares of estate vineyards now in bearing. Exports to Europe, the US, Singapore and Hong Kong.

Willespie Riesling

TTTT 2001 Light straw-green; a clean mix of mineral, herb and spice on the bouquet intensifies on the focused lime and citrus of the long palate. Impressive for a region which struggles with the variety; developing well. **rating: 89**

best drinking Now–2007 **drink with** Gravlax • $19

Willespie Verdelho

TTTY 2000 Light to medium yellow-green; the crisp and clean bouquet is developing slowly, with slightly grassy characters; the palate has similar herb and grass overtones, rather than the usual fruit salad, fleshing out on the finish. **rating: 84**

best drinking Now **drink with** Vegetable terrine • $23

Willespie Lot 9807 Cabernets

TTTTY NV Medium red-purple; the aromatic bouquet has a mix of cassis, cedar and earth, the light to medium-bodied palate a seamless mix of cedar, vanilla, sweet leather and cassis, finishing with fine, supple tannins. This unusual wine is a blend of 60 per cent Cabernet Franc, 40 per cent Cabernet Sauvignon, part of the Cabernet Franc coming from the 1997 vintage which spent 27 months in oak, while the 1998 components spent 18 months in oak. **rating: 90**

best drinking Now–2007 **drink with** Veal casserole • $25

Willespie Cabernet Sauvignon

TTTT 1998 Medium red-purple; bottle-developed secondary aromas provide a savoury mix with the underlying dark berry fruit; attractive blackcurrant fruit on the palate is joined by a nice touch of chocolate and ripe tannins to close. **rating: 88**

best drinking Now–2008 **drink with** Butterfly leg of lamb • $35

🍂 williams springs road NR

76 Dauncey Street, Kingscote, Kangaroo Island, SA 5223 **region** Kangaroo Island
phone (08) 8553 2053 **fax** (08) 8553 3042 **open** By appointment
winemaker Contract **est.** 1995
product range Chardonnay, Shiraz.
summary Roger and Kate Williams have established 11 hectares of chardonnay, cabernet sauvignon, shiraz and petit verdot. Most of the grapes are sold to Kangaroo Island Trading Co, with a small amount of chardonnay and shiraz made under the Williams Springs Road label. Cellar-door sales through the head office at Dauncey Street.

willow bridge estate ★★★★☆

Gardin Court Drive, Dardanup, WA 6236 **region** Geographe
phone (08) 9728 0055 **fax** (08) 9728 0066 **open** 7 days 11–5
winemaker Rob Bowen, David Crawford **production** 35 000 cases **est.** 1997

product range ($13.50–60 CD) Sauvignon Blanc Semillon, Chenin Blanc, Shiraz, Merlot, Cabernet Sauvignon; Winemaker's Reserve range of Sauvignon Blanc, Semillon Sauvignon Blanc, Chardonnay, Cabernet Rose, Black Dog Shiraz, Shiraz, Cabernet Sauvignon Merlot.

summary The Dewar family has followed a fast track in developing Willow Bridge Estate since acquiring their spectacular 180-hectare hillside property in the Ferguson Valley in 1996. Sixty hectares of chardonnay, semillon, sauvignon blanc, shiraz and cabernet sauvignon have already been planted, with tempranillo added in the spring of 2000, and another 10 hectares due to be planted over the next year or two. A state-of-the-art winery has been constructed which will be capable of handling the 1200 to 1500 tonnes expected from the estate plantings by 2004. Winemaker Rob Bowen has had a long and distinguished career, first as winemaker at Plantagenet and thereafter at Capel Vale. Exports to France, Germany, Canada, Singapore and Hong Kong.

Willow Bridge Estate Sauvignon Blanc Semillon

▼▼▼▼ 2002 Light straw-green; the clean, crisp and fresh bouquet has hints of herb and nettle, characters which come through on the lively mineral and herb palate. **rating:** 87

best drinking Now **best vintages** '00 **drink with** Fresh abalone • $14.50

Willow Bridge Estate Winemaker's Reserve Semillon Sauvignon Blanc

▼▼▼▼▼ 2000 Light to medium yellow-green; the single most outstanding feature of a high-quality wine is its great length and freshness, predominantly citrus and mineral, and with perfect balance. Having taken two and a half years to reach this point, there is no reason why the wine should not live for another 10 years, or whether it will ever be better is another issue. **rating:** 94

best drinking Now–2012 **best vintages** '00. '01 **drink with** Sugar-cured tuna • $21

Willow Bridge Estate The Black Dog Shiraz

▼▼▼▼▽ 2001 Medium to full red-purple; the savoury, spicy dark fruits and gentle oak of the bouquet give no hint of what is to come on the palate; here the 16° alcohol provides basic power, yet in a very strange way seems to diminish rather than enhance the array of ripe tannins and dark fruits. The wine got its name from a cellar hand remarking of the wine in barrel that it was 'as black as the inside of a dog'. Whether this all aids the marketability of the wine is another issue, but it does carry the alcohol far better than one might have expected, and does not heat up on the finish. Tamed in part by spending 18 months in oak. **rating:** 90

best drinking 2006–2016 **best vintages** '01 **drink with** Thick T-bone steak • $60

willow creek ★★★★

166 Balnarring Road, Merricks North, Vic 3926 **region** Mornington Peninsula
phone (03) 5989 7448 **fax** (03) 5989 7584 **open** 7 days 10–5
winemaker Phil Kerney **production** 10 000 cases **est.** 1989
product range ($15–35 CD) Sauvignon Blanc, Unoaked Chardonnay, Tulum Chardonnay, Tulum Reserve Chardonnay, Tulum Vintage Brut, Rose, Pinot Noir, Tulum Pinot Noir, Shiraz, Cabernet Sauvignon, Rutherglen Liqueur Muscat.
summary Yet another significant player in the Mornington Peninsula area, with 9 hectares of vines planted to cabernet sauvignon, chardonnay and pinot noir. Expansion of the cellar door was completed by January 1998, with a winery constructed for the 1998 vintage. The restaurant is open for lunch 7 days and Friday and Saturday nights for dinner. The wines are exported to the US and the UK.

Willow Creek Unoaked Chardonnay

▼▼▼▼ 2001 Light to medium yellow-green; stone fruit and faintly smoky aromas precede a light to medium-bodied palate offering fresh citrus and melon fruit; nice balance, no frills. **rating:** 85

best drinking Now **drink with** Vegetable terrine • $16

Willow Creek Tulum Chardonnay

▼▼▼▼▽ 2001 Light to medium yellow-green; very attractive melon and stone fruit aromas are complexed by good oak integration on the bouquet; a finely crafted and balanced palate, elegant and essentially fruit-driven, although the barrel-ferment French oak and lees contact have certainly helped shape the wine. Follows closely on the style and quality of the very good 2000 Tulum Chardonnay. **rating:** 91

best drinking Now–2007 **best vintages** '98, '01 **drink with** Fresh Tasmanian salmon • $25

Willow Creek Pinot Noir

▼▼▼▼ 2001 Light to medium purple-red; clean and fresh plum and spice aromas flow into a light to medium-bodied palate, with lively, zesty plum and cherry fruit; has length. **rating:** 87

best drinking Now–2005 **best vintages** '91, '94, '95, '97, '98 **drink with** Gently spiced Asian food • $25

Willow Creek Tulum Pinot Noir

ΥΥΥΥϘ 2001 Clear and lively red-purple; the bouquet has excellent fusion of dark plum, spice and oak, the powerful, tightly knit palate with good length and focus, albeit fractionally hard on the finish. The 2000 was superb. **rating: 90**

best drinking Now–2007 **best vintages** '00, '01 **drink with** Jugged hare • $35

Willow Creek Cabernet Sauvignon

ΥΥΥΥ 2001 Medium purple-red; clean, blackcurrant fruit is the driver of the bouquet, the oak influence minimal. The medium-bodied, supple palate offers smoothly textured blackcurrant fruit with earthy/savoury edges befitting the variety. Follows on the 2000 in different style, but similar quality. **rating: 87**

best drinking 2004–2009 **drink with** Braised veal • $25

willowvale wines   NR

Black Swamp Road, Tenterfield, NSW 2372 **region** Northern Slopes Zone
phone (02) 6736 3589 **fax** (02) 6736 3753 **open** 7 days 9–5
winemaker John Morley **production** 1200 cases **est.** 1994
product range ($14–25 CD) Federation Classic White, Ambrosia, London Bridge Chardonnay, Late Harvest Riesling, London Bridge Dry Red, London Bridge Soft Red, London Bridge Merlot, Bushranger Musket, Centenary of Federation Port.
summary John and Lyn Morley commenced establishing 1.8 hectares of vineyard of equal portions of chardonnay, merlot and cabernet sauvignon in 1994, with further planting in 1999 and 2000. The vineyard is at an altitude of 940 metres and was the first in the growing Tenterfield region. Advanced vineyard climatic monitoring systems have been installed, and a new winery building was constructed and equipped in time for the 2000 vintage.

will taylor wines   ★★★★

1B Victoria Avenue, Unley Park, SA 5061 **region** Warehouse
phone (08) 8271 6122 **fax** (08) 8271 6122 **open** By appointment
winemaker Various contract **production** 1400 cases **est.** 1997
product range ($20–40 R) Clare Valley Riesling, Hunter Valley Semillon, Adelaide Hills Sauvignon Blanc, Yarra Valley/Geelong Pinot Noir.
summary Will Taylor is a partner in the leading Adelaide law firm Finlaysons and specialises in wine law. Together with Suzanne Taylor, he has established a classic negociant wine business, having wines contract-made to his specification. Moreover, he chooses what he considers to be the best regions for each variety and added a Geelong/Yarra Valley Pinot Noir in 2000. Most of the wine is sold to restaurants, with small volumes sold to a select group of fine wine stores and mail order. Exports to the US.

Will Taylor Clare Valley Riesling

ΥΥΥΥΥ 2002 Light green-yellow; spotless, pure lime juice and apple aromas flow into a palate with great length and line; lovely acidity; bred to stay. **rating: 94**

best drinking 2005–2012 **best vintages** '00, '02 **drink with** Char-grilled octopus salad • $20.45

Will Taylor Hunter Valley Semillon

ΥΥΥΥ 2002 Light straw-green; a fresh, crisp, faintly grassy/herbal bouquet is followed by a palate which is painfully shy, needing a minimum of 5 years before it will even look like opening up. **rating: 87**

best drinking 2007–2012 **best vintages** '01 **drink with** Light pasta • $20.45

Will Taylor Yarra Valley/Geelong Pinot Noir

ΥΥΥΥ 2001 Medium red-purple; a complex bouquet with some faintly jammy fruit and a faint horsehair edge; the palate is much better, with cherry and plum fruit, subtle oak and brisk acidity. **rating: 87**

best drinking Now–2007 **best vintages** '00 **drink with** Jugged hare • $39.85

wilmot hills vineyard   NR

407 Back Road, Wilmot, Tas 7310 **region** Northern Tasmania
phone (03) 6492 1193 **fax** (03) 6492 1193 **open** 7 days 9–7
winemaker John Cole, Ruth Cole **est.** 1991
product range ($15–18 CD) Muller Thurgau, Pinot Noir, El Nino Pinot Noir, fruit wines and ciders.

summary The beautiful Wilmot Hills Vineyard is situated on the western side of Lake Barrington, not far from the Cradle Mountain road, with marvellous views to Mount Roland and the adjacent peaks. It is very much a family affair, established by John and Ruth Cole, and produces both wine and cider. John Cole spent 18 years in Melbourne participating in engineering design and some graphic art, Ruth working in the hospitality industry for 10 years and making fruit wines for 20 years. The neat on-site winery was both designed and built by the Coles, as was much of the wine and cider-making equipment.

wilson vineyard ★★★★

Polish Hill River, Sevenhill via Clare, SA 5453 **region** Clare Valley
phone (08) 8843 4310 **open** Weekends 10–4
winemaker John Wilson, Daniel Wilson **production** 4000 cases **est.** 1974
product range ($16–26.50 CD) Gallery Series Riesling, DJW Riesling, Chardonnay, Leucothea (sweet), Shiraz, Hippocrene Sparkling Burgundy, Zinfandel, Cabernet Sauvignon.
summary Dr John Wilson is a tireless ambassador for the Clare Valley and for wine (and its beneficial effect on health) in general. His wines were made using techniques and philosophies garnered early in his wine career and can occasionally be idiosyncratic but in recent years have been most impressive. The wines are sold through cellar door and retail in Sydney, Melbourne, Brisbane and Adelaide; no mailing list. Exports to the US and the UK.

Wilson Vineyard DJW Riesling

♥♥♥♥♥ **2002** Light straw-green; a spotlessly clean bouquet with lime and citrus, then a palate with excellent mouthfeel and balance of citrussy fruit. Already delicious, and headed upward. **rating:** 94
best drinking 2004–2014 **best vintages** '02 **drink with** Fresh asparagus • $18

Wilson Gallery Series Riesling

♥♥♥♥♥ **2002** Light straw-green; the moderately intense bouquet has attractive, floral, lime/lime blossom aromas which move into a smooth but intense palate with lime juice flavours balanced by cleansing acidity on the finish. **rating:** 94
best drinking Now–2010 **best vintages** '85, '90, '91, '92, '94, '96, '97, '99, '02 **drink with** Japanese cuisine • $19.50

Wilson Vineyard Zinfandel

♥♥♥♥ **NV** An interesting wine, coming mainly from the 2001 vintage, and fermented to 15.5° alcohol whereafter the yeast stopped working, leaving significant unfermented sugar. The dark berry aromas and flavours are thus offset by a moderately sweet finish, made in heaven for the cellar door. **rating:** 86
best drinking Now **drink with** An ice block • $24.50

Wilson Vineyard Cabernet Sauvignon

♥♥♥♥ **2000** Medium red-purple; clean, fresh and smooth cassis fruit aromas flow through directly to the opening of the palate, but fractionally green tannins lead to a slightly tart finish. One of the first to commercially release a Stelvin-capped red wine. **rating:** 85
best drinking 2004–2011 **drink with** Lamb Provençale • $22.50

wimbaliri wines ★★★

Barton Highway, Murrumbateman, NSW 2582 **region** Canberra District
phone (02) 6227 5921 **fax** (02) 6227 5921 **open** Weekends 10–5, or by appointment
winemaker John Andersen **production** 600 cases **est.** 1988
product range ($18–22 CD) Chardonnay, Pinot Noir, Merlot Cabernets, Cabernet Merlot.
summary John and Margaret Andersen moved to the Canberra district in 1987 and commenced the establishment of their vineyard at Murrumbateman in 1988; the property borders two highly regarded Canberra producers, Doonkuna and Clonakilla. The vineyard is close-planted with a vertical trellis system, with a total of 2.2 hectares planted to chardonnay, pinot noir, shiraz, cabernet sauvignon and merlot (plus a few vines of cabernet franc).

Wimbaliri Chardonnay

♥♥♥♥ **2001** Light to medium yellow-green; the moderately intense bouquet has good fruit and oak balance and integration, with some cashew aromas; the palate has quiet expression throughout, and, as with the 2000 vintage, the impact of 100 per cent barrel fermentation in French oak and prolonged lees contact is not immediately obvious. **rating:** 85
best drinking Now–2005 **drink with** Smoked trout • $18

Wimbaliri Pinot Noir
▼▼▼▼ **2001** Light to medium red with some purple remnants; the ripe plum fruit of the bouquet has some oak in support; a big wine (13.9° alcohol) in the mouth, having a mix of plum and more savoury notes; lacks line/persistence. **rating:** 86

best drinking Now–2005 **drink with** Wild mushroom risotto • $20

winbirra vineyard   NR

173 Point Leo Road, Red Hill South, Vic 3937 (PO Box 130, Red Hill South, Vic 3937) **region** Mornington Peninsula
phone (03) 5989 2109 **fax** (03) 5989 2109 **open** By appointment
winemaker Kevin McCarthy (Contract) **production** 450 cases **est.** 1990
product range ($28 ML) Pinot Noir Pinot Meunier.
summary Winbirra is a small, family-owned and run vineyard which has been producing grapes since 1990, between then and 1997 selling the grapes to local winemakers. Since 1997 the wine has been contract-made by Kevin McCarthy at T'Gallant and sold under the Winbirra label. There is 1.5 hectares of pinot noir (with three clones) and a 0.5 hectare of pinot meunier sourced from Best's vineyard at Great Western. In 1998 the wines were made at separate varietals, but in 1999 and 2000 a single wine composed of 70 per cent pinot noir and 30 per cent pinot meunier was made, both vintages producing wine of convincing quality.

🦘 winbourne wines   NR

Bunnan Road, Scone, NSW 2337 (PO Box 523, Scone) **region** Upper Hunter Valley
phone 0417 650 0834 **fax** (02) 6545 1636 **open** By appointment
winemaker John Horien, Stephen Hagan, Michael De Iuliis **production** 3000 cases **est.** 1996
product range ($12.50–19 ML) Semillon, Verdelho, Chardonnay, Shiraz, Merlot.
summary A legal contemporary of mine, who I have known for 40 years, is one of the faces behind Winbourne Wines. He still practises law at his law firm in Muswellbrook, but has also established a little under 50 hectares of vineyards planted to semillon, chardonnay, verdelho, shiraz, merlot and cabernet sauvignon. The lion's share of the production is sold as grapes, a little made into wine by several Hunter Valley winemakers. Says David White 'it could well be wondered why we are doing – have done – this'. I guess it simply proves that old lawyers are not necessarily wise lawyers.

windarra   NR

De Beyers Road, Pokolbin, NSW 2321 **region** Lower Hunter Valley
phone (02) 4998 7648 **fax** (02) 4998 7648 **open** Tues–Sun 10–5
winemaker Tom Andresen-Jung **production** 1650 cases **est.** 1985
product range ($8–32 CD) Semillon, Semillon Chardonnay, Chardonnay, Reserve Blue Bottle Chardonnay, Rose, Shiraz, White Liqueur Port, Old Tawny Port, Fair Dinkum Herbal Port, Mead, Gold Wine (Mead, with 22-carat gold flakes).
summary The Andresen family has 6 hectares of semillon, chardonnay and shiraz; the wines are contract made.

windermere wines   NR

Lot 3, Watters Road, Ballandean, Qld 4382 **region** Granite Belt
phone (07) 4684 1353 **fax** (07) 4684 1353 **open** 7 days 9.30–5
winemaker Wayne Beecham, Kate Beecham **production** 500 cases **est.** 1995
product range ($11–17 CD) Chardonnay, Lilybrook DW Chardonnay Semillon, Sangiovese Merlot Cabernet, Millroad DR Cabernet Merlot, Shiraz, Liqueur Muscat; a selection of liqueurs and fruit wines.
summary After spending 3 years travelling in Europe between 1983 and 1986, Wayne Beecham returned to Australia to take up a position with what was then Thomas Hardy Wines, and specifically to establish the RhineCastle wine distribution in Queensland. During the next seven and a half years he studied wine marketing at Roseworthy while working for Hardys, but in 1993 he, wife Julie and daughter Kate decided to move to the Granite Belt to establish Windermere Wines from the ground up. His long service with Hardys stood him in good stead, landing him a cellar position at Hardys Tintara in the 1994 vintage, working with winemaker David O'Leary. In typical Australian fashion, Wayne Beecham says they decided on the Granite Belt because 'if we were to succeed, we might as well do it in the toughest new region in the industry'.

windowrie estate ★★★

Windowrie, Canowindra, NSW 2804 **region** Cowra
phone (02) 6344 3234 **fax** (02) 6344 3227 **open** 7 days 10–6 at the Mill, Vaux Street, Cowra
winemaker John Holmes **production** 52 000 cases **est.** 1988
product range ($10–22 CD) Cowra Chardonnay, Cowra Cabernet Shiraz; The Mill range of Sauvignon Blanc, Verdelho, Chardonnay, Shiraz, Merlot, Cabernet Merlot; Family Reserve Chardonnay, Family Reserve Shiraz.
summary Windowrie Estate was established in 1988 on a substantial grazing property at Canowindra, 30 kilometres north of Cowra and in the same viticultural region. Most of the grapes from the 230-hectare vineyard are sold to other makers, with increasing quantities being made for the Windowrie Estate and The Mill labels, the Chardonnays enjoying show success. The cellar door is situated in a flour mill built in 1861 from local granite. It ceased operations in 1905 and lay unoccupied for 91 years until restored by the O'Dea family. Exports to the UK, The Netherlands, the US, Canada and Japan.

Windowrie Estate Platinum Series Cowra Chardonnay

▼▼▼▽ 2002 Light to medium yellow-green; the clean and fresh bouquet has light citrus and stone fruit aromas precisely replicated on the easy access palate. No oak. **rating:** 84
best drinking Now **drink with** Chicken takeaway • $9.99

Windowrie Estate The Mill Chardonnay

▼▼▼▽ 2002 Medium yellow-green; the melon and stone fruit of the bouquet has a subtle hint of oak in the background; the palate provides a replay, the oak barely perceptible, the fruit tracking the bouquet. **rating:** 84
best drinking Now **drink with** Pasta • $13

Windowrie Estate The Mill Cabernet Merlot

▼▼▼▼ 2001 Medium red-purple; the moderately intense bouquet has clean dark berry/olive/savoury aromas supported by subtle oak; the very substantial and ripe palate has the black fruits and complex tannins so seldom encountered in this region. A major, and pleasant, surprise. **rating:** 89
best drinking 2004–2010 **drink with** Braised lamb • $12

windsors edge   NR

McDonalds Road, Pokolbin, NSW 2320 **region** Lower Hunter Valley
phone (02) 4998 7737 **fax** (02) 4998 7737 **open** Fri–Mon 10–5, or by appointment
winemaker Monarch Wines (Contract), Tim Windsor, Jessie Windsor **production** 3500 cases **est.** 1996
product range ($14–18 CD) Semillon, Chardonnay, Rose, Shiraz, Sparkling Shiraz, Coonawarra Cabernet Sauvignon.
summary In 1995 Tim Windsor (a Charles Sturt graduate in winemaking) and wife Jessie (an industrial chemist) purchased the old Black Creek picnic racetrack at the northern end of McDonalds Road in Pokolbin. The first vines were planted in 1996, and planting has continued and to date 17 hectares of shiraz, semillon, chardonnay, tempranillo, tinta cao and touriga are in the ground. Three luxury cottages have been built, followed by a restaurant and cellar door, with a small winery beneath, and the range extended to include a Coonawarra Cabernet Sauvignon, a Chambourcin, and a Tasmanian Pinot. The winemaking, too, has been parceled out: the larger quantities are made by Monarch Wines; the smaller volumes of grapes sourced outside the Hunter are made by Tim and Jessie in the small winery below the restaurant; while the Tinta Cao and Touriga have been sent to the Peter Van Gent Winery in Mudgee to be fortified.

windy creek estate   NR

Stock Road, Herne Hill, WA 6056 **region** Swan Valley
phone (08) 9296 4210 **open** Tues–Sun 11–5
winemaker Tony Cobanov, Tony Roe **production** 10 000 cases **est.** 1960
product range ($6–10 CD) Chenin Blanc, Chardonnay, Sauvignon Blanc, Verdelho, Shiraz, Grenache, Cabernet Sauvignon.
summary A substantial family-owned operation (previously known as Cobanov Wines) producing a mix of bulk and bottled wine from 21 hectares of estate grapes. Part of the annual production is sold as grapes to other producers, including Houghton; part is sold in bulk; part sold in 2-litre flagons, and the remainder in modestly priced bottles.

windy ridge vineyard ★★★☆

Foster-Fish Creek Road, Foster, Vic 3960 **region** Gippsland
phone (03) 5682 2035 **open** Holiday weekends 10–5
winemaker Graeme Wilson **production** 300 cases **est.** 1978
product range ($15–39.50 CD) Traminer, Pinot Noir, Cellar Reserve Pinot Noir, Cabernet Sauvignon Malbec.
summary The 2.8-hectare Windy Ridge Vineyard was planted between 1978 and 1986, with the first vintage not taking place until 1988. Winemaker Graeme Wilson favours prolonged maturation, part in stainless steel and part in oak, before bottling his wines, typically giving the Pinot Noir 3 years and the Cabernet 2 years before bottling.

Windy Ridge Cellar Reserve Pinot Noir

▼▼▼▼ 2000 Medium red; the savoury/foresty bouquet is complex, and has ample dark plum varietal fruit to sustain that complexity. The palate has good structure and depth, the flavours totally consistent with the bouquet. The best for many years from Windy Ridge. **rating:** 88

best drinking Now–2007 **drink with** Wild mushroom risotto • $39.50

winewood NR

Sundown Road, Ballandean, Qld 4382 **region** Granite Belt
phone (07) 4684 1187 **fax** (07) 4684 1187 **open** Weekends and public holidays 9–5
winemaker Ian Davis **production** 1000 cases **est.** 1984
product range ($15–20 CD) Chardonnay, Chardonnay Marsanne, Shiraz Marsanne, MacKenzies Run (Cabernet blend), Muscat.
summary A weekend and holiday activity for schoolteacher Ian Davis and town-planner wife Jeanette; the tiny winery is a model of neatness and precision planning. The use of marsanne with chardonnay and semillon shows an interesting change in direction. Has 4.5 hectares of estate plantings, having added shiraz and viognier. All wine sold through cellar door; tutored tastings available.

winstead ★★★★

75 Winstead Road, Bagdad, Tas 7030 **region** Southern Tasmania
phone (03) 6268 6417 **fax** (03) 6268 6417 **open** By appointment
winemaker Neil Snare **production** 450 cases **est.** 1989
product range ($17–42 CD) Riesling, Pinot Noir, Reserve Pinot Noir.
summary The good news about Winstead is the outstanding quality of its extremely generous and rich Pinot Noirs, rivalling those of Freycinet for the abundance of their fruit flavour without any sacrifice of varietal character. The bad news is that production is so limited, with only 0.9 hectare of pinot noir and 0.3 hectare riesling being tended by fly-fishing devotee Neil Snare and wife Julieanne. Retail distribution in Melbourne.

Winstead Pinot Noir

▼▼▼▼ 2001 Medium red-purple; very ripe plummy fruit aromas, verging on jammy, are followed by a flavoursome palate, which introduces a touch of sweet and sour, for the spice and plum flavours have sappy counterpoints. A Curate's Egg. **rating:** 88

best drinking Now–2007 **best vintages** '96, '97, '98, '99, '00 **drink with** Saddle of hare • $29

wirilda creek ★★★

RSD 91, McMurtrie Road, McLaren Vale, SA 5171 **region** McLaren Vale
phone (08) 8323 9688 **fax** (08) 8323 9260 **open** 7 days 10–5
winemaker Kerry Flanagan **production** 1500 cases **est.** 1993
product range ($15–25 CD) Grape Pickers Verdelho, Evening Shadows (Sparkling Shiraz), Shiraz Trad, Shiraz Rare, Vine Pruners Blend, Cabernet Sauvignon Merlot, Old Sweet White Fortified Verdelho, Liqueur Port.
summary Wirilda Creek may be one of the newer arrivals in McLaren Vale but it offers the lot: wine, lunch every day (Pickers Platters reflecting local produce) and accommodation (four rooms opening onto a private garden courtyard). Co-owner Kerry Flanagan (with partner Karen Shertock) has had great experience in the wine and hospitality industries: a Roseworthy graduate (1980) he has inter alia worked at Penfolds, Coriole and Wirra Wirra and also owned the famous Old Salopian Inn for a period of time. A little under 4 hectares of McLaren Vale estate vineyards have now been joined with a little over 3 hectares of vineyards planted at Antechamber Bay, Kangaroo Island. Limited retail distribution in New South Wales and South Australia; exports to the US, Canada and Germany.

Wirilda Creek Evening Shadows Sparkling Shiraz

ŢŢŢŢ **NV** Medium red; the bouquet is gently earthy, with a background whisper of oak; the wine comes alive on the palate with very attractive chocolate and earth flavours, and is not too sweet, the failing of many sparkling reds. **rating:** 87

best drinking Now–2006 **drink with** Hors d'oeuvres • $23

Wirilda Creek Old Sweet White Fortified Verdelho

ŢŢŢŢ♀ **NV** The pale mahogany colour is testament to the age of the wine; the complex, nutty rancio aromas are fresh; the palate has complex nutty/cake flavours, and a clean aftertaste sustained by the excellent rancio. An old fortified Verdelho, a long-time specialty of the Langhorne Creek region. **rating:** 90

best drinking Now–2005 **drink with** Almond cake • $20

wirra wirra ★★★★☆

McMurtie Road, McLaren Vale, SA 5171 **region** McLaren Vale
phone (08) 8323 8414 **fax** (08) 8323 8596 **open** Mon–Sat 10–5, Sun 11–5
winemaker Samantha Connew **production** 100 000 cases **est.** 1969
product range ($14.50–69 R) Hand Picked Riesling, Sauvignon Blanc, Scrubby Rise (Semillon Sauvignon Blanc Chardonnay), Chardonnay, Sexton's Acre Unwooded Chardonnay, The Cousins (Sparkling Pinot Noir Chardonnay), Mrs Wigley Rose, The Anthem (Sparkling Shiraz), Late Picked Riesling, McLaren Vale Shiraz, Chook Block Shiraz, RSW Shiraz, McLaren Vale Grenache Shiraz, Scrubby Rise (Shiraz Cabernet Petit Verdot), Church Block (Cabernet Shiraz Merlot), Penley Coonawarra Cabernet Sauvignon, The Angelus Cabernet Sauvignon, fortifieds.
summary Long-respected for the consistency of its white wines, Wirra Wirra has now established an equally formidable reputation for its reds. Right across the board, the wines are of exemplary character, quality and style, The Angelus Cabernet Sauvignon and RSW Shiraz battling with each other for supremacy. Long may the battle continue under the direction of the highly respected Tim James, lured from his senior position at BRL Hardy late in 2000. The wines are exported to the US, the UK, Europe and Asia.

Wirra Wirra Adelaide Hills Sauvignon Blanc

ŢŢŢŢ♀ **2002** Light to medium yellow-green; a spotlessly clean and crisp bouquet ranges through herb, gooseberry and citrus; the ultra-crisp and tingling, lemony palate has mouth-puckering acidity, needing time to settle down. **rating:** 90

best drinking 2004–2006 **drink with** Blue swimmer crab • $21.50

Wirra Wirra Scrubby Rise

ŢŢŢŢ **2002** Light yellow-green; the clean, soft bouquet has predominantly citrus and some tropical aromas, the crisp and long palate more in a grassy/lemony spectrum. The 10 per cent barrel-ferment component adds to the texture, but is otherwise invisible. **rating:** 87

best drinking Now **drink with** Shellfish • $16.50

Wirra Wirra The Anthem

ŢŢŢŢ **NV** Light to medium red; earthy berry aromas and flavours are joined on the palate with a dash of chocolate; well balanced and not excessively sweet or phenolic. **rating:** 87

best drinking Now–2006 **drink with** Hors d'oeuvres • $29.50

Wirra Wirra Mrs Wigley Rose

ŢŢŢŢ **2002** Light red-purple; the fruit and spice of the bouquet lead into a palate with plenty of flavour and mid-palate fruit sweetness; the blend of Grenache and Petite Verdot is a decidedly strange one; perhaps the Petit Verdot component was the result of some juice run-off. **rating:** 86

best drinking Now **drink with** Cold meat salad • $18.50

Wirra Wirra McLaren Vale Shiraz

ŢŢŢŢŢ **2000** A perennial favourite which exceeded itself in 2000, not regarded as a particularly good vintage in McLaren Vale. Bright red-purple, the bouquet ranges through berry, earth, spice, cedar and regional chocolate, and the palate picks up all those characters. Supple and round, the mouthfeel is great, as is the overall flavour. **rating:** 95

best drinking 2004–2014 **best vintages** '99, '00 **drink with** Lamb shanks • $29.50

Wirra Wirra RSW Shiraz

ŢŢŢŢŢ **2000** Medium to full red-purple; a complex array of berry, blackberry and licorice fruit aromas flow into a concentrated, long and supple palate, fruit-driven, and not over-extracted. **rating:** 96

best drinking 2005–2015 **best vintages** '94, '95, '97, '98, '99, '00 **drink with** Smoked beef • $43

Wirra Wirra Church Block

ŸŸŸŸŸ **2001** An illustrious blend of 50 per cent cabernet sauvignon, 30 per cent shiraz and 20 per cent merlot which spends 18 months in French oak. Strong, bright red-purple; the solid bouquet has a mix of dark berry and regional chocolate fruit, the richly textured and structured palate with abundant flavour. Keeps the faith.   **rating:** 93

best drinking 2004–2009 **best vintages** '90, '91, '94, '98, '01 **drink with** Pasta bolognese • $21.50

Wirra Wirra The Angelus Cabernet Sauvignon

ŸŸŸŸŸ **2000** Medium red-purple; the bouquet has a mix of ripe blackberry, mulberry and spice, which flow through into the palate, with concentrated berry fruit and lingering tannins. Sixty per cent Coonawarra and 40 per cent McLaren Vale grapes; 20 months in French oak.   **rating:** 90

best drinking 2005–2015 **best vintages** '86, '90, '91, '92, '95, '96, '97, '98 **drink with** Spring lamb • $43

wise vineyards   ★★★☆

Lot 4 Eagle Bay Road, Dunsborough, WA 6281 **region** Margaret River
phone (08) 9756 8627 **fax** (08) 9756 8770 **open** 7 days 10–5
winemaker Bruce Dukes (Consultant), Andy Coppard, Amanda Kramer **production** 35 000 cases **est.** 1986
product range ($15–35 CD) Eagle Bay Semillon Sauvignon Blanc, Verdelho, Classic White, Unwooded Chardonnay, Pinot Noir, Classic Red, Eagle Bay Shiraz, Shiraz Cabernet Merlot, Cabernet Sauvignon.
summary Wise Vineyards, headed by Perth entrepreneur Ron Wise, brings together the 20.5-hectare Eagle Bay Vineyard at Meelup, the 10.3-hectare Donnybrook Valley Vineyard at Donnybrook, and the 8-hectare Bramley Estate Vineyard at Margaret River. The on-site restaurant is open daily for lunch, Friday and Saturday for dinner, and Saturday and Sunday for breakfast, and there are five chalets, variously sleeping 2–10 people all within 10 minutes walk from the restaurant.

Wise Vineyards Donnybrook Valley Chardonnay

ŸŸŸŸŸ **2001** Light to medium yellow-green; the delicate bouquet has neatly balanced melon and subtle oak, the melon and honeycomb palate with good length, and the promise of some cellaring ability.   **rating:** 91

best drinking Now–2005 **best vintages** '01 **drink with** Smoked eel • $24

witchmount estate   ★★★★

557 Leakes Road, Rockbank, Vic 3335 **region** Sunbury
phone (03) 9747 1088 **fax** (03) 9747 1066 **open** Wed–Sun 10–5
winemaker Tony Ramunno **production** 8000 cases **est.** 1991
product range ($9.50–35 CD) Summer White, Estate Chardonnay, Olivia's Paddock Chardonnay, Rose, Estate Shiraz (old vines), Lowan Park Shiraz (new vines), Estate Cabernet Sauvignon (old vines), Lowan Park Cabernet Sauvignon (new vines); Mt Cottrell range of Sauvignon Blanc Semillon, Shiraz.
summary Gaye and Matt Ramunno operate Witchmount Estate in conjunction with its on-site Italian restaurant and function rooms, which are open from Wednesday to Sunday inclusive for lunch and dinner. Over 20 hectares of vines have been established since 1991, varieties include nebbiolo, tempranillo and the rare northern Italian white grape picolit. The quality of the wines is consistently good, the prices very modest.

Witchmount Estate Olivia's Paddock Chardonnay

ŸŸŸŸ **2001** Light to medium yellow-green; complex but subtle barrel-fermentation characters are seamlessly folded into the fruit of the bouquet; the light to medium-bodied palate allows that gentle nectarine, melon and fig fruit free play.   **rating:** 88

best drinking Now–2006 **drink with** Pan-fried veal • $16

Witchmount Estate Shiraz

ŸŸŸŸŸ **2001** Bright, deep red-purple; the sweet and clean bouquet unfolds with blackberry, spice, raspberry and cherry aromas, the palate bringing distinct dark chocolate overtones to the abundant fruit play of the palate, adding complexity; balanced tannins to close.   **rating:** 92

best drinking 2004–2008 **best vintages** '01 **drink with** Marinated venison • $19.50

Witchmount Estate Lowan Park Shiraz

ŸŸŸŸ **2001** Medium to full red-purple; the clean bouquet offsets spicy savoury notes against dark fruits; the light to medium-bodied palate is fresh, with some chocolate joining the dominant dark fruit flavours; well handled oak.   **rating:** 89

best drinking 2005–2010 **drink with** Beef shashlik • $15

Witchmount Estate Cabernet Sauvignon

▼▼▼▼▽ 2001 Medium to full purple-red; the ripe mix of blackcurrant and blackberry fruit of the bouquet leads into abundant, rich dark berry flavours on the palate; the wine has good texture, structure and length. **rating:** 93

best drinking 2006–2016 **best vintages** '00, '01 **drink with** Bistecca Fiorentina • $19.50

Witchmount Estate Lowan Park Cabernet Sauvignon

▼▼▼▼ 2001 Medium red-purple; the clean bouquet mirrors that of the Lowan Park Shiraz, with earthy, savoury overtones to the core of blackcurrant/blackberry fruit. The palate has pleasing black fruit flavours, but a far lighter structure. **rating:** 87

best drinking 2005–2010 **drink with** Rack of lamb • $15

wj walker wines   NR

Burns Road, Lake Grace, WA 6353 **region** South West Australia Zone
phone (08) 9865 1969 **open** Not
winemaker Porongurup Winery **production** 1000 cases **est.** NA
product range ($10–15 R) Chardonnay, Shiraz, Cabernet Sauvignon, Port.
summary Lake Grace is 300 kilometres due east of Bunbury, one of those isolated viticultural outposts which are appearing in many parts of Australia these days. There are 1.5 hectares of shiraz and 0.5 hectare of chardonnay, and the wines are sold through local outlets.

wolf blass   ★★★★☆

Bilyara Vineyards, Sturt Highway, Nuriootpa, SA 5355 **region** Barossa Valley
phone (08) 8562 1955 **fax** (08) 8562 2156 **open** Mon–Fri 9.15–4.30, weekends 10–4.30
winemaker Chris Hatcher (Chief), Wendy Stuckey (White), John Glaetzer and Caroline Dunn (Red)
production NFP **est.** 1966
product range ($11–150 R) White wines under White, Yellow, Green and Gold labels, with emphasis on Riesling and blended Classic Dry White, Gold Label Riesling; red wines under Red, Yellow, Brown, Grey, Black and Platinum labels with emphasis on Cabernet Sauvignon, Shiraz and blends of these. Also sparkling and fortified wines. The Eaglehawk now roosts here, too, Eaglehawk Chardonnay, Eaglehawk Riesling, Eaglehawk Sauvignon Blanc, Eaglehawk Semillon Sauvignon Blanc, Traminer Riesling, Grenache Shiraz. The Blass range, with its red, minimalist labels in stark contrast to the usual baroque designs so loved by Wolf, is a more recent addition, Vintage Brut, Pinot Chardonnay Brut, Clare Valley Red Label Riesling, Semillon Sauvignon Blanc, Chardonnay,
summary Although merged with Mildara and now under the giant umbrella of Beringer Blass, the brands (as expected) have been left largely intact. The white wines (made by Wendy Stuckey) are particularly impressive, none more so than the Gold Label Riesling. After a short pause, the red wines have improved out of all recognition thanks to the sure touch (and top palate) of Caroline Dunn. All of this has occurred under the leadership of Chris Hatcher, who has harnessed the talents of the team and encouraged the changes in style. Worldwide distribution.

Eaglehawk Riesling

▼▼▼▼ 2002 Light green-yellow; a crisp mix of mineral, herb and citrus aromas, then a palate with good citrus/lime flavour, and in particular, finish. Good value; topped its class (49) at the 2002 National Wine Show. **rating:** 89

best drinking Now–2006 **best vintages** '90, '92, '93, '96, '01, '02 **drink with** Asparagus • $9.99

Wolf Blass South Australia Riesling

▼▼▼▼ 2002 Medium yellow-green; the clean and fresh bouquet offers ripe lime and citrus fruit, the easy-drinking palate neatly fleshed out with subliminal sweetness. The budget-priced version under the Wolf Blass label.
rating: 89

best drinking Now–2006 **drink with** Fresh asparagus • $11.99

Wolf Blass Semillon Sauvignon Blanc

▼▼▼▼ 2002 Light green-yellow; a light bouquet in the minerally/grassy spectrum and a light-bodied palate with lemon and fruit salad flavours; moderate length. Lacks intensity. **rating:** 85

best drinking Now **drink with** Fish and chips • $11.99

Wolf Blass Chardonnay Pinot Noir

▼▼▼▼ NV Good mousse; fragrant, citrussy chardonnay seems to make the major contribution on the bouquet, the impression reinforced by the crisp and lively palate, again with lemony/citrussy flavours. **rating:** 85

best drinking Now **drink with** Hors d'oeuvres • $12.50

Wolf Blass Platinum Label Adelaide Hills Shiraz

▼▼▼▼▽ **2000** Bright purple-red; the bouquet is flooded with sweet redcurrant, plum and blackcurrant fruit, the French oak impeccably balanced. The palate provides more of the same smooth, supple, sweet, red and black fruits, the oak once again in perfect harmony. Curiously, does not show its relatively cool-grown origins. The wine spent 20 months in new French oak. **rating:** 93

best drinking 2005–2012 **best vintages** '98, '00 **drink with** Yearling beef • $150

Wolf Blass Black Label Cabernet Sauvignon Shiraz

▼▼▼▼▼ **1999** Medium to full purple-red; both the bouquet and palate have an extra dimension of fruit complexity and depth, reflecting the fact that it is a blend of 10 components selected from 160 separate high-quality parcels earmarked for possible inclusion. The palate has a silky, supple smoothness, the oak evident but in no way excessive. The 53 per cent Cabernet Sauvignon component comes mainly from McLaren Vale, the 47 per cent Shiraz mainly from the Barossa, the balance from Langhorne Creek. **rating:** 95

best drinking 2004–2009 **best vintages** '86, '88, '90, '91, '95, '96, '97, '98, '99 **drink with** Steak with wild mushrooms • $125

Wolf Blass Grey Label Cabernet Sauvignon

▼▼▼▼▽ **2000** Medium red-purple; sweet and ripe red berry, plum and blackberry fruit with nicely integrated oak; the palate features fresh, pointed red berry fruits and lively acidity, the oak evident but by no means assertive. One hundred per cent Langhorne Creek; new French and American oak for 24 months. **rating:** 90

best drinking 2004–2010 **best vintages** '97, '99 **drink with** Mixed grill • $39

Wolf Blass Platinum Label Clare Valley Cabernet Sauvignon

▼▼▼▼▼ **2000** Deep red-purple; the bouquet is loaded with cassis and blackcurrant fruit, the French oak perfectly integrated; the blackcurrant fruit comes through in gloriously succulent form on the long, rippling palate. Here, too, both oak and tannins have been perfectly handled. Only a microscopic quantity available made, and only sold at the Wolf Blass cellar door. **rating:** 97

best drinking 2005–2020 **best vintages** '98, '00 **drink with** Spit-roasted leg of lamb • $150

woodlands   NR

Cnr Caves and Metricup Roads, Wilyabrup via Cowaramup, WA 6284 **region** Margaret River
phone (08) 9755 6226 **fax** (08) 9481 1700 **open** Weekends by appointment
winemaker David Watson, Mark Lane, Dorham Mann (Consultant) **production** 3000 cases **est.** 1973
product range ($20–45 R) Unwooded Chardonnay, Reserve Chloe Chardonnay, Cabernet Merlot, Margaret Cabernet Merlot, Reserve St Peter Cabernet Merlot,
summary The production (and visibility) of Woodlands have varied over the years, the core of the business lying with 6.8 hectares of cabernet sauvignon, more recently joined by merlot (1.2 ha), malbec (0.8 ha), cabernet franc (0.2 ha), pinot noir (0.2 ha) and chardonnay (0.8 ha), all now in bearing. Exports to the US.

woodonga hill   NR

Cowra Road, Young, NSW 2594 **region** Hilltops
phone (02) 6382 2972 **fax** (02) 6382 2972 **open** 7 days 9–5
winemaker Jill Lindsay **production** 4000 cases **est.** 1986
product range ($12.50–21 CD) Dry Rhine Riesling, Sauvignon, Chardonnay, Botrytis Semillon, Auslese Gewurztraminer, Meunier, Shiraz, Vintage Port, Cherry Liqueur Port.
summary Early problems with white wine quality appear to have been surmounted. The wines have won bronze or silver medals at regional wine shows in NSW and Canberra, and Jill Lindsay is also a successful contract-winemaker for other small producers.

wood park   NR

RMB 1139 Bobinawarrah–Whorouly Road, Milawa, Vic 3678 **region** King Valley
phone (03) 5727 3367 **fax** (03) 5727 3682 **open** At Milawa Cheese Factory
winemaker John Stokes **production** 3500 cases **est.** 1989
product range ($15–33 CD) Meadow Creek Chardonnay, Pinot Gris, Pinot Noir, Shiraz, Cabernet Shiraz.
summary The first vines were planted at Wood Park in 1989 by John Stokes as part of a diversification programme for his property at Bobinawarrah in the hills of the Lower King Valley to the east of Milawa. The bulk of the 8-hectare production is sold to Brown Brothers, with a further 8 hectares of vineyard being established for Southcorp. In an unusual twist, Stokes acquires his chardonnay from cousin John Leviny, one of the King Valley pioneers, who has his vineyard at Meadow Creek. To complicate matters further, all four vintages of Chardonnay ('95 to '98) were made by Rick Kinzbrunner. Exports to the US and Europe.

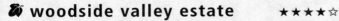 woodside valley estate ★★★★☆

Lots 40 and 41 Abbeyarm Road, Yallingup, WA 6282 (postal) **region** Margaret River
phone (08) 9345 4065 **fax** (08) 9345 4541 **open** Not
winemaker Kevin McKay **production** 500 cases **est.** 1998
product range ($30–45 ML) The Baudin Collection of: The Bailly Chardonnay, The Baptiste Shiraz, The Bissy Merlot, The Baudin Cabernet Merlot, The Baudin Cabernet Sauvignon.
summary Woodside Valley has been developed by a small syndicate of investors headed by Peter Woods. In 1998 they acquired 67 hectares of land at Yallingup, and have now established 19 hectares of chardonnay, sauvignon blanc, cabernet sauvignon, shiraz, malbec and merlot. The experienced Albert Haak is consultant viticulturist, and together with Peter Woods, took the unusual step of planting south-facing in preference to north-facing slopes. In doing so they indirectly followed in the footsteps of the French explorer Thomas Nicholas Baudin, who mounted a major scientific expedition to Australia on his ship *The Geographe*, and defied established views and tradition of the time in (correctly) asserting that the best passage for sailing ships travelling between Cape Leeuwin and Bass Strait was from west to east. It's a long bow, but it's a story for a winery which managed to produce some excellent wines from very young vines, as the 2000 The Baudin Cabernet Merlot handsomely demonstrates.

Woodside Valley Estate The Baudin Cabernet Merlot

♥♥♥♥♥ **2000** Medium red-purple; the bouquet exudes a striking mix of cassis cabernet and savoury/olivaceous merlot; the fine, elegant and supple palate has eaten up the oak coming from 20 months maturation in new French barrels even though the fruit is not particularly lush or over the top, simply all style. **rating:** 94
best drinking 2005–2020 **best vintages** '00 **drink with** Roast salt bush lamb • $39

woodsmoke estate   NR

Lot 2 Kemp Road, Pemberton, WA 6260 **region** Pemberton
phone (08) 9776 0225 **fax** (08) 9776 0225 **open** By appointment
winemaker Julie White **production** 1500 cases **est.** 1992
product range ($18–25 CD) Sauvignon Blanc, Semillon, Cabernet blend.
summary The former Jimlee Estate was acquired by the Liebeck family in July 1998 and renamed to WoodSmoke Estate. The original plantings of a little over 2 hectares of semillon, sauvignon blanc, cabernet franc and cabernet sauvignon were expanded with a further 2.5 hectares of cabernet franc and merlot in 2000.

woodstock   ★★★☆

Douglas Gully Road, McLaren Flat, SA 5171 **region** McLaren Vale
phone (08) 8383 0156 **fax** (08) 8383 0437 **open** Mon–Fri 9–5, weekends, holidays 12–5
winemaker Scott Collett **production** 30 000 cases **est.** 1974
product range ($9.95–33 CD) Riesling, Semillon, Douglas Gully Semillon Sauvignon Blanc, Verdelho, Chardonnay, Botrytis Sweet White, Five Feet (Dry Red), Shiraz, Grenache, Douglas Gully Malbec Cabernet Sauvignon Petit Verdot, Cabernet Sauvignon, Vintage Port, Very Old Tawny Port and Muscat. The Stocks Shiraz is a recently introduced flagship.
summary One of the stalwarts of McLaren Vale, producing archetypal, invariably reliable full-bodied red wines and showing versatility with spectacular botrytis sweet whites and high-quality (14-year-old) Tawny Port. Also offers a totally charming reception-cum-restaurant, which understandably does a roaring trade with wedding receptions. Has supplemented its 22 hectares of McLaren Vale vineyards with 10 hectares at its Wirrega Vineyard near Bordertown in the Limestone Coast Zone. The wines are exported to the UK, Switzerland, the US, Canada, New Zealand, Philippines, Malaysia and Singapore.

Woodstock Shiraz

♥♥♥♥ **2000** Medium red-purple; high-toned red and black fruit aromas drive the bouquet; some chocolate joins the flavour mix on the smooth palate; nicely balanced tannins and subtle oak throughout. A blend of Limestone Coast, McLaren Vale and Langhorne Creek shiraz. **rating:** 88
best drinking 2004–2010 **best vintages** '82, '84, '91, '92, '93, '94 **drink with** Steak in black bean sauce • $20

Woodstock Cabernet Sauvignon

♥♥♥♥ **2000** Light to medium red-purple; the bouquet is moderately aromatic, with a mix of earthy/savoury/cedary/spicy characters; the light to medium-bodied palate brings the latent redcurrant fruit more to the fore, with a background of the flavours promised by the bouquet. Pleasant but not exciting. **rating:** 85
best drinking 2004–2009 **best vintages** '82, '84, '91, '92, '94, '97 **drink with** Game pie • $20

woody nook ★★★☆

Metricup Road, Busselton, WA 6280 **region** Margaret River
phone (08) 9755 7547 **fax** (08) 9755 7007 **open** 7 days 10–4.30
winemaker Neil Gallagher **production** 5000 cases **est.** 1982
product range ($15–28 CD) Sauvignon Blanc, Kelly's Farewell (Sauvignon Blanc Semillon), Classique (Semillon Sauvignon Blanc Chardonnay), Chenin Blanc, Late Harvest, Shiraz, Merlot, Killdog Creek Cabernet Merlot, Cabernet Sauvignon, Nooky Delight; Gallagher's Choice Cabernet Sauvignon is top of the range.
summary This improbably named and not terribly fashionable winery has produced some truly excellent wines over the years, featuring in such diverse competitions as Winewise, the Sheraton Wine Awards and the Qantas West Australian Wines Show. Cabernet Sauvignon has always been its strong point, but it has the habit of bobbing up with excellent white wines in various guises. Since 2000 owned by Peter and Jane Baily, but Neil Gallagher continues as viticulturist, winemaker and minority shareholder. Exports to the UK and Hong Kong.

Woody Nook Kelly's Farewell

TTTY 2002 Light to medium yellow-green; the bouquet has abundant ripe, tropical fruit with some peachy notes, the medium-bodied palate picking up on the aromas of the bouquet, the only problem a slightly heavy finish. **rating: 84**

best drinking Now **drink with** Deep-fried calamari • $15

🐌 woongarra estate NR

Hayseys Road, Narre Warren East, Vic 3804 **region** Port Phillip Zone
phone (03) 9796 8886 **fax** (03) 9796 8580 **open** Thurs–Sun 9–5 by appointment only
winemaker Graeme Leith, Mal Stewart **production** 2000 cases **est.** 1992
product range ($12 CD) Sauvignon Blanc Semillon. Three Wise Men range of Pinot Noir and Shiraz also available.
summary Dr Bruce Jones, and wife Mary, purchased their Narre Warren East 16-hectare property many years ago; it falls within the Yarra Ranges Shire Council's jurisdiction and zoned 'Landscape', but because nearby Cardinia Creek does not flow into the Yarra River, it is not within the Yarra Valley wine region. Undeterred, they planted 0.66 hectare of MV6 clone pinot noir in 1986, but summer pruning by goats and sheep ensured no grapes appeared. In 1992 they chose another spot on the property, hired Andrew Clark as consultant, planting 1 hectare of sauvignon blanc, a small patch of shiraz and a few rows of semillon. Over 1 hectare of sauvignon blanc and pinot noir followed in 1996 (mostly MV6, some French clone 114 and 115) with yet more 114 and 115 pinot noir in 2000, lifting total plantings to 3.2 hectares of pinot noir, 1.4 hectares of sauvignon blanc and a splash of the other two varieties. The white grapes have had various purchasers and contract makers; the spectacular success has come with the Three Wise Men Pinot Noir (see separate entry).

Woongarra Estate Sauvignon Blanc

TTTY 2002 Developed yellow-green; the full bouquet has exotically ripe tropical fruit salad aromas, the palate similarly rich; ripe to the point of over-ripeness, and quite unusual. **rating: 84**

best drinking Now **drink with** Turkey breast • $12

Woongarra Estate Sauvignon Blanc Semillon

TTTT 2002 Light straw-green; clear varietal character, and all of the signs of highly protective winemaking leading to slight reduction in the bouquet; the palate is bright and fresh, the finish slightly grippy. The polar opposite of the Sauvignon Blanc. From Bendigo fruit. **rating: 85**

TTTT 2001 Light straw-green; the clean, firm and crisp bouquet has a range of lemon, grass and gooseberry aromas, the palate no less firm and intense. Yet another change of pace. Yarra Ranges region, whatever that may mean. **rating: 86**

best drinking Now **drink with** Mussels • $12

wordsworth wines NR

Cnr South Western Highway and Thompson Road, Harvey, WA 6220 **region** Geographe
phone (08) 9773 4576 **fax** (08) 9733 4269 **open** 7 days 10–5
winemaker Tim Mortimer **production** 2500 cases **est.** 1997
product range ($16–22 CD) Verdelho, Chardonnay, Daffodil Medium Dry White, Shiraz, Cabernet Merlot.
summary David Wordsworth has established a substantial business in a relatively short space of time. Thirty-three hectares of vines have been planted, with cabernet sauvignon (12 ha) and shiraz (5 ha) predominant, and lesser amounts of merlot, zinfandel, petit verdot, chardonnay, chenin blanc and verdelho. The winery features

massive jarrah beams, and the tasting room is built to size, with seating for 40 people. The wines have had show success in the limited period of time the winery has been operating, and the Verdelho is on the Tate Gallery's (London) wine list.

wyanga park   NR

Baades Road, Lakes Entrance, Vic 3909 **region** Gippsland
phone (03) 5155 1508 **fax** (03) 5155 1443 **open** 7 days 9–5
winemaker Graeme Little **production** 5000 cases **est.** 1970
product range ($12–18 CD) Sauvignon Blanc, Chardonnay, Miriam's Fancy Chardonnay, Rose, Boobialla (medium-sweet white), Pinot Noir, Shiraz Cabernet Sauvignon, fortifieds.
summary Offers a broad range of wines of diverse provenance directed at the tourist trade; one of the Chardonnays and the Cabernet Sauvignon are estate-grown. Winery cruises up the north arm of the Gippsland Lake to Wyanga Park are scheduled four days a week throughout the entire year.

wyndham estate   ★★★★

Dalwood Road, Dalwood, NSW 2335 **region** Lower Hunter Valley
phone (02) 4938 3444 **fax** (02) 4938 3422 **open** Mon–Fri 9.30–5, weekends 10–4
winemaker Brett McKinnon **production** NFP **est.** 1828
product range ($6.95–25 R) In ascending order: Bin TR2 Select White and Select Red; 1828 range of Semillon Sauvignon Blanc, Semillon Chardonnay, Unwooded Chardonnay, Vintage Brut, Cabernet Sauvignon Shiraz Ruby Cabernet; Bin 777 Semillon, Bin 111 Verdelho, Bin 222 Chardonnay, Bin 333 Pinot Noir, Bin 555 Shiraz, Bin 999 Merlot, Bin 888 Cabernet Merlot, Bin 444 Cabernet Sauvignon; Show Reserve range of Semillon, Chardonnay, Shiraz, Cabernet Merlot; Vintage Chardonnay Brut Cuvee.
summary Has risen to the challenge in recent years, its varietal wines smoothly dependable, the Show Reserves usually justifying their name (and price).

Wyndham Estate Show Reserve Chardonnay

TTTT **2001** Pale, bright straw-green; a clean, crisp, direct citrus-tinged bouquet with just a whiff of oak is effectively repeated on the crisp and clean palate understated rather than overstated.   **rating:** 88
best drinking Now–2006 **drink with** Smoked chicken • $19

Wyndham Estate Show Reserve Shiraz

TTTTY **1998** Medium red-purple; the savoury/earthy fruit aromas of the bouquet are balanced by well-judged vanilla oak, black fruits coming through on the attractive, smooth medium-bodied palate, finishing with gently savoury tannins.   **rating:** 90
best drinking Now–2008 **best vintages** '98 **drink with** Game pie • $25

wynns coonawarra estate   ★★★★☆

Memorial Drive, Coonawarra, SA 5263 **region** Coonawarra
phone (08) 8736 2225 **fax** (08) 8736 2228 **open** 7 days 10–5
winemaker Sue Hodder, Sarah Pidgeon **production** NFP **est.** 1891
product range ($12–89 R) Wynns Coonawarra Estate Riesling, Chardonnay, Shiraz, Cabernet Shiraz Merlot, Cabernet Sauvignon and Black Label Cabernet Sauvignon; Michael Shiraz, John Riddoch Cabernet Sauvignon.
summary The large-scale production has in no way prevented Wynns from producing excellent wines covering the full price spectrum from the bargain basement Riesling and Shiraz through to the deluxe John Riddoch Cabernet Sauvignon and Michael Shiraz. Even with steady price increases, Wynns offers extraordinary value for money.

Wynns Coonawarra Estate Riesling

TTTT **2002** Light to medium yellow-green; the clean, firm bouquet with predominantly mineral and herb aromas gives little indication of the quite intense and compact palate which follows, packed with flavour, even a little on the big side.   **rating:** 89
best drinking Now–2005 **best vintages** '90, '91, '93, '95, '96, '98, '99, '01 **drink with** King George whiting • $12

Wynns Coonawarra Estate Chardonnay

TTTT **2002** Medium green-yellow; the smooth bouquet has a mix of white peach and a touch of citrus fruit, the palate likewise focused on the fresh citrussy/peachy fruit. The malolactic influence is much less evident than in prior vintages, the oak subtle. Excellent value.   **rating:** 88
best drinking Now–2005 **best vintages** '92, '93, '94, '96, '97, '98, '99, '01 **drink with** Robe lobster • $12

Wynns Coonawarra Estate Shiraz

ŶŶŶŶ☨ 2001 Strong red-purple; ripe, aromatic plum, prune, blue berry and mulberry fruit to the bouquet lead into a palate with good depth and richness to the sweet fruit, reinforced by substantial tannins for the long haul. Good wine. **rating:** 91

best drinking 2005–2015 **best vintages** '54, '55, '62, '65, '70, '85, '86, '89, '90, '91, '93, '94, '96, '98, '01 **drink with** Spiced lamb • $18

Wynns Coonawarra Estate Cabernet Shiraz Merlot

ŶŶŶŶ☨ 2000 Full red-purple; rich dark berry, mulberry and plum fruit drives the bouquet, the palate with good depth and richness to the dark berry fruit flavours, the oak – as with the bouquet – in the background. A very good outcome for the vintage. **rating:** 91

best drinking 2005–2015 **best vintages** '86, '88, '90, '91, '92, '96 **drink with** Yearling beef • $18

Wynns Coonawarra Estate Black Label Cabernet Sauvignon

ŶŶŶŶ☨ 2000 Very good red-purple; firm, classic blackcurrant and earth varietal character in the mainstream of Coonawarra; the palate is powerful and rich, with blackberry, mulberry and blackcurrant fruit flavours held together in a strongly structured wine; plenty of tannins, and the oak is by no means overplayed. **rating:** 93

best drinking Now–2015 **best vintages** '82, '86, '88, '90, '91, '94, '95, '96, '97, '98, '99, '00 **drink with** Roast beef • $30

xanadu adelaide hills   NR

Grant's Gully Road, Clarendon, SA 5157 **region** Adelaide Hills
phone (08) 8383 5555 **fax** (08) 9322 4850 **open** Not
winemaker Natasha Mooney **production** NFP **est.** 1853
product range ($12–45 R) At the bottom Normans Encounter Bay, straight varietals coming from a blend of regions; next the Old Vine series of Grenache, Shiraz and Cabernet Sauvignon; and the flagship Chais Clarendon range of Shiraz and Cabernet Sauvignon, made only in the best years.
summary In October 2001 Xanadu Wines Limited purchased the key brands of Normans Wines, along with its Clarendon winery and vineyard, and packaged stock of premium wines. The business now trades under the name of Xanadu Wines Adelaide Hills, but many of the brands, noticeably Chais Clarendon at the top, continue.

Normans Chais Clarendon Shiraz

ŶŶŶŶ☨ 1999 Medium red-purple; ripe and smooth blackberry fruit aromas are swathed in quality oak; the rich and ripe palate has sweet blackberry fruit, dark chocolate, supple tannins, and the same quality oak of the bouquet. A blend of Barossa Valley and McLaren Vale Shiraz. **rating:** 92

best drinking 2004–2014 **best vintages** '99 **drink with** Rump steak • $45

xanadu wines   ★★★★

Boodjidup Road, Margaret River, WA 6285 **region** Margaret River
phone (08) 9757 2581 **fax** (08) 9757 3389 **open** 7 days 10–5
winemaker Jurg Muggli, Glenn Goodall **production** 100 000 cases **est.** 1977
product range ($14–70 R) Riesling, Semillon, Margaret River Show Reserve Semillon, Semillon Sauvignon Blanc, Secession Semillon Sauvignon Blanc, Chardonnay, Secession Chardonnay, Secession Rose of Cabernet, Secession Red, Shiraz, Frankland River Show Reserve Shiraz, Merlot, Secession Merlot, Cabernet Sauvignon, Lagan Estate Reserve Cabernet.
summary Xanadu, once a somewhat quirky, small family winery has reinvented itself with the arrival of substantial outside investment capital and the acquisition of the key brands of Normans Wines of South Australia. One hundred and thirty hectares of vineyard estate and much expanded winemaking facilities have been complemented by a large, open courtyard, a bar area, new cellar door and a cafe-style restaurant. Wine quality, led by outstanding Merlot, has also risen. Exports to all major markets.

Xanadu Semillon

ŶŶŶŶ 2001 Light straw-green; the clean and firm bouquet has faint nutty oak but is not (as yet) forthcoming or aromatic. The palate shows a very big wine, with the 14° alcohol quite obvious on the finish. Whole-bunch pressing, partial malolactic fermentation and barrel ageing all add to a wine very much in its own style. **rating:** 87

best drinking Now–2006 **best vintages** '96, '97, '98, '99, '00 **drink with** Richer fish dishes • $21

Xanadu Margaret River Show Reserve Semillon

▼▼▼▼ **2000** Excellent green-yellow; the bouquet is completely dominated by strong, spicy barrel-ferment oak inputs; complex oak is the driving force of the palate, and more fruit would have made a better wine. 500 cases made. **rating:** 87

best drinking Now–2007 **drink with** Marinated octopus • $35

Xanadu Semillon Sauvignon Blanc

▼▼▼▼▽ **2002** Medium yellow-green; the bouquet is complex, with an obvious touch of spicy barrel-ferment oak, the palate fruit-driven but with plenty of grass, herb and fruit salad flavours, the oak in diminuendo. **rating:** 90

best drinking Now–2005 **best vintages** '02 **drink with** Pan-fried scallops • $19

Xanadu Chardonnay

▼▼▼▼ **2001** Light to medium straw-green; a restrained bouquet with gentle cashew, fig, citrus and oak is followed by a delicate palate following the same track. Needed more fruit depth for top points, but could repay cellaring. **rating:** 87

best drinking Now–2006 **best vintages** '99, '00 **drink with** White-fleshed fish • $24

Xanadu Secession Chardonnay

▼▼▼▼▽ **2002** Light green-yellow; fresh, tangy stone fruit and citrus aromas introduce a palate with real length and life; unwooded chardonnay doesn't get much better than this; small wonder it won a gold medal at the Qantas West Australian Wine Show 2002. **rating:** 92

best drinking Now **drink with** Grilled fish • $14

Xanadu Frankland River Show Reserve Shiraz

▼▼▼▼ **2001** Medium red-purple; the moderately intense bouquet has spice and cedar, the light to medium-bodied palate lacking the expected concentration of fruit. Certainly, the wine is well made, and, certainly, it has elegance, but ultimately, this is not enough. **rating:** 86

best drinking 2004–2008 **drink with** Grilled steak • $45

Lagan Estate Reserve Cabernet

▼▼▼▼ **1998** Medium red-purple; the moderately intense bouquet has a fragrant mix of berry, spice, leaf and cedar, the palate picking up the pace with abundant fruit on entry, then equally abundant tannins towards the finish. Needs patience, but should repay it. **rating:** 89

best drinking 2005–2015 **drink with** Moroccan lamb • $70

yaldara wines   NR

Gomersal Road, Lyndoch, SA 5351 **region** Barossa Valley
phone (08) 8524 4200 **fax** (08) 8524 4678 **open** 7 days 9–5
winemaker Matt Tydeman **production** 500 000 cases **est.** 1947
product range ($10–45 R) A full range of wines under (in ascending order) the Lakewood, Earth's Portrait, Julians, and the super-premium The Farms label.
summary At the very end of 1999 Yaldara became part of the publicly listed Simeon Wines, the intention being that it (Yaldara) should become the quality flagship of the group. Despite much expenditure and the short-lived stay of at least one well known winemaker, the plan failed to deliver the expected benefits. In February 2002 McGuigan Wines made a reverse takeover for Simeon, and the various McGuigan brands will (presumably) fill the role intended for Yaldara.

yalumba   ★★★★☆

Eden Valley Road, Angaston, SA 5353 **region** Barossa Valley
phone (08) 8561 3200 **fax** (08) 8561 3393 **open** Mon–Fri 8.30–5, Sat 10–5, Sun 12–5
winemaker Brian Walsh, Alan Hoey, Louisa Rose, Peter Gambetta, Kevin Glastonbury, Natalie Fryar
production 900 000 cases **est.** 1849
product range ($6.50–120 CD) A clearly-structured portfolio arranged by price point, commencing at the bottom with Oxford Landing, then the Y series; next the Yalumba Barossa wines; then premium regional wines from the Eden Valley, Adelaide Hills, Clare Valley; Vinnovations Nebbiolo and Cienna; then at the top of the dry table wines are The Octavius Barossa Shiraz, The Signature Cabernet Sauvignon Shiraz, The Reserve Cabernet Sauvignon Shiraz; a newly added trio of Noble Pick sweet wines are rounded off with the Yalumba D sparkling wines and fortifieds.

summary Family-owned and run by Robert Hill-Smith; much of its prosperity in the late 1980s and early 1990s turned on the great success of Angas Brut in export markets, but the company has always had a commitment to quality and shown great vision in its selection of vineyard sites, new varieties and brands. It has always been a serious player at the top end of full-bodied (and full-blooded) Australian reds, and was the pioneer in the use of Stelvin screwcaps (for Pewsey Vale Riesling). While its 940 hectares of estate vineyards are largely planted to mainstream varieties, it has taken marketing ownership of Viognier. By way of postscript, tasting notes of 23 wines were written up for the 2004 database, far more than any other company. For space reasons, 6 were omitted. Exports to all major markets.

Yalumba Hand Picked Eden Valley Riesling

♥♥♥♥♡ **2002** Light to medium yellow-green; clear citrus, pear, apple and spice aromas come through on both bouquet and the attractive palate, which finishes with citrussy acidity. As yet, slightly atypical for the Eden Valley, but it may well be more lime juice flavours will develop with time in bottle. Postscript: in fact very similar to the 2000 vintage. **rating:** 93

best drinking 2005–2012 **best vintages** '00, '02 **drink with** Stuffed capsicum • $22.95

Yalumba Oxford Landing Sauvignon Blanc

♥♥♥♥ **2002** Very pale colour; clean herb and citrus aromas are followed by a very fresh and lively palate offering hints of passionfruit running through to a bright finish. Excellent value. **rating:** 87

best drinking Now **best vintages** '02 **drink with** Sugar-cured tuna • $7.95

Yalumba Eden Valley Viognier

♥♥♥♥♥ **2001** Yalumba has been on the Viognier learning curve for longer than any other producer (except for Elgee Park in the Mornington Peninsula). The smooth, enticing, seamless aromas of ripe fruit and spice flow into a palate with apricot, citrus and honey flavours which easily carry the 14.5° alcohol. A flavour bomb. **rating:** 94

best drinking Now **best vintages** '01 **drink with** Creamy pasta • $23

Yalumba The Virgilius

♥♥♥♥♡ **2001** Glowing yellow-green; the smooth, succulent and rich bouquet is as seamless as the Eden Valley varietal, the palate very powerful, intense and concentrated, but with a faintly phenolic finish. **rating:** 93

best drinking Now–2006 **best vintages** '99, '00, '01 **drink with** Pork neck • $49.95

Yalumba Antipodean Pinot Gris

♥♥♥♥ **2002** Light green-yellow; quite fragrant green apple and pear aromas lead into a similarly positive palate, with clear apple/nashi pear varietal flavours, and not too alcoholic or heavy (14° alcohol). **rating:** 87

best drinking Now–2005 **drink with** Lebanese hors d'oeuvres • $16.50

Yalumba Adelaide Hills Chardonnay

♥♥♥♥♥ **2001** Medium yellow-green; a lively, fruit-driven bouquet of citrus and nectarine is followed by an even more attractive palate with nectarine, melon, citrus and cashew flavours; precision, focus and elegance. Whole bunch-pressed, indigenous yeast fermentation and 11 months in new French oak. **rating:** 94

best drinking Now–2006 **best vintages** '01 **drink with** Sweetbreads • $30

Jansz Premium

♥♥♥♥♡ **NV** Light to medium yellow-green; the bouquet is clean, but quite complex, with some bready/yeasty aromas. The palate is lively, with a mix of citrus, white peach and pear; very good balance and length. A blend of cool-grown material from Tasmania, Victoria and South Australia. **rating:** 91

best drinking Now–2006 **drink with** Aperitif • $21.95

Yalumba Eden Valley Noble Pick Botrytis Riesling

♥♥♥♥♡ **2001** Glowing yellow-green; the clean bouquet has moderately intense lime juice aromas, the palate with fresh limey fruit, not particularly luscious, but with well-balanced acidity. More in auslese than beerenauslese style. **rating:** 91

best drinking Now–2007 **best vintages** '99, '01 **drink with** Tarte Tatin • $24.95

Yalumba Eden Valley Noble Pick Botrytis Semillon

♥♥♥♥♡ **2000** Golden orange; the soft bouquet offers peach, banana and cumquat, the complex palate tracking the bouquet and nicely tied off with good acidity. Drink asap. **rating:** 90

best drinking Now **drink with** Rich cream-based desserts • $24.95

Yalumba Coonawarra Shiraz

▼▼▼▼ **2000** Medium red-purple; a traditional, moderately intense blend of blackberry, black cherry, vanilla and earth aromas, then sweet berry/cherry fruit on the palate, complexed by a dash of savoury tannins. **rating:** 89

best drinking 2004–2010 **drink with** Irish stew • $24.95

Yalumba Octavius Shiraz

▼▼▼▼▽ **1998** Medium to full red-purple; a highly scented bouquet with a mix of ripe fruit and lashings of new oak, the palate in similar mode exuding massive fruit, oak and tannins. **rating:** 91

best drinking 2008–2018 **best vintages** '88, '90, '92, '93, '95, '96, '98 **drink with** The biggest steak imaginable • $89.95

Yalumba Barossa Valley Shiraz Viognier

▼▼▼▼▽ **1999** Medium red-purple; there are interesting spicy, savoury overtones to the red fruit of the bouquet, with similar spicy/savoury/chocolatey fruit on entrance to the palate, followed by a long finish with fine tannins. The influence of the Viognier is obvious throughout. **rating:** 93

best drinking 2004–2009 **best vintages** '98, '99 **drink with** Milk-fed lamb • $28.95

Yalumba Antipodean Petit Verdot

▼▼▼▼ **2001** Solid red-purple; moderately intense earthy black fruit aromas are followed by a wine with convincing structure; the black fruit flavours have fine, savoury tannins running throughout from start to finish. **rating:** 86

best drinking 2004–2007 **drink with** Barbecued beef • $16.50

Yalumba Coonawarra Merlot

▼▼▼▼▽ **2000** Medium red-purple; rich, ripe, redcurrant and raspberry fruit on the bouquet lead into a full-throated palate with abundant sweet, ripe fruit, subtle oak and soft tannins. Yet another face of Australian Merlot. **rating:** 90

best drinking 2004–2010 **drink with** Loin of lamb • $24.95

Yalumba Y Series Merlot

▼▼▼▼ **2002** Youthful, crimson purple; the light, clean bouquet has savoury redcurrant aromas proclaiming its varietal base; the palate has good texture, with some clever fruit handling to give sweetness to the back palate; comes together very well. **rating:** 86

best drinking Now–2005 **drink with** Anything you like • $9.00

Yalumba Tri-Centenary Grenache

▼▼▼▼ **2001** Medium red-purple; light, jammy/minty aromas are in the typical Yalumba style, but the palate has a greater depth of berry fruit and structure, which is all for the better. **rating:** 87

best drinking Now–2005 **drink with** Chinese stir-fried beef with Hoi Sin sauce • $28.95

Yalumba Signature Cabernet Shiraz

▼▼▼▼▼ **1998** Ross White. Medium red-purple; a wonderfully fragrant bouquet of raspberry, cassis and quality oak is followed by a palate which is elegant, but with a rich core of ripe, not jammy, fruit; good management of extract throughout. One of the best in the Signature range to date. **rating:** 94

best drinking 2005–2015 **best vintages** '62, '66, '75, '81, '85, '88, '90, '91, '92, '93, '95, '96, '97, '98 **drink with** Rare roast beef • $34.95

🐃 yalumba the menzies (coonawarra) ★★★☆

Riddoch Highway, Coonawarra, SA 5263 **region** Coonawarra
phone (08) 8737 3603 **fax** (08) 8737 3604 **open** 7 days 10–4.30
winemaker Kevin Glastonbury, Louisa Rose, Peter Gambetta **production** 4250 cases **est.** 2002
product range ($17.50–36.95 CD) The Menzies Cabernet Sauvignon; Mawson's range of Coonawarra Shiraz, Coonawarra Cabernet Franc, Coonawarra Cabernet Sauvignon Shiraz Merlot; and Smith & Hooper Wrattonbully range of Merlot, Cabernet Sauvignon Merlot.
summary Like many South Australian companies, Yalumba had been buying grapes from Coonawarra and elsewhere in the Limestone Coast Zone long before it became a landowner there. When it made the first vintage of The Menzies Cabernet Sauvignon in 1987, the grapes were contract-grown. In 1993 it purchased the 20-hectare vineyard which had provided the grapes outright, and a year later added a nearby 16-hectare block. Together, these vineyards now have 22 hectares of cabernet sauvignon and 4 hectares each of merlot and shiraz. The next step was the establishment of 82 hectares of vineyard in the Wrattonbully region, led by 34 hectares of

cabernet sauvignon, the remainder equally split between shiraz and merlot. The third step was to build The Menzies Wine Room and Vineyard on the first property acquired – named Menzies Vineyard – and to offer the full range of Limestone Coast wines through this striking rammed-earth tasting and function centre.

Smith & Hooper Limited Edition Merlot

ŸŸŸŸŸ **2000** Medium to full red-purple; a rich and complex bouquet with a range of red and dark small berry and cherry fruits plus well handled oak on the bouquet, then a palate built around a luscious core of sweet fruit and spice, and a long, lingering savoury finish supported by fine, silky tannins. Excellent wine. Ultra deluxe packaging which makes no mention of Yalumba. **rating: 93**

best drinking 2004–2014 **best vintages** '00 **drink with** Braised veal • $36.95

Yalumba Mawson's

ŸŸŸŸ **2000** Medium red-purple; ripe blackcurrant, plum and chocolate aromas are followed by a powerful palate with abundant tannins and extract, the oak somewhere in the background. A blend of Cabernet Sauvignon, Shiraz and Merlot in need of patience. **rating: 87**

best drinking 2005–2015 **best vintages** '98 **drink with** Barbecued steak • $18

Smith & Hooper Cabernet Sauvignon Merlot

ŸŸŸŸ **2000** Medium red-purple; clean blackberry, raspberry and mint aromas allied with a touch of oak spice lead into a palate with plenty of rich fruit and extract; vanilla oak and tannins round up a bargain-priced wine. **rating: 88**

best drinking Now–2008 **drink with** Lamb cutlets • $17.50

Yalumba The Menzies Cabernet Sauvignon

ŸŸŸŸ **1999** Medium red-purple; aromas of earth, chocolate and spice are more or less precisely reflected in the palate, with its mix of spice, chocolate and savoury blackberry fruit. **rating: 86**

best drinking 2004–2008 **best vintages** '90, '91, '94, '96, '98 **drink with** Topside steak • $35.95

yandoit hill vineyard ★★★

Nevens Road, Yandoit Creek, Vic 3461 **region** Bendigo
phone (03) 9379 1763 **fax** (03) 9379 1763 **open** By appointment (special open days for mail list customers)
winemaker Colin Mitchell **production** 300 cases **est.** 1988
product range ($19–25 CD) Arneis, Merlot, Cabernets, Nebbiolo Cabernet Sauvignon.
summary Colin and Rosa Mitchell commenced the development of Yandoit Hill with the first plantings in 1988 with merlot, and a little under a hectare each of cabernet franc and cabernet sauvignon followed by 0.5 hectare each of arneis (the first planting in Australia), and nebbiolo in 1995. The vineyard is situated 20 kilometres north of Daylesford, roughly halfway from Ballarat to Bendigo and, although situated on the north-facing slope of Yandoit Hill, is in an uncompromisingly cool climate. Colin Mitchell has already discovered that nebbiolo won't ripen to his satisfaction in most years but in vintages like 1988 makes a successful wine.

yangarra park ★★★☆

Kangarilla Road, McLaren Vale, SA 5171 **region** McLaren Vale
phone (08) 8383 7459 **fax** (08) 8383 7518 **open** By appointment
winemaker Peter Fraser **production** 100 000 cases **est.** 2000
product range ($14–28 R) Chardonnay, Shiraz, Merlot and Cabernet Sauvignon; Appellation Series McLaren Vale Shiraz, McLaren Vale Merlot, Coonawarra Cabernet Sauvignon.
summary This is the Australian operation of Kendall Jackson, one of the leading premium wine producers in California. In December 2000 Kendall Jackson acquired the 172-hectare Eringa Park vineyard from Normans Wines, 97 hectares are under vine, the oldest dating back to 1923. The name change to Yangarra Park provides the key estate base for the operation, but it intends to also buy grapes from all of the premium wine-growing regions in southeast Australia with the philosophy that regional blending can enhance both complexity and quality. It's early days yet; some better wines are in the pipeline. Exports to the US, the UK and Europe.

Yangarra Park Appellation Series McLaren Vale Shiraz

ŸŸŸŸ **2001** Medium to full red-purple; there is abundant ripe and sweet raspberry and blackberry fruit on the bouquet, backed by subtle French oak; a rich, full-bodied palate with lots of extract, adding coffee, vanilla and mocha to the generous berry fruit. **rating: 88**

best drinking 2005–2010 **drink with** Braised beef • $28

Yangarra Park Appellation Series McLaren Vale Merlot

YYYY 2001 Medium to full red-purple; quite plush, lush red fruit aromas are a sure sign of the plush, ripe, voluptuous fruit-driven palate. A very nice wine, but not particularly varietal. **rating:** 87

best drinking Now–2008 **drink with** Rack of lamb • $28

Yangarra Park Appellation Series Coonawarra Cabernet Sauvignon

YYYY 2001 Bright purple-red; the bouquet ranges through blackberry, blackcurrant, chocolate and earth, the medium-bodied palate fractionally angular in its texture and structure. **rating:** 86

best drinking 2004–2009 **drink with** Lamb casserole • $28

yanmah ridge   NR

Yanmah Road, Manjimup, WA 6258 **region** Manjimup
phone (08) 9772 1301 **fax** (08) 9772 1501 **open** By appointment
winemaker Peter Nicholas, John Wade (Consultant) **production** 3500 cases **est.** 1987
product range ($12.99–28 ML) Sauvignon Blanc, Chardonnay, Karrimont (Sparkling), Merlot, Reserve Merlot, Cabernet Merlot; Fishermans second label includes White, Fizz and Red.
summary Peter and Sallyann Nicholas have established 26 hectares of vineyards planted on elevated, north-facing slopes, with semillon, sauvignon blanc, chardonnay, pinot noir, sangiovese, merlot, cabernet franc and cabernet sauvignon. The property on which the vineyard is planted was identified by Peter Nicholas in 1986 as 'the perfect location' as the outcome of a study of grape growing regions in Western Australia. The project was the last requirement for Nicholas to complete his winemaking degree at Roseworthy Agricultural College. Their viticulture is environmentally friendly, with no residual herbicides or chemical pesticides. Although a new winery was built on-site in time for the 2001 vintage, the lion's share of the annual production is still sold (as grapes or wine) to other producers. Wholesale distribution through Working Wine, Victoria, Lionel Samson, Western Australia and Simsed Agencies, New South Wales and Queensland. Exports to England, Canada and Hong Kong.

yarrabank   ★★★★☆

38 Melba Highway, Yarra Glen, Vic 3775 **region** Yarra Valley
phone (03) 9730 1107 **fax** (03) 9739 0135 **open** 7 days 10–5
winemaker Claude Thibaut, Tom Carson, Darren Rathbone **production** 2000 cases **est.** 1993
product range ($30–35 CD) Cuvee, Creme de Cuvee, Brut Cuvee.
summary The 1997 vintage saw the opening of the majestic new winery established as part of a joint venture between the French Champagne house Devaux and Yering Station, and which adds another major dimension to the Yarra Valley. Until 1997 the Yarrabank Cuvee Brut was made under Claude Thibaut's direction at Domaine Chandon, but thereafter the entire operation has been conducted at Yarrabank. Four hectares of dedicated 'estate' vineyards have been established at Yering Station; the balance of the intake comes from other growers in the Yarra Valley and southern Victoria. Wine quality has been quite outstanding, the wines having a delicacy unmatched by any other Australian sparkling wines.

yarra brook estate   NR

Yarraview Road, Yarra Glen, Vic 3775 **region** Yarra Valley
phone (03) 9763 7066 **fax** (03) 9763 8757 **open** By appointment
winemaker Martin Williams MW (Contract) **production** 2000 cases **est.** 1997
product range ($15 CD) Chardonnay, Pinot Noir, Shiraz, Cabernet Sauvignon.
summary Beginning in 1997, Chris Dhar has established 26 hectares of vines, the lion's share being pinot noir (10.4 ha) and chardonnay (6.8 ha), the remainder equally shared between sauvignon blanc, merlot, shiraz and cabernet sauvignon. Most of the grapes are sold, but part of the production is made by Martin Williams MW. The prices ex the mail list are very reasonable, thanks to the exemption from WET for small wineries selling direct.

yarra burn   ★★★★

Settlement Road, Yarra Junction, Vic 3797 **region** Yarra Valley
phone (03) 5967 1428 **fax** (03) 5967 1146 **open** 7 days 10–5
winemaker Glenn James, Ed Carr, Stephen Pannell **production** 28 000 cases **est.** 1975
product range ($18–45.99 R) Sauvignon Blanc Semillon, Chardonnay, Pinot Noir, Chardonnay Pinot Noir, Shiraz, Cabernet Sauvignon, Sparkling Pinot, Chardonnay Pinot; Bastard Hill Chardonnay, Bastard Hill Pinot Noir.

summary Acquired by BRL Hardy in 1995 and, for the time being, the headquarters of Hardys' very substantial Yarra Valley operations, the latter centring on the large production from its Hoddles Creek vineyards. The new brand direction has largely taken shape. Care needs to be taken in reading the back labels of the wines other the Bastard Hill duo, for the majority are regional blends, albeit with a substantial Yarra Valley component. Exports to the UK and the US.

Yarra Burn Sauvignon Blanc Semillon

♥♥♥♥♡ 2002 Light green-yellow; clean and fresh, opening with herbs and then moving more to tropical; the medium-bodied palate has a lively mix of herb and lemon flavours; long, clean finish. No regional claim is made for the wine.   **rating:** 93

best drinking Now–2005 **best vintages** '02 **drink with** Light seafood • $17.99

Yarra Burn Chardonnay

♥♥♥♥ 2001 Light to medium yellow-green; discreet citrus and melon aromas emerge alongside subtle oak; the light to medium-bodied palate is distinctly citrussy/apply.   **rating:** 87

best drinking Now–2005 **best vintages** '97, '98, '00 **drink with** Grilled scampi • $19.99

Yarra Burn Bastard Hill Chardonnay

♥♥♥♥♡ 1998 Amazing, bright, light green-yellow; intense grapefruit, melon and barrel-ferment oak is followed by a still-youthful, long and lingering palate, focused and fruit-driven. Will seemingly live forever.   **rating:** 92

best drinking Now–2008 **best vintages** '95, '97, '98 **drink with** Richly sauced fish • $45.99

Yarra Burn Pinot Noir Chardonnay

♥♥♥♥♡ 2000 Light straw-green; a crisp, clean and fragrant bouquet of citrus and nectarine leads into a lively, fresh and well-balanced palate, which is quite delicate yet flavoursome and intense, doubtless due to the quality of the base material coming predominantly from the high altitude Hoddles Creek Vineyard in the Yarra Valley. Incidentally, there is a touch of Pinot Meunier in the blend.   **rating:** 92

best drinking Now–2006 **best vintages** '96, '97, '98, '99 **drink with** Sunshine • $23.99

Yarra Burn Pinot Noir

♥♥♥♥ 2001 Bright red-purple; the moderately intense bouquet has a mix of cherry, raspberry and strawberry with a savoury underlay. While the palate is not especially complex, it has good length, and will develop over the next few years.   **rating:** 89

best drinking Now–2006 **best vintages** '97, '00 **drink with** Ragout of venison • $23.99

Yarra Burn Shiraz

♥♥♥♥ 2000 Medium purple-red; strong ripe, juicy berry aromas are accompanied by controlled oak, moving into a very powerful palate where abrasive edges need to soften. A blend of Heathcote, Yarra Valley and Grampians material spending 18 months in French oak.   **rating:** 86

best drinking 2005–2010 **best vintages** '99 **drink with** Braised beef • $24

Yarra Burn Cabernet Sauvignon

♥♥♥♥ 2000 Medium red-purple; the bouquet has spicy overtones to blackberry fruit and balanced oak; the firm palate ranges through blackberry, earth and chocolate flavours, all helped by attractive oak. The back label is of no help in determining the region or regions of the wine.   **rating:** 88

best drinking 2004–2009 **best vintages** '98 **drink with** Marinated beef • $23.99

yarra edge   ★★★☆

PO Box 390, Yarra Glen, Vic 3775 **region** Yarra Valley
phone (03) 9730 1107 **fax** (03) 9739 0135 **open** At Yering Station, 7 days 10–5
winemaker Tom Carson, Darren Rathbone **production** 2000 cases **est.** 1984
product range ($30 CD) Chardonnay, Pinot Noir, Single Vineyard (Bordeaux blend).
summary Now leased to Yering Station, which makes the wines but continues to use the Yarra Edge brand for grapes from this estate. Tom Carson, Yering Station winemaker, was briefly winemaker/manager at Yarra Edge and knows the property intimately, so the rich style can be expected to continue.

Yarra Edge Chardonnay

♥♥♥♥ 2001 Medium yellow-green; pronounced charry/nutty barrel-ferment inputs on the bouquet, with the oak still evident and, indeed, dominant on the palate; nonetheless, there is good length to the nectarine fruit.   **rating:** 89

best drinking Now–2006 **best vintages** '92, '93, '94, '97, '98 **drink with** Smoked salmon pasta • $30

Yarra Edge Pinot Noir

ŦŦŦŦŸ **2001** Medium red-purple; fresh, clean, plummy aromas with a light touch of oak are followed by a fleshy and rich palate, with plenty of depth driven by ripe fruit. **rating:** 91

best drinking Now–2006 **best vintages** '01 **drink with** Wild mushroom risotto • $30

Yarra Edge Single Vineyard

ŦŦŦŦ **1998** Medium red-purple; the bouquet offers slightly simple red berry fruit and gentle oak, the light to medium-bodied palate with a distinctly savoury finish. A blend of Cabernet Sauvignon, Merlot, Malbec and Cabernet Franc. **rating:** 86

best drinking Now–2007 **drink with** Diced lamb • $30

yarraman estate ★★★

Yarraman Road, Wybong, NSW 2333 **region** Upper Hunter Valley
phone (02) 6547 8118 **fax** (02) 6547 8039 **open** 7 days 10–5
winemaker Angus Campbell **production** 25 000 cases **est.** 1967
product range ($15–28 R) Classic Hunter Series of Semillon, Chardonnay, Shiraz, Merlot; Black Cypress Series of Gewurztraminer, Chardonnay, Shiraz, Chambourcin, Cabernet Shiraz.
summary Ownership changes have come thick and fast at Yarraman Estate; following its recent acquisition by a small group of Sydney businessmen, and the appointment of Angus Campbell as winemaker/general manager and Richard Winchester as sales and marketing manager it is to be hoped a period of stability will follow. Exports to the UK and Canada.

Yarraman Estate Chardonnay

ŦŦŦŸ **2000** Developed yellow; quite complex bottle-developed characters are allied with peach on the bouquet; there is abundant, developed, peachy/buttery flavour, although the wine is perilously close to its use-by date. **rating:** 84

best drinking Now **drink with** Chicken nuggets • $25

Yarraman Estate Shiraz

ŦŦŦŦ **2000** Light to medium red-purple; clean cherry, plum, berry aromas are logically followed by a clean, soft cherry/berry palate, minimal oak, ripe tannins helping provide good balance. **rating:** 86

best drinking Now–2006 **drink with** Grilled yearling steak • $28

Yarraman Estate Merlot

ŦŦŦŦ **2000** Light to medium red-purple; spice, red berry, herb and olive aromas are followed by a light to medium-bodied palate, with clean, raspberry/red berry fruit and fine tannins. **rating:** 85

best drinking 2004–2008 **drink with** Milk-fed lamb • $28

Barrington Estate Pencil Pine Chambourcin

ŦŦŦŦ **2001** Medium purple-red; the light, spicy, savoury, plummy bouquet is followed by a palate with soft plummy fruit, a dash of dark chocolate and a soft finish. The region of origin is South East Australia, and the wine is said to come from old vines, which at the very least proves that old in this varietal context has a very elastic meaning. **rating:** 85

best drinking Now **drink with** Beef pie • $16

✿ yarrambat estate vineyard ★★★★☆

45 Laurie Street, Yarrambat, Vic 3091 (postal) **region** Yarra Valley
phone (03) 9717 3710 **fax** (03) 9717 3712 **open** Not
winemaker John Ellis (Contract) **production** 1500 cases **est.** 1995
product range ($25–35 ML) Chardonnay, Pinot Noir, Merlot Cabernet, Cabernet Sauvignon.
summary Ivan McQuilkin has a little over 2.6 hectares of chardonnay, pinot noir, cabernet sauvignon and merlot on his vineyard in the northwestern corner of the Yarra Valley, not far from the Plenty River which joins the Yarra River near Melbourne. The vineyard has been planted on an easterly slope, with north-south row orientation. It was in fact established by Hayden Gregson, from whom Ivan McQuilkin purchased the vineyard in 1997, and who continues to assist in the viticulture. In the first 2 years of production (1998 and 1999) the grapes were sold to Yering Station, but since that time the grapes have been vinified under the Yarrambat Estate label. It is very much an alternative occupation for McQuilkin, whose principal activity is as an international taxation consultant to expatriate employees. While the decision to make the wine was at least in part triggered by falling grape prices, hindsight proves it to have been a good one, because the red wines, in

particular, are outstanding. There are no cellar-door sales; the conditions of the licence are that wine sales can only take place by mail order or internet (www.yarrambat-estate.com), in the same fashion as Studley Park.

Yarrambat Estate Chardonnay

▼▼▼▼ 2001 Light to medium yellow-green; the bouquet has light, citrus melon fruit and smoky, slightly raw, oak, a combination which continues on the elegant light-bodied (in terms of fruit) palate, where the oak is somewhat aggressive. **rating: 86**

best drinking Now–2005 drink with Seared tuna • $25

Yarrambat Estate Pinot Noir

▼▼▼▼▽ 2001 Youthful red-purple, bright and clear; the clean bouquet offers gentle plum, cherry and spice, the oak subtle. The firm palate is built around dark cherry fruit, still softening and unfolding, but with considerable intensity. **rating: 92**

best drinking 2004–2008 best vintages '00, '01 drink with Barbecued quail • $30

Yarrambat Estate Merlot Cabernet

▼▼▼▼▽ 2000 Medium to full red-purple, bright and clear; the bouquet has voluminous, sweet red and blackcurrant fruit supported by well-handled oak; the palate is still very young, with intense, concentrated fruit and a lingering finish. Needs some years to soften. **rating: 92**

best drinking 2005–2012 best vintages '00 drink with Kangaroo fillet • $35

Yarrambat Estate Cabernet Sauvignon

▼▼▼▼▽ 2000 Bright purple-red; the clean and fresh bouquet has a classic mix of redcurrant, blackcurrant and cassis, fruit which comes through with equal clarity on the palate. In common with all of the Yarrambat wines, the style is youthful and guaranteeing repayment for those who are patient. **rating: 90**

best drinking 2005–2015 best vintages '00 drink with Lamb casserole • $35

yarra ridge ★★★☆

Glenview Road, Yarra Glen, Vic 3755 **region** Yarra Valley
phone (03) 9730 1022 **fax** (03) 9730 1131 **open** 7 days 10–5
winemaker Matt Steel **production** 45 000 cases **est.** 1983
product range ($16–42 R) Sauvignon Blanc, Chardonnay, Pinot Noir, Reserve Pinot Noir, Achilles Heel Pinot Noir, Shiraz, Reserve Shiraz, Merlot, Cabernet Sauvignon, Reserve Cabernet Sauvignon; Mount Tanglefoot has been introduced as a second range expressly made from grapes grown in regions other than the Yarra Valley.
summary Under the sole ownership and control of Beringer Blass, with a winery which is strained to its limits. Recent vineyard plantings in the Yarra Valley, and continued purchasing of Yarra Valley grapes, mean that the majority of the wines will continue to be Yarra Valley-sourced. That said, they have a commercial veneer, reliable rather than exciting.

Yarra Ridge Sauvignon Blanc

▼▼▼▼ 2002 Light straw-green; a soft bouquet with some tropical and passionfruit aromas which also make their mark on the plentiful, soft flavour of the palate. Becomes more focused and tight on the finish. **rating: 88**

best drinking Now drink with Fish and chips • $18

Yarra Ridge Chardonnay

▼▼▼▼ 2001 Pale green-yellow; the moderately intense bouquet offers well-balanced and integrated oak alongside light melon and stone fruit aromas; the palate lightens off significantly towards the finish, but may build a little more with a year or two in bottle. **rating: 86**

best drinking Now–2005 best vintages '90, '92, '93, '94, '96 drink with Scallops, mussels • $19

Yarra Ridge Pinot Noir

▼▼▼▼ 2001 Light to medium red-purple; both the bouquet and palate offer a mix of spice, forest, cherry and strawberry, the palate, however, firm rather than silky. **rating: 86**

best drinking Now best vintages '91, '92, '93, '96, '00 drink with Poultry • $20

Yarra Ridge Merlot

▼▼▼▼ 2000 Medium red-purple; the moderately intense bouquet ranges through a mix of spicy/savoury/earthy aromas on the one hand, and blackcurrant on the other; the light to medium-bodied palate is nicely rounded and soft. **rating: 87**

best drinking Now–2007 best vintages '95, '97 drink with Rack of veal • $20

Yarra Ridge Cabernet Sauvignon

▼▼▼▼♡ **2000** Bright, full red-purple; the bouquet has blackberry fruit with touches of anise and earth; the medium-bodied, smooth and supple palate has ripe red and black fruit flavours supported by subtle oak. **rating:** 90

best drinking 2004–2010 **best vintages** '00 **drink with** Rolled shoulder of lamb • $20

yarra track wines ★★★☆

518 Old Healesville Road, Yarra Glen, Vic 3775 **region** Yarra Valley

phone (03) 9730 1349 **fax** (03) 9730 1910 **open** Weekends and public holidays 10–5.30, most weekdays **winemaker** Martin Williams MW (Contract) **production** 800 cases **est.** 1989

product range ($24–26 CD) Chardonnay, Pinot Noir.

summary Jim and Diana Viggers began the establishment of their vineyard back in 1989; it now has 3.1 hectares of chardonnay and 3.4 hectares of pinot noir. The Viggers have chosen very competent winemaker (Martin Williams from 1999) and intend to increase wine production progressively while selling part of the grape production in the meantime. The wine is sold only through cellar door and through local restaurants.

yarra vale NR

Paynes Road, Seville, Vic 3139 **region** Yarra Valley

phone (03) 9735 1819 **fax** (03) 9737 6565 **open** Not

winemaker Domenic Bucci **production** 1500 cases **est.** 1982

product range ($13–26 R) Chardonnay, Rose, Merlot, Cabernet Sauvignon.

summary This is the second time around for Domenic Bucci, who built the first stage of what is now Eyton-on-Yarra before being compelled to sell the business in the hard times of the early 1990s. He has established 2 hectares of cabernet sauvignon and 0.5 hectare of merlot, supplemented by chardonnay which is supplied in return for his winemaking services to the grower. The wines have retail distribution in Melbourne through Sullivan Wine Agencies and exports via Rubins Productions.

🐌 yarra valley gateway estate NR

669 Maroondah Highway, Coldstream, Vic 3770 **region** Yarra Valley

phone (03) 9739 1184 **fax** (03) 9739 1184 **open** 7 days 9–5

winemaker Matt Aldridge (Contract) **production** 1200 cases **est.** 1993

product range ($19–22 R) Sauvignon Blanc, Chardonnay, Pinot Noir.

summary Rod Spurling extended his successful hydroponic tomato growing business by the planting of 6 hectares of sauvignon blanc, chardonnay and pinot noir in 1993. It is part of new grouping of so-called Micro Masters which have begun business in the Yarra Valley over the past few years.

yarra valley hills ★★★☆

c/- Dromana Estate, Harrison's Road and Bittern–Dromana Road, Dromana, Vic 3936 **region** Yarra Valley

phone (03) 5987 3177 **fax** (03) 5987 3977 **open** Not

winemaker Garry Crittenden, Rollo Crittenden **production** 10 000 cases **est.** 1989

product range ($17.50–21 CD) Sauvignon Blanc, Chardonnay, Pinot Noir, Cabernet Sauvignon.

summary The business of Yarra Valley Hills was acquired by Dromana Estate in 2000. Dromana has kept the Yarra Valley Hills brand, but sold the winery to a syndicate headed by Martin Williams, who will use it to both provide custom crush and make facilities for other Yarra Valley wineries, and (in the case of Martin Williams) to make his own Metier brand.

Yarra Valley Hills Sauvignon Blanc

▼▼▼▼ **2002** Light straw-green; the firm bouquet is primarily mineral, with touches of grass and herb; while uncompromisingly light bodied, the palate is quite fresh and well balanced, with a degree of intensity. **rating:** 87

best drinking Now **drink with** Fresh crab • $17

Yarra Valley Hills Chardonnay

▼▼▼▼♡ **2001** Medium yellow-green; complex smoky barrel-ferment overtones to the fig, cashew and melon of the bouquet are followed by a palate where fruit and malolactic influences (rather than oak) come more to the forefront; harmonious and well-made. **rating:** 91

best drinking Now–2006 **best vintages** '93, '94, '96, '01 **drink with** Crab, lobster • $19

Yarra Valley Hills Warranwood Pinot Noir

▼▼▼▼ **2001** Exceptionally deep red-purple; a powerful, concentrated bouquet with dark plum prominent is followed by a palate which simply expands on the bouquet, a huge wine, over-extracted and tannic, but very interesting. Who knows where it will be in 10 years. **rating:** 85

best drinking 2005–2012 **drink with** Leave it in the cellar • $20

yarra yarra ★★★★★

239 Hunts Lane, Steels Creek, Vic 3775 **region** Yarra Valley
phone (03) 5965 2380 **fax** (03) 5965 2086 **open** By appointment
winemaker Ian Maclean **production** NFP **est.** 1979
product range ($30–60 CD) Semillon Sauvignon Blanc, Merlot, Syrah, Cabernets, The Yarra Yarra (previously Reserve Cabernet Sauvignon).
summary Notwithstanding its production, the wines of Yarra Yarra have found their way onto a veritable who's who listing of Melbourne's best restaurants. This has encouraged Ian Maclean to increase the estate plantings from 2 hectares to over 7 hectares during the 1996 and 1997 seasons. The demand for the beautifully crafted wines continued to exceed supply, so the Macleans have planted yet more vines and increased winery capacity. Exports to the UK and Singapore.

Yarra Yarra Semillon Sauvignon Blanc

▼▼▼▼▼ **2000** Glowing yellow-green; a rich, spotlessly clean, complex weaving of fruit and oak (in that order) on the bouquet leads into an ultra-rich palate with notes of honey and peach; seamless, not phenolic, and good length. **rating:** 94

best drinking Now–2008 **best vintages** '97, '99, '00 **drink with** Wiener schnitzel • $35

Yarra Yarra Syrah

▼▼▼▼▽ **2001** Medium to full red-purple; fragrant spice and blackberry fruit with some French oak in the background are followed by a medium to full-bodied palate, with supple, mouthfilling fruit, ripe tannins and positive but harmonious oak. Ninety-eight per cent Shiraz and 2 per cent Viognier; 40 per cent new French oak. **rating:** 92

best drinking 2005–2012 **best vintages** '01 **drink with** Game pie • $40

Yarra Yarra Cabernets

▼▼▼▼▽ **2000** Excellent, bright red-purple; the clean, moderately intense bouquet has blackcurrant, cedar and a hint of mint; the fresh, focused and elegant palate turns around bright, black and redcurrant fruit; fine tannins, and good balance. A temperate 12.5° alcohol is a sheer pleasure. A blend of 77 per cent Cabernet Sauvignon, 13 per cent Cabernet Franc and 10 per cent Merlot. **rating:** 93

best drinking 2005–2010 **best vintages** '84, '86, '89, '90, '92, '95, '97, '00 **drink with** Osso buco • $45

The Yarra Yarra

▼▼▼▼▼ **2000** Medium to full red-purple; complex and rich black fruits with excellent, cedary French oak on the bouquet lead into a palate with blackcurrant and bitter chocolate flavours in abundance; excellent depth and texture; noticeably ripe tannins and a great aftertaste. A blend of 83 per cent Cabernet Sauvignon, 11 per cent Merlot and 6 per cent Cabernet Franc, formerly called Reserve Cabernet Sauvignon. **rating:** 96

best drinking 2006–2016 **best vintages** '97, '99, '00 **drink with** Braised beef • $60

yarra yering ★★★★★

Briarty Road, Coldstream, Vic 3770 (postal) **region** Yarra Valley
phone (03) 5964 9267 **fax** (03) 5964 9239 **open** Not open in 2002, usually first Saturday in May
winemaker Bailey Carrodus **est.** 1969
product range Dry White No 1 (Sauvignon Blanc Semillon), Chardonnay, Pinot Noir, Dry Red No 1 (Bordeaux-blend), Dry Red No 2 (Rhône-blend), Merlot (tiny quantities at $100 a bottle), Underhill Shiraz, Underhill 3 Year Cask Shiraz, Portsorts. The portfolio continues to expand, with Dry Red No. 3, Sangiovese and Viognier all making an appearance from the 1998 and/or '99 vintages.
summary Dr Bailey Carrodus makes extremely powerful, occasionally idiosyncratic wines from his 30-year-old, low-yielding unirrigated vineyards. Both red and white wines have an exceptional depth of flavour and richness, although my preference for what I believe to be his great red wines is well known. As he has expanded the size of his vineyards, so has the range of wines become ever more eclectic, none more so than the only Vintage Port being produced in the Yarra Valley. The wines are exported to the UK, the US, Switzerland, Germany, Hong Kong, Japan, Malaysia and Singapore.

yass valley wines NR

5 Crisps Lane, Murrumbateman, NSW 2582 **region** Canberra District
phone (02) 6227 5592 **fax** (02) 6227 5592 **open** Wed–Sun and public holidays 11–5, or by appointment
winemaker Michael Withers **production** 400 cases **est.** 1978
product range ($10–22 CD) Riesling, Semillon, Allegro (white blend), Chardonnay Semillon, Shiraz, Barbera, Merlot.
summary Michael Withers and Anne Hillier purchased Yass Valley in January 1991 and have subsequently rehabilitated the existing run-down vineyards and extended the plantings. Mick Withers is a chemist by profession and has completed a Wine Science degree at Charles Sturt University; Anne is a registered psychologist and has completed a Viticulture diploma at Charles Sturt. Crisps Lane Cafe is open weekends and public holidays from 11 am to 5 pm, with an emphasis on local produce. No recent tastings.

yaxley estate ★★★★

31 Dransfield Road, Copping, Tas 7174 **region** Southern Tasmania
phone (03) 6253 5222 **fax** (03) 6253 5222 **open** 7 days 10–6.30
winemaker Andrew Hood (Contract) **production** 330 cases **est.** 1991
product range ($19.80–25 CD) Sauvignon Blanc, Pinot Gris, Chardonnay, Pinot Noir.
summary While Yaxley Estate was established back in 1991, it was not until 1998 that it offered each of the four wines from its vineyard plantings, which total just under 2 hectares. Once again, the small batch handling skills (and patience) of contract-winemaker Andrew Hood have made the venture possible.

Yaxley Estate Pinot Noir

TTTTY **2001** Medium to full red, the purple starting to diminish; the complex bouquet with ripe plum, spice and forest aromas; the palate is undoubtedly from the big end of town, but has abundant flavour and potential style. Absolutely in the groove of the Yaxley style.　　　　　　　　　　　　　　　**rating: 93**

best drinking Now–2008 **best vintages** '00, '01 **drink with** Rare roast squab • $25

yellowglen ★★★☆

Whites Road, Smythesdale, Vic 3351 **region** Ballarat
phone (03) 5342 8617 **fax** (03) 5333 7102 **open** Mon–Fri 10–5, weekends 11–5
winemaker Charles Hargrave **production** 420 000 cases **est.** 1975
product range ($11–32 R) Grand Cuvee range of Pinot Noir Chardonnay, Brut Cremant, Brut Rose, Pinot Noir; Premium range of Vintage Brut, Y Premium, Y Sparkling Burgundy, Cuvee Victoria; also Yellow and Red.
summary Just as the overall quality of Australian sparkling wine has improved out of all recognition over the past 15 years, so has that of Yellowglen. Initially the quality lift was apparent at the top end of the range but now extends right to the non-vintage commercial releases.

Yellowglen Aged Release

TTTT **1999** Very pale straw-green, and strong mousse; the fragrant and lively bouquet has a mix of spice and citrus, the fine, very delicate and crisp palate with good length. The wine spent 30 months on lees, and is a blend of Pinot Noir, Chardonnay and a touch of Pinot Meunier.　　　　　　　　　　　　　　　**rating: 88**

best drinking Now–2005 **drink with** Oysters • $22

Yellowglen Vintage Cuvee Victoria

TTTTY **1999** Light green-straw, with strong mousse; the bouquet has abundant character, with strong Methode Champenoise baker's shop aromas and style; a lingering, lively and punchy palate is right on the button. Notwithstanding the name, which is a brand, the wine is a blend of Pinot Noir and Chardonnay sourced from the Adelaide Hills. Two gold medals to date are deserved.　　　　　　　　　　　**rating: 94**

best drinking Now–2006 **best vintages** '90, '91, '92, '95, '96, '99 **drink with** Aperitif • $32

Yellowglen Y

TTTY **NV** Light to medium green-straw; a quite concentrated fruit-driven bouquet with citrus, lemon and melon aromas, then a palate with lots of flavour, but a fraction grippy.　　　　　　　　　　**rating: 84**

best drinking Now **drink with** Aperitif • $22

🐦 yengari wine company NR

La Trobe University, Beechworth, Vic 3747 **region** Beechworth
phone (03) 5728 1438 **fax** (03) 5728 1505 **open** By appointment
winemaker Tony Lacy **production** 500 cases **est.** 2000

product range ($12–35 CD) Chardonnay, Shiraz, Merlot, Cabernet Sauvignon.

summary Tony Lacy and partner Trish Flores run an interesting grape and olive produce business, wines from the 2.4 hectares of shiraz, 1.2 hectares of chardonnay and 0.5 hectare of viognier forming but part of the range of products. Painted candles coloured with wine lees, stationery tinted using the same colour bases, wine soap (shiraz, chardonnay and cabernet sauvignon) and water colour paints (shiraz from 100 per cent sun-dried wine lees and chardonnay from sun-dried wine lees plus traces of natural water colour) are all produced and sold.

yeringberg ★★★★☆

Maroondah Highway, Coldstream, Vic 3770 **region** Yarra Valley
phone (03) 9739 1453 **fax** (03) 9739 0048 **open** By appointment
winemaker Guill de Pury **production** 1000 cases **est.** 1863
product range ($30–45 CD) Chardonnay, Marsanne/Roussanne, Pinot Noir, Yeringberg (Cabernet blend).
summary Makes wines for the new millennium from the low-yielding vines re-established on the heart of what was one of the most famous (and infinitely larger) vineyards of the 19th century. In the riper years, the red wines have a velvety generosity of flavour which is rarely encountered, yet never lose varietal character, while the Yeringberg White takes students of history back to Yeringberg's fame in the 19th century. The wines are exported to the UK, the US, Switzerland, Malaysia, Hong Kong, Indonesia and Singapore.

Yeringberg Marsanne Roussanne

♥♥♥♥♡ **2002** Light straw-green; spotlessly clean, firm, mineral, honeysuckle and apple aromas are followed by a palate with immaculate balance and mouthfeel; once again, there is a touch of honeysuckle and light spices; demands years. At 14°, fully ripe. **rating:** 92

best drinking 2006–2016 **best vintages** '94, '97, '98, '00, '02 **drink with** Snowy Mountains trout • $30

Yeringberg Chardonnay

♥♥♥♥♥ **2002** Light to medium yellow-green; a sophisticated, seamless marriage of melon, fig, citrus and oak on the bouquet leads into the elegant, understated but beautifully proportioned Chardonnay one has come to expect from Yeringberg. Here, too, years to go. **rating:** 94

best drinking 2004–2010 **best vintages** '88, '90, '91, '92, '93, '94, '97, '98, '00, '01, '02 **drink with** Sweetbreads • $30

Yeringberg Pinot Noir

♥♥♥♥ **2001** Light to medium red-purple; clean, light, cherry and strawberry aromas are followed by a relatively light-bodied palate, producing the same flavours, but not much depth. A pretty wine to be drunk as soon as possible. **rating:** 87

best drinking Now **best vintages** '97 **drink with** Squab • $45

Yeringberg Dry Red

♥♥♥♥♡ **2001** Medium red-purple; complex blackcurrant, blackberry, spice and cedar aromas are followed by a round, smooth, relatively soft palate, with attractive sweet berry fruit, touches of plum, and a low tannin profile. **rating:** 90

best drinking 2005–2010 **best vintages** '85, '86, '88, '90, '91, '93, '94, '97, '98, '99, '00 **drink with** Yarra Valley venison • $45

yering farm ★★★★

St Huberts Road, Yering, Vic 3770 **region** Yarra Valley
phone (03) 9739 0461 **fax** (03) 9739 0467 **open** 7 days 10–5
winemaker Alan Johns **production** 5000 cases **est.** 1989
product range ($20–30 CD) Sauvignon Blanc, Chardonnay, Pinot Noir, Shiraz, Merlot, Cabernet Merlot, Cabernet Sauvignon.
summary Former East Doncaster orchardists Alan and Louis Johns acquired the 40-hectare Yeringa Vineyard property in 1980; the property had originally been planted by the Deschamps family in the mid-19th century and known as Yeringa Cellars. The plantings now extend to 12 hectares, the first wines being made by Alan Johns in 1992. Since that time all of the wines have been made on-site, and have enjoyed consistent show success over the years, none greater, however, than the trophy at the 2002 Victorian Wines Show for Best Pinot Noir awarded to the 2000 Yering Farm Pinot Noir.

Yering Farm Sauvignon Blanc

TTTTY 2002 Very light straw-green; the clean and crisp bouquet has classic mineral, grass and spice aromas; the harmonious palate has good intensity and length, with citrus and gooseberry fruit coming through. Well made.

best drinking Now–2005 **best vintages** '02 **drink with** Shellfish • $20   **rating:** 90

Yering Farm Chardonnay

TTTT 2000 Light straw-green; the moderately intense bouquet has fresh stone fruit and touches of smoky oak, the light to medium-bodied palate nicely balanced, but lacks fruit intensity.   **rating:** 86

best drinking Now–2005 **drink with** Scampi • $23

Yering Farm Pinot Noir

TTTT 2001 Bright red-purple; clean, ripe strawberry aromas, not complex; a lively palate with a mix of strawberry and more stemmy flavours; fairly high acidity and needing to soften and round out.   **rating:** 87

TTTTY 2000 Bright red-purple, holding its hue particularly well; the clean bouquet has a mix of plum and black cherry complexed by balanced spicy oak; the firm palate has moderately ripe and pure plum fruit; although most of the 2000 Pinot Noirs are at their best, this trophy-winning wine has time in front of it.   **rating:** 90

best drinking Now–2006 **best vintages** '00 **drink with** Barbecued quail • $23

Yering Farm The Emerson Merlot

TTTTY 2000 Medium red-purple; clean, well articulated varietal aromas with gently ripe berry accompanied by touches of olive and spice lead into an elegant, well-balanced palate, gently savoury, finishing with fine tannins. True Merlot.   **rating:** 90

best drinking 2004–2009 **drink with** Roast veal • $25

Yering Farm Cabernet Merlot

TTTT 2000 Medium red-purple; the bouquet ranges through spice, earth, leaf and berry, the palate picking up on the berry component, sweet and juicy, and quite minty; not a lot of structure.   **rating:** 85

best drinking Now–2007 **drink with** Lamb chops • $25

Yering Farm The Grange Cabernet Sauvignon

TTTT 1999 Medium red-purple; the moderately intense bouquet mixes cedary/earthy notes with dark berry fruit; the tangy, blackberry-accented palate with fine savoury tannins needed just a touch more substance.   **rating:** 88

best drinking Now–2008 **drink with** Marinated beef • $25

yering range vineyard   NR

14 McIntyre Lane, Coldstream, Vic 3770 **region** Yarra Valley
phone (03) 9739 1172 **fax** (03) 9739 1172 **open** By appointment
winemaker Kevin Ryan, Margaret Ryan **production** 300 cases **est.** 1989
product range ($18 CD) Cabernet Sauvignon.
summary Yering Range has 2 hectares of cabernet sauvignon under vine, part being sold and part made under the Yering Range label by John Ellis at Hanging Rock. The tiny production is sold through a mailing list.

yering station   ★★★★☆

38 Melba Highway, Yarra Glen, Vic 3775 **region** Yarra Valley
phone (03) 9730 1107 **fax** (03) 9739 0135 **open** 7 days 10–5
winemaker Tom Carson, Dan Buckle, Darren Rathbone **production** 45 000 cases **est.** 1988
product range ($12.50–58 CD) Barak's Bridge Semillon Sauvignon Blanc, Chardonnay, Botrytis Semillon, Pinot Noir, Shiraz, Cabernet Blend; Yering Station Sauvignon Blanc, Marsanne, Chardonnay, Reserve Chardonnay, Pinot Gris Late Harvest, Pinot Gris Botrytis, Pinot Noir Rose ED, Pinot Noir, Shiraz, Merlot, Cabernet Sauvignon; also Verjuice in 375 ml bottles.
summary The historic Yering Station (or at least the portion of the property on which the cellar-door sales and vineyard are established) was purchased by the Rathbone family in January 1996 and is now the site of a joint venture with the French Champagne house Devaux. A spectacular and very large winery has been erected which handles the Yarrabank sparkling wines and the Yering Station and Yarra Edge table wines. Has immediately become one of the focal points of the Yarra Valley, particularly with the historic Chateau Yering next door, where luxury accommodation and fine dining is available. Yering Station's own restaurant is open every day for lunch, providing the best cuisine in the Valley. Since 2002, a sister company of Mount Langi Ghiran, now also owned by the Rathbone family. Exports to the US, Canada, the UK, Denmark, Sweden, Malaysia, Singapore, Hong Kong and Japan.

Yering Station Barak's Bridge Chardonnay

▼▼▼▼ **2001** Medium to full yellow-green; the moderately complex and tangy bouquet revolves around grapefruit and melon fruit; the palate has plenty of flavour, but has a slightly grippy finish. **rating:** 86

best drinking Now **drink with** Salmon salad • $15.50

Yering Station Reserve Chardonnay

▼▼▼▼ **2001** Medium yellow-green; extreme toasty/charry barrel-ferment aromas dominate the bouquet and play a major part in the palate; the wine has great character, and top-class fruit, but one has to question whether it will ever break free of the oak stranglehold. **rating:** 89

best drinking 2004–2009 **best vintages** '97, '99 **drink with** Pan-fried veal • $58

Yering Station Barak's Bridge Pinot Noir

▼▼▼▼ **2001** Light to medium red-purple; the light bouquet does have distinctive varietal character, plus a touch of stemminess which is quite appealing; while the palate does not have overmuch fruit, it is quite savoury and complex; fairly priced and, unlike most of the Barak's Bridge range, is entirely sourced from the Yarra Valley. **rating:** 87

best drinking Now **drink with** Pastrami • $15.50

Yering Station Merlot

▼▼▼▼▽ **2001** Strong and bright purple-red; the bouquet has smooth, sweet, red and blackcurrant fruit supported by a touch of quality French oak. The palate has depth, richness and structure, driven by quite sweet fruit, then held on the finish by gentle tannins. The sort of wine to give Merlot a good name, not a bad one. **rating:** 93

best drinking 2004–2010 **best vintages** '00, '01 **drink with** White Rocks veal • $23

Yering Station Reserve Cabernet Sauvignon

▼▼▼▼▽ **2000** Deep, bright red-purple; the bouquet offers a complex but seamless amalgam of blackcurrant and oak, including what seems to be a touch of barrel ferment; a powerful, long palate follows, finely structured, and which will live in part on its acidity. **rating:** 93

best drinking 2007–2017 **best vintages** '00 **drink with** Daube of lamb • $55

yokain vineyard estate ★★★☆

Worsley Back Road, Allanson, WA 6225 (postal) **region** Geographe
phone (08) 9725 3397 **fax** (08) 9725 3397 **open** Not
winemaker Camilla Vote **production** 1000 cases **est.** 1998
product range ($8–12 ML) Riesling, Verdelho, Chardonnay, Simply Red Shiraz Cabernet Sauvignon, Oaked Shiraz Merlot Cabernet Franc, Simply Red Cabernet Sauvignon Shiraz, Oaked Cabernet Sauvignon Merlot Cabernet Franc.
summary David and Julie Gardiner began the establishment of their 17-hectare vineyard in 1998, with all but 2 hectares planted in that year. Verdelho, chardonnay, semillon, shiraz, cabernet sauvignon, merlot and cabernet franc are in production; the 2000 plantings of riesling and zinfandel will produce their first grapes in 2003. Although they do not have a cellar door, they are in the process of establishing a wine bar at Dunsborough, and in the meantime are selling the wine by mail order for between $8 and $12 a bottle.

Yokain Vineyard Estate Riesling

▼▼▼▽ **2002** Pale colour; a clean, very light and discreet bouquet is followed by a palate with fairly light fruit, filled out and lengthened by a cleverly judged touch of residual sugar. **rating:** 84

best drinking Now **drink with** Summer salads • $10

Yokain Vineyard Estate Verdelho

▼▼▼▽ **2002** Medium straw-yellow; a quite fragrant, tropical bouquet is followed by an unusually bright, lively, lemony palate indicative of the fact that the wine was early picked, with only 10.5° alcohol. **rating:** 84

best drinking Now **drink with** Fish and chips • $8.50

Yokain Vineyard Estate Unwooded Chardonnay

▼▼▼▼ **2002** Light straw-green; lively, fresh and tangy citrus/stone fruit aromas are reflected on the palate, almost to the point of being slightly green. Nonetheless, it is the right side of the rainbow, and the wine is well above the average unwooded chardonnay. **rating:** 88

best drinking Now–2005 **drink with** Avocado and prawn salad • $8

Yokain Vineyard Estate Shiraz Merlot

ŢŢŢŢ 2001 Youthful purple-red; the bouquet has a mix of red fruits, earth and darker berry aromas, but seems to have been underworked; the palate is similarly all arms and legs, but has potential to settle down in bottle with its spice and blackberry flavours. **rating: 85**

best drinking 2004–2009 **drink with** Braised oxtail • $12

Yokain Vineyard Estate Cabernet Sauvignon Merlot Cabernet Franc

ŢŢŢŢ 2001 Medium to full red-purple; the moderately intense and clean bouquet has a mix of dark berry, black fruits, spice and cedar; the attractive dark berry fruit flavours of the palate are complemented by balanced tannins; the components are still softening and integrating, and this should be a lovely bottle in the years ahead. **rating: 89**

best drinking 2004–2010 **drink with** Moroccan lamb • $12

yrsa's vineyard ★★★☆

105 Tucks Road, Main Ridge, Vic 3928 **region** Mornington Peninsula
phone (03) 5989 6500 **fax** (03) 5989 6501 **open** By appointment
winemaker Craig McLeod, Judy Gifford (Contract) **production** 200 cases **est.** 1994
product range ($24–38 R) Single Vineyard Chardonnay, Single Vineyard Pinot Noir; Scion Label is due for release later in 2003 for the Australian market.
summary Yrsa's Vineyard is named after the lady from whom Steven and Marianne Stern acquired the property. She, in turn, was named after Yrsa Queen of Sweden, born in 565, whose story is told in the Norse sagas. Well known patent and trademark attorney, Steven Stern (whose particular area of expertise is in the wine and liquor business) and wife Marianne have established a little under 2.5 hectares each of pinot noir and chardonnay, and initially marketed the wines only in the UK. The tiny production has been further circumscribed by the loss of the 2002 vintage due to weather conditions. However, the wines are to be found on some icon Melbourne restaurant wine lists, including Lynch's, Sud and Bistro 1. A wine tasting studio available for small wine tastings (up to 10 people) is available by prior arrangement.

Yrsa's Single Vineyard Chardonnay

ŢŢŢŢ 2000 Developed yellow-green; a complex, with toast, honey and peach aromas, leads into a rich, mouthfilling palate, honey again making its appearance, balanced by brisk acidity on the finish. **rating: 89**
best drinking Now–2005 **drink with** Pan-fried veal • $38

Yrsa's Single Vineyard Pinot Noir

ŢŢŢŢ 2001 Light red; a light, savoury/foresty bouquet, then, as so often happens, a palate which offers more than either the colour or bouquet suggests. Spicy, savoury and long, the only thing it lacks is mid-palate fruit sweetness. **rating: 88**
best drinking Now–2006 **drink with** Braised quail • $28

yunbar estate NR

PO Box 64, Port Noarlunga, SA 5167 **region** Barossa Valley
phone (08) 8327 3987 **fax** (08) 8327 4087 **open** By appointment
winemaker The Bartiers **production** 1000 cases **est.** 1998
product range ($14–22 CD) Eden Riesling, Bushvines Semillon, Chaste Chardonnay, Sinners Shiraz, Miracle Merlot, Craig's Cabernet.
summary The intriguingly named Sinners Shiraz, the Merlot, Semillon, Riesling and Chardonnay are produced from a total of 8 hectares of contract-grown grapes, the Eden Riesling is made from contract-grown grapes. Sales via the website www.yunbar.com.

zappacosta estate wines NR

301 Kidman Way, Hanwood, NSW 2680 **region** Riverina
phone (02) 6963 0278 **fax** (02) 6963 0278 **open** 7 days 10–5
winemaker Dino Zappacosta **production** 50 000 cases **est.** 1956
product range ($12 CD) Riesling, Semillon, Dry White, Shiraz.
summary Zappacosta Estate, briefly known as Hanwood Village Wines, is a relatively new business, with the first release from the 1996 vintage, although the vineyard date back to 1956.

zarephath wines ★★★☆

Moorialup Road, East Porongurup, WA 6324 **region** Great Southern
phone (08) 9853 1152 **fax** (08) 9841 8124 **open** Mon–Sat 10–5, Sun 12–4
winemaker Robert Diletti **production** 3000 cases **est.** 1994
product range ($17–22 CD) Riesling, Unwooded Chardonnay, Chardonnay, Pinot Noir, Shiraz, Cabernet Sauvignon.
summary The 9-hectare Zarephath vineyard is owned and operated by Brothers and Sisters of The Christ Circle, a Benedictine community. They say the most outstanding feature of the location is the feeling of peace and tranquility which permeates the site, something I can well believe on the basis of numerous visits to the Porongurups. Exports to the US and the UK.

Zarephath Riesling

▼▼▼▼ 2002 Light straw-green; the light bouquet has faintly floral cosmetic/lanolin aromas which are not the least unpleasant; the palate tightens and brightens up, with citrus and spice flavours, good length and lively natural acidity. **rating:** 86
best drinking 2005–2010 **best vintages** '00 **drink with** Chinese prawns • $18

Zarephath Shiraz

▼▼▼▼ 2001 Medium purple-red; the moderately intense bouquet has distinct cool-grown earthy/gamey/spicy characters, opening up on the palate into tight but bright red fruit flavours, the brisk acidity giving the wine above-average length, but also suggesting that patience is required. **rating:** 86
best drinking 2006–2011 **drink with** Braised veal • $22

Zarephath Cabernet Sauvignon

▼▼▼▼▽ 2001 Dense red-purple; clean, concentrated blackcurrant and cedar aromas flow into a rich, concentrated and powerful palate, still tightly bound up, but sure to open up with time in bottle. **rating:** 90
best drinking 2006–2016 **best vintages** '01 **drink with** Rack of lamb • $22

zema estate ★★★★★

Riddoch Highway, Coonawarra, SA 5263 **region** Coonawarra
phone (08) 8736 3219 **fax** (08) 8736 3280 **open** 7 days 9–5
winemaker Tom Simons **production** 15 000 cases **est.** 1982
product range ($20–45 CD) Shiraz, Family Selection Shiraz, Merlot, Cluny (Cabernet-blend), Cabernet Sauvignon, Family Selection Cabernet Sauvignon.
summary Zema is one of the last outposts of hand-pruning in Coonawarra, the various members of the Zema family tending a 60-hectare vineyard progressively planted since 1982 in the heart of Coonawarra's terra rossa soil. Winemaking practices are straightforward; if ever there was an example of great wines being made in the vineyard, this is it. Exports to the UK, France, Malaysia, Thailand, Hong Kong and New Zealand.

Zema Estate Shiraz

▼▼▼▼▼ 2001 Medium red-purple; clean, smooth, dark berry fruit is allied with a touch of cedary oak on the bouquet; quite lovely and mouthfilling dark cherry and plum fruit drives the round, smooth and supple palate. Classic Zema fruit-driven style. **rating:** 94
best drinking 2005–2015 **best vintages** '84, '86, '88, '92, '94, '96, '97, '98, '01 **drink with** Bistecca Fiorentina • $25.65

Zema Estate Family Selection Shiraz

▼▼▼▼▼ 2000 Bright, clear but deep purple-red; sweet, dark plum and well-balanced and integrated oak coalesce on the bouquet, the palate ranging through chocolate, spice and berry flavours, with slightly more oak evident, but by no means oppressive. A typically, beautifully worked, wine. Multiple gold medal winner. **rating:** 94
best drinking 2004–2011 **best vintages** '00 **drink with** Italian style calf's liver • $45

Zema Estate Cluny

▼▼▼▼▽ 2001 Strong red-purple; sweet dark berry, plum and mulberry fruit aromas lead into a soft, round, fleshy mouthfilling palate, with exemplary oak and tannin management. A blend of Cabernet Sauvignon, Merlot, Cabernet Franc and Malbec. **rating:** 93
best drinking 2005–2015 **best vintages** '98, '99, '01 **drink with** Braised lamb • $25.65

Zema Estate Cabernet Sauvignon

▼▼▼▼▼ 2000 Zema Estate never disappoints with its wines, wines which truly express the terroir from which they come. Deep red-purple, the bouquet is redolent with sweet blackcurrant/cassis fruit; the harmonious texture and flavour caresses the mouth, with all the components of ripe cassis, gentle oak, and ripe, rounded tannins in perfect balance. **rating:** 95

best drinking 2004–2015 **best vintages** '84, '86, '88, '92, '93, '96, '97, '98, '00 **drink with** Barbecued leg of lamb • $25.65

Zema Estate Family Selection Cabernet Sauvignon

▼▼▼▼▽ 2000 Medium purple-red; fresh, ripe redcurrant/cassis aromas lead into a plush, ripe palate, with abundant cassis, blackcurrant and chocolate fruit flavours, supported by well-handled oak and tannins. **rating:** 93

best drinking 2005–2015 **best vintages** '97, '98 **drink with** Game • $45

ziebarth wines NR

Foleys Road, Goodger, Qld 4610 **region** South Burnett
phone (07) 4162 3089 **fax** (07) 4162 3084 **open** 7 days 10–5
winemaker John Crane (Contract) **production** 420 cases **est.** 1998
product range ($13.50–14.50 CD) Semillon, Fairview White, Rose, Shiraz Cabernet Franc.
summary The 4-hectare vineyard (with 1 ha each of semillon, cabernet sauvignon, merlot and chardonnay, together with 0.25 ha of chambourcin) is a minor diversification on a beef cattle property set on the edge of the Stuart Range, and which enjoys superb views. It is a small family operation with the aim of providing a wine experience for visitors, the wines being made for Ziebarth by John Crane at Crane Winery.

zig zag road NR

201 Zig Zag Road, Drummond, Vic 3461 **region** Macedon Ranges
phone (03) 5423 9390 **fax** (03) 5423 9390 **open** Weekends and public holidays
winemaker Alan Stevens, Deb Orton **production** 350 cases **est.** 1972
product range ($20–22 CD) Cabernet Sauvignon.
summary Alan Stevens and Deb Orton purchased the vineyard in 1988; it was then 16 years old, having been established way back in 1972 by Roger Aldridge. The dry-grown vines produce relatively low yields, and until 1996 the grapes were sold to Hanging Rock Winery. In 1996 the decision was taken to manage the property on a full-time basis, and to make the wine on-site, utilising 1 hectare each of shiraz and cabernet sauvignon, 0.5 hectare of pinot noir and 0.25 hectare of merlot.

zilzie wines ★★★

Lot 66 Kulkyne Way, Karadoc via Red Cliffs, Vic 3496 **region** Murray Darling
phone (03) 5025 8100 **fax** (03) 5025 8116 **open** Not
winemaker Bob Shields, Leigh Sparrow **production** 25 000 cases **est.** 1999
product range ($9.99–18.99 R) The wines are offered under three labels; the export-oriented Forbes Family range of Chardonnay, Shiraz, Merlot, Cabernet Sauvignon; in the middle come the Buloke Reserve Wines, with Sauvignon Blanc, Chardonnay, Shiraz, Petit Verdot, Sangiovese, Tempranillo, Merlot, Cabernet Merlot; Zilzie is the top of the range, with Chardonnay, Shiraz, Merlot, Cabernet Sauvignon, plus Show Reserves.
summary The Forbes family has been farming Zilzie estate since 1911; it is currently run by Ian and Ros Forbes, together with their sons Steven and Andrew. A diverse range of farming activities now include grape growing with 250 hectares of vineyards. Having established a position of a dominant supplier of grapes to Southcorp, Zilzie took the next step of forming a wine company in 1999 and built a winery in 2000 with a present capacity of 16 000 tonnes, but so designed that modules can be added to take it ultimately to 50 000 tonnes. The winery business includes contract storage, contract processing, contract winemaking, bulk wine production and bottled and branded wines. The wines are distributed nationally through Rutherglen Wine and Spirit Company Limited; exports to the UK.

Zilzie Show Reserve Chardonnay

▼▼▼▼ 2002 Light to medium yellow-green; the bouquet is clean, with some citrus fruit and subtle oak; the light to medium-bodied palate follows precisely along the line of the bouquet; not particularly intense, but gets there. Said to be barrel fermented and aged in French oak. **rating:** 85

best drinking Now **drink with** Yabbies • $18.99

Zilzie Buloke Reserve Shiraz

▼▼▼▽ 2002 Bright, deep purple-red; youthful blackberry fruit on the bouquet and palate certainly make a statement, although the overall texture and mouthfeel is a little on the rough side. **rating:** 84

best drinking 2004–2005 **drink with** Beef shashlik • $9.99

Zilzie Buloke Reserve Petit Verdot

▼▼▼▼ 2002 Bright, deep purple-red; blackcurrant and blackberry fruit aromas lead into a concentrated, quite tannic palate. As much grape juice as wine in character, but undoubtedly varietal. Good value. **rating:** 85

best drinking Now–2006 **drink with** Barbecue • $9.99

Zilzie Buloke Reserve Sangiovese

▼▼▼▽ 2002 Light to medium red-purple; light, savoury, spicy aromas lead into a light-bodied palate with savoury red fruits and emery board tannins. Should be drunk by the end of 2003 at the latest. **rating:** 84

best drinking Now **drink with** Spaghetti bolognese • $9.99

Zilzie Buloke Reserve Tempranillo

▼▼▼▽ 2002 Medium purple-red; the moderately intense bouquet has clean dark berry/plum fruit, the very youthful palate slightly callow and unworked, but has got more structure than many other young vine Tempranillos on the market in 2003. Could become more interesting once the vines reach maturity, particularly if yields are controlled. **rating:** 84

best drinking Now–2005 **drink with** Baby lamb • $9.99

Zilzie Merlot

▼▼▼▼ 2002 Strong purple-red; the mix of spice, leaf, herb and olive aromas are strongly varietal; the palate has considerable body and good extract, but is suddenly confronted with dark chocolate flavours which take the wine off in a different direction. A near miss, indeed. **rating:** 86

best drinking 2004–2007 **drink with** Braised veal • $13.99

index

MCLAREN VALE

JAMES HALLIDAY'S

wine

Odyssey

A year of wine, food and travel